Antique Trader ANTIQUES & COLLECTIBLES

2017 PRICE GUIDE • Eric Bradley

33rd Edition

Published by

Krause Publications, a division of F+W Media, Inc.
700 East State Street • Iola, WI 54990-0001
715-445-2214 • 888-457-2873
www.krausebooks.com

To order books or other products call toll-free 1-800-258-0929
or visit us online at www.krausebooks.com

ISSN 1536-2884
ISBN-13: 9781440246975
ISBN-10: 1440246971

Cover Design by Rebecca Vogel
Designed by Rebecca Vogel & Nicole MacMartin
Edited by Eric Bradley
Printed in the United States of America

10 9 8 7 6 5 4 3 2 1

FRONT COVER, CLOCKWISE FROM TOP LEFT:

Citrine, enamel, and gold brooch, Tiffany & Co., $11,250 (Heritage Auctions, ha.com)

Rookwood mat floral vase by Sallie Coyne, 1927, 10-5/8" h., $590 (Humler & Nolan, www.humlernolan.com)

Emilio Pucci handbag, 8-1/2" h. x 5" w., $338 (Capo Auction, ww.capoauctionnyc.com)

Edouard-Léon Cortès, "Flower Market at La Madeleine," circa 1950-1960, oil on canvas, 26" x 36", $42,500 (Heritage Auctions, ha.com)

Pennsylvania miniature paint-decorated side chair, 19th century, 16-1/2" h. overall, $726 (Conestoga Auction Co./Division of Hess Auction Group, www.conestogaauction.com)

BACK COVER:

Peach Blow plate, cup, and saucer, Gunderson Glass Works, circa 1950, plate 8" dia., $60 (Jeffrey S. Evans & Associates, www.jeffreysevans.com)

CONTENTS

LISTINGS

INTRODUCTION

WELCOME TO THE most complete visual reference to the world of fine art and collectibles available on the market today: Welcome to the *Antique Trader Antiques & Collectibles Price Guide*. With this 100 percent visual guide, you never have to second-guess what you're looking at or looking for. That's what's made this book the No. 1 selling reference book on the wide world of fine art and collectibles. Each entry is illustrated with a full-color photograph to make it easier than ever to compare and contrast it with the antiques you may find every day.

Each year, we scour the world of live auctions, online sales, dealers' booths, and group shops to show you what's hot and what's not. Some items will be very familiar – in fact, you may already own some of them – but there are others that are extraordinary and unique in their own right. Both examples are useful to help you understand where your collectible ranks in terms of condition, rarity, value, and eye appeal.

In addition to this annual guide and a host of reference books on the most important and popular segments of the collecting hobby, our staff produces *Antique Trader* magazine, which keeps a finger on the pulse of the market day in and day out. Like our informative magazine, this reference book is full of facts, history, and collecting advice you won't find anywhere else.

Since our last edition, we've documented a few trends in how collectors collect and which categories seem to be attracting greater interest.

Here are our annual picks of some of the hottest areas in the hobby:

Porcelain advertising signs in all conditions

Smalls (various collectibles no bigger than a breadbox and priced between $50 and $1,000)

Asian decorative prints

American folk art

Vintage LEGO sets

Sports memorabilia (with the exception of sports cards from 1974 and later)

Abraham Lincoln collectibles

Firearms

Curiosities or vintage objects that defy classification

Mid-Century Modern sculptures

Vintage Star Wars toys and action figures

Contemporary art by well-known artists

Beatles memorabilia

Vintage vinyl rock and roll records

High-grade comic books

Estate jewelry

Last year marked the first noticeable slowdown in the fine art and collectibles retail markets – a 7% decline from $68.2 billion to $63.8 billion. This cooling off is influenced by a number of global market conditions, but we've seen a few key elements contributing to it:

A NEW GENERATION OF BUYERS IS COLLECTING DIFFERENTLY

We see lots of young faces at antiques and collectibles shows all over the nation, but we don't see them accumulating as many examples of one category as previous generations once did. Today's buyers are satisfied with owning four or five truly excellent examples in top condition rather than 30 or 40 "middle of the road" examples. This becomes apparent when large collections re-enter the market for the first time in decades. The best examples in a collection fly out the door at astronomical prices, while the mid-range items languish. Low-priced items are also brisk sellers as people seek distinctive objects to decorate their homes.

EYE-APPEAL INFLUENCING VALUE

Eye-appeal is becoming a strong influence on values, however arbitrary that may be to some. Collectors are armchair historians by nature, but shoppers are increasingly influenced by a precious object's proportions, attractiveness, and composition. To fetch top dollar in today's market, a painting's subject matter should align with the artist's well-known visual focus. For example, a painting of Texas bluebonnets by Julian Onderdonk is preferred over his river bottom landscapes. The same is true with collectibles. A Darth Vader Star Wars action figure from 1977, still mounted on its display card rather than loose with its original cape and light saber, will almost always be worth more to a collector.

CROWDS GREET THE NEWLY DISCOVERED COLLECTIBLE

A new discovery - whether it has been resting happily in a private collection or hiding behind a wall for decades - is almost always greeted by an eager crowd. This can be a double-edged sword on values. If a newly discovered piece of early American pressed glass appears at auction, the price will predictably exceed expectations. But once the high price is shared around the world, the value may fall if other examples suddenly appear "out of the woodwork." That's why it's always important to buy from the most knowledgeable dealers, sellers, and auctioneers as possible. The truly rare antique or collectible is a rare thing itself these days, and the truly rare will always hold its value.

It may appear contradictory, but original examples of well-published or over-exposed items are also seeing a spike in values. The auction values for newly discovered examples of James Montgomery Flagg's iconic 1917 World War I recruitment poster depicting Uncle Sam above the words "I WANT YOU FOR U.S. ARMY" have more than doubled in value during the last decade (from $4,000 to $10,000+).

Rorimer-Brooks Art Deco desk/dressing table and stool, Cleveland, Ohio, birch plywood, figured maple, oak, and leather, compartmental letter holder in gilt paint with red interior with seven compartments on rectangular dark-stained birch plywood top over long drawer with circular pulls with silver linear painted accents, figural maple U-shape legs with silver ball feet, rectangular footstool upholstered in brown leather with conforming base, printed label reads, "Writing table & bench, wood with lacquer & silver leaf United States, made by Rorimer Brooks for Cleveland home in 1933. Loaned by Mrs. Warren Lahr," 27-1/2" h. x 39-1/2" w. x 19-1/2" d., compartment 11-1/2" h. x 39-1/4" w. x 6-1/4" d., footstool 19-1/2" h. x 20-1/2" w. x 13" d......... **$2,952**

Courtesy of Skinner, Inc., www.skinnerinc.com

PREMIUM PAID FOR UTILITY

Condition and rarity are still two leading factors behind today's values, but today's market is seeing buyers pay a premium for smaller, useful items rather than large decorative pieces. This is especially true for furniture. A small curio cabinet can be worth more than a large curio cabinet. This is especially true in large cities where living space is at a premium. Values can be increased even more if the furniture is functional, such as a pair of small cabinets or an attractive bookcase. These items are stronger sellers than a grand sideboard, which may seem ill suited for today's smaller dining rooms.

There is an important lesson here if you read between the lines. If you're looking to add furniture and art to your home, consider a visit to your local antiques shop or auction house before you visit your local big-box department store. The value of new items will certainly fall as soon as you cross the parking lot - who hasn't experienced this first-hand at your everyday garage sale? However, the value of a functional antique should remain steady or even increase over time. Sellers are making it easier than ever to either start a collection or add a unique item to your décor. Here are a few tips to keep in mind when you're looking to buy or sell in the coming year:

Abstract paintings from the 1960s and 1970s are hot commodities. Consider getting a second or even third opinion on a painting's value well before you sell it.

Collectibles valued between $50 and $500 are selling very well in today's market. It is very easy to collect vintage movie props, Art Deco gold rings, Loetz art glass, vintage travel posters, Russian icons, and vintage Tonka metal trucks, all for prices below $500 each. Many traditional and mid-range collectibles can now be found at this price point and it can be a solid starting point to build a stellar collection.

Alfonso Ossorio, "Fire and Ice," oil on Masonite abstract expressionist composition with heavy impasto, verso inscribed and dated "ossorio / io.viii.'55," with labels from Betty Parsons Gallery and Channel Thirteen Day Pass, dated May 14, 1982, overall good condition, light soiling throughout, 32" x 25-1/2". **$187,500**

Courtesy of Roland Auctioneers & Valuers, www.rolandauctions.com

As sad as it may be for some of us, the term **"vintage" is now being applied to items made or sold in the late 1980s and early 1990s**. It's not wise to move your 401(K) into vintage Furby toys, but vintage electronics, even vintage boomboxes, are hot collectibles in California and New York.

Pinbacks are making a comeback. Ranging from political buttons to fishing licenses from the 1920s to the 1950s, pinback buttons are being collected once again. A set of Pennsylvania fishing licenses recently sold for more than $1,500, and a complete set of 25 baseball pinbacks sealed in plastic from 1930s Cracker Jack boxes are fetching more than $1,000. This category is rife with reproductions, fakes, and fantasy pieces, so it's best to research before you buy or stick with a trusted dealer or auction house.

If any of the categories in this book pique your interest, there is one key task to keep in mind before you start buying or selling: Research. Research. Research.

And that's where this visual reference guide comes in. In this edition we've expanded and updated the most popular sections and added new ones, too. You'll notice special attention is drawn to the very best items pursued by collectors as **Top Lots!** Special features show why some categories are irresistible to collectors. We've also been on the road, like many of you, meeting dealers, auctioneers, collectors, and show managers who gave us the scoop on what's really happening in the hobby. You'll see their smiling faces along with their top tips, opinions, and collecting advice under the header **Inside Intel** located in various chapters across this new edition. We hope this helps you get to know the people behind the prices.

A book of this size and scope is a team project and many thanks are owed to editorial director Paul Kennedy and editor Mary Sieber; Antoinette Rahn, editor, online editor, and

Antique Trader

ABOUT ANTIQUETRADER.COM

We think you'll be impressed with the layout, sections, and information in this year's annual book. Because the antiques world (like everything else) is constantly changing, I invite you to visit AntiqueTrader.com and make it your main portal into the world of antiques.

Like our magazine, AntiqueTrader.com's team of collectors, dealers, and bloggers share information daily on events, auctions, new discoveries, and tips on how to buy more for less. Here's what you'll find at AntiqueTrader.com:

Free eNewsletters: Get a recap of the world of antiques sent to your inbox every week.

Expert Q&A columns: Learn how to value and sell your collections online and for the best prices.

The Internet's largest free antiques library: Dig into thousands of articles on research, prices, show reports, auction results, and more.

Blogs: Get vital how-to information about topics that include selling online, buying more for less, restoring pieces, spotting fakes and reproductions, displaying your collections, and finding hidden gems in your town!

Show guides: Check out the Internet's most visited antiques events calendar for links to more than 1,000 auctions, flea markets, conventions, and antiques shows worldwide.

Charles Lotton iridescent ruby and gold glass peacock table lamp, late 20th century, good condition, 23" h. **$8,125**

Courtesy of Heritage Auctions, ha.com

content manager of *Antique Trader* magazine; Karen Knapstein, print editor of *Antique Trader* magazine; designers Rebecca Vogel and Nicole MacMartin; and several specialists and contributors. Ever the professionals, they work year round to make this book the best it can be.

We also thank the numerous auction houses and their staffs for generously providing images. Their hard work and great ideas are always focused on one goal: selecting the topics, images, and features our readers will find the most fascinating. We hope you enjoy the results.

— *Eric Bradley*

Eric Bradley is the author of the critically acclaimed *Mantiques: A Manly Guide to Cool Stuff, Picker's Pocket Guide: Signs,* and *Picker's Pocket Guide: Toys,* and he is the editor of the annual *Antique Trader Antiques & Collectibles Price Guide.* A former editor of *Antique Trader* magazine and an award-winning investigative journalist with a degree in economics, he has appeared in *The Wall Street Journal, GQ, Four Seasons Magazine, Bottom Line/Personal* and *The Detroit News,* among others. He is a public relations associate at Heritage Auctions, ha.com, the world's largest collectibles auctioneer, and lives near Dallas with his wife and three children.

ADVERTISING

ADVERTISING ITEMS, WITH the exception of glass and ceramics, is the most diverse collecting category in all of collectibles. Before the days of mass media, advertisers relied on colorful product labels, containers, store displays, signs, posters, and novelty items to help set their product or service apart from competitors.

In the United States, advertising became an art form during the boom years after World War II until well into the mid-1970s. The rise of the middle class and freely flowing dollars left us with a plethora of items to collect. These items represent the work of America's skilled and talented writers and commercial illustrators and give us an entertaining look into everyday life of the 19th and 20th centuries.

The arrival of large, carefully curated collections at auctions and at specialty shows is also renewing interest in advertising items. Massive collections of tobacco tins, coffee tins, talcum powder containers, rarely seen syrup dispensers, and Coca-Cola memorabilia are being offered for sale. These large sales are increasingly offering grouped lots of up to 20 items, giving collectors the opportunity to purchase an interesting assortment of advertising items at one time.

The most popular pieces are sought after for one chief reason: eye appeal, according to William Morford, owner of William Morford Investment Grade Collectibles at Auction. Modern values "depend on the subject matter and the graphics - how powerful it is," he says. "The advanced collector who has the resources knows it's a smarter move to buy the best...and it's leaving all the lower end stuff behind," he says.

Morford said another emerging trend is the popularity of male-centric items bringing higher than expected prices at auction. "Hunting, fishing, oil, gas, and cars, gambling - pretty much all of them are popular now," he adds.

The most heavily collected advertising pieces remain signs, especially those with porcelain graphics. Lately this segment also has become dominated by items in exceptional condition and by obscure examples. However, unlike other segments, some auctioneers are reporting interest in signs in poor condition, even if sale prices are low. It seems new collectors entering the hobby are seeking rusty, chipped examples made popular on television programs such as "American Pickers."

For more information, see *Picker's Pocket Guide: Signs* (Krause Publications, 2014).

"A Morning of the New Era" for Edison Electric Appliance Co., Inc., chromolithographic transfer print on canvas advertisement, 27" h. x 19" w. overall with frame. **$24**

Courtesy of Clars Auction Gallery, www.clars.com

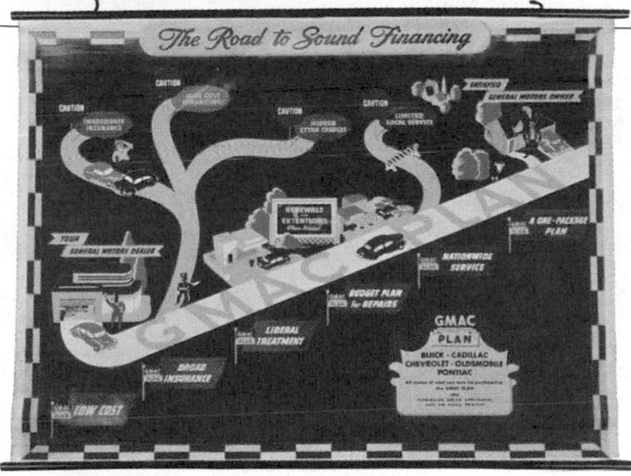

1940 GMAC Financing auto showroom canvas banner, very good-plus condition, light soiling and fading, no tears, 43" x 32". **$342**

Courtesy of Morphy Auctions, www.morphyauctions.com

Barber bust advertising figure, circa 1950s or later, near mint condition, 16-1/2" h. **$122**

Courtesy of Morphy Auctions, www.morphyauctions.com

W.S. Grinsfelder Co. Cigars calendar from 1906 with Japanese woman holding fan while another woman stands under parasol, basket turns to show months, calendar in good overall condition, minor damage to bottom and parasol, calendar 9-1/2" x 14" **$42**

Courtesy of North American Auction Co., www.northamericanauctioncompany.com

Vintage gemstone advertising clock with brass plaque that reads, "Your Birthstone in a W. W. W. Guaranteed Ring is here for you in endless variety at reasonable prices," 20" x 6" x 19" h. **$510**

Courtesy of Copake Auction Co., www.copakeauction.com

Sessions oak wall clock with reverse-painted advertising for "G.L. Harding / Jeweler and Optician / 7112 Lorain Ave., Cleveland, Ohio," excellent condition, 36" x 15". **$480**

Courtesy of Milestone Auctions, www.milestoneauctions.com

Dwinell Wright Co. Coffee wooden crate with paper advertising labels, good condition, labels with moderate wear and paper loss with staining, 21-1/4" x 15" x 16". **$122**

Courtesy of Morphy Auctions, www.morphyauctions.com

Two Colgate's talc advertising cutouts with images of baby, both double-sided, dated 1913, excellent condition, good colors, 14"................. **$132**

Courtesy of Milestone Auctions, www.milestoneauctions.com

Tin litho advertising globe for Whiteley Scotch, King's Ransom / "Round the World" Scotch, 15" h. x 20" w. x 7" d. **$295**

Courtesy of Turkey Creek Auctions, Inc., www.antiqueauctionsfl.com

▶ Miniature Kentucky stoneware advertising jug in brown and white glaze with stenciled blue inscription reading "Compliments of / C.A. Renaker / Cynthiana, Ky." with applied strap handle, fine condition, 3-1/4" h............. **$514**

Courtesy of Forsythes' Auctions, LLC, www.forsythesauctions.com

Rare Hoffritz & Keyer countertop advertising item made from wooden cigar box material, circa 1890, scroll-cut back with central oval chromolithograph of Victorian woman with surrounding stamped and blackened inscription reading "Hoffritz & Keyer / Manufacturers of / Cigar Boxes / Dayton, Ohio" with surrounding stamped and blackened scrollwork, small box on top labeled "MATCHES" and drawer below with brass handle with burled wood-grained paper covering, top shelf with two square recessed openings for containers for used matches, now missing, overall wear to paper covering on lower section and on portrait, some chips to the wood, 5" x 8-1/2" x 10-1/4" h. **$182**

Courtesy of Forsythes' Auctions, LLC, www.forsythesauctions.com

Old Crow Original Bourbon Whisky plastic countertop advertising figure, Advertising Novelty Sign Co. label underneath, excellent condition, no damage or repairs, 31" h. x 21" d. x 10" w....................................... **$277**

Courtesy of Nest Egg Auctions, www.nesteggauctions.com

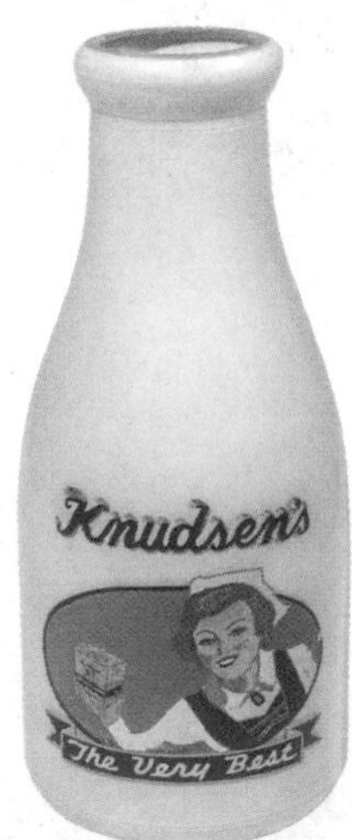

▲ Rare Knudsen's Milk advertising light, painted glass in form of milk bottle with woman in white and red uniform holding box of Knudsen's cottage cheese, "Knudsen's" above and "The Very Best" below, with light mounted on inside, cord through side, good condition, 19-3/4" h., 8" dia. **$1,029**

Courtesy of Forsythes' Auctions, LLC, www.forsythesauctions.com

Red Hawk Indian tin litho advertising plate made by Meek Co., very good condition, moderate paint wear and loss to edge, border with some areas of touch-up with some staining, 9-1/2" dia. **$61**

Courtesy of Morphy Auctions, www.morphyauctions.com

Original English Robin Starch advertising poster, numbered R21P, linen-backed color lithograph, 59-1/2" x 39-1/2".. **$188**

Courtesy of Material Culture, www.materialculture.com

Large Gill & Co. fire truck graphic puzzle, late 19th century, advertising premium from W.T. Gill 5 & 10 Cent Store, very good condition, few spots of missing paper, 63" x 8". **$204**

Courtesy of Material Culture, www.materialculture.com

Carnation Milk die-cut porcelain sign, very good condition with strong colors and minor chips. ... **$397**

Courtesy of Morphy Auctions, www.morphyauctions.com

Goodyear shoe porcelain sign with chip in field, 62" l. **$214**

Courtesy of Morphy Auctions, www.morphyauctions.com

Hires tin sign, very good condition, minor wear, 35-1/2" x 11"................... **$153**

Courtesy of Morphy Auctions, www.morphyauctions.com

Columbia Records porcelain sign, excellent-plus condition, staining and mild wear, light wear to edge, 20" x 30"... **$519**

Courtesy of Morphy Auctions, www.morphyauctions.com

The Robert Smith Ale Brewing Co. tin sign advertising Tiger brand ale, excellent condition, overall minor wear, 19-1/2" x 14".................. **$976**

Courtesy of Morphy Auctions, www.morphyauctions.com

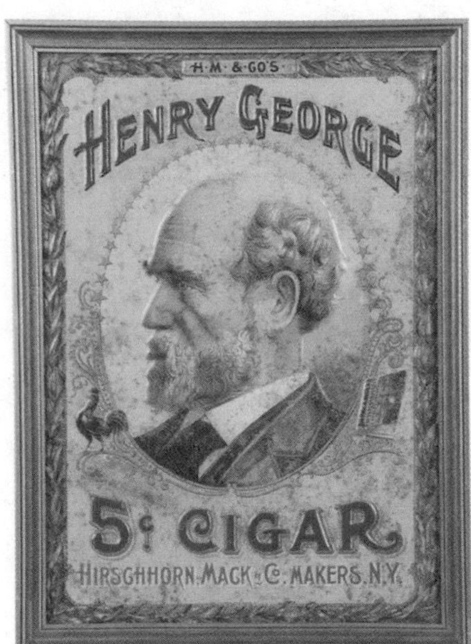

Henry George Cigar tin advertising sign by Tuscarora Advertising Co., embossed, framed without glass, good condition, 15-1/2" x 21-1/2" framed... **$580**

Courtesy of Morphy Auctions, www.morphyauctions.com

GE Fans flange sign, very good-plus condition, rubs and bubble wrap residue, 16-1/4" x 12". **$1,037**

Courtesy of Morphy Auctions, www.morphyauctions.com

Cooks Beer embossed cardboard sign, excellent-plus condition, few paint nicks, 13-1/2" x 10-3/4".. **$153**

Courtesy of Morphy Auctions, www.morphyauctions.com

Art Deco Curlee Clothes sign, hand-painted on tin, Lambertville, New Jersey, circa 1940, good condition, scratches and scuffs to surface, 48" x 96"... **$384**

Courtesy of Rago Arts and Auctions, www.ragoarts.com

Gillette die-cut tin sign, double-sided, good condition, one side with heavy rust and paint loss, other side with areas of oxidation and moderate rust on edges, 15" x 13-1/2"......................... **$580**

Courtesy of Morphy Auctions, www.morphyauctions.com

Cupid Ice Cream porcelain sign, good condition, overall wear and chips, 28" x 20"............ **$183**

Courtesy of Morphy Auctions, www.morphyauctions.com

Brooke Bond Tea porcelain sign, good condition, overall wear and chips, 40" x 60-1/2"............ **$183**

Courtesy of Morphy Auctions, www.morphyauctions.com

Rare hanging Gardner's bread sign in form of bagged loaf of bread with printed label reading "Gardner's Corn Top Enriched White Bread," with original chain hanger and hanger below reading "Bakery Department," very good condition, soiling and minor wear, 26" l. x 9" w., lower hanger 20" l. **$454**

Courtesy of Forsythes' Auctions, LLC, www.forsythesauctions.com

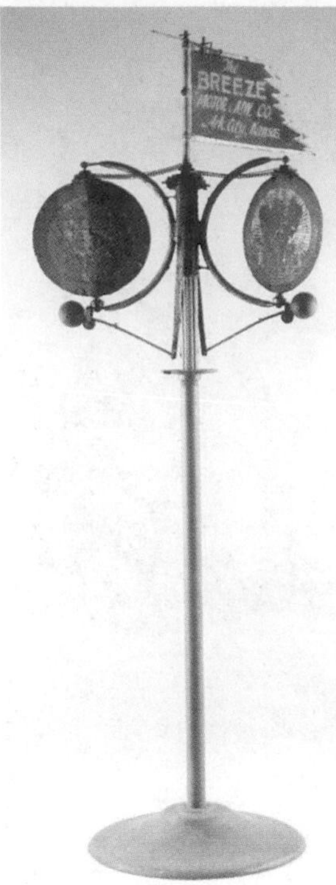

The Breeze Motor and Advertising Co. windmill sign, custom-made sample, all three signs turn manually, no motor present, good to very good condition, moderate wear to round signs with rust and paint loss, top sign with some rust and scrapes with some paint loss, 54" h......................... **$207**

Courtesy of Morphy Auctions, www.morphyauctions.com

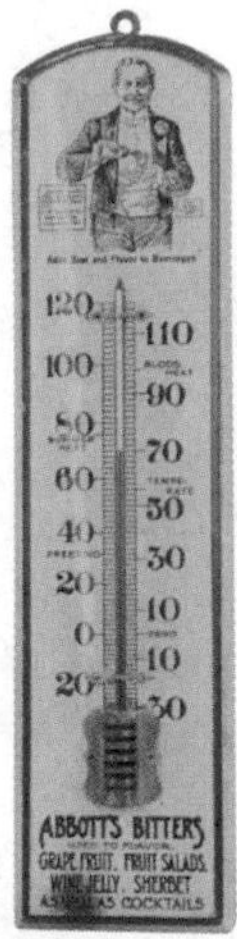

Abbott's Bitters wooden thermometer with working tube, very good condition, face with white stain running from top left edge to bottom of tube, minor stain on bottom left edge, edges and borders with nicks to paint and soiling, 21" l...................................... **$122**

Courtesy of Morphy Auctions, www.morphyauctions.com

Fountain Tobacco advertising tin, good condition, moderate wear with soiling and dings, 6-1/4" h. **$61**

Courtesy of Morphy Auctions, www.morphyauctions.com

The Boston Herald advertising tip tray, good condition, moderate oxidation, 3-1/2" dia. **$122**

Courtesy of Morphy Auctions, www.morphyauctions.com

Stegmaier Beer advertising tip tray, good condition, some dings and paint flecks, 6" x 4-1/2"............................... **$90**

Courtesy of Morphy Auctions, www.morphyauctions.com

Taka-Kola advertising tip tray, very good condition, mild edge wear with minor discoloration to field, 4" dia................... **$153**

Courtesy of Morphy Auctions, www.morphyauctions.com

top lot!

Buffalo Brewing Co. of Sacramento, California, glass sign, reverse-painted with textured silver foil-effect lettering, trademark buffalo galloping out of sunrise, horseshoe decorated with hops and grain, glass banded in copper-colored pressed tin and backed with wood, excellent condition, 19" dia..$29,280

COURTESY OF MORPHY AUCTIONS, WWW.MORPHYAUCTIONS.COM

Scarce Buddy L pressed steel private label Drewrys Extra Dry Beer truck, GMC-style cab with small chip on grill, excellent condition, 26" l...$630

Courtesy of Milestone Auctions, www.milestoneauctions.com

AMUSEMENTS

COLLECTIBLES THAT TICKLE our fancy, entertain us, and make us laugh are always winners. Among them are circus and amusement park memorabilia, magic and card tricks, parlor games, oddities, and all manner of good fun.

The 200th anniversary of Phineas Taylor Barnum's birth in 2010 triggered a renewed interest in collecting circus memorabilia. Collectibles range from broadsides announcing the circus is coming to town, to banners with brightly embellished visages of freakish sideshow acts, to windup tin toys depicting the lions, tigers, elephants, and clowns that no circus or sideshow would be complete without.

Magic is an ancient art with a rich history. The earliest reported magic trick – the ball and cups trick – began thousands of years ago, around 1700 B.C. Books on magic began to be published in the 16th century, and the first magic theater opened in London in 1873.

Collectors are interested in the history of magic as a performing art and the magicians who performed it. They collect books, posters, tokens, apparatus, printed ephemera (programs, tickets, broadsides, etc.) about magic as well as photos, letters, and other memorabilia about past and present performers.

Oddities fall into the "weird and wonderful" category of unusual items.

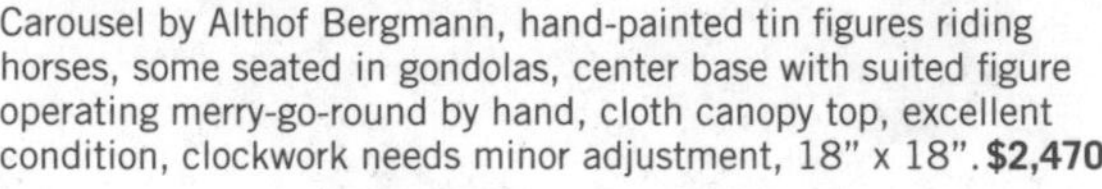

Carousel by Althof Bergmann, hand-painted tin figures riding horses, some seated in gondolas, center base with suited figure operating merry-go-round by hand, cloth canopy top, excellent condition, clockwork needs minor adjustment, 18" x 18". **$2,470**

Courtesy of Bertoia Auctions, www.bertoia.com

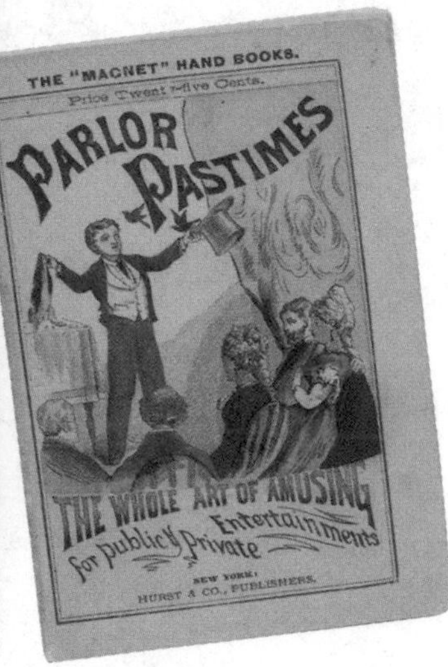

Raymond, Professor, *Parlor Pastimes – The Whole Art of Amusing for Public & Private Entertainments*, New York: Hurst & Co., 1875. Pictorial colored wraps, illustrations, diagrams, octavo, rebacked, minor wear around edges. $154

Courtesy of Potter & Potter Auctions, www.potterauctions.com

Rare early standing carousel goat, carved and painted by Charles I. D. Looff Co., Brooklyn, New York, circa 1895, full-bodied figure with raised forelegs and tasseled blanket, 56" h. x 67" w. x 11" d. on 66" brass pole with ball. **$6,000**

Courtesy of Phoebus Auction Gallery, www.phoebusauctions.com

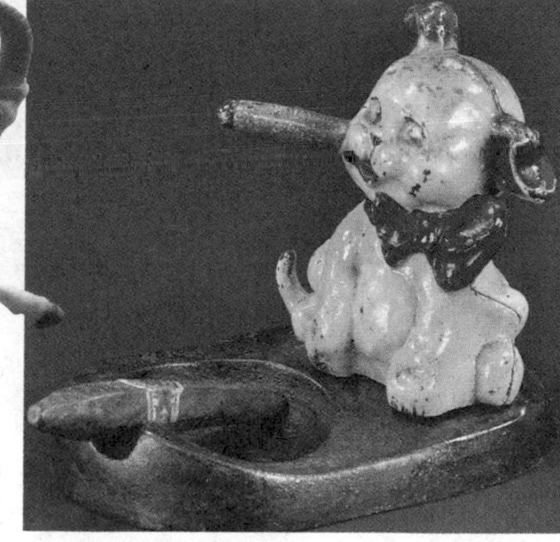

Cigar-smoking dog ashtray by Hubley, cast iron hand-painted white body with red bow, cast iron cigar resting in ashtray, excellent condition, 5-1/2" l. **$803**

Courtesy of Bertoia Auctions, www.bertoia.com

▶ Rabbit in top hat automaton by Roulette Decamp, circa early 20th century, when wound, music starts and rabbit slowly twists while emerging from top hat, chewing on carrot and occasionally raising his ears; excellent condition, 13-1/2" l. x 7-1/2" h. x 12-1/2" w. Unusual piece as rabbit is normally found in a cabbage or tree trunk. Often rabbit hair would fall into clockwork mechanism, causing sluggishness. **$3,050**

Courtesy of Morphy Auctions, morphyauctions.com

Hoffmann, Professor, *Drawing Room Amusements and Evening Party Entertainments*, London: George Routledge and Sons, 1879. Pictorial cloth stamped in gilt and black, illustrated, octavo, good condition, weak hinges. **$185**

Courtesy of Potter & Potter Auctions, www.potterauctions.com

Rabbit cart by Shimer, nickel-plated cast iron depiction of rabbit pulling cart with spoke wheels carrying smaller rabbit, excellent condition, 4-3/4" l. **$556**

Courtesy of Bertoia Auctions, www.bertoia.com

Imperial Shocker by Mills Novelty Co., circa 1902, tabletop electric shock machine with front castings of two female figures and roses, round dial with smiling female face reads, "Take a shock and look pleasant," one round-ended handle on each side allows operator to control how much electricity is released, unrestored excellent original condition, 23" x 16-1/2" x 12". $14,640

COURTESY OF MORPHY AUCTIONS, MORPHYAUCTIONS.COM

Dissected Map of the United States and Territories puzzle by J.H. Colton & Co., New York, 1865, lithographed map mounted on cardboard, lightly hand-colored, dissected into 30 pieces, with original color-lithographed two-part box, 11-3/4" x 13-1/2" assembled, box 5-1/2" x 6-3/4"................... **$584**

Courtesy of PBA Galleries, www.pbagalleries.com

Donald Duck amusement ride, fiberglass on wood base, electric but not coin operated, good condition, works, several cracks, 37" l. x 59" h. x 22" w...................................... **$363**

Courtesy of Richard Opfer Auctioneering, Inc., www.opferauction.com

RCA Victor Radio Floor Model 19k with walnut case, multi-band tube radio receiver with Magic Loop Antenna, input plug for television and records, serial No. 009958, excellent condition, 41" h. x 28" w. x 15" d. **$333**

Courtesy of Fontaine's Auction Gallery, www.fontainesauction.net

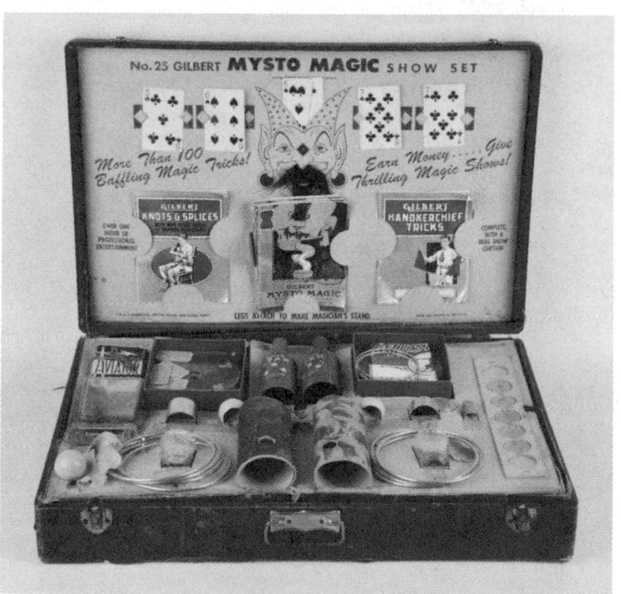

No. 25 Mysto Magic Show Set by A.C. Gilbert, original red pressboard box with insert, six different manuals showing various magic tricks, complete or near complete set, very good condition, tears and tape residue to box insert, 25" l................................. **$915**

Courtesy of Morphy Auctions, morphyauctions.com

10 Things You Didn't Know About **Bobbleheads**

Paul Bunyan, Canadian Mountie, Big Boy, Ben Casey, and another Paul Bunyan, excellent-plus condition, minor wear, largest 7-1/2" h. ....**$225 (excluding buyer's premium)**

Courtesy of Morphy Auctions, morphyauctions.com

1 Figurines with moving heads have many names. Some of those names include: bobbleheads, nodders, nodding heads, wobblers, and moving heads. Nodding figurine examples are made of composition, papier maché, porcelain, and plastic.

2 German nodders were made of ceramic and began production in the late 1700s/early 1800s. In the 20th century, commercialized bobblehead dolls were made of papier maché and then switched to the more durable ceramic.

3 A Russian short story published in 1842, titled "The Overcoat" (or "The Cloak") by Nicolai Gogol, describes the main character as having a neck "like the necks of those plaster cats which wag their heads, and are carried about upon the heads of scores of image sellers." (The short story can be read online at bit.ly/1RGJbVY.)

4 In 1960, Major League Baseball imported papier maché bobbleheads for each team to give away. Additional bobbleheads of specific players were made to commemorate the World Series. Those players were Roberto Clemente, Mickey Mantle, Roger Maris, and Willie Mays, although the "personalized" bobbleheads had the same faces as the generic team bobbleheads.

5 Bobbleheads reached the height of their popularity in the 1960s, but interest waned by the end of the 1970s. However, a limited Willie Mays giveaway by the San Francisco Giants on May 9, 1999, commemorating the 40th anniversary of Candlestick Park, is credited with breathing new life into bobblehead collecting.

6 If you can think of a subject, it is highly likely there is a bobblehead available. If you can't find one, there are many companies that make custom and personalized bobbleheads from photos (for less than $75). Here are a few options: www.bobblemaker.com; www.allbobbleheads.com; www.bobblemaker.com; www.bobbleheads.com.

7 In 2012, the TBS talk show "Conan" (teamcoco.com) produced one of the largest bobblehead dolls documented. Made primarily from high-density foam, the Conan O'Brien bobblehead stands 17 feet tall; O'Brien gifted the "bobble-statue" to the city of Chicago. After the Art Institute of Chicago rejected installation, the giant bobblehead found a home at Harold's Chicken Shack on Wabash Avenue. (View the "Conan" bobblehead installation video at https://youtu.be/I7UOV3sazQw.)

8 Antique Place, Hallandale, Florida, sold a German Shafer and Vater bisque figurine of two women with bobbleheads having tea and reading a book for $600 (excluding buyer's premium) in December 2015. The circa 1920 porcelain figurine, stamped "Made in Germany" on the bottom, measures 6" high.

9 Subscribers to the academic legal journal The Green Bag (http://www.greenbag.org) may receive bobbleheads of Supreme Court justices, although the editors "make no promises about when we will make them or who will get them." All prototypes of the Supreme Court Justice bobbleheads (and samples of all the production versions) are archived at the Lillian Goldman Law Library at the Yale Law School.

10 The National Bobblehead Hall of Fame and Museum opened in 2016 in Milwaukee.

– Compiled by Karen Knapstein

Sources: The Cardboard Connection (http://www.cardboardconnection.com); Bleacher Report (http://bleacherreport.com); www.bobbleheads.com; www.popculturespot.com; www.cbsnews.com; www.greenbag.org; Bobblehead Hall of Fame and Museum (http://www.bobbleheadhall.com).

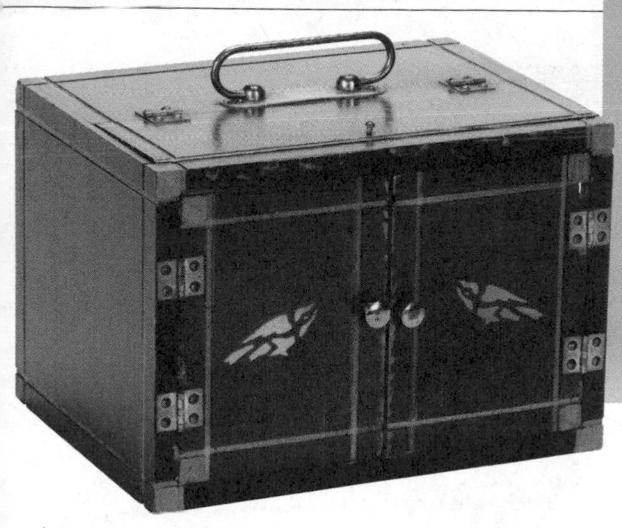

Scarce mahjong box by Sherms, Bridgeport, Connecticut, circa 1930, empty box from which great quantity of items, including framed picture, are magically produced, minor wear, 10" x 7" x 6-3/4"... **$277**

Courtesy of Potter & Potter Auctions, www.potterauctions.com

Cast aluminum clown novelty trash can cover by Game-Time, Litchfield, Michigan, good condition, original paint with significant wear, 26" h. x 24" dia.................................... **$214**

Courtesy of Morphy Auctions, morphyauctions.com

Percy the Penguin by Abbott's Magic Novelty Co., Colon, Michigan, circa 1948, wooden penguin figure dips his head into top hat to pick out selected card, lacquered in bright colors, with original instructions, precursor of Hamilton Card Duck, 14" high. **$215**

Courtesy of Potter & Potter Auctions, www.potterauctions.com

Simplified snake trick by Abbott's Magic Novelty Co., Colon, Michigan, circa 1955, imitation snake finds selected card by rising from woven basket, large wind-up model with original instructions, cards, duplicate snake, and oil can, basket woven on Potawatomi Indian reservation in southern Michigan, good working condition, basket 13" h... **$800**

Courtesy of Potter & Potter Auctions, www.potterauctions.com

Buffalo Bill's Wild West Sells Floto Circus poster, glued to board, moderate edge wear and chipping, small stains, discoloring, varnish applied overall, good condition, 35" x 22"........................... **$360**

Courtesy of Morphy Auctions, morphyauctions.com

Seils-Sterling Big 4 Ring Circus poster of circus owners with numerous lions and tigers surrounding them, framed, very good condition, 42" x 28". **$150**

Courtesy of Morphy Auctions, morphyauctions.com

Barnum & Bailey circus drum, one skin with Barnum & Bailey name with tiger, very good condition, 28-1/4" h.............**$1,140**

Courtesy of Morphy Auctions, morphyauctions.com

▲ Ringling Bros. and Barnum & Bailey circus poster, excellent condition, 42" x 28-1/2". **$90**

Courtesy of Morphy Auctions, morphyauctions.com

Crandall's Happy Circus cage wagon, wood with lithographed paper covering sliding door that reveals cage door with bars, rooftop and interior flooring grooved for placement of signs and animals, 16-3/4" l.........**$680**

Courtesy of Bertoia Auctions, www.bertoia.com

Framed stone lithographed poster advertising appearance at Alcazar d' Ete of Emma and Frank de Burgh, popular turn-of-century husband and wife attractions, 1890s, 28-1/2" w. x 37" h.......................... **$1,364**

Courtesy of Noel Barrett Antiques & Auctions, www.noelbarrett.com

Early CDV albumen photograph of Annie Oakley, circa 1880s, taken in front of circus tent or Wild West show tent, no identification on image except blue stamp on verso "Annie Oakley," 4-3/4" x 2-3/4"......**$2,200**

Courtesy of Heritage Auctions, ha.com

"Freaks" publicity still, MGM, 1932, vintage black and white, double weight, glossy 8" x 10"............**$750**

Courtesy of Heritage Auctions, ha.com

Buffalo Bill (Himself) and 101 Ranch Wild West Combined program, 1916, 28 pages of Wild West performers, cowboys, Indians, trick shooters, etc., 7-1/4" x 9-3/4"... **$325**

Courtesy of Heritage Auctions, ha.com

Schoenhut circus clowns, cloth-dressed painted wood figures, each in different original outfit, 8" h..........**$372**

Courtesy of Noel Barrett Antiques & Auctions, www.noelbarrett.com

ASIAN ART & ARTIFACTS

ASIAN ART (aka Eastern art) is highly prized by collectors. They are attracted by its fine workmanship and exquisite attention to detail, plus the undeniable lure of the exotic.

Often lumped under the generic header "Oriental," Asian art actually embraces a wide variety of cultures. Among the many countries falling under the Asian/Eastern art umbrella: Bali, Bhutan, Cambodia, China, India, Indonesia, Japan, Korea, Laos, Thailand, Tibet, Vietnam, and the Pacific Islands. Also in the mix: art forms indigenous to the native cultures of Australia and New Zealand, and works of art celebrating the traditions of such Eastern-based religions as Buddhism and Hinduism.

The influence of Eastern art on Western art is strong. As Western artisans absorbed the cultural traditions of the East, stylistic similarities crept into their work, whether subconsciously or deliberately. (The soft matte glazes popularized by Van Briggle Pottery, for example, resulted from founder Artus Van Briggle's ongoing quest to replicate the "dead" glazes of the Chinese Ming Dynasty.)

Chinese porcelain was one of the first representations of Asian art to entice buyers in the United States; export of the ware began in the 1780s.

Japanese porcelain, originally billed as Nippon, began to make its way to U.S. shores near the end of the 19th century. Early Chinese porcelain was often distinguished by a liberal use of blue and white; Japanese porcelain, by a similar reliance on floral and landscape motifs. Consumers found the products of both countries desirable, not only because of their delicacy, but also because pieces of comparable quality were not yet available domestically.

Porcelain was not the only outlet for Eastern creativity. Among the many other materials utilized: ivory, jade, bone, hardstone, marble, bronze, brass, gold, silver, wood, and fabric (primarily silk). Decorative treatments ranged from cloisonné (enamel sections in a pattern of metal strips) to intricate hand carving to the elaborate use of embroidery, gilt, and lacquer.

Asian art in any form offers a unique blend of the decorative and the functional. The richness of the materials and treatments utilized transforms even everyday objects into dazzling works of art. Among myriad items receiving this Cinderella treatment: bowls, vases, planters, chess sets, snuff bottles, rugs, robes, tapestries, tables, trays, jars, screens, incense burners, cabinets, and tea caddies. Even a simple item such as an oil lamp could be reborn through imaginative artistry: A Chinese version from the 1920s, its exterior worked in cloisonné, emerged as a colorful, ferocious dragon.

This multitude of products makes Asian art an ideal cross-collectible. Some may be interested only in the output of a specific country or region. Others may be drawn to a specific type of collectible (kimonos, snuff boxes, depictions of Buddha). There will even be those attracted solely to pieces created from a specific material, such as jade, ivory, or porcelain. Aficionados of any of these categories have a lifetime of collecting pleasure in store.

The timeline of Asian art is a long one, with value often determined by antiquity. Due to age and rarity, minor flaws (jade nicks, porcelain cracks, and chips) are not generally a detriment to purchase. Any restoration should only be done by a professional, and only after careful analysis as to whether or not restoration will affect value.

Asian art continues to be produced and imported today at an overwhelming rate (and often of "souvenir-only" quality). Collectors seeking museum-quality pieces are strongly advised to purchase only from reputable dealers, and to insist on proof of provenance.

Chinese hardwood horseshoe armchairs, late 19th century, heavy wear throughout indicative of age and use, 46" h. x 25-1/4" w. x 22" d....... **$250**

Courtesy of Heritage Auctions, ha.com

Wing Fat Chinese Export silver jardinière, Canton and Hong Kong, circa 1890, marked "HK," "WF," and two-character mark, supported by four cast dragons, each panel with different chased repoussé motif including battling dragons, bamboo forest, chrysanthemum blossoms, and landscape scene with figures, bottom plate silver-plated with loss of plating, surface scratches and wear commensurate with age and indicative of use, 4" x 8" x 6-1/4", 20.41 troy oz. including non-silver material. **$3,000**

Courtesy of Heritage Auctions, ha.com

Chinese Han Dynasty glazed earthenware figural temple offering stand, circa 220 AD, in temple form with pitched and channeled roof, rectangular body with two windows, exterior offering basket, on figural animal feet to front, wear commensurate with age, crazing, missing roof finials, chipping to feet, 21-3/4" h. x 20-1/2" w....................... **$1,875**

Courtesy of Heritage Auctions, ha.com

Chinese Export portrait porcelain plate depicting Martin Luther, after Frans Brun, circa 1750, grisaille plate with Luther in upper cartouche flanked by figural putti heads, lower cartouche depicting Christ and disciples, gilt tracery to rim, design derived from engraving by Brun published in Dutch Lutheran bible, good condition, wear to gilt, 9" dia. **$1,750**

Courtesy of Heritage Auctions, ha.com

Pair of Chinese Rose Medallion porcelain vases, 19th century, with everted rims, tapered necks, and elongated bodies, gilt figurative handles and relief to necks, painted panels of court, flower, and avian scenes to bodies, wear to gilt and paint, hairline crack to vase at base extending to underside, hairline crack under rim, wear commensurate with age, 23-1/2" h. **$1,250**

Courtesy of Heritage Auctions, ha.com

Pair of large Chinese patinated bronze imperial foo lions, 19th century, on raised stylized pedestals, lions sitting, resting paws on cloth balls, wearing ornate tasseled collars, open mouth snarls, and textured manes, patina to copper, wear commensurate with age, 21" h. x 11-1/2" w. x 18" d... **$938**

Courtesy of Heritage Auctions, ha.com

Miniature chinoiserie fitted cabinet, 19th century, two-door cabinet with painted countryside scenes to exterior case, five-drawer interior with bone and clay handles, houses and pagodas painted on drawer fronts, term feet, two drawer handles replaced, wear to paint, wear commensurate with age, 13" h. x 12" w. x 7" d. **$400**

Courtesy of Heritage Auctions, ha.com

Pair of Chinese hardwood with mother-of-pearl inlaid tabourets, late 19th century, missing some inlay to seats, 17-1/2" h., 13" dia.... **$325**

Courtesy of Heritage Auctions, ha.com

Small Chinese Export tobacco leaf pattern porcelain covered tureen, late 18th century, no mark to underside, good condition, 4-1/4" h. x 7-1/4" w. x 4-1/2" d.................. **$1,250**

Courtesy of Heritage Auctions, ha.com

Gray-painted Chinese Han Dynasty pottery cocoon jar, 1st-2nd century, decorated with everted rim and base, body with bands of decoration and scrolling throughout, wear commensurate with age, 9-3/4" h. **$1,000**

Courtesy of Heritage Auctions, ha.com

Carved Peking glass (overlay carved glass) covered ginger jar on splayed decorated foot, 18th century, semi-opaque red over opaque white ground, fisherman hooking carp, blossoming tree, willow tree, and oxen rider as part of relief decoration, reign mark of Qianlong Period incised into base and factory or other mark in relief on body, excellent condition, 3-1/2" h. x 3" w. x 2" dia................................ **$747**

Courtesy of Louis J. Dianni, LLC Antiques Auctions, louisjdianni.com

Pair of Japanese Meiji Period patinated bronze vases and censor, late 19th century, good condition, repair to figural dragon handle, handle loose, lacquering, damage to finial talon, intermittent scratching, 19-1/2" h. **$1,188**

Courtesy of Heritage Auctions, ha.com

Large Japanese Meiji Period bronze vase, 19th century, with flared neck depicting winged animal hybrids, body with cranes to obverse and predatory bird to reverse, sides decorated heavily in foliate motif, to reticulated avian base, on wooden stand, wear commensurate with age, 26-1/2" h. **$875**

Courtesy of Heritage Auctions, ha.com

Japanese lacquered wood and gilt bronze tray, Meiji Period, quatrefoil-form, depicting plum blossoms in vase, with gilt bronze gadrooned border, on four scroll and foliate feet, craquelure throughout tray, rubbing of gilt finish, surface wear commensurate with age, 1-1/4" x 13-1/4" x 9-3/4"...$413

Courtesy of Heritage Auctions, ha.com

Japanese bronze Meji Period teapot with dragons in relief, good condition, 11" h. **$244**

Courtesy of Bill Hood & Sons Art & Antiques Auctions, www.hoodauction.com

Antique Japanese Kutani hand-painted enameled porcelain charger with scene of warriors on horseback ambushing village in Doucai-colored style, red and gold tones to floral and geometric patterns in border, verso of phoenix birds with lotus blossoms in blue and white, bottom with blue six-character calligraphy Ming Chenghua reign mark, but likely made in Meji Period, 19th century, bottom with four pontil marks, with fitted wooden display stand, charger 24-3/8" dia., 7.35 kg. **$248**

Courtesy of Elite Decorative Arts, www.eliteauction.com

Antique Japanese hand-crafted wooden handled masu rice box mounted to wooden base, circa late Edo to Meiji Period, 19th century, 25" h. x 29" l. x 21" d. **$155**

Courtesy of Elite Decorative Arts, www.eliteauction.com

Japanese Imari porcelain umbrella/stick stand, circa 1890, with indented full-length grooves, indigo blue border at top and base, sides decorated in classical Imari colors of blue and reddish-brown and gold, with floral and foliate images and birds in tree, unmarked, excellent condition, 23" h., 8-3/4" dia. **$1,321**

Courtesy of Tradewinds Antiques & Auctions, www.tradewindsantiques.com

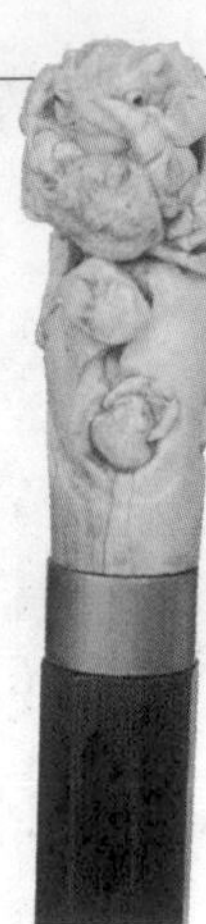

Japanese ivory cane of toads and crab, circa 1885, large toad with black jet eyes grappling with crab, second toad tries to assist large one, third toad in protective niche, 2/3" silver collar on octo-carved ebonized walnut shaft that terminates with 2-1/3" white metal and iron ferrule, very good condition with worn finish on shaft from usage, slight age bend, imported handle, 35-1/8" l. overall, ivory handle 3-1/4" h. x 1-1/4" w. **$908**

Courtesy of Tradewinds Antiques & Auctions, www.tradewindsantiques.com

Korean decorated stoneware jar, probably 18th/19th century, body with double blue ring at top over two sprays of red leaves, chips and roughness at rim and base ring, body with three star cracks and some glaze anomalies and stains, 10". **$248**

Courtesy of Brunk Auctions, www.brunkauctions.com

Bronze statue of Thai Buddha, circa 1700-1750, Buddha seated, eyes closed, 6-1/2" x 4-1/4" x 3", 820 g. **$688**

Courtesy of Material Culture, www.materialculture.com

Bronze oil lamp (sukunda), Nepal, 19th century, detailed presentation, 10-3/4" x 5-3/4" x 10-1/2". **$1,750**

Courtesy of Material Culture, www.materialculture.com

Copper repoussé ewer, Nepal, 19th century, fish/snake pattern, 8-1/4" x 6-1/2" x 8", 530 g. **$313**

Courtesy of Material Culture, www.materialculture.com

Rare bronze Tibetan teapot, circa 1750, dragon handle/ spout, with chain, 11" x 6-1/2" x 9", 1945 g. **$813**

Courtesy of Material Culture, www.materialculture.com

Two Indian village dancing bells for legs, circa 1800, bronze with flower design, with balls inside to create sound, larger bell 9" x 5-1/2" x 1-1/2", total weight 1435 g. **$188**

Courtesy of Material Culture, www.materialculture.com

top lot!

Chinese archaic bronze ritual wine vessel, trumpet-form neck above mid-section and base comprising geometrical designs and two cruciform apertures, inscription underneath, similar to Shang Dynasty examples, green patina, no evidence of damage or repair, 11-1/4" h., 6-1/8" dia. at upper rim. Provenance: From the collection of Mrs. G. G. Scranton, friend and patroness of Mrs. Dagny Carter, notable scholar of Chinese culture and art and author of three books on Chinese art and antiquities. The piece was purchased by Scranton subsequent to its discovery by Carter in 1931. The current owner's grandmother purchased all of Carter's art/artifact collection to enable Carter to leave China during the period of Japanese incursion (1937-1939) prior to World War II. $12,300

COURTESY OF DUMOUCHELLES,
WWW.DUMOUCHELLES.COM

Asiatic carved coco de mer, late 19th century, decorated with carved and repeating Asiatic motif raised on gilt paw feet, most likely originating from India (coco de mer is fruit of palm tree from Seychelles, famed as being largest seed in natural world and for its general similarity to female torso), gilt feet probable later additions, wear commensurate with age, 10" h. **$875**

Courtesy of Heritage Auctions, ha.com

Fine bronze shiva bowl, circa 1800, India, surrounded by faces and Ganesh forms and with Nandi bulls circling rim, 3-3/4" x 5" x 5", 1460 g. **$469**

Courtesy of Material Culture, www.materialculture.com

Rare bronze Radha statue, India, circa 1700-1750, patina, eight leaves, instrument in hand, hair in tight round bun, large breast, 7-1/4" h., 780 g. **$2,000**

Courtesy of Material Culture, www.materialculture.com

AUTOGRAPHS

IN *THE MEANING AND BEAUTY OF AUTOGRAPHS*, first published in 1935 and translated from the German by David H. Lowenherz of Lion Heart Autographs, Inc. in 1995, Stefan Zweig explained that to love a manuscript, we must first love the human being "whose characteristics are immortalized in them." When we do, then "a single page with a few lines can contain the highest expression of human happiness, and...the expression of deepest human sadness. To those who have eyes to look at such pages correctly, eyes not only in the head, but also in the soul, they will not receive less of an impression from these plain signs than from the obvious beauty of pictures and books."

John M. Reznikoff, founder and president of University Archives, has been a leading dealer and authority on historical letters and artifacts for more than 35 years years. He described the market for autographs as "very strong on many fronts."

Reznikoff suspects that Civil War items peaked after Ken Burns' series but that Revolutionary War documents, included those by signers of the Declaration of Independence and the Constitution, are still undervalued and can be purchased for under $500. Pop culture has come into its own. Reznikoff anticipates continued growth in memorabilia that includes music, television, movies, and sports. Babe Ruth, Lou Gehrig, and Ty Cobb are still good investments, but Reznikoff warns that authentication is much more of a concern in sports than in any other field.

The Internet allows for a lot of disinformation and this is a significant issue with autographs. There are two widely accepted authentication services: Professional Sports Authenticator (PSA/DNA) and James Spence Authentication (JSA). A dealer's reliability can be evaluated by seeing whether he is a member of one or more of the major organizations in the field: the Antique Booksellers Association of America, UACC Registered Dealers Program, and the National Professional Autograph Dealers Association (NPADA), which Reznikoff founded.

There is an additional caveat to remember and it is true for all collectibles: rarity. The value of an autograph is often determined less by the prominence of the signer than by the number of autographs he signed.

— Zac Bissonnette

Marilyn Monroe-signed black and white photograph, circa 1955, original print with matte finish, enlarged snapshot of star, signed in blue fountain pen ink on right side, from personal collection of James Collins, one of the "Monroe Six" – group of young children who followed Monroe around New York City so often that she knew their names.
....**$5,750**

Courtesy of Heritage Auctions, www.ha.com

The Chestnuts
Guildford
Jan. 4. 1876.

My dear Holiday,
I am delighted with these two pictures. What you are destined to come to at last I can't tell — but you seem to me to increase in powers of comic drawing at a most alarming rate. These pictures seem to me to have ten times as much fun in them as the scene on board ship, or the chase, in both of which the faces are so serious & earnest that the pictures are more likely

◄ ▼ Original pen and ink drawing by Lewis Carroll in illustration of *The Hunting of the Snark* with four-page autographed letter, dated Jan. 4, 1876, from him to book's illustrator, Henry Holiday, critiquing his designs, bound into copy of book, Macmillan & Co., London. **$24,600**

Courtesy of PBA Galleries, www.pbagalleries.com

"Golden Years" LP (RCA AFL 1-4792, 1983) signed by David Bowie in blue felt-tip pen while leaving The Four Seasons in Irving, Texas, on Oct. 13, 1995, on his way to Starplex Amphitheatre. **$2,250**

Courtesy of Heritage Auctions, www.ha.com

Poker-sized playing card signed by Harry Houdini, underlined "H. Houdini" with "01/1926" date, near fine condition, 2-1/4" h. x 3-1/2" w. **$2,337**

Courtesy of Potter & Potter Auctions, www.potterauctions.com

Michael Jordan hand-signed NBA Chicago Bulls basketball jersey. **$960**

Courtesy of J. Sugarman Auction Corp., www.jaysugarman.com

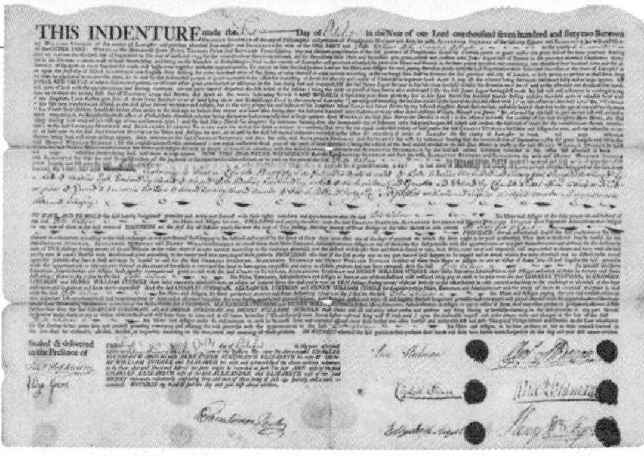

Signed sepia photograph of British Prime Minister Winston Churchill, circa 1940s, photographed by Harris and Ewing of Washington, signed "Winston S. Churchill" to lower portion of image, some light minor age wear to edges... **$3,940**

Courtesy of International Autograph Auctions, www.autographauctions.co.uk

Sealed & delivered in the Prefence of

Fra! Hopkinson

Eliza Grame

◄▲ Uncommon Colonial-era land deed for lot in new town of Manheim, Pennsylvania, issued Oct. 1, 1762, and signed "Fra. Hopkinson" by Francis Hopkinson, signer of the Declaration of Independence, among others, with six red wax seals, some light folds, and minimal intersection wear. **$2,214**

Courtesy of Early American History Auctions, www.earlyamerican.com

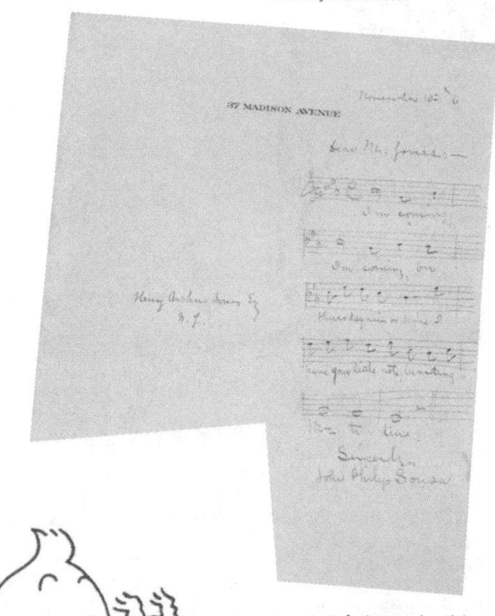

37 MADISON AVENUE

Sincerely,
John Philip Sousa

Framed photo of Thomas Edison, signed "To A J Desnoyer" by Edison, copyright Walter Scott Shinn, N.Y., some discoloration from moisture, 7-1/4" w. x 10" h. **$1,770**

Courtesy of Epic Auctions & Estate Sales, www.epicauctionsandestatesales.com

▲ Autograph with musical notes and lyrics to "Henry Arthur Jones Esq." from John Philips Sousa, on stationary marked "37 Madison Avenue" and dated "November 10th '6" (1906)............ **$1,045**

Courtesy of Alex Cooper Auctioneers, www.alexcooper.com

► Printed sketches of Tintin and Milou by George Prosper Remi, Belgian cartoonist who created "The Adventures of Tintin" series of comics, signed "Hergé" in blue ink at base of card. **$1,226**

Courtesy of International Autograph Auctions, www.autographauctions.co.uk

◀ Anton-Brenton model #AB-05 fiddle autographed by all members of country band Alabama, in black Sharpie ink on instrument's glossy finish, circa 1996, fine condition.................................... **$750**

Courtesy of Heritage Auctions, www.ha.com

Signed and inscribed postcard photograph of three brothers of famous Italian-French circus performing family The Fratellinis, with brothers in full clown costumes, signed in blue fountain pen ink near their printed names Alberto, Francois, and Paola, some age wear and slight damage to upper corners. **$478**

Courtesy of International Autograph Auctions, www.autographauctions.co.uk

▲ Photograph of playwright Tennessee Williams and actress Diana Barrymore, signed by Williams in blue ink in clear image of photo, "The roof is hot but the cats are cool! Love 10," some surface creasing to image, 8" x 10". **$773**

Courtesy of International Autograph Auctions, www.autographauctions.co.uk

American First Day Cover postmarked at Washington, D.C., on Nov. 4, 1968, signed by five noted artists of 20th century in blue or black ink: Norman Rockwell, Jamie Wyeth, Henriette Wyeth, Peter Hurd, and Jasper Johns.. **$295**

Courtesy of International Autograph Auctions, www.autographauctions.co.uk

▶ Partial autographed letter regarding adventures of Bonet brothers, natives of France, on African island of Madagascar, early 19th century, addressed to Francis Robinson, Strand, London............................. **$523**

Courtesy of PBA Galleries, www.pbagalleries.com

top lot!

World Champion 1927 New York Yankees team-signed baseball, signatures of eighteen members of squad preserved beneath vintage coating of shellac on ONL (Heydler) sphere, strong indication that ball was autographed during opening two games at Forbes Field in Pittsburgh; Ruth's 9/10 black fountain pen side panel signature underscored by his handwritten notation, "World Series 1927," sharing space with a single other signer, rare and important Miller Huggins, who died two years later; with five more Hall of Famers' signatures: Gehrig, Lazzeri, Pennock, Combs, and Hoyt, and other notables: Urban Shocker, Collins, Dugan, Meusel, Moore, and Ruether; with letter of examination from PSA/DNA, who assess average autograph quality as 7/10 and baseball itself as 4/10, adding extra half-point for aesthetics, for EX-MT 6 final grade. $65,725

"We won the World Series before it even got started," Babe Ruth explained years after one of the greatest baseball seasons in the history of the sport. "The Pirates were the other club, and the first two games were scheduled for Forbes Field. Naturally we showed up a day early and worked out in the strange park, and we won the Series during that workout. We really put on a show. Lou and I banged ball after ball into the right field stands, and I finally knocked one out of the park in right center. Bob Meusel and Tony Lazzeri kept hammering balls into the left field seats. One by one, the Pirates got up and left the park. Some of them were shaking their heads when we last saw them."

COURTESY OF HERITAGE AUCTIONS, HA.COM

Photograph of North American X-15 hypersonic rocket-powered aircraft in flight signed by astronaut Neil Armstrong in turquoise ink to clear area of image, circa 1960s, 9-1/2" w. x 7-1/2" h. Armstrong was one of 12 test pilots to fly the X-15 .... **$853**

Courtesy of International Autograph Auctions, www.autographauctions.co.uk

Official sheet of stamps issued by Israeli government with Tribes of Israel stained glass window design created by artist Marc Chagall for synagogue of Hebrew University's Hadassah Medical Centre in Jerusalem, signed by Chagall in blue ink along top margin and dated 1977... **$683**

Courtesy of International Autograph Auctions, www.autographauctions.co.uk

"Johnny Cash at San Quentin" LP signed by Cash in blue felt-tip pen at Dallas-area hotel sometime between 1986 and 1999............. **$875**

Courtesy of Heritage Auctions, www.ha.com

Full roll of Beatles wallpaper manufactured in 1964 by British wallpaper company Crown Wallcoverings, with images of each band member and first name autographs printed around posed images. **$500**

Courtesy of Heritage Auctions, www.ha.com

BANKS

MOST COLLECTIBLE BANKS were designed for one purpose: to encourage children to save money. How well the bank accomplished this task makes all the difference in making it collectible by later generations.

Manufactured from the late 1800s to the mid-1900s, mechanical, still, and register banks (which indicate the value of the coins deposited) are marvels of ingenuity made of tin, lead, or cast iron. Although banks come in all makes and functions, the most desirable banks employ a novelty or mechanical action when a coin is placed inside. Banks are sought after because they so efficiently represent the popular culture at the time they were made. This is evident in the wartime register banks sporting tin lithographic decorations of superheroes or animation characters or the cast iron figures that propagated racial stereotypes common from 1880 to 1930. Many early cast iron bank models have been reproduced during the years, especially in the 1950s and 1960s. A key indicator of a reproduction is fresh, glossy paint or dull details in the casting.

According to 10 years of sales data on LiveAuctioneers.com, most mechanical banks sell at auction for between $500 and $1,000. Morphy Auctions is the world leader in selling mechanical banks.

"There are a dozen or so collections that I know of that would bring over $1 million," said Dan Morphy, owner and founder of Morphy Auctions. "There are dozens of other bank collections that would fall in the six figure ranges."

Morphy says condition – like all other categories of collecting – is king. "Banks in top condition seem to be the trend these days," he said.

So, on the basis of affordability, now is the time to start a collection. "I always tell new collectors that they should buy what they like," Morphy said. "Even if you pay a little more than you should for a bank, the value in the enjoyment of owning it will more than offset the high price one may pay."

A top on Morphy's list to offer at auction is a Darkey & the Watermelon mechanical bank. Otherwise known as the Football Bank, it was designed and patented by Charles A. Bailey on June 26, 1888. Known as the leader in mechanical bank design, Bailey's Darkey & the Watermelon bank incorporated all of his imagination and design talents: When the right leg

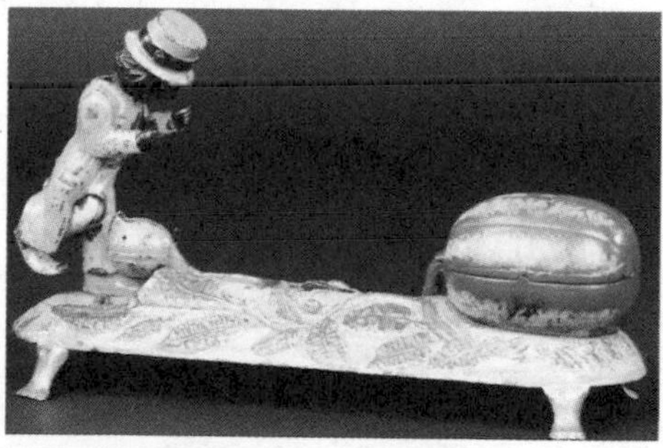

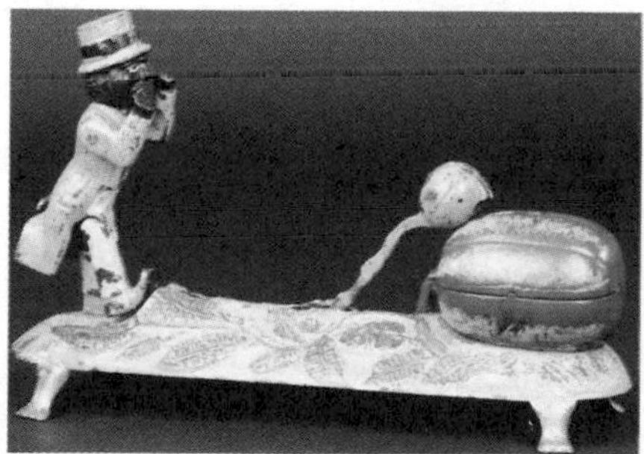

Darkey & the Watermelon mechanical bank by J. & E. Stevens Co., designed by Charles A. Bailey and patented in 1888, one of reportedly four known examples, sold for $225,000 (plus buyer's premium) in 2015 by Bertoia Auctions. The figure kicks a small watermelon into a larger one for coin deposit. Provenance: Wally Tudor, F. H. Griffith, Leon Perelman and Stan Sax Collections of a figure is pulled back into position, a coin is then placed in a small football; a lever in the figure's coattails is pressed and the football with coin is kicked over into a large watermelon. Only four of these banks are known to exist.

"That would be my dream bank," Morphy said, "in that I would also want to buy it!"

Like their predecessors crafted nearly 150 years ago, contemporary banks blur the line between tool and toy. Some modern banks that may make interesting collectibles in the future include digital register banks that tabulate coin and paper money deposits or those licensed by famous designers. But beware – antique banks are still being reproduced and can be found very cheaply at lesser-quality flea markets or sold online.

For more information on banks, see *The Official Price Guide to Mechanical Banks* by Dan Morphy, 2007, morphyauctions.com.

Always Did 'Spise a Mule mechanical bank, cast iron, in original box, original yellow base variation, J. & E. Stevens Co., excellent-plus to near mint working condition, tail missing from mule, 10" l. **$3,500**

Courtesy of Morphy Auctions, morphyauctions.com

Trick Pony mechanical bank, Shepard Hardware Co., excellent working condition, 7-1/2" l. **$2,196**

Courtesy of Morphy Auctions, morphyauctions.com

Elephant mechanical bank, cast iron, Hubley Manufacturing Co., excellent working condition, 5-1/2" h. **$122**

Courtesy of Morphy Auctions, morphyauctions.com

Uncle Sam mechanical bank, Shepard Hardware Co., excellent-plus working condition, 11-1/2" h. **$1,342**

Courtesy of Morphy Auctions, morphyauctions.com

top lot!

Panorama mechanical bank, J. & E. Stevens Co., designed by James D. Butter, MA, patented 1876, revolving picture roll at window changes after each coin deposit, excellent condition. $8,645

COURTESY OF BERTOIA AUCTIONS, WWW.BERTOIAAUCTIONS.COM

▲ Tank Savings Bank with wheels, cast iron still bank, Ferro Steel Corp., circa 1919. **$1,112**

Courtesy of Bertoia Auctions, www.bertoiaauctions.com

▶ Rooster mechanical bank, Kyser & Rex Co., circa 1880s, excellent condition; set coin in slot in rooster's tail, move lever downward, rooster moves head in crowing motion as coin falls into bank. **$803**

Courtesy of Bertoia Auctions, www.bertoiaauctions.com

Andy Gump still bank, cast iron, Arcade Manufacturing Co., all original, excellent-plus condition, 4-1/2" h. **$610**

Courtesy of Morphy Auctions, morphyauctions.com

10 Things You Didn't Know About **Banks**

Atlas Holding the World bank, Germany, circa 1915, scarce still bank in tin and lead, painted in silver overall, of god Atlas holding world money box on his back, key lock clasp, 5" h.... **$550**

Courtesy Bertoia Auctions, www.bertoiaauctions.com

1 Reportedly one of only three known examples, the Preacher in the Pulpit mechanical bank, manufactured by J. & E. Stevens Co., circa 1876, set a record when it sold for $263,550 (with buyer's premium) during an auction offered by Bertoia Auctions in November 2014.

2 The two types of banks are mechanical and still, and within those two groups are several styles.

3 It may be hard to believe, but archeological discoveries reveal that mechanical banks were in use in ancient Greece and Rome.

4 One of the best known examples of the late 19th century, The Blind Man and His Dog mechanical bank, designed by William H. Lotz and manufactured by J. & E. Stevens Co., sold for $49,200 (with buyer's premium) at a February 2014 auction presented by Morphy Auctions.

5 Mechanical bank collectors are in good company, as the Mechanical Bank Collectors of America (www.mechanicalbanks.org) demonstrates. The organization was founded in 1958 and its members include people from across the United States and in international locales as well.

6 If still banks are your thing, don't fret, there is also an international group of collectors who share your fondness for still banks: Still Bank Collectors Club of America (www.stillbankclub.com).

7 The Max Berry Collection, one of the most esteemed collections of mechanical and still banks ever amassed, realized more than $6 million (including buyer's premium) in a series of two auctions presented by Bertoia Auctions in 2014 and 2015.

Blind Man and Dog cast iron mechanical bank, (4460-A), yellow background, J. & E. Stevens Co., designed by William H. Lotz, patented Feb. 19, 1878, 6-3/4" l. **$49,200**

Courtesy of Morphy Auctions, morphyauctions.com

Preacher in the Pulpit mechanical bank, J. & E. Stevens Co., circa 1876, cast iron rarity, reportedly only three known examples; preacher standing at red-painted pulpit holds plate for coin placement, and as coin slides into bank, his head and arms lower and return to original pose; excellent condition. **$263,550**

Courtesy Bertoia Auctions, www.bertoiaauctions.com

Sources: http://www.virginiacaputo.com/Files/banks.html, Antique Trader *Antiques & Collectibles 2016 Price Guide*, and AntiqueTrader.com, LiveAuctioneers.com

8 Banks made in Germany, England, and the United States, between 1867 and 1928, are the big draw among seasoned collectors. During that time period, U.S. maker J. & E. Stevens Co. laid claim to producing the vast majority of cast iron mechanical banks.

9 Paint on a bank can reveal details of its past, including how old it is or isn't, and if all its parts are original. Compare paint shade and texture in multiple areas of a bank, and if it's similar across the board that's a good thing, but any differences should prompt further inspection.

10 Morphy Auctions, a longtime leader among firms bringing banks to auction, has presented more than 6,200 banks in the past 12-plus years.

– Compiled by Antoinette Rahn

Ives Palace still bank, circa 1885, crisp casting details, 7-1/2" x 8". **$2,259**

Courtesy of Bertoia Auctions, www.bertoiaauctions.com

Roller Skating cast iron mechanical bank, Kyser & Rex, near mint condition, 9" l..................... **$88,800**

Courtesy of Morphy Auctions, morphyauctions.com

Four Tower still bank, japanned finish, J. & E. Stevens Co., "BANK" on front, very good condition, 5-2/3" h....................................... **$155**

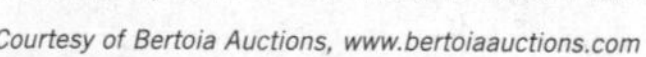

Courtesy of Bertoia Auctions, www.bertoiaauctions.com

Chimpanzee mechanical bank, lead, France, circa 1895, coin slot in back, weight of coin causes jaw to move, missing base plate........................... **$155**

Courtesy of Bertoia Auctions, www.bertoiaauctions.com

Punch & Judy still bank, tin, England, circa 1950, excellent condition, 4-1/4" h. **$247**

Courtesy of Bertoia Auctions, www.bertoiaauctions.com

Rutherford B. Hayes mechanical bank, place coin on Hayes' hand, he drops it into clear glass globe ballot box with paper ballot slips, weight of coin causes it to fall through slips and get funneled into drawer in base, pull knob and drawer slides open, restored, 6-3/4" x 4-1/2". **$6,250**

Courtesy of Heritage Auctions, ha.com

Eagle and eagletts mechanical bank, cast iron, American, "Pat. Jan 23 / 1883" on underside, wear to painted surface, 6-1/4" h.................... **$615**

Courtesy of Cowan's Auctions, www.cowanauctions.com

Plantation Darkey Savings Bank, American, Weeden's Mfg. Co., circa 1888, designed as tin home with coin-activated dancer and strumming banjo player, paper instructions on back, key not present, paint loss and scratches, 5-3/4" h...... **$738**

Courtesy of Cowan's Auctions, www.cowanauctions.com

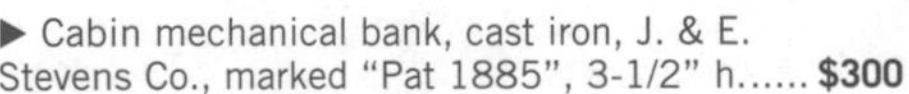

▶ Cabin mechanical bank, cast iron, J. & E. Stevens Co., marked "Pat 1885", 3-1/2" h...... **$300**

Courtesy of Cowan's Auctions, www.cowanauctions.com

Race car bank, silver, Tiffany & Co., New York, 2005, dents to wheels, scratches commensurate with age, 3" x 6-7/8" x 3-3/4", 9.57 troy oz. ... **$813**

Courtesy of Heritage Auctions, ha.com

Benjamin Butler Greenback Frog bank, cast iron, J. & E. Stevens Co., patented Nov. 13, 1878, trap door present, key missing, 6-1/2" h................ **$625**

Courtesy of Heritage Auctions, ha.com

Mary and Little Lamb penny bank, cast iron, early 20th century, very good condition with minor wear to painted surface, 4-1/2" h. **$240**

Courtesy of Jeffrey S. Evans & Associates, www.jeffreysevans.com

Beatles Ringo Starr "Yellow Submarine" figural bank, King Features/Pride Creations, 1968, King Features sticker on bottom, Pride Creations sticker partially torn off, very fine condition, 8" h. **$500**

Courtesy of Heritage Auctions, ha.com

Batman and Robin bank set, ceramic, Lego of Japan, 1966, very fine condition, 6-3/4" h. **$390**

Courtesy of Heritage Auctions, ha.com

Little Audrey figural bank, ceramic, American Bisque Co., third quarter 20th century, undamaged, 8-5/8" h. **$132**

Courtesy of Jeffrey S. Evans & Associates, www.jeffreysevans.com

Bonzo seated on tin bank, Germany, circa 1920, scarce, 5-1/4" h. **$247**

Courtesy of Bertoia Auctions, www.bertoiaauctions.com

Boy on Trapeze mechanical bank, cast iron, J. Barton Smith Co., Philadelphia, 1888, very good condition with paint loss on boy, 9" h. **$780**

Courtesy of Rich Penn Auctions, www.richpennauctions.com

Lion and Two Monkeys mechanical bank, cast iron, Kyser & Rex, patented July 17, 1883, very good working condition with some paint loss, 9" h. **$660**

Courtesy of Rich Penn Auctions, www.richpennauctions.com

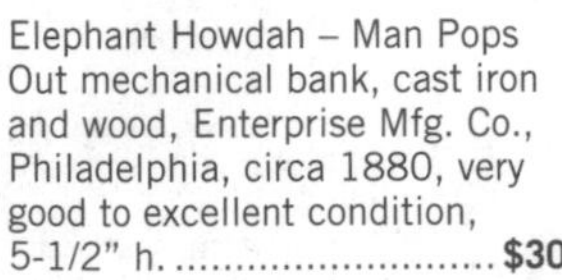

Elephant Howdah – Man Pops Out mechanical bank, cast iron and wood, Enterprise Mfg. Co., Philadelphia, circa 1880, very good to excellent condition, 5-1/2" h. **$300**

Courtesy of Rich Penn Auctions, www.richpennauctions.com

John Deere centennial bank, litho on metal to look like oil can with advertising, 1937, excellent condition, 3-1/2" h. **$300**

Courtesy of Rich Penn Auctions, www.richpennauctions.com

BARBIE

AT THE TIME of the Barbie doll's introduction in 1959, no one could have guessed that this statuesque doll would become a national phenomenon and eventually the most famous girl's plaything ever produced.

Over the years, Barbie and her growing range of family and friends have evolved with the times, serving as an excellent mirror of the fashion and social changes taking place in American society. Today, after 57 years of continuous production, Barbie's popularity remains unabated among both young girls and older collectors. Early and rare Barbie dolls can sell for remarkable prices, and it is every collector's hope to find a mint condition No. 1 Barbie.

1959 No. 1 blonde Ponytail Barbie with box, consistent light flesh color overall, hair still in original ponytail, original earrings, sunglasses, shoes, mini catalog, and instruction sheet included, excellent-plus condition, slight fading, minor loss to toenails, original stand in excellent condition, box lid with moderate fading to front, box bottom with two split corners, one repaired with tape, box 12" x 3"............................... **$4,880**

Courtesy of Morphy Auctions, www.morphyauctions.com

1959 No. 2 brunette Barbie in "Sweet Dreams" silhouette box, hair in original ponytail, original earrings and stand included, excellent condition, minor loss to nails, dressed in hard-to-find "Sweet Dreams" ensemble, missing mirror and brush, blue slippers have holes (to be worn by No. 1 Barbie), in original pink silhouette "Sweet Dreams" box with minor to moderate wear, box 12" x 3" **$6,710**

Courtesy of Morphy Auctions, www.morphyauctions.com

1960 No. 3 brunette Ponytail Barbie with box, hair in original ponytail, original earrings, sunglasses, shoes, stand, and mini catalog included, excellent-plus condition, slight discoloration to feet from shoe wear, two box rubs to back of calves; box lid with minor wear and small scrapes, box bottom with minor wear, original cardboard insert present, box 12" x 3"........................ **$1,342**

Courtesy of Morphy Auctions, www.morphyauctions.com

No. 4 brunette Ponytail Barbie in black and white striped bathing suit with original light blue hair band and Barbie and Ken booklet highlighting doll clothes for sale, right foot marked "Japan," backside reads "1958 B#135 Barbie Patents Pending by Mattel Inc," ears have some light green................................ **$288**

Courtesy of Philip Weiss Auctions, www.weissauctions.com

1961 brunette Bubblecut Barbie with early box, original red swimsuit, stand shoes, and mini catalog included, excellent-plus condition, in earliest bubblecut box with ponytail imagery and 1959 date, box with no wear or damage, cardboard insert present, box 12" x 3". **$549**

Courtesy of Morphy Auctions, www.morphyauctions.com

1962 brunette Ponytail Barbie with wrist tag, earrings, stand, shoes, catalog, and cardboard box inserts, near mint condition, undamaged box... **$488**

Courtesy of Morphy Auctions, www.morphyauctions.com

1962 brunette Bubblecut Barbie with box, original earrings, shoes, stand, and mini catalog included, foil wrist tag present but not attached, excellent-plus condition, box top and bottom with minor wear, box 12" x 3"............. **$244**

Courtesy of Morphy Auctions, www.morphyauctions.com

Limited edition Judith Leiber Barbie with miniature minaudière, brunette hair and blue eyes, gray lace corseted dress with white petticoat and matching gray sash, gray plastic heels, gold-tone enamel earrings with white crystal inlays, and gold and silver crystal evening bag with trademark B, in Judith Leiber box, very good to excellent condition, 6" w. x 12-1/4" h. x 6-1/2" d.......................... **$575**

Courtesy of Heritage Auctions, ha.com

BARBIE & FRIENDS

Blonde Ponytail Barbie and blonde flocked-hair Ken with assorted outfits, some incomplete or non-original, very good to excellent condition. **$200**

Courtesy of Morphy Auctions, www.morphyauctions.com

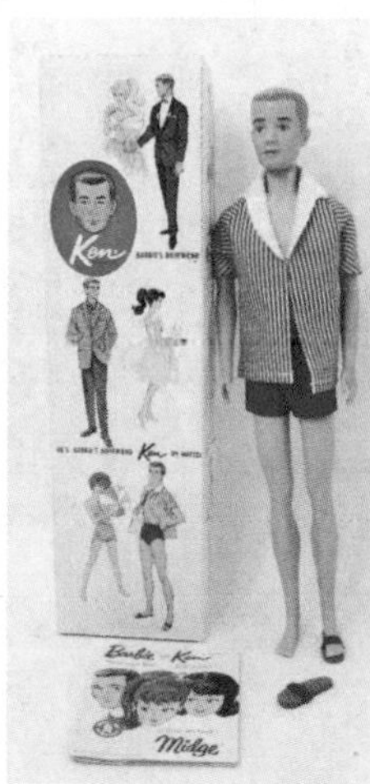

1961 blond painted-hair Ken with original box, original clothes, and sandals. **$55**

Courtesy of Pioneer Auction Gallery, www.pioneerantiqueauction.com

Bubblecut Barbie and Midge doll in carrying case with additional clothing and accessories, Midge model #860, Barbie model #860, Barbie with slightly greasy face, some outfits tagged Barbie......... **$190**

Courtesy of Morphy Auctions, www.morphyauctions.com

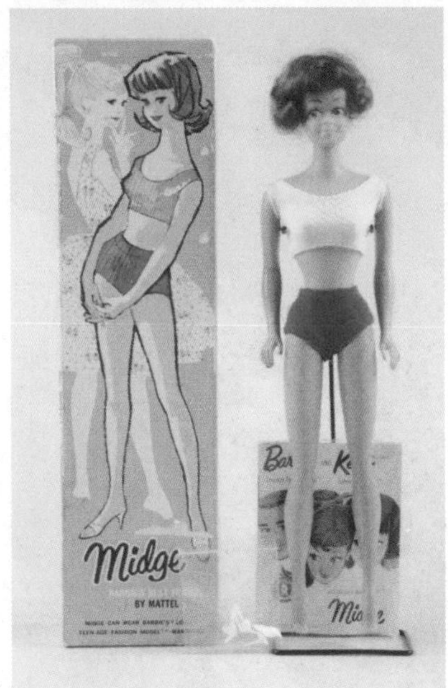

FAR LEFT: Midge, "Barbie's Best Friend," with original box and original instructions and book of various Barbie dolls, metal stand, doll excellent-near mint condition, box in excellent condition................**$50**

Courtesy of Morphy Auctions, www.morphyauctions.com

LEFT: 1968 Talking Julia in original box, #1128, curly black hair, brown eyes, rooted lashes, pink lips, bendable legs, and talking mechanism (not working), original silver and gold metallic jumpsuit, wrist tag, in original box, excellent condition. **$450**

Courtesy of Theriault's Antique Doll Auctions, www.theriaults.com

Circa 1960s Allan with original box and original swim outfit, sandals, other accessories and clothes, and booklet...**$40**

Courtesy of Pioneer Auction Gallery, www.pioneerantiqueauction.com

1962 Midge and 1963 Skipper dolls with Skipper case, Ideal Tammy "Ya Ya Ya" Beatles sweater, and Barbie, Skipper, and Ken clothes. **$200**

Courtesy of Kennedy's Auction Service, kennedysauction.com

BASKETS

THE NATIVE AMERICANS were the first basket weavers on this continent and, of necessity, the early Colonial settlers and their descendants pursued this artistic handicraft to provide essential containers for berries, eggs, and endless other items to be carried or stored.

Rye straw, split willow, and reeds are but a few of the wide variety of materials used. Nantucket baskets, plainly and sturdily constructed, along with those made by specialized groups, seem to draw the greatest attention to this area of collecting.

SHENANDOAH VALLEY BASKETS

Shenandoah Valley of Virginia stave and woven-splint miniature basket, first quarter 20th century, white oak, finely woven oblong form with oval wrapped rim, arched handle with V-shape supports, and rectangular bottom, original dry natural surface with very good patina, excellent condition, 4-1/8" h. overall, 4" x 5-1/2" dia. rim.. **$720**

Courtesy of Jeffrey S. Evans & Associates, www.jeffreysevans.com

Shenandoah Valley of Virginia painted rib-type woven-splint miniature basket, first quarter 20th century, white oak, finely woven kidney form with double wrapped rim and low arched handle, X-shape handle supports, original green-painted surface, very good condition with small losses to bottom, 3-1/2" h. overall, 4" dia. rim............. **$660**

Courtesy of Jeffrey S. Evans & Associates, www.jeffreysevans.com

Shenandoah Valley of Virginia woven pulled-rod basket, late 19th/first quarter 20th century, white oak, tall circular form with wrapped arched side handles with triangular attachments, excellent original dry natural surface, excellent condition, minor stains in base, 19-1/2" h. rim, 17" dia.. **$300**

Courtesy of Jeffrey S. Evans & Associates, www.jeffreysevans.com

NANTUCKET BASKETS

Nantucket Lightship basket signed "D. Bunker, 2d," 11-3/4" x 19-1/2" x 19-1/2". **$1,750**

Courtesy of Material Culture, www.materialculture.com

Nantucket woven basket purse, circa 1940-1960, Sherwin Porter Boyer (1907-1964), oval form with bail handle, wooden base, hinged cover with applied whale, under base with branded Boyer monogram and "Nantucket / Mass.," also with printed label, original dry surface, loss to end of whale's tail, woven hasp fraying, partial loss of one rim wrap at handle juncture, 11" h. overall, 5-1/2", 7-1/2" dia. rim. **$1,200**

Courtesy of Jeffrey S. Evans & Associates, www.jeffreysevans.com

Nantucket basket signed "A.O. Crawford," as found, 6" h. x 11" w. **$400**

Courtesy of Weiderseim Associates, Inc., www.weiderseim.com

NATIVE AMERICAN BASKETS

Native American round coiled basket with vertical imbrication to small loop handles, circa 1900-1920, excellent condition, 6-1/2" h. **$275**

Courtesy of Morphy Auctions, morphyauctions.com

Native American lidded basket, circa 1930, excellent condition, 5-1/2" h., 7" dia. **$183**

Courtesy of Morphy Auctions, morphyauctions.com

Apache basket with star in center, 10" x 10" x 2".. **$250**

Courtesy of Material Culture, www.materialculture.com

Alaskan Eskimo round smoked grass basket with carved caribou bone salmon figure in center, bone and faceted blue sea glass trade beads around edge, finely and tightly woven, good condition, 2" h., 5-1/4" dia.. **$83**

Courtesy of North American Auction Co., www northamericanauctioncompany.com

California Mission Washoe tribe basket woven from willow, red bud, and broken fern root, circa early 20th century, likely used for food/grain storage, minor losses near edge, structurally sound, 7" h., 11" dia. **$182**

Courtesy of Manor Auctions, www.manorauctions.com

Apache coil-built gathering basket with human and spirit figures, early 20th century, wear to rim, surface losses, bottom separating, 10" h., 12" dia. **$531**

Courtesy of Thomaston Place Auction Galleries, www.thomastonauction.com

Northwest Coast false embroidered basket, 3" h., 5" dia.. **$266**

Courtesy of Turkey Creek Auctions, Inc., www.antiqueauctionsfl.com

Yokuts/Mono coiled basket, sedge root background and red bud or iron boiled bracken fern root, butterfly pattern woven with contrasting elements, very good condition, 3" h., 6-1/2" dia. **$500**

Courtesy of DGW Auctioneers & Appraisers, www.dgwauctioneers.com

STORAGE BASKETS

Antique French vineyard storage basket, 31" x 21" x 18".. **$219**

Courtesy of Material Culture, www.materialculture.com

Pennsylvania rye straw coil storage basket with lid, 19th century, circular form with slightly bulbous sides, good condition with some soiling and losses, 17" h., 18" dia. **$182**

Courtesy of Conestoga Auction Co., www.conestogaauction.com

Pennsylvania rye straw coil storage basket with lid, 19th century, slightly bulbous form, tilted to one side, good condition with some soiling and losses, 19" h., 18" dia. **$182**

Courtesy of Conestoga Auction Co., www.conestogaauction.com

Large rectangular woven oak splint storage basket, carved bentwood handles, bentwood wrapped rim, carved wood cleats on base, good condition, some losses, remnants of gold paint on interior, 16-1/2" h. x 26" w. x 18" d...................................... **$218**

Courtesy of Conestoga Auction Co., www.conestogaauction.com

GATHERING BASKETS

American painted woven-splint gathering basket, probably ash, first quarter 20th century, rectangular form with wrapped rim, arched handle with carved grip and rim supports, and square open-weave bottom, original dry black and white painted surfaces, very good condition, one end with loss of some wraps repaired with string, 13-3/4" h. overall, 8" h. rim, 11-1/2" x 16" **$120**

Courtesy of Jeffrey S. Evans & Associates, www.jeffreysevans.com

◀ New England painted gathering basket, 19th century, original green paint, very good condition, age split where handle joins rings, 10" h. not including swing handle, 17" dia. **$554**

Courtesy of CRN Auctions, Inc., www.crnauctions.com

▲ Three-colored oak gathering basket with original surface with browns, blues and reds, 19th century, good condition with few breaks and losses, 11" h., 14-3/4" dia. **$272**

Courtesy of Conestoga Auction Co., www.conestogaauction.com

MISCELLANEOUS BASKETS

Hawkeye brand picnic basket/refrigerated cooler with woven wicker exterior with wooden handles, inside lined with galvanized metal, lidded compartment for ice storage, good condition, 9-3/4" x 21-1/2" x 14-1/2" h. **$107**

Courtesy of North American Auction Co., www.northamericanauctioncompany.com

American rib-type painted woven wicker basket, first half 20th century, deep chestnut-form with tightly wrapped rim and arched handle, original dry black- and bittersweet-painted surfaces, excellent condition, 15-1/2" h. overall, 10-3/4" h. rim, 10-1/4" x 11" rim. **$450**

Courtesy of Jeffrey S. Evans & Associates, www.jeffreysevans.com

BOOKENDS

BOOKENDS SERVE BOTH functional and decorative purposes. They not only keep a person's books in order, they look good while they're doing it.

Bookends are commonly made of a variety of metals - bronze, brass, pewter, or silver plate - as well as marble, wood, ceramic, and other natural or manmade materials. The art they feature represents many subjects, with wildlife, domesticated animals and pets, sports figures or items, nautical themes, and fantasy themes as favorites.

The value of an antique bookend is determined by its age, the material it is made from, what it represents, the company that created it, and how scarce it is.

Elephant bookends by Bradley & Hubbard, signed "B & H," excellent condition-plus, 9-1/4" h. **$519**

Courtesy of Morphy Auctions, morphyauctions.com

Cast iron Edgar Allen Poe cabin bookends by Bradley & Hubbard, excellent condition, 4" h. **$153**

Courtesy of Morphy Auctions, morphyauctions.com

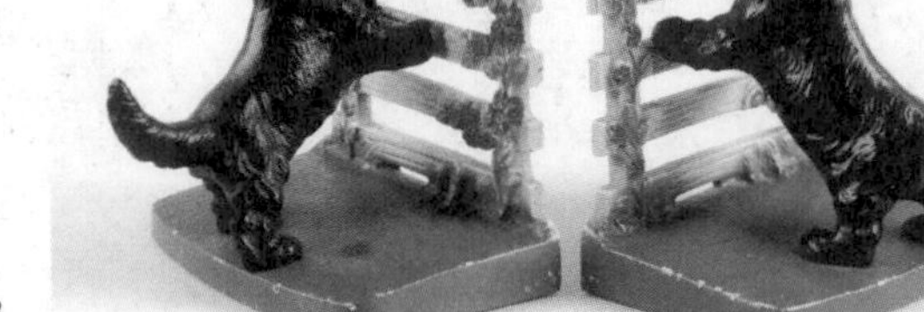

Cast iron Scotties by fence bookends by Hubley, excellent condition, 5" h. **$153**

Courtesy of Morphy Auctions, morphyauctions.com

Zebra bookends by Hubley, #3419, one of the most sought-after pair of bookends Hubley produced, very good condition, 5" h. **$183**

Courtesy of Morphy Auctions, morphyauctions.com

Quail bookends by Hubley, #461, Fred Everett, designer, excellent condition, 5-1/2" h. **$305**

Courtesy of Morphy Auctions, morphyauctions.com

Painted cast iron "Profanity" golfer bookends, 1928, Connecticut foundry, normal wear, good to very good condition, 5" h. **$61**

Courtesy of Richard Opfer Auctioneering, Inc., www.opferauction.com

Jayhawk bookends, University of Kansas mascot, marked "KU" on side of wing, rare, excellent condition, 5-1/2" h.................................... **$1,037**

Courtesy of Morphy Auctions, morphyauctions.com

Raggedy Ann and Andy bookends, signed "Copyright 1931 P.F. Volland & Co.," front of bases marked "Raggedy Ann" and "Raggedy Andy," highly sought-after and rare, near mint condition, 5-1/2" h....................................... **$397**

Courtesy of Morphy Auctions, morphyauctions.com

Art Deco patinated metal bookends of squirrels eating nuts, on marble bases, France, 20th century, 6" h.. **$768**

Courtesy of Rago Arts and Antiques, www.ragoarts.com

Bronze foo guardian dogs on rectangular plinths, China, 19th century, 7-1/4" h. **$640**

Courtesy of Rago Arts and Antiques, www.ragoarts.com

Cold painted bronze bookends of monks in red robes reading books, Austria, 7-1/4" h. x 4" w. x 4-1/2" d. **$154**

Courtesy of Kaminski Auctions, www.kaminskiauctions.com

Bronze Tiffany Studios zodiac pattern bookends, 5-3/4" h. **$456**

Courtesy of Philip Weiss Auctions, www.weissauctions.com

Bronze with jade insert bookends, turn of the 20th century, carved white jade gate to temple insert depicting bird of paradise, 4" h. overall, jade gate 3", 2269 g. **$124**

Courtesy of Elite Decorative Arts, www.eliteauction.com

Art Deco hand-painted bookends, 7" h. **$73**

Courtesy of William J. Jenack Estate Appraisers & Auctioneers, www.jenack.com

Art Deco flower motif bookends in orange and green, mint condition, 4-1/2" h. **$401**

Courtesy of Bertoia Auctions, www.bertoiaauctions.com

Rookwood flower motif bookends, XLI #2836, crazing, no chips or cracks, 3-1/2" x 5-1/2"................................**$72**

Courtesy of Philip Weiss Auctions, www.weissauctions.com

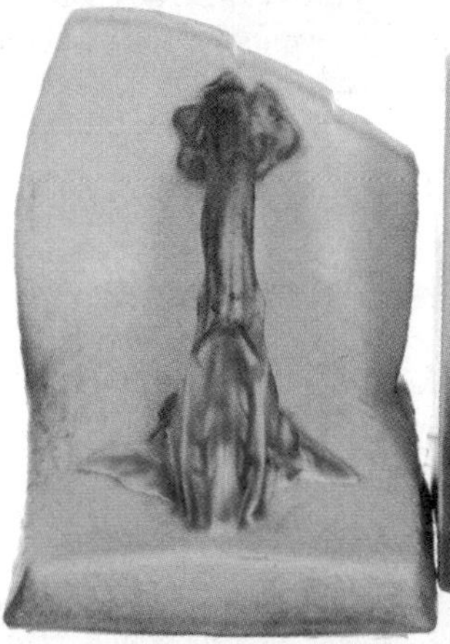

Roseville Bittersweet pattern bookends, 859, in gray and mauve tones, good condition, no chips, cracks, or repairs, 5-1/2" x 4-1/2"....................**$71**

Courtesy of Woody Auction, www.woodyauction.com

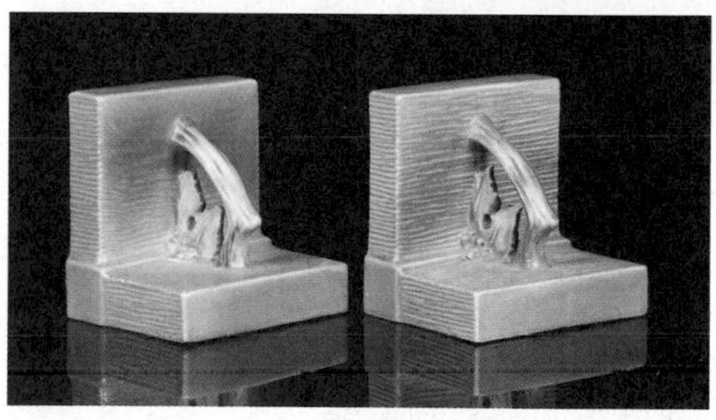

Roseville Bushberry pattern bookends, 5-1/4" h. x 5" w. x 4-1/8" d...........................**$154**

Courtesy of Kaminski Auctions, www.kaminskiauctions.com

Roseville Pinecone pattern bookends in brown tones, good condition, no chips, cracks, or repairs, 4-3/4" x 5"...........**$177**

Courtesy of Woody Auction, www.woodyauction.com

BOOKS

WITH AN EXCESS of 100 million books in existence, there are plenty of opportunities and avenues for bibliophiles to feed their enthusiasm and build a satisfying collection of noteworthy tomes without taking out a second mortgage or sacrificing their children's college funds. With so many to choose from, the true challenge is limiting a collection to a manageable size and scale, adding only volumes that meet the requirements of bringing the collector pleasure and holding their values.

What collectors are really searching for when they refer to "first editions" are the first printings of first editions. Every book has a first edition, each of which is special in its own right. As Matthew Budman points out in *Collecting Books* (House of Collectibles, 2004), "A first represents the launching of a work into the world, with or without fanfare, to have a great impact, or no impact, immediately or decades later. ... Holding a first edition puts you directly in contact with that moment of impact."

Devon Gray, director of Fine Books and Manuscripts at Skinner, Inc., www.skinnerinc.com, explains the fascination with collectible books: "Collectors are always interested in landmarks of human thought and culture, and important moments in the history of printing."

What makes a first edition special enough to be considered collectible is rarity and demand; the number of people who want a book has to be greater than the number of books available. So, even if there are relatively few in existence, there has to be a demand for any particular first edition to be monetarily valuable.

Author Richard Russell has been collecting and selling books since 1973; in his book, *Antique Trader Book Collector's Price Guide*, he explains that innovative (or perhaps even unpopular) books that are initially released in small printings "will eventually become some of the most sought after and expensive books in the collector's market." He gives as an example John Grisham's *A Time To Kill* (Wynwood Press, 1989), which had an initial print run of just 5,000 hardcover copies. The author bought 1,000 at wholesale with the plan to sell at retail and turn a bit of profit. When Grisham couldn't sell them at $10 apiece, he gave them away out of his law office.1 The book is valued at about $4,000 today.

Learning how to recognize first editions is a key to protecting yourself as a collector; you can't take it for granted that the person you are buying from (especially if he or she is not a professional bookseller) has identified the book properly. Entire volumes have been written on identifying first editions; different publishing houses use different means of identification, many utilizing differing methods and codes. However, according to the *Antique Trader Book Collector's Price Guide*, there are several details that will identify a first edition:

- The date on the title page matches the copyright date with no other printings listed on the copyright page (verso).
- "First Edition," "First Printing," "First Issue" or something similar is listed on the copyright page.
- A publisher's seal or logo (colophon) is printed on the title page, copyright page, or at the end of the text block.
- The printer's code on the copyright page shows a "1" or an "A" at one end or the other (example: "9 8 7 6 5 4 3 2 1" indicates first edition; "9 8 7 6 5 4 3 2" indicates second edition).

As is the case with many collectibles, condition is paramount. If a book was published with a dust jacket, it must be present and in great condition to attain the book's maximum value.

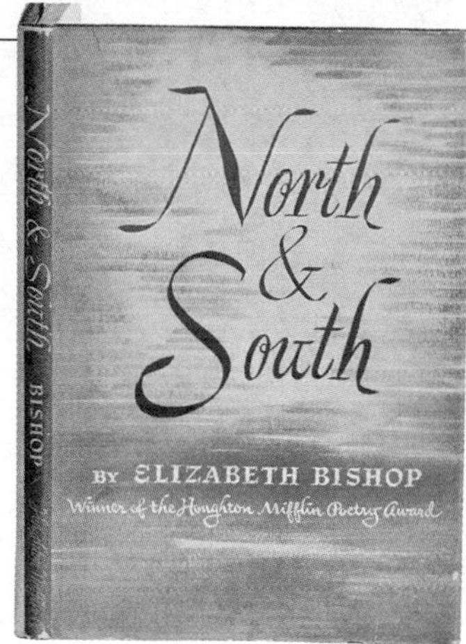

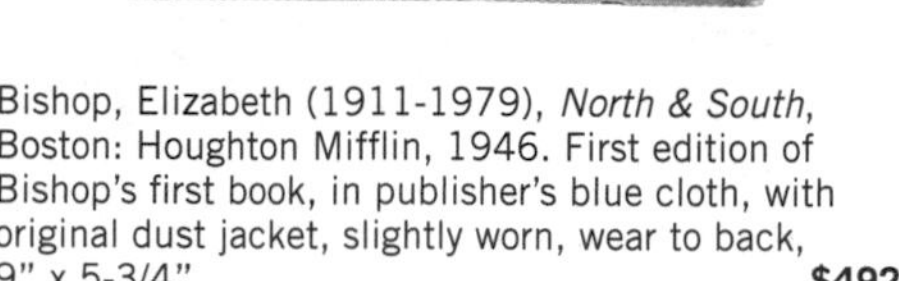

Bishop, Elizabeth (1911-1979), *North & South*, Boston: Houghton Mifflin, 1946. First edition of Bishop's first book, in publisher's blue cloth, with original dust jacket, slightly worn, wear to back, 9" x 5-3/4".. **$492**

Courtesy of Skinner, Inc., www.skinnerinc.com

Blue Book (Directory and Guide to Prostitutes in the Sporting District of New Orleans), New Orleans: no printer, no date, circa 1905. Tenth edition, small octavo, original tan wrappers printed in blue, text pages printed on coated stock in red and black, stapled; paper wraps breaking along joints, old tape repairs, 5-1/2" x 4-1/4". **$1,230**

Courtesy of Skinner, Inc., www.skinnerinc.com

Gray uses an example to illustrate the importance of condition.

"A book with a very large value basically has further to fall before it loses it all," she says. "A great example is the first edition of the printed account of the Lewis and Clarke expedition. In bad condition its value is in the four-figure range; in better condition, it gets up to five figures; and in excellent condition, six figures.

"Another example: The 1920 first American edition of T.S. Eliot's *Poems* sells for around $300 in poor condition with no dust jacket and $1,200 to $1,500 in good condition in a good dust jacket; the copy that Eliot gave to Virginia Woolf sold for 90,000 British pounds [approximately $136,000]; all the same edition."

A signature enhances a book's value because it often places the book in the author's hands. Cut signatures add slightly to a book's value because the author didn't actually sign the book – he or she may have never even held the book with the added cut signature. When the book itself is signed, even if with a brief inscription, it holds a slightly higher value. If the author is known for making regular appearances and accommodating all signature requests, the signature adds little to the value of the book because the supply for signed examples is plentiful.

"Real value potential comes into play with association material," Gray explains. "For example, a famous novelist's Nobel-winning story is based on a tumultuous affair he had with a famous starlet under his heiress-wife's nose, and you have the copy he presented to his wife, with her 'notes.'"

Even a title that has been labeled as "great," "important," or "essential" doesn't mean a particular edition – even a first edition – is collectible or monetarily valuable. After all, if a much-anticipated book is released with an initial print run of 350,000, chances are there will be hundreds of thousands of "firsts" to choose from – even decades after publication. Supply far outweighs demand, diminishing value.

The overly abundant supply of book club editions (which can be reprinted indefinitely) is just one of the reasons they're not valued by collectors. Some vintage book club editions were also made from inferior materials, such as high-acid paper using lower quality

Johnson, Samuel and George Steevens, editors, the plays of William Shakespeare in 15 volumes, fourth edition, London: Longman, et al., 1793. One of 25 fine paper copies illustrated with engravings published by E. and S. Harding, octavo volumes bound in uniform contemporary full dark blue straight-grained morocco, spines ruled and lettered in gilt; bindings rubbed, some chips to heads and tails, 8-1/2" x 5-1/4". **$1,169**

Courtesy of Skinner, Inc., www.skinnerinc.com

Hammett, Dashiell, *The Maltese Falcon* comic book adaptation illustrated by Rodlow Willard, Philadelphia: David McKay, 1946. Forty-eight pages, octavo, original pictorial side-stapled wrappers, minor creases; color throughout, housed in folding cloth portfolio with paper label reproducing cover image, No. 48 of Feature Books series released by McKay group and distributed by King Features Syndicate................................ **$344**

Courtesy of Swann Auction Galleries, www.swanngalleries.com

Wells, Herbert George (1866-1946), *The War of the Worlds*, New York: Harper & Brothers, 1898. First American edition, octavo, illustrated with frontispiece and 15 additional illustrated plates by Warwick Goble; bound in publisher's green cloth, front board stamped in black and green, spine and front board lettered in gilt; spine faded, rubbed, some surface grime to binding, 7-1/4" x 4-1/2"... **$308**

Courtesy of Skinner, Inc., www.skinnerinc.com

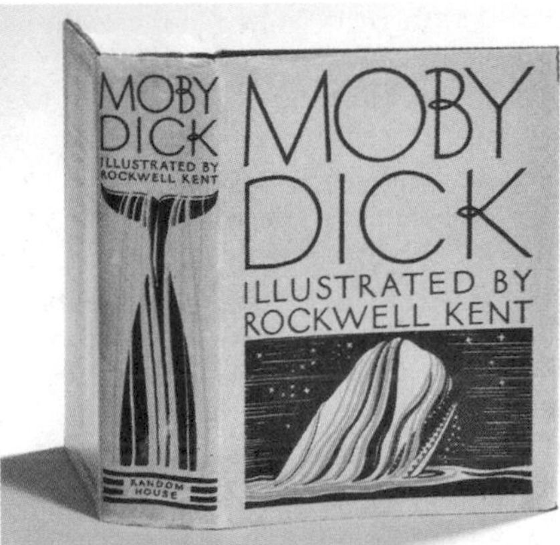

Melville, Herman (1819-1891), *Moby Dick*, illustrated by Rockwell Kent (1882-1971), New York: Random House, 1930. First trade edition, octavo, with original publisher's dust jacket, in black cloth publisher's binding blocked in silver, 7-1/4" x 5".. **$677**

Courtesy of Skinner, Inc., www.skinnerinc.com

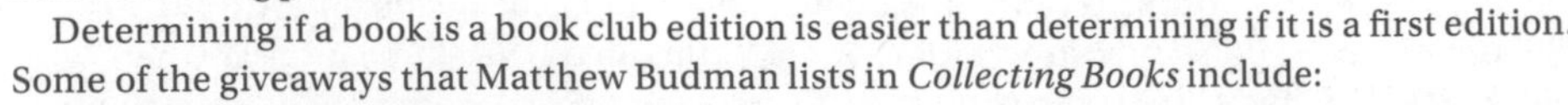

manufacturing processes.

Determining if a book is a book club edition is easier than determining if it is a first edition. Some of the giveaways that Matthew Budman lists in *Collecting Books* include:

- No price on dust jacket
- Blind stamp on back cover (small impression on the back board under the dust jacket); can be as small as a pinprick hole
- "Book Club Edition" (or similar notation) on dust jacket
- Books published by the Literary Guild after World War II are smaller format, thinner and

Poe, Edgar Allan, *Siope – A Fable in The Baltimore Book*, Baltimore: Bayly and Burns, 1838. Illustrated with six engravings, octavo, publisher's gilt and blind-stamped full morocco, recased with new endpapers, moderate wear; contemporary ownership inscription, contents foxed; housed in custom case (LMS book label). **$250**

Courtesy of Swann Auction Galleries, www.swanngalleries.com

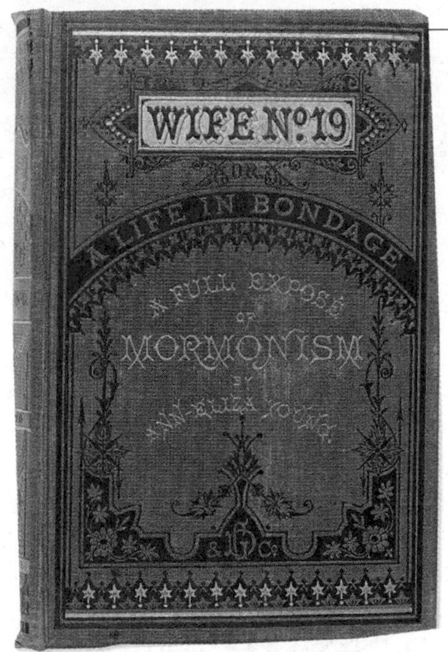

Mormons, group of 10 books on Mormons and early Utah (*Wife No. 19* shown), various sizes, bindings, and conditions, 1854-1890 and 1928. .... **$813**

Courtesy of Swann Auction Galleries, www.swanngalleries.com

printed on cheap paper.

Fledgling book collectors should also be aware of companies that built a burgeoning business of publishing a copious number of "classic" and best-seller reprints; just a few of the long list are Grosset & Dunlap, Reader's Digest, Modern Library, A.L. Burt, Collier, Tower and Triangle. Many of these companies' editions are valued only as reading copies, not as collectibles worthy of investment.

Proper care should be implemented early on when building a collection to assure the books retain their condition and value. Books should be stored upright on shelves in a climate-controlled environment out of direct (or even bright indirect) sunlight. Too much humidity will warp covers; high temperatures will break down glues. Arrange them so similar sized books are side-by-side for maximum support, and use bookends so the books don't lean, which will eventually cause the spines to shift and cause permanent damage.

A bookplate usually will reduce a book's value, so keep that in mind when you're thinking of adding a book with a bookplate to your collection, and avoid adding bookplates to your own volumes. Also, don't pack your volumes with high-acid paper such as newspaper clippings, and always be careful when placing or removing them from the shelf so you don't tear the spine.

Building a book collection – or any collection, for that matter – on a budget involves knowing more about the subject than the seller. Learning everything possible about proper identification of coveted books and significant authors involves diligence and dedication, but the reward is maximum enjoyment of collecting at any level.

— **Karen Knapstein** Print Editor, *Antique Trader*

[1]John Grisham's Favorite Mistake: Giving Away First Editions, http://www.thedailybeast.com/newsweek/2012/04/01/john-grisham-s-favorite- mistake-giving-away-first-editions.html

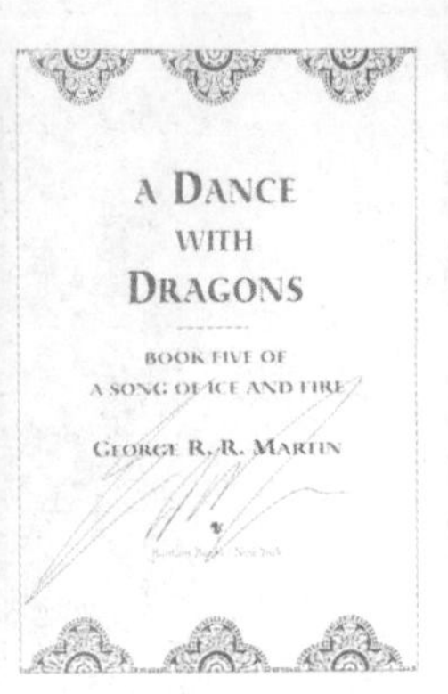

George R. R. Martin, *A Dance with Dragons*, New York: Bantam Books, 2011. First edition, signed by author, Book 5 of "A Song of Ice and Fire," inspiration for HBO's "Game of Thrones" series, publisher's gray paper over boards. **$62**

Courtesy of Heritage Auctions, ha.com

Edna Ferber, *Giant*, Garden City: Doubleday & Co., 1952. First edition, octavo, publisher's binding and dust jacket. **$251**

Courtesy of Heritage Auctions, ha.com

Ray Bradbury, group of four titles, New York: Knopf, various dates. First editions, inscribed by author, octavos, publisher's bindings and dust jackets. **$187**

Courtesy of Heritage Auctions, ha.com

Edgar Rice Burroughs, *Tarzan of the Apes*, New York: A. L. Burt Co., circa 1920. Early reprint edition, octavo, publisher's binding and original dust jacket, bookplate. **$60**

Courtesy of Heritage Auctions, ha.com

Wilson, Woodrow (1856-1924), *History of the American People*, New York & London: Harper & Brothers, 1902. Five octavo volumes, signed by Wilson in volume one while president-elect, dated "15 Feby. 1913," ex-libris Edward Mandell House (1858-1938), Wilson's chief advisor on European politics and diplomacy during World War I and at Paris Peace Conference of 1919, 8" x 5". **$1,230**

Courtesy of Skinner, Inc., www.skinnerinc.com

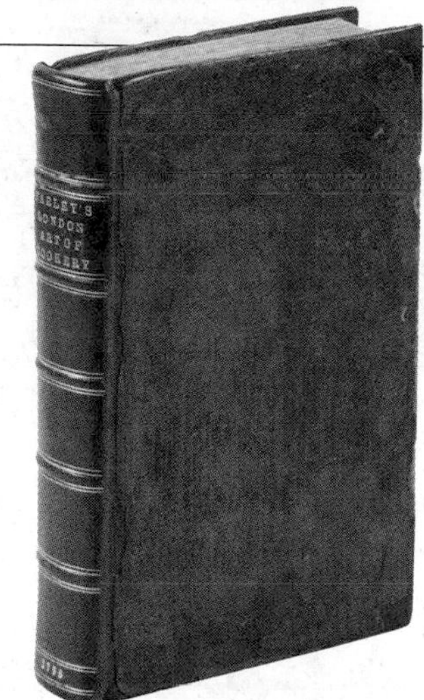

Farley, John, *The London Art of Cookery*, London publisher, printed for J. Scatcherd & H. Whitaker, et al., 1796. Eighth edition, 459 pages, copper-engraved frontispiece portrait, 12 copper-engraved plates showing bills of fare for each of 12 months, octavo, 8-1/4" x 4-3/4". This popular cookbook went through 12 editions between 1783 and 1811. .... **$160**

Courtesy of PBA Galleries, www.pba.com

Chao, Buwei Yang, *How to Cook and Eat in Chinese*, John Day, 1945-1949. Rare inscribed copy of Chinese-American cookbook that invented "stir-fry" and "pot stickers," inscribed on flyleaf, "Compliments of Buwei Y. Chao," with her additional signature in Chinese, and below that, a gift inscription by a later Chinese-American owner, "The key to your man's heart!" **$190**

Courtesy of PBA Galleries, www.pba.com

Craddock, Harry, *The Savoy Cocktail Book*, decorations by Gilbert Rumbold, New York: Richard R. Smith, 1930. Octavo, half cloth, decorated boards, about 700 recipes with additional information on punches, fizzes, and wines, illustrated with vignettes. Craddock was a legendary bartender at London's Savoy Hotel and later at the Dorchester. **$523**

Courtesy of Skinner, Inc., www.skinnerinc.com

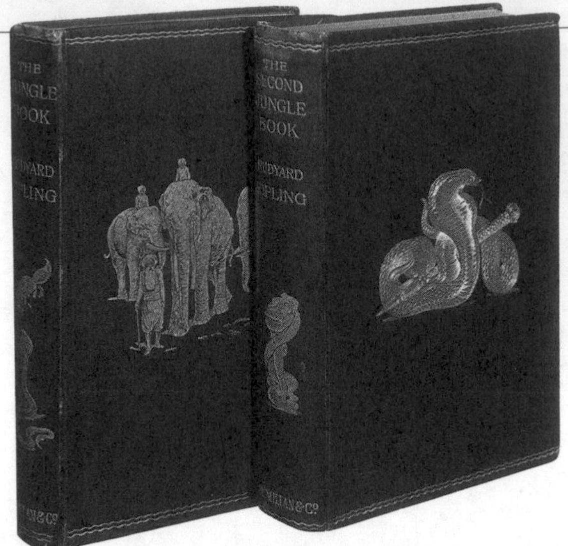

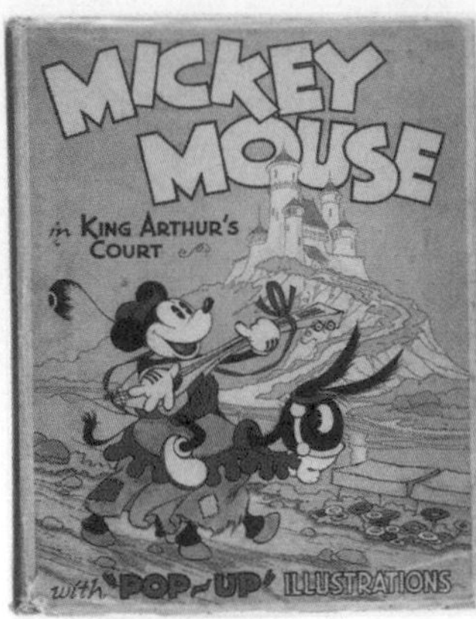

Kipling, Rudyard, *The Jungle Book* and *The Second Jungle Book*, London: Macmillan and Co., 1894, 1895. First English editions, illustrated, second title with two pages of advertisements at end, octavo, publisher's gilt-decorated blue cloth, all edges gilt, front corners bumped, contemporary ownership inscriptions, housed in custom cloth drop-back case. **$1,690**

Courtesy of Swann Auction Galleries, www.swanngalleries.com

Pop-Up Books, Walt Disney Studios, *Mickey Mouse in King Arthur's Court*, New York: Blue Ribbon Books, 1933. Octavo, publisher's binding and dust jacket. **$213**

Courtesy of Heritage Auctions, ha.com

Fleming, Ian, *Chitty Chitty Bang Bang: The Magical Car*, New York: Random House, 1964. First U.S. edition, association copy, octavo, publisher's binding in original dust jacket. **$275**

Courtesy of Heritage Auctions, ha.com

Plumly Thompson, Ruth, John R. Neill, illustrator, *The Hungry Tiger of OZ*, Chicago: The Reilly & Lee Co., 1926. First edition, illustrated, with 12 color plates by Neill, including frontispiece, publisher's dark green cloth, spine lettered in black, and color illustration mounted to front cover. **$138**

Courtesy of Heritage Auctions, ha.com

BOTTLES

Barber bottle, yellow green, 7-7/8", open pontil, sheared and tooled lip, 1885-1925 ....**$150-$200**

INTEREST IN BOTTLE collecting continues to grow, and more collectors are spending their free time digging through old dumps and foraging through ghost towns, digging out old outhouses, exploring abandoned mine shafts, and searching their favorite bottles or antiques shows, swap meets, flea markets, and garage sales. In addition, the Internet has greatly expanded, offering collectors numerous opportunities and resources to buy and sell bottles with many new auction websites, without even leaving the house. Many bottle clubs now have websites providing even more information for the collector. These new technologies and resources have helped bottle collecting to continue to grow and gain interest.

Most collectors, however, still look beyond the type and value of a bottle to its origin and history. Researching the history of a bottle is almost as interesting as finding the bottle itself.

There continues to be non-stop exciting action and major events happening in the world of bottle collecting. In addition to numerous bottle auctions, along with 15 to 20 antique bottle shows held each month by bottle clubs across the United States, England, Australia, and Europe, there have been major archeological finds, shipwreck discoveries in the Gulf of Mexico and the Baltic Sea, bottles found in attics, and of course many great bottle digs across the country.

All of this good news demonstrates that the hobby is not only strong but continues to gain popularity while bringing an overall greater awareness to a wider spectrum of antiques collectors. While attending shows and talking with collectors and dealers from across the country, the consensus is that the hobby is doing well and growing stronger.

Recent auctions continued to excite collectors. In 2015, Norm Heckler Auctions, Woodstock Valley, Connecticut, conducted five auctions that produced astonishing results. In March 2015, an early rare "G.W. Stone's Liquid - Cathartic & Family Physic - Lowell Mass" medicine bottle in medium yellow amber with an olive tone sold for $18,720. A rare and historically important deep emerald green "North Bend" - "Tippecanoe" Historical Cabin Bottle," in log cabin form, from Mount Vernon Glass Works, Vernon, New York, sold for $25,740.

Jeff Wichmann and his crew at American Bottle Auctions, Sacramento, California, were making some noise of their own with sales of bitters, sarsaparillas, and Western whiskeys. In April 2015, a rare olive yellow amber "Thos. Taylor & Co. Importers Viginia. N." Western whiskey sold for $10,500. A medium cobalt blue "Dr. Wynkoop's Katharismic Honduras Sarsaparilla New York" medicine sold for $8,500. A medium amber with olive tone "Dr. Wonser's USA Indian Root Bitters" sold for $13,500. A medium green "Alex Von Humboldt's Stomach Bitters" sold for $8,000. This bitters bottle is considered one of the rarest western "square"-shaped bitters and is the only true green example known.

Jim Hagenbuch and his crew at Glass Works Auction, East Greenville, Pennsylvania, were busy enticing bottle collectors with a selection of flasks, bitters, and medicine bottles. In March 2015, a rare yellowish "old" amber "New Granite Glass Works - Stoddard - N.H. - American Flag" flask sold for $21,500. A rare dark reddish amber "American Life Bitters - P.E. ILER - Manufacturer/Omaha, NEB - American Life Bitters" sold for $14,000. A medium blue green "DWD - E. Dexter Loveridge - Wahoo Bitters" PATD (motif of eagle with arrow) - "DWD" -E - Dexter Loveridge - Wahoo Bitters - 1863" sold for $20,000. In July 2015, a rare deep emerald green "Scott & Stewart - United States Syrup - New York" medicine sold for an astonishing $27,000.

For more information on bottles, see *Antique Trader Bottles Identification & Price Guide*, 8th edition, and *Picker's Pocket Guide: Bottles*, both by Michael Polak.

Barber bottle, medium cobalt blue, 8-1/4", pontil-scarred base, tooled rolled lip, 1885-1925. .... **$300-$400**

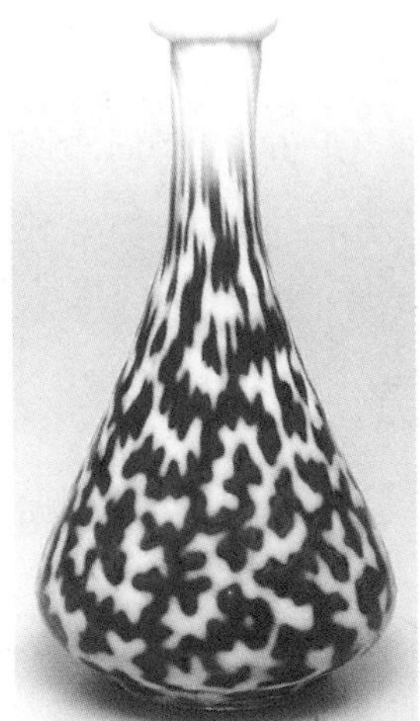

Barber bottle, fiery opalescent cranberry red, 6-7/8", white coral decoration, polished pontiled base, tooled top, scarce pattern and form, American, 1885-1925. **$300-$400**

Beer bottle, Boca (monogram B & B) Beer, amber, 11-1/2", quart, applied top, 1885-1900......................... **$250-$300**

Geo. W. Hoxsie's – Premium Beer bottle, dark olive amber, 7", smooth base, applied heavy collared top, Westford Glass Works, Westford, Connecticut, American, 1860-1873. **$350-$400**

Bitters bottle, Brady's Nerve Bitters, blue aqua, 9-1/4", smooth base, applied double collar top, rare, American, 1865-1875. .... **$1,400-$1,500**

Bitters bottle, Mills' Bitters – A. M. Gilman – Sole Proprietor, yellow amber, 11-1/4", lady's leg shape, smooth base, applied ring top, American, 1875-1885. .... **$2,200-$2,300**

Early canning jar, medium sapphire blue, quart, red iron pontil, applied top, utilized a cork closure, rare color, 1850-1860. .... **$250-$300**

Gin bottle, Gin Cocktail – S.M & Co. – N.Y. (on applied seal), medium yellow amber, 10-1/8", open pontil, applied double collar top, 1855-1870. .... **$600-$700**

Blown three-mold geometric ink bottle, yellow amber, 1-1/2", tubular open pontil, tooled disk mouth, 1815-1835. .... **$175-$200**

Ink bottle, S.O. Dunbar – Taunton, aqua, 2-3/8", eight-sided, open pontil, inward rolled lip, 1840-1860.. **$200-$250**

Cobalt blue medicine bottle, U.S.A. Hosp. Dept., (in oval), medium sapphire blue, 7", applied top, rare, 1860-1870. .... **$700-$1,000**

Medicine bottle, Dr. Convers Invigorating Cordial, deep blue aqua, 6-1/8", oval shape, open pontil, applied tapered collar top, 1840-1860.... **$125-$150**

Sarsaparilla bottle, Sands Sarsaparilla, aqua green, 8", applied top, American, 1885-1895.........................**$100-$125**

Sarsaparilla bottle, Log Cabin – Sarsaparilla – Rochester, N.Y., medium amber, 9", American, 1887-1895. ....**$100-$125**

Snuff bottle, medium yellow olive, 7-3/4", smooth base, tooled top, European, 1850-1870.........................**$200-$225**

Snuff bottle, dark yellow amber, 4-3/8", open pontil, tooled and flared-out lip, American, 1800-1825........................**$250-$275**

Soda bottle, Comstock, Gove & Co., teal blue, 7-1/8", ten-pin shape, applied blob top, 1855-1865........................**$200 $250**

Soda bottle, Steinke & Kornahrens – Soda Water – Return This Bottle, Charleston S.C., deep olive amber, 8-3/8", eight-sided, iron pontil, applied top, 1840 1860... **$2,500 $3,000**

Target ball, C. Bogardus Glass Ball Patd. Apr. 10th 1877, yellow amber, 2-5/8" dia., rough sheared top, American, 1877-1900, ... **$200-250**

Target ball, IRA Paines Filled Ball Oct 23, 1877, cobalt blue, 2-5/8" dia., American, 1877-1895.................. **$2,000-$2,100**

Target ball (motif of man shooting on two sides), medium amethyst, 2-5/8" dia., English, 1877-1895. ....**$200-$250**

Warner bottle, Warner's Kidney & Liver Cure – Toronto Can – Rochester N.Y. U.S.A. London England (85% label), deep amber, 9-1/2", American, 1885-1895. ....**$200-$225**

Handled whiskey, Star Whiskey – New York – W.B. Crowell Jr (inside embossed seal), dark amber, rib-pattern, 8-1/8", open pontil, applied double collar top, 1865-1875. .... **$1,000-$1,200**

Whiskey cylinder, Dyottville Glass Works Phila (on base), medium cherry puce, 11-1/2", applied tapered collar top, 1855-1870. ....**$200-$250**

BOXES

BOXES COME IN all shapes, sizes, and degree of antiquity—good news for the collector seeking a lifelong passion. Once early mankind reached the point where accumulation began, the next step was the introduction of containers designed especially to preserve those treasures.

Boxes have been created from every source material imaginable: wood, stone, precious metals, papier maché, porcelain, horn, and even shell. Among the most collectible:

Snuff boxes. These small, lidded boxes first came to favor in the 1700s. Although originally intended as "for use" items, snuff boxes are now prized for the elegant miniatures often painted on both the box exterior and interior.

Pillboxes. Like the snuffbox, these tiny boxes were as much in demand for their design as for their usefulness. Among the most desirable are 18th century pillboxes with enameled or repoussé (metal relief) decoration.

Match safes. In the days before safety matches, metal boxes with a striker on the base kept matches from inadvertently bursting into flame. Match safe material ranged from base metal to sterling silver. Although flat, hinged safes were the most common; novelty shapes, such as animal heads, also proved popular.

Lacquered boxes. Often classified as "Oriental" due to the 19th century fondness for decorating them with Asian motifs, lacquered boxes are actually found in almost every culture. Ranging anywhere from trinket- to trunk-sized, the common denominator is a highly polished, lacquered surface.

Folk art boxes. The diversity of available folk art boxes accounts for their modern collectibility. Folk art boxes were often the work of untrained artisans, created solely for their own needs from materials readily at hand. Among the many choices: wallpaper boxes, decoupage boxes, and "tramp art" boxes. Fueled by the imagination and ingenuity of their makers, the selection is both fascinating and limitless.

American tramp art box, late 19th/early 20th century, hinged lid and case in crazy quilt pattern with applied fabric divided by chip-carved strips, velvet-lined interior, original dry surfaces, 7" h. x 15-1/2" w. x 9" d. **$144**

Courtesy of Jeffrey S. Evans & Associates, www.jeffreysevans.com

Bank box, marked "Leap Frog" Toy Savings Bank, early dovetailed box, staining to front, lid and base are replacements, scarce find. **$803**

Courtesy of Bertoia Auctions, www.bertoiaauctions.com

Three graduated octagonal wooden storage boxes with decorative metal hinges and bale handles, 12", 15", and 18" h. with lids. **$168**

Courtesy of Phoebus Auction Gallery, www.phoebusauction.com

Chinese export silver box, Shanghai, late 19th/early 20th century, wooden interior, applied interlocking monogram, marks for Luen Wo, tests .900 or better, good condition, 6-1/8". **$434**

Courtesy of Phoebus Auction Gallery, www.phoebusauction.com

▲ Green-painted wooden treasure box by J.Y. Ayer, circa 1870s, hallmarked "WELLS FARGO" on front panel with stenciled white paint, thick wood with iron hardware on corners, hinges, and reinforcement, hand-forged iron latch with padlock and key, both stamped "W. F. & CO," leather handles on sides are missing (one stored inside box), inside stamped "Manufactured by J.Y. Ayer, 3740 Seventeenth St., S.F CAL," very good condition, 10" h. x 21" w. x 14-1/2" d. **$6,100**

Courtesy of Morphy Auctions, morphyauctions.com

◀ Hudson River decorated wooden box by Lew Hudnall of Englewood, Ohio, folk art town scenes in ovals on lid and front, yellow trim and florals painted on original surface, very good condition with light loss to base, 14-1/4" h. x 19" w. x 14" l. **$514**

Courtesy of Contestoga Auctions, www.conestogaauction.com

Paint-decorated wooden document box with strawberry and floral polychrome decoration on black background, square nail construction, 19th century, good condition with light surface wear, 5" h. x 9-1/2" w. x 17-1/2" l......................... **$121**

Courtesy of Contestoga Auctions, www.conestogaauction.com

Round bentwood paint-decorated box with wooden pegged construction and original painted surface, 19th century, good condition with wear to surface and light loss, 6-1/2" h., 14-1/2" dia........ **$133**

Courtesy of Contestoga Auctions, www.conestogaauction.com

Wooden painted hatbox with original red surface and floral applied decoration, 19th century, very good condition, 11-1/4" h., 15-1/2" dia...... **$109**

Courtesy of Contestoga Auctions, www.conestogaauction.com

Rare Russian gold and enamel snuffbox, St. Petersburg, circa 1784, circular form with fitted cover with translucent red enamel over engine-turned reeding interspersed with pellets, lid set with oval en plein enamel-painted plaque with pastoral scene of lovers and borders banded with enameled translucent green leaves and opaque white beads, interior hallmarked St. Petersburg with date 1784, 2-1/2" dia. **$11,520**

Courtesy of Jackson's International Auctioneers and Appraisers, jacksonsauction.com

American brilliant cut glass pillbox with ornate embossed sterling lid with Native American bust, good condition, no chips, cracks, or repairs, 2" dia.. .... **$325**

Courtesy of Woody Auction, www.woodyauction.com

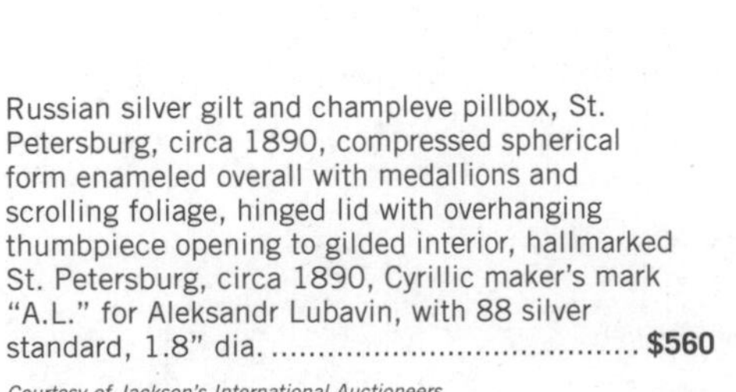

Russian silver gilt and champleve pillbox, St. Petersburg, circa 1890, compressed spherical form enameled overall with medallions and scrolling foliage, hinged lid with overhanging thumbpiece opening to gilded interior, hallmarked St. Petersburg, circa 1890, Cyrillic maker's mark "A.L." for Aleksandr Lubavin, with 88 silver standard, 1.8" dia. **$560**

Courtesy of Jackson's International Auctioneers and Appraisers, jacksonsauction.com

top lot!

Cartier Art Deco silver and enamel box, French, circa 1930, rectangular box with tapering legs with blue enamel top and rings, wooden liner, partial maker's mark, engraved on rim "Cartier Paris London New York" and "Made in France" for retailer, light scratches, small dents, .950 fine, 23.33 troy oz., 2-1/2 x 9". $19,840

COURTESY OF BRUNK AUCTIONS, WWW.BRUNKAUCTIONS.COM

Wallpaper-covered sewing box, 19th century, rectangular form, removable lid with pincushion top, tapered sides and lower full-width drawer, multicolor vertical striped wallpaper with white dot decoration, good condition, wear and losses, 3-3/4" h. x 6-1/2" w. x 5" d. **$484**

Courtesy of Conestoga Auctions, www.conestogaauction.com

Antique cast iron articulated bird match safe, good condition with minor pitting, 3-1/4" h. x 4-3/4" l. **$133**

Courtesy of Conestoga Auctions, www.conestogaauction.com

Circular wallpaper-covered box, 19th century, tan ground with blue, white, and maroon floral and geometric decoration, good condition with minor fading, 2" h., 3-1/8" dia. **$1,210**

Courtesy of Conestoga Auctions, www.conestogaauction.com

Two folk art inlaid ship ballot boxes, second half of 19th century, various hardwoods including rosewood, mahogany, satinwood, boxwood, and possibly maple, decoration of vessels in rectangular reserves on front and back, parquetry patterns to tops, one example with five-pointed star to each end, one example with lightship with "Galloper" inscribed to side, old possibly original fabric covering underside of each base, each retains old surface, 4-3/4" h. x 8-1/4" w. x 4-3/4" d. **$600**

Courtesy of Jeffrey S. Evans & Associates, www.jeffreysevans.com

New York or New England folk art paint-decorated poplar dome-top box with hinged lid over nailed case, second quarter 19th century, likely original paint-decorated surface with stenciled or stamped pinwheel/rosette-like devices, foliate sprays, and broken circles within black background reserve bordered by green, likely original hinges, lock, and hasp, newsprint-lined bottom with references to New York and Ohio cities, 13-1/2" h. x 30" w. x 13" d. **$900**

Courtesy of Jeffrey S. Evans & Associates, www.jeffreysevans.com

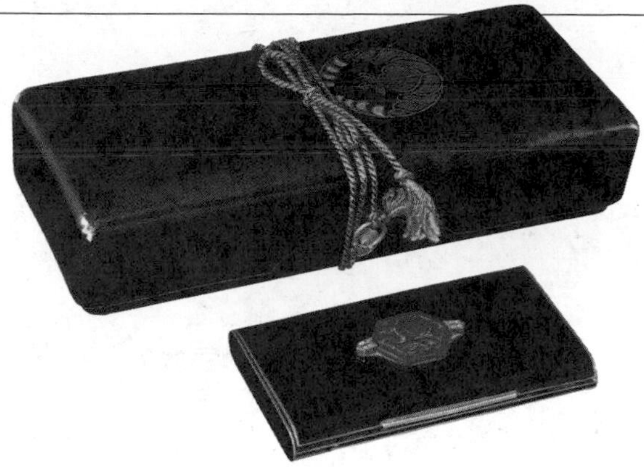

Rudolph Valentino boxes, circa 1925: Cigarette case, black enamel with red enamel emblem with marcasite detailing on lid, gold-washed interior; decorative box, possibly used for travel, wood and painted black with Art Nouveau floral image on top lid, bottom with rings on either side where attached string keeps box together; both pieces gifted by Valentino to Federico Beltran Masses, Spanish painter and close friend of Valentino, who painted two portraits of actor and lived with him in Los Angeles in 1925; clasp on cigarette case no longer works, chipping on corners of wooden box, cigarette case 2" x 3" x 1/4", bigger box 7" x 3" x 1-1/2". **$1,250**

Courtesy of Heritage Auctions, ha.com

Tiffany Studios glass and gilt bronze pine needle pattern card box, circa 1920, stamped TIFFANY STUDIOS, NEW YORK, 876, fine condition with original finish, surface wear commensurate with age, 4-3/8" h. **$1,500**

Courtesy of Heritage Auctions, ha.com

◀ Two Lalique clear and frosted glass powder boxes, Degas in original box, Duncan, post-1945, both engraved Lalique, France, good condition, Duncan 3-3/8" h. **$300**

Courtesy of Heritage Auctions, ha.com

Chinese lacquered tea caddy and work box, 19th century, dents and missing paint to lid of larger box, missing compartments to jewelry tray insert, broken locks and without keys to both, surface wear commensurate with age, taller box 6-5/8" x 12" x 9"............... **$325**

Courtesy of Heritage Auctions, ha.com

Chinese silver, enamel, and wood covered box with repoussé and enamel scene of three elders and child to central cartouche, bird and floral enamel border, inset with ebonized wood to base, sitting on four feet, marks: (chop marks), pin dents and minor loss of enamel, bent bevel to interior, scratches to wood, surface scratches commensurate with age, 4-3/4" x 10" x 10"..... **$1,875**

Courtesy of Heritage Auctions, ha.com

▲ Two decorative porcelain boxes from "Words and Music," Metro-Goldwyn-Mayer, 1948; both with square-shaped hinged lids, hand-painted with images of birds and flowers, interior painted with floral imagery, bottom of both with annotation reading in part "MGM XX5215"; 5" x 5" x 2-1/2". Provenance: Consigned by niece of Dorothy Ponedel, make-up artist at MGM and friend of Judy Garland, who gave these two decorative boxes to Ponedel as souvenirs. **$500**

Courtesy of Heritage Auctions, ha.com

Israeli silver and gilt etrog box, Hazorfim, Tel Aviv, Israel, circa 1900, marks: HAZORFIM, 925, surface wear commensurate with age, 5-5/8" x 6-1/4" x 4-3/4", 12.03 troy oz. **$531**

Courtesy of Heritage Auctions, ha.com

German silver luxury liner souvenir box, M.H. Wilkens & Sohne, Bremen-Hemelingen, Germany, circa 1902, box base engraved Souvenir of Princess Victoria Luise's Cruise to West-Indies 1902, marks: (crescent-crown), 800, WILKINS, overall surface wear commensurate with age, 1-1/8" h. x 2-1/2" w., 1.00 troy oz. **$138**

Courtesy of Heritage Auctions, ha.com

▲ Italian silver gilt and enamel box, 19th century, with British import marks: T.C. & SN. LTD., (crown in cross), (925), surface scratches commensurate with age, 1/2" x 3" x 2-1/8", 3.19 troy oz....**$2,750**

Courtesy of Heritage Auction, ha.coms

▶ Turnbridgeware box, early 20th century, fine condition with minor scratches commensurate with age, 6-3/4" h. x 7" w. **$138**

Courtesy of Heritage Auctions, ha.com

CERAMICS

belleek

THE NAME BELLEEK refers to an industrious village in County Fermanagh, Northern Ireland, on the banks of the River Erne, and to the lustrous porcelain wares produced there.

In 1849, John Caldwell Bloomfield inherited a large estate near Belleek. Interested in ceramics and having discovered rich deposits of feldspar and kaolin (china clay) on his lands, he soon envisioned a pottery that would use these materials, local craftspeople, and waterpower of the River Erne. He was also anxious to enhance Ireland's prestige with superior porcelain products.

Bloomfield had a chance meeting with Robert Williams Armstrong, who had established a substantial architectural business building potteries. Keenly interested in the manufacturing process, he agreed to design, build, and manage the new factory for Bloomfield. The factory was to be located on Rose Isle on a bend in the River Erne.

Bloomfield and Armstrong then approached David McBirney, a highly successful merchant and director of railway companies, and enticed him to provide financing. Impressed by the plans, he agreed to raise funds for the enterprise. As agreed, the factory was named McBirney and Armstrong, then later D. McBirney and Co.

Although 1857 is given as the founding date of the pottery, it is recorded that the pottery's foundation stone was laid by Mrs. J. C. Bloomfield on Nov. 18, 1858. Although not completed until 1860, the pottery was producing earthenware from its inception.

With the arrival of ceramic experts from the (William Henry) Goss Pottery in England, principally William Bromley, Sr. and William Wood Gallimore, Parian ware was perfected and by 1863, the wares we associate with Belleek today were in production.

With Belleek Pottery workers and others emigrating to the United States in the late 1800s

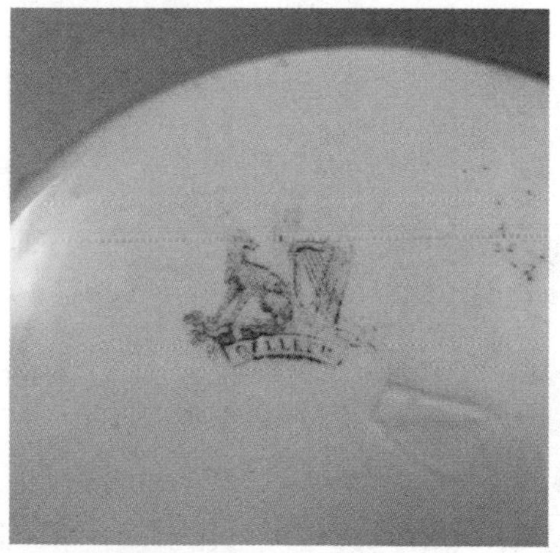

Belleek's black first mark, 1863-1890.

Courtesy of Belhorn Auctions LLC, belhornauctions.com

Belleek's black second mark, 1891-1926.

and early 1900s, Belleek-style china manufacture, known as American Belleek, commenced at several American firms, including Ceramic Art Co., Colombian Art Pottery, Lenox, Inc., Ott & Brewer, and Willets Manufacturing Co.

Throughout its Parian production, Belleek Pottery marked its items with an Irish harp and wolfhound and the Devenish Tower. Its second period began with the advent of the McKinley Tariff Act of 1891 and the (revised) British Merchandise Act as Belleek added the ribbon "Co. FERMANAGH IRELAND" beneath its mark in 1891. Both the first and second period marks were black, although they occasionally appeared in burnt orange, green, blue, or brown, especially on earthenware items. Its third period begin in 1926, when it added a Celtic emblem under the second period mark as well as the government trademark "Reg No 0857" granted in 1884. The Celtic emblem was registered by the Irish Industrial Development Association in 1906; it reads "Deanta in Eirinn" and means "Made in Ireland." The pottery is now utilizing its 13th mark, following a succession of three black marks, three green marks, one gold mark, two blue marks, and three green marks. The final green mark was used only a single year, in 2007, to commemorate its 150th anniversary. In 2008, Belleek changed its mark to brown. Early earthenware was often marked in the same color as the majority of its surface decoration. Early basketware has Parian strips applied to its base with the impressed verbiage "BELLEEK" and later on, additionally "Co FERMANAGH" with or without "IRELAND". Current basketware carries the same mark as its Parian counterpart.

The item identification scheme here appears in the works by Richard K. Degenhardt: *Belleek The Complete Collector's Guide and Illustrated Reference* (both first and second editions). Additional information, as well as a thorough discussion of the early marks, is located in these books.

MARKS

AMERICAN ART CHINA WORKS
R&E, 1891-1895

AAC (SUPERIMPOSED)
1891-1895

AMERICAN BELLEEK CO.
Company name, banner, and globe

CERAMIC ART CO.
CAC palette, 1889-1906

COLOMBIAN ART POTTERY
CAP, 1893-1902

COOK POTTERY
Three feathers with "CHC," 1894-1904

COXON BELLEEK POTTERY
"Coxon Belleek" in shield, 1926-1930

GORDON BELLEEK
"Gordon Belleek," 1920-1928

KNOWLES, TAYLOR & KNOWLES
"Lotusware" in circle with crown, 1891-1896

LENOX CHINA
Palette mark, 1906-1924

OTT & BREWER
Crown and shield, 1883-1893

PERLEE
"P" in wreath, 1925-1930

WILLETS MANUFACTURING CO.
Serpent mark, 1880-1909

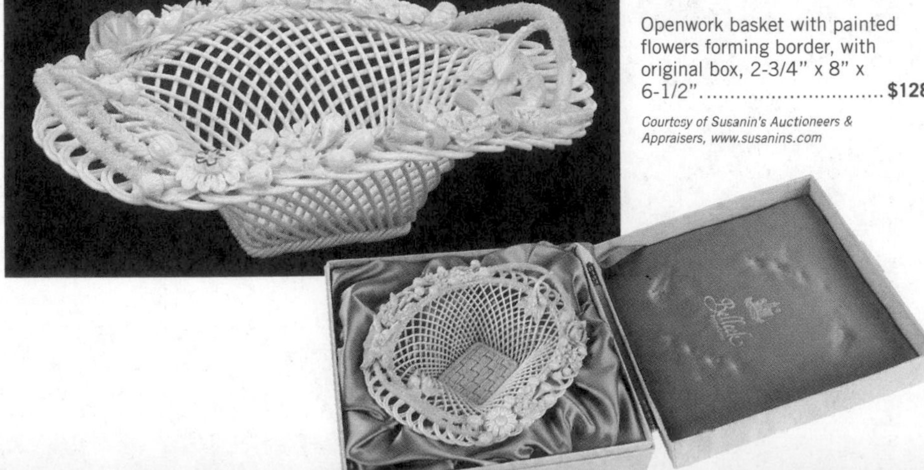

Openwork basket with painted flowers forming border, with original box, 2-3/4" x 8" x 6-1/2"............................... **$128**

Courtesy of Susanin's Auctioneers & Appraisers, www.susanins.com

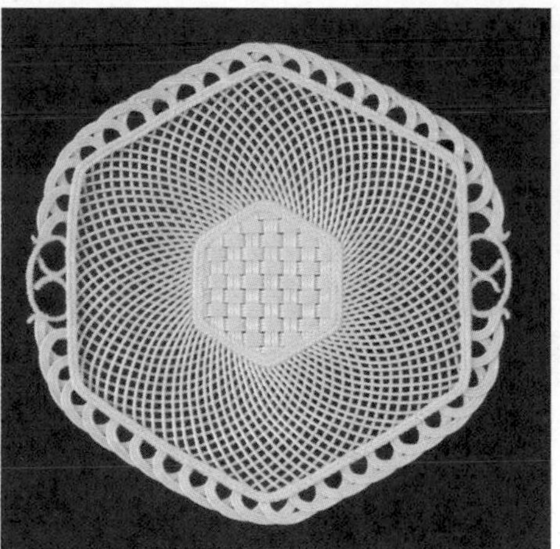

Open lattice hexagonal dish with tri-strand reticulated rim forming scalloped border over basketweave central pane, circa 1921-1954, impressed "Belleek, Co. Fermanagh, Ireland" to underside, excellent undamaged condition, 9-1/2" w. **$115**

Courtesy of Jeffrey S. Evans & Associates, www.jeffreysevans.com

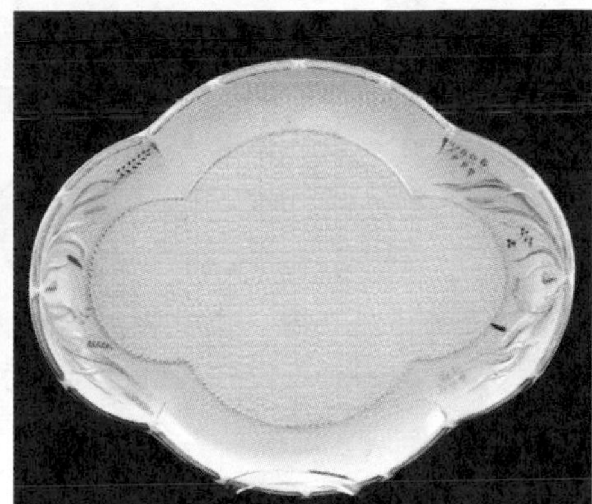

Grass Water pattern tray with impressed mark, no visible damage or repairs, 14-1/2" x 12". **$584**

Courtesy of Nest Egg Auctions, www.nesteggauctions.com

Vase in cream with pink rose and branch décor, brown mark, good condition, 6-3/4" h. **$6**

Courtesy of Woody Auction, www.woodyauction.com

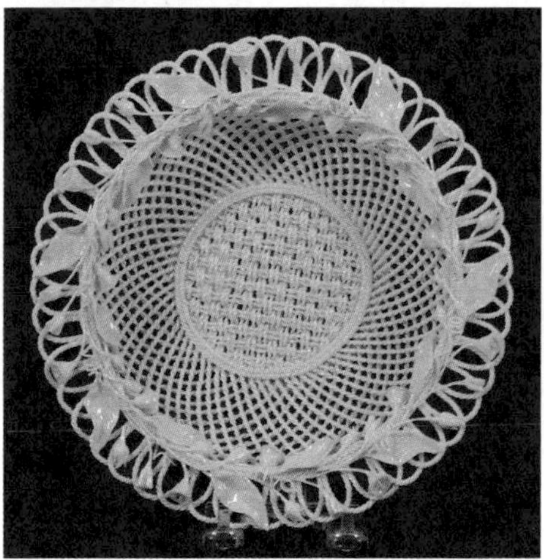

Convolvulus two-strand basketweave bowl with applied floral border, second mark (ribbon mark), no known damage, good condition, 2-1/4" x 9".**$472**

Courtesy of Woody Auction, www.woodyauction.com

Shamrock tri-foot jardiniere, shaped rim, body with applied flowers and clover leaves, three applied foliate motif feet, black mark on base, missing several clover leaves, 11" h. x 9" overall. **$531**

Courtesy of Burchard Galleries, www.burchardgalleries.com

Basket with four-strand weave and applied colored decorations, marked with Belleek (R) Co. Fermanagh, mint condition, 6-3/4" w. **$58**

Courtesy of Belhorn Auctions LLC, belhornauctions.com

Nile vase in white and green with gold trim, fourth mark (first green mark 1946-1955), mint condition, 9-5/8" h. **$207**

Courtesy of Belhorn Auctions LLC, belhornauctions.com

Hand holding shell vase in white and pink, black second mark (1891-1926), mint condition, 6-1/4" h. **$863**

Courtesy of Belhorn Auctions LLC, belhornauctions.com

Pitcher in white with green, black second mark (1891-1926), mint condition, 7-3/4" h. **$219**

Courtesy of Belhorn Auctions LLC, belhornauctions.com

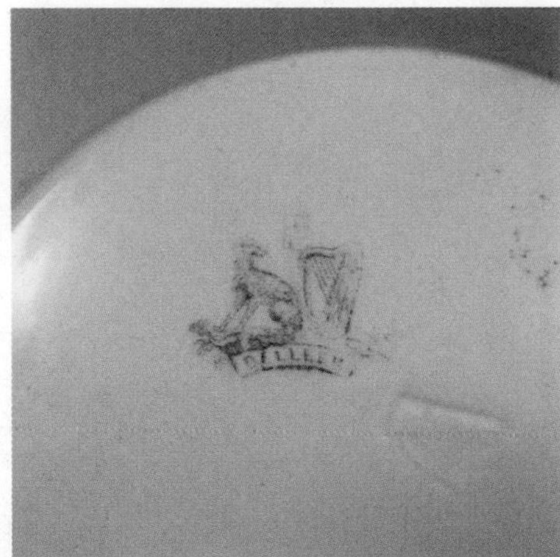

Earthenware pedestal dish with purple and gold trim, black first mark (1863-1890), small nicks around edge, 11-3/4" w. **$345**

Courtesy of Belhorn Auctions LLC, belhornauctions.com

CERAMICS

bennington pottery

BENNINGTON WARES, WHICH ranged from stoneware to parian and porcelain, were made in Bennington, Vermont, primarily in two potteries, one in which Captain John Norton and his descendants were principals, and the other in which Christopher Webber Fenton (also once associated with the Nortons) was a principal. Various marks are found on the wares made in the two major potteries, including J. & E. Norton, E. & L. P. Norton, L. Norton & Co., Norton & Fenton, Edward Norton, Lyman Fenton & Co., Fenton's Works, United States Pottery Co., U.S.P., and others.

The popular pottery with the mottled brown on yellowware glaze was also produced in Bennington, but such wares should be referred to as "Rockingham" or "Bennington-type" unless they can be specifically attributed to a Bennington, Vermont factory.

Glazed cup with raised peacock decoration, late 19th century, good condition, 3" h., 4" dia........ **$54**

Courtesy of Eldreds, www.eldreds.com

Four-gallon E. & L. P. Norton stoneware jug with bird decoration, impressed marked and 11" bird on leaf spray, bird's wings with dot decoration, very good condition, nick on lip, 18" h. **$889**

Courtesy of James D. Julia Auctioneers, Fairfield, Maine, www.jamesdjulia.com

Spittoon, shell-shape mold, good condition, no chips, cracks, or repairs, 4" x 9"....... **$47**

Courtesy of Woody Auction, www.woodyauction.com

Two Rockingham-glaze spaniels, one with chip to nose, one with chips to base, 10-1/2". **$116**

Courtesy of Strawser Auctions, www.strawserauctions.com

Rockingham-glaze candlestick, 8-3/4" h. **$46**

Courtesy of Strawser Auctions, www.strawserauctions.com

Flint-enamel pottery coachman bottle, circa 1849-1858, detailed gentleman with moustache holding bottle, cape with tassels, mottled brown with blue-green and some orange, unmarked, Lyman Fenton & Co., undamaged, 10-1/2" h. **$920**

Courtesy of Jeffrey S. Evans & Associates, www.jeffreysevans.com

Rockingham-glaze pottery coachman bottle, circa 1849-1858, mottled olive brown, chubby-face gentleman holding mug, cape without tassels, lightly impressed 1849 mark to underside, Lyman Fenton & Co., undamaged, 10-1/2" h. **$431**

Courtesy of Jeffrey S. Evans & Associates, www.jeffreysevans.com

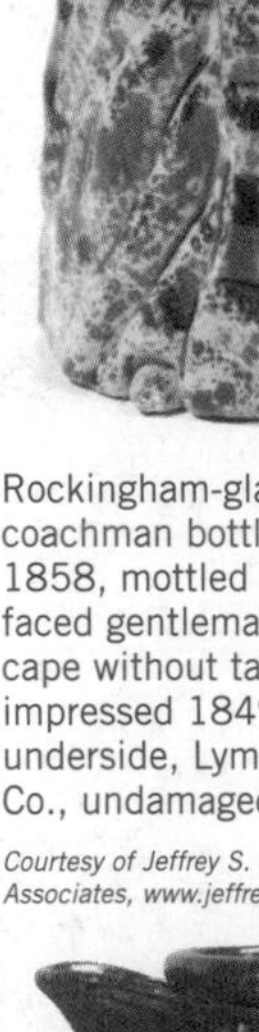

Rockingham-glaze pottery coachman bottle, circa 1849-1858, mottled brown, chubby-faced gentleman holding mug, cape without tassels, lightly impressed 1849 mark to underside, Lyman Fenton & Co., undamaged, 10-1/2" h. **$374**

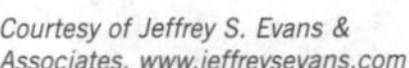

Courtesy of Jeffrey S. Evans & Associates, www.jeffreysevans.com

Two large Rockingham-glaze fish coffeepots, no lids, 9" h. **$75**

Courtesy of Strawser Auctions, www.strawserauctions.com

CERAMICS

buffalo pottery

INCORPORATED IN 1901 as a wholly owned subsidiary of the Larkin Soap Co., founded by John D. Larkin of Buffalo, New York, in 1875, Buffalo Pottery was a manufactory built to produce premium wares to be included with purchases of Larkin's chief product: soap.

In October 1903, the first kiln was fired and Buffalo Pottery became the only pottery in the world run entirely by electricity. In 1904 Larkin offered its first premium produced by the pottery. This concept of using premiums caused sales to skyrocket, and in 1905, the first Blue Willow pattern pottery made in the United States was introduced as a premium.

The Buffalo Pottery administrative building, built in 1904 to house 1,800 clerical workers, was the creation of a 32-year-old architect named Frank Lloyd Wright. The building was demolished in 1953.

By 1910 annual soap production peaked and the number of premiums offered in the catalogs exceeded 600. By 1915 this number had grown to 1,500. The first catalog of premiums was issued in 1893 and continued to appear through the late 1930s.

John D. Larkin died in 1926, and during the Great Depression the firm suffered severe losses, going into bankruptcy in 1940. After World War II, the pottery resumed production under new management, but its vitreous wares were generally limited to mass-produced china for the institutional market.

Among the pottery lines produced during Buffalo's heyday were Blue Willow (1905-1916), Gaudy Willow (1905-1916), Deldare Ware (1908-1909, 1923-1925), Abino Ware (1911-1913), historical and commemorative plates, and unique hand-painted jugs and pitchers. In the 1920s and 1930s the firm concentrated on personalized wares for commercial clients, including hotels, clubs, railroads, and restaurants.

For more information on Buffalo Pottery, see *Antique Trader Pottery & Porcelain Ceramics Price Guide, 7th edition.*

— *Phillip M. Sullivan*

Two pieces of Deldare Ware pottery, artist-signed "Ye Olden Times" bowl and "An Evening at Ye Lion Inn" charger, excellent condition, charger 13-1/2" dia. **$121**

Courtesy of Cottone Auctions, www.cottoneauctions.com

Pitcher, 1907, marked "Buffalo Pottery 1907 Underglaze Warranted" with small nick at end of spout, 6" h. **$23**

Courtesy of Belhorn Auctions LLC, belhornauctions.com

Deldare Ware emerald charger with center image of sheep and title "Lost" below image, initialed "SH" lower right, signed "Buffalo Pottery 1911" on back, very good condition, small flake to back of rim affects glaze, 13-1/2" dia. **$116**

Courtesy of Nest Egg Auctions, nesteggauctions.com

Deldare Ware pitcher in brown, 1939, marked "Made at Ye Buffalo Pottery Deldare Ware" in underglaze, excellent condition, 7-3/4" h........... **$58**

Courtesy of Belhorn Auctions LLC, belhornauctions.com

Pitcher marked "Buffalo Pottery Deer Hunt" with repaired handle and crack at tip of spout, 6-1/2" h.. **$12**

Courtesy of Belhorn Auctions LLC, belhornauctions.com

Dutch jug pitcher, marked "Buffalo Pottery 1907 Dutch Jug" with handle with hairline crack, 6-3/8" h. **$17**

Courtesy of Belhorn Auctions LLC, belhornauctions.com

CERAMICS

capodimonte

KING CHARLES OF Bourbon waxed passionate about porcelain upon wedding Maria Amalia, whose family was associated with the first hard paste porcelain factory in Europe: Meissen. The Meissen formula, which rivaled expensive, highly desirable Chinese porcelain, remained a closely guarded secret. Yet in 1743, after successfully creating pieces of equal quality, Charles founded a factory of his own, the Royal Capodimonte ("Top of the Mountain") Porcelain Factory in Naples, Italy.

According to Louise Phelps, associate director of the European Ceramics and Glass Department at Christie's auction house, "Though Capodimonte designs were inspired by Meissen production, their shapes tend to be slightly more flamboyant, and the porcelain, which is soft paste, is creamier and not as white as Meissen hard paste pieces.

"The most sought-after Capodimontes from this period were traditionally figures and groups modeled by Giuseppe Gricci, Antonio Flacone and others," Phelps said. "Italian comedy figures are especially attractive to collectors, as are figures of fishermen, spaghetti-eaters, and groups [that] show 'local' life." Many of these figurines feature characteristically small heads in proportion to their bodies.

While some Capodimonte figurines can be found for under $10,000 each, exceptional ones in prime condition command far more. Christie's reports that in 2005, the portrayal of a woman selling the bust of a warrior realized $130,000, while in 2011, a finely detailed depiction of Columbina and Punch realized nearly $150,000.

Non-figural pieces of this era, like enamel and gilt dresser boxes, wall plaques, covered jars, trinket boxes, and decorative vases, many of which feature brightly colored, high relief classic images or military scenes, are very collectible as well. While some are unmarked, others bear painted or impressed fleurs-de-lis in blue or gold.

During this period, Capodimonte, like other companies across Europe, also produced wildly popular, lifelike, handmade, applied porcelain flowers arranged in porcelain vases. Indeed, King Charles' Porcelain Room reputedly bloomed with bouquets of exquisite, hand-wrought, delicately tinted blossoms.

Due to their extreme age and fragility, however, few of these earliest non-figural Capodimontes have survived. In light of their rarity - and because this porcelain is considered the finest in Italy - they consistently command premium prices at auction.

In 2011, for example, Christie's auctioned a tiny, richly gilded, circa 1747-1752 marked Capodimonte teapot and cover, depicting hunter and hounds flanked by landscape vignettes on scroll and trelliswork supports, for

Marked, globular gilded teapot and cover with hunter and hounds, circa 1747-1752.
....**$209,189**

Courtesy Christie's Images Ltd., 2011, www.christies.com

nearly $210,000. Rare and unusual pieces may command even more.

From 1759 on, when Charles left Naples to become the king of Spain, the Royal Capodimonte factory continued production under direction of his son Ferdinand. Though Ferdinand's porcelains followed earlier shapes and styles, he favored classic, mythological, and significant historical decorative themes. During this era, his figurines, which often depicted royalty or the emerging middle class, became more lifelike. The Capodimonte blue crown over Neapolitan "N" trademark also came into use. With Napoleon's occupation of Naples in the early 1880s, however, the Golden Age of Capodimonte drew to a close.

According to Stuart Slavid, senior vice president and director of European Furniture & Decorative Arts, Ceramics, and Fine Silver at Skinner, Inc., "Rarely, if ever, do Ferdinand-period Capodimonte porcelains reach the market." The majority, along with earlier ones that have survived, reside in museums and private collections.

"Most Capodimontes available today, which are characterized by high relief, lots of colors and abundant gilding date to the mid-to-late 19th century," Slavid said.

Many were produced in the Majello factory, founded in 1867 by another Neapolitan reputedly inspired by love (for the daughter of a master ceramicist). Many pieces of this era, like a plaque portraying a golden Venus framed in black, a bowl adorned with swans and crane, or a ewer featuring three-dimensional dolphins, mermaids and Neptune, currently bring between $150 and $1,500 at auction.

Exceptional late 19th century Capodimontes, however, like a massive gilt and bronze chandelier, a 12-piece place setting featuring classic images, or a sizeable porcelain and bronze box displaying dense, enameled mythological or battle scenarios, may command considerably more.

As the fame of this unique porcelain spread during the 19th and 20th century, ceramic manufacturers across Italy began producing similar wares. Those labeled "in the Capodimonte style," however, vary greatly in technique, craftsmanship and value.

Moreover, since the original Capodimonte trademark was not fully protected, many bear misleading marks. Some may not even be porcelain. In recent years, for example, low quality knock-offs from the Far East have reached the market. So prior to purchase, collectors are advised to consult with qualified experts regarding a Capodimonte's material, age and origin.

People who are charmed by authentic Capodimontes – but not by their high cost – may consider collecting modern ones. "Today as of old, genuine Capodimonte porcelain is handcrafted exclusively in Naples and neighboring countries, through time-honored, traditional Neapolitan techniques," said Mena Castaldo, manager of Capodimonte's Finest located in Marano di Napoli (Naples), Italy. Due to high quality and workmanship, she said, these pieces are expected to hold or increase their value over time.

"At Capodimonte's Finest, porcelain centerpieces, which feature unique, hand-crafted flowers ranging from miniscule to several inches across, remain a traditional favorite," she said. "They range from about $200 to over $2,000 each, depending on their richness, refinement and size." Figurines of the Child Jesus, the Madonna or traditional Italian comedy characters like Pulchinello (Punch) and Arlecchino (Harlequin), for example, are generally within the same price range.

Beginning collectors, however, may find small, high-quality Capodimonte favors of interest. In Italy, these are customarily offered to guests to mark weddings, baptisms and other memorable occasions. Some, like an enticing slice of Neapolitan pizza or a miniature multicolor blossom atop an impossibly delicate white lace doily – all of handcrafted porcelain – cost up to $10 each. Larger ones, like a 6" highly detailed figure of Cupid or a pair of children in tender embrace, may top $200.

— Melody Amsel-Arieli

▲ Tankard, cylindrical shape with polychrome enameled high relief of entombment of Christ, angel finial mounted to hinged gilt bronze frame, 19th century, underglaze mark, 9-1/4" h. . **$461**

Courtesy Skinner, Inc., www.skinnerinc.com

Porcelain box with bronze mounts, circa 1880-1890, 4 1/2" h. x 8" w. x 4-1/2" d... **$2,800**

Courtesy Moss Antiques, www.1stdibs.com

▶ Figures of man on park bench feeding birds, man at brazier, and two men catching geese......................... **$125-$156**

Courtesy of Bonhams, www.bonhams.com

Oval casket with high relief panels of figures, 8.7" h......... **$206 (2007)**

Courtesy of Bonhams, www.bonhams.com

Mug and cover, circa 1890, 11-1/2" h., 6" dia. **$1,750**

Courtesy of Moss Antiques, www.1stdibs.com

"Statue Seller" figurine, woman with small head holding basket and bust of warrior, 1750-1753, 7-1/3" h. **$130,000**

Courtesy of Christie's Images Ltd., 2005, www.christies.com

Gilt bronze "cage" chandelier with Capodimonte porcelain characters, internal lighting and four lights, with drop, ball, and flower pendants, 1880, 33.46" h., 21.65" dia. **$5,403**

Courtesy of JLF-Jean Luc Ferrand, www.1stdibs.com

"Artemax" handcrafted Capodimonte tower of purple wisteria in hand-woven porcelain basket, approximately 14" x 10". **$1,100**

Courtesy of Capodimonte's Finest © 2015, www.capodimonte-porcelain.com

"Clio" handcrafted Capodimonte rose, daisy, and field flower centerpiece in porcelain decorative base, approximately 16" x 14". **$740**

Courtesy of Capodimonte's Finest © 2015, www.capodimonte-porcelain.com

CERAMICS

chinese export porcelain

LARGE QUANTITIES OF porcelain have been made in China for export to America from the 1780s, much of it shipped from the ports of Canton and Nanking. A major source of this porcelain was Ching-te-Chen in Kiangsi province, but wares were also made elsewhere. The largest quantities were blue and white. Prices fluctuate considerably, depending on age, condition, decoration, etc.

Nine blue and white hexagonal dishes, 17th/18th century, seven landscape scenes, one with woman in garden, one with peonies and rockery, most with small chips and minor wear along edges, some with hairlines, 9" dia. **$474**

Courtesy of James D. Julia Auctioneers, Fairfield, Maine, www.jamesdjuliacom

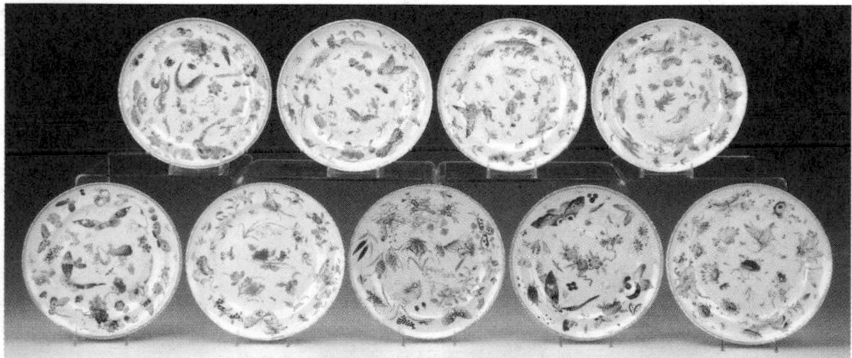

Nine famille rose dishes, 19th century, each with butterflies and various insects, five in good condition, one with hairline, one with small chip, and three restored, 8" dia. Provenance: According to family tradition, these items were brought back from China by Capt. Richard Alsager (1781-1841), a captain in the East India Co. and later MP (1835-1841) for Eastern Surrey in England. His last trip to China was in the mid-1820s. **$830**

Courtesy of James D. Julia Auctioneers, Fairfield, Maine, www.jamesdjuliacom

Four famille rose plates, Yongzheng Period (1723-1735), central design of peonies and Daoist accessories, minor rubbing to enamels, one with star fracture, remainder with minor wear, 9" dia. **$770**

Courtesy of James D. Julia Auctioneers, Fairfield, Maine, www.jamesdjuliacom

Large blanc de chine standing figure of Guanyin, late Qing Dynasty, with hands in prayer and wearing long flowing robes while standing on lotus leaf pedestal, left hand holding vase, good condition, 20" h. **$593**

Courtesy of James D. Julia Auctioneers, Fairfield, Maine, www.jamesdjuliacom

Famille rose porcelain panel inlay table screen, early 19th century, interior setting of noble with two beauties, mounted in wood stand, good condition, 15" h. Provenance: According to family tradition, this item was brought back from China by Capt. Richard Alsager (1781-1841), a captain in the East India Co. and later MP (1835-1841) for Eastern Surrey in England. His last trip to China was in the mid-1820s. **$2,370**

Courtesy of James D. Julia Auctioneers, Fairfield, Maine, www.jamesdjuliacom

Small blanc de chine Gu vase, 18th/19th century, typical form with thick-beaded waist, good condition, 5-1/2" h. **$948**

Courtesy of James D. Julia Auctioneers, Fairfield, Maine, www.jamesdjuliacom

Famille rose phoenix bowl, Guangxu mark and of period, with four phoenix in flight surrounded by vines and flowers, red and gilt band around top rim and foot, carved wood stand with openwork of same period, very good condition, one glaze pop at rim, 3-1/2" h., 8-1/4" dia. Provenance: From the estate of a midwestern public university chancellor who was invited to speak in China in the 1930s and visited Japan and India, where he acquired this item; he died in the late 1930s...**$8,888**

Courtesy of James D. Julia Auctioneers, Fairfield, Maine, www.jamesdjuliacom

Famille rose phoenix dish, Guangxu mark and of period, four phoenix in flight surrounded by vines and flowers encircled by red and gilt ring around rim, underside with three sprays of vines and flowers, very good condition, 10-3/4" dia. Provenance: From the estate of a midwestern public university chancellor who was invited to speak in China in the 1930s and visited Japan and India, where he acquired this item; he died in the late 1930s. **$7,703**

Courtesy of James D. Julia Auctioneers, Fairfield, Maine, www.jamesdjuliacom

Bottle-form vase, early 19th century, with polychrome and gilt decoration, neck with projecting collar continuing to bulbous body and footed base with two large cartouches with figural scenes, small scratches and areas of glaze loss on cartouches, 10-1/4" h......... **$615**

Courtesy of Skinner, Inc., www.skinnerinc.com

Teapot, early 19th century, domed lid with turned finial and flared edge above globular body with gilt crabstock spout and scrolled handle, lid with oval reserves with rose enamel landscapes within patterned gilt ground, body painted with domestic scenes within circular reserves on similar ground, shaped reserves with rose enamel landscapes, minor wear to gilt, 6-1/4" h................. **$984**

Courtesy of Skinner, Inc., www.skinnerinc.com

Pair of armorial soup plates, circa 1726, centering arms of Yonge and motto "TRIA JUNCTA IN UNO," border and cavetto in red and gilt with Taoist symbols, chips, 9" dia. **$3,567**

Courtesy of Skinner, Inc., www.skinnerinc.com

"The Declaration of Independence" punch bowl, circa 1920-1938, interior rim with floral garland centering floral arrangement at interior center, exterior polychrome-decorated with scenes of founding fathers and Declaration of Independence signers gathered at tables, loosely based on John Trumbull painting from circa 1817 showing presentation of document's first draft to Congress, figures surmounted by Union shield and spread-wing eagle clutching olive branch and arrows, his beak holding banner reading "THE DECLARATION OF INDEPENDENCE," and 13 blue stars above, minor rim chip, small rim repair with tight associated hairline crack through figures to right of eagle's shield on one side, minor wear to decoration, 4-1/2" h., 11-1/2" dia..... **$5,228**

Courtesy of Skinner, Inc., www.skinnerinc.com

"Glorious Victory at Culloden" mug, circa 1750, bulbous body and flared rim with large circular medallion of Duke of Cumberland wearing tricorn hat and red coat on crosshatched gray background, surrounded with lettering "Apl 16th 1746 In remembrance of Glorious Victory at Culloden" and scalloped border, flanked by large floral sprays, loop handle with molded terminal, horizontal hairline crack in body extending into portrait, glaze loss to sides of handle, 6-1/4". The battle at Culloden, in the Scottish highlands, was the final and decisive victory by English forces led by William Augustus, the Duke of Cumberland, over the Jacobite uprising of 1745. .... **$3,567**

Courtesy of Skinner, Inc., www.skinnerinc.com

Shaped platter, late 18th century, polychrome lattice border and phoenix at top, center with social scene, mounted in octagonal gilt frame with velvet liner, small rim chip, edge gilding worn with areas touched up with gold paint, plate 9-1/2" h. x 12" w. **$369**

Courtesy of Skinner, Inc., www.skinnerinc.com

Shaped serving dish, mid-18th century, square with shaped sides, enamel-decorated border with gilt edging and coat of arms at top center with rampant whippets flanking shield above banner lettered "Forward Ours," 9-1/4" w.... **$369**

Courtesy of Skinner, Inc., www.skinnerinc.com

Oval fruit basket, circa 1770, flared black enamel-decorated and parcel-gilt rim and gilt shaped handles above pierced latticework sides with applied flowers, interior bottom with shaped reserve of two men looking outward to harbor, one handle repaired, 3" h. x 8-1/4" w. **$277**

Courtesy of Skinner, Inc., www.skinnerinc.com

Famille rose lotus pattern punch bowl, circa 1760, exterior with three tiers of overlapping pink lotus petals and quatrefoil gilt medallions with lotus flower within, well with flower and vine pattern, minor imperfections, 5" h., 11" dia.......................... **$3,075**

Courtesy of Skinner, Inc., www.skinnerinc.com

Pair of rose medallion vases, 19th century, baluster forms with gilt monkey head faux handles, now fitted as lamps, on custom turned hardwood bases (unattached), one vase reconstructed, gilt wear, 17-1/4" h. to top of vase. **$461**

Courtesy of Skinner, Inc., www.skinnerinc.com

Famille rose umbrella stand, 19th century, surface wear and scratches, minor crack in base, 24-5/8" h., 9-1/2" dia. **$800**

Courtesy of Skinner, Inc., www.skinnerinc.com

Soup tureen and stand, 1770-1780, octagonal top above conforming basin with hog's head handles and deep stand, lid and sides of tureen and bottom center of stand polychrome-decorated with arms of Baillie impaling Campbell, borders of black enamel floral garlands and gilding, repaired break to body of tureen, gilt wear and loss, 9-3/4" h. overall, stand 14-1/2" l. **$369**

Courtesy of Skinner, Inc., www.skinnerinc.com

Bird-decorated platter, late 18th century, oval form with gilt and red enamel chain border and four floral sprays centering scene with five birds in marsh landscape, minor roughness to edge, minor wear to central image, 15-1/4" l. . **$400**

Courtesy of Skinner, Inc., www.skinnerinc.com

Polychrome platter, molded and shaped rim with polychrome four-part border, red, blue, and green outer edge, green band with black dots, red beading, and lavender scrollwork, red and blue cavetto centering crown surmounted by crossed flags of India and Great Britain, next to portrait within green foliate wreath above date 1757, 12-1/4" l. **$1,230**

Courtesy of Skinner, Inc., www.skinnerinc.com

Canton reticulated fruit basket and undertray, 19th century, with blue and white pagoda, river, and landscape scene, 3-3/4" h. x 9-1/8" w. **$492**

Courtesy of Skinner, Inc., www.skinnerinc.com

Famille rose decorated porcelain vase and cover, 19th century, polychrome enamel with cartouches of flowers within black ground with flowers and scrolled vines, very good condition throughout with no evidence of cracks, chips or restorations, 11" h. **$185**

Courtesy of Skinner, Inc., www.skinnerinc.com

Partial tea and chocolate service, mid-18th century, black floral and butterfly design with gilt highlights, bulbous teapot, two waste bowls, hexagonal dish, leaf-form dish, small cream jug, small plate, nine saucers, six tea bowls, and five handled chocolate cups, imperfections and repairs, teapot 5-1/2" h. x 7-3/4" l., leaf-form dish 7-1/4", bowls to 6" dia., cream jug 3-3/4" h. **$1,353**

Courtesy of Skinner, Inc., www.skinnerinc.com

Three graduated rose canton serving dishes, 19th century, minor wear, each with wear to rim gilding and enamel, largest with two repaired chips to underside of rim, medium with small rim nicks, smallest with wear to gilding and enamel, to 11-5/8" w. **$461**

Courtesy of Skinner, Inc., www.skinnerinc.com

CERAMICS

coalport

COALPORT PORCELAIN WORKS (John Rose & Co.) operated at Coalport, Shropshire, England, from about 1795 to 1926. In 1926, production was moved to Staffordshire. Since 1951 the firm has operated as Coalport China, Ltd., producing bone china.

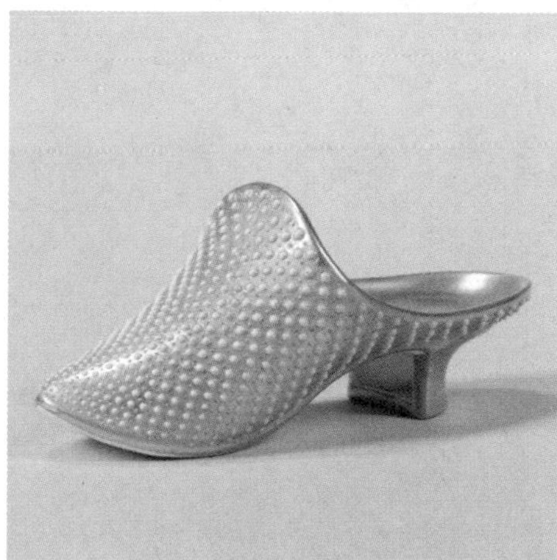

Jeweled porcelain slipper, England, late 19th century, allover gold ground with turquoise enamel jeweling, printed mark, several jewels with pitting, 5-1/4" l. **$554**

Courtesy of Skinner, Inc., www.skinnerinc.com

Pair of jeweled porcelain vases, England, late 19th century, bottle shape with mask handles to pale pink ground and turquoise enamel jeweling to gold field, printed marks, one vase with several jewels pitted, other vase in very good condition, 6-5/8" h. **$1,230**

Courtesy of Skinner, Inc., www.skinnerinc.com

Pair of jeweled porcelain vases and covers, England, late 19th century, each with yellow ground and gold field with turquoise enamel jeweling, printed marks, both covers heavily restored, one vase with several jewels touched up and one chipped, other vase with several jewels touched up, one missing, and two chipped, 7-3/4" h. **$615**

Courtesy of Skinner, Inc., www.skinnerinc.com

Jeweled porcelain box and cover, England, late 19th century, flat circular shape with turquoise enamel jeweling to gold ground, cover set with polychrome enameled simulated semiprecious medallion, printed crown mark, one jewel partially missing to cover, no pitting, 2-1/2" dia. **$461**

Courtesy of Skinner, Inc., www.skinnerinc.com

Jeweled porcelain box and cover, England, late 19th century, flat low-waisted circular shape, knop, cover, and box border decorated with simulated semiprecious stones to ivory ground with turquoise enamel jeweling to fields of gold, printed mark, knop jewel crazed, pitting to eight to 10 jewels, two jewels with chips, 2-1/4" h., 4" dia. **$1,046**

Courtesy of Skinner, Inc., www.skinnerinc.com

Jeweled porcelain egg-shaped box and cover, England, late 19th century, oval pink ground heavily gilded and decorated with turquoise enamel jeweling bordered with simulated semiprecious stones, printed mark, two jewels with pits, one chipped, 2-7/8" l. **$984**

Courtesy of Skinner, Inc., www.skinnerinc.com

Jeweled porcelain box and cover, England, late 19th century, kidney shape with gold ground and central simulated semiprecious stones surrounded by raised gold stars set with turquoise and white jeweling, printed mark, very good condition throughout, 3-5/8" l. **$800**

Courtesy of Skinner, Inc., www.skinnerinc.com

Jeweled porcelain ewer, England, late 19th century, scrolled foliate molded handle, yellow ground with turquoise enameled jeweling to gold field, shoulder with simulated red stones, printed mark, very good condition throughout, 7-1/2" h. **$923**

Courtesy of Skinner, Inc., www.skinnerinc.com

Jeweled porcelain shell-shaped box and cover, England, late 19th century, cover with simulated semiprecious stone centering gold ground adorned with turquoise jeweling, printed mark, very good condition throughout, 3-3/4" l. **$1,107**

Courtesy of Skinner, Inc., www.skinnerinc.com

Jeweled porcelain scent bottle, England, late 19th century, ovoid, with hinged cover and raised gold to polychrome enameled jeweling and stone-like free-form body, unmarked, very good condition throughout, 4-5/8" l. **$861**

Courtesy of Skinner, Inc., www.skinnerinc.com

Jeweled porcelain perfume bottle, England, late 19th century, heart shape with pink ground, shoulders with molded birds, central band with florets enamel decorated with simulated semiprecious stones, turquoise adorned jeweling to gold field at either side, hinged silver-plated cover, crazing to pink ground, slight patch of gilt wear to one side knop, several slight chips and pitting to jeweling, 4-1/8" l. **$1,169**

Courtesy of Skinner, Inc., www.skinnerinc.com

Jeweled porcelain perfume bottle, England, late 19th century, globular body with similarly shaped hinged cover, each with turquoise enamel jeweling to gold field with polychrome jeweled center band and atop cover, printed crown mark, slight crazing to each opal medallion, all jewels present, three to four with pitting, 3-3/4" h. **$677**

Courtesy of Skinner, Inc., www.skinnerinc.com

Jeweled porcelain scalloped box and cover, England, late 19th century, pink ground with polychrome decorated and jeweled star bands bordering turquoise jeweled gold fields, floral knop, printed mark, restored chip to inner collar of cover, base with tips of two jewels chipped, several jewels with pitting, 3-1/4" dia........... **$1,599**

Courtesy of Skinner, Inc., www.skinnerinc.com

Jeweled porcelain vase and cover, England, late 19th century, scrolled dolphin head and foliate molded handles to bottle shape with green ground and central polychrome enameled cartouches of landscapes and flowers beneath gold field adorned with turquoise jeweling, printed mark, vase in very good condition throughout, cover with finial repair to stem and touch up to one chip of enamel, 9-1/4" h. **$615**

Courtesy of Skinner, Inc., www.skinnerinc.com

Jeweled porcelain box and cover, England, late 19th century, square shape with rounded corners, gilded foliage bordering floriform gold medallion set with applied turquoise enamel jeweling centered with simulated enamel stone, printed crown mark, three turquoise jewels with pitting, 5" l. **$544**

Courtesy of Skinner, Inc., www.skinnerinc.com

Pair of jeweled porcelain vases and covers, England, late 19th century, each with molded lion head handles to ivory ground heavily gilded and decorated with turquoise enamel jeweling, band of simulated semiprecious stones about shoulder, printed mark, one cover with chip inside of inner collar, each vase with scattered abrasions to gilt ground, 6-3/4" h. **$738**

Courtesy of Skinner, Inc., www.skinnerinc.com

Jeweled porcelain covered bowl, England, late 19th century, with two foliate adorned side handles, pink ground with central band of stars with simulated semiprecious stones, surrounded by turquoise jewels set to gold field, printed mark, bowl with one turquoise jewel chipped and two with pitting, 4-7/8" h. overall. **$1,046**

Courtesy of Skinner, Inc., www.skinnerinc.com

Pair of Coalport porcelain plates, England, late 19th century, each with two-tone white and ivory ground, scalloped rim molded and decorated with shells, border with raised gold scrolled foliage and turquoise enameled florets, centers with scattered jeweling to scrolled foliage bordering central octagonal landscape cartouche, printed mark, each with light surface enamel and gilt wear, 9-1/2" dia.. **$277**

Courtesy of Skinner, Inc., www.skinnerinc.com

CERAMICS

contemporary

THE PROLIFIC TREND of contemporary ceramics appearing in museum exhibits, auctions, and at shows the last few years has not gone unnoticed. In many cases, American ceramic art is gaining increasing respect and preference as the medium of choice of many of today's most popular artists. The versatile and inexpensive material is easy to manipulate. The artist may express fine details of figurative sculptures or ugly mugs, such as popular face jugs, which were first made as early as the 14th century.

"We are just now adopting the perception of ceramics as fine art," said Leon Benrimon, New York Director of Modern & Contemporary Art at Heritage Auctions. "California gave rise to an active American ceramic art scene since the 1950s, and studio ceramics are getting a second glance from collectors as well."

It is always easy to find modern ceramics at garage sales and thrift stores, but it's not always easy to recognize the artist or an object's potential value upon first inspection. That fact almost cost the Caddo Indian Nation a rare piece of pottery that turned up in a Goodwill thrift store donation box. Goodwill placed the pear-form, 7-1/2" piece of pottery, decorated with two rows of symmetrical raised spikes, up for bids on shopgoodwill.com, the charity's online auction website. Buyers placed bids before a few astute historians alerted Goodwill of its potential historical value. Sure enough, tucked deep inside was a note that stated the item was "found in a burial mound near Spiro, Oklahoma, in 1970."

Historians think the simple ceramic pot originated from Oklahoma's Spiro Mounds archaeological site and could be thousands of years old. Members of the Caddo Indian Nation maintained a permanent settlement from approximately 800 to 1450, but they have inhabited the general area for 8,000 years. Goodwill returned the piece to the tribe.

Several 20th century modern and contemporary artists known more for their watercolors or oils expanded into ceramics. Collectors avidly pursue Wassily Kandinsky's glazed porcelain cups and saucers, which he produced in 1923. A pair recently sold for $1,250, an affordable sum compared to the artist's famed geometric and abstract paintings, which have sold for $1.6 million.

Cup and saucer painted in underglaze (hammer-scythe-cog), 1923, Wassily Kandinsky, 4-3/4" dia. **$1,250**

Courtesy of Heritage Auctions, ha.com

Contemporary ceramics dealer Marilyn Maddox seeks art pottery from the 1960s and 1970s. Collectors are drawn to vases, jugs, and decorative pieces popularly referred to as Fat Lava, a relatively new name used to describe chunky, brightly colored glazes.

"Young people love West German pottery," she said. "The more colors the better!" Small pitchers in red, brown, and azure drip glazes start at $75 and handled vessels in pockmarked glaze quickly sell for $65.

Perhaps the most famous 20th century contemporary artist to work with ceramics is Pablo Picasso, who began experimenting in the late 1940s. He produced more than 2,000 pieces after meeting Suzanne and Georges Ramié and visiting their Madoura Pottery workshop in Vallauris. Original vessels crafted by the master's hand can easily bring more than $300,000 at auction. It's unlikely to find an original at a garage sale, but that doesn't mean striking works by well-known artists are passed over all the time.

At a Crocker Farm stoneware auction in 2015, a face jug set a record after it was purchased at a garage sale for $1.50. The new owner posted the piece - made with kaolin eyes and teeth - on eBay, but when she became inundated with aggressive offers she turned to a specialist for help. Only then did she learn the rare, 5-1/2-inch tall, alkaline-glazed stoneware jug was made in Edgefield, South Carolina in 1860 and that it was worth a great deal more than $1.50. When the gavel fell, the small jug set a world record when it sold for $92,000.

– Eric Bradley

West German pottery with Fat Lava glazes in a variety of colors are hot sellers for dealer Marilyn Maddox, owner of Welcome Back Antiques. Young collectors are drawn to the unusual shapes and colors and like the fact that the collectibles can be used on the table.

Courtesy of Eric Bradley

"Sujet Poissin" red earthenware fish-form pitcher, 1962, Pablo Picasso (Spain, 1881-1973), pitcher conceived in 1952 and executed in 1962, one of 500... **$3,900**

Courtesy of A. B. Levy's, www.ablevys.com

"Madoura chouette" (wood owl) ceramic vase, 1969, Pablo Picasso, 11-1/2" h. **$16,800**

Courtesy of Los Angeles Auction House, www.laauctionhouse.com

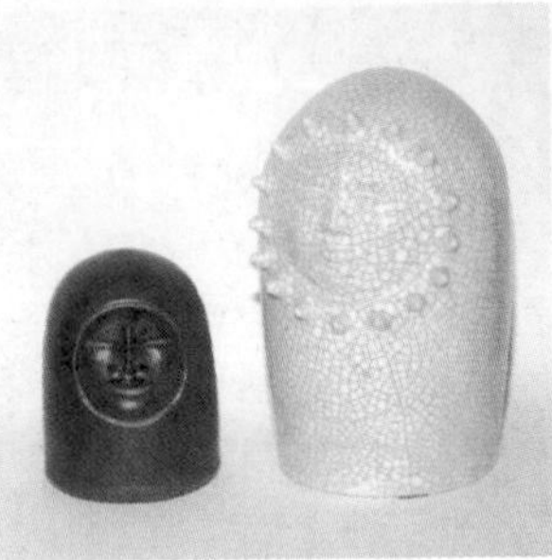

Sun and Moon sculptural domes, circa mid-20th century, Paul Bellardo (American, b. 1924), each signed, 9-1/2" h. **$175**

Courtesy of Doyle New York, www.doylenewyork.com

Florida Faience vase, 2004, signed "Last Great Pot Hand Made" on base, 13" h., 7-1/2" dia. **$120**

Courtesy of Turkey Creek Auctions, Inc., www.antiqueauctionsfl.com

Vase depicting African natives, elephant, and cat, 1988, W. Ledesma, 5-3/4" h. **$50**

Courtesy of Strawser Auction Group, www. strawserauctions.com

Porcelain fish, Hungary, marked Herend, 2-3/4" h.................. **$70**

Courtesy of Main Street Mining Co., www.mainstreetmining.com

Vase with painted woman and rooster, 20th century, Pillin Pottery, marked "Pillin," 6-1/4" h. x 3-3/4" w. **$200**

Courtesy of Main Street Mining Co., www.mainstreetmining.com

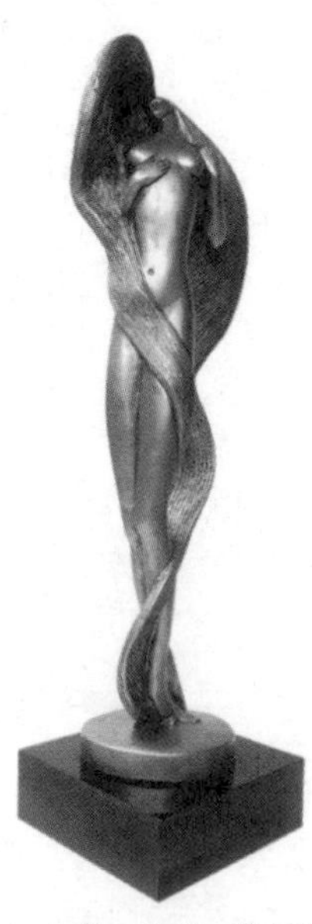

Sculpture, "Inspiration," 1987, David Fisher, marked "Fisher, Austin Prod Inc., AP3453, 1987," 30" h., base 3" h. **$30**

Courtesy of Main Street Mining Co., www.mainstreetmining.com

Figural set, "Wedding Ceremony" by Josepina Aguilar, nine pieces, all signed and marked. **$60**

Courtesy of Main Street Mining Co., www.mainstreetmining.com

Porcelain vase, Hawaiian, 20th century, marked "07, Dorothy Okuinate, Plumeria, K3," 4" h. **$15**

Courtesy of Main Street Mining Co., www.mainstreetmining.com

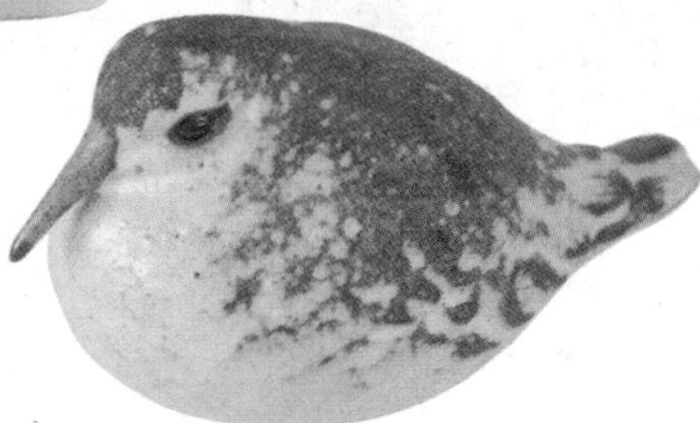

Bird, unmarked, 6" l. x 3-1/5" h. **$24**

Courtesy of Main Street Mining Co., www.mainstreetmining.com

"The Seasons" (Summer, Fall, Winter, and Spring) glazed earthenware sculptures, 1938, Viktor Schreckengost (American, 1906-2008), incised signature "VIKTOR SCHRECKENGOST" to each, 18" h. .... **$150,000-$250,000**

Courtesy of Heritage Auctions, ha.com

INSIDE INTEL *with* LEON BENRIMON

Leon Benrimon, New York Director of Modern & Contemporary Art, Heritage Auctions

COLLECTORS OF CONTEMPORARY CERAMICS SHOULD LOOK FOR THESE FIVE THINGS BEFORE BUYING:

- **LOOK FOR A SIGNATURE.** A signed piece is the first clue that you're holding an original work of art.
- **IS IT HANDMADE?** Telltale signs are grooves indicative of fingertips.
- **IS IT HAND-PAINTED?** Tiny imperfections or an artist's creative liberty can often be spotted in a piece of studio ceramics that has been hand-painted.
- **CONSIDER FORM AND FUNCTION.** The best works strike an artistic balance between the two: Handles are proportional and the piece is neither too heavy nor too light.
- **EYE APPEAL.** Is the piece attractive? Is it damaged?

"If you love it, buy it," Benrimon said. "Even if it's not worth more, you still get to live with a wonderful piece of original art."

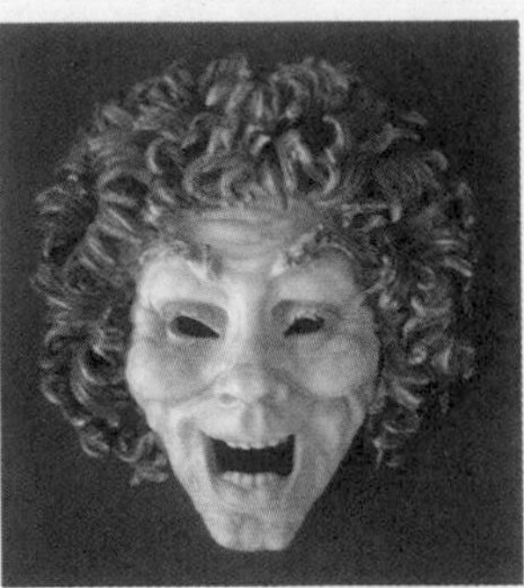
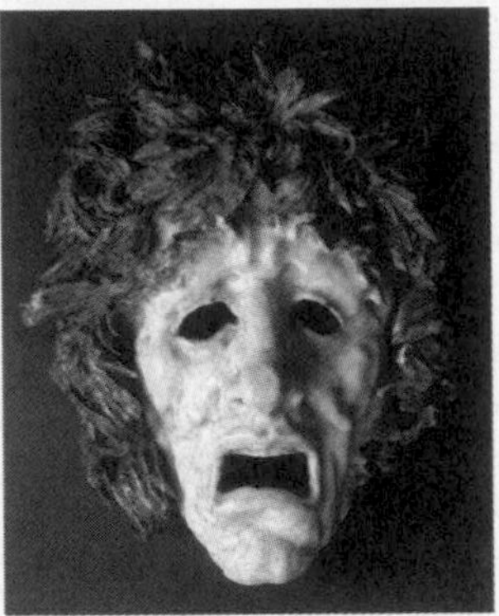

Five stylized glazed stoneware heads, circa 1945, Professor Eugenio Pattarino (Italian, 1885-1971), 11" h. x 9" w. x 4-1/2" d. **$3,250**

Courtesy of Heritage Auctions, ha.com

Movie star ceramic face masks, circa 1988, made by Clay Art of San Francisco, with Clay Art stickers and/or markings on back, set of 12: Humphrey Bogart, Marlon Brando, Charlie Chaplin, Joan Crawford, James Dean, Clark Gable, Clark Gable, Judy Garland, Elvis Presley, Elizabeth Taylor, John Wayne, and Mae West, all mostly 14" h. x 12" w. x 4" d. **$625**

Courtesy of Heritage Auctions, ha.com

Pair of Native American motif whiskey jugs, circa 1960s, Cheever Meaders, ash glaze, 8-1/2" h. **$13,200**

Courtesy of Slotin Folk Art Auction, www.slotinfolkart.com

Asian flattened body vase, 20th century, multiple color glazes, incised mark on bottom, 8" h., 16-1/2" dia. **$540**

Courtesy of Nadeau's Auction Gallery, www.nadeausauction.com

Acoma polychrome jar with feather and star designs with fingernail detailing, 20th century, Jay Vallo, marked "Jay Vallo, Acoma, N.M.," 10-3/4" h., 11" dia. **$225**

Courtesy of Allard Auctions, Inc., www.allardauctions.com

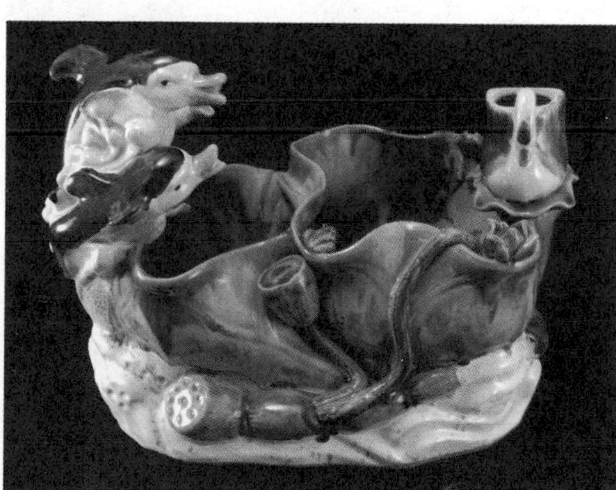

Sea life and swan freeform ceramic centerpiece, unmarked, 16" l. x 8-1/2" w. x 12" h. **$15**

Courtesy of Specialists of the South, Inc., www.specialistsofthesouth.com

Clown bust with mixed media attachments, marked 300/400, initialed LB, 22" h. **$250**

Courtesy of Auction Gallery of the Palm Beaches, West Palm Beach, Florida

▲ Bottle neck glazed stoneware vase, circa 1960, Paul Pressburger (American, 20th century), 11-3/4" h. **$375**

Courtesy of Heritage Auctions, ha.com

▶ Mermaid glazed ceramic figure, circa 1950, Scandinavian Modernist School, 20th century, 12-1/2" h..................................... **$375**

Courtesy of Heritage Auctions, ha.com

Ceramic baluster vase, Otto and Vivika Heino (American, 20th century), 3-3/4" h., 4" dia. Both artists signed their pots Vivika + Otto, regardless of who actually made them............................... **$575**

Courtesy of Heritage Auctions, ha.com

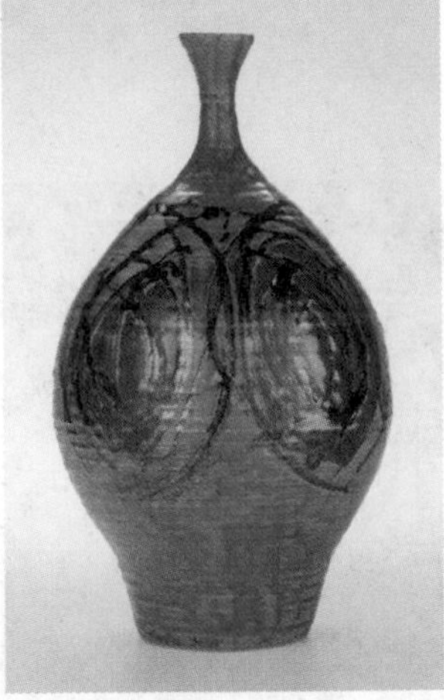

Bottle neck glazed stoneware vase, circa 1960, J.T. Abernathy (American, b. 1923), 16-1/2" h............... **$562**

Courtesy of Heritage Auctions, ha.com

CERAMICS

cowan

R. GUY COWAN opened his first pottery studio in 1912 in Lakewood, Ohio. The pottery operated almost continuously, with the exception of a break during World War I, at various locations in the Cleveland area until it was forced to close in 1931 due to financial difficulties.

Many of the 20th century's finest artists began with Cowan and its associate, the Cleveland School of Art. This fine art pottery, particularly the designer pieces, is highly sought after by collectors.

Many people are unaware that it was due to R. Guy Cowan's perseverance and tireless work that art pottery is today considered an art form and found in many art museums.

For more information on Cowan pottery, see *Antique Trader Pottery & Porcelain Ceramics Price Guide, 7th edition.*

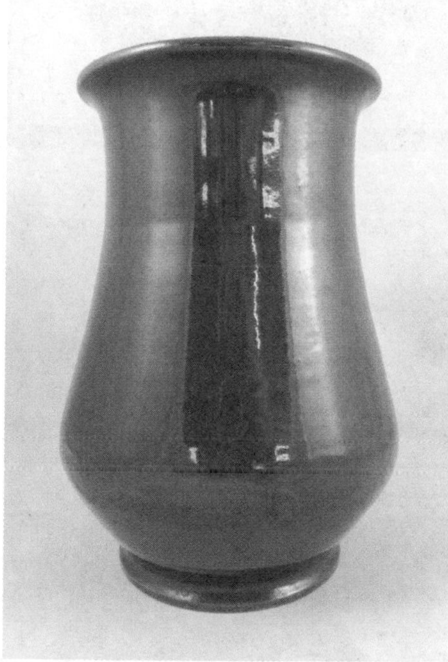

Vase, turquoise glaze, incised "R. Guy Cowan" with monogram on base, 8-1/2" h. **$1,029**

Courtesy of Rachel Davis Fine Arts, www.racheldavisfinearts.com

Squirrel vase, shape V-17, designed by Waylande Gregory, blue and light green high glazes, impressed "Cowan" with circular company logo on bottom, fine overall crazing, 8-1/2" h. **$190**

Courtesy of Mark Mussio, Humler & Nolan, www.humlernolan.com

top lot

Vase with scroll handles, shape V-99, scroll pattern painted by shape's designer, Viktor Schreckengost, Egyptian blue glaze, impressed circular Cowan logo, "Cowan" in block letters with shape number written in pencil, excellent original condition, 6" h. $3,200

COURTESY OF MARK MUSSIO, HUMLER & NOLAN, WWW.HUMLERNOLAN.COM

Console set, center bowl and pair of candlesticks, yellow glaze, all three pieces marked, bowl 5-1/2" h. x 16" w., candlesticks 4" h. **$48**

Courtesy of Rachel Davis Fine Arts, www.racheldavisfinearts.com

Console set, center bowl and two compotes, ivory glaze exterior, green interior, various sizes......................... **$48**

Courtesy of Rachel Davis Fine Arts, www.racheldavisfinearts.com

CERAMICS

dedham

DEDHAM POTTERY WAS originally organized in 1866 by Alexander W. Robertson in Chelsea, Massachusetts, and became A.W. & H. Roberson in 1868. In 1872, the name was changed to Chelsea Keramic Art Works and in 1891 to Chelsea Pottery, U.S.A. About 1895, the pottery was moved to Dedham, Massachusetts, and was renamed Dedham Pottery. Production ceased in 1943. High-fired colored wares and crackleware were specialties. The rabbit is said to have been the most popular decoration in blue on crackleware.

Assembled tea and coffee set, 21 pieces, each with crackleware glaze in rabbit pattern: eight associated teacups and saucers, tumbler, coffeepot, covered sugar, cream pitcher, and later teapot, largest 8-1/2" h. **$1,098**

Courtesy of Clars Auction Gallery, www.clars.com

Plate in polar bear pattern, 20th century, undamaged, 8-3/4" dia. **$240**

Courtesy of Eldreds, www.eldreds.com

Plate in duck pattern, 20th century, undamaged, 8-1/4" dia. **$204**

Courtesy of Eldreds, www.eldreds.com

Sixteen associated table items, each with crackleware glaze in floral patterns: three cereal bowls, teacup, saucer, two bread plates, two luncheon plates, and seven dessert plates, largest 10" dia. **$397**

Courtesy of Clars Auction Gallery, www.clars.com

Seven associated table items, each with crackleware glaze in various rare patterns: four bread plates, three in butterfly pattern and one in polar bear pattern, and three luncheon plates, two in mushroom pattern and one in turkey pattern, 10" dia. **$732**

Courtesy of Clars Auction Gallery, www.clars.com

Rabbit pattern coffeepot and cover, first quarter 20th century, blue and white with crackleware glaze, tall tapered form, faintly marked with blue rabbit stamp, hand-incised D5, two hairlines to lower terminal of handle, possibly as made, firing separation to underside of upper handle, 8-1/2" h. overall. **$115**

Courtesy of Jeffrey S. Evans & Associates, www.jeffreysevans.com

Five rabbit pattern plates, first half 20th century, blue and white with crackleware glaze, luncheon and charger sizes, each marked with blue rabbit stamp, charger with "Registered" below, undamaged, 8-1/2" and 12" dia. **$374**

Courtesy of Jeffrey S. Evans & Associates, www.jeffreysevans.com

Three grape pattern table items, first quarter 20th century, serving bowl, dinner plate, and luncheon plate, blue and white with crackleware glaze, each marked with blue rabbit stamp, undamaged, minor chip to underside of rim of luncheon plate, bowl with light interior stains/wear, bowl 4" h., 9" dia., plates 8-1/2" and 10" dia. **$127**

Courtesy of Jeffrey S. Evans & Associates, www.jeffreysevans.com

Six rabbit pattern luncheon plates, first quarter 20th century, blue and white with crackleware glaze, each marked with blue rabbit stamp, undamaged, 8-1/2" dia. **$345**

Courtesy of Jeffrey S. Evans & Associates, www.jeffreysevans.com

Four pieces: swan saucer, 5-3/4 dia.; magnolia bowl, 5-1/2" dia; and two rabbit plates, 6-1/4" and 8-1/2" dia., all with various marks, larger rabbit plate with staining beneath crackleware glaze. **$180**

Courtesy of Eldred's, www.eldreds.com

Two rabbit pattern items, first quarter 20th century, blue and white with crackleware glaze, sugar bowl with cover and tankard mug, each marked with blue rabbit stamp, mug hand-incised "Dedham Pottery," undamaged, flake to inner flange of cover, probably as made, mug with two short firing lines to foot rim, as made, 4-3/4" and 4" h. overall **$115**

Courtesy of Jeffrey S. Evans & Associates, www.jeffreysevans.com

Six rabbit pattern table items, first quarter 20th century, blue and white with crackleware glaze, covered sugar, creamer, cup and saucer, and salt and pepper shakers with "D.P." painted in blue, others marked with blue rabbit stamp, undamaged, light hairlines to interior of creamer, possibly as made, shakers 2-1/2" h. **$184**

Courtesy of Jeffrey S. Evans & Associates, www.jeffreysevans.com

Three assorted pattern plates, first half 20th century, blue and white with crackleware glaze, turkey and crab pattern luncheon plates and swan pattern dinner plate, each marked with blue rabbit stamp, swan with "Registered" below, undamaged, both with light wear to center, crab with two hairlines and flake to foot rim, swan and turkey 8-3/8" and 10" dia. **$207**

Courtesy of Jeffrey S. Evans & Associates, www.jeffreysevans.com

Eighteen table items, each with crackleware glaze in rabbit pattern: cereal bowl, two luncheon plates, eight dessert plates in various sizes, three bread plates, and four later cereal bowls. **$1,037**

Courtesy of Clars Auction Gallery, www.clars.com

Three serving bowls, each with crackleware glaze in rabbit pattern, largest 6" h., 12" dia. **$427**

Courtesy of Clars Auction Gallery, www.clars.com

Magnolia pattern cereal bowl, first quarter 20th century, blue and white with crackleware glaze, marked with blue rabbit stamp, undamaged, 2-5/8" h., 6" dia. **$81**

Courtesy of Jeffrey S. Evans & Associates, www.jeffreysevans.com

CERAMICS

delft

IN THE EARLY 17th century, Italian potters settled in Holland and began producing tin-glazed earthenwares, often decorated with pseudo-Oriental designs based on Chinese porcelain wares. The city of Delft became the center of this pottery production, and several firms produced the wares throughout the 17th and early 18th century. A majority of the pieces featured blue on white designs, but polychrome wares were also made. The Dutch Delftwares were also shipped to England, where eventually the English copied them at potteries in such cities as Bristol, Lambeth, and Liverpool. Although still produced today, Delft peaked in popularity by the mid-18th century.

For more examples of Delft pottery, see *Antique Trader Porcelain & Pottery Ceramics Price Guide,* 7th edition.

Polychrome charger, Holland, 18th century, with puce scroll line rim above border with flowers, surrounding center with palm among rockwork, peony and other foliage, underside with painted blue AB monogram mark, 13-1/2" dia. **$336**

Courtesy of Clars Auction Gallery, www.clars.com

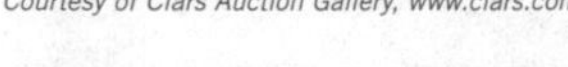

Polychrome decorated charger, Holland, mid-18th century, alternating floret and lattice border surrounding central floral landscape with bird, rim with numerous chips restored and age-typical glaze wear, 13-3/4" dia......................... **$369**

Courtesy of Skinner, Inc., www.skinnerinc.com

Two peacock chargers, Holland, 18th century, each with wide foliate border surrounding central urn with flowers, ochre enamel trim lines, De Klauw marks, each with age-typical rim chips and flaking, 13-3/4" dia. **$492**

Courtesy of Skinner, Inc., www.skinnerinc.com

Blue and white charger, England, probably Liverpool, mid-18th century, dot and lattice border to floral landscape with bird perched to one side, rim with areas of glaze repairs and scattered chipping, one surface chip along inner rim, 14" dia...... **$554**

Courtesy of Skinner, Inc., www.skinnerinc.com

Polychrome decorated charger, 18th century, zigzag and alternating floral and foliate border surrounding floral bouquet set in urn, age-typical edge chips and glaze flakes, 13-1/2" dia........................ **$431**

Courtesy of Skinner, Inc., www.skinnerinc.com

Dutch Pieter Paree charger, circa 1720-1740, painted in manganese, cobalt blue, ocher, and red with cell-and-diaper border with floral sprays in cartouches, pair of double blue lines enclosing large painting of vase of flowers, marked "MP" to underside, good condition with small chip, rim with minor chipping and flaking typical of ware, 13-1/2" dia. **$431**

Courtesy of Jeffrey S. Evans & Associates, www.jeffreysevans.com

Blue and white charger with detailed portrait of cavalier, floral and fruit border, artist signed, marked, good condition, 16" dia. **$118**

Courtesy of Woody Auction, www.woodyauction.com

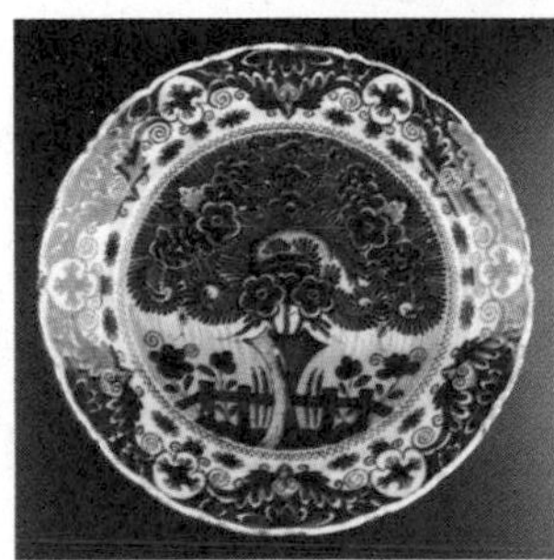

Dutch de Klauw charger with scallop-molded rim, circa 1750-1770, painted with cobalt blue monochrome enamel in Theeboom or Tea Plant pattern with full floral bouquet under border of lambrequins and scrolling foliate designs, underside with band of stylized designs near rim, marked with claw and 0617 to underside, very good condition, minor chipping and flaking typical of ware, 13-3/8" dia. **$575**

Courtesy of Jeffrey S. Evans & Associates, www.jeffreysevans.com

Dutch de Vergulde Blompot apothecary jars in molded cylindrical form with nearly flat covers, circa 1760-1780, bodies painted with "Myrrha" and "C. Boraginis" in reserve on shaped blue background with peafowl and baskets of fruit over putto's head and wings, and flowering sprays of fruit, marked "B.P" to underside, very good condition, minor chipping and flaking typical of ware, 9" h. **$316**

Courtesy of Jeffrey S. Evans & Associates, www.jeffreysevans.com

Dutch de Vergulde Blompot jar and cover of barrel-molded baluster-form with high-domed cover, 18th century, painted with lambrequins framing chinoiserie scenes before pavilion and pagoda, marked "B : P" to underside, jar lamped with drilled hole filled, collar rebuilt, and large section of cover rebuilt, 17-1/2" h... **$207**

Courtesy of Jeffrey S. Evans & Associates, www.jeffreysevans.com

Blue and white earthenware plaque, Holland, late 19th century, shield-shaped with male and female figure aboard horse-drawn cart, after painting by Otto Eerelman, good condition throughout, 22" h. x 15-1/2" w. **$800**

Courtesy of Skinner, Inc., www.skinnerinc.com

Dutch shaped oval plaque with scallop-molded border, circa 1950, centering boating and windmill scene, painted in shades of blue, various impressed, printed and hand-written marks to underside, excellent condition, glaze flakes to border, typical of ware, 11-1/2" x 13-3/4"............. **$161**

Courtesy of Jeffrey S. Evans & Associates, www.jeffreysevans.com

Dutch Makkum self-framed plaque of rectangular form, circa 1950, border painted with foliage and landscapes in rococo-shaped reserves, center with large view of windmill near water with woman walking in foreground, marked to underside, good condition, chip near bottom right-hand corner, minor flaking to corners and to inner edge, piece of Plexiglas glued to reverse for hanger, 9-1/2" x 12"........................ **$81**

Courtesy of Jeffrey S. Evans & Associates, www.jeffreysevans.com

Pair of blue and white plates with butterfly decoration, 18th century, 8-3/4" dia... **$86**

Courtesy of Pook & Pook, Inc., pookandpook.com

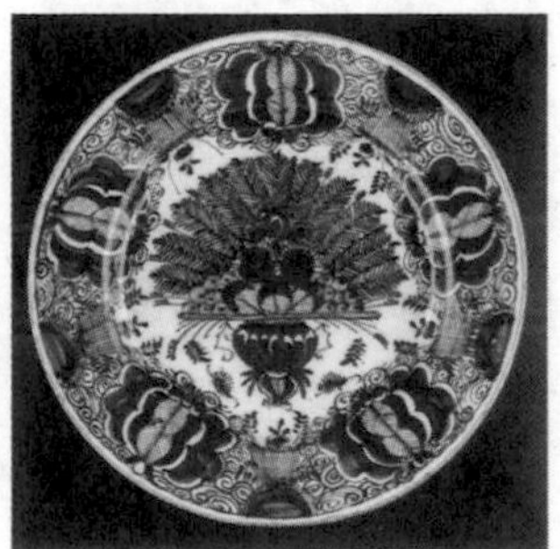

Dutch de Klauw dish or plate, circa 1750-1770, painted in Peacock pattern with ocher rim above border of lambrequins and stylized floral motifs, centering blooming vase of flowers, marked with claw and "LS" to underside, very good condition, minor chipping and flaking typical of ware, 10-1/4" dia. **$259**

Courtesy of Jeffrey S. Evans & Associates, www.jeffreysevans.com

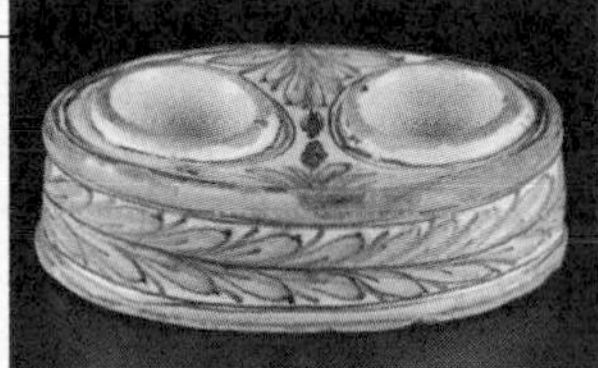

▲ Dutch triangular triple salt, circa 1690-1750, sides with molded hemisphere to mid-point, top with three wells with rolled collars, painted in manganese brown and blue, unmarked, good condition, minor chipping and flaking typical of ware, 1-3/4" h. x 6" x 6".... **$184**

Courtesy of Jeffrey S. Evans & Associates, www.jeffreysevans.com

◀ Dutch oval double salt, circa 1690-1750, molded with bands to top and bottom sides and with two collared wells to top, painted with lateral band of flowers in ocher, green, yellow, and cobalt blue residual dashes to wells, unmarked, good condition with chip to foot rim, flaking enamels, 1-5/8" h. x 5-5/8" x 3-1/2". **$138**

Courtesy of Jeffrey S. Evans & Associates, www.jeffreysevans.com

Polychrome standish, 18th century, 2-3/4" h. x 8" w. **$148**

Courtesy of Pook & Pook, Inc., pookandpook.com

Pair of manganese and white pottery covered garniture vases, 18th/19th century, faceted baluster bodies molded with leafy vines enclosing bird, rock, and flower scenes, faceted domed covers with "foo" dog finials, 13-1/2" h................ **$896**

Courtesy of Neal Auction, www.nealauction.com

Tile from de Porceleyne Fles (Delft) showing woman and child waving at plane above slogan "Voedsel – Vrede – Vryheid" (Food – Peace – Freedom) and dates April 29 to May 5, 1945, commemorating Allied food drops into Holland toward end of World War II, marked on reverse with company logo, excellent condition, 5-5/8" x 8-7/8". . **$150**

Courtesy of Mark Mussio, Humler & Nolan, www.humlernolan.com

Tile from de Porceleyne Fles (Delft) commemorating 1928 Olympic games held in Amsterdam, marked on reverse with company logo, excellent condition, 4-1/2" sq. **$225**

Courtesy of Mark Mussio, Humler & Nolan, www.humlernolan.com

Two early vases mounted as lamps, circa 1800, baluster-form with hexagonal bases with river scene on front panel, minor glaze chips on base and on high spots, one with chip at back of rim, 9-3/4" h.......... **$677**

Courtesy of Skinner, Inc., www.skinnerinc.com

CERAMICS

doulton and royal doulton

DOULTON & COMPANY, Ltd., was founded in Lambeth, London, in about 1858. It operated there until 1956 and often incorporated the words "Doulton" and "Lambeth" in its marks. Pinder, Bourne & Co. Burslem was purchased by the Doultons in 1878 and in 1882 became Doulton & Co., Ltd. It added porcelain to its earthenware production in 1884. The "Royal Doulton" mark has been used since 1902 by this factory, which is still in operation.

John Doulton, the founder, was born in 1793. He became an apprentice at the age of 12 to a potter in south London. Five years later he was employed in another small pottery near Lambeth. His two sons, John and Henry, subsequently joined their father in 1830 in a partnership he had formed with the name of Doulton & Watts. Watts retired in 1864 and the partnership was dissolved. Henry formed a new company that traded as Doulton and Co.

In the early 1870s the proprietor of the Pinder Bourne Co., located in Burslem, Staffordshire, offered Henry a partnership. The Pinder Bourne Co. was purchased by Henry in 1878 and became part of Doulton & Co. in 1882.

With the passage of time, the demand for the Lambeth industrial and decorative stoneware declined whereas demand for the Burslem manufactured and decorated bone china wares increased.

Doulton & Co. was incorporated as a limited liability company in 1899. In 1901 the company was allowed to use the word "Royal" on its trademarks by Royal Charter. The well-known "lion on crown" logo came into use in 1902. In 2000 the logo was changed on the company's advertising literature to one showing a more stylized lion's head in profile.

Today Royal Doulton is one of the world's leading manufacturers and distributors of premium grade ceramic tabletop wares and collectibles. The Doulton Group comprises Minton, Royal Albert, Caithness Glass, Holland Studio Craft, and Royal Doulton. Royal Crown Derby was part of the group from 1971 until 2000, when it became an independent company. These companies market collectibles using their own brand names.

Set of 11 plates, all excellent condition, 10-1/2" dia.. **$454**

Courtesy of Cottone Auctions, www.cottoneauctions.com

Turkey platter and 20 plates, stamped with manufacturer's marks and number D 5462, 21 pieces total, plates 10-1/2" dia., platter 21" l. x 17".. **$308**

Courtesy of DuMouchelles, www.dumouchelles.com

Vase with embossed bellflowers in cloisonné style, mottled crystalline glaze on lower half, marked with Royal Doulton lion and crown logo, numbers 8140 and 186 with incised artisan's mark, minor nicks to high points, 7-7/8" high............ **$157**

Courtesy of Humler & Nolan, www.humlernolan.com

Set of 12 plates, each decorated with image of different fish, perch, salmon, herring, pike, carp and others, gilt and moriage border, bases marked, 9" dia.................. **$277**

Courtesy of Kaminski Auctions, www.kaminskiauctions.com

Flambé scenic vase, oasis with Arabs and camels, good condition, no chips, cracks, or repairs, 12-1/2" h. **$354**

Courtesy of Woody Auction, www.woodyauction.com

Flambé pedestal bowl with farm scene, good condition, no chips, cracks, or repairs, 4-1/2" x 9-3/4"................. **$177**

Courtesy of Woody Auction, www.woodyauction.com

Chintz-type pattern D4031 table articles, circa 1920-1930, octagonal teapot and cover, plate, teacup and saucer, pair of flared-foot cylindrical vases with black handles, and vase, all transfer-printed with birds, trellis, and flowering vines on powder-blue grounds, with black lines and details; various impressed, printed, and hand-written marks to undersides; teapot, plate, and flat vase in excellent undamaged condition, one cylindrical vase cracked with small rim chip and both with some light crazing, cup and saucer with consistent crazing, 5-3/4" h. overall.................................. **$168**

Courtesy of Jeffrey S. Evans & Associates, www.jeffreysevans.com

Bowl with images of classical figures driving chariots in interior, green leaf-type decoration around rim, 5" h., 15" dia. **$86**

Courtesy of Kaminski Auctions, www.kaminskiauctions.com

Lidded tobacco jar with men playing golf, Kingsware series, inscribed "EGH from RLW," circa 1910, chip on inside of rim, 5" h. x 4-1/2" w., 4" dia., artwork 5" h. x 4-1/5" w., 4" dia. **$342**

Courtesy of Louis J. Dianni, LLC Antiques Auctions, louisjdianni.com

The Poacher toby jug, excellent condition, 3-3/4" h. **$30**

Courtesy of Milestone Auctions, www.milestoneauctions.com

Beer-style earthenware mug with raised pattern of golfers, circa 1910, no chipping, losses, or wear, 6" h. x 6" w. x 3" dia., artwork 6" h. x 6" w. **$436**

Courtesy of Louis J. Dianni, LLC Antiques Auctions, louisjdianni.com

Santa Claus toby jug, marked "Royal Doulton Tableware Limited 1983," good condition, no chips, cracks, or repairs, 7" **$71**

Courtesy of Woody Auction, www.woodyauction.com

Large pitcher and bowl set, strong colors on flower designs, near mint condition, no wear or damage, bowl 14-1/2" dia., pitcher 12" h. .... **$300-$600**

Courtesy of Morphy Auctions, morphyauctions.com

Vase, near mint condition, no wear, 16" h. .... **$150-$350**

Courtesy of Morphy Auctions, morphyauctions.com

Six assorted toothpick holders: two with birds, two with flowers, one with Dutch figures, and one with Bunnykins, first half 20th century, undamaged, one bird example with firing flaw to lower corner, as made, 1-3/4" to 2-1/2" h. **$84**

Courtesy of Jeffrey S. Evans & Associates, www.jeffreysevans.com

Tray, oblong flattened diamond shape with rounded corners, Babes in the Wood Series, center design of woman followed by girl holding woman's cloak, 13-1/2" l. **$1,000**

Vase, Titanian Ware, footed bulbous, slightly tapering body with flattened shoulder centering short flaring neck, celadon green ground decorated with small brown and white bird on flowering branch, decorated by H. Allen, marked "Royal Doulton Flambé – Titanian – Young White-Throat," 3-1/2" h. x 4" dia............................ **$489**

Vase, stoneware, small round foot supporting wide ovoid body tapering to short, wide and deeply rolled neck, wide body band in cream incised with cattle in meadow, cobalt blue shoulder decorated with incised pale blue scrolls, lower body and foot with lappet bands in cobalt blue, pale blue and brown, decorated by Hannah Barlow, 1887, Doulton-Lambeth, small glaze nick on top edge of rim, 6-3/8" h. **$1,093**

Vases, bulbous form with flaring neck, Babes in the Wood Series, one with design of girl looking into woman's basket, other with girl holding hem of woman's cloak, 9-1/2" h...................... **$2,500 pr.**

Teapot, covered, Lord of the Manor pattern, designed by Shane Ridge, limited edition of 1,500, introduced in 2003. ..... **$300**

CERAMICS

fiesta

THE HOMER LAUGHLIN China Co. originated with a two-kiln pottery on the banks of the Ohio River in East Liverpool, Ohio. Built in 1873-1874 by Homer Laughlin and his brother, Shakespeare, the firm was first known as the Ohio Valley Pottery and later Laughlin Bros. Pottery. It was one of the first white-ware plants in the country.

The company was awarded a prize for having the best white-ware at the 1876 Centennial Exposition in Philadelphia. Three years later, Shakespeare sold his interest in the business to Homer, who continued on until 1897. At that time, Homer sold his interest in the newly incorporated firm. Under new ownership in 1907, the headquarters and a new 30-kiln plant were built across the Ohio River in Newell, West Virginia, the present manufacturing and headquarters location.

In the 1920s, two additions to the Homer Laughlin staff set the stage for the company's greatest success: the Fiesta line. Dr. Albert V. Bleininger was hired in 1920. A scientist, author, and educator, he oversaw the conversion from bottle kilns to the more efficient tunnel kilns. Then, in 1927, the company hired designer Frederick Hurten Rhead, a member of a distinguished family of English ceramists. Having previously worked at Weller and Roseville potteries, he began to develop the artistic quality of the company's wares and to experiment with shapes and glazes. In 1935 this work culminated in his designs for the popular Fiesta line, which was produced until 1973, when waning popularity and declining sales forced the company to discontinue it. But renewed appreciation of Art Deco design, coupled with collectors scrambling to buy discontinued Fiesta on the secondary market, prompted the company to reintroduce the line on Fiesta's 50th anniversary in 1986, spawning a whole new generation of collectors.

For more information on Fiesta, see *Warman's Fiesta Identification and Price Guide* by Glen Victorey.

FIESTA COLORS

From 1936 to 1972, Fiesta was produced in 14 colors (other than special promotions). These colors are usually divided into the "original colors" of cobalt blue, light green, ivory, red, turquoise, and yellow; the "1950s colors" of chartreuse, forest green, gray, and rose (introduced in 1951); medium green (introduced in 1959); plus the later additions of Casuals, Amberstone, Fiesta Ironstone, and Casualstone ("Coventry") in antique gold, mango red, and turf green; and the striped, decal, and Lustre pieces. The colors that make up the "original" and "1950s" groups are sometimes referred to as "the standard 11." In many pieces, medium green is the hardest to find and the most expensive Fiesta color.

FIESTA COLORS AND YEARS OF PRODUCTION TO 1972

Antique Gold **1969-1972**
Chartreuse **1951-1959**
Cobalt Blue **1936-1951**
Forest Green **1951-1959**
Gray **1951-1959**
Green **1936-1951**
(often called light green when comparing it to other green glazes; also called "original" green)

Ivory **1936-1951**
Mango Red **(same as original red)** **1970-1972**
Medium Green **1959-1969**
Red .... **1936-1944 and 1959-1972**
Rose **1951-1959**
Turf Green **1969-1972**
Turquoise **1937-1969**
Yellow **1936-1969**

Set of seven nesting bowls, all marked, overall light to moderate wear commensurate with age, smallest with fleabites to rim, largest red bowl with fleabites and glaze loss to rim, some abrasions and bruising, tallest 7-1/2" h., 11" dia. **$640**

Courtesy of Rago Arts and Auctions, www.ragoarts.com

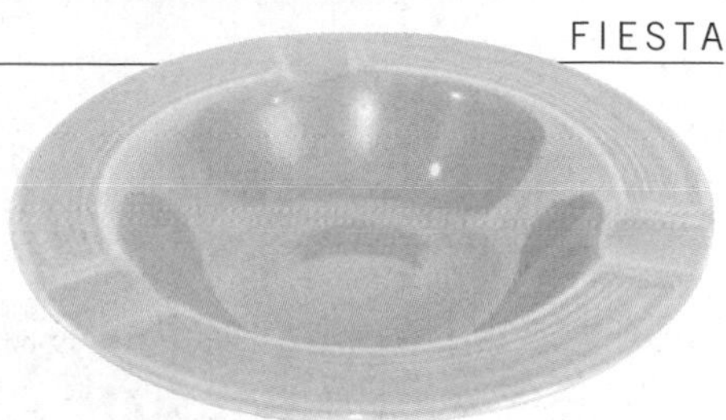

Medium green ashtray. **$121**

Courtesy of Strawser Auctions, www.strawserauctions.com

Rare turquoise covered onion soup. **$4,114**

Courtesy of Strawser Auctions, www.strawserauctions.com

Cobalt footed salad bowl. **$303**

Courtesy of Strawser Auctions, www.strawserauctions.com

Medium green dessert bowl, 6" dia. **$206**

Courtesy of Strawser Auctions, www.strawserauctions.com

Red fruit bowl, 11-3/4" dia. **$145**

Courtesy of Strawser Auctions, www.strawserauctions.com

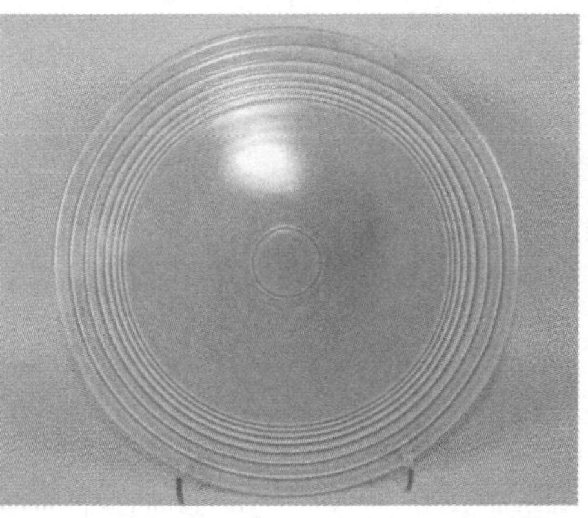

Green cake plate, minor nick. **$242**

Courtesy of Strawser Auctions, www.strawserauctions.com

Individual cream and sugar set: red creamer (minor hairline), yellow sugar, and cobalt figure-eight tray. **$109**

Courtesy of Strawser Auctions, www.strawserauctions.com

Cobalt tripod candleholders. **$242**

Courtesy of Strawser Auctions, www.strawserauctions.com

Rare ivory with red stripe #4 mixing bowl, minor rim wear. **$6,050**

Courtesy of Strawser Auctions, www.strawserauctions.com

Medium green cream and sugar...................... **$145**

Courtesy of Strawser Auctions, www.strawserauctions.com

Charteusse coffee pot.................................... **$109**

Courtesy of Strawser Auctions, www.strawserauctions.com

Three-tier tidbit tray. **$18**

Courtesy of Strawser Auctions, www.strawserauctions.com

BOTTOM MARKS

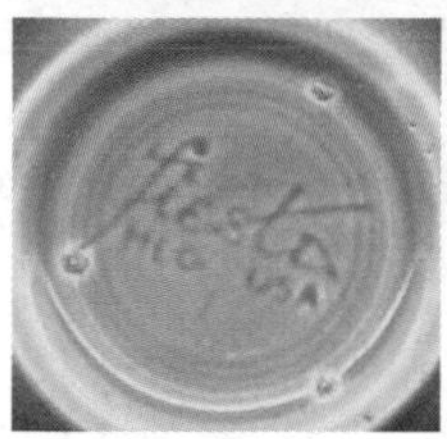

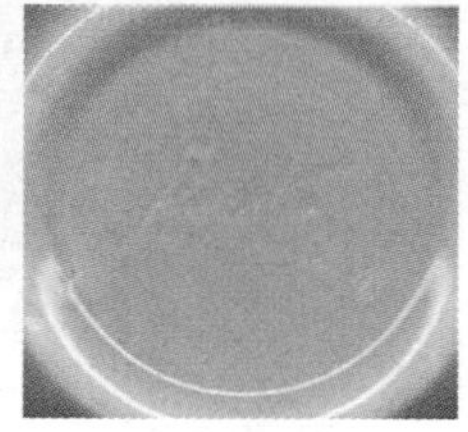

Bottom of No. 1 mixing bowl in green, showing sagger pin marks, the "Fiesta/HLCo. USA" impressed mark, and the faint "1" size indicator. The impressed size mark on the bottom of the No. 2 mixing bowl in yellow is too faint to be seen in this image.

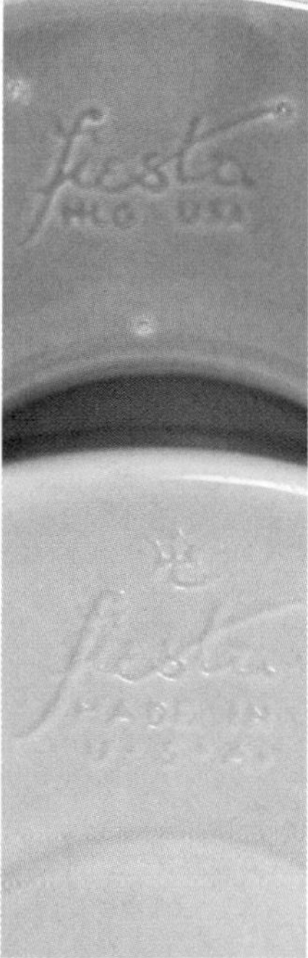

Two different impressed marks on the bottoms of relish tray inserts.

An ink stamp on the bottom of a piece of Fiesta.

Notice the different bottoms of two ashtrays. The top one has a set of rings with no room for a logo. The bottom ashtray has rings along the outer edge, opposite of the ring pattern on the ashtray above. The red example is an older example. The yellow ashtray with the logo can be dated to after 1940.

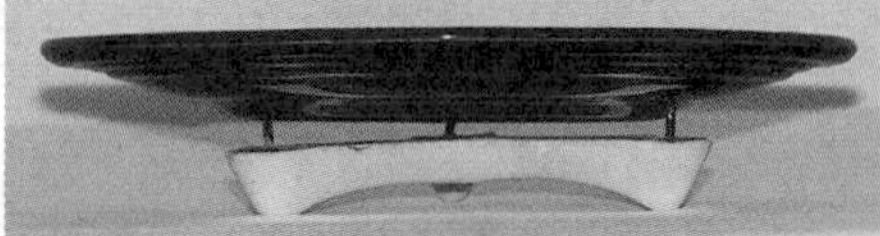

A 9" cobalt blue plate rests on a stilt with sagger pins to show the basic idea of how it worked. Please note that this stilt is not the exact one that would have been used by Homer Laughlin China Co., but rather an updated style in use today by many ceramic studios.

Bottom of a teacup saucer in turquoise, showing sagger pin marks and the "Genuine Fiesta" stamp.

Bottom of 6" bread plate in turquoise, showing "Genuine Fiesta" stamp.

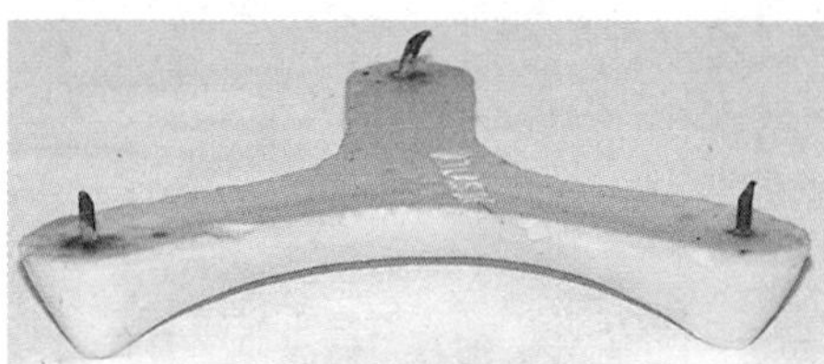

Fiesta pieces were glazed on the underside, so before being fired, each piece was placed on a stilt to keep it off the floor of the kiln. The stilt was made up of three sagger pins positioned an equal distance from each other to form three points of a triangle. If you inspect the underside of any piece of Fiesta, which has a completely glazed bottom, you will notice three small blemishes in a triangular pattern. Later in Fiesta's production run, the undersides of pieces were glazed and then wiped, creating a dry foot, before going into the kiln to be fired.

Examples of impressed Fiesta bottom marks.

Relish tray, ivory tray with all six original colors. **$182**

Courtesy of Strawser Auctions, www.strawserauctions.com

Water set, turquoise disc water pitcher and six original water tumblers.................................. **$303**

Courtesy of Strawser Auctions, www.strawserauctions.com

Juice set, yellow disc juice pitcher and six original juice tumblers... **$272**

Courtesy of Strawser Auctions, www.strawserauctions.com

Juice set, Jubilee celadon pitcher and pink, gray, and beige tumblers....................................... **$206**

Courtesy of Strawser Auctions, www.strawserauctions.com

Red sauceboat with rare red ironstone tray, minor wear.. **$91**

Courtesy of Strawser Auctions, www.strawserauctions.com

Yellow French casserole................................. **$133**

Courtesy of Strawser Auctions, www.strawserauctions.com

Gray plate with metal handle, 9" dia., and rose fruit bowl with carrier, 4-3/4" dia.................... **$454**

Courtesy of Strawser Auctions, www.strawserauctions.com

Red vase, 12" h. **$575**

Courtesy of Strawser Auctions, www.strawserauctions.com

Turquoise vase, minor glaze miss to rim, 12" h. **$424**

Courtesy of Strawser Auctions, www.strawserauctions.com

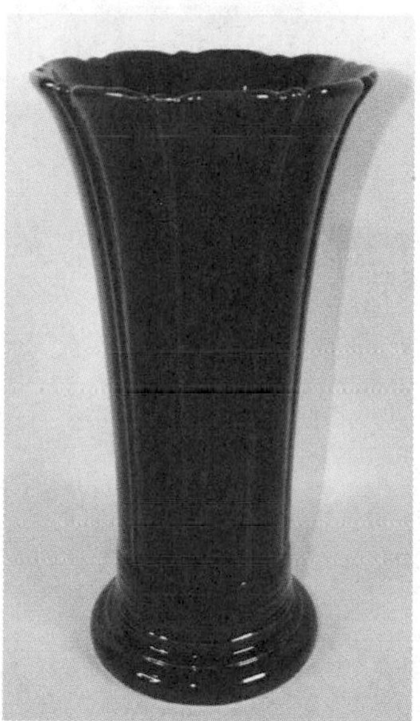

Cobalt vase, 12" h...................**$787**

Courtesy of Strawser Auctions, www.strawserauctions.com

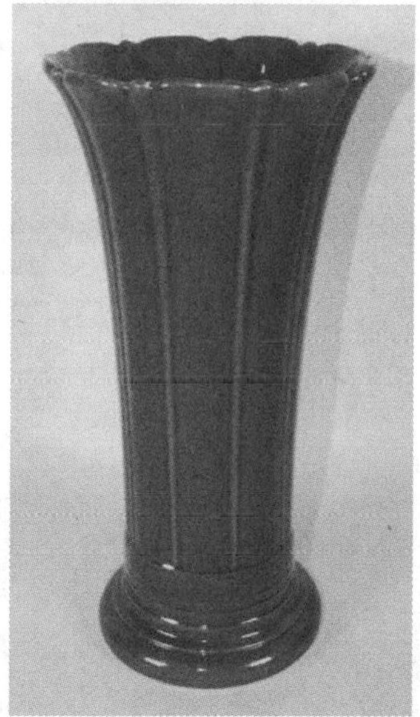

Red vase, no damage visible, 12" h. **$502**

Courtesy of Turkey Creek Auctions, Inc., www.antiqueauctionsfl.com

! top lot

Twenty-three Looney Tunes Post-'86 pieces in various colors. **$333**

Courtesy of Strawser Auctions, www.strawserauctions.com

Twelve Post-'86 lilac pieces, scratch to big platter. **$303**

Courtesy of Strawser Auctions, www.strawserauctions.com

Ten assorted Post-'86 apricot pieces. **$847**

Courtesy of Strawser Auctions, www.strawserauctions.com

CERAMICS

frankoma

JOHN FRANK STARTED his pottery company in 1933 in Norman, Oklahoma, but when he moved the business to Sapulpa, Oklahoma, in 1938, he felt he was home. Still, he could not know the horrendous storms and trials that would follow him. Just after his move, on Nov. 11, 1938, a fire destroyed the entire operation, which included the pot and leopard mark he had created in 1935. Then in 1942, the war effort needed men and materials, so Frankoma could not survive. In 1943, John and Grace Lee Frank bought the plant as junk salvage and began again.

The time in Norman had produced some of the finest art ware that John would ever create and most of the items were marked either Frank Potteries, Frank Pottery, or to a lesser degree, the "pot and leopard" mark. Today these marks are avidly and enthusiastically sought by collectors. Another elusive mark wanted by collectors: Firsts Kiln Sapulpa 6-7-38. The mark was used for one day only and denotes the first firing in Sapulpa. It has been estimated that perhaps 50 to 75 pieces were fired on that day.

The clay Frankoma used is helpful to collectors in determining when an item was made. Creamy beige clay known as "Ada" clay was in use until 1953. Then a red brick shale was found in Sapulpa and used until about 1985 when, with the addition of an additive, the clay became a reddish pink.

Rutile glazes were used early in Frankoma's history. Glazes with rutile have caused more confusion among collectors than any other glazes. For example, a Prairie Green piece shows a lot of green but it also has some brown. The same is true for the Desert Gold glaze; the piece shows a sandy-beige glaze with some brown. Generally speaking, Prairie Green, Desert Gold, White Sand, and Woodland Moss are the most puzzling to collectors.

In 1970 the government closed the rutile mines in America, and Frankoma had to buy it from Australia. It was not the same, so the results were different. Values are higher for the glazes with rutile. Also, the pre-Australian Woodland Moss glaze is more desirable than that created after 1970.

After John Frank died in 1973, his daughter Joniece Frank, a ceramic designer at the pottery, became president of the company. In 1983 another fire destroyed everything Frankoma had worked so hard to create. They rebuilt, but in 1990, after the IRS shut the doors for nonpayment, Joniece, true to the Frank legacy, filed for Chapter 11 bankruptcy so she could reopen and continue the work she loved.

Figural Native American ashtray in white glaze, marked, good condition, 6". **$47**

Courtesy of Woody Auction, www.woodyauction.com

In 1991 Richard Bernstein purchased the pottery, and the name was changed to Frankoma Industries. The company was sold again in 2005 to Det and Crystal Merryman. Yet another owner, Joe Ragosta, purchased the pottery in 2008.

Frankoma Pottery was closed for good in 2010 with a factory closeout auction in Oklahoma in 2011.

Will Rogers plaque, paper label verso, 6" x 5-1/4"..**$24**

Courtesy of Rachel Davis Fine Arts, www.racheldavisfinearts.com

▲ Advertising/dealer sign, mint condition, 7" w. . **$12**

Courtesy of Belhorn Auctions LLC, belhornauctions.com

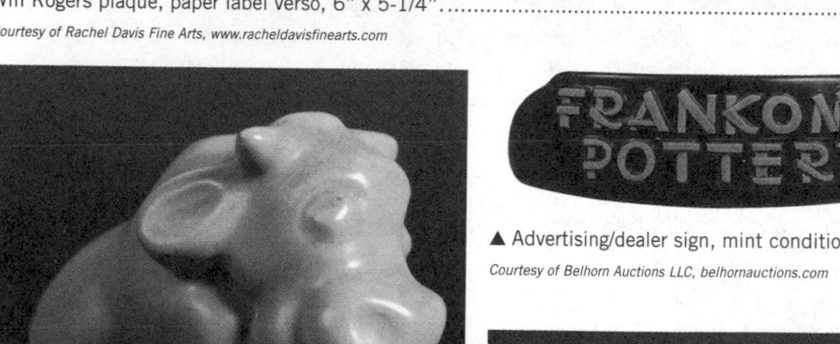

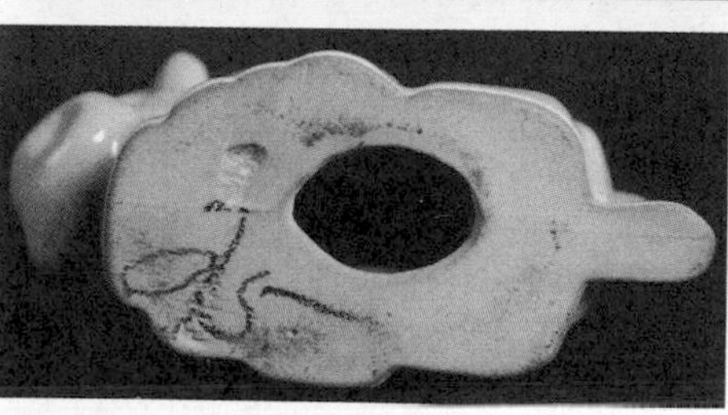

Early Ada clay bull figurine, impressed block letter mark on base, very good condition, 2" h. x 3-1/4" l. **$290**

Courtesy of Dirk Soulis Auctions, www.dirksoulisauctions.com

CERAMICS

fulper pottery

FROM THE "GERM-PROOF Filter" to enduring Arts & Crafts acclaim - that's the unlikely journey of Fulper Pottery, maker of the early 20th century uniquely glazed artware that's become a favorite with today's collectors.

Fulper began life in 1814 as the Samuel Hill Pottery, named after its founder, a New Jersey potter. In its early years, the pottery specialized in useful items such as storage crocks and drainpipes fashioned from the area's red clay. Abraham Fulper, a worker at the pottery, eventually became Hill's partner, purchasing the company in 1860. Renamed after its new owner, Fulper Pottery continued to produce a variety of utilitarian tile and crockery. By the turn of the 20th century, the firm, now led by Abraham's sons, introduced a line of fire-proof cookware and the hugely successful "Germ-Proof Filter." An ancestor of today's water cooler, the filter provided sanitary drinking water in less-than-sanitary public places, such as offices and railway stations.

In the early 1900s, Fulper's master potter, John Kunsman, began creating various solid-glaze vessels, such as jugs and vases, which were offered for sale outside the pottery. On a whim, William H. Fulper II (Abraham's grandson, who'd become the company's secretary/treasurer) took an assortment of these items to exhibit at the 1904 Louisiana Purchase Exposition - along with, of course, the Germ-Proof Filter. Kunsman's artware took home an honorable mention.

Since Chinese art pottery was then attracting national attention, Fulper saw an opening to produce similarly styled modern ware. Dr. Cullen Parmelee, who headed the ceramics department at Rutgers, was recruited to create a contemporary series of glazes patterned after those of ancient China. The Fulper Vasekraft line of art pottery incorporating these

Four miniature pitchers, shape 38B, referred to as "dipstick" in Fulper catalog: two in Famille Rose glaze, marked with Fulper racetrack ink stamp, both in excellent condition; one in blue flambé glaze, marked with rectangular Fulper ink stamp, glaze skips at foot ring; and one in green flambé glaze with mahogany at rim, marked with rectangular Fulper ink stamp, excellent condition; all 4-3/8" h. **$190**

Courtesy of Mark Mussio, Humler & Nolan, www.humlernolan.com

glazes made its debut in 1909. Unfortunately, Parmelee's glazes did not lend themselves well to mass production because they did not result in reliable coloration. Even more to their detriment, they were expensive to produce.

In 1910, most of Parmelee's glazes disappeared from the line. A new ceramic engineer, Martin Stangl, was given the assignment of revitalizing Vasekraft. His most notable innovation: steering designs and glazes away from reinterpretations of ornate Chinese classics and toward the simplicity of the burgeoning Arts & Crafts movement. Among his many Vasekraft successes: candleholders, bookends, perfume lamps, desk accessories, tobacco jars, and even Vasekraft lamps. Here, both the lamp base and shade were of pottery; stained glass inserts in the shades allowed light to shine through.

Always attuned to the mood of the times, William Fulper realized that by World War I the heavy Vasekraft stylings were fading in popularity. A new and lighter line of Fulper Pottery Artware, featuring Spanish Revival and English themes, was introduced. Among the most admired Fulper releases following the war were Fulper Porcelaines: dresser boxes, powder jars, ashtrays, lamps, and other accessories designed to complement the fashionable boudoir.

Fayence, a popular line of solid-color, open-stock dinnerware eventually known as Stangl Pottery, was introduced in the 1920s. In 1928, following William Fulper's death, Martin Stangl was named company president. The artware that continued into the 1930s embraced Art Deco as well as Classical and Primitive stylistic themes. From 1935 onward, Stangl Pottery became the sole Fulper output. In 1978, the Stangl assets came under the ownership of Pfaltzgraff.

Unlike wheel-thrown pottery, Fulper was made in molds; the true artistry came in the use of exceptionally rich, color-blended glazes. Each Fulper piece is one-of-a-kind. Because of glaze divergence, two Fulper objects from the same mold can show a great variance. While once a drawback for retailers seeking consistency, that uniqueness is now a boon to collectors: Each Fulper piece possesses its own singular visual appeal.

Figural pottery perfume lamp in form of parrot perched on stump with green and orange mottled glaze, marked on underside, 9-1/2" h. **$305**

Courtesy of Clars Auction Gallery, www.clars.com

Rare tulip vase, shape 588, in Mirrored Black glaze with silver crystals throughout, marked on bottom with raised Fulper vertical oval mark, excellent original condition, 11-1/2" h. **$1,700**

Courtesy of Mark Mussio, Humler & Nolan, www.humlernolan.com

Buttress vase in Wisteria glaze, marked on bottom with Fulper racetrack ink stamp, grinding chips at base, 8-1/4" h. **$190**

Courtesy of Mark Mussio, Humler & Nolan, www.humlernolan.com

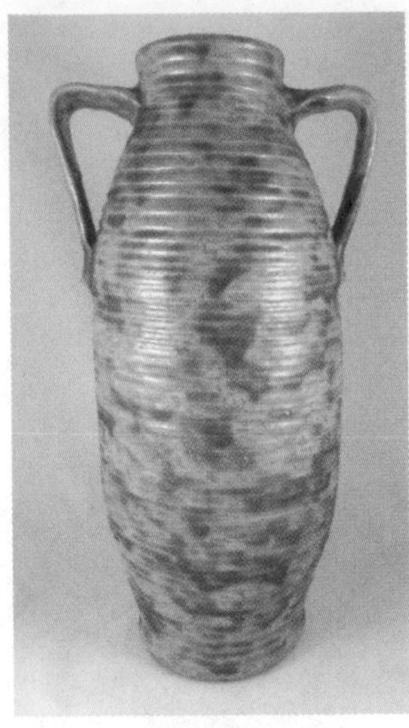

Floor vase, large two-handled free hand coiled design with Leopard Skin glaze, marked, 21" h. **$665**

Courtesy of Rachel Davis Fine Arts, www.racheldavisfinearts.com

Rolled rim dish, green matte glaze, marked, good condition, 5" dia................................ **$177**

Courtesy of Woody Auction, www.woodyauction.com

▲ Blue bowl, 9-3/4" dia........ **$58**

Courtesy of Strawser Auctions, www.strawserauctions.com

◀ Vase with five small buttresses between rim and shoulder, in thick green flambé glaze over oatmeal, impressed oval Fulper logo, excellent original condition, 5" h. **$200**

Courtesy of Mark Mussio, Humler & Nolan, www.humlernolan.com

Vase, ribbed bulbous form, stamped Fulper and marked "827" on bottom, 3-1/2"h. ... **$85**

Courtesy of Rachel Davis Fine Arts, www.racheldavisfinearts.com

Double-handled vase in green glaze, marked Fulper, mint condition, 8-3/8" w............. **$138**

Courtesy of Belhorn Auctions LLC, belhornauctions.com

Fulper Stangl Pottery advertising sign in blue glaze, marked Stangl/Fulper Collector's Club / June 1998, mint condition, 6-1/2" h. **$12**

Courtesy of Belhorn Auctions LLC, belhornauctions.com

CERAMICS

grueby

FINE ART POTTERY was produced by the Grueby Faience and Tile Co. established in Boston in 1891. Choice pieces were created with molded designs on a semi-porcelain body. The ware is marked and often bears the initials of the decorators. The pottery closed in 1907.

Vase with leaves, circa 1905, circular pottery stamp, incised ERF 4-6, excellent glaze, flecks to high points, several small burst glaze bubbles, 8-1/2" x 5-1/2"............................ **$2,500**

Courtesy of Rago Arts and Auctions, www.ragoarts.com

◀ Vase with leaves in curdled mustard glaze, circa 1905, circular stamp, incised RE for Ruth Erickson, several glaze misses, chips and flecks to high points, 10" x 6"....... **$1,920**

Courtesy of Rago Arts and Auctions, www.ragoarts.com

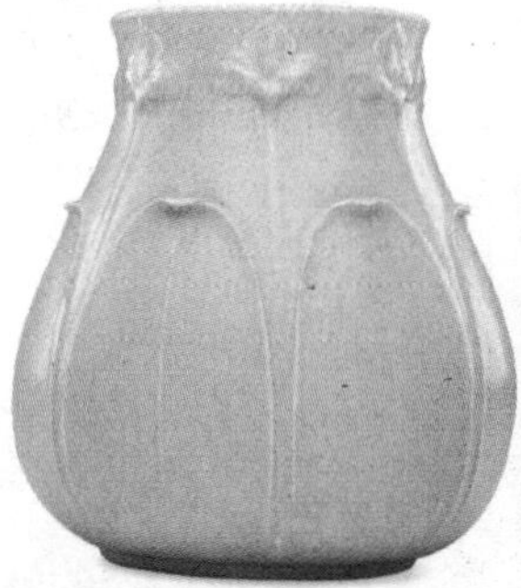

Vase with irises in rare oatmeal glaze, circa 1905, circular pottery stamp, incised W.P. for Wilhelmina Post, small chips and flecks to high points, 8-1/2" x 7"..................... **$4,480**

Courtesy of Rago Arts and Auctions, www.ragoarts.com

top lot!

Early floor vase with leaves and buds, circa 1905, partial circular faience stamp, flecks to high points, professional restoration to chip at rim, 23" x 8"..................................... $10,000

COURTESY OF RAGO ARTS AND AUCTIONS, WWW.RAGOARTS.COM

◀ Lamp base with leaves, circa 1905, circular faience stamp and rare paper label "GRUEBY POTTERY PAN AMERICAN EXPOSITION 1901," excellent condition, vase base 6-1/2" x 8"................................ **$6,875**

Courtesy of Rago Arts and Auctions, www.ragoarts.com

▶ Gourd vase with leaves, circa 1905, circular pottery stamp/224/artist initials, excellent condition, 7-3/4" x 4-1/2"........................... **$5,938**

Courtesy of Rago Arts and Auctions, www.ragoarts.com

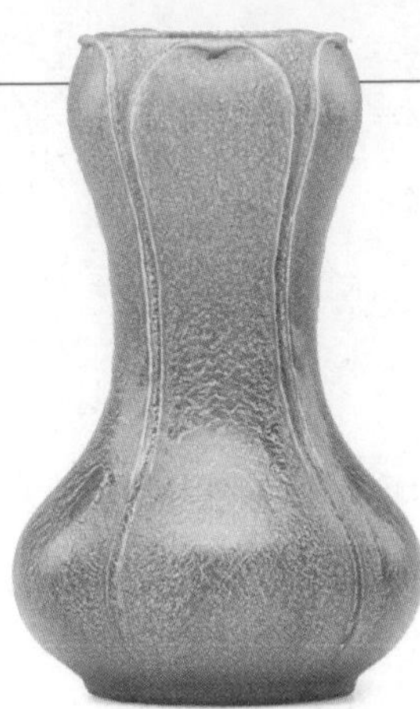

Oval portrait tile in white and blue, marked "1913 by W. H. Grueby No. 58" on back and "W. Clark Noble So. 1913" on front, excellent condition, 5-1/2" h. **$63**

Courtesy of Belhorn Auctions LLC, belhornauctions.com

Tile with goat and flowers, circa 1905, original paper label, excellent condition, small glaze flake to one back corner, light overall surface wear, 6" sq. **$2,125**

Courtesy of Rago Arts and Auctions, www.ragoarts.com

Copper-mounted tile in cuenca with seagulls, circa 1905, probable mark obscured by mount, excellent condition, light wear to high points, 4" sq. **$1,063**

Courtesy of Rago Arts and Auctions, www.ragoarts.com

Glazed ceramic tile in cuerda seca with penguins, 1910s, brass frame, tile monogrammed O.C., excellent condition, tile 4" sq., 1-1/2" x 5" sq. overall. **$3,000**

Courtesy of Rago Arts and Auctions, www.ragoarts.com

CERAMICS

haeger

SLEEK, SINUOUS, COLORFUL and cutting edge, timeless, trim of line, and, above all, thoroughly modern. That's the hallmark of Haeger Potteries. Since its 1871 founding in Dundee, Illinois, the firm has successfully moved from the utilitarian to the decorative. Whether freshly minted or vintage, Haeger creations continue to provide what ads called "a galaxy of exquisite designs...visual achievements symbolizing expert craftsmanship and pottery-making knowledge."

Today's collectors are particularly captivated by the modernistic Haeger output of the 1940s and '50s – from panther TV lamps and figurines of exotic Asian maidens to statuary of rearing wild horses and snorting bulls. But the Haeger story began long before then, with the Great Chicago Fire of 1871.

Founder David Haeger had recently purchased a budding brickyard on the banks of Dundee's Fox River. Following the fire, his firm produced bricks to replace decimated Chicagoland structures. For the next 30 years, industrial production remained the primary emphasis of the Haeger Brick and Tile Co. It wasn't until 1914 that the company, now under the guidance of Edmund Haeger, noted the growing popularity of the Arts & Crafts movement and turned its attention to artware.

From the beginning, Haeger was distinguished by its starry roster of designers. The first: J. Martin Stangl, former glaze wizard for Fulper. The design emphasis of Stangl and his early Haeger successors was on classically simple, uncluttered Arts & Crafts stylings. Haeger's roster of pots, jugs, vases, bowls, and candleholders all proved big hits with buyers.

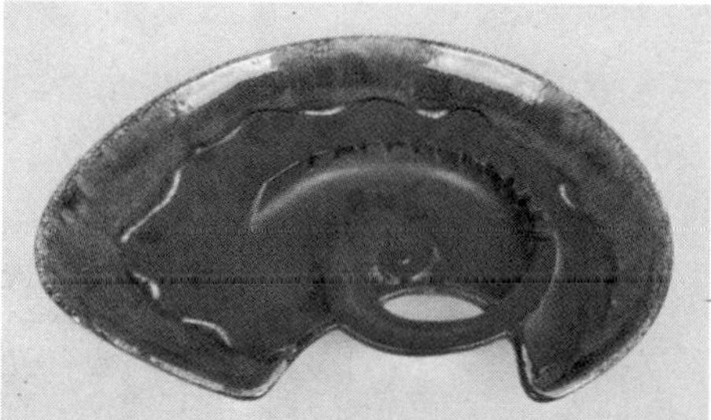

▲ Royal Haeger ashtray, good to excellent condition, small chip, 16" x 11"....................... **$12**

Courtesy of Milestone Auctions, www.milestoneauctions.com

◀ Royal Haeger Orange Peel pottery pitcher, marked "Royal Haeger U.S.A., The Haeger Potteries Inc., Dundee, Ill." on felt-lined bottom, 10-1/2" h. x 9-1/2" w. at base......................... **$80**

Courtesy of Stephenson's Auctioneers & Appraisers, www.stephensonsauction.com

Royal Haeger pitcher, excellent condition, light scratches, 19" h. **$30**

Courtesy of Milestone Auctions, www.milestoneauctions.com

An early zenith was reached with a pavilion at the 1934 Chicago World's Fair. In addition to home environment settings accented with Haeger, there was an actual working factory. Once fair-goers had viewed the step-by-step pottery production process, they could purchase a piece of Haeger on the way out. The World's Fair brought Haeger to America's attention – but its grandest days of glory were still ahead.

The year 1938 saw the promotion of Edmund Haeger's forward-thinking son-in-law, Joseph Estes, to general manager, the arrival of equally forward-thinking designer Royal Arden Hickman, and the introduction of the popular Royal Haeger line.

The multi-talented Hickman, snapped up by Haeger after stays at J. H. Vernon, Kosta Crystal, and his own Ra Art, quickly made his mark. Earlier Haeger figurals were generally of animals and humans at rest. Under the guidance of Hickman and the soon-to-follow Eric Olsen, motion was key: leaping fish, birds taking wing, and a ubiquitous snarling black panther. The energetic air of underlying excitement in these designs was ideally suited to the action-packed atmosphere of World War II and the postwar new day that followed.

In 1944, Hickman left Haeger following a dispute over lamp production, returning only for occasional free-lance assignments. The 1947 arrival of his successor, Eric Olsen, coincided with the official celebration of Haeger's Diamond Jubilee; that's when much of the Olsen line made its debut. From towering abstract figural lamps to long-legged colts, self-absorbed stalking lions, and mystic pre-Columbian priests, his designs were ideal for the soon-to-be-ultra-current "1950s modern" décor.

After nearly 150 years, most recently under the leadership of Joseph Estes' daughter, Alexandra Haeger Estes, Haeger Potteries ceased production in 2016 due to financial difficulties.

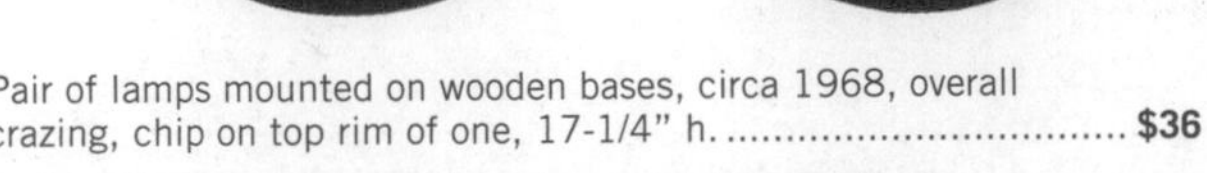

Pair of lamps mounted on wooden bases, circa 1968, overall crazing, chip on top rim of one, 17-1/4" h. **$36**

Courtesy of Stephenson's Auctioneers & Appraisers, www.stephensonsauction.com

Royal Haeger conch shell vase, marked "Royal Haeger R-321 Royal Hickman USA" on bottom, excellent condition, 7-5/8" h. **$6**

Courtesy of Belhorn Auctions LLC, belhornauctions.com

Royal Haeger covered bowl, 6-3/4" h. x 7-1/2" w. **$5**

Courtesy of Martin Auction Co., martinauctionco.com

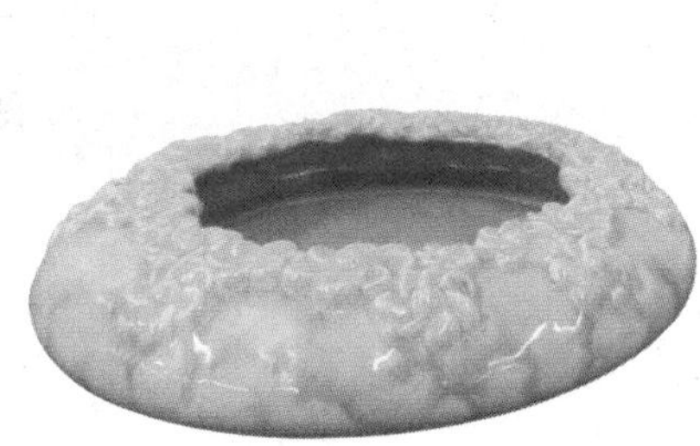

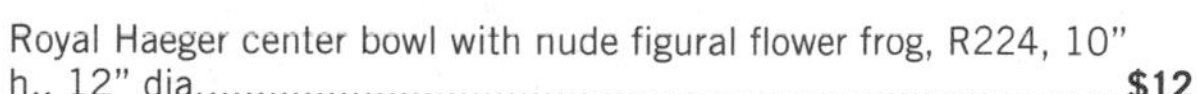

Royal Haeger center bowl with nude figural flower frog, R224, 10" h., 12" dia. **$121**

Courtesy of William J. Jenack Estate Appraisers & Auctioneers, www.jenackauctions.com

Pair of Royal Haeger figurines of peasants, #R-382 and #R-383, marked "Royal Haeger R-382, R-383 USA" on bottom, good condition, 16-1/2" h. **$35**

Courtesy of Rachel Davis Fine Arts, www.racheldavisfinearts.com

Haeger advertising sign in bronze, marked with Haeger label, excellent condition, 8-3/8" w. **$12**

Courtesy of Belhorn Auctions LLC, belhornauctions.com

▲ Pair of mid-century Royal Haeger vases, fern agate glaze, antelope form, overall good condition, approximately 14" h. x 8" w. **$150**

Courtesy of Premier Auction Galleries, Chesterland, Ohio

◀ Royal Haeger vessel in brown and orange, marked "Royal Haeger USA" on bottom, excellent condition, 7-1/2" h............................ **$46**

Courtesy of Belhorn Auctions LLC, belhornauctions.com

CERAMICS

hampshire pottery

HAMPSHIRE POTTERY was made in Keene, New Hampshire, where several potteries operated as far back as the late 18th century. The pottery now known as Hampshire Pottery was established by J. S. Taft shortly after 1870. Various types of wares, including art pottery, were produced through the years. Taft's brother-in-law, Cadmon Robertson, joined the firm in 1904 and was responsible for developing more than 900 glaze formulas while in charge of all manufacturing. His death in 1914 created problems for the firm, and Taft sold out to George Morton in 1916. Closed during part of World War I, the pottery was later reopened by Morton for a short time and manufactured white hotel china. From 1919 to 1921, mosaic floor tiles became the main production. All production ceased in 1923.

Pedestal jardinière in Art Nouveau style, late 19th/early 20th century, allover matte green glaze, squared rim over rounded bombe body relief-decorated with calla lilies and plain ovoid reserves, similarly decorated pedestal base, unmarked, 40" h. x 16" w. x 16" d. overall................. **$1,020**

Courtesy of John Moran Auctioneers, johnmoran.com

Six pieces green-glazed art pottery, 20th century, all with matte glaze, all marked Hampshire Pottery: lamp base with water lily design, 0018, electrified, hairline at top, 16-3/4"; narcissus bowl, star crack to base, 3-1/4" x 9-7/8"; bowl, 151 and M cipher within circle, star crack in base, 3-1/4" x 5"; bowl, 2211, good condition, 2-1/2" x 5-1/4"; cylindrical vase, 17/2, base irregularities, 6"; vase, surface scratches, 8"... **$1,178**

Courtesy of Brunk Auctions, www.brunkauctions.com

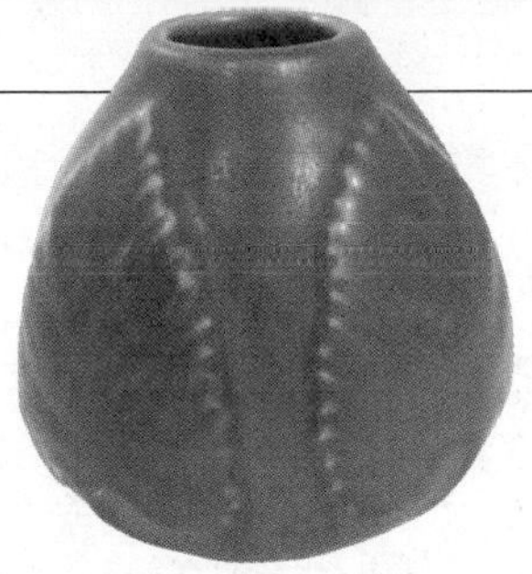

Vase with green glaze finish over leaf design, impressed with Hampshire Pottery marks on base, 3-5/8" h. **$120**

Courtesy of Main Street Mining Co., mainstreetmining.com

Vase with off-white matte glaze with leaf design, impressed with Hampshire Pottery marks on base, 3-5/8" h. **$90**

Courtesy of Main Street Mining Co., mainstreetmining.com

Teapot in brown with gold trim, marked Hampshire Pottery, 9" h.. **$6**

Courtesy of Belhorn Auctions LLC, belhornauctions.com

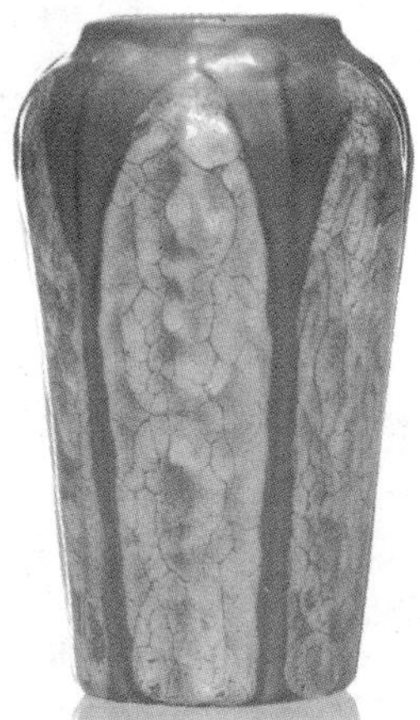

Vase with molded leaf design in dark brown mat glaze with lighter brown accent, marked on bottom Hampshire Pottery, "Emoretta" mark, and shape number 33, minor roughness at base, 6-1/2". **$350**

Courtesy of Mark Mussio, Humler & Nolan, www.humlernolan.com

◀ Hooded candleholder, form #0029, matte green glaze, small chip to rim of base, 6-1/2" h. **$60**

Courtesy of John McInnis Auctioneers, www.mcinnisauctions.com

Two vases, both marked, low form example with molded leaves in blue glaze with suffused areas of green, 2-1/2" h., 4-1/2" dia., and tall example with molded pedals in pale orange glaze, 6-1/2" h. **$347**

Courtesy of Butterscotch Auctioneers & Appraisers, www.butterscotchauction.com

Lamp base, Mission/Arts & Crafts style, circa 1900-1905, semi-gloss green glaze on squat form with gourd-like ribbing, factory drilled, brass electric insert with two original Hubbell sockets with acorn chain pulls, brass lyre-form finial, impressed "Hampshire" with M in circle cipher, original paper label with model number 601 in pencil, pottery 7" x 11", 23-1/2" h. overall with adjustable height stem........ **$767**

Courtesy of Thomaston Place Auction Galleries, www.thomastonauction.com

Lamp base, Mission/Arts & Crafts style, circa 1900-1905, semi-gloss green glaze on slender form with inverted tulip stem decoration, garlic mouth, hollow base with divot for cord, brass stem with two original Hubbell sockets with acorn chain pulls, brass urn-form finial on replaced adjustable-height stem, impressed script "Hampshire" and marked with model no 0014, original paper label with same number, pottery 11-1/2" x 7-3/4", 25" h. overall. **$826**

Courtesy of Thomaston Place Auction Galleries, www.thomastonauction.com

CERAMICS

herend

THE HEREND PORCELAIN Manufactory, which is located near Budapest, Hungary, originally produced earthenware pottery. By 1839, like many enterprising companies across Europe, it manufactured wildly popular white, translucent, hard paste porcelain. Almost immediately, Herend creations earned accolades at industrial art exhibitions, world exhibitions, and world fairs in Paris, London, Vienna, St. Petersburg, St. Louis, and Chicago.

As a result, Hungarian and European aristocracy, long used to dining on Meissen, Sèvres or pieces imported from the Far East, now purchased sets of sumptuous Herend porcelain. In fact, several Herend design patterns, among them "Rothschild Bird" and "Queen Victoria," featuring brightly colored butterflies flitting amid flowering branches, were named for these early, distinguished customers. Other notable customers have included Franz Joseph I and Empress Elisabeth, both of Austria.

"Herend's extensive traditional floral and fauna patterns continue to be most popular," according to Laszlo Szesztay, the commercial director of Herend Porcelain Manufactory Ltd. "Production time is typically eight weeks from start to finish, though certain pieces may take up to eight months." This is because each butterfly's wing, each tiny petal, each delicate finial, is shaped and hand-painted by highly skilled craftsmen. Everything is of the highest quality.

According to Matilda Burn, a specialist at Christie's European Ceramics & Glass Department, buyers tend to buy sets of Herend tableware porcelain to use and enjoy. Moreover, those in perfect condition often find new owners through auction houses. In her experience, the "Rothschild Bird" pattern, which comes up most frequently, tends to do consistently well at auction. The estimated range for a reasonably sized service currently runs around $7,600 to more than $12,000, but prices achieved can vastly exceed this. For example, a service that was sold in October 2014 achieved a price above $34,000. The popular "Queen Victoria" pattern can also achieve similar prices.

The "Cornucopia" pattern, which is rarer, can also be highly collectible. "Tea and coffee services, though considerably smaller, tend to follow the same rules," Burn said. "A decent-sized 'Rothschild Bird' pattern tea service might carry an estimate of some $3,000 to $4,500." Herend is also a good investment. Some antique sets dating to the 1840s, for example, currently sell for many times their original price.

In recent years, Herend has been redesigning centuries-old patterns by changing colors and motifs. These modernized Herend services, with enamels and patterns that are often bright and decorative, appeal to contemporary tastes. Elegant Herend dinnerware sets, for instance, are frequently featured in bridal registries. A variety of private and trade clients, from individuals and decorators making purchases for new homes to professionals who purchase for resale, also seek Herend services.

Contemporary Herend sets vary considerably in price, dependent on their pattern, condition, and number of components. A table service featuring multiple tureens, serving dishes, and sauce-boats as well as 12-each dinner plates, soup plates and side plates may command as much as $7,600. Services that feature the ever-popular "Queen Victoria" pattern

"Rothschild Bird" porcelain, fourth quarter 20th century, hand-painted with birds and insects on molded ground, service plate/charger, 11" dia.; dinner plate, 10" dia.; six flat cups, 2-1/4" h.; six saucers, 6-1/4" dia.; two sugar bowls, 4-1/4" dia., one with matching cover with yellow rose knop; two mini tureens with lemon knops, 3-1/2" h. x 5" w.; open sauce boat, 3" h. x 9-1/4" w.; medium ginger jar with yellow rose knop, 5-3/4" h., 6-1/4" dia.; five open-weave baskets, 4-1/2" dia.; three open-weave baskets, 3-1/2" dia.; cachepot, 6" h., 7-3/4" dia.; three round scalloped dishes, 4-3/4" dia.; two fan-shaped hors d'oeuvres dishes, 6" w. x 3-1/2" d.; two pots with pink rose lids, 2" h., 2-1/2" dia.; four oval baskets, 3" w.; two oval bowls, 7-3/4" w.; two round vegetable bowls, 10-1/2" dia.; and vase, 6" h., 5-1/4" dia.; scalloped-edge vase with chip at base. **$1,845**

Courtesy of New Orleans Auction Galleries, www.neworleansauction.com

may bring more than $12,000. Those featuring Herend's "Rothschild Bird" pattern may bring even more.

Herend's signature fishnet motif originated in 1874, according to Isabelle Kohler, product manager at Herend USA, an independent importer and distributor of Herend porcelain exclusively in the United States. "That occurred when one of their artists, intrigued with a Chinese plate's fish scale design, painted it onto a rooster figurine's breast to imitate feathers," she said.

Though Herend "Fish Scale" dinnerware is rimmed with diminutive fishnets, prominent ones adorn an array of their figurines, especially animal figurines.

Herend's endearing fishnet-menagerie boasts numerous tender and terrifying creatures, from bears, birds and bugs to rodents and roosters. Their prices vary widely, depending on size and detail. Frog aficionados, for example, can choose between a Frog on Lily Pad at $235, a gold-crowned Frog Prince at $350, or an assemblage of Tree Frogs on Leaves at $1,595. Farming fans may opt for a Dapper Duck at $285, The Cow Jumped Over the Moon at $295 or Standing Foal & Mare at $3,740. Because Herend has become synonymous with bunnies, however, fishnet bunnies of all description, at $225 to $2,050, are most popular. Many fishnet figurines are available in black, rust, green, pink or yellow. Blue, however, is the all-time favorite.

Items in Herend USA's exclusive, limited edition Reserve Collection, which are meticulously crafted for connoisseurs, are more costly yet. Their hand-painted, rust-color fishnet giraffe, which towers at more than 15 inches and arrives in a luxury case, for example, commands $4,170. Herend's alluring, highly detailed, non-fishnet Geisha commands $7,330.

Herend USA also offers a wide selection of home accessories, charming items for children, and dinnerware. Several of the firm's patterns bear names that differ from their European equivalents, however. Americans know "Apponyi Fleur," which features a stylized peony amid garlands of leaves, for example, as "Chinese Bouquet." They know luxuriously gilded "Tupini" as "Cornucopia" and delicate "Nyon" as "Morning Glory." Because Herend USA does not stock all versions of Herend Hungary patterns, however, collectors might want to explore off- or online auctions.

Beginning collectors, who generally purchase Herend items for decorative purposes, often start with something small, like a gold-rimmed candy box or a cachepot (a container for plants) dating to the 19th century. Some prefer contemporary Herend collectibles like a gold-banded teacup and saucer at $85, or another featuring the "Queen Victoria" design at $240. Others might find Herend's small bowls, coasters or place card holders, which start at about $50 apiece, appealing. Bonbonnieres, perennial favorites, featuring exquisitely crafted bunny, butterfly, rose, or strawberry finials on their lids, are another possibility. These begin at around $100 each.

Each Herend product, which begins as a white porcelain blank, bears a complicated back stamp featuring a number of digits, a slash, and color-code letters. Above this appears the company's signature blue mark, which indicates its form and pattern number.

The Herend Porcelain Manufactory, which has been in existence for nearly two centuries, constantly introduces new motifs, but it never discontinues a pattern, so collectors and delighted diners alike can always complete sets or replace damaged pieces.

— Melody Amsel-Ariel

Monumental pair of "Rothschild Bird" ginger jars, fourth quarter 20th century, hand-painted birds and scattered insects, marked on bottom, fine condition, 24-1/2" h., 10-1/4" dia................ **$1,599**

Courtesy of New Orleans Auction Galleries, www.neworleansauction.com

"Rothschild Bird" tableware, 20th century, birds and butterflies and basketweave rim, manufacturer's marks on reverse, eight dinner plates, all with scattered knife marks to enamel, five dessert plates in fine condition, dinner plate 10-1/4" dia., dessert plates 7-1/2" dia.......................... **$800**

Courtesy of Skinner, Inc., www.skinnerinc.com

"Indian Basket/East Indies Flowers" oval soup tureen, circa 1915-1930s, with basket of peonies and other flowers and molded basketweave border, twig-form handles and applied roses, knop in form of putto holding bow, marked in overglaze blue, fine condition, 13-1/4" h. x 12-3/4" w. x 7" d. **$984**

Courtesy of New Orleans Auction Galleries, www.neworleansauction.com

Pair of guinea fowl, 20th century, model #1129 after J.J. Kandler model for Meissen, underside with blue shield mark and impressed uppercase marks, 6-1/2" h. Provenance: From the Birmingham Museum of Art........................... **$397**

Courtesy of Clars Auction Gallery, www.clars.com

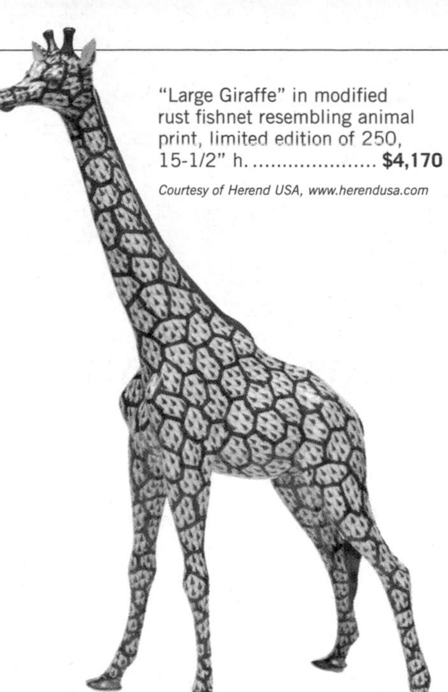

"Large Giraffe" in modified rust fishnet resembling animal print, limited edition of 250, 15-1/2" h. **$4,170**

Courtesy of Herend USA, www.herendusa.com

"Carnival Man" and "Carnival Woman" figurines from 1988 Carnival Series designed by Imre Schrammel and issued in limited edition of 100 each (man No. 23/100, woman, first edition, No. 3/100), excellent overall condition, woman 15" h. **$1,793**

Courtesy of Heritage Auctions, ha.com

Set of three "Chinamen" figures, 6", 4-1/4", and 2-3/4" h. **$186**

Courtesy of Strawser Auctions, www.strawserauctions.com

"Ducks," late 20th century, marked with Herend logo and impressed "HEREND 5035," good condition with minimal wear, 8-1/4" h. **$2,000**

Courtesy of Heritage Auctions, ha.com

◄ "Henry the Rooster" in rust fishnet design, contemporary, 5-1/4" x 7"....................... **$950**

Courtesy of Herend USA, www.herendusa.com

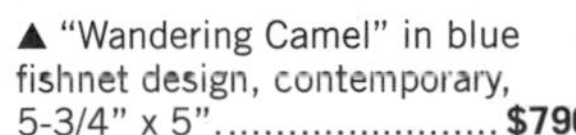

▲ "Wandering Camel" in blue fishnet design, contemporary, 5-3/4" x 5"....................... **$790**

Courtesy of Herend USA, www.herendusa.com

CERAMICS

hull pottery

IN 1905, Addis E. Hull purchased the Acme Pottery Co. of Crooksville, Ohio. In 1917, the A.E. Hull Pottery Co. began making art pottery, novelties, stoneware, and kitchenware, later including the famous Little Red Riding Hood line. Most items had a matte finish with shades of pink, blue, and brown predominating.

After a flood and fire in 1950, the factory reopened in 1952 as the Hull Pottery Co. New pieces, mostly with a glossy finish, were produced. The firm closed in 1985.

Pre-1950 vases are marked "Hull USA" or "Hull Art USA" on the bottom. Many also retain their paper labels. Post-1950 pieces are marked "Hull" in large script or "HULL" in block letters.

Each pattern has a distinctive letter or number, e.g., Wildflower has a "W" and a number; Water Lily, "L" and number; Poppy, numbers in the 600s; Orchid, numbers in the 300s. Early stoneware pieces are marked with an "H."

For more information on Hull Pottery, see *Warman's Hull Pottery Identification and Price Guide* by David Doyle.

Teapot, Bow Knot pattern, professional spout repair, 6-1/2" x 11". **$71**

Courtesy of Woody Auction, www.woodyauction.com

Two-handle vase in Bow Knot pattern, excellent condition, 9" h. **$48**

Courtesy of Milestone Auctions, www.milestoneauctions.com

Double cornucopia vase in Bow Tie pattern, #B13-13", 8" x 13". **$83**

Courtesy of Woody Auction, www.woodyauction.com

Dogwood pattern pitcher, front and back, 14" h............................**$71**

Courtesy of California Auctioneers & Appraisers, www.californiauctioneers.com

LEFT: Magnolia pattern vase in yellow and dusty rose, 1946-1947, marked on bottom USA 3-8-1/2, 8" h. **RIGHT:** Wildflower pattern vase stamped on base W-6-7-1/2"..**$54**

Courtesy of Premier Auction Galleries, Chesterland, Ohio

Magnolia pattern double-handle vase, front and back, marked Hull Art USA 7-8 1/2". **$58**

Courtesy of Vero Beach Auction, www.verobeachauction.com

Ewer in highly desirable Tulip pattern, front and back, 1938-1940, part of exclusive Sueno Line, matte pastel satin finish, Hull base designation 109-33-12, bottom marked with Hull, USA and 109-33-13, mint condition, 7-1/2" x 5" x 13-1/2" h. **$36**

Courtesy of Accurate Auctions, Sheffield, Alabama

Two vases, #I 27-12" double cornucopia vase in Water Lily pattern and #W-1 5-1/2" two-handled vase, two angles shown, good condition..**$106**

Courtesy of Woody Auction, www.woodyauction.com

Two Wildflower pattern vases, front and back, both with maker's mark on bottom: Hull Art, W-6-7-1/2", excellent condition, taller vase 7-1/2" h..**$90**

Courtesy of Morphy Auctions, www.morphyauctions.com

Woodland pattern tea set, front and back: teapot, creamer, and sugar. **$81**

Courtesy of Vero Beach Auction, www.verobeachauction.com

CERAMICS

ironstone

DURABILITY: WHEN INTRODUCED in the early 1800s, that was ironstone china's major selling point. Durability also accounts for the still-ready availability of vintage ironstone china, literally centuries after it first captivated consumers. Unlike its fragile porcelain contemporaries, this utilitarian earthenware was intended to withstand the ravages of time - and it has.

Ironstone owes its innate sturdiness to a formula incorporating iron slag with the clay. Cobalt, added to the mix, eliminated the yellowish tinge that plagued earlier attempts at white china. The earliest form of this opaque dinnerware made its debut in 1800 England, patented by potters William and John Turner. However, by 1806 the Turner firm was bankrupt.

Ironstone achieved its first real popularity in 1813, when Charles Mason first offered for sale his "Patent Ironstone China." Mason's white ironstone was an immediate hit, offering vessels for a wide variety of household uses, from teapots and tureens to washbowls and pitchers.

Although the inexpensive simplicity of white ironstone proved popular with frugal householders, by the 1830s in-mold and transfer patterns were providing a dose of visual variety. Among the decorative favorites: Oriental motifs and homey images such as grains, fruits, and flowers.

Mason's patented formula for white ironstone lasted 14 years. Upon its expiration, numerous other potteries jumped into the fray. By the 1840s, white ironstone found its way across the ocean, enjoying the same success in the United States and Canada as it had in England. By the 1880s, however, the appeal of white ware began to fade. Its successor, soon overtaking the original, was ironstone's most enduring incarnation, Tea Leaf, which was popular into the early 1900s.

English ironstone covered soup tureen and undertray, 19th century, green ground with gilt decoration and painted floral reserves, marked, 10-1/2" h. overall x 14-1/4" l. **$300**

Courtesy of Neal Auction, www.nealauction.com

English blue and white ironstone foot basin, Ridgeway & Morley, circa 1840, marked ARCHIPELAGO/IMPROVED GRANITE CHINA, 8-5/8" h. x 19" w. x 13-1/4" d. **$1,830**

Courtesy of Neal Auction, www.nealauction.com

Four Blue Willow ironstone platters, 19th century, largest 14-1/4" l. x 18" w. **$221**

Courtesy of Pook & Pook, Inc., pookandpook.com

Fifty-five pieces of Elsmore & Forster white wheat ironstone, 19th century, dinner plates, salad plates, serving platters, gravy pitchers, covered tureens, water pitcher, and waste bowls................................. **$455**

Courtesy of Pook & Pook, Inc., pookandpook.com

Set of three graduated ironstone serving dishes, 20th century, largest 4-3/4" h., 11-1/4" dia. **$98**

Courtesy of Pook & Pook, Inc., pookandpook.com

English ironstone cake stand, mid-19th century, marked REAL IRONSTONE CHINA, 5-3/8" h., 14-3/8" dia... **$800**

Courtesy of Neal Auction, www.nealauction.com

Centerpiece ironstone bowl, 20th century, 7" h., 15-3/4" dia. **$62**

Courtesy of Pook & Pook, Inc., pookandpook.com

Mason's ironstone tureen and stand, Allsup / No.16 / St Paul's Church Yard, London. **$261**

Courtesy of Strawser Auctions, www.strawserauctions.com

Pair of Mason's ironstone platters, 11". **$319**

Courtesy of Strawser Auctions, www.strawserauctions.com

Imari-palette ironstone platter, England, 19th century, 22" w. x 18" h. **$369**

Courtesy of Skinner, Inc., www.skinnerinc.com

English Wedgwood Flow Blue Chapoo pattern ironstone pitcher, circa 1840-1865, transfer printed, of hexagonal paneled, molded form, pattern under floral and stylized geometric border, printed mark to underside, good condition, light crazing at foliate molding to front under spout, 5-3/4" h. **$207**

Courtesy of Jeffrey S. Evans & Associates, www.jeffreysevans.com

White ironstone two-handled covered slop jar with fruit finial, good condition, no chips, cracks, or repairs, 13-1/2". .. **$35**

Courtesy of Woody Auction, www.woodyauction.com

English ironstone storage jar, 19th century, reserve with scene from Uncle Tom's Cabin, 3-3/4" h. **$350**

Courtesy of Neal Auction, www.nealauction.com

CERAMICS

kpm

KPM PLAQUES are highly glazed, enamel paintings on porcelain bases that were produced by Konigliche Porzellan Manufaktur (KPM), the King's Porcelain Factory, in Berlin, Germany, between 1880 and 1901.

Their secret, according to Afshine Emrani, dealer and appraiser at www.some-of-my-favorite-things.com, is KPM's highly superior, smooth, hard-paste porcelain, which could be fired at very high temperatures.

"The magic of a KPM plaque is that it will look as crisp and beautiful 100 years from now as it does today," he said. Even when they were introduced, these plaques proved highly collectible, with art lovers, collectors, tourists, and the wealthy acquiring them for extravagant sums.

"First Snow" framed plaque, 19th century, woman in doorway holding child in swaddling clothes, standing beside young girl in snow, after painting by Georg Fredrick Bischoff (German, 1819-1873), KPM mark impressed vérso, 19" h. x 15" w. overall. **$3,965**

Courtesy of Clars Auction Gallery, www.clars.com

Plaque of barefoot girl with tambourine and harp in landscape, 19th century, scene from biblical reference in Exodus, Chapter 15, verse 19, KPM mark verso, 7" h. Provenance: From the Birmingham Museum of Art. **$915**

Courtesy of Clars Auction Gallery, www.clars.com

KPM rarely marketed painted porcelain plaques itself, however. Instead, it usually supplied white, undecorated ones to independent artists who specialized in this genre. Not all artists signed their KPM paintings, however.

While most KPM plaques were copies of famous paintings, some, commissioned by wealthy Americans and Europeans in the 1920s, bear images of actual people in contemporary clothing. These least collectible of KPM plaques command between $500 and $1,500 each, depending on the attractiveness of their subjects.

Gilded, hand-painted plaques featuring Middle Eastern or female Gypsy subjects and bearing round red "Made in Germany" stamps were produced just before and after World War I for export. They command between $500 and $2,000 each. Plaques portraying religious subjects, such as the Virgin Mary or the Flight into Egypt, command higher prices but are less popular.

Popular scenes of hunters, merrymakers, musicians, etc., generally fetch less than $10,000 apiece because they have been reproduced time and again. Rarer, more elaborate scenes, however, like "The Dance Lesson" and "Turkish Card Players" may be worth many times more.

Highly stylized portraits copied from famous paintings - especially those of attractive children or décolleté women - allowed art lovers to own their own "masterpieces." These are currently worth between $2,000 and $20,000 each. Romanticized portrayals of cupids and women in the nude, the most desirable KPM subjects of all, currently sell for up to $40,000 each. Portraits of men, it must be noted, are not only less popular, but also less expensive.

Size also matters. A 4" x 6" inch plaque whose subject has been repeatedly reproduced may sell for a few thousand dollars. Larger ones that portray the same subject will fetch proportionately more. A "Sistine Madonna" plaque, fashioned after the original work by Rafael and measuring 10" x 7-1/2", might cost $4,200. One featuring the identical subject but measuring 15" x 11" might cost $7,800. A larger plaque, measuring 22" x 16", might command twice that price.

The largest KPM plaques, measuring 22" x 26", for example, often burst during production. Although no formula exists for determining prices of those that have survived, Emrani said that each may sell for as much as $250,000. Rare plaques like these are often found in museums.

The condition of a KPM plaque also affects its price. Most, since they were highly glazed and customarily hung instead of handled, have survived in perfect condition. Thus, those that have sustained even minor damage, like scratches, cracks, or chips, fetch considerably lower prices. Those suffering major damage are worthless.

KPM painted plaques arouse so much interest and command such high prices that, over the last couple of years, unscrupulous dealers have entered the market. According to dealer Balazs Benedek, KPM plaques are "the mother of all fakes. About 90 percent of KPM plaques are mid-to-late-20th century reproductions. And about 70 percent are not hand painted."

Collectors should be aware that genuine KPM paintings always boast rich, shiny, glazes that preserve their colors, and though subject matter may vary, they typically feature nude scenes, indoor portraits of women, or group gatherings in lush settings. Anything wildly different should raise suspicion.

Genuine KPMs, on their backs or edges, feature small icons of scepters deeply set in the porcelain, over the letters KPM. These marks are sometimes accompanied by an "H" or some other letter, which may indicate their production date or size. Some are imprinted with the size of the plaque as well, which facilitated sorting or shipping. Shallow or crooked imprints may reveal a fake.

— *Melody Amsel-Arieli*

top lot

Plaque of woman and child by open window, late 19th/early 20th century, signed "L. Sturm" with KPM marks and inscription on reverse, framed, very good condition throughout, 18-7/8" h. x 11-3/8" w. $14,760

COURTESY OF SKINNER, INC., WWW.SKINNERINC.COM

Framed plaque of Victorian woman in gold skirt with matching jacket and blue floral bustle swag holding tennis racket, in gold frame, impressed K.P.M. and scepter mark, very good to excellent condition, frame repainted, plaque 5-1/4" w. x 7-1/4" h., frame 17" w. x 19" h. overall....... **$3,259**

Courtesy of James D. Julia Auctioneers, Fairfield, Maine, www.jamesdjuliacom

Plaque after painting titled "Reception of an Ambassador" by Frederick Arthur Bridgman, Jesus speaking to ambassador while gesturing to infirm man and his daughter, artist initials "C.R.M." in lower right corner, impressed K.P.M. and scepter mark along with letter H on back, unframed, very good to excellent condition, 16-1/4" w. x 12-3/8" h.. **$2,963**

Courtesy of James D. Julia Auctioneers, Fairfield, Maine, www.jamesdjuliacom

Plaque of long-haired woman, late 19th/early 20th century, impressed KPM mark on reverse with scepter, framed, very good condition throughout, plaque 13-1/8" h. x 7-7/8" w. **$6,150**

Courtesy of Skinner, Inc., www.skinnerinc.com

"To Be Good" plaque of woman with long hair wearing green kimono, late 19th/early 20th century, inscribed "Bien Etre" on reverse, very good condition throughout, 12-3/8" h. x 7-1/4" h. (sight). **$6,765**

Courtesy of Skinner, Inc., www.skinnerinc.com

Plaque of woman in red gown with rose, late 19th/early 20th century, impressed KPM and scepter mark on reverse, framed, very good condition, 10-3/8" h. x 8-1/4" (sight). **$1,046**

Courtesy of Skinner, Inc., www.skinnerinc.com

Plaque of maiden seated in garden, late 19th/early 20th century, later frame, indistinct signature, impressed KPM scepter mark on verso, very good condition, plaque 7-1/2" x 13". **$11,070**

Courtesy of Skinner, Inc., www.skinnerinc.com

▶ "The Fates" plaque of Clotho, Lachesis, and Atropus after F. P. Thumann, late 19th/early 20th century, inscribed "Die drei Parzen. w/ Prof Thumann/made in Germany" with impressed KPM and scepter mark, very good condition, plaque 10-1/2" x 12-1/2". **$4,920**

Courtesy of Skinner, Inc., www.skinnerinc.com

Oval plaque of Saint Anthony in polychrome green tones, 19th century, with wood frame, impressed KPM and scepter mark on reverse, nicks to plaque under frame, plaque 10-1/2" h. x 8-3/4" w. **$984**

Courtesy of Skinner, Inc., www.skinnerinc.com

Plaque of children in wheelbarrow, late 19th/early 20th century, inscribed "Wanderlust nach C. Lasch" with Royal Vienna mark and impressed mark, signed, framed, plaque in very good condition, frame damaged, plaque 8-3/4" x 11". **$2,337**

Courtesy of Skinner, Inc., www.skinnerinc.com

CERAMICS

limoges

"LIMOGES" HAS BECOME the generic identifier for porcelain produced in Limoges, France, and the surrounding vicinity. Over 40 manufacturers in the area have, at some point, used the term as a descriptor of their work, and there are at least 400 different Limoges identification marks. The common denominator is the product itself: fine hard-paste porcelain created from the necessary components found in abundance in the Limoges region: kaolin and feldspar.

Until the 1700s, porcelain was exclusively a product of China, introduced to the Western world by Marco Polo and imported at great expense. In 1765, the discovery of kaolin in St. Yrieixin, a small town near Limoges, made French production of porcelain possible. (The chemist's wife credited with the kaolin discovery thought at first that it would prove useful in making soap.)

Limoges entrepreneurs quickly capitalized on the find. Adding to the area's allure: expansive forests, providing fuel for wood-burning kilns; the nearby Vienne River, with water for working clay; and a workforce eager to trade farming for a more lucrative pursuit. Additionally, as the companies would operate outside metropolitan Paris, labor and production costs would be significantly less.

By the early 1770s, numerous porcelain manufacturers were at work in Limoges and its environs. Demand for the porcelain was high because it was both useful and decorative. To meet that demand, firms employed trained as well as untrained artisans for the detailed hand painting required. (Although nearly every type of Limoges has its fans, the most sought-after - and valuable - are those pieces decorated by a company's professional artists.) At its industrial peak in 1900, Limoges factories employed over 8,000 workers in some aspect of porcelain production.

Myriad products classified as Limoges flooded the marketplace from the late 1700s onward. Among them were tableware pieces, such as tea and punch sets, trays, pitchers, compotes, bowls, and plates. Also popular were vases and flower baskets, dresser sets, trinket boxes, ash receivers, figural busts, and decorative plaques.

Although produced in France, Limoges porcelain was soon destined for export overseas; eventually over 80 percent of Limoges porcelain was exported. The United States proved a particularly reliable customer. Notable among the importers was the Haviland China Co.; until the 1940s, its superior, exquisitely decorated china was produced in Limoges and then distributed in the United States.

By the early 20th century, many exporters in the United States were purchasing porcelain blanks from the Limoges factories for decoration stateside. The base product was authentically made in France, but production costs were significantly lower: Thousands of untrained porcelain painters put their skills to work for a minimal wage. Domestic decoration of the blanks also meant that importers could select designs suited to the specific tastes of target audiences.

Because Limoges was a regional designation, rather than the identifier of a specific manufacturer, imported pieces were often marked with the name of the exporting firm, followed by the word "Limoges." Beginning in 1891, "France" was added. Some confusion

top lot!

Pair of "Uncle Tom's Cabin" figural vases, circa 1852-1865, each formed on oval base with flaring scarlet ground scattered with gilt stars, scalloped upper rim, sides molded with parcel-gilt palm, lily, and banana leaves in high relief to sides, fronts molded with high-relief biscuit figural groups of "Tom et Evangeline" and "La Fruite d'elise," each with realistic botanical elements to lower part of parcel gilt bases, both with incised script N or NO to interior bases, excellent condition, Eliza vase with chip to parcel gilt foliage, front left, Uncle Tom vase with section of palm front lacking and two leaves near basket with broken tips, wear to gilding, foliage and stars, 18-5/8" and 19" h. Provenance: Deaccessioned by the Strong Museum, Rochester, New York. Literature: Parallels Fenichell, "Fragile Lessons," Ceramics in America, 2006.

Note: Among the most important anti-slavery, pre-Civil War objects produced in Europe for the American market, these vases are unique in coloration. Per Fenichell, reference 1, of larger-size figural vases, this pair lacks both polychrome enamel landscape and waterscape views based on Bour's and Bettenier's prints and found on other examples. Further, this pair lacks Bohemian-influenced extensive gilding found on pairs such as those at Newark. This pair is painted in "the" fashionable color of the 1850s, called "Solferino," a fine purple-red color. Mary Todd Lincoln visited the firm of Haughwout & Dailey at 540 Broadway, New York, to order both her services of china, the first visit recorded in 1861. Haughwout & Dailey was also the firm known to decorate to order many articles of Haviland and Limoges porcelain in their upstairs decorating atelier, where women from Staffordshire, eastern France, and Western Germany worked as painters. Based on the thematic decoration of vases in this group, the effect was meant to attract the wealthy and patriotic anti-slavery homeowner, whether living in New York, Boston, Philadelphia, or Washington, D.C. $7,475

COURTESY OF JEFFREY S. EVANS & ASSOCIATES, WWW.JEFFREYSEVANS.COM

has arisen from products marked "Limoges China Co." (aka "American Limoges"). This Ohio-based firm, in business from 1902-1955, has no connection to the porcelain produced in France.

The heyday of quality French Limoges lasted roughly into the 1930s. Production continues today, but after World War II, designs and painting techniques became much more standardized.

Vintage Limoges is highly sought-after by today's collectors. They're drawn to the delicacy of the porcelain as well as the colors and skill of decoration; viewing a well-conceived Limoges piece is like seeing a painting in a new form. Valuation is based on age, decorative execution, and, as with any collectible, individual visual appeal.

For more information on Limoges, see *Antique Trader Pottery and Porcelain Ceramics Price Guide, 7th edition.*

Partial gilt and polychrome decorated vase, shouldered form with raised gilt sprays flanking oval reserves decorated with birds in naturalistic setting, 13" h. x 7" w. **$214**

Courtesy of Clars Auction Gallery, www.clars.com

Jardiniere, exterior hand-painted with polychrome sunflowers, base signed "M. Crane" and dated 1903, 9-1/2" h. x 11" w. **$92**

Courtesy of Clars Auction Gallery, www.clars.com

Set of 12 hand-painted service plates, circa 1900-1932, made by Guerin, cobalt borders with gilt scrollwork, center panels with hand-painted floral bouquets, each with two marks, indicating Guerin produced blanks and executed decoration, overall excellent condition, one plate with small chip to foot rim, 11" dia. **$1,845**

Courtesy of New Orleans Auction Galleries, www.neworleansauction.com

Porcelain and gilt-bronze hand-painted centerpiece, circa 1891-1896, pink ground with hand-painted panel of fishing couple in 18th century dress, border with panels of flowers with gilt trim, pierced scrollwork bronze base with matching handles and border around upper edge, marked by Mark Redon of Limoges, with spurious "Sèvres" mark, 6" h. x 17" w. x 9" d. **$554**

Courtesy of New Orleans Auction Galleries, www.neworleansauction.com

Set of 11 raised gilt cabinet plates, circa 1894-1930, cobalt borders with raised gilt scrollwork surrounding central panel with hand-painted flowers, marked by Charles Ahrenfeldt, artist-signed "Hiceille", 8-1/2" dia. **$584**

Courtesy of New Orleans Auction Galleries, www.neworleansauction.com

Large tankard with floral decoration on stand, circa 1900, 18-1/2" h. **$148**

Courtesy of Pook & Pook, Inc., pookandpook.com

Charger with game birds, artist signed Muville, good condition, 13" dia. **$207**

Courtesy of Woody Auction, www.woodyauction.com

◀ Two-handled vase in cream and blue with large orange poppies, gold highlights, artist signed Kimmel, marked with letters JPL, good condition, 13-1/2".. **$207**

Courtesy of Woody Auction, www.woodyauction.com

Two-part punch bowl on stand, multicolor with vintage motif and heavy gold highlights, marked, good condition, 9" x 14"................................ **$649**

Courtesy of Woody Auction, www.woodyauction.com

Two-part jardiniere on base, green tones with pink and yellow roses, base with strong gold trim, good condition, 11-1/4" x 11". **$531**

Courtesy of Woody Auction, www.woodyauction.com

CERAMICS

majolica

IN 1851, an English potter was hoping that his new interpretation of a centuries-old style of ceramics would be well received at the Great Exhibition of the Industries of All Nations set to open May 1 in London's Hyde Park.

Potter Herbert Minton had high hopes for his display. His father, Thomas Minton, founded a pottery works in the mid-1790s in Stoke-on-Trent, Staffordshire. Herbert Minton had designed a "new" line of pottery, and his chemist, Leon Arnoux, had developed a process that resulted in vibrant, colorful glazes that came to be called "majolica."

Trained as an engineer, Arnoux also studied the making of encaustic tiles, and had been appointed art director at Minton's works in 1848. His job was to introduce and promote new products. Victorian fascination with the natural world prompted Arnoux to reintroduce the work of Bernard Palissy, whose naturalistic, bright-colored "maiolica" wares had been created in the 16th century. But Arnoux used a thicker body to make pieces sturdier. This body was given a coating of opaque white glaze, which provided a surface for decoration.

Italian urn in Classical form with figural handles, centered with scenic reserve of Cupid beside young woman, on circular base, 24-1/2" h....... **$366**

Courtesy of Clars Auction Gallery, www.clars.com

Pieces were modeled in high relief, featuring butterflies and other insects, flowers and leaves, fruit, shells, animals, and fish. Queen Victoria's endorsement of the new pottery prompted its acceptance by the general public.

When Minton introduced his wares at Philadelphia's 1876 Centennial Exhibition, American potters also began to produce majolica.

For more information on majolica, see *Warman's Majolica Identification and Price Guide* by Mark F. Moran.

Italian urn with stylized foliate handles flanking central reserve with genre scene of wine harvesters and oxen in naturalistic setting, on white ground, 26" h., 20" dia......................... **$366**

Courtesy of Clars Auction Gallery, www.clars.com

Italian vase, 20th century, in baluster form, two relief lion faux handles, centering foliate reserve of grape clusters, 22" h., 20" dia. **$214**

Courtesy of Clars Auction Gallery, www.clars.com

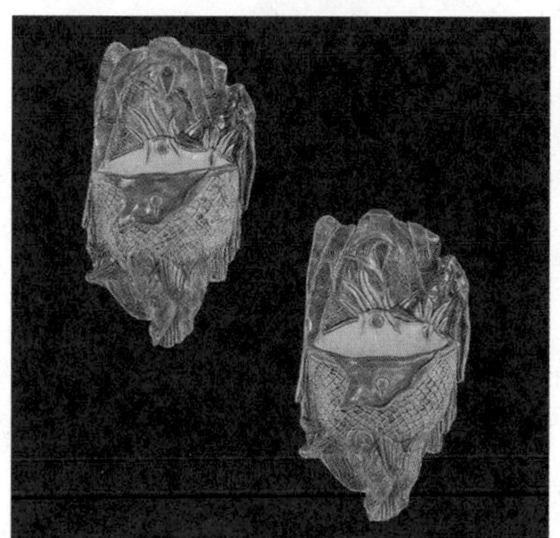

Pair of French wall pockets in form of game baskets, fourth quarter 19th century, molded with leather straps on backplate, rabbit to one side and clutch of game birds on bottom, impressed "1501" on back, 14-1/2" h. x 8" w. x 3-3/4" d.**$431**

Courtesy of New Orleans Auction Galleries, www.neworleansauction.com

George Jones Victorian cheese dish, fourth quarter 19th century, twig-molded stand with turquoise-ground dome with raspberries, molded cow knop on top, overall good condition, chips to foot and rim of base, manufacturing cracks to interior of dome, hairline crack to base of dome with no separation, 13-1/4" h., 11-1/2" dia. **$1,230**

Courtesy of New Orleans Auction Galleries, www.neworleansauction.com

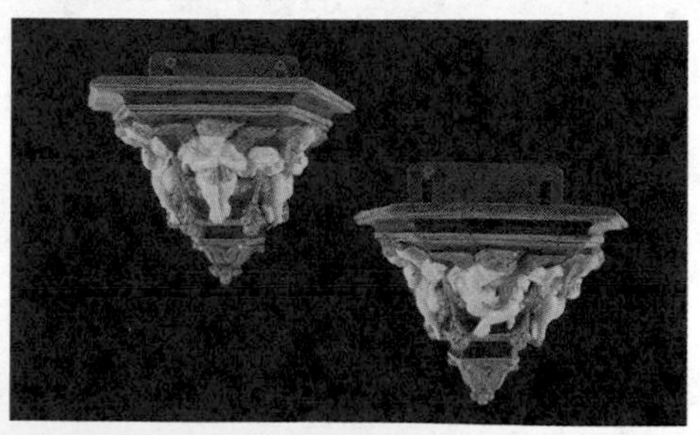

Pair of English wall brackets, possibly George Jones, fourth quarter 19th century, molded with putti on cobalt ground, stamped "putti" indistinctly on interior, bodies of shelves in overall excellent condition, minor nicks to surfaces, minor color bleed throughout, glaze in overall good condition, both tops with small drill hole and crack, back plate hardware mounted well, tops sturdy and visible, 5-1/4" h. x 8" w. x 5-1/2" d.**$431**

Courtesy of New Orleans Auction Galleries, www.neworleansauction.com

Large pair of Aesthetic Movement vases, probably French, fourth quarter 19th century, with molded cranes in front of bamboo-form vases with stalks, branches, and leaves, one vase with crane's head professionally reattached, some restoration and short hairline to top rear center vase, tight vertical hairline to rear of largest vase, bamboo branch bridging gap between two vases reattached, 25-1/2" h. x 9-1/2" w. x 7" d. **$2,214**

Courtesy of New Orleans Auction Galleries, www.neworleansauction.com

Large Aesthetic Movement baluster vase, probably early 20th century, molded with dragon and cloud on blue ground, 25-3/4" h. **$750**

Courtesy of Neal Auction Co., www.nealauction.com

Venetian charger, second quarter 18th century, blue and yellow with villas in garden with rabbits, birds, and insects, marked "S.6.I.B" on reverse, scattered flakes and nicks along outer rim, three top side chips and one underside chip to rim, 13-3/4" dia. **$1,722**

Courtesy of New Orleans Auction Galleries, www.neworleansauction.com

Austrian jardinere on pedestal, third quarter 19th century, dual-handled oblong jardiniere atop conforming segmented pedestal, each allover with C and S scrolls, rocaille, and faux grillage, hand-painted in blue over white ground with gilt highlights, raised maker's mark "WS&S" for Majolikafabrik Wilhelm Schiller & Sohn, inscribed "Made in Austria" and impressed "8084", 52-1/4" h. x 27-1/4" w. x 12-1/2" d. **$625**

Courtesy of John Moran Auctioneers, www.johnmoran.com

Monumental Joseph Holdcroft cachepot and matching underplate, circa 1870-1885, London, with molded Greek key borders on cobalt ground, in Aesthetic Movement style with prunus branches, water lilies, and fish, interior turquoise glazed, impressed "J. Holdcroft" on underside of underplate, minor chips to plate rim and foot rim, scuffs and abrasions to underside, structurally sound, professional repair to base above foot rim with subsequent inpainting, scattered losses to flowers, vertical hairline crack to center of cachepot, blue ground and interior reglazed with pigment slips on branches and flora, 15-1/2" h., 18" dia. **$584**

Courtesy of New Orleans Auction Galleries, www.neworleansauction.com

Square planter, late 19th century, 8-3/4" h. x 7-3/4" w. **$246**

Courtesy of Pook & Pook, Inc., pookandpook.com

Large Continental rooster vase, early 20th century, inscribed "Louis Carrier Belleuse," 21-1/2" h. **$935**

Courtesy of Pook & Pook, Inc., pookandpook.com

George Jones cachepot on stand, circa 1875, molded with lily of valley against pink ground, 9-1/2" h. **$800**

Courtesy of Strawser Auctions, www.strawserauctions.com

Two Castelli plaques, Italy, 18th century, each with polychrome decoration of Biblical scenes, in ebonized and gilded frames, each with edge chip, each 7-3/8" to 8-3/8" h. x 9-3/8" to 11-1/4" w. **$1,046**

Courtesy of Skinner, Inc., www.skinnerinc.com

George Jones grape server, circa 1875, pink oval dish with large green vine leaf, handle formed as fox peering into bowl with tail appearing on mottled underside, 11" w. **$461**

Courtesy of Strawser Auctions, www.strawserauctions.com

George Jones iris pitcher, circa 1875, shape number 2509, lilac ground body molded with irises and water lilies, 5-1/2" h. **$554**

Courtesy of Strawser Auctions, www.strawserauctions.com

top lot

Rare George Jones putti vintners pitcher, circa 1875, straight-sided cobalt blue body molded with grapevines and putti dancing around barrel with putto atop, raising glass, 9" h. $2,460

COURTESY OF STRAWSER AUCTIONS, WWW.STRAWSERAUCTIONS.COM

Geranium platter, 11-1/2". **$148**

Courtesy of Strawser Auctions, www.strawserauctions.com

Cobalt water lily and bullrush basket, excellent condition, 9" w. x 7" h.................................. **$209**

Courtesy of Strawser Auctions, www.strawserauctions.com

Rare George Jones swift and nest pitcher, circa 1875, modeled as mottled green and brown nest with turquoise interior and large black and white swift forming handle, 4-1/2" h. **$1,169**

Courtesy of Strawser Auctions, www.strawserauctions.com

George Jones covered claret beer jug, circa 1875, shape number 3228, cobalt body with turquoise panels of foxes and hounds, with riding crop forming handle and pewter mounted lid with fox finial, 12" h. **$1,968**

Courtesy of Strawser Auctions, www.strawserauctions.com

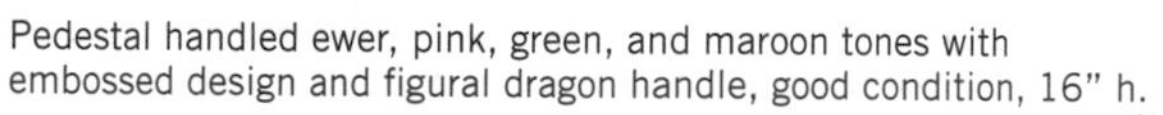

Pedestal handled ewer, pink, green, and maroon tones with embossed design and figural dragon handle, good condition, 16" h. **$35**

Courtesy of Woody Auction, www.woodyauction.com

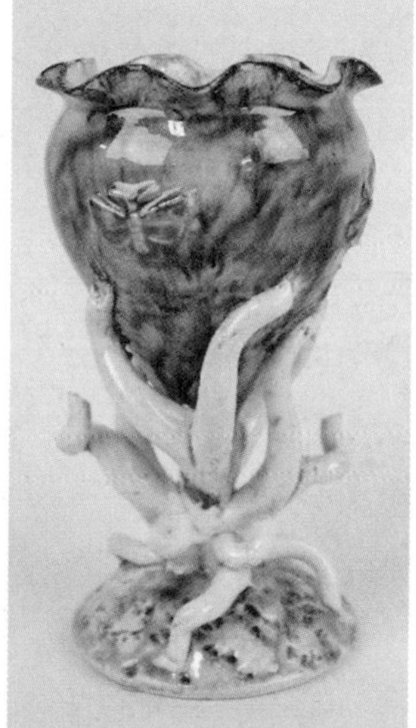

Thomas Sergent Palissy vase, 5-1/2" h. **$93**

Courtesy of Strawser Auctions, www.strawserauctions.com

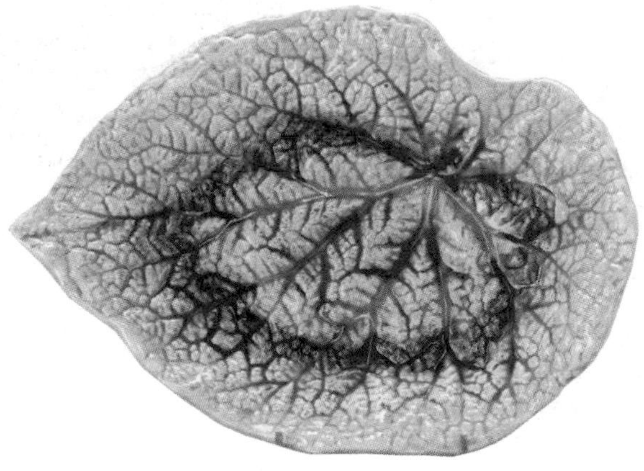

Begonia leaf tray, 11". **$49**

Courtesy of Strawser Auctions, www.strawserauctions.com

CERAMICS

marblehead

MARBLEHEAD POTTERY WAS organized in 1904 by Dr. Herbert J. Hall as a therapeutic aid to patients in a sanitarium he ran in Marblehead, Massachusetts. It was later separated from the sanitarium and directed by Arthur E. Baggs, a fine artist and designer, who bought out the factory in 1916 and operated it until its closing in 1936. Most wares were hand-thrown and decorated and carry the company mark of a stylized sailing vessel flanked by the letters M and P.

Vase with repeating floral design at shoulder, impressed Marblehead ship logo on bottom, excellent original condition, 4-1/4" h. **$850**

Courtesy of Mark Mussio, Humler & Nolan, www.humlernolan.com

Vase with ring of flowers in green and red against speckled blue ground, impressed Marblehead ship logo on base, excellent original condition, 2-1/2" h., 4" dia.. **$600**

Courtesy of Mark Mussio, Humler & Nolan, www.humlernolan.com

Chamber stick in blue mat glaze, impressed Marblehead ship logo on bottom, excellent original condition, 2" h., 5" dia.. **$90**

Courtesy of Mark Mussio, Humler & Nolan, www.humlernolan.com

Rare vase in blue mat glaze, impressed Marblehead logo on bottom, excellent original condition, 3-1/2" h............. **$150**

Courtesy of Mark Mussio, Humler & Nolan, www.humlernolan.com

Vase with geometric design, 1910s, impressed ship mark and MP, incised HT, excellent condition, one small stilt pull visible on side, 6" x 3-1/4". **$3,250**

Courtesy of Rago Arts and Auctions, www.ragoarts.com

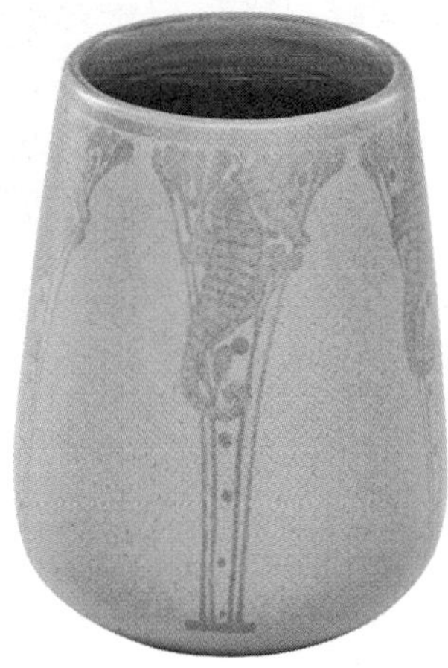

Vase with seahorses, 1910s, stamped ship mark and MP, professional restoration to part of rim, 7" x 5". **$3,375**

Courtesy of Rago Arts, www.ragoarts.com

◀ Vase in gray and blue speckled mat glaze, impressed Marblehead logo on bottom, excellent original condition, 10-1/4" h. **$325**

Courtesy of Mark Mussio, Humler & Nolan, www.humlernolan.com

▲ Vase in blue mat glaze, signed, 3" h. **$151**

Courtesy of Strawser Auctions, www.strawserauctions.com

Uncommon wall pocket in dark green mat glaze, impressed Marblehead ship logo and original Marblehead Pottery label on back, excellent original condition, 5" h. **$120**

Courtesy of Mark Mussio, Humler & Nolan, www.humlernolan.com

CERAMICS

martin brothers

MARTINWARE, THE TERM used for this pottery, dates from 1873 and is the product of the Martin brothers - Robert, Wallace, Edwin, Walter, and Charles - and is often considered the first British studio potters. From first to final stages, the hand-thrown pottery was completely the work of the team. The early wares may be simple and conventional, but the Martin brothers built their reputation by producing ornately engraved, incised, or carved designs as well as rather bizarre figural wares. The amusing face jugs are considered some of their finest work. After 1910, the work of the pottery declined and can be considered finished by 1915, though some attempts were made to fire pottery as late as the 1920s.

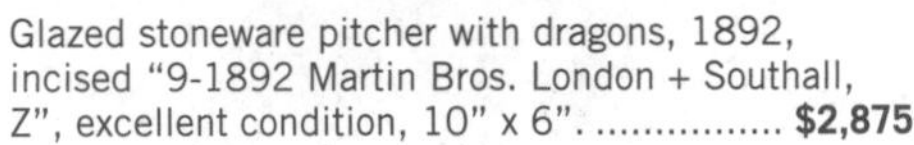

Glazed stoneware pitcher with dragons, 1892, incised "9-1892 Martin Bros. London + Southall, Z", excellent condition, 10" x 6". **$2,875**

Courtesy of Rago Arts and Auctions, www.ragoarts.com

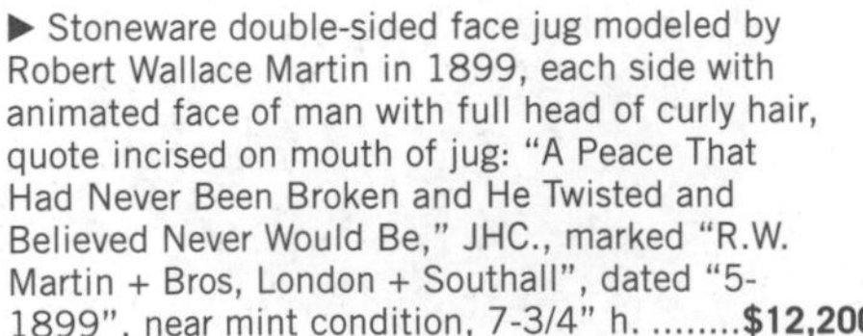

▶ Stoneware double-sided face jug modeled by Robert Wallace Martin in 1899, each side with animated face of man with full head of curly hair, quote incised on mouth of jug: "A Peace That Had Never Been Broken and He Twisted and Believed Never Would Be," JHC., marked "R.W. Martin + Bros, London + Southall", dated "5-1899", near mint condition, 7-3/4" h. **$12,200**

Courtesy of Morphy Auctions, morphyauctions.com

top lot!

Glazed stoneware bird tobacco jar, 1898, signed "9-1898 Martin Bros London + Southall" on base, signed "Martin Bros 3-1898 London + Southall" on head, professional restoration to head, small reglued chip near beak, 10-1/2" x 5"........................**$31,250**

Courtesy of Rago Arts and Auctions, www.ragoarts.com

Stoneware wally bird jar and cover, marked "Martin Bros, London + Southall" on rim of head and on base, dated "1-1898" on head and base, near mint condition, 10-5/8" h..$57,950

COURTESY OF MORPHY AUCTIONS, MORPHYAUCTIONS.COM

Glazed ceramic creature, circa 1900, with partial signature, excellent condition, 2-1/2" x 3" x 4". **$5,313**

Courtesy of Rago Arts and Auctions, www.ragoarts.com

Stoneware monster spoon warmer, marked "R W Martin, London + Southall", incised 21, near mint condition, 5-3/16" h. x 7" l. x 6-1/2" w. **$45,750**

Courtesy of Morphy Auctions, morphyauctions.com

CERAMICS

mccoy pottery

THE FIRST MCCOY with clay under his fingernails was W. Nelson McCoy. With his uncle, W. F. McCoy, he founded a pottery works in Putnam, Ohio, in 1848, making stoneware crocks and jugs.

That same year, W. Nelson's son, James W., was born in Zanesville, Ohio. James established the J. W. McCoy Pottery Co. in Roseville, Ohio, in the fall of 1899. The J. W. McCoy plant was destroyed by fire in 1903 and was rebuilt two years later.

The first examples of Loy-Nel-Art wares were produced at this time. The line's distinctive title came from the names of James McCoy's three sons, Lloyd, Nelson, and Arthur. Like other "standard" glazed pieces produced at this time by several Ohio potteries, Loy-Nel-Art has a glossy finish on a dark brown-black body, but Loy-Nel-Art featured a splash of green color on the front and a burnt-orange splash on the back.

Tankard pitcher with drunken sailor design, 1926, bottom marked with "6" inside shield inside circle, good condition with no visible damage, 6" dia., 8" h. $42

Courtesy of North American Auction Co., www.northamericanauctioncompany.com

George Brush became general manager of J. W. McCoy Pottery Co. in 1909. The company then became Brush-McCoy Pottery Co. in 1911, and in 1925 the name was shortened to Brush Pottery Co. This firm remained in business until 1982.

Separately, in 1910, Nelson McCoy, Sr. founded the Nelson McCoy Sanitary and Stoneware Co., also in Roseville. By the early 1930s, production had shifted from utilitarian wares to art pottery, and the company name was changed to Nelson McCoy Pottery.

Designer Sydney Cope was hired in 1934 and was joined by his son, Leslie, in 1936. The Copes' influence on McCoy wares continued until Sydney's death in 1966. That same year, Leslie opened a gallery devoted to his family's design heritage and featuring his own original art.

Nelson McCoy, Sr. died in 1945 and was succeeded as company president by his nephew, Nelson McCoy Melick.

A fire destroyed the plant in 1950, but company officials – including Nelson McCoy, Jr., then 29 – decided to rebuild, and the new Nelson McCoy Pottery Co. was up and running in just six months.

Nelson Melick died in 1954. Nelson, Jr. became company president and oversaw the company's continued growth. In 1967, the operation was sold to entrepreneur David Chase. At this time, the words "Mt. Clemens Pottery" were added to the company marks. In 1974, Chase sold the company to Lancaster Colony Corp., and the company marks included a stylized "LCC" logo. Nelson, Jr. and his wife, Billie, who had served as a products supervisor, left the company in 1981. In 1985, the company was sold again, this time to Designer Accents. The McCoy pottery factory closed in 1990.

For more information on McCoy pottery, see *Warman's McCoy Pottery, 2nd edition*, by Mark F. Moran.

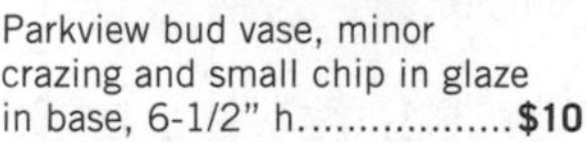

Parkview bud vase, minor crazing and small chip in glaze in base, 6-1/2" h. **$10**

Courtesy of Apple Tree Auction Center, www.appletreeauction.com

Turtle flower sprinkler in green, marked McCoy USA, excellent condition, 9-5/8" l. **$24**

Courtesy of Belhorn Auctions LLC, belhornauctions.com

Vase in green with bust of woman design, rare signed example of Navarre, a line based on J. B. Owens Pottery Co.'s forms and designs purchased by McCoy when Owens went out of business; impressed with shape number 030 and green ink stamp Navarre logo with fleur-de-lis and chapeau, light crazing and touch-up to base chip and top edge of rim, 6-5/8" h. **$375**

Courtesy of Mark Mussio, Humler & Nolan, www.humlernolan.com

Loy-Nel-Art vase with butterflies in standard glaze, unmarked, small nick on bottom, 8-1/4" h. **$23**

Courtesy of Belhorn Auctions LLC, belhornauctions.com

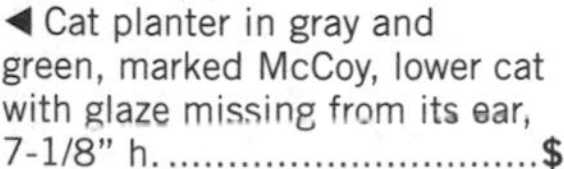

◀ Cat planter in gray and green, marked McCoy, lower cat with glaze missing from its ear, 7-1/8" h. **$9**

Courtesy of Belhorn Auctions LLC, belhornauctions.com

Zuni pattern art vase with colored decorations, unmarked, mint condition, 4" h. **$86**

Courtesy of Belhorn Auctions LLC, belhornauctions.com

Spring Wood pattern vase in white with pink flowers, marked McCoy USA, mint condition, 9-1/4" h. **$15**

Courtesy of Belhorn Auctions LLC, belhornauctions.com

Blossomtime pattern vase in white with green, pink and brown, marked McCoy, mint condition with label, 8-1/8" h. **$10**

Courtesy of Belhorn Auctions LLC, belhornauctions.com

Brush-McCoy turtle planter in green and brown, marked B493 USA, mint condition, 7-1/4" l. **$26**

Courtesy of Belhorn Auctions LLC, belhornauctions.com

Figural planter, green with yellow bird design, hairline crack near bird, 5" x 10" **$18**

Courtesy of Woody Auction, www.woodyauction.com

Brush-McCoy pottery frog, 11" l. **$40**

Courtesy of Apple Tree Auction Center, www.appletreeauction.com

Crocodile planter in green, marked McCoy USA, excellent condition, 9-3/4" l. **$15**

Courtesy of Belhorn Auctions LLC, belhornauctions.com

Brush-McCoy frog planter in green and brown, unmarked, excellent condition, 5-3/4" l. . **$15**

Courtesy of Belhorn Auctions LLC, belhornauctions.com

J. W. McCoy Olympia pattern vase, unmarked, excellent condition, 8-3/4" h. **$58**

Courtesy of Belhorn Auctions LLC, belhornauctions.com

Pigeon or dove miniature planter in green, unmarked, excellent condition, 4" l. **$18**

Courtesy of Belhorn Auctions LLC, belhornauctions.com

Bananas wall pocket in green and yellow, marked NM, excellent condition, 7-1/4" h. **$25**

Courtesy of Belhorn Auctions LLC, belhornauctions.com

◀ Brush-McCoy amaryllis vase in white, unmarked, excellent condition, 2-7/8" h. **$17**

Courtesy of Belhorn Auctions LLC, belhornauctions.com

CERAMICS

meissen

KNOWN FOR ITS finely detailed figurines and exceptional tableware, Meissen is recognized as the first European maker of fine porcelain.

The company owes its beginnings to Johann Friedrich Bottger's 1708 discovery of the process necessary for the manufacture of porcelain. "Rediscovery" might be a better term, since the secret of producing hard paste porcelain had been known to the Chinese for centuries. However, Bottger, a goldsmith and alchemist, was the first to successfully replicate the formula in Europe. Soon after, The Royal Saxon Porcelain Works set up shop in Dresden. Because Bottger's formula was highly sought after by would-be competitors, in 1710 the firm moved its base of operations to Albrechtburg Castle in Meissen, Saxony. There, in fortress-like surroundings, prying eyes could be successfully deflected. And because of that move, the company name eventually became one with its locale: Meissen.

The earliest Meissen pieces were red stoneware, reminiscent of Chinese work and incised with Chinese characters. Porcelain became the Meissen focus in 1713; early releases included figurines and teasets, the decorations reminiscent of baroque metal. In 1719, after Bottger's death, artist J. J. Horoldt took over the firm's direction. His Chinese-influenced designs, which employed a lavish use of color and decoration, are categorized as chinoiserie.

By the 1730s, Meissen employed nearly 100 workers, among them renowned modelers J. G. Kirchner and J. J. Kandler. The firm became known for its porcelain sculptures; subjects included birds, animals, and familiar figures from commedia dell'arte. Meissen dinnerware also won acclaim; in earlier attempts, the company's white porcelain had only managed to achieve off-white. Now, at last, there were dazzling white porcelain surfaces that proved ideal for the exquisite, richly colored decoration that became a Meissen trademark.

Two polychrome enameled figures, late 19th/early 20th century, flower vendor in 18th century dress holding basket of flowers on shaped circular base and gentleman in 18th century attire holding black tricorn hat on circular base, with blue crossed swords mark and incised numbers R137 and R138, 10" h.. **$2,196**

Courtesy of Clars Auction Gallery, www.clars.com

Following Horoldt's retirement in the mid-1700s, Victor Acier became Meissen's master modeler. Under Acier, the design focus relied heavily on mythological themes. By the early 1800s, however, Meissen's popularity began to wane. With production costs mounting and quality inconsistent, changes were instituted, especially technical improvements in production that allowed Meissen to operate more efficiently and profitably. More importantly, the Meissen designs, which had remained relatively stagnant for nearly a century, were refurbished. The goal: to connect with current popular culture.

Meissen's artists (and its porcelain) proved perfectly capable of adapting to the prevailing tastes of the times. The range was wide: the ornate fussiness of the Rococo period; the more subdued Neoclassicism of the late 1700s; the nature-tinged voluptuousness of early 20th century Art Nouveau; and today's Meissen, which reinterprets, and builds on, all of these design eras.

Despite diligent efforts, Meissen eventually found its work widely copied. A crossed-swords trademark, applied to Meissen pieces from 1731 onward, is a good indicator of authenticity. However, even the markings had their imitators. Because Meissen originals, particularly those from the 18th and 19th centuries, are rare and costly, the most reliable guarantee that a piece is authentic is to purchase from a reputable source.

Meissen porcelain is an acquired taste. Its gilded glory, lavish use of color, and almost overwhelmingly intricate detailing require just the right setting for effective display. Meissen is not background décor. These are three-dimensional artworks that demand full attention. Meissen pieces also often tell a story (although the plots may be long forgotten): a cherub and a woman in 18th century dress read a book, surrounded by a bevy of shepherdesses; the goddess Diana perches on a clock above a winged head of Father Time; the painted inset on a cobalt teacup depicts an ancient Dresden cathedral approached by devout churchgoers. Unforgettable images all, and all part of the miracle that is Meissen.

Vase with cobalt blue ground flanked by upright scroll handles, 20th century, painted with loose bouquet on socle foot and square base, 11-1/2" h. Provenance: From the Birmingham Museum of Art. **$488**

Courtesy of Clars Auction Gallery, www.clars.com

Pair of vases in English style, circa 1850, baluster form with frill rim, cross-hatch molded ground painted with bouquets and applied scrolling cartouches, splayed foot molded as shells and acanthus, underside with blue cross swords, incised model number, press number 74, 8-1/2" h. Provenance: From the Birmingham Museum of Art. **$1,220**

Courtesy of Clars Auction Gallery, www.clars.com

► Jewel box with serpentine front and hinged lid, 19th century, hand-painted couples styled after Watteau on sides, lid and interior, underside with blue cross swords mark, 3" h. x 6" w. x 4-1/2" d. Provenance: From the Birmingham Museum of Art. **$1,220**

Courtesy of Clars Auction Gallery, www.clars.com

top lot!

"Elements" ewer personifying water, circa 1850-1900, after model by Johann Joachim Kandler (1706-1775), base with dolphins, mermaid pursuing trio of hippocampi through water, fleet of ships in background raised in bas relief, Neptune sitting in shell overlooking sight, against ground of hand-painted insects, handle in form of bundled water reeds connecting to shell-molded spout, marked with pommel-ended crossed swords underglaze blue mark, with two cancellation lines underneath, good condition, half-glazed interior body with area of firing cracks down body visible from exterior shell between and below four hippocampi, all professionally restored, one tail below handle restored and with surface nick, foot interior incised with number 320 and small impressed number 99 or 66 in underglaze, 23-3/4" h. x 14" w. x 8" d. $19,680

COURTESY OF NEW ORLEANS AUCTION GALLERIES, WWW.NEWORLEANSAUCTION.COM

◀ Partial dinner service with various hand-painted flowers, circa 1857-1872: soup tureen, 10" h. x 12-1/4" w. x 7-1/2" d.; pair of oval platters, 14" w. x 11" d.; oval platter, 10-3/4" w. x 8-3/4" d.; pair of low round bowls, 10" dia.; round chop plate, 12-1/2" dia.; oval open vegetable bowl, 11" w. x 7-1/2" d.; pair of square open bowls, 4" h. x 10-1/2" w. x 10-1/2" d.; single open square bowl, 2-3/4" h. x 9" w. x 9" d.; 25 dinner plates, 10" dia.; 14 soup plates, 9-1/2" dia.; 13 salad/dessert plates, 8" dia.; 14 bread and butter plates, 7" dia.; pair of covered mustard pots, 3-1/4" h.; pair of covered sugar bowls, 3-1/4" h.; three salt dishes, 1-3/4" dia.; 12 demitasse cups, 2" h., and 14 saucers, 4-1/4" dia.; and sauceboat on integral stand, 7-1/2" h. x 9" w., like-new condition, one bread and butter plate with flake chip at rim, all pieces (except for two plates) with double cancellation marks..**$2,706**

Courtesy of New Orleans Auction Galleries, www.neworleansauction.com

▲ Dessert service for 12, 72 pieces, plates circa 1924-1934, cups and saucers circa mid-20th century, each piece with gilt-painted scalloped rim and hand-painted floral sprays on white ground: 12 pierced latticework-rim dessert plates, 1" h., 8-1/4" dia.; 12 crescent-shaped salad plates, 1" h. x 8-1/2" w.; 12 teacups, 2" h. x 4-1/2" w., 3-3/4" dia.; 12 saucers, 7/8" h., 5-7/8" dia.; 12 demitasse cups, 1-5/8" h. x 3-3/8" w. x 2-7/8" d.; 12 demitasse saucers, 3/4" h., 4-3/4" dia.; each with blue underglaze crossed swords mark, cups and saucers each with dual incised lines denoting second choice, overall good condition, light scratches commensurate with occasional handling. **$1,200**

Courtesy of John Moran Auctioneers, johnmoran.com

◀ Octagonal dish with polychrome and partial gilt-painted blossoms and foliate reserves, circa 1725, paneled border at rim, underside with blue Caduceus mark, impressed Drehlers to foot rim, 4-1/2" w. Provenance: From the Birmingham Museum of Art. **$854**

Courtesy of Clars Auction Gallery, www.clars.com

▶ Figure of Stehende Dame Mit Facher, circa 1929, attributed to Paul Scheurich, modeled in white, in contemporary costume with lily on her shoulder, arms crossed, holding large plumed fan, on shaped square base, blue crossed swords mark on back, inscribed "Scheurich 29" on side, underside with incised number A1224, impressed number 156 with crossed swords mark, very good condition, 18-3/8" h. **$2,337**

Courtesy of Skinner, Inc., www.skinnerinc.com

▲ Apollo and Daphne figural, late 19th/early 20th century, impressed numbers F 9, 121, and factory mark, fingers of two raised hands restored, one lower hand restored and missing one finger, piece to end of flowing hair broken and repaired, corner to base repaired and discolored, 14" h. **$1,476**

Courtesy of Skinner, Inc., www.skinnerinc.com

▲ Vase in Rococo style with Schneeballen cover, circa 1824-1850, in two pieces, with painted fluting and bands, and swags of sculpted flowers, "daub" crossed swords mark of period, 17" h., 6-1/4" dia. .. **$523**

Courtesy of New Orleans Auction Galleries, www.neworleansauction.com

Pierced oval centerpiece on tapered foot, third quarter 19th century, oval bowl pierced with anthemia and flowers in Aesthetic taste, sides set with satyr-head handles with scrolled horns, marked with underglaze blue cross swords and overglaze 12A in aquamarine-colored rope trim, 10-1/4" h. x 13-1/4" w. x 8-1/2" d. **$800**

Courtesy of New Orleans Auction Galleries, www.neworleansauction.com

▶ Male polychrome Pagoda figure with nodding head, tongue, and hands, 19th/early 20th century, seated cross-legged, blue crossed swords mark, incised numbers 956 and 93, flake at side terminal to one hand support, 5-3/4" h. **$3,075**

Courtesy of Skinner, Inc., www.skinnerinc.com

Partial dinner service, early 20th century, 72 pieces, each gilt and scalloped basketweave-rim plate hand-painted with variety of floral sprays on white ground: 36 dinner plates, 1-1/4" h., 10-1/4" dia.; 12 rimmed soup bowls, 1-3/4" h., 9-1/8" dia.; and 24 salad plates, 1" h., 8-1/2" dia.; each with blue underglaze crossed swords mark and impressed and painted numerical marks verso, overall good condition, scattered light scratches commensurate with occasional handling. **$2,400**

Courtesy of John Moran Auctioneers, johnmoran.com

Blue Onion porcelain tureen and undertray, 10" h. x 19" w. **$258**

Courtesy of Pook & Pook, Inc., pookandpook.com

Figural vases, late 19th/early 20th century, each with polychrome decoration and gilded highlights, trio of draped putti suspending urn with floral garland and scenes of amorous couples, on scrolling bases, factory marks, one with repair to collar support for vase, one with gilt rim wear to collar support and chip to one foot of cherub, 8" h. **$1,476**

Courtesy of Skinner, Inc., www.skinnerinc.com

Floral tray, late 19th/early 20th century, white ground with central polychrome bouquet, gilded rocaille shells at corners and handholds, with crossed blue swords mark, second quality mark, 15-5/8" l. x 15-1/2" w. **$738**

Courtesy of Skinner, Inc., www.skinnerinc.com

Platter with horses, hay wagon, adults, and children, 14-3/4" l. x 17-1/4" w. **$209**

Courtesy of Pook & Pook, Inc., pookandpook.com

Marcolini period hand-painted cabbage-form tureen and underplate, circa 1774-1817, with gilt-trimmed framboise-colored leaves and panels of hand-painted flower bouquets, marked in underglaze blue with crossed swords over star, overall good condition, light wear to gilding pigment, small chip to inside of tureen foot rim, tureen 7-1/2" h., 7" dia., underplate 9-3/4" dia. **$738**

Courtesy of New Orleans Auction Galleries, www.neworleansauction.com

CERAMICS

mettlach

CERAMICS WITH THE name Mettlach were produced by Villeroy & Boch and other potteries in the Mettlach area of Germany. Villery & Boch's finest years of production are thought to be from about 1890-1910.

Four half-liter steins with inlay lids: Design number 1796 with tipsy jester, signed C. Worth; 2035 with soiree of mythical creatures and nudes; 2025 with nude youths and cherubs; and 2057 with women and men in celebration; all with Castle and Mettlach impressions, Geschützt and other marks below bases, minor interior stains, all in very good condition...................... **$650**

Courtesy of Mark Mussio, Humler & Nolan, www.humlernolan.com

Lidded jar in gray with blue and white, marked Mettlach 3451, small nick at top, 3" h. . **$6**

Courtesy of Belhorn Auctions LLC, belhornauctions.com

Two beer steins, .4-liter number 1909 pug-type with transfer decoration and pewter lid and half-liter number 2012 mosaic-type with inlay lid, first marked with number and date only, second with printed and impressed markings, marked for 1889 and 1902, undamaged, 5-1/2" and 8" h. to top of lid.. **$288**

Courtesy of Jeffrey S. Evans & Associates, www.jeffreysevans.com

Pair of Villeroy & Boch half-liter steins, each with hops, wheat, and flowers, factory marks and impressed number 1909, good condition throughout, 8-1/2" h..................................... **$338**

Courtesy of Skinner, Inc., www.skinnerinc.com

Villeroy & Boch punch bowl set, late 19th/early 20th century, lidded bowl with fruit-decorated border above reserves of gnome genre scenes, annotated with German phrases, together with undertray and six coasters, punch bowl 15" h. **$305**

Courtesy of Clars Auction Gallery, www.clars.com

Mettlach stein numbered 1370, 6" h. **$74**

Courtesy of Pook & Pook, Inc., pookandpook.com

Massive charger with gnome and goblet in flowering tree with large insects, signed by designer Heinrich Schlitt on front, signed Mettlach 2113 on back, excellent condition with minor wear to gold trim, holes cast into foot ring for hanging, 16-1/4" dia..**$500**

Courtesy of Mark Mussio, Humler & Nolan, www.humlernolan.com

CERAMICS

minton

THOMAS MINTON ESTABLISHED the Minton factory in England in 1793. The factory made earthenware, especially the blue-printed variety, and Thomas Minton is sometimes credited with the invention of the blue Willow pattern. For a time, majolica and tiles were also important parts of production, but bone china soon became the principal ware.

Nineteen Dynasty pattern cobalt and gilt bone china items, one serving platter, two oval rimmed servers, lidded tureen with undertray, serving bowl, sauce boat, and 12 teacups, three with saucers, largest 16-1/2" l............. **$1,342**

Courtesy of Clars Auction Gallery, www.clars.com

Buckingham K-159 pattern partial bone china dinner service, circa 1951-2009, with raised gilt borders on ivory ground, 12 dinner plates, 10-1/2" dia.; 12 salad/dessert plates, 8" dia.; 12 bread and butter plates, 6" dia.; 11 cups, 2-1/4" h.; and 12 saucers, 4-3/4" dia. **$2,460**

Courtesy of New Orleans Auction Galleries, www.neworleansauction.com

Chocolate set, 27 pieces, chocolate pot, eight demitasse cups and eight saucers, five larger cups and five saucers, purple maker's mark under foot.. **$150**

Courtesy of O'Gallerie, www.ogallerie.com

Cabinet plate with hand-painted underwater scene with fish, signed A. H. Wright, 9-1/4" dia........................... **$74**

Courtesy of Pook & Pook, Inc., pookandpook.com

Dynasty pattern cobalt and gilt bone china partial dinner service, circa 1951-2009, assembled service of eight dinner plates, 10-1/2" dia.; eight salad/dessert plates, 7-1/2" dia.; eight bread and butter plates, 6" dia.; eight footed cups, 4" dia.; 15 saucers, 5-1/2" dia.; eight cream soup bowls, 4-1/4" dia.; one cream soup bowl with flaring rim, 4-1/2" dia.; and eight cream soup bowl stands, 6" dia., very good condition, raised gilding intact, one cream soup bowl lacks foot, one saucer with damage. **$2,337**

Courtesy of New Orleans Auction Galleries, www.neworleansauction.com

Eleven bone china dessert plates with raised gilt scrollwork on apple-green ground and hand-painted signed floral panels on ivory ground, circa 1928, with Minton mark, incorporating retailer, St. Louis Glass and Queensware Co., impressed date marks, 9" dia. **$677**

Courtesy of New Orleans Auction Galleries, www.neworleansauction.com

Parian figure of William Shakespeare, signed John Bell, 17-3/4" h. **$357**

Courtesy of Pook & Pook, Inc., pookandpook.com

Two Parian figures, "Clorinda" and "Dorothea," John Bell (British, 1812-1895), 1848, both marked, signed and dated, taller 14" h. **$450**

Courtesy of Neal Auction, www.nealauction.com

Rare majolica posy vase, circa 1875, two yellow and pink pomegranates supported by twigs and leaves on gray rocky ground, 6" h................ **$2,583**

Courtesy of Strawser Auctions, www.strawserauctions.com

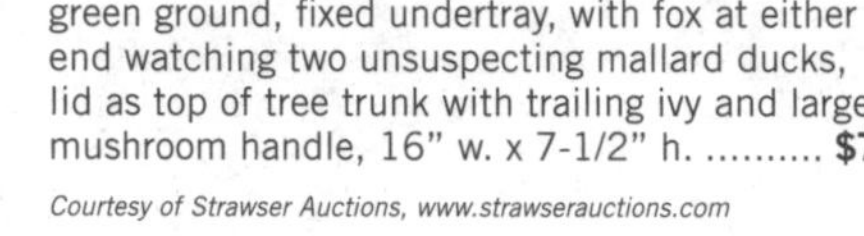

Rare and important majolica mushroom tureen, circa 1875, oval fern and ivy tree trunk with leafy green ground, fixed undertray, with fox at either end watching two unsuspecting mallard ducks, lid as top of tree trunk with trailing ivy and large mushroom handle, 16" w. x 7-1/2" h. **$7,688**

Courtesy of Strawser Auctions, www.strawserauctions.com

Majolica shell and vine wine cooler, circa 1875, cobalt blue gadrooned body with two arched branch and vine leaf handles, scrolling green lip, circular conch shell pedestal base, 9-1/2" h. ... **$246**

Courtesy of Strawser Auctions, www.strawserauctions.com

Hand-painted tile with swans and cygnets, marked "Minton Stoke On Trent," minor edge nicks, 8" sq. **$30**

Courtesy of Woody Auction, www.woodyauction.com

CERAMICS

mochaware

MOCHA DECORATION IS found on basically utilitarian creamware or yellowware articles and is achieved by a simple chemical reaction. A color pigment of brown, blue, green, or black is given an acid nature by infusion of tobacco or hops. When this acid nature colorant is applied in blobs to an alkaline ground color, it reacts by spreading in feathery seaweed designs. This type of decoration is usually accompanied by horizontal bands of light color slip.

Produced in many Staffordshire, England, potteries from the late 18th until the late 19th centuries, its name is derived from the similar markings found on mocha quartz. In addition to the seaweed decoration, mocha wares are also seen with earthworm and cat's-eye patterns or a marbleized effect.

Creamware quart mug, England, circa 1810, body with alternating bands of brown and yellow slip separated by two wide green-glazed bands in center, hairline crack at rim, staining, 5-5/8" h. **$492**

Courtesy of Skinner, Inc., www.skinnerinc.com

Creamware half-pint mug, England, circa 1800, top and bottom edges with red and blue slip bands, body with horizontal and vertical lines filled with black slip, minor imperfections, small chip and minor roughness on mouth, hairline cracks in side, base, and handle, 3-1/2" h.. **$492**

Courtesy of Skinner, Inc., www.skinnerinc.com

Creamware pint mug, England, circa 1830, body with cable decoration on light blue slip band bordered by narrow brown slip bands, no chips, cracks, or evidence of repair, 4-7/8" h..**$615**

Courtesy of Skinner, Inc., www.skinnerinc.com

Creamware pint mug, England, circa 1820, body decorated with dendritic fan decoration of alternating heights over gray and brown slip bands, wear on base, staining on interior, 4-3/4" h. **$554**

Courtesy of Skinner, Inc., www.skinnerinc.com

Creamware pint mug, England, circa 1810-1820, body with two wide orange slip bands with dendritic decoration and narrow brown slip bands, three small chips on underside of base, 4-5/8" h. **$1,076**

Courtesy of Skinner, Inc., www.skinnerinc.com

Pearlware pint mug, England, circa 1830, body with cable and cat's-eye decoration on wide gray slip band bordered by bands of brown and blue slip, minor roughness on rim, 4-7/8" h. **$554**

Courtesy of Skinner, Inc., www.skinnerinc.com

top lot

Pearlware pint mug, England, circa 1830, body with cat's-eye twigs on wide gray slip band, bordered by double narrow bands of brown slip, two hairline cracks in rim, 4-7/8" h. $2,337

COURTESY OF SKINNER, INC., WWW.SKINNERINC.COM

Large pearlware pitcher, England, circa 1810, body with wide gray slip bands with cable and cat's-eye decoration, narrow brown bands and rouletted green shoulder band, star-shaped stress crack in base, staining, 7-1/2" h. **$554**

Courtesy of Skinner, Inc., www.skinnerinc.com

Small pearlware pitcher, England, circa 1830, body with yellow slip and cable decoration below wide green band, bottom impressed with number 7, minor roughness on spout, 4-1/2" h. **$1,169**

Courtesy of Skinner, Inc., www.skinnerinc.com

Pearlware pint mug, England, circa 1810-1820, body decorated with alternating bands of brown and blue slip between wide green-glazed borders, two small chips on base and impact mark on rim, 4-5/8" h. **$923**

Courtesy of Skinner, Inc., www.skinnerinc.com

Yellowware double-handled bowl, 19th century, with dendritic decoration over alternating brown and white slip bands, applied strap handles on sides and raised foot on bottom, no chips, cracks, or evidence of repair, 8" dia., 4" h. ... **$677**

Courtesy of Skinner, Inc., www.skinnerinc.com

CERAMICS

moorcroft

WILLIAM MOORCROFT was first employed as a potter by James Macintyre & Co., Ltd. of Burslem, Staffordshire, England, in 1897. He established the Moorcroft pottery in 1913. Walter Moorcroft, William's son, continued the business upon his father's death and made wares in the same style. The majority of the art pottery wares were hand thrown, resulting in a great variation among similarly styled pieces. Colors and marks are keys to determining age. The company initially used an impressed mark, "Moorcroft, Burslem"; a signature mark, "W. Moorcroft," followed. Modern pieces are marked simply "Moorcroft," with export pieces also marked "Made in England."

Florian Ware vase, tapered form with peacock feather designs, signed on underside in green, 15" h. **$7,930**

Courtesy of Clars Auction Gallery, www.clars.com

Macintyre Florian Ware vase with floral decoration, marked on bottom with Florian Ware ink stamp in brown, W. Moorcroft des in green, M869 in brown and incised P, fine overall crazing, 5-1/4" h...... **$450**

Courtesy of Mark Mussio, Humler & Nolan, www.humlernolan.com

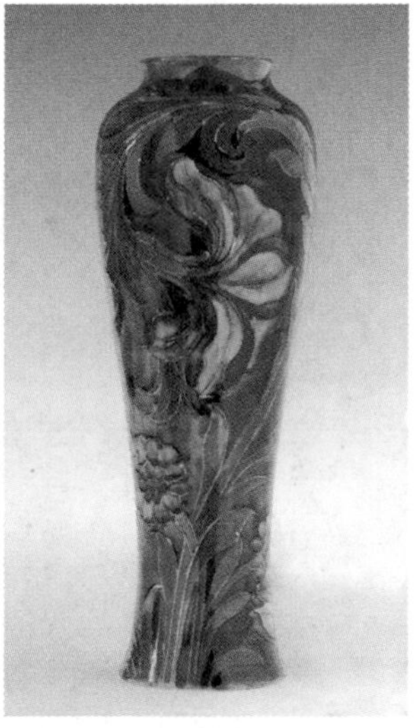

Spanish design vase, early 20th century, signed, excellent condition, glaze wear to rim, 12" h. **$1210**

Courtesy of Cottone Auctions, www.cottoneauctions.com

Uncommon "Waving Corn" vase in rose and maize, mid-1930s, impressed factory mark with facsimile signature, 1928-1949, and painted signature, excellent original condition, 6-1/8" h. **$200**

Courtesy of Mark Mussio, Humler & Nolan, www.humlernolan.com

Plaque with moonlit scene designed by Rachel Bishop, made by slip trailing, 2008, tile marked "Moorcroft Made in Stoke on Trent England" with date and artisan marks, label for frame reads: "Framed For Moorcroft by Frame Workshop Marsh St North, Hanley, Staffs., ST1 5HR," excellent original condition, with original Moorcroft presentation box, plaque approximately 4" x 12"......... **$600**

Courtesy of Mark Mussio, Humler & Nolan, www.humlernolan.com

Small flowerpot, 3-1/2"......... **$70**

Courtesy of Strawser Auctions, www.strawserauctions.com

Plaque titled "Tree Sparrows" done by slip trailing, 2014, marked with Moorcroft logo date and several artisan marks, framed, excellent original condition, approximately 4" x 12"................................ **$250**

Courtesy of Mark Mussio, Humler & Nolan, www.humlernolan.com

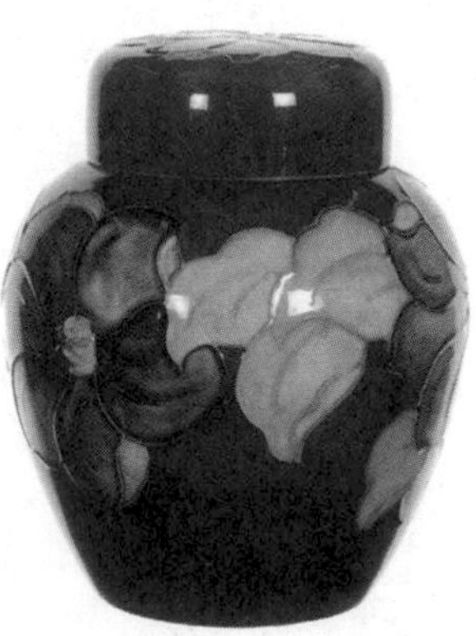

Covered jar, green with floral decor, marked, original paper labels on jar and lid, good condition, no chips, cracks, or repairs, 6"........................... **$94**

Courtesy of Woody Auction, www.woodyauction.com

"River Traffic" vase, Paul Hilditch design, made in 2013, with "Moorcroft Made in Stoke on Trent England" logo and Hilditch's painted signature along with other artisan marks and symbols, in excellent condition, 12-1/4" h........... **$700**

Courtesy of Mark Mussio, Humler & Nolan, www.humlernolan.com

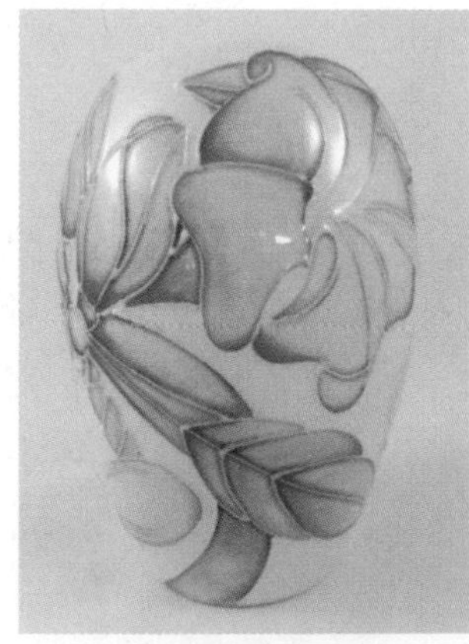

Vase, marked on bottom, dated 1999, good condition, 5-1/4" h....................................... **$97**

Courtesy of Rachel Davis Fine Arts, www.racheldavisfinearts.com

CERAMICS

newcomb college

THIS POTTERY WAS established in the art department of Newcomb College in New Orleans in 1897. Each piece was hand-thrown and bore the potter's mark and decorator's monogram on the base. It was always studio business and never operated as factory. Its pieces are, therefore, scarce, with the early wares eagerly sought. The pottery closed in 1940.

▲ Bowl with floral decoration at shoulder by Sadie Irvine, 1924, marked with Newcomb logo, shape number 265, date code for 1925 (OO 42), letters JM for potter Joseph Meyer, and Irvine's monogram, excellent condition, professional repair at rim, 3-5/8" h., 11" dia., with unmarked Newcomb flower frog, 1-3/8" h., 4-3/8" dia. **$600**

Courtesy of Mark Mussio, Humler & Nolan, www.humlernolan.com

◀ Hand-thrown wall plaque with peacock feather decoration by unknown artist, 1915, incised and painted in blue, green and cream, two pierced holes on backside for hanging, marked with Newcomb College logo, date code for 1915 (HE 38), impressed initials of potter Joseph Meyer, and A in circle indicating type of clay body, excellent original condition, 8-1/4" dia., with rare copy of Ormond and Irvine's *Louisiana's Art Nouveau / The Crafts of the Newcomb Style* in which it is pictured on page 109................................ **$2,800**

Courtesy of Mark Mussio, Humler & Nolan, www.humlernolan.com

▲ Carved mat glaze scenic vase with cypress trees and Spanish moss by Anna Frances Simpson, 1925, marked with Newcomb logo, impressed date code for 1925 (OP 52), impressed letters JM for potter Joseph Meyer, shape number 250, and incised monogram of artist, original Newcomb Pottery paper label on which is written date code, title "Cypress," and price of $12, excellent condition, professional restoration to rim, 8-1/8" h. **$1,800**

Courtesy of Mark Mussio, Humler & Nolan, www.humlernolan.com

top lot

Monumental high glaze vase with incised and modeled irises by Harriet Coulter Joor, 1902, dark blue, green, and white underglaze, base marked with Newcomb cipher, decorator's mark, Joseph Meyer's potter's mark, registration number S7, and letter U for buff clay body, 12-1/4" h., 8-1/2" dia. $33,550

COURTESY OF NEAL AUCTION, WWW.NEALAUCTION.COM

Mat glaze low bowl with band of carved fruit blossoms on shoulder by Sadie Irvine, 1925, marked with Newcomb logo, date code for 1925 (OU 51), incised number 6, and incised monogram of artist, excellent condition with faint crazing, 2-3/4" h. x 4-3/4" w. **$600**

Courtesy of Mark Mussio, Humler & Nolan, www.humlernolan.com

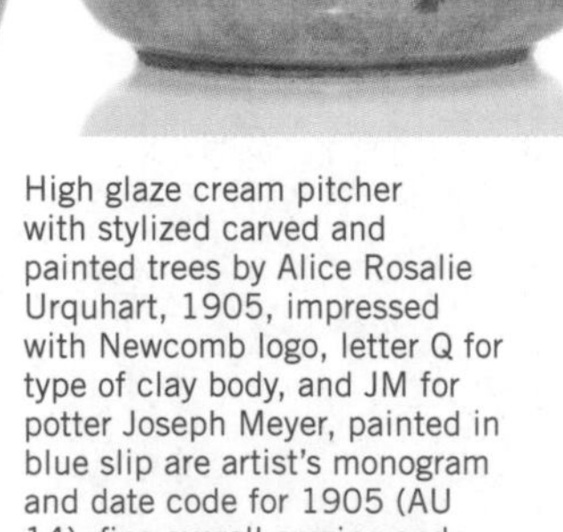

High glaze cream pitcher with stylized carved and painted trees by Alice Rosalie Urquhart, 1905, impressed with Newcomb logo, letter Q for type of clay body, and JM for potter Joseph Meyer, painted in blue slip are artist's monogram and date code for 1905 (AU 14), fine overall crazing and professional restoration to rim chip, 3-3/4" h. **$850**

Courtesy of Mark Mussio, Humler & Nolan, www.humlernolan.com

Gourd vase in green mat glaze, impressed with Newcomb College logo, letter M and incised 215 beneath, very good condition, open glaze blisters and glaze grinding on base, 6-7/8" h. **$400**

Courtesy of Mark Mussio, Humler & Nolan, www.humlernolan.com

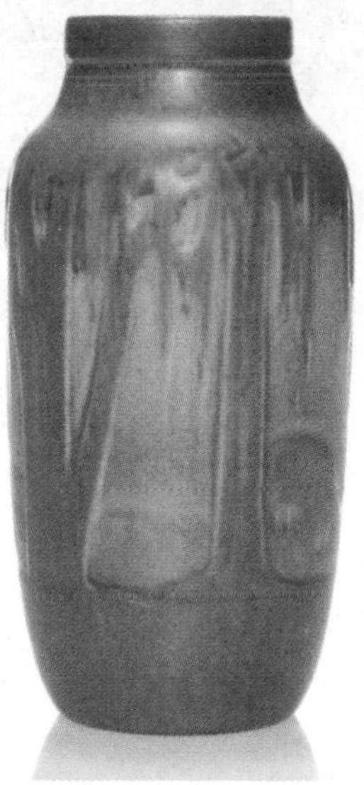

Scenic vase with high relief trees, Spanish moss, and red evening sky by Sadie Irvine, 1928, marked with Newcomb logo, date code for 1928 (RA 28), shape number 19, impressed monogram of potter Joseph Meyer, and incised monogram of artist, excellent original condition, uncrazed, 6-1/4" h. **$3,200**

Courtesy of Mark Mussio, Humler & Nolan, www.humlernolan.com

Bowl with relief-carved Cherokee roses by Anna Frances Simpson, 1930, matte glaze with blue, green, white, and yellow underglaze, base marked with Newcomb cipher, decorator's mark, Jonathan Hunt's potter's mark, registration number SG26, and shape number 49, 6" h., 8" dia. **$3,750**

Courtesy of Neal Auction, www.nealauction.com

Matte glaze low bowl with bas relief-molded rim on blue ground by Anna Frances Simpson (1880-1930) and potted by Joseph Meyer (1848-1931), circa 1914, New Orleans, marked NC for Newcomb College, JM for Joseph Meyer, and 1914 registration number 6Y81, letter C in circle identifying clay, numbers 256 and 301, one of which identifies shape, overall very good condition, crazing and light staining to inside glaze, 3-3/4" h., 6-1/4" dia. **$1,353**

Courtesy of New Orleans Auction Galleries, www.neworleansauction.com

High glaze jardiniere with incised irises by Marie Medora Ross, 1905, blue and green underglaze, base marked with Newcomb cipher, decorator's mark, Joseph Meyer's potter's mark, registration number AR81, and letter Q for buff clay body, 5-1/4" h., 5-1/2" dia **$3,200**

Courtesy of Neal Auction, www.nealauction.com

High glaze vase with incised mock orange design by Mazie T. Ryan, 1904, blue underglaze, base marked with Newcomb cipher, decorator's mark, Joseph Meyer's potter's mark, and registration number SS12, 7-3/8" h. **$6,250**

Courtesy of Neal Auction, www.nealauction.com

Vase in Moon and Moss design by Anna Frances Simpson, 1930, matte glaze with blue and green underglaze, base marked with Newcomb cipher, decorator's mark, Jonathan Hunt's potter's mark, registration number SG91, and shape number 157, 9-1/2" h., 6-1/2" dia....................... **$7,000**

Courtesy of Neal Auction, www.nealauction.com

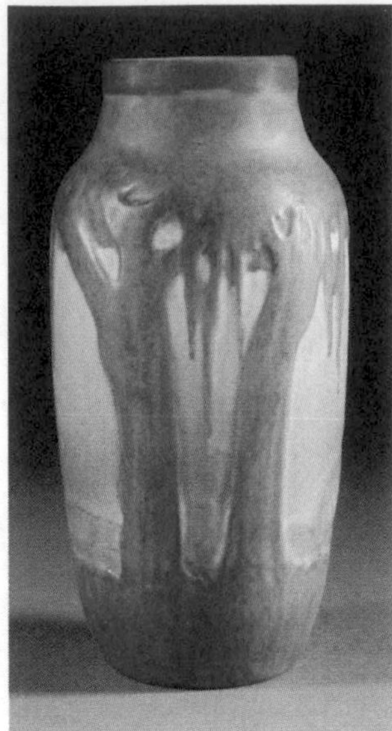

Vase with relief-carved "twilight" moss-laden oak design by Sadie Irvine, 1928, matte glaze with blue, green, and pink underglaze, base marked with Newcomb cipher, decorator's mark, registration number RA64, and shape number 19, lip repair, 6-5/8" h. **$2,800**

Courtesy of Neal Auction, www.nealauction.com

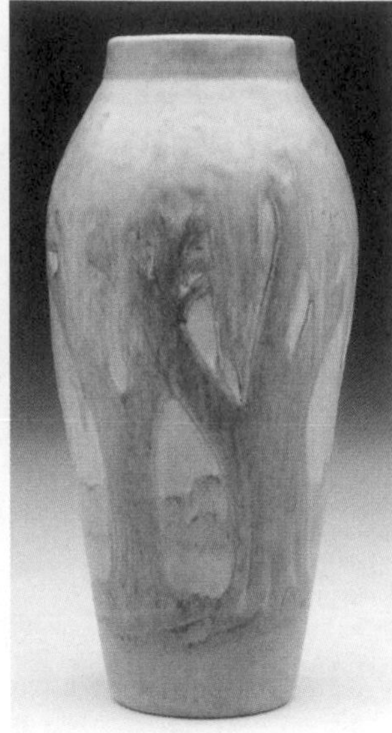

Vase with blue trees with green foliage and moss in relief against light blueish-gray and green background by Anna F. Simpson, signed with impressed conjoined NC and numbered ND19 on underside, impressed with number 82 and artist initials, very good to excellent condition, 8-1/2" h. **$5,036**

Courtesy of James D. Julia Auctioneers, Fairfield, Maine, www.jamesdjuliacom

High glaze vase with incised Aztec lily design in blue by Marie Medora Ross, 1904, blue-green and mustard yellow underglaze, base marked with Newcomb cipher, decorator's mark, Joseph Meyer's potter's mark, and registration number AB 98, retains partial original paper label, 10-1/4" h. ...**$14,030**

Courtesy of Neal Auction, www.nealauction.com

Three high glaze plates with three incised crawfish in blue underglaze by Marie Levering Benson, 1907, marked with Newcomb cipher, decorator's mark, Joseph Meyer's potter's mark, and registration numbers BT 86, BT 88, and BT 91, 7-1/2" dia..... **$18,300**

Courtesy of Neal Auction, www.nealauction.com

Vase in Moon and Moss design by Aurelia Arbo, matte glaze with blue, green, and yellow underglaze, base marked with Newcomb cipher, decorator's mark, Francis Ford's potter's mark, and registration number V34, 5" h., 6" dia. **$2,700**

Courtesy of Neal Auction, www.nealauction.com

CERAMICS

niloak

NILOAK POTTERY IS famous for its marbleized swirls of red, blue, gray, white, and other clay colors. Once produced in Benton, Arkansas, it has achieved center stage in national auctions. Rago Arts' auctions in recent years have seen the values paid for Niloak demonstrate a pottery that holds its value.

The pottery, founded by the Hyten family, derived its name from the backwards spelling of the clay type known as kaolin. In regular production from 1910 to 1934, Niloak was produced as vases, penholders, kitchenware, ewers, creamers, sand jars to douse cigarettes, umbrella jars, and even limited special-order production as tile. The family pottery produced housewares with the name "Hyten Brothers" and "Eagle Pottery" on it.

Charles "Bullet" Hyten was born in Benton in 1877. His father died while he was a child. Hyten learned the pottery trade from his stepfather, Frank Woosley. Woosley worked for the elder Hyten and cared for him until his death, while also keeping the family business going. Woosley married Bullet's mother, Harriet, in 1882.

In 1895, Woosley sold the family business to Bullet, who was 18. Soon after, tragedy struck. A fire consumed one of the kilns. Bullet almost lost the business.

In time, he and other potters in the area noticed the amazing colors of clay in the local ground. He had a business connection with a potter in Hot Springs. Together, they discovered that kiln heat burned out the unique colors of Saline County clays. They found a way to add chemicals and colors that duplicated the color of what was in the ground. He had a business connection with a potter in Hot Springs. Together, they discovered that kiln heat burned out the unique colors of Saline County clays. They found a way to add chemicals and colors that duplicated the color of what was in the ground.

Hyten started to experiment seriously in 1909. In 1910 the Niloak process was perfected. Confident of success, Hyten sought financing for his company in 1911. Then fire destroyed the pottery a year later. Undaunted, Hyten built a brick factory alongside the railroad tracks, capitalizing on the rail line for ease of shipping and tourist traffic. At full strength, about 35 people worked there full-time, including four to five potters.

The Niloak pottery manufactured Eagle brand pottery and red clay flowerpots, thriving through World War I and the early 1920s recession years. But the company couldn't survive the Great Depression. Official Niloak production ceased in 1934. Then some Little Rock businessmen bought the business and Hyten worked for them.

The new pottery sold Hywood, which was a glazed cast ware, and produced Niloak in limited quantities. In time, the factory sold all pottery under the Niloak name because the brand was marketable.

Wartime limits on materials in the 1940s hurt the quality of production, and the factory closed in the 1950s.

Figural woman in hoop skirt, pink and green mottled tones, unmarked, good condition, 9-3/4" h. **$30**

Courtesy of Woody Auction, www.woodyauction.com

— *John J. Archibald*

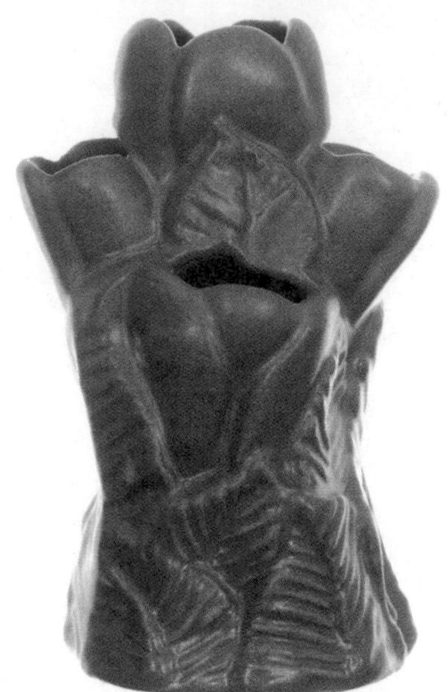

Figural tulip five-section vase, pink/mauve tones, marked, good condition, 7" h. **$24**

Courtesy of Woody Auction, www.woodyauction.com

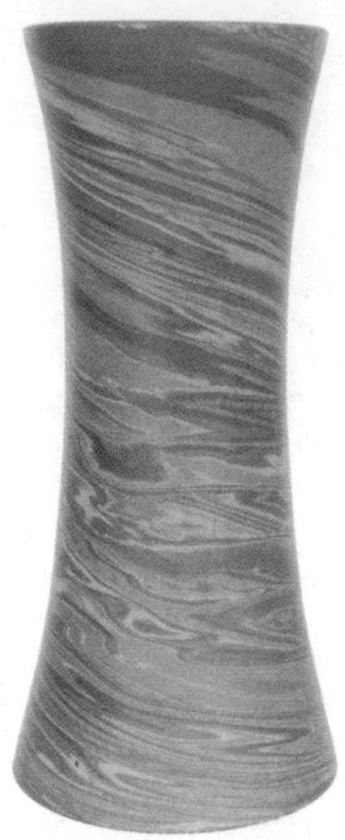

Corset-shaped vase, traditional swirled color design, small base chip, 10" h. **$71**

Courtesy of Woody Auction, www.woodyauction.com

Vase, traditional swirled color design, marked, good condition, 8" h. **$177**

Courtesy of Woody Auction, www.woodyauction.com

Vase, traditional swirled color design, marked, good condition, 14" h. **$266**

Courtesy of Woody Auction, www.woodyauction.com

Vase, traditional swirled color design, marked, good condition, 12" h. **$266**

Courtesy of Woody Auction, www.woodyauction.com

CERAMICS

nippon

"NIPPON" IS A term used to describe a wide range of porcelain wares produced in Japan from the late 19th century until about 1921. It was in 1891 that the United States implemented the McKinley Tariff Act, which required that all wares exported to the United States carry a marking indicating their country of origin. The Japanese chose to use "Nippon," their name for Japan. In 1921 the import laws were revised and the words "Made in" had to be added to the markings. Japan was also required to replace the "Nippon" with the English name "Japan" on all wares sent to the United States.

Many Japanese factories produced Nippon porcelain, much of it hand-painted with ornate floral or landscape decoration and heavy gold decoration, applied beading, and slip-trailed designs referred to as moriage. Be aware that a number of Nippon markings have been reproduced and used on new porcelain wares.

Two-handled vase in pink with floral and lattice highlights, medallion farm scene décor, green wreath mark, good condition, 10" h................ **$118**

Courtesy of Woody Auction, www.woodyauction.com

Urn with handles and floral decoration, 17-1/4" h. **$74**

Courtesy of Pook & Pook, Inc., pookandpook.com

Two-handled vase in cream and yellow with medallion portrait of recamier, gold highlights, marked, good condition, 7" h. **$177**

Courtesy of Woody Auction, www.woodyauction.com

Chocolate pot with floral bands, 9-1/2" h. **$12**

Courtesy of Strawser Auctions, www.strawserauctions.com

► Pair of two-handled vases in cream tones with cottage and evergreen sunset scenic décor, flower mark, good condition, 12" h. **$71**

Courtesy of Woody Auction, www.woodyauction.com

Footed two-handled vase, light amethyst background with shield-shaped lake scene, floral and gold highlights, green wreath mark, good condition, 13" h. **$148**

Courtesy of Woody Auction, www.woodyauction.com

◄ Two-handled squat vase in white and cream with rose décor, heavy gold highlights, blue maple leaf mark, good condition, 6-1/2" h. **$35**

Courtesy of Woody Auction, www.woodyauction.com

Square two-handled vase in green with Egyptian sailboat scenic décor, gold trim highlights, blue maple leaf mark, good condition, 12-1/2" h. **$177**

Courtesy of Woody Auction, www.woodyauction.com

Square two-handled vase with pale brown background and scenic field décor, ornate gold highlights, green wreath mark, good condition, 10" h. **$106**

Courtesy of Woody Auction, www.woodyauction.com

Two-handled vase, circa 1920, round mouth flaring with straight sides to quatre-lobed foot, painted with large spray of peonies on tan to brown ground, band of yellow below rolled rim with geometric motifs, green marks to underside, excellent condition, 12-1/4" h. **$58**

Courtesy of Jeffrey S. Evans & Associates, www.jeffreysevans.com

CERAMICS

george ohr

GEORGE OHR, THE eccentric potter of Biloxi, Mississippi, worked from about 1883 to 1906. Some think him to be one of the most expert throwers the craft will ever see. The majority of his works were hand-thrown, exceedingly thin-walled items, some of which have a crushed or folded appearance. He considered himself the foremost potter in the world and declined to sell much of his production, instead accumulating a great horde to leave as a legacy to his children. In 1972 this collection was purchased for resale by an antiques dealer.

Pitcher, squat body with pinched rim and spout, green glaze, circa 1883-1898, impressed mark, 3-3/4" h. x 6-3/8" w. **$3,438**

Courtesy of Neal Auction, www.nealauction.com

Gourd-shaped vase in black glaze with gray highlights, faint "Geo. E. Ohr Biloxi" impressed mark, excellent condition, 3-1/8" h. **$1,800**

Courtesy of Mark Mussio, Humler & Nolan, www.humlernolan.com

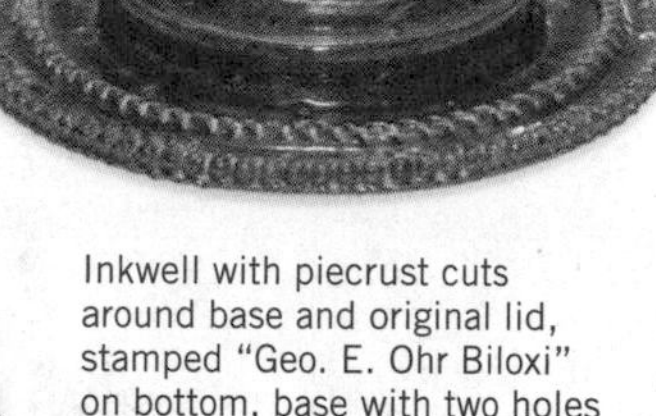

Inkwell with piecrust cuts around base and original lid, stamped "Geo. E. Ohr Biloxi" on bottom, base with two holes punched through damp clay, apparently so inkwell can be mounted to desk, excellent condition, 1-5/8" h. x 5-1/8" w. **$2,100**

Courtesy of Mark Mussio, Humler & Nolan, www.humlernolan.com

Unusual bottle-shaped vase with jagged rim in tan, green, and brown high glazes, impressed "G.E. Ohr Biloxi" on bottom, tiny chips at rim and base and two stilt pulls on bottom, 4-7/8" h. **$750**

Courtesy of Mark Mussio, Humler & Nolan, www.humlernolan.com

Bowl with folded rim in green and speckled brown glaze, circa 1883-1898, impressed mark, 1-5/8" h., 5" dia. **$1,098**

Courtesy of Neal Auction, www.nealauction.com

Vase, baluster form with ringed neck and pinched rim, plum and blue glaze, circa 1883-1898, impressed mark, 4-1/4" h. **$3,782**

Courtesy of Neal Auction, www.nealauction.com

CERAMICS

overbeck

THE OVERBECK STUDIO pottery was founded by four sisters, Hannah, Mary Francis, Elizabeth, and Harriet, in the Overbeck family home in Cambridge City, Indiana, in 1911. A fifth sister, Margaret, who worked as a decorator at Zanesville Art Pottery in 1910, was the catalyst for establishing the pottery, but she died the same year.

Launching at the tail end of the Arts & Crafts movement and believing "borrowed art is bad art," the sister potters dedicated themselves to producing unique quality pieces with original design elements, which often were inspired by the natural world. Pieces can also be found in the Art Nouveau and Art Deco styles, as well as unique figurines and grotesques. The studio used several marks through the years, including an incised O and incised OBK, often accompanied by the artist's initials. The pottery ceased production in 1955.

Figure of robin feeding nest of chicks, impressed on bottom with Overbeck logo, excellent original condition, 3-1/2" h. **$665**

Courtesy of Mark Mussio, Humler & Nolan, www.humlernolan.com

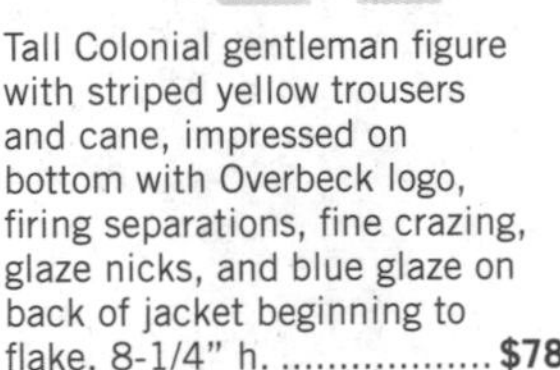

Tall Colonial gentleman figure with striped yellow trousers and cane, impressed on bottom with Overbeck logo, firing separations, fine crazing, glaze nicks, and blue glaze on back of jacket beginning to flake, 8-1/4" h. **$787**

Courtesy of Mark Mussio, Humler & Nolan, www.humlernolan.com

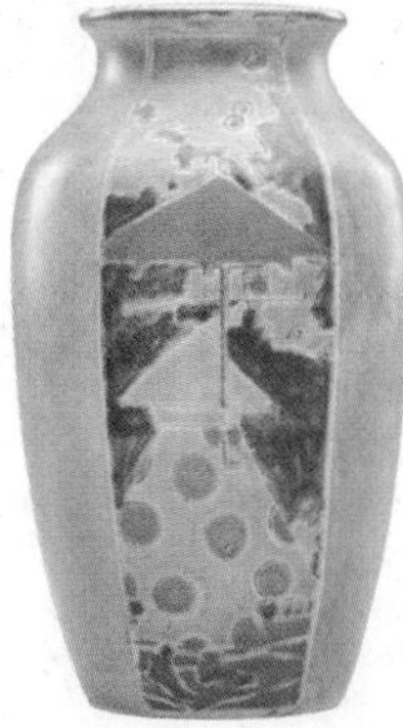

◀ Vase, Elizabeth Overbeck (1875-1936) and Mary Francis Overbeck (1878-1955), incised with women holding umbrellas, circa 1920, incised "OBK/E/F" on bottom, professional restoration to chip at rim, 7" x 3-3/4"................................ **$5,625**

Courtesy of Rago Arts and Auctions, www.ragoarts.com

▶ Blue pottery vase, broad with flared lip, white carved scene of man walking with animal by his side, repeated five times, marked "OBK E F" on bottom, lip with old repair, 9" h. **$4,680**

Courtesy of Manifest Auctions, www.manifestauctions.com

CERAMICS

owens

OWENS POTTERY was the product of the J. B. Owens Pottery Co., which operated in Ohio from 1890 to 1929. In 1891 it was located in Zanesville and produced art pottery from 1896, introducing Utopian wares as its first art pottery. The company switched to tile after 1907. Efforts to rebuild after the factory burned in 1928 failed, and the company closed in 1929.

Standard glaze vase, 13-1/2" h. **$116**

Courtesy of Strawser Auctions, www.strawserauctions.com

Lotus vase with small school of fish by Charles Chilcote, signed on side by artist and marked with impressed Owens torch on bottom along with shape number 1243, fine overall crazing and faint bruise at foot, 10-1/4" h. **$375**

Courtesy of Mark Mussio, Humler & Nolan, www.humlernolan.com

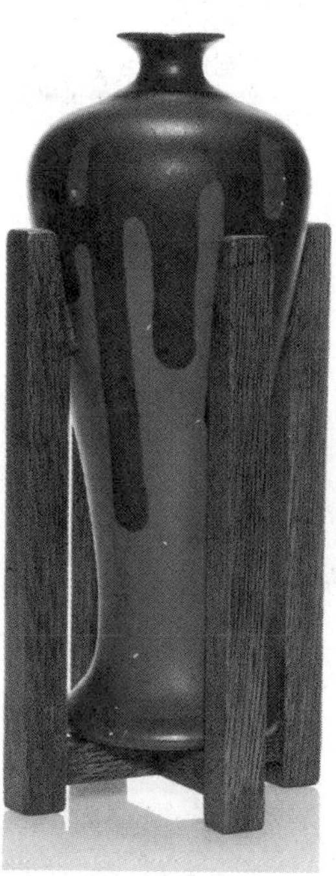

Rare drip glaze Mission vase with oak stand, circa 1905, impressed Owens logo along with shape number 1118, marked "306 S Mission Pottery" in black slip; Owens Mission pottery was cold painted by August Hutaf and as in most examples, there are several small nicks to paint, oak stand wobbly but rare, ceramic portion 11-1/8" h., with stand 12-1/4" h. **$650**

Courtesy of Mark Mussio, Humler & Nolan, www.humlernolan.com

Creamware grapes mug in white with gold trim, unmarked, mint condition, 4-5/8" h. **$40**

Courtesy of Belhorn Auctions LLC, belhornauctions.com

Aqua Verdi candleholder made as advertising item for Owens' Zanesville Tile Co. in 1906, Art Nouveau holder in form of vines marked "Let Your Light B(urn?) Baltimore Feb 13, 06 Zanesville Tile Co. J.B. Owens", excellent original condition with minor open bubbles, 5-3/8" h. **$225**

Courtesy of Mark Mussio, Humler & Nolan, www.humlernolan.com

Clover vase in standard glaze, marked "Owens 05," mint condition, 10-1/2" h. **$75**

Courtesy of Belhorn Auctions LLC, belhornauctions.com

Lotus vase with mushroom decoration, impressed "Owens Lotus 227" on bottom, fine overall crazing, glaze nick at bottom and dark line at rim, 7-3/4" h. **$225**

Courtesy of Mark Mussio, Humler & Nolan, www.humlernolan.com

Utopian footed vase with J. B. Owens mark, signed by artist, nick at rim, 6-1/2" h. **$35**

Courtesy of Belhorn Auctions LLC, belhornauctions.com

Rare matte glaze tile with leaves in two colors in new barn wood frame, impressed "Owens" and "Zanesville" on back, excellent original condition, 5-7/8" x 8-7/8". . **$250**

Courtesy of Mark Mussio, Humler & Nolan, www.humlernolan.com

Vase in dark brown glaze with pink floral blossoms, artist signed, good condition, 8" h. **$266**

Courtesy of Woody Auction, www.woodyauction.com

Lightweight mug with image of Native American male painted by Anna Fulton Best, bottom incised with Owens logo, shape number 830, and Best's monogram, fine overall crazing, 7-1/2" h. **$550**

Courtesy of Mark Mussio, Humler & Nolan, www.humlernolan.com

CERAMICS

red wing pottery

VARIOUS POTTERIES OPERATED in Red Wing, Minnesota, starting in 1868, the most successful being the Red Wing Stoneware Co., organized in 1877. Merged with other local potteries through the years, it became known as Red Wing Union Stoneware Co. in 1906 and was one of the largest producers of utilitarian stoneware items in the United States.

After a decline in the popularity of stoneware products, an art pottery line was introduced to compensate for the loss. This was reflected in a new name for the company, Red Wing Potteries, Inc., in 1936. Stoneware production ceased entirely in 1947, but vases, planters, cookie jars, and dinnerware of art pottery quality continued in production until 1967, when the pottery ceased operation altogether.

For more information on Red Wing pottery, see *Warman's Red Wing Pottery Identification and Price Guide* by Mark F. Moran.

STONEWARE

Ten-gallon stoneware crock marked "10" with 6" wing logo, "Red Wing Union Stoneware Co. Red Wing, Minn." in oval, good condition, one hairline crack, 15-1/2" dia., 16-1/4" h.................... **$95**

Courtesy of North American Auction Co., www.northamericanauctioncompany.com

Fifeen-gallon salt-glazed stoneware crock with large wing logo, "Red Wing Union Stoneware Co. Red Wing, Minn." in oval, good overall condition, chip near base, bale handles missing, 18" dia., 18" h................................ **$95**

Courtesy of North American Auction Co., www.northamericanauctioncompany.com

Thirty-gallon salt-glazed crock with four leaves, marked "30" with "Red Wing Union Stoneware Co. Red Wing, Minn." in oval, good condition, no cracks or chips, factory bumps in finish, 22-1/2" dia., 23" h............................ **$387**

Courtesy of North American Auction Co., www.northamericanauctioncompany.com

Five-gallon crock with bale handles, good condition. **$111**

Courtesy of Bunte Auction Services, Inc., www.bunteauction.com

Stoneware water cooler crock for Virginia School Supply, 17" h. **$885**

Courtesy of Richard D. Hatch & Associates, www.richardhatchauctions.com

Stoneware five-gallon water cooler, flake chip on inside rim, spider crack on base, missing lid, 14" h.. .... **$73**

Courtesy of Conestoga Auction Co., www.conestogaauction.com

Early three-gallon stoneware jug marked with faint "3" and "D," slightly textured glaze, good overall condition, 9" dia., 17" h. **$71**

Courtesy of North American Auction Co., www.northamericanauctioncompany.com

Three-gallon signed stoneware jug with white flint glaze, very good condition, 15" h. **$121**

Courtesy of Conestoga Auction Co., www.conestogaauction.com

Five-gallon salt-glazed stoneware jug with 4" wing logo, marked "5" with "Red Wing Union Stoneware Co. Red Wing, Minn." in oval, good condition, large crack near base and several chips throughout, 11-1/2" dia., 17-1/2" h. **$83**

Courtesy of North American Auction Co., www.northamericanauctioncompany.com

Rare half-gallon advertising whiskey jug, circa 1880, reads, "Joe Matteucci / Wholesale Liquors / Great Falls, Mont.," chip around edge under brown shoulder and score mark across back, no cracks, 9" h., 6" dia. **$268**

Courtesy of North American Auction Co., www.northamericanauctioncompany.com

Advertising stoneware whiskey jug from Adolf Goldhammer Wholesale Wines and Liquors, circa 1890, commissioned by Red Wing Union Stoneware but not marked as such, paint or stamp marked on front, "Adolf Goldhammer / Wholesale Wines and Liquors / 2633 W. Colfax Ave. / Phone Main 7761 - - Denver, Colo.," good condition, slight wear, hairline crack or glaze craze across center, bottom with chip, 9" h., 5-3/4" dia. **$119**

Courtesy of North American Auction Co., www.northamericanauctioncompany.com

Rare advertising stoneware jug, late 1800s, "RWS Co" marked on bottom, "From Goodkind Bros. / Wholesale Wines, / Liquors And Cigars / Helena, – Mont." on front, good condition, hairline crack across front bottom edge, 6" dia., 8-1/2" h. **$357**

Courtesy of North American Auction Co., www.northamericanauctioncompany.com

Stoneware presentation money bank, circa 1890, Bristol slip-glazed, globular form with two-tier finial, pronounced foot, and vertical coin slot on shoulder, sponged cobalt wreath encircling "Cora" below slot, additional cobalt rings spaced on body and finial, possibly Red Wing Pottery, small chip to foot, 5" h., 2-1/8" dia. base. **$360**

Courtesy of Jeffrey S. Evans & Associates, www.jeffreysevans.com

Stoneware flowerpot, salt-glazed, conical pot with drain hole and attached saucer, rouletted decorative bands and three cobalt-filled incised rings, probably Minnesota Stoneware Co. (Red Wing, Minnesota) or White's Utica (New York), late 19th/early 20th century, small chip and flake to outer edge of rim, 5 1/4" h., 5 3/8" dia. rim. **$132**

Courtesy of North American Auction Co., www.northamericanauctioncompany.com

top lot

Rare advertising stoneware jug, late 1800s, "From Goodkind Bros. / Wholesale Wines, / Liquors And Cigars / Helena, – Mont." marked across front, very good condition with slight chip of glaze at top, 7-1/4" dia., 11" h. The Goodkind Bros. building at Sixth and Main streets in Helena has been a historic location since 1884 when the business began. The building was created by architect Francis Dickson Lee (1826-1885), who was also a developer of Confederate torpedo boats and spar torpedoes during the Civil War......... $1,428

COURTESY OF NORTH AMERICAN AUCTION CO., WWW.NORTHAMERICANAUCTIONCOMPANY.COM

ART POTTERY & MISCELLANEOUS

Pottery vase in light green glaze, marked "1168 Red-Wing USA" on bottom, good condition, two hairline cracks on interior, 2-1/2" x 8" x 6-3/4" h. **$41**

Courtesy of North American Auction Co., www.northamericanauctioncompany.com

Ashtray, approximately 7-1/4" x 8"........ **$15**

Courtesy of Pioneer Auction Gallery, www.pioneerantiqueauction.com

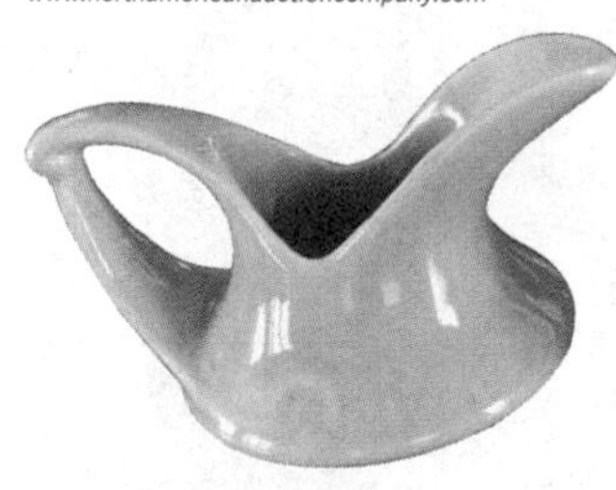

Creamer and sugar "snack set" in Plain pattern, Gypsy Trail line, late 1930s-1943, pastel pink/peach, creamer marked "Red Wing," excellent condition, creamer 3" h. x 4" w., 2-3/4" dia., sugar 2" h. x 3-1/2" w., 2-3/4" dia. .... **$15-$30**

Two vases, no. 1197 in blue glaze with embossed fleur de lis and M-1443 in turquoise glaze with embossed houses, birds, fruit and flowers, designed by Charles Murphy, both marked on bottom; and Hospitality Ware pitcher in green glaze with embossed flowers, unmarked with old sticker remnants, good condition, 9" h., 8-1/2" h., and 9-1/4" h........ **$48**

Courtesy of Rachel Davis Fine Arts, www.racheldavisfinearts.com

CERAMICS

redware

RED EARTHENWARE POTTERY was made in the American colonies from the late 1600s. Bowls, crocks, and all types of utilitarian wares were turned out in great abundance to supplement pewter and hand-made treenware. The ready availability of the clay, the same used in making bricks and roof tiles, accounted for the vast production. The lead-glazed redware retained its reddish color, although a variety of colors could be obtained by adding various metals to the glaze. Interesting effects occurred accidentally through unsuspected impurities in the clay or uneven temperatures in the firing kiln, which sometimes resulted in streaks or mottled splotches. Redware pottery was seldom marked by the maker.

▶ Large Pennsylvania redware double-handled crock, 19th century, numbered 31 and initialed on underside, 13-1/4" h. **$86**

Courtesy of Pook & Pook, Inc., www.pookandpook.com

◀ Contemporary Wisconsin redware pottery table lamp, 12" h. **$246**

Courtesy of Pook & Pook, Inc., www.pookandpook.com

Bread tray with manganese splash decoration, 19th century, 2-3/4" l. x 11-1/2" w., with mold and shallow bowl. **$135**

Courtesy of Pook & Pook, Inc., www.pookandpook.com

Breininger loaf dish, 13-1/2" h. x 19-1/2" w. **$197**

Courtesy of Pook & Pook, Inc., www.pookandpook.com

Continental colander, 19th century, 4-1/4" h., 10" dia.. **$98**

Courtesy of Pook & Pook, Inc., www.pookandpook.com

Massive Breininger charger decorated with dragoon, 21-1/2" dia. **$455**

Courtesy of Pook & Pook, Inc., www.pookandpook.com

Five I. S. Stahl mugs dated 1940 and 1941, tallest 4-1/4" h. **$172**

Courtesy of Pook & Pook, Inc., www.pookandpook.com

▲ Pennsylvania or Maryland redware mixing bowl with yellow and green slip decoration, 19th century, 4" h., 12" dia................................. **$172**

Courtesy of Pook & Pook, Inc., www.pookandpook.com

◀ Large Pennsylvania redware shallow bowl, 19th century, 4" h., 16-1/2" dia............................ **$172**

Courtesy of Pook & Pook, Inc., www.pookandpook.com

Pennsylvania redware shaving mug, 19th century, 4" h. **$123**

Courtesy of Pook & Pook, Inc., www.pookandpook.com

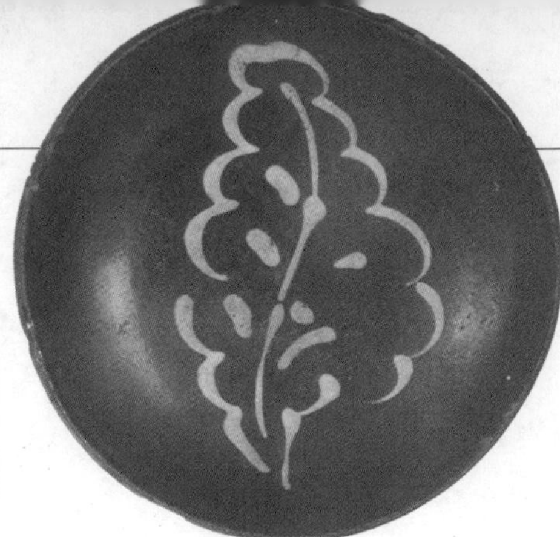

Pennsylvania redware plate, 19th century, with yellow slip leaf decoration, 10" dia. **$600**

Courtesy of Pook & Pook, Inc., www.pookandpook.com

I. S. Stahl flowerpot, signed and dated 1938, 5" h. **$135**

Courtesy of Pook & Pook, Inc., www.pookandpook.com

Pennsylvania redware plate with slip decorated splotches, early 19th century, 8" dia. **$381**

Courtesy of Pook & Pook, Inc., www.pookandpook.com

Pennsylvania redware flowerpot with manganese splotching, 19th century, impressed CS on underside, 5" h. **$246**

Courtesy of Pook & Pook, Inc., www.pookandpook.com

Pennsylvania redware plate with slip decorated wavy lines, early 19th century, 8-1/4" dia. **$283**

Courtesy of Pook & Pook, Inc., www.pookandpook.com

top lot!

Pennsylvania redware monkey man and jug match holder, 19th century, 6-1/2" h. $7,200

COURTESY OF POOK & POOK, INC., WWW.POOKANDPOOK.COM

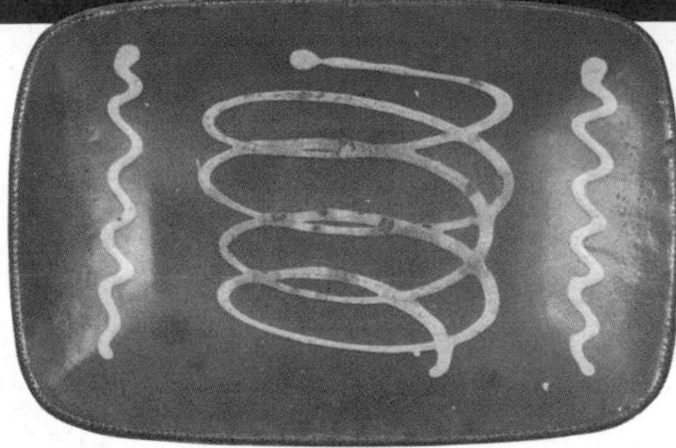

New England redware loaf dish with yellow slip decoration, 19th century, 8" h. x 11-3/4" w..... **$504**

Courtesy of Pook & Pook, Inc., www.pookandpook.com

Redware figure of recumbent cat on slab base, 19th century, with incised features, 3" h. x 5-1/4" w. **$1,440**

Courtesy of Pook & Pook, Inc., www.pookandpook.com

Pennsylvania redware spouted bowl with manganese decoration, 19th century, 4-1/4" h., 8-1/2" dia.. **$308**

Courtesy of Pook & Pook, Inc., www.pookandpook.com

CERAMICS

rockingham

THE MARQUIS OF ROCKINGHAM first established an earthenware pottery in the Yorkshire district of England around 1745, and it was occupied afterward by various potters. The well-known mottled brown Rockingham glaze was introduced about 1788 by the Brameld Brothers and became immediately popular. Production of true porcelain began at the factory in the 1920s and continued to be made until the firm closed in 1842.

Since that time the so-called Rockingham glaze has been used by various potters in England and the United States, including some famous wares produced in Bennington, Vermont (see Bennington Pottery). Similar glazes were also used by potteries in other areas of the United States, including Ohio and Indiana, but only wares specifically attributed to Bennington should use that name. The following listings include wares featuring the dark brown mottled glaze produced at various sites here and abroad.

American Rockingham glaze pottery flask, second half 19th century, mottled dark brown over yellowware body, flattened ovoid form, both sides with two men seated at table drinking, within blackberry vine border, unmarked, undamaged, 6" h. **$138**

Courtesy of Jeffrey S. Evans & Associates, www.jeffreysevans.com

Three nesting Rockingham glaze mixing bowls, late 19th century, two with ribbed sides, some minor roughage to glaze, 9-1/4" to 11" dia... **$72**

Courtesy of Eldred's, www.eldreds.com

American Rockingham glaze pottery seated spaniel, probably Ohio, second half 19th century, mottled brown over yellowware body, collar lock and free-standing front legs, rectangular base with ovolo corners and molded foliate and shell decoration on front and sides, unmarked, small chip to front and underside of base, 10-1/2" h., 6-1/2" x 8-3/4" base. **$219**

Courtesy of Jeffrey S. Evans & Associates, www.jeffreysevans.com

American Rockingham glaze pottery seated spaniel, probably Ohio, second half 19th century, mottled brown over pumpkin-color body, closed legs, seated on oval cushion raised on three-step rectangular base with beaded lower edges, unmarked, excellent condition, nose with professional restoration and two glaze flakes, 7" h., 6-1/4" x 3-3/4" base. **$288**

Courtesy of Jeffrey S. Evans & Associates, www.jeffreysevans.com

CERAMICS

rookwood

MARIA LONGWORTH NICHOLS founded Rookwood Pottery in 1880. The name, she later reported, paid homage to the many crows (rooks) on her father's estate and was also designed to remind customers of Wedgwood. Production began on Thanksgiving Day 1880 when the first kiln was drawn.

Rookwood's earliest productions demonstrated a continued reliance on European precedents and the Japanese aesthetic. Although the firm offered a variety of wares (Dull Glaze, Cameo, and Limoges for example), it lacked a clearly defined artistic identity. With the introduction of what became known as its "standard glaze" in 1884, Rookwood inaugurated a period in which the company won consistent recognition for its artistic merit and technical innovation.

Rookwood's first decade ended on a high note when the company was awarded two gold medals: one at the Exhibition of American Art Industry in Philadelphia and another later in the year at the Exposition Universelle in Paris. Significant, too, was Maria Longworth Nichols' decision to transfer her interest in the company to William W. Taylor, who had been the firm's manager since 1883. In May 1890, the board of a newly reorganized Rookwood Pottery Co. purchased "the real estate, personal property, goodwill, patents, trade-marks... now the sole property of William W. Taylor" for $40,000.

Under Taylor's leadership, Rookwood was transformed from a fledgling startup to successful business that expanded throughout the following decades to meet rising demand.

Throughout the 1890s, Rookwood continued to attract critical notice as it kept the tradition of innovation alive. Taylor rolled out three new glaze lines - Iris, Sea Green, and Aerial Blue - from late 1894 into early 1895.

At the Paris Exposition in 1900, Rookwood cemented its reputation by winning the Grand Prix, a feat largely due to the favorable reception of the new Iris glaze and its variants.

Over the next several years, Rookwood's record of achievement at domestic and international exhibitions remained unmatched.

Throughout the 1910s, Rookwood continued in a similar vein and began to more thoroughly embrace the simplified aesthetic promoted by many Arts & Crafts figures.

Limoges-style vase with ferns and bamboo by artist with unfamiliar cipher, 1882, marked on bottom Rookwood Pottery in mold, impressed with 1882 date and anchor mark, artist's mark of S with vertical line in slip on side of vase, blisters in black glaze, nicks to high points of heavy slip decoration, 10-1/2" h. **$400**

Courtesy of Mark Mussio, Humler & Nolan, www.humlernolan.com

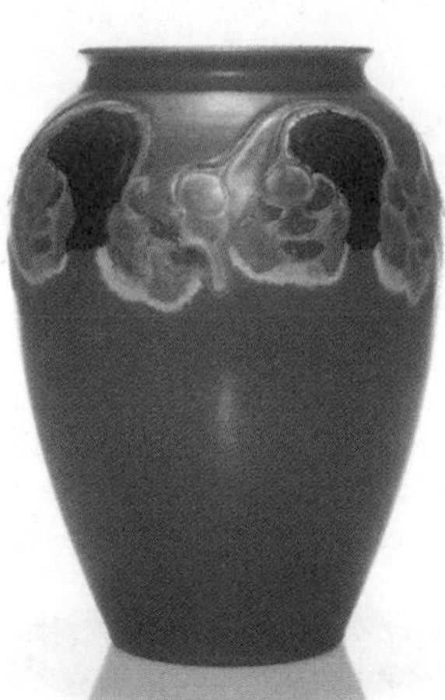

Carved and painted Decorated Mat vase by C.S. Todd, 1918, with repeating passages of leaves and fruit, marks: Rookwood logo, date, shape 581E, and artist's incised initials, professional repair to small rim chip, 9-1/2" h. **$425**

Courtesy of Mark Mussio, Humler & Nolan, www.humlernolan.com

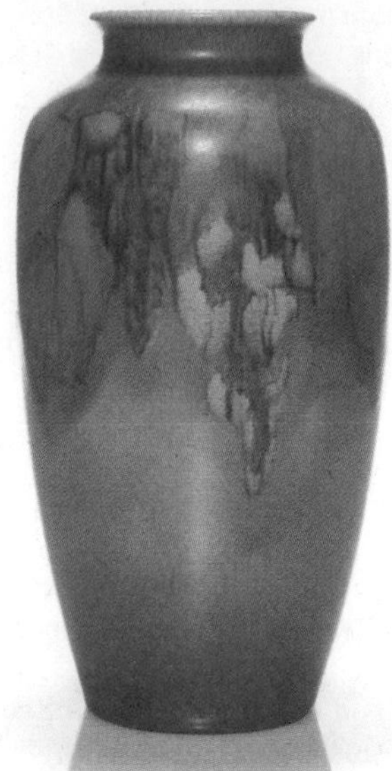

Mat Glaze vase with floral design by Sallie Coyne, 1927, marks: Rookwood logo, date, shape 614 D, and artist's monogram in blue slip, no crazing, professional repair to chip at base, 10-5/8" h....... **$500**

Courtesy of Mark Mussio, Humler & Nolan, www.humlernolan.com

Mat Glaze handled vase by Jens Jensen, 1929, maroon magnolias and buds over mottled backdrop of cobalt blue and chestnut brown, interior in dark blue, marks: company logo, date, shape 6114C, and cipher of artist in black slip, excellent condition, 11" h... **$800**

Courtesy of Mark Mussio, Humler & Nolan, www.humlernolan.com

Tall Standard Glaze tankard with spaniel by E.T. Hurley, 1901, marks: Rookwood logo, date, shape 775, and artist's initials, fine overall crazing, 7-1/2" h. **$900**

Courtesy of Mark Mussio, Humler & Nolan, www.humlernolan.com

GE double lightbulb advertising ashtray in maroon glaze, 1949, marks: company logo, date, and circular GE logo, uncrazed, 1-1/4" h. x 6-5/8" l. **$250**

Courtesy of Mark Mussio, Humler & Nolan, www.humlernolan.com

Production of the Iris line, which had been instrumental in the firm's success at the Paris Exposition in 1900, ceased around 1912. Not only did the company abandon its older, fussier underglaze wares, but the newer lines the pottery introduced also trended toward simplicity.

The collapse of the stock market in October 1929 and the ensuing economic depression dealt Rookwood a severe blow, leading to bankruptcy in April 1941. It was purchased by a group of investors led by automobile dealer Walter E. Schott and his wife, Margaret. Production started once again. In the years that followed, Rookwood changed hands a number of times before moving to Starkville, Mississippi, in 1960. It finally closed its doors there in 1967. In the 1980s, Dr. Arthur Townley, a Michigan art pottery collector, spent his life savings acquiring Rookwood's assets from a group of Florida investors. In 2006, The Rookwood Pottery Co. purchased the assets from Townley and eventually returned the company to Cincinnati, where it currently produces artisan wares.

ROOKWOOD MARKS

Rookwood employed a number of marks on the bottom of its vessels that denoted everything from the shape number, to the size, date, and color of the body, to the type of glaze to be used.

COMPANY MARKS

1880-1882

In this early period, a number of marks were used to identify the wares.

1. "ROOKWOOD" followed by the initials of the decorator, painted in gold. This is likely the earliest mark, and though the wares are not dated, it seems to have been discontinued by 1881-1882.
2. "ROOKWOOD / POTTERY. / [DATE] CIN. O." In Marks of American Potters (1904), Edwin AtLee Barber states, "The most common marks prior to 1882 were the name of the pottery and the date of manufacture, which were painted or incised on the base of each piece by the decorator."
3. "R. P. C. O. M. L. N." These initials stand for "Rookwood Pottery, Cincinnati, Ohio, Maria Longworth Nichols," and were either painted or incised on the base.
4. Kiln and crows stamp. Barber notes that in 1881 and 1882, the trademark designed by the artist Henry Farny was printed beneath the glaze.
5. Anchor stamp: Barber notes that this mark is "one of the rarest."
6. Oval stamp.
7. Ribbon or banner stamp: According to Barber, "In 1882 a special mark was used on a trade piece... the letters were impressed in a raised ribbon.
8. Ribbon or banner stamp II: A simpler variation of the above stamp, recorded by Herbert Peck.

1883-1886

1. Stamped name and date.
2. Impressed kiln: Appears only in 1883.

1886-1960

Virtually all of the pieces feature the conjoined RP monogram. Pieces fired in the anniversary kilns carry a special kiln-shaped mark with the number of the anniversary inside of it.

1955

A diamond-shaped mark that reads: "ROOKWOOD / 75th / ANNIVERSARY / POTTERY" was printed on wares.

1960-1967

Occasionally pieces are marked "ROOKWOOD POTTERY / STARKVILLE MISS"; from 1962 to 1967 a small "®" occasionally follows the monogram.

top lot

Monumental Dull Glaze vase with frogs and ducks by Rookwood founder Maria Longworth Nichols, 1883, six ducks, 10 frogs, and grasses in heavy enamel glazes on mat ground with band of nailhead patterns at collar and base by Fannie Auckland, several frogs appear to hold hands, marked with Rookwood in block letters, date, and G for ginger clay, several places where incised outline of animals is still visible, enamel not applied all the way to edge, excellent original condition, 20" h. In 1883 there were only three artists who were allowed to work on vases this large: Nichols, Matthew Daly, and Albert Valentien, and of these three, the only one who could get away with not signing the piece was company founder Nichols. Daly and Valentien were rigid about signing their work, and both were more accomplished than Nichols, who may be considered an outsider artist because of her naive style.. **$28,000**

COURTESY OF MARK MUSSIO, HUMLER & NOLAN, WWW.HUMLERNOLAN.COM

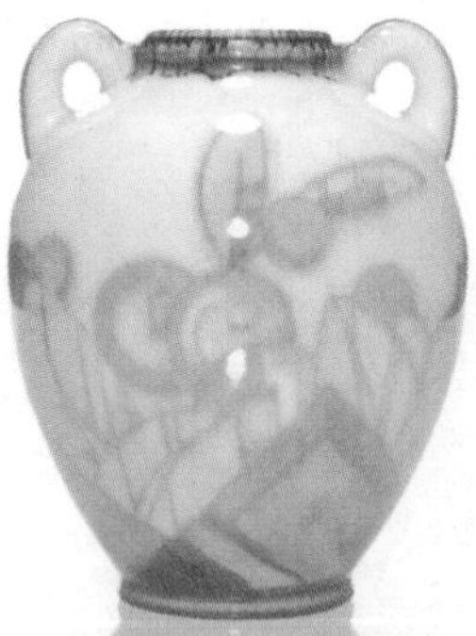

Porcelain vase with stylized flower garden by Lorinda Epply, 1930, interior in Annversary Glaze introduced around time of company's 50th anniversary, marked with Rookwood logo, date, fan-shaped esoteric mark used during Rookwood's 50th anniversary, shape number 2640 E, and artist monogram in black slip, no crazing, 8-3/4" h. **$2,500**

Courtesy of Mark Mussio, Humler & Nolan, www.humlernolan.com

DATE MARKS

Unlike many of their contemporaries, Rookwood seems very early on to have adopted a method of marking its pottery that was accurate and easy to understand.

From 1882-1885, the company impressed the date, often with the company name, in block letters (see 1883-86, No. 1).

Although the date traditionally given for the conjoined RP mark is June 23, 1886, this marks the official introduction of the monogram rather than the first use.

Stanley Burt, in his record of the Rookwood at the Cincinnati Museum noted two pieces from 1883 (Nos. 2 and 3) that used the monogram. The monogram was likely designed by Alfred Brennan, since it first appears on his work.

From 1886 on, the date of the object was coded in the conjoined "RP" monogram.

1886: conjoined "RP" no additional flame marks.

1887-1900: conjoined "RP" with a flame added for each subsequent year. Thus, a monogram with seven flames would represent 1893.

1900-1967: conjoined "RP" with 14 flames and a Roman numeral below the mark to indicate the year after 1900. Thus, a monogram with 14 flames and the letters "XXXVI" below it signifies 1936.

CLAY-TYPE MARKS

From 1880 until around 1895, Rookwood used a number of different colored bodies for production and marked each color with a letter code. These letters were impressed and usually found grouped together with the shape number, sometimes following it, but more often below it.

The letter "S" is a particularly vexing designation since the same initial was used for two other unrelated designations. As a result, it is particularly important to take into account the relative position of the impressed letter.

R = Red
Y = Yellow
S = Sage
G = Ginger
W = White
O = Olive
P = From 1915 on, Rookwood used an impressed "P" (often found perpendicular to the orientation of the other marks) to denote the soft porcelain body.

SIZE AND SHAPE MARKS

Almost all Rookwood pieces have a shape code consisting of three or four numbers, followed by a size letter. "A" denotes the largest available size, "F" is the smallest. According to Herbert Peck, initial designs were given a "C" or "D" designation so that variations could be made. Not every shape model, however, features a variation in every size.

GLAZE MARKS

In addition to marking the size, shape and year of the piece, Rookwood's decorators also used a number of letters to designate the type of glaze to be used upon a piece. Generally speaking, these marks are either incised or impressed.

"S" = Standard Glaze to be used. (Incised.)
"L" = Decorators would often incise an "L" near their monogram to indicate that the light variation of the Standard Glaze was to be used. (Incised.)
"SG" = Sea Green Glaze to be used.
"Z" = from 1900-1904 designated any piece with a Mat Glaze. (Impressed)
"W" = Iris Glaze to be used.
"V" = Vellum Glaze to be used; variations include "GV" for Green Vellum and "YV" for Yellow Vellum.

Z-Line tray with incised web and spider in red and brown mat glazes, 1902, impressed on bottom with Rookwood logo, date, and shape number 363 Z, excellent original condition, uncrazed, 3/4" h. x 5-3/4" x 4"................................ **$1,000**

Courtesy of Mark Mussio, Humler & Nolan, www.humlernolan.com

Standard Glaze vase with yellow irises by Frederick Rothenbusch, 1900, marked with Rookwood logo indicating date, shape number 808, and Rothenbusch's incised monogram, fine overall crazing, 7-1/2" h.......................... **$550**

Courtesy of Mark Mussio, Humler & Nolan, www.humlernolan.com

Standard Glaze bud vase with fruit blossoms by Anna Valentien, 1894, marked with company logo indicating date, shape number 686, impressed W for white clay, and artist's incised initials, light crazing and minor scratches, 3-3/8" h. x 4-1/2" w. **$160**

Courtesy of Mark Mussio, Humler & Nolan, www.humlernolan.com

Plaque with winter scene of snow-covered meadow with pine trees and mountains against winter sky, signed in lower right corner with conjoined initials "FR" for Frederick Rothenbusch, marked on reverse with impressed flame marked and dated 1913, in heavy quarter-sawn oak frame, very good to excellent condition with some crazing, plaque 10-1/2" w. x 8-1/2" h., frame 15-5/8" w. x 13-3/4" h. **$3,851**

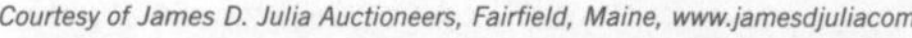

Courtesy of James D. Julia Auctioneers, Fairfield, Maine, www.jamesdjuliacom

Vellum Glaze scenic vase with trees and peach-colored sky with lake in background by Lorinda Epply, 1916, marked with Rookwood logo, date, shape number 2040 E, impressed V and incised V for Vellum, and Epply's incised monogram, excellent original condition, uncrazed, 7-5/8" h. **$1,400**

Courtesy of Mark Mussio, Humler & Nolan, www.humlernolan.com

top lot

Sea Green glaze vase by Sturgis Laurence, 1900, sailing vessel with full sails on choppy seas with detailed waves, two men visible on deck with lifeboats and rigging, rim, base, and back in black glaze, marked with Rookwood logo, date, shape number 900 C, incised G for Sea Green glaze, and incised initials of artist, light crazing, 7-5/8" h. $10,000

COURTESY OF MARK MUSSIO, HUMLER & NOLAN, WWW.HUMLERNOLAN.COM

Ashtray with fox in light blue high glaze, 1945, marked with Rookwood logo, date, and shape number 2647, glaze skip and some minor peppering, no crazing, fox's ears intact, 2-1/4" h., 6-1/2" dia.. **$150**

Courtesy of Mark Mussio, Humler & Nolan, www.humlernolan.com

Letter holder with first U.S. postage stamp in blue high glaze, 1956, impressed with Rookwood symbol, date, and "Rookwood Cinti, O." on base, excellent original condition, no crazing, 3" x 4-1/4".. **$70**

Courtesy of Mark Mussio, Humler & Nolan, www.humlernolan.com

Circular tray with Rookwood Pottery building and gates in Aventurine glaze, 1958, front marked with name "Rookwood," Rookwood logo, date, and "Rookwood Cinti O" on back, no crazing, minor stilt pulls on bottom, 5/8" x 5-1/2"................ **$100**

Courtesy of Mark Mussio, Humler & Nolan, www.humlernolan.com

CERAMICS

roseville pottery

ROSEVILLE IS ONE of the most widely recognizable of potteries across the United States. Having been sold in flower shops and drug stores around the country, its art and production wares became a staple in American homes through the time Roseville closed in the 1950s.

The Roseville Pottery Co., located in Roseville, Ohio, was incorporated on Jan. 4, 1892, with George F. Young as general manager. The company had been producing stoneware since 1890, when it purchased the J. B. Owens Pottery, also of Roseville.

The popularity of Roseville Pottery's original lines of stoneware continued to grow. The company acquired new plants in 1892 and 1898, and production started to shift to Zanesville, just a few miles away. By about 1910, all of the work was centered in Zanesville, but the company name was unchanged.

Young hired Ross C. Purdy as artistic designer in 1900, and Purdy created Rozane – a contraction of the words "Roseville" and "Zanesville." The first Roseville artwork pieces were marked either Rozane or RPCO, both impressed or ink-stamped on the bottom.

In 1902, a line was developed called Azurean. Some pieces were marked Azurean, but often RPCO. In 1904 at the St. Louis Exposition, Roseville's Rozane Mongol, a high-gloss oxblood red line, captured first prize, gaining recognition for the firm and its creator, John Herold.

Azurean pattern vase with oversized bouquet of blackberries and leaves across front, painted and signed by Walter Myers, impressed "RP Co, 950" beneath, excellent condition, fine overall crazing, 7-3/4" x 7-1/2" w.. **$275**

Courtesy of Mark Mussio, Humler & Nolan, www.humlernolan.com

Baneda pattern vase in green, shape number 596, shape number marked on bottom in orange crayon, excellent original condition, 9-1/8" h... **$425**

Courtesy of Mark Mussio, Humler & Nolan, www.humlernolan.com

Many Roseville lines were a response to the innovations of Weller Pottery, another Zanesville pottery, and in 1904 Frederick Rhead was hired away from Weller as artistic director. He created the Olympic and Della Robbia lines for Roseville. His brother Harry took over as artistic director in 1908, and in 1915 he introduced the popular Donatello line.

By 1908, all handcrafting ended except for Rozane Royal. Roseville was the first pottery in Ohio to install a tunnel kiln, which increased its production capacity.

Frank Ferrell, who was a top decorator at the Weller Pottery by 1904, was Roseville's artistic director from 1917 until 1954. This Zanesville native created many of the most popular lines, including Pine Cone, which had scores of individual pieces.

Many collectors believe Roseville's circa 1925 glazes were the best of any Zanesville pottery. George Krause, who in 1915 became Roseville's technical supervisor responsible for glaze, remained with Roseville until the 1950s.

Company sales declined after World War II, especially in the early 1950s when cheap Japanese imports began to replace American wares, and a simpler, more modern style made many of Roseville's elaborate floral designs seem old-fashioned.

In the late 1940s, Roseville began to issue lines with glossy glazes. The company also tried to offset its flagging artware sales by launching a dinnerware line - Raymor - in 1953. The line was a commercial failure.

Roseville issued its last new designs in 1953. On Nov. 29, 1954, the facilities of Roseville were sold to the Mosaic Tile Co.

For more information on Roseville, see *Warman's Roseville Pottery*, 2nd edition, by Denise Rago.

Baneda pattern vase in pink, shape number 592, original Roseville Pottery foil sticker on bottom, excellent original condition, faint crazing, 7-1/8" h. **$250**

Courtesy of Mark Mussio, Humler & Nolan, www.humlernolan.com

Falline pattern vase in brown, shape number 644-6", excellent condition, 6" h. **$275**

Courtesy of Mark Mussio, Humler & Nolan, www.humlernolan.com

Ferella pattern vase in red with green accents, shape number 509-8", excellent condition, 8" h. **$375**

Courtesy of Mark Mussio, Humler & Nolan, www.humlernolan.com

Futura Aztec pattern bowl in brown and turquoise, shape number 188-8", marked in pencil "$2.50" and "Jog X" beneath, excellent original condition, 4" h. x 8" l. **$200**

Courtesy of Mark Mussio, Humler & Nolan, www.humlernolan.com

Futura pattern stilted half-egg vase in tan shading to blue, shape number 197-6", excellent condition, 5-1/8" h. **$450**

Courtesy of Mark Mussio, Humler & Nolan, www.humlernolan.com

Fuchsia pattern wall pocket in green, shape number 1282-8", marked on bottom Roseville 1282-8", fine overall crazing, 8-3/8" h. **$150**

Courtesy of Mark Mussio, Humler & Nolan, www.humlernolan.com

Futura pattern box vessel in blue, shape number 190-3-1/2", unmarked, fine overall crazing, 3-5/8" h. **$160**

Courtesy of Mark Mussio, Humler & Nolan, www.humlernolan.com

Montacello pattern candlesticks in brown, shape number 1085-4-1/2, both partially marked with shape number in red crayon beneath, excellent condition, 4-3/4" h. **$200**

Courtesy of Mark Mussio, Humler & Nolan, www.humlernolan.com

Morning Glory pattern bowl, shape number 271-12", unmarked, scattered crazing, 5-1/8" h. x 13" from handle to handle. **$206**

Courtesy of Mark Mussio, Humler & Nolan, www.humlernolan.com

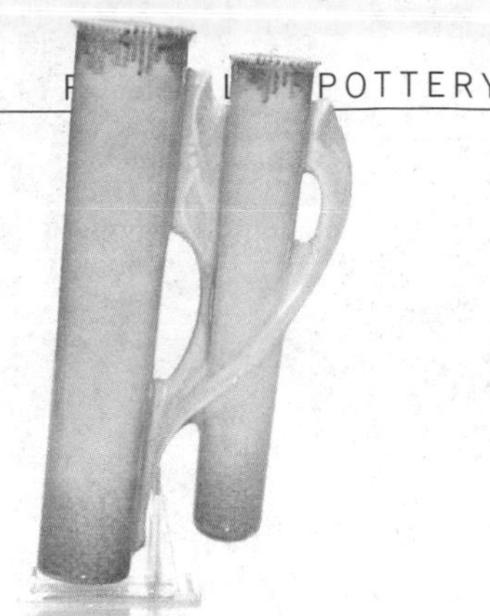

Orian pattern wall pocket in blue and teal, shape number 1276-8", marked with original Roseville Pottery foil sticker, excellent original condition, 8-1/4" h. **$300**

Courtesy of Mark Mussio, Humler & Nolan, www.humlernolan.com

Panel pattern vase with nudes posing with trees in brown and orange, marked on bottom with Rv ink stamp, fine overall crazing, 11-3/8" h.............. **$600**

Courtesy of Mark Mussio, Humler & Nolan, www.humlernolan.com

Pauleo pattern vase in raspberry glaze shading into dark purple with allover crackle pattern, marked "130" in crayon beneath, minor surface rubs, patches of light glaze covering, 9" h. x 7" w. **$375**

Courtesy of Mark Mussio, Humler & Nolan, www.humlernolan.com

Pine Cone pattern vase in blue, shape number 709-10", marked 709 in orange crayon with silver Roseville Pottery foil sticker on bottom, 10-1/4" h. **$484**

Courtesy of Mark Mussio, Humler & Nolan, www.humlernolan.com

Rozane pattern fish ornament, shape number 1, in blue and brown high glaze, marked "Roseville U.S.A. 1" on bottom, excellent original condition, 5" h. **$550**

Courtesy of Mark Mussio, Humler & Nolan, www.humlernolan.com

! top lot

Large Sunflower pattern jardiniere on pedestal, jardiniere unmarked, faint overall crazing, nicks on stems, two tight lines descending from rim, pedestal unmarked and in excellent condition, pedestal 18-3/8" h., jardiniere 10" h., 13" dia., combined 28-1/4" h. $1,800

COURTESY OF MARK MUSSIO, HUMLER & NOLAN, WWW.HUMLERNOLAN.COM

Sunflower pattern vase, shape number 494-10", unmarked, excellent original condition, faint crazing, 10-1/4" h. **$800**

Courtesy of Mark Mussio, Humler & Nolan, www.humlernolan.com

Vista pattern floor vase, shape number 121 under glaze beneath base, excellent condition, 15" h. **$550**

Courtesy of Mark Mussio, Humler & Nolan, www.humlernolan.com

Vista pattern umbrella stand, unmarked, fine overall crazing and small glaze skips, no damage or repairs, 19-3/4" **$950**

Courtesy of Mark Mussio, Humler & Nolan, www.humlernolan.com

CERAMICS

r.s. prussia

ORNATELY DECORATED CHINA marked "R.S. Prussia" and "R.S. Germany" continues to grow in popularity. According to the Third Series of Mary Frank Gaston's *Encyclopedia of R.S. Prussia* (Collector Books, Paducah, Kentucky), these marks were used by the Reinhold Schlegelmilch porcelain factories located in Suhl in the Germanic regions known as "Prussia" prior to World War I, and in Tillowitz, Silesia, which became part of Poland after World War II. Other marks sought by collectors include R.S. Suhl, R.S. steeple or church marks, and R.S. Poland.

The Suhl factory was founded by Reinhold Schlegelmilch in 1869 and closed in 1917. The Tillowitz factory was established in 1895 by Erhard Schlegelmilch, Reinhold's son. This china customarily bears the phrase "R.S. Germany" and "R.S. Tillowitz". The Tillowitz factory closed in 1945, but it was reopened for a few years under Polish administration.

Prices are high and collectors should beware of the forgeries that sometimes find their way onto the market. Mold names and numbers are taken from Gaston's books.

The "Prussia" and "R.S. Suhl" marks have been reproduced, so buy with care. Later copies of these marks are well done, but the quality of porcelain is inferior to the production in the 1890-1920 era.

Collectors are also interested in the porcelain products made by the Erdmann Schlegelmilch factory. This factory was founded by three brothers in Suhl in 1861. They named the factory in honor of their father, Erdmann Schlegelmilch. A variety of marks incorporating the E.S. initials were used. The factory closed circa 1935. The Erdmann Schlegelmilch factory was an earlier and entirely separate business from the Reinhold Schlegelmilch factory. The two were not related to each other.

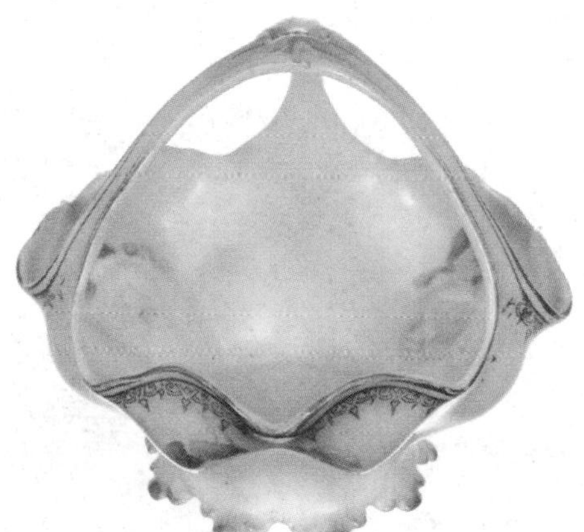

Three-handled miniature basket, white, green, and brown satin finish with pink rose décor, good condition, 4-3/4"................ **$148**

Courtesy of Woody Auction, www.woodyauction.com

Bowl, green and cream tones with Easter lily décor, good condition, 10-3/4" dia.................. **$71**

Courtesy of Woody Auction, www.woodyauction.com

Icicle mold cake plate, cream center with floral décor, medallion highlights with hanging baskets, gold tapestry border, good condition, 11" dia............................... **$207**

Courtesy of Woody Auction, www.woodyauction.com

Chickens creamer, circa 1900, 4" h. **$172**

Courtesy of Pook & Pook, Inc., pookandpook.com

Melon Eaters water pitcher, circa 1900, 11-1/2" h. **$480**

Courtesy of Pook & Pook, Inc., pookandpook.com

Covered cracker jar with gold-painted, -stenciled, and -stippled decoration, late 19th/ first quarter 20th century, mold 508, with pink lustre finish to rim and shoulder, divided by pearlized finish flowers in panels of satin ground, with printed Dice Throwers decoration to body, cover with satin finish to rim and pearlized finish flowers, red and green Prussia wreath and star printed mark, undamaged with some wear, irregularities as made, 7-1/4" h. overall............. **$2,990**

Courtesy of Jeffrey S. Evans & Associates, www.jeffreysevans.com

Snow birds with cabin plate, circa 1900, 8-1/2" dia........ **$443**

Courtesy of Pook & Pook, Inc., pookandpook.com

Footed cracker jar, green and white satin finish with pink floral décor, good condition, 7" h. **$177**

Courtesy of Woody Auction, www.woodyauction.com

Mold #343 plate, white background with spring season keyhole portrait, pink highlights, good condition, 9" dia................................ **$266**

Courtesy of Woody Auction, www.woodyauction.com

Winter portrait plate, circa 1900, 8-3/4" dia................ **$689**

Courtesy of Pook & Pook, Inc., pookandpook.com

Portrait shaving mug, circa 1900, 3-1/2" h. **$467**

Courtesy of Pook & Pook, Inc., pookandpook.com

Three-piece portrait tea service, circa 1900, teapot 4-1/4" h....... **$480**

Courtesy of Pook & Pook, Inc., pookandpook.com

Mill scene tray, circa 1900, 12-1/2" w. **$148**

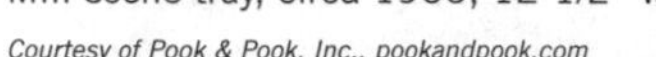

Courtesy of Pook & Pook, Inc., pookandpook.com

Swan relish tray, circa 1900, 9-3/4" w. **$148**

Courtesy of Pook & Pook, Inc., pookandpook.com

Portrait tray, circa 1900, 11-1/2" w. **$664**

Courtesy of Pook & Pook, Inc., pookandpook.com

Tiger vase, circa 1900,
6-1/4" h. **$1,132**

Courtesy of Pook & Pook, Inc., pookandpook.com

Ostrich vase, circa 1900,
7-1/4" h. **$135**

Courtesy of Pook & Pook, Inc., pookandpook.com

CERAMICS

satsuma

VIBRANTLY AND PAINSTAKINGLY crafted, Meiji Satsuma earthenware reflects Japanese artistry, history and culture, from the featured themes and motifs to the art form's minute liquid gold embellishments and ivory to yellow fine-crackled glazes.

Although created expressly for export, Satsuma are richly hand-painted works with stylized Japanese themes that reflect how their creators believed Westerners perceived their country – or how they wanted it to be perceived.

The Satsuma art form was created during the Meiji Dynasty (1868-1912) in Kyushu, a historic ceramics center in southern Japan. By the late 19th century, Japan's artists began participating in the Great International Fairs, for the first time promoting contact with the outside world. Their massive pairs of Satsuma vases, bowls and jardinières, meticulously detailed and featuring subjects foreign to Western taste, caused an immediate sensation in America and Europe. To satisfy this craze, Satsuma techniques spread from Kyushu studios to those in Kyoto, Osaka, Nagoya, Tokyo, Yokohama, and elsewhere.

Many master painters, eager for business and fame, signed the bases of their creations with Japanese Kanji marks, often in cartouche. Some cleverly included their names or the names of their studios in their artwork, for example, written on scrolls. In this way, Sozan, Kinkozan, Kozan, and Ryozan became known for their characteristic techniques, style, subject matter, and harmony between form and design.

Noted for their dense ornamentation, Satsuma can be embellished with borders of varying types and patterns, including enamel, geometric, brocade, scroll, latticework, and lush florals. Many Satsuma reflect the Japanese love of nature by including flocks of birds, sprays of wisteria, flowering trees, and winding streams. Others display picnics, market scenes, holidays, celebrations, processions, and the many festivals that enrich Japanese life. Themes can even include Samurai epics, Asian mythological representations, or elements of demonology.

Dressed in brocaded kimonos, the human subjects include geishas, Noh actors, musicians, and wise men who are shown strolling, flying kites, conversing, playing flutes, offering gifts, reading scrolls, bestowing blessings, or observing the moon.

Although rendered with miniature brush strokes – perhaps, at times, with single hairs from rats – the subjects' facial expressions reflect the full range of human emotions. Several personalities have actually been identified.

Serious collectors seek pieces by Osakan Yabu Meizan, which are distinguished by their extremely fine work, or by Nakamura Baikei, which are very rare. Baikei's pieces, which feature skillfully enameled, imaginative motifs varying from whimsical dancing monkeys to violent archers, always include lengthy inscriptions extolling the merits of his work and how much effort they took to paint.

"Fortunately, the time required to reproduce something that even remotely resembles a quality piece of Satsuma has kept reproductions out of the higher end of the market," dealer Matthew Baer of Ivory Tower Antiques said. The very low end, however, is riddled with reproductions from China that bear little resemblance to Satsuma. They are often stamped "Royal Satsuma" or "Satsuma Made in China" in English.

Figural and sculpted Satsuma are purely decorative. Vari-shaped incense burners, vases, boxes, flowerpots, plates, and tea caddies, though modeled after functional objects, were intended to be decorative as well. This is because earthenware, which is fired at a lower temperature than porcelain, stains with usage.

Satsuma vases, which often come in pairs and measure several feet high, may be divided into three or four panels. A single vase commonly depicts contrasting themes, such as a warrior scene, harmonious nature scene, beautiful geishas, and a hanging basket with a puppy eyeing a butterfly.

Working with a knowledgeable dealer is a great way to take the step from reading about Satsuma to actually handling the pieces and eventually purchasing them. Good dealers are happy to work with new collectors, teaching them how to recognize good pieces.

Prices for entry-level pieces will generally be in the hundreds of dollars. Very nice quality items will generally run from about $2,000 to $5,000. At the very top end, prices tend to increase almost exponentially, with true masterpieces running from $25,000 through $50,000 and more. Of course, there will always be the proverbial sleeper found somewhere for much less, but one can search for a lifetime without discovering it.

"Satsuma prices are primarily determined by the quality of their artwork, their artists, condition, form, and motifs," Baer said. "Satsuma is all about detail, and a truly fine piece will look even better under the scrutiny of a loupe than to the naked eye. A masterpiece will have good proportions in the figures, and the details will not only show up in the focal point of the scenes, but also in the periphery and in the background. Pieces that include unusual subject matters, such as animals or mythological creatures, are generally more desirable, but this certainly does not exclude well-executed, more common themes. Some very fine pieces exhibit a great deal of artistic restraint, which requires an even greater sense of balance to achieve the desired outcome."

— Melody Amsel-Arieli

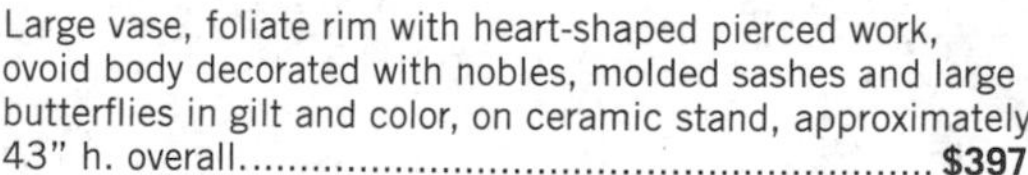

Large vase, foliate rim with heart-shaped pierced work, ovoid body decorated with nobles, molded sashes and large butterflies in gilt and color, on ceramic stand, approximately 43" h. overall.. **$397**

Courtesy of Clars Auction Gallery, www.clars.com

Urn and cover, early 20th century, 15-3/4" h................ **$98**

Courtesy of Pook & Pook, Inc., pookandpook.com

Pair of double-gourd bottle vases, probably Meiji Period (1868-1912), decorated with bird and chrysanthemum panels and textile scrolls, 11-3/4" h. **$175**

Courtesy of Neal Auction, www.nealauction.com

Jar and cover, early 20th century, 8-1/2" h................. **$37**

Courtesy of Pook & Pook, Inc., pookandpook.com

Shell-form bowl, probably Meiji Period (1868-1912), sea life-encrusted exterior, interior with figures in mountainous landscape, 3-1/2" h. x 14-3/8" w. **$200**

Courtesy of Neal Auction, www.nealauction.com

Two bowls, smaller one with butterflies to interior and chrysanthemums to exterior, base recess marked "Shozan" with Shimazu clan crest, larger one with butterflies surrounded by chrysanthemums, marked "Juzando-do" on recessed base, 3-1/2" h., 8-1/2" dia. **$458**

Courtesy of Clars Auction Gallery, www.clars.com

CERAMICS

saturday evening girls (paul revere)

PAUL REVERE POTTERY may appear sporadically in today's auction market, but there is no mistaking it once you get a glimpse.

The playful designs - sometimes with wisdom-infused illustrations, depictions of nature, and daily life of the early 20th century - and practical quality construction seem to be what defines this form of pottery, but there is much more to it.

Paul Revere Pottery is, in fact, a glorious extension of a greater educational effort that began with three women in late 19th century Boston. In the midst of tremendous social and cultural change and economic disparity among people, Edith Brown (1872-1932), Edith Guerrier (1870-1958), and Helen Storrow (1864-1944) came together to provide young immigrant women in the North End neighborhood of Boston with opportunities to experience various facets of life, and in turn gain new skills.

The Saturday Evening Girls (SEG) Club grew out of the Saturday Evening Girls Story Hour, which was established by Guerrier in 1899 as part of the North Bennet Street Industrial School (NBSIS). The school was established to train newly arrived immigrants in the North End neighborhood (largely Italian and Jewish families) in skilled trades. Not only was the Boston Public Library branch of the NBSIS the place where the Saturday Evening Girls Club took shape, it was the first trade school in America, according to the book *Saturday Evening Girls* by Meg Chalmers and Judy Young (Schiffer Publications).

Four circular glazed ceramic trivets, 1920s, all marked, two glazed-over markings, trees tile: firing line to bottom edge and wear to surface; Paul Revere: bruise to bottom edge; house and trees: bruise to top edge; swan: some peppering; 4-1/4" dia. ea. Provenance: From the collection of actress Penny Marshall, Los Angeles................................**$1,024**

Courtesy of Rago Arts and Auctions, www.ragoarts.com

Guerrier (a librarian and writer) and Brown (an artist) met while attending the Museum School of Boston's Museum of Fine Arts. In the early 20th century, the two women, who were living together by this time, met Helen Osborne Storrow, a longtime philanthropist in Boston. With a shared focus of social and political reform, empowerment of women, and the importance of honing various skills and creative endeavors, the three formed a bond that would change the lives of many and eventually bring Paul Revere Pottery into existence.

In the early years the club incorporated lessons in practical business and trade skills, with creative programs such as storytelling and dance. Following a trip to Europe in 1906, Guerrier and Brown began researching the possibility of incorporating pottery-making classes into their club curriculum. Upon

Rare glazed ceramic milk pitcher in cuerda seca with turtle and hare, Rose Bacchini, 1910, body incised "SLOW BUT SURE", base signed 333 6/10 S.E.G./R.B., excellent condition, 5" x 4-1/4". Provenance: From the collection of actress Penny Marshall, Los Angeles.
.... **$3,200**

Courtesy of Rago Arts and Auctions, www.ragoarts.com

seeing some of the early pieces the group created, Storrow purchased a home in the North End of Boston, near the Old North Church. This provided space to designate individual rooms for the pottery-making process, an area to sell the pottery, and rooms for club meetings. On the upper floor were apartments, including one where Guerrier and Brown lived.

Given that this new "headquarters" was located near the Old North Church, where Paul Revere had instructed his fellow Sons of Liberty to hang lanterns to signal movement of British troops ahead of the American Revolution, the brand would become Paul Revere Pottery.

While the SEG Club continued to offer its original programming for younger girls, the pottery was specifically the work of older teenage girls and young women. The SEG pottery-making curriculum was filled with valuable lessons, including day-to-day business practices, operation and maintenance of equipment, and the importance of mentoring and exposure to a variety of creative interests.

By 1915, Paul Revere Pottery by Saturday Evening Girls was attracting widespread interest, and expansion of the program and its operation was necessary. The group moved from its original Hull Street location to Brighton, Massachusetts, where the kiln, furnace, workrooms, and sales space were built according to the designs of Brown and Guerrier. Until this point, pottery production was handled by a group of more than 50 SEG members working part-time and a small number of decorators working full-time. With the incorporation of the Paul Revere Pottery Co. in 1916, it became a full-time business and remained as such until operations ceased in 1942.

The expansion of the business was a chance to put the things the young women were learning into a full-time career on a larger scale. And for directors Brown, Guerrier, and Storrow, it created a platform to demonstrate the SEG's effectiveness in incorporating various reforms in the workplace and having an even longer-lasting impact on the lives of its participants.

One example of this can be seen in the life of Sara Galner Bloom, one of the most prolific of the SEG artists. She was a familiar face in NBSIS programs, having attended a variety of club offerings over the years, according to Nonie Gadsden, author of *Art and Reform: Sara Galner, the Saturday Evening Girls, and the Paul Revere Pottery.* (Gadsden is also the Katharine Lane Weems Senior Curator of American Decorative Arts and Sculpture at the Museum of Fine Arts, Boston, and is currently working on a book about a Tiffany window, circa 1890s, which was gifted to the museum.)

Upon completing her required schooling, which at the time lawfully concluded at the age of 14, some of Galner's teachers attempted to help her continue with her education. However, as was the case for many immigrant youths, her parents were depending on her to enter the workforce and add to the family's income, Gadsden explained. While working first as a department store clerk and then a dressmaker, Galner continued her work at the SEG pottery. Eventually she chose to enroll in evening high school classes (much to her father's dismay) but also remained an active SEG member. A few years into her pottery work, Galner was offered a full-time position at the pottery by Brown. An offer she turned down because the rate of pay ($4 per week) was less than what she earned as a dressmaker. A counter-offer by Brown and a negotiation by Galner resulted in a salary of $7 per week for her and the rest of the SEG pottery artists, Gadsden said.

This was in addition to the already positive work conditions at the pottery for this time. In addition to receiving a wage that was greater than many other factory wages of the day, employees of the Paul Revere Pottery Co. worked eight-hour workdays instead of the usual 12-plus hours, Saturday was a half-day, and they received paid vacations, according to the book *Saturday Evening Girls.*

"It was a clean, healthy, and educational work environment for girls who didn't get much handed to them in life," Gadsden said. "Brown and Guerrier took these girls under their wings and exposed them to a variety of experiences and opportunities, but that's not to say the girls didn't work for it."

Galner's work is some of the most acclaimed of the Paul Revere Pottery legacy. One of the most recognizable aspects of her work is the use of floral designs, as well as the popular bread and milk children's sets. Not only was she an accomplished pottery artist, but later she went on to manage a Paul Revere Pottery shop in Washington, D.C.

The simple and relatable designs developed by Brown and other SEG artists, and elevated by Galner, are part of the appeal this pottery enjoys today.

Interest in Paul Revere Pottery, as limited as its exposure may be, is represented in prices paid at auction. Having brought many examples to auction - including a record-setting glazed ceramic fireplace depicting a wooded landscape by Saturday Evening Girls artists Fannie Levine, Albina Mangini, and Brown that sold for $219,750 (with buyer's premium) in 2013 - David Rago, principal of Rago Arts and Auctions, explained some of what sets this style of pottery apart.

"Little material better describes the Arts & Crafts [movement] in America," Rago said. "Conceived by women, decorated by women, focusing on kitchen ware, centered on designs that are both sophisticated and simple, the intent of SEG was to better the lives of women who needed a boost by involving them in the arts."

In February 2015, during a sale by Rago, an SEG wall pocket with a poppies design measuring 6" x 4" sold for $2,750. In Chalmers & Young's book, samples of 1921 Paul Revere Pottery catalog pages show that a wall pocket of this size sold for between $2.50 and $4, depending on the design.

"The appeal of Saturday Evening Girls Paul Revere Pottery

Tall vase in cuerda seca with wooded landscape, Sara Galner, 1917, signed SEG 21-17/S.G., overall excellent condition, burst glaze bubbles to body, 10" x 5-1/4".................. **$3,456**

Courtesy of Rago Arts and Auctions, www.ragoarts.com

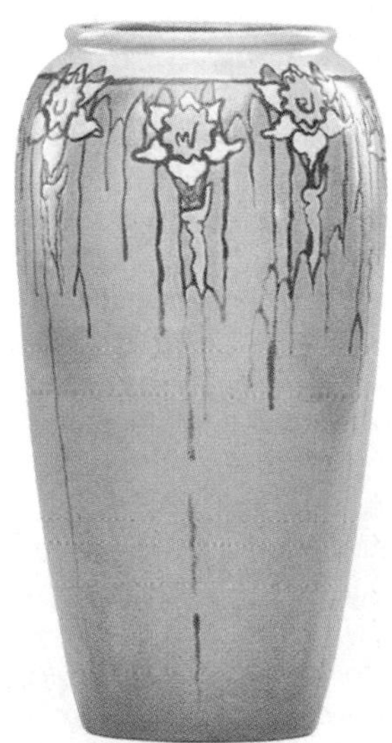

Tall vase in cuerda seca with daffodils, Sara Galner, 1915, signed 5-15/S.E.G./S.G., extensive professional restoration, 10-3/4" x 5-1/2". **$2,688**

Courtesy of Rago Arts and Auctions, www.ragoarts.com

is tied in with the general interest in Arts & Crafts pottery because it is handmade, often hand-thrown and decorated by a known person," said Riley Humler, principal of Humler & Nolan. "The main appeal still has to do with the quality of the art, and often, although simple in design, the better pieces are stunning in execution and composition, and most often done in soft, matte glazes."

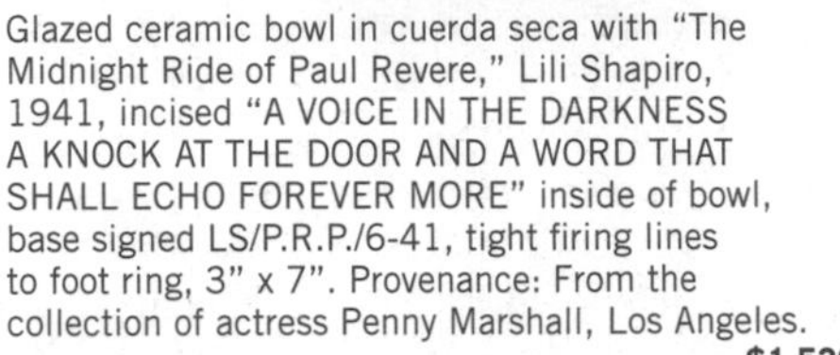

Glazed ceramic bowl in cuerda seca with "The Midnight Ride of Paul Revere," Lili Shapiro, 1941, incised "A VOICE IN THE DARKNESS A KNOCK AT THE DOOR AND A WORD THAT SHALL ECHO FOREVER MORE" inside of bowl, base signed LS/P.R.P./6-41, tight firing lines to foot ring, 3" x 7". Provenance: From the collection of actress Penny Marshall, Los Angeles. **$1,536**

Courtesy of Rago Arts and Auctions, www.ragoarts.com

Eventually Galner married Morris Bloom and had three children. The children didn't know much at all about their mother's time as an SEG, according to Gadsden, who met Galner's son and daughter-in-law during a lecture at the Museum of Fine Arts in Boston. It was clear from their first meeting that Galner's son, Dr. David L. Bloom, was a fan, although he knew less about it than one might expect. As Gadsden explained, at the time many people - especially those who immigrated to the United States - spoke less of the past and focused more on the future. It was by chance at an exhibition that Dr. Bloom saw a pot on display in the MFA exhibition "The Art That is Life" like the one his mother had. The pot had the familiar "S.E.G." signature and Galner's initials on the bottom. That sparked his fascination not only in the pottery, but its social history and his mother's role in it.

"What initially shocked me was how little he knew about his mother's life and work with the SEGs," Gadsden said. "However, he had met his mother's fellow artists and spent time with them (at regular SEG reunions) and knew they were special to her, but not a lot about that connection. That intrigued me."

That led to a sharing of information between Dr. Bloom and Gadsdsen and deeper dialogue about SEG, which led Gadsden to request one or two examples of the Paul Revere Pottery that Bloom had acquired in the years following his mother's death, to display at the Museum of Fine Arts in Boston. Instead, Dr. Bloom donated part of the collection to the museum and the rest is a promised gift. In all, more than 130 items of Paul Revere Pottery became part of the museum collection in 2006.

Although Galner may not have regaled her children with stories of her years as an artist at Paul Revere Pottery, she passed on much of the practical sensibilities, work ethic, appreciation, and engagement in a creative and culturally diverse community, and a progressive mindset to her children. For the retired Dr. Bloom, who became one of the nation's leading radiologists, he credits his success and the person he is to his mother, said Gadsden, whose telling of the events surrounding this family intrigued Frederic Sharf, a trustee of the Museum of Fine Arts so much so that he underwrote her book.

To sum up the lessons and influences the SEG Club and development of Paul Revere Pottery brought forth is a challenge, Gadsden said, when asked what valuable insights people today can take away from the program and product.

"There is talent and skill in all areas of society," she said. "It just needs to be given the opportunity to flourish. Every work of art has a personal story behind it, about the people who created it and the experiences they encountered. There is remarkable value in that."

Today the market for Paul Revere Pottery is thin as pieces are scarce, according to Rago and Humler. As the market for early 20th century decorative art has narrowed, it has pushed the cream to the top, Rago said. This is true of most of the pottery from the Arts & Crafts period, he added.

Large glazed ceramic mug in cuerda seca with ships and monogram C.R.S., Albina Mangini, 1912, signed AM/224-4-12/S.E.G., excellent condition, 4-3/4" x 5-1/2". Provenance: From the collection of actress Penny Marshall, Los Angeles. **$3,712**

Courtesy of Rago Arts and Auctions, www.ragoarts.com

Lidded pitcher in blue and white with circle containing duck with initials BH above on yellow field and W below in green field, marked "SEG" on bottom in black slip with date 7-18, excellent original condition, spot near base where glaze is thin, 9-1/2" h......... **$350**

Courtesy of Mark Mussio, Humler & Nolan, www.humlernolan.com

"That prices for the best, rarest work have risen so dramatically hasn't necessarily translated to more pieces coming to market," Rago said. "The people who own it, love it because it is truly fine and lovable ware, spiritually wrought and well designed, and they remain loathe to sell it."

The seldom-seen scenic pieces with no lettering are most sought-after or garner the most interest at auctions, Humler said.

"Lots of pieces were made for children's breakfast sets with bowl, pitcher, mug or plate, and often these have dates and children's names included with the design," he said. "The best pieces will be scenic or floral pieces that do not reference anyone. And as in most art pottery, if an item is of great quality, big is better than small."

During an auction presented by Humler & Nolan in early 2015, a three-piece SEG children's breakfast set (mug, bowl and plate) featuring an illustration of racing rabbits and the name "Joan Audrey Carlson" on each piece commanded $350. In the 1921 Paul Revere Pottery catalog, a similar set purchased new would have cost $8.

One aspect of Paul Revere Pottery that lends itself to identification, and, in turn, avoiding reproductions, is the signature and markings on each piece.

"Because the work is almost always signed, artist signed, and dated, this makes determining (the period of a) piece a fairly easy matter," Rago said.

Becoming as familiar as possible with the subject of Paul Revere Pottery, or any work for that matter, is a primary step before buying anything, advised Humler and Rago. In addition to being well-versed in the various types of signatures, gaining knowledge about the materials used in the development of the pottery and attributes of the different periods, along with seeking out reputable people to buy from, go a long way toward ensuring the opportunities one has to acquire SEG works are positive.

"I cannot emphasize enough the importance of scholarship when being a collector," Humler said. "Know your area better than the people from whom you buy, and you should be way ahead of the game."

Although it's been more than 105 years since the first Saturday Evening Girls pottery was created by the hands of young immigrant women of Boston's North End, as a result of the tireless commitment of Guerrier, Brown, and Storrow, the influence and impact of this educational and empowering experience lives on in the pottery enjoyed by many, and through the descendants of the women artisans who transformed simple clay into something spectacular.

— Antoinette Rahn

CERAMICS

CERAMICS

sèvres

SÈVRES PORCELAIN, THE grandest of ultimate luxury, artistic ceramics, was favored by European royalty, the aristocracy of the 19th century, and great 20th century collectors. Its story begins in 1708, when, following frenzied experimentation, German alchemist Johann Bottger discovered the formula for strong, delicate, translucent hard-paste porcelain. Unlike imported white chinaware, Bottger's porcelain could also be painted and gilded. Soon potteries across Europe were producing decorative items with fashionable gilt and flowers.

French potters lacked an ample source of kaolin, a requisite for hard paste porcelain, however. So from clay and powdered glass, they developed a soft paste formula. Soft-paste, though more fragile, could be fired at a lower temperature than hard-paste. This allowed a wider variety of colors and glazes.

Baluster-form vase with flaring waved mouth above silver-clad shoulders, late 19th/early 20th century, enameled and hand-painted with yellow and purple poppies on green ground, clad within conformingly decorated silver base on undulating rocaille foot, underglaze signature to base "Milet" for Paul Milet (1870-1950), marked with number 64 and incised with number 24, signature on body "[?] vost" partially obscured by silver overlay, mount with first standard Minerva mark denoting .950 fineness and illegible maker's mark, overall good condition, general minor rubbed wear and tarnishing to silver mounts commensurate with age, scattered minute inherent glaze flaws, 9-3/4" h., 4" dia. **$1,625**

Courtesy of John Moran Auctioneers, johnmoran.com

The Sèvres porcelain factory was originally founded at Chateau de Vincennes in 1738. Its soft-paste porcelain was prized for its characteristic whiteness and purity. By the time this workshop relocated to Sèvres in 1756, its craftsmen were creating small porcelain birds, figurals of children in white or delicate hues, and innovative pieces with characteristic rosy-hued backgrounds. They also produced detailed allegorical and thematic pieces like "Flute Lesson," "Jealousy," and "Justice and the Republic," which sparkle with transparent, colorless glazes.

The introduction of unglazed, natural-toned "biscuit" porcelain, a favorite of Madame de Pompadour, the mistress of Louis XV, followed. Many of these molded sculptures portray lifelike sentimental or Classical scenes. Biscuit porcelain is extremely fragile.

Madame de Pompadour also adored Sèvres' porcelain flowers, the most delicate item produced during these early years. Legend has it that, to further the company's production, she once presented Louis XV with a profusion of Sèvres vases abloom with colorful porcelain pretties, petal upon tinted petal atop cunningly wired "stems."

When Louis XV assumed full control of Sèvres porcelain in 1759, he insisted on flawless, extravagant creations, many of which he commissioned for his personal collection. In his travels, he also spread the Sèvres reputation for opulent ornamentation, vivid colors, and fine glazes.

The renowned Sèvres mark, elaborate blue interlaced Ls, was born of his royal patronage and helps determine dates of production. Other marks, either painted or incised, indicate specific Sèvres painters, gilders, sculptors, and potters by name.

Louis XV's successor, Louis XVI, continued to support the royal Sèvres tradition. He not only set prices and arranged exhibitions, but also marketed pieces personally.

Although kaolin deposits were discovered near Limoges in 1768, Sèvres began producing hard-paste porcelain commercially only from 1773. During this period, they continued to produce soft-paste items as well.

Pair of ormolu mounted porcelain covered urns, 19th century, each of baluster form flanked by upright bracket handles, painted after Boucher with amorous couples, reverse with watery landscape, 17-1/2" h. Provenance: From the Birmingham Museum of Art. **$1,952**

Courtesy of Clars Auction Gallery, www.clars.com

After suffering financial ruin during the French Revolution, Sèvres, in addition to creating traditional pieces for the luxury market, began producing simpler, less expensive items. During this period, its craftsmen also abandoned their old-fashioned soft-paste formula for hard-paste porcelain.

Sèvres porcelain regained its former glory under Napoleon Bonaparte, who assumed power in 1804. He promoted elaborately ornamented pieces in the classical style. The empire's richly decorated, themed dinner sets, for example, were enjoyed by distinguished guests, visiting rulers, and Napoleon himself. These pieces typically feature florals, landscapes, or cameo portraits framed by solid gold edging accented with stylized palm fronds, the ancient Greek symbol of victory.

Along with dinner sets and coffee services, tea services were among Sèvres' most popular creations. During the early 1800s, when passion for that luxury potion peaked, Greek or Etruscan pottery inspired the design of many Sèvres teapots. These were valued not only for their beauty, but also because, as porcelain, they could withstand the heat.

Many Sèvres shapes, which range from simple cylindrical vases to elaborate perforated potpourri jars, were innovative for their times. Some, like a gondola-shaped vase designed to hold aromatic petals or another with elephant-head handles fitted as candle arms, serve a double purpose. Sèvres also created a wide selection of decorative utilitarian objects, including tobacco jars, lidded ewers and basins, painted plaques, punch bowls, sorbet coolers, and milk jugs.

The range of Sèvres creations is extensive, varying in shape, historical styles, motifs, and ornamentation. Vases typically feature double round, oval, or elliptical finely painted scenes edged in white against pastel backgrounds. One side portrays figures, while the other features flower bouquets. Their lavish gilding, a royal touch reserved especially for Sèvres creations, is often embellished with engraved detail, like flowers or geometric motifs. Many fine pieces like these are still found in pristine condition, if rarely or never used.

Simple plates and tea wares can be found for a few hundred dollars. Because large numbers were made to accompany dessert services, quite a few Sèvres biscuit porcelains have also survived. These fragile pieces command $3,000 to $70,000 apiece.

Sceau a verre and shell-shaped dish, late 18th century, gilt oeil-de-perdrix decoration added in 19th century, with blue interlaced Ls enclosing date letters HH and painter's M:X for Mme Xrouet, dish 8-1/2" dia. **$427**

Courtesy of Clars Auction Gallery, www.clars.com

Fourteen hand-painted porcelain plates with partial blue ground and loose floral bouquets, overglazed intertwined double-L mark verso, centering "v" mark corresponding to year 1774, 8-1/2" dia. **$519**

Courtesy of Clars Auction Gallery, www.clars.com

Assembled 20-piece collection of white and gold porcelain: eight dinner plates with Louis-Philippe's initials and ivy border, blanks dated 1849, with "Chateau de St. Cloud" decorator's marks, 9" dia.; teapot with Napoleon III's crest, with blank mark for 1853 and decorator's mark for 1855; five coffee cups and six saucers with molded ribbing and gilt initials, blank marks dated 1886 and decorator's marks for 1889, 2-1/4" h., 4-1/4" dia.; overall very good condition with gilding largely intact, small surface chip to teapot spout rim, two dinner plates with small losses to rims, third dinner plate with wear to foot rim, one saucer with minor manufacturing flaw to gilding. **$677**

Courtesy of New Orleans Auction Galleries, www.neworleansauction.com

According to Errol Manners, author, lecturer, and proprietor of London's H & E Manners: Ceramics and Works of Art, the Sèvres market has strengthened considerably in recent years. "Pieces linked directly to the Court and very early experimental wares, which appeal to more serious and academic collectors, command the highest prices of all," he said. "Major pieces can command a few hundred thousand dollars. A set of Sèvres vases can command over $1 million."

Manners recommends that would-be collectors visit museums and consult serious dealers and collectors before purchasing a Sèvres piece. "And read the books," he said. "There are really no shortcuts. It takes serious study."

Collecting Sèvres porcelain is, in his experience, "a minefield for the unwary, since many fakes and pastiches - showy, decorative 'Sèvres-style' imitations - abound. These were produced during the 19th century in the style of the 18th century, but not by Sèvres," he said.

"While Sèvres-style pieces are not authentic Sèvres, they may be authentic antiques," according to Edan Sassoon, representing the Artes Antiques and Fine Art Gallery in Beverly Hills, California. "If they faithfully imitate Sèvres pieces in quality, style, and opulence, they may not only have decorative value, but may also be quite expensive. In today's market, a piece of Sèvres-style porcelain, depending on its color, condition, size, and quality, may command hundreds of thousands of dollars."

– Melody Amsel-Arieli

Turquoise-ground monteith (seu crenelle), porcelain 18th century, decoration 19th century, oval form with scalloped rim, painted after Boucher with vignette of shepherd in landscape reserve, verso with putti among grapevines in clouds within elaborate gilt surround, rim similarly enriched, 5" h. x 11-1/2" w. x 8" d. Provenance: From the Birmingham Museum of Art................................ **$488**

Courtesy of Clars Auction Gallery, www.clars.com

Gilt and lapis ground partial coffee set, circa 1892-1922, 27 pieces with painted sprigs of flowers: coffeepot, 8-3/4" h., 5" dia.; cream jug, 3-3/4" h., 2-3/4" dia.; sugar bowl, 4-1/2" h., 3-3/4" dia.; and 12 demitasse cups, 2" h., with 12 matching saucers, 4-1/2" dia.; marked with various blank marks dating 1892-1922, with various decorator's initials including "BB" and "HP"; overall very good condition with minor rubbing to gilt, wear and indications of age and use, two cups and one saucer with flake to rim, bottom edge of spout of coffeepot with fleabite/tiny chip on underside...................... **$1,046**

Courtesy of New Orleans Auction Galleries, www.neworleansauction.com

Hand-painted pedestal covered urn, Art Nouveau woman in fancy dress on gold field surrounded by chrysanthemum décor, attributed to Alphonse Mucha, marked, lid with professional restoration, 22" h. **$1,298**

Courtesy of Woody Auction, www.woodyauction.com

Three-part pedestal urn, cobalt blue with courting scene on front panel, reverse panel with scene of lake and ruins, gold enamel highlights, elaborate gilt fitting with handles depicting women's heads, marked, good condition, 29" x 12-1/2"......................... **$2,006**

Courtesy of Woody Auction, www.woodyauction.com

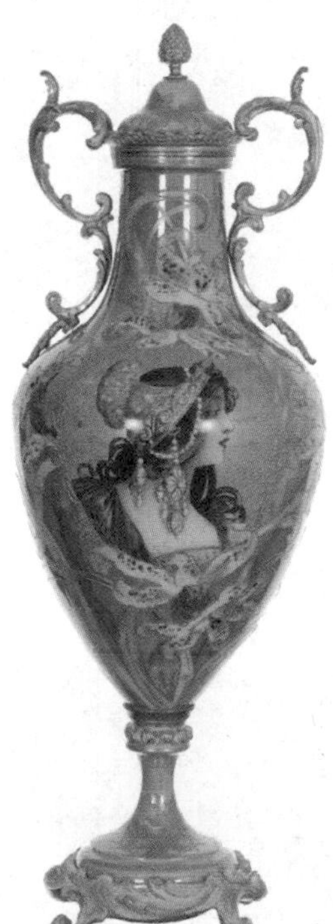

Hand-painted pedestal covered urn, Art Nouveau design of woman in elaborate dress on gold field with orchid highlights, decoration attributed to Alphonse Mucha, marked, good condition, 21" h. **$1,888**

Courtesy of Woody Auction, www.woodyauction.com

CERAMICS

spatterware

SPATTERWARE TAKES ITS name from the "spattered" decoration, in various colors, used to trim pieces hand-painted with rustic center designs of flowers, birds, houses, etc. Popular in the early 19th century, most was imported from England.

Related wares, called stick spatter, had freehand designs applied with pieces of cut sponge attached to sticks, hence the name. Examples date from the 19th and early 20th centuries and were produced in England, Europe, and America.

Some early spatter-decorated wares were marked by the manufacturers, but not many. Twentieth century reproductions are also sometimes marked, including those produced by Boleslaw Cybis.

Red peafowl pattern cup and saucer, 19th century...................... **$135**

Courtesy of Pook & Pook, Inc., pookandpook.com

Red and green rainbow bull's-eye pattern plate, 19th century, 9-1/2" dia.......................... **$344**

Courtesy of Pook & Pook, Inc., pookandpook.com

Child's blue six-piece fort pattern tea service, 19th century, teapot 4-1/2" h. **$455**

Courtesy of Pook & Pook, Inc., pookandpook.com

Child's green nine-piece peafowl pattern tea service, 19th century, teapot 4-1/2" h. **$295**

Courtesy of Pook & Pook, Inc., pookandpook.com

Red and blue criss-cross pattern plate, 19th century, 8-1/2" dia.......................... **$295**

Courtesy of Pook & Pook, Inc., pookandpook.com

Two red peafowl pattern soup bowls, 19th century, 9-3/4" dia. **$234**

Courtesy of Pook & Pook, Inc., pookandpook.com

Three blue peafowl pattern plates, 19th century, 9" dia. and 8-1/2" dia. **$295**

Courtesy of Pook & Pook, Inc., pookandpook.com

Red peafowl pattern waste bowl, 19th century, 3-1/4" h., 6-1/4" dia. **$49**

Courtesy of Pook & Pook, Inc., pookandpook.com

Three peafowl pattern plates, 19th century, one red example, 9-1/4" dia., and two blue examples, 9-1/2" dia...**$209**

Courtesy of Pook & Pook, Inc., pookandpook.com

Red peafowl pattern sugar bowl, 19th century, 8" h. **$98**

Courtesy of Pook & Pook, Inc., pookandpook.com

Blue peafowl pattern sugar bowl, 19th century, 5-1/4" h. **$86**

Courtesy of Pook & Pook, Inc., pookandpook.com

Blue peafowl pattern teapot, 19th century, 6-1/2" h. **$98**

Courtesy of Pook & Pook, Inc., pookandpook.com

Red peafowl pattern teapot, 19th century, 7-1/4" h. **$197**

Courtesy of Pook & Pook, Inc., pookandpook.com

CERAMICS

spongeware

SPONGEWARE: THE NAME says it all. A sponge dipped in colored pigment is daubed onto a piece of earthenware pottery of a contrasting color, creating an overall mottled, "sponged" pattern. A clear glaze is applied, and the piece fired. The final product, with its seemingly random, somewhat smudged coloration, conveys an overall impression of handmade folk art.

Most spongeware, however, was factory-made from the mid-1800s well into the 1930s. Any folk art appeal was secondary, the result of design simplicity intended to facilitate maximum production at minimum cost. Although mass-manufacturing produced most spongeware, it did in fact originate in the work of independent potters. Glasgow, Scotland, circa 1835, is recognized as the birthplace of spongeware. The goal: the production of utilitarian everyday pottery with appeal to the budget-conscious. Sponged surface decorations were a means of adding visual interest both easily and inexpensively.

Since early spongeware was quickly made, usually by amateur artisans, the base pottery was often insubstantial and the sponging perfunctory. However, due to its general usefulness, and especially because of its low cost, spongeware quickly found an audience. Production spread across Great Britain and Europe, finally reaching the United States. Eventually, quality improved, as even frugal buyers demanded more for their money.

The terms "spongeware" and "spatterware" are often used interchangeably. Spatterware took its name from the initial means of application: A pipe was used to blow colored pigment onto a piece of pottery, creating a spattered coloration. Since the process was tedious, sponging soon became the preferred means of color application, although the "spatterware" designation remained in use. Specific patterns were achieved by means of sponge printing (aka "stick spatter"): A small piece of sponge was cut in the pattern shape desired, attached to a stick, then dipped in color. The stick served as a more precise means of application, giving the decorator more control, creating designs with greater border definition. Applied colors varied, with blue (on white) proving most popular. Other colors included red, black, green, pink, yellow, brown, tan, and purple.

Because of the overlap in style, there really is no "right or wrong" in classifying a particular object as "spongeware" or "spatterware"; often the manufacturer's advertising designation is the one used. Spatterware, however, has become more closely identified with pottery in which the mottled color pattern (whether spattered or sponged) surrounds a central image, either stamped or painted free-hand. Spongeware usually has no central image; the entire visual consists of the applied "splotching." Any break in that pattern comes in the form of contrasting bands, either in a solid color matching the mottling, or in a portion of the base earthenware kept free of applied color. Some spongeware pieces also carry stampings indicating the name of an advertiser, or the use intent of a specific object ("Butter," "Coffee," "1 Qt.").

Much of what is classified as spatterware has a certain delicacy of purpose: tea sets, cups and saucers, sugar bowls, and the like. Spongeware is more down-to-earth, both in intended usage and sturdiness. Among the many examples of no-nonsense spongeware: crocks, washbowl and pitcher sets, jugs, jars, canisters, soap dishes, shaving mugs, spittoons, umbrella stands, washboards, and even chamber pots. These are pottery pieces that mean business; their shapes, stylings, and simple decoration are devoid of fussiness.

Spongeware was usually a secondary operation for the many companies that produced it and was marketed as bargain-priced service ware; it's seldom marked. Today, spongeware is an ideal collectible for those whose taste in 19th century pottery veers away from the overly detailed and ornate. Spongeware's major appeal is due in large part to the minimalism it represents.

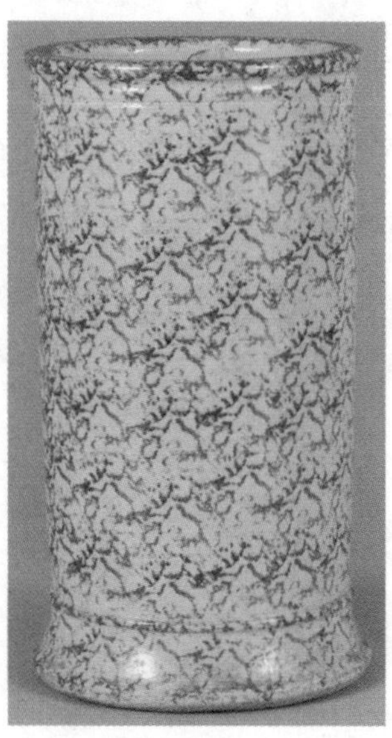

▲ Three mixing bowls, late 19th century, largest 5-3/4" h., 12-3/4" dia. **$135**

Courtesy of Pook & Pook, Inc., pookandpook.com

◄ Blue decorated umbrella stand, circa 1900, 17-3/4" h. **$713**

Courtesy of Pook & Pook, Inc., pookandpook.com

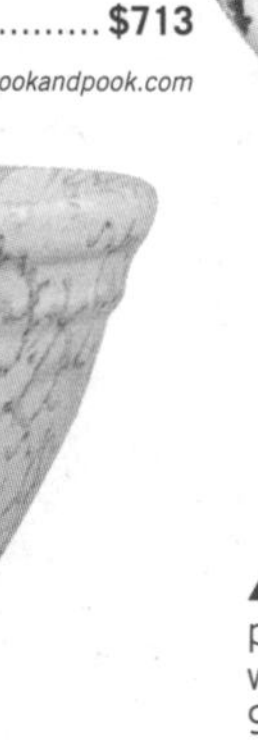

▲ Chicken wire blue decorated pitcher, very good condition, wear to spout and tight hairline, 9" h. **$61**

Courtesy of Conestoga Auction Co., www.hessauctiongroup.com

Chicken wire blue decorated bowl, good condition with tight hairline, 6" h., 13" dia. **$85**

Courtesy of Conestoga Auction Co., www.hessauctiongroup.com

Five blue and white handled pitchers, late 19th/early 20th century, cracks and foot chip, minor roughness, 9 h." **$960**

Courtesy of Eldred's, www.eldreds.com

CERAMICS

staffordshire

STAFFORDSHIRE FIGURES and groups made of pottery were produced by the majority of the Staffordshire, England, potters of the 19th century and were used as mantle decorations or "chimney ornaments" as they were sometimes called. Pairs of dogs were favorites and were turned out by the carload, and 19th century pieces are still readily available. Well-painted reproductions also abound, and collectors are urged to exercise caution before purchasing.

The process of transfer-printing designs on earthenware developed in England in the late 18th century, and by the mid-19th century, most common ceramic wares were decorated in this manner, most often with romantic European or Asian landscape scenes, animals or flowers. The earliest transferwares were printed in dark blue, but later, light blue, pink, purple, red, black, green, and brown were used. A majority of these wares were produced at various English potteries until the turn of the 20th century, but French and other European firms also made similar pieces, and all are quite collectible.

The best reference on this area is Petra Williams' *Staffordshire Romantic Transfer Patterns - Cup Plates and Early Victorian China* (Fountain House East, 1978).

TRANSFERWARE

"Fair Mount Near Philadelphia" and "Upper Ferry Bridge over the River Schuylkill" blue transferware shallow bowl and plate, 19th century, 9-3/4" dia. and 8-3/4" dia. **$270**

Courtesy of Pook & Pook, Inc., pookandpook.com

Two "Peace and Plenty" blue transferware plates, 19th century, 7-3/4" dia. and 10-1/2" dia. **$197**

Courtesy of Pook & Pook, Inc., pookandpook.com

Pearlware transferware platter, 19th century, incised mark, scenic decoration with figures and cattle, 19" x 14-3/4". **$400**

Courtesy of Neal Auction, www.nealauction.com

Boston State House blue transferware plate, 19th century, 8-3/4" dia. **$123**

Courtesy of Pook & Pook, Inc., pookandpook.com

Park Theatre, New York blue transferware plate, 19th century, 10" dia. **$135**

Courtesy of Pook & Pook, Inc., pookandpook.com

"Landing of General Lafayette" blue transferware plate, 19th century, 8-7/8" dia. **$160**

Courtesy of Pook & Pook, Inc., pookandpook.com

Blue transferware platter, 19th century, depicting naval engagement of Chesapeake and Shannon ships, 14-3/4" x 19-1/2". **$1,968**

Courtesy of Pook & Pook, Inc., pookandpook.com

"Niagara from the American Side" blue transferware platter, 19th century, 11-3/4" l. x 14-3/4" w. **$172**

Courtesy of Pook & Pook, Inc., pookandpook.com

Large blue transfer-decorated platter, Joseph Stubbs, Longport, Burslem, England, circa 1825, with shell motif in center and floral border, minor rim chip, 18-1/2" w. x 15-1/4" h. **$677**

Courtesy of Skinner, Inc., www.skinnerinc.com

Blue transfer-printed pearlware platter on stand, 19th century and later, depicting river with temple and fort in distance, Tiber pattern, on accompanying later stand, platter 19-1/8" w. **$923**

Courtesy of Skinner, Inc., www.skinnerinc.com

William Adams "Caledonia" two-color transferware pitcher, circa 1840-1860, scallop- and panel-molded body with red reserve surrounded by green border patterns, unmarked, good condition with chip to spout and shallow vertical stress lines to interior near handle, 9-1/4" h. **$288**

Courtesy of Jeffrey S. Evans & Associates, www.jeffreysevans.com

Blue transferware pitcher, 10-3/4" h., and bowl, 4-1/4" h., 13" dia., 19th century. **$86**

Courtesy of Pook & Pook, Inc., pookandpook.com

"Canova" transferware ewer and wash basin in blue, circa 1840, scalloped border with alternating floral cartouches and scenic reserves, central imagery of urn in Italianate landscape, marked in blue to underside of each for T. Mayer, undamaged, ewer 9-5/8" h., basin 4-1/4" h., 12-3/4" dia.**$345**

Courtesy of Jeffrey S. Evans & Associates, www.jeffreysevans.com

Transferware child's egg in black, circa 1830-1840, depicting boy taking flute lessons and boy with his dog and basket of birds, lettered "A PRESENT FOR / A GOOD BOY" between scenes, two glaze nicks and light wear, 2-1/2" l. x 2" d. **$403**

Courtesy of Jeffrey S. Evans & Associates, www.jeffreysevans.com

FIGURES

Pair of spaniels, 19th century, 8-1/2" h. **$258**

Courtesy of Pook & Pook, Inc., pookandpook.com

Parr-Kent zebra figures, circa 1920-1930, each painted with black stripes on white bodies, standing on grassy mound encrusted with dried clay "grass" painted realistically, on orange-brown bases, very good condition, one with losses to grass, 5-1/8" h. **$127**

Courtesy of Jeffrey S. Evans & Associates, www.jeffreysevans.com

◀ The Four Seasons Lusterware figures, Dixon, Austin & Co., circa 1820-1826, luster and polychrome-decorated gowns and bases, season marked on each appropriate figure, impressed "DIXON, AUSTIN & CO." mark on each base, wear, 9" h. **$3,690**

Courtesy of Skinner, Inc., www.skinnerinc.com

Spaniel figure molded as seated dog with curly tail, collar, lock and chain-form leash, yellow eyes, black muzzle, and red mouth, 19th century, unmarked, good condition, typical crazing to glaze throughout, 11-5/8" h. . **$69**

Courtesy of Jeffrey S. Evans & Associates, www.jeffreysevans.com

Earthenware Antony and Cleopatra figures, late 18th century, possibly Neale & Co., each overglaze enamel decorated and modeled reclining atop free-form naturalistically decorated earth and floral base, each with minor abrasions to enameling, Antony with professionally restored piece out of front and rim chip repairs surrounding foot rim, Cleopatra with restored hairlines to front and backside and rim chip repairs surrounding foot rim, 12" l.. **$308**

Courtesy of Skinner, Inc., www.skinnerinc.com

◀ Busts of children after Meissen original, 20th century, girl and boy with pink and green headdresses, orange-brown hair, ruddy checks, red collar or tie, girl with cross on chain, both with blue dress with gold highlights, on socketed, shaped, and waisted cylindrical bases and flaring, rounded-rectangular plinths, very good condition, undamaged, crazing, 8-1/4" h. **$81**

Courtesy of Jeffrey S. Evans & Associates, www.jeffreysevans.com

Lead-glazed creamware tea canister and cover, circa 1765, attributed to William Greatbatch, translucent polychrome glazes to molded rectangular form with fruit above basketweave banded foot, cover with professionally restored rim chip, canister top collar with internal and external rim chip and staining, 4" h.. **$677**

Courtesy of Skinner, Inc., www.skinnerinc.com

White salt-glazed stoneware camel teapot, mid-18th century, slip-cast figure with chinoiserie molded howdah, missing cover, pot with rim chip repairs to howdah and top lip of camel's mouth, lightly crazed throughout, 7-1/2" l. overall x 5-1/4" h. **$400**

Courtesy of Skinner, Inc., www.skinnerinc.com

MISCELLANEOUS

Pearlware nesting hen tureen, circa 1830-1860, cover modeled as seated Polish hen with red and black feathers with chick on back, lower section modeled as lower body with five chick heads emerging from under feathers, good condition, hen's beak broken off and glued back into place, overpainted hairline, firing crack in base original to manufacture, 7" h. **$1,265**

Courtesy of Jeffrey S. Evans & Associates, www.jeffreysevans.com

Figural bud vases depicting ram and ewe standing near tree, marked, good condition, 5" h. **$94**

Courtesy of Woody Auction, www.woodyauction.com

Nesting hen tureen, circa 1950, cover modeled as speckled hen with gray, black, and red feathers, seated on grassy mound above eggs, lower section modeled as basket, unmarked, hen in good condition with some flaking to enamels, 7-3/4" h. **$173**

Courtesy of Jeffrey S. Evans & Associates, www.jeffreysevans.com

CATEGORY

teco pottery

TECO POTTERY was the line of art pottery introduced by the American Terra Cotta and Ceramic Co. of Terra Cotta (Crystal Lake), Illinois, in 1902. Founded by William D. Gates in 1881, American Terra Cotta originally produced only bricks and drain tile.

Because of superior facilities for experimentation, including a chemical laboratory, the company was able to develop an art pottery line, favoring a mat green glaze in the earlier years but eventually achieving a wide range of colors including a metallic luster glaze and a crystalline glaze. Although some hand-thrown pottery was made, Gates favored a molded ware because it was less expensive to produce. By 1923, Teco Pottery was no longer being made, and in 1930 American Terra Cotta and Ceramic Co. was sold.

For more information on Teco Pottery, see *Teco: Art Pottery of the Prairie School* by Sharon S. Darling (Erie Art Museum, 1990).

Twin-handled vase in mat green glaze with charcoaling, impressed on bottom with Teco logo and shape number 297, excellent original condition, glaze thin on handle edges, 5-1/2" h. **$475**

Courtesy of Mark Mussio, Humler & Nolan, www.humlernolan.com

Vase with molded floral design in mat green glaze, impressed Teco on bottom, professional repair to rim, 8-5/8" h. **$350**

Courtesy of Mark Mussio, Humler & Nolan, www.humlernolan.com

Twin-handled vase, shape number 407, in light mat green glaze, impressed on bottom with Teco logo, professional restoration to chip at rim, 8-1/2" h. **$350**

Courtesy of Mark Mussio, Humler & Nolan, www.humlernolan.com

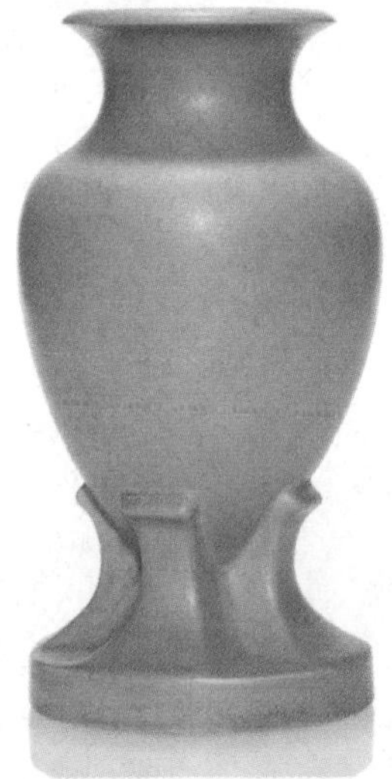

Vase with mat green glaze with charcoaling, impressed Teco on bottom, professional repair to base, 9-1/2" h................... **$900**

Courtesy of Mark Mussio, Humler & Nolan, www.humlernolan.com

! top lot

Large gray elephant figure, unmarked, body of animal in excellent condition, restoration to several chips out of plinth, 17" h., plinth 20" l. The elephant was made for the exterior of the manager's office at the Westinghouse powerplant in Berwyn, Illinois. When the building was razed years ago, the elephant and a companion piece were saved. $2,200

COURTESY OF MARK MUSSIO, HUMLER & NOLAN, WWW.HUMLERNOLAN.COM

Vase in mat green glaze with charcoaling, impressed Teco on bottom, small chip at base, 4-3/4" h. **$150**

Courtesy of Mark Mussio, Humler & Nolan, www.humlernolan.com

Unusual buttress vase in mat red glaze, impressed with Teco logo on bottom, excellent original condition, single glaze nick on one buttress, 5-5/8" h. **$800**

Courtesy of Mark Mussio, Humler & Nolan, www.humlernolan.com

Buttress vase in mat green glaze, impressed Teco on base, minor nicks on buttress edges and professional repair at base, 6-1/4" h. **$750**

Courtesy of Mark Mussio, Humler & Nolan, www.humlernolan.com

◀ Low bowl in mat taupe glaze, impressed with Teco logo on bottom, curdling in glaze due to light application, 1" h., 4-1/4" dia. **$130**

Courtesy of Mark Mussio, Humler & Nolan, www.humlernolan.com

CERAMICS

teplitz/amphora pottery

ANTIQUE DEALERS AND COLLECTORS often refer to Art Nouveau-era art pottery produced in the kaolin-rich Turn-Teplitz region of Bohemia (today Teplice region, Czech Republic) collectively as Teplitz. Over the years, however, this area boasted many different potteries. To add to the confusion, they opened, closed, changed owners, merged or shared common designers against a background of changing political borders.

Although all produced pottery, their techniques and products varied. Some ceramicists, like Josef Strnact and Julius Dressler, produced brightly glazed faience and majolica earthenware items. According to Elizabeth Dalton, Furniture and Decorative Arts Specialist at Michaan's Auctions, Alameda, California, a strong earthenware body rather than delicate, brittle porcelain allowed more unusual manipulation of the ceramic surface of their vases, flowerpots, and tobacco jars.

Alfred Stellmacher, who founded the Imperial and Royal Porcelain Factory in 1859, produced fanciful, sculptural creations noted for their fine design and quality. Many feature applied natural motifs, Mucha and Klimt-like portraits, or simulated jewels.

"The most collectible Teplitz pieces of all, however, are those manufactured by the Riessner, Stellmacher and Kessel Amphora Porcelain Works (RStK), which was founded in 1892," said Stuart Slavid, vice president and director of European furniture, decorative arts and fine ceramics at Skinner Auctions, Boston.

Archeology and history buffs may recognize amphoras as ceramic vessels used for storage and transport in the ancient world. Art collectors and dealers, however, know amphoras as RStK pieces that incorporate undulating, asymmetrical Art Nouveau interpretations of flora and fauna - both natural and fanciful - in their designs. Many RStK artists honed their skills at the Teplitz Imperial Technical School for Ceramics and Associated Applied Arts. Others drew on the fine ceramics manufacturing tradition of nearby Dresden.

Producing Amphora was time-consuming and prohibitively expensive. Each piece began with an artist's drawing, which would typically include lifelike images of snakes, sea creatures, dragons, maidens, flora, or fauna. Once approved, each drawing was assigned a style number, which would subsequently appear on the bottom of identically shaped pieces, along with the word "Amphora."

Using these drawings as their guides, craftsmen carved and fired clay models from which they created smooth plaster-of-paris molds. These molds were then lined with

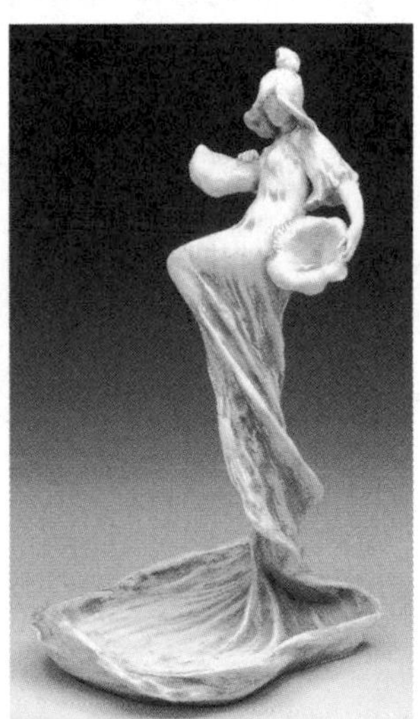

Amphora receiving card tray with figure of Art Nouveau maiden amid large flowers, long gown forming tray, cream-colored glaze with brown shadowing, signed on underside with impressed "Amphora" signature in oval, numbered 800721, and stamped "Turn Teplitz Bohemia Made in Austria" in red, very good to excellent condition with professional repair to small stem on back of figure, 17-1/4" h. **$2,666**

Courtesy of James D. Julia Auctioneers, Fairfield, Maine, www.jamesdjuliacom

top lot

Monumental Amphora 1900 Paris Exposition gold medal-winning vase in shaded blue and green glaze with gilt highlights, Art Nouveau maiden leaning on side and reaching for flower dangling from lip of vase, neck of vase decorated with three Art Nouveau maidens' faces with hair flowing down side of neck, bulbous body of vase with root design, maiden's gown flowing onto oval pedestal foot, signed on front of vase with artist initials "E.S.T" for Eduard Stellmacher, signed "Amphora Austria, Turn, Paris 1900 RSTK" on underside, very good to excellent condition, two small roots on side of vase with cracks, possibly occurring during firing, 23-3/4" h. $10,665

COURTESY OF JAMES D. JULIA AUCTIONEERS, FAIRFIELD, MAINE, WWW.JAMESDJULIACOM

thin layers of clay. Once the clay dried and the molds removed, the resulting Amphoras were fine-carved, hand-painted, and glazed. Finally they were refired, sometimes as many as 10 times. Since each was decorated in a unique way, no two Amphoras were exactly alike. Since their manufacture was so complex, reproducing one is nearly impossible.

RStK's innovative pieces earned international acclaim almost immediately. After winning prizes at both the Chicago and St. Louis world's fairs, exclusive establishments, including Tiffany & Co., marketed them in the United States.

Pair of Julius B. Dressler Amphora handled ewers, molded, blue matte background with gold stencil highlights, marked, good condition, 19-1/2" h. **$590**

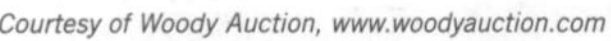

Courtesy of Woody Auction, www.woodyauction.com

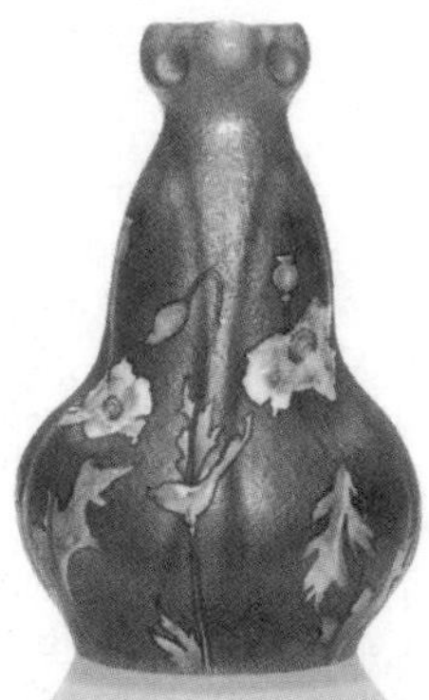

Amphora vase with iridescent ground and painted white poppies in enamel, marked with crown and "Amphora Austria" on bottom, excellent original condition with minor wear to gold trim, 12-1/2" h. **$160**

Courtesy of Mark Mussio, Humler & Nolan, www.humlernolan.com

In addition to lavish Amphoras, Riessner, Stellmacher and Kessel also produced highly detailed, intricately crafted female busts, both large and small. Virgins, nymphs, and dancers, reflecting fashionable literary, religious, and mythological motifs and themes of the day, were popular choices. Larger busts, because they were so complex and so rarely made, were expensive from the start. Today these 100-year-old beauties, especially those that escaped the ravages of time, are extremely desirable.

In 1894, leading Viennese porcelain retailer Ernst Wahliss purchased the RStK Amphora. Paul Dachsel, a company designer and Stellmacher's son-in-law, soon left to open his own pottery. Dachsel was known for adorning fairly simple forms with unique, intricate, stylized Art Nouveau embellishments, as well as modern-looking applied handles and rims. These, along with his Secessionist works - those influenced by Austrian exploration of innovative artistic forms outside academic and historical traditions - are highly collectible today.

After Wahliss' death, the Amphora Porcelain Works - now known as the Alexandra Porcelain Works Ernst Wahliss - became known for Serapis-Wahliss, its fine white earthenware line that features intricate, colorful, stylized natural forms.

When Stellmacher established his own company in 1905, the firm continued operating as the Riessner and Kessel Amphora Works. After Kessel left five years later, Amphora Werke Riessner, as it became known, continued to produce Amphora pottery through the 1940s. In 1945, Amphora Werke Riessner was nationalized by the Czechoslovakian government.

Although many Amphoras retail for under $1,000, some are quite costly. Rare, larger pieces, probably commissioned or created expressly for exhibition, were far more prone to breakage in production and display, so they command far more.

Do Teplitz pieces make good investments? According to Stuart Slavid, "Considering their rarity, quality, and decorative appeal, there's still plenty of room for growth, especially at the higher end of the market. I personally think that higher-end Amphoras are exceptional. History says you can't go wrong buying the very best. There will always be collectors at that level."

— Melody Amsel-Arieli

Two Teplitz portrait porcelain vases, late 19th/early 20th century, one tapered, 6-3/4" h., and one bulbous, 5-1/4" h., each vessel with blue and green ground, gilding to rims and long-haired maiden among stylized trees and water, stamped "TURN TEPLITZ BOHEMIA/R St. K/MADE IN AUSTRIA" in red with incised "11 76" mark, each in very good condition with slight gilt wear along rims.. **$1,046**

Courtesy of Skinner, Inc., www.skinnerinc.com

Large Riessner, Stellmacher & Kessel Amphora vase with two loop handles and poppy decoration with faux jewels for centers, impressed "Amphora" in oval and impressed with early conjoined "R.St. & K" logo, excellent original condition, 15-1/2" h.................................... **$375**

Courtesy of Mark Mussio, Humler & Nolan, www.humlernolan.com

CERAMICS

van briggle pottery

THE VAN BRIGGLE POTTERY was established by Artus Van Briggle, who formerly worked for Rookwood Pottery in Colorado Springs, Colorado, at the turn of the 20th century. He died in 1904, but the pottery was carried on by his widow and others. From 1900 until 1920, the pieces were dated. It remains in production today, specializing in art pottery.

"Shell Girl" mulberry glaze figurine, circa 1930s, designed by William Higman, 7-1/2" h. **$109**

Courtesy of Rachel Davis Fine Arts, www.racheldavisfinearts.com

Maroon bee flower bowl with flower frog, 9" dia.............. **$116**

Courtesy of Strawser Auctions, www.strawserauctions.com

Early maroon leaf molded vase, 4-1/4"................................ **$87**

Courtesy of Strawser Auctions, www.strawserauctions.com

Maroon vase with Native American heads, 11-1/2" h. **$377**

Courtesy of Strawser Auctions, www.strawserauctions.com

Blue flowerpot with flower frog, reticulated leaf rim, 4".......... **$58**

Courtesy of Strawser Auctions, www.strawserauctions.com

top lot!

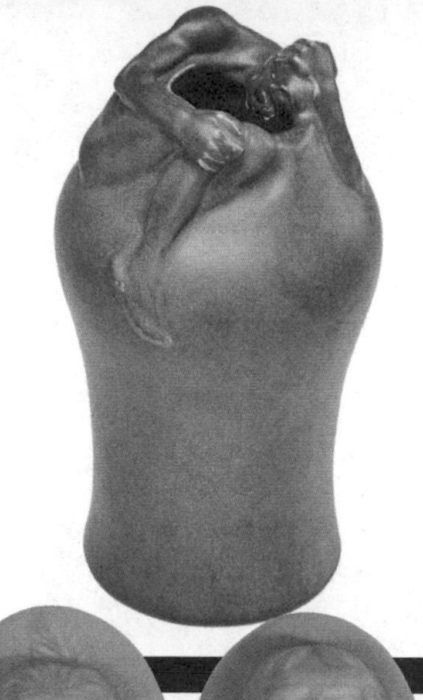

Important early Despondency vase, 1902, incised "AA VAN BRIGGLE 1902 III" in Artus Van Briggle's hand, overall excellent condition, minor dark scuffs to body, glazed-over firing lines to foot ring and base during production, 13-1/2" x 6-1/2". **$87,500**

COURTESY OF RAGO ARTS AND AUCTIONS, WWW.RAGOARTS.COM

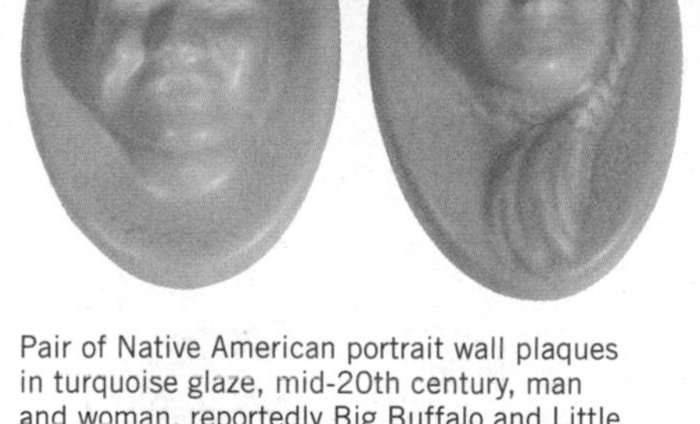

Pair of Native American portrait wall plaques in turquoise glaze, mid-20th century, man and woman, reportedly Big Buffalo and Little Star, each marked on reverse for Van Briggle Art Pottery, Colorado Springs, Colorado, along with "TE" (possible artist's mark), very good condition with light overall crazing and possible hairline to edge of female example, each 5-1/2" h. x 3-5/8" w. .. **$115**

Courtesy of Jeffrey S. Evans & Associates, www.jeffreysevans.com

Early blue/green fern mold vase, 8"............................ **$186**

Courtesy of Strawser Auctions, www.strawserauctions.com

Blue/green Art Nouveau lady vase, 11"........................... **$377**

Courtesy of Strawser Auctions, www.strawserauctions.com

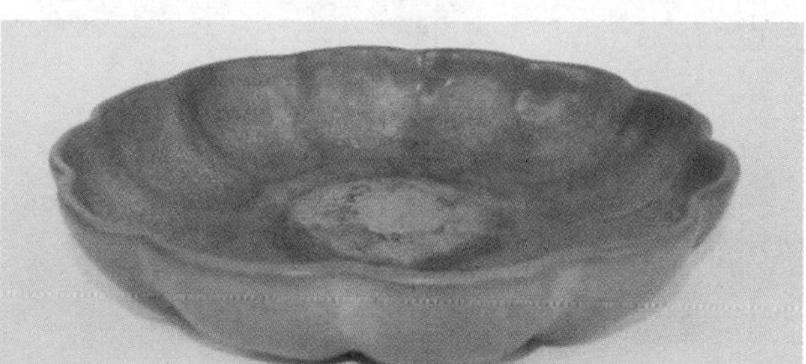

◄ Mt. Craig glaze console bowl, 9-1/2"................................ **$93**

Courtesy of Strawser Auctions, www.strawserauctions.com

10 Things You Didn't Know About **Van Briggle Pottery**

Artus and Anne Van Briggle on the job.

Courtesy of www.veniceclayartists.com

1 More than a century after Artus and Anne Van Briggle began handcrafting American art pottery for sale, 21st century artisans of Van Briggle Pottery & Tile have carried on the tradition, being mindful of the aesthetic awareness and approach the Van Briggles set forth while creating pieces that reveal both innovation and tradition. The company is reportedly the oldest active pottery in the United States, established in 1899. However, it "temporarily paused production" recently as change in ownership takes place, according to an automated email response from the company.

2 Van Briggle pottery is represented in museum exhibitions and historical collections around the world. The Colorado Springs Pioneers Museum (www.cspm.org) in Colorado Springs, Colorado, features an exhibition devoted to Van Briggle Pottery, as do the Pasadena Museum of History (www.pasadenahistory.org) in Pasadena, California, and the Farnsworth Art Museum (www.farnsworthmuseum.org) in Rockland, Maine.

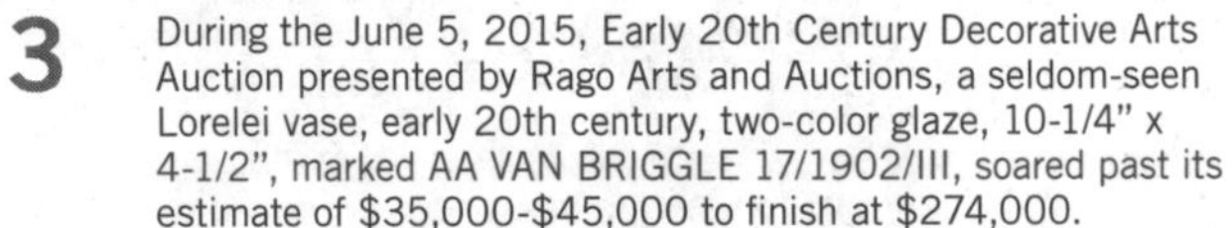

3 During the June 5, 2015, Early 20th Century Decorative Arts Auction presented by Rago Arts and Auctions, a seldom-seen Lorelei vase, early 20th century, two-color glaze, 10-1/4" x 4-1/2", marked AA VAN BRIGGLE 17/1902/III, soared past its estimate of $35,000-$45,000 to finish at $274,000.

Lorelei vase by Van Briggle realized $274,000 at auction.

Courtesy Rago Arts and Auctions, www.ragoarts.com

4 In addition to traditional pottery pieces, Van Briggle artisans also produce bookends and tiles. More traditional items sometimes include figures and elements of nature. For example, a grouping of five low bowls sporting seven flower frogs, with Persian Rose and Ming Blue glazes, 1910-1928, marked with various Van Briggle makers' marks, sold for $937.50 at auction on March 27, 2015 at Rago Arts and Auctions.

5 Artus Van Briggle began his creative journey as a renowned painter, studying in Europe. But it was pottery that captured his attention and became his passion. He and his wife, Anne, became respected pottery artists while working at Rookwood Pottery in Ohio. This is where they honed their craft and Artus began exploring the possibility of creating satin matte glazes using natural minerals in various colors. Although this type of glaze was evident in ancient Chinese pottery, it was not seen in modern art pottery.

6 A pair of stunning and detailed owl bookends featuring Van Briggle's Ming Blue and Mountain Crag glazes, circa 1910, realized $312.50 during an auction offered by Rago Arts and Auctions on March 27, 2015. There was some crazing present on the bookends, but overall they were deemed to be in nice condition, and measured 5-1/4" x 5-1/2" x 3-1/4".

Grouping of low bowls and flower frogs, 1910-1928, topped $937 at auction in 2015.

Courtesy Rago Arts and Auctions, www.ragoarts.com

7 For those who collect Van Briggle pottery or seek to do so, the Van Briggle Collector Society may serve as a helpful resource. Membership in the club comes with the opportunity to own a limited edition creation by Van Briggle Pottery, a commemorative tile, *Collector's Quarterly* newsletter, and the "Official Van Briggle Pottery Dating Guide." Learn more online: bit.ly/AT10THNGS33016.

Sources: www.vanbriggle.com;; www.manitouspringsheritagecenter.org; www.justartpottery.com/pages/pottery-newsletter/2004-04/; www.artpotteryblog.com; www.justartpottery.com; www.veniceclayartists.com

8 The Van Briggles decision to move to Colorado Springs may have seemed a bit odd, given that both of them were enjoying successful artistic careers working for Rookwood Pottery in Cincinnati, a region of the country noted for innovative and tremendous production of art pottery between the late 19th and the mid-20th centuries. However, the couple made the move in hopes of easing Artus' suffering related to tuberculosis, by living in a different climate and altitude.

9 Artus Van Briggle was just 35 years old when he died from tuberculosis in 1904, just three years into the production of Van Briggle Pottery. Anne Van Briggle remained at the helm of Van Briggle Pottery, leading the artisans and having a hand in producing items herself until 1912.

Van Briggle plate with goose heads in yellow glaze, 1906, marked, 1" x 5-1/2"; it sold at auction for $1,062.50.

Courtesy Rago Arts and Auctions, www.ragoarts.com

10 As with any pottery, the makers' marks of Van Briggle pottery not only aid in proper identification, but they tell a bit of the company's history. The primary symbol on the bottom of each piece is a double side-by-side letter "A" and the "Van Briggle" name. Early pieces often included Roman numerals indicating years of production, and after ceasing that practice in 1906, "Colorado Springs" or "Colo Springs" was added. This has evolved over the years, but the double-A symbol and "Van Briggle" name have been constant.

– Compiled by Antoinette Rahn

Three vases in light green, turquoise, and mulberry, first half 20th century, two with leaf motif, possibly shape 510, and one with oak leaf and acorn motif, each with conjoined A mark and script "Van Briggle / Colo. Spgs." mark, undamaged, turquoise example with crazing throughout, oak leaf example with some dust residue, 3-1/4" to 3-3/4" h. **$138**

Courtesy of Jeffrey S. Evans & Associates, www.jeffreysevans.com

Three vases in turquoise, first half 20th century, early daffodil vase with script "Van Briggle" mark and two different smaller floral vases, one with water lily motif, both with script "Van Briggle / Colo. Spgs" mark, each with conjoined A mark, crazing throughout, tall daffodil example with minor chip to base edge, remainder undamaged, 4-3/4" to 9 3/4" h...................................... **$161**

Courtesy of Jeffrey S. Evans & Associates, www.jeffreysevans.com

Three vases in mulberry with blue accents, first half 20th century, tall bottle-form example with scroll or loop double handles, example with double handles and floral band around middle, and shape 859 leaf vase, each with conjoined A mark and script "Van Briggle / Colo. Spgs" mark, undamaged, 5-5/8" to 9-3/4" h. **$259**

Courtesy of Jeffrey S. Evans & Associates, www.jeffreysevans.com

Two dragonfly bowls, blue example and pink/mulberry example, first quarter 20th century, each with conjoined A and "Van Briggle" script mark to underside, undamaged, 8-1/4" to 8-1/2" dia., each 2" h. **$138**

Courtesy of Jeffrey S. Evans & Associates, www.jeffreysevans.com

Three vases in pink/mulberry, conch shell example, stylized floral motif example, and pinched-rim example with vertical twists, each with conjoined A mark and script "Van Briggle / Colo Spgs." mark, mid-20th century, undamaged, crazing throughout floral motif example, 3-3/4" to 5" h. **$115**

Courtesy of Jeffrey S. Evans & Associates, www.jeffreysevans.com

Plate in green to purple glaze with floral or foliate decoration around rim, first quarter 20th century, conjoined A mark, script "Van Briggle" with illegible date, possibly 1906, and impressed "60 / A" shape or similar mark, undamaged, 8" dia. **$748**

Courtesy of Jeffrey S. Evans & Associates, www.jeffreysevans.com

CERAMICS

wedgwood

IN 1754, JOSIAH WEDGWOOD and Thomas Whieldon of Fenton Vivian, Staffordshire, England, became partners in a pottery enterprise. Their products included marbled, agate, tortoiseshell, green glaze, and Egyptian black wares.

In 1759, Wedgwood opened his own pottery at the Ivy House works, Burslem. In 1764, he moved to the Brick House (Bell Works) at Burslem. The pottery concentrated on utilitarian pieces.

Between 1766 and 1769, Wedgwood built the famous works at Etruria. Among the most-renowned products of this plant were the Empress Catherina of Russia dinner service (1774) and the Portland vase (1790s). The firm also made caneware, unglazed earthenwares (drabwares), piecrust wares, variegated and marbled wares, black basalt (developed in 1768), Queen's or creamware, and Jasperware (perfected in 1774).

Bone china was produced under the direction of Josiah Wedgwood II between 1812 and 1822, and was revived in 1878. Moonlight Lustre was made from 1805 to 1815. Fairyland Lustre began in 1920. All Lustre production ended in 1932.

A museum was established at the Etruria pottery in 1906. When Wedgwood moved to its modern plant at Barlaston, North Staffordshire, the museum was expanded.

Pair of rare Auro basalt vases, circa 1880s, raised gilt and bronze lilies and leaves, inscribed "Lilium Auratum S. 513" on base with impressed "WEDGWOOD" in all capital letters, 9-1/4" h., 4-1/4" dia. Auro ware was an experimental line Wedgwood sold in the 1880s. **$1,722**

Courtesy of New Orleans Auction Galleries, www.neworleansauction.com

Rare Auro basalt vase, circa 1880s, bronze and gilt lilies and leaves, impressed "WEDGWOOD" in all capital letters, hand-inscribed "S. 513 Lilium Auro Ware", overall very good condition, small loss to one raised flower stamen (anther), light scuffs to bottom of foot rim consistent with use, 9" h., 3-1/2" dia. opening. Auro ware was an experimental line Wedgwood sold in the 1880s. **$2,337**

Courtesy of New Orleans Auction Galleries, www.neworleansauction.com

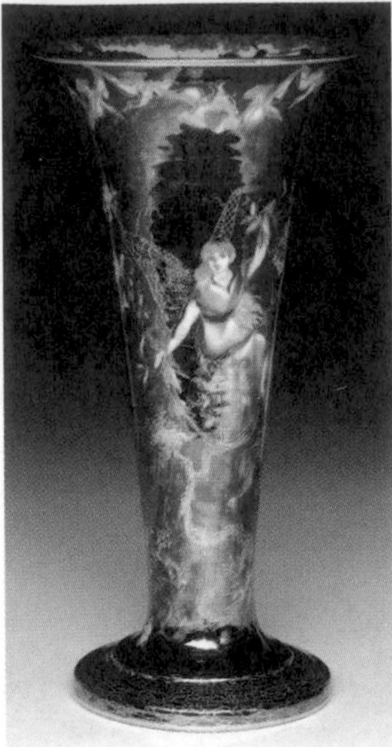

Fairyland Lustre vase in Butterfly Women pattern with butterfly women on front and back dressed in blue gowns with gilded wings and sitting on tree branch, band of birds in flight around flaring lip, Midnight Lustre background, interior with band of fairies in flight against Pearl Lustre background, signed on underside with "Wedgwood England Z4968" brown Portland Vase mark, very good to excellent condition, 9-3/8" h. **$3,792**

Courtesy of James D. Julia Auctioneers, Fairfield, Maine, www.jamesdjuliacom

Pair of Fairyland Lustre baluster vases with mottled orange interiors, circa 1915-1929, exteriors with polychrome hummingbirds with gilt outline, upper edge with gilt cranes, marked "Wedgwood, Made in England, 11, Z5294", 5" h., 5-1/2" dia. **$554**

Courtesy of New Orleans Auction Galleries, www.neworleansauction.com

Commemorative octagonal bowl in Fairyland Lustre Woodland Bridge pattern on both interior and exterior panels, interior against daylight sky, exterior against midnight sky, with original paperwork and box, signed "Fairyland Lustre WOODLAND BRIDGE Based upon an original design by Daisy Makeig-Jones Wedgwood designer 1914-1931 Number 85 In a Limited Edition of 100 Wedgwood Bone China Made in England" on underside, very good to excellent condition, box with torn corner, 9" dia. at widest. **$2,074**

Courtesy of James D. Julia Auctioneers, Fairfield, Maine, www.jamesdjuliacom

Fairyland Lustre vase in Firbolgs IV pattern with brown firbolgs against dark red background with gilded outlines and details, signed on underside with "Wedgwood England Z5200" gold Portland Vase mark, very good to excellent condition, 8" h. **$1,007**

Courtesy of James D. Julia Auctioneers, Fairfield, Maine, www.jamesdjuliacom

Fairyland Lustre commemorative plaque in The Enchanted Palace design with torch-illuminated stairway leading from water's edge to palace above, golden snake with bird's head climbing tree toward bird's nest with chicks against blue star-filled sky, in original wooden frame, marked "The Enchanted Palace Based upon an original Wedgwood design in Fairyland Lustre produced in 1922 No. 205 in a Limited Edition of 250 Wedgwood Bone China Made in England" on backside, with original paperwork and original box, plaque in very good to excellent condition, box torn at two corners with yellowed tape on two ends, plaque 8" w. x 11-3/4" h., 10-1/2" w. x 14-1/4" h. overall................ **$1,778**

Courtesy of James D. Julia Auctioneers, Fairfield, Maine, www.jamesdjuliacom

Pair of black Jasper covered urns with "Dancing Hours" decoration, 20th century, marked "Wedgwood, Made in England, 66", overall excellent condition, fine line of grout residue at socle of one urn, 10-1/2" h., 4" dia. **$1,169**

Courtesy of New Orleans Auction Galleries, www.neworleansauction.com

Fairyland Lustre vase and cover, circa 1920, pattern Z5157 Candlemas to covered vase shape 2046, printed mark, vase collar with rim chip professionally restored, 11" h. **$4,305**

Courtesy of Skinner, Inc., www.skinnerinc.com

▲ Six Imari palette plates, 19th century, 8 1/4" dia. **$62**

Courtesy of Pook & Pook, Inc., pookandpook.com

► Tricolor Jasper dip diceware cup and cover, late 18th/early 19th century, with foliate molded handle and relief to cover, black ground with terra-cotta-colored quatrefoils to white engine-turned dicing, impressed mark, cover with replaced ball finial, cup with restored handle and firing flaw to rim, 3" h..................... **$1,353**

Courtesy of Skinner, Inc., www.skinnerinc.com

Tricolor Jasper dip diceware sugar bowl and cover, 19th century, cylindrical shape with applied white foliate relief to domed cover and bowl bordering dark blue ground with green quatrefoils to white engine-turned dicing, impressed mark, very good condition, 3-1/2" h............ **$984**

Courtesy of Skinner, Inc., www.skinnerinc.com

Dark blue Jasper dip incense burner and cover, early 19th century, applied white foliate festoons to blue bowl mounted atop tails of three dolphins set on triangular base bordered with laurel and berries, with reticulated cover and solid white jasper insert disc, impressed mark, firing line to tail of one dolphin, small chip to upper lip of dolphin, 5" h. **$1,599**

Courtesy of Skinner, Inc., www.skinnerinc.com

CERAMICS

weller pottery

WELLER POTTERY WAS made from 1872 to 1945 at a pottery established originally by Samuel A. Weller at Fultonham, Ohio, and moved in 1882 to Zanesville, Ohio.

Weller's famous pottery slugged it out with several other important Zanesville potteries for decades. Cross-town rivals such as Roseville, Owens, La Moro, and McCoy were all serious fish in a fairly small and well-stocked lake. While Weller occasionally landed some solid body punches with many of his better art lines, the prevailing thought was that his later production ware just wasn't up to snuff.

Samuel Weller was a notorious copier and, it is said, a bit of a scallywag. He paid designers such as William Long to bring their famous discoveries to Zanesville. He then attempted to steal their secrets, and, when successful, renamed them and made them his own.

After World War I, when the cost of materials became less expensive than the cost of labor, many companies, including the famous Rookwood Pottery, increased their output of less expensive production ware. Weller Pottery followed along in the trend of production ware by introducing scores of interesting and unique lines, the likes of which have never been created anywhere else, before or since.

◀ Dickens Ware II vase with female golfer, impressed "Weller Dickens Ware, X, 355" and "W" on bottom, artist initials "EW" on side of piece in brown slip, excellent original condition, 7-3/8" h. **$450**

Courtesy of Mark Mussio, Humler & Nolan, www.humlernolan.com

◀ Dickens Ware II vase with male golfer, impressed "Weller Dickens Ware, 607" and "W." on bottom, artist initial "Z" incised along side of piece, two areas where glaze flaked off golfer's legs, 11-1/4" h. **$450**

Courtesy of Mark Mussio, Humler & Nolan, www.humlernolan.com

▲ Etched Matt jardiniere with large pink tulip on either side, incised and painted "Weller" on bottom, nick on one etched line, hand-carved, 8-1/8" h. x 11-1/4" w. **$1,000**

Courtesy of Mark Mussio, Humler & Nolan, www.humlernolan.com

In addition to a number of noteworthy production lines, Weller continued in the creation of hand-painted ware long after Roseville abandoned them. Some of the more interesting Hudson pieces, for example, are post-World War I pieces. Even later lines, such as Bonito, were hand painted and often signed by important artists such as Hester Pillsbury. The closer you look at Weller's output after 1920, the more obvious the fact that it was the only Zanesville company still producing both quality art ware and quality production ware.

For more information on Weller pottery, see *Warman's Weller Pottery Identification and Price Guide* by Denise Rago and David Rago.

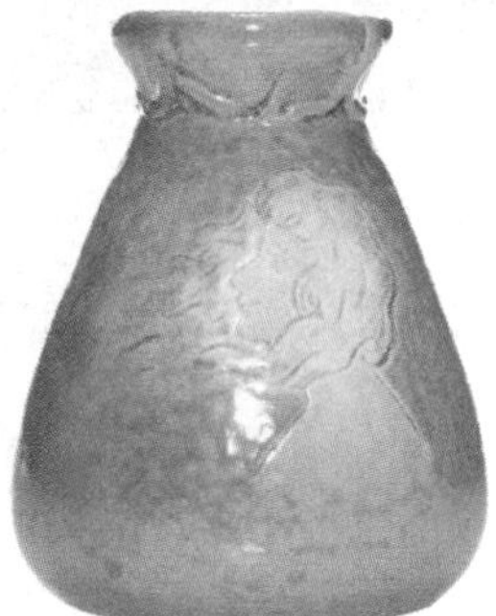

Etched Matt vase with profile of young woman on side, glossy finish, possibly trial or experimental piece, collar and rim hand-applied and twisted, incised "Weller Etched Matt 53" on bottom, label affixed to bottom from "The Rare, The Unusual, The Seldom Seen Weller Pottery Museum Exhibition" seminal show held in conjunction with publication of book by same name, work of Allan Wunch and Linda Carrigan............................ **$475**

Courtesy of Mark Mussio, Humler & Nolan, www.humlernolan.com

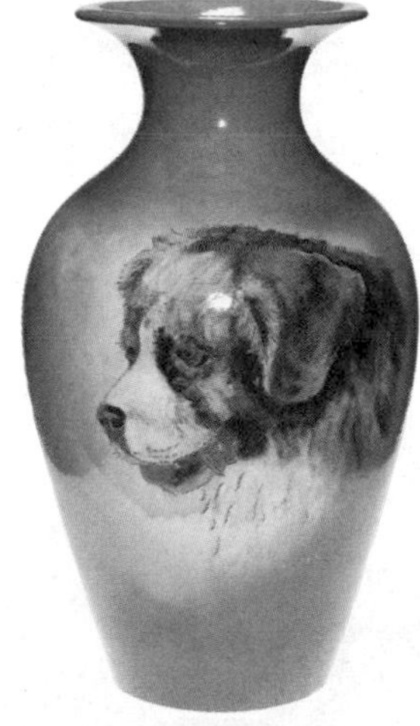

Rare Etched Ware vase with nearly life-size head of Saint Bernard etched into body of vase and slip painted by Albert "Doghead" Wilson, high glaze over green background, signed "A. Wilson after Landseer" on front and "Weller Decorative Etched Ware" on bottom, restoration to glaze loss mostly inside rim and to some lifting glaze, 27-3/8" h............. **$1,000**

Courtesy of Mark Mussio, Humler & Nolan, www.humlernolan.com

Fudzi vase with orchid-like flowers in shiny and dull glazes, impressed "X" with three hard-to-read numbers, excellent original condition, 7-1/2" h....................... **$1,100**

Courtesy of Mark Mussio, Humler & Nolan, www.humlernolan.com

Hudson gray vase with portrait of cat poised in front of full moon, impressed "Weller" on bottom, damaged in back, 7-3/4" h........................... **$450**

Courtesy of Mark Mussio, Humler & Nolan, www.humlernolan.com

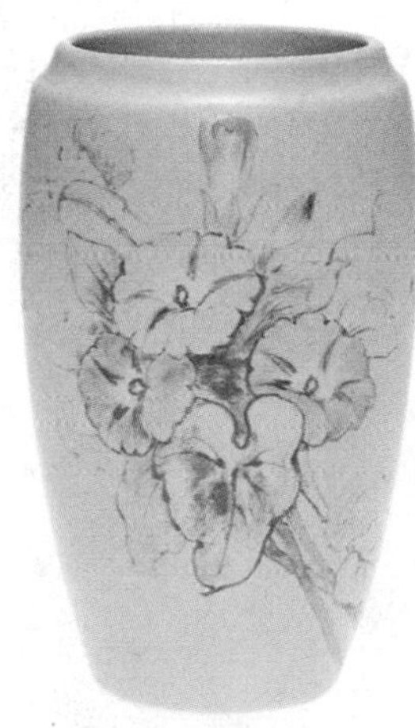

Hudson Perfecto vase with morning glory decoration, impressed "Weller" in large block letters on bottom, not artist signed, fine overall crazing, 7-1/2" h............... **$160**

Courtesy of Mark Mussio, Humler & Nolan, www.humlernolan.com

Hudson vase with dogwood decoration by M. Yinger, impressed "Weller" in large block letters and signed by artist on foot ring, fine overall crazing, glaze bubbles and small skip at foot ring, 8-5/8" h. **$100**

Courtesy of Mark Mussio, Humler & Nolan, www.humlernolan.com

Hudson vase with nasturtiums and leaves about shoulder by Sarah Reed McLaughlin, artist signed near base, excellent condition, 9-1/2" h............... **$300**

Courtesy of Mark Mussio, Humler & Nolan, www.humlernolan.com

Hudson scenic vase with windmills, houses, and sailboats by Sarah Reid McLaughlin, hand thrown, signed by artist in black slip on side and incised "Weller Pottery" on bottom, uncrazed, 8-1/8" h. **$1,000**

Courtesy of Mark Mussio, Humler & Nolan, www.humlernolan.com

Louwelsa vase with twin rust-colored lilies on long leafy stems, artist signed by Albert Haubrich on side, company impressed mark beneath, drill hole in bottom, flat base rim chip underneath, overall crazing and several body nicks, 13-1/2" h. x 9" w. **$250**

Courtesy of Mark Mussio, Humler & Nolan, www.humlernolan.com

Louwelsa scenic vase with two wading birds foraging among reeds by Levi Burgess, impressed marks beneath with number 324, conjoined artist monogram on side, excellent condition, fine overall crazing, 10-3/4" h. **$550**

Courtesy of Mark Mussio, Humler & Nolan, www.humlernolan.com

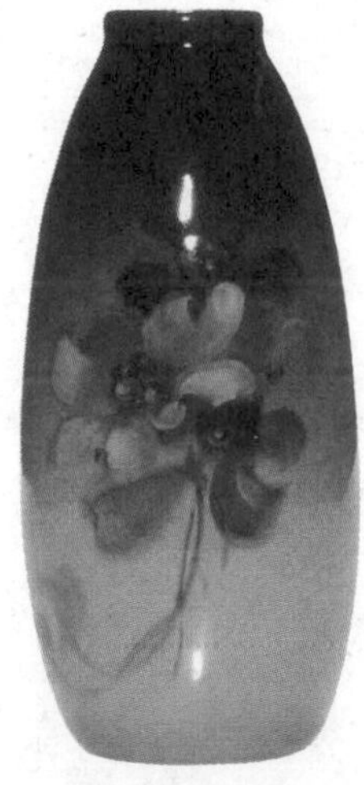

Blue Louwelsa vase with dogwood, marked with full circle "Louwelsa Weller" stamp, fine overall crazing and small bruise on top side of rim, 8-5/8" h. **$200**

Courtesy of Mark Mussio, Humler & Nolan, www.humlernolan.com

Rhead Faience tankard slip- and squeeze bag-decorated with trees with green foliage outlined in white, incised "Weller Faience, Rhead, E 580" with professional restoration to interior of rim and middle of handle, surface abrasions, fine overall crazing, 11" h. **$950**

Courtesy of Mark Mussio, Humler & Nolan, www.humlernolan.com

Tall Rochelle vase (Hudson variant) with woodbine by Hester Pillsbury with artist initials to side of piece in brown slip, incised "Weller" on base, fine overall crazing and glaze nick on top edge of rim, 13-1/8" h. **$250**

Courtesy of Mark Mussio, Humler & Nolan, www.humlernolan.com

Sicard buttressed bowl with floral design on exterior and purple luster on interior, unmarked, faint crazing and two nicks at rim, 2-1/2" h., 6-1/2" dia.......................... **$140**

Courtesy of Mark Mussio, Humler & Nolan, www.humlernolan.com

Souvenir vase from 1904 St. Louis World's Fair, incised and slip decorated with young entertainer wearing white cap, shirt, knickers and shoes, long green case slung across his back, marked "L.P.E. (Louisiana Purchase Expo), 1904, St Louis" in white slip on side, excellent condition, 5" h. **$160**

Courtesy of Mark Mussio, Humler & Nolan, www.humlernolan.com

Rare garden gnome with feather, unmarked, several restored breaks, overall roughness of glaze in production, 14-5/8" h......... **$600**

Courtesy of Mark Mussio, Humler & Nolan, www.humlernolan.com

Pan garden ornament with major damage, broken at knees and chest, flute broken and lost, and broken section of green vegetation on which he sits, incised "Weller Pottery" on base, 16" h........................ **$650**

Courtesy of Mark Mussio, Humler & Nolan, www.humlernolan.com

CERAMICS

zsolnay

ZSOLNAY POTTERY was made in Pecs, Hungary, in a factory founded in 1862 by Vilmos Zsolnay. Utilitarian earthenware was originally produced with an increase in art pottery production from as early as 1870. The highest level of production employed more than 1,000 workers.

The Art Nouveau era produced the most collectible and valuable pieces in today's marketplace. Examples are displayed in major art museums worldwide. Zsolnay is always well marked and easy to identify. One specialty was the metallic eosin glaze.

With more than 10,000 different forms created over the years, and dozens of glaze variations for each form, there is always something new being discovered in Zsolnay. Today the original factory size has been significantly reduced with pieces being made in a new factory.

Green eosin-glazed vase, 20th century, printed factory mark, drilled base, small areas of black irregularities to glaze about body, 17-1/4" h......... **$480**

Courtesy of Eldred's, www.eldreds.com

Moorish-style covered urn, late 19th/early 20th century, allover reticulated strapwork design in cream, brown, and pale yellow with gilded accents, gilt five churches mark and impressed factory marks, cover with extensive polychrome-enameled restorations, finial restored, crazing, 12" h..................... **$72**

Courtesy of Eldred's, www.eldreds.com

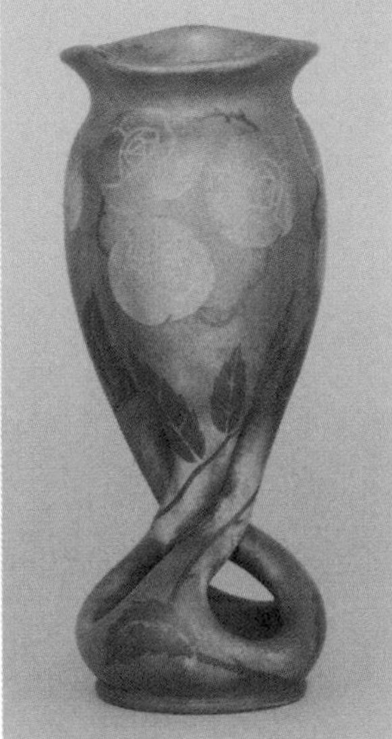

Eosin-glazed ceramic vase, circa 1900, flutter rim, organic body and twisted tripartite base, with stylized flowering rose vines in green, orange, and purple, five churches mark and impressed M 23 6181, scattered crazing, 9" h..... **$3,900**

Courtesy of Eldred's, www.eldreds.com

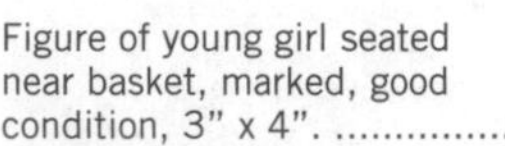

Figure of young girl seated near basket, marked, good condition, 3" x 4". **$30**

Courtesy of Woody Auction, www.woodyauction.com

Green eosin-glazed figure of woman undressing and preparing to bathe, 20th century, printed five churches mark and impressed 12, good condition, 9-3/4" h............ **$270**

Courtesy of Eldred's, www.eldreds.com

Two Moorish-style porcelain vases, late 19th/early 20th century, both in stylized bottle form with allover reticulated strapwork design in green, cream, brown, and pale yellow with gilded accents, both with crazing and age-typical wear; one with two C-scroll handles, gilded five churches and impressed factory marks, and numbered 2775, 6-3/4" h.; and one with impressed five churches factory mark, numbered "2_63" with traces of paper label, 7-1/2" h. **$330**

Courtesy of Eldred's, www.eldreds.com

Persian-style vase, late 19th/early 20th century, in Mosque lamp form with polychrome decoration of rooster and hen amid flowering shrubs, stylized geometric designs at rim and base, gilded accents, underglaze blue five churches mark and impressed 495(?), age-typical wear/loss to gilding, 8-1/4" h. **$960**

Courtesy of Eldred's, www.eldreds.com

Green eosin-glazed figure of Meditazione, circa 1933, modeled as standing monk gazing at ground while holding book behind his back, titled on base, base also inscribed "A Szentfoldi ut Emlekere-1933", printed gilded five churches mark, impressed factory mark and numbered 8154, surface abrasions to glaze, 15" h..... **$570**

Courtesy of Eldred's, www.eldreds.com

Three small vessels, late 19th/early 20th century, all decorated with Persian design of polychrome flowers and gilded accents, all with various underglaze blue and impressed factory marks, all with crazing and age-typical loss/wear to gilding, ewer with repaired foot rim chip, jug with reglued break to handle with small piece missing, vase in good condition, ewer 9-3/4" h., jug 8-1/4" h., and vase 7-3/4" h.. **$450**

Courtesy of Eldred's, www.eldreds.com

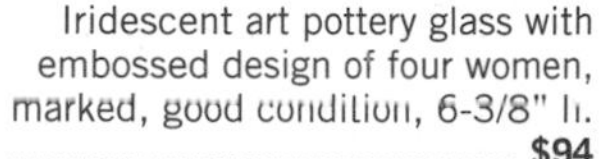

Iridescent art pottery glass with embossed design of four women, marked, good condition, 6-3/8" h. **$94**

Courtesy of Woody Auction, www.woodyauction.com

CHRISTMAS COLLECTIBLES

CHRISTMAS COLLECTIBLES REPRESENT the holiday celebrating the birth of Jesus Christ. Collectibles include ornaments, kugels, feather trees, candy containers, household décor, art, games, cards, and a plethora of other items from every corner of the world.

Original pen and watercolor illustration for *Snow Before Christmas*, Tasha Tudor (Oxford University Press, 1941, Hare S-61), two children on snow horses with hills in background, signed "T. Tudor" in image at lower right, image in near fine condition, adhesive evidence to most of verso, small marginal stain at upper left and lower right corners, sheet 9" x 8-1/4"........................... **$3,933**

Courtesy of Quinn's Auction Galleries, www.quinnsauction.com

"Two Children With Christmas Tree," Tasha Tudor, original watercolor with ink and graphite, basis for Christmas card, signed "T. Tudor" in image at lower left, framed under glass, Norman Rockwell Museum in Stockbridge, Massachusetts sticker on back of frame, 7-1/2" x 4" within matting. ... **$2,904**

Courtesy of Quinn's Auction Galleries, www.quinnsauction.com

"Christmas Cheer for Old Fort Dearborn," Paul Strayer (American, 1885-1981), oil on canvas, signed lower right, impression from stretcher bar visible, pattern of craquelure throughout, strokes of inpainting in background and foreground, possible inpainting surrounding standing figure on far right, 7-1/2" x 4" within matting. Provenance: From the collection of Illinois Governor Jim Thompson, Chicago. **$2,250**

Courtesy of Treadway Gallery, Inc., www.treadwaygallery.com

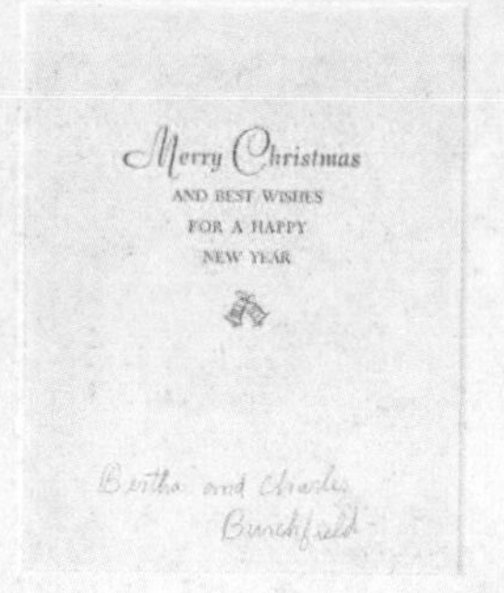

Christmas card, "The Night Before Christmas" by Charles E. Burchfield (American, 1893-1967), signed "Bertha and Charles Burchfield," 6-1/4" h. x 10-1/2" w.. **$787**

Courtesy of Cottone Auctions, www.cottoneauctions.com

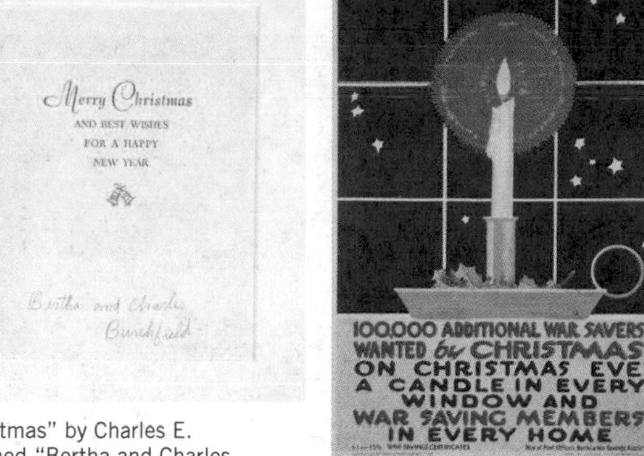

"100,000 Additional War Savers Wanted by Christmas" poster, monogram, Scotland, borders trimmed, original folds, 30" x 19-1/2"................... **$219**

Courtesy of Guernsey's, www.guernsey.com

When Santa Claus Was Young, Helen Reid Cross, first edition, London, Humphrey Milford, circa 1920, 48 pages, color frontispiece and black and white illustrations in text, 8vo, original wrappers, ribbon bound, publisher's original two-part box, scarce, near fine condition, light wear to box, ribbon frayed..................... **$123**

Courtesy of PBA Galleries, www.pbagaleries.com

Nine assorted blown-molded Christmas lights in various colors, fourth quarter 19th/first quarter 20th century, each with diamond pattern including one square example with bust of Queen Elizabeth on each side and anchor and registration markings under base, and one with embossed plain shield, ground and rough-broken rims, together with tin-frame example with various colored glass panels, 3-1/4" to 4" h...**$1,200**

Courtesy of Jeffrey S. Evans & Associates, www.jeffreysevans.com

Walt Disney Mickey Mouse light set, Noma Electric Corp., eight lights with different decals of Mickey, Minnie, and other Disney characters, in original box marked "Walt Disney Ent.," cover with Mickey and Minnie Mouse decorating Christmas tree with lights, excellent condition, matching box insert with creasing and wear, 16-1/4" x 6"..................... **$244**

Courtesy of Morphy Auctions, morphyauctions.com

Fourteen Crummles English limited edition Christmas boxes, enamel on copper, each with nutcracker Christmas motif and all #90 out of 100, with original fitted boxes and descriptive tags, each approximately 2-1/4" dia..**$185**

Courtesy of Kaminski Auctions, www.kaminskiauctions.com

Five KPM porcelain Christmas collector's plates, decoration in cobalt blue and gilt with legend "Wiehnachten" (Christmas) 1972, 1973, 1976, 1976, and 1977, with three original boxes, each marked with KPM globe and scepter, 7-1/2" dia.**$61**

Courtesy of Clars Auction Gallery, www.clars.com

Vintage Coloramic Christmas tree stand with box, tin with graphics of winter scene, with original box, excellent condition. **$30**

Courtesy of Milestone Auctions, www.milestoneauctions.com

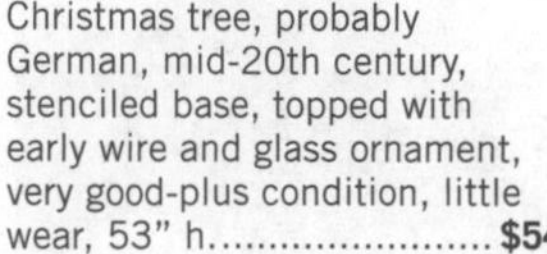

Christmas tree, probably German, mid-20th century, stenciled base, topped with early wire and glass ornament, very good-plus condition, little wear, 53" h........................**$549**

Courtesy of Morphy Auctions, morphyauctions.com

"Extra Fancy Miniature Tree Decorations," cardboard box with 24 assorted blown-glass ornaments for miniature tree, in original cotton padded box with Shackman, New York label, ornaments in excellent condition, box 9-1/2" x 3"... **$148**

Courtesy of Frasher's Doll Auctions, Oak Grove, Missouri

Three mercury glass ornaments, German, matching man and woman with exaggerated heads and pipe form, 4" each. **$696**

Courtesy of Dirk Soulis Auctions, www.dirksoulisauctions.hibid.com

Rare red ribbed blown glass ball-form German kugel, very good condition, 3-3/4" dia. **$7,865**

Courtesy of Conestoga Auction Co., www.conestogaauction.com

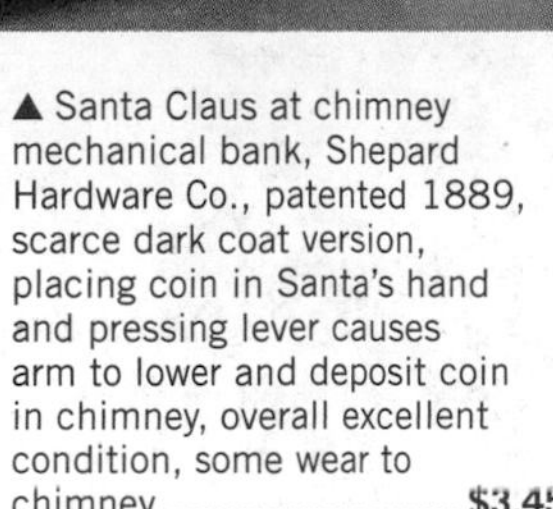

▲ Santa Claus at chimney mechanical bank, Shepard Hardware Co., patented 1889, scarce dark coat version, placing coin in Santa's hand and pressing lever causes arm to lower and deposit coin in chimney, overall excellent condition, some wear to chimney. **$3,451**

Courtesy of Bertoia Auctions, www.bertoiaauctions.com

Antique German kugel, cobalt blue blown-glass geometric cluster of grapes, very good condition, 4-1/2" h. **$6,500**

Courtesy of Conestoga Auction Co., www.conestogaauction.com

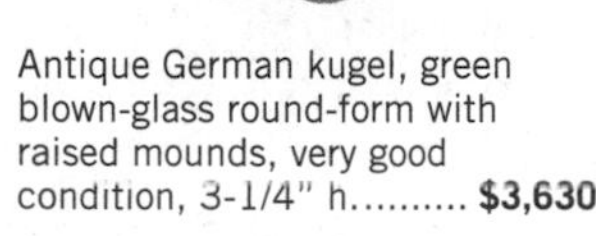

Antique German kugel, green blown-glass round-form with raised mounds, very good condition, 3-1/4" h. **$3,630**

Courtesy of Conestoga Auction Co., www.conestogaauction.com

Figural Santa Claus match holder and striker, Royal Bayreuth, red jacket, blue mark, good condition, no chips, cracks, or repairs, 4-1/4". **$2,478**

Courtesy of Woody Auction, www.woodyauction.com

Carved wooden Santa Claus countertop display figure, found in Pennsylvania, restoration to feet, 35" h..................... **$2,040**

Courtesy of Copake Auction, Inc., www.copakeauction.com

"The Old Elf" carving, John L. Heatwole (Shenandoah Valley of Virginia, 1948-2006), Santa Claus in red suit wearing mittens, holding teddy bear, and carrying side satchel, polychrome paint, base inscribed with title on reverse and "JL Heatwole VA. '98" on one side, 1998, 9-1/2" h., 2-3/8" x 2-1/4" base. **$1,200**

Courtesy of Jeffrey S. Evans & Associates, www.jeffreysevans.com

Early German windup composition Santa Claus holding small feather-style tree, all original with original "Made in Germany" decal on foot, excellent condition, windup works well, 10" high..........**$1,920**

Courtesy of Milestone Auctions, www.milestoneauctions.com

Tin litho Santa Claus by Arnold, mechanical, working, excellent to near mint condition, original box missing top, 3-3/4" h.... **$847**

Courtesy of Richard Opfer Auctioneering, Inc., www.opferauction.com

◀ Santa Claus on sleigh battery-operated toy, Japan, 1950s, lithographed tin and vinyl reindeer and Santa head, very good working condition, 17" l. **$154**

Courtesy of Potter & Potter Auctions, www.potterauctions.com

▶ Celluloid and tin windup "Santa Claus on Sled" pulled by reindeer, with box, all original, excellent working condition, 8"....................... **$78**

Courtesy of Milestone Auctions, www.milestoneauctions.com

top lot!

Tin litho Santa Claus automobile, Tippco, German, full-figured lithographed Santa driver, original tree in rear, dry cell makes tree light up, marked "Dunlop Cord" on tin litho tires, excellent near mint condition, 12-1/4" l. x 10-1/4" h. $30,000

COURTESY OF MORPHY AUCTIONS, MORPHYAUCTIONS.COM

Christmas tin, early 20th century, marked on base "Carr's & Co. Biscuit Manufacturer Carlisle," wear to surface all around, dents and dings, 7-1/2" h. **$62**

Courtesy of Nest Egg Auctions, www.nesteggauctions.com

Vintage tinsmith-made Christmas village decoration with three steeples including clock tower, red painted roof, white sand-textured painted surface, good condition, wear, losses and dents, 14 1/4" h. x 26-1/2" w. **$393**

Courtesy of Conestoga Auction Co., www.conestogaauction.com

Marx Nativity Set in box, lithographed metal stable with 13 figures, Christmas story booklet, electric light, and cord, near mint condition, box with edge wear, box 11" l. **$92**

Courtesy of Morphy Auctions, morphyauctions.com

Waldo Peirce (New York/Maine/Massachusetts, 1884-1970), "Letters to Florida," two decorated Christmas envelopes in one frame, pen and ink with watercolor, burro from Tucson in 1957 and elephant named Phil in 1962, airmail borders, good condition, 4" x 9-1/2" each, 19" x 18-3/4" overall. **$480**

Courtesy of Thomaston Place Auction Galleries, www.thomastonauction.com

R. H. Palenske (American, 1884-1954), "Christmas Travelers" etching, signed in pencil, mat burn and tape remnants throughout edges, toning to verso, 10" x 7-7/8". **$36**

Courtesy of Rachel Davis Fine Arts, www.racheldavisfinearts.com

"A Merry Christmas and A Happy New Year" advertising tin, very good condition, minor soiling and scraping throughout, 3-1/2" h........... **$122**

Courtesy of Morphy Auctions, morphyauctions.com

Elihu Vedder (American, 1836-1923), "Peace on Earth, Good Will to Man" Christmas card design, circa 1882, watercolor on board, 8-7/8" x 7" sight. **$4,500**

Courtesy of Heritage Auctions, ha.com

Six vintage Christmas candy containers, painted pressed cardboard with glitter and crepe paper, three with feather hair tufts, "Made in Western Germany" stamped on inside of neck, very good condition, smallest snowman with paint loss and missing piece on backside, largest snowman with paint flaking on hat, 6" and smaller............ **$72**

Courtesy of Stephenson's Auction, www.stephensonsauction.com

WE GIVE
CHRISTMAS CLUB
THRIFTIES
REDEEMABLE IN CASH
at CHRISTMAS

"We Give Christmas Club Thrifties" double-sided tin sign marked "A-M Sign Co. Lynchburg, VA 4-54," with rust and loss, some bubbled paint, 20" x 28"......................... **$102**

Courtesy of Mark Mattox Auctioneer & Real Estate Broker, Inc., mattoxauctions.com/auctions

C.D. Kenny advertising tray with child in Christmas clothes, good condition, paint nicks to border and edges, main field with abrasions and paint chips, 9-1/4" dia........................... **$61**

Courtesy of Morphy Auctions, morphyauctions.com

▲ Christmas stocking costume jewelry brooch, yellow metal with enamel and rhinestone-accented gifts, marked "Weiss" on back, 2-3/4" l................. **$54**

Courtesy of Main Street Mining Co. Auctions, mainstreetmining.com

◀ Christmas tree costume jewelry brooch, pink and white rhinestones, unmarked, 3-1/4" l. **$72**

Courtesy of Main Street Mining Co. Auctions, mainstreetmining.com

top lot!

John McCrady (American/New Orleans, 1911-1968), "Christmas Near Oxford, Mississippi," 1949, gouache on board, unsigned, "Caller-Times Art Exhibit and Sale" label, "Arts & Crafts Club" stamp and handwritten authentication inscription by Mary Basso McCrady en verso, accompanied by copy of letter of authentication dated Dec. 8, 1980, signed by Mary Basso McCrady, 19-1/4" x 26-1/4"........................$53,760

COURTESY OF NEAL AUCTION CO., WWW.NEALAUCTIONS.COM

CIVIL WAR COLLECTIBLES

THE CIVIL WAR began on April 12, 1861, at Fort Sumter, the Confederates surrendered at Appomattox Courthouse on April 9, 1865, and all official fighting ceased on May 26, 1865.

Between the beginning and end of the Civil War, the way wars were fought and the tools soldiers used changed irrevocably. When troops first formed battle lines to face each other near Bull Run Creek in Virginia on June 21, 1861, they were dressed in a widely disparate assemblage of uniforms. They carried state-issued, federally supplied, or brought-from-home weapons, some of which dated back to the Revolutionary War, and marched to the orders and rhythms of tactics that had served land forces for at least the previous 100 years.

Four short years later, the generals and soldiers had made major leaps in the art of warfare on the North American continent, having developed the repeating rifle, the movement of siege artillery by rail, the extensive employment of trenches and field fortifications, the use of ironclad ships for naval combat, the widespread use of portable telegraph units on the battlefield, the draft, the organized use of African-American troops in combat, and even the levying of an income tax to finance the war.

For some Civil War enthusiasts, collecting war relics is the best way to understand the heritage and role of the thousands who served. Collecting mementoes and artifacts from the Civil War is not a new hobby. Even before the war ended, people were gathering remembrances. As with any period of warfare, the first collectors were the participants themselves. Soldiers sent home scraps of flags, collected minie-ball shattered logs, purchased privately marketed unit insignias, or obtained a musket or carbine for their own

Civil War captain's coat and sash, circa 1861-1865, blue broadcloth body with Eagle I buttons, infantry captain's shoulder straps, black velvet lining in collar, green silk lining, cotton sleeve lining with blue stars and stripes, and officer's sash. **$2,829**

Courtesy of Skinner, Inc., www.skinnerinc.com

Civil War artillery shell jacket, circa 1861-1865, size four blue broadcloth body with red worsted tape, brass general service buttons, brass hardware for shoulder scales, heavy gray jean cloth lining, and cotton sheeting in sleeves. .. **$1,722**

Courtesy of Skinner, Inc., www.skinnerinc.com

South Carolina Confederate veteran's uniform jacket, gray wool with navy blue standup collar, cotton twill lining, nine-button front, eight (of nine) 19 mm South Carolina brass buttons with "Waterbury Companies Inc." back marks, "New York Clothing House / Baltimore" tailor's tag on inside. **$1,062**

Courtesy of Heritage Auctions, ha.com

Enlisted kepi, blue wool, 1870s-1880s, leather chin strap, eagle-insignia buttons, front with M1872 infantry insignia with numbers "34," interior with partially restitched leather sweat band, no head liner. **$350**

Courtesy of Heritage Auctions, ha.com

Civil War forage cap with original insignia, standard issue federal kepi, applied infantry bugle over "104" on top of hat, which appears original to use, leather visor and chin strap, eagle side buttons, no lining, contract paper label in top of crown reads, "Size No. 6 71/2 U.S. ARMY, T. G. & Co.," period calling card found in hat reads "Capt John Foley" along with two calling cards that read "Mrs John Foley." **$1,750**

Courtesy of Heritage Auctions, ha.com

use after the war. Civilians wrote to prominent officers asking for autographs, exchanged photographs (*carte de visites*) with soldiers, or kept scrapbooks of items that represented the progress of the conflict.

After the war, the passion for owning a piece of it did not subside. Early collectors gathered representative weapons, collected battlefield-found relics, and created personal or public memorials to the veterans. Simultaneously, surplus sales emerged on a grand scale. This was the heyday of Civil War collecting. Dealers such as Francis Bannerman made hundreds of Civil War relics available to the general public.

Following World War II, a new wave of collecting emerged. Reveling in the victories in Japan and in Europe, Americans were charged with a renewed sense of patriotism and heritage. At the same time, newspapers started to track the passing of the last few veterans of the Civil War. As the nation paid tribute to the few survivors of the Rebellion, it also acknowledged that the 100-year anniversary of the war was fast upon them. In an effort to capture a sense of the heritage, Civil War buffs began collecting in earnest.

During the Civil War Centennial in the 1960s, thousands of outstanding relics emerged from closets, attics, and long-forgotten chests, while collectors eagerly bought and sold firearms, swords, and uniforms. It was during this time that metal detectors first played a large role in Civil War collecting, as hundreds donned headphones and swept battlefields and campsites, uncovering thousands of spent bullets, buttons, belt plates, and artillery projectiles.

By the 1970s, as this first wave of prominent and easily recognized collectibles disappeared into collections, Civil War buffs discovered carte-de-visites, tintypes, and ambrotypes. Accoutrements reached prices that far outstretched what surplus dealers could have only hoped for just a few years prior. The demand for soldiers' letters and diaries prompted people to open boxes and drawers to rediscover long-forgotten manuscript records of battles and campaigns.

By the end of the 20th century, collectors who had once provided good homes for the objects began to disperse their collections, and Civil War relics reemerged on the market. It is this era of Civil War relic reemergence in which we currently live. The fabulous collections assembled in the late 1940s and early 1950s are reappearing.

It has become commonplace to have major sales of Civil War artifacts by a few major auction houses, in addition to the private trading, local auctions, and Internet sales of these items. These auction houses handle the majority of significant Civil War items coming to the marketplace.

The majority of these valuable items are in repositories of museums, universities, and colleges, but many items were also traded between private citizens. Items that are being released by museums and from private collections make up the base of items currently being traded and sold to collectors of Civil War material culture. In addition, many family collections acquired over the years have been recently coming to the marketplace as new generations have decided to liquidate some of them.

Collectors in the same fashion as any material cultural item now acquire Civil War items. Individuals interested in antiques and collectibles find items at farm auction sales, yard sales, estate sales, specialized auctions, private collectors trading or selling items, and the Internet and online auction sales.

Provenance is important in Civil War collectibles - maybe even more important than with most other collectibles. Also, many Civil War items have well-documented provenance as they come from family collections or their authenticity has been previously documented by auction houses, museums, or other experts in the field.

For more information on Civil War memorabilia, see *Warman's Civil War Collectibles Identification and Price Guide*, 3rd edition, by Russell L. Lewis.

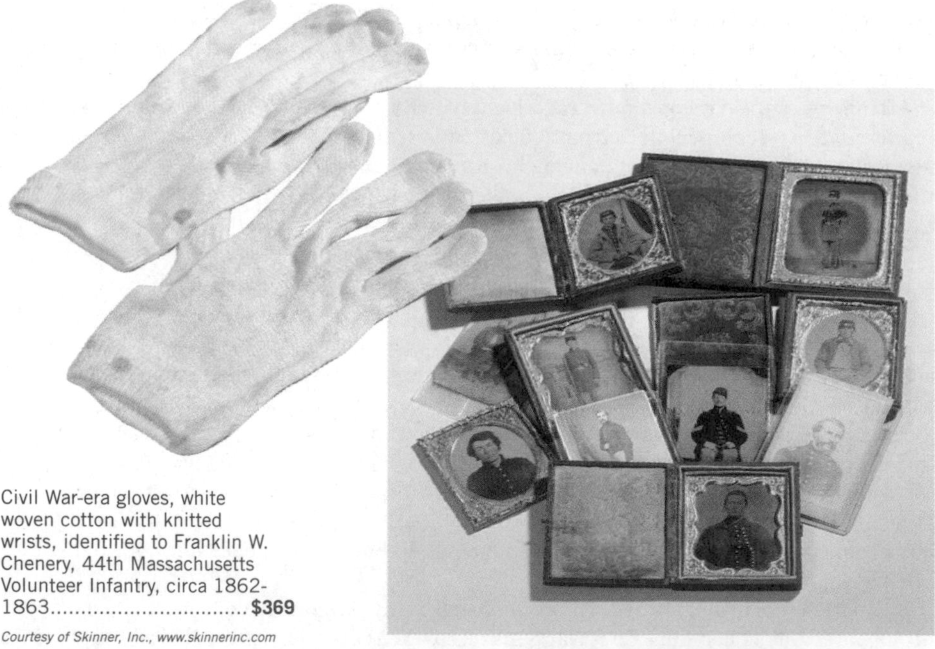

Civil War-era gloves, white woven cotton with knitted wrists, identified to Franklin W. Chenery, 44th Massachusetts Volunteer Infantry, circa 1862-1863................................ **$369**

Courtesy of Skinner, Inc., www.skinnerinc.com

Ten Civil War images, circa 1861-1865, tintypes and carte-de-visites of soldiers in various poses and uniforms............**$738**

Courtesy of Skinner, Inc., www.skinnerinc.com

Civil War 36 caliber pistol, serial No. 4258, barrel 5-3/4" l., overall 13-1/2" l. **$200**

Courtesy of Mosby & Co. Auctions, www.mosbyauctions.net

Civil War-era encased Tranter revolver, mid-19th century, 5-3/4" octagon .44 caliber barrel, five-shot percussion pistol, engraved frame, serial No. 20720, stamped "Tranter's Patent" on frame and loading lever, double-action with pass-through spur trigger, checkered wood grip, original fitted mahogany case with accoutrements of brass powder flask, bullet mold, cleaning rod, caps, slugs, balls and jelly, case 2-1/2" h. x 15" x 7-3/4", overall 12-1/2". **$2,500**

Courtesy of Burchard Galleries, www.burchardgalleries.com

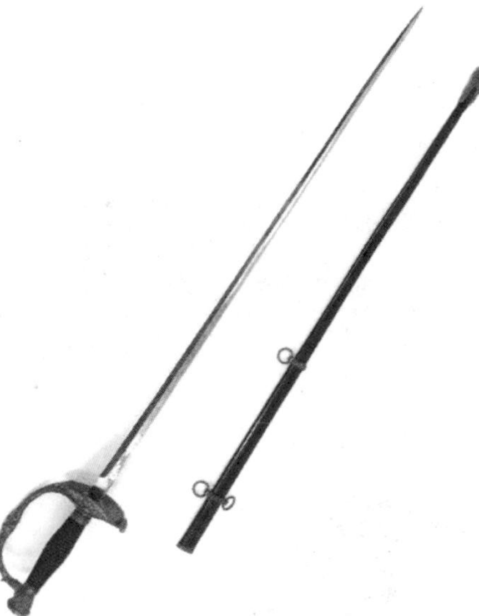

U.S. Civil War staff and field officer's parade sword in scabbard, by Hartley & Graham, maker's mark on ricasso, etched blade with eagle and U.S., leather-and-wire-wrapped grip, with folding guard, blade 30" l., 38" l overall. **$210**

Courtesy of Stephenson's Auction, www.stephensonsauction.com

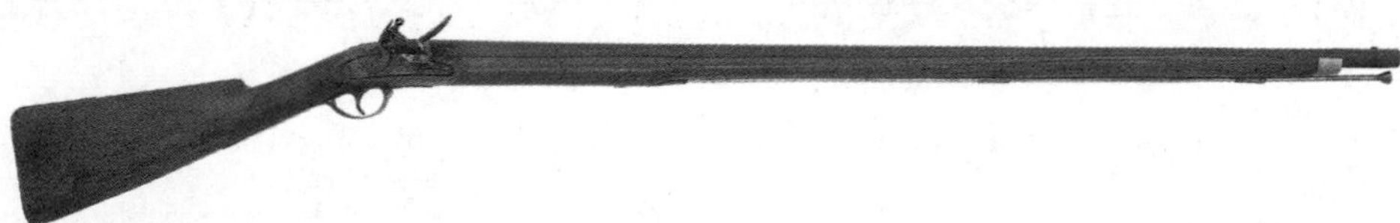

New England Militia flintlock musket gun, marked at breech with "US," "JM" and "P" proofs, British-made lock marked "John" with illegible last name and "Warranted," functioning action, butt tang sparsely engraved, walnut stock, 57" overall with 41-3/4" round smoothbore barrel. **$562**

Courtesy of Heritage Auctions, ha.com

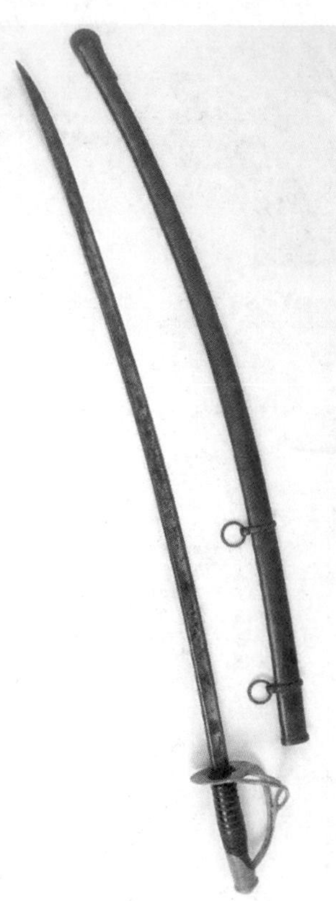

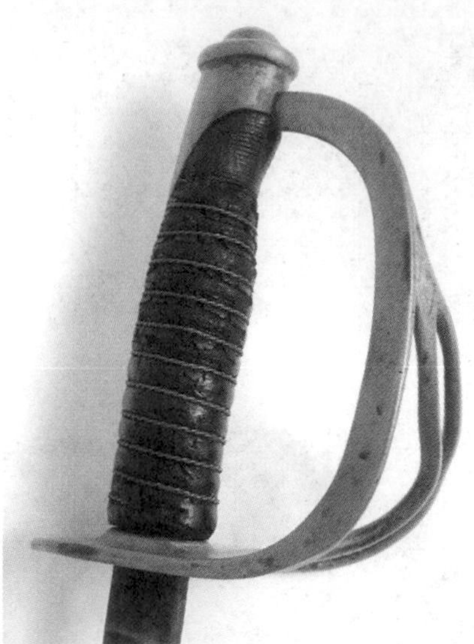

U.S. Civil War 1864 cavalry sword in scabbard, impressed on right ricasso "U.S.," "J.C.W.," and "864," by Mansfield & Lamb, maker's mark stamped on left ricasso, leather-and-wire-wrapped grip, blade 34-1/2" l., 42-3/4" l. overall.......... **$425**

Courtesy of Stephenson's Auction, www.stephensonsauction.com

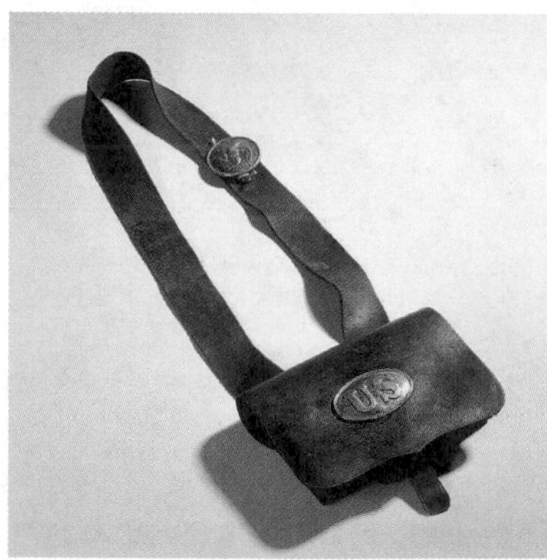

Civil War cartridge box, circa mid-to-late 19th century, black leather box with lead-filled brass plate marked "US," tin cartridge inserts inside box, leather shoulder strap with lead-filled brass eagle breastplate. **$677**

Courtesy of Skinner, Inc., www.skinnerinc.com

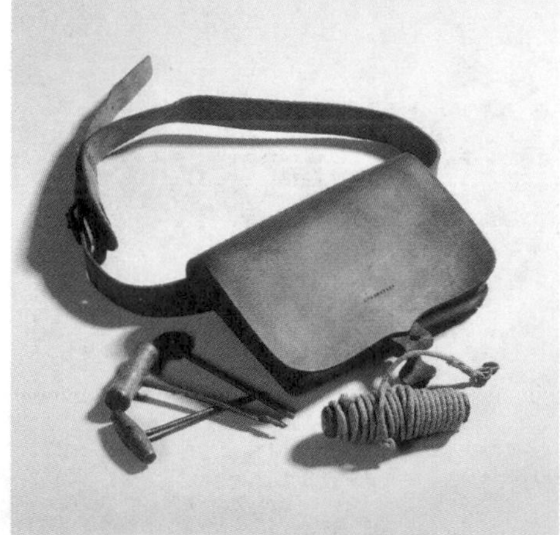

Civil War artillery gunner's pouch, belt, and tools, circa 1861-1865, leather belt with iron roller buckle, marked on inside "H. Richardson / Co. E. 1st Arty. N.Y.S.V.," marked inside flap "H. Richardson / Co. E. 1st Arty. N.Y.S.V.," pouch holds vent-clearing punch, lanyard, and two gimlets. **$1,046**

Courtesy of Skinner, Inc., www.skinnerinc.com

Cowpens-style flag, circa mid-to-late 19th century, red and white machine-sewn wool bunting stripes, blue wool bunting canton with 12 hand-sewn white cotton stars in circle with one star in center, coarse linen hoist with some repairs and hand-sewn grommets, with attached note, "Civil War flag brought in by Dr. Hart, will get data on it later," 51" h. x 89" l. **$923**

Courtesy of Skinner, Inc., www.skinnerinc.com

Civil War medal identified to Samuel K. Thompson, 5th Kansas Cavalry and 54th United States Colored Troops, circa 1865, 14k gold with rectangular bar at top, front marked "5th Kas: Cav: & 54th U.S.C.T.," back of bar marked "Samuel K. Thompson," shield below bar marked with battles fought in 1863 with pair of applied crossed sabers, bottom crescent and star (VII Corps badge) engraved with crossed muskets and other battles and central Masonic device, back engraved with additional battles. **$2,829**

Courtesy of Skinner, Inc., www.skinnerinc.com

Paint-decorated seaman's chest, 19th century, hinged lid with schooner near shore, foliate decoration on sides, front identified with James F. Whitten, Civil War sailor who served on CSS Virginia II, 8-1/2" h. x 20-1/2" x 11".. **$200**

Courtesy of Burchard Galleries, www.burchardgalleries.com

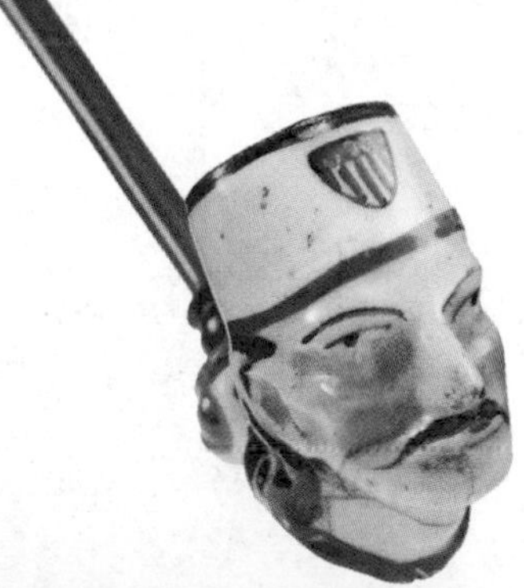

Civil War-period hand-painted ceramic patriotic pipe, bowl with image of Zouave wearing fez centered on American shield, 7-3/4" overall......... **$100**

Courtesy of Heritage Auctions, ha.com

Civil War-period brass box bleeder in original pasteboard box partially recovered in cloth, working and complete with all of its iron blades, brass case 1-5/8" x 1-1/2" x 1-1/4" h..............**$250**

Courtesy of Heritage Auctions, ha.com

Original Civil War sheet iron Sibley stove attributed to Union Army 6th Corps Camp at Battle of Antietam, blacksmith-made warming tray made from iron keg hoop, small rounded opening at base to assist ventilation, stove 29" h., 18" dia. base tapering to 4" opening at top, hinged iron door 8" x 8". Originally designed to warm the circular Sibley tent, these unusual, portable, and durable iron stoves became a staple of Union Army camp life and were used for warmth and cooking both inside and outside a variety of shelters............. **$400**

Courtesy of Heritage Auctions, ha.com

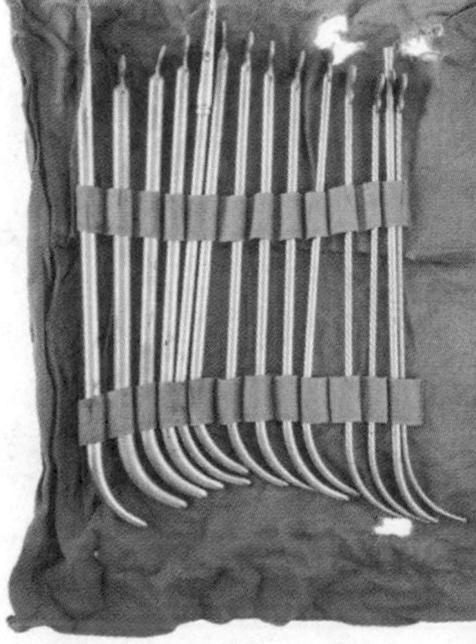

▲ Civil War-period catheter set, 13 pieces, marked "Leur Paris" along with sizes, nickel-plated and housed in cloth roll-up, pieces range in size from 10 to 30, 9-3/4" to 11-1/2". **$275**

Courtesy of Heritage Auctions, ha.com

◀ Civil War-period snare drum and drumsticks, excellent hide heads and snares, interior label reads, "Made by White Brothers 86 Tremont Street Boston," four leather tighteners, maple shell and loops, drum 11" h., 14" dia., matching rosewood drumsticks 14-7/8". **$1,125**

Courtesy of Heritage Auctions, ha.com

CLOCKS

THE MEASUREMENT AND recording of time has been a vital part of human civilization for thousands of years, and the clock, an instrument that measures and shows time, is one of the oldest human inventions.

Mechanical, weight-driven clocks were first developed and came into use in the Middle Ages. Since the 16th century, Western societies have become more concerned with keeping accurate time and developing timekeeping devices that were available to a wider public. By the mid-1600s, spring-driven clocks were keeping much more accurate time using minute and seconds hands. The clock became a common object in most households in the early 19th century.

Clocks are a prime example of form following function. In its earliest incarnations, the functionality of a timepiece was of paramount importance. Was it telling the time? More importantly, was it telling the correct time? Once those basic questions had been answered, designers could experiment with form. With the introduction of electronics in the 20th century, almost all traditional clockwork parts were eliminated, allowing clocks to become much more compact and stylistically adaptable.

In lavish Art Deco styles of the 1920s and 1930s, clocks featured the same attention to exterior detail as a painting or sculpture. Fashioned of materials ranging from exotic woods to marble, bronze, and even wedges of Bakelite, Art Deco clocks were so lovely that it was actually an unexpected bonus if they kept perfect time. The Parisian firm, Leon Hatot, for instance, offered a clear glass stunner with hands and numerals of silver.

For the budget-conscious, particularly during the 1930s Depression years, inexpensive novelty clocks found favor. Prominent among these were molded-wood clocks by Syroco (Syracuse Ornamental Co.). Offering the look of hand-carving at a fraction of the cost, Syroco clocks featured an interior mechanism by Lux.

Also popular: affordable clocks ideally suited for a specific room in the home, such as the Seth Thomas line of kitchen-ready "Red Apple" clocks. Other companies specialized in attractively priced clocks with added whimsy. Haddon's "Ship Ahoy" clock lamp had a sailboat rocking on its painted waves, while MasterCrafters ceramic clocks replicated a pendulum effect with moving figures, such as children on swings or old folks in rocking chairs. Another bestseller, still in production today, is the "Kit-Cat Clock" with pendulum tail and hypnotic moving eyes.

And possessing an irresistible kitschy charm: "souvenir" clocks from locales as diverse as New York and Las Vegas. What better way to travel back in time than with a "Statue of Liberty Clock" (complete with glowing torch) or a sparkly Vegas version with casino dice marking the hours?

After the production restraints of World War II, postwar clock designers found inspiration in fresh shapes and materials. Among the most unusual: "clock lamps" by San Francisco's Moss Manufacturing. These Plexiglas eye-poppers exhibit a mastery of multi-purposing. They tell time. They light up. They hold flowers. Many even include a rotating platform: flick the switch, and a ceramic figurine (often by a prominent design name, such as deLee, Hedi Schoop, or Lefton) begins to twirl.

Equally modern yet less over-the-top were fused glass clocks by Higgins Glass Studio of Chicago. Although artisans such as Georges Briard also designed glass clocks, those by Michael and Frances Higgins are among the mid-century's most innovative. Clocks were a natural outgrowth for these pioneers of practical design, whose decorative housewares ran the gamut from cigarette boxes to candleholders.

According to Michael Higgins, “We try to make things which may be thought beautiful. But we are not ashamed if our pieces are useful. It makes them easier to sell.”

A 1954 Higgins clock for GE, featuring ball-tipped rays radiating outward on the glass face, is as unexpectedly glorious as an alien sun. A later line of glass-on-glass clocks was created for Haddon during the Higgins' stay at Dearborn Glass Co. The hours are indicated by colorful glass chunks fused to a vibrantly patterned glass slab. While from the mid-century, a Higgins clock is not of the mid-century. Simplicity and clarity of line, coupled with a bold use of color, make Higgins clocks right at home in any age.

There's no time like the present to explore the limitless treasure trove of mid-20th century clocks. Which will be your favorite? Only time will tell.

MANTEL CLOCKS

Charles X patinated bronze and siena marble mantel clock, circa 1830, 11-3/4" h. x 13-1/2" w. x 5-1/4" d.. **$500**

Courtesy of Sotheby's, www.sotheby.com

Charles X patinated bronze and siena marble mantel clock, circa 1830, dial flanked by rams' heads joined by garlands, 20" h. x 12-1/4" w. x 9-3/4" d.
.... **$500**

Courtesy of Sotheby's, www.sotheby.com

Charles X patinated bronze and siena marble mantel clock, circa 1830, surmounted by a tazza, 21" h. x 8-1/2" w. x 6-3/4" d........................ **$125**

Courtesy of Sotheby's, www.sotheby.com

Tiffany Art Deco marble mantel clock, circa 1920, marked "Tiffany & Co." on face, beveled front and back glass, 10" h. **$580**

Courtesy of Morphy Auctions, morphyauctions.com

top lot!

E. Howard & Company No. 61 regulator clock, Boston, circa 1875-1885, carved walnut case with pitched pediment and central carved and turned finial, full-length glass door flanked by carved ornament, full-length glass sides, molded flat base with raised moldings enclosing decorative grained panels, 14" silvered brass engraved dial marked "E. Howard & Co./Boston, Mass.," dial reading seconds at top, hours below and minutes around perimeter with original blued steel hands, brass damascened movement marked "E. Howard & Co./ Boston" with deadbeat escapement, jeweled pallets, maintaining power, Geneva stops and all mounted to heavy iron bracket attached to backboard, seconds beating, faceted glass vial and invar or lead temperature-compensating pendulum with painted wooden rod attached to iron backplate and beating against highly figured walnut backboard, silvered beat scale, key and holder, all powered by brass-cased weight, 94" h $52,275

COURTESY OF SKINNER, INC., WWW.SKINNERINC.COM

German gilt metal mounted walnut "swinging cherub" mantel timepiece, Lenzkirch, Germany, circa 1905, small single-train going barrel movement with inverted wheel train regulated by upside-down anchor escapement connected via brass wire-cranked armature to back-and-forth swinging pendulum pivoted beneath movement, backplate stamped with "Lenzkirch A.U.G., 1 Million" trademark over serial No. 13463, silvered Arabic numeral dial decorated with rosette to center with cartouche numerals within applied gilt bezel, case of architectural form with concave-sided pediment surmounted by vase finial and applied with foliate cast panel mount to front, over ogee cornice and gilt stud-decorated shaped panel around dial, base with baluster-turned columns flanking recess enclosing pendulum with bob cast as child on swing fronting foliate gilt surrounding decorated back panel flanked by incised scroll-shaped side projections capped with gilt finials, on ogee-molded plinth base with curved side sections and disc feet, 17" h...... **$1,080**

Courtesy of Dreweatts & Bloomsbury, www.bloomsburyauctions.com

DESK-TYPE CLOCKS

Modern Cartier polished steel and shagreen desk timepiece, model number 180891GD, with onyx set carrying handle and alarm stop feature, 3-1/2" h. x 4-1/4" w. **$625**

Courtesy of Sothey's, www.sotheby.com

Cast iron Sambo clock, all original, clean clock face, 16" h............ **$1,586**

Courtesy of Morphy Auctions, morphyauctions.com

U.S. Navy ship clock by Chelsea Clock Co. of Boston, circa 1942, in Bakelite case, 10-1/4" dia. **$580**

Courtesy of Morphy Auctions, morphyauctions.com

L'Emeraude Art Deco clock, Lausanne, Switzerland, circa 1930, clock face with Arabic numerals set in chrome frame with triangular decorations of rose onyx on black plastic base with onyx feet, marked "A L'Emeraude Lausanne," 8-1/4" h. x 10-1/4" w. x 3-1/2" d. **$1,476**

Courtesy of Skinner, Inc., www.skinnerinc.com

Viennese enamel clock, circa 1880, depicts young couple in love, 4-1/2" h. x 2" w. **$488**

Courtesy of Morphy Auctions, morphyauctions.com

Lalique clear and frosted glass cat clock, late 20th century, engraved "Lalique, France," 7-3/4" h.. .... **$375**

Courtesy of Heritage Auctions, ha.com

WALL CLOCKS

Miniature Vienna wall regulator clock, full-length glazed door with engaged turned half-columns, Roman numeral porcelain dial with brass bezel, eight-day time and strike, spring-powered movement, with gridiron pendulum, 24" h....... **$123**

Courtesy of Skinner Inc., www.skinnerinc.com

Mid-century Howard Miller sunburst spike wall clock, maker marked, 19" x 19"..................... **$308**

Courtesy of Don Presley Auction, www.donpresley.com

Coca-Cola lighted clock, hard-to-find item, 18" h. x 18" l.. **$800**

Courtesy of Morphy Auctions, morphyauctions.com

Pepsi advertising clock, 1961, excellent condition, 16" x 16". **$150**

Courtesy of Morphy Auctions, morphyauctions.com

LONGCASE/GRANDFATHER/STANDING CLOCKS

Grandfather clock, circa 1850, brass finials and heavily painted phase, signed "Adam Middelnich" on dial, very good-plus condition, missing or broken veneer pieces, 91" h **$1,220**

Courtesy of Morphy Auctions, morphyauctions.com

William Rust japanned longcase clock, Bury, England, circa 1760, gilt and green-painted japanned case with remnants of raised decoration, arched hood with engaged quarter-columns flanking composite brass dial with boss in arch reading, "Willm Rust Bury," silvered Roman numeral chapter ring, engraved center, subsidiary seconds dial and date aperture, tombstone-shaped waist door over step-molded base and bun feet, eight-day time and hour strike movement, regulated by pendulum and two lead weights, 89" h...................................... **$861**

Courtesy of Skinner, Inc., www.skinnerinc.com

Rare Gustav Stickley grandfather clock, Eastwood, New York, circa 1915, branded, hammered amber glass panels in door and late painted dial, works, weights, and pendulum all original, very good original finish and color with minor edge wear and two short gouges, 71" x 18-1/4" x 12"............................**$12,160**

Courtesy of Rago Arts and Auctions, www.ragoarts.com

W. Wilkinson mahogany and oak-veneered longcase clock, Leeds, England, circa 1800, bellflower-inlaid swan's neck pediment, cast brass Corinthian capital on reeded columns flanking painted iron dial reading "W. Wilkinfon Leeds," with moon's age in arch, and floral spandrels, seconds and calendar dials, shell-inlaid panel above cyma-shaped waist door with urn-inlaid center, raised bottom panel with central and corner petal inlay, bracket feet, eight-day time and hour strike movement, pendulum and two lead weights, 90" h. **$615**

Courtesy of Skinner, Inc., www.skinnerinc.com

Louis XV-style marquetry and gilt bronze bracket clock and pedestal, Tiffany & Co., New York, circa 1970, clock surmounted by child playing horn above pad top with foliate inlay, arched glazed door with brass border, raised on gilt bronze bracket feet, gilt dial with inset Roman numeral tablets, with conforming rosewood and satinwood pedestal, marks to face: "Tiffany, MADE IN ITALY," 45" h. **$2,875**

Courtesy of Heritage Auctions, ha.com

COCA-COLA

& Other Soda Pop Collectibles

COLLECTIBLES PROVIDE A nostalgic look at our youth and a time when things were simpler and easier to understand. Through collecting, many adults try to recapture this time loaded with fond memories.

The American soft drink industry has always been part of this collectible nostalgia phenomenon. It fits all the criteria associated with the good times, fond memories, and fun. The world of soda pop collecting has been one of the mainstays of modern collectibles since the start of the genre.

Can soda pop advertising be considered true art? Without a doubt! The very best artists in America were an integral part of that honorary place in art history. Renowned artists like Rockwell, Sundbloom, Elvgren, and Wyeth helped take a quality product and advance it to the status of an American icon and all that exemplifies the very best about America.

This beautiful advertising directly reflects the history of our country: its styles and fashion, patriotism, family life, the best of times, and the worst of times. Nearly everything this country has gone through can be seen in these wonderful images.

Organized Coca-Cola collecting began in the early 1970s. The Coca-Cola Co., since its conception in 1886, has taken advertising to a whole new level. This advertising art, which used to be thought of as a simple area of collecting, has reached a whole new level of appreciation. So much so, that it has been studied and dissected by scholars as to why it has proved to be so successful for more than 120 years.

For more information on Coca-Cola collectibles, see *Petretti's Coca-Cola Collectibles Price Guide*, 12th edition, by Allan Petretti.

Round tin clock, 1950s, 18" dia. **$252**

Courtesy of Philip Weiss Auctions, www.weissauctions.com

"Basic Training Program for Route Salesmen" training kit with nine Coca-Cola training records, books, and nine Coca-Cola films........... **$148**

Courtesy of Rockabilly Auction Co., www.rockabillyauction.com

COCA-COLA

"Pause Here" wooden sign, circa 1930-1940s, 12-1/2" x 37". **$1,380**

Courtesy of Philip Weiss Auctions, www.weissauctions.com

Diner set, round table with Coca-Cola logo and four red vinyl-upholstered chairs with Coca-Cola logo on backrest, table trimmed in chrome with chrome legs, chrome legs on chairs, very good used condition with minor scuffs and scratches. **$295**

Courtesy of Rockabilly Auction Co., www.rockabillyauction.com

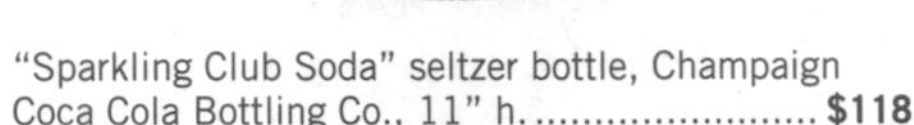

"Sparkling Club Soda" seltzer bottle, Champaign Coca Cola Bottling Co., 11" h. **$118**

Courtesy of Philip Weiss Auctions, www.weissauctions.com

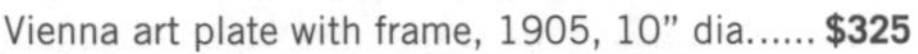

Vienna art plate with frame, 1905, 10" dia...... **$325**

Courtesy of Philip Weiss Auctions, www.weissauctions.com

Scarce aluminum bottle carrier with Masonite bottom, "Drink Coca Cola in Bottles" embossed on two sides, "Property of Coca Cola Bottling Company" engraved on both ends, original condition with scuffs and scratches................ **$183**

Courtesy of Rockabilly Auction Co., www.rockabillyauction.com

Candy Films porcelain sign, excellent original condition with minor scuffs, chips, and scratches. **$708**

Courtesy of Rockabilly Auction Co., www.rockabillyauction.com

Bottle rack with round base and four attached hanging brackets, double-sided tin marquee sign at top reads "Drink Coca Cola / Take home a carton / 25¢ plus deposit," "Drink Coca Cola" stamped on base, with three wooden Coca-Cola carriers, one with break in handle, very good condition, 57" h. x 13" w.............................. **$458**

Courtesy of Morphy Auctions, morphyauctions.com

Vendor badge, excellent condition. **$14**

Courtesy of Central Texas Coins and Collectibles, Round Rock, Texas

Fountain Service header sign, porcelain, used on Coca-Cola fountain service signs, original condition with scuffs, scratches, and porcelain chips. **$354**

Courtesy of Rockabilly Auction Co., www.rockabillyauction.com

"Take a case home Today" single-sided advertising sign, tin, excellent condition, 19-1/2" x 28".... **$976**

Courtesy of Morphy Auctions, morphyauctions.com

Art Deco Coca-Cola bottle sign. **$540**

Courtesy of Mecum Auctions, www.mecum.com

Metal bowl with three metal Coca-Cola bottles as legs, 9-1/2" dia. **$244**

Courtesy of Morphy Auctions, morphyauctions.com

Cooler with bottle opener on side, 34" h. **$519**

Courtesy of Morphy Auctions, morphyauctions.com

"Join the friendly circle" advertising poster, 1954, framed in glass, 32-1/4" x 21"...................... **$580**

Courtesy of Morphy Auctions, morphyauctions.com

Select Vend V 83 conversion bottle vending machine with keys, very good condition, 64" h. **$915**

Courtesy of Morphy Auctions, morphyauctions.com

Button with Sprite Boy, excellent condition, 16" dia.. **$1,952**

Courtesy of Morphy Auctions, morphyauctions.com

Scarce cross sign, tin litho with beveled edges, two factory holes on top and one hole in lower center, good condition, some bends, moderate soiling, scattered paint loss, 6" x 6"............ **$2,075**

Courtesy of Morphy Auctions, morphyauctions.com

PEPSI-COLA

Pepsi-Cola menu board, 30" x 19-1/2"........... **$266**

Courtesy of Bright Star Antiques Co., www.brightstarantiques.com

National Cash Register with Pepsi Cola advertising, 1916, restored............................ **$278**

Courtesy of Rockabilly Auction Co., www.rockabillyauction.com

top lot

"Enjoy Pepsi-Cola / Hits the Spot" sign. $5,400

COURTESY OF MECUM AUCTIONS, WWW.MECUM.COM

Pepsi-Cola picnic cooler, 1951, original blue paint, very good to excellent condition, 12" h. x 18" w. x 9" d. **$210**

Courtesy of Rich Penn Auctions, www.richpennauctions.com

OTHER SODA BEVERAGES

Richardson Root Beer embossed metal advertising sign, 8-1/2" x 23-1/2". **$156**

Courtesy of Material Culture, www.materialculture.com

Muscadine Thrill soda sign, tin, 1930s, 11-3/4" x 23-3/4". **$208**

Courtesy of North American Auction Co., www.northamericanauctioncompany.com

▲ Magnus Root Beer soda fountain, main barrel insulated to hold ice and soda water, metal holders on both sides hold 15" glass syrup dispensers, front with two taps for syrup and central tap for soda water over metal drip tray, "Magnus Root Beer / It's Fine in the Stein" on back, very good condition, 33" h. x 32" w. x 31" d............................. **$855**

Courtesy of Morphy Auctions, morphyauctions.com

Thirsty? JUST
WHISTLE
MORNING-NOON-NIGHT

Whistle soda fountain sign, tin, original condition with scuffs, scratches, and small holes, 27" w. x 12-1/2" h. **$255**

Courtesy of Rockabilly Auction Co., www.rockabillyauction.com

Brunswick orange soda single-sided tin advertising sign, some areas of repainting to edges where wear has occurred, good condition, 13-3/4" x 42". ... **$305**

Courtesy of Morphy Auctions, morphyauctions.com

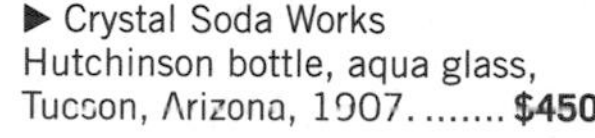

▶ Crystal Soda Works Hutchinson bottle, aqua glass, Tucson, Arizona, 1907. .... **$450**

Courtesy of Holabird-Kagin Americana, www.holabirdamericana.com

COIN-OPS

DID YOU KNOW coin-operated dispensers date back to ancient times when they were used in houses of worship to deliver holy water? You'd be hard-pressed to find one of those offered at auction today, but many other types of coin-operated gadget-like gizmos certainly come up for sale, and there are always eager buyers lining up to add them to collections.

Coin-ops, as they're often referenced by both marketers and aficionados, come in all shapes and sizes and fall into three main categories: gambling, including slot machines and trade stimulators; vending machines with service devices like scales and shoe shiners as a subcategory; and arcade machines. From simple post-World War II gumball and peanut machines that can usually be found for under $100, to rare antique arcade machines that bring to mind the fortune teller amusement working magic in the popular movie "Big" starring Tom Hanks, these are all considered collectible.

Today one of those talking fortune-teller machines can easily bring five figures at auction. Other interesting models without talking features can be purchased more reasonably, in the $1,000-$5,000 range, but none of them come cheap when they're in good working order.

Amusements such as these originated in penny arcades of the late 1800s. There were machines allowing patrons to demonstrate their skill at bowling, shooting or golf, among other pastimes, along with the familiar strength testers that sprang to life at a penny a pop. Some machines known as "shockers" were marketed as medical devices. In fact, one made by Mills, a huge manufacturer of coin-ops, was actually named "Electricity is Life," and it would supposedly cure what ails you, according to Bill Petrochuk, an avid collector actively involved with the Coin Operated Collectors Association (http://coinopclub.org). Another lung tester, which operated by blowing into a mouthpiece attached to a hose causing water to rise in the device as a measurement tool, was eventually banned, ironically, due to the spread of tuberculosis.

There are also those aforementioned trade stimulators, some of which skirted gambling laws, according to Larry DeBaugh, a frequent consultant for Morphy Auctions, who knows his stuff when it comes to devices powered by pocket change. These machines stimulated the trade of businesses like tobacco stores and bars by offering patrons a chance to win products, many times by spinning reels or playing a game. Later machines dispensed gum on the side for each coin spent. Customers received something for their money, and presto, law enforcement couldn't technically deem it gambling.

The earliest trade stimulators were cigar machines with no gambling involved, however. They were truly cigar dispensers, and for a nickel a customer would get a cigar. What made it different from buying from the guy down the block is that you might get two or three for the same nickel using the machine. Petrochuk adds that these were used to free up some of the tobacco shop clerk's time as well. When taxes were imposed on cigars, requiring that they be sold from original boxes, these machines were no longer serviceable. They're now considered rare collectibles and sell for $10,000 and up in most instances, when you can find them.

There were also slot machines designed for use outside casinos that would vend a pack of mints, or do a bit of fortune telling, in the same way as later trade stimulators. These machines were fought by authorities for decades, according to DeBaugh. Finally, in the 1950s and 1960s, vending-style gambling machines of this sort were outlawed, and their makers concentrated their marketing efforts on Las Vegas going forward.

Traditional slot machines are quite popular today as well, and collectors like DeBaugh, who've studied, bought and sold these types of items for 35-40 years, have seen a bit of everything including those in pretty rough shape.

"An average machine, one that's seen a lot of play from the '40s or late '30s and is basically worn out, will run about $1,000. But they won't be worth anything unless they are restored. After they're running, you might have a $3,000 machine."

Petrochuk notes that collectors of coin-ops in general look for "nice, clean, original machines," but a very small percentage fall into that category. He likes to use the term "preservation" when referring to giving old coin-ops new life, as in keeping things as original as possible. He sees restoration as more of a redo that might require totally new paint or extensive re-plating. "These old machines took a real beating. A few battle scars are acceptable," he adds.

Preserving coin-ops means using as many original parts as possible to replace those that are worn and fabricating new ones out of appropriate materials when needed. DeBaugh supplies Rick Dale of the History Channel's hit television series "American Restoration" with many parts salvaged from old slot machines that can't be repaired. He also notes that it's tough to find older slots from the early 1900s in anything but poor condition. The wood usually needs work, and sometimes the nickel or copper finishes will need to be re-plated as well.

Other unusual coin-ops beyond the familiar "one-armed bandits" include devices that sold matchbooks, collar buttons, and sprays of perfume. Going even further into the unimaginable zone are machines that actually dispensed live lobsters via a game of sorts. Others even provided live bait for fishing excursions.

Nut and gum dispensers are the most common vending models, but unusual brands in this category most definitely appeal to advertising collectors in addition to coin-op enthusiasts. In fact, many coin-ops are direct extensions of advertising collectibles since vending machines made in the 1920s and '30s, unlike those that dispense multiple types of snacks today, usually focused on a single brand. Hershey's machines dispensed chocolate bars. Wrigley's dispensers rotated to deliver packs of gum. There were even coin-operated dispensers for Dixie Cups. Add an unusual shape or size to the equation and advanced collectors will pay big bucks to own them.

Even those old-fashioned red, white, and blue stamp dispensers used in post offices 30-40 years ago appeal to collectors of newer machines, and those can be found for less than $100. If you want a slot machine for use in a "man cave" or game room, DeBaugh suggests looking at a Mills machine from the 1940s or '50s. Both high top and half-top models can be found for around $1,000 in good working order. What's even better, they're dependable and reliable for home use for hours of coin-op fun.

— *Pamela Y. Wiggins*

Bally Mfg. Co. poker hand little disks trade stimulator, 5¢ coin-op, 1932....................... **$1,003**

Courtesy of H.G. Webber Antiques and Auctions, www.hgwebber.com

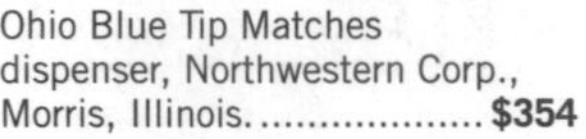

Ohio Blue Tip Matches dispenser, Northwestern Corp., Morris, Illinois. **$354**

Courtesy of Epic Auctions, www.epicauctionsandestatesales.com

Rowntree's Fruit Pastilles skill vendor, used for Rowntree candy, 31-1/2" x 19". **$390**

Courtesy of Milestone Auctions, www.milestoneauctions.com

U.S. Postage Stamps machine with keys. **$108**

Courtesy of Milestone Auctions, www.milestoneauctions.com

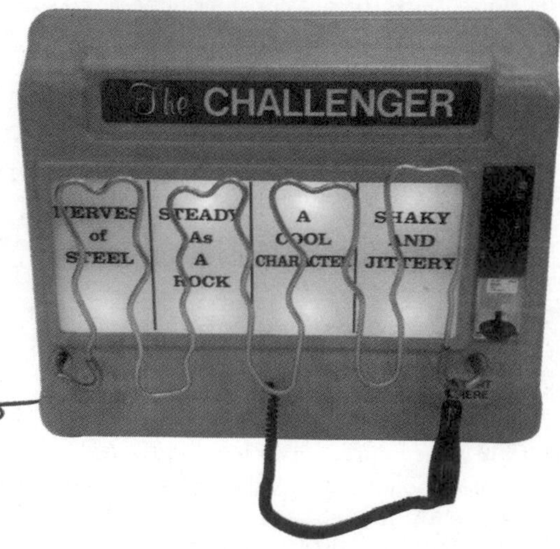

The Challenger skill game, 9" h. x 23-1/4" w. x 10" d. **$236**

Courtesy of Epic Auctions, www.epicauctionsandestatesales.com

Daval Penny Pack trade simulator, 14 pounds, 9" x 8-1/2" x 11". **$560**

Courtesy of Coinop Warehouse, www.coinopwarehouse.com

Penny Smoke coin-op, 1¢, Dandy Vendor, cast metal, three-of-a-kind wins one package of cigarettes, 12" h. **$363**

Courtesy of Richard Opfer Auctioneering, www.opferauction.com

Adams Gum dispenser, 1¢, nickel-plated with six slots, 16" h. **$170**

Courtesy of Richard Opfer Auctioneering, www.opferauction.com

Whiz Ball countertop coin-op game, 1¢, cast metal and wood, restored, 14-1/2" h. .. **$272**

Courtesy of Richard Opfer Auctioneering, www.opferauction.com

Floor model candy dispenser, German, separate column and coin insert for either candy or a surprise, 66" h. **$1,830**

Courtesy of Morphy Auctions, morphyauctions.com

Regina Musical Automaton, nickel-operated floor-standing music box, 71" h. x 23" w. x 13" d. **$3,872**

Courtesy of Briggs Auction Inc., www.briggsauction.com

Shyver's Multi-Phone DJ music selector, communicator allowed customer to request music from disk jockey, 16" h. **$671**

Courtesy of Morphy Auctions, morphyauctions.com

The Roovers Name Plate Machine, patented April 7, 1891, No. 26268, by Roover Bros., Inc., 56" x 16" x 12-1/2". **$732**

Courtesy of Morphy Auctions, morphyauctions.com

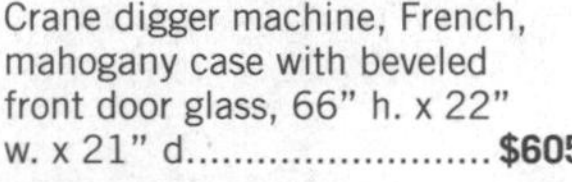

Crane digger machine, French, mahogany case with beveled front door glass, 66" h. x 22" w. x 21" d. **$605**

Courtesy of Fontaine's Auction Gallery, www.fontainesauction.net

Hunting-themed floor model arcade machine, "La Chasse a Courre" by Forestry, French, horse and hound chasing buck through forest, 66" h. **$2,318**

Courtesy of Morphy Auctions, morphyauctions.com

◀ Bally Mfg. Co. 10¢ bowling arcade game, circa 1950s, printed Formica-branded playing field, 104" x 25" x 88". **$336**

Courtesy of Morphy Auctions, morphyauctions.com

Hershey's candy bar vending machine, 1¢, 25" h. **$206**

Courtesy of Richard Opfer Auctioneering, www.opferauction.com

top lot!

Columbia Steamer arcade machine, rare operating boat model in lighted wood and glass display showcase, insert coin to play music box and see model operate, with keys and two related images, excellent condition, 14" x 42" x 27". $15,250

COURTESY OF MORPHY AUCTIONS, MORPHYAUCTIONS.COM

Kicker and Catcher skill game, Baker Novelty Co., 1930s, 1¢, 17-1/2" x 14" x 8". **$600**

Courtesy of Stephenson's Auctioneers & Appraisers, www.stephensonsauction.com

Magic Clock arcade penny fortune-teller, scarce dial with fruit instead of numbers.................... **$116**

Rockabilly Auction Co., www.rockabillyauction.com

Callie Ben Hur counter wheel slot machine, circa 1908, European coin system but will play on U.S. half dollar, 16" x 10" x 25". **$1,020**

Courtesy of Morphy Auctions, morphyauctions.com

Exhibit Supply Co. drop card viewer, 19 pounds, 11-1/4" x 8-1/4" x 13"................................. **$280**

Courtesy of Coinop Warehouse, www.coinopwarehouse.com

COINS

WHAT MAKES A COIN VALUABLE?

Rarity, collector demand, and condition drive value in the collectible coin market. Specific date and mint mark combinations with low mintages within a particular series are known as key dates. For example, the U.S. Mint produced only 52,000 1916 Standing Liberty quarters, making it the key date in the series. But it's not enough for a coin to just be rare; there must collector demand for it too. The Standing Liberty quarter is considered one of the most beautiful U.S. coins ever produced and is one of the most popularly collected U.S. coins. Thus, demand for a key date like the 1916 outpaces supply.

CONDITION IS KEY

Condition, or grade, is key to any coin's value. The higher the condition, the higher the value, particularly among scarce coins like key dates. Grades are usually expressed in a combination of terms and numbers. For example, uncirculated coins - those showing no signs of wear - are described as "mint state" and are assigned numbers ranging from 60 to 70. The higher the number, the higher the grade. A coin graded MS-65, for example, is better than a coin graded MS-63.

Coins showing wear ("circulated" coins) are described as either about uncirculated (AU), extremely fine (EF or XF), very fine (VF), fine (F), very good (VF), or good (G), from best to worst. Specific numbers are again added to these adjectives to further designate a coin's grade. Proof coins are struck by a special process and receive their own grading designation (proof-65, proof-55, proof-45, and so on).

Many coins today are graded by professional grading services, who encapsulate the coin in plastic holders with their grades attached. The holders were nicknamed "slabs" and are a common sight at coin shows and shops. Prominent among the grading services are the Professional Coin Grading Service and the Numismatic Guaranty Corp.

For more information on U.S. coins, see *Warman's Companion U.S. Coins and Currency*, 3rd edition, by Arlyn G. Sieber.

NGC: *Numismatic Guaranty Corp.*
PCGS: *Professional Coin Grading Service*

U.S. COINS

1882 Indian cent, MS-66, PCGS. **$999**

Courtesy of Heritage Auctions, ha.com

1937 Lincoln cent, proof-65, NGC. **$1,939**

Courtesy of Heritage Auctions, ha.com

1959 Lincoln cent, proof-68, PCGS. **$1,645**

Courtesy of Heritage Auctions, ha.com

1916-D dime, AU-58, NGC. **$9,400**

Courtesy of Heritage Auctions, ha.com

1875-CC 20-cent, MS-64, PCGS. **$3,760**

Courtesy of Heritage Auctions, ha.com

1935-S quarter, MS-67, PCGS. **$1,293**

Courtesy of Heritage Auctions, ha.com

1946 quarter, MS-67, PCGS. **$1,116**

Courtesy of Heritage Auctions, ha.com

1999-S quarter, Georgia, silver, proof-70, PCGS. **$1,208**

Courtesy of Heritage Auctions, ha.com

1976-S Kennedy half dollar, 40 percent silver, proof-70, PCGS. **$400**

Courtesy of Heritage Auctions, ha.com

1972-S Eisenhower dollar, 40 percent silver, proof-70, PCGS. **$494**

Courtesy of Heritage Auctions, ha.com

1859 gold $3, MS-64, PCGS. **$8,225**

Courtesy of Heritage Auctions, ha.com

1904 gold $5, MS-67, PCGS. **$15,275**

Courtesy of Heritage Auctions, ha.com

1925-D gold $20, MS-63. .... **$7,344**

Courtesy of Heritage Auctions, ha.com

WORLD COINS

Canada, 1859 cent, AU-53, PCGS, with double punched narrow 9, Type I. **$423**

Courtesy of Heritage Auctions, ha.com

Canada, 1947 50 cents, curved 7, maple leaf, AU-50, PCGS. **$2,585**

Courtesy of Heritage Auctions, ha.com

Canada, 1957 dollar, Ottawa Mint, MS-65, PCGS. **$645**

Courtesy of Heritage Auctions, ha.com

China, Szechuan Republic, 200 cash, year 2 (1913), VF. **$165**

Courtesy of Heritage Auctions, ha.com

Great Britain, gold noble, 1361-1369, Edward III, London Mint, AU-58, PCGS........................ **$4,465**

Courtesy of Heritage Auctions, ha.com

Great Britain, 1819 crown, George III, Royal Mint, "LIX" on edge, MS-65, PCGS. **$3,055**

Courtesy of Heritage Auctions, ha.com

Great Britain, 1887 crown, Queen Victoria, Royal Mint, MS-64, NGC.. **$541**

Courtesy of Heritage Auctions, ha.com

Great Britain, 1993 gold five pounds, gem cameo proof, commemorates 40th anniversary of Queen Elizabeth II's coronation.............................. **$2,115**

Courtesy of Heritage Auctions, ha.com

Mexico, 1808 gold 8 escudos, Charles IV, Mexico City Mint, VF. **$1,410**

Courtesy of Heritage Auctions, ha.com

Mexico, Republic Cagallito, 1913 peso, Mexico City Mint, MS-66, NGC. **$2,233**

Courtesy of Heritage Auctions, ha.com

Mexico, 1864 10 centavos, Mexico City Mint, MS-64, NGC.. **$470**

Courtesy of Heritage Auctions, ha.com

COMICS

BACK IN 1993, Sotheby's auctioned a copy of *Fantastic Four #1* (1961) that was said to be the finest copy known to exist. It sold for $27,600, which at the time was considered an unheard-of price for a 1960s comic. A few years ago Heritage Auctions sold that same copy for $203,000 ... and it's not even the finest known copy anymore.

It used to be that only comics from the 1930s or 1940s could be worth thousands of dollars. Now, truly high-grade copies of comics from the Silver Age (1956-1969 by most people's reckoning) can sell for four, five, or even six figures. Note I said truly high-grade. Long gone are the days when a near mint condition copy was only worth triple the price of a good condition copy. Now near mint is more like 10-20 times good, and sometimes it's as much as a factor of 1,000.

A trend of the last couple of years has been that the "key" issues have separated even further from the pack, value-wise. Note that not every key is a "#1" issue – if you have *Amazing Fantasy #15, Tales of Suspense #39*, and *Journey into Mystery #83*, you've got the first appearances of Spider-Man, Iron Man, and Thor. (Beware of reprints and replica editions, however.)

The most expensive comics of all remain the Golden Age (1938-1949) first appearances, like Superman's 1938 debut in *Action Comics #1*, several copies of which have sold for $1 million or more. However, not every comic from the old days is going up in value. Take Western-themed comics. Values are actually going down in this genre as the generation that grew up watching Westerns is at the age where they're looking to sell, and there are more sellers than potential buyers.

Comics from the 1970s and later, while increasing in value, rarely reach anywhere near the same value as 1960s issues, primarily because in the 1970s, the general public began to look at comics as a potentially

Sad Sack's Army Life Parade file copy long box group (Harvey, 1969-76), average near mint-minus condition, includes one to five file copies each of issues #23-48, 51, 52, 54-58, and 61............................ **$777**

Courtesy of Heritage Auctions, ha.com

valuable collectible. People took better care of them and in many cases hoarded multiple copies.

What about 1980s favorites like *The Dark Knight Returns* and *Watchmen*? Here the demand is high, but the supply is really high. These series were heavily hyped at the time and were done by well-known creators, so copies were socked away in great quantities. We've come across more than one dealer who has 20-30 mint copies of every 1980s comic socked away in a warehouse, waiting for the day when they're worth selling.

I should mention one surprise hit of the last couple of years. When Image Comics published *The Walking Dead #1* in 2003, it had a low print run and made no particular splash in the comics world. Once AMC made it into a television series, however, it was a whole different story. High-grade copies of #1 have been fetching $1,000 and up lately.

If you've bought comics at an auction house or on eBay, you might have seen some in CGC holders. Certified Guaranty Co., or CGC, is a third-party grading service that grades a comic book on a scale from 0.5 to 10. These numbers correspond with traditional descriptive grades of good, very fine, near mint and mint, with the higher numbers indicating a better grade. Once graded, CGC encapsulates the comic book in plastic. The grade remains valid as long as the plastic holder is not broken open. CGC has been a boon to the hobby, allowing people to buy comics with more confidence and with the subjectivity of grading taken out of the equation. Unless extremely rare, it's usually only high-grade comics that are worth certifying.

One aspect of collecting that has exploded in the last 20 years has been original comic art, and not just art for the vintage stuff. In fact, the most expensive piece Heritage Auctions has ever sold was from 1990: Todd McFarlane's cover art for *Amazing Spider-Man #328*, which sold for more than $650,000. It's not unusual for a page that was bought for $20 in the 1980s to be worth $5,000 now.

If you want to get into collecting original comic art, McFarlane would not be the place to start unless you've got a really fat wallet. I suggest picking a current comic artist you like who isn't yet a major "name." Chances are his originals will be a lot more affordable. Another idea is to collect the original art for comic strips. You can find originals for as little as $20, as long as you're not expecting a Peanuts or a Prince Valiant. Heritage Auctions (HA.com) maintains a free online archive of every piece of art it has sold, and it is an excellent research tool.

As expensive as both comic books and comic art can be at the high-end of the spectrum, in many ways this is a buyer's market. In the old days you might search for years to find a given issue of a comic; now you can often search eBay and see 10 different copies for sale. Also, comics conventions seem to be thriving in almost every major city, and while the people in crazy costumes get all the publicity, you can also find plenty of dealers of vintage comics at these shows. From that point of view, it's a great time to be a comic collector.

– *Barry Sandoval*

Barry Sandoval is Director of Operations for Comics and Comic Art, Heritage Auctions. In addition to managing Heritage's Comics division, which sells some $20 million worth of comics and original comic art each year, Sandoval is a noted comic book evaluator and serves as an advisor to the *Overstreet Comic Book Price Guide*.

COMICS

◄ *Giant-Size X-Men* #1 illustrated by Dave Cockrum with color comic art throughout, quarto comic book format, stapled pictorial wrappers, first edition, first appearances of X-men's most popular characters, including Storm, Nightcrawler, Colossus, and Thunderbird, first issue (1975) of X-men to feature Wolverine and his second full-length appearance in any comic book; slight wear to wrappers, slight page yellowing........... **$900**

Courtesy of PBA Galleries, www.pbagalleries.com

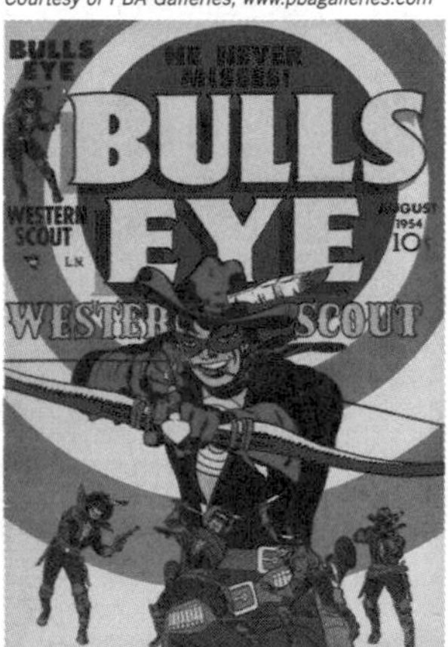

Bulls Eye #1 (Mainline Publications, 1954), CGC VG 4.0, Joe Simon and Jack Kirby cover and art...................... **$155**

Courtesy of Heritage Auctions, ha.com

◄ *Batman* #227 (DC, 1970), CGC VF+ 8.5, Neal Adams' classic cover swipe of Detective Comics #31, Robin backup story, with hanging panels, Irv Novick, Dick Giordano, and Mike Esposito art................ **$382**

Courtesy of Heritage Auctions, ha.com

► *Doctor Strange* #169 (Marvel, 1968), CGC VF+ 8.5, first appearance of Doctor Strange in his own title, origin retold, Dan Adkins cover and art. **$382**

Courtesy of Heritage Auctions, ha.com

◀ *Marvel Comics Super Special KISS*, two volumes, illustrated throughout with color comic art, quartp, stapled pictorial wrappers, first editions. *Marvel Super Special* Volume 1, No. 1, illustrated by John and Sal Buscema and others (1977) and *Marvel Super Special* Volume 1, No. 5, illustrated by John Buscema, with fold-out color poster (1978); slight wear to wrappers at staples, inside near fine or better condition. First appearances of KISS as superheroes battling classic villains such as Dr. Doom and Mephisto, and first issue reportedly printed with real blood from the members of KISS mixed with red ink at printer, as detailed in issue. **$100**

Courtesy of PBA Galleries, www.pbagalleries.com

More Fun Comics No. 25, illustrated throughout with color comic art, quarto, comic book format, stapled pictorial wrappers, first edition (1937), featuring Siegel and Shuster's Dr. Occult among other classic characters; very good or better condition, moderate wear and soiling to wrappers, previous owner's name written in pen or colored pencil at top of front cover, some yellowing to pages. *More Fun Comics* was originally titled *New Fun: The Big Comic Magazine*; it was an American comic book anthology that introduced several major superhero characters and was the first American comic book series to feature solely original material rather than reprints of newspaper comic strips. It was the first publication of the company that would become DC Comics. **$350**

Courtesy of PBA Galleries, www.pbagalleries.com

◀ *The Avengers* #58 (Marvel, 1968), CGC VF/NM 9.0, the Vision's origin revealed, he joins the Avengers, featuring Captain America, Thor, Iron Man, Hawkeye, Goliath, and Black Panther, John Buscema cover and art. **$143**

Courtesy of Heritage Auctions, ha.com

Thor #166 (Marvel, 1969), CGC NM 9.4, second full appearance of Him (aka Adam Warlock), Jack Kirby cover and art........ **$335**

Courtesy of Heritage Auctions, ha.com

The Amazing Spider-Man #76 (Marvel, 1969), CGC VF 8.0, Spider-Man versus the Lizard, Human Torch appearance, John Romita, Sr. cover, John Buscema and Jim Mooney art................ **$62**

Courtesy of Heritage Auctions, ha.com

COMIC ART

◀ Carl Barks, "Dam Disaster at Money Lake" signed limited edition lithograph print #226/345 (Another Rainbow, 1986), Uncle Scrooge McDuck, Donald Duck and nephews witness bursting dam at Money Lake (caused by Beagle Boys) and watch Uncle Scrooge's fortune wash down stream; eighth Barks lithography in series by Another Rainbow Publishing, based on a story in Dell's Four Color #356; excellent condition, 25" x 21-1/2"....**$359**

Courtesy of Heritage Auctions, ha.com

"Society Dog Show" Mickey Mouse and Pluto animation drawing (Walt Disney, 1939), chaos ensues when fire breaks out at dog show, Pluto (on skates) and Mickey save the day; two-character original 12 field five-peghole animation drawing from Bill Roberts-directed short, drawn in graphite with orange pencil highlights with number 142 in bottom right corner, fine condition, 4" x 5"...............**$598**

Courtesy of Heritage Auctions, ha.com

"Alpine Climbers" Mickey Mouse animation drawing (Walt Disney, 1938), mountain climber Mickey, eagle egg in hand, looks in mother eagle's direction; original 12 field five-peghole animation drawing in graphite with blue pencil highlights, number 88 written in lower right corner, fine condition....................**$263**

Courtesy of Heritage Auctions, ha.com

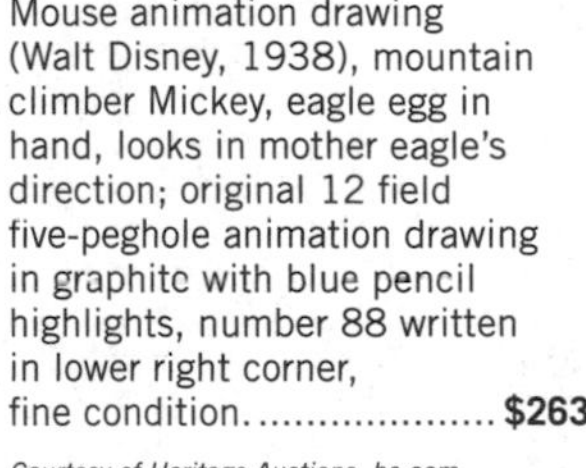

Otto Messmer, "Felix the Cat," original work on paper, circa 1990s, signed by Messmer, very good condition, 12-1/2" x 11-3/4".........................**$1,300**

Courtesy of Auctionata U.S., auctionata.com

"Oz Politicians" limited edition giclee on paper by Dan Piraro, creator of comic strip "Bizarro!", framed, numbered and hand-signed by artist with certificate of authenticity, good condition, image 15" x 8", 22" x 15" with frame..........**$350**

Courtesy of Seized Assets Auctioneers, www.seizedassetsauctioneers.com

Dan Barry and Bob Fujitani, "Flash Gordon" daily comic strip original art dated 4-6-85 through 4-15-85 (King Features Syndicate, 1985), eight consecutive dailies (Sundays not included) in ink over graphite on Bristol board, excellent condition, slight tanning, glue residue, occasional text correction, image 13" x 3-3/4". **$1,016**

Courtesy of Heritage Auctions, ha.com

Al Capp (American, 1909-1979), "Li'l Abner" ink on paper comic strip drawing, 1967, signed lower right, three panels published by News Syndicate, no certificate of authenticity, good condition, stain in center panel, artist corrections within each panel, 6" h. x 19" w., 10" x 23" framed. **$150**

Courtesy of Leonard Auction, Inc., www.leonardauction.com

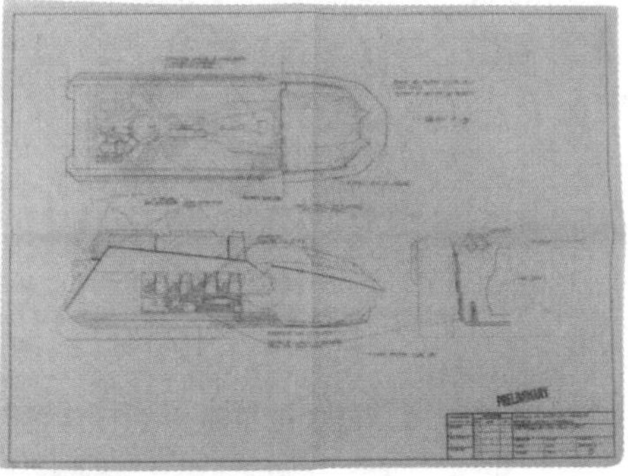

Three Leonard Starr original blueprints for "Thunder Cats" comics, 17" w. x 22" h. Provenance: From Connecticut estate of Leonard Starr.................... **$125**

Courtesy of Greenwich Auction, www.greenwichauction.net

▲ Bruce Timm, "Batman Superman" animation cel, circa 1990, signed by Timm in lower center, 25-1/2" x 21" with frame.................................... **$300**

Courtesy of Auctionata U.S., auctionata.com

◀ Barry Smith's "Tupenny Conan" portfolio, six black and white plates in stiff pictorial paper folder, outer pictorial manila envelope, No. 236 of 1,000 copies, first edition, signed by artist on first plate at limitation, with certificate of authenticity, date-stamped and signed by publisher, slight wear to outer envelope and edges of folder, plates in fine condition, 15" x 11". **$110**

Courtesy of PBA Galleries, www.pbagalleries.com

Black Americana framed comic book art, pages framed under glass, excellent condition, each print 7" x 9", 28-1/4" x 14-1/2" framed........... **$100**

Courtesy of Morphy Auctions, morphyauctions.com

MISCELLANEOUS

Four early newspaper advertising comic pins: New York Sunday American Maggie and Jiggs, 1-1/4" dia., Evening Ledger Comics Harold Teen and Babe Bunting, 1-1/4" dia., plus three others. **$30**

Courtesy of Ron Rhoads Auctioneers, www.ronrhoads-auction.com

▲ *E.C. Comics' The Complete Mad*, four volumes, color illustrations throughout, quarto, pictorial boards, pictorial slipcase, first Russ Cochran edition, reproductions of original classic EC comics from 1950s, published 1986-1987, fine condition, slight scuffing to slipcase. **$100**

Courtesy of PBA Galleries, www.pbagalleries.com

Five volumes of *The Spirit*, illustrated by author throughout, pictorial stapled wrappers, various dates: *The Spirit: The First 93 Dailies*, signed by Eisner on inner cover, Richton Park, Illinois, Funny Paper Book Store, 1977, first edition; *The Spirit Volume 2 – 200 Dailies*, signed by Eisner on first page, Richton Park, Illinois, Funny Paper Book Store, 1978, first edition; *The Spirit Volume 2: 200 Dailies*, signed by Eisner on first page, Park Forest, Illinois: Ken Pierce, 1980, second printing; *The Spirit Volume 3: 200 More Dailies*, signed by Eisner on first page, Park Forest, Illinois, Ken Pierce, 1980, first edition; and *The Spirit Volume 4: The Last 245 Dailies*, signed by Eisner on first page, Park Forest, Illinois: Ken Pierce, 1980, first edition; near fine condition, some wear to wrappers, previous owner's name sometimes in pen on inner covers. **$160**

Courtesy of PBA Galleries, www.pbagalleries.com

COOKIE JARS

COOKIE JARS EVOLVED from the elegant British biscuit jars found on Victorian-era tables. These 19th century containers featured bail handles and were often made of sterling silver and cut crystal.

As the biscuit jar was adapted for use in America, it migrated from the dining table to the kitchen, and by the late 1920s it was common to find a green (or pink or clear) glass jar, often with an applied label and a screw-top lid, on kitchen counters in the typical American home.

During the Great Depression – when stoneware was still popular but before the arrival of widespread electric refrigeration – cookie jars in round and barrel shapes arrived. These heavy-bodied jars could be hand-painted after firing. These decorations were easily worn away by eager hands reaching for Mom's baked goodies. The lids of many stoneware jars typically had small tapering finials or knobs that also contributed to cracks and chips.

American Bisque Little Audrey with printed "LITTLE / AUDREY" to front, impressed "USA" above base, American Bisque Co., third quarter 20th century, undamaged, some scattered crazing, primarily to underside of cover, 13-1/2" h............. **$1,050**

Courtesy of Jeffrey S. Evans & Associates, www.jeffreysevans.com

The golden age of cookie jars began in the 1940s and lasted for less than three decades, but the examples that survive represent an exuberance and style that have captivated collectors.

It wasn't until the 1970s that many collectors decided – instead of hiding their money in cookie jars – to invest their money in cookie jars. It was also at this time that cookie jars ceased to be simply storage vessels for bakery and evolved into a contemporary art form.

The Brush Pottery Co. of Zanesville, Ohio, produced one of the first ceramic cookie jars in about 1929, and Red Wing's spongeware line from the late 1920s also included a ridged, barrel-shaped jar. Many established potteries began adding a selection of cookie jars in the 1930s.

The 1940s saw the arrival of two of the most famous cookie jars: Shawnee's Smiley and Winnie, two portly, bashful little pigs who stand with eyes closed and heads cocked, he in overalls and bandana, she in flowered hat and long coat. A host of Disney characters also made their way into American kitchens.

In the 1950s, the first television-influenced jars appeared, including images of Davy Crockett and Popeye. This decade also saw the end of several prominent American potteries, including Roseville, and the continued rise of imported ceramics.

A new collection of cartoon-inspired jars was popular in the 1960s, featuring characters drawn from the Flintstones, Yogi Bear, Woody Woodpecker, and Casper the Friendly Ghost. Jars reflecting the race for space included examples from McCoy and American Bisque. This decade also marked the peak production era for a host of West Coast manufacturers, led by twin brothers Don and Ross Winton.

For more information on cookie jars, see *Warman's Cookie Jars Identification and Price Guide* by Mark F. Moran.

Three American Bisque brownie cookie jars, small chip to mouth of one with blue bottom, nice overall condition reflecting normal age ware. **$300**

Courtesy of Philip Weiss Auctions, www.weissauctions.com

American Bisque Casper the Ghost, marked "Harvey Publications," crazing, no chips or cracks. **$360**

Courtesy of Philip Weiss Auctions, www.weissauctions.com

American Bisque Popeye head, all original including pipe, slight chipping to mouith of jar, 10-1/2" h. including lid. **$408**

Courtesy of Philip Weiss Auctions, www.weissauctions.com

Regal China Alice in Wonderland, incised to underside "WALT DISNEY PRODUCTIONS" arched over "ALICE IN WONDERLAND," Regal China Co., mid-20th century, undamaged, minute flakes to glaze on hair bow, collar, and spot of roughness to interior of base rim, possibly as made, 13-1/4" h. **$720**

Courtesy of Jeffrey S. Evans & Associates, www.jeffreysevans.com

Regal China Dutch Girl with blue hat and red skirt, Regal China Co., second half 20th century, impressed "54-200" to underside, otherwise unmarked, undamaged, 11" h. **$450**

Courtesy of Jeffrey S. Evans & Associates, www.jeffreysevans.com

McCoy jack-o-lantern, orange and green with embossed "MCCOY / USA" to underside, Nelson McCoy Pottery Co., third quarter 20th century, undamaged with minor crazing to interior base, 8-1/2" h. **$510**

Courtesy of Jeffrey S. Evans & Associates, www.jeffreysevans.com

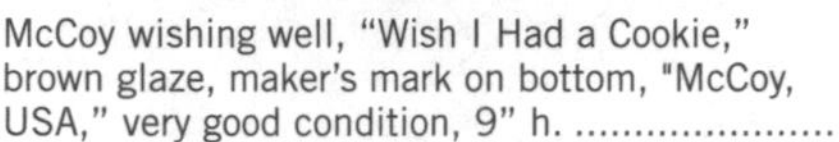

McCoy wishing well, "Wish I Had a Cookie," brown glaze, maker's mark on bottom, "McCoy, USA," very good condition, 9" h. **$12**

Courtesy of Morphy Auctions, morphyauctions.com

McCoy birdhouse with bird. **$75**

Courtesy of Strawser Auctions, www.strawserauctions.com

McCoy chicken, signed, excellent condition, all original with no chips, 10" h. **$36**

Courtesy of Milestone Auctions, www.milestoneauctions.com

Early McCoy touring car, signed, excellent condition. **$40**

Courtesy of Omega Auction Corp., www.omegaauctioncorp.com

Appleman Buick Roadmaster, underside signed "Appleman" and dated 1980, further inscribed "PR IIII," underside of lid impressed "PR IV," 8" h. x 16" l. **$372**

Courtesy of Midwest Auction Galleries, www.midwestauctioninc.com

Metlox Little Red Riding Hood, Metlox Potteries, third quarter 20th century, pressed to underside "MADE IN / POPPYTRAIL / CALIF. / USA" with outline of state of California, 12-1/2" h. **$390**

Courtesy of Jeffrey S. Evans & Associates, www.jeffreysevans.com

Robinson-Ransbottom Whale, Robinson-Ransbottom Pottery Co., third quarter 20th century, impressed "R.R.P. CO. / ROSEVILLE, O." surrounding "USA" to underside, 8-1/4" h. **$300**

Courtesy of Jeffrey S. Evans & Associates, www.jeffreysevans.com

Treasure Craft Dracula, limited edition 507/1000, with certificate of authenticity, near mint condition, 14" h. **$72**

Courtesy of Milestone Auctions, www.milestoneauctions.com

top lot

5 FASCINATING FACTS ABOUT AMERICAN BISQUE COOKIE JARS

1. American Bisque was a prolific producer of cookie jars, believed to be second only to McCoy Pottery.
2. Often the jars bear a simple U.S.A. mark and perhaps a mold number, while some jars include a maker's mark consisting of the company abbreviation: A.B. Co.
3. Most American Bisque pottery pieces have two uncommon wedge shapes on the bottom that are helpful in authentication.
4. Reproduction cookie jars are often smaller than originals, and the design details may not be as defined.
5. Before becoming a champion of cookie jars, the American Bisque Pottery Co. was best known for producing the famous Kewpie dolls of the mid-20th century.

SOURCES: *AMERICAN BISQUE COLLECTOR'S GUIDE* BY MARY JANE GIACOMINI; WWW.COOKIEJARSTORE.COM; COLLECTIBLES.ABOUT.COM

American Bisque Baby Huey, various colors, "BABY HUEY" written across front, American Bisque Co., third quarter 20th century, excellent condition overall with moderate crazing to base and interior base, glazed over chip to cover rim, as made, 13-3/4" h. $1,320

COURTESY OF JEFFREY S. EVANS & ASSOCIATES, WWW.JEFFREYSEVANS.COM

Calirox clear glass cookie jar with lid, marked "Property of Calirox Never Sold," used as counter display at a mercantile in early 1900s, good overall condition, chip on back side, 10-1/2" dia., 15-1/2" h. **$179**

Courtesy of North American Auction Co., www.northamericanauctioncompany.com

Robinson-Ransbottom Frosty the Snowman, various colors, impressed "ROSEVILEE, OHIO / USA / R.R.P. CO" under base, Robinson-Ransbottom Pottery Co., third quarter 20th century, undamaged with minute crazing to interior base, 13-5/8" h. overall.............. **$192**

Courtesy of Jeffrey S. Evans & Associates, www.jeffreysevans.com

Shawnee Puss 'N Boots with transfer-printed decoration, impressed "PATENTED / PUSS 'N BOOTS / USA" to underside, Shawnee Pottery Co., mid-20th century, undamaged, 10-1/4" h. overall. **$96**

Courtesy of Jeffrey S. Evans & Associates, www.jeffreysevans.com

Treasure Craft Wolfman, limited edition 403/750, with certificate of authenticity, near mint condition, 14" h. **$102**

Courtesy of Milestone Auctions, www.milestoneauctions.com

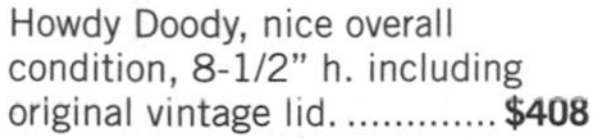

Howdy Doody, nice overall condition, 8-1/2" h. including original vintage lid. **$408**

Courtesy of Philip Weiss Auctions, www.weissauctions.com

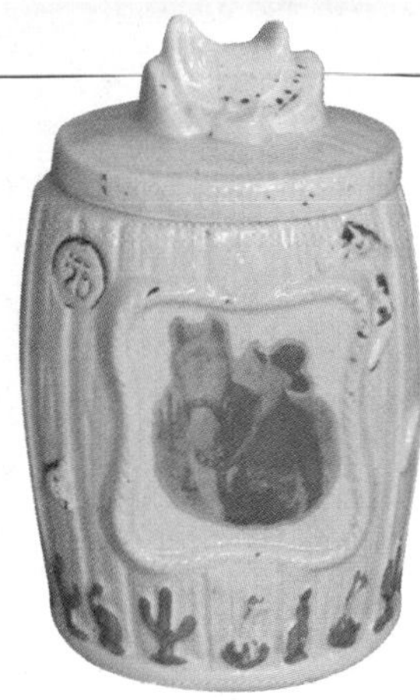

Hopalong Cassidy, circa 1950, paint loss, crack to lid, 11-1/2" h. from base to top of lid. **$324**

Courtesy of Philip Weiss Auctions, www.weissauctions.com

Peter Pan Products Hopalong Cassidy, Chicago, 1950, glazed pottery with raised decorations, decal of Hopalong and Topper, original label on bottom, fine condition, approximately 8" diameter at widest.... **$123**

Courtesy of PBA Galleries, www.pbagalleries.com

Transformers, hard to find, all original, excellent condition, 9" h. **$90**

Courtesy of Milestone Auctions, www.milestoneauctions.com

◀ Roseville Pottery Zephyr Lily pattern, with maker's mark on bottom: Roseville, USA 5-8", very good condition, 10-1/2" h. **$210**

Courtesy of Morphy Auctions, morphyauctions.com

▶ Roseville Pottery two-handled Freesia pattern, No. 4-8", brown tones, good condition, no chips, cracks, or repairs. **$207**

Courtesy of Woody Auction, www.woodyauction.com

Roseville Pottery blue Magnolia pattern, No. 2-8"..................**$64**

Courtesy of Strawser Auctions, www.strawserauctions.com

Roseville Pottery two-handled Water Lily pattern, No. 1-8", pink tones, chip repair under rim..................................**$148**

Courtesy of Woody Auction, www.woodyauction.com

Roseville Pottery Clematis pattern, No. 3-8", blue tones, good condition, no chips, cracks, or repairs...............**$177**

Courtesy of Woody Auction, www.woodyauction.com

Fry Sunnybrook black pressed glass, original cover and wrapped bail handle, H. C. Fry Glass Co., first half 20th century, 7-1/4" h. overall. **$48**

Courtesy of Jeffrey S. Evans & Associates, www.jeffreysevans.com

Shawnee Muggsy with cold-painted and transfer-printed decoration, Shawnee Pottery Co., mid-20th century, impressed "PATENTED / MUGGSY / USA" to underside, undamaged, with some irregularities as made, firing flaw to cover flange interior, some wear to printed decoration, 11" h. **$420**

Courtesy of Jeffrey S. Evans & Associates, www.jeffreysevans.com

Pair of Shawnee Pottery pigs with banks incorporated in lids, boy and girl pigs dressed in brown with green, good condition, no chips, cracks, or repairs, 11" h. **$325**

Courtesy of Woody Auction, www.woodyauction.com

Hull Pottery Red Riding Hood, good condition, no chips, cracks, or repairs, 13" h...... **$236**

Courtesy of Woody Auction, www.woodyauction.com

Warner Bros. Tweety Bird, licensed, excellent condition..**$35**

Courtesy of Omega Auction Corp., www.omegaauctioncorp.com

Big Sky Carvers ranger station log cabin with bears and moose, very good condition, 8-1/2" x 7-1/2" x 10" h........**$30**

Courtesy of North American Auction Co., www.northamericanauctioncompany.com

Christopher Radko Dapper Hare Carriage, 2002, porcelain, original tag and box, 13-1/2" h. x 13-1/2" l. **$182**

Courtesy of William J. Jenack Estate Appraisers & Auctioneers, www.jenack.com

Homer Laughlin China Co. Fiesta Post-'86 dancing lady........................ **$145**

Courtesy of Strawser Auctions, www.strawserauctions.com

COUNTRY STORE

FEW CATEGORIES OF fine collectibles are as fun and colorful as country store memorabilia. The staple of quality antiques shows and shops nationwide, the phrase often refers to such an expansive field of items that it's often difficult to decide where "country store collectibles" begin and "advertising collectibles" end. However, that's one of the very reasons why the category remains so popular and one of the two reasons why this market is growing in value and appeal.

Country store collectibles are associated with items in use in general or frontier retail establishments dating from the mid-1800s and well into the 1940s. The country store was a natural evolution of the pioneer trading post as the more affordable source of day-to-day living items, baking and cooking supplies, or goods for general household and home garden use. Country store furniture is rare, but larger pieces usually include retail countertops and dry goods bins.

The appeal of country store memorabilia has never really waned during the last 40 years, however, the emergence of online trading in the late 1990s redefined items dealers once described as rare. Much like how mid-20th century rock and roll and entertainment memorabilia is used to decorate Applebee's Bar and Grill restaurants, so have country store collectibles been used to line the walls of Cracker Barrel Restaurant and Old Country Store establishments to evoke big appetites for comfort food.

Among items in high demand are original and complete store displays in top condition. These displays were originally intended to hold the product sold to customers and were not generally available for private ownership. Those that survive are highly sought after by collectors for their graphic appeal and their rarity. Until recently, restoration of these items would negatively impact auction prices. However, recent auction results show strong prices for these items if they are rare and retain most of the original graphics.

A great deal of time, talent, and production value was invested in these store displays. Think of them as the Super Bowl commercials of their day. With limited counter space and a captive audience, marketers used every technique and theme available to catch customers' eyes. And here is where the appeal of country store collectibles crosses over so many different categories of collectibles. A fine paper poster advertising DeLaval Cream Separators may appeal to those who collect farming items, cows, and country maidens in addition to

Cast iron coffee grinder, Landers, Frary & Clark, New Britain, Connecticut, wooden crank, nickel-plated top, original paint, "20-1/2" on front, good condition, 18" h. with 8-1/2" wheels. **$2,596**

Courtesy of A-1 Auction, www.a-1auction.net

country store items. The same principal applies to store displays. Are they collected as country store items or as well-preserved examples of vintage advertising, or both?

This category was extremely popular between the late 1970s and the mid-1990s. It appears the hobby is reaching a point at which longtime collectors are ready to begin a new phase of their lives – one that requires fewer items and less space – and are offering these collections for the first time in decades. So if the old adage, "The best time to buy an antique is when you see it" is true, the country store collectibles category stands grow as these large collections come to market and the crossover appeal catches the attention of a wide variety of collectors.

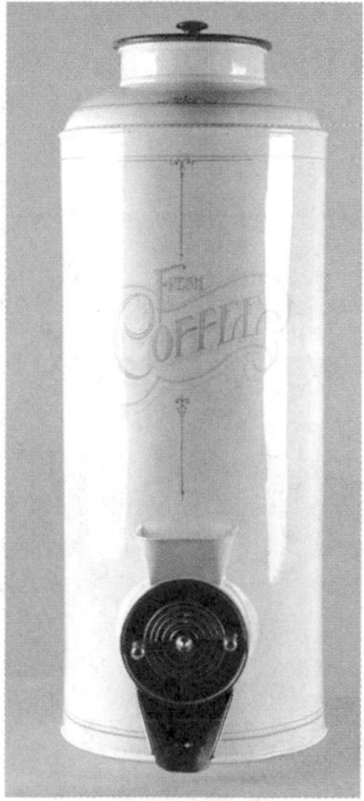

Tabletop coffee dispenser, white with lavender and blue pinstriping, "Fresh Coffee" on front, brass turning handle and spout with wooden lid, restored, paint in excellent condition, 34" x 16".......................... **$214**

Courtesy of Morphy Auctions, www.morphyauctions.com

Oak display cabinet with nine glass-front display drawers that open from back for product storage, excellent condition, 44-1/2" x 25" x 34"... **$793**

Courtesy of Morphy Auctions, www.morphyauctions.com

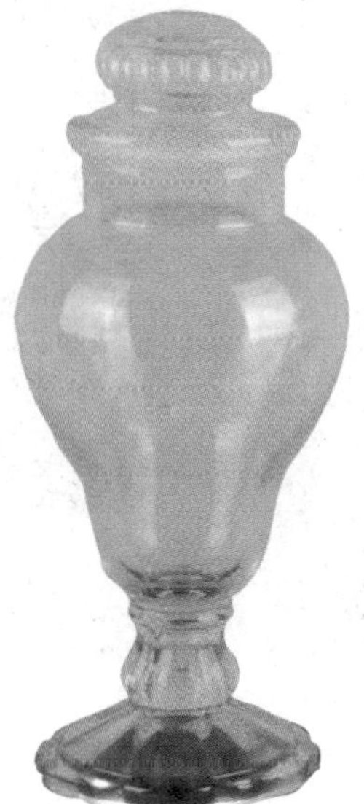

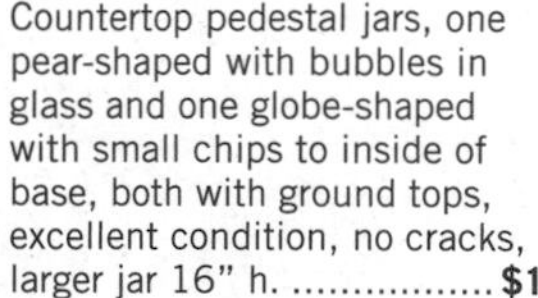

Countertop pedestal jars, one pear-shaped with bubbles in glass and one globe-shaped with small chips to inside of base, both with ground tops, excellent condition, no cracks, larger jar 16" h. **$183**

Courtesy of Morphy Auctions, www.morphyauctions.com

top lot

Rare pagoda spice bin, American Can Co., six-sided tin tower with revolving base, dispenses six different spices, excellent original paint, 36" h. x 27" dia. $3,300

COURTESY OF SHOWTIME AUCTION SERVICES, WWW.SHOWTIMEAUCTIONS.COM

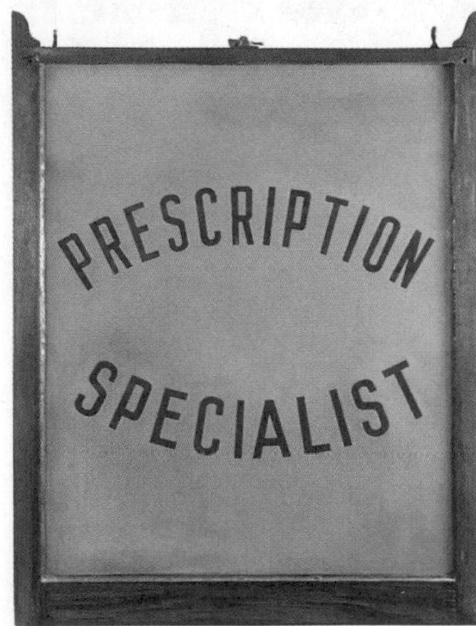

Drugstore window, "Prescription Specialist," frosted glass in wood frame with decorative metal latch at top, hooks for hanging, excellent condition, 43-1/4" h. x 34-1/2" w. x 1-1/2" d.. **$360**

Courtesy of Rich Penn Auctions, www.richpennauctions.com

Coin changer, hardwood with Eastlake design, pressed front reads "F.R. Rice & Co., St. Louis," brass plate with "Hopkins & Robinson Mfg. Co., Louisville, KY, patd Nov 20, 1883," lift top with 1¢ to $1 coin chutes, unusual, very good condition with original surface, 17" h. x 14" w. **$1,080**

Courtesy of Rich Penn Auctions, www.richpennauctions.com

Police Liniment drugstore display cabinet, slanted front glass door, five shelves for display, split/missing wood on top, 50-1/2" h., 18" x 11" w. **$230**

Courtesy of Vero Beach Auction, www.verobeachauction.com

Oscillating octagon nuts and bolts cabinet, turn-of-the-20th century, rare piece with 80 pull-out triangle-shaped drawers with round porcelain knobs, front of each drawer shows size of bolt or nut, top with cut piece of marble in octagonal shape to match cabinet, overall good condition for its age, 36" h., 22-1/2" dia. **$1,666**

Courtesy of North American Auction Co., www.northamericanauctioncompany.com

Uncle Sam Peanut Warmer, circa 1900, all original paint and glass, very good-plus condition, 21-1/2" h........... **$458**

Courtesy of Morphy Auctions, www.morphyauctions.com

Sack rack, Mack's Fancy Bag Rack, stenciled wood with iron string holder, very good condition, 20-1/2" h. x 7-1/2" w. x 16-1/4" d.................... **$480**

Courtesy of Rich Penn Auctions, www.richpennauctions.com

Pine country store desk, 25" x 20". **$48**

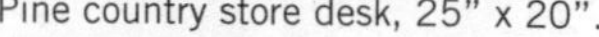

Courtesy of Saco River Auction Co., www.sacoriverauction.com

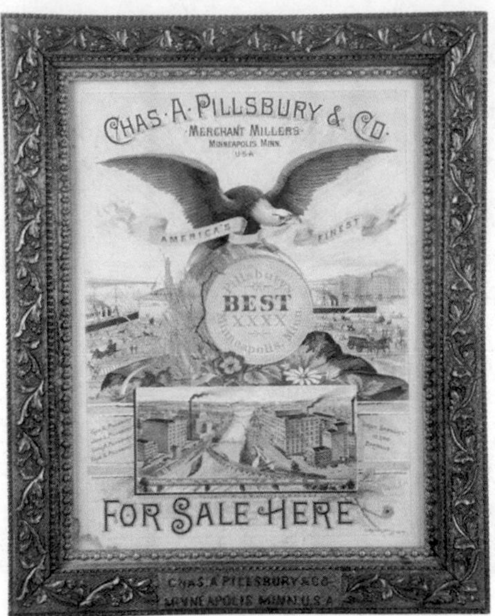

Pillsbury Mills advertising poster in original gesso frame marked Chas. A. Pillsbury & Co., 1880s, frame with original gold paint, center of poster with eagle perched on top of barrel of Pillsbury flour or grain with image of New York harbor and Liverpool docks showing product being transported, poster most likely hung in upscale general store in late 1880s, excellent condition, minor soiling and small stain in bottom left corner, framed 24" x 30". **$2,196**

Courtesy of Morphy Auctions, www.morphyauctions.com

Cash register, National No. 313 with original marble shelf, excellent working condition, 17" h. x 9-1/2" w. x 16" d.. **$840**

Courtesy of Rich Penn Auctions, www.richpennauctions.com

Mother's Best Flour reverse-on-glass curved light-up glass sign with metal frame and hanger, minor paint loss on frame, excellent working condition, 17" dia. **$1,440**

Courtesy of Rich Penn Auctions, www.richpennauctions.com

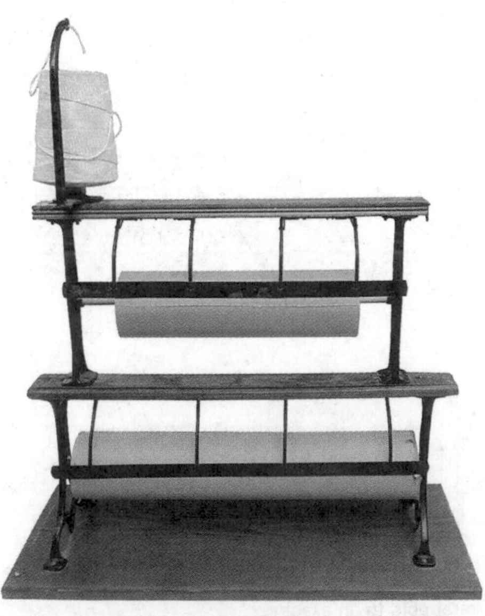

Country store paper roller with string holder, wood and metal, excellent condition, 34-1/2" h. x 31" w. x 8" d.. **$270**

Courtesy of Rich Penn Auctions, www.richpennauctions.com

Glass GrapeOla syrup dispenser, circa 1940s, ceramic reservoir, glass with metal spigot, "GrapeKola 5¢" embossed on reservoir, excellent condition, 7-1/2" w. x 7-1/2" d. x 20-1/2" h. **$1,020**

Courtesy of Morphy Auctions, morphyauctions.com

Bell wall-mount coffee grinder, cast iron, glass, and wood with intricate casting design on face of grinder, turn crank, hardware and glass cup, very good condition, 8" w. x 5-1/2" d. x 17" h. **$660**

Courtesy of Morphy Auctions, morphyauctions.com

Advertising clock, Mihalovitch's Hungarian Blackberry Juice, fourth quarter 19th century, blue acid-cut to colorless glass, original wind-up mechanism with last patent date of 1891, brass hanging chain, excellent condition, operational, some minor edge roughness likely as made, 12" d. **$450**

Courtesy of Jeffrey S. Evans & Associates, www.jeffreysevans.com

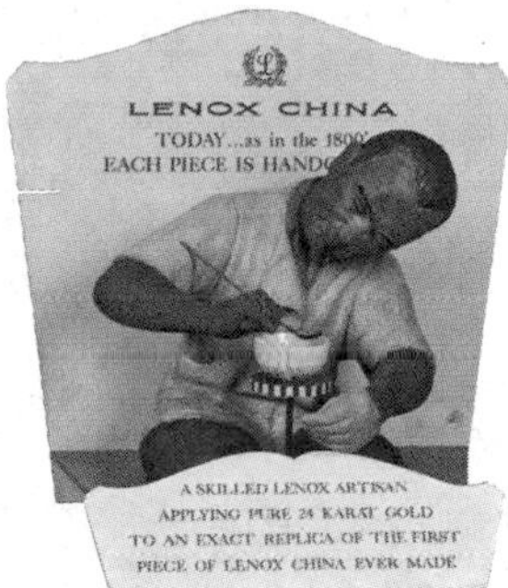

Electric animated display of figural man painting teacup, teacup with spinning motion, Lenox China, "Today...as in the 1800s, each piece is handcrafted" and "A skilled Lenox artisan applying pure 24 karat gold to an exact replica of the first piece of Lenox ever made" printed on two areas on display, very good condition, working order, 20" w. x 16" d. x 20" h. **$780**

Courtesy of Morphy Auctions, morphyauctions.com

Tin coffee containers: Pilot-Knob, Bowers Brothers, Inc., Richmond, Virginia, and Mammy's Favorite Brand, C.D. Kenny Co., Baltimore, first half 20th century, four-pound size containers, Kenny container with original lid and bail handle, very good condition with wear spots, Pilot-Knob in fine condition with light rust to lid, 8-1/2" h. and 10-3/4" h., respectively....... **$390**

Courtesy of Jeffrey S. Evans & Associates, www.jeffreysevans.com

Eskimo Pie container counter display, "The Magic Jar," circa 1920-1930s, orange lithographed tin core with pie images and letter on face, polished brass lid, plated base with three figural Eskimos serving as feet; scratches and loss of litho, 16" h.............. **$525**

Courtesy of Philip Weiss Auctions, www.weissauctions.com

DESK ACCESSORIES

IMAGINE SURLY MR. Potter behind his desk in Frank Capra's "It's a Wonderful Life" (RKO, 1949). In addition to his own portrait and not one, but two busts of Napoleon, Henry Potter's office is filled with expensive-looking accessories, although one can only speculate what a miniature decorative skull positioned on an executive's desk means. One thing is certain: All the decorative details in Potter's office support that he is king of his domain.

Desk accessories are available in designs as diverse as the characters in Capra's movie. In the late 19th and early 20th century, a time when a lavish desk commanded attention in a personal library or executive's office, it was only proper for the accessories to fit the desk and the person sitting behind it.

Tiffany and Bradley & Hubbard are familiar makers of collectible antique desk sets. However, lesser-considered makers of desk accessories are Art Metal Works of New York City and Newark, New Jersey (the company that would eventually become Ronson and specialize in making lighters) and the near-obscure Heintz Art Metal Works of Buffalo, New York.

TIFFANY: AN OBSESSION WITH QUALITY

Collectors of Tiffany desk accessories are in good company. Tiffany's grapevine desk objects were at home on President Woodrow Wilson's desk, while President George Bush preferred the firm's Zodiac items. The Tiffany name is synonymous with quality. According to Bill Holland, author of *Tiffany Desk Sets* (Schiffer, 2008), Louis Comfort Tiffany was obsessed with his creations: "The amount of time and effort that went into them is incredible. Tiffany was obsessed to make things that were beautiful for other people."

The introduction to the book *Tiffany Desk Treasures* (Hudson Hills Press, 2002), by George Kemeny and Donald Miller, spells out the allure of Tiffany accessories to middle economic classes: "Desk items may be collected at a fraction of the cost of almost anything else the Tiffany Studios created. Relatively speaking, these objects are still easily available and are particularly desirable for anyone wishing to own period Tiffany pieces."

Holland, a Tiffany collector for 35 years and dealer for the last 32, agrees. "Desk pieces are a great place to start [collecting Tiffany] because if you're starting out on a budget and you want to spend $500 to $1,000,

Brass elephant-form desk clock, France, circa 1890, Asian elephant on rococo-style base with 3" white porcelain Roman numeral dial with pierced brass hands, eight-day spring-powered time and strike movement regulated by pendulum, surmounted by seated cherub, 16" h. **$1,680**

Courtesy of Skinner, Inc., www.skinnerinc.com

you can buy three, four, or even five pieces. You get a lot more for your money when buying desk pieces. [They] have a lot of character for minimum money. And they're varied enough that you won't get bored."

The most popular pieces, according to Holland, "are ones that incorporate Tiffany metal and glass," such as the Grapevine and Pine Needle patterns. The least popular patterns were never popular. For example, Royal Copper, which used copper plating over brass, wasn't Tiffany's best work and never did really well.

Tiffany desk sets could be ordered from Tiffany with as few as six items from the company catalog. Common items include a pen, pen tray, letter opener (paper knife), book rack or bookends, paperweight, blotter corners or ends, rocker blotter, and inkstand with inkwell insert, to name but a few. Some of the uncommon items include a letter scale, cigar cutter, string holder, and clock. The Bookmark pattern even has a box for rubber bands; it is the only pattern to include this accessory. Tiffany produced 24 desk accessory patterns - patterns that accommodated every décor - and up to 100 items were made in some of those patterns, making it a real challenge for collectors who believe in acquiring complete sets.

BRADLEY & HUBBARD: SMITHSONIAN RESIDENT

Among the familiar firm Bradley & Hubbard's diverse catalog of high-quality metal items are bookends, letter holders, lamps, clocks...all the components one could imagine for a stylish and impressive desk set.

The Meriden, Connecticut, firm began as Bradley, Hatch & Co., and was founded in 1852 in Meriden to manufacture clocks. According to the Smithsonian Institute (www.si.org), "By the 1890s, the Bradley and Hubbard name was synonymous with high quality and artistic merit."

In 1940, the Charles Parker Co., famous for its Parker sporting shotgun, purchased the Bradley & Hubbard Manufacturing Co., establishing the Bradley and Hubbard Division. As a division of the Charles Parker Co., Bradley and Hubbard produced brass and bronze items, as well as lighting fixtures and goods.

Bradley & Hubbard products were sold in its own showrooms in New York, Boston, Chicago, and Philadelphia. Retailers Marshall Field, Sears and Roebuck, and Montgomery Ward also carried B&H products, and a force of traveling salesmen guaranteed public exposure to the firm's artistic - yet functional - metalwares.

Bradley and Hubbard designers made sure to create objects for every taste, too. One elaborate example exhibited in the Smithsonian's Castle Collection of Bradley & Hubbard items is a circa 1885 brass-plated cast iron letter holder, measuring 6" h. x 9" w. x 5" d. The letter holder (marked B&H / 3549 / 7030) displays elaborate cartouches and a stag leaping over a fence chased by two dogs. Slightly less pristine examples are selling in online auctions for roughly $50 or less.

Striking designs are also used in the firm's Arts & Crafts and Art Nouveau lines, of course, but prices follow along the same affordable lines as the Victorian examples. Single common pieces can be purchased for less than $50, and entire sets can sometimes be found for less than $200. In May 2015, DuMouchelle's (Detroit) sold a 10-piece bronze desk set in polished finish and in good condition for $185, including buyer's premium.

RONSON: MUCH MORE THAN LIGHTERS

According to *Ronson Art Metal Works* (Schiffer, 2001), authored by Stuart Schneider, Art Metal Works (the precursor of Ronson, which became famous as a cigarette lighter manufacturer after World War II) was founded by Louis Aronson in the 1880s and became a leader in metal casting in Newark, New Jersey, in the early 20th century.

From the early 1900s until the early 1940s, Art Metal Works/Ronson produced a vast array of bookends and desk accessories, utilizing nearly 30 different finishes. The company's output was so prolific that an impressive collection can be built of AMW bookends alone. In addition to bookends, Art Metal Works also produced clocks, crucifixes, penholders, and desk sets.

Tiffany Studios bronze paper rack in Venetian pattern with design of flowers, circles, and scrolls with small animals on bottom border, gold patina, signed on underside "Tiffany Studios New York 1644," very good to excellent condition, 10" w. x 6-1/4" h. **$1,007**

Courtesy of James D. Julia Auctioneers, Fairfield, Maine, www.jamesdjuliacom

Black Forest carved dog inkwell, late 19th/early 20th century, hinged head opening to glass inset inkwell, paws on hollowed log, 4" h. **$960**

Courtesy of Skinner, Inc., www.skinnerinc.com

According to Schneider, when it comes to identifying pieces made by the company, "Several different marks were used on Art Metal Works' products. One can find AMW, Art Metal Works, L.V. Aronson, Ronson, and Ronson Metal Art Wares. The name Ronson, a shortened form of Aronson, was trademarked in 1910." When hunting online for prospective purchases, no single search will do; collectors should search for all these terms for the most complete results.

Although many pieces are marked, dating Art Metal Works items can be confusing; copyright dates on items can lead collectors (and some dealers) to believe that is the date of the item. "Copyright notations refer to design elements and not the finished product," Schneider explained in *Ronson Art Metal Works.* For example, an elephant figure may have been copyrighted and used on an incense burner in the 1910s and then used later on a bookend in the 1920s. "The same copyright date on both pieces may confuse a collector who is not familiar with what exactly was copyrighted," Schneider said.

Art Metal Works designs incorporate attractive elements that easily fit into vintage-themed décor; their ready availability and low prices make them a good choice for decorative accents.

HEINTZ: A WELL-KEPT SECRET

More obscure but arguably more distinctive than those previously mentioned are desk items produced by the Heintz Art Metal Shop. Author Kevin McConnell first wrote an article on Heintz for the August 1990 edition of *The Antique Trader Price Guide to Antiques* at the behest of its editor, Kyle Husfloen. McConnell includes part of that research in his book, *Heintz Art Metal, Silver-on-Bronze Wares* (Schiffer, 1990), which is an invaluable research and educational resource for devotees of the Arts & Crafts movement as well as American bronze wares.

Producing Arts & Crafts, Art Nouveau, and other finely executed decorative and utilitarian items in Buffalo, New York, for just 24 years, Heintz used a sintering process to bond silver designs to bronze objects, creating strikingly elegant designs. The shop's designs are simple but well executed and of truly high quality.

Heintz design motifs include geometrics, florals, and animals. Some also included enameling.

Heintz items are more limited in availability and higher-priced than either Bradley & Hubbard or Ronson Art Metal Works, but they are not as limited or as expensive as one

top lot!

Tiffany Studios patinated bronze inkwell, circa 1910, in form of crab with hinged shell, holding ink pot between its claws, stamped "Tiffany Studios / New York / 856," overall good condition with general marks, scratches, rubbed wear, and verdigris commensurate with age, scattered dings to inkwell body and rim, lacking seashell-inset inkwell cover and antenna, 2-5/8" h. x 7-1/2" w., 7-1/4" dia. $5,400

COURTESY OF JOHN MORAN AUCTIONEERS, WWW.JOHNMORAN.COM

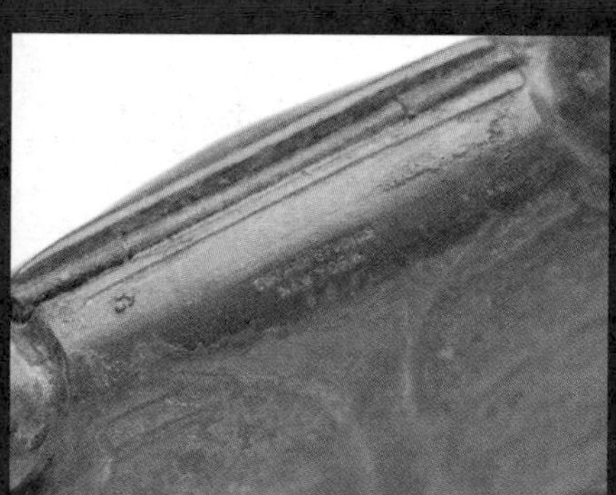

might think. For example, a floral-decorated (production #1003) five-piece Heintz desk set including a calendar holder, inkwell (no glass insert), blotter, pen rest, and letter opener sold for $335 in a January 2016 online auction.

One thing all these manufacturers have in common: All their wares are well made and meant to be used; they are all made to hold up to regular use if properly cared for.

Tiffany items should be cleaned with a soft, damp cloth, according to Bill Holland, who said the best pieces will "hold up pretty well without doing much to them," but don't over clean, don't drop, and don't polish. "Most pieces that are not shiny were not meant to be shiny," he said.

Stuart Schneider also recommends gentle care, but with stronger conviction. When asked about warnings he would give when using and caring for Ronson's Art Metal pieces, Schneider said, "Tell your cleaning people, if you have them, not to use any product on your pieces; it may take the finish off. The finishes on a lot of the pieces are pretty solid finishes, but chemicals have the potential to cause damage."

Whether you're looking for one piece or to complete an entire 100-piece set, with countless items and unlimited designs to choose from, well-made vintage and antique desk accessories can portray whatever character the collector chooses without breaking the bank – or passing a hat.

— *Karen Knapstein* Print Editor, *Antique Trader Magazine*

Art Deco figural desk clock, Paris, circa 1925, Belgian slate and alabaster with seated spelter and composite female figure and standing peacock, hexagonal dial with Arabic numerals and pierced hands within tetradecagon (13-sided) alabaster and black slate case, eight-day time and count-wheel strike movement with platform escapement, marked "The Friedlander Co., France" and "Fini Paris J.S. 46448" on back plate, alabaster and black slate base, 13" h. x 28" w. **$1,200**

Courtesy of Skinner, Inc., www.skinnerinc.com

Engraved cast metal and glass inkwell and scale, circa 1860, with snail-shaped molded milk glass ink jars on scrolled rotating arms, center shaft with scale marked 0-8, shaped base with foliate engraving, traces of blue paint throughout, unmarked, 8-1/4" h. **$861**

Courtesy of Skinner, Inc., www.skinnerinc.com

Four Tiffany Studios desk pieces: Calendar frame with acid etched Pine Needle pattern design on sides with caramel slag glass backing, gold patina, original spring clip, 4-1/2" w. x 3-1/2" d.; playing card case with acid-etched Pine Needle pattern sides, back, top and bottom with caramel slag glass backing, gold patina, holds two decks of cards, 4-1/4" h.; round inkwell with acid-etched Pine Needle pattern on side and top with caramel slag glass backing, gold patina, with glass insert, 3-3/4" dia., 2-1/2" h.; and square inkwell with acid-etched Grapevine pattern on sides and top with caramel slag glass backing, copper patina, with glass insert, 3-1/4" sq. x 3" h.; all pieces signed on underside "Tiffany Studios New York" and numbered, all in very good to excellent condition with minor wear and discoloration to patina on calendar frame, screw missing from underside of Pine Needle inkwell. **$830**

Courtesy of James D. Julia Auctioneers, Fairfield, Maine, www.jamesdjuliacom

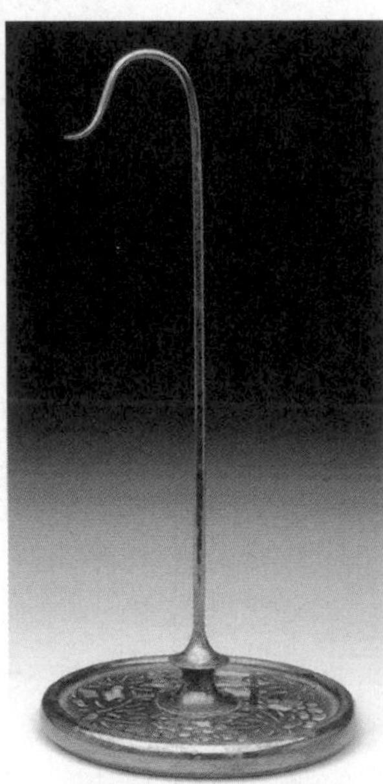

Rare Tiffany Studios silver-plated bill hook in acid-etched Grapevine pattern with clam broth glass backing, silvered patina, signed "Tiffany Studios New York" on underside, very good to excellent condition, 7-1/4" h. **$948**

Courtesy of James D. Julia Auctioneers, Fairfield, Maine, www.jamesdjuliacom

Tiffany Studios Bookmark pattern desk set with large blotter ends, bookends, octagonal inkwell, matchbox holder, pen tray, rocker blotter, and letter rack, with Tiffany Studios Zodiac pattern desk lamp, all pieces in gold dore, all pieces stamped "Tiffany Studios New York" and numbered, very good to excellent condition with minor wear to patina, lamp with replacement switch, rewired with contemporary plastic cord, blotter ends 19-1/4" l. **$2,370**

Courtesy of James D. Julia Auctioneers, Fairfield, Maine, www.jamesdjuliacom

Mephistopheles-form bronze inkwell, Continental, 19th century, cast as bust of demon with hinged lid to back of head, circular black slate base, unmarked, 6-1/2" h. **$210**

Courtesy of Skinner, Inc., www.skinnerinc.com

Bronze hound head letter opener, impressed with AR monogram for Arthur Rubinstein/Aust-Reich Foundry, "F. Gornik," "MADE IN AUSTRIA," and indistinctly numbered, 12-7/8" l. **$780**

Courtesy of Skinner, Inc., www.skinnerinc.com

Green onyx and ormolu inkwell, 19th century, square with central covered inkwell surrounded by four pen rests, mounted with reticulated gilt-metal scrolling foliage and garlands, four toupie feet, unmarked, 9" l. **$240**

Courtesy of Skinner, Inc., www.skinnerinc.com

Tiffany Studios Pine Needle pattern bronze bookends, acid-etched pine needle design with caramel slag glass backing, gold patina, signed "Tiffany Studios New York 1024," pine needle panel on one bookend slightly loose in slot on base plate, glass panel with crack at bottom corner, patina with minor wear and discoloration, 5-1/2" w. x 6" h. **$533**

Courtesy of James D. Julia Auctioneers, Fairfield, Maine, www.jamesdjuliacom

Austrian Art Nouveau bronze figural letter holder, circa 1910, marked "Hering," 13-1/8" x 12" x 5".......... **$2,750**

Courtesy of Heritage Auctions, ha.com

DISNEY

COLLECTIBLES THAT FEATURE Mickey Mouse, Donald Duck, and other famous characters of cartoon icon Walt Disney are everywhere. They can be found with little effort at flea markets, garage sales, local antiques and toys shows, and online as well as through auction houses and specialty catalogs.

Of Disney toys, comics, posters, and other items produced from the 1930s through the 1960s, prewar Disney material is by far the most desirable.

Mickey Mouse "Steamboat Willie" original production drawing, Ub Iwerks, number "325" at lower right corner, from scene six minutes into cartoon where Mickey uses mallets to play bull's teeth like a musical instrument, 3-1/4" x 3-3/4"............................ **$1,403**

Courtesy of Hake's Americana & Collectibles, www.hakes.com

Mickey Mouse large store display, Old King Cole, Inc., 1935, painted composition, 23-1/2" x 40" x 3".......... **$1,150**

Courtesy of Hake's Americana & Collectibles, www.hakes.com

Minnie Mouse "shy" porcelain figurine, Rosenthal, Germany, circa 1932, #556 in series, 3-1/4" h......................... **$3,061**

Courtesy of Hake's Americana & Collectibles, www.hakes.com

Mickey Mouse button for RKO Kiddie Klub, 1930s, no maker name or back paper, 1-1/4". **$582**

Courtesy of Hake's Americana & Collectibles, www.hakes.com

Mickey Mouse Cocoa tin container, Sweetacres, Australia, 1930s, one-pound can, 6" dia., 2-1/2" h. **$209**

Courtesy of Hake's Americana & Collectibles, www.hakes.com

"Snow White and the Seven Dwarfs" color concept original art, circa 1936, 5-1/2" x 7-3/4".. **$2,151**

Courtesy of Hake's Americana & Collectibles, www.hakes.com

Mickey Mouse and Friends "Atlantic City" small sand pail and shovel, Ohio Art, 1930s, 4-1/4" h. **$5,376**

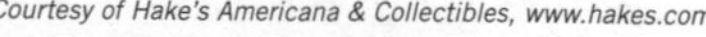

Courtesy of Hake's Americana & Collectibles, www.hakes.com

Horace Horsecollar and Clarabelle Cow bookshelf, Kroehler Manufacturing Co., 11-1/2" x 21-1/4" x 52". **$2,783**

Courtesy of Hake's Americana & Collectibles, www.hakes.com

top lot

Mickey and Minnie Mouse riding motorcycle, Tipp & Co., Germany, circa 1930s, with working clockwork mechanism, all original, right side of toy in best condition, lithography with moderate wear and scratches with some oxidation to left side of toy, wheels generally clean with some blemishes and oxidation, 9-1/4" l. $58,663

COURTESY OF BERTOIA AUCTIONS, WWW.BERTOIAAUCTIONS.COM

Mickey Mouse wristwatch, US Time, circa 1947, with original box. **$153**

Courtesy of Morphy Auctions, morphyauctions.com

Pinocchio doll, R. John Wright, No. 246 of 500, with original box, 11-1/4" x 4-1/4" x 6-1/4". **$1,100**

Courtesy of Morphy Auctions, morphyauctions.com

Mickey Mouse Washer tin litho toy washing machine, Ohio Art, 8" h. **$214**

Courtesy of Morphy Auctions, morphyauctions.com

Snow White and the Seven Dwarfs radio, Emerson, 8" l. **$1,830**

Courtesy of Morphy Auctions, morphyauctions.com

Musical Pluto tin litho wind-up, Marx, 1960s, made in Japan, with built-in key and three tunnels, 8-1/4" x 8-1/4" x 2-3/4". **$266**

Courtesy of Hake's Americana & Collectibles, www.hakes.com

G-E Mazda Lamps lightbulbs store display with Mickey and Minnie Mouse and Pluto, 1941, General Electric, die-cut cardboard display, 20-1/2" x 41". **$455**

Courtesy of Hake's Americana & Collectibles, www.hakes.com

Dopey and Doc Fisher-Price platform toy, paper on wood, No. 770, 12" l. **$153**

Courtesy of Morphy Auctions, morphyauctions.com

Donald Duck lollipop display, French or Canadian, 1940s, wood backing with 14 holes for lollipops, composition bust, 5-3/4" x 8". **$1,341**

Courtesy of Hake's Americana & Collectibles, www.hakes.com

Disneyland large biscuit tin, Belgium, circa 1940, J. Schuybroek S.A. Hoboken-Anvers, Silly Symphonies characters pictured, 7-3/4" x 12-3/4" x 2-1/2". **$443**

Courtesy of Hake's Americana & Collectibles, www.hakes.com

Davey Crockett Indian fighter boots, Trimfoot, circa 1955, children's size 13-1/2, leather with leather fringe and fur trim. **$230**

Courtesy of Hake's Americana & Collectibles, www.hakes.com

Mickey Mouse and Donald Duck electricity safety poster for Duquesne Light Co., Pittsburgh, Pennsylvania, Walt Disney Productions, circa 1939, 16" x 21"............... **$225**

Courtesy of Hake's Americana & Collectibles, www.hakes.com

Mickey Mouse tin litho tea set, Ohio Art, marked "Walt Disney Enterprises," original box. **$793**

Courtesy of Morphy Auctions, morphyauctions.com

Walt Disney Character Lites, Paramount, seven different characters, original box, 10-1/2" l. **$122**

Courtesy of Morphy Auctions, morphyauctions.com

Walt Disney Comics and Stories, Vol. 1, No. 7, April 1941................................ **$480**

Courtesy of Philip Weiss Auctions, www.weissauctions.com

RPM Motor Oil advertising sign with Donald Duck, marked "Walt Disney Productions," 1940, 24" dia. **$6,710**

Courtesy of Morphy Auctions, morphyauctions.com

Mickeys' Mousekemovers moving van with box, Linemar, Japan, 12-3/4" l. **$512**

Courtesy of Bertoia Auctions, www.bertoiaauctions.com

Dopey walker, Marx, 1938, tin litho wind-up with original box, 8-1/4" h. **$278**

Courtesy of Bertoia Auctions, www.bertoiaauctions.com

Walt Disney Company award with Jiminy Cricket, 1978, 12" x 7" x 7". **$500**

Courtesy of Heritage Auctions, ha.com

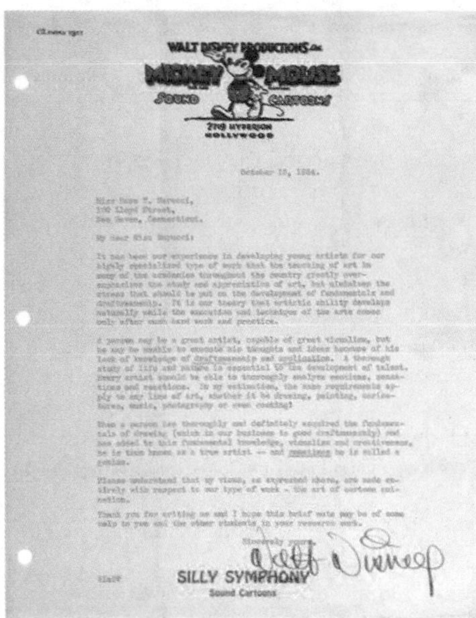

WALT DISNEY PRODUCTIONS
MICKEY MOUSE
SOUND CARTOONS
2719 HYPERION
HOLLYWOOD

[illegible]

SILLY SYMPHONY
Sound Cartoons

Walt Disney signed letter on company letterhead, 1934, 11" x 8-1/2"................................... **$5,625**

Courtesy of Heritage Auctions, ha.com

Mickey Mouse stock poster, United Artists, 1935, one sheet, 27" x 41"...............................**$11,950**

Courtesy of Heritage Auctions, ha.com

Honest John the Fox, 1939, Walt Disney Studios, gouache on trimmed celluloid, 8-1/3" x 13"..........**$3,750**

Courtesy of Leslie Hindman Auctioneers, www.lesliehindman.com

DOORSTOPS

DOORSTOPS HAVE BEEN around as long as there have been doors. They were originally improvised from garden stones, wedges of wood, pieces of furniture, or any other objects heavy enough to prop doors open to ensure air circulation. Early decorative ones, which date from the late 1700s, were generally round and made of sand-cast brass or metal with flat, hollow backs.

By the early 19th century, scores of French and English households boasted fashionable three-dimensional iron doorstops in the shape of animals, flowers, and figurines. Some, called door porters, incorporated convenient long handles that were used to lift and place them easily.

Homes with French double doors often featured matching pairs, like matching eagles or horse hooves, Punch and Judy, or lions opposing unicorns. Today these sets range from $400-$900 each, depending on condition and themes.

Doorstops migrated to American shores after the Civil War, where due to Yankee frugality, they became smaller and lighter than European models.

During the height of their popularity - the 1920s through the mid-1940s - American homemakers could purchase doorstops, or coordinated sets that included doorknockers and bookends, for pennies in gift stores and through mail-order catalogs. Fashionable Art Deco, circus, and nursery rhyme themes, along with figures like organ grinders, dapper gentlemen, Southern belles and flappers, reflected the times.

Cheery flower and flower-basket doorstops featuring bouquets of tulips, zinnias, pansies, black-eyed Susans or sunflowers, for example, celebrated the arrival of spring. Although some currently start at around $100 apiece, those that have survived with original paint in prime condition may fetch many times that amount.

Hubley's dog breed doorstops, which portray lifelike, highly detailed Doberman pinschers, German shepherds, cocker spaniels, French bulldogs, beagles and various types of terriers, and more, were also extremely popular. So were arched, curled, springing, or sleeping cats.

John and Nancy Smith, avid collectors and leading doorstop and figural cast iron authorities, as well as authors of *The Doorstop Book: An Encyclopedia of Doorstop Collecting*, find that beginners generally concentrate on certain themes like flowers, animals, people, or wildlife. Some seek doorstops produced by a particular foundry, including Albany, National, Eastern Specialty, Judd, Wilton, Litto, Virginia Metalcrafters, Waverly, or Spencer.

As their collections grow, however, many explore other themes as well. Nautical

Full-figured Scottie dog doorstop in standing position, Hubley Manufacturing Co., Lancaster, Pennsylvania, cat # 305, with original leather collar, mint condition, 9" h.............................**$216**

Courtesy of Bertoia Auctions, www.bertoiaauctions.com

enthusiasts may collect clipper ship, sailor, lighthouse, and anchor doorstops. Sports fans may seek skiers, golfers, caddies, or football players. Animal lovers may populate menageries with Hubley honey bears and horses or Bradley & Hubbard parrots. Some prefer pets portrayed in character, like rabbits in evening dress, Peter Rabbits chomping on carrots, and strutting ducks in tophats. These fancies currently sell from $300-$2,000.

Other collectors search for bright, sassy, desirable and pricey Anne Fish Art Deco pieces like bathing beauties, Charleston dancers, and parrots, or Taylor Cook's brightly colored elephant on barrels, koalas, or fawns.

"In addition to their beauty," observes Lewis Keister, proprietor of East Meets West Antiques based in Los Angeles, "the historical value of many of these doorstops can be significant. One highly desirable doorstop, the yellow-slickered Old Salt fisherman, for example, is very appealing to both antique collectors and folk art collectors." So are the nostalgic, mellow-hued stagecoach, Conestoga wagon, Aunt Jemima, Victorian lady, fruit basket, horns of plenty, and cozy, rose-covered cottage doorstops. Even when doorstops outnumber doors, home decorators, charmed by their appeal, often display them as colorful accent pieces, bookends, or works of art lined up in custom-built shelving, antique cupboards, or along staircases.

Doorstops that feature outstanding sculptural quality, form and character are the most desirable of all. If they also bear identifying stamps, signatures, copyrights, studio names or production numbers (which often appear on their backs), their values rise even further.

In addition to desirability, rarity - possibly due to high production costs, short foundry existence, or even bad design - raises the value of vintage doorstops. Condition, however, determines their ultimate worth. Collectors should certainly buy doorstops that they like within a price range that they find comfortable. But they should be in the very best condition that they can afford. According to experts, only these will retain or increase in value over time. And some may increase considerably.

Today, for example, a rare, unusual, desirable doorstop that is also in mint condition - perhaps a vintage Uncle Sam, Halloween Girl, or Whistling Jim - may command as much as $10,000.

Cast iron cockatoo doorstop, Taylor Cook, model #4, circa 1930, 10-1/2" h. **$690**

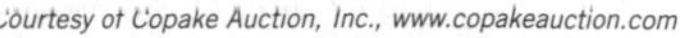

Courtesy of Copake Auction, Inc., www.copakeauction.com

Cast iron modernistic cat doorstop, Hubley Foundry, Lancaster, Pennsylvania, cat #308, circa 1920, 10-1/2" h.. .... **$1,680**

Courtesy of Copake Auction, Inc., www.copakeauction.com

Because doorstops are cast objects, however, caution the Smiths, they lend themselves to reproduction. In addition to reuse of old molds, new designs are continually in production. "Older doorstops usually have smoother, more refined castings than reproductions, which are rougher or pebbly. Seams, if any, are usually tighter. Originals feature slotted screws or rivets, while reproductions, if cast in two or more pieces, are usually assembled with Philips-head screws. Moreover, artists generally painstakingly smoothed mold marks of vintage castings with hand files. Reproductions, however, are finished in minutes with power tools and tumblers. These leave coarser grinding marks."

Collectors should also look carefully at the wear patterns on possible buys. Most old doorstops were used for their original purpose – holding doors open. So potential buyers are advised to look for wear in the logical places: on their tops, where they were handled, and around their bases, where they were scuffed along the floor. Reproductions rarely resemble the real thing.

By studying as many collections as possible – by actually handling as many doorstops as possible, beginners can learn to differentiate between vintage pieces and reproductions.

Doorstops are readily found at antique shows, shops, and auctions. It is recommended, however, to purchase them from reputable dealers who not only specialize in cast iron items, but also guarantee their authenticity.

Cast iron elephant doorstop, Bradley & Hubbard Foundry, Meriden, Connecticut, circa 1920, marked "B & H, 7799" on backside, 10-1/2" h. **$570**

Courtesy of Copake Auction, Inc., www.copakeauction.com

Cast iron penguin doorstop, penguin looking upward, painted in Art Deco colors of red and yellow, marked "No. 1, copyright 1930, Taylor Cook," excellent condition, 10" h. **$3,050**

Courtesy of Morphy Auctions, morphyauctions.com

Cast iron sitting fox doorstop, Hubley Manufacturing Co., Lancaster, Pennsylvania, full-figure, three-piece casting, rare and desirable, overpainted with gold highlight wash, very good condition. **$3,660**

Courtesy of Morphy Auctions, morphyauctions.com

Cast iron rooster doorstop signed "Spencer," double-sided casting, very good condition, small tip of tail feather broken off, 13-1/2" h. **$1,220**

Courtesy of Morphy Auctions, morphyauctions.com

Cast iron doorstop, squirrel with nut, Bradley & Hubbard, Meriden, Connecticut.......... **$570**

Courtesy of Copake Auction, Inc., www.copakeauction.com

Footmen doorstop (smaller version), Hubley Foundry, Lancaster, Pennsylvania, circa 1920, marked "272" on backside, "Fish" on front of base, designed by Anne Fish, rarer of the two footmen models, 9-1/4" h. **$690**

Courtesy of Copake Auction, Inc., www.copakeauction.com

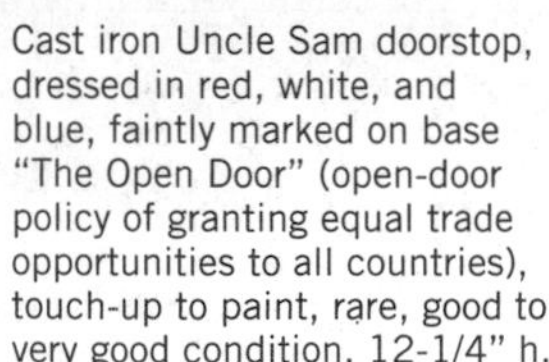

Cast iron Uncle Sam doorstop, dressed in red, white, and blue, faintly marked on base "The Open Door" (open-door policy of granting equal trade opportunities to all countries), touch-up to paint, rare, good to very good condition, 12-1/4" h. **$976**

Courtesy of Morphy Auctions, morphyauctions.com

Wine merchant doorstop, solid casting, full figure of merchant in green, blue, and red overloaded with inventory, carrying bottles of red and white wines, rare, pristine condition, 9-3/4" h.......... **$3,396**

Courtesy of Bertoia Auctions, www.bertoiaauctions.com

Parlor maid doorstop, Hubley Foundry, Lancaster, Pennsylvania, circa 1920, marked "268" on backside and "FISH" on front of base, designed by Anne Fish, 9" h. **$1,140**

Courtesy of Copake Auction, Inc., www.copakeauction.com

Cast iron Charleston dancers doorstop, Art Deco designed form with two intertwined dancers, Hubley Manufacturing Co., Lancaster, Pennsylvania, marked "Copyright Fish, 270," designed by Anne Fish, good condition, 9" h.................. **$793**

Courtesy of Morphy Auctions, morphyauctions.com

Bird of paradise doorstop, L.A.C.S. #765, multicolored bird flying with wavy plumed tail on curvy base, near mint condition, 13-3/8" h........ **$2,347**

Courtesy of Bertoia Auctions, www.bertoiaauctions.com

Cast iron jayhawk doorstop, Castrite, Topeka, University of Kansas mascot, excellent condition, 8-1/2" h. **$793**

Courtesy of Morphy Auctions, morphyauctions.com

Cast iron rabbit doorstop, Littco Products, rabbit in overalls pushing wheelbarrow full of assorted goodies, strong colors, 11-5/8" h. **$1,162**

Courtesy of Bertoia Auctions, www.bertoiaauctions.com

Cast iron Art Deco poppies doorstop, good to very good condition, 6-1/2" h. **$230**

Courtesy of Richard Opfer Auctioneering, Inc., www.opferauction.com

Cast iron "Whistlin' Jim" doorstop, 17" h. **$1,560**

Courtesy of Copake Auction, Inc., www.copakeauction.com

Cast iron dachshund on base doorstop, Bradley & Hubbard, Meriden, Connecticut, double-sided, rubber bumpers intact, excellent condition, 10" h. **$2,440**

Courtesy of Morphy Auctions, morphyauctions.com

Cast iron pig doorstop with original paint, good condition with minor wear, 5-3/4" h. x 8-3/4" l **$1,210**

Courtesy of Conestoga Auction Co., www.conestogaauction.com

Rare Boston terrier cast iron doorstop, Bradley & Hubbard, Meriden, Connecticut, circa 1920, untouched original paint and condition, 9" h. x 11-1/2" w. **$420**

Courtesy of Stanton Auctions, www.stantonauctions.com

Reclining sheep stoneware doorstops, Pfaltzgraff Pottery Co., York, Pennsylvania, circa 1920-1930, molded with Bristol slip-glazed surfaces and brushed cobalt details, ram with hand-modeled and applied clay horns, shallow chips to underside of muzzle and tail and to tip of each horn of ram, 8-1/2" l. **$369**

Courtesy of Crocker Farm, www.crockerfarm.com

"Mary, Mary Quite Contrary" cast iron doorstop, standing figure of woman watering her garden, circa 1930, Littco Products, original paint, partial paper label affixed to reverse, excellent condition, 12-1/2" h. **$484**

Courtesy of Fontaine's Auction Gallery, www.fontainesauctions.com

Five cast iron cat doorstops: Small cast iron black-painted cat with yellow eyes attributed to National Foundry Co., silver-painted cat with bow and textured surface, white-painted Art Deco Hubley Manufacturing Co. cat, Judd Co. cat with painted green eyes, and small painted solid cast iron cat with white highlights and yellow-painted eyes, early 20th century, overall paint wear on most, from 5-5/8" to 10" h. **$861**

Courtesy of Case Antiques, Inc. Auctions & Appraisals, caseantiques.com

Seated Punch doorstop (from Punch and Judy puppetry fame), hand-painted brass casting, circa 1910, facing right with small dog seated beside him, original painted finish in very good condition, 12" h. **$786**

Courtesy of Fontaine's Auction Gallery, www.fontainesauctions.com

◀ Three cast iron doorstops: Peacock and urn by Hubley Manufacturing Co., Lancaster, Pennsylvania, peacock by Albany, and Polly parrot by Hubley, some paint wear, very good condition overall, 8-1/8" h. **$420**

Courtesy of Morphy Auctions, morphyauctions.com

Large lion cast iron doorstop, circa 1880, hollow back, stepped rectangular base, detailed mane and muscles in legs, overall good condition, 8-1/2" h. x 11-1/2" w. **$431**

Courtesy of Dirk Soulis Auctions, www.dirksoulisauctions.com

Cast iron doorstop inspired by development of *New York Times* crossword puzzles, figure with jacket that simulates puzzle, books strewn at feet on base, body illustrates theme of piece: "Crossed Out," overall excellent-plus condition, 7-3/8" h. **$1,560**

Courtesy of Morphy Auctions, morphyauctions.com

Turkey cast iron doorstop with detailed feathers, dropped wings, and open tail feathers, early 20th century, Bradley & Hubbard, Meriden, Connecticut, rubber bumpers intact, overall excellent-plus condition, 12-1/2" h........ **$3,300**

Courtesy of Morphy Auctions, morphyauctions.com

◀ Parrot motif bronze and enamel doorstop, detailed casting with folded wings, contour feathers, muscular claws, realistic coloring on head and body, Bradley & Hubbard, Meriden, Connecticut, good condition overall, 7" l. x 2-1/2" w. x 8" h. **$180**

Courtesy of Greenwich Auction, www.greenwichauction.net

Mythological form cast iron doorstop, cold painted red and gold, rarely seen folk art structure with detailed design of face appearing to be adorned in type of mask, 8" h. x 8" w. x 9" d. **$307**

Courtesy of Greenwich Auction, www.greenwichauction.net

◀ "The Pingree House" doorstop designed by sculptor Sarah Symonds, based on actual Gardner-Pingree House at 128 Essex St., Salem, Massachusetts, built in 1805 by one of region's most noted architects and carvers, John Gardner, base of doorstop signed "The Pingree House, Salem, Mass., Sarah W. Symonds," overall excellent condition, 6-1/2" h......... **$1,560**

Courtesy of Morphy Auctions, morphyauctions.com

FARM TOOLS

The joke goes: A farmer recently won $1 million in the lottery. When asked what he was going to do with the money, he replied, "I'll keep farming until it runs out."

The same is true with farm tool collectors: It doesn't matter how much money they have, there's always a new tool or discovery to add to the collection and deplete your bank account. Thankfully, the hobby's bright future and solid prices may mean collectors could end up ahead of the millionaire farmer in the end.

Farm tool collectors can easily spend their entire lives finding unique discoveries on a regular basis and make a nice display in a workshop or outbuilding.

Courtesy of Eric Bradley

"Farm tools are definitely hot," according to Richard Backus, editor in chief of *Farm Collector*, a monthly magazine spanning small engines, tractors, and hand tools. One of the magazine's most popular articles is "Ten Agricultural Inventions that Changed the Face of Farming in America." It mirror's some of the most popularly collected tools and drives home the relevance of the hobby – without farm tools the United States would not be the prosperous country we know and love today (warts and all). History comes alive in farm tools in ways decorative arts can rarely show.

Take, for instance, the cotton gin. By the turn of the 19th century, slavery in the American South seemed to be on the wane. In practical terms, slavery lacked economic viability. In

Cotton gin, circa first quarter 19th century, circular metal wheels with teeth in addition to wood drums with teeth, working, on display from 1944 through 2004 at the Atlanta Museum. .... **$10,000+**

Courtesy of Heritage Auctions, ha.com

1792, the South was selling roughly 138,000 pounds of raw cotton to mostly English mills. Two decades later, after the invention of the cotton gin by Eli Whitney, that number had increased to 62 million – a 450-fold increase. The cotton gin revolutionized American agriculture and can be directly credited for extending the life of America's "peculiar institution" for another 50 years and ensuring a bitter Civil War. Despite their widespread use, cotton gins themselves remain scarce collectibles and have fetched between $15,000 and $75,500 at auction during the last decade.

Backus compares the tool-making farmers of the 18th and 19th centuries to the fast-moving tech moguls behind the 1990s dot com boom and today's digital apps. Like today's iPhone app developer, a 19th century farmer who might be handy with a forge labored to invent a time-saving tool for himself and one that could possibly be marketed and make his family wealthy. Farm toolmakers were, in a sense, the original hackers. "They were very much the same," Backus said. "These tools revolutionized life and a farmer could double or quadruple his productivity. He could set up an engine to take care of a chore and run off and do something else."

American farm tool production occurred primarily on a small scale until the Industrial Revolution. Literally thousands of different manufacturers came and went until the late 1920s, Backus said, all of them vying for a slice of the growing and lucrative agricultural machinery market.

"We used to be a country that made things all the time, that was the norm," Backus said. "Farms had all these different implements and each one required special tools. And possibilities existed to create an accessory for it to make it work differently or even make it better than its original purpose. Without hesitation, there are a lot of one-of-a-kind items to be collected."

Most of these inventions were agricultural hand tools, and this is the category that dominates the antique farm tool hobby today. As small-town garages or commercial shops pushed for new ways to make more with less, countless tools were developed with ingenious uses. One of the most popular features in Backus' magazine is its "Mystery Farm Tools" column, in which subscribers submit photos of attic finds and barn thingamajigs hoping someone out there can explain its original use.

Farm tool collectors can easily spend their entire lives finding unique discoveries on a regular basis. Some collectors specialize, such as Dean Stump of Waterloo, Iowa. He spent 40 years collecting what was called the finest private John Deere literature and memorabilia collection ever assembled.

Resources: *Farm Collector* is a monthly magazine dedicated to the preservation of antique farm equipment. To subscribe, visit FarmCollector.com or call 866-624-9388.

Hay stacker wrench, open end, cast iron, embossed "Dain Mfg Co / Carrollton Mo" in large letters, 10" l......................................**$4,750**

Courtesy of Rich Penn Auctions, www.richpennauctions.com

When more than 500 lots from his collection crossed the block in 2015, the hammer prices of wrenches surpassed that of high-end advertising. An early hay stacker open-end wrench embossed "Dain Mfg Co / Carrollton Mo" turned out a top bid of $4,750. Joseph Dain invented the inclined hay stacker, and his company, Dain Manufacturing Co., had close ties with John Deere starting in the mid-1890s. The relationship evolved into Dain selling its implements through Deere dealers in Minneapolis and elsewhere before the firm merged with John Deere in 1911.

"These are the things people can hold, and that can be a lot of fun," Backus said. "We see continued interest in tools and tool collecting. In general, we sense nothing but a continuing increase in values. They are certainly not going down."

— *Eric Bradley*

American Home & Farm Cyclopedia, 1883, by author Horace R. Alden, published by W.H. Thompson, Philadelphia, hardcover, 1,033 pages, 100 chapters, Victorian-era reference farm and household guide, 2,000 custom color illustrations of common and necessary farm tools of the day, 9-1/2" h. x 6-1/2" w....................**$3,000-$4,000**

Courtesy of Neetmok, eBay

▲ John Deere clevis fasteners, circa early 1900s: Part No. 164A; Part No. 2835 from 19th century walking plow; and Part No. G878A, all embossed cast iron, 8" l.......................**$50**

Courtesy of Rich Penn Auctions, www.richpennauctions.com

◀ 1926 Ford Model T/tractor conversion, Pullford conversion, 30:1 gear reduction system, 27 Ford in-cowl gas tank, shortened frame, lug wheels and native oak fenders/platform (converting Model T Fords to tractors became a common practice in the late 1920s and 1930s), rare, 12' l. **$4,800**

Courtesy of Rich Penn Auctions, www.richpennauctions.com

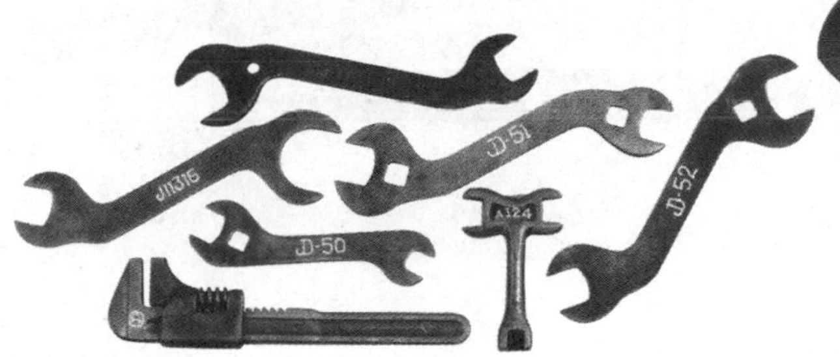

John Deere brand wrenches, set of seven: Part No. J11316 for snapping oil adjustment stud used on #15 and #25A corn pickers, circa 1939; Part Nos. JD-50, JD-51, and JD-52; Part No. 10007 with "Deere" stamped both sides; Part No. A124, t-shaped; and Part No. HZ6758 pipe wrench, 4-1/8" w. x 9" l. **$550**

Courtesy of Rich Penn Auctions, www.richpennauctions.com

Dain three-wheel corn cutter seat, circa 1900, left, part no. SS37, cast iron, 11" l........... **$80**

Courtesy of Rich Penn Auctions, www.richpennauctions.com

Five assorted tools made by Lanz: Oil pan plug; Part No. 821F32 with 17 and 19 mm ends; Part No. 995; Part No. 985 with 22 and 27 mm ends; and wrench with 28 and 33 mm ends, all cast iron, wrenches 6-3/4" to 12" l. **$200**

Courtesy of Rich Penn Auctions, www.richpennauctions.com

John Deere dinner bell, embossed "John Deere Plow Co." on one side of yoke, "St. Louis and Dallas, TX" on opposite side, attached to special-made roller cart, rare, 29" h. x 24" w., 16" dia.. **$4,000**

Courtesy of Rich Penn Auctions, www.richpennauctions.com

Hay stacker wrench, cast iron, marked "Dain Mfg Co. / Ottumwa IA," open end, embossed, cast iron, 10" l. **$450**

Courtesy of Rich Penn Auctions, www.richpennauctions.com

Two manure spreader handles, Deere & Co., cutout shaft marked K5, rare, 35" l., and K5 embossed Deere & Co., spreader handle with broken end and missing wire to attach spring, rare, 31" l. **$550**

Courtesy of Rich Penn Auctions, www.richpennauctions.com

John Deere wagon seat, wood, original paint, 21" h. x 40" w. **$950**

Courtesy of Rich Penn Auctions, www.richpennauctions.com

John Deere buggy step, cast iron, brass inlay, 8" h. **$500**

Courtesy of Rich Penn Auctions, www.richpennauctions.com

◀ Rotary drop corn planter box, Deere & Mansur, circa 1870s, wood and embossed cast iron, #148L, 9" h. x 14-1/2" w. x 11" d. **$1,400**

Courtesy of Rich Penn Auctions, www.richpennauctions.com

▼ Row marker, circa 1912, narrow track sower, Part No. H 39 M, cast metal, very good condition, 39-1/2" l. **$200**

Courtesy of Rich Penn Auctions, www.richpennauctions.com

John Deere Pea Attachment pea planter and brochure, Y2848-B, steel with cast iron gears, spring-loaded lid, raised bands at top of canister, Miester Garage brochure, "Cost-Reducing Equipment for Canning Peas," A-169-35-5, attachment 7" h., 6" dia., brochure 9" h. x 4" w. folded.. **$100**

Courtesy of Rich Penn Auctions, www.richpennauctions.com

Van Brunt grain drill measurer, John Deere, embossed numbers on back gears, bottom gear shows breakout.................... **$50**

Courtesy of Rich Penn Auctions, www.richpennauctions.com

Hay harpoon, circa late 1890s, made by Nellis, Model #7-28, rare, 33" l., 11 lbs. Harpoons were used with rope and pulleys to lift heavy hay bales as well as loose hay up to the barn loft. **$80**

Courtesy of Lang's Auctions, www.langsauction.com

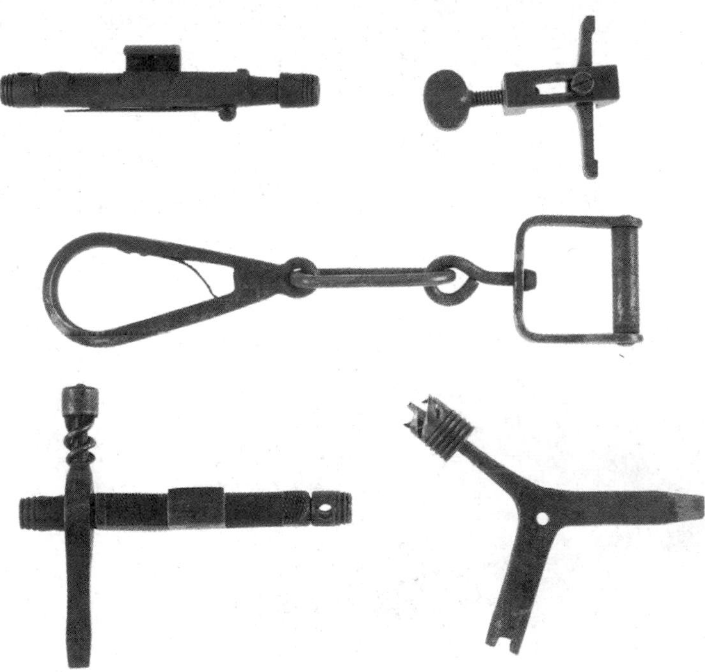

Assorted farm tools including nipple wrenches, picks, and carbine sling hook. **$84**

Courtesy of Heritage Auctions, ha.com

Butchering tools, circa 1880s, manufactured by and marked "Foster Bros.": cleaver, 16" overall; 9" cleaver with Foster Bros. Diamond Arrow trademark, 16-3/4" overall; clip blade heavy butcher knife with blade marked with Diamond Arrow trademark, 17-1/2" l. **$187**

Courtesy of Heritage Auctions, ha.com

Drill press, "PAT JAN 1872", pivot guide allowed angled holes, 28" h. x 27" w. **$100**

Courtesy of Pangaea Auctions, gopangaea.com

"The Old Cultivator" by Ray Swanson (American, 1937-2004), oil on board, 30" x 22". **$1,792**

Courtesy of Heritage Auctions, ha.com

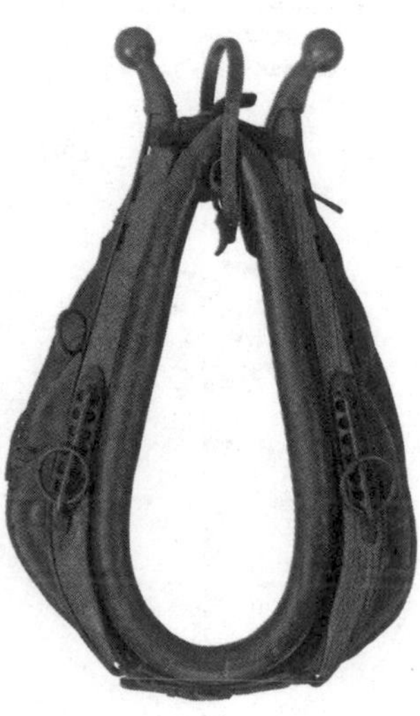

Horse collar, leather and steel harness, with wagon and plow attachments, 25" h. x 18" w. ....**$100-$150**

Courtesy of Pangaea Auctions, gopangaea.com

◀ ▼ Antique branding iron rod with letter R, 36" l. **$95**

Courtesy of Pangaea Auctions, gopangaea.com

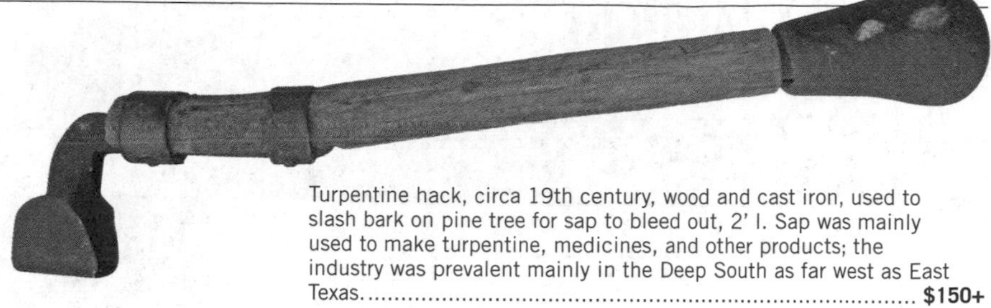

Turpentine hack, circa 19th century, wood and cast iron, used to slash bark on pine tree for sap to bleed out, 2' l. Sap was mainly used to make turpentine, medicines, and other products; the industry was prevalent mainly in the Deep South as far west as East Texas. .... **$150+**

Courtesy of Farm Collector *magazine, www.farmcollectormagazine.com*

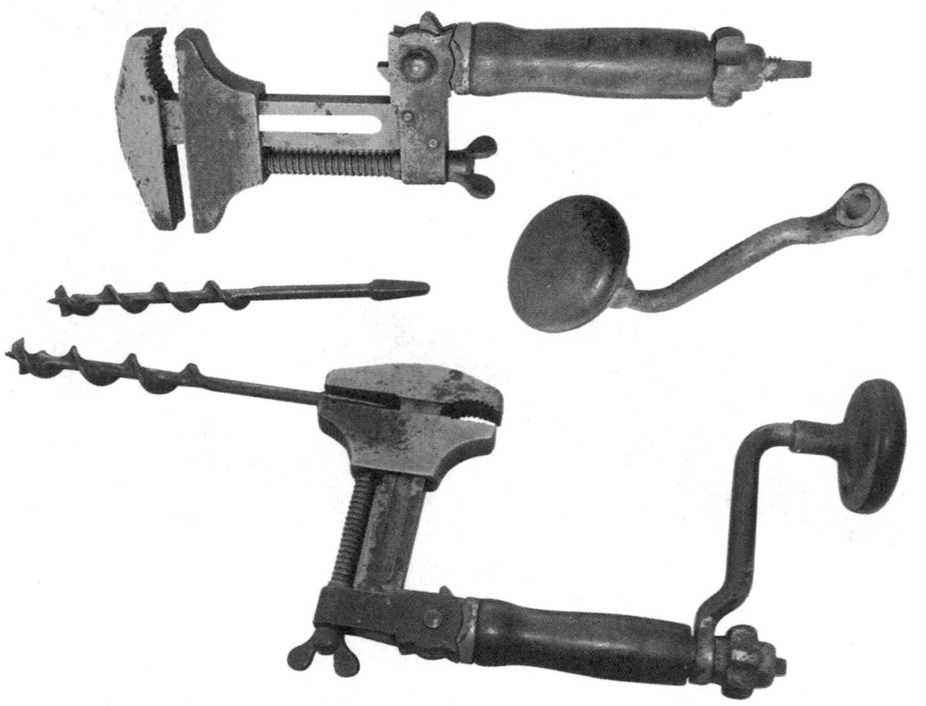

Combination tool, circa 1894, with interchangeable and adjustable accessories including wrench, screwdriver, carpenter's brace, bench vice, glass cutter, and drill, patent awarded to Samuel J. Johnston, Leesburg, Virginia, May 21, 1901, 12" l. .... **$50-$100+**

Courtesy of Farm Collector *magazine, www.farmcollectormagazine.com*

Eight gear-driven food tools: meat juicer, Hinckley-Scott apple parer, Turner-Seymour pea sheller, Enterprise cherry stoner, Goodell apple peeler, Nu-way potato peeler, #36 Raisin tool, and lightning flask clamp, longest 12 1/2" l. **$120**

Courtesy of Eldred's Auctioneers & Appraisers, www.eldreds.com

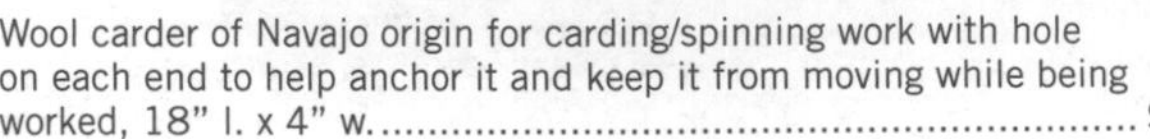

Wool carder of Navajo origin for carding/spinning work with hole on each end to help anchor it and keep it from moving while being worked, 18" l. x 4" w. **$20**

Courtesy of Desert West Auction Service, www.desertwestauction.com

Bead breaker, circa 1940s-1950s, used to fix flat tires by breaking bead of tire away from rim, fits tires 15" to 1" dia. ....**$5-$100**

Courtesy of Farm Collector *magazine, www.farmcollectormagazine.com*

Traction device or lug, steel with leather belts, added traction when strapped to rear wheel of Model T tire stuck in mud or snow, 10" l. ....**$50+**

Courtesy of Farm Collector *magazine, www.farmcollectormagazine.com*

FINE ART

DESPITE A FLUCTUATING global economy, the art market continues to see an expansion of its buyer pool and growth of some genres, with modern art commanding attention in the leader spot in terms of popularity and prices paid, especially among the world's wealthiest buyers.

Ernie Barnes (American, 1938-2009), "Football Players," oil on board, signed lower right "Ernie Barnes," good overall condition, light overall surface grime with accretions, 30" x 40". **$8,750**

Courtesy of Heritage Auctions, ha.com

Roughly $53.9 billion changed hands in 2014 in transactions involving fine and decorative art. The figure marks the first time such sales neared the pre-recession record of $51 billion in 2007.

Rich Americans are pouring new profits into modern and post-war and contemporary art with absolutely no end in sight, according to the annual *TEFAF Art Market Report* by Art Economics.

According to Holly Sherratt, a consignment director of modern and contemporary art at Heritage Auctions, Dallas, "Despite longstanding rumors of an art bubble, the contemporary art market continues to be strong, mostly driven by top-performing artists in the market and the trendsetting galleries that promote them."

The global hub for all art sales is the United States (39% of all transactions) and specifically New York, where post-war and contemporary art lead sales at auction houses and galleries. China, however, remains the largest emerging market although sales are still haunted by non-paying bidders and a high percentage of unsold lots. In some cases the rate of unsold lots in China surpasses half of all lots offered.

Online sales are also a leading driver of fine art sale, which may surprise some. But collectors and dealers are comfortable making purchases with only a website between them. This segment is expected to grow a whopping 25 percent per year and is estimated to reach $10 billion in five years.

Although multi-million dollar auction records tend to capture the most headlines, the market is seeing more art in general sold and at faster rates, and the market is currently growing by six percent a year, according to Arts Economics' annual report.

These customers are much more selective about what they buy. So as condition sets the market for collectibles, the best examples of an artist's work influences prices. An artist's key works continue to bring the best prices as collectors remain mindful of both aesthetics and resale.

"Collectors are looking for established names such as Andy Warhol, Roy Lichtenstein,

Jasper Johns, Robert Rauschenberg, and Frank Stella," Sherratt said. "American artists like Jeff Koons, Jean Michel Basquiat, Christopher Wool, and Richard Prince top the charts. U.K. artists Peter Droig and Damien Hirst are also at the top of the list along with German artist Martin Kippenberg, and Chinese artists Zeng Fanzhi, Luo Zhongli, Chen Yifei, and Zhang Xioagang."

In the middle market, post-war art is still very strong and less speculative than contemporary art, Sherratt said. The Art Economics report shows sales that take place in this middle market are mainly valued between $1,000 and $50,000.

"Prints account for many of these sales and provide an easier entry point and safer investment for many collectors," Sherratt said. "But even in this market, there is strong demand for star contemporary artists like Jeff Koons and Takashi Murakami, often in the form of editions."

With so few contemporary artists dominating the market, a lot of great art remains at reasonable prices, said Sherratt, who also points out robust demand on the West Coast. The region offers a substantial market and a source of very good art that has not yet fully maximized its enthusiast base.

"In the United States, Los Angeles is experiencing an art renaissance with international galleries like Hauser, Wirth & Schimmel opening satellite offices, superstar dealers like Larry Gagosian operating galleries, and The Broad museum opening in 2015," she said. "The California art community is incredibly strong, but with exception of a few artists like Ed Ruscha, Chris Burden, and John Baldessari, most California artists have not sold for their potential.

"California art offers great investment opportunities for investors and dealers alike," she said. "With so much wealth, celebrity, and fashion concentrated in one area, I wouldn't be surprised to see prices for West Coast art increase in the coming years."

The Master of the Parrot (Flemish, active Antwerp, circa 1520), "The Virgin Nursing the Christ Child," oil on panel, light frame wear with abrasions, accretions, and flakes of loss, faint craquelure, light overall surface grime with tiny accretions, 11" x 8-1/4". **$25,000**

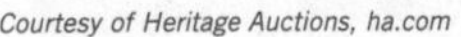

Courtesy of Heritage Auctions, ha.com

Edward Brian Seago (British, 1910-1974), "A Street in Wanchai, Hong Kong," oil on Masonite, signed lower left "Edward Seago," titled verso "Street in Wanchai – / Hong Kong," possible flake of loss to right of awning at lower left edge, loss to impasto of pale pink sheet at center of work, 26" x 20". **$55,000**

Courtesy of Heritage Auctions, ha.com

top lot!

Alfonso Ossorio, "Fire and Ice," oil on Masonite abstract expressionist composition with heavy impasto, verso inscribed and dated "ossorio / io.viii.'55," with labels from Betty Parsons Gallery and Channel Thirteen Day Pass, dated May 14, 1982, overall good condition, light soiling throughout, 32" x 25-1/2"..........................$187,500

COURTESY OF ROLAND AUCTIONEERS & VALUERS, WWW.ROLANDAUCTIONS.COM

Fauvist-style, "Two Men in Suits," oil on canvas, signed left center, "K.O. 13," two tears on right, paint loss, canvas loose on stretchers, surface abrasions, 45-1/2" h x 33" w. **$6,875**

Courtesy of Roland Auctioneers & Valuers, www.rolandauctions.com

Georgi Alexandrovich Lapchine (Russian, 1885-1950), "Still Life with Flowers," oil on canvas, signed lower right, 42" h. x 28" w...................... **$9,150**

Courtesy of Clars Auction Gallery, www.clars.com

Edouard-Léon Cortès (French, 1882-1969), "Flower Market at La Madeleine," circa 1950-1960, oil on canvas, signed lower left "Edouard Cortès," pinhole in upper left corner and where painting is unvarnished at edges, 26" x 36"..**$42,500**

Courtesy of Heritage Auctions, ha.com

Michele Cascella (Italian, 1892-1989), "Fenêtre à Portofino," 1957, oil on canvas, signed, dated, and inscribed lower left "Michele Cascella Portofino 1957," titled verso "Fenêtre à Portofino," very good condition, slight buckling at upper right corner, small areas with light craquelure, 59" x 36".....**$12,500**

Courtesy of Heritage Auctions, ha.com

Andrew Newell Wyeth (American, 1917-2009), "The Mill" study, 1959, watercolor and pencil on paper, signed lower right "A. Wyeth," excellent condition, light paper discoloration with faint mat burn along extreme edges, light abrading at center right edge, crease at upper right corner, small abrasion in lower right corner, 4-5/8" x 9"..**$21,250**

Courtesy of Heritage Auctions, ha.com

Frederik Hendrik Kaemmerer (Dutch, 1839-1902), "By the Skating Pond," oil on canvas, signed lower right "F.H. Kaemmerer," inscribed lower left "C.," light overall craquelure, faint stretcher creases, minor overall surface grime with possible accretions, 43-1/2" x 25-3/4"..........**$18,750**

Courtesy of Heritage Auctions, ha.com

Michele Cascella (Italian, 1892-1989), "Portofino Boat Works," oil on canvas, signed lower right "Michele Cascella," light craquelure, accretions scattered throughout, 30" x 50"..............................**$9,375**

Courtesy of Heritage Auctions, ha.com

Jozef Gabryel Bakos (American, 1891-1977), "Portrait of a Lady with Dog," oil on canvas, signed "Bakos" upper right, overall unframed 34" h. x 26" w. **$976**

Courtesy of Clars Auction Gallery, www.clars.com

Vincente Viudes (Spanish, 1916-1984), oil on canvas depicting flowers, staining, paint loss, sight 33" h. x 33" w. **$813**

Courtesy of Roland Auctioneers & Valuers, www.rolandauctions.com

Hughes Claude Pissarro (French, b. 1935), "La Casa Flores" (Home Flowers – Venice), pastel, with certificate, 20" x 14-1/2". **$3,450**

Courtesy of Vero Beach Auction, www.verobeachauction.com

John Raphael Smith (British, 1752-1812), "Mrs. Eliza Draper," oil on canvas, unsigned, artist plaque lower center on frame, 15" h. x 11-1/2" w. **$2,318**

Courtesy of Clars Auction Gallery, www.clars.com

Percy Gray (American, 1869-1952), "Spring Landscape," 1911, watercolor on paper laid on board, signed and dated lower right "Percy Gray 1911," good condition, minor paper discoloration and light surface grime with mat burn along edges, bumps and abrasions along extreme edges, 15-1/8" x 10-7/8"............................ **$5,250**

Courtesy of Heritage Auctions, ha.com

Reginald Marsh (1898-1954), "New York Skyline," 1936, watercolor and pencil on paper, signed and dated lower right "R. Marsh 1936," 14" x 19-3/4"... **$4,250**

Courtesy of Heritage Auctions, ha.com

Wifredo Lam (Cuban, 1902-1982), no title, watercolor on paper, 36" x 28-1/2".............. **$6,490**

Courtesy of Omega Auction Corp., www.omegaauctioncorp.com

Etienne Adolphe Piot (French, 1850-1910), "A Seated Italian Beauty Holding Flowers," unsigned, oil on canvas, 20th century, original stretcher and tacking edge, some looseness of canvas upper right with bulge, possible retouch, 35-1/2" x 26". **$4,960**

Courtesy of Brunk Auctions, www.brunkauctions.com

SCULPTURE

Antoine-Louis Barye (French, 1796-1875), "Thésée Combatant le Minotaure," second version, 1845, bronze with brown patina, inscribed on base "Barye," stamped underside "44," light rubbing on areas of high relief, scratches to patina, rubbing at corners of base, 18" h. ...**$15,000**

Courtesy of Heritage Auctions, ha.com

Raymond Leon Rivoire (French, 1884-1966), "Susse Freres Eviteures Paris," bronze sculpture of woman walking dog, silvered bronze, base marked, 29" h. x 32" l. x 7-1/2" w. **$7,073**

Courtesy of Kaminski Auctions, www.kaminskiauctions.com

▲ Bronzed metal dancer after Demetre Chiparus, circa 1930, dents and warping of base, repair to behind of figure, 17-1/2" x 23" x 6-1/4"...**$1,188**

Courtesy of Heritage Auctions, ha.com

◀ Mathurin Moreau (1822-1912), bronze depicting standing woman with laurel leaves, signed on base "Moreau Math. Sept," good condition, no foundry marks, 10-1/2" w. x 7" d. x 20-3/4" h.....**$1,625**

Courtesy of Roland Auctioneers & Valuers, www.rolandauctions.com

top lot

Bronze of two Greek male athletes, Continental, 19th century, one standing with his arm on other's shoulder, both carrying torches, with freestanding caryatid, on naturalistic base with part of swagged column, 19-7/8" h........$273,000

COURTESY OF SKINNER, INC., WWW.SKINNERINC.COM

Cold-painted Vienna bronze pheasant sculpture in manner of Franz Bergman, first half 20th century, marked "AUSTRIA," very good condition, minor marks to paint, 4" x 8-1/2"............... **$277**

Courtesy of Nest Egg Auctions, www.nesteggauctions.com

Large Meiji Period bronze elephant, Japanese, late 19th/early 20th century, tusks removed, signed in oval cartouche on belly, very good condition, 16" h. x 22" l. x 9" w. **$2,460**

Courtesy of Nest Egg Auctions, www.nesteggauctions.com

FOLK ART/AMERICANA

FOR A NATION that takes deep pride in calling itself a nation of immigrants, American folk art and Americana acts like the ribbon tying our collective heritage together. Rich with evidence of German woodworking, Scottish ship-carving, or perhaps African tribal motifs, each work is one-of-a-kind and stands on its own, backed by good ol' American individuality. The fact that most works were completed by self-taught artists who had little to no formal training enhances the appeal to collectors of American folk art and Americana. In one sense, the vernacular charm symbolizes the country's reputation for ambition, ingenuity, and imagination. There's little wonder why American folk art and Americana is more popular than ever.

The last few years saw several large folk art and Americana collections come to market with spectacular results. It also saw preservationists and scholars take major steps to ensure folk art remains an important art form in our national heritage.

Sotheby's presentation of the Ralph Esmerian collection of American folk art in early 2014 generated the highest proceeds ever for an American folk art collection. The 228-lot selection from the former chairman emeritus of the American Folk Art Museum was as noteworthy as its owner was notorious. Esmerian is serving a six-year federal sentence for fraud associated with the sale of jewelry and collectibles worth millions. The collection was ordered to be sold to provide restitution to victims and generated more than $10.5 million.

The collection held true American treasures. The top lot was a carved figure of Santa Claus by master carver Samuel Robb, the last figure he ever carved, in fact. Famous for his cigar store American Indian figures, Robb completed the 38" Santa in 1923 as a Christmas present to his daughter, Elizabeth. The figure more than doubled its pre-auction estimate to hammer for $875,000.

Two ceramic bowling pins, 20th century, each painted in alternating white, gray, red, and black stripes, height to 10-1/2"............................... **$369**

Courtesy of Skinner, Inc., www.skinnerinc.com

The sale meant that two Samuel Robb-carved figures achieved world records within just months of each other. The Maryland-based auction firm of Guyette, Schmidt and Deeter sold a rare Robb cigar store American Indian princess, circa 1880, in late 2013 for a record $747,000.

Another sign of this category's growing interest with collectors and the general public is the popularity of the only museum dedicated to the scholarly study and exhibition of the country's self-taught artisans. In 2013, the American Folk Art Museum had record attendance with over 100,000 visitors. The museum's more than 5,000 items were collected almost entirely through gifts. Collectors cheered in December 2013 when the museum digitized and gave away free 118 issues of *Folk Art* magazine (formerly *The Clarion*), originally published between winter 1971 and fall 2008. The trove may be accessed online (as of 2015) at issuu.com/american_folk_art_museum.

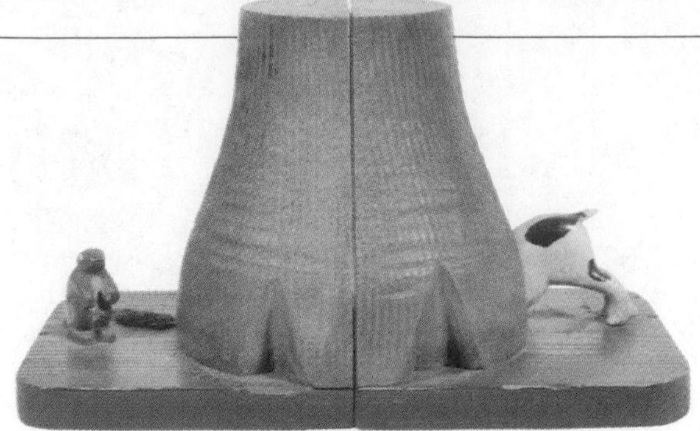

Carved and painted wooden bookends with dog running into tree stump and squirrel standing by tree stump, good condition with minor wear, 6-3/4" h. x 5-1/2" w. x 6" d. **$157**

Courtesy of Conestoga Auction Co., www.conestogaauction.com

Carved standing female figure, circa 1930, with arms crossed and wearing blue dress with white yoke and cuffs, on square base, 17" h. x 5-1/2" w. x 4-1/4" d. **$305**

Courtesy of Clars Auction Gallery, www.clars.com

Wooden man on tractor whirligig, 20th century, fair condition with weathering, incomplete, 9-1/2" h. x 17" l. **$121**

Courtesy of Conestoga Auction Co., www.conestogaauction.com

Carved wooden cribbage board, 19th century, one side centering bas relief lion with floral sprays above and below, other with curtains, roses, stag, bird, and woman's hand holding cards, edges of board carved with trailing vines, 1/2" h. x 10-3/4" l. x 4" d................. **$305**

Courtesy of Clars Auction Gallery, www.clars.com

Carved and painted wooden Civil War soldier in full uniform, 19th century, standing at attention in front of American flag holding musket with bayonet, wood platform base with wire fencing, good condition with wear, right foot missing, 9-3/4" h. x 5" w. x 4" d............................ **$545**

Courtesy of Conestoga Auction Co., www.conestogaauction.com

◀ Barber pole of carved and painted wood, executed circa 1860, 95" x 9-1/2" x 9-1/2". .... **$15,000-$25,000**

Courtesy of Sotheby's, www.sothebys.com

Carved man on horseback, circa 1900, polychrome piece with man in hat and blue suit sitting astride gray horse, on shaped base, in acrylic display box, 11" h. x 11" w. x 6-1/2" d. **$336**

Courtesy of Clars Auction Gallery, www.clars.com

▶ Carved and painted wooden paper knife, human head effigy finial, in modern custom-made stand, good condition with minor wear, 14" h. **$73**

Courtesy of Conestoga Auction Co., www.conestogaauction.com

American eagle, John Haley Bellamy (1836-1914), carved and painted pine wall plaque with traces of gold leaf, executed in Kittery Point, York County, Maine, circa 1890, 27" x 96"............**$600,000-$800,000**

Courtesy of Sotheby's, www.sothebys.com

▲ Swordfish painted sword, possibly made from front appendage of swordfish, blade painted on one side with images of anchor, ship's steering wheel, compass, swordfish, American eagle with flag, ocean liner, two sailboats, and dingy; grip, pommel, and guard of bentwood and three-wood marquetry; titled "Swordfishing" at far end, signed by artist "C. D. Sigsbee 1884," excellent condition, 44" l. **$875**

Charles Dwight Sigsbee (1845-1923) served in the navy on and off from 1862 to 1907 when he retired. His specialty was hydrography. He invented the Sigsbee Sounding Machine, which attained the status of a standard piece of deep-water oceanographic equipment for five decades. He is perhaps best known as the commander of the battleship Maine when it exploded in Havana harbor in February 1898. He and his officers were exonerated by a court of inquiry. He was promoted to rear admiral in 1903 and is buried at Arlington National Cemetery.

Courtesy of Heritage Auctions, ha.com

▲ Punched tin lampshade, Pennsylvania, very good condition, 10" dia. **$182**

Courtesy of Conestoga Auction Co., www.conestogaauction.com

Finely carved and painted boy on rooster figural pipe, 19th century, head removes to expose tin-lined smoking bowl, very good condition with minor wear, missing stem, 3-3/8" h................ **$575**

Courtesy of Conestoga Auction Co., www.conestogaauction.com

Carved bird tree with mushrooms, late 19th/early 20th century, five polychrome painted birds perched on tree branches, six painted mushrooms mounted on platform base, good condition with wear and losses, 12-1/4" h. x 13-1/4" w. x 8" d... **$908**

Courtesy of Conestoga Auction Co., www.conestogaauction.com

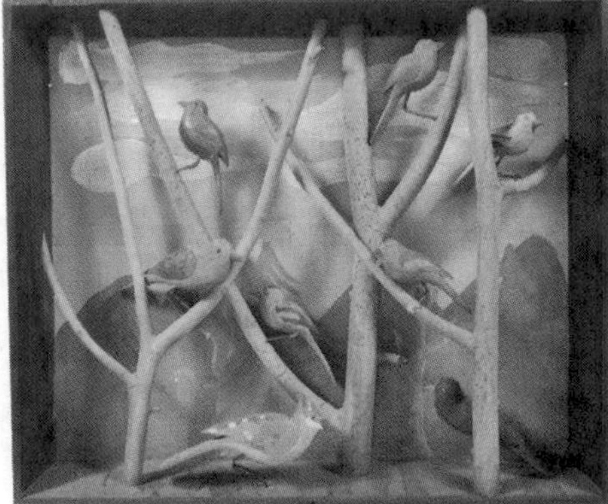

Shadowbox with carved birds in tree branches, Elizabethtown, Lancaster County, Pennsylvania, early 20th century, eight various bird species mounted in dovetailed shadowbox frame, original paint, good condition, minor fading, 24-3/4" h. x 28-3/4" w. x 5" d..................................... **$1,331**

Courtesy of Conestoga Auction Co., www.conestogaauction.com

"Home for Thanksgiving," Grandma (Ann Robertson) Moses (American, 1860-1961), oil on canvasboard, signed lower right "Moses," 12" x 16"... **$17,500**

Courtesy of Heritage Auctions, ha.com

Barbara Strawser painting of farmstead, 1974, very good condition, 10" x 12".................... **$333**

Courtesy of Conestoga Auction Co., www.conestogaauction.com

Wisconsin folk art painting, mid-19th century, with woman in front of log cabin and river, in black frame, sight size 11" x 14-1/2"........... **$1,046**

Courtesy of Skinner, Inc., www.skinnerinc.com

Sheet metal running horse weathervane, good condition with light loss, 14-3/4" h. x 24" w. **$272**

Courtesy of Conestoga Auction Co., www.conestogaauction.com

Lady golfer weathervane, copper repoussé and cast zinc weathervane with directional, cast circa 1900, 44" x 38-1/2" x 15". .... **$500,000-$700,000**

Courtesy of Sotheby's, www.sothebys.com

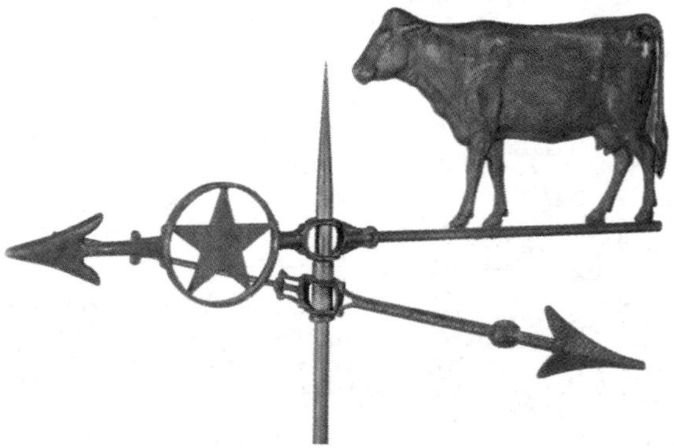

Cow weathervane, Upstate New York, late 19th/early 20th century, stamped galvanized tin cow on arrow directional with cast iron elements, mounted on copper rod and twisted iron bracket, remnants of paint, 55-1/2" x 30" x 14"..**$1,125**

Courtesy of Material Culture, www.materialculture.com

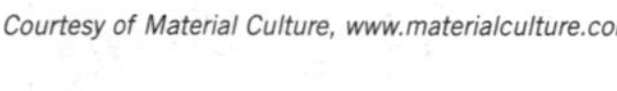

Carved pine sewing/work box from Augusta County, Shenandoah Valley of Virginia, first half 20th century, covered example with fitted interior and applied foliate devices, old refinished surface with mellow color, very good condition overall with minor wear and cracks, 9" h. x 11-3/4" w. x 8" d. overall. **$510**

Courtesy of Jeffrey S. Evans & Associates, www.jeffreysevans.com

Log cabin-form jewelry box, 19th century, diamond-shingled room on log-form body with front door and window, opening to marquetry inlaid interior lid with mirror and three compartments, front door opening to two marquetry-faced drawers, 11-1/2" h. x 14-1/4" w. x 9" d.. **$677**

Courtesy of Skinner, Inc., www.skinnerinc.com

◀ Lamp composed of Popsicle sticks and glass marbles, 1960s, excellent condition, 15" h. **$30**

Courtesy of Morphy Auctions, morphyauctions.com

▲ Carved, turned, and painted plant stand, circa 1920-1930, with elements of Art Deco stylization and four bird figures, baluster-form legs, and various applied elements, old red-painted surface, good condition overall with areas of wear and small losses to bird figures and other applied elements, 32-3/4" h. x 17" w. x 17" d. overall. **$450**

Courtesy of Jeffrey S. Evans & Associates, www.jeffreysevans.com

Hooked rug made of wool and cotton fabrics on burlap, American, first half 20th century, two facing roosters on polychrome checkerboard ground, professionally mounted, very good condition with minor wear, 31" x 46" overall. **$228**

Courtesy of Jeffrey S. Evans & Associates, www.jeffreysevans.com

Early primitive Windsor chair with old red paint surface, deaccessioned from American Folk Art Museum of New York, seat 16" h., 36" h. overall. **$1,440**

Courtesy of Copake Auction, Inc., www.copakeauction.com

Pictorial hooked rug made of wool and cotton fabrics on burlap, American, first quarter 20th century, three dogs parading across horizontal center band surrounded by floral elements and geometric sawtooth-type border, professionally mounted, very good condition with minor fading and areas of wear, 24-1/2" x 45-1/2" overall. .. **$840**

Courtesy of Jeffrey S. Evans & Associates, www.jeffreysevans.com

10 Things You Didn't Know About **Johannes Spitler**

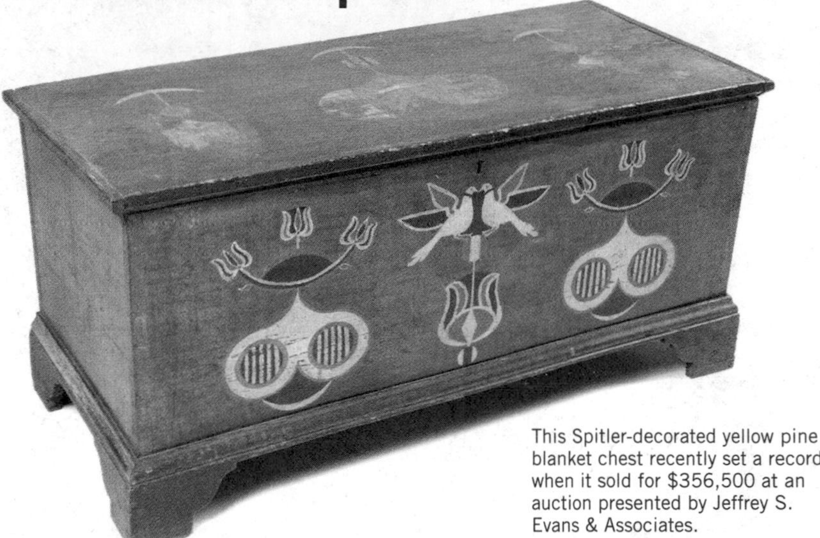

This Spitler-decorated yellow pine blanket chest recently set a record when it sold for $356,500 at an auction presented by Jeffrey S. Evans & Associates.

Courtesy of Jeffrey S. Evans & Associates, www.jeffreysevans.com

1 An unusual practice among folk artists of the time, Johannes Spitler (1774-1837) initialed and numbered the things he created. This has allowed researchers to more easily establish a catalog of his work and aids collectors in authenticating pieces.

2 Despite making his home first in the rural area of Shenandoah County, Virginia, and then a German community in Ohio, his works challenged the perception of what a "rural artist" represented and the type of materials he/she used.

3 Spitler's work often included themes commonly seen in German-American culture and art, but the designs were a mix of traditional and modern. One of the techniques often recognized in his work is the use of similar designs, such as a broken scroll pediment, in clocks and chests constructed within the same year.

4 With few pieces by this renowned furniture decorator actually crossing the auction block, when one does there is potential for a history-making event. Such was the case on June 20, 2015 during an auction presented by Jeffrey S. Evans & Associates. A yellow pine chest, circa 1800, claimed top lot status at the sale, setting an auction record for a blanket chest decorated by Spitler when it sold for $356,500. The chest was made for a family that settled in the same area as Spitler's ancestors, Massanutten, during the 18th century, and it had been passed down from one family member to the next in the six decades since it was constructed.

5 In creating the uniquely progressive designs he is known for, research reveals that the colors often seen in his work – rich blue, red ochre, lampblack, and white lead pigments – were available but limited in access. Consistent use of these pigments in multiple works, along with the use of stencils and templates, was a much more modern approach to craftsmanship than was normally seen in Shenandoah County (now Page County) where Spitler honed his craft.

6 Examples of Spitler's work, which include mostly blanket chests and some clocks, are on exhibition in various museums around the United States. A circa 1800-1809 Spitler-decorated chest acquired by the Museum of the Shenandoah Valley in 2012 was among 50 items by Shenandoah Valley artists selected for a special exhibition as part of the museum's 10th anniversary celebration in 2016.

7 Historians, collectors, museum curators, and nearly anyone familiar with Spitler's work remain mystified as to why the acclaimed young folk artist ceased to expand his portfolio once his family moved to Ohio in 1809. Although research has shown he created a few pieces with ties to the Ohio region in which he lived and farmed, it was a considerable drop from the 25-per-year rate research shows he was producing while in Virginia.

Spitler blanket chest, late 18th century, featured in a current exhibition at the Winterthur Museum in Wilmington, Delaware.

Courtesy of Winterthur Museum, Gift of John A. and Judith C. Herdeg, 2011.32

8 One of the first documented examinations of Spitler's work was an article by Donald Walters, "Johannes Spitler: Shenandoah County, Virginia, Furniture Decorator," which appeared in *The Magazine Antiques* in October 1975. Author and decorative arts expert Elizabeth Davison is reportedly in the process of researching Spitler and his body of work.

9 A Spitler blanket chest, circa 1797, sparked a bit of a "family reunion" of sorts in 2011, when a curator with the Winterthur Museum, Garden & Library in Wilmington, Delaware, posted a blog titled "The Chest of Many Mysteries," which was recently gifted to the museum. In the comments section of the post, four different people shared notes about their connection to Spitler and expressed interest in learning what the curator discovered about the chest.

10 The Spitler blanket chest that set a record at auction in June 2015 wasn't the first time Jeffrey S. Evans & Associates assisted with a record-setting sale of Spitler folk art. In 2004, the Mt. Crawford, Virginia, auction house presented a Modisett family hanging cupboard decorated by Spitler. The piece sold for $962,500, the current record holder for the sale of American folk art paint-decorated furniture at auction.

– Compiled by Antoinette Rahn

Sources: Donald Walters, "Johannes Spitler: Shenandoah County, Virginia, Furniture Decorator," *The Magazine Antiques*, Vol. 108, No. 4 (October 1975), Selftaughtgenius.org; www.museumblog.winterthur.org; www.themsv.org; Jeffrey S. Evans & Associates; www.elizabethadavison.com
http://cool.conservation-us.org/coolaic/sg/wag/1992/WAG_92_shelton.pdf
http://museumblog.winterthur.org/2011/09/02/the-chest-of-many-mysteries/
http://selftaughtgenius.org/reads/johannes-spitler
http://themsv.org/news-room/msv-open-special-10th-anniversary-exhibition-april-28

FURNITURE STYLES

american

PILGRIM CENTURY 1620–1700

MAJOR WOOD(S): Oak

GENERAL CHARACTERISTICS:

- **Case pieces:** Rectilinear low-relief carved panels; blocky and bulbous turnings; splint-spindle trim
- **Seating pieces:** Shallow carved panels; spindle turnings

WILLIAM AND MARY 1685–1720

MAJOR WOOD(S): Maple and walnut

GENERAL CHARACTERISTICS:

- **Case pieces:** Paint-decorated chests on ball feet; chests on frames; chests with two-part construction; trumpet-turned legs; slant-front desks
- **Seating pieces:** Molded, carved crest rails; banister backs; cane, rush (leather) seats; baluster, ball and block turnings; ball and Spanish feet

QUEEN ANNE 1720–1750

MAJOR WOOD(S): Walnut

GENERAL CHARACTERISTICS:

- **Case pieces:** Mathematical proportions of elements; use of the cyma or S-curve broken-arch pediments; arched panels, shell carving, star inlay; blocked fronts; cabriole legs and pad feet
- **Seating pieces:** Molded yoke-shaped crest rails; solid vase-shaped splats; rush or upholstered seats; cabriole legs; baluster, ring, ball and block-turned stretchers; pad and slipper feet

CHIPPENDALE 1750–1785

MAJOR WOOD(S): Mahogany and walnut

GENERAL CHARACTERISTICS:

- **Case pieces:** Relief-carved broken-arch pediments; foliate, scroll, shell, fretwork carving; straight, bow or serpentine fronts; carved cabriole legs; claw and ball, bracket or ogee feet
- **Seating pieces:** Carved, shaped crest rails with out-turned ears; pierced, shaped splats; ladder (ribbon) backs; upholstered seats; scrolled arms; carved cabriole legs or straight (Marlboro) legs; claw and ball feet

FEDERAL (HEPPLEWHITE) 1785–1800

MAJOR WOOD(S): Mahogany and light inlays

GENERAL CHARACTERISTICS:

- **Case pieces:** More delicate rectilinear forms; inlay with eagle and classical motifs; bow, serpentine or tambour fronts; reeded quarter columns at sides; flared bracket feet
- **Seating pieces:** Shield backs; upholstered seats; tapered square legs

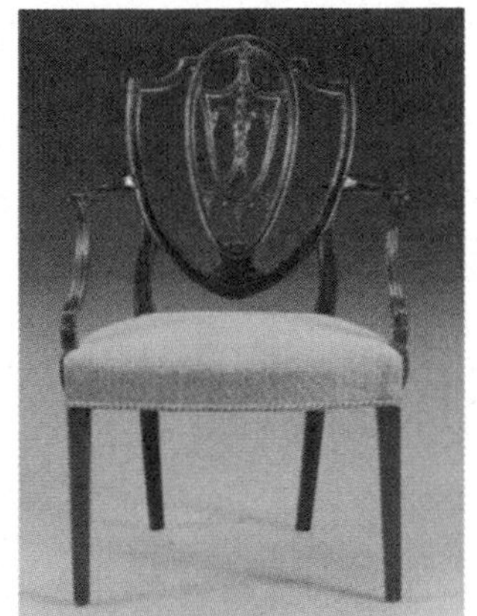

FEDERAL (SHERATON) 1800–1820

MAJOR WOOD(S): Mahogany, mahogany veneer, and maple

GENERAL CHARACTERISTICS:

- **Case pieces:** Architectural pediments; acanthus carving; outset (cookie or ovolu) corners and reeded columns; paneled sides; tapered, turned, reeded or spiral-turned legs; bow or tambour fronts; mirrors on dressing tables
- **Seating pieces:** Rectangular or square backs; slender carved banisters; tapered, turned or reeded legs

CLASSICAL (AMERICAN EMPIRE) 1815–1850

MAJOR WOOD(S): Mahogany, mahogany veneer, and rosewood

GENERAL CHARACTERISTICS:

- **Case pieces:** Increasingly heavy proportions; pillar and scroll construction; lyre, eagle, Greco-Roman and Egyptian motifs; marble tops; projecting top drawer; large ball feet, tapered fluted feet or hairy paw feet; brass, ormolu decoration
- **Seating pieces:** High-relief carving; curved backs; out-scrolled arms; ring turnings; sabre legs, curule (scrolled-S) legs; brass-capped feet, casters

VICTORIAN – EARLY VICTORIAN 1840–1850

MAJOR WOOD(S): Mahogany veneer, black walnut, and rosewood

GENERAL CHARACTERISTICS:

- **Case pieces:** Pieces tend to carry over the Classical style with the beginnings of the Rococo substyle, especially in seating pieces.

VICTORIAN – GOTHIC REVIVAL 1840–1890

MAJOR WOOD(S): Black walnut, mahogany, and rosewood

GENERAL CHARACTERISTICS:

- **Case pieces:** Architectural motifs; triangular arched pediments; arched panels; marble tops; paneled or molded drawer fronts; cluster columns; bracket feet, block feet or plinth bases
- **Seating pieces:** Tall backs; pierced arabesque backs with trefoils or quatrefoils; spool turning; drop pendants

VICTORIAN – ROCOCO (LOUIS XV) 1845–1870

MAJOR WOOD(S): Black walnut, mahogany, and rosewood

GENERAL CHARACTERISTICS:

- **Case pieces:** Arched carved pediments; high-relief carving, S- and C-scrolls, floral, fruit motifs, busts and cartouches; mirror panels; carved slender cabriole legs; scroll feet; bedroom suites (bed, dresser, commode)
- **Seating pieces:** High-relief carved crest rails; balloon-shaped backs; urn-shaped splats; upholstery (tufting); demi-cabriole legs; laminated, pierced and carved construction (Belter and Meeks); parlor suites (sets of chairs, love seats, sofas)

VICTORIAN – RENAISSANCE REVIVAL 1860–1885

MAJOR WOOD(S): Black walnut, burl veneer, painted and grained pine

GENERAL CHARACTERISTICS:

- **Case pieces:** Rectilinear arched pediments; arched panels; burl veneer; applied moldings; bracket feet, block feet, plinth bases; medium and high-relief carving, floral and fruit, cartouches, masks and animal heads; cyma-curve brackets; Wooton patent desks
- **Seating pieces:** Oval or rectangular backs with floral or figural cresting; upholstery outlined with brass tacks; padded armrests; tapered turned front legs, flared square rear legs

VICTORIAN – LOUIS XVI 1865–1875

MAJOR WOOD(S): Black walnut and ebonized maple

GENERAL CHARACTERISTICS:

- **Case pieces:** Gilt decoration, marquetry, inlay; egg and dart carving; tapered turned legs, fluted
- **Seating pieces:** Molded, slightly arched crest rails; keystone-shaped backs; circular seats; fluted tapered legs

VICTORIAN – EASTLAKE 1870–1895

MAJOR WOOD(S): Black walnut, burl veneer, cherry, and oak

GENERAL CHARACTERISTICS:

- **Case pieces:** Flat cornices; stile and rail construction; burl veneer panels; low-relief geometric and floral machine carving; incised horizontal lines
- **Seating pieces:** Rectilinear; spindles; tapered, turned legs, trumpet-shaped legs

VICTORIAN JACOBEAN AND TURKISH REVIVAL 1870–1890

MAJOR WOOD(S): Black walnut and maple

GENERAL CHARACTERISTICS:

- **Case pieces:** A revival of some heavy 17th century forms, most commonly in dining room pieces
- **Seating pieces:** Turkish Revival style features: oversized, low forms; overstuffed upholstery; padded arms; short baluster, vase-turned legs; ottomans, circular sofas
- **Jacobean Revival style features:** heavy bold carving; spool and spiral turnings

VICTORIAN – AESTHETIC MOVEMENT 1880–1900

MAJOR WOOD(S): Painted hardwoods, black walnut, ebonized finishes

GENERAL CHARACTERISTICS:

- **Case pieces:** Rectilinear forms; bamboo turnings, spaced ball turnings; incised stylized geometric and floral designs, sometimes highlighted with gilt
- **Seating pieces:** Bamboo turning; rectangular backs; patented folding chairs

ART NOUVEAU 1895–1918

MAJOR WOOD(S): Ebonized hardwoods, fruitwoods

GENERAL CHARACTERISTICS:

- **Case pieces:** Curvilinear shapes; floral marquetry; whiplash curves
- **Seating pieces:** Elongated forms; relief-carved floral decoration; spindle backs, pierced floral backs; cabriole legs

TURN-OF-THE-CENTURY (EARLY 20TH CENTURY) 1895–1910

MAJOR WOOD(S): Golden (quarter-sawn) oak, mahogany, hardwood stained to resemble mahogany

GENERAL CHARACTERISTICS:

- **Case pieces:** Rectilinear and bulky forms; applied scroll carving or machine-pressed designs; some Colonial and Classical Revival detailing
- **Seating pieces:** Heavy framing or high spindle-trimmed backs; applied carved or machine-pressed back designs; heavy scrolled or slender turned legs; Colonial Revival or Classical Revival detailing such as claw and ball feet

MISSION (ARTS & CRAFTS MOVEMENT) 1900–1915

MAJOR WOOD(S): Oak

GENERAL CHARACTERISTICS:

- **Case pieces:** Rectilinear through-tenon construction; copper decoration, hand-hammered hardware; square legs
- **Seating pieces:** Rectangular splats; medial and side stretchers; exposed pegs; corbel supports

COLONIAL REVIVAL 1890–1930

MAJOR WOOD(S): Oak, walnut and walnut veneer, mahogany veneer

GENERAL CHARACTERISTICS:

- **Case pieces:** Forms generally following designs of the 17th, 18th, and early 19th centuries; details for the styles such as William and Mary, Federal, Queen Anne, Chippendale, or early Classical were used but often in a simplified or stylized form; mass-production in the early 20th century flooded the market with pieces that often mixed and matched design details and used a great deal of thin veneering to dress up designs; dining room and bedroom suites were especially popular.
- **Seating pieces:** Designs again generally followed early period designs with some mixing of design elements.

ART DECO 1925–1940

MAJOR WOOD(S): Bleached woods, exotic woods, steel, and chrome

GENERAL CHARACTERISTICS:

- **Case pieces:** Heavy geometric forms
- **Seating pieces:** Streamlined, attenuated geometric forms; overstuffed upholstery

MODERNIST OR MID-CENTURY 1945–1970

MAJOR WOOD(S): Plywood, hardwood, or metal frames

GENERAL CHARACTERISTICS: Modernistic designers such as the Eames, Vladimir Kagan, George Nelson, and Isamu Noguchi led the way in post-war design. Carrying on the tradition of Modernist designers of the 1920s and 1930s, they focused on designs for the machine age that could be mass-produced for the popular market. By the late 1950s many of their pieces were used in commercial office spaces and schools as well as in private homes.

- **Case pieces:** Streamlined or curvilinear abstract designs with simple detailing; plain round or flattened legs and arms; mixed materials including wood, plywood, metal, glass, and molded plastics
- **Seating pieces:** Streamlined or abstract curvilinear designs generally using newer materials such as plywood or simple hardwood framing; fabric and synthetics such as vinyl used for upholstery with finer fabrics and real leather featured on more expensive pieces; seating made of molded plastic shells on metal frames and legs used on many mass-produced designs

DANISH MODERN 1950–1970

MAJOR WOOD(S): Teak

GENERAL CHARACTERISTICS:

- **Case and seating pieces:** This variation of Modernistic post-war design originated in Scandinavia, hence the name; designs were simple and restrained with case pieces often having simple boxy forms with short rounded tapering legs; seating pieces have a simple teak framework with lines coordinating with case pieces; vinyl or natural fabric were most often used for upholstery; in the United States dining room suites were the most popular use for this style although some bedroom suites and general seating pieces were available.

FURNITURE STYLES

english

JACOBEAN MID-17TH CENTURY

MAJOR WOOD(S): Oak, walnut

GENERAL CHARACTERISTICS:

- **Case pieces:** Low-relief carving; geometrics and florals; panel, rail and stile construction; applied split balusters
- **Seating pieces:** Rectangular backs; carved and pierced crests; spiral turnings ball feet

WILLIAM AND MARY 1689-1702

MAJOR WOOD(S): Walnut, burl walnut veneer

GENERAL CHARACTERISTICS:

- **Case pieces:** Marquetry, veneering; shaped aprons; 6-8 trumpet-form legs; curved flat stretchers
- **Seating pieces:** Carved, pierced crests; tall caned backs and seats; trumpet-form legs; Spanish feet

QUEEN ANNE 1702–1714

MAJOR WOOD(S): Walnut, mahogany, veneer

GENERAL CHARACTERISTICS:

- **Case pieces:** Cyma curves; broken arch pediments and finials; bracket feet
- **Seating pieces:** Carved crest rails; high, rounded backs; solid vase-shaped splats; cabriole legs; pad feet

GEORGE I 1714–1727

MAJOR WOOD(S): Walnut, mahogany, veneer, and yew wood

GENERAL CHARACTERISTICS:

- **Case pieces:** Broken arch pediments; gilt decoration, japanning; bracket feet
- **Seating pieces:** Curvilinear forms; yoke-shaped crests; shaped solid splats; shell carving; upholstered seats; carved cabriole legs; claw and ball feet, pad feet

GEORGE II 1727–1760

MAJOR WOOD(S): Mahogany

GENERAL CHARACTERISTICS:

- **Case pieces:** Broken arch pediments; relief-carved foliate, scroll and shell carving; carved cabriole legs; claw and ball feet, bracket feet, ogee bracket feet
- **Seating pieces:** Carved, shaped crest rails, out-turned ears; pierced shaped splats; ladder (ribbon) backs; upholstered seats; scrolled arms; carved cabriole legs or straight (Marlboro) legs; claw and ball feet

GEORGE III 1760–1820

MAJOR WOOD(S): Mahogany, veneer, satinwood

GENERAL CHARACTERISTICS:

- **Case pieces:** Rectilinear forms; parcel gilt decoration; inlaid ovals, circles, banding or marquetry; carved columns, urns; tambour fronts or bow fronts; plinth bases
- **Seating pieces:** Shield backs; upholstered seats; tapered square legs, square legs

REGENCY 1811–1820

MAJOR WOOD(S): Mahogany, mahogany veneer, satinwood, and rosewood

GENERAL CHARACTERISTICS:

- **Case pieces:** Greco-Roman and Egyptian motifs; inlay, ormolu mounts; marble tops; round columns, pilasters; mirrored backs; scroll feet
- **Seating pieces:** Straight backs; latticework; caned seats; sabre legs, tapered turned legs, flared turned legs; parcel gilt, ebonizing

GEORGE IV 1820–1830

MAJOR WOOD(S): Mahogany, mahogany veneer, and rosewood

GENERAL CHARACTERISTICS: Continuation of Regency designs

WILLIAM IV 1830–1837

MAJOR WOOD(S): Mahogany, mahogany veneer

GENERAL CHARACTERISTICS:

- **Case pieces:** Rectilinear; brass mounts, grillwork; carved moldings; plinth bases
- **Seating pieces:** Rectangular backs; carved straight crest rails; acanthus, animal carving; carved cabriole legs; paw feet

VICTORIAN 1837–1901

MAJOR WOOD(S): Black walnut, mahogany, veneers, and rosewood

GENERAL CHARACTERISTICS:

- **Case pieces:** Applied floral carving; surmounting mirrors, drawers, candle shelves; marble tops
- **Seating pieces:** High-relief carved crest rails; floral and fruit carving; balloon backs, oval backs; upholstered seats, backs; spool, spiral turnings; cabriole legs, fluted tapered legs; scrolled feet

EDWARDIAN 1901–1910

MAJOR WOOD(S): Mahogany, mahogany veneer, and satinwood

GENERAL CHARACTERISTICS: Neo-Classical motifs and revivals of earlier 18th century and early 19th century styles

FURNITURE

antique furniture

FURNITURE COLLECTING HAS been a major part of the world of collecting for more than 100 years. It is interesting to note how this marketplace has evolved.

In past decades, 18th century and early 19th century furniture was the mainstay of the American furniture market, but in recent years there has been a growing demand for furniture manufactured since the 1920s. Factory-made furniture from the 1920s and 1930s, often featuring Colonial Revival style, has seen a growing appreciation among collectors. It is well made and features solid wood and fine veneers rather than the cheap compressed wood materials often used since the 1960s. Also much in demand in recent years is furniture in the Modernistic and Mid-Century taste, ranging from Art Deco through quality designer furniture of the 1950s through the1970s (see "Modern Furniture" later in this section).

These latest trends have offered even the less well-heeled buyer the opportunity to purchase fine furniture at often reasonable prices. Buying antique and collectible furniture is no longer the domain of millionaires and museums.

Today more furniture is showing up on Internet sites, and sometimes good buys can be made. However, it is important to deal with honest, well-informed sellers and have a good knowledge of what you want to purchase.

As in the past, it makes sense to purchase the best pieces you can find, whatever the style or era of production. Condition is still very important if you want your example to continue to appreciate in value in the coming years. For 18th century and early 19th century pieces, the original finish and hardware are especially important as it is with good furniture of the early 20th century Arts & Crafts era. These features are not quite as important for most manufactured furniture of the Victorian era and furniture from the 1920s and later. However, it is good to be aware that a good finish and original hardware will mean a stronger market when the pieces are resold. Of course, whatever style of furniture you buy, you are better off with examples that have not had major repair or replacements. On really early furniture, repairs and replacements will definitely have an impact on the sale value, but they will also be a factor on newer designs from the 20th century.

As with all types of antiques and collectibles, there is often a regional preference for certain furniture types. Although the American market is much more homogenous than it was in past decades, there still tends to be a preference for 18th century and early 19th century furniture along the Eastern Seaboard, whereas Victorian designs tend to have a larger market in the Midwest and South. In the West, country furniture and "western" designs definitely have the edge except in major cities along the West Coast.

Whatever your favorite furniture style, there are still fine examples to be found. Just study the history of your favorites and the important points of their construction before you invest heavily. A wise shopper will be a happy shopper and have a collection certain to continue to appreciate as time marches along.

For more information on furniture, see *Antique Trader Furniture Price Guide* by Kyle Husfloen.

BEDROOM

Rare American Rococo carved and ebonized mahogany bedstead, mid-19th century, attributed to purveyor Prudent Mallard, New Orleans, scrolled pediment, crest with central urn and flowers above cabochon cartouche, paneled headboard, turned finials with gadrooned edge, reeded posts, shaped footboard, paneled foot and side rails with rounded corners, acanthus and shell carved skirt, acanthine bracket feet, casters, 74-5/8" h. x 81" l. x 64" w. **$7,040**

Courtesy of Neal Auction Co., www.nealauctions.com

Large oak Murphy bed on wheels with carved detail on front with knobs, bed folds out, very good condition, 54-1/2" x 20-1/2" x 52"...... **$3,355**

Courtesy of Morphy Auctions, www.morphyauctions.com

▲ American Rococo carved mahogany full tester bed, mid-19th century, marked "C. Lee" and numbered "281" on bottom of post, arched crest with central cabochon and shell, molded paneled headboard, turned tapered posts, molded tester with egg-and-dart edge, shaped rails and foot board, disc feet, 108-1/2" h. x 77" l. x 64-1/2" w. **$3,840**

Courtesy of Neal Auction Co., www.nealauctions.com

◀ American Classical carved mahogany poster bed, circa 1830, Philadelphia, carved cornucopia and shell crest, paneled headboard, spiral-turned posts with tobacco leaves, turned feet, brass cuffs, 87" h. x 74" l. x 56" w. **$2,176**

Courtesy of Neal Auction Co., www.nealauctions.com

top lot!

Rare and important Louisiana inlaid cherrywood and cypress armoire, circa 1810, molded cornice, inlaid frieze centered by monogram "HR," Heloise Aurora Roland (b. 1795), inlaid doors with pierced brass escutcheon, fiche hinges, interior with shelves and medial belt of drawers, paneled sides scalloped and spurred apron, cabriole legs, chamfered corner stiles extending to cornice and hoof terminals on cabriole, 79-7/8" h. x 56-1/2" w. x 24-1/2" d.
.... $76,800

COURTESY OF NEAL AUCTION CO., WWW.NEALAUCTIONS.COM

SEATING

Pennsylvania miniature paint-decorated side chair, 19th century, hoop back with shaped splat, ovoid seat with turned splayed legs and stretcher supports, yellow floral decoration with green and black highlights, light green ground, original label under seat reads, "Frank Polis 329 South Street, Philadelphia, Children's Carriages and Small Chairs, George Polis Chair & Furniture Warerooms," good condition, all original paint, some wear and losses, 16-1/2" h. overall......... **$726**

Courtesy of Conestoga Auction Co., www.conestogaauction.com

Rare pair of American Gothic Revival oak hall chairs, probably New Orleans, crafted by unknown "Stanton Hall Master," mid-19th century, tall backs supported by pierced and carved stiles terminating in crocketed spires, central pierced and carved splats with additional carved spire, plank seats, and pierced front legs, 68" h....**$12,500**

Courtesy of New Orleans Auction Galleries, Inc., www.neworleansauction.com

Edwardian upholstered oak and wicker chaise lounge, early 20th century, light wear to newer upholstery, wormholing throughout base and headboard, no holes or damage to wicker, 32-1/2" h. x 63" w. x 33-1/4" d........................ **$625**

Courtesy of Heritage Auctions, ha.com

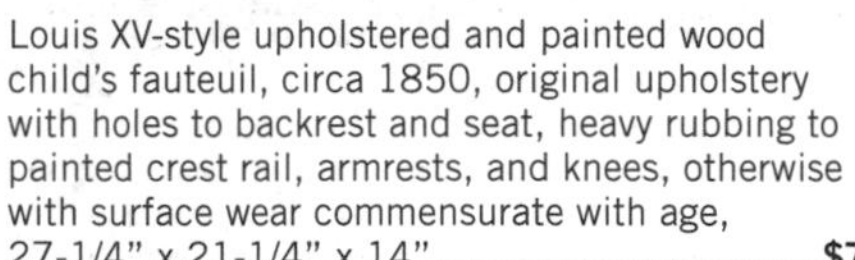

Louis XV-style upholstered and painted wood child's fauteuil, circa 1850, original upholstery with holes to backrest and seat, heavy rubbing to painted crest rail, armrests, and knees, otherwise with surface wear commensurate with age, 27-1/4" x 21-1/4" x 14"............................... **$750**

Courtesy of Heritage Auctions, ha.com

Pair of Louis XVI-style upholstered walnut armchairs, circa 1900, with oval backs, carved ribbon and quatrefoil borders to seat back, serpentine arm rails and apron, raised on fluted tapering legs, upholstered in silk brocade material, stain to seat of one chair, light kick marks to legs, consistent wear indicative of use, 36-3/4" h. x 23-1/2" w. x 20" d.................... **$550**

Courtesy of Heritage Auctions, ha.com

DESK • DISPLAY • SIDEBOARD • STORAGE

Painted Carlton desk, circa 1890, satinwood veneers, floral and avian figural-painted decoration throughout, upper tier with six dovetailed drawers and two flanking document boxes, central cabinet painted with two putti, downswept lidded stationery boxes to each side with female portrait cartouches, top inset with tooled brown leather writing surface, to three drawers decorated with floral garlands, on tapering legs with faux foliate inlay, terminating on brass casters, wear to leather writing surface, wear to finish, wear to apron, commensurate with age, 40" h. x 48" w. x 24" d. **$8,750**

Courtesy of Heritage Auctions, ha.com

American Rococo carved and laminated rosewood etagere, mid-19th century, attributed to John Henry Belter, New York, crest centered with federal shield surrounded by floral cascades, arched mirrored back, shaped graduated mirrored shelves, lotus-carved supports, serpentine marble top, leaf and floral carved base, acanthine turned feet, 90-1/2" h. x 58-1/2" w. x 16-1/2" d.... **$18,560**

Courtesy of Neal Auction Co., www.nealauctions.com

Napoleon III giltwood oval wall mirror, circa 1870, surmounted by carved ruffled bow and pair of putti with flanking scrolling foliage, high relief floral border around pane, repair throughout bow and to one putti, rubbing of gilt finish and some flaking exposing gesso, 45-1/2" h. x 31" w. **$750**

Courtesy of Heritage Auctions, ha.com

Louis XVI-style gilt bronze and mahogany vitrine with marble top, circa 1900, electrified vitrine with rosso giallo marble top, gilt beading to molding, frieze panels of scrolling foliate designs flanking central frieze with goats and nymph head motif, doors with finely reeded gilt borders to glass, bronze rose garland mounts to shoulders, three-shelf interior, down to lower gilt molding, floral mounts to apron, tapering fluted feet with cup sabots, leg reglued, electrified, minor abrasions and scratches to veneer, chip to marble top to rear, 56" h. x 41" w.. ....**$22,500**

Courtesy of Heritage Auctions, ha.com

Rare and important Kentucky Federal figured cherry and tambour-door sideboard, 1800-1810, oak, cherry, ash, poplar and other mixed secondary woods, serpentine "cupid's bow" façade set with four dovetailed drawers with period eagle-decorated brass pulls, lower drawer flanked by two serpentine tambour-door cabinets further flanked by two inlaid cabinet doors, flame cherry veneers, tapered square legs inlaid with figured walnut panels outlined in line inlay, good condition overall, one section of tambour door replaced, brass possibly original, front legs with evidence of small braces at back with some later glue, 40-1/2" x 70-1/2" x 23-1/2"..............**$19,840**

Courtesy of Brunk Auctions, www.brunkauctions.com

American Late Federal carved mahogany sideboard, circa 1830-1845, paneled frieze drawers, recessed central paneled doors, side cupboards with laurel appliqués flanked by scrolled supports with acanthus molding, brass ball front feet, scrolled back feet, poplar secondary wood, 44-3/4" h. x 61-7/8" w. x 24" d.. .... **$6,400**

Courtesy of Neal Auction Co., www.nealauctions.com

Very fine and rare Soap Hollow miniature blanket chest dated 1856, stenciled with stylized pineapple and floral motifs, red ground with black trim and yellow highlights, molded lid, applied trim surrounding full-width dovetailed drawer, molded bracket base, very good condition, all original decoration, age crack on lid and minor wear to surface, 15-3/4" h. x 22-1/2" w. x 12-3/4" d. **$19,360**

Courtesy of Conestoga Auction Co., www.conestogaauction.com

East Tennessee painted poplar food/pie safe, probably Greene, Jefferson, or Washington Counties, circa 1840, rectangular top with applied cut-out gallery above two chamfered-edge dovetailed drawers and two hinged doors, on turned feet, each door set with large tin panel made up of four smaller tins, each hand-punched in pattern depicting Masonic arch enclosing candlestick with two stars above and triple diamond ornaments to each side, each top corner with quarter fan, each end set with panel made up of 2-1/2 tins with matching decorative devices, poplar secondary wood, case in scraped-down mustard paint, tins with remnants of mustard paint, 53-1/2" h. overall, 46-1/2" h. top x 53-1/2" l. x 18-1/2" d. **$1,800**

Courtesy of Jeffrey S. Evans & Associates, www.jeffreysevans.com

Walnut cellaret on stand, Roanoke River Basin, 1790-1810, dovetailed box with original dividers for 12 bottles, conforming original stand set with drink slide over single dovetailed drawer, pierced knee returns on tapered legs, yellow pine secondary, very good condition overall, top with minor shrinkage cracks and one strip at front, original rear corner brackets, front brackets replaced, brass bail handle replaced, 37" x 19" x 15-1/4". **32,240**

Courtesy of Brunk Auctions, www.brunkauctions.com

TABLES

American Rococo Revival carved rosewood and marble turtle-top table attributed to John Henry Belter, New York, circa 1860, original white cartouche-form marble top on conforming carved skirt on scrolled and stylized dolphin-carved legs on scrolled feet, cross-stretchers set with fruit-carved ornament, casters, probably original marble top with minor edge crack and other stains and abrasions, cracks and repairs at two scrolled feet, scattered chips to carved elements, 29-1/2" x 40" x 32"..**$22,320**

Courtesy of Brunk Auctions, www.brunkauctions.com

Napoleon III gilt bronze-mounted mahogany single-drawer side table with marble top, circa 1865, round rouge marble tabletop with banded and fluted bronze border above continuous gilt bronze scrolling foliage plaques, medial shelf joining fluted, tapering legs with gilt bronze mounts and feet, minor kick marks to legs and expected rubbing of gilt bronze, minor missing flakes of veneer to edge of tabletop, 28-5/8" h., 17-1/4" dia... **$2,250**

Courtesy of Heritage Auctions, ha.com

Rare Charleston Queen Anne mahogany candlestand, South Carolina, 1755-1775, circular top with batten support on baluster-turned stand with tripod base, 24" top split and repaired with two plugged holes at center, batten replaced, pedestal inset into batten... **5,890**

Courtesy of Brunk Auctions, www.brunkauctions.com

French gilt bronze-mounted mahogany demilune side tables, 19th century, marble tops over two drawers with gilt bronze escutcheon and laurel wreath-form handles, ebonized stringing to each drawer and to sides of table, cabriole legs with gilt bronze feet at front, original hardware and locks, light missing flakes and chips to marble tops, scratching to veneer from handles, small missing flakes to veneer throughout, kick marks to legs, 30" x 25-3/4" x 14"... **$938**

Courtesy of Heritage Auctions, ha.com

FURNITURE

modern furniture

MODERN DESIGN IS everywhere, evergreen and increasingly popular. Modernism has never gone out of style. Its reach into the present day is as deep as its roots in the past. Just as it can be seen and felt ubiquitously in the mass media of today - on film, television, in magazines, and department stores - it can be traced to the mid-1800s post-Empire non-conformity of the Biedermeier Movement, the turn of the 20th century anti-Victorianism of the Vienna Secessionists, the radical reductionism of Frank Lloyd Wright and the revolutionary post-Depression thinking of Walter Gropius and the Bauhaus school in Germany.

"The Modernists really changed the way the world looked," said John Sollo, a partner in the former Sollo Rago Auction of Lambertville, New Jersey. Sollo's former partner in business, and one of the most recognizable names in the field, David Rago, took Sollo's idea a little further by saying that Modernism is actually more about the names behind the design than the design itself, at least as far as buying goes.

No discussion of Modern can be complete, however, without examining its genesis and enduring influence. Modernism is everywhere in today's pop culture. Austere Scandinavian furniture dominates the television commercials that hawk hotels and mutual funds. Post-war American design ranges across sitcom set dressings to movie sets patterned after Frank Lloyd Wright houses and Hollywood Modernist classics set high in the hills.

You only have to look at the dorm rooms of college students and the apartments of young people whose living spaces are packed with the undeniably Modern mass-produced products of IKEA, Target, Design Within Reach, and the like.

There can be no denying that the post-World War II manufacturing techniques and subsequent boom led to the widespread acceptance of plastic and bent plywood chairs along with low-sitting coffee tables, couches and recliners.

"The modern aesthetic grew out of a perfect storm of post-war optimism, innovative materials, and an incredible crop of designers," said Lisanne Dickson, director of 1950s/ Modern Design at Treadway-Toomey.

"I think that the people who designed the furniture were maybe ahead of society's ability to accept and understand what they were doing," Sollo said. "It's taken people another 30 to 40 years to catch up to it."

There are hundreds of great Modern designers, many who worked across categories - furniture, architecture, fine art, etc. - and many contributed to the work of other big names without ever seeking that glory for themselves.

For more information on Modernism, see *Warman's Modernism Furniture & Accessories Identification and Price Guide* by Noah Fleisher.

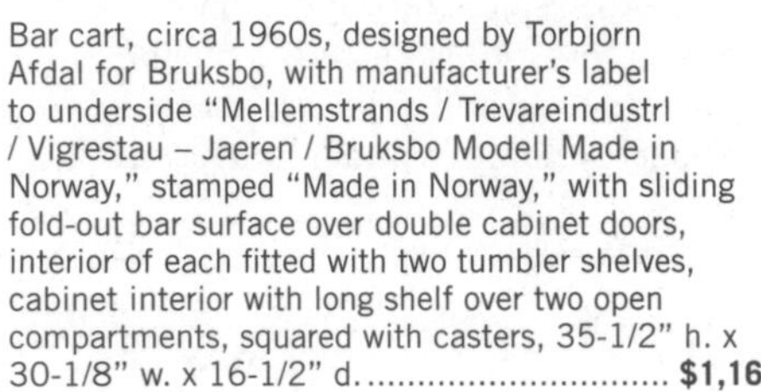

Bar cart, circa 1960s, designed by Torbjorn Afdal for Bruksbo, with manufacturer's label to underside "Mellemstrands / Trevareindustrl / Vigrestau – Jaeren / Bruksbo Modell Made in Norway," stamped "Made in Norway," with sliding fold-out bar surface over double cabinet doors, interior of each fitted with two tumbler shelves, cabinet interior with long shelf over two open compartments, squared with casters, 35-1/2" h. x 30-1/8" w. x 16-1/2" d. **$1,169**

Courtesy of John Moran Auctioneers, www.johnmoran.com

Mid-century bar in manner of Weinberg, United States, circa 1950, ivory-colored plastic laminate top with aluminum edging on wrought iron frame with slanted legs supporting box faced on three sides with slates of teak wood, open side with two shelves, unmarked, 40-1/2" h. x 42" w. x 18" d. **$277**

Courtesy of Skinner, Inc., www.skinnerinc.com

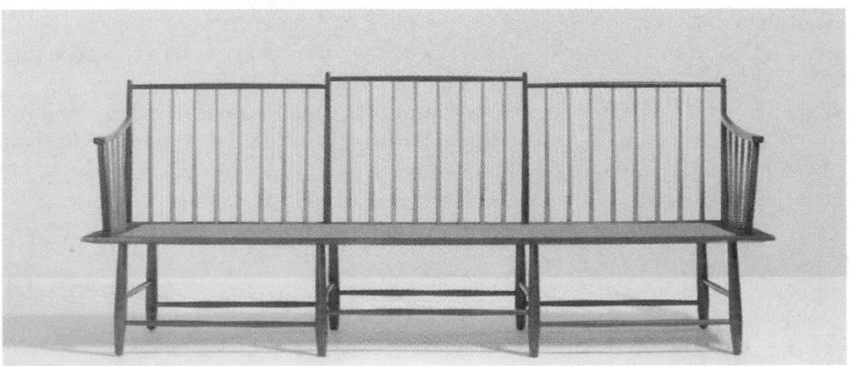

Rare Edward Wormley bench, model 4871, American, 1948, walnut, cherry, Henning Watterston upholstery, leather, 87" w. x 25" d. x 34-1/4" h. **$35,840**

Courtesy of Wright, www.wright20.com

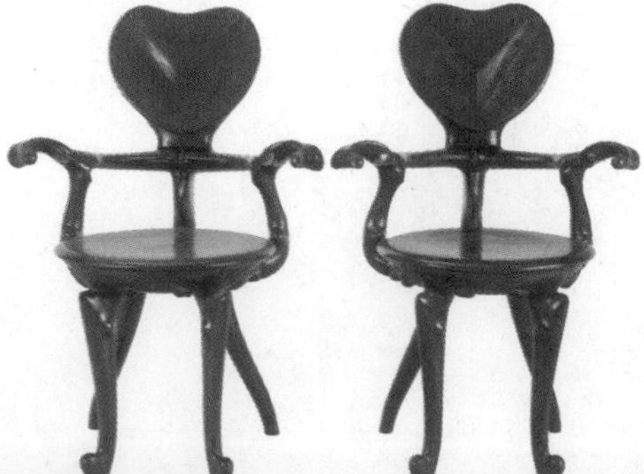

Pair of oak chairs, circa 1970, Casa Calvet, after Antoni Gaudí (Spanish, 1852-1926), incised to underside "XXX/CL," good condition, back right leg loose on one chair, minor kick marks to legs, 39" x 25-1/2" x 20".................................. **$4,750**

Courtesy of Heritage Auctions, ha.com

Pair of oak and maple wingback chairs, 20th century, contrasting wood stains to curved sides and arms, sides and back constructed of oak and interior of maple, channeled upholstery to seat and back, one upholstered in khaki suede, other in khaki velvet, on tapered feet, plaque to reverse of apron inscribed "CITY ANTIQUES REPRODUCTIONS LOG ANGELES," some wear and discoloration to upholstery from use, 38" h. x 31" w. x 33" d. **$2,375**

Courtesy of Heritage Auctions, ha.com

Seven grass-seated chairs, circa 1960 with one later production, black walnut and woven sea grass, underside of one chair marked "Nakashima, 7-9-04" in marker, light white paint streaks to legs of two chairs, light wear to woven seats and minor kick marks to legs indicative of use, 26-1/2" x 23-3/8" x 18". **$10,000**

Courtesy of Heritage Auctions, ha.com

Six dining chairs, two armchairs and four side chairs, 1960s, Tommi Parzinger (1903-1981), Parzinger Originals, New York, stained and lacquered ash, upholstery, unmarked, armchairs 32-1/2" x 22" x 22", side chairs 31-1/2" x 19" x 22". **$6,250**

Courtesy of Rago Arts and Auctions, www.ragoarts.com

Pair of New Hope chairs, 1960s, Phil Powell (1919-2008), New Hope, Pennsylvania, sculpted walnut, upholstery, unmarked, 30" x 29" x 34". **$23,750**

Courtesy of Rago Arts and Auctions, www.ragoarts.com

Easy chair, upholstered back and seat with cushions, tapered legs, 36" h. x 34" w. x 38" d. **$677**

Courtesy of Capo Auction, www.capoauctionnyc.com

!top lot

Rare Marcel Breuer chaise lounge, Isokon Furniture Co. for Heal & Sons, Hungary/England, 1936, molded and cut maple plywood, upholstery, 55" w. x 23-1/2" d. x 32-1/4" h. $83,200

COURTESY OF WRIGHT, WWW.WRIGHT20.COM

Pair of Hans Wegner armchairs – "the chair" or "the round chair" – circa 1950s, light brown finish with black leather seats, likely early contract furniture, unmarked except for 1950s-era Upholsters International Unions label and "J. G. Furniture Company Inc NYC" inspection and contents tags, light wear, scratching to finish, small scratches to leather, wear on one rear foot, chrome glides, 29-1/2" h. x 25" w. x 20" d. . **$1,722**

Courtesy of Kaminski Auctions, www.kaminskiauctions.com

Pair of chairs, Finn Juhl (1912-1989) for Baker Furniture Co., Armchair No. 48, 1960s, United States, teak, leather, unsigned, constructed with one screw to vertical support at back, original finish, original upholstery, original hardware intact, 27-1/2" w. x 25" d. x 32" h. **$5,312**

Courtesy of Treadway Gallery, Inc., www.treadwaygallery.com

Gilbert Rohde chest, United States, 1940-1949, hardwood veneers, rectangular top with shaped front over two cabinet doors, interior fitted with median shelf, circular pulls, some finish wear, 29-5/8" h. x 23" w. x 14" d. **$923**

Courtesy of Skinner, Inc., www.skinnerinc.com

Chest, light green and white finish, branded in drawer "Kittinger Buffalo," 33-1/2" h. x 45-1/2" w. x 21" d........... **$615**

Courtesy of Kaminski Auctions, www.kaminskiauctions.com

◀ George Nakashima chest of drawers, 1957, New Hope, Pennsylvania, dark walnut with gray sap, horizontal rectangular top with exposed joinery over two banks of drawers, three deeper drawers on each side protected by two special order sliding doors in book-matched grain, 31-1/8" h. x 72" w. x 20" d. **$13,530**

Courtesy of Skinner, Inc., www.skinnerinc.com

◀ Mastercraft custom-made sideboard credenza buffet cabinet, cream color with faux leather overlay design and gilt metal appliqué, base crafted of gilt brass with Asian motif, 32-3/4" h. x 72-1/2" l. x 20-3/8" d. **$3,100**

Courtesy of Elite Decorative Arts, www.eliteauction.com

◀ Laminate desk with two faux drawer fronts and slide-forward top concealing mold-formed divided red acrylic interior, lower door at right side conceals file drawer and two shallow drawers, left side with adjustable two-shelf bookcase, top right drawer with "DF2000 / Made in France" label, wear throughout with detached non-structural leg element, 61" w. x 21" d. x 30-3/4" h. **$1,063**

Courtesy of Roland Auctioneers & Valuers, www.rolandauctions.com

◀ Rorimer-Brooks Art Deco desk/dressing table and stool, Cleveland, Ohio, birch plywood, figured maple, oak, and leather, compartmental letter holder in gilt paint with red interior with seven compartments on rectangular dark-stained birch plywood top over long drawer with circular pulls with silver linear painted accents, figural maple U-shape legs and silver ball feet, rectangular footstool upholstered in brown leather with conforming base, printed label reads, "Writing table & bench, wood with lacquer & silver leaf United States, made by Rorimer Brooks for Cleveland home in 1933. Loaned by Mrs. Warren Lahr," 27-1/2" h. x 39-1/2" w. x 19-1/2" d., compartment 11-1/2" h. x 39-1/4" w. x 6-1/4" d., footstool 19-1/2" h. x 20-1/2" w. x 13" d.................................. **$2,952**

Courtesy of Skinner, Inc., www.skinnerinc.com

Room divider, Evans Clark, designed circa 1949, Glenn of California, closed 60" x 32" x 16", open 60" x 64" x 8".. **$9,600**

Courtesy of Los Angeles Modern Auctions, www.lamodern.com

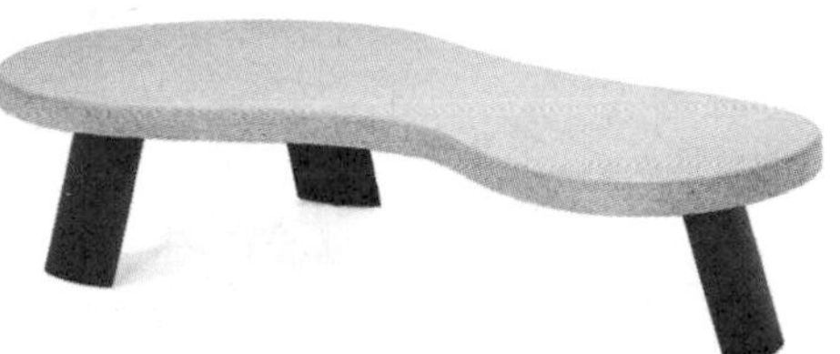

Amoeba coffee table (No. 5028), Paul Frankl (1886-1958), 1940s, Johnson Furniture Co., Grand Rapids, Michigan, enameled cork, stained and lacquered mahogany, stenciled model number, excellent condition, 14" x 72" x 36". **$10,240**

Courtesy of Rago Arts and Auctions, www.ragoarts.com

Chrome and Formica kitchen table and chairs by Stoneville Furniture Co., four matching chrome and turquoise Naugahyde chairs with one leaf for oval table, good to fair condition, table surface scuffed, three chairs with small tears, 29" h. x 48" l. x 36" w. **$189**

Courtesy of Leonard Auction, www.leonardauction.com

Three-piece Tomlinson Sophisticate, pair of slipper chairs and revolving cocktail table, circa 1961, High Point, North Carolina; chairs with fruitwood frames and caned backs, loose seat cushions, date at underside "October 1961," typical light surface wear and abrasions, upholstery in generally good condition, 28"; circular cocktail table with inlaid rotating top and pedestal base, underside with label "Sophisticate by Tomlinson," top slightly loose, surface wear and abrasions, minor cracks at feet, 18" x 42". **$2,108**

Courtesy of Brunk Auctions, www.brunkauctions.com

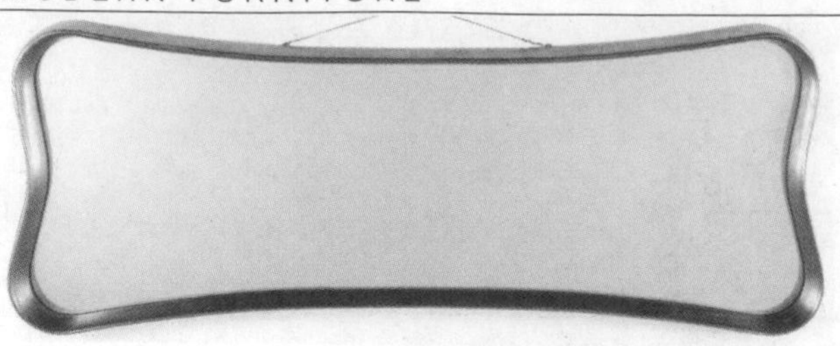

Giltwood dog bone mirror,
19-1/2" x 49-1/2".............. **$438**

Courtesy of Material Culture, www.materialculture.com

Kitchen table with leaf, chrome legs with cream-colored Formica top, good condition, 30" h. x 47" w. x 36" d........ **$41**

Courtesy of Leonard Auction, www.leonardauction.com

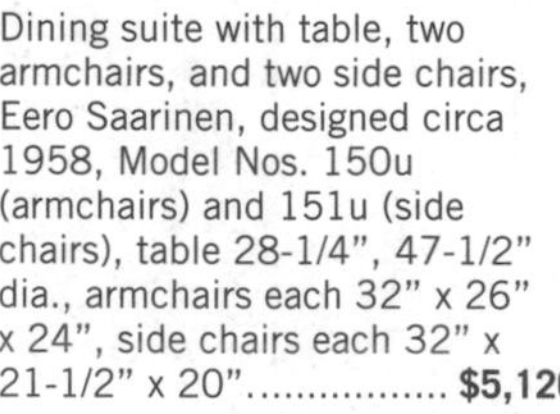

Dining suite with table, two armchairs, and two side chairs, Eero Saarinen, designed circa 1958, Model Nos. 150u (armchairs) and 151u (side chairs), table 28-1/4", 47-1/2" dia., armchairs each 32" x 26" x 24", side chairs each 32" x 21-1/2" x 20"................. **$5,120**

Courtesy of Los Angeles Modern Auctions, www.lamodern.com

Pierre Jeanneret sofa from Punjab University, Chandigarh, France/ India, circa 1955, teak, upholstery, 64" w. x 32" d. x 33" h. .. **$35,840**

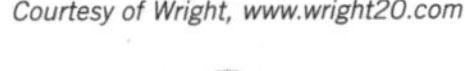

Courtesy of Wright, www.wright20.com

Poet sofa, Finn Juhl (1912-1989), 1950s, Niels Vodder, Denmark, teak, upholstery, unmarked, 34" x 51" x 31"............................. **$8,750**

Courtesy of Rago Arts and Auctions, www.ragoarts.com

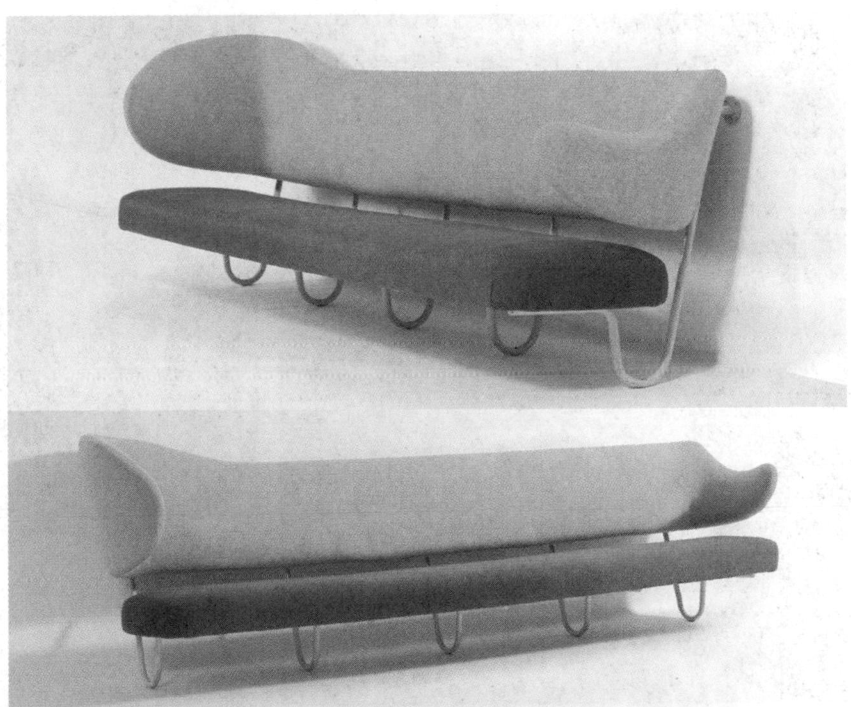

Finn Juhl custom wall-mounted sofa from Villa K. Kokfeldt, Hellerup, Denmark, Niels Vodder, Denmark, 1953, upholstery, enameled steel, with Juhl's original floor plan and elevation of form, 130" w. x 32" d. x 39-1/4" h. **$76,800**

Courtesy of Wright, www.wright20.com

GLASS

american brilliant cut glass

CUT GLASS IS made by grinding decorations into glass by means of abrasive-carrying metal or stone wheels. An ancient craft, it was revived in 1600 by the Bohemians and spread through Europe to Great Britain and America.

American cut glass came of age at the Centennial Exposition in 1876 and the World Columbian Exposition in 1893. America's most significant output of high-quality glass occurred from 1880 to 1917, a period now known as the Brilliant Period. Glass from this period is the most eagerly sought by collectors.

Known for its exquisite cut glass, the Libbey Glass Co. became synonymous with the Brilliant Period. Punch bowls are considered some of Libbey's most cherished pieces and include the Grand Prize pattern from the 1904 St. Louis World's Fair and the Stars and Stripes pattern presented to President William McKinley. Libbey was, as Edward Atlee Barber described in his 1900 publication American Glassware, "world-famous for the depth and richness of their cut designs, their simplicity and complexity of pattern, purity of color and prismatic brilliancy."

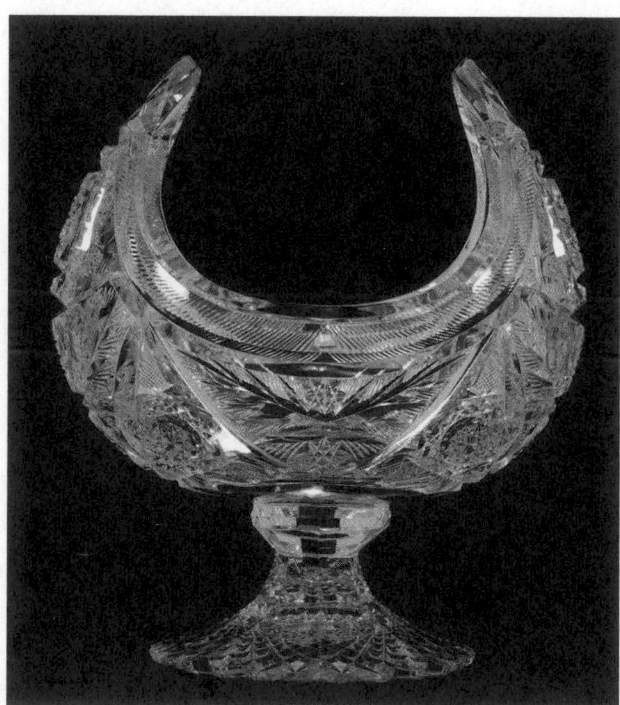

Crescent vase, Libbey Diana pattern, signed, large scalloped petticoat hobstar base, no chips, cracks or repairs, 10-1/2" x 9". **$67,850**

Courtesy of Woody Auction, www.woodyauction.com

Trumpet vase with double stars and hobnails, late 19th/early 20th century, 16-1/2"......... **$544**

Courtesy of Neal Auction, www.nealauction.com

Pedestal punch bowl in Propeller pattern by Marshall Field, large 6" hobstar base, facet-cut ball stem, no chips, cracks or repairs, 9-3/4" x 12-1/2". **$1,121**

Courtesy of Woody Auction, www.woodyauction.com

Fish-shaped vase with large hobstar clusters, cane, Strawberry Diamond and Prism motif, hobstar base, thick blank, no chips, cracks or repairs, 14-1/2" h. **$1,180**

Courtesy of Woody Auction, www.woodyauction.com

Footed vase, possibly Pairpoint, with hobstars and diapered triangles, late 19th/early 20th century, 13 5/8"................. **$320**

Courtesy of Neal Auction, www.nealauction.com

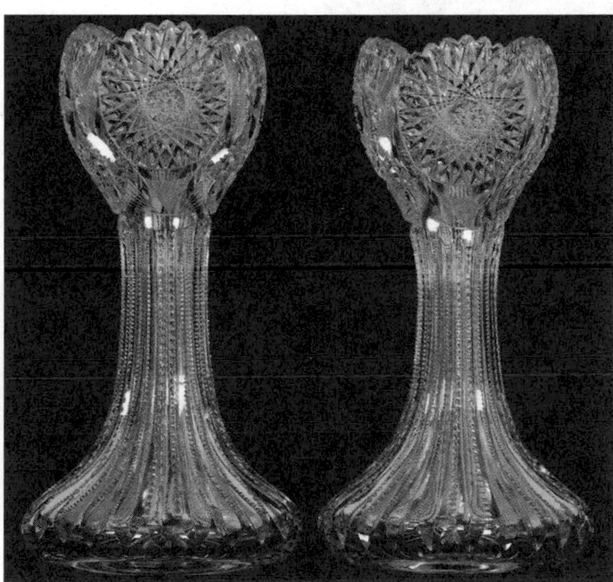

Pair of corset-shaped vases with prism-cut bodies with large Hobstar, Strawberry Diamond and Fan highlights, ray cut bases, extra thick and heavy blanks, no chips, cracks or repairs, 14" x 7-1/4".......**$1,534**

Courtesy of Woody Auction, www.woodyauction.com

Five-part banquet lamp in Ellsmere pattern, signed Libbey, fully pattern-cut globe, fully pattern-cut font, long stem body and pattern-matched skirted base, marked Bradley & Hubbard metal works, replacement pattern cut chimney, no chips, cracks or repairs, 37" x 8". **$10,325**

Courtesy of Woody Auction, www.woodyauction.com

Monumental Mt. Washington lamp, Strawberry Diamond and Button motif, fully cut pattern shade and font, figural silver-plate base with winged horses, electrified, metal ring that holds lampshade not attached to lamp arms, 23" x 12-1/2". **$2,950**

Courtesy of Woody Auction, www.woodyauction.com

Table lamp in Harvard pattern, circa 1900-1910, mushroom shade, baluster base, cut glass prisms, electrified, 24-1/2" h., 12-1/2" dia..................... **$1,536**

Courtesy of Neal Auction, www.nealauction.com

Rare Strawberry dome table lamp, pattern #129 by Fry, Hobstar, Vesica, Strawberry Diamond, Prism and Fan motifs, shade with frosted background with star and fan highlights, no chips, cracks or repairs, 13-1/2" x 9-1/2". ... **$885**

Courtesy of Woody Auction, www.woodyauction.com

Table lamp with mushroom shade, Hobstar Vesica, Prism, Cane and Fan motifs, pattern matched base, two lights, large cut prisms, no chips, cracks or repairs, 23-1/2" x 12". **$1,003**

Courtesy of Woody Auction, www.woodyauction.com

Special-order vase with engraved chrysanthemum décor with pattern-cut base, attributed to Tuthill, no chips, cracks or repairs, 18-1/4". **$2,714**

Courtesy of Woody Auction, www.woodyauction.com

Pair of decanters with morning glory floral décor, pattern-cut stoppers, no chips, cracks or repairs, 12" h. **$1,121**

Courtesy of Woody Auction, www.woodyauction.com

Two pitchers in Russian pattern with star-cut buttons, triple-notched handles, silver with elaborate embossed designs, finials appear polished down, signed Tiffany silver collars and lids marked "7769 TIFFANY COMPANY MAKERS L," 9" h. **$1,416**

Courtesy of Woody Auction, www.woodyauction.com

Tankard with modified Russian cut body with Strawberry Diamond, long Thumbprint and notched prism motif, elaborate signed Tiffany sterling spout and collar, no chips, cracks or repairs, 14-1/2" h. **$1,888**

Courtesy of Woody Auction, www.woodyauction.com

Two-part punch bowl, hobstar and hobstar cluster motif, Strawberry Diamond highlights, excellent condition, no chips, cracks or repairs, 13-1/2" x 15"..**$1,652**

Courtesy of Woody Auction, www.woodyauction.com

Vase in Adam pattern by Sinclaire, rare size, no chips, cracks or repairs, 22-1/2" x 9". **$2,242**

Courtesy of Woody Auction, www.woodyauction.com

Large punch bowl in Ozella pattern with expanding stars, fan shapes, and diamond panels, signed Libbey, excellent condition, 14" dia. **$363**

Courtesy of Fontaine's Auction Gallery, fontainesauction.com

Fourteen-piece Colonna pattern punch bowl set, Libbey Glass Co., late 19th/early 20th century, signed, two-part bowl, 9-1/2" h., 13-1/2" dia.; 12 cups, 2-1/8"; and Gorham silver-plate and cut glass ladle, 13" l. **$1,792**

Courtesy of Neal Auction, www.nealauction.com

Ice cream tray, Brunswick stars and hobstars, late 19th/early 20th century, 13-3/4" l....... **$768**

Courtesy of Neal Auction, www.nealauction.com

Round tray in Ellsmere pattern, signed Libbey, no chips, cracks or repairs, 11-3/4"................. **$1,534**

Courtesy of Woody Auction, www.woodyauction.com

Round tray in Vintage pattern by Tuthill, signed, no chips, cracks or repairs, 12". **$649**

Courtesy of Woody Auction, www.woodyauction.com

Round scalloped tray, pattern similar to Claremont by Bergen, no chips, cracks or repairs, 14"...... **$531**

Courtesy of Woody Auction, www.woodyauction.com

Bowl, green cut to clear with engraved Cherry and Apple décor, wide Gorham sterling gilt rim, attributed to Pairpoint, no chips, cracks or repairs, 3-1/4" x 12".. **$944**

Courtesy of Woody Auction, www.woodyauction.com

GLASS

baccarat

BACCARAT GLASS HAS been made by Cristalleries de Baccarat, France, since 1765. The firm has produced various glassware of excellent quality as well as paperweights. Baccarat's Rose Tiente is often referred to as Baccarat's Amberina.

Molded and cut-glass eight-light chandelier, 20th century, recently cleaned, no prisms missing, 52" h. x 42" d. **$3,125**

Courtesy of Heritage Auctions, ha.com

Pair of antique French table chandeliers, gilt bronze structure, opalescent, amethyst, and clear crystals with three lights and beaded shades, excellent condition, 20-1/4" h. **$1,045**

Courtesy Last Chance by Live Auctioneers, www.liveauctioneers.com

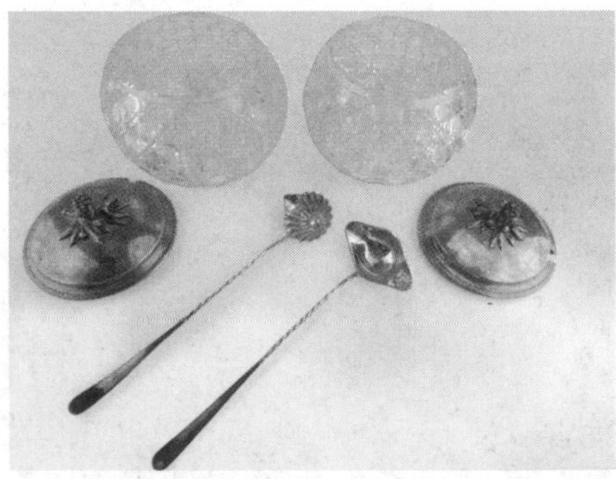

Cut crystal bowls with ladles and silver plate lids with finials, ladles marked Christofel, bowls marked Baccarat, 9" h. x 8" w. **$615**

Courtesy of Don Presley Auctions, www.donpresley.com

French cut glass with sulphide goblet, colorless lead glass, conical bowl with encapsulated bust of Minerva surrounded by strawberry diamond and fan cutting, on hexagonal baluster-form tiered stem and ray-cut foot, probably Baccarat, second half 19th century, 7-7/8" h., 3-1/4" dia....................... **$1,200**

Courtesy of Jeffrey S. Evans & Associates, www.jeffreysevans.com

Cut glass bowl with gilt bronze and enamel base, cherubs with enamel blue and white flowers, good condition, 11-1/2" h. x 10-1/4" dia.. **$984**

Courtesy of Westport Auction, www.westportauction.com

Cranberry cut to clear art glass vase, floral overlay with acid-cut background, nick to base, 6" h. x 5" w....................... **$590**

Courtesy of Woody Auction, www.woodyauction.com

Salvador Dali (Spanish, 1904-1989) for Baccarat, pair of "Castor and Pollux"-1973 crystal candlesticks, from edition of 500, each in original Baccarat red boxes, marked with manufacturer's stencil mark and incised with Dali signature, one incised "CASTOR 154/500 Baccarat Audouin," other incised "POLLUX 154/500 Baccarat Audouin," 10-1/4" h. x 6-3/4" w. x 4-3/4" d............. **$2,232**

Courtesy of Ahlers & Ogletree Auction Gallery, www.aandoauctions.com

Pair of gilt bronze and cut glass wall sconces (one shown), scrolled arms, floriform candlecups with pendeloque pendants, 19th century, 14" h. x 12" w. **$640**

Courtesy of Neal Auction Co., www.nealauction.com

Frosted art glass nautilus shell with label and original box, circa 20th century, 7" h. x 5" w. **$396**

Courtesy of Bill Hood & Sons, www.hoodauction.com

Group of six perfume bottles (three shown) in Amberina red to clear transition glass with twisted ribbed form glass, good condition, 5-1/2" h., 2-1/4" dia. **$246**

Courtesy of Peachtree & Bennett, www.peachtreebennett.com

Fifty-five piece glass service (five samples shown) with vine and animal decoration in matte style, circa 1900, seven red wine glasses, 12 white wine glasses, eight sweet wine glasses, four champagne glasses, 15 liquor glasses, and nine glasses, inscribed with Baccarat, ranging in size from 5-1/2" h. to 4-1/4" h. **$1,028**

Courtesy of Schuler Auktionen, www.schulerauktionen.ch

Concentric pink, yellow, white and green millefiore paperweight, signed with Baccarat logo, good condition, 3" dia............................... **$186**

Courtesy of Kodner Galleries, www.kodner.com

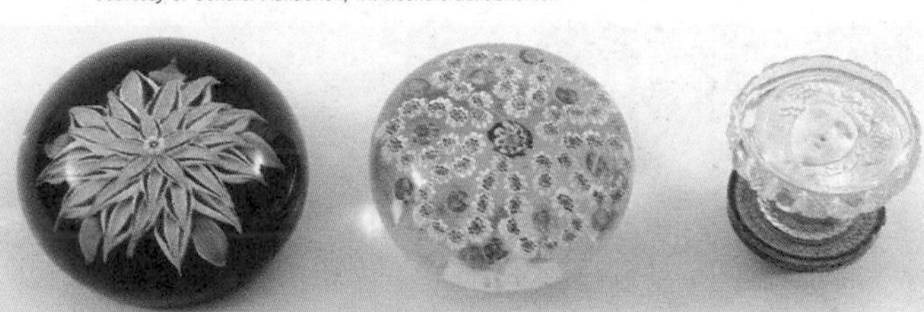

Two paperweights and sulfide door knob: contemporary Baccarat dahlia paperweight, circa 1972; antique Clichy clear glass paperweight with millefiori center flower; and sulfide door knob, mid-19th century, 2-1/4" l. x 2" dia. **$1,062**

Courtesy of Burchard Galleries, www.burchardgalleries.com

Pair of Ormolu mounted vases, circa 19th century, 13" h... **$5,312**

Courtesy of Distinction Auctions, www.distinctionauctions.com

Emerald cut to clear Baccarat cologne bottle, French, cut in Russian pattern with vesicas and fine diamonds, with possibly unmatched sterling repoussé stopper depicting Venus with cherubs, probably Irian pattern, light wear to base of bottle, small dent to edge of silver stopper and wear to decoration; and Thomas G. Hawkes cut and engraved Gravic Glass perfume bottle, early 20th century, thick blank with deeply carved pattern of chrysanthemums, possibly unmatched gold stopper with circular gold wreath of flowers with alternating pearls and rubies, 4-1/2" w. **$496**

Courtesy of Brunk Auctions, www.brunkauctions.com

GLASS

bride's baskets

THESE BERRY OR fruit bowls were popular late Victorian wedding gifts, hence the name. They were produced in a variety of quality art glass wares and sometimes were fitted in ornate silver-plate holders.

Bride's basket with floral decoratlon on Wllcox quadruple silver-plate centerpiece with three cherub or putti figures, scene atop centerpiece of cherub in swan boat with birds and foliage, dimples to ruffled edge, wear to gilding on ruffled edge, basket 10-1/2" dia., 5-3/4" h..... **$1,625**

Courtesy of Clarke Auction Gallery, www.clarkeny.hibid.com

Square bride's basket, pink and white satin diamond-quilted mother-of-pearl glass, ruffled rim with applied blue glass trim, on Tufts silver-plate stand, good condition. **$206**

Courtesy of Woody Auction, www.woodyauction.com

Daisy and Button pattern bride's basket, circular blue bowl fitted in large ornate quadruple-plate stand marked with Toronto Silver-Plate Co. and numbered 180, late 19th century, excellent condition overall, three pattern chips to bowl, area of scuffing on stand, 12-3/8" h. overall, bowl 4" h., 10" dia..................**$420**

Courtesy of Jeffrey S. Evans & Associates, www.jeffreysevans.com

Cranberry and white overlay handgrip ruffled baskets with optic windows and enamel floral décor, on Meriden Britannia silver-plate frame with woman atop pedestal and cutout cherub medallions..... **$2,478**

Courtesy of Woody Auction, www.woodyauction.com

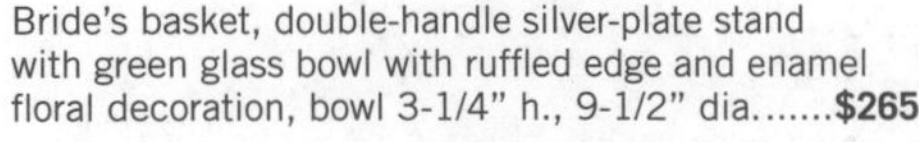

Bride's basket, double-handle silver-plate stand with green glass bowl with ruffled edge and enamel floral decoration, bowl 3-1/4" h., 9-1/2" dia.......**$265**

Courtesy of Burchard Galleries, www.burchardgalleries.com

Double pigeon blood ruffled bride's basket with enamel floral décor on marked Pairpoint silver-plate frame with cherubs riding on turtles, good condition, 15-3/4" h. x 22" w...................... **$2,006**

Courtesy of Woody Auction, www.woodyauction.com

Four Victorian bride's baskets and silver-plate table baskets: Silver-plated Aesthetic and floral décor frame with pierced crane motif on each leg and fold-over ruffled rim pink satin glass bowl enameled with flowering vines, 13" h.; Aesthetic frame with green satin bowl with stylized ruffled edge in frame with ring, 12" h.; and two small Forbes Silver Co. plated baskets with repoussé borders and pierced handles, 6" h.; glass bowls not original to frames................ **$212**

Courtesy of Austin Auction Gallery, www.austinauction.com

Two Cabbage pattern oval clear glass bride's baskets on Tufts silver-plate frames, 10" h., 10" dia. **$177**

Courtesy of Woody Auction, www.woodyauction.com

Middletown bride's basket, white metal with leaping stag on base, pattern #714 marked on base, enamel blue glass bowl with floral motif, repair to one tooth, 15-1/2" h., 10-3/4" dia. **$177**

Courtesy of Burchard Galleries, www.burchardgalleries.com

Victorian bride's basket, shallow pale yellow-green cased opal bowl with swirled and ruffled rim, enameled decorated interior, ground pontil mark, loosely fitted in quadruple-plate stand with steer-head handles, marked for Reed & Barton and numbered 895, late 19th century, 5-1/4" h., 11-1/4" dia.. **$132**

Courtesy of Jeffrey S. Evans & Associates, www.jeffreysevans.com

Lattice bride's basket, cranberry opalescent, square rim with upright ruffles and down-turned corners, fitted in quadruple-plate stand with anchor mark, Northwood Glass Co. and others, circa 1890, stand re-silvered with minor soldering on handle junctures, 13" h., 7-1/2" dia. **$156**

Courtesy of Jeffrey S. Evans & Associates, www.jeffreysevans.com

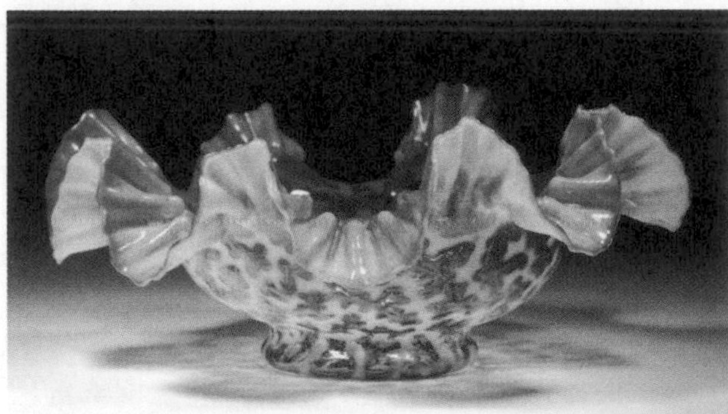

Seaweed pattern bride's bowl in cranberry opalescent, ruffled and crimped rim, circa 1890, 4" h., 10" dia.................................. **$120**

Courtesy of Jeffrey S. Evans & Associates, www.jeffreysevans.com

Bride's basket, amber opalescent with enameled floral decoration in silver-plate Victorian stand, good condition, silver-plate with some losses, 12" h., 12" dia.**$103**

Courtesy of Kennedy Auction Service, www.kennedysauction.com

Bride's basket, hand-blown Mt. Washington cased pink over opal glass octagonal-lobed bride's bowl with burgundy daisies and Art Nouveau gilded cobalt florals, double crimp bowl with deep pontil ground and inverted base in lieu of Bohemian everted applied seats, circa 1890, proper 1894-1902 Benedict Mfg. Co. quadruple-plate basket, signed, 10-1/2" h., 10-1/2" dia..**$191**

Courtesy of Accurate Auctions, www.accurateauctions.com

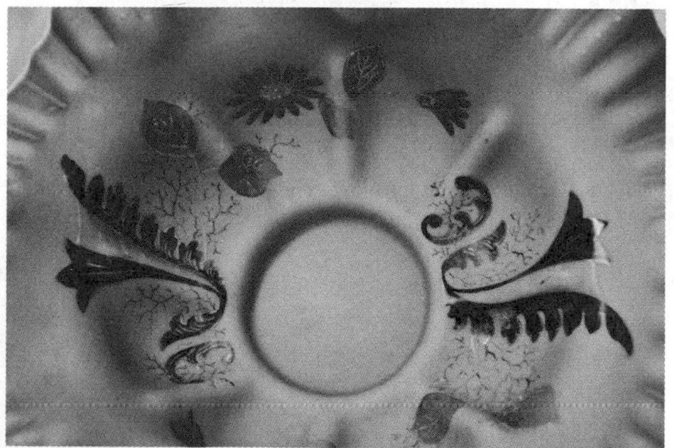

GLASS

cambridge glass

THE CAMBRIDGE GLASS Co. was founded in Ohio in 1901. Numerous pieces are now sought, especially those designed by Arthur J. Bennett, including Crown Tuscan. Other productions included crystal animals, "Black Amethyst," "blanc opaque," and other types of colored glass. The firm was finally closed in 1954. It should not be confused with the New England Glass Co. of Cambridge, Massachusetts.

Emerald and gilded thistle covered marmalade and dual-handled spooner, circa 1914, Near Cut pattern, which first appeared in 1905 (signed pieces that sold for premium dollars during the St. Louis World's Fair helped develop awareness and appreciation for the pattern and design), 7-1/2" x 4-1/2" x 6-3/4"..**$56**

Courtesy of Accurate Auctions, www.accurateauctions.com

Pair of emerald pressed glass gilded bowls, 1900-1915, Near Cut dual-handled thistle sugar bowl, Cambridge Glass Co., and gilded rose and arches serving bowl, excellent condition, minor gilt wear, sugar bowl 7-1/2" x 4-1/2" x 4", serving bowl 9" x 9". **$30**

Courtesy of Accurate Auctions, Sheffield, Alabama

Ruby-stained water pitcher, colorless with gilt decoration, Near Cut Daisy pattern, circa 1910-1920, 10" h. **$360**

Courtesy of Jeffrey S. Evans & Associates, www.jeffreysevans.com

Ruby-stained Daisy pattern table articles, covered butter dish, creamer and spooner, colorless, circa 1910-1920, very good condition overall, flake to underside of one rim point of butter dish, chip to one foot on creamer, chip to rim point of spooner, 4-5/8" to 5-3/4" h. **$132**

Courtesy of Jeffrey S. Evans & Associates, www.jeffreysevans.com

Rose Point pattern etched glass service ware, 23 pieces: lobed plates, footed dishes, one large spoon, relish dishes, handle dish, covered dishes, sugar and creamer pots, pitcher and candelabra, 3-3/4" to 12-1/4". **$272**

Courtesy of Austin Auction Gallery, www.austinauction.com

Rose Point pattern etched glassware (not all shown): 12 water goblets, 12 plates, sauce bowl and plate, compote, two cream and sugar sets, and two salt and pepper sets, goblets 8-1/2" h. **$142**

Courtesy of Leonard Auction, www.leonardauction.com

Rose Point pattern 34-piece collection: punch bowl, large tray, ladle, 12 cups, 14 cocktail glasses, centerpiece bowl, cocktail shaker, candlesticks, and footed vase, 4-1/4" to 13-1/2" h., 2-1/2" to 17-1/2" dia................ **$3,075**

Courtesy of Kaminski Auctions, www.kaminskiauctions.com

Two green cologne bottles and one stopper, one bottle with extra glass at pontil and one with small flake on rim, stopper with minor imperfections, 5-7/8" to 7-1/2" h... **$186**

Courtesy of Green Valley Auctions, www.greenvalleyauctions.com

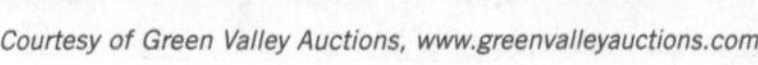

Pinched Black Amethyst decanter, glasses, and swizzle sticks, one from One Fifth Avenue and other with twist hook, circa 1930s. **$126**

Courtesy of Charleston Estate Auctions, www.charlestonestateauctions.com

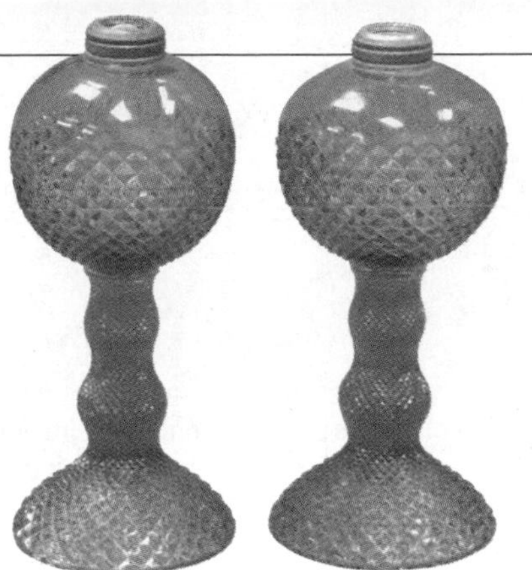

Diamond pattern amber-colored vintage fluid glass lamps, 9-1/2" h. **$73**

Courtesy of William J. Jenack Estate Appraisers & Auctioneers, www.jenack.com

Twelve etched crystal wine glasses, early 20th century, 8-1/4" h. **$151**

Courtesy of King Galleries, www.kinggalleriesauction.com

Four lidded hen-shaped saltcellars, early 20th century, 2-1/2" **$18**

Courtesy of Omega Auction Corp., www.omegaauctioncorp.com

Carmen (ruby) Japonica fluted footed bowl, four feet and edges fluted, unusual form, marked with Japonica logo on bottom, circa 1930, nicks around edges and some enamel loss, 11" x 10" x 5-1/2". **$2,124**

Courtesy of Manor Auctions, www.manorauctions.com

Five pressed swans, colorless, two different model examples, circa 1920s, bowls 3" to 10" dia. **$122**

Courtesy of Jeffrey S. Evans & Associates, www.jeffreysevans.com

Etched Samovar, vaseline (uranium), circa 1927, plate etched 695, factory-polished rim, fitted in plated-metal stand, 12-1/2" h. **$390**

Courtesy of Jeffrey S. Evans & Associates, www.jeffreysevans.com

GLASS

carnival art glass

CARNIVAL GLASS IS what is fondly called mass-produced iridescent glassware. The term "carnival glass" has evolved through the years as glass collectors have responded to the idea that much of this beautiful glassware was made as give-away glass at local carnivals and fairs. However, more of it was made and sold through the same channels as pattern glass and Depression glass. Some patterns were indeed giveaways, and others were used as advertising premiums, souvenirs, etc. Whatever the origin, the term "carnival glass" today encompasses glassware that is usually pattern molded and treated with metallic salts, creating that unique coloration that is so desirable to collectors.

Early names for iridescent glassware, which early 20th century consumers believed to have all come from foreign manufacturers, include Pompeian Iridescent, Venetian Art, and Mexican Aurora. Another popular early name was "Nancy Glass," as some patterns were believed to have come from the Daum, Nancy, glassmaking area in France. This was at a time when the artistic cameo glass was enjoying great success. While the iridescent glassware being made by such European glassmakers as Loetz influenced the American market place, it was Louis Tiffany's Favrile glass that really caught the eye of glass consumers of the early 1900s. It seems an easy leap to transform Tiffany's shimmering glassware to something that could be mass produced, allowing what we call carnival glass today to become "poor man's Tiffany."

Carnival glass is iridized glassware that is created by pressing hot molten glass into molds, just as pattern glass had evolved. Some forms are hand finished, while others are completely formed by molds. To achieve the marvelous iridescent colors that carnival glass collectors seek, a process was developed where a liquid solution of metallic salts was put onto the still hot glass form after it was unmolded. As the liquid evaporated, a fine metallic surface was left which refracts light into wonderful colors. The name given to the iridescent spray by early glassmakers was "dope."

Many of the forms created by carnival glass manufacturers were accessories to the china American housewives so loved. By the early 1900s, consumers could find carnival glassware at such popular stores as F. W. Woolworth and McCrory's. To capitalize on the popular fancy for these colored wares, some other industries bought large quantities of carnival glass and turned them into "packers." This term reflects the practice where baking powder, mustard, or other household products were packed into a special piece of glass that could take on another life after the original product was used. Lee Manufacturing Co. used iridized carnival glass as premiums for its baking powder and other products, causing some early carnival glass to be known by the generic term "Baking Powder Glass."

Classic carnival glass production began in the early 1900s and continued about twenty years, but no one really documented or researched production until the first collecting wave struck in 1960

It is important to remember that carnival glasswares were sold in department stores as well as mass merchants rather than through the general store often associated with a young America. Glassware by this time was mass-produced and sold in large quantities by such enterprising companies as Butler Brothers. When the economics of the country soured in the 1920s, those interested in purchasing iridized glassware were not spared. Many of the leftover inventories of glasshouses that hoped to sell this mass-produced glassware found their way to wholesalers who in turn sold the wares to those who offered the glittering glass as prizes at carnivals, fairs, circuses, etc. Possibly because this was the last venue people associated the iridized glassware with, it became known as "carnival glass."

For more information on carnival glass, see *Warman's Carnival Glass Identification and Price Guide,* 2nd edition, by Ellen T. Schroy.

No. 474 pattern four-piece punch set, marigold, two-piece pedestal punch bowl and three punch cups, Imperial Glass Co., first quarter 20th century, flake to one scallop on pedestal base, one punch cup with significant crack, remainder undamaged, 2-1/2" to 9" h. overall, 12" dia. punch bowl.. **$48**

Courtesy of Jeffrey S. Evans & Associates, www.jeffreysevans.com

CARNIVAL GLASS COMPANIES

Much of vintage American carnival glassware was created in the Ohio valley, in the glasshouse-rich areas of Pennsylvania, Ohio, and West Virginia. The abundance of natural materials, good transportation, and skilled craftsmen that created the early American pattern glass manufacturing companies allowed many of them to add carnival glass to their production lines. Brief company histories of the major carnival glass manufacturers follow:

CAMBRIDGE GLASS CO. (CAMBRIDGE)

Cambridge Glass was a rather minor player in the carnival glass marketplace. Founded in 1901 as a new factory in Cambridge, Ohio, it focused on producing fine crystal tablewares. What carnival glass it did produce was imitation cut-glass patterns.

Colors used by Cambridge include marigold, as well as few others. Forms found in carnival glass by Cambridge include tablewares and vases, some with its trademark "Near-Cut."

DIAMOND GLASS CO. (DIAMOND)

This company was started as the Dugan brothers (see Dugan Glass Co.) departed the carnival glass-making scene in 1913. However, Alfred Dugan returned and became general manager until his death in 1928. After a disastrous fire in June of 1931, the factory closed.

Dugan Glass Co. (Dugan)

The history of the Dugan Glass Co. is closely related to Harry Northwood (see Northwood Glass Co.), whose cousin, Thomas Dugan, became plant manager at the Northwood Glass Co. in Indiana, Pennsylvania, in 1895. By 1904, Dugan and his partner W. G. Minnemayer bought the former Northwood factory from the now defunct National Glass conglomerate and opened as the Dugan Glass Co. Dugan's brother, Alfred, joined the company and stayed until it became the Diamond Glass Co. in 1913. At this time, Thomas Dugan moved to the Cambridge Glass Co., later Duncan and Miller and finally Hocking, Lancaster. Alfred left Diamond Glass, too, but later returned.

Understanding how the Northwood and Dugan families were connected helps collectors understand the linkage of these three companies. Their productions were similar; molds were swapped, retooled, etc.

Colors attributed to Dugan and Diamond include amethyst, marigold, peach opalescent, and white. The company developed deep amethyst shades, some almost black.

Forms made by both Dugan and Diamond mirrored what other glass companies were producing. The significant contribution by Dugan and later Diamond were feet - either ball or spatula shapes. They are also known for deeply crimped edges.

Fenton Art Glass Co. (Fenton)

Frank Leslie Fenton and his brothers, John W. Fenton and Charles H. Fenton, founded this truly American glassmaker in 1905 in Martins Ferry, Ohio. Early production was of blanks, which the brothers soon learned to decorate themselves. They moved to a larger factory in Williamstown, West Virginia.

By 1907, Fenton was experimenting with iridescent glass, developing patterns and the metallic salt formulas that it became so famous for. Production of carnival glass continued at Fenton until the early 1930s. In 1970, Fenton began to reissue carnival glass, creating new colors and forms as well as using traditional patterns.

Colors developed by Fenton are numerous. The company developed red and Celeste blue in the 1920s; a translucent pale blue, known as Persian blue, is also one of its more distinctive colors, as is a light yellow-green color known as vaseline. Fenton also produced delicate opalescent colors including amethyst opalescent and red opalescent. Because the Fenton brothers learned how to decorate their own blanks, they also promoted the addition of enamel decoration to some of their carnival glass patterns.

Forms made by Fenton are also numerous. What distinguishes Fenton from other glassmakers is its attention to detail and hand finishing processes. Edges are found scalloped, fluted, tightly crimped, frilled, or pinched into a candy ribbon edge, also referred to as 3-in-1 edge.

IMPERIAL GLASS CO. (IMPERIAL)

Edward Muhleman and a syndicate founded the Imperial Glass Co. at Bellaire, Ohio, in 1901, with production beginning in 1904. It started with pressed glass tableware patterns as well as lighting fixtures. The company's marketing strategy included selling to important retailers of its day, such as F. W. Woolworth and McCrory and Kresge, to get glassware into the hands of American housewives. Imperial also became a major exporter of glassware, including its brilliant carnival patterns. During the Depression, it filed for bankruptcy in 1931, but was able to continue on. By 1962, it was again producing carnival glass patterns. By April 1985, the factory was closed and the molds sold.

Colors made by Imperial include typical carnival colors such as marigold. It added interesting shades of green, known as helios, a pale ginger ale shade known as clambroth, and a brownish smoke shade.

Forms created by Imperial tend to be functional, such as berry sets and table sets. Patterns vary from wonderful imitation cut glass patterns to detailed florals and naturalistic designs.

MILLERSBURG GLASS CO. (MILLERSBURG)

John W. Fenton started the Millersburg Glass Co. in September 1908. Perhaps it was the factory's more obscure location or the lack of business experience by John Fenton, but the company failed by 1911.

The factory was bought by Samuel Fair and John Fenton, and renamed the Radium Glass

Co., but it lasted only a year.

Colors produced by Millersburg are amethyst, green, and marigold. Shades such as blue and vaseline were added on rare occasions. The company is well known for its bright radium finishes.

Forms produced at Millersburg are mostly bowls and vases. Pattern designers at Millersburg often took one theme and developed several patterns from it. Millersburg often used one pattern for the interior and a different pattern for the exterior.

NORTHWOOD GLASS CO. (NORTHWOOD)

Englishman Harry Northwood founded the Northwood Glass Co. He developed his glass formulas for carnival glass, naming it "Golden Iris" in 1908. Northwood was one of the pioneers of the glass manufacturers who marked his wares. Marks range from a full script signature to a simple underscored capital N in a circle. However, not all Northwood glassware is marked.

Colors that Northwood created were many. Collectors prefer its pastels, such as ice blue, ice green, and white. It is also known for several stunning blue shades. The one color that Northwood did not develop was red.

Forms of Northwood patterns range from typical table sets, bowls, and water sets to whimsical novelties, such as a pattern known as Corn, which realistically depicts an ear of corn.

UNITED STATES GLASS CO. (U.S. GLASS)

In 1891, a consortium of 15 American glass manufacturers joined together as the United States Glass Co. This company was successful in continuing pattern glass production, as well as developing new glass lines. By 1911, it had begun limited production of carnival glass lines, often using existing pattern glass tableware molds. By the time a tornado destroyed the last of its glass factories in Glassport in 1963, it was no longer producing glassware.

Colors associated with US Glass are marigold, white, and a rich honey amber.

Forms tend to be table sets and functional forms.

WESTMORELAND GLASS CO. (WESTMORELAND)

Started as the Westmoreland Specialty Co., Grapeville, Pennsylvania, in 1889, this company originally made novelties and glass packing containers, such as candy containers. Researchers have identified its patterns being advertised by Butler Brothers as early as 1908. Carnival glass production continued into the 1920s. In the 1970s, Westmoreland, too, begin to reissue carnival glass patterns and novelties. However, this ceased in February of 1996 when the factory burned.

Colors originally used by Westmoreland were typical carnival colors, such as blue and marigold.

Forms include tablewares and functional forms, containers, etc.

—Ellen T. Schroy

Blackberry Block pattern pitcher and six tumblers, white, Fenton Art Glass Co., circa early 20th century, good condition, some sickness to recesses of bottom of pitcher, light wear, pitcher 11" h. .... **$4,000-$6,000**

Courtesy of Rago Arts and Antiques, www.ragoarts.com

Bushel Basket pattern bowl, aqua opalescent, raised on four feet, signed, Northwood Glass Co., first quarter 20th century, undamaged, 4-3/4" h. **$144**

Courtesy of Jeffrey S. Evans & Associates, www.jeffreysevans.com

Butterfly and Berry pattern seven-piece berry set, marigold, Fenton Art Glass Co., good condition, no chips, cracks or repairs. **$59**

Courtesy of Woody Auction, www.woodyauction.com

Carolina Dogwood pattern bowl, blue opalescent and iridescent, ruffled and scalloped rim, Westmoreland Glass Co., first quarter 20th century, undamaged, base with striations as made, minute wear to interior, 2-3/4" h. overall, 8-5/8" dia. overall. **$132**

Courtesy of Jeffrey S. Evans & Associates, www.jeffreysevans.com

Butterfly and Berry pattern four-piece table set, marigold, covered sugar bowl, creamer, spooner, and covered butter dish, Fenton Art Glass Co., first quarter 20th century, creamer and spooner undamaged, sugar and butter bases undamaged, sugar cover with flake to finial, butter cover with some roughness and minute flakes to rim, 4-1/2" to 6-1/4" h. overall.. **$120**

Courtesy of Jeffrey S. Evans & Associates, www.jeffreysevans.com

! top lot

Dragon and Lotus pattern ruffled bowl, red, good condition, no chips, cracks or repairs, 9" dia. $944

COURTESY OF WOODY AUCTION, WWW.WOODYAUCTION.COM

Drapery pattern rose bowl, aqua opalescent, beaded rim, Northwood Glass Co., first quarter 20th century, undamaged, 3-1/2" h. overall, 5" dia. overall. **$180**

Courtesy of Jeffrey S. Evans & Associates, www.jeffreysevans.com

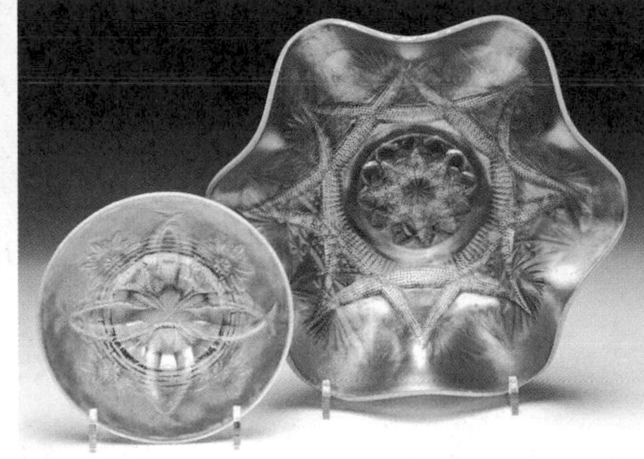

Four Flowers pattern plate and Ski Star pattern bowl, both in peach opalescent, Dugan Glass Co., first quarter 20th century, 1" and 3-3/4" h., 6-1/2" and 11" dia. overall. **$84**

Courtesy of Jeffrey S. Evans & Associates, www.jeffreysevans.com

▲ Good Luck pattern bowl, marigold, ribbed exterior, Northwood Glass Co., good condition, no chips, cracks or repairs, 9". **$94**

Courtesy of Woody Auction, www.woodyauction.com

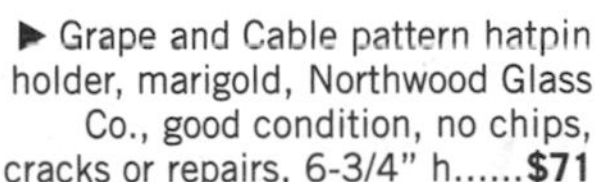

▶ Grape and Cable pattern hatpin holder, marigold, Northwood Glass Co., good condition, no chips, cracks or repairs, 6-3/4" h...... **$71**

Courtesy of Woody Auction, www.woodyauction.com

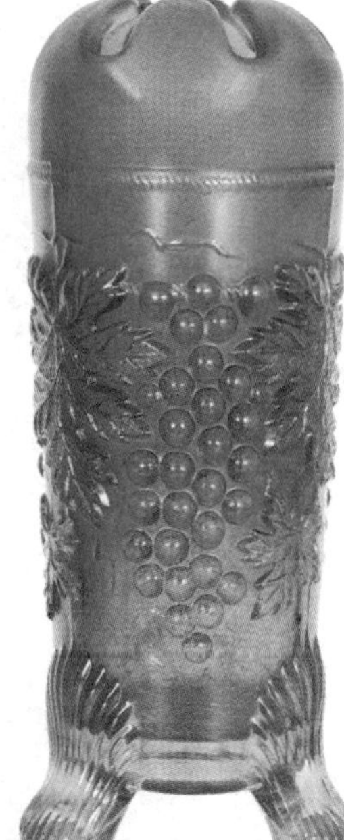

Grape and Cable pattern covered sweetmeat, amethyst, Northwood Glass Co., first quarter 20th century, excellent condition overall with flake to cover rim, minor area of post-production polishing to base rim, 8-3/4" h. overall, 5-1/4" dia. rim. **$108**

Courtesy of Jeffrey S. Evans & Associates, www.jeffreysevans.com

Grape and Cable pattern orange bowl, Northwood Glass Co., signed, 7" h. x 10-1/8" w. **$153**

Courtesy of Bill Hood & Sons Art & Antiques Auctions, Inc., www.hoodauction.com

Grape Arbor pattern decanter set with three matching and two non-matching glasses, marigold, Northwood Glass Co., unmarked, good condition, decanter stopper broken on bottom and one non-matching glass with chipped bottom, decanter 10-1/2" h., matching glasses 4" h....... **$42**

Courtesy of Premier Auction Galleries, www.premierauction.com

Hearts and Flowers pattern compote with ruffled rim, aqua opalescent, Northwood Glass Co., circa 1912, undamaged, 6" h. overall.................... **$228**

Courtesy of Jeffrey S. Evans & Associates, www.jeffreysevans.com

Heavy Iris pattern water pitcher, marigold, with applied colorless handle, Dugan Glass Co., first quarter 20th century, undamaged, 11" h.......... **$84**

Courtesy of Jeffrey S. Evans & Associates, www.jeffreysevans.com

Holly pattern hat bowl, red with some vaseline in foot, ruffled rim, Fenton Art Glass Co., first quarter 20th century, 3-1/8" h., 6-1/4" dia. overall... **$156**

Courtesy of Jeffrey S. Evans & Associates, www.jeffreysevans.com

Inverted Strawberry pattern chalice-shaped compote, green, Cambridge Glass Co., good condition, no chips, cracks or repairs, 6" x 5-1/4"......... **$295**

Courtesy of Woody Auction, www.woodyauction.com

Leaf and Beads pattern compote, amethyst, Northwood Glass Co., circa 1905, undamaged, 3-5/8" h., 7-3/4" dia. overall........................... **$48**

Courtesy of Jeffrey S. Evans & Associates, www.jeffreysevans.com

Orange Tree/No. 921 pattern bowl with upright scalloped rim and collared foot, blue, Fenton Art Glass Co., first quarter 20th century, undamaged, 2-1/2" h., 8-1/8" dia. rim.................... **$72**

Courtesy of Jeffrey S. Evans & Associates, www.jeffreysevans.com

Peacock at the Fountain pattern pitcher and tumbler set, blue, Northwood Glass Co., excellent condition with no chips or cracks, largest 8" h.. **$458**

Courtesy of Morphy Auctions, morphyauctions.com

Persian Medallion pattern plate, white, Fenton Art Glass Co., first quarter 20th century, undamaged, 9" dia............ **$510**

Courtesy of Jeffrey S. Evans & Associates, www.jeffreysevans.com

Rays and Ribbons pattern bowl in amethyst and Peacock and Urn pattern bowl in green, Millersburg Glass Co., first quarter 20th century, Rays and Ribbons undamaged, Peacock and Urn with scattered minute flaking to rim, 9-1/2" and 9" dia. overall and 2-7/8" and 2-3/4" h. **$270**

Courtesy of Jeffrey S. Evans & Associates, www.jeffreysevans.com

Round-Up pattern ruffled bowl, amethyst, Dugan Glass Co., first quarter 20th century, undamaged, 2-1/2" h. overall, 8-1/2" dia. overall. **$204**

Courtesy of Jeffrey S. Evans & Associates, www.jeffreysevans.com

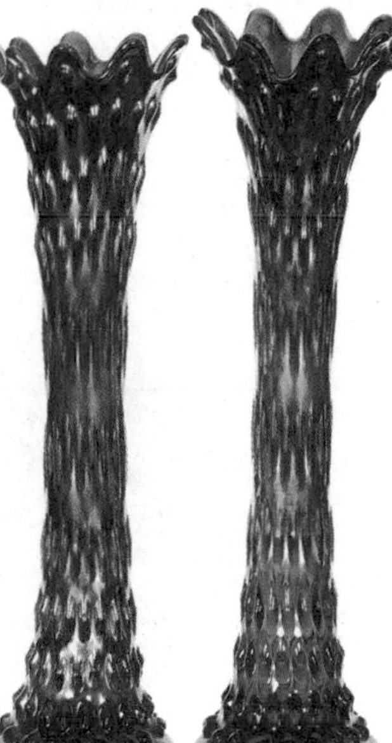

Pair of Rustic pattern vases, blue, Fenton Art Glass Co., good condition, no chips, cracks or repairs, 16" h....... **$106**

Courtesy of Woody Auction, www.woodyauction.com

Two Singing Birds pattern mugs, olive green, Northwood Glass Co., good condition, no chips, cracks or repairs, 3-1/2" h. **$94**

Courtesy of Woody Auction, www.woodyauction.com

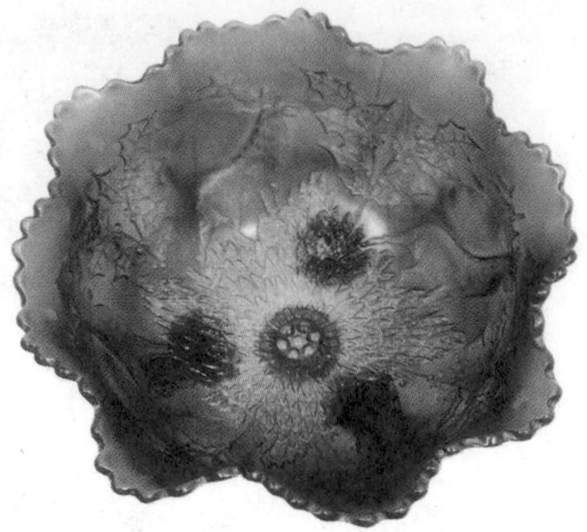

▲ Stag and Holly pattern three-footed ruffled bowl, blue, Fenton Art Glass Co., good condition, no chips, cracks or repairs, 9-1/2" h. **$94**

Courtesy of Woody Auction, www.woodyauction.com

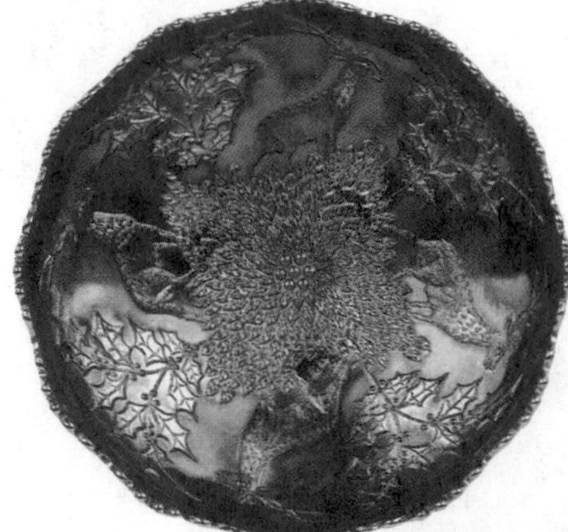

◀ Stag and Holly pattern three-footed bowl, blue, Fenton Art Glass Co., good condition, no chips, cracks or repairs, 4" x 10". **$148**

Courtesy of Woody Auction, www.woodyauction.com

Stork and Rushes pattern punch bowl and four cups with handles, marigold, Dugan Glass Co./Diamond Glass Co., bowl 4-1/2" h. x 9-5/8" w. .... **$200-$400**

Courtesy of Kaminski Auctions, www.kaminskiauctions.com

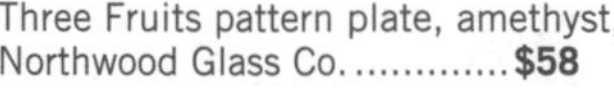

Three Fruits pattern plate, amethyst, Northwood Glass Co. **$58**

Courtesy of Strawser Auctions, www.strawserauctions.com

Tiger Lily/No. 484 pattern seven-piece water set, marigold, water pitcher and six tumblers, Imperial Glass Co., first quarter 20th century, undamaged, 4-3/8" to 8-3/4" h. **$108**

Courtesy of Jeffrey S. Evans & Associates, www.jeffreysevans.com

Windmill pattern seven-piece water set, water pitcher and six tumblers, marigold with colorless and frosted panels, Imperial Glass Co., each with maker's mark in base, 4-1/8" to 8-1/2" h. **$60**

Courtesy of Jeffrey S. Evans & Associates, www.jeffreysevans.com

Two Tree Trunk pattern vases, Northwood Glass Co., pattern introduced 1912: green standard-size vase with rayed base, 10-1/2" h., 3-5/8" dia. base, and amethyst mid-size vase with unpatterned base and 10-petal rim, 11-3/8" h., 4-3/4" dia. base, each with N-in-circle trademark, green vase undamaged, amethyst vase with light flake to two rim points.................................... **$108**

Courtesy of Jeffrey S. Evans & Associates, www.jeffreysevans.com

Wishbone and Spades pattern plate, dark amethyst/purple with strong iridescence, plain rim and exterior, Dugan Glass Co., first quarter 20th century, 6-1/2" dia. **$108**

Courtesy of Jeffrey S. Evans & Associates, www.jeffreysevans.com

GLASS

consolidated glass

THE CONSOLIDATED LAMP & Glass Co. of Coraopolis, Pennsylvania, was founded in 1894. For a number of years it was noted for its lighting wares but also produced popular lines of pressed and blown tableware. Highly collectible glass patterns of this early era include the Cone, Cosmos, Florette, and Guttate lines.

Lamps and shades continued to be good sellers, but in 1926 a new "art" line of molded decorative wares was introduced. This "Martelè" line was developed as a direct imitation of the fine glassware being produced by Renè Lalique of France, and many Consolidated patterns resembled their French counterparts. Other popular lines produced during the 1920s and 1930s were Dancing Nymph, the delightfully Art Deco Ruba Rombic introduced in 1928, and the Catalonian line, which debuted in 1927 and imitated 17th century Spanish glass.

Although the factory closed in 1933, it was reopened under new management in 1936 and prospered through the 1940s. It finally closed in 1967. Collectors should note that many later Consolidated patterns closely resemble wares of other competing firms, especially the Phoenix Glass Co. Careful study is needed to determine the maker of pieces from the 1920-1940 era.

A book that will be of help to collectors is *Phoenix & Consolidated Art Glass, 1926-1980*, by Jack D. Wilson (Antique Publications, 1989).

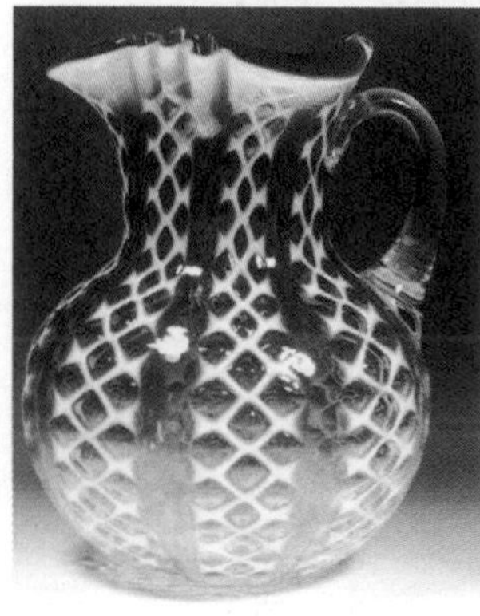

Criss-Cross pattern water pitcher, circa 1888, rubina opalescent, applied colorless handle, polished pontil mark, minor spalling associated with pontil mark, 8-1/2" h....... **$1,560**

Courtesy of Jeffrey S. Evans & Associates, www.jeffreysevans.com

Guttate four-piece table set, cranberry, covered butter dish, sugar bowl, creamer, and spooner, circa 1894, creamer with crack to upper terminal of handle, cover of sugar bowl with flaking to interior rim, each piece with roughness to rims as made, 2-5/8" to 5-1/4" h. **$540**

Courtesy of Jeffrey S. Evans & Associates, www.jeffreysevans.com

Paragon kerosene parlor lamp shade, crystal satin and polychrome-enameled decoration, floral design, original stamped brass shade ring, circa 1902, normal roughness to fitter, 9-1/2" h., 4" dia................................ **$180**

Courtesy of Jeffrey S. Evans & Associates, www.jeffreysevans.com

Pink Lattice Cone pattern biscuit jar, late 19th century, fitted with silverplate mount and lid, 9" h. **$72**

Courtesy of Farmer Auctions, www.farmer-auctions.com

Cherub parlor lamp, fourth-quarter 19th century, ruby satin with matching pattern ball-form shade, "305" embossed on cast iron base, brass decorative font crown, brass drop-in font with complete working mechanics including "Royal" embossed flame spreader with slip chimney, minor bruise to shade fitter, isolated scratches to shade, 23-1/2" h. to top of shade, 14-5/8" h. to shade ring, 6-3/4" sq. base, 9-1/2" h. shade, 4" dia. **$300**

Courtesy of Jeffrey S. Evans & Associates, www.jeffreysevans.com

Olive pattern serving plate with green wash and four frosted colorless Dancing Nymph pattern plates, four with factory polished rims, second quarter 20th century, 8-1/4", 10-1/4", and 11-1/4" dia. ... **$70**

Courtesy of Jeffrey S. Evans & Associates, www.jeffreysevans.com

Guttate, Pineapple, and Shell & Seaweed patterns of toothpick holders, circa 1894, blue Guttate example with rim ground and polished, green Shell & Seaweed example with check to rim, as made, 2-1/4" to 2-1/2" h... **$216**

Courtesy of Jeffrey S. Evans & Associates, www.jeffreysevans.com

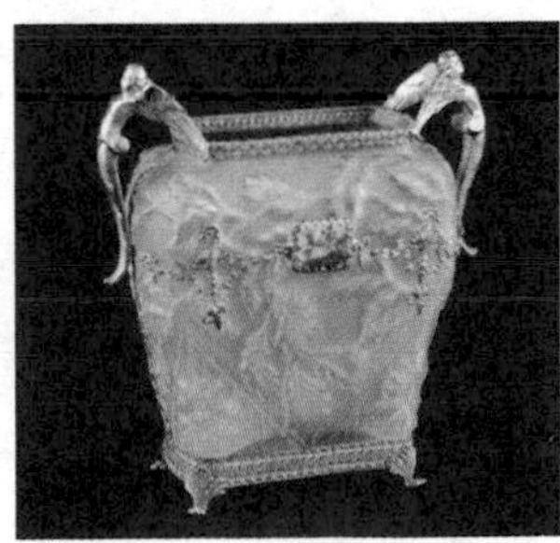

Frosted art glass vase with ormolu and porcelain mounts in French Empire style, very good condition, light gilt loss to mounting, 11" h. x 10" w. x 4" d................................. **$277**

Courtesy of Nest Egg Auctions, www.nesteggauctions.com

top lot

Embossed Basketweave pattern miniature lamp, circa 1894, cased blue with satin finish, square-form font with matching ribbed umbrella-form shade and period collar, fitted with period Nutmeg burner, colorless chimney, excellent condition, scattered minute flakes and roughness to exterior layer of glass, with some light spots, 7" h. to top of shade, 3-1/4" h. to top of collar, 2" sq. base................**$2,760**

COURTESY OF JEFFREY S. EVANS & ASSOCIATES, WWW.JEFFREYSEVANS.COM

▶ ▼ Spanish Lace and Poinsettia pattern shakers, late 19th century, tallest 4-3/8" h. **$835**

Courtesy of Farmer Auctions, www.farmerauctions.com

Ruba Rombic pattern ashtray, circa 1930, No. 829, 2" h. x 4" d. **$102**

Courtesy of Ewbank's Auctions, www.ewbankauctions.co.uk

Blackberry and Cricket pattern vase, gray glass molded overall with figure designs, interior fitted with bulb and brass cap at top, rim chips and flakes under brass cap, 18"............................ **$124**

Courtesy of Brunk Auctions, www.brunkauctions.com

Ruba Rombic pattern toilet bottle, circa 1930, mold blown lilac colored glass, designed by Reuben Haley, with conforming stopper and cased interior, 7-1/2" h............................. **$1,094**

Courtesy of Doyle New York, www.doylenewyork.com

Guttate pattern water pitcher, early 20th century, opaque white with gilt decoration, applied handle with pressed-leaf design to upper terminal, polished pontil mark, with 20th century yellow tankard, 9" h. **$36**

Courtesy of Jeffrey S. Evans & Associates, www.jeffreysevans.com

Amberina sugar shaker, late 19th century, cranberry to light yellow, decorated with enameled florals, berries, stems, and leaves, small firing flaw on base, 5-1/4" h. **$204**

Courtesy of Farmer Auctions, www.farmerauctions.com

GLASS

custard glass

CUSTARD GLASS CAME on the American scene in the 1890s, more than a decade after similar colors were made in Europe and England. The Sowerby firm of Gateshead-on-Tyne, England had marketed its patented "Queen's Ivory Ware" quite successfully in the late 1870s and early 1880s.

There were many glass tableware factories operating in Pennsylvania and Ohio in the 1890s and early 1900s, and the competition among them was keen. Each company sought to capture the public's favor with distinctive colors and, often, hand-painted decoration. That is when "custard glass" appeared on the American scene.

The opaque yellow color of this glass varies from a rich, vivid yellow to a lustrous light yellow. Regardless of intensity, the hue was originally called "ivory" by several glass manufacturers who also used superlative sounding terms such as "Ivorina Verde" and "Carnelian." Most custard glass contains uranium, so it will "glow" under a black light.

The most important producer of custard glass was certainly Harry Northwood, who first made it at his plants in Indiana, Pennsylvania, in the late 1890s and, later, in his Wheeling, West Virginia, factory. Northwood marked some of his most famous patterns, but much early custard is unmarked. Other key manufacturers include the Heisey Glass Co., Newark, Ohio; the Jefferson Glass Co., Steubenville, Ohio; the Tarentum Glass Co., Tarentum, Pennsylvania; and the Fenton Art Glass Co., Williamstown, West Virginia.

Custard glass fanciers are particular about condition and generally insist on pristine quality decorations free from fading or wear. Souvenir custard pieces with events, places, and dates on them usually bring the best prices in the areas commemorated on them rather than from the specialist collector. Also, collectors who specialize in pieces such as cruets, syrups, or salt and pepper shakers will often pay higher prices for these pieces than would a custard collector.

Key reference sources include William Heacock's *Custard Glass from A to Z*, published in 1976 but now out of print, and the book *Harry Northwood: The Early Years*, available from Glass Press. Heisey's custard glass is discussed in Shirley Dunbar's *Heisey Glass: The Early Years* (Krause Publications, 2000), and Coudersport's production is well-documented in Tulla Majot's book, *Coudersport's Glass 1900-1904* (Glass Press, 1999). The Custard Glass Society holds a yearly convention and maintains a web site: www.homestead.com/custardsociety.

— *James Measell*

Grape and Cable fernery, custard with nutmeg stain, on three scrolled feet, with N-in-circle trademark, Northwood Glass Co., circa 1906, undamaged with three areas of wear to interior, 4-1/2" h., 7-3/4" dia. **$60**

Courtesy of Jeffrey S. Evans & Associates, www.jeffreysevans.com

Argonaut Shell/Nautilus pattern six-piece water set with gilt decoration, pitcher with script "Northwood" trademark under base, and five tumblers with factory polished bases, Northwood Glass Co., circa 1900, 3-3/4" to 8-3/8" h. **$120**

Courtesy of Jeffrey S. Evans & Associates, www.jeffreysevans.com

Three-piece blue custard glass set, enameled Coralline decoration, square covered box with rim chip, 3-3/4" w. x 8" h.................................... **$12**

Courtesy of Hudson Valley Auctions, www.hudsonvalleyauctioneers.com

Four cruets with polychrome-enamel and gilt decoration, three Ring Band pattern and one Carnelian/Everglades pattern example with pressed facet stopper that is frozen, circa late 19th/early 20th century, 6-3/4" to 7-1/8" h. **$180**

Courtesy of Jeffrey S. Evans & Associates, www.jeffreysevans.com

Chrysanthemum Sprig pattern cream pitcher, ribbed body, gold enamel decoration, Northwood Glass Co., 4-1/2" h.. .... **$12**

Courtesy of Early Auction Co., www.earlyauctionco.com

Twelve assorted articles, each with enamel and gilt decoration, including Intaglio pattern covered butter dish, Louis XV pattern master berry bowl and two tumblers, and Geneva pattern spooner, late 19th/early 20th century, minor crack to one foot of Georgia Gem pattern breakfast creamer, 1-1/2" to 6-1/2" h..................... **$180**

Courtesy of Jeffrey S. Evans & Associates, www.jeffreysevans.com

Pitcher and six glasses, good condition, pitcher 9-1/2" h., glasses 6-1/2" h................ **$330**

Courtesy of Pace Auctions, www.paceauctions.com

Grape and Cable pattern pedestal punch bowl, pink stain with custard, N-in-circle trademark on pedestal and bowl, circa 1906, Northwood Glass Co., bowl 6" h., 11" dia., pedestal 5-1/4" h., 6-1/4" dia. base. **$390**

Courtesy of Jeffrey S. Evans & Associates, www.jeffreysevans.com

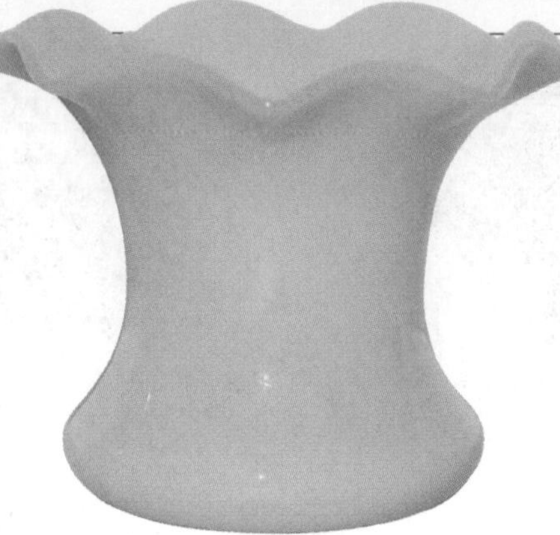

Flared vase, 4" h. **$48**

Courtesy of Stanton Auctions, www.stantonauctions.com

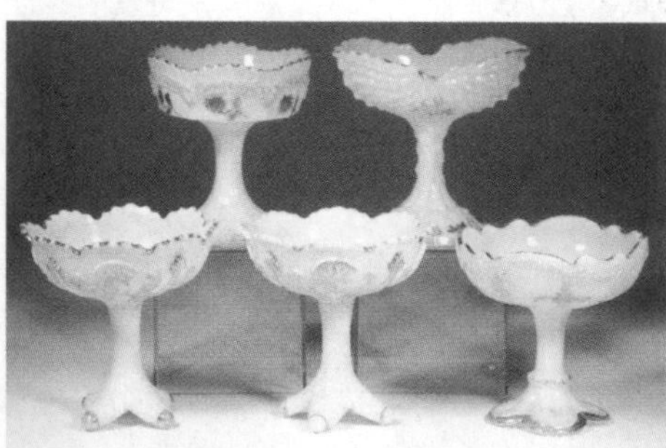

Five jelly compotes in Inverted Fan and Feather, Argonaut Shell, Chrysanthemum Sprig, and Itaglio patterns, circa late 19th/early 20th century, Northwood Glass Co./Dugan Glass Co., flake to rim of Intaglio example, minute flake to underside of one foot of Inverted Fan example, 4-3/4" to 5" h. **$96**

Courtesy of Jeffrey S. Evans & Associates, www.jeffreysevans.com

Tree trunk vase with nutmeg stain, slightly flared 12-petal rim, circular foot, N-in-circle trademark to base, circa first quarter 20th century, Northwood Glass Co./Dugan Glass Co., 13-3/8" h., 7-3/4" dia. rim, 5-1/4" dia. base **$540**

Courtesy of Jeffrey S. Evans & Associates, www.jeffreysevans.com

Four Paris porcelain cups or tasse bouillon and covers, painted with insects, one inscribed "B Potter 40 Christopher Potter" in underglaze blue, 11-1/2" h. Originally a Cambridgeshire landowner and army victualler, by 1789 Potter resided in Paris, likely as a result of the scandal surrounding his unseating from the parliamentary constituency of Colchester for corrupt practices. **$531**

Courtesy of Dreweatts & Bloomsbury, www.dreweatts.com

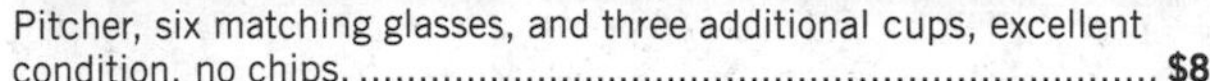

Pitcher, six matching glasses, and three additional cups, excellent condition, no chips. **$82**

Courtesy of Milestone Auctions, www.milestoneauctions.com

Iris miniature lamp, compressed globular-form font, dark yellow/butterscotch matching patterned chimney-shade, No. 1 clinch collar, fitted with Plume & Atwood Hornet burner, New Martinsville Glass Co., circa 1904, undamaged lamp and burner, normal roughness to rims as made, collar with repair, 8-3/8" h. to top of chimney shade, 3-5/8" h. to top of collar, 3-1/4" dia. base. **$24**

Courtesy of Jeffrey S. Evans & Associates, www.jeffreysevans.com

Inverted Fan and Feather pattern four-piece table set, colorless opalescent with gilt decoration, covered butter dish, covered sugar bowl, creamer, and spooner, Northwood Glass Co., circa 1899, significant crack to butter base, minor bruise to sugar bowl cover finial, 4-1/2" to 6-3/4" h. **$192**

Courtesy of Jeffrey S. Evans & Associates, www.jeffreysevans.com

Nine items including creamer, sugar, vase, two spooners, berry dish, and Oriental ivory scuttle mug, five in Louis XV pattern. **$95**

Courtesy of Woody Auction, www.woodyauction.com

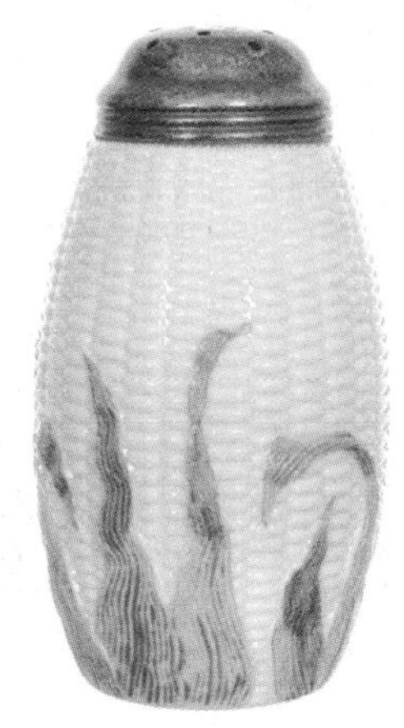

Maize pattern sugar shaker with colored highlights, Libbey glass, good condition, 6"..... **$118**

Courtesy of Woody Auctions, www.woodyauctions.com

GLASS

cut glass

CUT GLASS IS made by grinding decorations into glass by means of abrasive-carrying metal or stone wheels. An ancient craft, it was revived in 1600 by Bohemians and spread through Europe to Great Britain and America.

American cut glass came of age at the Centennial Exposition in 1876 and the World Columbian Exposition in 1893. America's most significant output of high-quality glass occurred from 1880 to 1917, a period now known as the Brilliant Period. Glass from this period is the most eagerly sought glass by collectors.

Late Regency cut glass eight-light chandelier, scalloped and fan cut vase with shaped corona and canopy, hung with faceted cut glass drops above vase shaped with eight scrolling strawberry and prismatic cut branches hung with conforming drops, receiver bowl with acorn pendant finial. **$13,672**

Courtesy of Dreweatts & Bloomsbury, www.dreweatts.com

Set of cut glass decanters with broad band of cut diamonds, nine large and nine small, below tapering step cut necks, early 20th century, 11-1/3" h. x 9-3/4" d..**$7,975**

Courtesy of Dreweatts & Bloomsbury, www.dreweatts.com

French gilt-bronze glass tantalus with hinged compartment fitted with four gilt-embossed glass stoppered bottles in removable stand with 16 gilt-embossed glass cups, chamfered diamond-cut plinth, on gadrooned and molded base, bracket feet and applied at sides with handles, probably Baccarat, 12" h. x 14" w. x 12" d. **$9,840**

Courtesy of A.B. Levy's, www.ablevys.com

▲ Bohemian engraved and cut beaker/tumbler, second half 19th century, colorless non-lead glass, cylindrical form with 12 small titled allegorical reserves below rim, each with cherub above four medial reserves, each engraved with scene from young couple's life, on six feet, additional swags and pendants, shallow chip to side of one foot, 5" h., 3-1/4" dia. **$7,800**

Courtesy of Jeffrey S. Evans & Associates, www.jeffreysevans.com

Four European cut and molded decanters in colorless lead glass, quart Russian Imperial Glass example with vertical pillars and encrusted suphide cartouche with gold and red foil drapery centering "AM" initials, non-original stopper, and two English cylinder examples with broad flute cuttings, appropriate stoppers, first half 19th century, 5" h. to 14" h. **$3,900**

Courtesy of Jeffrey S. Evans & Associates, www.jeffresevans.com

Early American Brilliant cut glass punch bowl, cut and engraved in Vintage pattern, Tuthill, two-piece construction with original matching base, good condition overall with minor flakes, 13" h. x 14" w. **$5,535**

Courtesy of Hill Auction Gallery, www.hillauctiongallery.com

American Brilliant cut glass bowl on stand with hobstars and pineapples, scalloped rim, splayed foot, 13-5/8" h., 15" dia. **$448**

Courtesy of Neal Auction Co., www.nealauction.com

Amethyst cut to clear glass pitcher, stylized Feather and Cross Hatching design, Stevens & Williams, possibly designed by Frederick Carder, 9" h. x 9" w................................... **$4,235**

Courtesy of Cottone Auctions, www.cottoneauctions.com

► Victorian-style silver-plate and cut glass centerpiece and plateau, oval form with acanthus feet, ivy banding and conforming mirrored plate, Royal Castle, Sheffield, with reclining Bacchic figures with gadrooned knopped standard and vintage banded capital, bowl 15" h. x 15-1/4" w., 13-1/2" dia., plate 29-1/2" x 22-1/2"......................... **$5,750**

Courtesy of New Orleans Auction Galleries, www.neworleansauction.com

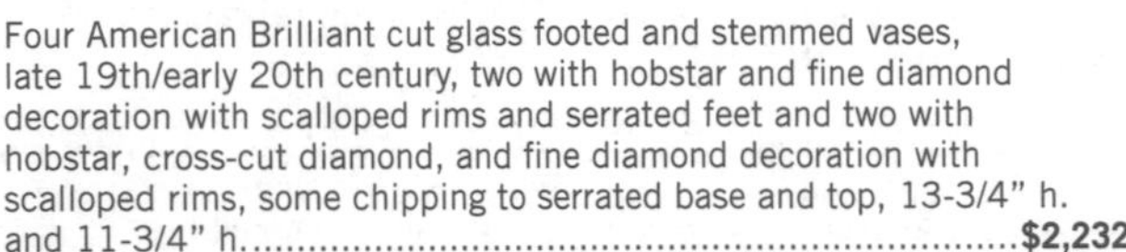

Four American Brilliant cut glass footed and stemmed vases, late 19th/early 20th century, two with hobstar and fine diamond decoration with scalloped rims and serrated feet and two with hobstar, cross-cut diamond, and fine diamond decoration with scalloped rims, some chipping to serrated base and top, 13-3/4" h. and 11-3/4" h. **$2,232**

Courtesy of Case Antiques Auctions & Appraisals, www.caseantiques.com

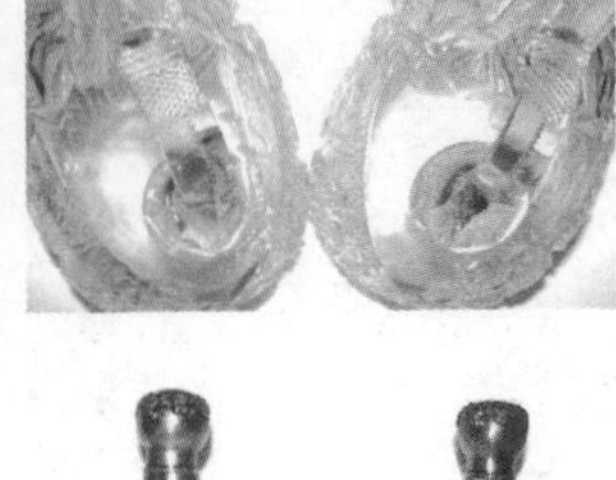

▲ Matched pair of handled cologne/cruets or carafe bottles with monogrammed stoppers, oblong/ovoid/flat-sided form with finger handle and flat cut surface for thumb, very good condition, monogrammed sterling tops with dents, cork needs to be replaced, 8-1/2" h. x 3-1/2" w., 6" dia. **$276**

Courtesy of Premiere Auction Galleries, www.premiereauctiongalleries.com

American Brilliant cut glass pedestal urn, Lyra pattern, square pattern cut base, 11" h. x 7-1/2" w. **$885**

Courtesy of Woody Auction, www.woodyauction.com

American Brilliant cut glass punch bowl on stand, late 19th century, bowl with minor chips to rim and chips to shaft that fits into base, 11-1/2" h., 10" dia. **$230**

Courtesy of Kennedy's Auction Service, www.kennedysauction.com

American Brilliant cut glass tankard, Hobstar, Cane, Prism, Vesica, Strawberry Diamond and Fan motif, 13-1/2" h. ... **$649**

Courtesy of Woody Auction, www.woodauction.com

◀ Pair of Bohemian cut glass five-light table torchiers with four shaped brass arms with crystal prism drops, center light, hurricane-style cut glass shades, 42" h., 18" dia. .. **$2,360**

Courtesy of Burchard Galleries, www.burchardgalleries.com

GLASS

daum nancy

DAUM NANCY FINE glass, much of it cameo, was made by Auguste and Antonin Daum, who founded the factory in 1875 in Nancy, France. Most of their cameo and enameled glass was made from the 1890s into the early 20th century.

Cameo glass is made by carving into multiple layers of colored glass to create a design in relief. It is at least as old as the Romans.

Glass coupe, acid-etched enameled cameo with geranium design, circa 1900s, base etched Daum Nancy with Crois de Lorraine, excellent condition, light-colored line throughout leaf design, 7" h. x 6-1/2" w. **$8,960**

Courtesy of Rago Arts and Auctions, www.ragoarts.com

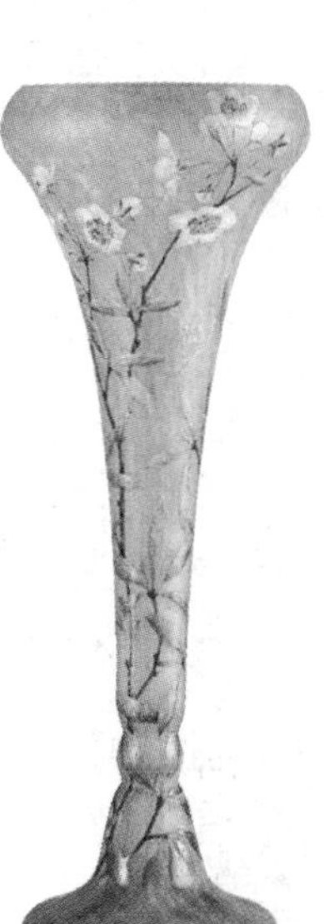

Glass vase with cherry blossom design, enameled cameo, circa 1900, etched Daum Nancy on body with Croix de Lorraine, excellent condition, two flecks to rim, 17" h. x 6" w..... **$7,680**

Courtesy of Rago Arts and Auctions, www.ragoarts.com

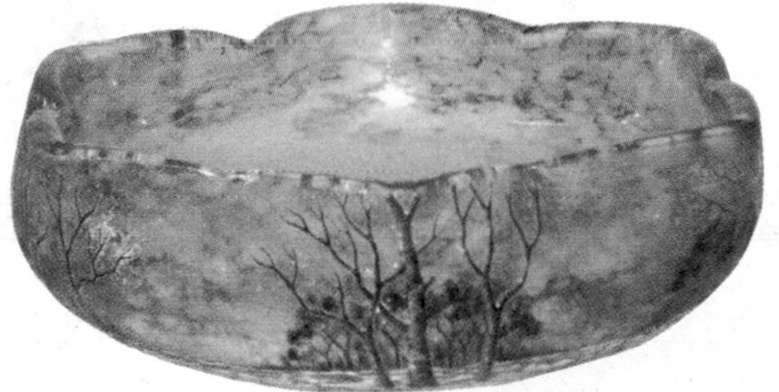

Ovoid form bowl with six-point star rim in orange and yellow mottled glass, winter forest scene of snow-covered meadow with brown trees, signed Daum Nancy, 8" w.......... **$3,025**

Courtesy of Jaremos Estate Liquidators, www.jaremos.com

! top lot

French Art Noveau-style covered jar, cameo cut floral and leaf decoration, signed Daum Nancy on bottom, circa 1920, 3" h. x 5" l. x 4-1/2" w.........$13,400

COURTESY OF BRUHNS AUCTION GALLERY, INC., WWW.BRUHNSAUCTION.COM

Scenic glass pitcher with purple summer landscape, signed Daum Nancy on bottom of base, circa early 20th century, 7-1/2" h........ **$5,850**

Courtesy of Manifest Auctions, www.manifestauctions.com

Glass lamp with acid-etched cameo landscape, circa 1900, base and shade signed Daum Nancy with Croix de Lorraine, slight bend to arm, 20" h. x 11" w. **$7,040**

Courtesy of Rago Arts and Auctions, www.ragoarts.com

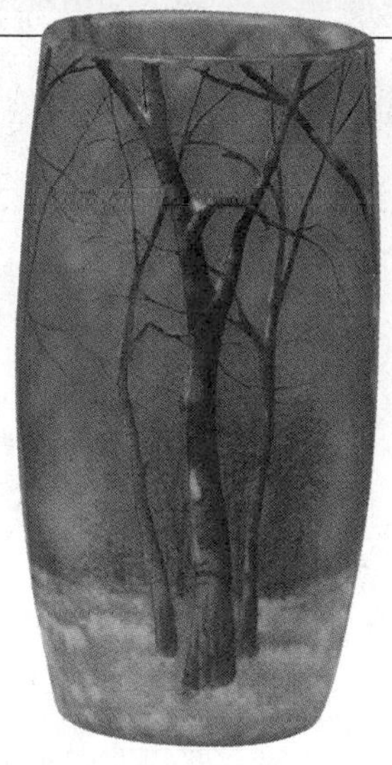

▲ Vase, colorless cut glass with layers of orange-yellow powdered, overlay, circumferential wintry woodland landscape in polychrome enamel painting, polished and etched, partially decorated with frosted glass effect, signed Daum Nancy, 12 cm at bottom, 4-3/4" h. **$1,820**

Courtesy of Henry's Auktionshaus, www.henrys.de

Perfume bottle with pink blossoms and green leaves, cameo glass with gilded paint on lid and rim, small nicks around rim, marked Daum Nancy, 4" h. x 2-1/2" w. .. **$2,125**

Courtesy of The Popular Auction, www.thepopularauction.com

Pair of cameo glass and sterling silver bottles, repoussé-decorated with fruiting raspberry vines over silver-clad neck opening to rounded-shouldered cylindrical body of green cut back to clear glass, overall good condition with general light marks, scratches, wear and tarnishing to silver commensurate with age, 6-1/4" h. x 3" d. **$1,476**

Courtesy of John Moran Auctioneers, www.johnmoran.com

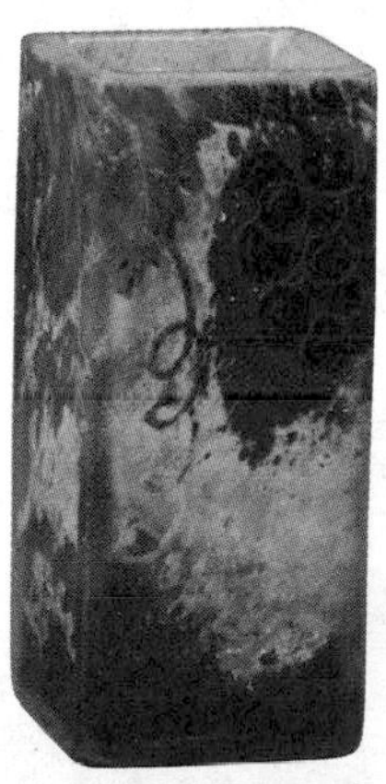

Floral décor vase with grapes and painted autumn foliage, colorless layer glass, yellow and purple powdered, red-purple and green overlay, cut, polished and etched, signed, partially fire polished, 4-3/4" h. **$2,826**

Courtesy of Henry's Auktionshaus, www.henrys.de

Vase with floral motif, enameled and martel glass, circa 1900, signed Daum Nancy with Croix de Lorraine/No. 32, 8" h. x 7-3/4" w. **$2,944**

Courtesy of Rago Arts and Auctions, www.ragoarts.com

Squat vase with cameo bleeding hearts with brown and green leaves, green base, marked Daum Nancy on side above cross of Lorraine, flea bite on top of rim, 3-3/4" h. x 3-1/2" w. **$1,200**

Courtesy of Farmer Auctions, www.farmer-auctions.com

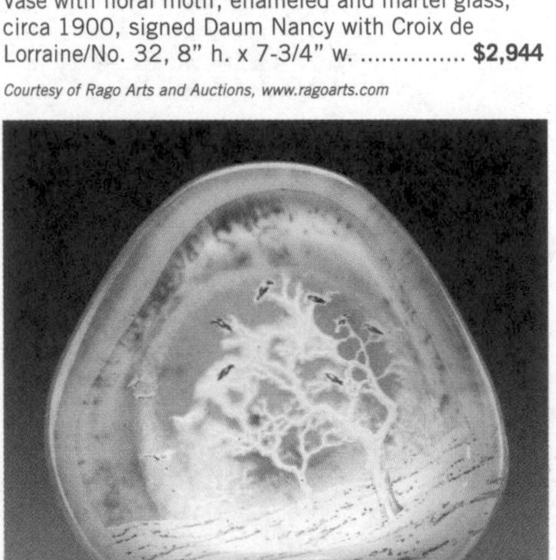

Etched and enameled glass Blackbird vide poche, circa 1900, marked Nancy Daum, 1-1/2" h. x 6" w. x 6" d.. **$1,063**

Courtesy of Heritage Auctions, ha.com

▲ Sterling silver-mounted cameo glass vase wheel-carved with azaleas, circa 1900, silver stamped with hallmarks, base acid-etched Daum Nancy with Croix de Lorraine, excellent condition, small scratch to one flower, 7-1/4" h. x 4-1/2" w. **$10,240**

Courtesy of Rago Arts and Auctions, www.ragoarts.com

◀ Purple cameo cut vase with iris decoration on taupe ground with gilt highlight, marked on bottom, 4-1/2" h. x 5" w. **$242**

Courtesy Treasure Seeker Auctions, www.treasureseekerauction.com

GLASS

depression glass

DEPRESSION GLASS IS the name of colorful glassware collectors generally associated with mass-produced glassware found in pink, yellow, crystal, or green in the years surrounding the Great Depression in America.

The homemakers of the Depression-era were able to enjoy the wonderful colors offered in this new inexpensive glass dinnerware because they received pieces of their favorite patterns packed in boxes of soap, or as premiums given at "dish night" at the local movie theater. Merchandisers, such as Sears & Roebuck and F. W. Woolworth, enticed young brides with the colorful wares that they could afford even when economic times were harsh.

Because of advancements in glassware technology, Depression-era patterns were mass-produced and could be purchased for a fraction of what cut glass or lead crystal cost. As one manufacturer found a pattern that was pleasing to the buying public, other companies soon followed with their adaptation of a similar design. Patterns included several design motifs, such as florals, geometrics, and even patterns that looked back to Early American patterns like Sandwich glass.

As America emerged from the Great Depression and life became more leisure-oriented again, new glassware patterns were created to reflect the new tastes of this generation. More elegant shapes and forms were designed, leading to what is sometimes called "Elegant Glass." Today's collectors often include these more elegant patterns when they talk about Depression-era glassware.

Depression-era glassware is one of the best-researched collecting areas available to the American marketplace. This is due in large part to the careful research of several people, including Hazel Marie Weatherman, Gene Florence, Barbara Mauzy, Carl F. Luckey, and Kent Washburn. Their books are held in high regard by researchers and collectors today.

Regarding values for Depression glass, rarity does not always equate to a high dollar amount. Some more readily found items command lofty prices because of high demand or other factors, not because they are necessarily rare. As collectors' tastes range from the simple patterns to the more elaborate patterns, so does the ability of their budget to invest in inexpensive patterns to multi-hundreds of dollars per form patterns.

For more information on Depression glass, see *Warman's Depression Glass Identification and Price Guide*, 6th Edition, or *Warman's Depression Glass Field Guide*, 5th Edition, both by Ellen T. Schroy.

PATTERN SILHOUETTE Identification Guide

Depression-era glassware can be confusing. Many times a manufacturer came up with a neat new design, and as soon as it was successful, other companies started to make patterns that were similar. To help you figure out what pattern you might be trying to research, here's a quick identification guide. The patterns are broken down into several different classifications by design elements.

ART DECO

Ovide

BASKETS

Lorain

BEADED EDGES

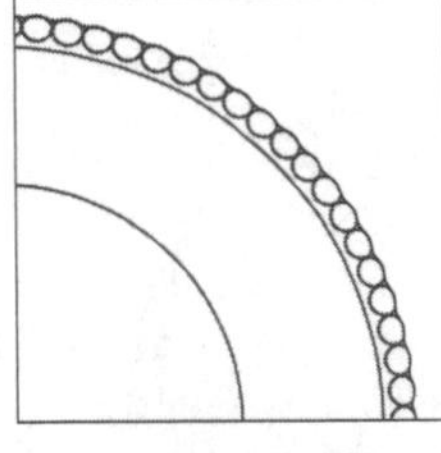

Beaded Edge

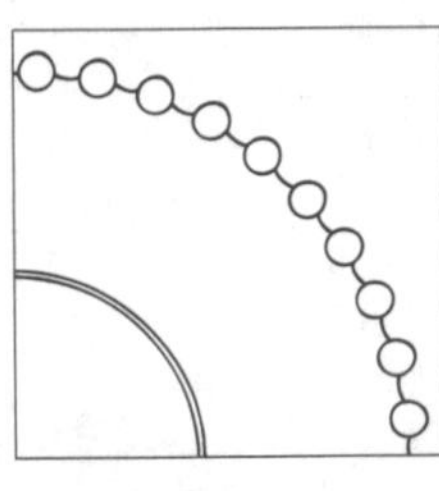

Candlewick

BIRDS

Delilah

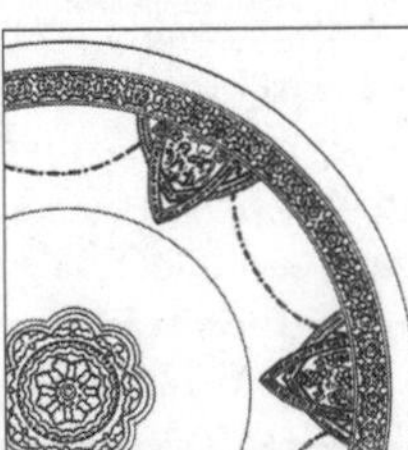

Georgian

Parrot

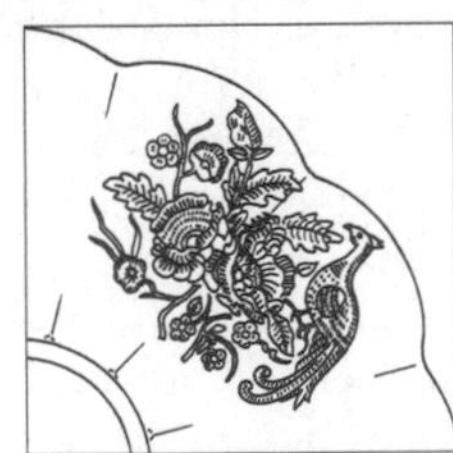

Peacock & Wild Rose

BLOCKS

Beaded Block

Colonial Block

BOWS

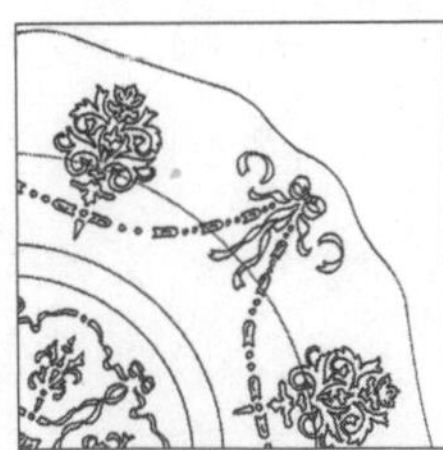

Bowknot

COINS

Coin

CUBES

American

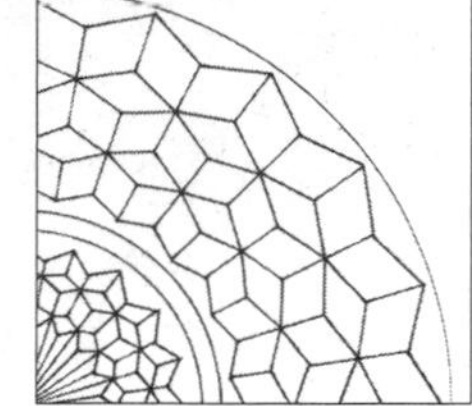

Cube

DIAMONDS

Cape Cod

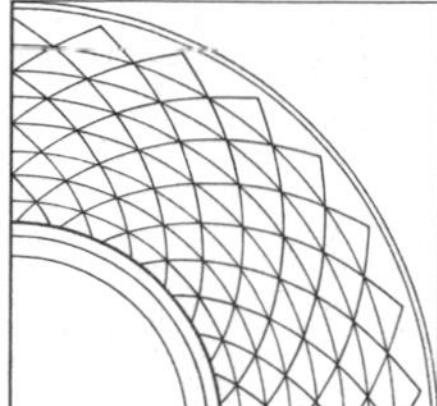

Diamond Quilted

English Hobnail

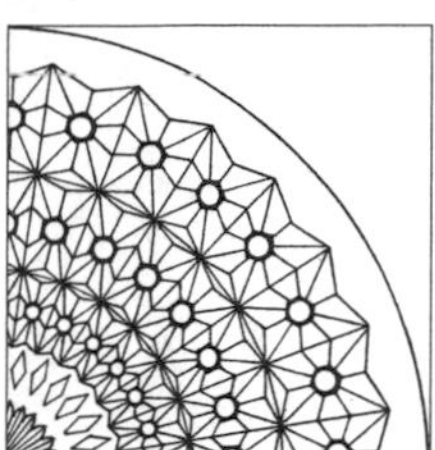

Holiday

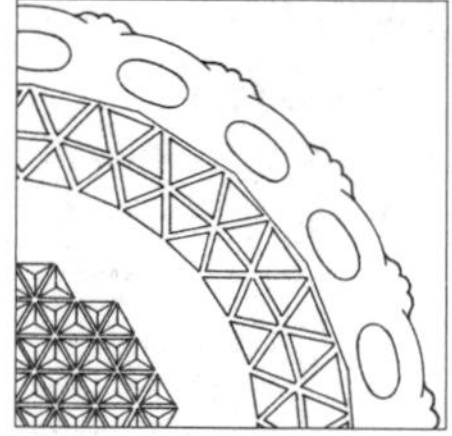

Laced Edge

Miss America

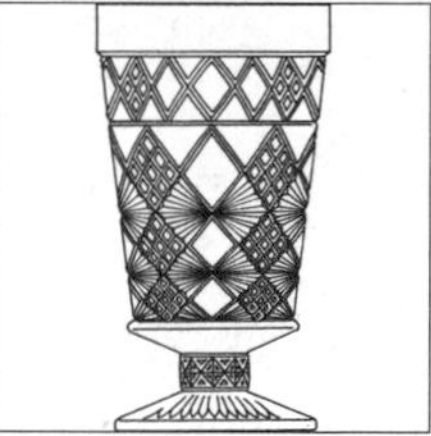

Peanut Butter

Waterford

Windsor

ELLIPSES (FANS)

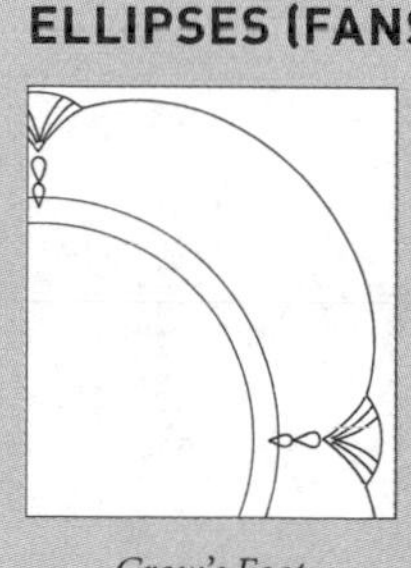

Crow's Foot

Newport

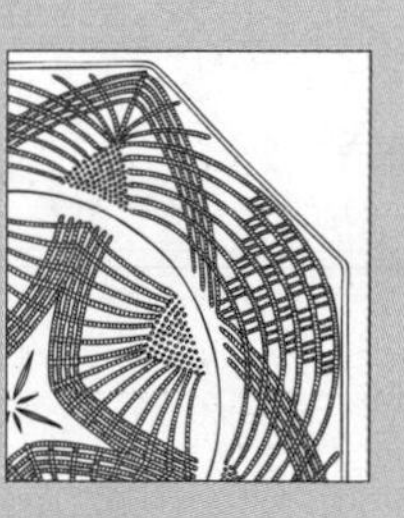

Romanesque

FIGURES

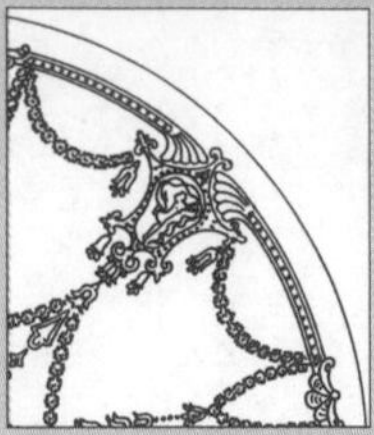

Cameo

Cupid

FLORALS

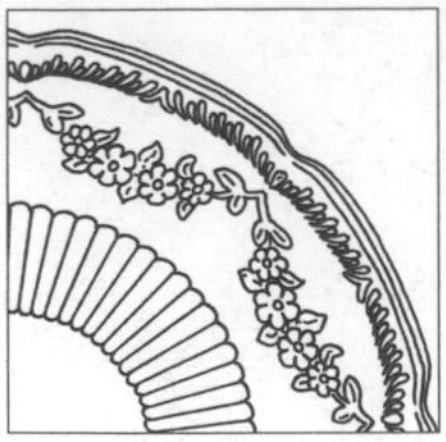

Alice

Cherry Blossom

Cloverleaf

Daisy

Dogwood

Doric

Doric & Pansy

Floragold

Floral

Floral and Diamond Band

Flower Garden with Butterflies

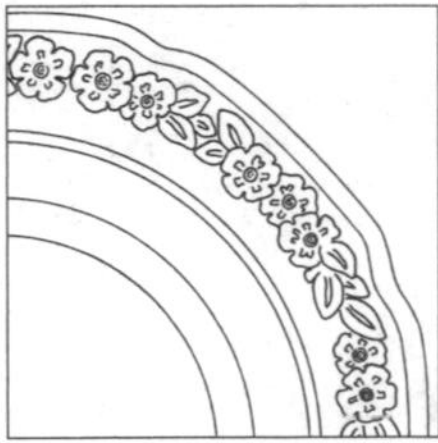

Indiana Custard

Iris

Jubilee

FLORALS *continued*

Mayfair (Federal)

Mayfair (Open Rose)

Normandie

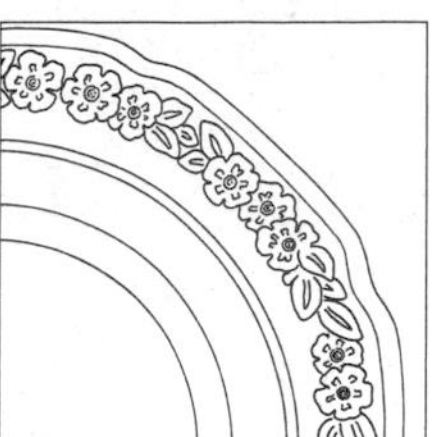
Orange Blossom

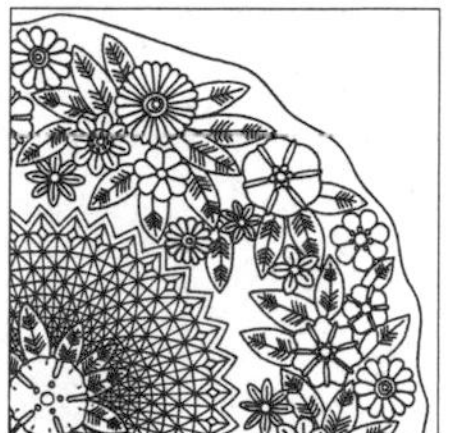
Pineapple & Floral

Primrose

Rosemary

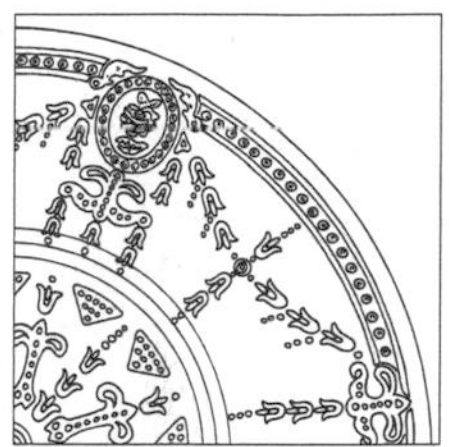
Rose Cameo

Royal Lace

Seville

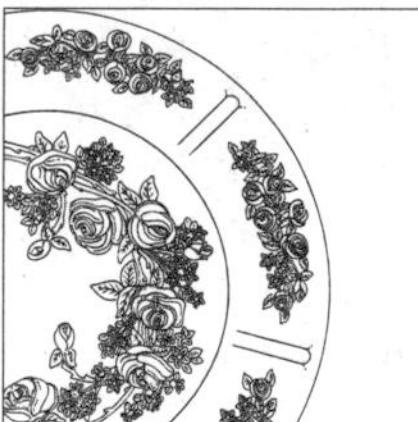
Sharon

Sunflower

Thistle

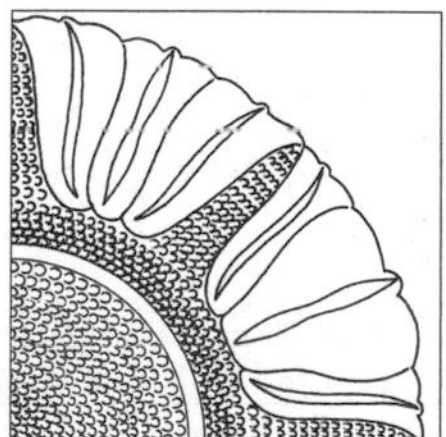
Tulip

Vitrock

Wild Rose

FRUITS

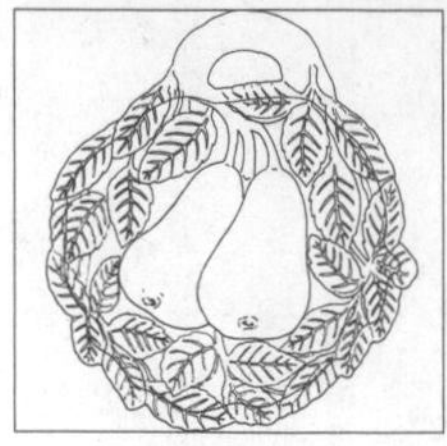

Avocado

Cherryberry

Della Robbia

Fruits

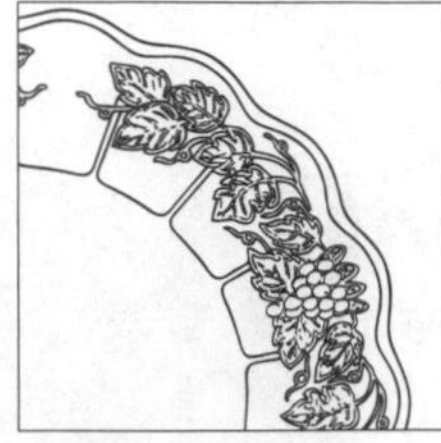

Paneled Grape

Strawberry

GEOMETIC & LINE DESIGNS

Cracked Ice

Cape Cod

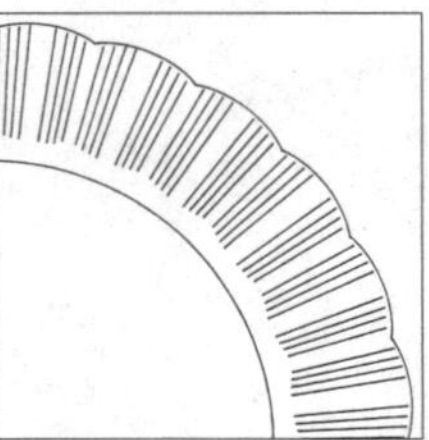

Cremax

Early American Prescut

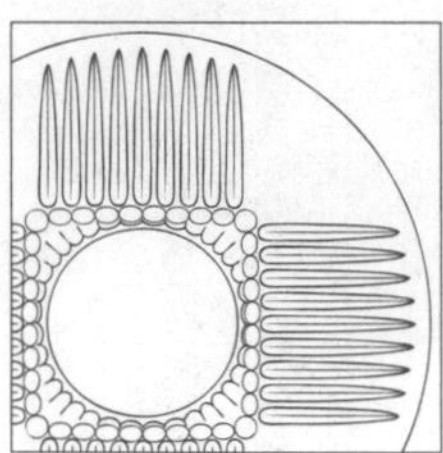

Park Avenue

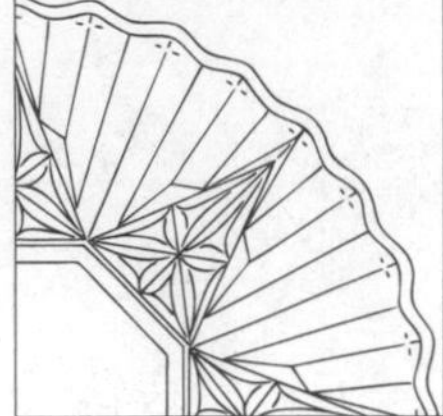

Pioneer

Sierra

Star

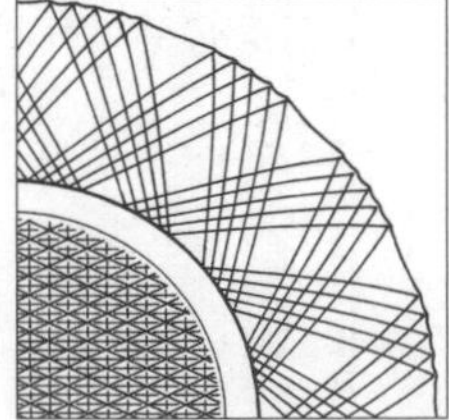

Starlight

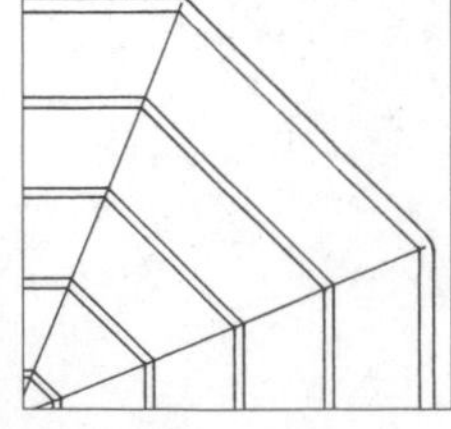

Tea Room

HONEYCOMB

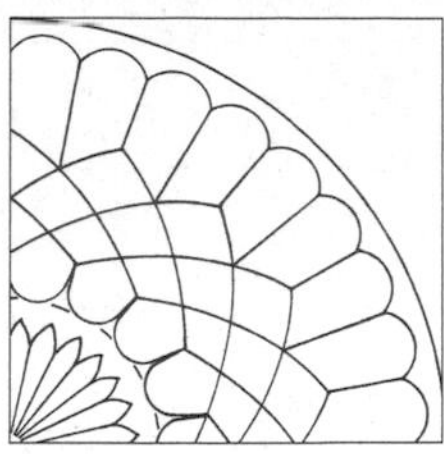

Aunt Polly

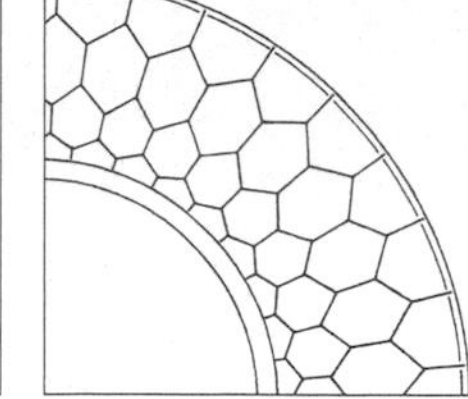

Hex Optic

HORSESHOE

Horseshoe

LEAVES

Laurel Leaf

Sunburst

LACY DESIGNS

Harp

Heritage

S-Pattern

Sandwich (Duncan Miller)

Sandwich (Hocking)

Sandwich (Indiana)

LOOPS

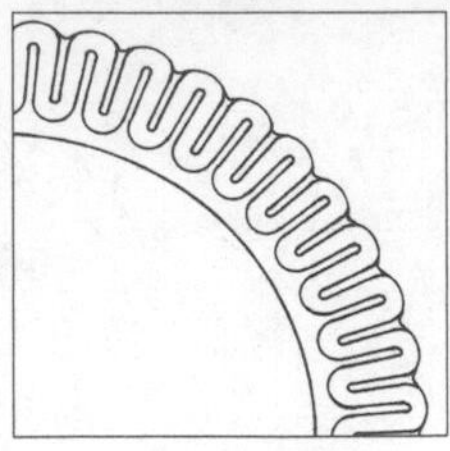

Christmas Candy

Crocheted Crystal

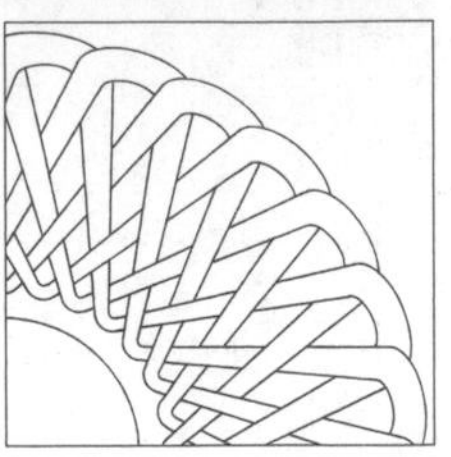

Pretzel

PETALS

Aurora

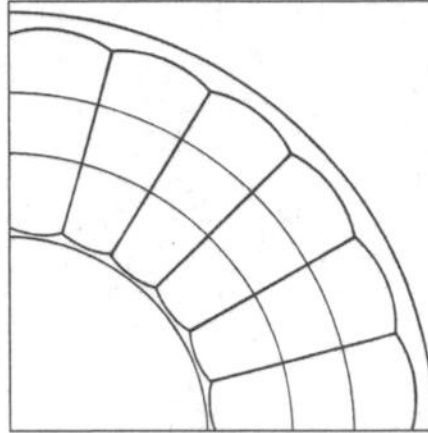

Block Optic

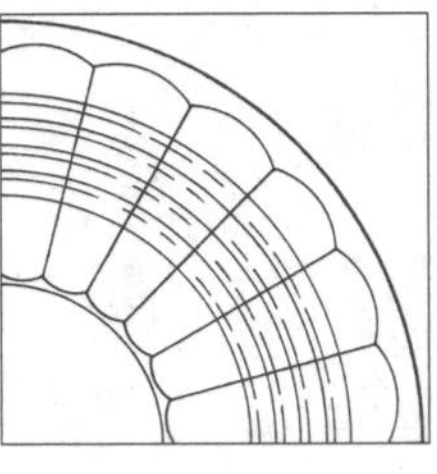

Circle

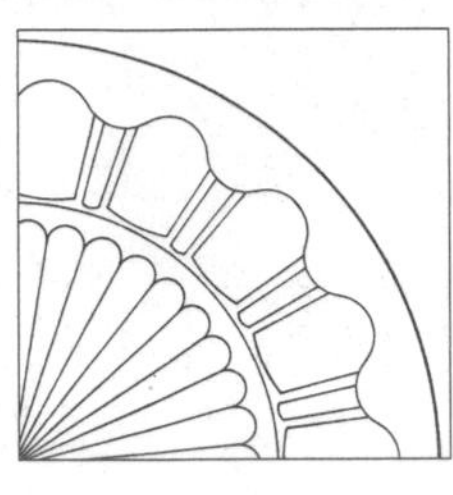

Colonial

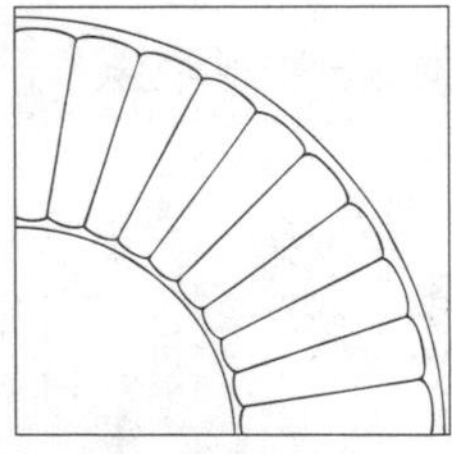

National

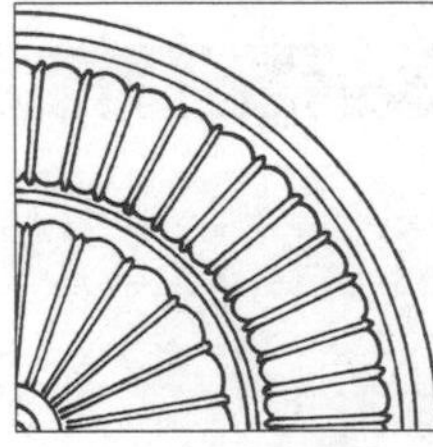

New Century

Old Café

Ribbon

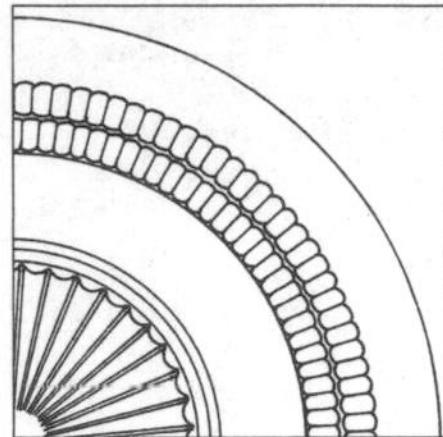

Roulette

Round Robin

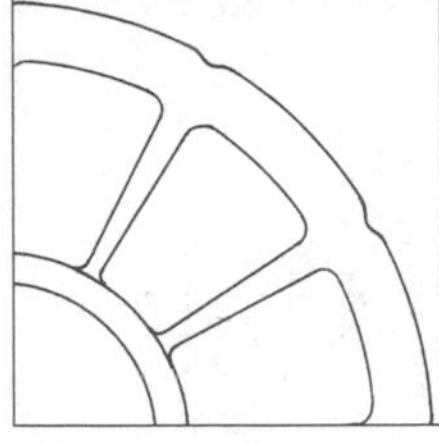

Victory

PETALS/RIDGES WITH DIAMOND ACCENTS

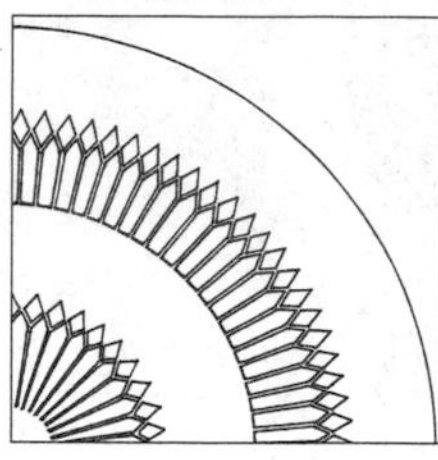
Anniversary

Coronation

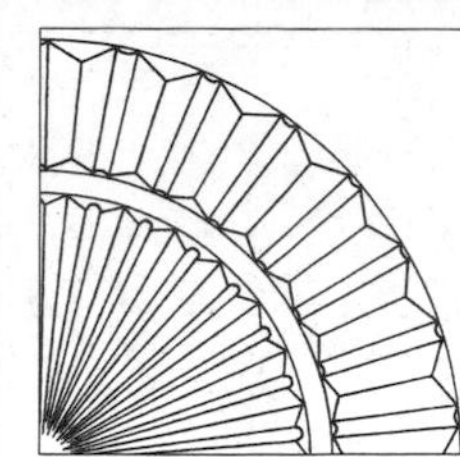
Fortune

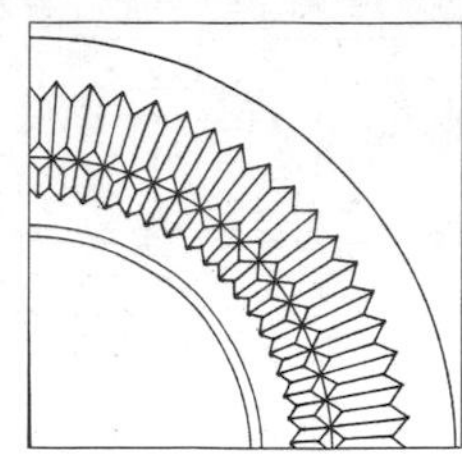
Lincoln Inn

Petalware

Queen Mary

PLAIN

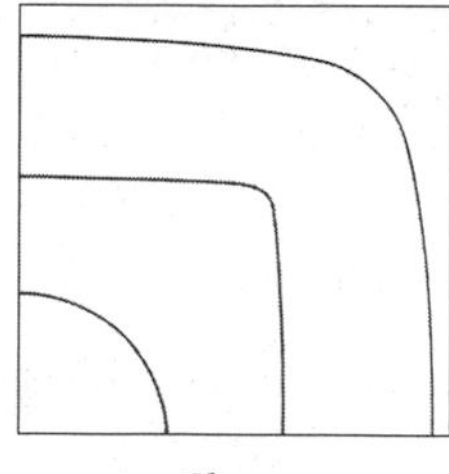
Charm

Mt. Pleasant

PYRAMIDS

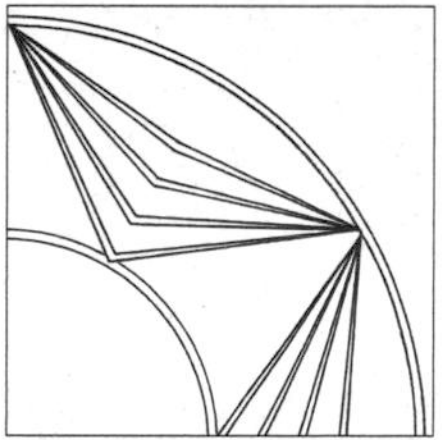
Pyramid

RAISED BAND

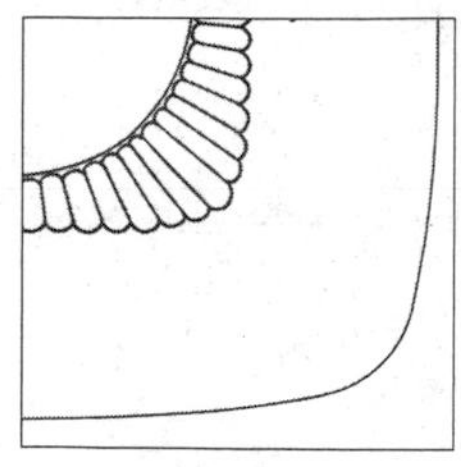
Charm

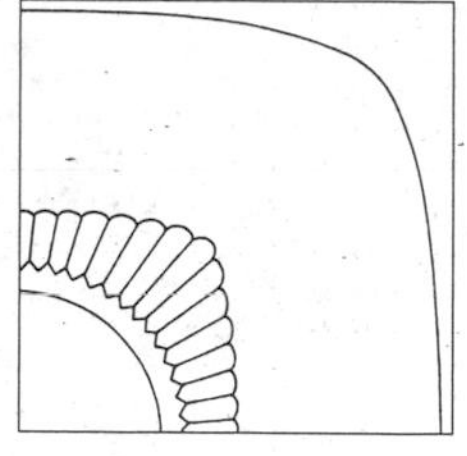
Forest Green

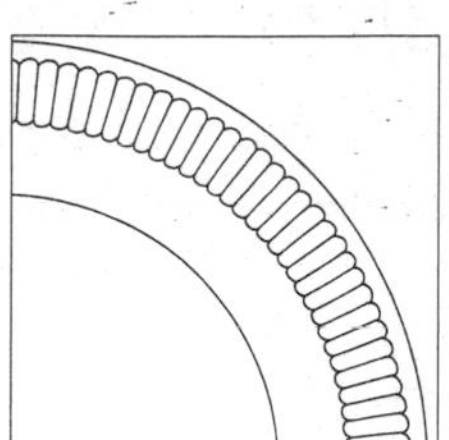
Jane Ray

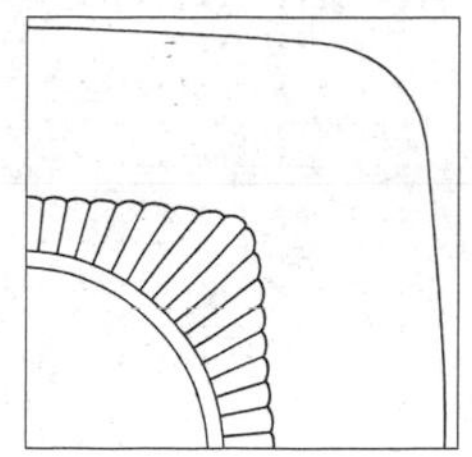
Royal Ruby

RAISED CIRCLES

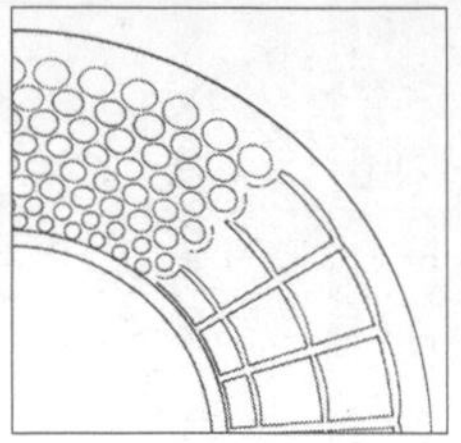
American Pioneer

Bubble

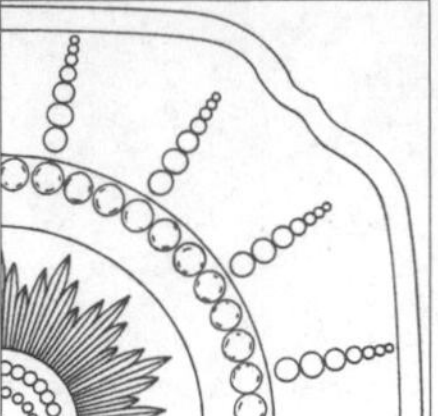
Columbia

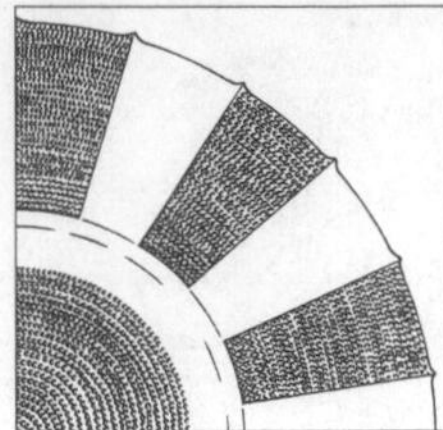
Dewdrop

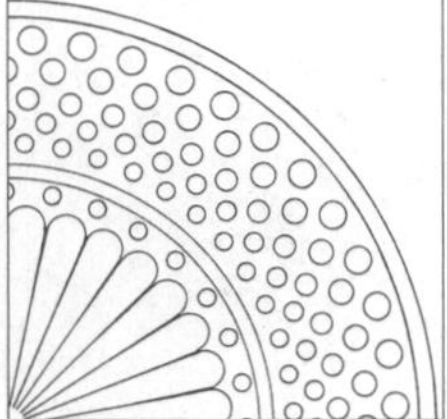
Hobnail

Moonstone

Oyster & Pearl

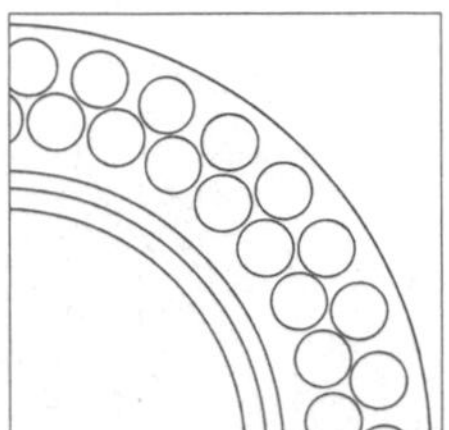
Raindrops

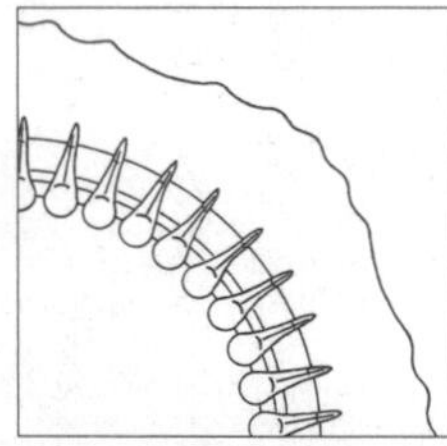
Radiance

Ships

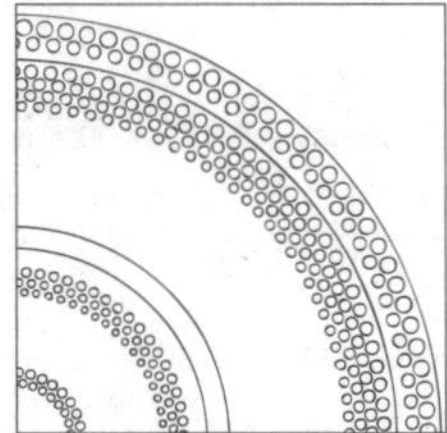
Teardrop

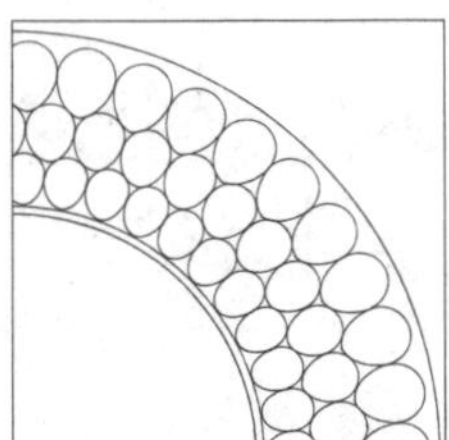
Thumbprint

RIBS

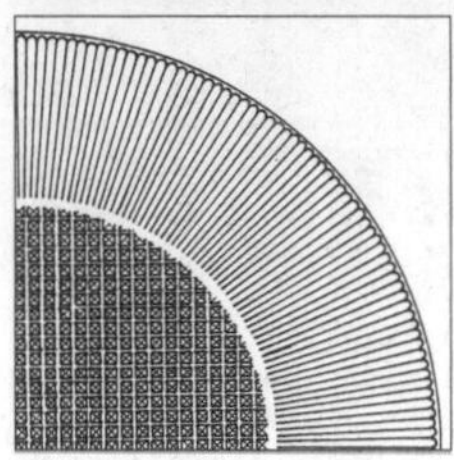
Homespun

RINGS (CIRCLES)

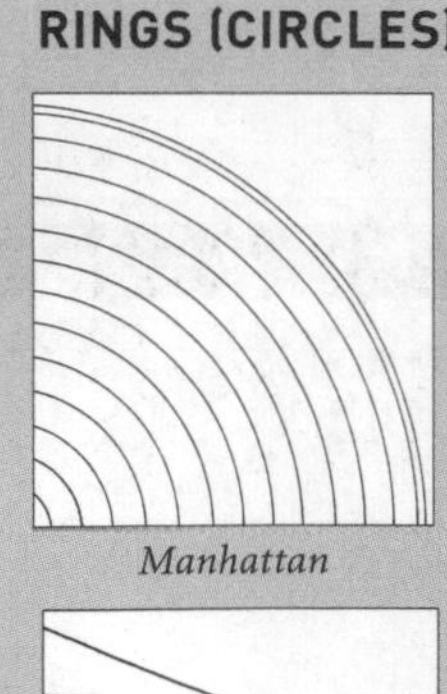
Manhattan

Moderntone

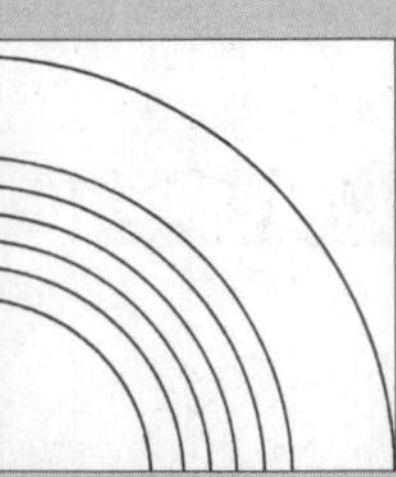
Moondrops

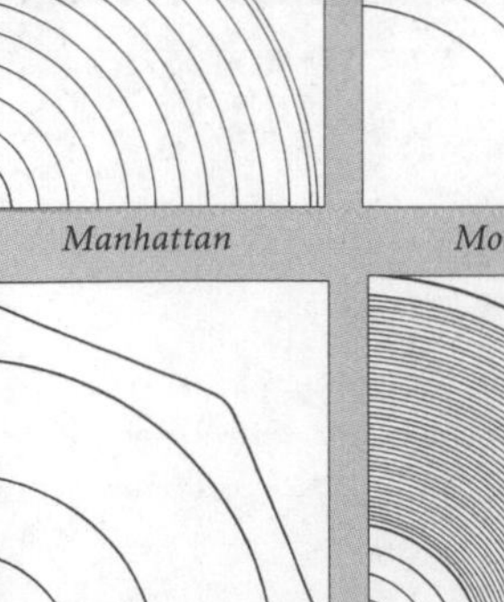
Moroccan Amethyst

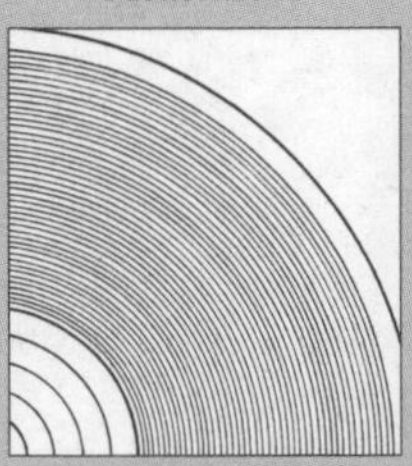
Old English

Ring

SCENES

Chinex Classic

Lake Como

SCROLLING DESIGNS

Adam

American Sweetheart

Florentine No. 1

Florentine No. 2

Madrid

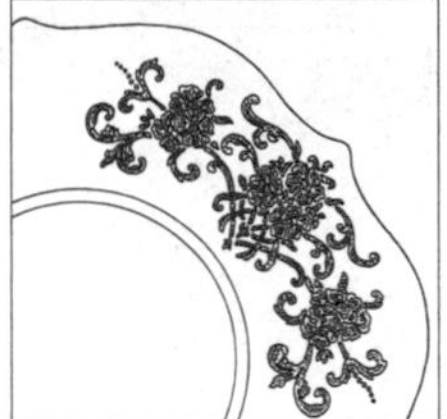
Patrick

Philbe

Primo

Princess

Rock Crystal

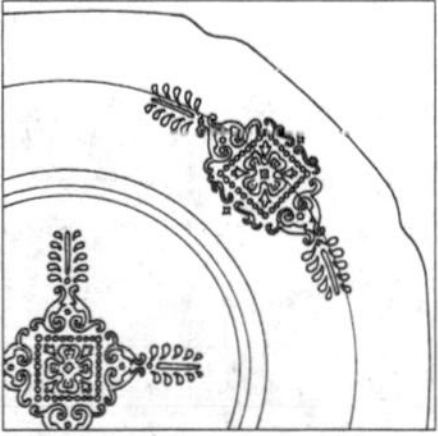
Roxana

Vernon

SWIRLS

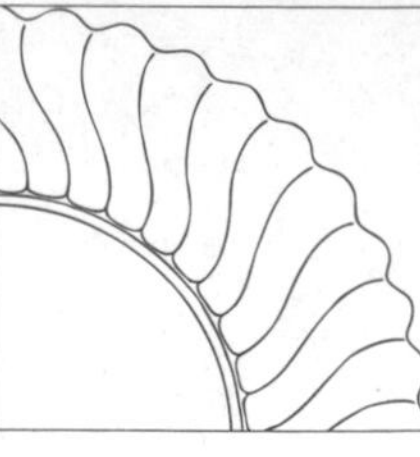

Colony

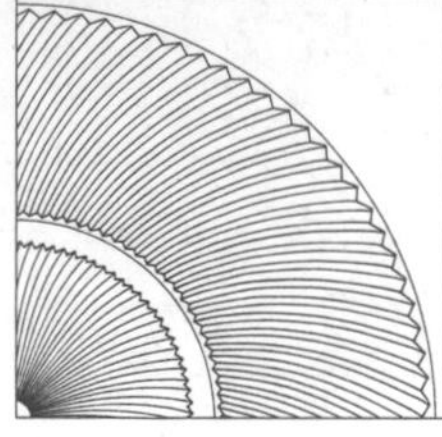

Diana

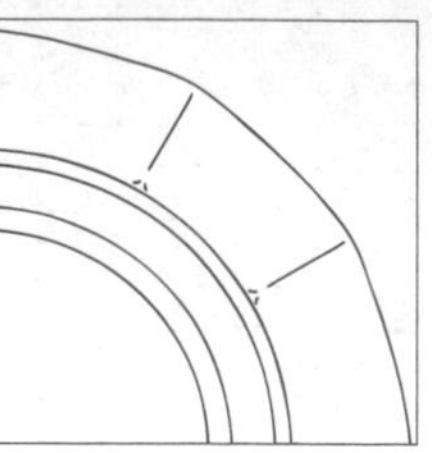

Fairfax

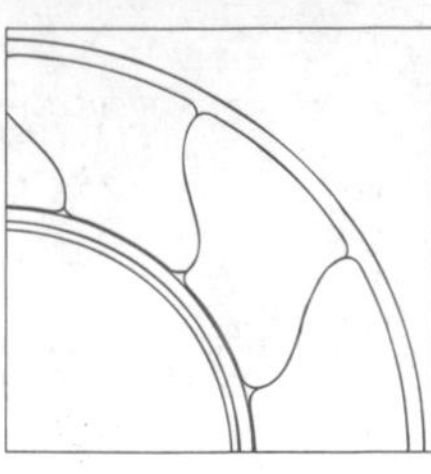

Jamestown

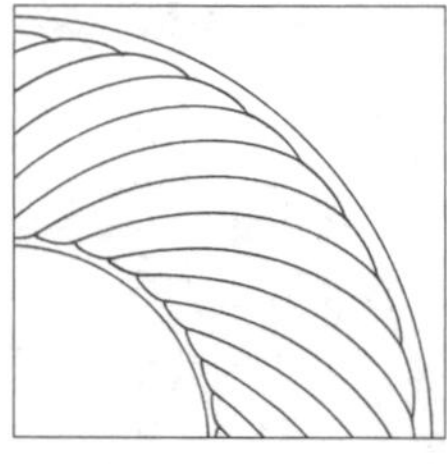

Spiral

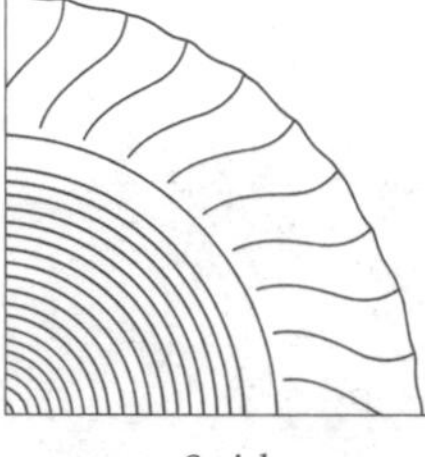

Swirl

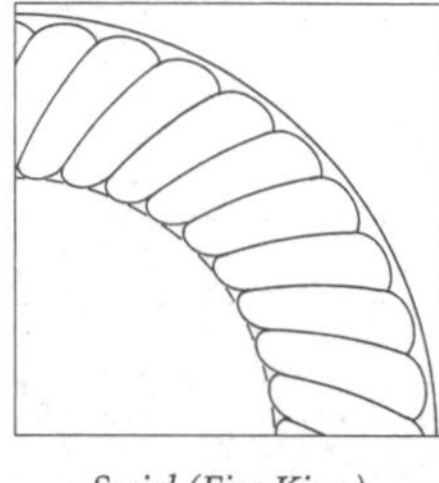

Swirl (Fire King)

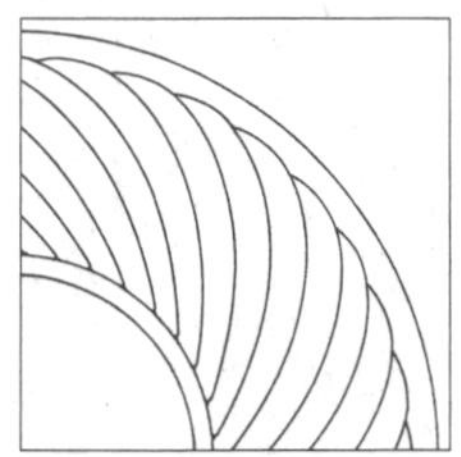

Twisted Optic

TEXTURED

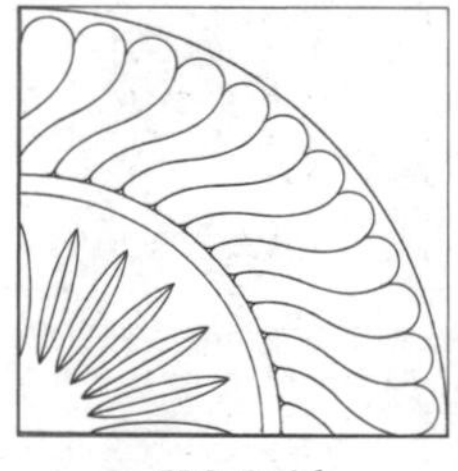

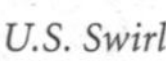

U.S. Swirl

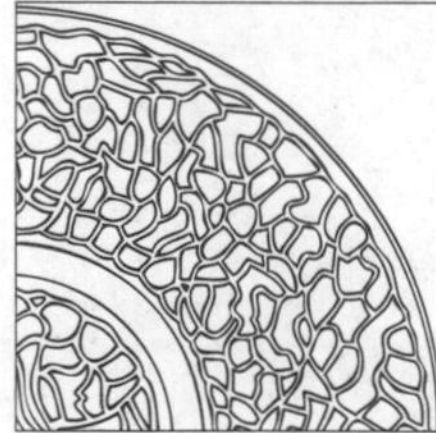

By Cracky

Twiggy

American pattern punch bowl in crystal, Fostoria Glass Co., 1915-1986, good condition, chip to base, 8-1/2" h., 19" dia. **$48**

Courtesy of Estate Auction Co., www.estateauctionco.com

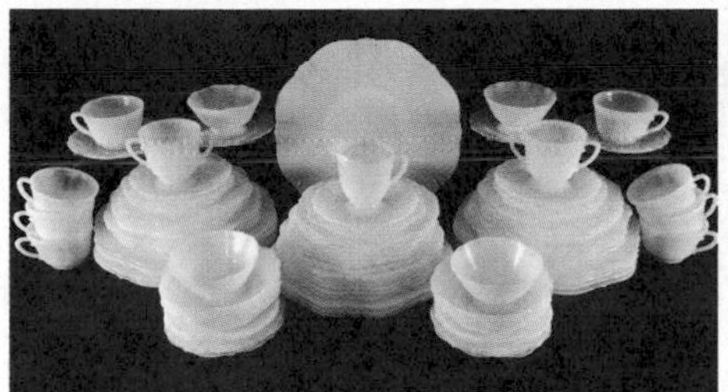

Ninety pieces of American Sweetheart pattern in Monax, MacBeth-Evans Glass Co., 1930-1936, some plates with center decoration, expected wear appropriate to age.. **$798**

Courtesy of Specialists of the South, www.specialistsofthesouth.com

Original box with American Sweetheart pattern 16-piece luncheon set in pink, MacBeth-Evans Glass Co., 1930-1936, never used, four place settings with tumblers, cups, saucers, and luncheon plates, with American Sweetheart extras not in boxes: four cups, four saucers, three dinner plates, and two tumblers, all in mint condition; box label reads "Free Gift from Stevens Clothes / Toledo, Ohio." **$135**

Courtesy of Stony Ridge Auction Gallery, www.stonyridgeauction.com

Cameo pattern sandwich server with center handle in green, Hocking Glass Co., 1930-1934, rare, one of only four recorded examples, undamaged, 4" h. overall, 10" dia...................... **$5,000-$6,000**

Courtesy of Jeffrey S. Evans & Associates, www.jeffreysevans.com

Cherry Blossom pattern platter in green, Jeanette Glass Co., circa 1930-1939, 13" x 9-3/4" x 1-3/4"... **$58**

Courtesy of Charleston Auction Co., Charleston Estate Auctions, www.charlestonestateauctions.com

Cube pattern bowl in pink (shown), Jeannette Glass Co., 1929-1933, 2-3/4" x 7-1/2", and 4-1/2" bowl. **$12**

Courtesy of LeMar Auctions and Estate Services, www.lemarauctions.com

Five Dogwood pattern luncheon plates in green and three in pink, MacBeth-Evans Co., 1929-1932, good condition, 8"................................ **$17**

Courtesy of LeMar Auctions and Estate Serv ces, www.lemarauctions.com

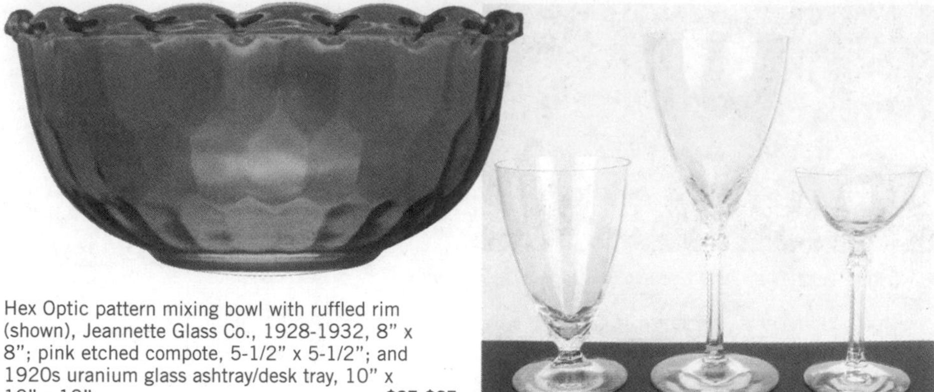

Hex Optic pattern mixing bowl with ruffled rim (shown), Jeannette Glass Co., 1928-1932, 8" x 8"; pink etched compote, 5-1/2" x 5-1/2"; and 1920s uranium glass ashtray/desk tray, 10" x 10" x 10".. **$65-$85**

Courtesy of Charleston Auction Co., Charleston Estate Auctions, www.charlestonestateauctions.com

Fairfax pattern glasses and goblets in blue (three shown), Fostoria Glass Co., 1927-1944, 10 stemmed wine glasses, eight shallow goblets, seven water glasses, vase, and glass teacup. **$62**

Courtesy of Louis J. Dianni, LLC Antiques Auctions, louisjdianni.com

Iris pattern pitcher with six cone-shaped tumblers in iridescent, Jeannette Glass Co., 1928-1932, 1950s, 1970s.. **$45**

Courtesy of EJ's Auction & Consignment, www.ejsauction.com

Jade-ite ware, Anchor Hocking Glass Corp. under Fire King trademark, early 1930s, four salad plates, four dessert plates, and tea container, good condition, plates 9" and 7-3/4" dia., tea container 4-1/2" h... **$84**

Courtesy of Premier Auction Galleries, www.pag4u.com

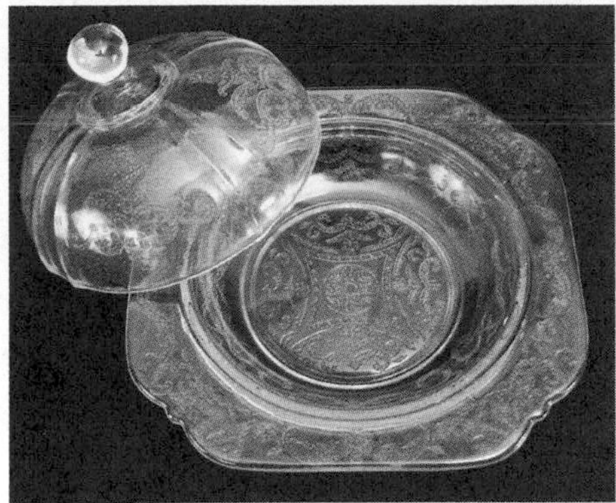

Madrid pattern covered butter dish in crystal, Federal Glass Co., 1932-1939, condition appropriate to age, 7" w. **$40**

Courtesy of Specialists of the South, www.specialistsofthesouth.com

Five Manhattan pattern pieces in pink by Anchor Hocking Glass Co., 1938-1943, two 5" compotes, one creamer, one sugar, and one 6-1/2" footed bowl, good condition. **$59**

Courtesy of Woody Auction, www.woodyauction.com

Mayfair/Open Rose pattern bowl in pink, Hocking Glass Co., 1931-1937, normal wear for age, 11-1/2" w. x 3" h. **$24**

Courtesy of Desert West Auction Service, www.desertwestauction.com

Five Moderntone pattern cups and saucers in cobalt blue (two shown) and Moderntone pattern oval glass platter in cobalt blue, Hazel Atlas Glass Co., 1934-1942 and late 1940s to early 1950s, with cobalt blue glass grape cluster, platter 11"-12". **$29**

Courtesy of LeMar Auctions and Estate Services, www.lemarauctions.com

National pattern salad bowl in crystal, 4" h., 9-1/2" dia., and National pattern footed round plate, 12", Jeannette Glass Co., late 1940s to mid-1950s. **$17**

Courtesy of LeMar Auctions and Estate Services, www.lemarauctions.com

Princess pattern serving bowl in pink, Hocking Glass Co., 1931-1935, good condition, 9-1/4"x 4".. **$29**

Courtesy of LeMar Auctions and Estate Services, www.lemarauctions.com

Royal Ruby pattern dishes (part shown), Anchor Hocking Glass Corp., 1938-1967, and other patterns in red, possibly Oyster and Pearl, footed tumblers, cordials, platter, dinner plates, salad plates, creamer and sugar bowl, cups, bowls, etc.......... **$81**

Courtesy of Vero Beach Auction, www.verobeachauction.com

Seven-piece Royal Ruby pattern lemonade set, Anchor Hocking Glass Corp., 1938-1967, good condition, pitcher 7" h., glasses 4-1/4" h.................. **$46**

Courtesy of Martin Auction Co., martinauctionco.com

Oyster and Pearl pattern dishes in pink, Anchor Hocking Glass Corp., 1938-1940, 10-1/2" dia. bowl with 13-1/2" dia. underplate, sauce pitcher, two 12" l. tab-handled divided relish dishes, and small tab-handled bowl, expected wear. **$29**

Courtesy of Specialists of the South, www.specialistsofthesouth.com

Princess pattern dishes in pink, Hocking Glass Co., 1931-1935, never used (received as wedding gift in 1933), two 16-piece sets in original boxes with original packing and "Fostoria Ohio" shipping labels, four each cups and saucers, footed tumblers, and grill plates; with additional Princess pattern cookie jar, candy jar, lidded sugar and creamer, and open vegetable bowl; mint condition, no reproductions, salt and pepper shakers were used and show discolorations to lids............................... **$243**

Courtesy of Stony Ridge Auction Gallery, www.stonyridgeauction.com

Sandwich pattern bowl in amber (shown), Indiana Glass Co., 1920s to 1980s, and unknown pattern rectangular candy dish, unmarked, bowl 3" h., 6-1/2" dia.. **$6**

Courtesy of Main Street Mining Co. Auctions, mainstreetmining.com

Depression glass candlesticks in pink, possibly Spiral or Swirl pattern by Hocking Glass Co. or Anchor Hocking Glass Corp., excellent condition, 8" h. **$48**

Courtesy of Milestone Auctions, www.milestoneauctions.com

Ten Swirl pattern luncheon plates in pink, Jeannette Glass Co., 1937-1938, good condition, 8" dia.. **$12**

Courtesy of Premier Auction Galleries, www.pag4u.com

Ships/Sailboats pattern pitcher and five tumblers in blue and white, Hazel Atlas Glass Co., late 1930s, with small windmill bucket, expected wear appropriate to age, four tumblers 5" h. **$114**

Courtesy of Specialists of the South, www.specialistsofthesouth.com

Seven Versailles pattern glasses (one shown) in green, Fostoria Glass Co., three with chips to foot, 5-1/4" h., 3-1/4" dia. mouth, 2-3/4" dia. foot. .. **$59**

Courtesy of Appraisal & Estate Sale Specialists, Inc., estatesalemandan.webs.com

GLASS

duncan and miller

DUNCAN & MILLER Glass Co., a successor firm to George A. Duncan & Sons Co., produced a wide range of pressed wares and novelty pieces during the late 19th century and into the early 20th century. During the Depression era and after, the company continued making a wide variety of more modern patterns, including mold-blown types, and also introduced a number of etched and engraved patterns. Many colors, including opalescent hues, were produced during this era, and especially popular today are the graceful swan dishes they produced in the Pall Mall and Sylvan patterns.

The numbers in the photograph descriptions indicate the original factory pattern number. The Duncan factory was closed in 1955.

Two Block and Rosette pattern punch bowls, No. 50, colorless, circa 1902, 5-1/2" and 9" h., 10-3/4" and 12" dia. **$180**

Courtesy of Jeffrey S. Evans & Associates, www.jeffreysevans.com

Water goblet, clear pattern, Duncan & Miller Glass Co., early 20th century, 3" h. x 2-3/4" w. **$30**

Courtesy of World of Antiques, www.worldofantiques.net

Block and Rosette pattern table set, No. 50, circa 1902, seven pieces including ruby-stained butter cover, creamer with gilt decoration, spooner and celery vase, colorless, individual sauce/berry bowls with scattered flaking/roughness to rims, 1-1/2" to 6" h....... **$72**

Courtesy of Jeffrey S. Evans & Associates, www.jeffreysevans.com

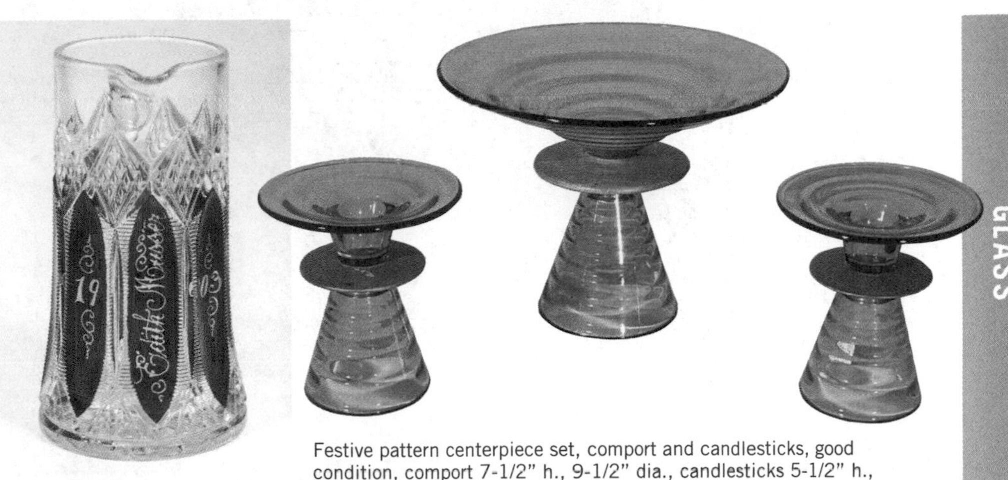

Ladder pattern with diamond variant water pitcher, pattern introduced in 1904, ruby stained, colorless, applied handle, with souvenir letter, 9-1/4" h. **$228**

Courtesy of Jeffrey S. Evans & Associates, www.jeffreysevans.com

Festive pattern centerpiece set, comport and candlesticks, good condition, comport 7-1/2" h., 9-1/2" dia., candlesticks 5-1/2" h., 5" dia.. **$85**

Courtesy of Rachel Davis Fine Arts, www.racheldavisfinearts.com

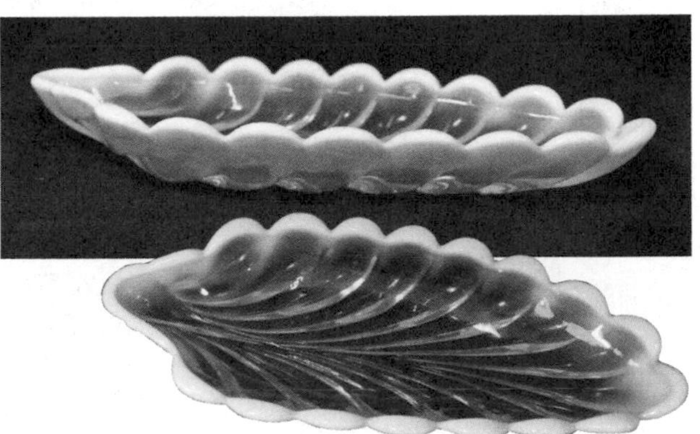

Sanibel pattern vaseline opalescent clamshell candy dish, later 1920s to mid-1930s, 13 oz., 9-1/2" h. x 4" w. x 1-1/2" d...**$46**

Courtesy of Accurate Estate Auctions, www.accurateauctions.com

Twelve amber-stained articles, No. 35, colorless with engraved decoration, first quarter 20th century, three compotes and handled sandwich server, sherbet cups, 1/2" to 7" h., 8-1/2" dia. **$168**

Courtesy of Jeffrey S. Evans & Associates, www.jeffreysevans.com

Candlesticks, No. 1-41, circa 1940, colorless, each with bobeche, screw connector, and prisms, 9-3/4" h.................. **$48**

Courtesy of Jeffrey S. Evans & Associates, www.jeffreysevans.com

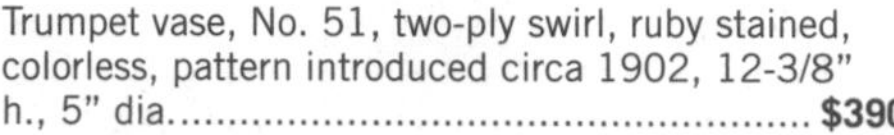

Trumpet vase, No. 51, two-ply swirl, ruby stained, colorless, pattern introduced circa 1902, 12-3/8" h., 5" dia.. **$390**

Courtesy of Jeffrey S. Evans & Associates, www.jeffreysevans.com

Star-in-Square pattern water pitcher, ruby-stained, colorless, with applied handle, early 20th century, minor wear and pattern roughness, 8-3/8" h. ... **$108**

Courtesy of Jeffrey S. Evans & Associates, www.jeffreysevans.com

Sweet Sixty-One pattern ruby-stained four-piece table set, No. 61, circa 1906, colorless, covered butter dish, sugar bowl, creamer and spooner, 4-1/8" to 6" h... **$156**

Courtesy of Jeffrey S. Evans & Associates, www.jeffreysevans.com

Set of 12 blue opalescent hobnail water goblets, circa 1940s, condition good, 4" h. x 2-1/2" w.... **$54**

Courtesy of Premiere Auction Galleries, www.pag4u.com

Maiden's Blush-stained pattern 10-piece punch set, No. 51, early 20th century, two-ply swirl, colorless, two-piece pedestal punch bowl and nine punch cups, with factory polished base, 2-1/4" to 11-1/2" h., punch bowl 15" dia...................... **$390**

Courtesy of Jeffrey S. Evans & Associates, www.jeffreysevans.com

Four Star-in-Square pattern ruby-stained articles, No. 75, circa 1912, colorless, cruet with gilt decoration, salt and pepper shakers with period lids, and toothpick holder, moderate wear to toothpick holder, 2-3/8" to 6-3/4" h................ **$300**

Courtesy of Jeffrey S. Evans & Associates, www.jeffreysevans.com

GLASS

durand

FINE DECORATIVE GLASS similar to that made by Tiffany and other outstanding glasshouses of its day was made by Vineland Flint Glass Works Co. in Vineland, New Jersey, first headed by Victor Durand, Sr. and subsequently by his son, Victor Durand, Jr., in the 1920s.

Lady Gray Rose touchier shade, ovoid form in iridescent red with platinum King Tut pattern, amber and marigold interior, very good condition, 8" h., fitter 3-1/4" w. **$847**

Courtesy of Jaremos Estate Liquidators, www.jaremos.com

Pair of King Tut pattern art glass vases, baluster form, unsigned, iridescent interior, one with crack on foot, 6-1/4" h. x 4-1/2" w. .. **$708**

Courtesy of Burchard Galleries, www.burchardgalleries.com

King Tut pattern footed bowl, blue lustre with opal King Tut decoration, applied gold lustre foot, polished pontil mark, unsigned, early 20th century, 5" h., 8-3/8" dia. **$1,200**

Courtesy of Jeffrey S. Evans & Associates, www.jeffreysevans.com

Pair of King Tut pattern trumpet-form lamps with gold shades with green and gold iridescence, molded bronze bases with leaf-molded shade holders, now electrified, excellent condition, metal with some wear to surface and spots of patina, 15-1/2" h., 5-1/4" dia......................... **$984**

Courtesy of New Orleans Auctions, www.neworleansauction.com

Crackle vase, iridescent, footed base with ruffled rim, very good condition, light dirt accumulation and color loss, 9-1/2" h. **$413**

Courtesy of Leonard Auction, www.leonardauction.com

Moorish crackle lamp shade, silver blue foliage pattern over gray and gold ground, very good condition, chips around lower cut rim, very good condition, tiny chips around lower cut rim, 8" h. x 6" w. **$354**

Courtesy of Leonard Auction, www.leonardauction.com

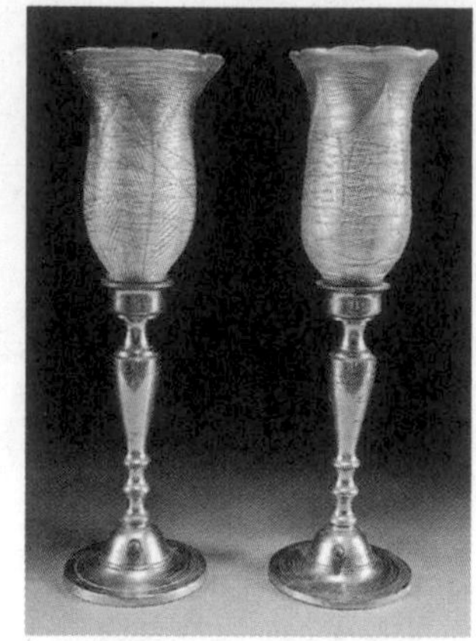

Pair of American Favrile glass and brass candlesticks, gold iridescence with pulled feather and glass thread, 20th century, attributed to Durand, electrified, 16-1/2" h. **$437**

Courtesy of Neal Auction Co., www.nealauction.com

Four-piece set, cranberry and green pulled feather pattern charger and bowl, and green and cranberry cordial stems, charger 14-1/4" dia., bowl 3-3/8" h., 8-1/4" dia., stems 4-1/4" h., 3-1/2" dia. **$324**

Courtesy of Burchard Galleries, www.burchardgalleries.com

Experimental peacock feather pattern vase, circa 1924-1931, red lustre with platinum design, applied foot and polished pontil mark, signed "2028, XX, Durand", 8-1/8" h. **$2,520**

Courtesy of Jeffrey S. Evans & Associates, www.jeffreysevans.com

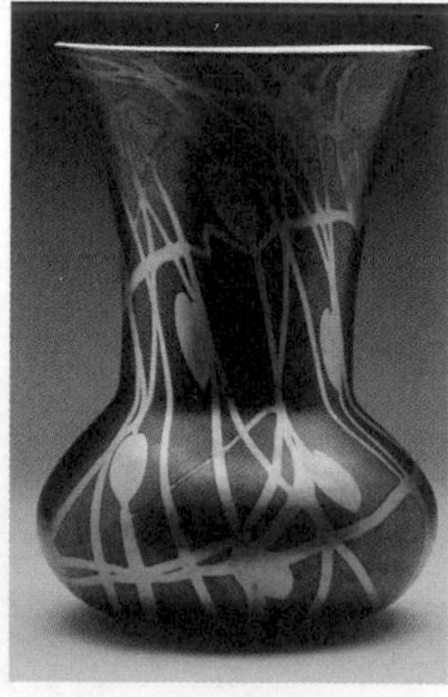

Vase with black background and blue leaves and vines, marked Durand, excellent condition, no chips or cracks, 12" h. **$1,037**

Courtesy of Morphy Auctions, morphyauctions.com

Threaded Leaf pattern glass shade boudoir lamp, cast brass figural putti base, gold thread and leaf decoration on shade, 12-3/4" h. x 5" dia............. **$177**

Courtesy of Burchard Galleries, www.burchardgalleries.com

Gold threaded squat vase with flared rim, bulbous body, gold lustre with threads, marked on base 1700-10, loss of threads, repaired drill hole to base, overall 9-3/4" h., 8" dia...... **$767**

Courtesy of Burchard Galleries, www.burchardgalleries.com

Art glass vase, blue iridescent with heart and vine motif with applied threading, not signed, in style of Durand, losses to threading, 7" h., 5" dia...... **$554**

Courtesy of DuMouchelles, www.dumouchelles.com

Vase, blown glass, iridescent green and gold swirl, signed "Durand 17" on underside, 7" h. x 5-1/2" w., 5-1/2" dia.................................... **$625**

Courtesy of Concept Art Gallery, www.conceptgallery.com

Threaded glass vase with smaller threaded vase, larger vase signed Durand, small vase unsigned, some accumulation of surface dirt to smaller vase, 10-1/4" h. x 4" h................ **$500**

Courtesy of Concept Art Gallery, www.conceptgallery.com

GLASS

fenton art glass

THE FENTON ART Glass Co. was founded in 1905 by Frank L. Fenton and his brother John W. in Martins Ferry, Ohio. They initially sold hand-painted glass made by other manufacturers, but it wasn't long before they decided to produce their own glass. The new Fenton factory in Williamstown, West Virginia, opened on Jan. 2, 1907. From that point on, the company expanded by developing unusual colors and continued to decorate glassware in innovative ways.

Two more brothers, James and Robert, joined the firm. But despite the company's initial success, John W. left to establish the Millersburg Glass Co. of Millersburg, Ohio, in 1909. The first months of the new operation were devoted to the production of crystal glass only. Later iridized glass was called "Radium Glass." After only two years, Millersburg filed for bankruptcy.

Fenton's iridescent glass had a metallic luster over a colored, pressed pattern and was sold in dime stores. It was only after the sales of this glass decreased and it was sold in bulk as carnival prizes that it came to be known as carnival glass.

Fenton became the top producer of carnival glass, with more than 150 patterns. The quality of the glass and its popularity with the public enabled the new company to be profitable through the late 1920s. As interest in carnival glass subsided, Fenton moved on to stretch glass and opalescent patterns. A line of colorful blown glass (called "off-hand" by Fenton) was also produced in the mid-1920s.

During the Great Depression, Fenton survived by producing functional colored glass tableware and other household items, including water sets, table sets, bowls, mugs, plates, perfume bottles and vases. Restrictions on European imports during World War II ushered in the arrival of Fenton's opaque colored glass, and the lines of "Crest" pieces soon followed. In the 1950s, production continued to diversify with a focus on milk glass, particularly in

Holly and Berry pattern carnival glass plate, blue, 9-1/2" dia... **$64**

Courtesy of Strawser Auctions, www.strawserauctions.com

Lotus pattern carnival glass footed bowl, blue..... **$52**

Courtesy of Strawser Auctions, www.strawserauctions.com

hobnail patterns. In the third quarter of Fenton's history, the company returned to themes that had proved popular to preceding generations and began adding special lines such as the Bicentennial series.

Innovations included the line of Colonial colors that debuted in 1963, including amber, blue, green, orange, and ruby. Based on a special order for an Ohio museum, Fenton in 1969 revisited its early success with "Original Formula Carnival Glass." Fenton also started marking its glass in molds for the first time.

Stag & Holly pattern carnival glass footed bowl, blue.......... **$81**

Courtesy of Strawser Auctions, www.strawserauctions.com

The star of the 1970s was the yellow and blushing pink creation known as Burmese. This was followed closely by a menagerie of animals, birds, and children. In 1975, Robert Barber was hired by Fenton to begin an artist-in-residence program, producing a limited line of art glass vases in a return to the off-hand, blown-glass creations of the mid-1920s. Shopping at home via television was a phenomenon in the late 1980s when the "Birthstone Bears" became the first Fenton product to appear on QVC. In August 2007, Fenton discontinued all but a few of its more popular lines, and the company ceased production altogether in 2011.

For more information on Fenton Art Glass, see *Warman's Fenton Glass Identification and Price Guide*, 2nd edition, by Mark F. Moran.

No. 1700 (OMN) / Lincoln Inn pattern seven-piece Depression glass water set, blue iridescent, water pitcher and six tumblers, Fenton Art Glass Co., circa 1928, undamaged, 4-1/2" to 7-1/4" h. **$192**

Courtesy of Jeffrey S. Evans & Associates, www.jeffreysevans.com

No. 1653 five-piece ice tea set, green opalescent, pitcher with triangular crimped rim and four ice tea glasses, Fenton Art Glass Co., second quarter 20th century, 5-3/8" to 9-3/4" h. overall. **$180**

Courtesy of Jeffrey S. Evans & Associates, www.jeffreysevans.com

Coin Dot pattern six-piece beverage set, blue opalescent, pitcher with applied colorless pinched handle and five tumblers, Fenton Art Glass Co., second quarter 20th century, tumblers undamaged, pitcher with moderate bruise to body, 4-1/8" to 4-7/8" h................ **$72**

Courtesy of Jeffrey S. Evans & Associates, www.jeffreysevans.com

Coinspot water pitcher, blue opalescent, flared star-crimped rim, applied blue handle, Fenton Art Glass Co., circa 1910, undamaged, 9-1/4" h. overall. **$156**

Courtesy of Jeffrey S. Evans & Associates, www.jeffreysevans.com

Coinspot pattern seven-piece water set, green opalescent, water pitcher with crimped rim and six pressed tumblers, Fenton Art Glass Co., circa 1910, undamaged, 4" to 9-1/2" h............................. **$120**

Courtesy of Jeffrey S. Evans & Associates, www.jeffreysevans.com

Footed candy dish, large, 1950s, signed..................... **$18**

Courtesy of Omega Auction Corp., www.omegaauctioncorp.com

◀ No. 1653 Coinspot pattern seven-piece ice tea set, colorless opalescent, water pitcher with applied handle and six ice tea glasses, Fenton Art Glass Co., second quarter 20th century, two tumblers with two chips to rim, remainder undamaged, 5-3/8" to 9-3/4" h. overall. **$84**

Courtesy of Jeffrey S. Evans & Associates, www.jeffreysevans.com

Twelve Cherry and Scale pattern tumblers, custard with nutmeg stain, Fenton Art Glass Co., circa 1908, undamaged, 4" h. **$36**

Courtesy of Jeffrey S. Evans & Associates, www.jeffreysevans.com

Hand-painted lamp, signed on bottom, chip to shade, 19" h. **$115**

Courtesy of Vero Beach Auction, www.verobeachauction.com

Pink hobnail vintage barber bottle, Victorian era, unmarked, with spout, minus cork, near mint condition, 8-1/2" h. **$153**

Courtesy of Morphy Auctions, morphyauctions.com

Six Waterlily With Cattails pattern tumblers, blue opalescent, Fenton Art Glass Co., circa 1908, one with chip near base, remainder undamaged, some with minor pattern roughness as made, 3-7/8" h. **$72**

Courtesy of Jeffrey S. Evans & Associates, www.jeffreysevans.com

Cranberry opalescent hobnail hurricane lamp, 24" h. **$139**

Courtesy of Strawser Auctions, www.strawserauctions.com

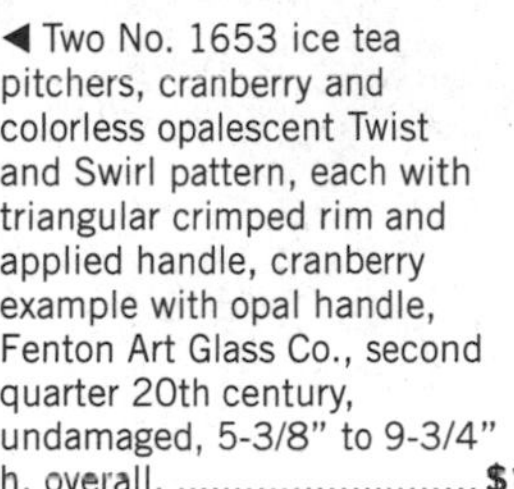

◀ Two No. 1653 ice tea pitchers, cranberry and colorless opalescent Twist and Swirl pattern, each with triangular crimped rim and applied handle, cranberry example with opal handle, Fenton Art Glass Co., second quarter 20th century, undamaged, 5-3/8" to 9-3/4" h. overall. **$132**

Courtesy of Jeffrey S. Evans & Associates, www.jeffreysevans.com

Emerald green opalescent hobnail two-piece punch bowl and 12 cups (with hooks) with glass ladle, part of Connoisseur Collection #226, 11-1/2" h., 13-1/2" dia........................ **$406**

Courtesy of Strawser Auctions, www.strawserauctions.com

Cactus pattern three-piece water set, topaz/vaseline (uranium) opalescent, water pitcher with applied Vaseline (uranium) reeded handle and original sticker and two goblets, Fenton Art Glass Co., circa 1959, 6-3/8" to 11-1/4" h. overall. **$168**

Courtesy of Jeffrey S. Evans & Associates, www.jeffreysevans.com

Honeycomb and Clover pattern six-piece berry set, green opalescent, master berry bowl and five individual berry dishes, Fenton Art Glass Co., circa 1909, two dishes with minor bruises to feet, 5-3/8" to 8-5/8" dia. overall. **$60**

Courtesy of Jeffrey S. Evans & Associates, www.jeffreysevans.com

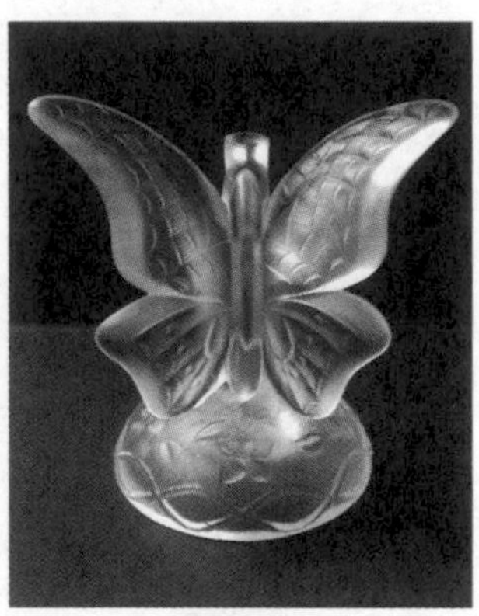

Frosted glass butterfly, signed.**$24**

Courtesy of Omega Auction Corp., www.omegaauctioncorp.com

▲ Opalescent Swirl pattern five-piece water set, colorless opalescent, water pitcher with applied cobalt blue reeded handle and four tumblers, each signed twice, one signature states "Fenton/80th," Fenton Art Glass Co., undamaged, 5" to 9-3/4" h. **$96**

Courtesy of Jeffrey S. Evans & Associates, www.jeffreysevans.com

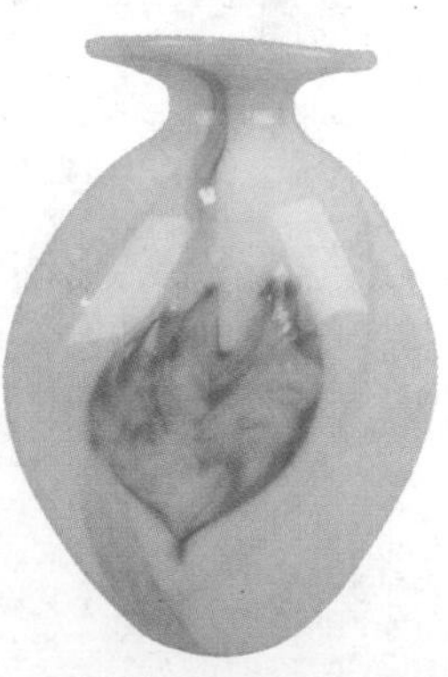

Art glass vase, 1976, 9-1/2" h. **$319**

Courtesy of Strawser Auctions, www.strawserauctions.com

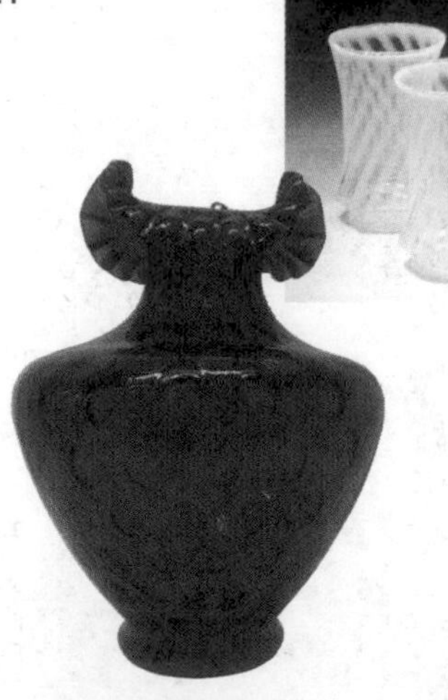

Cranberry glass vase............. **$52**

Courtesy of Teel Auction Services, www.teelauctionservices.com

GLASS

fostoria

THE FOSTORIA GLASS CO., founded in 1887, produced numerous types of fine glassware over the years. Its factory in Moundsville, West Virginia, closed in 1986.

Approximately 165-piece Chintz pattern elegant glassware set (part shown), tall water glasses with stems, low water goblets, cocktail, champagne, red wine, white wine, and juice glasses, and tri-footed torte plate, cigarette vase, and ashtray, 8" h. to 3-3/4" h. **$885**

Courtesy of Burchard Auction Galleries, www.burchardgalleries.com

Five brocaded ice blue cocktail glasses with stems, some wear to gold trim, 6" h. **$144**

Courtesy of Kennedy Auction Service, www.kennedysauction.com

Coin pattern punch bowl and 42 cups, 10 cups have minor roughness, punch bowl 14" w., 6-3/4" h., punch cups 2-1/2" h. **$73**

Courtesy of Ron Rhodes Auctioneer, www.ronrhoads-auction.com

Suite of stemware and serving pieces, eight red wine glasses, eight champagne couples, seven sherry glasses, eight aperitifs, eight sherbets, eight cordials, pitcher, candlesticks, two-section dish, folded tray, compote, and footed bowl, from 6-1/4 h. to 9-3/4" h. **$523**

Courtesy of Michaan's Auctions, www.michaans.com

Four-piece No. 1819 Dandelion pattern ruby-stained table set, circa 1911, colorless with gilt decoration, covered butter dish, sugar bowl, creamer, and spooner, slight flake to edge of one panel of creamer, 4" h. to 6" h. overall **$360**

Courtesy of Jeffrey S. Evans & Associates, www.jeffreysevans.com

Tantalus bar with bottles etched "Gin," "Rye," and "Scotch," mid-20th century, chrome bar, Fostoria glass bottles, good condition with minor oxidation and scuffing to metal bar and minor scratching to glass, 11" h. x 12-3/4" w. x 4-1/4" d. **$250**

Courtesy of Concept Art Gallery, www.conceptgallery.com

Heart and Vine pattern shades with iridescent interiors, unsigned, nicks and light chipping to upper rims, light crazing to underside, 4-3/4" h., 4-3/4" dia. **$861**

Courtesy of Westport Auction, www.westportauction.com

U.S. Senate glass ashtray with frosted center medallion marked "United States Senate," circa 1960, 1-3/4" h., 9-3/4" dia. **$125**

Courtesy of Neal Auction Co., www.nealauction.com

Eight Needlepoint pattern tumblers, green with opalescent rims, marked on underside, slight wear to pattern, 3" h., 3-1/2" dia. **$109**

Courtesy of Manor Auctions, www.manorauctions.com

Rose pattern miniature lamp, circa 1900, opaque white with green staining and polychrome decoration, ball-form font with footed base, matching pattern and decorated ball-form chimney shade, fitted with Plume & Atwood Hornet burner, roughness on chimney shade rim, as made, light denting to thumbwheel, 10" h. to top of chimney shade, 4-5/8" h. to top of collar, 2-3/4" dia. base. **$216**

Courtesy of Jeffrey S. Evans & Associates, www.jeffreysevans.com

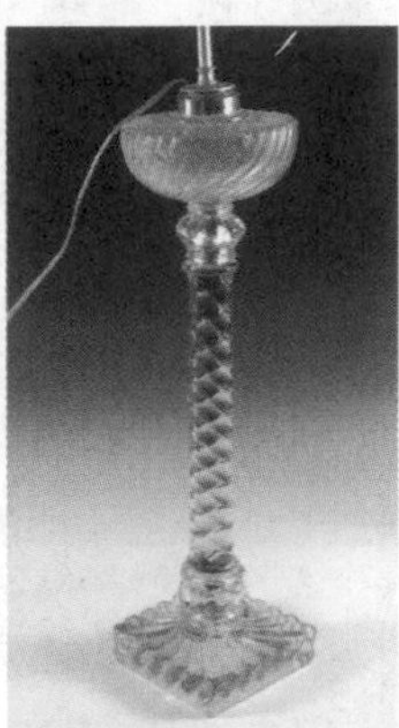

Queen Anne/Colony pattern massive oil banquet lamp, electrified, with cloth shade, fine condition, 38" h., 6" sq. vase, 16" dia. shade. **$300**

Courtesy of Thomaston Place Auction Galleries, www.thomastonauction.com

◀ No. 500 Atlanta/Square Lion pattern banana stand, circa 1895, colorless with faint purple tint to plate, produced from salver/cake stand, 10" h. overall **$420**

Courtesy of Jeffrey S. Evans & Associates, www.jeffreysevans.com

◀ Heirloom pattern large opal yellow epergne, circa 1960-1961, 3-3/4" h., 4-1/2" dia. **$328**

Courtesy of Accurate Auctions, www.accurateauctions.com

George Sakier tall compote, circa 1920s, green glass, unmarked, 5-3/4" h. **$30**

Courtesy of Main Street Mining Co. Auctions, www.mainstreetmining.com

GLASS

gallé

GALLÉ GLASS WAS made in Nancy, France, by Emile Gallé, founder of the Nancy School and leader in the Art Nouveau movement in France. Much of his glass, both enameled and cameo, is decorated with naturalistic motifs. The finest pieces were made in the last two decades of the 19th century and the opening years of the 20th.

Pieces marked with a star preceding the name were made between 1904, the year of Gallé's death, and 1914.

Vase in green with cameo bleeding heart flowers, stems, and leaves descending from top of vase, acid-textured background, three-sectioned top, closed top with open sides, signed "Gallé" on side in cameo, engraved "Nancy Depose Ges Gesck" on underside, 13" h. **$6,814**

Courtesy of James D. Julia, Inc., www.jamesdjulia.com

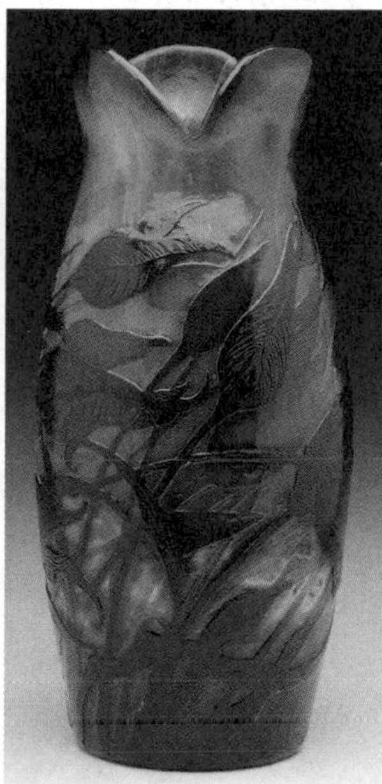

Vase with floral cameo acid-cut decoration in brown, purple, and white against amber background with tortoiseshell appearance, fire polished, irregular rim, signed on back in cameo with Oriental-style "Gallé" signature, 11-1/4" h. **$11,850**

Courtesy of James D. Julia, Inc., www.jamesdjulia.com

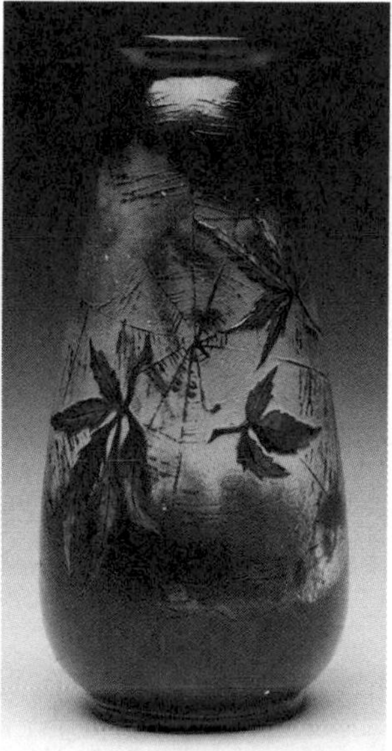

Vase with cameo spider web on front with fallen leaves in red cameo with blue opalescence caught in web, two red falling cameo leaves on back, acid-textured clear shading to red background, signed on underside with blue opalescence signature "E. Gallé" with fallen leaf, 6-1/2" h. **$5,036**

Courtesy of James D. Julia, Inc., www.jamesdjulia.com

top lot

Vase with grapevine and spider web design in yellow and lavender with white background and dark lavender cameo carved overlay, 12" h. $14,160

COURTESY OF WOODY AUCTION, WWW.WOODYAUCTION.COM

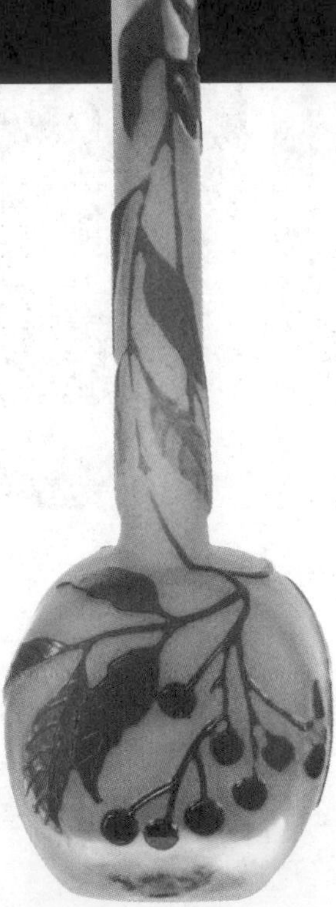

Stick vase, yellow background with cameo carved cranberry overlay with leaf and berry décor, 6-3/4" h. **$767**

Courtesy of Woody Auction, www.woodyauction.com

Vase with red acid-cut cameo flower, stems, and leaves against frosted pastel yellow background, windowpane technique where frosted area is not applied behind flowers, signed "Gallé" on side in cameo, 6-1/2" h. **$2,133**

Courtesy of James D. Julia, Inc., www.jamesdjulia.com

French cameo egg-shaped covered box in white, yellow, orange and green, with vintage motif, 5" h...................... **$3,540**

Courtesy of Woody Auction, www.woodyauction.com

Mold-blown and overlay vase with pomegranates and leaves of fuchsia and lavender, signed, 11-1/2" h. **$10,980**

Courtesy of Royal Crest Auctioneers, Redondo Beach, California

Vase with crocus design, colorless glass with opaque white and yellow, light blue and purple overlay, cut, polished and etched, partially fire polished, circa 1910, signed, 5" h. **$2,542**

Courtesy of Henry's Auktionshaus, www.henrys.de

Dragonfly cameo vase, amber to frosted clear with dragonfly, pond, and water lilies, flared rim, tapered neck, bulbous body, 23" h., 8-1/4" dia... **$5,015**

Courtesy of Burchard Galleries, www.burchardgalleries.com

Two-handled vase in white, yellow, and red with cameo leaf and berry design, signed *Gallé, 5-1/2" h...**$2,124**

Courtesy of Woody Auction, www.woodyauction.com

Acid-etched cameo bowl with flowers, circa 1910, signed "Gallé" on body, 3-1/4" h., 4-1/2" dia....................... **$1,024**

Courtesy of Rago Arts and Auctions, www.ragoarts.com

Pair of enameled cabinet vases with antelope, circa 1890s, both with enameled Gallé signature to base, overall very good condition, minor nicks to enamel and light scratches to both, 4" h., 2-1/2" dia........ **$768**

Courtesy of Rago Auctions, www.ragoarts.com

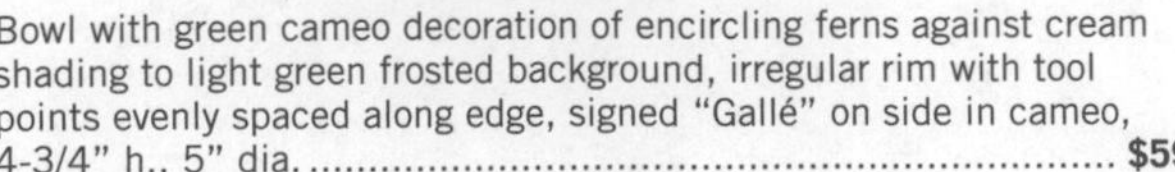

Bowl with green cameo decoration of encircling ferns against cream shading to light green frosted background, irregular rim with tool points evenly spaced along edge, signed "Gallé" on side in cameo, 4-3/4" h., 5" dia. **$592**

Courtesy of James D. Julia, Inc., www.jamesdjulia.com

Scenic cameo vase, hand blown and cut, converted into lamp, circa 1905, 6" h. **$484**

Courtesy of Bruhn's Auction Gallery, www.bruhnsauction.com

GLASS

heisey

NUMEROUS TYPES OF FINE GLASS were made by A.H. Heisey & Co., Newark, Ohio, from 1895. The company's trademark, an H enclosed within a diamond, has become known to most glass collectors. The company's name and molds were acquired by Imperial Glass Co., Bellaire, Ohio, in 1958, and some pieces have been reissued.

Orchid pattern elegant glassware, approximately 36 pieces including 64 oz. jug, square covered butter dish, large salad bowl, low water goblets, flat iced tea, plates, sherbet dishes, creamer, sugar, and pair of candleholders, 5-3/8" h. to 11-1/2" h. **$472**

Courtesy of Burchard Galleries, www.burchardgalleries.com

Prince of Wales pattern seven-piece water set, colorless with traces of gilt decoration, water pitcher and six tumblers with factory polished base, each piece with H-in-diamond trademark, first quarter 20th century, pitcher with pattern chip, flake and minor bruise, minute refracting spide mark on spout as made, 4" to 8-3/4"....**$108**

Courtesy of Jeffrey S. Evans & Associates, www.jeffreysevans.com

No. 335/Prince of Wales pattern ruby-stained four-piece water set, colorless, pitcher and three tumblers with factory polished base, circa 1920, each etched with H-in-diamond trademark, 3-7/8" to 8-3/4" h.......................................**$420**

Courtesy of Jeffrey S. Evans & Associates, www.jeffreysevans.com

Two toothpick holders, one colorless with gilt decoration and one signed Prison Stripe pattern example, circa 1901 and 1906, 2-3/8" h. and 2-1/2" h...**$168**

Courtesy of Jeffrey S. Evans & Associates, www.jeffreysevans.com

Prison Stripe pattern straw holder, excellent condition, 10" h. **$366**

Courtesy of Morphy Auctions, morphyauctions.com

▲ No. 1280/Winged Scroll pattern seven-piece berry set, circa 1900, custard with gilt decoration, master bowl and six sauce/berry bowls, 1-1/4" to 3-3/8" h. **$108**

Courtesy of Jeffrey S. Evans & Associates, www.jeffreysevans.com

Two No. 1280/Winged Scroll pattern table articles, custard with gilt decoration, cruet with pressed-facet topper and celery vase, circa 1900, 5" h. and 6" h.. **$48**

Courtesy of Jeffrey S. Evans & Associates, www.jeffreysevans.com

No. 1220/Punty Band pattern ruby-stained cruet, colorless, pressed-facet stopper, souvenir lettering, 1896-1910, 5-7/8" h. **$132**

Courtesy of Jeffrey S. Evans & Associates, www.jeffreysevans.com

Two perfume bottles, colorless with floral and foliate etched designs and original stoppers, larger bottle with etching of bird, very good condition, 8-3/4" h. and 5-1/2" h. **$85**

Courtesy of Conestoga Auction Co./Hess Auction Group, www.hessauctiongroup.com

◀ Glass and silver shaker, silver floral motifs over body and silver trim to top and bottom, three-part design, stopper, eye shield, and body, marked "41" underneath stopper and under shaker, very good condition, 12" h. x 3-1/2" w. **$500**

Courtesy of Auctionata, www.auctionata.com

Twelve cocktail glasses with figural seahorse stems (two shown), six amber, six clear, signed with H-in-diamond trademark, 6-7/8" h......... **$1,888**

Courtesy of Burchard Galleries, www.burchardgalleries.com

GLASS

imperial

FROM 1902 UNTIL 1984, Imperial Glass Co. of Bellaire, Ohio, produced handmade glass. Early pressed glass production often imitated cut glass and may bear the raised "NUCUT" mark in the interior center. In the second decade of the 1900s, Imperial was one of the dominant manufacturers of iridescent or carnival glass. When glass collecting gained popularity in the 1970s, Imperial again produced carnival glass and a line of multicolored slag glass. Imperial purchased molds from closing glasshouses and continued many lines popularized by others including Central, Heisey, and Cambridge. These reissues may cause confusion, but they were often marked.

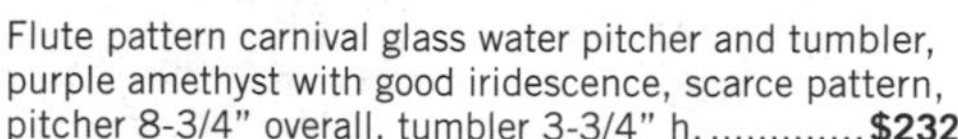

Flute pattern carnival glass water pitcher and tumbler, purple amethyst with good iridescence, scarce pattern, pitcher 8-3/4" overall, tumbler 3-3/4" h. **$232**

Courtesy of Green Valley Auctions & Moving, Inc., www.greenvalleyauctions.com

Zipper Loop pattern carnival glass kerosene footed finger lamp, marigold, first quarter 20th century, No. 1 Taplin-Brown collar fitted with period No. 0 slip burner and colorless chimney with serrated scalloped top, 4-3/4" h. to top of collar, foot 3-5/8" dia. **$240**

Courtesy of Jeffrey S. Evans & Associates, www.jeffreysevans.com

◀ Four assorted Hobnail/Dew Drop pattern items, circa 1970s, one in uranium, three in opalescent, bowl, compote with goffered rim, signed pedestal covered dish with milk glass cover and foot, and box with factory-polished rim, lacking cover, 2-3/4" h. to 7-3/4" h. overall, bowl 10" dia. **$60**

Courtesy of Jeffrey S. Evans & Associates, www.jeffreysevans.com

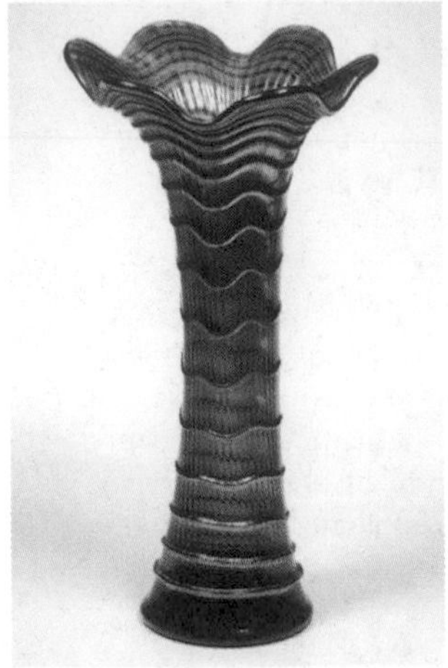

Ripple pattern carnival glass vase with ruffled rim, first half of 20th century, amethyst iridescent, 13-1/8" h., 3-7/8" dia.......................... **$108**

Courtesy of Jeffrey S. Evans & Associates, www.jeffreysevans.com

No. 2 Scroll Americana pattern decanter, circa 1960, turquoise, with original stopper, 10-1/2" h. overall. **$72**

Courtesy of Jeffrey S. Evans & Associates, www.jeffreysevans.com

Bundling/Pattern No. 9 miniature finger oil lamp, fourth quarter 19th century, crystal/colorless, pattern base with handle and matching umbrella shade, period burner and chimney, 7-7/8" h. to top of shade, 3-1/2" h. base to top of collar. **$120**

Courtesy of Jeffrey S. Evans & Associates, www.jeffreysevans.com

Pair of ruby flash Cape Cod pattern decanters, both with residue build-up in inner portions and minor wear, one with small chips on inner top rim and stopper, 9-1/4" h...... **$48**

Courtesy of Barry S. Slosberg, Inc. Auctioneers, www.bssauction.com

Three-in-one marmalade/jam jar, Vaseline (black lighted), first half 20th century, undamaged with minute roughness to cover rim, as made, 6-1/2" h. overall. **$96**

Courtesy of Jeffrey S. Evans & Associates, www.jeffreysevans.com

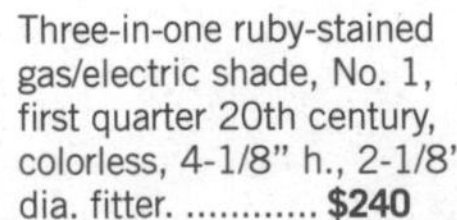

Three-in-one ruby-stained gas/electric shade, No. 1, first quarter 20th century, colorless, 4-1/8" h., 2-1/8" dia. fitter. **$240**

Courtesy of Jeffrey S. Evans & Associates, www.jeffreysevans.com

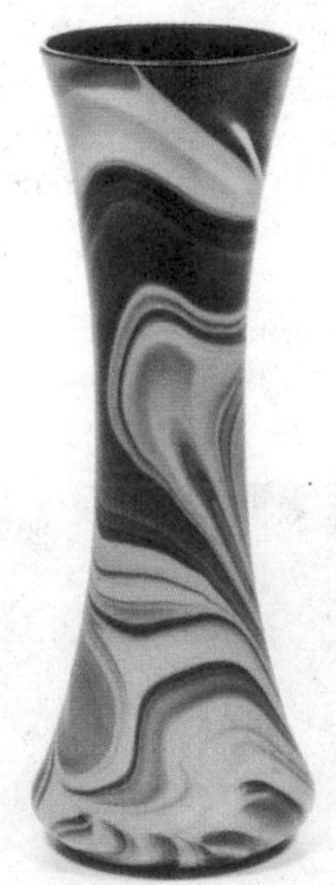

Lead lustre vase, shape number 622, circa 1925, marbled medium to light blue, cobalt blue interior, polished pontil mark, 10-1/4" h.................. **$240**

Courtesy of Jeffrey S. Evans & Associates, www.jeffreysevans.com

GLASS

lalique

RENÉ JULES LALIQUE was born on April 6,1860, in the village of Ay, in the Champagne region of France. In 1862, his family moved to the suburbs of Paris.

In 1872, Lalique began attending College Turgot where he began studying drawing with Justin-Marie Lequien. After the death of his father in 1876, Lalique began working as an apprentice to Louis Aucoc, who was a prominent jeweler and goldsmith in Paris.

Lalique moved to London in 1878 to continue his studies. He spent two years attending Sydenham College, developing his graphic design skills. He returned to Paris in 1880 and worked as an illustrator of jewelry, creating designs for Cartier, among others. In 1884, Lalique's drawings were displayed at the National Exhibition of Industrial Arts, organized at the Louvre.

At the end of 1885, Lalique took over Jules Destapes' jewelry workshop. Lalique's design began to incorporate translucent enamels, semiprecious stones, ivory, and hard stones. In 1889, at the Universal Exhibition in Paris, the jewelry firms of Vever and Boucheron included collaborative works by Lalique in their displays.

In the early 1890s, Lalique began to incorporate glass into his jewelry, and in 1893 he took part in a competition organized by the Union Centrale des Arts Decoratifs to design a drinking vessel. He won second prize.

Lalique opened his first Paris retail shop in 1905, near the perfume business of François Coty. Coty commissioned Lalique to design his perfume labels in 1907, and he also created his first perfume bottles for Coty.

In the first decade of the 20th century, Lalique continued to experiment with glass manufacturing techniques and mounted his first show devoted entirely to glass in 1911.

During World War I, Lalique's first factory was forced to close, but the construction of a new factory was soon begun in Wingen-sur-Moder, in the Alsace region. It was completed in 1921, and still produces Lalique crystal today.

In 1925, Lalique designed the first "car mascot" (hood ornament) for Citroën, the French automobile company. For the next six years, Lalique would design 29 models for companies such as Bentley, Bugatti, Delage, Hispano-Suiza, Rolls Royce, and Voisin.

Lalique's second boutique opened in 1931, and this location continues to serve as the main Lalique showroom today.

René Lalique died on May 5, 1945, at the age of 85. His son, Marc, took over the business at that time, and when Marc died in 1977, his daughter, Marie-Claude Lalique Dedouvre, assumed control of the company. She sold her interest in the firm and retired in 1994.

For more information on Lalique, see *Warman's Lalique Identification and Price Guide* by Mark F. Moran.

(Editor's Note: In some of the descriptions of Lalique pieces that follow, you will find notations like "M p. 478, No. 1100" or "Marcilhac 952, pg. 428." This refers to the page and serial numbers found in *René Lalique, maître-verrier, 1860-1945: Analyse de L'oeuvre et Catalogue Raisonné,* by Félix Marcilhac, published in 1989 and revised in 1994. Printed entirely in French, this book of more than 1,000 pages is the definitive guide to Lalique's work, and listings from auction catalogs typically cite the Marcilhac guide as a reference.)

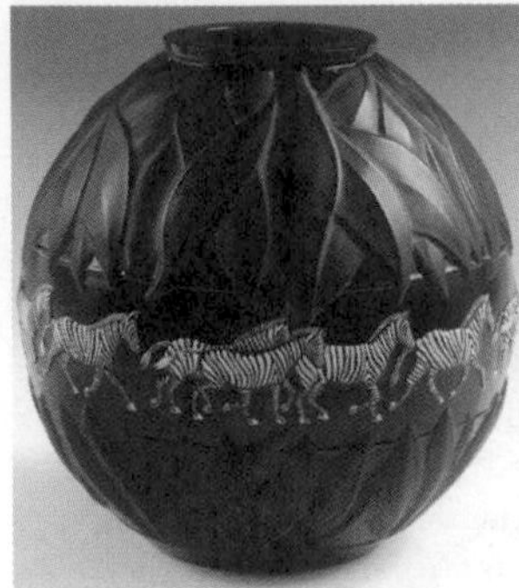

Tanzania black crystal vase with zebra images encircling center of body, engraved signature on polished glass base, 8-1/2" h. x 7-1/2" d. **$2,784**

Courtesy of Dirk Soulis Auctions, www.dirksoulisauctions.com

Scent bottle with deeply impressed dahlia flowers on each flat side, frosted glass in light green patination, frosted mushroom-shaped stopper, signed on underside "R. Lalique France" in etched block letters, 8-1/4" h........................... **$1,185**

Courtesy of James D. Julia, Inc., www.jamesdjulia.com

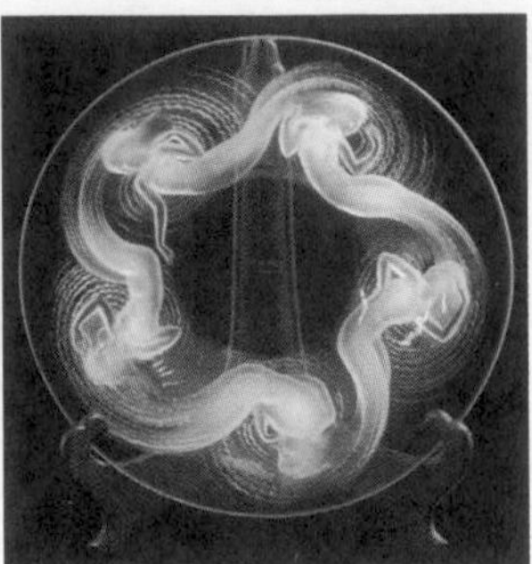

Calypso pattern molded plate, circa 1930, Marcilhac 413, iridescent glass, 14-1/2" d. **$2,722**

Courtesy of A.N. Abell Auction Co., www.abell.com

Monnaie du Pape pattern vase, circa 1914, molded frosted dark amber with leaf decoration, impressed "R. Lalique" on center base, overall very good condition, outer rim edge with two polished areas, 9-1/4" h. x 6-1/2" d... **$4,464**

Courtesy of Case Antiques Auction & Appraisal, www.caseantiques.com

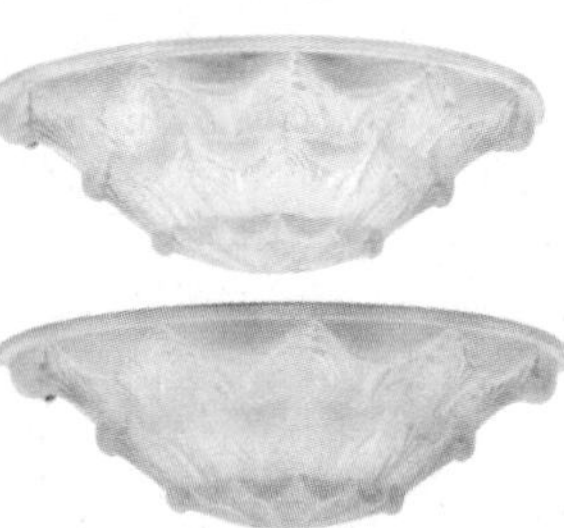

Pair of frosted Gaillon wall scones, circa 1927, very good condition, chipping near holes where bracket attaches to reverse, chipping to rim edges to side facing wall, 5-3/8" h. x 17-3/4" w. **$5,500**

Courtesy of Heritage Auctions, ha.com

Uncommon Perruches vase, form 876, circa 1919, rare butterscotch color, engraved R. Lalique signature, 10-1/4" h. x 9-1/2" w. x 9-1/2" d.......**$15,990**

Courtesy of Le Shoppe Too, www.leshoppe.net

Miro Dena glass perfume counter sign, circa 1925, molded glass with self-easel, Lalique mark, 6-1/8" h. ... **$8,610**

Courtesy of Perfume Bottles Auction, www.perfumebottlesauction.com

Flora Bella blue glass coupe, circa 1930, "R Lalique France" marking, good condition, moderate scratches to bowl and surface, fleabites and two chips to rim, large chip to floral decoration, repaired chip, 15-1/2" d. **$3,750**

Courtesy of Heritage Auctions, ha.com

Goblet-shaped vase, wheel cut topaz glass, six caryatid-type relief figures around body, inscribed "R. Lalique", 7-7/8" h. **$2,460**

Courtesy of Alex Cooper Auctioneers, www.alexcooper.com

Laurier pattern vase with high relief opalescent leaves and berries encircling body, signed with carved signature "R. Lalique France" on side near foot, marked "No. 947" on underside, 7" h. **$474**

Courtesy of James D. Julia, Inc., www.jamesdjulia.com

top lot!

Oiseau de Feu clear and frosted decorative object, circa 1922, illumination possible, molded "R. Lalique" signature, 17" w. **$51,660**

COURTESY OF A.B. LEVY'S, WWW.ABLEVYS.COM

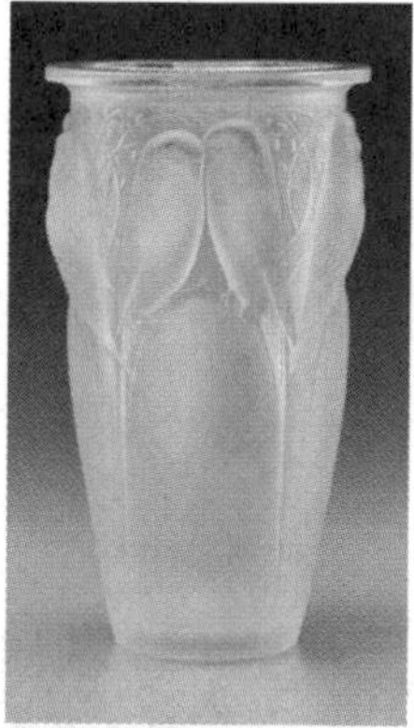

Ceylan opalescent vase, wheel carved "R. Lalique France" signature, engraved No. 905, scuffing to rim and base, two fleabites to underside, 9-1/2" h. **$35,000**

Courtesy of Heritage Auctions, ha.com

Papillons clear, frosted, and polished vase with blue patina, circa 1936, acid-stamped "R. Lalique", 9" h. **$20,910**

Courtesy of A.B. Levy's, www.ablevys.com

Clear crystal horse head sculpture, 20th century, acid-stamped Lalique, 20" h... **$8,757**

Courtesy of Cottone Auctions, www.cottoneauctions.com

Lievres vase in blue, circa 1923, molded "R. Lalique" mark, good condition, fleabite and minor wax residue to underside, 6-1/2" w. **$6,562**

Courtesy of Heritage Auctions, ha.com

GLASS

libbey glass

IN 1878, William L. Libbey obtained a lease on the New England Glass Co. of Cambridge, Massachusetts, changing the name to the New England Glass Works, W. L. Libbey and Son, Proprietors. After his death in 1883, his son, Edward D. Libbey, continued to operate the company at Cambridge until 1888, when the factory was closed.

Edward Libbey moved to Toledo, Ohio, and set up the company subsequently known as Libbey Glass Co. During the 1880s, the firm's master technician, Joseph Locke, developed the now much desired colored art glass lines of Agata, Amberina, Peach Blow, and Pomona. Renowned for its cut glass of the Brilliant Period, the company continues in operation today as Libbey Glassware, a division of Owens-Illinois, Inc.

Two low bowls, one in Cluster pattern, one in Gem pattern, some tooth roughness on Gem pattern bowl, 8-3/4" h. **$224**

Courtesy of Woody Auction, www.woodyauction.com

Cologne bottle, footed, four-petaled lip, shading from ruby at top to topaz, conforming original stopper, marked "Amberina/Libbey" on base of bottle, plug, and stopper, repair to dauber, one of four Amerbina perfume/cologne bottle models issued by Libbey Cut Glass Co. in 1918 in commemoration of company anniversary, 8-1/2" h. **$868**

Courtesy of Brunk Auctions, www.brunkauctions.com

Hand-painted open salt, 19th century, made for Columbian World's Fair, marked Libbey Cut Glass, Toledo, Ohio, 1-1/4" h. x 2" w. **$84**

Courtesy of Main Street Mining Co. Auctions, www.mainstreetmining.com

Silhouette center bowl with moonstone elephant-stem and foot, factory polished base, second quarter 20th century, 7-5/8" h., 11" dia. overall. **$1,320**

Courtesy of Jeffrey S. Evans & Associates, www.jeffreysevans.com

Ice bucket, good condition with age appropriate wear, tiny nicks, 6-1/2" h., 6-1/2" dia. **$780**

Courtesy of Milestone Auctions, www.milestoneauctions.com

Five-piece glass set, circa 1886, ball-form Spot-Optic pattern water pitcher with square-form rim and applied colorless handle and four Diamond-Optic pattern tumblers, Pomona etching, colorless with light amber iridescence and light blue staining, cornflower garland decoration, each with polished pontil mark, New England Glass Works, 3-3/4" h. to 7" h... **$144**

Courtesy of Jeffrey S. Evans & Associates, www.jeffreysevans.com

Biscuit jar in Nash Series pattern, early 20th century, with Oxford pattern sterling collar, lid, and foot, marked "Tiffany & Company" on foot, 11" h. Provenance: Past association with noted businessman and philanthropist Diamond Jim Brady............................. **$2,950**

Courtesy of Woody Auction, www.woodyauction.com

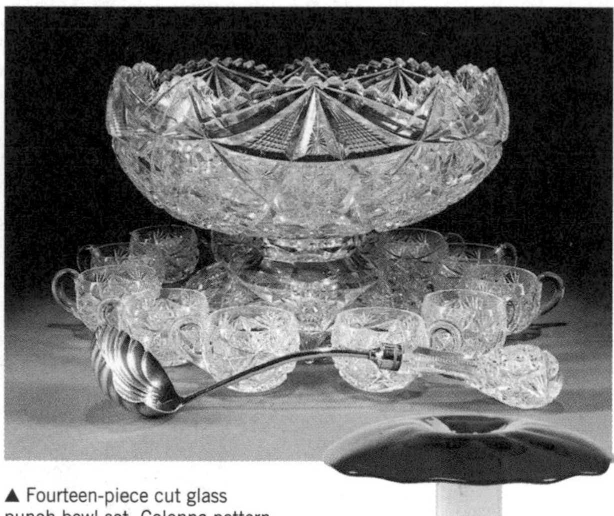

▲ Fourteen-piece cut glass punch bowl set, Colonna pattern, late 19th/early 20th century, signed, two-part bowl, 9-1/2" h., 13-1/2" dia.; 12 cups, 2-1/8" h.; and Gorham silver-plate and cut glass ladle, 13" l. **$1,792**

Courtesy of Neal Auction Co., www.nealauction.com

◀ Cut glass flower center bottle, textured diamond pattern on short neck with faceted ring collar, body alternating hobstar and stylized cut pattern, radiant cut foot, likely Libbey Cut Glass Co., some surface wear, some very minor flaking overall, 6" h. x 8" w......................... **$212**

Courtesy of Austin Auction Gallery, www.austinauction.com

Rib-optic mushroom-form vase with flanged fuchsia rim, polished pontil mark with "Amberina/Libbey" marking, etched "Libbey Glass Co. Circa 1917" signature, 2-7/8" h. overall, 2-7/8" dia. base, 6" dia. rim........................ **$192**

Courtesy of Jeffrey S. Evans & Associates, www.jeffreysevans.com

GLASS

mary gregory

GLASS ENAMELED IN white with silhouette-type figures, primarily of children, is now termed "Mary Gregory" and was attributed to the Boston and Sandwich Glass Co. However, recent research has proven conclusively that this was not decorated by Mary Gregory nor was it made at the Sandwich plant. Gregory was employed by Boston and Sandwich Glass Co. as a decorator; however, records show her assignment was the painting of naturalistic landscape scenes on larger items such as lamps and shades but never the charming children for which her name has become synonymous. Further, in the inspection of fragments from the factory site, no paintings of children were found.

It is now known that all wares called "Mary Gregory" originated in Bohemia beginning in the late 19th century and were extensively exported to England and the United States well into the 20th century.

For further information, see *The Glass Industry in Sandwich, Volume 4* by Raymond E. Barlow and Joan E. Kaiser, and *Mary Gregory Glassware, 1880-1900* by R. & D. Truitt.

Glass decanter, 19th century, 10" h.........**$39**

Courtesy of Sheppard's Irish Auction House, www.sheppards.ie

Seven tumblers including three pseudo-cameo, two spatter, and one ribbed spiral with spatter decoration, likely Mary Gregory, late 19th/early 20th century, 3-3/4" h. to 4-1/4" h. **$216**

Courtesy of Jeffrey S. Evans & Associates, www.jeffreysevans.com

Cranberry fruit bowl in enamel with two cherubs, four gilt-trimmed clear glass feet, 5-1/2" h., 5" sq. **$300**

Courtesy of Farmer Auctions, www.farmer-auctions.com

Enameled glass candleholder, 26-1/4" h. x 9" w. x 9" d............ **$232**

Courtesy of Vogt Appraisers & Auctioneers, www.vogtauction.com

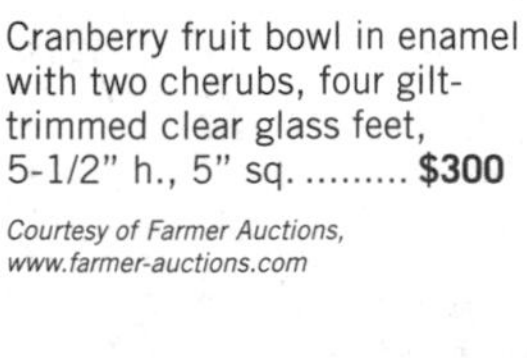

◀ Pair of cranberry glass vases with covers, woman with companion, 9-2/3" h. **231**

Courtesy of Mossgreen Auctions, www.mossgreen.com.au

Pair of Bohemian amethyst vases, baluster form with gilt accents to neck and foot, one with enamel decoration of man with butterfly net and one with woman feeding birds, one marked "26" and other "13" on underside, 10-7/8" h.......... **$248**

Courtesy of Ahlers & Ogletree Auction Gallery, www.aandoauctions.com

Hinged jewel box with enamel décor of young boy with flower, gilt metal trim, 4-1/2" h. x 4-1/2" w. **$106**

Courtesy of Woody Auction, www.woodyauction.com

Pair of barber tonic bottles, cobalt blue example with girl playing tennis, amethyst example with girl in garden with basket, cobalt with damaged ceramic spout, amethyst bottle with metal spout, both 9" h... **$213**

Courtesy of Morphy Auctions, morphyauctions.com

GLASS

milk glass

"MILK GLASS" IS a general term for opaque colored glass. Though the name would lead you to believe it, white wasn't the only color produced.

According to *Warman's Depression Glass* author and expert Ellen Schroy, "Colored milk glasses, such as opaque black, green, or pink, usually command higher prices. Beware of reproductions in green and pink. Always question a milk glass pattern found in cobalt blue. Swirled colors are a whole other topic and very desirable."

The number of patterns, forms, and objects made is limited only by the imagination. Commonly found milk glass items include dishes (especially the ever-popular animals on nests), vases, dresser sets, figurines, lanterns, boxes, and perfume bottles.

After World War I, the popularity of milk glass waned but production continued. Milk glass made during the 1930s and 1940s is often considered of lower quality than other periods because of the economic Depression and wartime manufacturing difficulties.

"The milk glass made by Westmoreland, Kemple, Fenton, etc., was designed to be used as dinnerware," Schroy said. "Much of the milk glass we see at flea markets and antique shows and in shops now is coming out of homes and estates where 1940-1950s-era brides are disposing of their settings.

"Care should be taken when purchasing, transporting, and using this era of milk glass as it is very intolerant of temperature changes," Schroy said. "Don't buy a piece at a flea market unless you can protect it well for its trip to your home. And when you get it home, let it sit for several hours so its temperature evens out to what your normal home temperature is. It's almost a given if you take a piece of cold glass and submerge it into a nice warm bath, it's going to crack. And never, ever expose it to the high temps of a modern dishwasher."

So how do you tell the old from the new? Schroy said getting your hands on it is often the only way to tell. "Milk glass should have a wonderful silky texture. Any piece that is grainy is probably new," she said. "The best test is to look for the 'ring of fire', which will be easy to see in the sunlight. Hold the piece of milk glass up to a good light source (I prefer natural light) and see if there is a halo of iridescent colors right around the edge, look for reds, blues, and golds. This ring was caused by the addition of iridized salts into the milk glass formula. If this ring is present, it's probably an old piece." However, 1950s-era milk glass does not have this telltale ring, she said.

Old milk glass should also carry appropriate marks and signs, like the "ring

Two covered duck-shaped dishes, Atterbury & Co., one with amethyst head and blue eyes, one with mottled opaque blue head and ruby eyes, each embossed "PATD MARCH 15-1887" on base, minute loss to one eye, minor flaking to tail, and minor mold roughness as made to amethyst-headed example, minor mold roughness as made to blue-headed example, 4-3/4" h. x 4" w. x 9" d. **$300**

Courtesy of Jeffrey S. Evans & Associates, www.jeffreysevans.com

Steer's head covered dish with applied black eyes, Challinor, Taylor & Co., circa 1885-1893, excellent overall condition, sliver chip to front of one ear, base with annealing lines and manufacturing imperfection to underside as made, flaking to rim, 5" h. overall x 5-1/4" w., base 7-7/8" dia. **$2,400**

Courtesy of Jeffrey S. Evans & Associates, www.jeffreysevans.com

Four-piece opalescent table set with monkey figures, possibly Valley Glass Co., Beaver Falls, Pennsylvania, circa 1890, covered butter dish, covered sugar bowl, creamer, and spooner, each piece with rayed base, butter undamaged with minute flake to cover rim, sugar base with minute flake to one scallop and moderate spall to table ring, creamer with crack running from lower terminal of handle, 5" h. to 7-1/4" h. overall. **$2,040**

Courtesy of Jeffrey S. Evans & Associates, www.jeffreysevans.com

The Family Creamer, opaque white, floral headdress and original red eyes, fourth quarter 19th century, 5" h., 4-1/8" dia. **$330**

Courtesy of Jeffrey S. Evans & Associates, www.jeffreysevans.com

of fire"; appropriate patterns for specific makers are also something to watch for, such as Fenton's Hobnail pattern. Collectors should always check for condition issues such as damage and discoloration. According to Schroy, there is no remedy for discolored glass, and cracked and chipped pieces should be avoided, as they are prone to further damage.

— *Karen Knapstein* Print Editor, *Antique Trader Magazine*

Westmoreland banana boat footed compote with Doric lace edge, 8-1/2" h. x 12" l. x 6-3/8" d.... **$30**

Courtesy of King Galleries, wwwkinggalleriesauction.com

Bohemian lusters with hand-painted rosettes, gold luster on trim, 10 prisms, 12-1/2" h....... **$270**

Courtesy of John McInnis Auctioneers, www.mcinnisauctions.com

Chinese Gu Yue Xusan-style famille rose painted snuff bottle, likely 19th century, with water birds and flowering plants, stopper lacking spoon, 2-1/4" h................. **$960**

Courtesy of Neal Auction Co., www.nealauction.com

Crown-shaped gasoline pump globe, near mint condition, 17" h. **$324**

Courtesy of Milestone Auctions, www.milestoneauctions.com

White eagle gasoline pump globe, blunt nose on eagle figure, excellent condition, old tight hairline crack from tail to talon on one side, 21" h... **$1,800**

Courtesy of Rich Penn Auctions, www.richpennauctions.com

Two scent bottles: Late Victorian silver-capped scent bottle in case, unmarked, hinged rounded cover chased with scrolls and foliage, spherical shape, 2-3/4" h., and porcelain tapered scent bottle with brass screw cover, painted in gilt with butterfly and flowers on white ground, 6-1/4" l...................... **$253**

Courtesy of Dreweatts & Bloomsbury, www.dreweatts.com

GLASS

mt. washington

A WIDE DIVERSITY of glass was made by the Mt. Washington Glass Co. of New Bedford, Massachusetts, between 1869 and 1900. It was succeeded in 1900 by the Pairpoint Manufacturing Co. Throughout its history, the Mt. Washington Glass Co. made different types of glass including pressed, blown, art, lava, Napoli, cameo, cut, Albertine, Peachblow, Burmese, Crown Milano, Royal Flemish, and Verona.

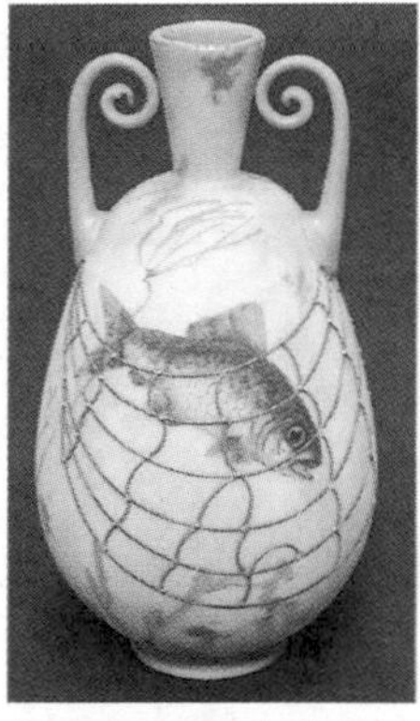

Burmese vase, shaded body with "Fish in a Golden Net" motif of three fish and variety of aquatic plants overlaid with gold enamel fishing net, double applied handles, 10" h. **$5,747**

Courtesy of Early Auction Co., www.earlyauctionco.com

Burmese ribbed-barrel mustard pot, fourth quarter 19th century, glossy finish, period quadruple-plate hinged lid and spoon, 4-3/8" h. **$192**

Courtesy of Jeffrey S. Evans & Associates, www.jeffreysevans.com

Burmese ribbed cruet with floral decoration and fitted stopper, 6-1/2" h. x 4" w. ... **$413**

Courtesy of Woody Auction, www.woodyauction.com

Colonial Ware vase with dancing Colonial woman, fourth quarter 19th century, opaque white with gilt and polychrome enamel decoration, bulbous base with elongated neck and flared rim, factory polished base, 9-7/8" h. **$132**

Courtesy of Jeffrey S. Evans & Associates, www.jeffreysevans.com

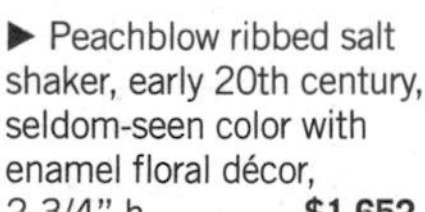

► Peachblow ribbed salt shaker, early 20th century, seldom-seen color with enamel floral décor, 2-3/4" h. **$1,652**

Courtesy of Woody Auction, www.woodyauction.com

◄ Crown Milano vase with ruffled rim, bulbous body with acorns and oak leaves, and gilt trim, 8-1/2" h. **$744**

Courtesy of Case Antiques Auctions, www.caseantiques.com

Pink and yellow hat-shaped toothpick holder, enamel floral décor, 2-1/4" h. **$354**

Courtesy of Woody Auction, www.woodyauction.com

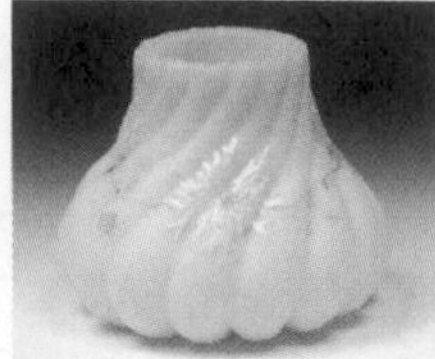

Swirled bead-top toothpick holder, circa 1890, opal with blue shading and polychrome decoration, beaded rim, 2" h. **$228**

Courtesy of Jeffrey S. Evans & Associates, www.jeffreysevans.com

Crown Milano No. 850 vase, fourth quarter 19th century, bulbous form with swirled body, floral design, opaque white with cream exterior with blue and green staining and gold enamel decoration, polished pontil mark, 5-3/4" h............... **$660**

Courtesy of Jeffrey S. Evans & Associates, www.jeffreysevans.com

Royal Flemish vase with owls on branches against moon, squared body with cutout mouth and curling applied handles, gold enamel highlights, cutout mouth reduced in size, 8-1/2" h.... **$1,180**

Courtesy of Early Auction Co., www.earlyauctionco.com

Melon ribbed biscuit jar, cream-colored glass, spatter blue with pink roses and jeweled stamens, missing three jewels, 7" w. **$181**

Courtesy of Jaremos Estate Liquidators, www.jaremos.com

Rare 1882 Mt. Washington/Pairpoint Georgian-style biscuit barrel, late 19th century, poppies theme with pink drapery relief medallion borders and heavy enamel floral accents with ruby cabachons, two-line style and batch designation and early underlined P in diamond mark denoting Pairpoint, 8-1/2" h. x 6-1/2" w. x 6-1/2" d. **$247**

Courtesy of Accurate Auctions, www.accurateauctions.com

Five toothpick holders, fourth quarter 19th century, various overlaid colors with polychrome decoration, each with satin finish and polished pontil mark, two examples with applied colorless rims, 2-1/2" h. to 3-1/2" h. **$570**

Courtesy of Jeffrey S. Evans & Associates, www.jeffreysevans.com

Three-piece glass condiment set, blue and cream ribbed salt and pepper shaker with pink mustard jar set on silver-plate frame. **$324**

Courtesy of Woody Auction, www.woodyauction.com

Scarce fig/beet mucilage pot, circa 1893-1900, cased cranberry with polychrome spider mum decoration, satin finish, quadruple-plate cap with attached original brush, 3" h.....**$1,200**

Courtesy of Jeffrey S. Evans & Associates, www.jeffreysevans.com

GLASS

murano glass

IN THE 1950S, the American home came alive with vibrant-colored decorative items, abstract art, and "futuristic"-designed furniture. The colorless geometry of the 1930s was out.

Over the last decade, mid-century design has once again gained favor with interior decorators, magazines, shows, and stores dedicated solely to this period. The bold colors and free-form shapes of mid-century modern Italian glass are emblematic of 1950s design. This distinctive glass has become a sought-after collectible.

Prices realized at auction for 1950s glass have seen a resurgence. However, there are still many items readily available and not always at a premium.

Italian glass can be found in many American homes. In fact, it is likely that some of the familiar glass items you grew up with were produced in Italy - the candy dish on the coffee table with the bright colors, the ashtray with the gold flecks inside. Modern glass objects from Italy were among the most widely distributed examples of 1950s design.

As with any decorative art form, there are varying levels of achievement in the design and execution of glass from this period. While you should always buy what you love, as there is never a guarantee return on investment, buying the best representation of an item is wise. In considering modern Italian glass, several points make one piece stand above another.

Italy has a centuries-old tradition of glassmaking, an industry whose center is the group of islands known as Murano in the lagoon of Venice. The most recognized and desirable Italian glass comes from three companies: Seguso, Venini, and Barovier & Toso.

Italy offers a vast array of talented glass artists. Top end collectors seem to favor Carlo Scarpa from Venini, Napoleone Martinuzzi (who worked at Venini from 1925-1932), and Dino Martens of Aureliano Toso. You can expect to pay several thousand dollars for a fine piece by one of these artists.

For slimmer collecting budgets, good quality examples by other artists are available and more affordable. Alfredo Barbini and Fulvio Biaconi (for Venini) are two of them. While some of their work does command top dollar, many of their pieces are priced for the novice collector.

A few mid-century designs can still be found that could prove to be sleepers in the near future. Look for Inciso vases by Venini, Aborigeni pieces by Barovier & Toso, and Soffiati examples by Giacomo Cappellin. Each of these designs is

Commedia dell'Arte glass figurine "Pantalone," Fulvio Bianconi (1915-1996), circa 1950, three-line acid stamp "VENINI MURANO ITALIA," excellent condition, 15" x 4". **$960**

Courtesy of Rago Arts and Auctions, www.ragoarts.com

totally different from the other, yet all are reasonably priced in today's market.

Collectors should be aware that the most popular glass form is the vase, with glass sculpture following next in line. Popular sculptural forms include male or female nude figurals and pasta glass animals by Fulvio Biaconi.

Reproductions of the most famous forms of Italian glass are rampant. Some are marketed as such, while others are made to fool unsuspecting buyers. Also, and perhaps more confusing, many Italian glass designs are being produced to this day. The most common example of this is the Handkerchief vase. Originally produced by Piero Chiesa in 1937 for Fontana Arte, it was called the Paper Bag vase due to its crumpled shape. In the 1950s, Bianconi designed his own version for Venini. Since that time, generic manufacturers throughout Murano have produced countless unsigned imitations for the tourist trade. Almost all Venini handkerchief vases were signed, except for a few very valuable examples by Dino Martens.

Whether from the original manufacturer or another firm, Murano glass now being reproduced includes Sommerso designs, Barbini glass aquariums, and bowls along with Oriente designs. Venini lamps have also been reproduced. No doubt there will be more reproductions to come.

Pulegoso vase with applied handles, Napoleone Martinuzzi (1892-1977), circa 1930s, four-line acid-stamp "Venini Murano MADE IN ITALY," excellent condition, 12-1/2" x 8-1/2"..........**$19,200**

Courtesy of Rago Arts and Auctions, www.ragoarts.com

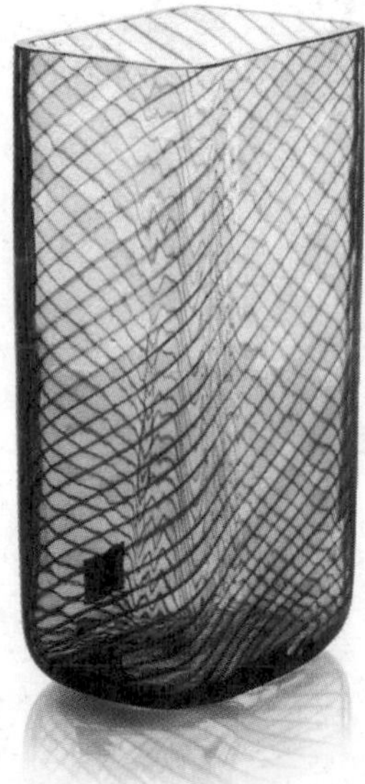

Tartan glass vase, circa 1950s-1960s, original paper Murano label, flecks and chip to rim, minor scratches to body, 9-3/4" x 5" x 3-1/2".......... **$702**

Courtesy of Rago Arts and Auctions, www.ragoarts.com

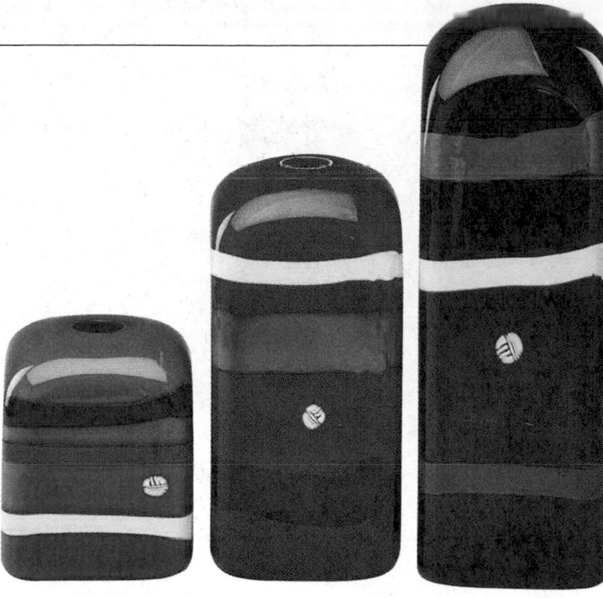

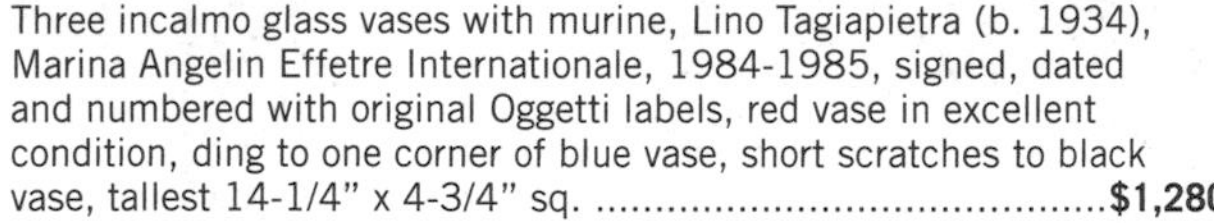

Three incalmo glass vases with murine, Lino Tagiapietra (b. 1934), Marina Angelin Effetre Internationale, 1984-1985, signed, dated and numbered with original Oggetti labels, red vase in excellent condition, ding to one corner of blue vase, short scratches to black vase, tallest 14-1/4" x 4-3/4" sq. **$1,280**

Courtesy of Rago Arts and Auctions, www.ragoarts.com

Vase, Lino Tagliapietra (b. 1934), Effetre Internationale, 1982, etched LINO TAGLIAPIETRA F31 MURANO 93/100 1982, original Oggetti decal label, overall excellent condition, some short minor scratches, 9-1/2" x 6". **$1,280**

Courtesy of Rago Arts and Auctions, www.ragoarts.com

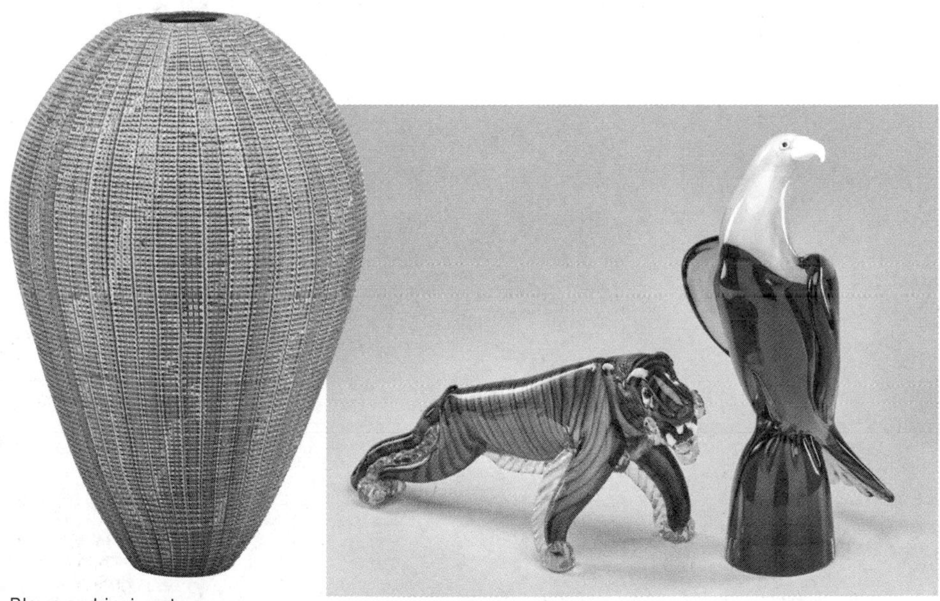

Blown and inciso glass vase, Massimilliano Schiavon (b. 1971), signed, 13-1/2" x 8-1/4"........................... **$2,500**

Courtesy of Rago Arts and Auctions, www.ragoarts.com

Glass eagle and tiger tabletop sculptures with gold foil inclusions, Livio Seguso (b.1930), late 20th century, eagle with etched signature, rough spot on end of tiger's tail, minor scuff to base of eagle, taller sculpture 15" x 7" x 4"..**$1,520**

Courtesy of Rago Arts and Auctions, www.ragoarts.com

Fluted pink to white vase, good condition, 8-1/2" w. x 20" h....... **$469**

Courtesy of Clarke Auctioneers & Appraisers, www.clarkeny.com

Doppio incalmo vase, Lino Tagliapietra (b. 1934), blown and battuo glass, signed and dated 1991, excellent condition with some accidental spots to lowest ring of clear glass, small polished chip under foot, possibly incurred in development, 17" x 4-1/4". **$5,760**

Courtesy of Rago Arts and Auctions, www.ragoarts.com

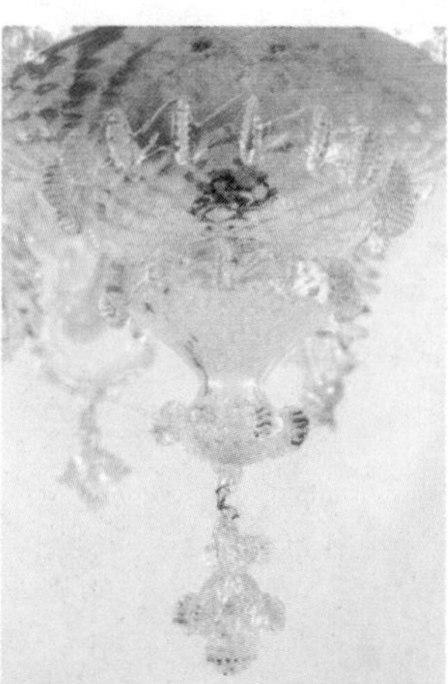

Blown glass clear chandelier with gold aventurine, attributed to Barovier & Toso, 20th century, baluster-shaped structure with gold leaf tip, diamond optic pattern, and six scrolled spiral candle arms ending in bowl-form bobeches, tapering ruffled base hung with tassel, 43" x 36"...**$2,108**

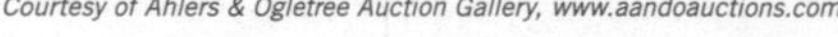

Courtesy of Ahlers & Ogletree Auction Gallery, www.aandoauctions.com

Blue parrot with red beak, Avventura wraps body, perched on clear leafy stump, excellent original condition, 11-3/4" x 5-1/2"............................... **$400**

Courtesy of Mark Mussio, Humler & Nolan, www.humlernolan.com

Pair of cranberry birds perched on clear serpentine branch balanced on gold foil base with gilded leaves applied, in style of Archimede Seguso, excellent condition, 9" x 4" across base. **$100**

Courtesy of Mark Mussio, Humler & Nolan, www.humlernolan.com

Aerial teardrop sculpture, possibly Salviati & Co., bubbles floating within, partial foil sticker where Murano can be read, excellent condition, scratches to bottom, 13" h. x 6-1/2" w., 15 lbs................. **$80**

Courtesy of Mark Mussio, Humler & Nolan, www.humlernolan.com

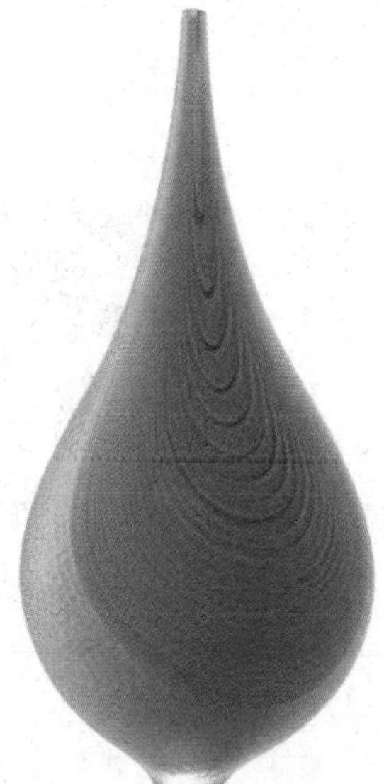

Battuto glass vase, Lino Tagliapietra (b. 1934), 1998, etched "Lino Tagliapietra 1998 X," 21-1/2" x 9-1/2" x 5-1/2". **$19,200**

Courtesy of Rago Arts, www.ragoarts.com

Murrine glass vase, Gianni Versace (1946-1997), Venini, 2001, etched "Versace Venini 2001," original Venini decal label, 10-1/2" x 6".......... **$1,920**

Courtesy of Rago Arts, www.ragoarts.com

Battuto glass vase, Vittorio Ferro (b. 1932), Fratelli Pagnin, 2000, etched Vittorio Ferro Pagnin 2000, 13" x 6". **$1,536**

Courtesy of Rago Arts, www.ragoarts.com

GLASS

northwood glass co.

NORTHWOOD GLASS CO. was founded by Harry Northwood, son of prominent English glassmaker John Northwood, who was famous for his expertise in cameo glass.

Harry migrated to America in 1881 and, after working at various glass manufacturers, formed the Northwood Glass Co. in 1896 in Indiana, Pennsylvania. In 1902 he created H. Northwood and Co. in Wheeling, West Virginia. After Northwood died in 1919, H. Northwood and Co. began to falter and eventually closed in 1925.

Northwood produced a wide variety of opalescent, decorated, and special effect glasses, and colors like iridescent blue and green, which were not widely seen at the time.

Arabian Nights pattern water pitcher, blue opalescent, ruffled circular rim, applied blue handle with pressed-fan design to upper terminal, possibly Beaumont Glass Co./Northwood Glass Co., circa 1895, 9" h. **$600**

Courtesy of Jeffrey S. Evans & Associates, www.jeffreysevans.com

Chrysanthemum Swirl pattern cruet, cranberry opalescent, applied colorless handle and pressed-facet stopper, Northwood Glass Co./Buckeye Glass Co., circa 1890, 6-1/2" h. .. **$450**

Courtesy of Jeffrey S. Evans & Associates, www.jeffreysevans.com

Chrysanthemum Swirl pattern water pitcher, cranberry opalescent, applied handle with faint pressed fan design at upper terminal, Northwood Glass Co./Buckeye Glass Co., circa 1890, 9" h...... **$1,440**

Courtesy of Jeffrey S. Evans & Associates, www.jeffreysevans.com

Two Alaska pattern table items, Vaseline opalescent, banana boat and master berry bowl, Northwood Glass Co./Dugan Glass Co., circa 1897, 3" and 3-1/4" h. overall, banana boat 10" w. x 6" h. **$1,020**

Courtesy of Jeffrey S. Evans & Associates, www.jeffreysevans.com

Chrysanthemum Sprig pattern pagoda seven-piece water set, opaque blue with blue stain and gilt decoration, water pitcher and six tumblers, circa 1899, 3-3/4" h. to 8" h. **$360**

Courtesy of Jeffrey S. Evans & Associates, www.jeffreysevans.com

Daisy and Drape pattern carnival glass vase, aqua opalescent, on three feet, first quarter 20th century, 6-1/4" h. **$360**

Courtesy of Jeffrey S. Evans & Associates, www.jeffreysevans.com

Diamond Spearhead pattern water pitcher, Vaseline opalescent, tankard form, circa 1902, 9-7/8" h. **$228**

Courtesy of Jeffrey S. Evans & Associates, www.jeffreysevans.com

No. 263 Leaf Umbrella pattern water pitcher, cased turquoise/ blue (glossy), applied colorless handle, circa 1889, 8-3/4" h. **$180**

Courtesy of Jeffrey S. Evans & Associates, www.jeffreysevans.com

Opaline Brocade/ Spanish Lace pattern water pitcher, Vaseline opalescent, shouldered form with three-section crimped and ruffled rim, applied reeded handle, circa 1899, 9-1/2" h. **$600**

Courtesy of Jeffrey S. Evans & Associates, www.jeffreysevans.com

Miniature lamp, Parian Swirl pattern, amber with opal spatter, matching patterned ball-form shade, brass collar, fitted with E. Miller & Co. Nutmeg burner, colorless chimney, pattern introduced circa 1895, 6-1/4" h. to top of shade, 3" h. to top of collar, 2-3/8" dia. base. . **$450**

Courtesy of Jeffrey S. Evans & Associates, www.jeffreysevans.com

No. 287 Royal Ivy pattern four-piece table set, cased yellow-green and pink spatter, covered butter dish, covered sugar bowl, creamer, and spooner, pattern introduced in 1890, 3-1/2" h. to 6" h. **$900**

Courtesy of Jeffrey S. Evans & Associates, www.jeffreysevans.com

Water pitcher, blue opalescent with polychrome-enamel decoration, Northwood Glass Co./Dugan Glass Co., circa 1897, 7-1/2" h. **$270**

Courtesy of Jeffrey S. Evans & Associates, www.jeffreysevans.com

Four-piece table set, circa 1899, inverted fan and feather design, gilt decoration, covered butter dish, covered sugar bowl, creamer, and spooner, 4-1/2" h. to 6-3/4" h. **$192**

Courtesy of Jeffrey S. Evans & Associates, www.jeffreysevans.com

Ribbed opal lattice toothpick holder, cranberry opalescent with satin finish, factory polished rim, possibly Northwood Glass Co., circa 1888, 2-1/8" h. **$270**

Courtesy of Jeffrey S. Evans & Associates, www.jeffreysevans.com

GLASS

opalescent glass

OPALESCENT GLASS IS one of the most popular areas of glass collecting. The opalescent effect was attained by adding bone ash chemicals to areas of an item while still hot and refiring the object at tremendous heat. Both pressed and mold-blown patterns are available to collectors. *Opalescent Glass from A to Z* by the late William Heacock is the definitive reference book for collectors.

Three ribbed tumblers in Christmas Snowflake pattern, circa 1895, cranberry opalescent, each with factory-polished rim, Northwood Glass Co./Dugan Glass Co., 3-3/4" h. **$390**

Courtesy of Jeffrey S. Evans & Associates, www.jeffreysevans.com

Chrysanthemum Swirl pattern tall salt shaker, circa 1890, cranberry opalescent, period lid, Northwood Glass Co./Buckeye Glass Co., 3-1/8" h.......**$330**

Courtesy of Jeffrey S. Evans & Associates, www.jeffreysevans.com

Coral Reef Seaweed pattern barber's bottle, late 19th/early 20th century, cranberry opalescent, circular tapered form, period spout, polished pontil mark, Hobbs, Brockunier & Co. and Beaumont Glass Co., 10-1/4" h. overall, bottle 9" h................**$480**

Courtesy of Jeffrey S. Evans & Associates, www.jeffreysevans.com

Coin Spot pattern water tankard, late 19th/early 20th century, cranberry opalescent, tapered-form, applied colorless reeded handle, 9-1/8" h... **$1,200**

Courtesy of Jeffrey S. Evans & Associates, www.jeffreysevans.com

No. 323 Dew Drop pattern water pitcher, circa late 19th century, canary opalescent, square form rim, applied handle and polished pontil mark, Hobbs, Brockunier & Co., 7-1/2" h.............**$192**

Courtesy of Jeffrey S. Evans & Associates, www.jeffreysevans.com

Diamond Spearhead pattern four-piece table set, circa 1900-1904, cobalt blue opalescent, covered butter dish, covered sugar bowl, creamer, and spooner, National Glass Co./Dugan Glass Co., sugar base with two pattern flakes and roughness, 4-3/8" h. to 6-3/4" h. overall. **$840**

Courtesy of Jeffrey S. Evans & Associates, www.jeffreysevans.com

Diamond Spearhead pattern open compote, circa 1902, Vaseline opalescent, gauffered rim, Northwood Glass Co./ National Glass Co., 8" h., 8-1/2" dia... **$600**

Courtesy of Jeffrey S. Evans & Associates, www.jeffreysevans.com

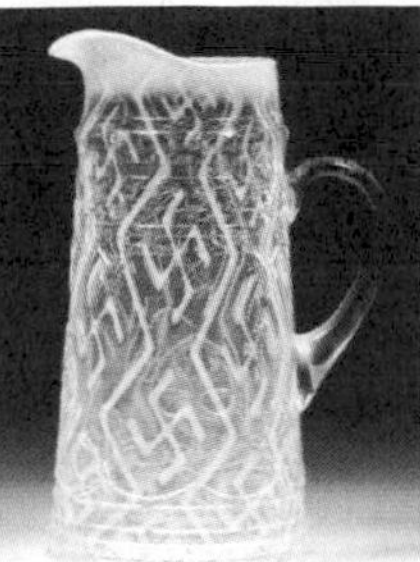

Diamonds and Clubs pattern water pitcher, early 20th century, colorless opalescent, tankard form, applied colorless handle, Dugan Glass Co., 11-1/4" h. **$420**

Courtesy of Jeffrey S. Evans & Associates, www.jeffreysevans.com

Reverse Swirl pattern collard water pitcher, circa 1888-1902, Vaseline opalescent with applied handle, Buckeye Glass Co./ Model Flint Glass Co., 9" h. **$180**

Courtesy of Jeffrey S. Evans & Associates, www.jeffreysevans.com

Swirl Melon Rib pattern syrup pitcher, late 19th/ early 20th century, cranberry opalescent, eight-lobed body, scrolling eye design at rim, applied colorless handle, period lid, split on collar and lid hinge detached on one side, 5" h........ **$840**

Courtesy of Jeffrey S. Evans & Associates, www.jeffreysevans.com

Vase, 20th century, opalescent purple glass with layered pink, green and cream-colored glass forming vines and flowers, John Lotton Studio, signed and dated at underside, 6-3/4" h. **$492**

Courtesy of DuMouchelles, www.dumouchelles.com

Jar and cover in baluster form, ground of raised flower heads, faceted finial, Sabino, engraved signature to base, 4" dia. **$207**

Courtesy of Aalders Auctions, www.aaldersauctions.com

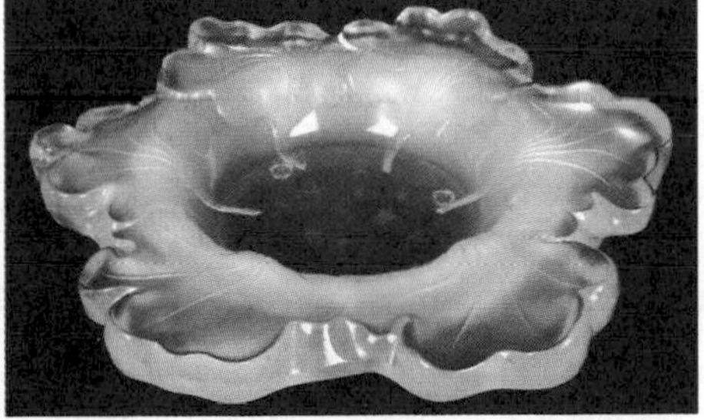

▲ Bowl with six opalescent leaves around perimeter, engraved Lalique, France, 2-3/4" h., 12" dia...... **$448**

Courtesy of Kamelot Auction House, www.kamelotauctions.com

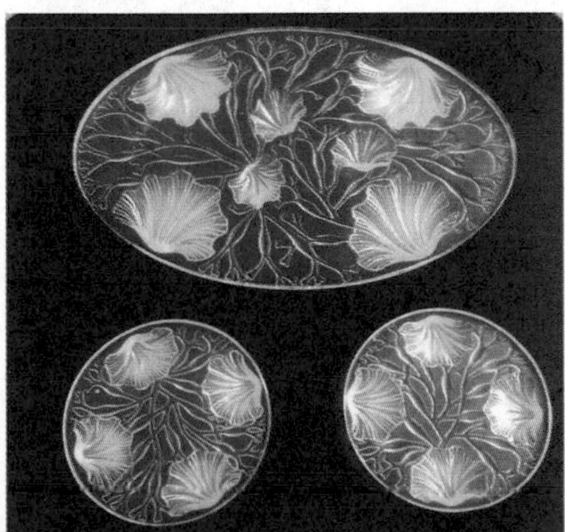

◀ Three Art Deco opalescent glass trivet trays, each with shell and coral motif, signed Verlys, France, oval tray 11-3/4" l. x 8" w. x 1" h., round trays 4-7/8" dia., 3/4" h. **$190**

Courtesy of Klein James, www.kleinjames.com

GLASS

pairpoint

ORIGINALLY ORGANIZED IN New Bedford, Massachusetts, in 1880 as the Pairpoint Manufacturing Co. on land adjacent to the famed Mount Washington Glass Co., Pairpoint first manufactured silver and plated wares. In 1894, the two famous factories merged as the Pairpoint Corp. and enjoyed great success for more than 40 years.

The company was sold in 1939 to a group of local businessmen and eventually bought out by one of the group, who turned the management over to Robert M. Gundersen. Subsequently, it operated as the Gundersen Glass Works until 1952 when, after Gundersen's death, the name was changed to Gundersen-Pairpoint. The factory closed in 1956.

Subsequently, Robert Bryden took charge of this glassworks, at first producing glass for Pairpoint abroad and eventually, in 1970, beginning glass production in Sagamore, Massachusetts. Today the Pairpoint Crystal Glass Co. is owned by Robert and June Bancroft. They continue to manufacture fine quality blown and pressed glass.

Examples of Pairpoint glass designs are displayed in museums across the country, including New York's Metropolitan Museum of Art and Boston's Museum of Fine Arts. "Puffy" lamps with ornate polychrome glass shades are probably the most recognized Pairpoint items, selling for thousands of dollars at auction. **For more Pairpoint lamps, please see the "Lamps & Lighting" section.**

Fine cut centerpiece bowl on bronze and onyx base with three cherubs surrounding controlled bubble, 12" h., 9" dia. **$461**

Courtesy of Echoes Antiques & Auction Gallery Inc., www.echoesauctions.net

Six tavern glass plates, colorless, shape No. D1521 with hand-painted polychrome No. 281 whale decoration, circa 1924-1930, several with polished pontil marks and enameled numbers to reverse, 8" h., 8-1/4" dia. **$270**

Courtesy of Jeffrey S. Evans & Associates, www.jeffreysevans.com

Two blue cornucopias, clear controlled bubble base, 8" h. x 4" w. **$152**

Courtesy of Bill Hood & Sons Art & Antique Auctions, www.hoodauction.com

Amethyst candlesticks, each with polished pontil mark, circa 1925, 8" h. **$204**

Courtesy of Jeffrey S. Evans & Associates, www.jeffreysevans.com

Ten plates with cornucopia decoration and serving plate with floral decoration, early 20th century, probably Pairpoint Manufacturing Co., 8-1/2" dia. **$215**

Courtesy of Alex Cooper Auctioneers, www.alexcooper.com

Cut glass table utensils with floral decoration, pitcher, celery dish, candy dish, nut bowl, and serving tray (part shown), probably Pairpoint Manufacturing Co., tallest item 10" h.............. **$154**

Courtesy of Alex Cooper Auctioneers, www.alexcooper.com

Crystal controlled bubble inkwell with enameled silver-plate top decorated with bird, cracks in enamel and scratches on base, 3" h. x 2-1/2" w. **$48**

Courtesy of Barry S. Slosberg, Inc. Auctioneers, www.bssauction.com

Engraved glass articles, shape No. A-294 comport, shape No. 1600 candlestick, both in Grapes pattern, stick-vase insert in No. 154 pattern, and finger bowl in Vintage pattern, late 19th/first quarter 20th century, 3" h. to 12" h. **$72**

Courtesy of Jeffrey S. Evans & Associates, www.jeffreysevans.com

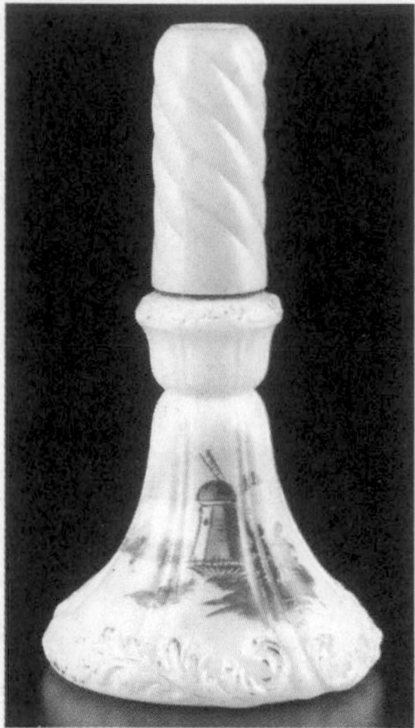

Swedish oil burning candle, No. 87, opaque white with green enamel and gilt depicting windmill with possible artist initials to lower right corner, panels with acanthus leaf and scroll embossing to base of font, marked "87/126" on underside of base, appropriate opal with cream ground candle-form swirled shade, period collar with scalloped shoulder edge, 6-1/4" h. to top of shade, 3" h. to top of collar, 4-7/8" d. base. **$660**

Courtesy of Jeffrey S. Evans & Associates, www.jeffreysevans.com

Cologne bottle cut in Savoy pattern with scalloped base and matching stopper, late 19th century, good condition with small chips to stopper, small rim chip, and scratches to base, 9-1/2" h.................... **$186**

Courtesy of Brunk Auctions, www.brunkauctions.com

Venetti blown and etched trumpet vase, early 20th century, with flared rim with floral and lattice decoration on latticino twist stem above etched flared foot, 12-3/4" h. **$416**

Courtesy of Jackson's, www.jacksonsauction.com

Punch bowl, Brilliant Period cut glass, on stand with conforming ladle, glass most likely Pairpoint Manufacturing Co., bowl 6-5/8" h., 12" dia., stand 5-3/4" h. **$246**

Courtesy of Kaminski Auctions, www.kaminski.com

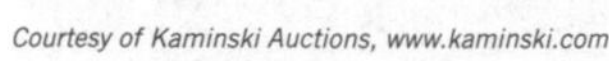

Dresser box, circular form, with three leafy floral stalk images on hinged lid with silver-plate collar numbered 3 on interior hinge, probably Pairpoint Manufacturing Co., 3-1/4" h., 3-1/4 lbs. **$302**

Courtesy of Austin Auction Gallery, www.austinauction.com

Six-knob glass handle bell with twisted blue and white ribbon, 20th century, excellent condition, 11" h................. **$150**

Courtesy of Morphy Auctions, morphyauctions.com

Peach Blow bell with applied swirled handle with blown teardrop bell, circa 1973, limited edition of 200, signed "P" and "CB" for Pairpoint Manufacturing Co., and Cynthia Bryden (Pairpoint decorator in 1970s), 11-1/2" h.............. **$108**

Courtesy of Jeffrey S. Evans & Associates, www.jeffreysevans.com

LAMPS

Puffy dogwood lamp on signed base with acanthus leaf pattern, signed "Pairpoint 3083," overpainted, retains "Pat. Applied For" stencil, replaced sockets, interior repainted, very good condition, shade with nicks to bottom rim, 19-3/4" h., 12-1/2" dia... **$1,500**

Courtesy of Milestone Auctions, www.milestoneauctions.com

Table lamp with Lansdowne shade with bucolic scene on fluted base, 1910s-1920s, signed "H. Hisher" and "The Pairpoint Corp'n" on shade, stamped "PAIRPOINT P D3058" on base, shade in overall excellent condition with minor streaks to paint, base with two replaced sockets and one replaced pull chain, minor overall water drips and minor oxidation to original dark green patina, minor losses to patina on ball of heat cap, 22" x 18". **$1,536**

Courtesy of Rago Arts and Auctions, www.ragoarts.com

Puffy boudoir lamp, lilac tree shade with butterflies, 1910s-1920s, reverse-painted frosted glass, patinated and enameled metal, single socket, marked "THE PAIRPOINT CORP" on shade, stamped "PAIRPOINT MFG CO" on base, overall excellent original condition, minor oxidation to base, rewired, original plug, 16-3/4" x 9".................. **$2,560**

Courtesy of Rago Arts and Auctions, www.ragoarts.com

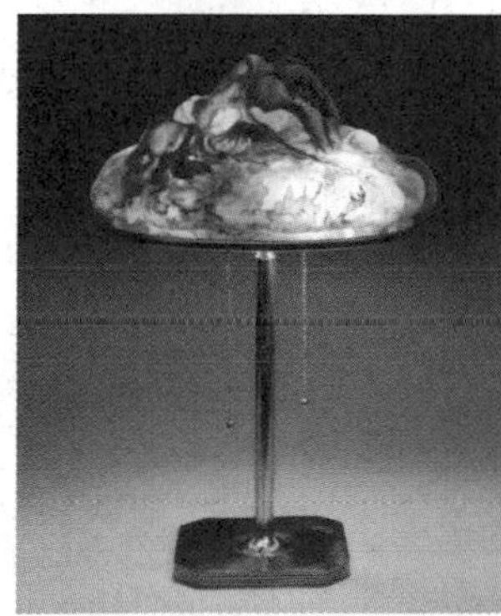

Puffy poppy lamp, reverse-painted molded shade, signed Pairpoint, brass and chrome base #3085, engraved body, double-socket fixture, minor rim chips to shade, fitter ring neck screws stripped, 16-1/2" h. x 12-1/4", shade 7" h. x 14-1/2", fitter rim 11-3/4".... **$9,145**

Courtesy of Burchard Galleries, www.burchardgalleries.com

GLASS

pattern glass

THOUGH IT HAS never been ascertained whether glass was first pressed in the United States or abroad, the development of the glass-pressing machine revolutionized the glass industry in the United States, and this country receives the credit for improving the method to make this process feasible. The first wares pressed were probably small flat plates of the type now referred to as "lacy," the intricacy of the design concealing flaws.

In 1827, both the New England Glass Co., Cambridge, Massachusetts, and Bakewell & Co., Pittsburgh, took out patents for pressing glass furniture knobs; soon other pieces followed. This early pressed glass contained red lead, which made it clear and resonant when tapped (flint). Made primarily in clear, it is rarer in blue, amethyst, olive green, and yellow.

By the 1840s, early simple patterns such as Ashburton, Argus, and Excelsior appeared. Ribbed Bellflower seems to have been one of the earliest patterns to have had complete sets. By the 1860s, a wide range of patterns was available.

In 1864, William Leighton of Hobbs, Brockunier & Co., Wheeling, West Virginia, developed a formula for "soda lime" glass that did not require the expensive red lead for clarity. Although "soda lime" glass did not have the brilliance of the earlier flint glass, the formula came into widespread use because glass could be produced cheaply.

SOURCING ENGLISH PRESSED GLASS

My wife, Brenda, and I collect British pressed glass made between 1837 and 1937, and our trips to England combine the fun of being in a land new to us with the thrill of the hunt that collectors enjoy. We attend antique shows (called "fairs" or "fayres" in England) and visit antique shops. You might think that most items in our collection were found in England, and you would be correct. But some of our most interesting and significant British-made items were found right here in the United States.

How does British glass get to the United States? Imports and exports have been important areas of economic activity on both sides of "the pond" for many years, so it should not be surprising to find American-made glass in Britain and vice-versa. Moreover, our nearby neighbor to the north, Canada, was part of the British Commonwealth for many years, and people from Britain immigrated to Canada while others traveled back and forth, whether doing business or visiting relatives. Canadian citizens often work or live in the United States, and

◀ Purple malachite covered sugar basin with inscription as quoted in article. **$400-425**

▼ Purple malachite butter dish with portrait of the Marquis of Lorne. .. **$475-$500**

▲ Blue malachite creamer with portrait of the Marchioness of Lorne............. **$160-$175**

antique dealers from Canada do shows in the States, so the "pipeline" from Canada also became a means for British glass to come to the States.

Most British pressed glassware from the 19th century is either decorative or utilitarian, and special categories within these classifications are "novelty" and "commemorative" glass. Novelty items can range from match holders and items that might hold pins to miniature versions of objects such as wheelbarrows or coaches. Commemoratives were created to celebrate specific events and/or particular people, especially royalty or important political figures.

Henry Greener & Co. operated the Wear Flint Glass Works at Sunderland in northeast England on the coast of the North Sea. The Greener firm's roots go back to the first quarter of the 19th century, and it is credited with many patterns and unique designs, including pressed glass

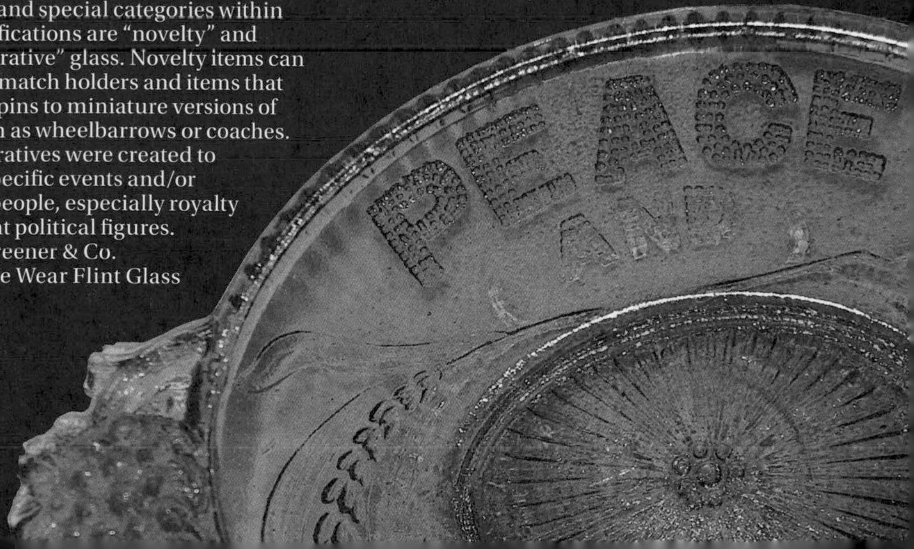

Crystal coach novelty, 7" l. **$150-$175**

Rare Greener tankard pitcher in dark cobalt blue. ..... **$275-$300**

Blue Gladstone mug.............. **$75**
Amethyst Peabody mug. **$95**

commemorative pieces honoring politician John Bright or British Prime Minister William Ewart Gladstone, as well as Anglo-American philanthropist George Peabody.

Greener items may bear the firm's trademark – a roaring lion with a battle-axe or star above its right forepaw. Additionally, items may have a British registry mark. This sort of mark designates that which is similar to a U.S. patent, letting others know that the design of the article is protected by law, just as with a copyright. Registry marks may be diamond in shape with numbers or Roman numerals at each corner, or they may be a simple "Rd." followed by a number.

Politician John Bright is best remembered for his campaign in favor of the repeal of the Corn Laws. The Greener items that honor him always have the phrase "Peace and Plenty" in large letters. You may see articles in crystal, such as plates, cream jugs or sugar basins, and there are several sizes of dishes that are oval in shape. Items in any transparent color are rather hard to find.

There are four pressed glass items created by Greener to honor a famous British husband and wife who share significant places in Canadian history, as well as other items made by the same glass company. Princess Louise (fourth daughter of Queen Victoria and Prince Albert) married John Sutherland Campbell, the Duke of Argyll, on March 21, 1871. This was the first marriage of a British royal to a commoner since the early 1500s. The Duke was a member of Parliament (MP), and he also had the title Marquis of Lorne, so his bride Louise became known as the Marchioness of Lorne. In 1878, the Marquis was appointed Governor General of Canada, an honorary post making him head of state and the official representative of Queen Victoria. The Marquis and Marchioness left England for Canada in November 1878. At some point when the appointment to Canada was known, the British glassmaking firm Greener & Co. decided to produce commemorative glassware.

There are four items in the commemorative set honoring the Marquis and Marchioness of Lorne: covered butter dish, footed creamer, footed sugar basin with cover, and footed spooner. All are pressed glass with foliage and symbolic elements for England (rose), Ireland

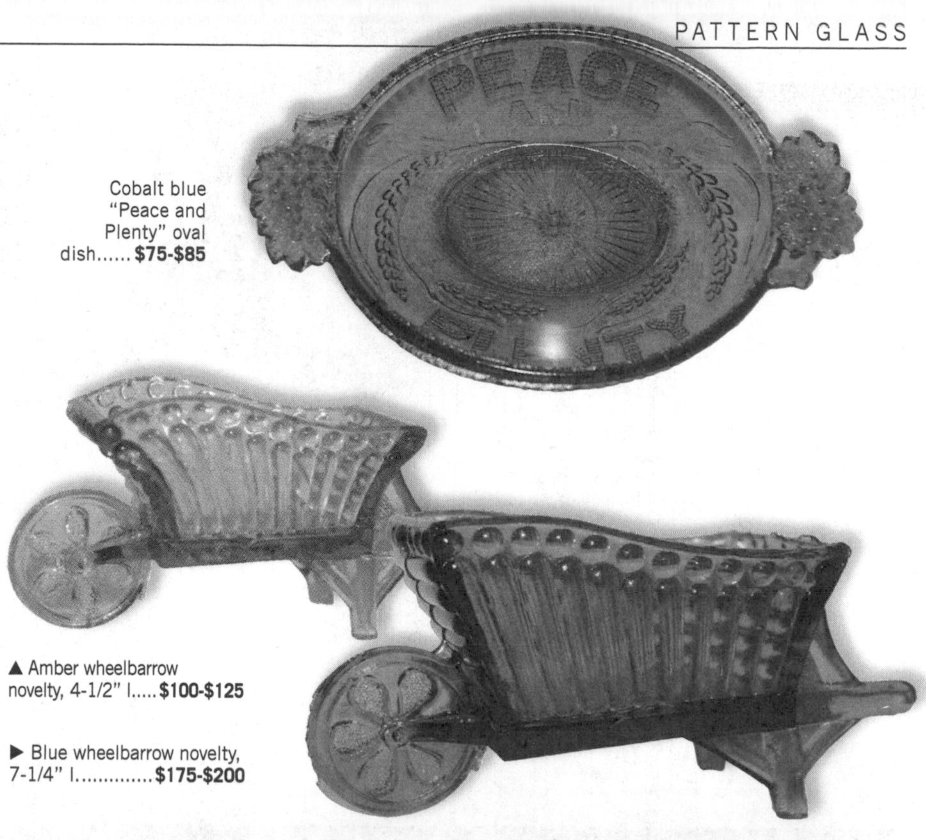

Cobalt blue "Peace and Plenty" oval dish...... **$75-$85**

▲ Amber wheelbarrow novelty, 4-1/2" l..... **$100-$125**

► Blue wheelbarrow novelty, 7-1/4" l............. **$175-$200**

(shamrock), and Scotland (thistle) in low relief on their surface areas. Portraits of the Marquis and the Marchioness and an inscription are distinctive features. This inscription appears in embossed letters on the cover of the butter dish and sugar basin and on the side of the sugar basin: "marquis & marchioness of lorne landed at halifax n. s. 25th novr 1878." The inscription is framed by the shape of a shield as an outline consisting of small raised beads. The skilled moldmaker managed to get the words within the available area by using the abbreviations "N. S." for Nova Scotia and "novr" for November.

All four Marquis and Marchioness of Lorne items can be found in transparent amber or crystal as well as opaque white, but the opaque "malachite" or "slag" colors are most desirable. Blue malachite is a mixture of cobalt blue and opaque white, green malachite consists of opaque green and opaque white, and purple malachite combines dark amethyst with opaque white. Many collectors use the term "slag" when speaking of malachite glass.

In any of the malachite colors, the creamer and spooner will sell in the $160 to $185 price range; the covered sugar basin and covered butter dish will bring $425 to $500 or more. Opaque white articles will sell for somewhat less. The transparent amber and crystal examples are very hard to find, so it's difficult to establish prices for them.

The Greener firm made some other items in milk glass, and the "Hanlan mug" is surely one of the most interesting. The mug commemorates a dramatic contest between two oarsmen in a challenge race. The winner, Edward Hanlan, is depicted on the front of the mug directly opposite the handle, and there is a great deal of lettering in low relief: "Edward Hanlan Champion of the World Nov. 15th 1880 Beat Trickett of N. S. W."

There are several other pressed glass factories of note in Britain. In the meantime, don't hesitate to look for British glass right here in the United States.

– James Measell

Anglo-Irish Strawberry Diamond pattern cut glass bowl on stand, first half 19th century, colorless lead glass, in two sections, shallow bowl with allover pattern including base, scalloped rim, hollow stand with matching pattern and horizontal prisms, narrow prisms to underside of foot, undamaged except for shallow chip to one rim scallop, top edge of foot possibly repolished, 9-1/8" h., 11" dia. rim, 8-3/8" dia. foot.......... **$720**

Courtesy of Jeffrey S. Evans & Associates, www.jeffreysevans.com

Anglo-Irish Strawberry Diamond pattern cut glass urn/compote and cover, first half 19th century, colorless lead glass, hemispherical bowl with roll-over rim, faceted compressed-knop stem and square stepped foot with conforming pattern to underside, interior-fitting domed cover with button-like finial, chip to one foot corner, 9-1/2" h. overall, 8-1/2" dia. overall. **$450**

Courtesy of Jeffrey S. Evans & Associates, www.jeffreysevans.com

Hobbs No. 335/Hexagon Block pattern ruby-stained seven-piece water set, colorless, tankard pitcher with applied colorless handle and six tumblers with factory polished bases, Hobbs, Brockunier & Co., Wheeling, West Virginia, pattern introduced in 1889, one tumbler with chip under base, two others with minor spall under base as made, remainder undamaged, 3-7/8" to 12-7/8" h. **$108**

Courtesy of Jeffrey S. Evans & Associates, www.jeffreysevans.com

Petticoat/National (OMN) pattern four-piece table set, Vaseline, covered butter dish, covered sugar bowl, creamer, and spooner, Riverside Glass Works, pattern introduced 1899, sugar undamaged, butter with flake to base rim, remainder with scattered chipping to feet, 4-1/4" to 6-3/4" h. overall. **$120**

Courtesy of Jeffrey S. Evans & Associates, www.jeffreysevans.com

Iris and Meander/Iris (OMN) pattern four-piece table set, circa 1903, blue opalescent, covered butter dish, covered sugar bowl, creamer, and spooner, Jefferson Glass Co., sugar and butter base undamaged, butter cover and spooner with minute pattern flake to each, creamer with scattered pattern flaking/roughness, 4-1/2" to 6-3/4" h. overall....................................... **$204**

Courtesy of Jeffrey S. Evans & Associates, www.jeffreysevans.com

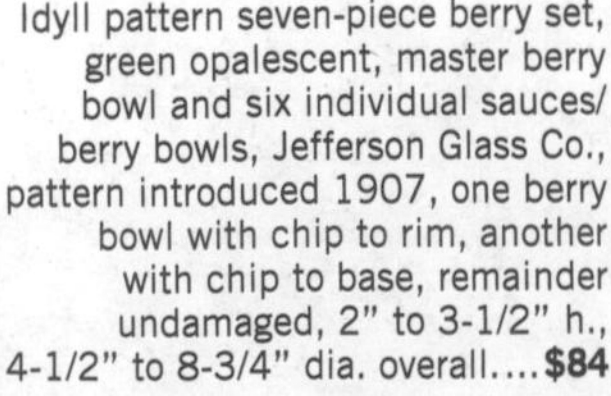

Idyll pattern seven-piece berry set, green opalescent, master berry bowl and six individual sauces/berry bowls, Jefferson Glass Co., pattern introduced 1907, one berry bowl with chip to rim, another with chip to base, remainder undamaged, 2" to 3-1/2" h., 4-1/2" to 8-3/4" dia. overall.... **$84**

Courtesy of Jeffrey S. Evans & Associates, www.jeffreysevans.com

New York (OMN)/Beaded Shell pattern seven-piece water set, colorless opalescent, water pitcher and six tumblers, Dugan Glass Co., pattern introduced 1904, undamaged, 3-3/4" to 8-1/4" h. **$108**

Courtesy of Jeffrey S. Evans & Associates, www.jeffreysevans.com

Prince of Wales pattern seven-piece water set, first quarter 20th century, colorless with traces of gilt decoration, water pitcher and six tumblers with factory polished base, each piece with H-in-diamond trademark, Heisey Glass Co., pitcher with pattern chip, flake, and minor bruise and minute refracting spider mark on spout as made, one tumbler with flake to base, remainder undamaged, 4" to 8-3/4" h. overall........**$108**

Courtesy of Jeffrey S. Evans & Associates, www.jeffreysevans.com

Duncan & Miller No. 61/Sweet Sixty-One pattern ruby-stained four-piece table set, colorless, covered butter dish, covered sugar bowl, creamer, and spooner, Duncan & Miller Glass Co., pattern introduced in 1906, flake to sugar cover rim, 4-1/8" to 6" h. overall. **$132**

Courtesy of Jeffrey S. Evans & Associates, www.jeffreysevans.com

Hobbs No. 339/Leaf and Flower pattern amber-stained three-piece table set, colorless, covered butter dish, creamer, and spooner, Hobbs, Brockunier & Co., Wheeling, West Virginia, pattern introduced in 1890, spooner with minute roughness, remainder undamaged, 3-1/2" to 4-3/4" h. overall..**$108**

Courtesy of Jeffrey S. Evans & Associates, www.jeffreysevans.com

Thousand Eye/Adams No. 130 pattern salver/cake stand, circa 1891, Vaseline, closed rim, Adams & Co., undamaged, 7-1/2" h. overall, 11" dia. overall...**$156**

Courtesy of Jeffrey S. Evans & Associates, www.jeffreysevans.com

Unlisted Hobbs No. 319/Polka Dot pattern three-piece champagne set, rubina verde, water tankard with applied Vaseline reeded handle and two tall, tapered tumblers with factory-polished rims, Hobbs, Brockunier & Co., pattern introduced circa 1884, undamaged, tankard pitcher with scattered interior scratching, 5-5/8" to 10-5/8" h...... **$1,800**

Courtesy of Jeffrey S. Evans & Associates, www.jeffreysevans.com

Pattern-molded compote, circa 1820-1845, colorless lead glass with applied cobalt blue rim, deep hemispherical bowl with 12 molded flutes and flared rim, raised on hollow baluster-form stem and thick circular foot with polished pontil mark, Pittsburgh region and others, undamaged with hint of wear, 8" h., 8" dia. rim, 4-3/4" dia. foot............... **$960**

Courtesy of Jeffrey S. Evans & Associates, www.jeffreysevans.com

Pressed glass store display stand, fourth quarter 19th century, blue, three-step form with high back embossed with Daisy and Button-type pattern and word "Perfumery", different pattern on sides and lower front, top of each step embossed with wood-like texture, chip to lower corner and minor mold roughness, 10" h. x 6-1/2" w. x 5-3/4" d. **$748**

Courtesy of Jeffrey S. Evans & Associates, www.jeffreysevans.com

Poinsettia pattern five-piece water set, circa 1903, blue opalescent, water pitcher and four tumblers with pressed interior pattern, each tumbler signed with N-in-circle trademark, H. Northwood Co., pitcher with short crack to upper terminal of handle, tumblers undamaged, 4" to 9-1/2" h. overall................. **$120**

Courtesy of Jeffrey S. Evans & Associates, www.jeffreysevans.com

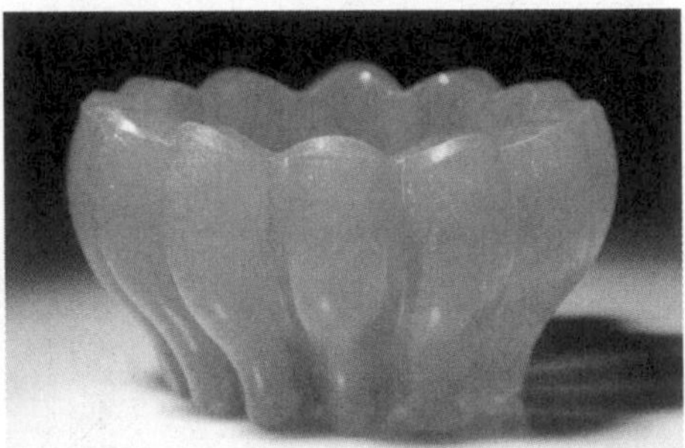

Heavy ribbed pressed open salt, 1840-1860, translucent starch blue, circular form with 12 vertical ribs, excellent condition, 1-3/4" h., 3-1/8" dia.. **$184**

Courtesy of Jeffrey S. Evans & Associates, www.jeffreysevans.com

BT-2 "Pittsburgh" steamboat pressed open salt, 1830-1845, purple blue/cobalt, embossed on stern, rope table ring, rare, Stourbridge Flint Glass Works, Pittsburgh, rim with chip to paddle wheel, chip to stern, and loss of sawtooth, light crack off rim, 1-1/2" h. x 1-7/8" x 3-5/8". **$288**

Courtesy of Jeffrey S. Evans & Associates, www.jeffreysevans.com

GLASS

peach blow

SEVERAL TYPES OF glass lumped together by collectors as Peach Blow were produced by half a dozen glasshouses. Hobbs, Brockunier & Co., Wheeling, West Virginia, made Peach Blow as a plated ware that shaded from red at the top to yellow at the bottom and is referred to as Wheeling Peach Blow. Mt. Washington Glass Works produced a homogeneous Peach Blow shading from rose at the top to pale blue in the lower portion. The New England Glass Works' Peach Blow, called Wild Rose, shaded from rose at the top to white. Gundersen-Pairpoint Co. also reproduced some of the Mt. Washington Peach Blow in the early 1950s, and some glass of a somewhat similar type was made by Steuben Glass Works, Thomas Webb & Sons, and Stevens & Williams of England. New England Peach Blow is one-layered glass and the English is two-layered.

Another single-layered shaded art glass was produced early in the 20th century by New Martinsville Glass Mfg. Co. Originally called Muranese, collectors today refer to it as New Martinsville Peach Blow.

Cased vase with hand-painted enamel florals and butterfly, excellent condition, 7-3/4" h. x 4" w., 4" dia. **$108**

Courtesy of Accurate Auctions, www.accurateauctions.com

Double gourd cased glass vase, unsigned, 10-1/2" h. . **$42**

Courtesy of Main Street Mining Co. Auctions, www.mainstreetmining.com

Satin pitcher with tall handle, gold enamel with flowers and dragonfly, Mt. Washington Glass Works, 10-1/2" h. ... **$348**

Courtesy of Strawser Auctions, www.strawserauctions.com

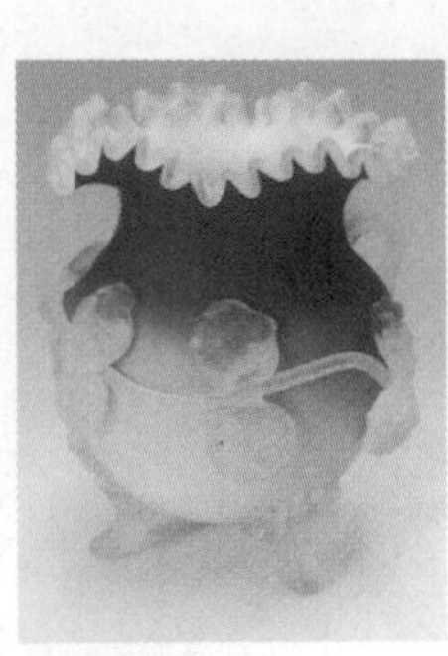

Footed vase with ruffled rim, body with applied frosted foliate and floral decoration, on three frosted feet, Stevens & William, 9-1/4" h., 7-1/2" dia....... **$206**

Courtesy of Burchard Galleries, www.burchardgalleries.com

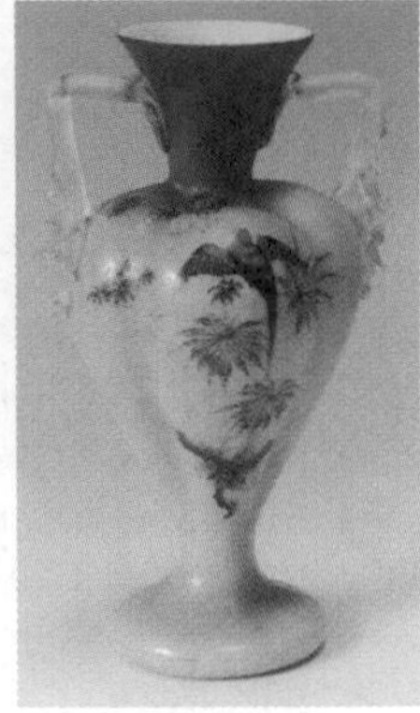

Victorian vase with enameled decoration and satin glass handles, possibly Mt. Washington Glass Works, 11" h., 6" dia. **$118**

Courtesy of Burchard Galleries, www.burchardgalleries.com

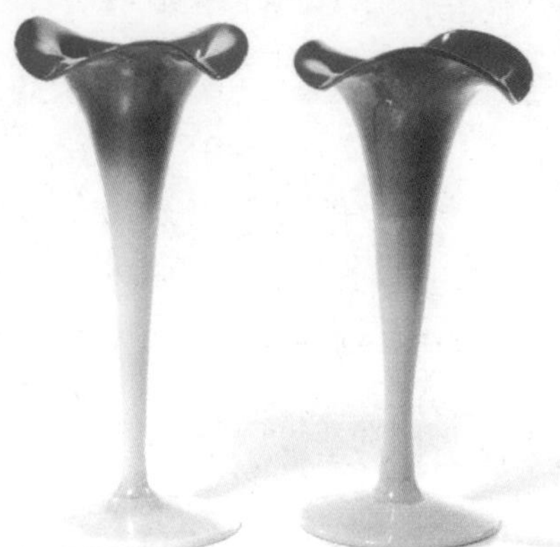

Pair of lily-shaped vases, circa 1886-1888, deep rose to peach with glossy finish, each with gauffered three-petal rim, polished pontil mark, and worn original label, New England Glass Co., 7" h. **$270**

Courtesy of Jeffrey S. Evans & Associates, www.jeffreysevans.com

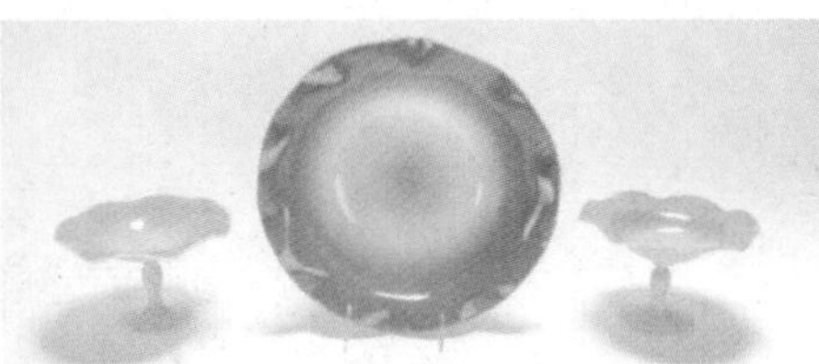

Pair of compotes and bowl, ruffled rims, ground pontil, unsigned, bowl 11-1/2" dia.................... **$69**

Courtesy of Wickliff Auctioneers, www.wickliffauctioneers.com

Three items in deep rose to pink with plush finish, circa 1950, plate, cup with applied reeded handle and foot, and saucer, Gunderson Glass Works, plate 8" dia. **$60**

Courtesy of Jeffrey S. Evans & Associates, www.jeffreysevans.com

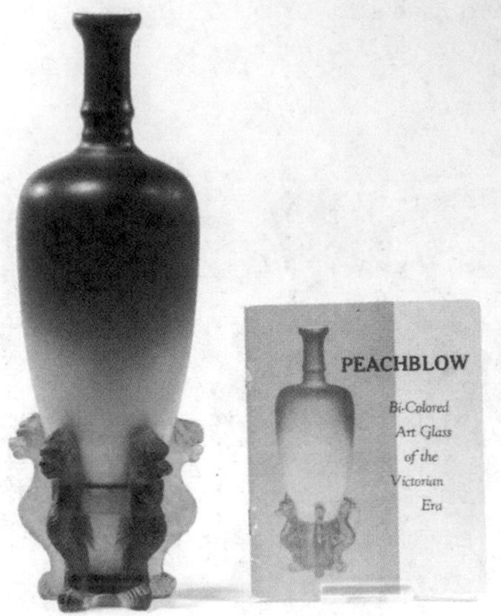

Hobbs No. 22 Morgan vase, circa 1886, plush/satin finish, polished pontil mark, and original satin amber five-griffin stand, Hobbs, Brockunier & Co, 10" h. **$510**

Courtesy of Jeffrey S. Evans & Associates, www.jeffreysevans.com

Rose bowl with polychrome and gilt decoration of spider mums, fourth quarter 19th century, rough pontil mark, probably Mt. Washington Glass Works, 3-5/8" h.............. **$132**

Courtesy of Jeffrey S. Evans & Associates, www.jeffreysevans.com

GLASS

phoenix glass

THE PHOENIX GLASS Co. of Beaver, Pennsylvania, was established in 1880. Known primarily for commercial glassware, the firm also produced a molded, sculptured, cameo-type line from the 1930s until the 1950s.

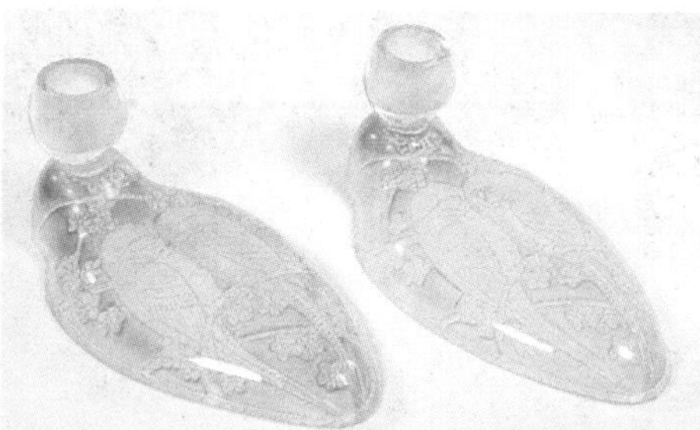

Lovebirds pattern candleholders, light green washed colorless, shoe-form with single socket at heel and factory-polished table ring, Phoenix Glass Co. and Consolidated Lamp & Glass Co., circa second quarter 20th century, 3" h. x 4" w. x 7-3/8" d. **$390**

Courtesy of Jeffrey S. Evans & Associates, www.jeffreysevans.com

Nailsea/Venetian Thread pattern fairy lamp, opal loops on red satin finish, fairy-size dome fitted on colorless Clarke's lamp cup and matching flower-trough base with upturned fluted rim, probably Phoenix Glass Co., circa fourth quarter 19th century, 5-1/2" h., 6-1/4" dia. base. **$510**

Courtesy of Jeffrey S. Evans & Associates, www.jeffreysevans.com

Overshot Peloton pattern water pitcher, colorless with applied polychrome canes, bulbous form, square rim, applied handle with polished pontil mark, Phoenix Glass Co., circa 1885, 7-7/8" h. **$216**

Courtesy of Jeffrey S. Evans & Associates, www.jeffreysevans.com

Spot-Optic pattern pitcher, ruby die-away to opal sensitive crystal, applied handle and polished pontil mark, circa 1883-1888, 7-3/4" h.......... **$196**

Courtesy of Jeffrey S. Evans & Associates, www.jeffreysevans.com

Spot-Optic pattern tankard, blue opalescent, applied blue handle and polished pontil mark, probably Phoenix Glass Co., circa 1883-1888, 9" h. overall...**$805**

Courtesy of Jeffrey S. Evans & Associates, www.jeffreysevans.com

Spot-Optic pattern water pitcher, ruby die-away to opal sensitive amber, triangular-form fully crimped rim, applied colorless reeded handle, polished pontil mark, circa 1883-1888, 9" h. overall. ... **$540**

Courtesy of Jeffrey S. Evans & Associates, www.jeffreysevans.com

Spot-Optic pattern water pitcher, ruby die-away in opal sensitive blue with opalescent diamond pattern, ball form with circular plain rim, blue applied handle with opal and ruby die-away to lower terminal, polished pontil mark, circa 1883-1885, undamaged except for some minute high-point wear to body, 6-3/4" h........**$374**

Courtesy of Jeffrey S. Evans & Associates, www.jeffreysevans.com

Spot-Optic pattern water pitcher, colorless with mica, opal, and red flakes, shouldered form with crimped top, U-shape spout, applied colorless reeded handle, and polished pontil mark, fourth quarter 19th century, undamaged, uneven base, 8" h. overall. **$138**

Courtesy of Jeffrey S. Evans & Associates, www.jeffreysevans.com

Spot-Optic Craquelle pattern cruet, cranberry opalescent, ball-form with triangular ruffled rim, applied colorless handle, polished pontil mark, circa 1883-1888, 6-1/2" h. overall.................... **$259**

Courtesy of Jeffrey S. Evans & Associates, www.jeffreysevans.com

Swirl pattern pitcher, cranberry to blue opalescent, ball form with circular rim and applied blue reeded handle, probably Phoenix Glass Co., circa late 19th/early 20th century, polished pontil mark, 7-7/8" h. **$900**

Courtesy of Jeffrey S. Evans & Associates, www.jeffreysevans.com

Zig Zag Optic pattern glass pitcher and tumblers set, square eight-lobed pitcher with applied colorless handle and satin blue tumblers, Phoenix Glass Co., circa 1889, overall very good condition, one tumbler with smooth chip to rim, bubble burst and small bruise, pitcher with small bruise to rib, pitcher 8-1/2" h., tumblers 3-3/4" h................................ **$372**

Courtesy of Ahlers & Ogletree Auction Gallery, www.aandoauctions.com

Molded glass vase with dancing nude female motif, original label on underside, 11-1/2" h.... **$246**

Courtesy of DuMouchelles, www.doumouchelles.com

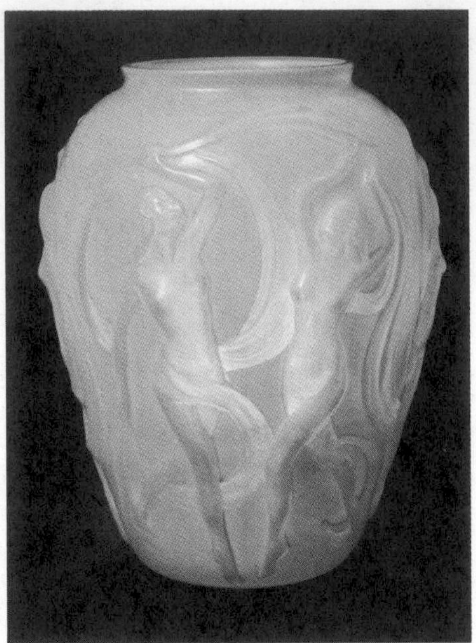

Vase with molded frosted glass figures of dancing nude maidens on hard-to-find lavender ground, Phoenix Glass Co., 11-1/2" h. x 9" w. **$413**

Courtesy of Burchard Galleries, www.burchardgalleries.com

Five vases in green, yellow, and frosted color glass with seagulls, goldfish, grass with grasshoppers, and flying geese, probably Phoenix Glass Co., good condition, some chips to rim of vases, 10" h. x 4-1/2" w. x 2-1/2" dia. **$246**

Courtesy of Westport Auction, www.westportauction.com

GLASS

pressed

PRESSED GLASS IS one of the largest collecting categories in all of antiques, and the number of pieces sold at auction each year easily surpasses more than 3,500 examples in today's market.

Pressed glass was originally produced to imitate expensive cut glass owned mainly by the wealthy. It is made by pressing molten glass either mechanically or manually into textured molds. Unless removed by hand, each piece will retain mold lines, even on pieces with extensive detailing.

In recent years, three lots stunned the collecting community and refocused attention on a category many had not thought about in years. Each gives in inside look at how the hobby is changing as longtime collections are finally offered after years in private hands.

A bidding war broke out over a 2-1/4" high x 3-1/8" wide pressed glass rectangular salt made by the Providence Flint Glass Works of Providence, Rhode Island. The diminutive blue salt is signed "Providence" on the base and its auctioneers, the Hess Auction Group, dated the piece sometime between 1831 and 1833. A conservative absentee bid of $200 opened the lot and then things got interesting. Floor bidders used $100 increments to push the salt to $2,500 before Internet bidders advanced the pace to $3,750. But it was a paddle on the floor that claimed it at $4,720, fully 10 times its low estimate of $400.

The lovely salt was from the private collection of renowned glass and china specialist Corinne Machmer, a familiar face at many Pennsylvania shows and shops. Machmer's lifelong collection also turned out a unique dark purple salt in the form of a boat, which sold to a phone bidder for $7,316. One of a group offered in the auction, the 1-1/2" high x 3-3/4" wide boat salt is signed on the stern "Pittsburgh" and was produced by the Sturbridge Flint Glass Works of Pittsburgh, Pennsylvania, between 1828 and 1835.

A few months later, Skinner, Inc. auctioned a rare pair of marbleized blue pressed glass tulip vases from the Boston

Blue salt, Providence Flint Glass Works, Providence, Rhode Island, circa 1831-1833, signed "Providence" on base, unique, 2-1/4" h. x 3-1/8" w. **$4,720**

Courtesy of Hess Auction Group, www.hessauctiongroup.com

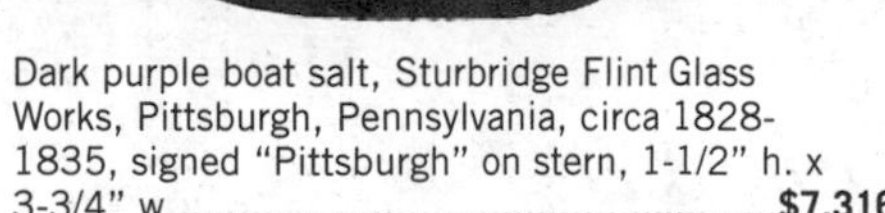

Dark purple boat salt, Sturbridge Flint Glass Works, Pittsburgh, Pennsylvania, circa 1828-1835, signed "Pittsburgh" on stern, 1-1/2" h. x 3-3/4" w. **$7,316**

Courtesy of Hess Auction Group, www.hessauctiongroup.com

& Sandwich Glass Co. of Sandwich, Massachusetts, for $23,370. The 9-7/8" tall pair was estimated to bring between $2,000 and $3,000, but the sale marked the first time the circa 1845-1865 vases were offered at auction in nearly 50 years. The set was last purchased at an auction held by noted early American glass auctioneer Richard A. Bourne in November 1967.

"The American glass market overall began to stabilize in 2015 and we are seeing that trend continue in 2016," said Jeffrey S. Evans, the nation's leading specialist early American pressed glass auctioneer. "Certain categories like 19th century free-blown wares and bottles/flasks continue to draw strong demand and are performing well."

Evans's firm made headlines after a pair of brilliant peacock green pressed loop/leaf vases sold for $11,400. The pair was fashioned in a seven-loop bowl and raised on a seven-loop circular foot, likely by the Boston & Sandwich Glass Co. between 1845 and 1860. It is only one of two pairs Evans has ever offered, the other being from the 50-year collection of the late Lois Hirschmann of Marion, Massachusetts (sold to benefit the Sandwich Glass Museum's Endowment Fund).

However, examples of early American pressed glass commanding four and five figures at auction are only 2% of the overall market (according to historical sale data available on LiveAuctioneers, BidSquare, and Invaluable). Extremely rare examples continue to take top lot honors when they appear, but auctioneers like Evans are busy these days, overseeing the sale of thousands of pieces of glass each year. Collectors such as Machmer and Hirschmann are revealing their treasures after decades of enjoyment at a time when most examples of pressed glass sell for less than $100 and exemplary pieces can be had for between $100 and $5,000.

"Pressed glass and Victorian glass has seen increased interest," Evans said, "but demand is still having a hard time keeping up with the large volume of material coming onto the market."

Rather than lament over the generally lower prices for mid-range examples in less than mint condition, we see the pressed glass hobby as an ideal time to begin collecting and learning about America's diverse history of glass making. On every front, the hobby is welcoming new students: Once expensive reference books are now affordable; online auction hosting sites make it easy to buy functional and historical American glassware made during the late 1700s and 1800s for less than $75; and newcomers to the hobby can still learn a great

Sixteen hen on nest motif items, mid-20th century, assortment of serving tureens/condiment jars/sugar bowls/salt cellars, tallest 8-3/4" h. **$150**

Courtesy of Greenwich Auction, www.greenwichauction.net

Covered compote, green opalescent hobnail, 9" h. **$35**

Courtesy of Specialists of the South, Inc., www.specialistsofthesouth.com

deal from a generation that researched glassmaking and founded glass museums more than any other.

"There are numerous active glass pages on Facebook," Evans said, "including several established glass clubs that are contributing to market growth and drawing new collectors. This bodes well for the future of the glass market."

— Eric Bradley

COLLECTOR FACT:

One of two complete original sets, this particular dish and undertray (PICTURED LEFT) is a perfect illustration of the transition from the pressed lacy period to the pressed pattern period in American glass. Its form is based on the Gothic Arch and Heart rectangular covered dishes with undertrays produced between 1835 and 1845 at the Boston & Sandwich Glass Co. It is likely that this horn of plenty dish was the initial form produced in the pattern and among the first pieces of EAPG ever manufactured.

Dish and tray, circa 1845-1855, Boston & Sandwich Glass Co., horn of plenty/comet (OMN) rectangular covered honey dish or casket with undertray, colorless lead glass, domed cover with pattern on interior and octagonal finial, dish with even-scallop rim, smooth base edge, and inverted diamond-point pattern in base, tray with same even-scallop rim and base pattern, Horn of Plenty pattern modified to fit on shoulder, rare and important, dish 5-1/2" h. x 4" x 6-1/2", tray 4-5/8" x 7".. **$4,750**

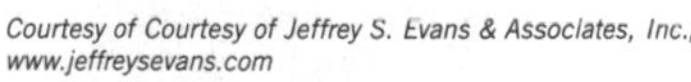

Courtesy of Courtesy of Jeffrey S. Evans & Associates, Inc., www.jeffreysevans.com

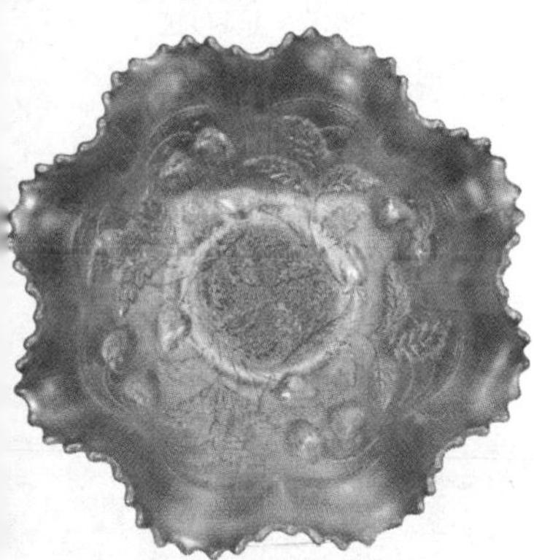

Carnival glass ruffled bowl, Stippled Strawberry pattern, ice blue, with basket weave back, possibly unique, 9" w......**$18,000**

Courtesy of Seeck Auctions, www.seeckauction.com

Amethyst vertical rib blown glass cruet, applied loop handle with foliate terminal and original stopper, 7-1/4" h. **$8,260**

Courtesy of Hess Auction Group, www.hessauctiongroup.com

Vases, circa 1845-1860, Boston & Sandwich Glass Co., deep peacock green, each deep seven-loop bowl with conforming rim, raised on seven-loop circular foot, wafer construction, 9-1/2" h., 4-7/8" dia. rim, 3-3/4" dia. foot.. **$9,500**

Courtesy of Jeffrey S. Evans & Associates, Inc., www.jeffreysevans.com

Tumbler, colorless non-lead glass, mid-19th century, eight-panel form embossed with "LOUIS N. BONAPARTE PRESIDENT" arched above profile bust, reverse with "R. F. / 1848" within cartouche with flags and battle axes, polished table ring, 3-1/2" h., 2-3/4" dia. rim. **$40**

Courtesy of Jeffrey S. Evans & Associates, Inc., www.jeffreysevans.com

Last Supper tray, amber, Indiana Glass Co., 11" l. x 7" w. **$5**

Courtesy of Main Street Mining Co. Auctions, www.mainstreetmining.com

Two casters, colorless, fourth quarter 19th/early 20th century, molded swirl and Zipper panel examples, each fitted in signed and numbered quadruple-plate stand, makers unverified, 6-3/4" and 10".... **$70**

Courtesy of Jeffrey S. Evans & Associates, Inc., www.jeffreysevans.com

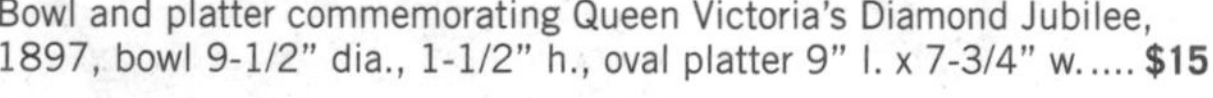

Bowl and platter commemorating Queen Victoria's Diamond Jubilee, 1897, bowl 9-1/2" dia., 1-1/2" h., oval platter 9" l. x 7-3/4" w..... **$15**

Courtesy of Heritage Auctions, ha.com

Ale set, five-piece colorless hobnail with cranberry and yellow staining, fourth quarter 19th century, pitcher with applied handle and applied prunt to lower terminal, four ale glasses with factory polished bases, probably European, 7" to 10-3/4" h. **$120**

Courtesy of Jeffrey S. Evans & Associates, Inc., www.jeffreysevans.com

top lot!

Pair of marbleized blue tulip vases with octagonal bases, circa 1845-1865, Boston & Sandwich Glass Co., Sandwich, Massachusetts, originally purchased from Richard A. Bourne in November 1967, 9-7/8" h **$23,370**

COURTESY OF SKINNER, INC. WWW.SKINNERINC.COM

Carnival glass bowl, ribbon-edge iridescent leaf and grape design, 7-1/2" dia. **$50**

Courtesy of Specialists of the South, Inc., www.specialistsofthesouth.com

Five swan bowls, colorless, Cambridge Glass Co., circa 1920s, #1044 and four #1040 examples, 3" to 10" dia. **$110**

Courtesy of Jeffrey S. Evans & Associates, Inc., www.jeffreysevans.com

◀ Cruet, chrysanthemum swirl pattern, colorless opalescent with satin finish, Northwood Glass Co./Buckeye Glass Co., circa 1890, applied handle with pressed plume design to upper terminal, paneled stopper, 6-3/4" **$50**

Courtesy of Jeffrey S. Evans & Associates, Inc., www.jeffreysevans.com

▶ Cruet, beaded circle, H. Northwood & Co., circa 1904, custard with gilt and floral polychrome-enamel decoration, later pressed facet custard stopper, 6-7/8" **$50**

Courtesy of Jeffrey S. Evans & Associates, Inc., www.jeffreysevans.com

Compote, vaseline art glass, optic-patterned bowl with factory polished rim, possibly Czech, first half 20th century, Vaseline (black lighted) circular twisted stem with applied ruby crimped decoration, figural vaseline and ruby decorative flower, ruby foot with pressed fan design, 8" h., 6-1/2" dia. bowl rim. **$475**

Courtesy of Jeffrey S. Evans & Associates, Inc., www.jeffreysevans.com

Vase, medium green, Boston & Sandwich Glass Co., circa 1845-1865, deep hexagonal bowl with pulled and flared six-petal rim and ovoid lower bull's-eyes, hexagonal flared foot, polished pontil mark, single-piece construction, 6-1/4" h., 3-3/4" dia. rim, 2-3/4" dia. foot. **$850**

Courtesy of Jeffrey S. Evans & Associates, Inc., www.jeffreysevans.com

Vase, medium honey amber, Boston & Sandwich Glass Co., circa 1840-1860, small-size version, hexagonal bowl with flared six-scallop rim, no reinforcement ridge to scallops, five lines through each upper loop, hexagonal foot with factory polished lower mold lines and table ring, single-piece construction, 4-3/4" h., 3-1/4" dia. rim, 2-5/8" dia. foot..... **$850**

Courtesy of Jeffrey S. Evans & Associates, Inc., www.jeffreysevans.com

Candlesticks, Dolphin Double-Step pattern, rare set of four, likely Boston & Sandwich Glass Co., circa 1845-1870, electric/copper blue, each six-petal socket with lower extension, medium dolphin-form standard and square base, wafer construction, 9-7/8" h., 3-5/8" sq. base......................... **$4,000**

Courtesy of Jeffrey S. Evans & Associates, Inc., www.jeffreysevans.com

Pitcher, spatter, colorless with cranberry and opal flakes, Northwood Glass Co., fourth quarter 19th century, circular-form crimped rim, applied colorless handle with pressed-fan design to upper terminal, 8-1/2"............................... **$50**

Courtesy of Jeffrey S. Evans & Associates, Inc., www.jeffreysevans.com

Rare and important basket, deep fiery opalescent, Boston & Sandwich Glass Co., circa 1840-1855, bowl with 32-point rim above 16 vertical staves, 34-point star under slumped conical base, hexagonal knop and flared base, wafer construction, 8" h., 8-1/4" dia. rim, 5-1/4" dia. foot. **$7,000**

Courtesy of Jeffrey S. Evans & Associates, Inc., www.jeffreysevans.com

Vase, deep amethyst with applied opal rim, Boston & Sandwich Glass Co., circa 1840-1860, small conical bowl with six loops twisted to right and gauffered eight-petal rim, ring-top hexagonal baluster-form standard and panel-top circular foot, wafer construction, rare, 8" h., 4-1/2" dia. rim, 4" dia. base. **$5,000**

Courtesy of Jeffrey S. Evans & Associates, Inc., www.jeffreysevans.com

Crucifix form candlestick, New England Glass Co., circa 1870-1890, cobalt blue, hexagonal socket above crucifix standard embossed "INRI" at top, stepped hexagonal base, single-piece construction, made by numerous companies, 9-7/8" h., 4" dia. base. **$225**

Courtesy of Jeffrey S. Evans & Associates, Inc., www.jeffreysevans.com

Compote, grapevine and acanthus leaf form, circa 1860-1875, colorless lead glass, shallow bowl with wide, flared 12-petal rim, hollow pillar and leaf stem and circular foot, wafer construction, 7" h., 8-1/2" dia., 5-1/4" dia. foot. **$20**

Courtesy of Jeffrey S. Evans & Associates, Inc., www.jeffreysevans.com

Sweetmeat dish, colorless lead glass, Boston & Sandwich Glass Co., circa 1840-1865, 17 loops with conforming cover, seven-loop foot, wafer construction, 8-1/2", 6-1/2" dia., 4-1/4" dia. foot... **$60**

Courtesy of Jeffrey S. Evans & Associates, Inc., www.jeffreysevans.com

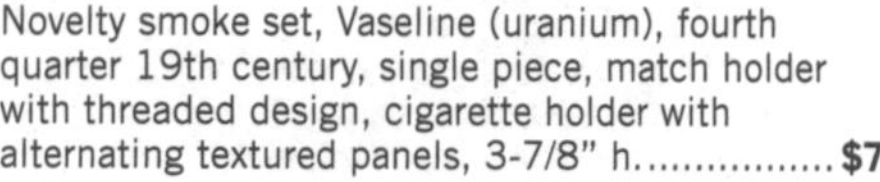

Novelty smoke set, Vaseline (uranium), fourth quarter 19th century, single piece, match holder with threaded design, cigarette holder with alternating textured panels, 3-7/8" h. **$70**

Courtesy of Jeffrey S. Evans & Associates, Inc., www.jeffreysevans.com

Sugar bowl, cobalt blue octagonal form, probably made by New England Glass Co. or possibly by Curling, Robertson & Sons of Pittsburgh, California, circa 1850-1870, two different alternating scroll and acanthus leaf designs in panels, circular foot with pattern underneath, lacking cover, 3-7/8" h., 4-7/8" dia. rim, 3" dia. foot.. **$50**

Courtesy of Jeffrey S. Evans & Associates, Inc., www.jeffreysevans.com

Lacy hairpin square dish, Boston & Sandwich Glass Co., circa 1830-1840, colorless, center with leaf-like quatrefoil enclosing four-petal blossom set within background of tiny diamonds in squares, scallop and point rim, rare and important with seven examples known, 1-1/4" h., 7-3/8" x 7-3/4"... **$1,300**

Courtesy of Jeffrey S. Evans & Associates, Inc., www.jeffreysevans.com

Tumbler with Civil War motif, circa 1865, colorless lead glass, one side embossed with cannon, trench mortar, tamping rod, and cannon balls with flag flying above, reverse with spread-wing American eagle with breast shield, one talon holding long sword and other with flagpole and unfurled 34-star flag, liberty pole with cap covers both mold lines, polished table ring, 4-5/8" h. . **$250**

Courtesy of Jeffrey S. Evans & Associates, Inc., www.jeffreysevans.com

Opalescent figural boat inkstand with pewter hinged lid, New England Glass Co., circa 1870-1890, lightly embossed "PAT'D AUG. 9. 1870", 2-3/8" h. x 5-1/2" l. **$150**

Courtesy of Jeffrey S. Evans & Associates, Inc., www.jeffreysevans.com

Esther pattern amber-stained seven-piece water set, Riverside Glass Works, 1896, colorless with polychrome-enamel decoration, pitcher with applied colorless handle with pressed feather design to upper terminal, six tumblers with factory polished bases, 3-3/4" to 10-1/8" h. **$150**

Courtesy of Jeffrey S. Evans & Associates, Inc., www.jeffreysevans.com

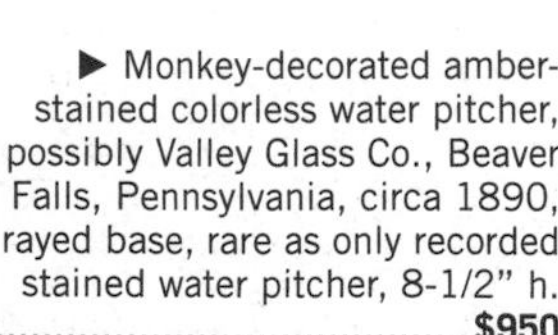

▶ Monkey-decorated amber-stained colorless water pitcher, possibly Valley Glass Co., Beaver Falls, Pennsylvania, circa 1890, rayed base, rare as only recorded stained water pitcher, 8-1/2" h. **$950**

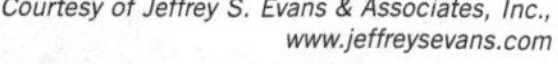

Courtesy of Jeffrey S. Evans & Associates, Inc., www.jeffreysevans.com

Lighthouse-shaped rectangular covered honey/butter dish, colorless, Canton Glass Co., fourth-quarter 19th century, cover with lighthouse on one side and sinking ship on other, shaped star and button finial, base with two handles, knife rack and four feet, likely unique, 7-1/4" h. x 4" x 4-7/8" cover, 6-1/2" x 8-1/4" base. **$2,000**

Courtesy of Jeffrey S. Evans & Associates, Inc., www.jeffreysevans.com

▲ Waisted loop cologne bottle, probably Boston & Sandwich Glass Co., circa 1840-1870, medium green with original gilt decoration, medium-size hexagonal bottle with panel-cut neck, factory polished lip and pontil mark, original flower-form stopper with gilt decoration, each unit numbered 28, 5-5/8" h. overall, bottle 3-5/8" h., 3-1/8" dia. base. **$250**

Courtesy of Jeffrey S. Evans & Associates, Inc., www.jeffreysevans.com

GLASS

quezal

IN 1901, Martin Bach and Thomas Johnson, who had worked for Louis Tiffany, opened a competing glassworks in Brooklyn, New York, called the Quezal Art Glass and Decorating Co. Named for the quetzal, a bird with brilliantly colored features, Quezal produced wares closely resembling those of Tiffany until the plant closed in 1925. In general, Quezal pieces are more defined than Tiffany glass, and the decorations are brighter and more visible.

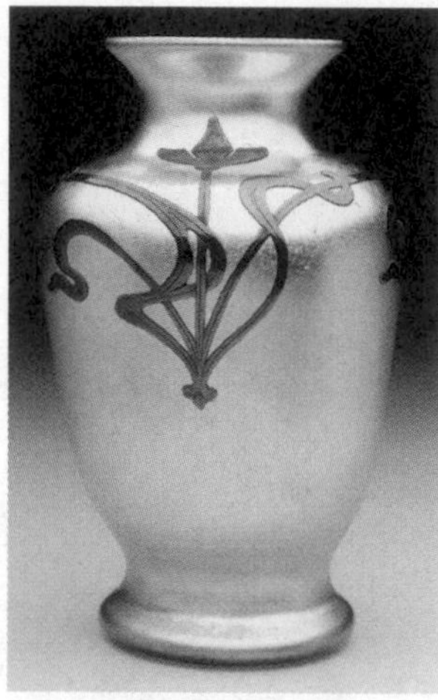

Vase in iridescent gold with pink and blue flashes around foot, silver overlay around shoulder and design of stylized flower and scrolling leaves, signed "Quezal" in polish pontil, very good condition, silver overlay lifting in places and one flower missing, 6-3/4" h. **$267**

Courtesy of James D. Julia Auctioneers, Fairfield, Maine, www.jamesdjulia.com

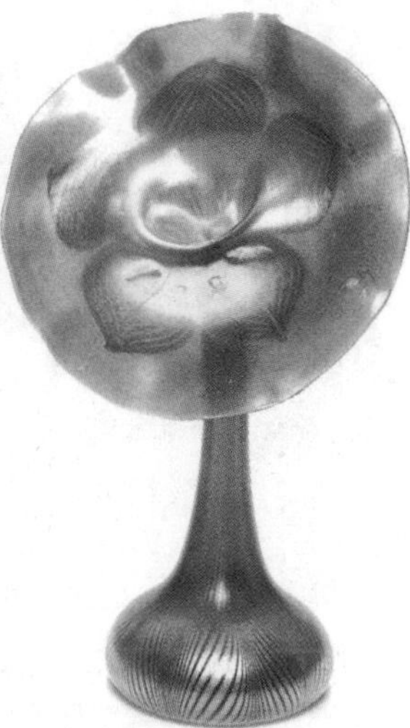

Jack-in-the-pulpit vase, iridescent gold body in five green pulled feathers design extending up body with strong iridescent tones, undulating open face with factory burst bubble, signed "Quezal" on pontil, 14-3/4" h. **$2,662**

Courtesy of James D. Julia Auctioneers, Fairfield, Maine, www.jamesdjulia.com

Vase with dragged loop design from foot to top of shoulder and iridescent gold zipper pattern from foot to lip against cream-colored background, very good to excellent condition, 7" h. **$533**

Courtesy of James D. Julia Auctioneers, Fairfield, Maine, www.jamesdjulia.com

Vase with butterscotch background and iridescent green heart and vine décor, 6-3/4" h. **$767**

Courtesy of Woody Auction, www.woodyauction.com

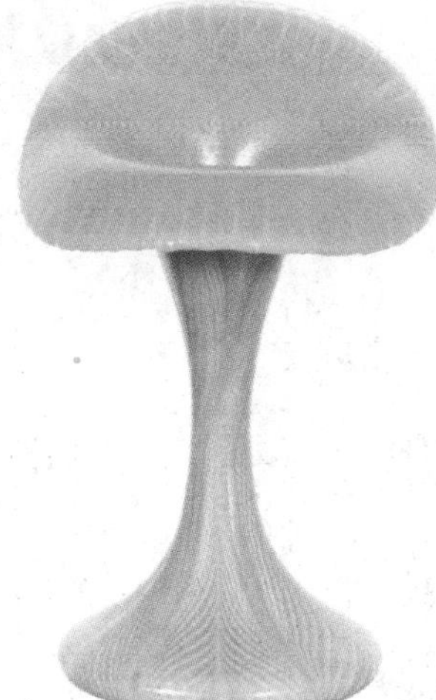

Jack-in-the-pulpit vase, green and gold with pulled feather design and white highlights and gold interior, 5" h. **$1,534**

Courtesy of Woody Auction, www.woodyauction.com

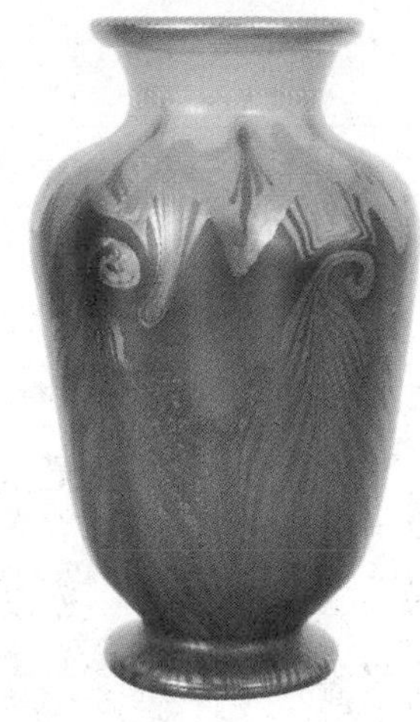

Vase, dark green with silver pulled leaf design and gold and white highlights, inscribed "C937" on base, excellent color, 5-1/4" h. **$1,180**

Courtesy of Woody Auction, www.woodyauction.com

Vase in iridescent green and yellow with blue and rose shades and leaf décor with end volutes, rounded bole and flared neck, early 20th century, signed "Quezal" on base, 6" h.........**$927**

Courtesy of IEGOR, www.iegor.net

▲ Vase with opal body with cinched neck and heavy decoration of gold pulled feathers tipped in green, signed "Quezal C 97" on pontil, 4" h........... **$726**

Courtesy of Early Auction Co., www.earlyauctionco.com

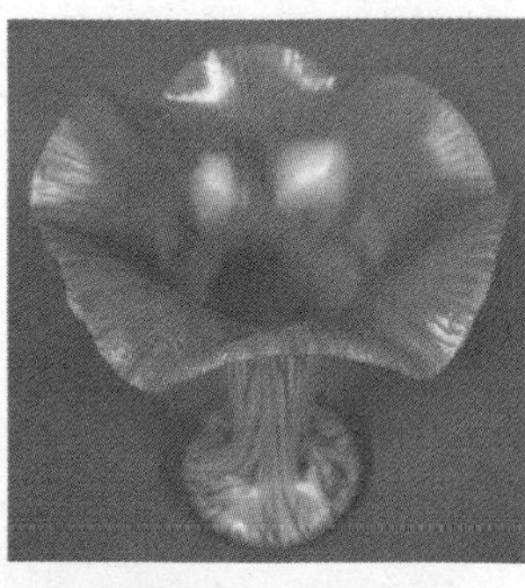

◀ Vase in iridescent green pulled feather design with gold highlights, iridescent gold interior, "555" inscribed on base with "Bailey Banks & Biddle" paper label, 9-1/4" h., 7-1/2" dia....................... **$1,003**

Courtesy of Woody Auction, www.woodyauction.com

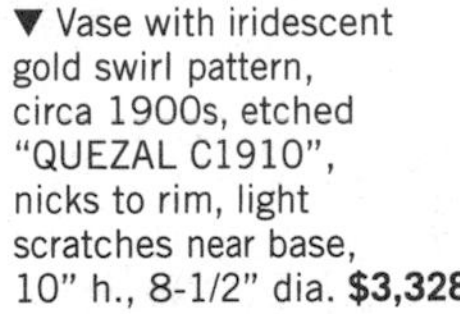

▼ Vase with iridescent gold swirl pattern, circa 1900s, etched "QUEZAL C1910", nicks to rim, light scratches near base, 10" h., 8-1/2" dia. **$3,328**

Courtesy of Rago Arts and Auctions, www.ragoauctions.com

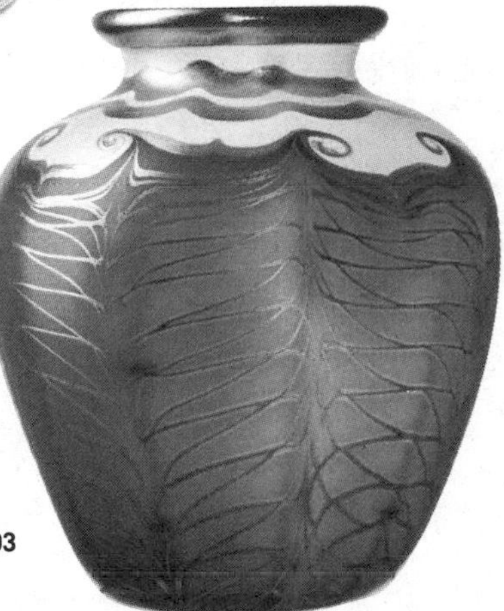

Arts & Crafts chandelier with Quezal shades, circa 1900s, patinated metal, four sockets and shades, etched "QUEZAL" on shades, rewired, frame in good original condition and original shades in excellent condition, fixture 15" h., 19" dia., shades 5-1/4" h., 5" dia. **$1,280**

Courtesy of Rago Arts and Auctions, www.ragoauctions.com

◀ Four blue shades in pulled feather design, lobed bodies, iridescent gold interiors, early 20th century, marked Quezal, 5-1/2" h. **$1,536**

Courtesy Neal Auction Co., www.nealauction.com

Three shades with hooked feather design, good condition, signed, 3-1/4" h., 3-3/4" dia. **$615**

Courtesy of Westport Auction, www.westportauction.com

Four shades, gold aurene in bell form and etched "Quezal" along inner lip of each, 5" h., 4-1/4" dia. **$406**

Courtesy of New Orleans Auction, www.neworleansauction.com

Vase in iridescent green and gold with pulled feather design, gold interior, and tri-fold rim, marked "P613" on base, 9-1/4" h. **$1,180**

Courtesy of Woody Auction, www.woodyauction.com

GLASS

sandwich glass

NUMEROUS TYPES OF glass were produced at the Boston & Sandwich Glass Co. in Sandwich, Massachusetts, on Cape Cod, from 1826 to 1888. Founded by Deming Jarves, the company produced a wide variety of wares in differing levels of quality. The factory used free-blown, blown three-mold, and pressed glass manufacturing techniques. Both clear and colored glasses were used.

Jarves served as general manager from 1826-1858, and after he left, emphasis was placed on mass production. The development of a lime glass (non-flint) led to lower costs for pressed glass. Some free-blown and blown-and-molded pieces were made. By the 1880s the company was operating at a loss, and the factory closed on Jan. 1, 1888.

Three free-blown and decorated smoke bells, opal with polychrome floral decoration, each with gaufered rims and period metal caps and brass ring hangers, Boston & Sandwich Glass Co. and others, circa 1850-1888, 3-1/4" h., 3-3/4" dia. **$480**

Courtesy of Jeffrey S. Evans & Associates, www.jeffreysevans.com

Pressed Ashburton quart bar decanter, deep amethyst lead glass, Prussian form with applied collared bar lip and polished pontil mark, Boston & Sandwich Glass Co. and others, circa 1840-1880, 10" h. **$720**

Courtesy of Jeffrey S. Evans & Associates, www.jeffreysevans.com

Footed rectangular salt dish, opalescent light blue with diamond, scroll, and floral motifs, Boston & Sandwich Glass Co., labeled William J. Elsholz Collection, circa 1840-1880, good condition with pin nips, 2" h. x 3-1/2" w. **$3,025**

Courtesy of Conestoga Auction Co., www.conestogaauction.com

top lot

Pressed Four-Printie Block whale oil/fluid stand lamps, deep amethyst, each with dome-top conical font with hexagonal knop extension, hexagonal compressed knop and flared foot, with wafer construction, each fitted with pewter fine-line collars, Boston & Sandwich Glass Co. and possibly others, circa 1840-1850, excellent condition overall, flake to foot of one, other with three flakes to rim of foot, one with slightly loose collar, 11-1/4" h., 5-1/4" dia. **$5,100**

COURTESY OF JEFFREY S. EVANS & ASSOCIATES, WWW.JEFFREYSEVANS.COM

Three candlesticks, colorless, all near matching, and two pink curtain tie-backs, circa mid-19th century, candlesticks 7" h. **$84**

Courtesy Hyde Park Country Auctions, www.hpcountryauctions.com

Pressed Dolphin double-step candlesticks, starch blue over alabaster/clambroth, shiny surfaces, each six-petal socket with lower extension, raised on medium dolphin-form standard and square base, wafer construction, probably Boston & Sandwich Glass Co., circa 1845-1870, 9-3/4" h. x 3-5/8" sq. base. **$1,725**

Courtesy of Jeffrey S. Evans & Associates, www.jeffreysevans.com

Pressed hexagonal socket and loop candlesticks, violet blue, each thick-lipped urn-form socket with compressed knop lower extension, raised on hexagonal knop and seven-loop circular base with rough pontil mark, wafer construction, circa 1840-1860, undamaged, 6-3/4" h., 4-3/8" dia. base. **$1,955**

Courtesy of Jeffrey S. Evans & Associates, www.jeffreysevans.com

Pressed hexagonal candlestick, medium amber, standard size, urn-shape socket with double-knop lower extension, raised on hexagonal base with ringed standard, wafer construction, probably Boston & Sandwich Glass Co., circa 1840-1860, 9" h., 4-1/2" dia. overall base.........**$1,495**

Courtesy of Jeffrey S. Evans & Associates, www.jeffreysevans.com

Pressed hexagonal and square candlesticks, yellow (uranium), each thick-lipped hexagonal socket with lower knop extension, raised on octagonal baluster-form standard and square base with lemon-squeezer interior, wafer construction, Boston & Sandwich Glass Co. and others, 1840-1860, one with sliver chip to one upper base corner, other with glued socket, 7-1/2" h. x 3" sq. base.... **$92**

Courtesy of Jeffrey S. Evans & Associates, www.jeffreysevans.com

Pressed hexagonal candlesticks, yellow (uranium), each thin-lipped socket with lower knop extension, raised on hexagonal knop and oversized flared base, wafer construction, Boston & Sandwich Glass Co. and possibly others, 1840-1860, undamaged, 7-1/2" h., 5-1/2" dia. overall base. **$207**

Courtesy of Jeffrey S. Evans & Associates, www.jeffreysevans.com

Glass candlesticks, yellow, in molded hexagonal form, minor flakes to base, 7-1/2" h....... **$173**

Courtesy of Thomaston Place Auction Galleries, www.thomastonauction.com

Pressed flattened sawtooth font, Dolphin base whale oil/fluid stand lamps, colorless, each dome-top slightly conical font with short lower extension, raised on medium-size dolphin standard and concave-sided hexagonal base with three concentric rings underneath, wafer construction, near matching No. 1 brass collars fitted with matching brass double-tube fluid burners, original chains and caps, circa 1840-1860, excellent overall condition, 11-1/2" h. to top of collar, 4-1/2" dia. overall base. **$1,150**

Courtesy of Jeffrey S. Evans & Associates, www.jeffreysevans.com

Pressed Heart stand lamps, translucent starch blue over alabaster/clambroth, each dome-top hexagonal font raised on hexagonal baluster-form standard and base, wafer construction, matching brass fine-line collars and four-tube vapor burners, Boston & Sandwich Glass Co. and possibly others, 1845-1860, one with flake to lower base corner, other with crack to font, 10" h. to top of collar, 4-1/2" dia. overall base. **$1,265**

Courtesy of Jeffrey S. Evans & Associates, www.jeffreysevans.com

Pressed Four-Printie Block stand lamps, yellow, each dome-top conical font with hexagonal knop extension, raised on hexagonal compressed knop and flared base, wafer construction, pewter fine-line collars and double-tube fluid burners with chains and caps, Boston & Sandwich Glass Co. and possibly others, 1840-1850, flake to outer edge of one base, 11" h. to top of collars, 5-1/4" dia. overall base. **$1,265**

Courtesy of Jeffrey S. Evans & Associates, www.jeffreysevans.com

Frosted Madonna standards, colorless, each figural Madonna stem on ribbed and scalloped foot, with two appropriate metal screw mounts (one lacking female part) and turban-form ring sleeve, with two bobeches and nine prisms of unknown association, circa 1870-1887, one undamaged, other with shallow chip under base standards, 10-1/2" h., 6" dia. base. **$207**

Courtesy of Jeffrey S. Evans & Associates, www.jeffreysevans.com

GLASS

steuben

FREDERICK CARDER, an Englishman, and Thomas G. Hawkes of Corning, New York, established the Steuben Glass Works in 1903 in Steuben County, New York. In 1918, the Corning Glass Co. purchased the Steuben company. Carder remained with the firm and designed many of the pieces bearing the Steuben mark. Probably the most widely recognized wares are Aurene, Verre De Soie, and Rosaline, but many other types were produced. The firm operated until 2011.

Shade with reddish/brown hooked loop design descending from fitter with matching pulled feather ascending from ruffled rim, cream-colored background with yellow interior and light iridescence, signed in fitter with silver fleur-de-lis "Steuben" mark, very good to excellent condition, shallow flake on top of fitter, 5-1/4" h. **$830**

Courtesy of James D. Julia Auctioneers, Fairfield, Maine, www.jamesdjulia.com

Bell-shaped shade with butterscotch exterior, dark to light gradient from top to rim, case white interior, unsigned, roughness to top edge of shade from making, 8" h., 16-3/8" dia. **$474**

Courtesy of James D. Julia Auctioneers, Fairfield, Maine, www.jamesdjulia.com

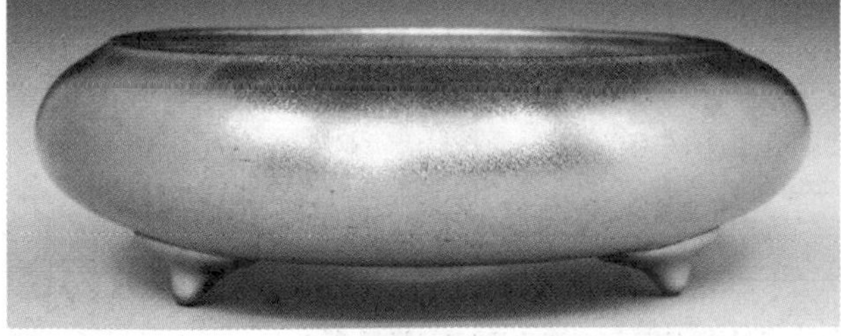

Aurene bowl with rolled rim and three applied free-form feet, gold iridescence with subtle pink highlights, signed "Aurene 2536" on underside, very good condition, minor staining to interior, 6" d. ... **$208**

Courtesy of James D. Julia Auctioneers, Fairfield, Maine, www.jamesdjulia.com

top lot

Asian-influenced vase in Rouge Flambé, unsigned, with remnants of original Steuben paper label, small cinder inclusion at lip from making, very good to excellent condition, 6" h. $9,480

COURTESY OF JAMES D. JULIA AUCTIONEERS, FAIRFIELD, MAINE, WWW.JAMESDJULIA.COM

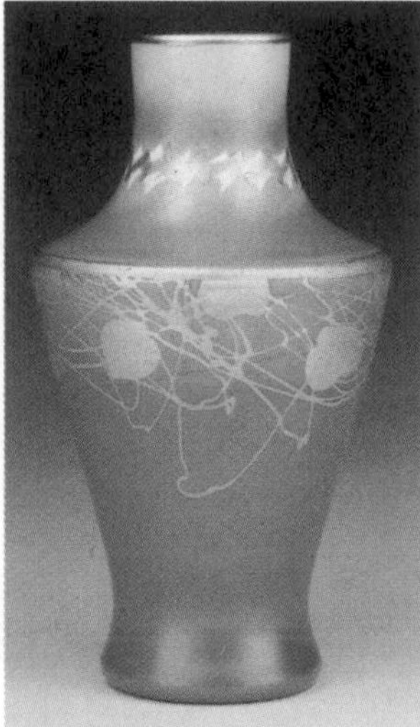

Tyrian pattern vase with gold iridescent heart and vine design surrounding shoulder and intarsia border encircling neck, shade gradient from light green at top to bluish/purple at bottom, applied gold iridescent lip, etched signature "Tyrian" on underside, 8-1/2" h..... **$4,444**

Courtesy of James D. Julia Auctioneers, Fairfield, Maine, www.jamesdjulia.com

Vase with acid cutback Rosaline stylized flowers, stems and leaves encircling body against acid-textured alabaster background, 9-1/2" h. **$1,185**

Courtesy of James D. Julia Auctioneers, Fairfield, Maine, www.jamesdjulia.com

▲ Moss agate vase in green, amber, red, and brown with gold flecks throughout, bottom of vase drilled and plugged with cork, bottom of foot with small chips, bottom interior of vase with staining, 7" h.............. **$830**

Courtesy of James D. Julia Auctioneers, Fairfield, Maine, www.jamesdjulia.com

◀ Vase with alabaster body with two applied black jade leaf-and-vine-design handles, 8" h. **$948**

Courtesy of James D. Julia Auctioneers, Fairfield, Maine, www.jamesdjulia.com

Pair of wine glasses, each with inverted saucer foot and hollow blown stem with ribbed disc at top of stem supporting bowl that is intaglio carved with panels containing fern leaf and floral garland, top of wine in flashed cranberry glass with engraved ribbon, one with etched script signature "Steuben" on underside, one unsigned, 7-1/2" h. **$1,185**

Courtesy of James D. Julia Auctioneers, Fairfield, Maine, www.jamesdjulia.com

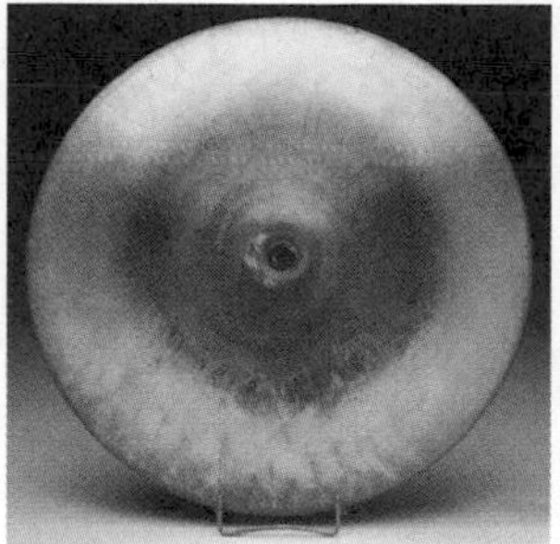

Gold Aurene rondel with iridescence shading from gold to platinum in center with blue and red highlights on front side, backside with platinum iridescence at edge and gold iridescence shading to red at center with lightly polished pontil, light scratches to iridescence, 12-1/4" h........ **$415**

Courtesy of James D. Julia Auctioneers, Fairfield, Maine, www.jamesdjulia.com

Wine glass with clear inverted saucer foot with opalescent rim and opalescence at bottom and top of clear twisted stem, Oriental jade cup with swirling bands of white opalescence, 7-1/4" h. **$711**

Courtesy of James D. Julia Auctioneers, Fairfield, Maine, www.jamesdjulia.com

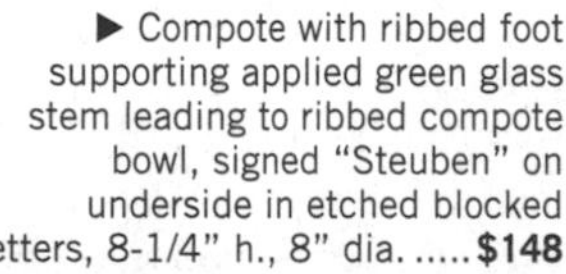

▶ Compote with ribbed foot supporting applied green glass stem leading to ribbed compote bowl, signed "Steuben" on underside in etched blocked letters, 8-1/4" h., 8" dia. **$148**

Courtesy of James D. Julia Auctioneers, Fairfield, Maine, www.jamesdjulia.com

Covered amber jar with pedestal foot and chalice-shaped body with original amber glass lid with glass apple and leaf finial, very good to excellent condition, flake to inside rim of lid and minor roughness to lid rim, 10-1/2" h. **$356**

Courtesy of James D. Julia Auctioneers, Fairfield, Maine, www.jamesdjulia.com

Chandelier with Arts & Crafts fixture and hammered inverted dome suspended from four heavy chains, hammered ceiling cap, hammered shade holders suspended from upper lip of dome, vertically ribbed with gold iridescence with strong pink and platinum highlights, one shade with remnants of silver fleur-de-lis mark in fitter, others are unsigned, two shades with flakes to fitters, 24-1/2" h. **$3,259**

Courtesy of James D. Julia Auctioneers, Fairfield, Maine, www.jamesdjulia.com

Clear crystal rock sculpture with gold vermeil thistle rising from top of rock, designed by James Houston, circa 1967, etched signature "Steuben" on underside, 7-1/2" h. **$3,851**

Courtesy of James D. Julia Auctioneers, Fairfield, Maine, www.jamesdjulia.com

GLASS

tiffany glass

TIFFANY & CO. was founded by Charles Lewis Tiffany (1812-1902) and Teddy Young in New York City in 1837. Originally called Tiffany, Young and Ellis, the name was shortened to Tiffany & Co. in 1853 when Charles Tiffany took control and shifted the firm's focus to jewelry.

By the 1860s, Tiffany & Co. had established itself as America's most prestigious and reputable firm, first by importing the best of European goods and then by manufacturing its own wares of the highest quality. From 1867 until the end of the century, Tiffany exhibited and won medals at international expositions in Paris and the United States.

Charles' son, Louis Comfort Tiffany (1848-1933), was an American artist and designer who worked in the decorative arts and is best known for his work in stained glass. This outstanding American glass designer established Tiffany Glass Co. in 1885, and in 1902 it became known as Tiffany Studios, producing glass until the early 1930s.

Tiffany revived early techniques and devised many new ones. His work in large part defined both the Art Nouveau and Aesthetic movements. In the world of antiques and collectibles, his name is ubiquitous - even those who do not collect Tiffany Studios items know who he is and what his work looks like.

Because Tiffany Studios' glass is so widely loved and collected, there is a significant market in fakes, especially at the higher end of the spectrum, most specifically in lamps. This makes verification the most important thing to look for when it comes to Tiffany Studios.

For more Tiffany lamps, please see the "Lighting" section.

Cypriot vase with bubbled gold iridescent surface, areas of strong blue, purple, and green, signed "L.C. Tiffany-Favrile 9759J" on underside, very good to excellent condition, 5-1/2" h...........**$11,850**

Courtesy of James D. Julia Auctioneers, Fairfield, Maine, www.jamesdjulia.com

Flower-form vase with vertically ribbed inverted saucer foot with green pulled feather decoration extending up from stem and onto side of bowl, set against cream-white background with wide flaring ruffled and stretched rim with gold iridescence and red highlights, signed "L.C. Tiffany-Favrile 8824 C" on underside, very good to excellent condition, 7-1/2" h., 8-7/8" dia.................. **$1,185**

Courtesy of James D. Julia Auctioneers, Fairfield, Maine, www.jamesdjulia.com

Cabinet vase with gold Cypriot finish and lava-like band flowing around body, bluish/green interior, signed "L.C. Tiffany-Favrile 4959E" on underside, very good to excellent condition, 3-1/2" h. **$11,257**

Courtesy of James D. Julia Auctioneers, Fairfield, Maine, www.jamesdjulia.com

Art glass shade with faint pulled feather decoration descending from fitter against gold iridescent translucent background with faint diamond quilted pattern, numbered S11108 in fitter, very good to excellent condition, small flake to edge of fitter, 5" h. **$948**

Courtesy of James D. Julia Auctioneers, Fairfield, Maine, www.jamesdjulia.com

Tel el Amarna vase with gold iridescent body with pink and purple highlights on shoulder, applied neck with intarsia band of gold iridescent pulled feather design overlaid with cream-colored zigzag line, bronze iridescent background, signed "L.C. Tiffany-Favrile 4586 H" on underside, 5-7/8" h..... **$5,925**

Courtesy of James D. Julia Auctioneers, Fairfield, Maine, www.jamesdjulia.com

Jack-in-the-Pulpit vase with bulbous foot, long slender neck, and wide flaring and lightly ruffled face with stretched rim, gold iridescence with strong pink and green highlights, gold iridescence shading on foot and transparent amber on neck, signed "L.C. Tiffany-Favrile 5804 G" on underside, 18-1/4" h......**$11,257**

Courtesy of James D. Julia Auctioneers, Fairfield, Maine, www.jamesdjulia.com

Gold Favrile glass vase, circa 1908, etched "2448C L.C. Tiffany – Favrile," moderate wear and scratches to interior, 16-1/4" h. x 9-1/2" w...... **$1,920**

Courtesy of Rago Arts, www.ragoarts.com

Gold iridescent vase with strong pink and blue highlights at neck and platinum highlights at shoulder, signed "L.C. Tiffany-Favrile 3619 L" on underside, 16" h. **$1,066**

Courtesy of James D. Julia Auctioneers, Fairfield, Maine, www.jamesdjulia.com

Gold Favrile flower-form vase with vertically ribbed inverted saucer foot and body with ribs twisting slightly at top, gold iridescence with purple and green highlights on ribbing, top of vase glows red when backlit, signed "L.C. Tiffany-Favrile 3728D" on underside, very good condition, some inconsistencies in iridescent finish near bottom of vase, 17-7/8" h. **$1,125**

Courtesy of James D. Julia Auctioneers, Fairfield, Maine, www.jamesdjulia.com

Flower-form vase with translucent gold iridescent inverted saucer foot with green pulled feather design beginning at foot and extending to lip of vase, cream-white opaque background at top, iridescent foot with strong red, green, and blue highlights, signed "L.C.T. R9789" on underside, very good condition, some minor roughness to lip caused by open bubbles from making, 13" h................. **$7,500**

Courtesy of James D. Julia Auctioneers, Fairfield, Maine, www.jamesdjulia.com

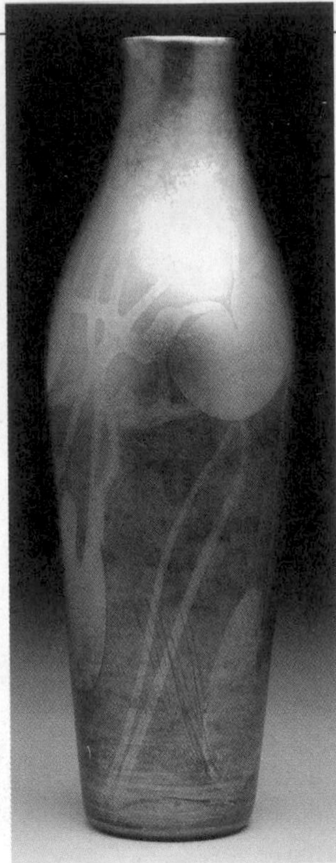

Dark gold iridescent vase with lighter gold leaf and vine decoration surrounding body, blue, purple, and pink highlights within iridescence, signed "L.C. Tiffany-Favrile H 4716 C" on underside and retains original Tiffany-Favrile Glass paper label on button pontil, very good to excellent condition, 13-1/2" h........ **$3,550**

Courtesy of James D. Julia Auctioneers, Fairfield, Maine, www.jamesdjulia.com

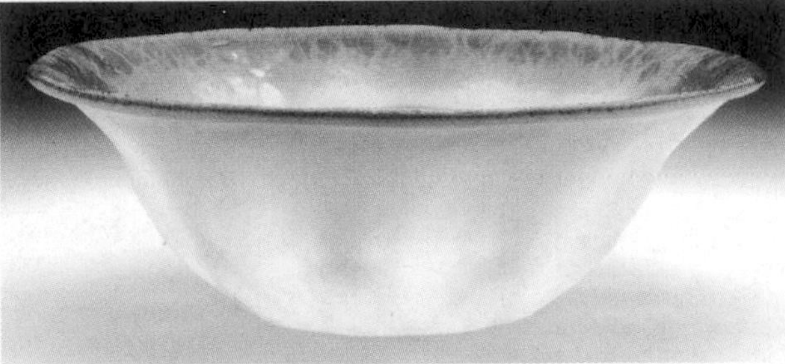

Deep blue iridescent bowl with stretched rim, white and pastel yellow opalescent vertical bands lead to clear bottom with white opalescent center, exterior of bowl in white and pastel yellow opalescent with intaglio-carved butterfly image on rim and intaglio-carved flower covering polish pontil, signed with engraved signature "L.C. Tiffany-Inc. Favrile" on underside, 9-1/4" d. **$830**

Courtesy of James D. Julia Auctioneers, Fairfield, Maine, www.jamesdjulia.com

top lot!

Vase with textured lava-like exterior and decorated with random free-form bands of smooth gold iridescence surrounding body, interior in robin's egg blue that shows through somewhat when vase is backlit, signed "L.C.T. R1849" on underside, 3-1/2" h. $17,775

COURTESY OF JAMES D. JULIA AUCTIONEERS, FAIRFIELD, MAINE, WWW.JAMESDJULIA.COM

Candle shade with gold iridescent damascene design, light pink and platinum highlights, small ruffled rim, unsigned, numbered H2522, 3-1/4" h. **$827**

Courtesy of James D. Julia Auctioneers, Fairfield, Maine, www.jamesdjulia.com

Cabinet vase with green leaf and vine decoration with white highlighting within each green leaf, gold iridescent background with pink and blue highlights, signed "L.C. Tiffany Inc. Favrile 1036-6525M" on underside, 2-7/8" h. **$1,185**

Courtesy of James D. Julia Auctioneers, Fairfield, Maine, www.jamesdjulia.com

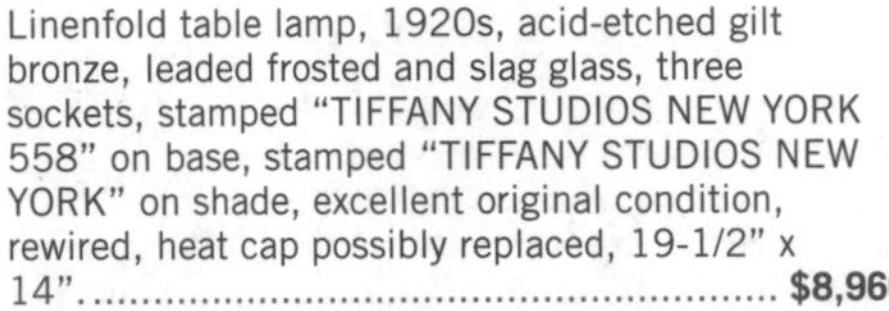

Linenfold table lamp, 1920s, acid-etched gilt bronze, leaded frosted and slag glass, three sockets, stamped "TIFFANY STUDIOS NEW YORK 558" on base, stamped "TIFFANY STUDIOS NEW YORK" on shade, excellent original condition, rewired, heat cap possibly replaced, 19-1/2" x 14".. **$8,960**

Courtesy of Rago Arts and Auctions, www.ragoarts.com

Arrowroot-design leaded glass table lamp, three-light metal base with leaded stained glass shade in green, yellow, and red floral Arrowroot pattern, marked "Tiffany Studios, New York" on shade, base not marked, very good condition, shade 20" dia.. **$3,146**

Courtesy of Briggs Auction, Inc., www.briggsauction.com

Bronze and Favrile glass 10-light lily lamp, circa 1910, stamped "TIFFANY STUDIOS, NEW YORK 381" on base, engraved "L.C.T." on shades, base with all original elements, one nozzle loose and in need of repair, one shade unsigned, internal fracture to socket rim, 21-1/8" h. **$20,000**

Courtesy of Heritage Auctions, ha.com

Leaded glass and bronze Poinsettia table lamp on Mushroom base, circa 1905, stamped "TIFFANY STUDIOS NEW YORK, 394 S197; 1557-8" on shade, cracking throughout shade toward border and foliage, strengthening to one border tile interior, original sockets and pull chains, rewired, 22-1/2" h., 16" dia. **$30,000**

Courtesy of Heritage Auctions, ha.com

Signed turtleback lamp with original marked Tiffany Studios three-panel shield shade with green slag panels and amethyst "turtleback" iridized medallions set on marked Tiffany Studios base, electrified, Bryant fittings, good condition, 15-1/2" x 8-1/2". **$5,310**

Courtesy of Woody Auction, www.woodyauction.com

Table lamp signed Tiffany Studios, New York and numbered 419, signed "LCT" on green iridescent art glass shade, excellent condition, 13-3/4" h., shade 7" dia. **$6,710**

Courtesy of Morphy Auctions, www.morphyauctions.com

Bronze and gold Favrile glass four-light newel post lamp, Corona, New York, circa 1910, marked "TIFFANY STUDIOS, NEW YORK (CDTCO cypher), 315" on base, marked "L.C.T. Favrile" on shades, good condition, 23-1/2" h. excluding shades. **$9,376**

Courtesy of Heritage Auctions, ha.com

GLASS

tiffin

A WIDE VARIETY of fine glasswares were produced by the Tiffin Glass Co. of Tiffin, Ohio. Beginning as a part of the large U.S. Glass Co. early in the 20th century, the Tiffin factory continued making a wide range of wares until its final closing in 1984. One popular line is now called Black Satin and includes various vases with raised floral designs. Many other acid-etched and hand-cut patterns were also produced over the years and are collectible today. The three *Tiffin Glassmasters* books by Fred Bickenheuser are the standard references for Tiffin collectors.

Eight wine glasses etched with laurel leaf wreath, very good condition, 6" h. x 3-1/4" w., 3-1/4" dia.............................. **$153**

Courtesy of Charleston Auction Co., www.charlestonauctions.com

Shield pedestal sign for Tiffin Glass Collectors Club convention, circa 1980s, etched "Honoring Plant #" on base, 6" h. x 3-1/4" w. x 3-1/4" d. **$29**

Courtesy of Accurate Auctions, www.accurateauctions.com

Forty-eight glasses of "Psyche-Green" stemware in four sizes (part shown), etched with dancing nude figure, Tiffin-Franciscan, 8-3/4" h. **$413**

Courtesy of Leonard Auction, www.leonardauction.com

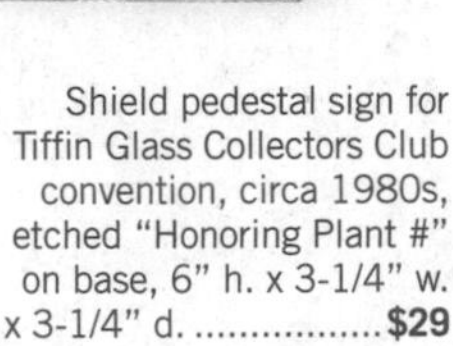

Hand-blown holiday parade cane with large hollow bulb and pulled and pointed end, late 1920s/early 1930s, Latticino interwoven spiral of cobalt blue and line green threads with brown around golden thread, 3-1/2" w. x 44" l................. **$19**

Courtesy of Accurate Auctions, www.accurateauctions.com

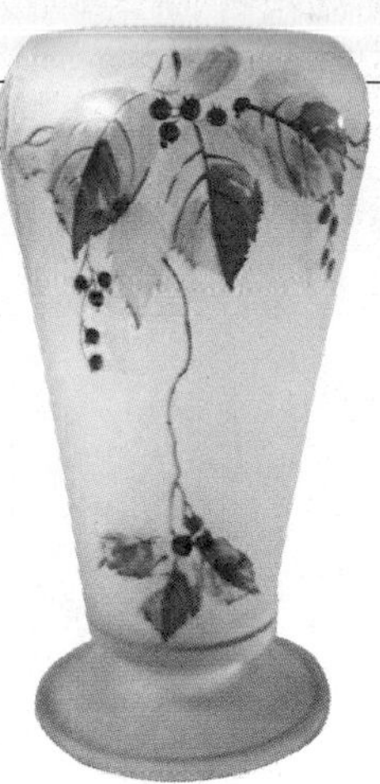
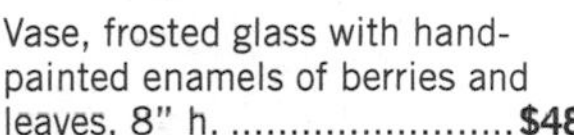

Vase, frosted glass with hand-painted enamels of berries and leaves, 8" h. **$48**

Courtesy of Klein James, www.kleinjames.com

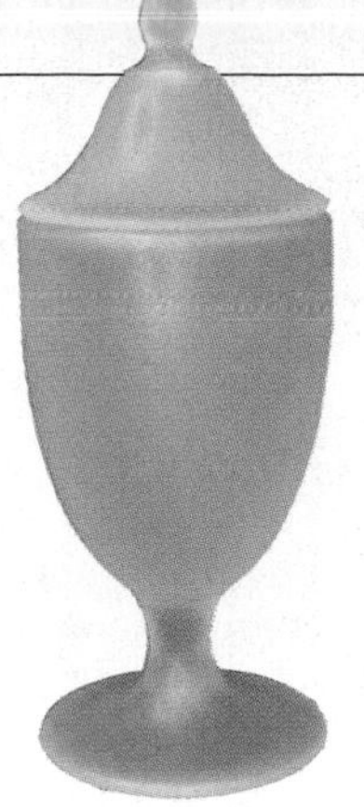

Covered candy jar, mid-1920s, topaz iridescent satin #179, soft tapered top, 9-3/4" h. x 3-1/2" w., 3-1/2" dia.......... **$111**

Courtesy of Accurate Auctions, www.accurateauctions.com

Assortment of Black Satin glass, circa 1920s: high crimped vase, 10" h.; candlesticks, 8" h.; and dresser box with gold floral accents, 6-1/4" h. x 3-1/2" w. x 2" d. . **$53**

Courtesy of Charleston Auction Co., www.charlestonauctions.com

Twenty-four pieces of Tiffin glass, early 20th century, 20 salad plates with gold encrusted rim, two different patterns, 10 plates in each pattern, octagon serving bowl, serving bowl, dessert plate, and serving dish, 6" dia. to 13" dia... **$115**

Courtesy of Shelly's Auction Gallery, www.liveauctioneers.com/shelleys-auction-gallery

Wine bottle, circa 1920s, Vaseline with traces of gilt decoration, etched grapevine design, fitted in unmarked mental stand, 10-1/2" h. **$84**

Courtesy of Jeffrey S. Evans & Associates, www.jeffreysevans.com

Pair of figural owl glass shades with threaded bases, probably Tiffin/U.S. Glass Co., 7-1/4" h., 3" dia.............. **$96**

Courtesy of Ron Rhodes Auctioneers, www.ronrhoads-auction.com

GLASS

wave crest

NOW MUCH SOUGHT after, Wave Crest was produced by the C. F. Monroe Co., Meriden, Connecticut, in the late 19th and early 20th centuries. It was made from opaque white glass blown into molds, then hand-decorated in enamels, and metal trim was often added. Boudoir accessories such as jewel boxes, hair receivers, etc., predominated.

Victorian-era hand-painted glass plaque with cast metal and gilt mounted ormolu frame, very good condition, 9-1/2" x 6-1/2" overall.................. **$2,460**

Courtesy of Nest Egg Auctions, www.nesteggauctions.com

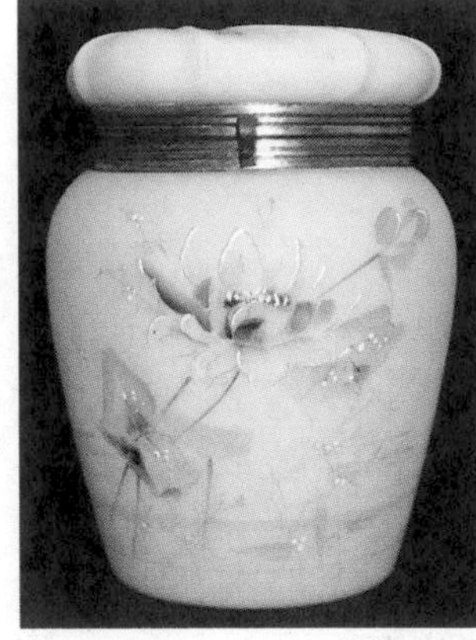

Hand-decorated cigar humidor with multicolored daisies, slight green-bluish tone on opal ware, lid in blown-out shell form, 7-1/2" h. x 6" w. **$338**

Courtesy of The Auction Gallery of Boca Raton, www.agobr.com

Tobacco jar in cobalt blue, scarce color and design, 6-1/4" h. **$826**

Courtesy of Professional Appraisers & Liquidators LLC, www.charliefudge.com

Small metal-mounted open pin tray with satin lining and green painted floral exterior, signed WAVE CREST, 5-1/2" w., and twist-form floral decorated biscuit jar with silver-plated lid and handle, unsigned, 7" h. x 6" w., both in good overall condition. **$307**

Courtesy of Nest Egg Auctions, www.nesteggauctions.com

Everted tapered and ribbed biscuit jar with lavender daisies and hand-beaded accents, 1906-1908, daisy and arches silver-plate band and handle, excellent condition, 6-1/2" x 6-1/2" x 10-1/2"................ **$121**

Courtesy of Accurate Auctions, www.accurateauctions.com

Rare Rococo relief Mt. Washington/Rodefer Glass women's trinket box in waisted round flattened form with blue florals, circa 1898-1902, later custom ornate pedestal base, 3-1/4" x 4"........................ **$230**

Courtesy of Accurate Auctions, www.accurateauctions.com

Helmschmied Swirl pattern Mt. Washington/Rodefer Glass opal glass round dresser box blank, circa 1896-1898, with pink spring floral spray and concave bluebell floral border, banner and shield Wave Crest Trade Mark stamp, excellent condition, 6-1/2" x 6-1/2" x 4" h.......... **$178**

Courtesy of Accurate Auctions, www.accurateauctions.com

Rare baluster vase, opal glass blank in spring floral spray with ormolu seahorse handles, circa 1898-1900, excellent condition, block script "Wave Crest Trade Mark" stamp, 4" x 4" x 9-1/2" h..................... **$178**

Courtesy of Accurate Auctions, www.accurateauctions.com

Rare blown-out Baroque shell Mt. Washington opal glass round valuables box blank with pink spring floral spray and blue lobes, circa 1894-1896, working lock, banner and shield Wave Crest Trade Mark block script stamp, excellent condition (with orifinal liner), 7-1/4" x 7-1/4" x 3-1/2" h.. **$230**

Courtesy of Accurate Auctions, www.accurateauctions.com

Women's boudoir box, circa 1900-1902, with interlocking scrolls border, cherry blossom theme, deep relief design, Wave Crest marking, excellent condition with original liner with some wear, 4" h. x 7-1/2" w. x 7-1/2" d...................... **$287**

Courtesy of Accurate Auctions, www.accurateauctions.com

◀ Scenic-decorated dresser box, late 19th/early 20th century, opal, circular form with cream-colored ground, pale green and rose highlighting, top transfer-decorated with Venetian scene, faint signature under base, 2-3/4" h. x 4-3/8" d.............**$144**

Courtesy of Jeffrey S. Evans & Associates, www.jeffreysevans.com

GLASS

webb

THOMAS WEBB & Sons of Stourbridge was one of England's most prolific glasshouses. Many types of glass, including cameo, have been produced by this firm through the years. The company also produced various types of novelty and art glass during the late Victorian period.

◄ Art glass vase, circa 1890, enameled cranberry opalescent with floral decoration, ribbed sides, three-footed base, 7-1/2" h., 8" dia.............. **$181**

Courtesy of Bruhns Auction Gallery, www.bruhnsauction.com

▲ Vase in gilt-decorated cased satin, late 19th century, 7-1/4" h....... **$635**

Courtesy of Mossgreen Auctions, www.mossgreen.com.au

Cameo glass figural scent bottle modeled as swan's head in cranberry glass overlaid in white glass and cut through, silver screw cap marked Gorham, inner stopper, two small spots in white layer, 6" h. **$5,842**

Courtesy of Perfume Bottle Auctions, www.perfumebottleauctions.com

Lidded jar shaded from dark to light pink with raised enameled gold gilt decoration of vines, florals, and butterfly, 4-1/2" h............. **$324**

Courtesy of Farmer Auctions, www.farmer-auctions.com

Cameo vase with shaped rim and body, green ground cameo cut red poinsettia flower motif with gilt accents, signed "Thomas Webb & Sons" on base, 6-3/4" h. x 5-3/4" w. x 4-1/2" d.......................... **$472**

Courtesy of Burchard Galleries, www.burchardgalleries.com

Cameo vase with purple floral motif, signed "Webb" near base, good condition, 8-1/4" h., 6" dia. **$523**

Courtesy of Peachtree & Bennett, www.peachtreebennett.com

Cameo vase with citrine background and white cameo carved floral overlay, 3-1/2" h. ..**$472**

Courtesy of Woody Auction, www.woodyauction.com

Biscuit jar of rose glass with white floral and butterfly decoration, silver-plated lid with floral finial hallmarked R.F.E. & Co Ltd., fixed handle, 8-1/2" h. **$615**

Courtesy of CRN Auctions, www.crnauctions.com

Four-layer cameo bottle, circa 1902, opal over red over lemon over opal, primrose and butterfly, English silver repoussé screw cap, marks for Birmingham, good condition, loss to opal, silver with minor wear, 4-1/2" h. **$2,232**

Courtesy of Brunk Auctions, www.brunkauctions.com

Cameo bowl, frosted white ground with pink floral designs and pinched sides, 2-3/4" h., 5-1/4" dia. **$413**

Courtesy of Burchard Galleries, www.burchardgalleries.com

Vase, alabaster glass core with exterior of enamel and parcel gilt design, raised floral elements arranged in diamond shapes, surrounded in black and white enamel dots, floral and foliage motifs, 8-1/8" h. x 6-1/2" w., 6-1/2" dia. **$184**

Courtesy of Peachtree & Bennett, www.peachtreebennett.com

Vase in deep blue shaded to pale blue with gold enamel decoration, red propeller signature, early 20th century, 9" h. **$108**

Courtesy of Jeffrey S. Evans & Associates, www.jeffreysevans.com

Overlay floral cameo glass bowl, circa 1890, marked, good condition, 2-1/8" h., 4-3/4" dia. **$325**

Courtesy of Heritage Auctions, ha.com

Decanters with hobnail and diamond cut decoration, with original stoppers, 14-1/4" h. x 6-2/3" w. **$1,394**

Courtesy of Dreweatts & Bloomsbury, www.dreweatts.com

Pair of vases with ruffled rims, powder blue to white with enameled bird on branch decoration and gilt trim, 11" h. x 7-1/2" w. **$325**

Courtesy of Hudson Valley Auctions, www.hudsonvalleyauctions.com

HUNTING & FISHING COLLECTIBLES

FOR DIE-HARD HUNTERS, there's nothing better than spending time surrounded by vintage examples of the brands and tools they use in the field and on the water. The market for vintage hunting and fishing collectibles has seen prices creep ever northward out of the hundreds and into the thousands in recent years. The diverse category touches on thousands of different items and price points, with even nominally priced items finding new homes every day.

Crow decoy, carved single-piece body with open beak and glass eyes, craquelure painted finish, steel legs, good condition, paint in very good condition, 15" x 4" x 10" h........................ **$1,150**

Courtesy of Forsythe's Auctions, LLC, www.forsythesauctions.com

Decoys are one of the most popular collectibles. Collectors may be drawn to derelicts or those carved by the most well-respected artisans in North America. "There has been established, over the past 40 years or so, a 'pecking order' of the most collectible carvers of old decoys," said Stan VanEtten, publisher of *Hunting & Fishing Collectibles Magazine.* "But by no means is there within our hobby/business an agreed-upon list of these renowned artisans; and, in fact, there is no universal agreement as to what is old."

Hunting and fishing ephemera is among the scarcest of all collectibles in this category. It doesn't always have to be paper, as the word is so often associated. Ephemera, including wooden boxes, labels, hunting tags and licenses, and even specialty magazines, all find a price among hunting and fishing collectors.

Hunting- and fishing-themed advertising items are among the most sought-after today. The market bull's-eye still revolves around the biggest names in advertising displays: Winchester, Peters, Remington, and Western Powder. Even pieces in compromised condition are bringing very good prices on eBay.

Demand is so great for early Winchester paper that aluminum signs are being mass-produced by the thousands in the United States - not overseas. These fakes and fantasy pieces are designed after 19th century cartridge boards. Rectangular signs measure 12-1/2" x 16" and 16" x 8-1/2", and circular signs are often 11" or 12" in diameter. The popularity of these signs is overwhelming, mostly because prices are less than $10 shipped and lots of collectors really want a piece of Winchester lore and history.

Perhaps unsurprisingly, a nice collection of vintage lures spanning a full century can be assembled for less than $500. Most lures sell at auction for between $1 and $100. Lures valued greater than $1,000 are generally early examples, uncataloged examples, in excellent condition, rare finds with original boxes, or prototypes.

HUNTING COLLECTIBLES

Tin mallard drake decoy, fair condition with overall wear, rust and corrosion, 7" h. x 16-1/2" l....... **$121**

Courtesy of Conestoga Auction Co., www.conestogaauction.com

Scrimshaw carved powder horn with domed hardwood plug, carved and stepped spout, and engraved hunting dog and "TIP" on side, fine untouched condition, 8-1/2" l......................... **$182**

Courtesy of Forsythe's Auctions, LLC, www.forsythesauctions.com

Pair of duck decoys, early 20th century, larger decoy 7" x 15" x 5"...................................... **$375**

Courtesy of Material Culture, www.materialculture.com

Polychrome painted decoy marked "Cedar IS Gun Club" on underside, 18-1/2" l. x 10" h. **$690**

Courtesy of Copake Auction, Inc., www.copakeauction.com

Early polychrome painted wooden goose decoy, 32" l. x 19-1/2" h....................................... **$480**

Courtesy of Copake Auction, Inc., www.copakeauction.com

Preening tundra swan confidence decoy, early 20th century, carved and painted timber, 15" x 33" x 12".. **$1,125**

Courtesy of Material Culture, www.materialculture.com

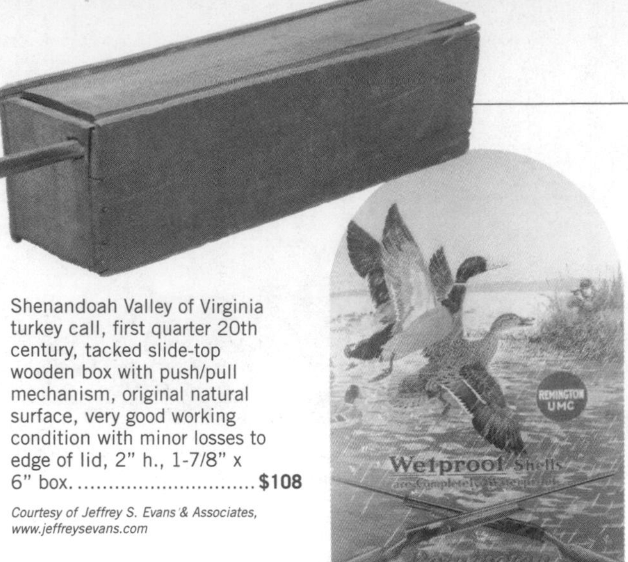

Shenandoah Valley of Virginia turkey call, first quarter 20th century, tacked slide-top wooden box with push/pull mechanism, original natural surface, very good working condition with minor losses to edge of lid, 2" h., 1-7/8" x 6" box. **$108**

Courtesy of Jeffrey S. Evans & Associates, www.jeffreysevans.com

Remington die-cut cardboard store display sign, 1922, wet-proof shells with image of ducks by artist Lynn Bogue Hunt, centerfold crease and minor stain at bottom right corner, framed under glass, 26" x 39-1/2" image only. **$1,200**

Courtesy of Showtime Auction Services, www.showtimeauctions.com

Rare early handcrafted, full-size duck blind boat with oars, built in 1917, tongue and groove construction and original paint, good overall condition. **$476**

Courtesy of North American Auction Co., www.northamericanauctioncompany.com

Scarce Winchester mountain lion poster advertising Winchester cartridges and rifles, illustration by Lynn Bogue Hunt, excellent condition, unfaded colors, minor wear, fold lines with professional touch-up, framed, 62-3/4" x 10-3/4"........... **$6,710**

Courtesy of Morphy Auctions, morphyauctions.com

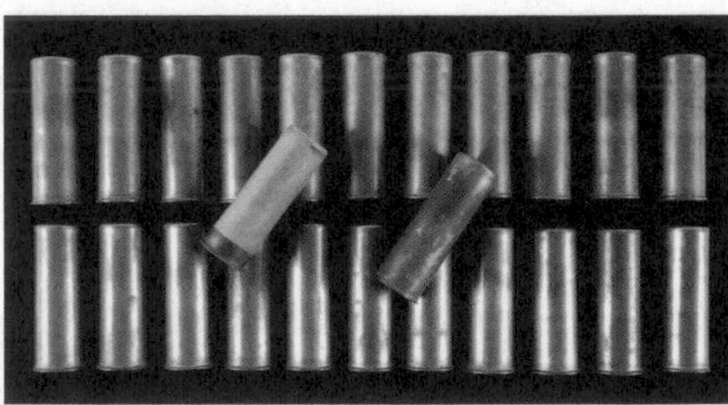

Rare early Winchester brass shotgun shells with box, circa 1890-1900: 23 live unfired original Winchester No. 12 brass cartridges with heads stamped "Winchester No. 12" and one No. 12 US Climax paper and brass shell, box marked "25 Shells, Shotgun / 12 Gauge, Brass / Smokeless Powder / No. 00 Buckshot / For Use in Hunting Small Game / Lot W.R.A. -22005," each shell 2-1/2" l. x 7/8" w., box 4-1/2" x 4" x 2-1/2". **$167**

Courtesy of North American Auction Co., www.northamericanauctioncompany.com

FISHING COLLECTIBLES

Tightly woven wicker fishing creel with original leather latch, 19th century, very good condition with minor breaks and losses, replaced leather shoulder strap, 8-1/4" h. x 11" l. x 6" d. **$55**

Courtesy of Conestoga Auction Co., www.conestogaauction.com

Metal fishing creel painted green, hinged top and hinged fish hole, maker and vintage unknown, good condition, missing part of latch, no strap, paint in very good-plus to excellent-minus condition, 12" w. at base x 9-1/4" h. x 6-1/2" d. **$366**

Courtesy of Morphy Auctions, morphyauctions.com

Fish decoys by Hans Janner, Sr., 13" l. **$2,783**

Courtesy of William J. Jenack Estate Appraisers & Auctioneers, www.jenack.com

Heddon #401 fish decoy, four-point fins, metal tail, rainbow, rough condition. **$458**

Courtesy of Morphy Auctions, morphyauctions.com

Series #400 fish decoy, James Heddon's Sons, Dowagiac, Michigan, glass eyes, green fancy back, marked four-point fins, metal tail, and inchworm line tie, with original wrapping tissue and circa 1919/1920 "error" box with ice decoy paper end label, unmarked for color, decoy in excellent condition with minor varnish flaking. **$3,050**

Courtesy of Morphy Auctions, morphyauctions.com

Frog fish decoy, weighted, with old Oliver's Auction tag, 8" **$92**

Courtesy of Morphy Auctions, morphyauctions.com

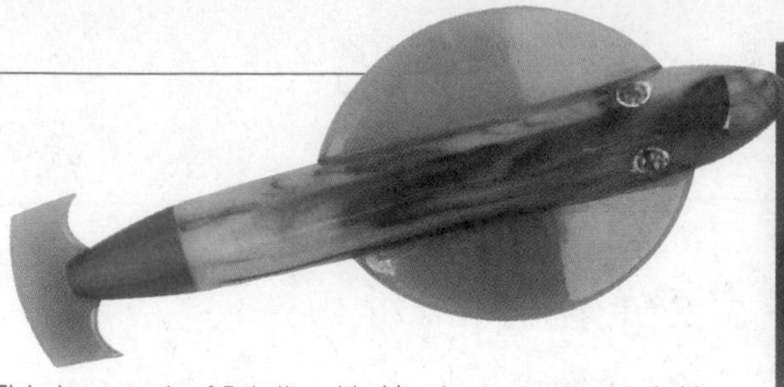

Fish decoy made of Bakelite with rhinestone eyes, mounted side fins and tail, inserted three-hole line tie marked "PAT MOD B17," unknown maker, excellent condition, with original Oliver's Auction tag, 4-3/4" l. **$244**

Courtesy of Morphy Auctions, morphyauctions.com

▲ Hardy Silex #2 two-fly reel in rare size of 3-1/8", circa 1913, steel and brass, smooth brass foot and ivorine twin cranks, inside engraved "RWX" for Hardy employee, some tarnish to metal surface, light scratching, mild discoloration, 3-1/4" h. x 1-1/4" w. x 3" d. **$187**

Courtesy of Louis J. Dianni, LLC Antiques Auctions, louisjdianni.com

Rare Oscar Peterson patent model hand-carved wooden bait, hand-blended paint pattern, striped and spotted details (near match to Peterson's patent #1,627,455, granted May 3, 1927, for artificial fishing bait), excellent condition, 2-3/4" l. **$4,270**

Courtesy of Morphy Auctions, morphyauctions.com

Pair of early fishing reels, one marked Appleton & Bassett/Julius Vom Hofe, one unmarked ball-handle model. **$214**

Courtesy of Morphy Auctions, morphyauctions.com

J.C. Higgins tackle box with assorted wood and plastic baits and miscellaneous fishing tackle. **$92**

Courtesy of Morphy Auctions, morphyauctions.com

top lot!

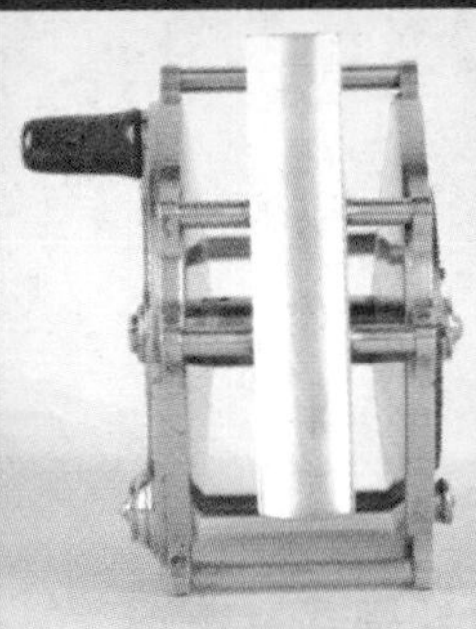

Rare Philbrook & Paine marbleized raised pillar salmon reel, circa 1880, orange and black marbleized hard rubber with German silver accent, sold by and marked "William Mills & Son NY," excellent condition, strong echoing click, full-length unaltered foot, clean spool and crisp slotted screws, used little, 3-3/4", highly sought-after model by reel collectors. $12,200

COURTESY OF MORPHY AUCTIONS, MORPHYAUCTIONS.COM

◀ Early leather tackle case with original trays and fishing-related items including hooks. **$244**

Courtesy of Morphy Auctions, morphyauctions.com

▶ Large green tackle box and handmade baits from Charles Mizner of Euclid, Ohio, approximately 76 wood baits with large slot of metal baits, all believed to have been made by Mizner, condition of baits ranges from good fished to excellent condition, with letter of provenance and Mizner's 1951 Ohio muskalonge license, box 24" x 7" x 8".............. **$549**

Courtesy of Morphy Auctions, morphyauctions.com

Vintage wood tackle box with small assortment of salt water and salmon fishing tackle...... **$31**

Courtesy of Morphy Auctions, morphyauctions.com

▲ Rare *Winchester Fishing Tackle* catalog with chromolithographed cover, dated 1924, 8vo, 5-1/2" x 8-1/2" with 32 illustrated pages advertising rods, reels, hooks, flies, lures, leaders, lines, tackle boxes and other fishing-related items, last illustrated page shows Winchester pocketknife, flashlight, hatchet and pump-action rifle, fine condition, minor wear to paper wraps... **$121**

Courtesy of Forsythe's Auctions, LLC, www.forsythesauctions.com

South Bend and Oreno Fishing Tackle display framed in shadow box, circa 1930, image of young boy with his numerous catches and pictures of fish caught by South Bend lures, very good-plus condition, minor soiling and some light stains, 35" h. x 55" l. x 7" w...... **$3,965**

Courtesy of Morphy Auctions, morphyauctions.com

▶ Cardboard Pflueger Fishing Tackle advertising sign illustrating three different types of fish being caught with Pflueger hooks, professionally framed, excellent condition, slight fading, mild wear, 35-3/4" x 41-3/4" framed... **$580**

Courtesy of Morphy Auctions, morphyauctions.com

Seven tin fish bait holders and tackle boxes. **$153**

Courtesy of Morphy Auctions, morphyauctions.com

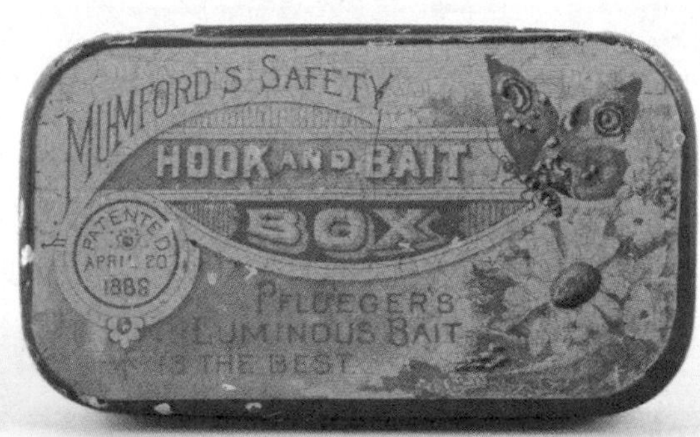

Mumford's Safety Hook and Bait box, pre-1900, patented April 20, 1889, decorated with butterfly, flowers, and Victorian-style print and design, "Pflueger's Luminous Bait is the Best," 2-1/2" x 1-1/2". This painted, hinged tin box was mounted to a fishing rod and used to store a small bait or hook while still attached to the line. **$1,525**

Courtesy of Morphy Auctions, morphyauctions.com

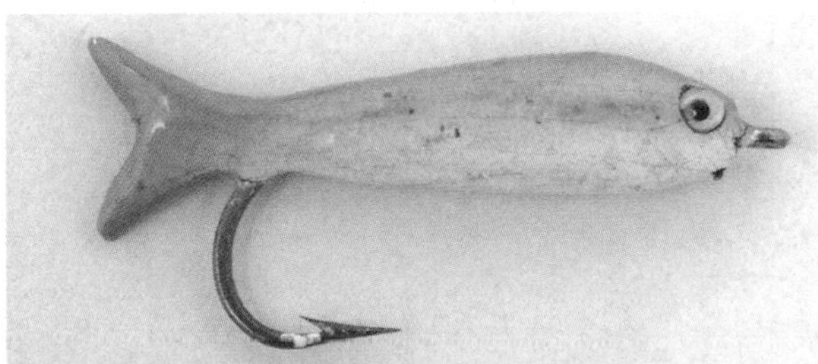

Fly rod minnow bait, Wright & McGill Fishing Tackle, Denver, with glass eyes, blended green and yellow body and white belly, excellent, uncleaned condition, 1-5/8" **$2,220**

Courtesy of Morphy Auctions, morphyauctions.com

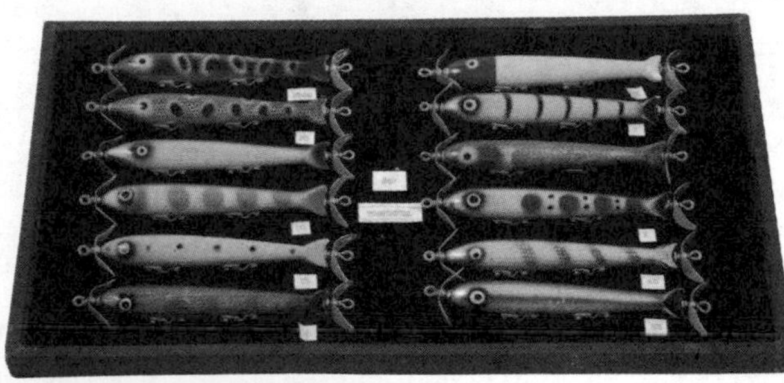

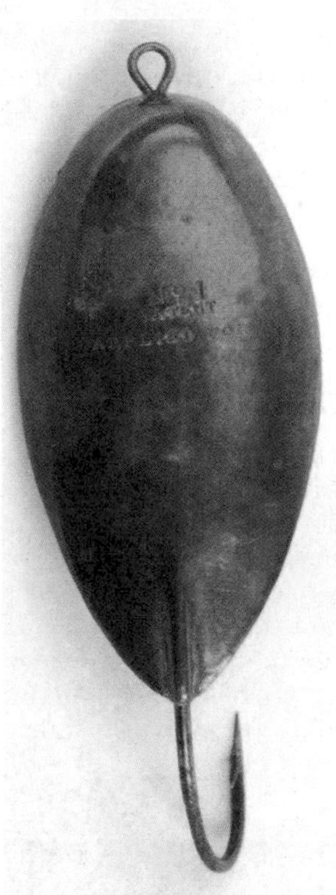

▲ J. T. Buel's Patent Applied For Hook to Spoon bait, Julio T. Buel, Whitehall, New York, marked "No.1 Patent Applied For" on front copper side and "J. T. Buel Whitehall, NY" on interior silver side, 2-1/2", one of few known examples and one of the rarest and most important metal baits in U.S. history. **$2,440**

Courtesy of Morphy Auctions, morphyauctions.com

◀ Original 8-1/4" x 15" factory tray of painted-eye Barracuda-brand Torpecudas from Florida Fishing Tackle Mfg. Co., Inc., most in excellent condition, all unrigged, all with surface rig and marked props, missing two color labels. **$458**

Courtesy of Morphy Auctions, morphyauctions.com

ILLUSTRATION ART

EXPOSURE PLAYS AN important role in collector demand and values for illustration art, which has proven itself over the last decade as one of the most popular and dynamic art genres in the country.

Take for instance "Hello Everybody!," a calendar illustration originally produced for Brown & Bigelow in the late 1920s. Artist Rolf Armstrong created the carefree pastel on board of a young lady with a bright smile at the nexus of the Roaring '20s and the Great Depression. Popular reaction was enthusiastic. The artwork appeared as a calendar illustration, on playing cards, puzzles, a die-cut advertising sign for Orange Kist soda pop, and as the cover for the March 1929 edition of *College Humor* magazine. According to Janet Dobson's *Pin Up Dreams: The Glamour Art of Rolf Armstrong*, early works such as "Hello Everybody!" defined the vision of feminine beauty for the next 40 years and earned Armstrong the title of "Father of the Pin-Up Artists." The exposure and reputation of the artist generated strong demand when the original work finally came up for auction when its sale price was pushed to $30,000.

"Hello Everybody!" represents the type of subject matter that is attracting mainstream attention.

"It's really what we think of as classic images in all genres that speak directly and powerfully to a specific time period - whether it's a 1940s *Saturday Evening Post* cover, 1950s science-fiction paperback cover, or 1960s Gil Elvgren calendar pin-up," said Todd Hignite, director of illustration art at Heritage Auctions, the world's largest auctioneer of illustration art and related works.

Interestingly, as the market for illustration art matures, auctioneers are reclassifying works as American fine art and offering works by artists with household names along with other artists such as Grandma Moses, Leroy Neiman, or by the Wyeths. Norman Rockwell's works now routinely bring in excess of $2 million at auction, but his early illustration art, steeped in sentimentality and strong national pride, may be found for less than $100,000.

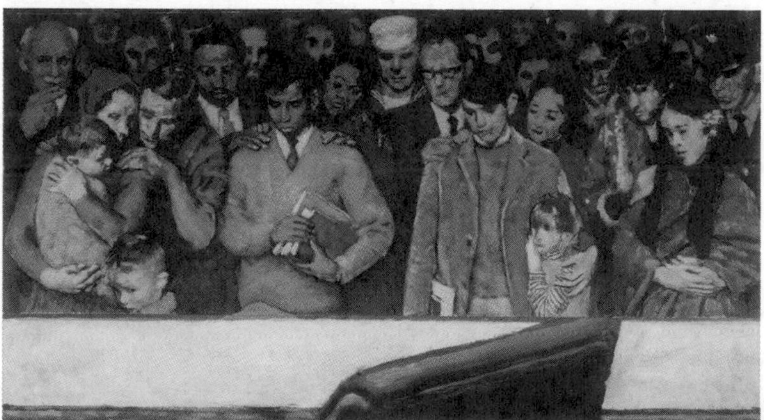

Norman Rockwell (American, 1894-1978), "The Right to Know," 1968, oil on photographic paper laid on joined panel, *Look* magazine preliminary, signed, titled, and inscribed lower right: "color sketch for 'Right to Know' picture. To Allen and Bill Loos / sincerely / Norman / Rockwell," 10-1/2" x 18-1/2". **$106,250**

Courtesy of Heritage Auctions, ha.com

"Well-known artists such as Rockwell did indeed work in advertising – many illustrators did – and it's certainly less expensive than a magazine cover by the same artist," Hignite said.

Although industry watchers are excited to see many illustration artists make the leap from illustration art to American fine art, there are dozens, perhaps thousands, of artists whose identity is still lost but whose art lives on. Currently these works are anonymously attributed simply as "American artist," but that doesn't mean research has stopped looking into the identity of these artists. Scholars have been given a boost in recent years thanks to collectors who remain fascinated by various styles.

"The scholarship and research in the field is very active and between exhibitions, publications, and more dealers handling the work, is increasing all the time, but there's still a lot of work to be done in terms of identifying art," Hignite said. "Oftentimes artists didn't sign their paintings, and if their style isn't immediately identifiable, there's a good deal of digging to do. Much of the best research actually comes from devoted fans and collectors, who doggedly put together extensive checklists and track down publication histories, check stubs from publishers, biographies, etc., to try and enhance our understanding of the history."

This confluence of awareness, appreciation, and a growing nostalgia for mid-century works have more than doubled values for pieces offered just a few short years ago. Hignite credits the increase to a matter of supply and demand. "I think simply the opportunity to see a steady supply of great art by Elvgren has increased the demand," he said. "If you see one of his paintings in person, there's no question of his painting talent, and collector confidence increases as we see such a steady growth and consistent sales results."

Kay Rasmus Nielsen (Denmark, 1886-1957), "The Nightingale – and when I go back, I hear the nightingale, sing – ," 1923, to illustrate "The Nightingale" in a collection of Hans Christian Andersen stories published by Hodder & Stoughton in 1924; watercolor on artist's board with traces of pencil, Chinese maiden at foot of willow tree beside river, within decorative foliate border in pencil, signed and dated in pencil to lower right border, mounted, together with backboard from original frame with large manuscript title label in Nielsen's hand (rubbed but legible), and other labels denoting provenance, board 14-1/2" x 10-3/4"..........**$46,938**

Courtesy of Dominic Winter Auctioneers, www.dominicwinter.co.uk

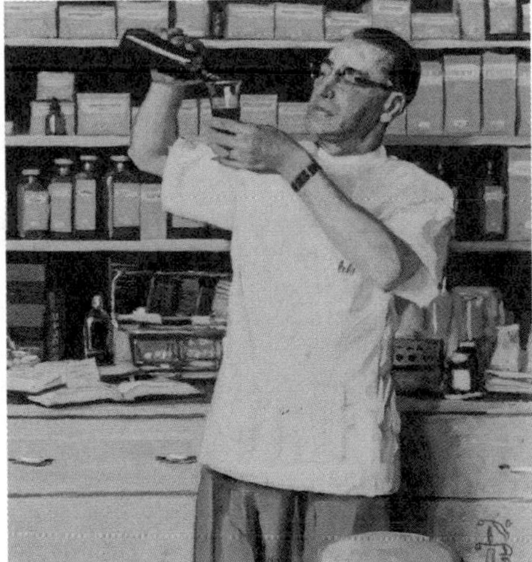

Norman Rockwell (American, 1894-1978), "Study for The Pharmacist," oil on photographic paper laid on board, Upjohn Pharmaceuticals advertisement, 1955, initialed lower right "N / R," sheet 10-1/2" x 9". **$27,500**

Courtesy of Heritage Auctions, ha.com

10 Things You Didn't Know About **J.C. Leyendecker**

J.C. Leyendecker

1 During his career, it's reported that J.C. Leyendecker's magazine covers totaled more than 400, with many appearing on the Saturday Evening Post.

2 Born in Montabaur, Germany in 1874, Leyendecker arrived in America with his family at the age of eight. At the age of 15 he began working days at J. Manz & Co. Engraving in Chicago, and in the evening he studied at the Chicago Art Institute.

3 He was added to the Society of Illustrators' Hall of Fame posthumously in 1977. Leyendecker died of a heart attack in 1951.

4 Leyendecker and his brother, Frank, both studied at the illustrious Académie Julian in Paris, and upon their return to the United States in 1898, they opened an art studio in Chicago, and then relocated their company to New York at the turn of the 20th century.

5 "Man With Narrow Tie" oil on canvas laid on panel, a circa 1910 Cluett Shirts Arrow Collar advertisement by Leyendecker, commanded $56,250 during an auction on May 10, 2014 at Heritage Auctions. The piece, which measures 19-3/8" x 16-7/8", has Cluett, Peabody & Co., Inc. copyright labels verso. Leyendecker's "Arrow Collar Man" is considered by many to be one of his iconic works.

Original oil painting by J.C. Leyendecker, used for Cluett Shirts Arrow Collar advertisement, circa 1910. It sold for $56,250 at auction in 2014.

Courtesy of Heritage Auctions, ha.com

The Saturday Evening Post original cover art from January 1915, featuring "New Year's Baby (Cleaning Up)" by J.C. Leyendecker, signed, which sold for $137,000 during a Heritage Auctions sale in November 2014.

Courtesy of Heritage Auctions, ha.com

Source: AskArt.com; www.illustratedgallery.com; www.saturdayeveningpost.com; www.liveauctioneers.com; www.nrm.org; www.americanillustrators.com; http://www.artcyclopedia.com; http://hagginmuseum.org/Collections/JCLeyendecker http://www.americanillustrators.com/travel/norman-rockwell-and-his-mentor-j-c-leyendecker/
AskArt.com; www.illustratedgallery.com; www.saturdayeveningpost.com; www.liveauctioneers.com; www.nrm.org; www.americanillustrators.com; http://www.artcyclopedia.com; http://hagginmuseum.org/Collections/JCLeyendecker

6 In the summer of 2015, the Norman Rockwell Museum hosted an exhibition titled "J.C. Leyendecker and *The Saturday Evening Post*." Although Rockwell is largely considered the preeminent illustrator of *The Saturday Evening Post*, Leyendecker preceded him in setting the tone of the magazine and was one of Rockwell's idols. It's reported that Rockwell closely observed and at times sought to imitate some elements of Leyendecker's approach to his work. Rockwell's 1960 biography, *My Adventures as an Illustrator*, includes a chapter about Leyendecker's influence.

7 Leyendecker's covers were a significant part of how *The Saturday Evening Post* acknowledged holidays in the early 20th century. Circulation trends of the period reflected how the covers contributed to the magazine's appeal. Leyendecker's holiday covers helped grow circulation to two million copies a week.

8 He was among a group of about 30 artists considered to be the leaders of the "Golden Age of American Illustration." During the period between 1800 and the 1920s, Leyendecker, Howard Pyle, Jessie Willcox Smith, Maxfield Parrish, Violet Oakley, Walter Crane, and Beatrix Potter, among others, established new avenues in book and magazine illustration.

9 More than 10 museums within the United States have permanent displays or have hosted exhibitions featuring Leyendecker's work over the years. The Haggin Museum in Stockton, California, features nearly 60 original pieces by Leyendecker, all acquired during the 1950s. Through the efforts of then-museum director Earl Rowland, the paintings were gifted to the museum from companies that had employed Leyendecker, as well as from friends and family of the artist. It is said to be the largest collection of works by Leyendecker on permanent display in a museum.

10 One of the most recognizable illustrations of Leyendecker's storied career is the varied New Year Baby series he designed for the cover of *The Saturday Evening Post*. The last painting in that series was done in 1943, which was also the last cover Leyendecker designed for that magazine.

– Compiled by Antoinette Rahn

Saul Tepper (American, 1899-1987), "Loose Lips Sink Ships," oil on canvas, 1944, Stetson advertisement, signed upper right "Saul / Tepper," 28" x 33"............ **$7,500**

Courtesy of Heritage Auctions, ha.com

LeRoy Neiman (American, 1921-2012), "Admiring the View," oil on Masonite, *Playboy*, 1965, signed and dated lower center: LeRoy Neiman '65, 30" x 22-1/2". **$47,500**

Courtesy of Heritage Auctions, ha.com

Stevan Dohanos (American, 1907-1994), "Mutually Beneficial Friendship," gouache on board, *Saturday Evening Post* cover, Oct. 11, 1958, signed lower left: Stevan Dohanos, light overall surface grime with accretions, faint mat burn along edges, light creasing in corners, notches and bumps along extreme edges, minuscule flakes of loss, most notably in crates, small spots of discoloration below far right figure's right foot, 28-3/4" x 26-1/4"....................**$31,250**

Courtesy of Heritage Auctions, ha.com

Anton Loeb (American, 20th century), "Wizard of Oz," gouache on board, published as inside cover of Allan Chaffee's adaption of *Wizard of Oz* by L. Frank Baum, Random House, 1950, signed twice lower right, 12-3/4" x 17-3/4" (sight)........... **$1,875**

Courtesy of Heritage Auctions, ha.com

Tom Beecham (American, 1926-2000), "Hunting in the Valley of Death," oil and gouache on board, *Fury* magazine cover, December 1955, signed lower right, 18" x 15" (image)....................... **$325**

Courtesy of Heritage Auctions, ha.com

Everett Shinn, "Rip Van Winkle," gouache and watercolor on board, for story published in *Coronet Magazine*, 1939, signed in image, lower left, 16" x 11-3/8". ....**$10,000-$15,000**

Courtesy of Swann Auction Galleries, www.swanngalleries.com

Charles Addams, "The dark side of 'Little Annie'," watercolor, ink, and gouache on Whatman board, cover art for *Show: The Magazine of the Arts*, April 1962, signed in image, lower left and inscribed, signed, and dated in upper right, slight watercolor streaking at lower left of image into margin, 21-1/4" x 17-1/4"......................... **$6,000-$9,000**

Courtesy of Swann Auction Galleries, www.swanngalleries.com

Harry Parkhurst, *Complete Detective Novel* magazine cover, oil on canvas, for February 1931 issue featuring "Murder Across the Footlights" by Madelon St. Denis, signed lower left, framed, 28" x 22". .... **$3,500-$5,000**

Courtesy of Swann Auction Galleries, www.swanngalleries.com

Frederick Blakeslee, cover art for October 1935 issue of *Dare-Devil Aces* magazine, oil on canvas, signed lower right, mounted to stretcher and framed, with copy of magazine, 29-1/2" x 20-3/4".. **$4,000-$6,000**

Courtesy of Swann Auction Galleries, www.swanngalleries.com

Edward Gorey, "Dead By Now," pen and ink on board, circa 1954, proposed cover and spine illustration for *The Crime Club Selection Dead By Now* by Margaret Erskine, signed in ink, lower right margin, 9-3/8" x 7-1/2".................. **$3,000-$4,000**

Courtesy of Swann Auction Galleries, www.swanngalleries.com

Hjalmar "Cappy" Amundsen, cover art for *Motor Boating* magazine, oil on canvas, November 1944, U.S. Navy escort carrier with three Grumman F6F Hellcat fighters overhead, signed lower right, craquelure on upper third of composition, two small punctures and one short tear repaired on verso, mounted on original stretcher and framed, with copy of magazine, 28-1/2" x 26-1/2". .... **$2,000-$3,000**

Courtesy of Swann Auction Galleries, www.swanngalleries.com

Vanessa Bell, "Some Poems of Mallarmé," watercolor and pencil on board, study for dust jacket illustration for *Some Poems of Mallarmé by Roger Fry and Charles Mauron*, published by Chatto & Windus, London, 1936, archivally matted and framed, 8-5/8" x 5-3/4" (image). .... **$3,000-$4,000**

Courtesy of Swann Auction Galleries, www.swanngalleries.com

Walter Crane, "Goody Two Shoes," watercolor on paper, circa 1874, cover design for *Goody Two Shoes,* Crane's Toy Books Shilling Series, Volume 71, similar to final design published by George Routledge and Sons, tape along all borders, verso, scattered foxing, 12-1/8" x 10-1/2".. **$2,000-$3,000**

Courtesy of Swann Auction Galleries, www.swanngalleries.com

JEWELRY

JEWELRY HAS HELD a special place for humankind since prehistoric times, both as an emblem of personal status and as a decorative adornment worn for its sheer beauty. This tradition continues today. We should keep in mind, however, that it was only with the growth of the Industrial Revolution that jewelry first became cheap enough so that even the person of modest means could win a piece or two.

Only since around the mid-19th century did certain forms of jewelry, especially pins and brooches, begin to appear on the general market as a mass-produced commodity and the Victorians took to it immediately. Major production centers for the finest pieces of jewelry remained in Europe, especially Italy and England, but less expensive pieces were also exported to the booming American market and soon some American manufacturers also joined in the trade. Especially during the Civil War era, when silver and gold supplies grew tremendously in the U.S., did jewelry in silver or with silver, brass or gold-filled (i.e. gold-plated or goldplate) mounts begin to flood the market here. By the turn of the 20th century all the major mail-order companies and small town jewelry shops could offer a huge variety of inexpensive jewelry pieces aimed at not only the feminine buyer but also her male counterpart.

Inexpensive jewelry of the late 19th and early 20th century is still widely available and often at modest prices. Even more in demand today is costume jewelry, well-designed jewelry produced of inexpensive materials and meant to carefully accent a woman's ensemble. Today costume jewelry of the 20th century has become one of the most active areas in the field of collecting and some of the finest pieces, signed by noted designers and manufacturers, can reach price levels nearly equal to much earlier and scarcer examples.

Jewelry prices, as in every other major collecting field, are influenced by a number of factors including local demand, quality, condition and rarity. As market prices have risen in recent years it has become even more important for the collector to shop and buy with care. Learn as much as you can about your favorite area of jewelry and keep abreast of market trends and stay alert to warnings about alterations, repairs or reproductions that can be found on the market.

For more information on jewelry, see *Warman's Jewelry Identification and Price Guide*, 5th edition, by Christie Romero or *Warman's Costume Jewelry Identification and Price Guide* by Pamela Y. Wiggins.

jewelry styles

Jewelry has been a part of every culture throughout time, reflecting the times as well as social and aesthetic movements. Jewelry is usually divided into periods and styles. Each period may have several styles, with some of the same styles and types of jewelry being made in both precious and non-precious materials. Elements of one period may also overlap into others.

Georgian, 1760-1837. Fine jewelry from this period is quite desirable, but few good-quality pieces have found their way to auction in recent years. Sadly, much jewelry from this period has been lost.

Victorian, 1837-1901. Queen Victoria of England ascended to the throne in 1837 and remained queen until her death in 1901. The Victorian period is a long and prolific one,

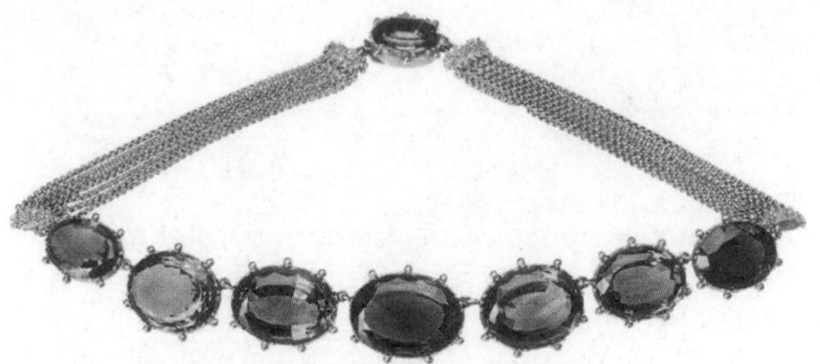

Late Georgian amethyst and bloomed gold necklace with seven oval faceted amethysts in beaded cut-down collets with seven-strand multi-chain with cannetille details and foil-backed amethyst box clasp, 15k bloomed gold, unmarked, retailed by Marshall Field & Co., Antique Jewelry Collection, box with description, 16" l., 37.9 dwt. **$2,944**

Courtesy of Rago Arts and Auctions, www.ragoarts.com

Victorian slide necklace with seed pearls, 14k yellow gold, intricate border, two gold tassels, missing one seed pearl, 57" l., 47.0 dwt..... **$2,829**

Courtesy of Skinner, Inc., www.skinnerinc.com

abundant with many styles of jewelry. It warrants being divided into three sub-periods: Early or Romantic period dating from 1837-1860; Mid or Grand period dating from 1860-1880; and Late or Aesthetic period dating from 1880-1901.

Sentiment and romance were significant factors in Victorian jewelry. Often, jewelry and clothing represented love and affection, with symbolic motifs such as hearts, crosses, hands, flowers, anchors, doves, crowns, knots, stars, thistles, wheat, garlands, horseshoes and moons. The materials of the time were also abundant and varied. They included silver, gold, diamonds, onyx, glass, cameo, paste, carnelian, agate, coral, amber, garnet, emeralds, opals, pearls, peridot, rubies, sapphires, marcasites, cut steel, enameling, tortoiseshell, topaz, turquoise, bog oak, ivory, jet, hair, gutta percha and vulcanite.

Sentiments of love were often expressed in miniatures. Sometimes they were representative of deceased loved ones, but often the miniatures were of the living. Occasionally, the miniatures depicted landscapes, cherubs or religious themes.

Hair jewelry was a popular expression of love and sentiment. The hair of a loved one was placed in a special compartment in a brooch or a locket, or used to form a picture under a glass compartment. Later in the mid-19th century, pieces of jewelry were made completely of woven hair. Individual strands of hair would be woven together to create necklaces, watch chains, brooches, earrings and rings.

In 1861, Queen Victoria's husband, Prince Albert, died. The queen went into mourning for the rest of her life, and Victoria required that the royal court wear black. This atmosphere spread to the populace and created a demand for mourning jewelry, which is typically black. When it first came into fashion, it was made from jet, fossilized wood. By 1850, there were dozens of English workshops making jet brooches, lockets, bracelets and necklaces. As the supply of jet dwindled, other materials were used such as vulcanite, gutta percha, bog oak and French jet.

By the 1880s, somber mourning jewelry was losing popularity. Fashions had changed and the clothing was simpler and had an air of delicacy. The Industrial Revolution, which had begun in the early part of the century, was now in full swing and machine-manufactured jewelry was affordable to the working class.

Edwardian, 1890-1920. The Edwardian period takes its name from England's King Edward VII. Though he ascended to the throne in 1901, he and his wife, Alexandria of Denmark, exerted an influence over the period before and after his ascension. The 1890s were known as La Belle Epoque. This was a time known for ostentation and extravagance. As the years passed, jewelry became simpler and smaller. Instead of wearing one large brooch, women were often found wearing several small lapel pins.

In the early 1900s, platinum, diamonds and pearls were prevalent in the jewelry of the wealthy, while paste was being used by the masses to imitate the real thing. The styles were reminiscent of the neo-classical and rococo motifs. The jewelry was lacy and ornate, feminine and delicate.

Edwardian compact necklace, monogrammed compact with pink and white enameling and floral border, on 14k gold chain, chain 18" l., compact 1-1/2" dia., 10.9 dwt. **$523**

Courtesy of Skinner, Inc., www.skinnerinc.com

Arts & Crafts, 1890-1920. The Arts & Crafts movement was focused on artisans and craftsmanship. There was a simplification of form where the material was secondary to the design. Guilds of artisans banded together. Some jewelry was mass-produced, but the most highly prized examples of this period are handmade and signed by their makers. The pieces were simple and at times abstract. They could be hammered, patinated and acid etched. Common materials were brass, bronze, copper, silver, blister pearls, freshwater pearls, turquoise, agate, opals, moonstones, coral, horn, ivory, base metals, amber, cabochon-cut garnets and amethysts.

Art Nouveau, 1895-1910. In 1895, Samuel Bing opened a shop called "Maison de l'Art Nouveau" at 22 Rue de Provence in Paris. Art Nouveau designs in the jewelry were characterized by a sensuality that took on the forms of the female figure, butterflies, dragonflies, peacocks, snakes, wasps, swans, bats, orchids, irises and other exotic flowers. The lines used whiplash curves to create a feeling of lushness and opulence.

Art Nouveau 14k gold, diamond, and emerald pendant designed as articulated stylized flower with emerald and diamond drop on 18k gold chain, pendant 4" l. x 2" w., 20.8 dwt. **$1,599**

Courtesy of Skinner, Inc., www.skinnerinc.com

1920s-1930s. Costume jewelry began its steady ascent to popularity in the 1920s. Since it was relatively inexpensive to produce, it was mass-produced. The sizes and designs of the jewelry varied. Often, it was worn a few times, disposed of and then replaced with a new piece. It was thought of as expendable, a cheap throwaway to dress up an outfit. Costume jewelry became so popular that it was sold in both upscale and "five and dime" stores.

During the 1920s, fashions were often accompanied by jewelry that drew on the Art Deco movement, which got its beginning in Paris at the "Exposition Internationale des Arts Décoratifs et Industriels Modernes" held in 1925. The idea behind this movement was that form follows function. The style was characterized by simple, straight, clean lines, stylized motifs, and geometric shapes. Favored materials included chrome, rhodium, pot metal, glass, rhinestones, Bakelite, and celluloid.

One designer who played an important role was Coco Chanel. Though previously reserved for evening wear, the jewelry was worn by Chanel during the day, making it fashionable for millions of other women to do so, too.

With the 1930s came the Depression and the advent of World War II. Perhaps in response to the gloom, designers began using enameling and brightly colored rhinestones to create whimsical birds, flowers, circus animals, bows, dogs and just about every other figural form imaginable.

top lot

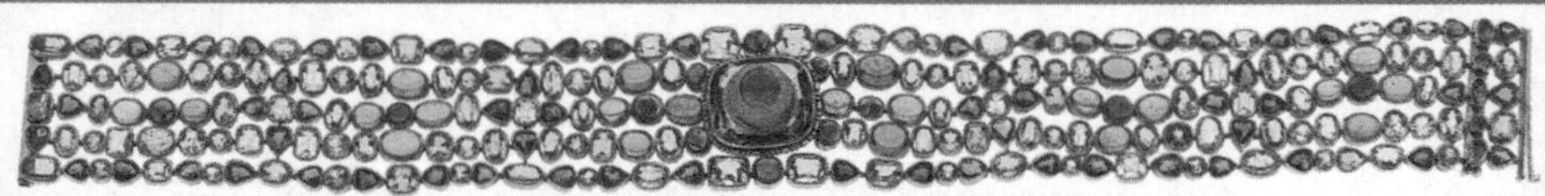

Antique multi-stone and gold collar necklace attributed to Paulding Farnham, with original photo of Lucia James Madill, Farnham's sister-in-law, wearing necklace (not shown); pink tourmaline cabochon measuring 8.85 mm atop green tourmaline cabochon measuring 16.45 mm, supported by cushion-shaped citrine measuring 23.70 mm x 20.40 mm, with heart-shaped citrines weighing approximately 25.15 carats, square and oval-shaped topaz weighing approximately 26.85 carats, pear-shaped and round-cut quartz weighing approximately 14.40 carats, oval-shaped green tourmaline cabochons weighing approximately 27.60 carats, round and oval-shaped pink tourmaline cabochons weighing approximately 8.25 carats, set in 18k gold, removable half-inch extender, not marked, gross weight 200.60 grams, 13-1/2" x 1-7/16".. .... **$45,000**

COURTESY OF HERITAGE AUCTIONS, HA.COM

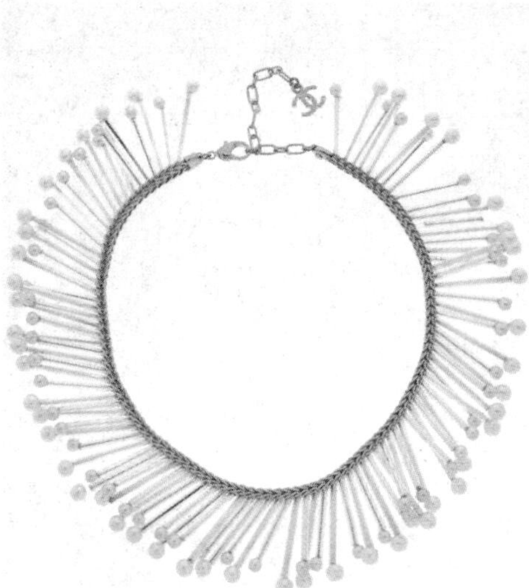

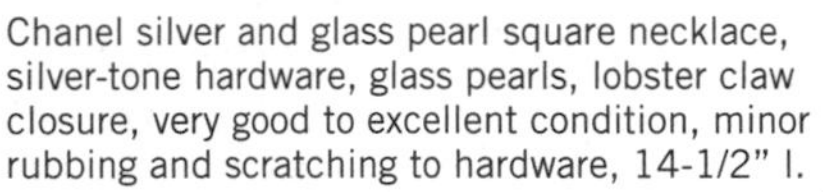

Chanel silver and glass pearl square necklace, silver-tone hardware, glass pearls, lobster claw closure, very good to excellent condition, minor rubbing and scratching to hardware, 14-1/2" l. **$625**

Courtesy of Heritage Auctions, ha.com

Miriam Haskell cultured pearl and rhinestone necklace and earrings set, 1930s, necklace signed. **$261**

Courtesy of Strawser Auctions, www.strawserauctions.com

Retro Modern, 1939-1950. Other jewelry designs of the 1940s were big and bold. Retro Modern had a more substantial feel to it and designers began using larger stones to enhance the dramatic pieces. The jewelry was stylized and exaggerated. Common motifs included flowing scrolls, bows, ribbons, birds, animals, snakes, flowers, and knots.

Sterling silver now became the metal of choice, often dipped in a gold wash known as vermeil.

Designers often incorporated patriotic themes of American flags, the V-sign, Uncle Sam's hat, airplanes, anchors, and eagles.

Post-War Modern, 1945-1965. This was a movement that emphasized the artistic approach to jewelry making. It is also referred to as Mid-Century Modern. This approach was occurring at a time when the Beat Generation was prevalent. These avant-garde designers created jewelry that was handcrafted to illustrate the artist's own concepts and ideas. The materials often used were sterling, gold, copper, brass, enamel, cabochons, wood, quartz, and amber.

Crown Trifari set: bracelet and clip earrings, 1950s, one stone missing from bracelet, 7" l..... **$26**

Courtesy of Omega Auction Corp., www.omegaauctioncorp.com

1950s-1960s. The 1950s saw the rise of jewelry that was made purely of rhinestones: necklaces, bracelets, earrings and pins. The focus of the early 1960s was on clean lines: Pillbox hats and A-line dresses with short jackets were a mainstay for the conservative woman. The large, bold rhinestone pieces were no longer the must-have accessory. They were now replaced with smaller, more delicate gold-tone metal and faux pearls with only a hint of rhinestones.

At the other end of the spectrum were psychedelic-colored clothing, Nehru jackets, thigh-high miniskirts and go-go boots. These clothes were accessorized with beads, large metal pendants and occasionally big, bold rhinestones. By the late 1960s, there was a movement back to Mother Nature and the "hippie" look was born. Ethnic clothing, tie-dye, long skirts, fringe and jeans were the prevalent style, and the rhinestone had, for the most part, been left behind.

Simulated coral, gold-tone, and crystal costume jewelry in manner of Van Cleef & Arpels, Panetta brooch 2-1/4" l., Ciner earclips with simulated emeralds, 1-1/2" l. **$215**

Courtesy of New Orleans Auction Gallery, www.neworleansauction.com

BRACELETS

Art Deco diamond and platinum bracelet with emerald-cut diamond measuring 8.31 mm x 6.13 mm x 3.86 mm and weighing 1.58 carats, emerald-cut diamond measuring 8.46 mm x 6.03 mm x 3.73 mm weighing 1.54 carats, baguette and square-cut diamonds weighing 12.25 carats, full-cut diamonds weighing approximately 9.00 carats, set in platinum, total diamond weight approximately 24.37 carats, 72.00 grams, 6-1/2" x 3/4". **$25,000**

Courtesy of Heritage Auctions, ha.com

Antique garnet and gold bracelet with oval-shaped garnet cabochons weighing approximately 43.10 carats set in 18k gold, 33.40 grams, 6-3/4" x 15/16". **$3,125**

Courtesy of Heritage Auctions, ha.com

Victorian 14k gold and pearl braided buckle bracelet, buckle set with seed pearls, good condition, clasp missing three pearls, 9-1/2" l., 10.5 dwt. . **$492**

Courtesy of Skinner, Inc., www.skinnerinc.com

Arts & Crafts amethyst and sterling silver bracelet attributed to Laurence Foss, hand-made links alternating between squares and rectangles with acorns and leaves set with amethysts, marked "L/F Sterling" on back, 6-3/4" l., 1.5 troy oz. Provenance: From the collection of the late Christie Romero, historian of antique, period, and vintage jewelry as well as certified gemologist, lecturer, instructor and consultant, director of the Center for Jewelry Studies, author of *Warman's Jewelry Identification & Price Guide*, and appraiser on PBS's "Antiques Roadshow." **$738**

Courtesy of Skinner, Inc., www.skinnerinc.com

BROOCHES & PINS

Antique citrine, enamel, and gold brooch, Tiffany & Co., early 20th century, round-cut citrine measuring 14.30 mm x 14.00 mm x 11.20 mm and weighing approximately 10.70 carats, citrine cabochons, enamel applied on 18k gold, marked Tiffany & Co., 24.30 grams, 1-3/4" dia. **$11,250**

Courtesy of Heritage Auctions, ha.com

Shell cameo pendant brooch, 18k gold, dated 1849, depicting scene of romantic couple in woods, signed Lamont, tubular frame with engraved accents, "S.G. Lamont 1849" hand-engraved on back of shell, small crack to back of shell, 3" h. x 2-1/2" w., 21.1 dwt. **$1,046**

Courtesy of Skinner, Inc., www.skinnerinc.com

Antique coral cameo brooch depicting Bacchante, gold mount, 14k or slightly less, slightly loose in setting, 1-5/8" l. **$554**

Courtesy of Skinner, Inc., www.skinnerinc.com

Antique gold, pearl, and diamond initial brooch with seed pearls and rose-cut diamonds, initials "EH," 1-1/4" l. **$246**

Courtesy of Skinner, Inc., www.skinnerinc.com

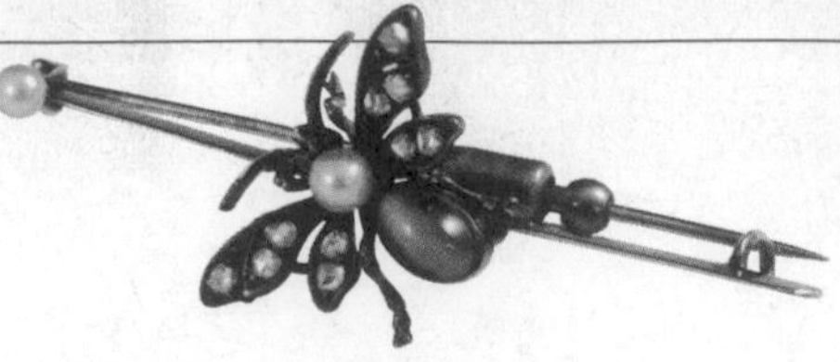

Antique bug brooch, 14k gold with agate and pearl body and rose-cut diamond-set wings, 2-1/8" l., 3.3 dwt. **$461**

Courtesy of Skinner, Inc., www.skinnerinc.com

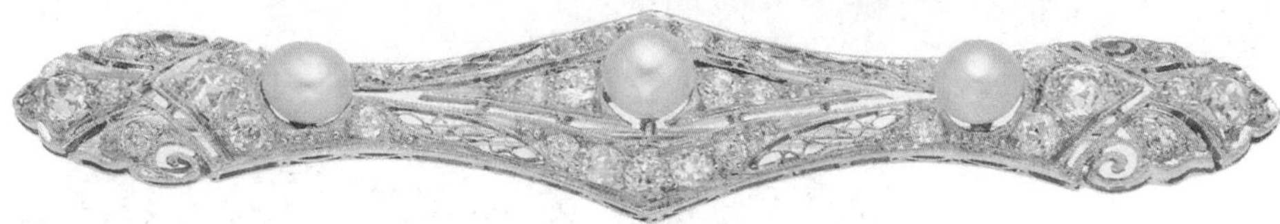

Art Deco diamond, cultured pearl, platinum, and white gold brooch, European-cut diamonds weighing approximately 1.75 carats, cultured pearls ranging in size from 5.00 mm to 5.35 mm, set in platinum with 14k white gold pinstem and catch, 8.00 grams. 2-7/8" x 1/2". **$350**

Courtesy of Heritage Auctions, ha.com

Antique citrine and gold brooch, oval-shaped citrine measuring 24.60 mm x 19.00 mm x 11.00 mm and weighing approximately 27.25 carats, set in 18k gold, 14.80 grams, 1-5/16" x 1-1/8". **$225**

Courtesy of Heritage Auctions, ha.com

Antique amethyst, diamond, seed pearl, and gold brooch, round-cut amethyst measuring 23.25 mm x 23.25 mm x 12.15 mm and weighing approximately 31.25 carats, seed pearls, and rose-cut diamonds weighing approximately 0.10 carat, set in 14k gold, 25.70 grams, 2" x 1-7/8". **$875**

Courtesy of Heritage Auctions, ha.com

Antique beryl, quartz, diamond, and silver-topped gold brooch, oval-shaped faceted foil-back quartz measuring 8.90 mm x 6.40 mm, round- and cushion-cut green beryls weighing approximately 1.00 carat, rose- and single-cut diamonds weighing approximately 0.70 carat, set in silver-topped 18k gold, 15.40 grams, 1-7/8" x 1-5/8". **$625**

Courtesy of Heritage Auctions, ha.com

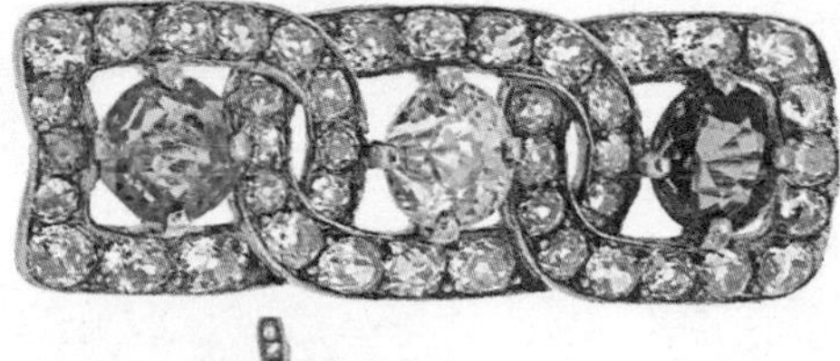

Antique sapphire, emerald, diamond, and platinum-topped gold brooch, round-cut pink sapphire measuring 6.95-7.23 mm x 4.04 mm and weighing approximately 1.60 carats, round-cut yellow sapphire measuring 6.78-6.99 mm x 7.04 mm and weighing approximately 2.65 carats, round-cut emerald measuring 6.85-7.03 mm x 5.99 mm and weighing approximately 1.55 carats, mine-cut diamonds weighing approximately 3.65 carats, set in platinum-topped 14k gold, 6.00 grams, 3/8" x 1-1/2"........... **$3,750**

Courtesy of Heritage Auctions, ha.com

Antique diamond, seed pearl, and platinum-topped gold pendant-brooch, European-cut diamonds weighing approximately 1.10 carats, rose-cut diamonds weighing approximately 1.15 carats, seed pearls, set in platinum-topped gold, 12.00 grams, 2-5/8" x 1-1/2". **$625**

Courtesy of Heritage Auctions, ha.com

EARRINGS

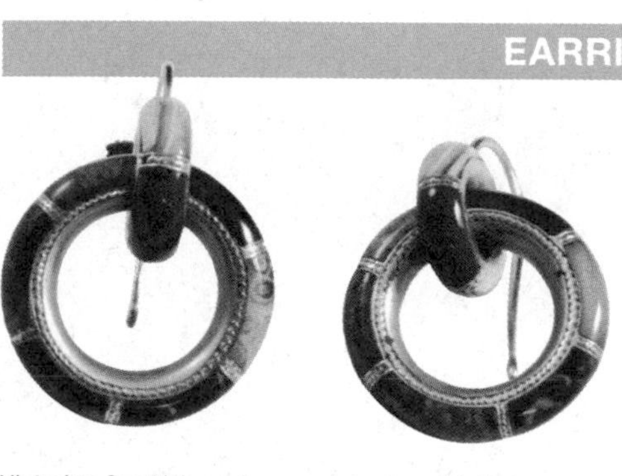

Victorian Scottish agate earpendants, each hoop set with various agates, low-karat gold mounts, 1-1/8" l. **$523**

Courtesy of Skinner, Inc., www.skinnerinc.com

Antique pearl earpendants, 14k gold, pearls set amidst multi-tier leaf motif, visible clear stringing on back, 2" l., 3.6 dwt. **$677**

Courtesy of Skinner, Inc., www.skinnerinc.com

Victorian snake earpendants, applied and engraved snakes coiled around elongated gold drops with ruby eyes, 10k gold, 2-1/2" l., 5.1 dwt. Provenance: From the collection of the late Christie Romero, historian of antique, period, and vintage jewelry as well as certified gemologist, lecturer, instructor and consultant, director of the Center for Jewelry Studies, author of *Warman's Jewelry Identification & Price Guide*, and appraiser on PBS's "Antiques Roadshow."........ **$461**

Courtesy of Skinner, Inc., www.skinnerinc.com

NECKLACES & PENDANTS

Georgian woven high carat yellow gold necklace, circa 1880, finely woven wire chain apportioned by cannetille stations and closure, girandole ornament suspending three drops, two with later shepherd's hook wire backs for use as earrings, unmarked, 17" l. **$2,176**

Courtesy of Rago Arts and Auctions, www.ragoarts.com

Antique moonstone, diamond, and platinum-topped gold necklace, moonstone cabochons weighing approximately 1.70 carats, single- and full-cut diamonds weighing approximately 0.70 carat, set in platinum-topped gold, 14.20 grams, pendant 2-1/4" x 1-5/8", chain 19" l. **$1,250**

Courtesy of Heritage Auctions, ha.com

Victorian necklace with shield-form 14k yellow gold and enamel pendant set with pearls, two gold tassels on either side, chain with fancy links, with box, necklace 18" l., 32.6 dwt. **$1,476**

Courtesy of Skinner, Inc., www.skinnerinc.com

Antique garnet and gold necklace, oval-shaped garnets ranging in size from 19.10 mm x 14.30 mm x 6.55 mm to 16.20 mm x 12.75 mm x 5.65 mm, set in 22k gold, 53.50 grams, 17" x 7/8". **$7,188**

Courtesy of Heritage Auctions, ha.com

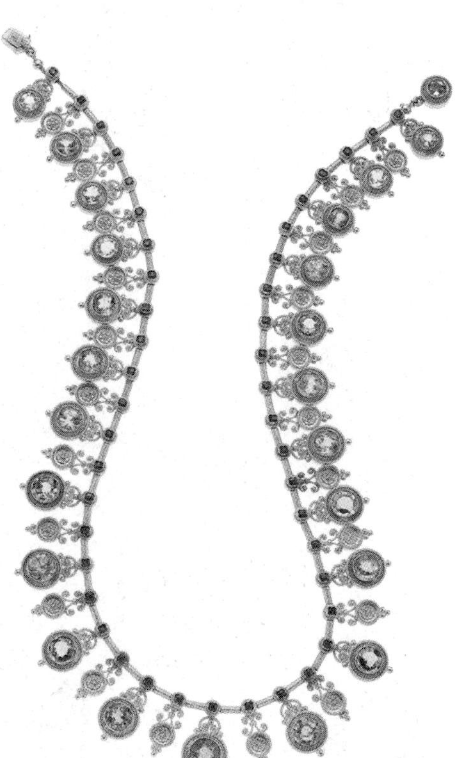

Etruscan Revival peridot, ruby, and gold necklace, Successori Marchesini, circa 1870, graduated round-cut peridots weighing approximately 25.00 carats, round-cut rubies weighing approximately 1.80 carats, set in 18k gold, with applied plaque marked Successori Marchesini, 57.20 grams, 15-3/4" l. **$15,000**

Courtesy of Heritage Auctions, ha.com

Art Nouveau 14k yellow gold and pearl plique-a-jour pendant, French, early 20th century, shield-form pendant with decoration of amorous couple on front and tree on reverse, with French inscription and date, edges with pearl floral motif, 1-1/2" l., 4.2 dwt. **$584**

Courtesy of Skinner, Inc., www.skinnerinc.com

Art Nouveau platinum, diamond, and sapphire clover pendant with diamond and sapphire leaves and scrolling stem on platinum chain, pendant 1-1/4" h. x 3/4" w., 4.1 dwt. **$984**

Courtesy of Skinner, Inc., www.skinnerinc.com

Antique jadeite jade, diamond, and gold pendant, carved jadeite jade measuring 22.00 mm x 13.63 mm x 13.82 mm, full-cut diamonds weighing approximately 0.40 carat, set in 14k gold, 7.20 grams, 1-5/8" x 15/16". **$1,625**

Courtesy of Heritage Auctions, ha.com

Victorian Scottish agate and gold pendant with panels of Victorian Scottish agate set in 14k gold, 8.60 grams, 2-11/16" x 1". **$425**

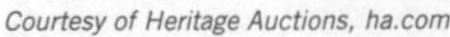

Courtesy of Heritage Auctions, ha.com

Antique aquamarine and gold pendant, oval-shaped aquamarine measuring 31.00 mm x 25.30 mm x 15.90 mm and weighing approximately 64.90 carats, set in 18k gold, 14k gold bale, 23.44 grams, 1-15/16" x 1-1/4". **$2,500**

Courtesy of Heritage Auctions, ha.com

RINGS

Edwardian diamond and platinum-topped gold ring, European-cut diamonds weighing approximately 0.25 carat with rose-cut diamonds set in platinum-topped 18k gold, 2.80 grams, size 7 (sizeable).... **$275**

Courtesy of Heritage Auctions, ha.com

Art Deco 14k white gold and diamond ring set with five large round-cut diamonds and eight smaller diamonds, size 7, 4.3 dwt. **$738**

Courtesy of Skinner, Inc., www.skinnerinc.com

Antique opal, diamond, and silver-topped gold ring, navette-shaped opal surrounded by European-cut diamonds weighing approximately 1.20 carats, set in silver-topped 18k gold, 5.01 grams, size 6-1/4. .... **$875**

Courtesy of Heritage Auctions, ha.com

Art Deco platinum, diamond, and sapphire ring, size 6-1/2, 2.8 dwt. **$923**

Courtesy of Skinner, Inc., www.skinnerinc.com

Art Deco 14k white gold and diamond ring, cluster-set with diamonds, size 8, 2.4 dwt. .. **$338**

Courtesy of Skinner, Inc., www.skinnerinc.com

Antique 14k gold, porcelain, and diamond ring, small painted porcelain plaque of woman surrounded by rose-cut diamonds, size 6-1/2, 2.4 dwt. **$615**

Courtesy of Skinner, Inc., www.skinnerinc.com

Antique cameo ring depicting Cupid and Psyche, some scratches to ring band, size 8-1/2........... **$554**

Courtesy of Skinner, Inc., www.skinnerinc.com

SETS

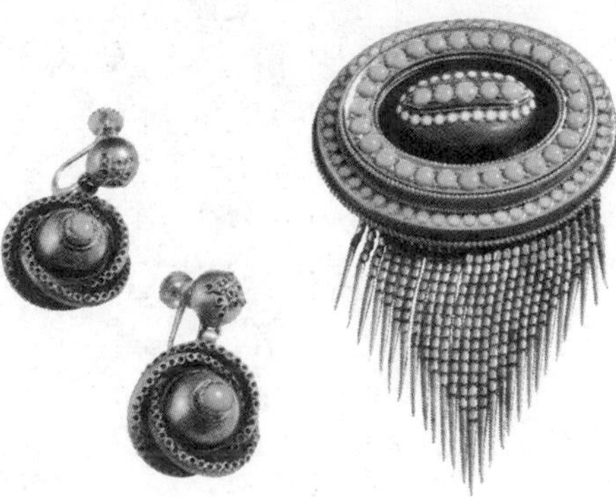

Antique gold and turquoise brooch and earrings: 18k gold knot-form earrings with center turquoise and 14k gold post, 17.5 dwt., and 14k gold, turquoise, and enameled brooch with articulated fringe and glass back, small chip to turquoise stone in brooch, fringe intact and secure, back with some repairs, brooch with fringe 3" l. x 1-3/4" w.. **$1,107**

Courtesy of Skinner, Inc., www.skinnerinc.com

Antique gold and garnet carbuncle suite: approximately 15k gold brooch and earpendants each set with carbuncle, applied wirework accents, 1-1/2" l. x 1-3/8", 15.8 dwt............. **$861**

Courtesy of Skinner, Inc., www.skinnerinc.com

COSTUME JEWELRY

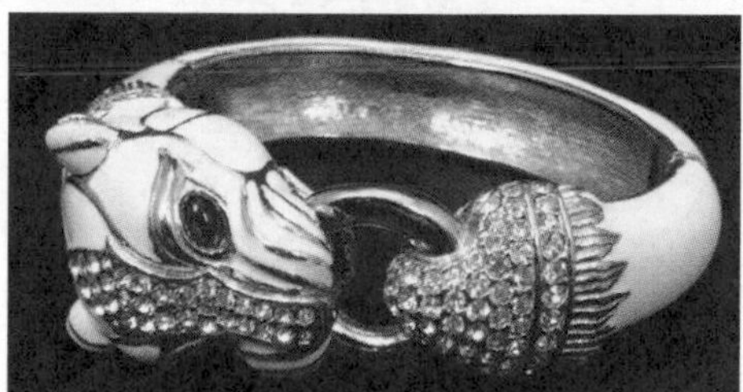

Vintage Ciner enameled panther bracelet with red glass eyes and rhinestone decorations over white enamel, 2-1/2" dia., 108g. **$215**

Courtesy of Elite Decorative Arts, www.eliteauction.com

Vintage Ciner enameled cheetah bracelet with green glass eyes and rhinestone decorations over black and gold enamel, 2-1/2" dia., 103g........ **$215**

Courtesy of Elite Decorative Arts, www.eliteauction.com

Three-piece Ciner suite in manner of David Webb, gold-tone with large simulated onyx and diamond links centering cabochon simulated ruby, diamond or emerald, with ear clips en suite, 1-1/2" w., necklace 18" l., bracelet 7" l. (wearable linked together as single 25" necklace). **$369**

Courtesy of New Orleans Auction Gallery, www.neworleansauction.com

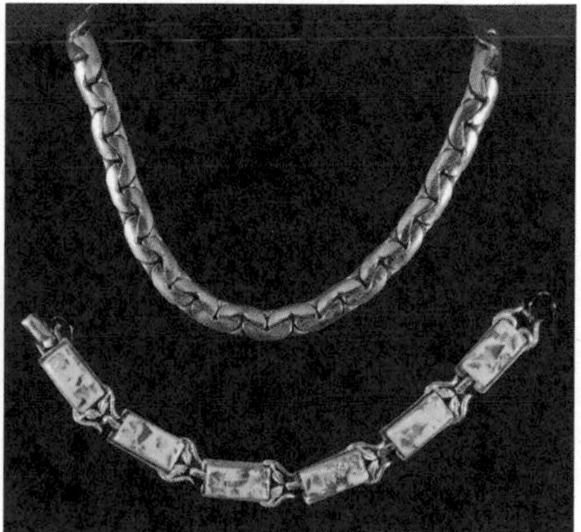

Vintage Coro necklace and bracelet, silver finish link necklace, bracelet with bluish colored stones. **$46**

Courtesy of Specialists of South, www.specialistsofthesouth.com

Vintage Miriam Haskell green glass necklace, circa 1920s, approximately 11" l.................... **$156**

Courtesy of Premier Auction Galleries, www.pag4u.com

Frank Hess for Miriam Haskell flower brooch, circa 1938, flower with red, blue, green, and clear strass centers, green pressed glass leaves, embossed in plate Miriam Haskell.................. **$288**

Courtesy of Rago Arts and Antiques, www.ragoarts.com

Miriam Haskell jade and pearl double-strand necklace, gold-tone clasp with raised marks, 15-1/4" l., 78.6 grams. **$93**

Courtesy of Elite Decorative Arts, www.eliteauction.com

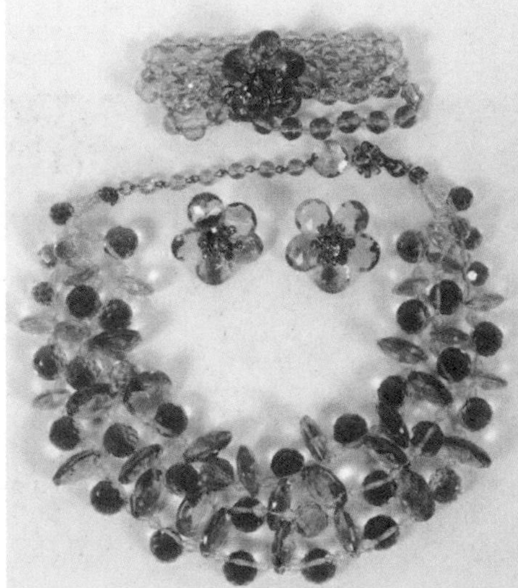

Miriam Haskell signed three-piece set, brilliant-cut pink-rose crystal, good condition: triple-strand necklace, 16" l.; four-strand bracelet, 19.5 mm l.; earrings, clip clasp, 3.5 mm dia................. **$369**

Courtesy of DuMouchelles, www.dumouchelle.com

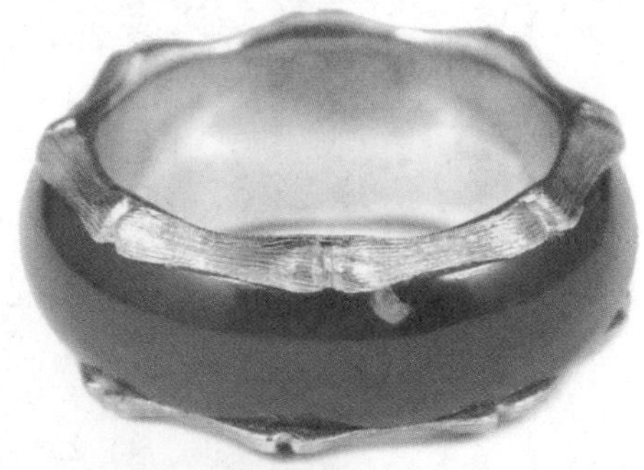

Vintage Hobé jade bamboo ring, mid-20th century, 14k yellow gold, signed Hobé, lady's size 7, approximately 4 dwt................................. **$434**

Courtesy of Elite Decorative Arts, www.eliteauction.com

Hobé 1940s-1950s sterling silver floral bracelet, signed "Hobe Sterling Design Pat'd," 7-1/2" x 1-1/2", 73.17 g. **$206**

Courtesy of DuMouchelles, www.dumouchelle.com

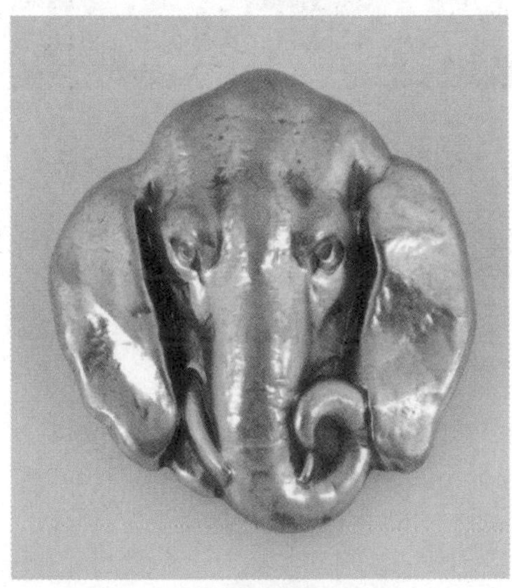

Joseff of Hollywood elephant brooch, gold-tone, signed, fair condition. **$122**

Courtesy of Morphy Auctions, morphyauctions.com

◀ Kenneth Jay Lane faux pearl necklace comprised of two matching necklaces each with faux jet beads, together with faux pearl necklace with faceted faux jet and clear stones, one necklace stamped "Kenneth Lane," overall very good condition.. **$63**

Courtesy of Leslie Hindman Auctioneers, www.lesliehindman.com

Vintage Kenneth Jay Lane bracelet, 75" x 3-1/4" x 2-3/4". **$250**

Courtesy of Material Culture, www.materialculture.com

Kenneth Jay Lane faux amber cabochon hinged bracelet with pavé rhinestones and tiger-eye cabochons, stamped K.J.L............................... **202**

Courtesy of Leslie Hindman Auctioneers, www.lesliehindman.com

Carved ivory figural poodle brooch with rhinestone collar by Jomaz, 1-1/2"................................ **$142**

Courtesy of Richard D. Hatch & Associates, www.richardhatchauctions.com

Two Mazer Bros. brooches: sword brooch with lion heads and jeweled crown, 2-3/4" l. and 4" l. ... **$272**

Courtesy of William J. Jenack Estate Appraisers & Auctioneers, www.jenack.com

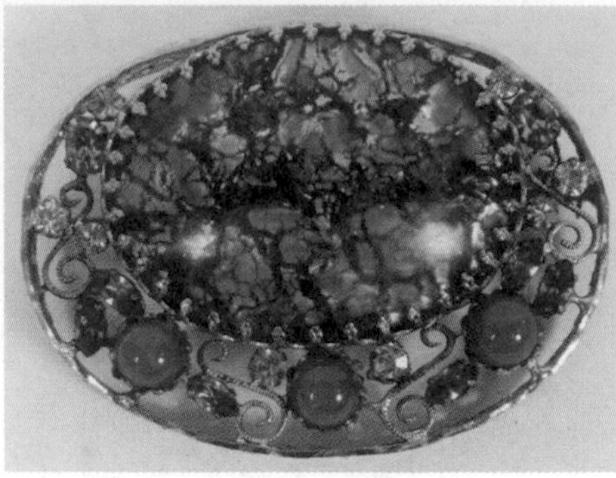

Schreiner New York blue and green stone brooch, good condition, 2-1/4" w. x 1-3/4" l. .. **$154**

Courtesy of DuMouchelles, www.dumouchelle.com

Vintage Trifari sterling silver designer figural crown brooch pin, fully hallmarked "TRIFARI STERLING" and numbered 137542 to verso, 1-3/4" h. x 2" w., 22.6 grams. **$161**

Courtesy of Elite Decorative Arts, www.eliteauction.com

Trifari feather-shaped pin with moonstones and paste stones, 4" l. **$176**

Courtesy of Butterscotch Auction Gallery, www.butterscotchauction.com

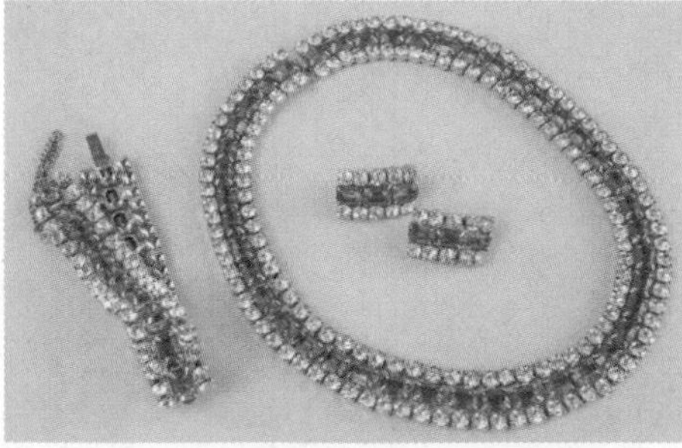

Rhinestone and simulated emerald suite: necklace, bracelet, and earrings, necklace 15" l. **$25**

Courtesy of Capo Auction, www.capoauctionnyc.com

Trifari gold-tone aqua enamel and rhinestone demi parure: choker necklace and earclips, each stamped "Crown Trifari." **$139**

Courtesy of Leslie Hindman Auctioneers, www.lesliehindman.com

KITCHENWARE

EVERYONE KNOWS THAT the kitchen is the hub of the home. So when the wildly successful "Downton Abbey" series started streaming across television screens, the show's Edwardian kitchen became a visual primer on class and comfort in our increasingly uncertain times.

That vision not only riveted viewers to each "Downton Abbey" installment, but the show's anti-snobbery theme created a new market niche for antique kitchen collectibles.

When stoic butler Mr. Carson chides housekeeper Mrs. Hughes about a new-fangled electric toaster, antique dealers nationwide said vintage toasters flew off the shelves.

"We simply could not believe how much interest 'Downton Abbey' sparked in antique kitchen utensils," said Rege Woodley, a retired antique dealer in Washington, Pennsylvania. "I sold one of my antique rolling pins to my neighbor for $100 because it looked like the one used by Mrs. Patmore, the cook in 'Downton Abbey.'"

Pat Greene, owner of Nothing New Antiques, said she was excited about all the "Downton Abbey" fuss and hoped her antique kitchenwares fetched some lasting prices, too. "My rolling pins usually go for $5 to $10, but I'm seeing a big rush on my cookie cutters," said Greene of Pittsburgh.

Mary Kirk of New Alexandria, Pennsylvania, collects antique cookbooks and was especially interested in trying to prepare some of the food served in the "Downton Abbey" show. "I am extremely interested in trying to prepare the eggs poached with spinach – a dish that poor young kitchen maid Daisy had to prepare during one show scene," said Kirk, a

Hoosier-style American oak kitchen cabinet in two sections, first quarter 20th century, upper section with three hinged doors and tambour roll-up, lower section with porcelain top, breadboard pull-out, and lower tin-lined breadbox drawer, original hardware, old refinished surface, backboard to upper section replaced, lacking sifter and possibly other interior components, 70-1/2" h. x 41" w. x 27-1/2" d. **$270**

Courtesy of Jeffrey S. Evans & Associates, www.jeffreysevans.com

Art Deco Hoosier paint-decorated kitchen cabinet in two pieces, first quarter 20th century, top with three doors above tambour concealing two tin dispensing bins and revolving spice rack with bottles, base with porcelain adjustable top, two over three drawers and door, original painted and decorated surfaces, original interior labels and instructions, excellent condition, 70" h. x 40-1/2" w. x 26-1/2" d. **$228**

Courtesy of Jeffrey S. Evans & Associates, www.jeffreysevans.com

Tansu kitchen chest, 59-3/4" h. x 35" w. x 15-3/4" d. **$378**

Courtesy of Leslie Hindman Auctioneers, www.lesliehindman.com

retired librarian. Because of the show's lengthy shooting schedule, producers reported that most of the food served during production consisted of light salads.

Jimmy Roark of Nashville, Tennessee, said he has not seen as large a rush for his kitchen collectibles as a result of the show. "What I see is a more gradual demand for these items," said Roark, who operates a small antique collectibles shop in his garage. "I sell a lot of my cookie cutters, antique wooden bowls, and vintage mixer beaters during the holidays."

Still, the "Downton Abbey" magic continues to seed interest in a broad swath of antique kitchen utensils and artifacts from Bennington mixing bowls to turn-of-the-century tiger wood rolling pins.

Stephen White of White & White Antiques & Interiors of Skaneateles, New York, said interest in antique kitchenware remains steady. He was quick to feature his rare whale ivory-crested Nantucket rolling pin valued at $425. "I have unusual kitchen antiques from hand food choppers to copper pots," he said.

"When you think of Pittsburgh, you can't escape the long history that the H.J. Heinz Co. has here," said Toni Bahnak of Candlewood Antiques in Ardara, Pennsylvania. "We have rare old vinegar bottles and ketchup bottles that denote an era when the Heinz Co. made its own glass," Bahnak said.

Painted cut-out folk art spice cabinet made by Charles F. Ohlrich (1881-1961), Cleveland, circa 1900-1920, mixed woods including some from cigar boxes, multi-tier cathedral form with hinged lid behind upper pediment, four levels of small drawers flanked by side shelf, lower full-length drawer, drawer faces with applied carved ornaments and original porcelain knobs, original red paint with old varnished surface, 22" h. overall x 17" w. x 7" d.................................. **$420**

Courtesy of Jeffrey S. Evans & Associates, www.jeffreysevans.com

Industry experts say ketchup and pickle collectibles rose in value because of the business deal that saw the H.J. Heinz Co. purchased by Warren Buffett's Berkshire Hathaway and 3G Capital, which was co-founded by Jorge Lemann, one of Brazil's richest men. Even before the blockbuster deal was announced, some Heinz memorabilia collectors reported that their antique bottles and jars were fetching higher prices than normal.

"I had one of my antique vinegar bottles sell for about $225 and I think I could have gotten more for it," said Ruth Oslet, an antiques collector from Waynesburg, Pennsylvania. She sold it to a marketing executive who collects business memorabilia.

Tom Purdue, a longtime collector of food company antiques, said history and nostalgia play an important role in what people remember and want to save for their modern kitchens. "I can remember the distinct smell of my grandmother's old pickle jars and Heinz horseradish in her musty old kitchen where she used a hand pump to wash dishes," said Purdue, an 89-year-old former blacksmith from Wheeling, West Virginia.

The ever-expanding business reaches back to 1869 when Henry John Heinz and neighbor L. Clarence Noble began selling grated horseradish, bottled in clear glass to showcase its purity. It wasn't until 1876 that the company introduced its flagship product, marketing the country's first commercial ketchup.

Not all history, though, is tied to corporate America. Family memories still stoke the embers of home cooking although many young people today find fast food the fuel of the future.

"I still have my family's old cornbread recipe and I use it all the time," said Elizabeth Schwan, gallery director for Aspire Auctions in Pittsburgh.

Schwan, who scans the country for antiques, admits she has a soft spot for old kitchen utensils. "Flower-sifters, antique copper mixing bowls, and rolling pins were all part of my heritage because my family grew up on a Kentucky farm," Schwan said. "I can still smell the homemade bread and jams."

And like most farm families, the kitchen served as a meeting place and refuge from a long day's work. "Between verbal debates about what to plant on the south flats, we would help our parents churn butter and chop wood for the old country stove," said Myrtle Bench, 91, of Washington, Pennsylvania.

But as a young America turned from the agricultural frontier in the late 1890s and began to embrace a manufacturing economy, automation replaced handcrafts, and the kitchen became a new testing ground for a variety of modern gizmos like the automatic dishwasher.

The automatic dishwasher was a toy for the rich when an electric model was introduced in 1913 by Willard and Forrest Walker, two Syracuse, New York brothers who ran a hardware store when they were not tinkering with kitchen machines. The new dishwasher sold for $120 (the equivalent of $1,429 in today's dollars), a hefty premium over the $20 the Walkers charged for their popular hand-cranked model and also more expensive than a gasoline-powered washer the brothers put on the market in 1911.

"You can still find some of the old hand-crank washers, but I like to spend my time finding kitchen utensils that reflect how people prepared their food," said Dirk Hayes, a freelance cook from Uniontown, Pennsylvania. "I loved watching 'Downton Abbey' because the kitchen scenes really gave you a flavor of how the food was prepared. I never had that kind of staff, but it's fun to dream," said Hayes, who collects rolling pins and antique carving knives.

— Chriss Swaney

Fire King jadite green mixing bowl, refrigerator bin, cereal jar, flour jar, and sugar shaker, chip to cereal jar. **$1**

Courtesy Vero Beach Auction, www.verobeachauction.com

French meat or juice press, nickel-plated cast iron, Depose-France cast on bottom, fancy feet and scrolling, excellent condition, 15" h. x 11" w.... **$780**

Rich Penn Auctions, www.richpennauctions.com

H.J. Heinz Co. blue and white salt-glazed ceramic crock, "H. J. HEINZ CO." trademark to front, Albany slip-glazed interior, possibly used for pickling, fourth quarter 19th/first quarter 20th century, 5-1/2" h. x 6-1/2" d. **$168**

Courtesy of Jeffrey S. Evans & Associates, www.jeffreysevans.com

Meat press/sausage stuffer, cast iron and brass, unusual design in excellent condition, 24" h. x 13-1/2" w. x 17-1/4" d....... **$120**

Rich Penn Auctions, www.richpennauctions.com

▲ Wooden dough bin on iron wheels, circa 1840, fine original condition, 30" h. x 27" w. x 60" l. Dough bins held flour and yeast and were used for making bread; portable bins allowed the baker to move it to the warmest part of room so the dough could rise. ... **$1,875**

Courtesy of Guernsey's, www.guernseys.com

▶ Blue slip-decorated stoneware six-gallon butter churn attributed to Shenfelder Pottery, Reading, Pennsylvania, 19th century, trailing floral and foliate blue slip decoration surrounding date 1869, No. 6 at base representing gallon size, unsigned, good condition, 1" x 2" pop-out on back side of churn, missing lid and plunger, 21-1/2" h. **$1,029**

Courtesy of Conestoga Auction Co., www.conestogaauction.com

Shaker mixed wood butter churn, 19th century, natural varnished finish, vertical staves with interlocking tapered support bands with elongated handle and plunger, good condition with use and age wear, 52-3/4" h. overall. **$333**

Courtesy of Conestoga Auction Co., www.conestogaauction.com

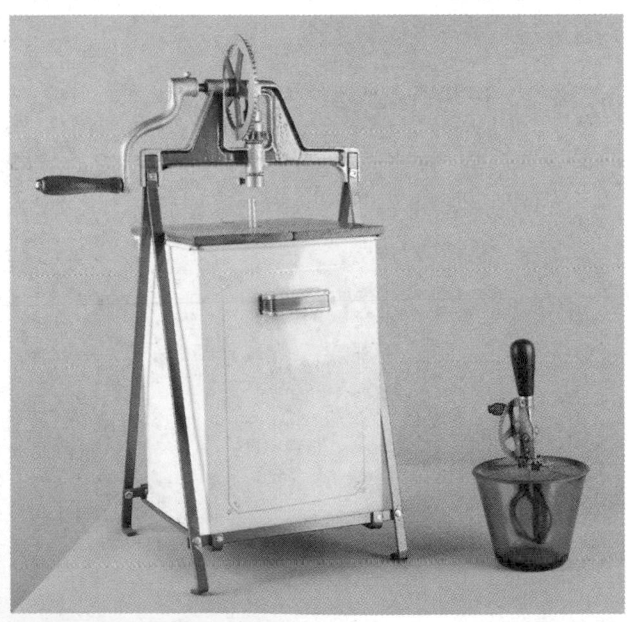

Large metal butter churn with wooden lid and mechanical mixer with glass jar, excellent condition, churn 25" h.......... **$90**

Courtesy of Morphy Auctions, morphyauctions.com

Cast iron string holder of woman in white dress gazing into mirror, Judd Co., #1468, reverse side holds string with small feed cast under woman's elbow for dispensing, 7-3/4" h. **$309**

Courtesy of Bertoia Auctions, www.bertoiaauctions.com

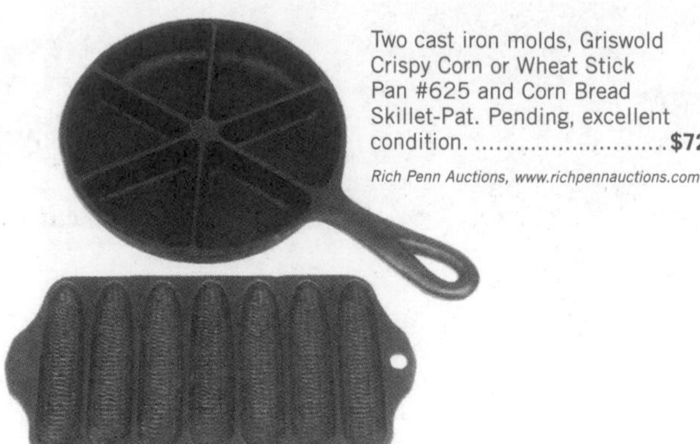

Two cast iron molds, Griswold Crispy Corn or Wheat Stick Pan #625 and Corn Bread Skillet-Pat. Pending, excellent condition. **$72**

Rich Penn Auctions, www.richpennauctions.com

Five pieces of 19th century wooden kitchenware including saltbox, 9" h., and small divided cutlery box with heart-shaped handle, 7-1/2" w. **$400**

Courtesy of Wiederseim Associates, Inc., www.wiederseim.com

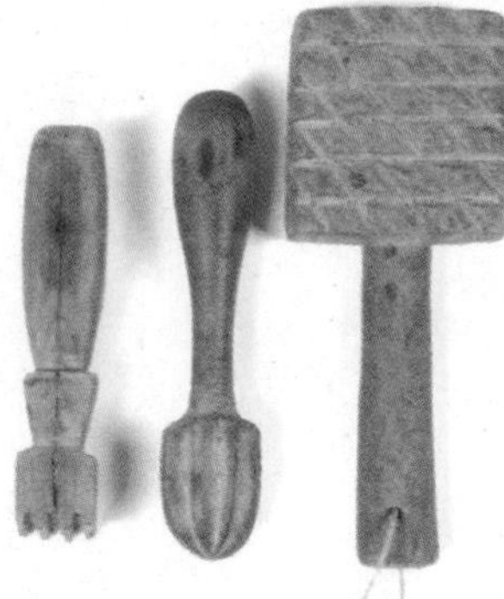

Three American carved treen kitchen implements, second half 19th century, paddle-style two-sided butter print with large and small diamond designs, excellent condition original dry surfaces, square tool with crack to one side, others in very good condition with expected wear, butter print 7-1/4" l. **$48**

Courtesy of Jeffrey S. Evans & Associates, www.jeffreysevans.com

Fifteen wooden kitchen utensils: two mandolin slicers, six cutting boards (two pig-shaped), one bread paddle, two rolling pins, one dough scraper, two spoons, and one bowl with handle; cutting boards show signs of use with multiple cut marks, especially pig boards.. **$454**

Courtesy of Quinn's Auction Galleries, www.quinnsauction.com

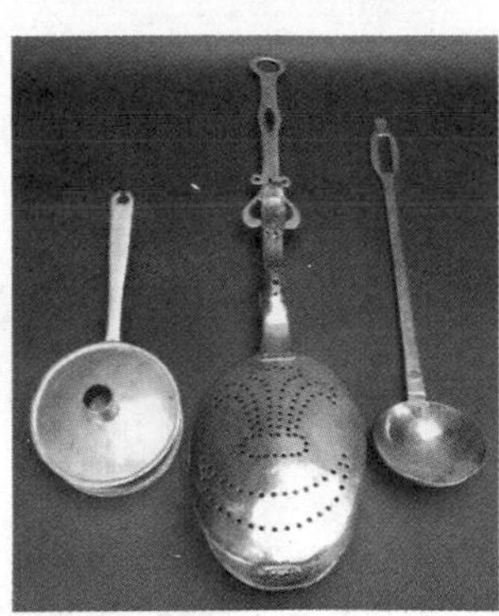

Brass kitchen tools, 19th century, brass ladle, tinderbox, and chestnut roaster, ladle fastened to handle with brass nails, tinder box with candle holder attached to lid, typical wear from use, slight pitting and dark spotting along surface of pieces, mild denting along lid of tinder box and to handle of roaster, 24-1/2" h. x 5-1/2" w. x 3" d. **$50**

Courtesy of Jouis J. Dianni, LLC Antiques Auctions, louisjdianni.com

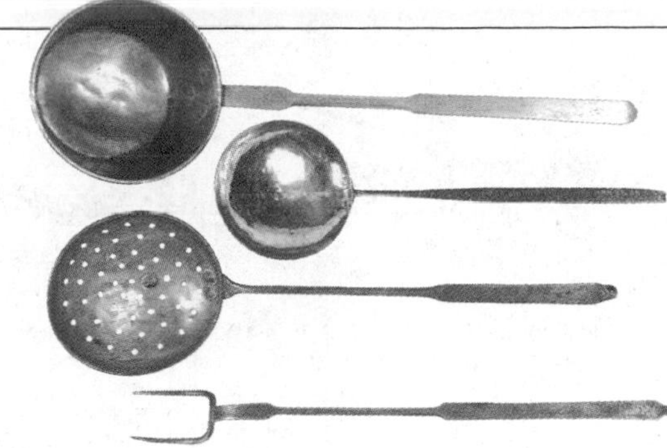

Four kitchen utensils, 19th century: copper bowl ladle, 15" l.; copper bowl dipper, 21" l.; brass bowl skimmer, 18" l.; and iron meat fork, 17" l., fair to good condition with some pitting and rust. **$194**

Courtesy of Conestoga Auction Co., www.conestogaauction.com

▲ Two bird-form tin cookie cutters, 19th century, fair to good condition with some rust and corrosion, 5-1/2" and 6-3/4" l. **$666**

Courtesy of Conestoga Auction Co., www.conestogaauction.com

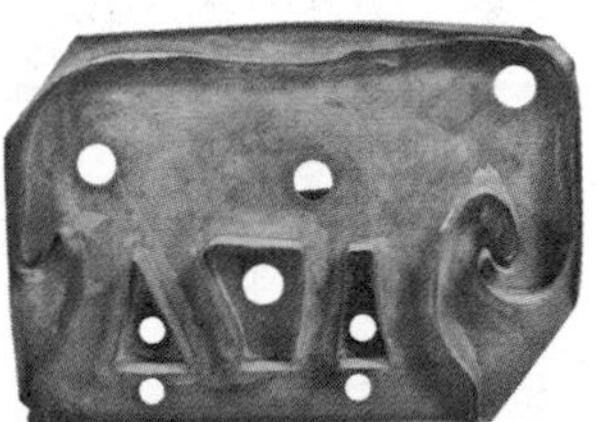

▲ Large elephant-form tin cookie cutter, signed "G. Endriss 700 N St. Phila." on handle, good condition with wear and minor dents, 7-3/8" h. x 10-1/2" w. **$1,150**

Courtesy of Conestoga Auction Co., www.conestogaauction.com

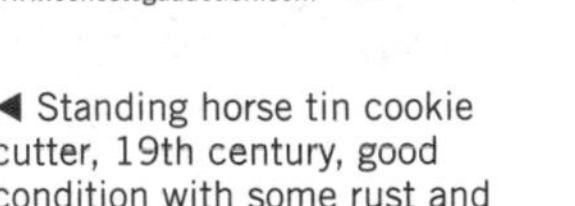

◀ Standing horse tin cookie cutter, 19th century, good condition with some rust and corrosion, 5" h. x 9-1/2" w. . **$847**

Courtesy of Conestoga Auction Co., www.conestogaauction.com

Rolling pin with whalebone caps, roller with alternating bands of varied wood, 19th century, one band of wood with age split, 15" l. **$677**

Courtesy of CRN Auctions, Inc., www.crnauctions.com

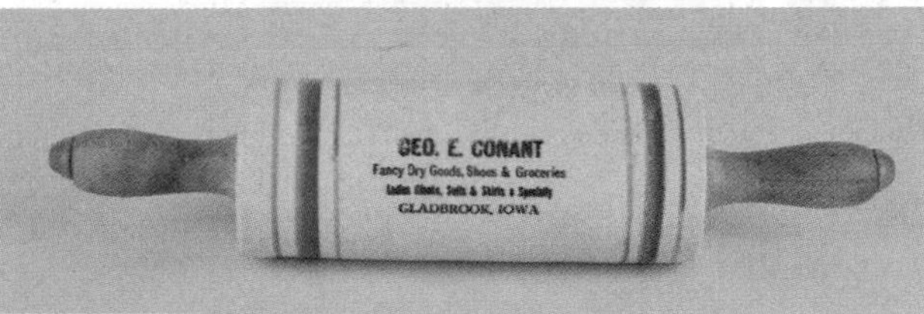

Early ceramic rolling pin with wooden handles, advertises George E. Conant dry goods store in Gladbrook, Iowa, excellent condition, 14-1/2" l. **$336**

Courtesy of Morphy Auctions, morphyauctions.com

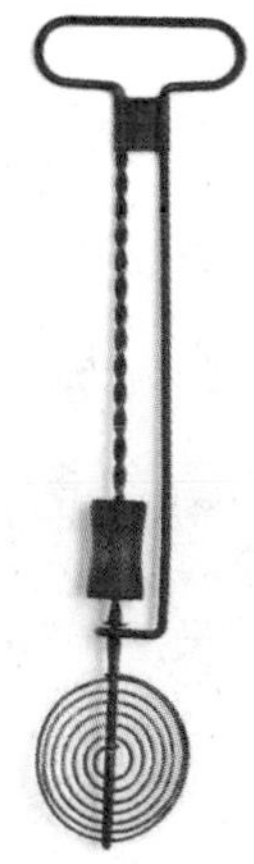

Antique egg beater, 12" h. .. **$270**

Courtesy of John McInnis Auctioneers Appraisers, www.mcinnisauctions.com

Seven graduated copper cooking pots with blacksmith wrought iron copper-riveted handles, not marked, probably American-made antiques, largest 15" l. x and 6-3/4" h., 7-1/4" dia., smallest 5-1/2" l. x 3" h., 2-5/8" dia. **$238**

Courtesy of North American Auction Co., www.northamericanauctioncompany.com

Antique cloisonne enamel on copper teapot with dragon handle, overall good condition, 11" w. x 6-1/2" d. x 8-3/4" h. **$154**

Courtesy of Roland Auctioneers & Valuers, www.rolandauctions.com

Three French heavy hammered copper ragout pots, 19th century, two marked "E. Dehillerin, 8 Rue Coquilliere, Paris" and "L'Industrie Hotelliere, 13 Rue Gambetta, Nancy," each with dovetail construction, 8" to 9" h., 14-1/2" to 17" dia. **$688**

Courtesy of New Orleans Auction Gallery, www.neworleansauction.com

◀ Aesthetic Movement teakettle stand with tray, circa 1875, wrought iron, copper, brass, and transfer-painted porcelain, wooden tray stamped "FEP" with shield and blue K, teapot stamped 2R, 48" x 18" x 22" overall **$1,280**

Coutesy of Rago Arts and Antiques, www.ragoarts.com

Cherry and pewter coffee grinder, 19th century, iron crank handle and mechanism, pewter hopper, dovetailed cherry case and beaded drawer and brass mushroom pull, good condition with some age cracks, dents to pewter and use wear, 10" h. overall **$73**

Courtesy of Conestoga Auction Co., www.conestogaauction.com

Tea caddy, circa 1820, mahogany with pine secondary wood, exterior with fine marquetry fish-scale pattern of mahogany and birch with center top of rosewood, four brass feet **$718**

Courtesy of Jouis J. Dianni, LLC Antiques Auctions, louisjdianni.com

top lot!

Copper teakettle, circa 1785-1814, Lancaster, Pennsylvania, signed Schaum, arched swing handle mounted on curved chevron, brass mushroom finial, domed lid, gooseneck spout and crimped seam tabs, good condition with dents and creases, 12-1/2" h. overall. $2,178

COURTESY OF CONESTOGA AUCTION CO., WWW.CONESTOGAAUCTION.COM

LAMPS & LIGHTING

LIGHTING DEVICES HAVE been around for thousands of years, and antique examples range from old lanterns used on the farm to high-end Tiffany lamps. The earliest known type of lamp was the oil lamp, which was patented by Aimé Argand in 1784 and mass-produced starting in the 19th century. Around 1850 kerosene became a popular lamp-burning fluid, replacing whale oil and other fluids.

In 1879 Thomas A. Edison invented the electric light, causing fluid lamps to lose favor and creating a new field for lamp manufacturers. Decorative table and floor lamps with ornate glass lampshades reached their height of popularity from 1900-1920, due to the success of Tiffany and other Arts & Crafts lamp makers such as Handel.

EARLY NON-ELECTIC LIGHTING

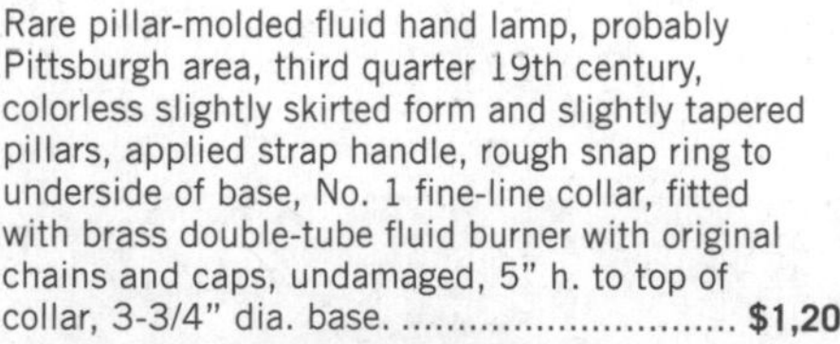

Rare pillar-molded fluid hand lamp, probably Pittsburgh area, third quarter 19th century, colorless slightly skirted form and slightly tapered pillars, applied strap handle, rough snap ring to underside of base, No. 1 fine-line collar, fitted with brass double-tube fluid burner with original chains and caps, undamaged, 5" h. to top of collar, 3-3/4" dia. base. **$1,200**

Courtesy of Jeffrey S. Evans & Associates, www.jeffreysevans.com

Saucer base miniature finger lamp, fourth quarter 19th/early 20th century, light blue conical-form font with ringed shoulder, saucer base with single flat-tab handle, underside embossed "PAT. APPLIED FOR," period collar, fitted with period Hornet-type burner, colorless chimney, undamaged lamp and setup, lamp and chimney rims with normal mold roughness, 3" h. to top of collar, 4-1/2" dia. base. **$510**

Courtesy of Jeffrey S. Evans & Associates, www.jeffreysevans.com

Bull's-eye loop handle kerosene footed finger lamp, Diamond Glass Co., 1890-1902, colorless font, light blue opalescent base, opaque light blue molded handle, No. 1 Taplin-Brown collar, undamaged, collar with electrical fitting sleeve, 5-7/8" h. to top of collar, 4" sq. foot. **$780**

Courtesy of Jeffrey S. Evans & Associates, www.jeffreysevans.com

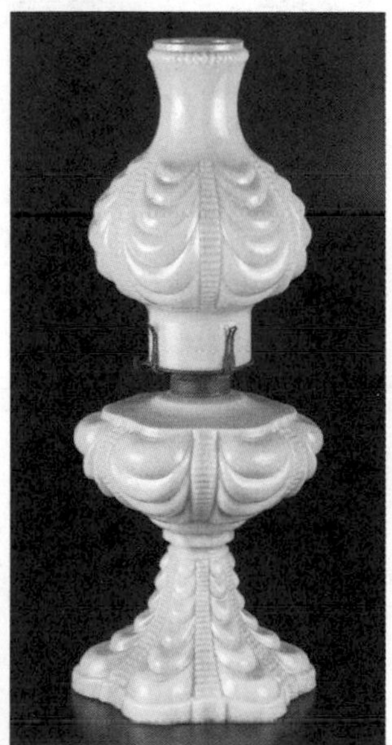

Victorian kerosene banquet lamp, late 19th/early 20th century, cased light blue font molded with shells, brass stem with jasperware insert and square base, fitted with non-period Duplex double-wick burner, chimney, and shade, 17" h. to top of collar, undamaged, slightly tilted. .. **$168**

Courtesy of Jeffrey S. Evans & Associates, www.jeffreysevans.com

◀ Coolidge Drape/Bellevue pattern (OMN) kerosene stand lamp, Pittsburgh Lamp, Brass & Glass Co., fourth quarter 19th century, opaque blue with mottling to base, No. 2 Taplin-Brown collar, matching patterned translucent light blue chimney shade, fitted with period No. 2 slip burner, undamaged lamp, chimney shade with minor normal roughness to each rim and minor flake to fitter, one drape with broken bubble, as made, burner undamaged, 18-7/8" h. to top of chimney shade, 9-1/2" h. to top of collar, 7-1/4" dia. foot. **$1,200**

Courtesy of Jeffrey S. Evans & Associates, www.jeffreysevans.com

Victorian cherub and bird banquet lamp, 20th century, elements together by association, cast-metal lattice and floral font vase with later paint, figural cherub and bird stem, cast-metal floral band foot embossed B&H/5023, brass drop-in font with signed B&H flame spreader and oil cap, crystal satin Honeycomb and Medallion pattern shade with non-period chimney, font vase with minor loss and 2-3/8" split running from rim with possible repairs, shade and chimney with normal roughness to fitters, 34" h. overall, 12-1/4" h. shade ring, 7" sq. base. **$240**

Courtesy of Jeffrey S. Evans & Associates, www.jeffreysevans.com

Panel-optic art glass miniature lamp, late 19th/early 20th century, pink opalescent globular-form font with apple green (uranium) and pink opalescent applied floral ornamentation, font within four bud vases depicting thorned branches and large flower with foliage, apple green (uranium) applied scalloped eight-point star base, dark to light pink opalescent panel-optic shade and scallop rim, period collar, fitted with Wild & Wessel Kosmos burner, colorless chimney, excellent condition, flake to one base star point, one bud vase with small area of undissolved metal to interior, as made, collar with some light denting, setup undamaged, 9-7/8" h. overall to top of shade, 5" h. to top of collar, 5" dia. base. **$1,560**

Courtesy of Jeffrey S. Evans & Associates, www.jeffreysevans.com

Panel-optic art glass miniature lamp, late 19th/early 20th century, amberina egg-form font, amber applied base with five large leaves encircling font over five tapered and raised foot tips, matching patterned umbrella-form shade, period collar, fitted with Plume & Atwood Nutmeg burner, colorless chimney, excellent condition, font undamaged, three foot tips with expected minute flakes/roughness, shade undamaged and with normal fitter roughness, as made, collar with light splits, burner deflector with damage, chimney top with minute flake, 8" h. overall to top of shade, 4-5/8" h. to top of collar, 3-1/4" dia. base. **$300**

Courtesy of Jeffrey S. Evans & Associates, www.jeffreysevans.com

American gilt metal figural solar lamp, circa 1850, classical female figure on stepped marble base, cut-glass shade with waffle and pinwheel design, marked "Cornelius & Baker/Philadelphia," 28" h., 8-1/2" dia....................... **$1,408**

Courtesy of Neal Auction Co., www.nealauctions.com

Antique bronze sinumbra lamp, mid-19th century, patinated nymph emerges from ormolu-mounted white marble column, domed frosted shade with floral garlands, 28-1/2" h. **$2,304**

Courtesy of Neal Auction Co., www.nealauctions.com

American gilt brass hanging sinumbra lamp, circa 1840, bulbous period shade cut with lyre motifs, in gilded mounts, suspended by chain below smoke bell, marked "Manufactured by H. N. Hooper & Co. Boston," 25" h., 12" dia.......................... **$4,800**

Courtesy of Neal Auction Co., www.nealauctions.com

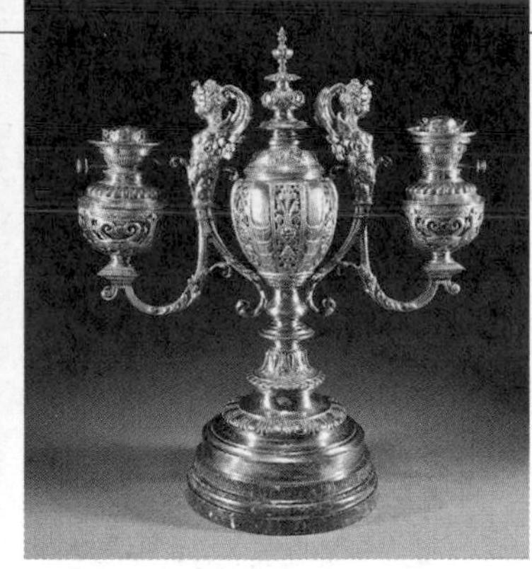

Antique English brass double-arm newell post lamp, circa 1900, reticulated standard, female terms, now on conforming marble base, fonts marked "Messengers/Patent," 29" h. x 25" w. 11" dia... **$1,024**

Courtesy of Neal Auction Co., www.nealauctions.com

Millefiori art glass floral oil lamp with cobalt base with lattice design, hurricane shade, 18-1/8" h. **$372**

Courtesy of Elite Decorative Arts, www.eliteauction.com

ELECTRIC LIGHTING

Art Nouveau leaded glass and silver-plate figural table lamp, shade by Bent Glass Novelty Co., New York, stylized butterfly form-shaped slag glass shade in red and orange glass with applied spiral-patterned wiring, flanked with green leaf border, surmounting Criaghead & Kintz cocatoo and turtle figural silver-plate standard, 27-1/2" h. **$4,270**

Courtesy of Clars Auction Gallery, www.clars.com

Handel Arts & Crafts leaded glass table lamp, shade with geometric reserves alternating from green to red with caramel glass frieze, surmounting three-socket cluster on patinated floral decorated base, 24" h. x 20" w. **$1,464**

Courtesy of Clars Auction Gallery, www.clars.com

Handel leaded glass table lamp, early 20th century, triangular caramel slag glass panels with vertical apron of red medallions and pale yellow ovals, two-light abstract lotus-form patinated metal base, bulbous at bottom rising to tapered neck, green felt on base with cloth label for "HANDEL/Lamps," no observed marks on shade, cracks to four yellow ovals, two red medallions, and two caramel slag glass panels, 26-1/4" h. to top of finial, shade 22" dia.. **$806**

Courtesy of Brunk Auctions, www.brunkauctions.com

Handel hanging light fixture, #5219, hammered copper and slag glass, with four original chains suspending pyramidal shade with band of square cutouts, repoussé decoration, signed with tag, minor wear to original patina, glass intact without cracks, one missing square glass inset, lacking ceiling cap, shade 22-1/4" sq. x 14-1/2" h..................... **$2,375**

Courtesy of Treadway Gallery, Inc., www.treadwaygallery.com

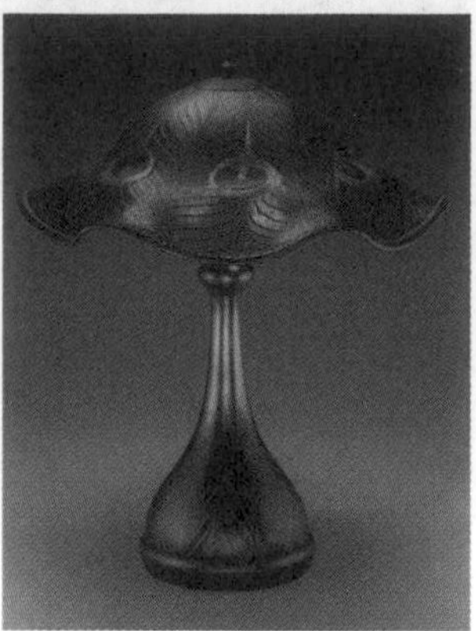

Charles Lotton iridescent ruby and gold glass peacock table lamp, late 20th century, good condition, 23" h............. **$8,125**

Courtesy of Heritage Auctions, ha.com

Pairpoint scenic table lamp, serial No. D 3042, Exeter floral shade surmounting patinated metal urn-form base, Pairpoint and serial number marked to base, 23" h. x 17-1/2" w. **$1,098**

Courtesy of Clars Auction Gallery, www.clars.com

Pairpoint Puffy lotus table lamp with yellow lotus blossom at peak surrounded by buds and green foliage, base with ornamental triplet stems and acanthus leaves on top of foot, impressed "Pairpoint Mfg. Co" with Pairpoint logo and 3083 form number beneath, base with Harvey Hubbell light socket with ball chain, green cloth cord, excellent condition, shade 6" h. x 13" w., combined 20" h........ **$4,840**

Courtesy of Humler & Nolan, www.humlernolan.com

Pairpoint Puffy apple tree table lamp, open-top shade with butterflies, apple blossoms, bumblebees, and apples, gold stamped "Pairpoint Mfg Corp, 1902" at rim's edge, touch-up areas inside lower rim, tree trunk base with moss green finish, "Pairpoint Mfg Co," Pairpoint logo, and form number 3092 impressions beneath, some wear, original Harvey Hubbell light sockets with acorn pulls, original lacquered paper sticker, shade 8" h. x 16" w., combined 25" h........................... **$9,680**

Courtesy of Humler & Nolan, www.humlernolan.com

Tiffany Studios leaded glass and bronze apple blossom table lamp on ribbed mushroom base, circa 1910, base stamped "TIFFANY STUDIOS, NEW YORK, 6861," shade stamped but not numbered, original electrical components and cap, shade sits flush but with approximately 20 small hairline cracks throughout, minor scratches to cap, patina to base, 23" h., 15-3/4" dia. **$16,250**

Courtesy of Heritage Auctions, ha.com

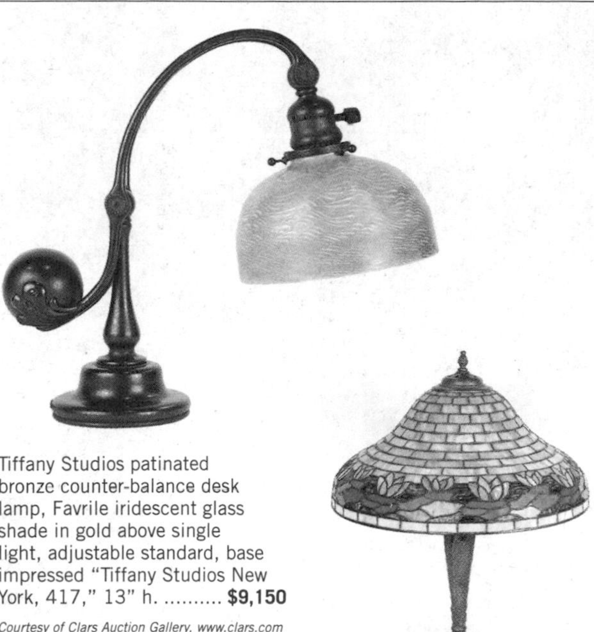

Tiffany Studios patinated bronze counter-balance desk lamp, Favrile iridescent glass shade in gold above single light, adjustable standard, base impressed "Tiffany Studios New York, 417," 13" h. **$9,150**

Courtesy of Clars Auction Gallery, www.clars.com

▲ Wilkinson Arts & Crafts leaded glass table lamp, dome shade with stylized foliate designs in green, red, and blue on mottled ground, surmounting two-socket cluster, baluster-form standard terminating on circular base marked 1737, 23" h. x 18" w. **$3,355**

Courtesy of Clars Auction Gallery, www.clars.com

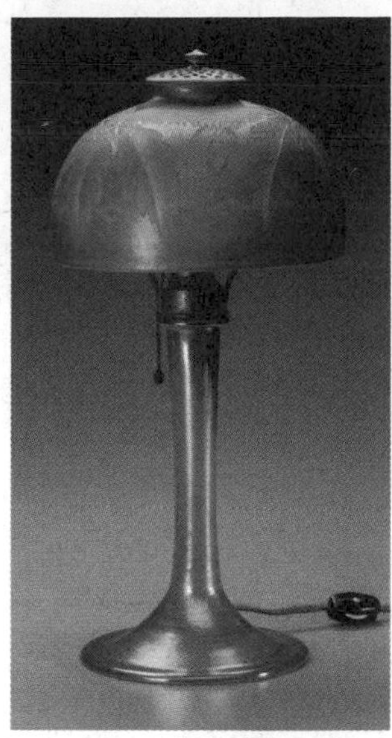

Tiffany Studios engraved green Favrile glass palm desk lamp, circa 1905, engraved "L.C. Tiffany, Favrile, 20212" to shade, original cap with strong patina matching harp and hardware, light onion-skin texture to edge of shade, strong coloration through base, good condition, 15" h. **$7,500**

Courtesy of Heritage Auctions, ha.com

◀ Tiffany & Co. bronze floor lamp base with Tiffany leaded glass shade, early 20th century, white dogwood blossoms and green leaves on blue ground, applied beaded border, underside rim with plaque stamped "Tiffany Studios New York" applied later, circular copper cap, three-light bronze base with swirl decoration, spiral gas line, pierced platform base with four acanthus leaf paw feet and stamped "Tiffany & Co." and "175," seven pieces of stained glass with cracks, corrosion to bronze base, shade 10-1/2" x 22", 69-1/2" h. overall........... **$9,300**

Courtesy of Brunk Auctions, www.brunkauctions.com

Wilkinson leaded glass and bronzed metal rose table lamp, circa 1910, verdigris patina to base, hairline cracks around border of shade, lamp base does not sit flush because of replacement nut and bolt, 27" h., 22" dia. **$6,000**

Courtesy of Heritage Auctions, ha.com

top lot

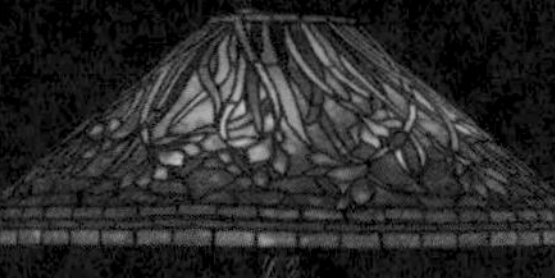

Tiffany Studios leaded glass and bronze daffodil table lamp on twisted vine base, circa 1905, stamped "TIFFANY STUDIOS NEW YORK, 1497-8; 443," four stable hairline cracks to shade, updated electrical wiring with original cap and light sockets, good verdigris patina to base and edge of cap, 27-1/2" h., 20-1/2" dia..$68,750

COURTESY OF HERITAGE AUCTIONS, HA.COM

Triennale floor lamp of Carrera marble, leather, enameled metal, and aluminum by Gino Sarfatti (Italian, 1912-1984), circa 1950, Arredoluce, stamped "MADE IN ITALY," light scuffing to enameled shades, 69-1/2" h. **$5,000**

Courtesy of Heritage Auctions, ha.com

Akari lamp of Washi paper, bamboo ribbing, and metal by Isamu Noguchi (American, 1904-1988), designed 1951, signed along base, good condition, small tear near bottom, 49-1/2" h. **$300**

Courtesy of Heritage Auctions, ha.com

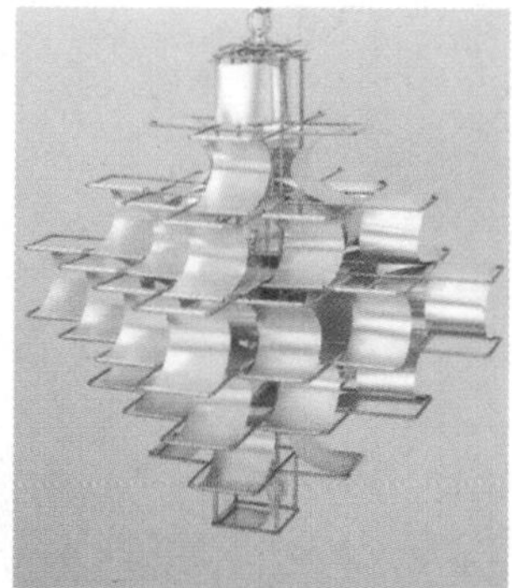

Cassiopé chandelier of brushed aluminum and steel wire by Max Sauze (French, b. 1933), designed 1969, good condition, missing screw, light oxidation to hanging fixture, 25-5/8" h. **$1,188**

Courtesy of Heritage Auctions, ha.com

LUXURY GOODS

ALTHOUGH THERE IS little question whether handbags are continuing their reign on the luxury accessories market, additional types of items and interested bidders in this high-end market also continue to grow.

In addition to the booming luxury handbag market, luxury accessories auctions also often feature luggage and trunks, dinner china, jewelry, watches, vintage clothing, and surfboards, rare vintage bicycles and binoculars. For instance, Leslie Hindman Auctioneers hosts multiple luxury accessories and vintage fashion auctions each year, and while handbags are largely represented, so too are couture fashions from designers including Chanel, Christian Dior, Yves Saint Laurent, and Alexander McQueen, just to name a few.

This speaks to one of the most significant developments to come from the rise in luxury accessory auctions, the increase in collecting among women.

"Collectibles and collecting have traditionally been male-dominated pursuits," said Matt Rubinger, director of Heritage Auctions' Luxury Accessories category, as reported in *Warman's Antiques & Collectibles 2015.* "No one in the business was looking at these very high-quality pieces of enduring haute couture as having value beyond being arm candy. This assumption effectively dismissed half the potential population of collectors, that is, women."

In recent years, Heritage Auctions has added luxury accessories to its list of record-setting categories. In 2015, fine jewelry and luxury accessories combined for a solid year, with more than $26 million in combined auction totals ($15+ million in jewelry and $11+ million in luxury accessories).

In fact, in September 2014, an Hermes Extraordinary Collection 30cm diamond matte Himalayan Nilo crocodile Birkin bag realized $185,000 at auction, which put it squarely in second place for the highest price paid for a handbag at auction. The world record, set in 2011,

Louis Vuitton special-order monogram Macassar canvas cave whiskey trunk with crystal and silver service, originally designed in 1955, with whiskey bar, monogram-coated canvas with black leather trim, silver-plated brass hardware, one black leather top handle, and double flip clasp and pinchlock closure; interior with four crystal coupelle whiskey glasses separated into compartments in red taiga leather with crystal coupelle bottle with silver twist cap; silver flap clasp on either side of case opens second compartment in matching red taiga leather with silver ice bucket and two crystal coupelle coaster trays; taiga leather box with silver ice tongs and silver case with eight swizzle sticks; with black leather luggage tag and two keys with black leather cord connected to handle; excellent condition, 13" w. x 16" h. x 8" d................**$10,625**

Courtesy of Heritage Auctions, ha.com

is also a diamond Birkin, which sold for $203,150 through Heritage Auctions.

As one may expect, brand name is said to play a part in the appeal of luxury accessories and goods. However, as Seung Yoon Rhee of the Hankuk Academy of Foreign Studies in South Korea discovered in "A Study of Why Luxury Goods Sell and their Effect on the Economy," it's not the only factor.

"Many luxury goods exhibit superior quality compared to goods from other brands," Rhee stated. "In these cases, luxury goods can be seen as worthwhile investments for people buying them."

Whatever the reason, based on the addition or expansion of existing luxury accessories departments within auction houses, the record-setting prices being paid at auction, and the evolving array of items being consigned, the appeal of luxury accessories is more than "skin deep."

HANDBAGS/LUGGAGE/CARRYING CASES

Louis Vuitton classic monogram canvas trunk, monogram coated canvas, top handle and leather accents, three brass belt closures, interior in beige leather with removable tray and straps to secure contents, good condition, 24" w. x 18 h. x 8-1/2" d. **$1,000**

Courtesy of Heritage Auctions, ha.com

◀ Antique diamond, emerald, and half pearl mesh purse, 18k gold frame with European-cut diamonds weighing approximately 0.25 carat, oval-shaped, cushion-shaped, and emerald-cut emeralds weighing approximately 1.60 carats, half pearls measuring 5.65 mm and 5.90 mm, gold mesh with 18k gold chain, good condition, purse 8-1/2" x 5-1/2", chain 10" l., 174.50 g. **$4,750**

Courtesy of Heritage Auctions, ha.com

Gucci crocodile and canvas dragon evening bag by Tom Ford, exterior in green and black crocodile with canvas sides, jeweled dragon clasp with green enamel, gold and green enamel bamboo chain, interior in green satin with one slip pocket, with dustbag, excellent condition, small dent where clasp touches body of bag, 9" w. x 4" h. x 1.5" d.**$1,313**

Courtesy of Heritage Auctions, ha.com

Vintage Judith Leiber handbag, patent leather and paisley.... **$275**

Courtesy of Bill Hood & Sons Art & Antique Auctions, www.hoodauction.com

Gucci brown alligator briefcase with small rolled handle and two securing straps with silver buckle closures, Gucci logo set in bottom of bag, interior with three main compartments and two additional compartments that can be opened up, luggage tag, good condition, scratching to skin throughout, scratching throughout hardware, edges of base and sides show wear, interior with wear, vintage odor, 18" w. x 12" h. x 3-1/2" d. . **$813**

Courtesy of Heritage Auctions, ha.com

FASHION ACCESSORIES

Antique diamond and gold earrings with European-cut diamonds, 7.81-7.83 mm x 4.64 mm and 7.85-7.88 mm x 4.54 mm, weighing approximately 1.65 carats each, and mine-cut diamonds, 5.40 mm x 5.00 mm, set in 14k white and yellow gold, 1" x 5/16", 3.59 g. **$21,250**

Courtesy of Heritage Auctions, ha.com

▲ Vintage-style garnet jewelry group, 18k yellow gold necklace of graduated round clusters set with approximately 363 round garnets from 2.0 mm to 4.0 mm, estimated combined 33.0 carats, 17" l., 45.7 g.; 14k yellow gold pendant, prong- and bezel-set with 47 round garnets ranging from 3.0 mm to 6.0 mm, estimated combined 16.0 carats, 32.5 mm dia., 8.9 g.; and 18k yellow gold ring centering marquise-cut garnet with 35 round-cut garnets, estimated combined 1.75 carats, size 8, 5.2 g.; with appraisals and receipt from Italy, good condition.. **$1,240**

Courtesy of Brunk Auctions, www.brunkauctions.com

◀ Miriam Haskell lily-of-the-valley set: two brooches, one necklace, and set of earclips, necklace and large pin stamped, earclips and smaller pin unstamped, overall good condition, one earclip needs to have center floral beads reattached, necklace 14" x 2", large brooch 6-1/2" x 5", smaller brooch 4-1/2" x 3", earclips 3" x 1-1/2". **$500**

Courtesy of Leslie Hindman Auctioneers, www.lesliehindman.com

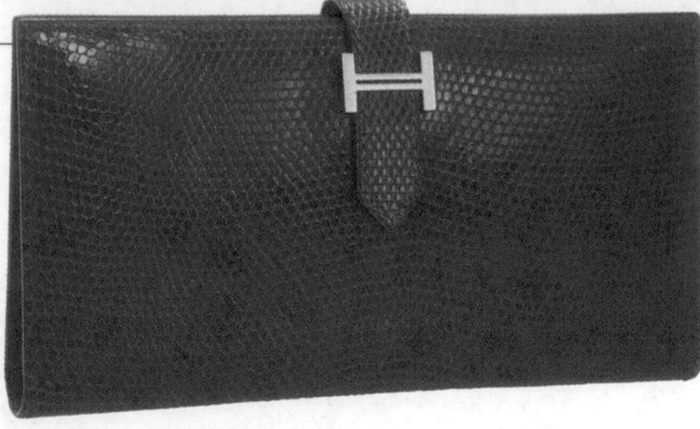

Hermès braise lizard Bearn wallet with palladium hardware, bi-fold design with belt closure, interior in braise chevre leather, top half of interior with long zip pocket with long slip pocket behind for paper currency, bottom half of interior with five card pockets, two long slip pockets, and gusseted slip pocket behind, excellent condition, some scratching to hardware, 7" w. x 3-1/2" h. x 1/2" d. **$3,000**

Courtesy of Heritage Auctions, ha.com

Chanel black quilted lambskin leather glasses case with small gold CC logo, interior lined in black canvas, very good condition, exterior with light indentations and nicks typical of lambskin leather, interior with gold residue from printed Chanel logo, 3" w. x 6" h. x 1/4" d. **$138**

Courtesy of Heritage Auctions, ha.com

Two Edwardian sterling silver-mounted green alligator skin cases, both Birmingham, 1898-1899 Mappin & Webb coin purse, kidskin interior with five accordion compartments, central one with locking bar, 4" x 2", and 1902-1903 Charles Penny Brown wallet, kidskin interior with two accordion pouches and two coin slots, 5-1/4" x 4"........................ **$500**

Courtesy of New Orleans Auction Gallery, www.neworleansauction.com

Patek Philippe diamond and 18k white gold woman's Gemma watch with pink alligator strap, white gold casing, diamond set bezel, sides, and lugs, 1.10 cttw. faceted sapphire crystal, transparent case back, mother-of-pearl dial with black minute indexes, pavé diamond set center, and blue baton hands; movement is caliber 16-250, 18 jewels, manual wind, with Geneve quality hallmark; band in pink alligator with 18k white gold buckle with diamond set buckle; excellent condition, light wear to back of strap and back of face, small black dot on band by casing.. **$11,875**

Courtesy of Heritage Auctions, ha.com

Lady's silk jacket and chinchilla stole: silk brocaded fur-trimmed jacket, probably chinchilla, in Indian motif pattern, Lord & Taylor label, padded shoulders, size medium, 30" l., and chinchilla stole with floral lace lining, 78" x 11", both in good condition.......... **$1,240**

Courtesy of Brunk Auctions, www.brunkauctions.com

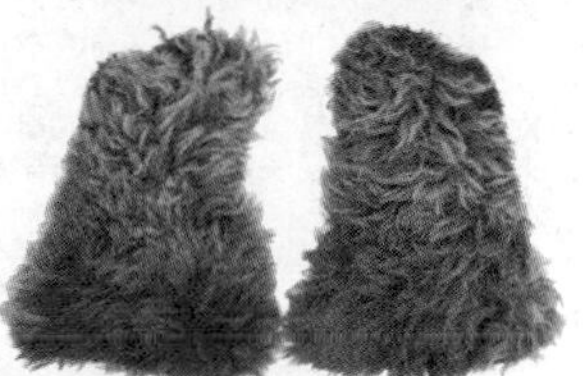

▲ Carved ivory rabbit cane, late 19th century, ebonized wood standard surmounted by carved ivory rabbit in prone position, good condition, appropriate age-related cracking to ivory, sticker residue to front of cane, scuffing to point, 38" h.......... **$1,250**

Courtesy of Heritage Auctions, ha.com

◀ Buffalo coat and gloves, golden brown fur-covered coat lined with black cotton, approximately size large, with five black tin buttons and loops, lined collar, original tag reading "PATTERSON & STEVENSON CO. MINNEAPOLIS, MINN.," with large pair of felt-lined gloves of slightly lighter color, coat in very good to fine condition, well preserved, some split seams at collar and sleeve joint, gloves in fine condition.......... **$938**

Courtesy of Heritage Auctions, ha.com

GENERAL GOODS

Napoleon III boulle and gilt glass cave à liqueur, circa 1870, case with brass and painted faux tortoiseshell boullework to top and serpentine front, front lifting to reveal four liqueur decanters with stoppers and 14 liqueur stems with gilt decoration within fitted interior, surface wear commensurate with age and indicative of use, missing two liqueur stems, minor rubbing to gilt glass, flaking of paint throughout front and lid of case, some lifting of brass, missing flakes of paint to sides, 10-1/4" h. x 14" w. x 10-1/4" d. ... **$2,000**

Courtesy of Heritage Auctions, ha.com

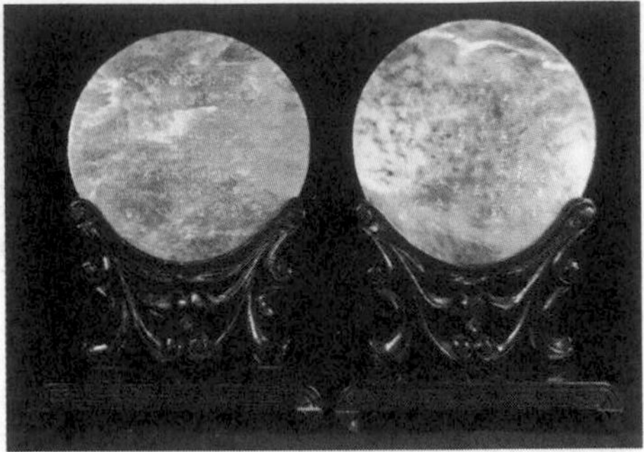

Pair of nephrite jade table screens with stands, Chinese school, circa 1900, Chinese calligraphy highlighted in gilt, stands of mahogany with Greek key design, good condition, wear to gilding, re-gluing of joint where foot meets base, 11-1/2" h. x 14" w. x 7-3/4" d.. **$374**

Courtesy of Louis J. Dianni, LLC, Antiques Auctions, louisjdianni.com

Six fine press first editions by Joyce Carol Oates, all in fine condition: *Fertilizing the Continent*, cloth-backed decorative boards, one of 12 signed copies, designed by Herb Yellin, proprietor of Lord John Press, signed by Oates on title page, Northridge, California, Santa Susana Press, 1976; *Invisible Woman*, red cloth with silver lettering on cover and spine, copy No. 101 of 300 copies, signed by Oates at colophon, Princeton, New Jersey, Ontario Review Press, 1982; *Queen of the Night*, cloth-backed decorative boards, presentation copy, as issued, matching issue of 300 numbered copies, signed by Oates at colophon, Northridge, California, Lord John Press, 1979; *Queen of the Night*, full red leather, gilt-lettered spine, publisher's copy, as issued, matching deluxe issue of 50 numbered copies, signed by Oates at colophon, Northridge, California, Lord John Press, 1979; *Luxury of Sin*, leather-backed decorative boards, letter "x" of 26 deluxe lettered copies, signed by Oates at colophon, Northridge, California, Lord John Press, 1984; *Time Traveler*, full green cloth with gilt lettering on spine, No. 15 of 150 numbered copies, signed by Oates on half title page, Northridge, California, Lord John Press, 1987.. **$369**

Courtesy of PBA Galleries, www.pbagalleries.com

Steuben silver and gold letter opener with glass paperweight base, Excalibur sword-form paperknife with 18k rope handle in faceted glass paperweight, designed by James Houston, Corning, New York, circa 1965, marked "Steuben, 18K, STERLING," in original fitted leather and velvet case, light surface scratches to base of paperweight, surface scratches commensurate with age to paperknife, 8" x 4-1/2" x 3-1/4", 3.46 troy oz. **$1,063**

Courtesy of Heritage Auctions, ha.com

Two Dupont silver-plated lighters in original cases, circa 1970, light surface wear commensurate with age, 4-1/4" h. **$1,438**

Courtesy of Heritage Auctions, ha.com

Louis Vuitton limited edition letter opener with display case, mahogany with iridescent mother-of-pearl monogram inlay, excellent condition, light scratching to monogram, 1/2" w. x 7" l. **$425**

Courtesy of Heritage Auctions, ha.com

MAGIC: THE GATHERING

THE MULTI-PLAYER CARD game Magic: The Gathering will celebrate its 25th anniversary in 2018 (the first year to be officially deemed "vintage" in collecting circles), although a strong secondary market for rare cards has existed for some time. Cards now trade daily on online marketplaces and prices can range from a few cents to more than $30,000.

Designed by Dr. Richard Garfield, Magic: The Gathering (commonly called "MTG" or just "Magic") caused an immediate sensation when it debuted in 1993 and it continues to thrive, with approximately 20 million players as of 2015. It is credited with inspiring numerous early imitators and such famous successors as Pokemon and Yu-Gi-Oh!

Magic: The Gathering can be played by two or more players in various formats, the most common of which uses a deck of 60 or more cards. Each game represents a battle between wizards known as "planeswalkers" who employ spells, artifacts, and creatures depicted on individual Magic cards to defeat their opponents.

Ben Bleiweiss

Courtesy of StarCityGames.com

Collectors seek out rare cards and those from early editions but values are constantly in flux, said Ben Bleiweiss, General Manager of Acquisitions at StarCityGames.com, the world's largest Magic: The Gathering store, with an inventory that includes an extensive selection of out-of-print sealed product and over 20 million individual cards. Here Bleiweiss outlines why values fluctuate and how the secondary market for cards and related memorabilia has evolved during the past 25 years.

ANTIQUE TRADER (AT): How has this amazing game created a lasting impact on worldwide culture and generated popular spin-offs?

BEN BLEIWEISS (BB): Magic combines several elements of popular games and cultural touchstones, plus it is both portable and timeless. It combined the elements of sports card collecting (putting together complete sets/one of each), gamesmanship (the cards have a use - playing a game), and a fantasy art element (heavy influence in classic fantasy works). Since all you need is a single deck of Magic cards to play, it's a very portable game - and one that has found a lot of popularity with U.S. military personnel for this very reason.

One of the reasons Magic has endured and

◀ GURU Island promotional cards (non-foil), near-mint/mint condition. .... **$300-$350**

Courtesy of StarCityGames.com

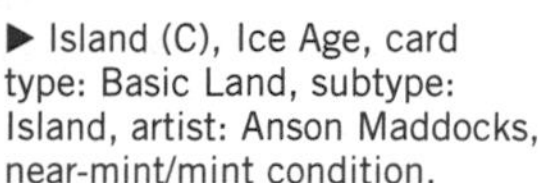

▶ Island (C), Ice Age, card type: Basic Land, subtype: Island, artist: Anson Maddocks, near-mint/mint condition. .... **50¢ to $1**

Courtesy of StarCityGames.com

thrived for nearly 25 years is because the cards have an intrinsic use in and of themselves beyond collection purposes. The values of individual cards are constantly in flux because newly printed cards can affect the play value (and therefore demand) on all previously printed cards. There is a very healthy tournament structure around Magic (giving out several million dollars of prize money annually between official and unofficial events), which drives a value on the cards even further.

AT: Do collectors find more value in owning a single card from these early printings or do they look to own an entire set?

BB: In my estimation, true collectors (people who purchase Magic for the sole purpose of collecting cards, and do play with them or buy them as investments) probably make up less than 1% of the total number of people who are involved in Magic. However, this is because many of the early Magic sets are extremely expensive. A near-mint condition Alpha set, for instance, will set you back at least $150,000 at this point. So the people who are true collectors A) tend to have a lot more disposable capital than the average player, and B) tend to try to put together complete sets. There are even a few collectors who collect graded sets (usually from BGS), where they only include cards that are graded 9.0 or higher.

AT: Was Magic an instant success when it debuted in 1993? How rare are the first published cards?

BB: Magic was an instant success when it debuted at Gen Con in 1993. The initial (Alpha) print run sold out immediately, as did the Beta (second printing of Alpha) and Unlimited (third printing of Alpha) print runs. While Wizards no longer releases print run information on cards, Stephen D'Angelo collected some early print run numbers that were discussed by Wizards employees. There were initially 2.6 million Alpha cards printed (enough to make 1,100 copies of each Alpha Rare, or 1,100 total possible Alpha sets), with the number rising to 7.8 million for Beta (3,200 of each Rare/possible sets) and 40 million for Unlimited (18,500 of each Rare/possible sets). The first few expansion sets (Arabian Nights, Antiquities, Legends, and The Dark) all had very low print run numbers; starting with Revised (the first reprint set after Unlimited) and Fallen Empires (the first expansion set after The Dark), print run numbers were much higher and were enough to meet demand.

AT: Can you explain what the "Reserved List" is and how it impacted the collectibility and market for certain cards?

BB: Early Magic sets were printed way below demand. While Alpha/Beta/Unlimited had near-identical contents (Beta and Unlimited each had a third picture of each of the five

Exclusive "Pinny Arcade" Elspeth pin first debuted at PAX Prime in 2013. .... **$20**

Courtesy of StarCityGames.com

Magic: The Gathering 3rd Edition/Revised Booster Box, sealed. Revised Edition of basic set released in April 1994 with 306 cards; white-bordered set cleaned up several rules and graphical oversights from previous Unlimited basic set; each factory-sealed display box contains 36 booster packs, rare. .... **$1,500-$2,000**

Courtesy of Dave & Adam's, dacardworld.com

basic lands added, along with Circle of Protection: Black and Volcanic Island, which were accidentally left off the Alpha print sheets), Revised removed many problematic cards (ones which were too powerful, too weak, or too confusing), and substituted many cards from Arabian Nights and Antiquities. The 4th Edition (the next reprint set after Revised) rotated out even more cards and added in multiple cards from Legends and The Dark. Wizards then printed another separate reprint set (Chronicles), which reprinted even more cards from Arabian Nights, Antiquities, Legends, and The Dark.

These reprints (especially the ones in 4th Edition and Chronicles) caused a market panic, as the price of reprinted cards dropped sharply. In order to boost consumer confidence, Wizards established a list of cards that they would never reprint in a tournament-legal or tournament-functional form (i.e., they wouldn't try to skirt the Reserved List by printing a functionally identical card under a different card name). Initially this list was of all cards that had not yet been reprinted as of 4th Edition. Later, all Commons and Uncommons were removed from the list, and only select cards from new sets were added. Starting with the Mercadian Masques expansion set (October 1999), Wizards announced that no future cards would be added to the Reserved List.

AT: I've learned that several specific early cards tend to be the most valuable in today's market (e.g., the "Power Nine" – Ancestral Recall, Black Lotus, Mox Emerald, Mox Jet, Mox Pearl, Mox Ruby, Mox Sapphire, Time Walk, Timetwister). Why are collectors drawn to own these cards? How high have you seen prices climb for examples in near mint-mint condition?

BB: One of the innovations of Magic cards is the introduction of rarity within a pack of cards. A typical Magic pack contains 15 cards. In Alpha/Beta/Unlimited, these would include one Rare card, three Uncommon cards, and 11 Common cards. For Beta/Unlimited, there were 117 Rare, 95 Uncommon, and 75 Common cards in the set (one fewer Common and one fewer Rare in Alpha, due to Circle of Protection: Black and Volcanic Island being omitted from the print sheet). In order to get a complete set of Beta cards, assuming no duplication, a player would have to open a minimum of 117 packs of cards (one of each Rare), and likely you'd have to open many more than that due to duplication.

The Power Nine cards (listed above) were all Rare cards in Alpha/Beta/Unlimited. These are among the nine most powerful cards for game play ever printed and were among the cards discontinued in the Revised printing of Magic due to being too powerful. The most powerful (and expensive) of these is Black Lotus. An Alpha Black Lotus is basically the most valuable/desired regular-print Magic card (one that isn't a misprint or from an unofficial release). I'd equate it to an Action Comics #1 or T-206 Honus Wagner card, as far as the status it holds within the Magic-collecting community. A near-mint condition Alpha Black Lotus is worth at least $20,000, and likely would fetch two to five times that amount if graded BGS 9.0 or higher.

AT: What would you say are the most beloved or nostalgic cards for those who first played the game in the mid-1990s?

BB: This is a tricky question because as stated above, many people collect different cards for different reasons. For those who like the art of Magic, Serra Angel is likely one of the most iconic/nostalgic cards from Magic's early days. From a player's perspective, maybe something like Shivan Dragon, Atog, or Swords to Plowshares. From a collector's perspective, the Power Nine and the original Dual Lands (Badlands, Bayou, Plateau, Savannah, Scrubland, Taiga, Tropical Island, Tundra, Underground Sea, Volcanic Island from Alpha/Beta/Unlimited/Revised).

AT: Does the same sense of nostalgia for these same cards appear in today's players, or do today's players have their own unique set of characters and cards dear to their hearts?

BB: A little of each. There are many tournament formats in Magic. The most popular one, Standard, only allows cards printed within the past three expansion blocks (approximately 18 months' worth of cards; each block is two sets, and each set is released quarterly). For formats that allow older cards all the way back to the original set releases (Legacy/Vintage), there's a very healthy dose of nostalgia for these very same cards. For newer players, there's generally a sense of attachment to whatever cards either A) the person first started playing with or B) had the most fun building a deck around. It's best to say that players more often than not do get a sense of nostalgia about Magic cards, but the exact card they become attached to is extremely varied.

AT: How have fans responded to the appearance of the original art from these cards appearing for sale online or at auction?

BB: The market for original Magic artwork has exploded within the past two years. Pieces from the first few sets (Alpha through The Dark) have started commanding exorbitant prices. The original artwork of Alpha/Beta/Unlimited Rares command a minimum $10,000 price tag, with iconic pieces hitting the $50,000+ range. People have really started collecting Magic cards in earnest, and those that either A) are the most popular cards or B) have really standout artwork demand a much higher price tag. Unpopular pieces usually sell in the $300-$1,000 range, depending on the artist and size of the piece.

AT: Can you share an example of how some cards with the same name but made at different times with different

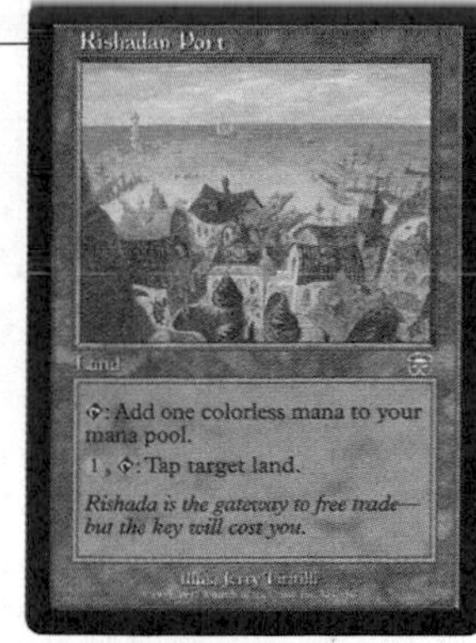

Card, Rishadan Port, Mercadian Masques (foil), card type: Land, artist: Jerry Tiritilli, near-mint/mint condition, rarity: rare. ....**$550-$600**

Courtesy of StarCityGames.com

Card, A Display of My Dark Power, Archenemy Schemes, card type: Scheme, artist: Jim Nelson, rarity: common. **$1.99**

Courtesy of StarCityGames.com

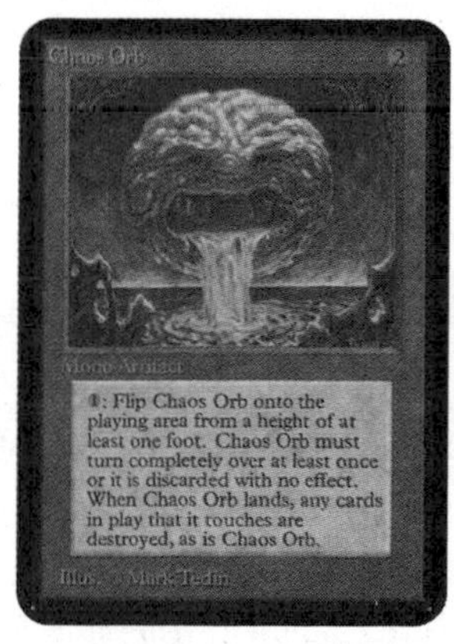

Chaos Orb, Alpha, card type: Artifact, artist: Mark Tedin, near-mint/mint condition, rarity: rare..................**$650-$700**

Courtesy of StarCityGames.com

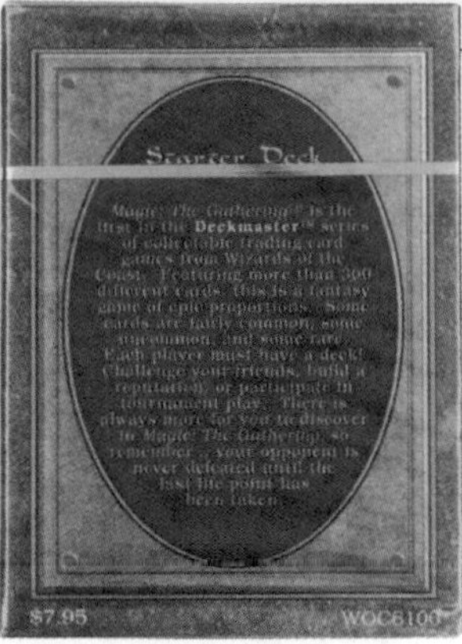

3rd Edition/Revised Starter Deck, sealed. Revised Edition was released in order to clean up a number of rules problems that Limited Edition and Unlimited Edition rules had. Cards still had white borders and no expansion symbol, but art was lightened considerably. Cards were available from mid-April 1994 through mid-April 1995, rarity: rare. .... **$200-$250**

Courtesy of Dave & Adam's, dacardworld.com

Card, Lord of Atlantis (Beta), graded BGS 9.5 GEM MINT, card type: Creature, creature type: Merfolk, artist: Melissa Benson, rarity: rare. ....**$500-$550**

Courtesy of StarCityGames.com

◀ Card, Black Lotus (SCAN 232-LEA-10), Alpha, card type: Artifact, artist: Christopher Rush, rarity: rare. ....**$20,000-$30,000**

Courtesy of StarCityGames.com

▶ Card, Shivan Dragon, Alpha, creature: Dragon, artist: Melissa Benson, near-mint/mint condition, rarity: rare................**$950-$1,000**

Courtesy of StarCityGames.com

art have different values in price?

BB: As stated earlier, the Reserve List stopped having cards added to it starting in 1999. This means that any cards that were printed since that time can be reprinted whenever Wizards of the Coast wants to reprint them. In general, Wizards doesn't reprint cards for the sake of reprinting them. They only reprint if the card makes sense within the context of a set they are releasing. A good example of this is Lightning Bolt, a card first printed in Alpha (1993) and most recently reprinted in Modern Masters 2015 Edition.

Lightning Bolt has been printed in eight booster-pack sets (Alpha, Beta, Unlimited, Revised, 4th Edition, Magic 2010 Edition, Magic 2011 Edition, and Modern Masters 2015 Edition), two box sets (Anthologies and Betadown), and two rare releases (Summer Magic and Alternate 4th Edition). In addition, there have been six premium printings of Lightning Bolt (ones with a foil finish): Magic 2010 Edition, Magic 2011 Edition, Modern Masters 2015 Edition, Premium Deck Series: Fire and Lightning box set, and two promotional printings.

There are three artworks for Lightning Bolt: Christopher Rush version, a Christopher Moeller version, and a Veronique Meignaud version.

Christopher Rush was the original artist of Lightning Bolt (Alpha version). Here are the values of the ones with his artwork:

Alpha: $120 (rarest regular release)

Card, Badlands, Beta, card type: Land, subtype: Swamp Mountain, artist: Rob Alexander, near-mint/mint condition, rarity: rare. **$1,200**

Courtesy of StarCityGames.com

Card, Mox Emerald, Unlimited, card type: Artifact, artist: Dan Frazier, near-mint/mint condition, rarity: rare. .... **$1,300+**

Courtesy of StarCityGames.com

Card, Mox Ruby (Unlimited), card type: Artifact, graded BGS 9 MINT, artist: Dan Frazier, near-mint/mint condition, rarity: rare........... **$1,600-$1,625**

Courtesy of StarCityGames.com

◀ Card, Demonic Tutor, Beta, card type: Sorcery, artist: Douglas Schuler, near-mint/mint condition, rarity: uncommon................ **$200-$250**

Courtesy of StarCityGames.com

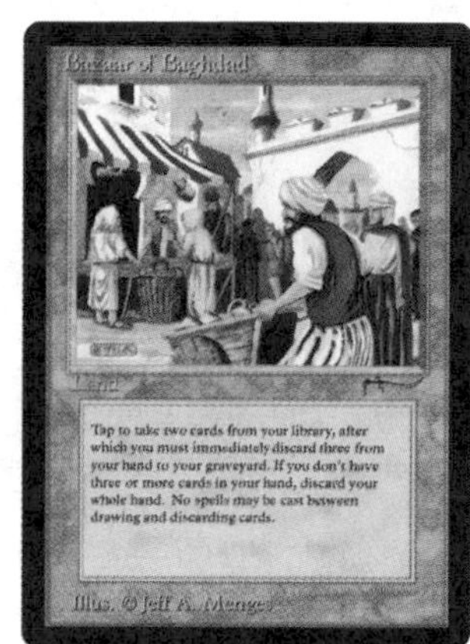

▶ Card, Bazaar of Baghdad (Arabian Nights), card type: Land, graded BGS 9 MINT, artist: Jeff A. Menges, near-mint/mint condition, rarity: uncommon. ....**$850-$900**

Courtesy of StarCityGames.com

Beta: $100
Unlimited: $10
Revised Edition: $4
4th Edition: $4
Anthologies: $6
Beatdown: $5
Alternate 4th Edition: $10
Summer Magic: $1,500 (Rarest unofficial release)
Promo Version #1: $250 (given only as a gift to judges who officiated early Magic tournaments)

All Christopher Rush Lightning Bolts that were in Booster Packs were printed at a Common rarity.

Christopher Moeller:
Magic 2010: $4
Magic 2011: $4
Modern Masters 2015 Edition: $5
Magic 2010 Foil: $12
Magic 2011 Foil: $10

Card, Ancestral Recall (Unlimited), card type: Instant, graded BGS 9 MINT, artist: Mark Poole, near-mint/mint condition, rarity: rare. .... $2,000-$2,200

Courtesy of StarCityGames.com

Card, Serra Angel, Alpha, card type: Creature, creature type: Angel, artist: Douglas Schuler, near-mint/mint condition, rarity: uncommon. .... $170+

Courtesy of StarCityGames.com

Card, Diamond Valley, Arabian Nights, card type: Land, artist: Brian Snoddy, rarity: uncommon....................... $200+

Courtesy of StarCityGames.com

Modern Masters 2015 Edition Foil: $10

Premium Deck Series: Fire and Lightning: $6

The Modern Masters 2015 Edition version of Lightning Bolt was printed at an uncommon rarity; this is why it is valued slightly higher than the Magic 2010/2011 versions (which were printed at the common rarity).

Veronique Meignaud

Promo Version #2: $60 (given to players as a mailing reward for playing in a certain number of tournament events).

The value of each of these Lightning Bolts is primarily driven by the rarity/print run of each version of this card.

AT: Are Magic collectors plagued by fakes and reproductions? If so, where do these come from and how can a collector protect their investment and collection from "bad cards?"

BB: Over the past three years there has been a very marked increase in the number and quality of counterfeit cards being introduced into the market, primarily from China. The good news is that none of these cards is of high-enough quality that anyone who works with Magic cards for a living should be fooled by it. I'd always recommend sending cards to an official grading service (such as Beckett Grading Service) because Beckett will not only grade the cards, but also certify their authenticity.

– Eric Bradley

FRONT

BACK

Playmat, "Shadows over Innistrad – Archangel Avacyn / Avacyn, the Purifier," made by Ultra Pro, double-sided, near-mint/mint condition, 24" h. x 13-1/2" w......................... $30+

Courtesy of StarCityGames.com

Illustration art, "Hornet Sting," Magic: The Gathering card illustration, 2011, artist Matthew Stewart, oil on paper laid on board, initialed and dated 2000, 8-1/5" w. x 11-1/2" h. **$400**

Courtesy of Heritage Auctions, ha.com

Illustration art, Magic: The Gathering, 7th Edition, Card #24, "Knight Errant" (Wizards of the Coast, 1999), artist Matthew D. Wilson, 10-3/4" h. x 8" w. **$382**

Courtesy of Heritage Auctions, ha.com

Coin, $2, 2014, Jace, the Mind Sculptor, limited edition, silver, .999 silver, 33 mm x 55 mm, obverse with original color artwork of Jace by Jason Chan (art was used on powerful Jace, the Mind Sculptor Planeswaker card from Magic: The Gathering Worldwake release) against relief-engraved background and border design, reverse with Ian Rank-Broadley effigy of Her Majesty Queen Elizabeth II, mintage: 5,000, issued by New Zealand Mint as legal tender, under authority of Niue. .... **$150+**

Courtesy of New Zealand Mint

Illustration art, "Penumbra Spider," Magic: The Gathering card illustration, 2006, artist Jeff Easley (American, 20th century), acrylic on board, 14" w. x 18" h. **$550**

Courtesy of Heritage Auctions, ha.com

Illustration art, Magic: The Gathering, "Cryptwailing" card illustration original art (Wizards of the Coast, 1993), artist Nick Percival, acrylic on textured paper, 15-1/2" h. x 11-1/2" w. **$334**

Courtesy of Heritage Auctions, ha.com

MAPS & GLOBES

MAP COLLECTING IS growing in visibility thanks to discoveries and sales of historically important maps. It remains a surprisingly affordable hobby when one considers most maps made in the early 19th century are hand-colored and represent the cutting-edge scientific knowledge at the time. Most examples from the last 400 years are available for less than $500, and engravings depicting America or its states may be owned for less than $150. Larger maps are usually worth more to collectors.

Globes, or terrestrial globes, have been around for centuries, dating back to the 1400s, when owning a globe was a rarity and reserved for only those with titles and/or riches. As time passed, globes became more widely available. Today antique globes offer collectors a unique view of the world as it existed in history.

MAPS

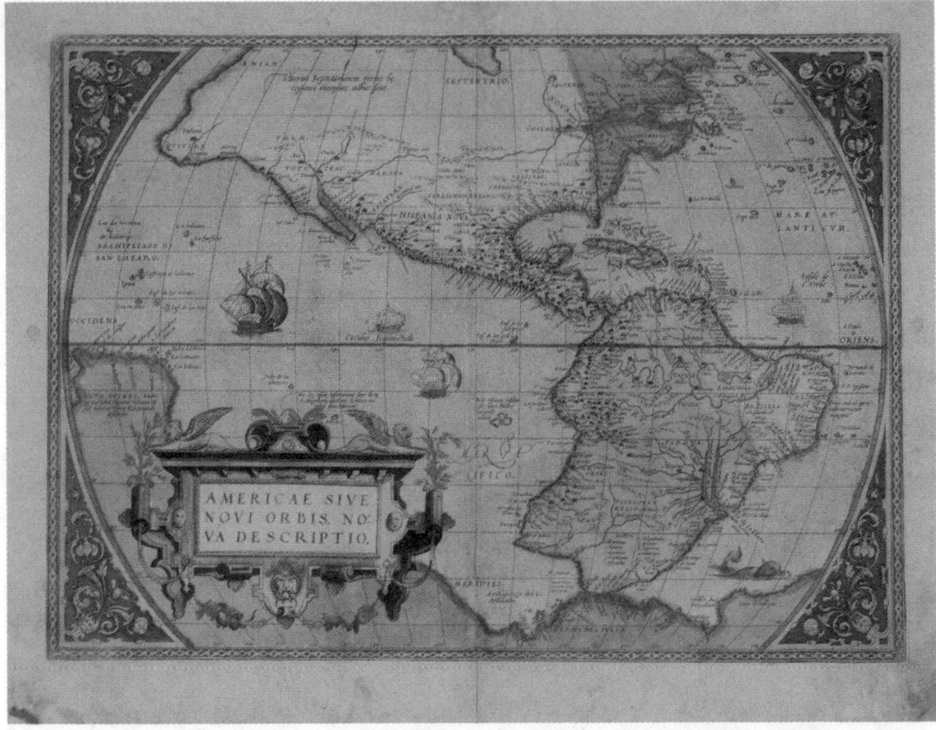

"Americae Sive Novi Orbis Nova," Abrahamus Ortellius, Amsterdam, 1573, from Ortelius' "Theatrum Orbis Terranus," first modern world atlas, one of the most seminal and sought after maps of the New World, later hand-coloring, in very good condition with slight scattered soiling around margins, paper repair to bottom corners and top corner of centerfold, 15-1/2" w. x 21" h. **$3,146**

Courtesy of Brunk Auctions, www.brunkauctions.com

top lot!

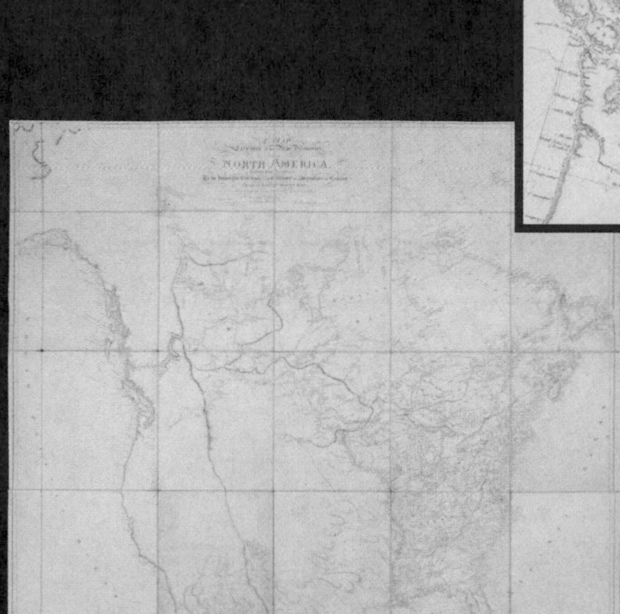

"A Map Exhibiting all the New Discoveries in the Interior Parts of North America. Inscribed by permission to the Honorable Governor and Company of Adventurers of England Trading...in testimony of their liberal communications to Aaron Arrowsmith, 1802"; engraved, colored in outline, mounted on linen, used in planning of Lewis and Clark expedition and carried along on expedition, very good condition with moderate toning and slight soiling. **$86,100**

COURTESY OF PBA GALLERIES, WWW.PBAGALLERIES.COM

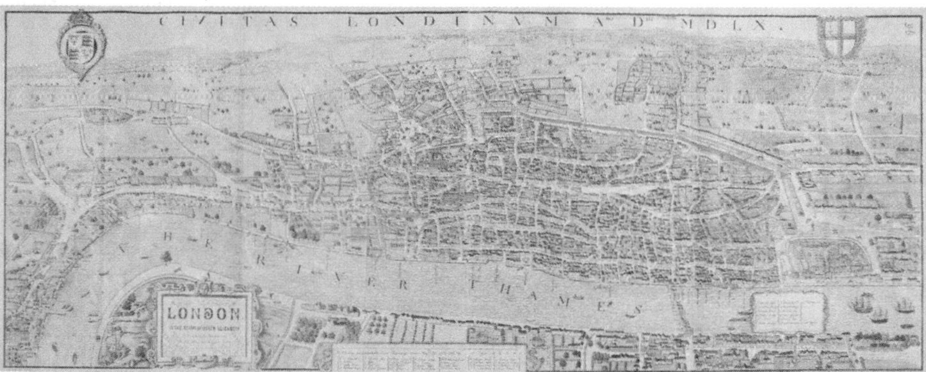

Hand-colored lithographed map of two sheets of London by Edward Weller, issued by *The Weekly Dispatch*, 1863, with decorative title cartouche on lower left, key panel lower center, and arms above, faint old vertical folds, short marginal splits, 17-3/4" w. x 48-1/4" l. **$422**

Courtesy of Dreweatts & Bloomsbury, www.dreweatts.com

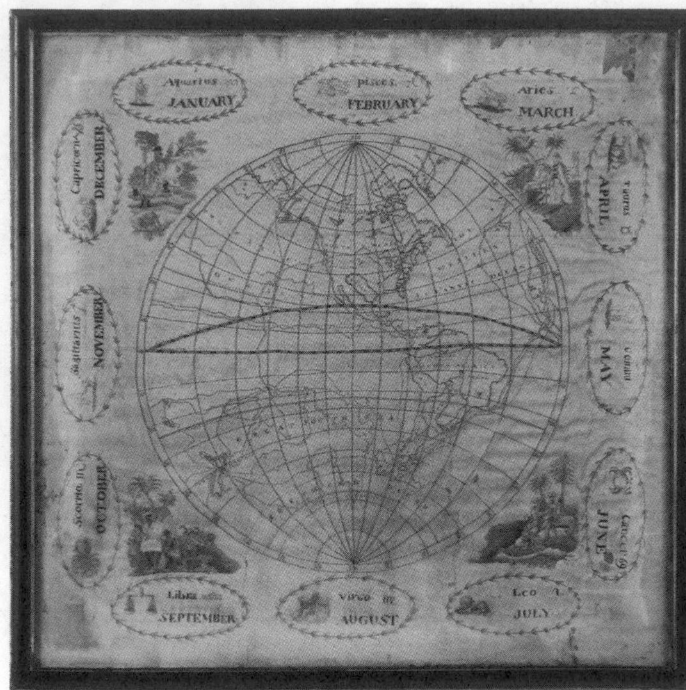

Hand-made embroidered map on silk of Western Hemisphere, 18th century, with color vignettes in corners, signs of zodiac embroidered around border, also tracks of Cook's exploration, some darkening and discoloration to fabric and light staining, 20-3/4" w. x 20-1/2" h.......... **$615**

Courtesy of PBA Galleries, www.pbagalleries.com

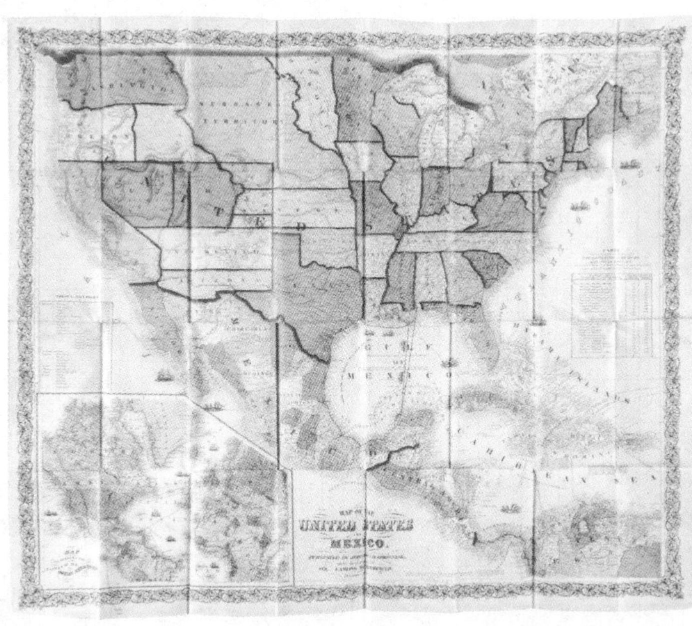

Hand-colored lithographed double-page map, tipped to rear endpaper, located within "United States and Mexican Mail Steamship Line and Statistics of Mexico" by Carlos Butterfield, Washington, 1860, New York, J.A.H Hasbrouck & Co. Printers, with full-page autographed letter from Butterfield to Salem Gazette and plans to connect gulf ports of United States and Mexico by steamship, 8-3/4" w. x 5-1/2" h. **$3,075**

Courtesy of PBA Galleries, www.pbagalleries.com

Five Carey and Lea southern state maps including 1822 Tennessee and Georgia, hand-colored, circa 1825 for Georgia and Florida, slight toning to both, Georgia map 17-7/8" w. x 22-1/4" h., Florida map 21-1/4" w. x 24-3/8" h. **$726**

Courtesy of Brunk Auctions, www.brunkauctions.com

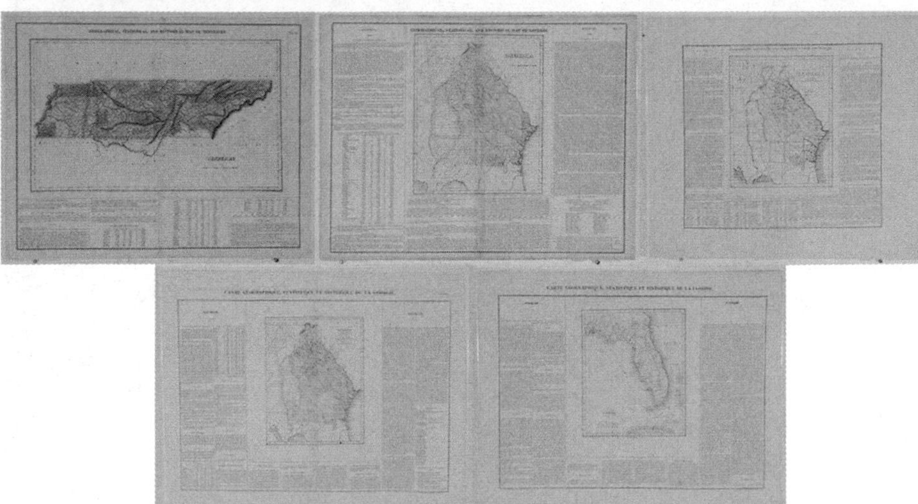

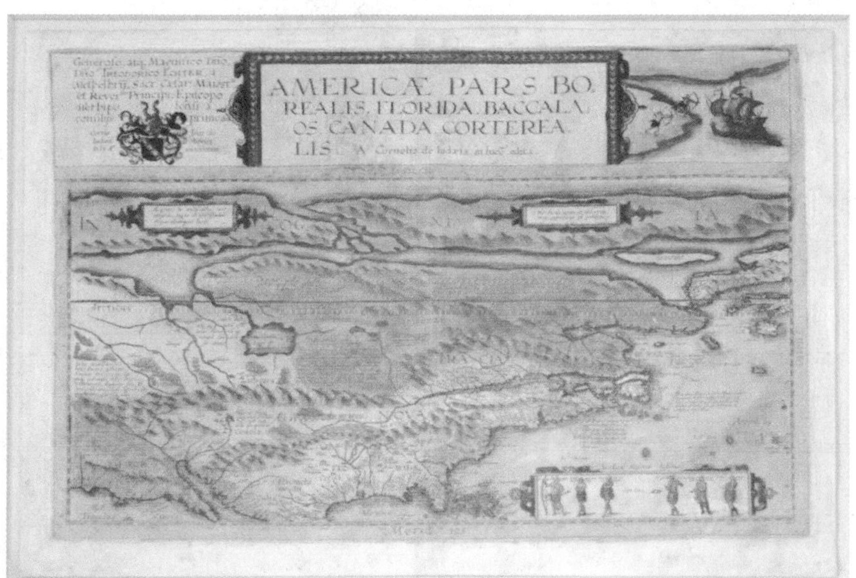

"Ameriae Pars Borealis, Florida, Bacalaos, Canada," Cornelis de Jode, Antwerp, 1593, engraved with original hand-color in full, only edition of de Jode's map of North America showing Northwest Passage and Florida, 16" w. x 21" h. **$31,250**

Courtesy of Arder Gallery, www.aradergalleries.com

Five Vuillemin maps (one shown): Russia and Europe, 1856; Spain and Portugal, 1860; Great Britain, 1860; Holland and Belgium, 1860; Spain and Portugal, 1885; all printed in Paris or New York, toning and scattered foxing on each, smallest 35-1/4" w. x 25-1/2" h., largest 27-1/2" w. x 40" h. **$242**

Courtesy of Brunk Auctions, www.brunkauctions.com

Map of United State of America, two copies, Arbuckle Bros., New York, 1889, with 48 chromolithographic pictorals, one representing each state, bound in pictorial paper covers, string-tied, originally issued as trade cards for Arbuckles' Coffee, one copy in very good condition with little wear at extremities, other in good condition with some pages disconnected from string ties, 7" w. x 11" h. **$363**

Courtesy of Brunk Auctions, www.brunkauctions.com

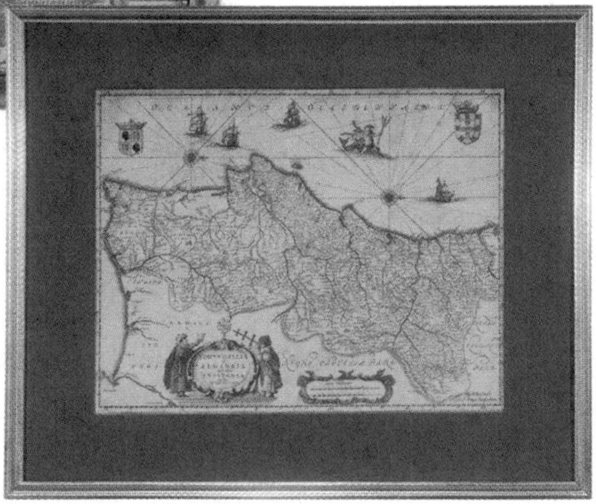

Two maps: Map of Portugal "Portugallia et Algarbia quae olim Lusitania," circa 1646, hand-colored mostly in outline, engraved map by Jansson with decorative title cartouche, in very good condition with overall toning, 15" w. x 19-1/4" h., and map of Spain, circa 1579, by Hondius with eight city plans at top and 12 decorative panels with costumed figures on left and right margins, in very good condition, some underdeveloped hand-coloring, 16-1/4" w. x 23-3/4" h. **$242**

Courtesy of Brunk Auctions, www.brunkauctions.com

"La Terre Sainte 1703" hand-colored engraving of Holy Lands, Twelve Tribes and territories, 18th/19th century, inscribed "1703, To Majesty and Dauphin" in French on plate, uneven age toning and matte burn, 9-1/8" w. x 12-1/8" h.......... **$200**

Courtesy of Roland Auctions, www.rolandauctions.com

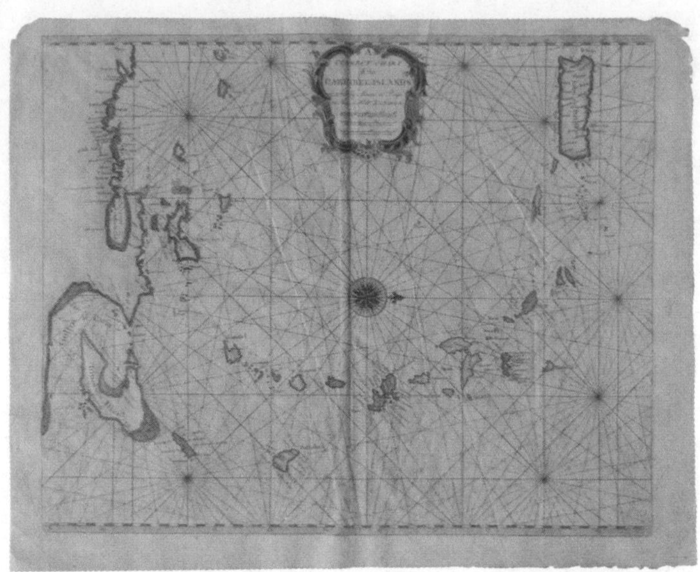

English Atlas of Sea Chart, covers Mediterranean and North America, Mount & Page's English Pilot, Fourth Book, 18th century, with detail of Windward Islands, including Grenada, Saint Vincent, Martinique and Dominica, 18-3/4" w. x 23" h. **$1,100**

Courtesy of Last Chance by LiveAuctioneers, www.liveauctioneers.com

GLOBES

Terrestrial globe mounted on polychrome scroll-legged pod and platform, 20th century, 65" h. **$1,557**

Courtesy of Sheppard's Irish Auction House, www.sheppards.ie

Austro-Hungarian terrestrial globe, circa 1840, Bernard Biller, mounted on molded mahogany stand, with "SCHLOSS LIECHTENSTEIN" label, made of 18 lithographed paper gores and two polar calottes, 12-1/2" dia. **$5,000**

Courtesy of Arder Gallery, www.aradergalleries.com

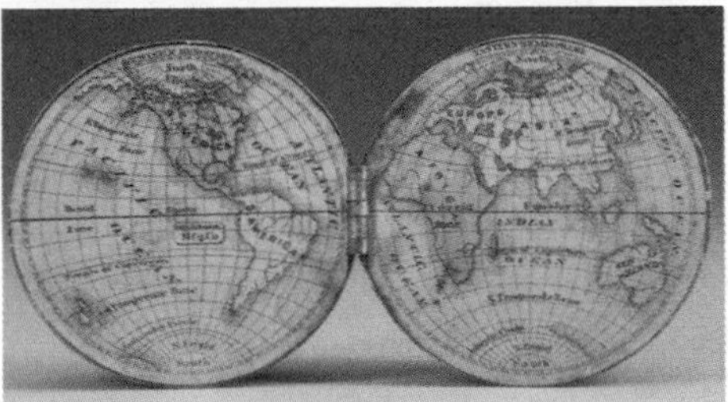

Hinged terrestrial pocket globe, Holbrook's Apparatus Mfg. Co., Wethersfield, Connecticut, mid-19th century, foxing throughout, minor loss of paper to edges, slight buckling of paper to interior, 2-7/8" dia. **$1,625**

Courtesy of Heritage Auctions, ha.com

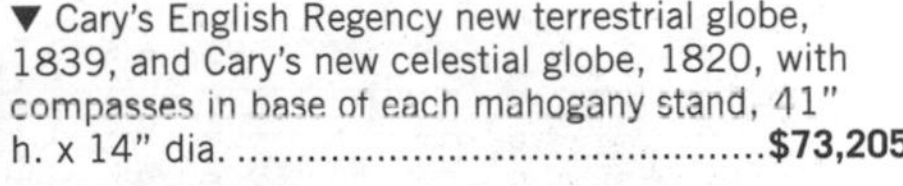

▼ Cary's English Regency new terrestrial globe, 1839, and Cary's new celestial globe, 1820, with compasses in base of each mahogany stand, 41" h. x 14" dia. **$73,205**

Courtesy of Northgate Gallery, Inc., www.northgateauctions.com

Terrestrial and celestial globes, "Cary's New Terrestrial globe delineated from best authority's extent exhibiting different tracks of Captain Cook and new discoveries made by him and other circumnavigators," London, J. & W. Cary, Strand, 1800; new celestial globe with upwards of 3,500 stars from most accurate observations of 1800, excellent condition, old restoration to surface of spheres and painted horizon rings, cracks to center cross-brace support of one stand, 17-1/4" h. **$13,640**

Courtesy of Brunk Auctions, www.brunkauctions.com

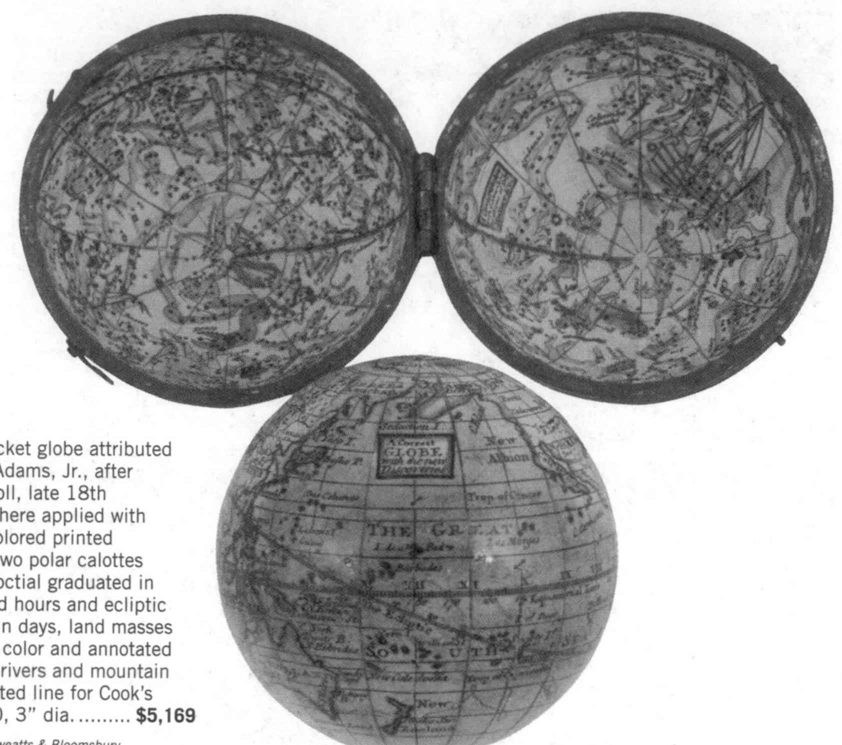

English pocket globe attributed to George Adams, Jr., after Herman Moll, late 18th century, sphere applied with 12 hand-colored printed gores and two polar calottes with equinoctial graduated in degrees and hours and ecliptic graduated in days, land masses outlined in color and annotated with major rivers and mountain ranges, dotted line for Cook's Track 1760, 3" dia.......... **$5,169**

Courtesy of Dreweatts & Bloomsbury, www.dreweatts.com

Globe covered with 12 copper-engraved paper gores with original full and outline hand coloring, mid-19th century, Josiah Loring, original four-legged stand with mahogany horizon ring, maple stretchers, brass meridian, and brass hour pointer, with tracks of explorers such as James Cook, Charles Wilkes, La Perouse and others, professionally conserved, 19" h. x 18" dia. overall........ **$2,460**

Courtesy of PBA Galleries, www.pbagalleries.com

MID-CENTURY DECORATIVE ARTS

IF THERE'S ONE THING Ralph Alter has in his booth that no one else has, it's this: young buyers.

Ralph and his wife, Shelli, sell under the name dinnerpARTy at more than 30 antiques and collectible shows a year, and their core customer is female, age 25-45, and looking for unique mid-century decorative arts for her home. It's a trend that's picked up in recent years and his high turnover of large, abstract paintings and small, organic sculptures is proof.

"We can't keep enough abstract paintings in stock," he said. "If it's priced between $400 and $4,000, it's gone just as soon as we put it on display. People are looking for unique items, and nothing says mid-century modern more than an abstract painting."

Two blue glass boxes, one hinged box with Murano sticker, 4-3/4" x 3" x 3-1/2", one box unmarked, hinged 2-1/2" x 2-3/4" x 2"........................... **$350**

Courtesy of Main Street Mining Co., www.mainstreetmining.com

Mid-century decorative arts have been a strong market for the last decade or so, but auction houses and dealers are seeing an uptick among affluent members of the millennial generation. They are looking past IKEA and Target and are seeking original artworks and pieces by big-name designers such as Eames, Saarinen, and Nakashima.

Often labeled as mid-century modern or "Moderne," the phrase has evolved into a marketing slogan that immediately conjures images of furniture with straight lines, organic sculptures (often nudes from the era of the sexual revolution), and ceramics made in the United States, Scandinavia, and South America.

Auctioneers are offering such design in specialty auctions labeled "20th century auctions" or "20th century art and design." Sales offer design-forward pieces from the Bauhaus Movement of the 1920s to practically anything made of chrome during the 1970s.

A sculpture-front screen designed by Paul Evans in 1969 brought $135,750 at a Rago Auctions' Modern Design sale in 2015. The important example of the artist's work spent most of the last decade on display at various museum exhibitions and was in the private collection of craftsman Dorsey Reading, who fatefully went to work for Evans in New Hope, Pennsylvania, while still a high school student.

— *Eric Bradley*

Floor sculpture in form of sheep, brass and teakwood, India, longhair Peruvian wool overlay, 23" h. x 29" l.................................. **$100**

Courtesy of Main Street Mining Co., www.mainstreetmining.com

top lot

"Working for Paul Evans was like an adventure every day – you never knew what was coming that morning or when he walked through that door," Reading told Todd Merrill, author of *The New Americana: Furniture 1946-1996*. "It was a fun day."

Like Evans, most mid-century craftsman took calculated risks with their artworks, always pushing the limits of what could be discovered at the intersection of raw materials and imagination. American artist and furniture designer Charles Hollis Jones used acrylic and Lucite to craft furniture that appeared as brittle as glass but was as solid as wood. Still creating, his acrylic tables, chairs, lamps, and étagères made in the 1970s regularly sell for between $5,000 and $10,000 at auction.

Perhaps collectors of mid-century decorative arts are searching for a piece of that adventure and risk-taking by owning beautiful, useful things.

"The label has expanded to include design mainly from the 1930s to the early 1970s," Ralph Alter said. "Brown furniture is dead – absolutely dead. I hear so many dealers complaining, but you have to change with people's tastes. We subscribe to the décor magazines our customers read, watch the shows they watch, and we look for items that would look at home in those environments. We do our homework."

Sculpture-front screen, 1969, Paul Evans (1931-1987), New Hope, Pennsylvania, welded, forged, torch-cut, and polychromed steel, bronze, 23k gold leaf, signed "Paul Evans 69 D," 82-1/2" h. x 36" w. x 4" d. $135,750

COURTESY OF RAGO ARTS AND AUCTIONS, WWW.RAGOARTS.COM

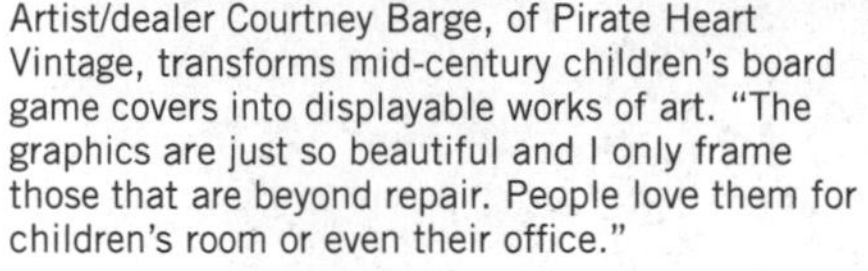
Artist/dealer Courtney Barge, of Pirate Heart Vintage, transforms mid-century children's board game covers into displayable works of art. "The graphics are just so beautiful and I only frame those that are beyond repair. People love them for children's room or even their office."

Courtesy of Eric Bradley

Reticulated crab ashtray, 1960s, brass, hinged claws, 10" l. x 9" w. **$10**

Courtesy of Main Street Mining Co., www.mainstreetmining.com

Sterling leaf-form serving dish, circa 1960s, 12-1/2" l. x 6" w., 291 g. **$100**

Courtesy of Main Street Mining Co., www.mainstreetmining.com

Female bronze sculpture, unmarked, 21-3/4" h. x 7-3/4" w. **$60**

Courtesy of Main Street Mining Co., www.mainstreetmining.com

Penguin form silver-plate cocktail shaker, 1936, Napier Co., designed by Emil A. Schuelke, marked "Napier Patents Pend. #284, "12-1/2" h. **$550**

Courtesy of Main Street Mining Co., www.mainstreetmining.com

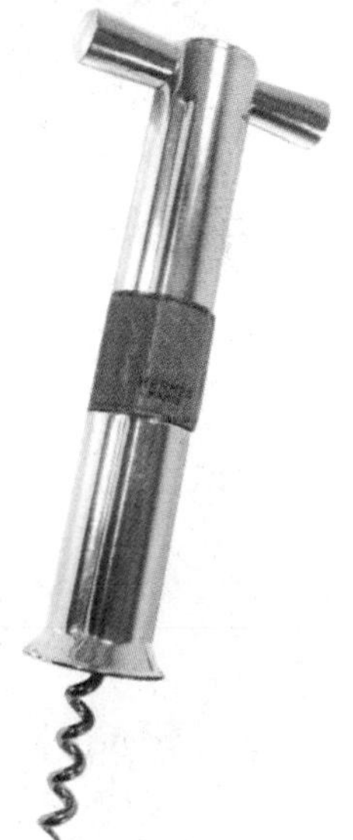

Corkscrew, Hermés, marked "Hermés Paris," 8-1/4"....... **$300**

Courtesy of Main Street Mining Co., www.mainstreetmining.com

Mystery clock (hands move without any visual mechanical force), LeCoultre Co., marked 439 LeCoultre Co., Swiss, face 7-1/4" dia. **$180**

Courtesy of Main Street Mining Co., www.mainstreetmining.com

Sunburst wall clock, Syroco, eight-day run time, working, 16" w. **$40**

Courtesy of Main Street Mining Co., www.mainstreetmining.com

Bibendum chairs, circa mid-20th century, designed by Eileen Gray, original red wool fabric upholstery, chrome base, 27" h. **$475**

Courtesy of Specialists of the South, Inc., www.specialistsofthesouth.com

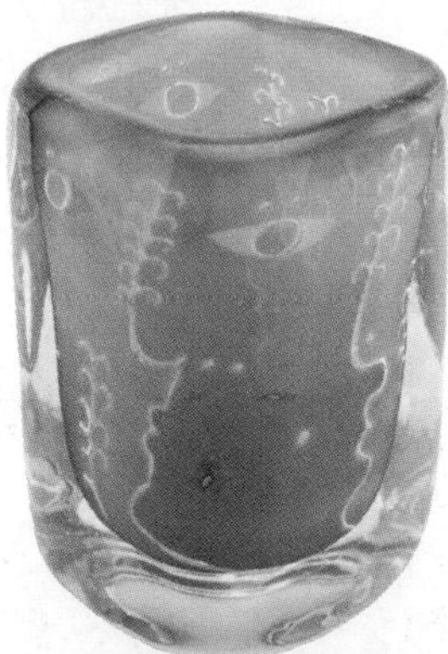

Ariel "Faces" vase, circa 1970, Ingeborg Lundin (Sweden, for Orrefors), olive green and clear, made in Cubist style, 2-3/4" h.................... **$3,480**

Courtesy of Los Angeles Auction House, www.laauctionhouse.com

Armchair, circa 1960s, George Nakashima (Japanese/American, 1905-1990), walnut frame, grass seat, 27-3/4" h. x 23-1/4" w. x 19" d.. **$2,250**

Courtesy of Ahlers & Ogletree, www.aandoauctions.com

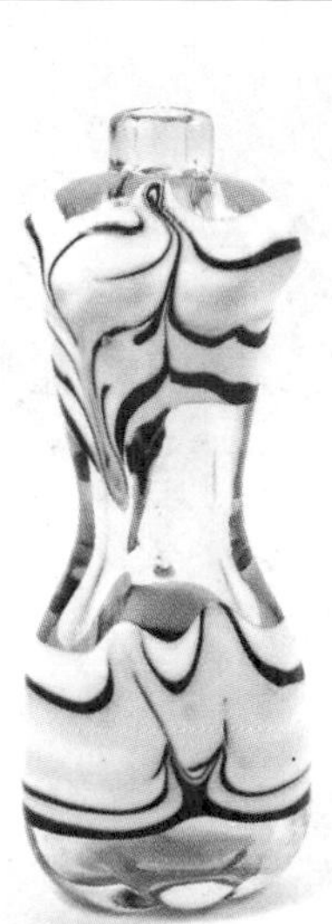

Bikini figural vase, mid-20th century, Fulvio Bianconi (Italy, 1915-1996) for Venini, 14-1/2" h. **$12,500**

Courtesy of Ahlers & Ogletree, www.aandoauctions.com

Iron rocking chair sculpture, circa 1950, in style of Henry Moores (1898-1986), unsigned, 12-1/4" h. x 15" w. **$350**

Courtesy of Pangaea Auctions, gopangaea.com

Office desk/work station, Bruce Burdick for Herman Miller, circa 1970s, 10' polished aluminum beam mounted to top and bottom with 12 attachments: five magazine or book racks; two hanging files with two drawers each (one deep for files); rectangular book rest or shelf; three rectangular file/paper trays; one small swiveling rectangular tray or stand; polished aluminum legs with pad feet, 60" w. x 35-3/4" d. **$1,600**

Courtesy of Ahlers & Ogletree, www.aandoauctions.com

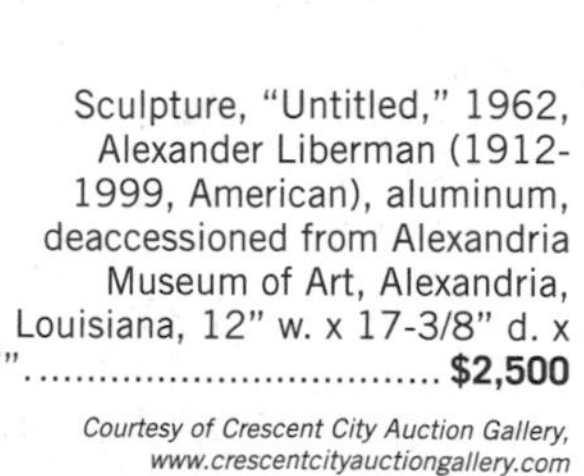

Sculpture, "Untitled," 1962, Alexander Liberman (1912-1999, American), aluminum, deaccessioned from Alexandria Museum of Art, Alexandria, Louisiana, 12" w. x 17-3/8" d. x 7" **$2,500**

Courtesy of Crescent City Auction Gallery, www.crescentcityauctiongallery.com

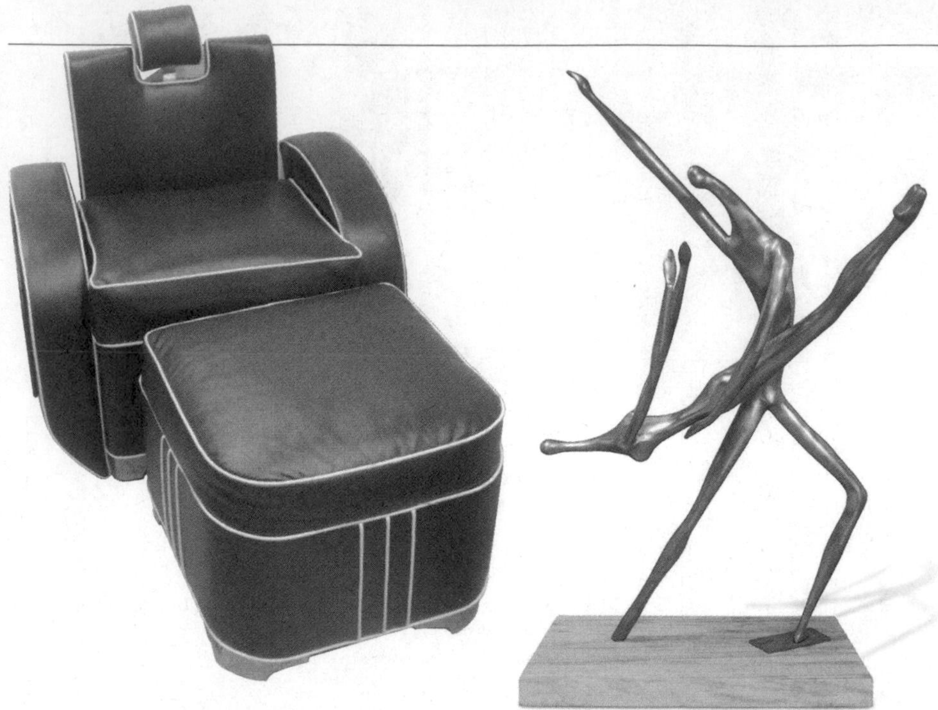

Reclining chair with headrest and matching footstool, circa mid-20th century, Royalchrome Distinctive Furniture, Royal Metal Manufacturing Co., Chicago, New York, Los Angelas, 31" h. x 31" w. **$450**

Courtesy of Nadeau's Auction Gallery, www.nadeausauction.com

"Dancers" sculpture, bronze on stone base, Manuel Carbonell (Cuban, b. 1918), signed MC and inscribed 1/1, 47-1/2" h. x 31" w. x 18" d. **$1,875**

Courtesy of Doyle New York, www.doylenewyork.com

Folding chairs, 1928-1929, Marcel Breuer (Hungarian, 1902-1981), two sets of four connected folding chairs, one set of two connected folding chairs, from Andy Warhol Museum, Pittsburgh, largest 34" h. x 7'-10" w. x 19" d. **$3,125**

Courtesy of Doyle New York, www.doylenewyork.com

Bronze sculpture, mid-20th century, figurehead of winged goddess, possible architectural mount, unsigned, 13" h. x 18" w. **$1,200**

Courtesy of Pangaea Auctions, gopangaea.com

INSIDE INTEL *with* RALPH ALTER

Co-owner of dinnerpARTy, mid-century art and design, with wife Shelli Alter, *(317) 815-0868, maximumralph@yahoo.com*

WHAT'S HOT: Small, mid-century sculptures and abstract paintings. "All people are looking for unique items for their home, but especially young shoppers. They want something totally unique and are willing to pay for it."

WHAT'S NOT: Brown mid-century furniture. "You just can't move it. It's all about color right now. People want to blend lots of color and are always looking for pairs of unique chairs. That's the No. 1 rule when buying: Always buy in pairs. But if you see an unusual single chair you should never pass it up.

Many dealers and collectors are classifying mid-century decorative arts as items made between the mid-1930s and the mid-1970s, a period that produced exquisite and challenging designs, according to dealer Ralph Alter.

Courtesy of Eric Bradley

Palloni waste basket, circa mid-20th century, Piero Fornasetti (Italian, 1913-1988), transfer print on metal and brass, stamped "Fornasetti Milano, Made in Italy," 11" h. x 10-1/4" dia.................... **$1,375**

Courtesy of Doyle New York, www.doylenewyork.com

Brass poodle sculpture with nodding head, circa 1960s, 13" h. **$10**

Courtesy of Specialists of the South, Inc., www.specialistsofthesouth.com

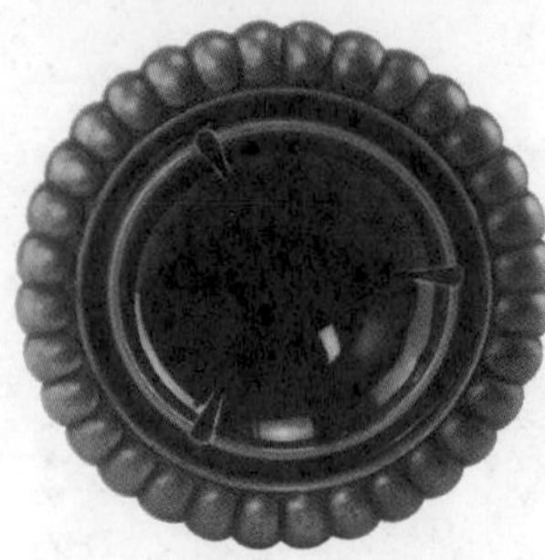

Ceramic ashtray with green glazed porcelain ash receiver, marked "Anthony" in script and "USA 227"..................... **$40**

Courtesy of Pangaea Auctions, gopangaea.com

Sculpture with cubist influence, circa mid-20th century, casting material over metal wire, unknown artist, possibly Russian, 23" h. x 16" w... **$1,800**

Courtesy of Pangaea Auctions, gopangaea.com

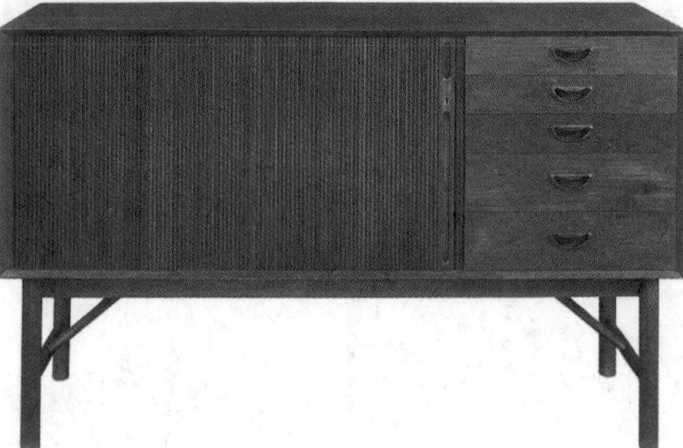

Teak cabinet, circa mid-20th century, Peter Hvidt and Orla Molgaard-Nielsen (Danish, 1916-1986 and 1907-1993), tambour door cabinet, model 26025, "Made in Denmark" stamp, 34" h. x 53" w. x 19" d.. **$2,000**

Courtesy of Doyle New York, www.doylenewyork.com

Wall clock, circa mid-20th century, marked "Sessions Electric Self-Starting Wall Clock," 16" sq. **$50**

Courtesy of Eldred's, www.eldreds.com

Storage system, circa 1950s, walnut, aluminum, laminate and enameled aluminum, designed by George Nelson & Associates, famed CSS (Comprehensive Storage System) for Herman Miller, 7'-8" h. x 10'-10" w. x 30" d. **$3,000**

Courtesy of Doyle New York, www.doylenewyork.com

Egg-form lighter, wooden with brass accents, circa 1940s, Evans, mounted eagle, rare, 6" h. x 3" w. **$40**

Courtesy of Pangaea Auctions, gopangaea.com

Snowball aluminum and enameled aluminum light fixture, Poul Henningsen (Danish, 1894-1967), designed 1958, produced 1983, for Louis Poulson, 16" h., 15" dia...................... **$1,063**

Courtesy of Doyle New York, www.doylenewyork.com

RAR rocker for Herman Miller, circa 1950, Charles Eames (American, 1907-1978) and Ray Kaiser Eames (American, 1912-1988), fiberglass shell, zinc wire, walnut, 27" h. x 25" w. x 27" d. **$375**

Courtesy of Heritage Auctions, ha.com

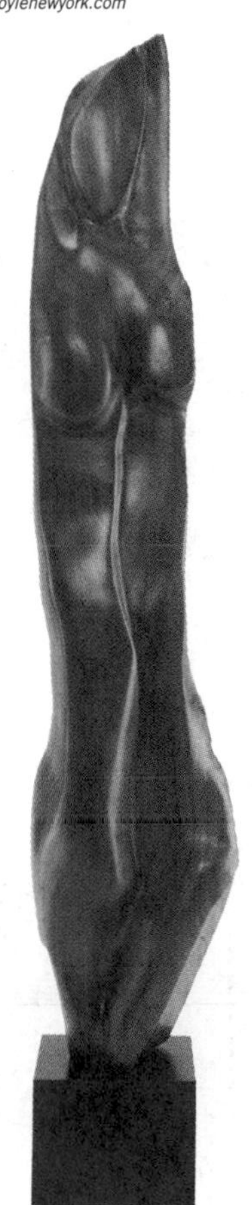

Convertible teak coffee/dining table, circa mid-20th century, Danish design, 28" h. as dining table x 57" w. x 35-1/4" d................. **$1,250**

Courtesy of Doyle New York, www.doylenewyork.com

Wood female form sculpture, circa mid-20th century, unknown artist, 25" h. x 6" w. **$125**

Courtesy of Pangaea Auctions, gopangaea.com

MUSIC MEMORABILIA

THE STATE OF the hobby for those who collect music and related memorabilia is healthy. Before the economy went south in 2008, multiple buyers have been in the market for a pricey item, such as a fully signed photo of The Beatles. The resulting bidding battle could drive the price up to $10,000. These days, fewer people are looking for that type of item to begin with, and those who are interested likely would pay less for it, too. Instead, buyers are gravitating toward low- to mid-price lots that previously might not have been considered for auction. And the acts that buyers are interested in aren't necessarily your parents' favorites.

Artists from the late 1970s and 1980s, especially hard rock, heavy metal and pop acts, are poised to be the next generation of headlining acts for collectors. Guns N' Roses, Motley Crüe, Bon Jovi, U2, Prince, and Madonna as prime examples.

And just as the desired artists are changing, so, too, are some of the items that are being collected. Concert posters are practically nonexistent because there isn't much of a need for them anymore. Also on the endangered species list: ticket stubs, printed magazines, handbills, and promotional materials.

On the other hand, T-shirts have come into their own. And those reports you've heard about the pending demise of vinyl records in the wake of digital formats? Don't believe them. Vinyl is far from dead. Among collectors of 1960s artists, vinyl is a prime collectible, and collectors of '80s bands or artists are just as intrigued and as interested in vinyl as the previous generation.

One key piece of advice: Don't look at music memorabilia as an investment. Build a collection around your passion, be it punk music, concert posters, or all things Neil Diamond.

Here are some tips on collecting music memorabilia: Strive to acquire items that are in the best condition possible and keep them that way. Put a priority on provenance. Weigh quantity and rarity. Take advantage of opportunities geared toward collectors, such as Record Store Day. Refine the focus of your collection and don't try to collect everything. And think before you toss. Good-condition, once-common items that date back before World War II – like advertising posters, Coca-Cola bottles, 78 RPM records, and hand tools – are cherished by collectors today.

Unused ticket to Beatles' final commercial concert at San Francisco's Candlestick Park on Aug. 29, 1966, headshots of each man, admits one to upper stand reserve, near mint condition, 5-3/4" x 2-1/2".. **$625**

Courtesy of Heritage Auctions, ha.com

BEATLES

Set of four Beatles Remco dolls (U.S., 1964), 5" rubber dolls with rooted hair, black suits, and individual musical instruments, George and Ringo in original boxes, dolls in very good or better condition with light wear, Ringo box in overall fair condition with general wear, soiling, and loose lid, George box in very good condition............. **$400**

Courtesy of Heritage Auctions, ha.com

Beatles record brooches by Invicta Plastics (UK, 1964), complete 1964 set with original display box, plastic with paper photos encased under Perspex cover, one of each Beatle and one of group, all in very good condition with slight surface scratches and small stains on scalloped-edge white display cards, Ringo card slightly faded with two small pinholes near center, box in very good condition, brooches 1-3/4" dia......................... **$625**

Courtesy of Heritage Auctions, ha.com

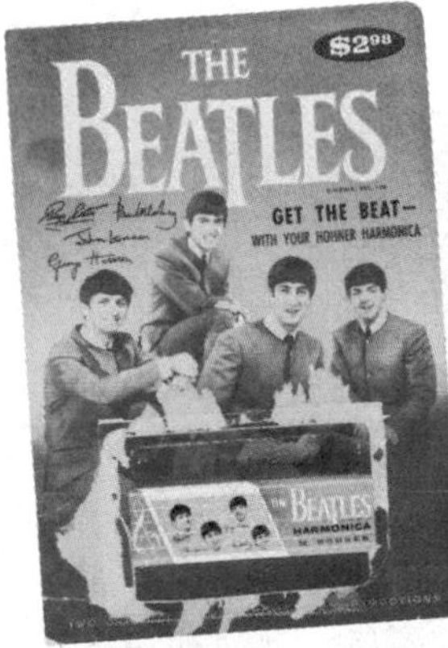

Beatles harmonica in box with original display card (U.S., 1964), standard metal Hohner harmonica in box with headshots of Beatles and facsimile signatures, photos and autographs for George Harrison and Paul McCartney reversed and later corrected, 7-1/2" x 11" fold-over display card with collarless suit images of Beatles, inside is written music to "Little Child" and "Please, Please Me," both songs in which John Lennon played harmonica, back of card with photo of Lennon and instructions on how to get started playing, harmonica and box in excellent condition, display card with creasing and paper loss where blister pack was torn off, harmonica 4", box 4" x 1-1/4" x 1".............. **$3,000**

Courtesy of Heritage Auctions, ha.com

◄ Beatles gumball machine with set of Beatles Capitol Records gumball charms (U.S., 1964), black plastic record-shaped charm with photo of each Beatle, various song titles on reverse, 3" x 4" signage from 1964-1965 taped inside clear top says, "Get Your BEATLES! BUTTONS HERE!", very good condition, no key, approximately 15" h. **$275**

Courtesy of Heritage Auctions, ha.com

Beatles 45 RPM record box (Air Flite, U.S., 1964), green singles case covered in deep textured paper over cardboard, overall fair condition, scuffs, tears, and stains on surface, seam splits throughout, tape residue near images, original brass clasp and hinges and top handle in excellent working condition, approximately 7-3/4" x 8-1/2" x 5"........... **$113**

Courtesy of Heritage Auctions, ha.com

Four polychrome ceramic tile portraits of Beatles from 1960s, framed together, marked "hand enameled by bernice '65", 10-3/8" x 31-3/4" framed..**$576**

Courtesy of Julien's Auctions, www.juliensauctions.com

◀ Smile #2, second printing, Haight-Ashbury Pedigree (Kitchen Sink, 1971), CGC NM- 9.2 white pages, President Richard Nixon and John Lennon cover, adult content, Fogel's 2015 Underground Price & Grading Guide NM- 9.2 value = $15. CGC census-3/16: 1 in 9.2, none higher. **$227**

Courtesy of Heritage Auctions, ha.com

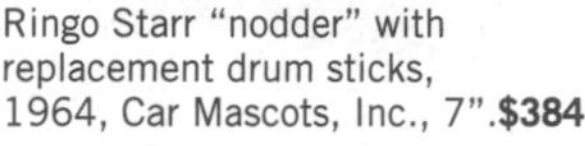

Ringo Starr "nodder" with replacement drum sticks, 1964, Car Mascots, Inc., 7".**$384**

Courtesy of Julien's Auctions, www.juliensauctions.com

▶ Blue cotton jersey sweatshirt made to promote Ringo Starr's 1969 film "The Magic Christian" that reads, "I Am A Magic Christian. Funny You Don't Look It!" **$875**

Courtesy of Julien's Auctions, www.juliensauctions.com

GENERAL ITEMS

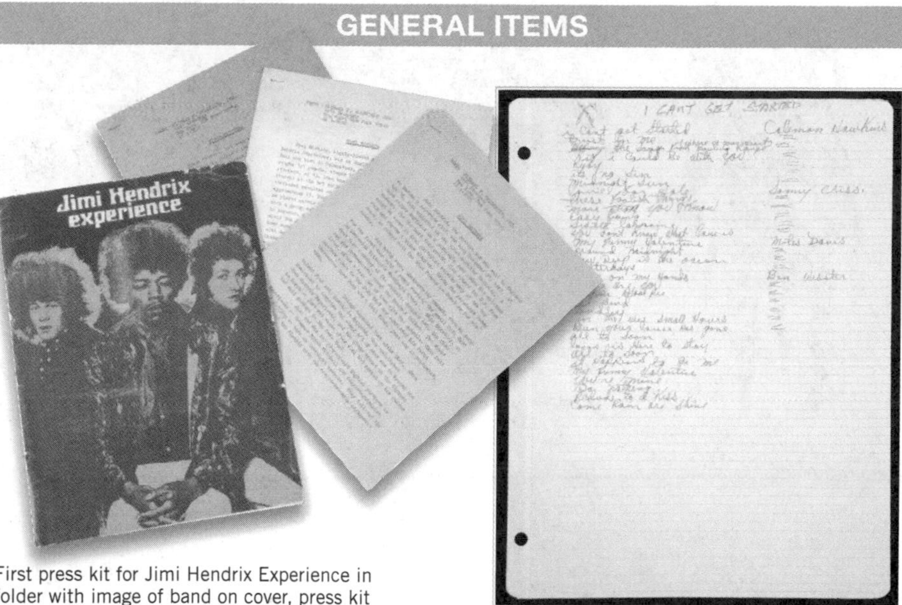

First press kit for Jimi Hendrix Experience in folder with image of band on cover, press kit consists of six printed pages outlining musical careers of Jimi Hendrix, Mitch Mitchell, and Noel Redding, 12" x 9". **$512**

Courtesy of Julien's Auctions, www.juliensauctions.com

B.B. King handwritten list of songs and names of artists who performed them, in black ink on lined paper, page titled "I Can't Get Started," which is also first song on list, 11" x 8-1/2". **$768**

Courtesy of Julien's Auctions, www.juliensauctions.com

Elvis Presley Enterprises (EPE) record case gifted to Ken Moore by Presley, brown case with image of Presley on cover playing guitar and image of hound dog, "Card Missing" written at top right corner of case in unknown hand, with letter of authenticity from EPE Archives, 7-3/4" x 7-3/4" x 2-1/4". Moore worked for Presley's security team and was traveling aboard the USS Lurline with Presley in 1957 for his concerts in Oahu, Hawaii. Provenance: From estate of Ken Moore. **$768**

Courtesy of Julien's Auctions, www.juliensauctions.com

Set of eight lobby cards for Elvis Presley film "Live a Little, Love a Little" (MGM, 1968), each 11" x 14". **$256**

Courtesy of Julien's Auctions, www.juliensauctions.com

Black silk moire custom-made jacket stage worn by Heart vocalist Ann Wilson, velvet collar, puffed sleeves, jet-like buttons and exaggerated tails, embellished with iridescent glass and beadwork. Provenance: From Collection of Ann and Nancy Wilson. **$576**

Courtesy of Julien's Auctions, www.juliensauctions.com

Jacksons Victory Tour program, signed "Michael Jackson" on cover in black pen, 14 x 11". **$896**

Courtesy of Julien's Auctions, www.juliensauctions.com

KISS original debut album Casablanca Records promotional poster, only issued with white label promotional releases of 1974 KISS debut album, one of few machine-folded posters made, 23" x 35"......................... **$784**

Courtesy of Backstage Auctions, www.backstageauctions.com

Guitar autographed by members of The Rolling Stones. **$1,000**

Courtesy of Mecum Auctions, www.mecum.com

Stephen Pearcy 1986 tour-used RATT road case used for rack mountable components, official RATT logo stenciled to one side, with Hollywood address, top and bottomed stenciled SL (Stage Left), back of case stenciled "Stephen Pearcy" with large "Riot Brides" sticker, case 26" x 12" x 20". Provenance: From private collection of Stephen Pearcy. **$695**

Courtesy of Backstage Auctions, www.backstageauctions.com

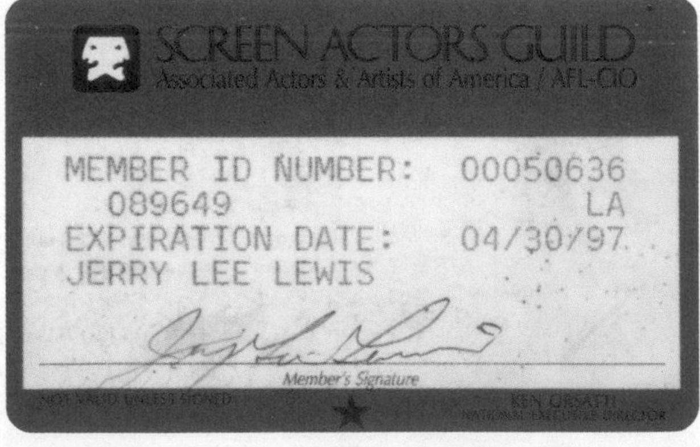

Screen Actors Guild card belonging to Jerry Lee Lewis and signed by Lewis, expiration date listed as April 30, 1997, 2-1/4" x 3-1/2".. **$768**

Courtesy of Julien's Auctions, www.juliensauctions.com

The Runaways Lita Ford rare "Queens of Noise" Japan Tour 1977 jacket, exclusively made for original five band members; white denim, slight discoloration, back with patchwork and embroidery, signed by Ford, size small, 20" from pit-to-pit and 25" from top of collar to bottom. Legendary Japanese concert promoter Udo (Artists, Inc.) welcomed The Runaways to Japan in 1977 with a set of these rare tour jackets. Provenance: From private collection of Lita Ford. **$863**

Courtesy of Backstage Auctions, www.backstageauctions.com

Capitol Records Fiftieth Anniversary promotional book and CD box set (1992) spanning years 1942-1992, with artists and discographies of entire period, still-sealed, eight-CD box set of 163 recordings divided into thematic categories and sampler CD with selection of hits, book limited to 1000 copies, this book with gold stamp numbers "001" indicating first of run, 11-1/2" x 11-1/2"............. **$300**

Courtesy of Heritage Auctions, ha.com

Guitar pick used by Jimmy Page, guitarist and founder of rock band Led Zeppelin....... **$115**

Courtesy of Ewbank's Auctions, www.ewbankauctions.co.uk

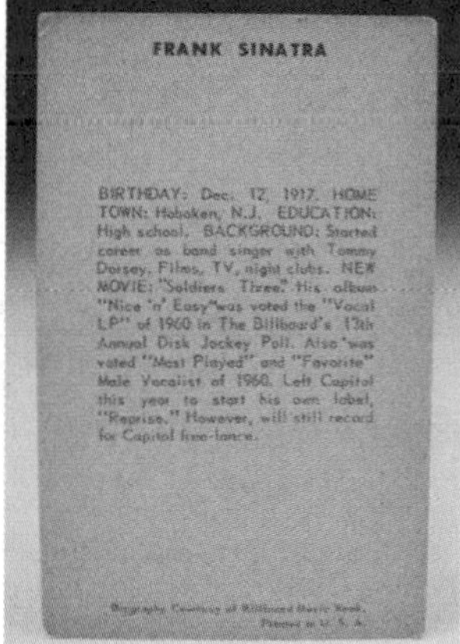

Frank Sinatra collector's card, "Sincerely, Frank Sinatra." **$50**

Courtesy of Christiana Auction Gallery, www.christianaauctiongallery.com

NATIVE AMERICAN ART & ARTIFACTS

INTEREST IN NATIVE American material cultural artifacts has been long-lived. In recent years it has become commonplace to have important sales of these artifacts by at least four major auction houses in addition to private trading, local auctions, and Internet sales.

The majority of valuable items are held in repositories of museums, universities, and colleges, but many items that were traded to private citizens are now being sold to collectors and can be acquired in the same fashion as any material cultural item: at farm auction sales (an especially good place for farm family collections to be dispersed), yard sales, estate sales, specialized auctions, and from private collectors trading or selling items. The most wonderful of all sources is the Internet, especially online auction sales.

However, Native American artifacts may be more difficult to locate for a variety of reasons: scarcity of items; legal protection of the items being traded; more vigorous collecting of artifacts by numerous international, national, state, regional, and local museums and historical societies; frailties of the items themselves, as most were made of organic materials; and a more limited distribution network through legitimate secondary sales.

However, it is still possible to find some types of Native American items through the traditional sources of online auctions, auction houses in local communities, antique stores and malls, flea markets, trading meetings, estate sales, and similar venues. The most likely items to find in these ways are items made of stone, chert, flint, obsidian, and copper. Most organic materials will not have survived the rigors of a marketplace unless they were recently released from some estate or collection and their value was unknown to the previous owner.

For more information on Native American collectibles, see *Warman's North American Indian Artifacts Identification and Price Guide* by Russell E. Lewis.

Original hand-tinted photograph, circa 1930-1940, of well-known Montana Crow Chief Max Big Man (born in 1886), 22-1/2" x 16-1/4", 26-3/4" x 31-3/4" framed.................... **$100**

Courtesy of North American Auction Co., www.northamericanauctioncompany.com

Three Mescalero Apache burden baskets, late 19th century, to 12" h.... **$338**

Courtesy of Skinner, Inc., www.skinnerinc.com

Haida mask plaque in carved bone, 19th century or earlier, frog on forehead, drilled to suspend from cord, probably part of a Shaman's fetish necklace, 5-1/4" x 4"...... **$2,200**

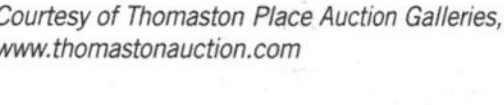

Courtesy of Thomaston Place Auction Galleries, www.thomastonauction.com

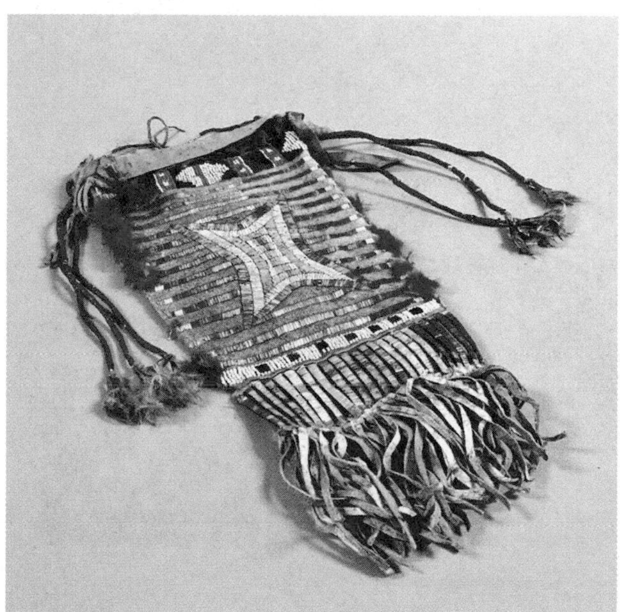

Lakota beaded and quilled hide bag, late 19th century, front with multicolored spiderweb design, some fading to quillwork, 15" l. **$1,230**

Courtesy of Skinner, Inc., www.skinnerinc.com

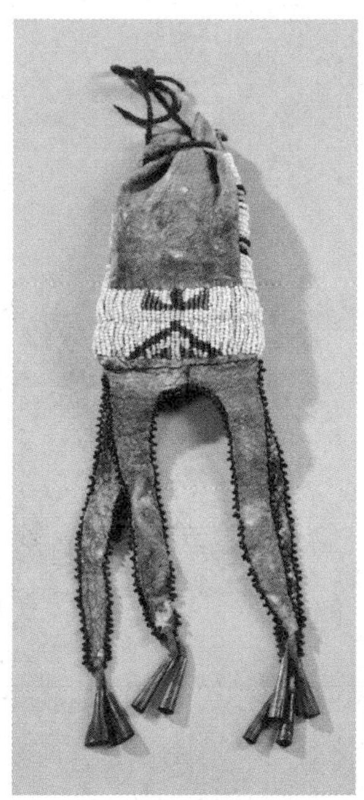

Cheyenne beaded hide paint bag, circa last quarter 19th century, traces of yellow pigment overall, with four long tabs and tin cone danglers at bottom, 8" l. **$984**

Courtesy of Skinner, Inc., www.skinnerinc.com

top lot

Large Yokuts polychrome serving basket or tray, turn of 20th century, coiled construction with three bands of polychrome rattlesnake diamond design and additional polychrome design elements to rim and center, 22-3/4" dia., 3-3/4" h. $4,800

COURTESY OF CASE ANTIQUES AUCTIONS & APPRAISALS, WWW.CASEANTIQUES.COM

Lakota quilled and beaded hide half cradle, circa last quarter 19th century, with quilled slats and fringe at upper back and roll-beaded edging, 11-1/2" h. **$861**

Courtesy of Skinner, Inc., www.skinnerinc.com

Navajo Yei rug, circa 1940, native handspun wool, aniline dyes, 36" x 35-1/4" **$625**

Courtesy of Heritage Auctions, ha.com

Navajo silver and turquoise squash blossom necklace, mid-to-late 20th century, 25" l. **$738**

Courtesy of Skinner, Inc., www.skinnerinc.com

Plains beaded moccasins, circa 1890 to 1900, lane-stitched with sinew in opaque and translucent beads, each decorated on vamp with red, white, and blue chevrons, similar motifs in teepee shapes encircling foot, rawhide soles and upper instep and tongue, 10-1/2" l. **$500**

Courtesy of Artemis Gallery Live, www.artemisgallerylive.com

Five Plains pipe bowls, four of catlinite, one with incised Indian head decoration with older black clay bowl, longest 8" l. **$308**

Courtesy of Skinner, Inc., www.skinnerinc.com

Navajo regional rug, Ganado, Arizona, circa 1940, native handspun wool, aniline dye.. **$813**

Courtesy of Heritage Auctions, ha.com

Nez Perce flat-twined cornhusk bag, Columbia Plateau, circa 1875, contrasting woven design programs on each side, diamond pattern of red, orange, blue, and green on natural background on one side, verso with repeated triangular motif of red, blue, pink, and lavendar on natural ground with two tan leather loops through which a strap could be threaded, light beige leather and suede trim with plaited cording attached along rim of bag, 16-1/2" x 11".....**$350**

Courtesy of Artemis Gallery Live, www.artemisgallerylive.com

Oil on canvas portrait of Plains chief by Troy Denton (1949-), period-style frame, 33" x 29". **$3,125**

Courtesy of Heritage Auctions, ha.com

Plains pipe, circa last quarter 19th century, with ribbed catlinite T-bowl, ash stem with incised crosses on raised sections, 29-1/2" l. overall........ **$677**

Courtesy of Skinner, Inc., www.skinnerinc.com

Seneca hand-crafted wood paddle with large concave receptacle and short handle, circa 19th century, 9" l....... **$100**

Courtesy of Artemis Gallery Live, www.artemisgallerylive.com

◀ Native American, possibly Sioux, full-beaded moccasins, late 19th/early 20th century, white ground with beaded geometric designs in red, orange, green, and blue and beaded tongues with feather and metal accents, parfleche soles, 11" l. **$375**

Courtesy of Case Antiques Auctions & Appraisals, www.caseantiques.com

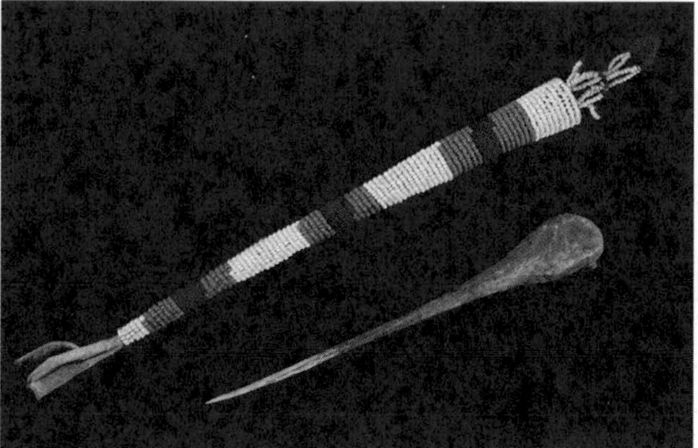

Sioux beaded awl case with antler or bone awl, case in white, green, and red with early 1800s glass trade seed beads on parfleche case with cut fringe, top of case with fancy beaded edge, finely carved awl in well-preserved condition with sharp point used to punch holes in leather or hide, case 12-1/4" l., awl 7" l.................................... **$375**

Courtesy of North American Auction Co., www.northamericanauctioncompany.com

Southwest polychrome pottery olla, early 20th century, wavy line decoration around rim, geometric and line decoration to body, 9-3/4" h............... **$400**

Courtesy of Case Antiques Auctions & Appraisals, www.caseantiques.com

Zuni ring, Southwest United States, circa 1930 to 1950, sterling silver and petit point oval and pear-shaped turquoise stones and one jet stone, hand-cut by Zuni lapidarist, signed "TXX" on underside, size 8-1/4 to 8-1/2 with central motif 1-1/8" dia........................ **$125**

Courtesy of Artemis Gallery Live, www.artemisgallerylive.com

Native American beaded pouch with dogs, circa 1860 to 1880, 10" x 8-1/2"..................... **$250**

Courtesy of Morphy Auctions, www.morphyauctions.com

Native American tomahawk, 19th century, constructed of ash or walnut and decorated with brass nail heads, 16-1/4" l. x 7" w. **$1,600**

Courtesy of Wooten & Wooten Auctioneers & Appraisers, www.wootenandwooten.com

Original chalk painting by Syd Shores, 1953, signed and dated by Shores in lower image area, 11" x 13"..**$131**

Courtesy of Heritage Auctions, ha.com

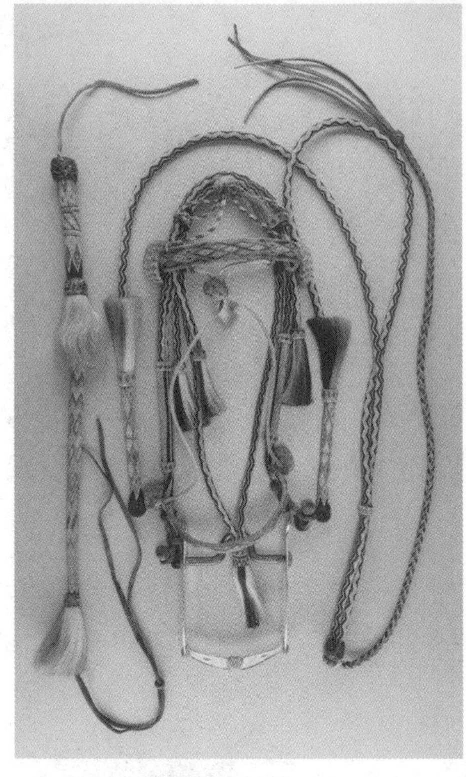

Native-made horsehair bridle, quirt, and reins, circa 1900, dyed horsehair, commercial leather, bridle 20", quirt 45" overall, reins 87". **$2,750**

Courtesy of Heritage Auctions, ha.com

Beaded trade purse, 19th century, sailing ship, possibly made for trade or sailor-made, 9-5/8" h. x 7" w. **$300**

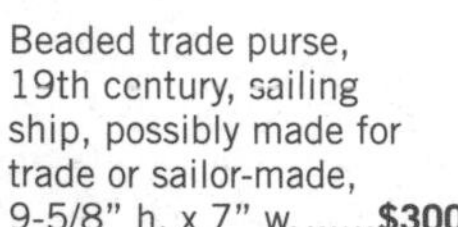

Courtesy of Wooten & Wooten Auctioneers & Appraisers, www.wootenandwooten.com

OCCUPIED JAPAN

OCCUPIED JAPAN (OJ) is the mark, sticker, or stamp used on a vast variety of objects produced during the seven- to 10-year period during and after the United States occupation of Japan, immediately following World War II. These items were mainly produced for export to U.S. consumers. From 1946 to 1947, Japan's primary economic driver was the carefully controlled manufacturing and exporting of consumer goods.

Because anti-Japanese sentiment was especially high following the war, some reports show that at least 50 percent of all goods produced during the period were specifically marked "Made in Occupied Japan" or "Occupied Japan" to prove the goods had been produced under American influence. By 1948, restrictions were relaxed, but export items were still marked as such until as late as 1955.

Collectors mainly focus on figures, china, toys, cameras, and comic character novelties. The world's Occupied Japan Club has existed for nearly 30 years and flourished during the 1980s and 1990s, thanks to comprehensive reference books by author and club director Florence Archambault and to Baby Boomers, who grew up with the term "Occupied Japan" as a household phrase, finally reaching the "money years" of their 40s and 50s.

The top of the OJ market is difficult to determine. Nikon cameras made during the period can bring $40,000 or more, but it's unlikely such cameras are collected specifically for the metal base plates engraved "MADE IN OCCUPIED JAPAN." Most of the OJ goods produced were of general low quality with many exceptions. Depending on the maker, the level of detail and form of some porcelain and bisque potteries are impressive. Paulux, Andrea, Maruyama, Moriama, Chubu, and Lefton are prime choices. Maruni is the lacquerware leader by far and can be found in future-forward, minimalist designs that would not look out of place in a 2017 edition of *Elle Décor Magazine.*

These bisque figures and porcelain centerpieces can be highly complex and detailed, and retain a glimmer of the immense talent and reputation Japanese ceramic craftsman earned during

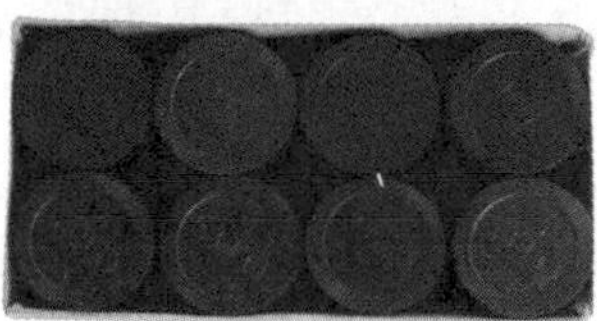

Checkers, wood, El Gee, made by Snappy, marked "Made in Occupied Japan" #216, original box with 24 game pieces. .... **$8-$10**

Courtesy of Kathy Gardner, facebook.com/theoccupiedjapancollectors

Pigeon Finest Quality Tooth Picks, sealed with approximately 750 flat picks. .... **$8-$10**

Courtesy of Kathy Gardner, facebook.com/theoccupiedjapancollectors

"Doll" figurine, porcelain, marked "Occupied Japan" and "American Children" (copy of Hummel No. 34, "Little Mother"), 45 different variations known to exist from American Children line, 5-1/2" .... **$30-$50**

Courtesy of Kathy Gardner, facebook.com/theoccupiedjapancollectors

Pocket knife, multi-blade, marked "Occupied Japan," 5-3/4" l. .... **$25-$28**

Courtesy of Kathy Gardner, facebook.com/theoccupiedjapancollectors

the centuries before the war. OJ porcelain and bisque makers most often replicated the delicate Colonial motifs of Chelsea porcelain figures made in the 18th century and Staffordshire figures made in the early 19th century.

"One thing we have all wondered for years: Why so many Colonials?" said Kathy Gardner, who has collected OJ items for the last 30 years. Gardner owns and runs the Washington Street Inn, a Bluffton, Indiana, bed and breakfast, where her 2,050-piece collection is one of the country's largest year-round displays of its kind (220 E. Washington St., Bluffton, IN 46714, 260-824-9070, klgardner45@yahoo.com).

Gardner works closely with California-based collector Shoko Tanaka and the Occupied Japan Collectors community to share information and highlight special pieces. Tanaka has made it a mission to research kiln and pottery sites and introduce the collectibles to a new generation of Japanese. A busy Facebook page titled "Occupied Japan Collectors" boasts more than 1,000 followers and information is shared daily.

Other than the occasional discovery of a rare comic character or a sports figure toy that commands a few thousand dollars at auction, porcelain and bisque figures and china have become the bulk of this hobby. Besides Colonial figures, Occupied Japan ceramics makers introduced American Children figures, which are either copies or variations of M.I. Hummel figurines.

"There are 45 of them," Gardner said. "They are marked OJ and each has a title. There was fierce competition to get them all and we were willing to pay $100-plus 10 years ago. We still want them, but now consider $25-$40 an excellent price."

The current market for OJ has produced an impressive entry-level collectible across dozens of categories. Values published in the early 1970s show a Maruni red lacquerware vase with a metal base selling for $20 (the equivalent to $107 in 2015 dollars). A search online shows the same vase can be had today for $80-$100. A massive, 20-inch long porcelain figural group of a team of four white horses pulling a chariot and female nymph rider can be found for $150 to $200; a Paulux pastel blue demitasse cup/saucer set can be had for $12 or less.

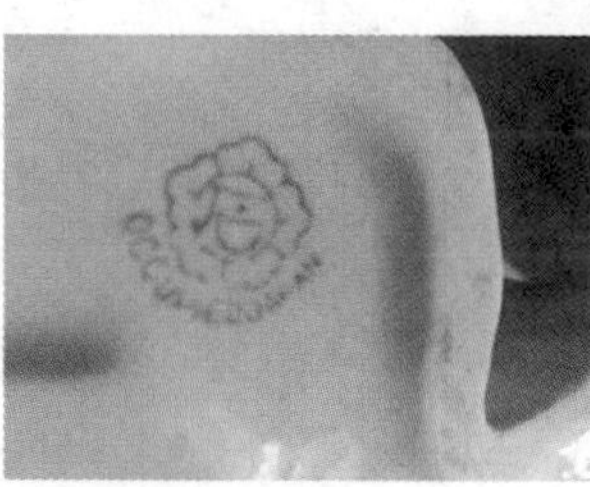

LD mark of Sekkaen, Seto, Aichi Prefecture, Japan.

Paulux mark, a highly desirable manufacturer.

"Values used to be fairly absolute, but are not anymore," Gardner said. "What I know is this: We can't let history slip away. Because once these things are gone, they're gone, and someone has to keep around what will never be again, especially the pieces we call 'big and beautiful.' I would add novelties and toys to that list!"

— *Eric Bradley*

Sources .... Join the Occupied Japan Collecting Club: Contact Kathy Gardner, 260-824-9070, klgardner45@yahoo.com, or editor Shoko Tanaka, shoko1122@gmail.com or 1312 Marina Circle, Davis, CA 95616.

Old postman figurine, porcelain, marked "Occupied Japan", LD mark of Sekkaen, Seto, Aichi Prefecture, Japan, referred to these as "LD kids", 9-1/4" h. .... **$22.50-$27.50**

Courtesy of Kathy Gardner, facebook.com/theoccupiedjapancollectors

Porcelain centerpiece of woman with two shells, marked "Occupied Japan" and "Ardalt," 14" h. ....**$175-$225**
One shell rather than two. ....**$200-$225**

Courtesy of Kathy Gardner, facebook.com/theoccupiedjapancollectors

Boy pulling pig figurine, porcelain, marked "Occupied Japan", LD mark of Sekkaen, Seto, Aichi Prefecture, Japan, referred to these as "LD kids", 7-1/2" h. .... **$22.50-$27.50**

Courtesy of Kathy Gardner, facebook.com/theoccupiedjapancollectors

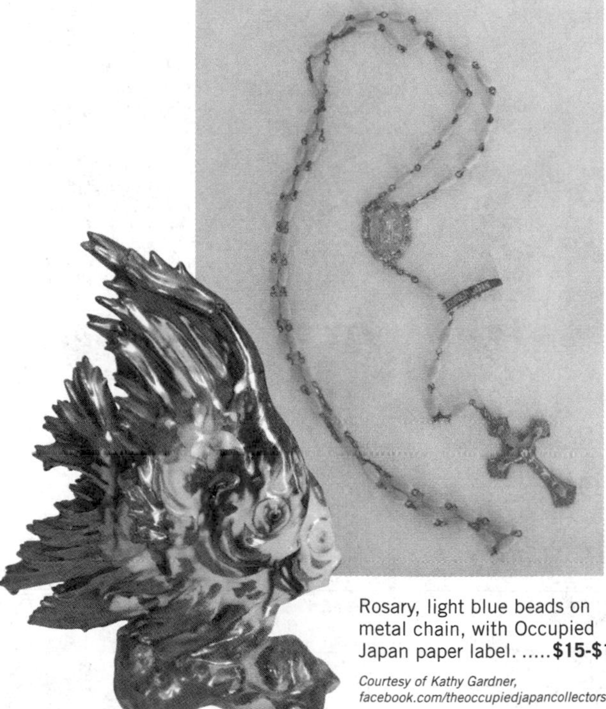

Rosary, light blue beads on metal chain, with Occupied Japan paper label. .....**$15-$17.50**

Courtesy of Kathy Gardner, facebook.com/theoccupiedjapancollectors

Rare fish figurine, porcelain, one side decorated in gold and blue, reverse decorated in pink and gold, 12" h. .... **$100+**

Courtesy of Kathy Gardner, facebook.com/theoccupiedjapancollectors

"Bowing Couple" figurines, porcelain, man and woman, marked "Occupied Japan" with Isihara mark, 8" h. .... **$60-$70**

Courtesy of Kathy Gardner, facebook.com/theoccupiedjapancollectors

Figurine, bisque, man, woman, dog, and sheep, marked "Occupied Japan" with Paulux mark, 11" h. .... **$150+**

Courtesy of Kathy Gardner, facebook.com/theoccupiedjapancollectors

Figurine, bisque, two figures and coach on metal base, marked "Occupied Japan", base may be American in origin, 13" h. overall................. **$150+**

Courtesy of Kathy Gardner, facebook.com/theoccupiedjapancollectors

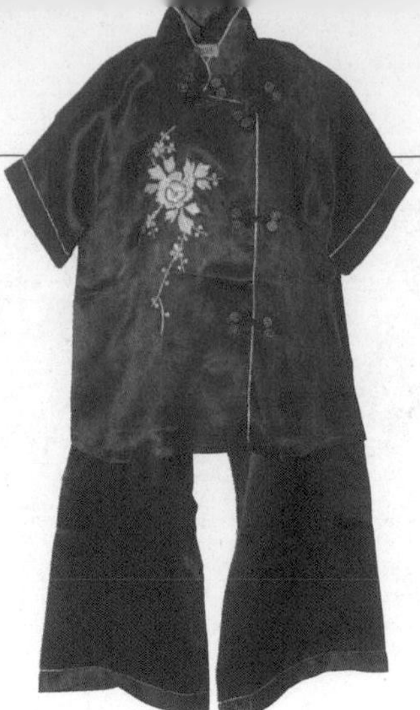

Children's pajamas, orange, size 17, with original cloth label in neck identifying it as Occupied Japan. .... **$20-$25**

Courtesy of Kathy Gardner, facebook.com/theoccupiedjapancollectors

Rare figurines, bisque, peasant woman and man on bases, heavy, marked "Occupied Japan" with Ardalt symbol, 20" h. ....**$375-$400/pair**

Courtesy of Kathy Gardner, facebook.com/theoccupiedjapancollectors

Horse and plow figurine, two horses with two men on base, 13" l. x 7" h. ....**$175-$200**

Courtesy of Kathy Gardner, facebook.com/theoccupiedjapancollectors

Highly detailed figurine, bisque, father holding doll and playing with two girls and boy on base, marked "Occupied Japan" with Ardalt mark, 11-1/4" h. .... **$180-$190**

Courtesy of Kathy Gardner, facebook.com/theoccupiedjapancollectors

Highly detailed figurine, bisque, woman holding baby with two children at feet with puppy on base, marked "Occupied Japan", 10-1/4" h. .....**$180-$190**

Courtesy of Kathy Gardner, facebook.com/theoccupiedjapancollectors

Figurine, bisque, girl and boy on base, marked "Occupied Japan" with Paulux mark, highly desirable manufacturer, 9-1/4" h. .... **$45-$55**

Courtesy of Kathy Gardner, facebook.com/theoccupiedjapancollectors

Figurine, bisque, two-horse coach with woman and man figure, original reins, marked "Occupied Japan" with Paulux mark, highly desirable manufacturer, 6-1/4" h. ....**$90-$110**

Courtesy of Kathy Gardner, facebook.com/theoccupiedjapancollectors

Liqueur bottle of figural centaur playing mouth harp, marked "Occupied Japan", presumably souvenir or gift shop item, value may increase if bottle is still full or unopened, 3-1/2" h...... **$20-$30**

Courtesy of Kathy Gardner, facebook.com/theoccupiedjapancollectors

Figural owl bank, porcelain, marked "Occupied Japan" and "Souvenir of Montreal" (many Occupied Japan export souvenir items were sent to Canada), 4-1/2" h................................ **$18-$20**

Courtesy of Kathy Gardner, facebook.com/theoccupiedjapancollectors

Figurines, porcelain, Native American man and woman on bases, marked "Occupied Japan", 9-3/4" h. .... **$35-$40**

Courtesy of Kathy Gardner, facebook.com/theoccupiedjapancollectors

Figural horse creamer (at least six to eight different figural animal creamers are known to exist), marked "Occupied Japan", 4-1/2" h. **$20-$25**

Courtesy of Kathy Gardner, facebook.com/theoccupiedjapancollectors

Salt and pepper shakers, bisque chicken figurals, marked "Occupied Japan", 3" h. .... **$18-$20**

Courtesy of Kathy Gardner, facebook.com/theoccupiedjapancollectors

Dog figurine, porcelain, marked "Occupied Japan", 6-1/2" h. ..**$15-$20**

Courtesy of Kathy Gardner, facebook.com/theoccupiedjapancollectors

Multiplier & Divider Pencil Box, wood, with sliding top, knob operates paper on "dowel" that reveals answers for multiplication and division problems, paper instructions included, marked "Occupied Japan", 9-3/4" l. ....**$20-$25**

Courtesy of Kathy Gardner, facebook.com/theoccupiedjapancollectors

Pencil sharpener, "Julian" brand by Yamamuro & Co., Ltd., Tokyo, marked "Made in Occupied Japan", passage on sharpener reads, "Needed by every pencil user everywhere, sharpens all standard size pencils, Will not break the lead, place fixed cover case will be altered thrice." ....**$30-$35**

Courtesy of Kathy Gardner, facebook.com/theoccupiedjapancollectors

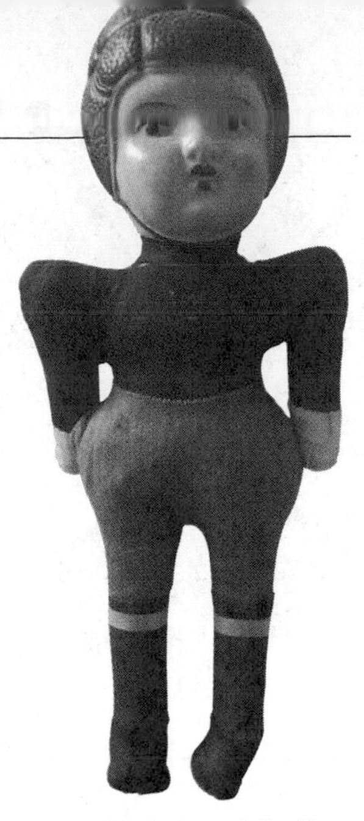

Stuffed football player doll with celluloid head, 10" h. **$17.50-$20**

Courtesy of Kathy Gardner, facebook.com/theoccupiedjapancollectors

Shookum doll with papoose, paper Occupied Japan label, 5" h. ....**$17.50-$20**

Courtesy of Kathy Gardner, facebook.com/theoccupiedjapancollectors

Eight glass swizzle sticks, two each of four animals, paper label, 5-1/2" l. .... **$17.50-$20**

Courtesy of Kathy Gardner, facebook.com/theoccupiedjapancollectors

Cricket cage, replica, possibly salesman sample, paper included reads "Singing Cricket Cage," 3" h. .... **$20-$25**

Courtesy of Kathy Gardner, facebook.com/theoccupiedjapancollectors

INSIDE INTEL

CARE FOR OCCUPIED JAPAN PORCELAIN:

"Use soap and a little water and an artist's brush if it is a complicated piece; soap won't hurt anything.

"Many times all it needs is a little water, but be careful. On occasion you may mistake the color on a piece for dirt, so always look close before you wash. Bisque is washable, just be a tad more careful."

Kathy Gardner, Bluffton, Indiana, a 30-year collector of Occupied Japan

▲ Figurine, porcelain, two ladies play cards while gentleman watches, often-used Colonial theme, marked "Occupied Japan" with Paulux mark, 8-1/2" h. .... **$65-$80**

Courtesy of Kathy Gardner, facebook.com/theoccupiedjapancollectors

◀ Pair of rare figurines, roosters or fighting cocks, marked "Occupied Japan," 5" h. and 6" h. .. **$35-$40**

Courtesy of Kathy Gardner, facebook.com/theoccupiedjapancollectors

Leather woman's belt, marked "Made in Occupied Japan", 28" l. .... **$30-$35**

Courtesy of Kathy Gardner, facebook.com/theoccupiedjapancollectors

Figurine, porcelain, girl/woman hitting boy with rolling pin, 5" h....................................... **$12-$15**

Courtesy of Kathy Gardner, facebook.com/theoccupiedjapancollectors

Figurine, porcelain, girl feeding two calves on base, 6" h... **$15-$17.50**

Courtesy of Kathy Gardner, facebook.com/theoccupiedjapancollectors

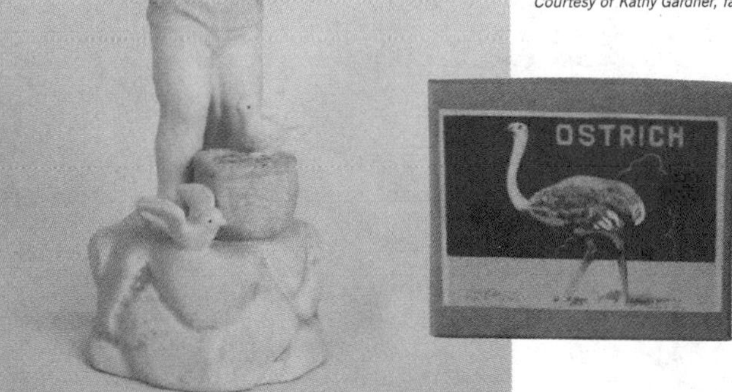

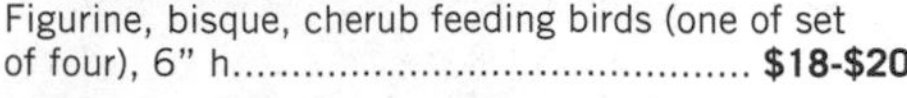

Figurine, bisque, cherub feeding birds (one of set of four), 6" h... **$18-$20**

Courtesy of Kathy Gardner, facebook.com/theoccupiedjapancollectors

Wind-up ostrich toy with original box, marked "Made in Japan", 5-1/4" h. .... **$90-$100**

Courtesy of Kathy Gardner, facebook.com/theoccupiedjapancollectors

Figurine, barefoot mother and boy with shoes on base, 7" h.. **$17.50-$22**

Courtesy of Kathy Gardner, facebook.com/theoccupiedjapancollectors

Figurine, bisque, swinging cherub on bowed branch (two porcelain variations exist and each one shows two Hummel-style children on swing), 7" h. .... **$25-$28**

Courtesy of Kathy Gardner, facebook.com/theoccupiedjapancollectors

Children's tea set, porcelain, cups, saucers, sugar and teapot, each with transfer of Walt Disney's Donald Duck, boxed example, marked "Made in Occupied Japan, WDP", 1/2" x 10-1/2". **$550**

Courtesy of Hake's Americana & Collectibles, www.hakes.com

Figurine, bisque, seated woman with standing cherub and book, 7-1/4" h. .... **$70-$75**

Courtesy of Kathy Gardner, facebook.com/theoccupiedjapancollectors

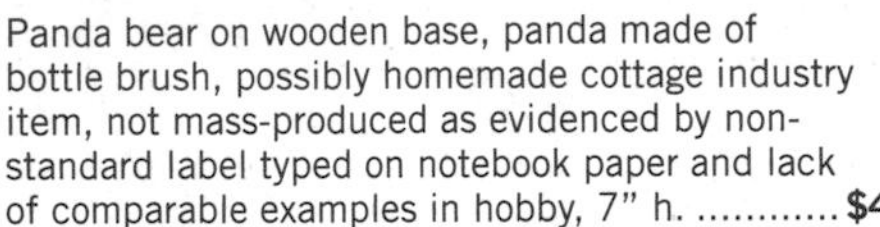

Panda bear on wooden base, panda made of bottle brush, possibly homemade cottage industry item, not mass-produced as evidenced by non-standard label typed on notebook paper and lack of comparable examples in hobby, 7" h. **$40**

Courtesy of Kathy Gardner, facebook.com/theoccupiedjapancollectors

Men's rayon Pali Brand Aloha shirt, circa 1950, made in post-war Occupied Japan, (Pali means cliff), commonly found in blue but also in yellow. .... **$400-$600**

Courtesy of VintageAlohaShirts.com

Toy nodder, pink donkey form, celluloid, 5-3/4" h. .... **$15-$20**

Courtesy of Kathy Gardner, facebook.com/theoccupiedjapancollectors

Movie poster, "The Philadelphia Story" (MGM, post-war, 1946), early Japanese poster with Motion Picture Export Association (MPEA) seal in upper left corner (paper was scarce in Occupied Japan so posters were smaller), 14-1/4" x 20". **$3,883**

Courtesy of Heritage Auctions, ha.com

PAPERWEIGHTS

ANTIQUE PAPERWEIGHTS MADE in the 19th century captured floral designs, reptiles and millefiori canes in very traditional Victorian styles encased in a solid sphere of clear crystal.

Artists of the 19th century generally produced paperweights in factory settings along with other decorative glass objects. Rarely signed by individual artists, most antique paperweights are attributed to a factory by motif, color palette, canes and shape. Little is known about individual artists who created the work.

In a 19th century society with fancy desks and paper, paperweights were functional objects of art. Flowers were a large part of Victorian society and both ladies and gentleman of the time were attracted to fauna and flora. Paperweights were considered fascinating objects of art and conversation pieces in Victorian homes.

Factories producing paperweights were primarily located in France, Italy, Czechoslovakia, America, and China. Factory-made paperweights often had similar motifs. Factories would also produce special pieces. These rare designs showcased fantastic capabilities and secret techniques only known to each factory. Today these special pieces bring staggering auction results.

In the mid-20th century there was a revival in modern paperweights. At first artists began creating updated versions using glass-working techniques of antique traditions. This revival began alongside the studio art glass movement in America. Individual glass artists opened homegrown studios in garages and basements. The pioneer and dean of the American paperweight revival was Charles Kaziun of Brockton, Massachusetts. Kaziun set new artistic standards and methods for creating paperweights at that time. He worked alone in his own small home studio creating the path that all subsequent contemporary paperweight artists followed.

Contemporary artists making paperweights introduced several differences from the past: They worked alone or with an assistant in private home studios; concentrated only on paperweights; developed individual styles and methods of making the work; and always signed the artwork and often numbered editions.

In the early years of collecting paperweights, few collectors knew much about paperweights and even less about how they were made. In 1955 Paul Jokelson, an avid antique paperweight collector and importer, founded the Paperweight Collectors Association. He promoted paperweights and created a forum for educating collectors and helping artists like Kaziun show and sell their new work. Jokelson published many early books on paperweights; other authors followed, creating a library of books on paperweights. The PCA has biannual paperweight conventions.

Today many artists all over the world are creating fine paperweights. The finest modern paperweights have made their way into private and

Large glass paperweight with footed base, late 19th century, 13" h. x 5" w.................... **$123**

Courtesy of Wiederseim Associates, Inc., www.weiderseim.com

Rookwood cat paperweight designed by William Hentschel, cast in 1911, gray-green mat glaze, marked with Rookwood logo, date, and shape number 1883, wheel-ground X due to glaze being light in places, nick on plinth, 5-3/8" h. **$275**

Courtesy of Mark Mussio, Humler & Nolan, www.humlernolan.com

Five Saturday Evening Girls glazed ceramic paperweights by Tillie Block and Sara Galner, Boston, 1910s-1920s, three marked, Block and Galner geese paperweights in excellent condition, chip to base of tulip, bruise to yellow swan, glaze miss to last, 2-1/2" dia. ea. **$1,280**

Courtesy of Rago Arts and Auctions, www.ragoarts.com

Amalric Walter pâte-de-verre bird paperweight, Nancy, France, 1920s, molded signature "A. WALTER NANCY" and artist initial "B," excellent condition, 4" x 4" x 3". ... **$1,920**

Courtesy of Rago Arts and Auctions, www.ragoarts.com

Rookwood turtle paperweight cast in 1923, brown over tan mat glazes, marked with Rookwood logo, date, and shape number 1686, uncrazed, excellent original condition, 2-1/4" h. **$850**

Courtesy of Mark Mussio, Humler & Nolan, www.humlernolan.com

Grueby Faience Co. molded Arts & Crafts scarab-shaped paperweight in dark green glaze, first quarter 20th century, Boston, impressed circular maker's mark and remnant of paper label to underside, 1-1/4" h. x 2-3/4" w. x 3-7/8" d..................... **$750**

Courtesy of John Moran Auctioneers, www.johnmoran.com

museum art collections. The Bergstrom-Mahler Museum of Glass in Neenah, Wisconsin, houses one of the world's largest collections of paperweights in the United States. It's second only to the holdings of the Corning Museum of Glass in New York. Other institutions such as The Chicago Art Institute, Museum of Fine Arts in Boston, and The Currier Museum of Art in Manchester, New Hampshire, among others, also have modern paperweights on view.

Today's paperweight artists have stepped beyond the traditional form and are creating new works of contemporary art glass. They truly enjoy their work and continue to be motivated by their love of art.

Collectors love paperweights because, unlike other forms of art, collectors can hold them in their hands and be drawn into a fascinating miniature world.

– Courtesy of James D. Julia Auctioneers,

Fairfield, Maine, www.jamesdjulia.com, and Debbie Tarsitano Studios

top lot

Rare Rookwood Mouse paperweight by Kitaro Shirayamadani, cast in 1937, blue over brown high glazes, marked with Rookwood logo, date, and shape number 6618, uncrazed, excellent condition, 3-1/8" h. **$2,800**

COURTESY OF MARK MUSSIO, HUMLER & NOLAN, WWW.HUMLERNOLAN.COM

Claycraft Potteries teal and blue glazed art pottery scarab-form paperweight, circa 1920s-1930s, very good condition with minor wear, 3-1/8" l. **$218**

Courtesy of Conestoga Auction Co., www.conestogaauction.com

Rookwood "Potter at the Wheel" paperweight with Coromandel glaze, cast in 1935, marked with Rookwood logo and date, uncrazed, excellent original condition, 3-5/8" dia.......... **$325**

Courtesy of Mark Mussio, Humler & Nolan, www.humlernolan.com

Rookwood cat paperweight designed by Louise Abel, cast in 1945, Wine Madder Glaze, impressed with Rookwood logo, date, shape number 6182, and Abel's mold monogram, uncrazed, excellent original condition, 6-5/8" h. **$170**

Courtesy of Mark Mussio, Humler & Nolan, www.humlernolan.com

Rookwood cocker spaniel paperweight cast in 1953, Jet Black glaze, marked with Rookwood logo, date, and shape number 7024, uncrazed, excellent original condition, 4-1/8" h. **$300**

Courtesy of Mark Mussio, Humler & Nolan, www.humlernolan.com

Tom Philabaum Studio art glass paperweight with yellow filigree dome design, dated 1983, good condition, 2-5/8" h. **$145**

Courtesy of Conestoga Auction Co., www.conestogaauction.com

St. Louis modern French paperweight with encased upright bouquet, triple overlay in white, powder blue, and brown with flowers in red, cobalt blue, white, yellow, and orange with green leaves, signed in white flower center with partial cane 1983, with original fitted box, very good to excellent condition, 2-3/4" dia. **$918**

Courtesy of James D. Julia Auctioneers, Fairfield, Maine, www.jamesdjuliacom

Josh Simpson studio art glass paperweight with multiple techniques in the style of Simpson's Inhabited Planet series, dated 3.25.06, signed on base, 3-1/2" dia. **$172**

Courtesy of Pook & Pook, Inc., pookandpook.com

Richard Satava paperweight with translucent Passion Moon Jellyfish with thread-like tentacles free swimming within, engraved "Satava, 788-11" beneath, excellent original condition, 6" h. **$300**

Courtesy of Mark Mussio, Humler & Nolan, www.humlernolan.com

Victor Trabucco multi-faceted studio art glass paperweight with red and white wild roses, signed "Trabucco 1985" on side, marked "VT" on a leaf back, 4-1/2" dia. **$443**

Courtesy of Pook & Pook, Inc., pookandpook.com

PERFUME BOTTLES

ALTHOUGH THE HUMAN sense of smell isn't nearly as acute as that of many other mammals, we have long been affected by the odors in the world around us. Science has shown that scents or smells can directly affect our mood or behavior.

No one knows for certain when humans first rubbed themselves with some plant or herb to improve their appeal to other humans, usually of the opposite sex. However, it is clear that the use of unguents and scented materials was widely practiced as far back as Ancient Egypt.

Some of the first objects made of glass, in fact, were small cast vials used for storing such mixtures. By the age of the Roman Empire, scented waters and other mixtures were even more important and were widely available in small glass flasks or bottles. Since that time glass has been the material of choice for storing scented concoctions, and during the past 200 years some of the most exquisite glass objects produced were designed for that purpose.

It wasn't until around the middle of the 19th century that specialized bottles and vials were produced to hold commercially manufactured scents. Some aromatic mixtures were worn on special occasions, while many others were splashed on to help mask body odor. For centuries it had been common practice for "sophisticated" people to carry on their person a scented pouch or similar accoutrement, since daily bathing was unheard of and laundering methods were primitive.

Commercially produced and brand name perfumes and colognes have really only been common since the late 19th and early 20th centuries. The French started the ball rolling during the first half of the 19th century when D'Orsay and Guerlain began producing special scents. The first American entrepreneur to step into this field was Richard Hudnut, whose firm was established in 1880. During the second half of the 19th century most scents carried simple labels and were sold in simple, fairly generic glass bottles. Only in the early 20th century did parfumeurs introduce specially designed labels and bottles to hold their most popular perfumes. Coty, founded in 1904, was one of the first to do this, and they turned to Rene Lalique for a special bottle design around 1908. Other French firms, such as Bourjois (1903), Caron (1903), and D'Orsay (1904) were soon following this trend.

People collect two kinds of perfume bottles—decorative and commercial. Decorative bottles include any bottles sold empty and meant to be filled with your choice of scent. Commercial bottles are any that were sold filled with scent and usually have

Cartier yellow metal perfume bottle, marked Cartier, very good condition, 3-7/8" x 1-1/4", 165.90 g... **$138**

Courtesy of Heritage Auctions, ha.com

▲ Richard Hudnut frosted glass three-flowers perfume display bottle, circa 1910, good condition, chip missing to neck and fleabites to stopper, expected wear and sun staining to label, 23-3/8" h. **$125**

Courtesy of Heritage Auctions, ha.com

◀ Baccarat glass Le Roy Soleil perfume bottle by Salvador Dali, acid-etched, 97/3000, with necklace and spray bottle housed in lower compartment, bottle empty, very good condition, bottle 5-1/2" h. **$400**

Courtesy of Heritage Auctions, ha.com

the label of the perfume company.

The rules of value for perfume bottles are the same as for any other kind of glass—rarity, condition, age, and quality of glass.

The record price for perfume bottle at auction is something over $310,000, and those little sample bottles of scent that we used to get for free at perfume counters in the 1960s can now bring as much as $300 or $400.

For more information on perfume bottles, see *Antique Trader Perfume Bottles Price Guide* by Kyle Husfloen.

(**Editor's Note:** In some of the descriptions of Lalique bottles that follow, you will find notations like "M p. 478, No. 1100" or "Marcilhac 952, pg. 428." This refers to the page and serial numbers found in *René Lalique, maître-verrier, 1860-1945: Analyse de L'oeuvre et Catalogue Raisonné,* by Félix Marcilhac, published in 1989 and revised in 1994. Printed entirely in French, this book of more than 1,000 pages is the definitive guide to Lalique's work, and listings from auction catalogs typically cite the Marcilhac guide as a reference.)

R. Lalique enameled glass Le Lys perfume bottle and powder box for D'Orsay, circa 1922, molded R. LALIQUE, (M p. 935 and 968, No. D'ORSAY 19 and 4), good condition, small chip to underside of powder box lid, sticker residue to underside, scuffing and slight abrasions to underside of bottle, sticker residue to bottle, bottle 7" h. **$400**

Courtesy of Heritage Auctions, ha.com

R. Lalique gilt and clear glass Pierre Précieuse perfume for Lionceau, cap with enameled intertwined LP, circa 1927, stamped LIONCEAU - R. LALIQUE, PARIS, FRANCE 232, (M p. 943, No. Lionceau-Pierce), glass in good condition, missing chip to top right corner, stopper appears to be lodged, rubbing to gilt patina to each corner, 3-3/4" h. This model is the only flacon designed for Parfums Lionceau and was also referred to as Diamont. Lionceau provided 13 available scents for this model, including Parfum pour Blondes and Poème Araba. **$2,375**

Courtesy of Heritage Auctions, ha.com

Vintage Lalique signed perfume bottle................**$65**

Courtesy of Omega Auction Corp., www.omegaauctioncorp.com

Lalique Le Baiser perfume bottle, sealed, signed on bottom, 4-1/2" h. **$215**

Courtesy of Capo Auction, www.capoauctionnyc.com

Two Lalique "Ambre D'Orsay" perfume bottles, black glass, France (des. 1911 M p. 933, no. 1), molded LALIQUE AMBRE D'ORSAY, etched 629 and 92, one stopper etched 92; bottle 629: stopper stuck, chips to all corners, flecks and chip to base; bottle 92: chips and flecks to stopper and bottle; 5-1/4" x 1-1/2" ea. **$832**

Courtesy of Rago Arts and Antiques, www.ragoarts.com

Pair of Jacob Petit porcelain perfume bottles, late 19th century, pseudo JP mark, missing piece to one lid, 17-1/2" h. **$625**

Courtesy of Heritage Auctions, ha.com

Steuben jade glass fluted perfume bottle, circa 1903-1930, stenciled STEUBEN with fleur-de-lis, fleabites to base of stopper, light scuffing to underside of bottle, very good condition, 3-3/4" h...................... **$81**

Courtesy of Heritage Auctions, ha.com

Czech cut crystal perfume bottle, excellent-plus condition, no wear or damage, 9-1/2" h....... **$200-$400**

Courtesy of Morphy Auctions, morphyauctions.com

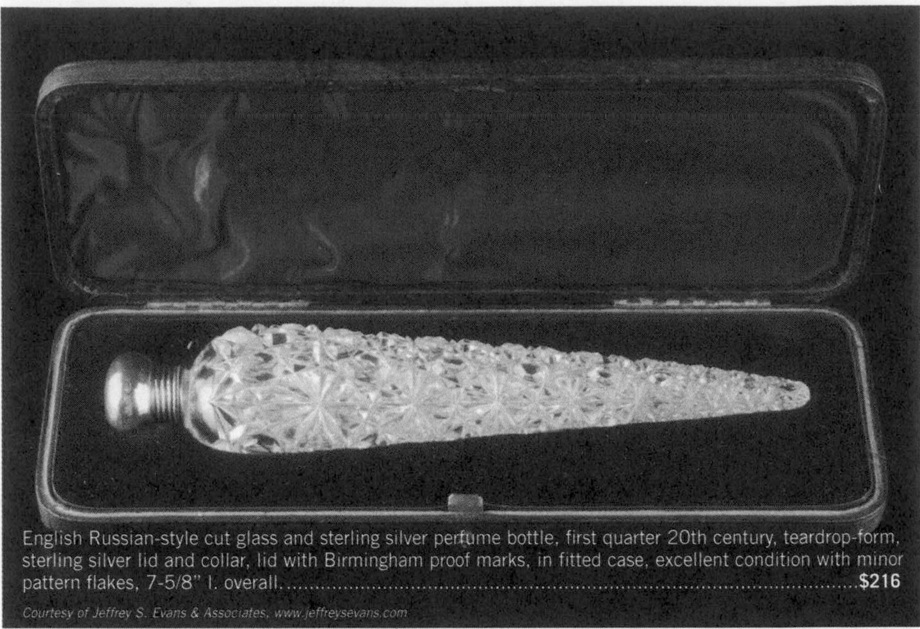

English Russian-style cut glass and sterling silver perfume bottle, first quarter 20th century, teardrop-form, sterling silver lid and collar, lid with Birmingham proof marks, in fitted case, excellent condition with minor pattern flakes, 7-5/8" l. overall.......... **$216**

Courtesy of Jeffrey S. Evans & Associates, www.jeffreysevans.com

Czech crystal perfume bottle with stopper in nude female form, good condition, 8" h. x 6-1/2" w.. **$308**

Courtesy of DuMouchelles, dumouchelles.com

Vigny Golliwogg French perfume bottle and box, circa 1925, original box with some warping and no lid, bottle with original labels to front and underside, very good condition, 6-1/8" h. **$425**

Courtesy of Heritage Auctions, ha.com

French figural walnut with brass miniature sewing kit and perfume bottle, mid-19th century, natural finish, hinged cover with white silk lining, seven compartments within engraved brass plate, each fitted with gilded implement: bodkin, cut ruby perfume bottle with hinged cover, funnel, needle case, scissors, stiletto, and thimble, very good condition overall, implements with expected wear to gilding, does not close completely, bottom lacks closure snap, 1-7/8" h. x 2-1/8" x 1-1/2"..........**$840**

Courtesy of Jeffrey S. Evans & Associates, www.jeffreysevans.com

French D'artgental cameo perfume/scent bottle, late 19th/early 20th century, ruby to yellow/green (uranium) and shaded ruby ground, sterling cap with pressed hallmark with "L" and "B" separated by bottle, cap also pressed "Argent/COTY/Paris," 6-1/4" h. overall....................**$330**

Courtesy of Jeffrey S. Evans & Associates, www.jeffreysevans.com

Two drugstore perfume bottles, one marked Cologne and the other marked White Rose, with etched words and patterns, White Rose with significant cracks from neck into jar, Cologne in excellent condition, 16" and 18" h......................................**$155**

Courtesy of Rich Penn Auctions, www.richpennauctions.com

PETROLIANA

GASOLINE- AND OIL-RELATED collectibles are called petroliana. The category is dominated by signs, but it also includes posters, cans, premiums, lights, and service station items. Pieces are collected for display and a premium is placed on eye appeal and condition.

As with all advertising items, factors such as brand name, intricacy of design, color, age, condition, and rarity drastically affect value. Signs enjoying the hottest demand are those measuring 30 to 42 inches, in near mint condition, and with interesting graphics and bright colors.

Reproductions, fantasy pieces, and fakes have plagued petroliana collectors for decades. The relatively recent boon in the category has ushered in a new and diverse tidal wave of merchandise designed for fast profit, particularly porcelain signs. Brands such as Sinclair, Indian, Oilzum, and Mobilgas are actively sold on websites and at flea markets across the nation. These mass-produced signs are getting increasingly more difficult to distinguish from authentic, vintage survivors of the early 20th century.

The only way to avoid reproductions is experience: making mistakes and learning from them; talking with other collectors and dealers; finding reputable resources (including books and websites), and learning to invest wisely, buying the best examples you can afford.

Marks can be deceiving, paper labels and tags are often missing, and those that remain may be spurious. Adding to the confusion are "fantasy" pieces that are often made more for visual impact than deception. There is another important factor to consider. A contemporary maker may create a "reproduction" sign or gas globe in tribute of the original, and sell it for what it is: a legitimate copy. Many of these are dated and signed by the artist or manufacturer, and these legitimate copies are highly collectible today. Such items are not intended to be frauds.

But a contemporary piece may pass through many hands between the time it leaves the maker and wind up in a collection. When profit is the only motive of a reseller, details about origin, ownership, and age can become a slippery slope of guesses, attribution, and – unfortunately – fabrication.

A FEW TIPS TO KEEP IN MIND WHEN PURCHASING PETROLIANA SIGNS:

1. No two porcelain signs are ever truly identical. The original process used to make them was imperfect to begin with – each color layer of enamel was added and baked on in a special kiln at temperatures specific to each

Sinclair Productos Gasolina with rooster image DSP die-cut sign, in original mounting frame, marked made in U.S.A., very good condition, small chips in fields, 58" x 52". **$22,836**

Courtesy of Morphy Auctions, morphyauctions.com

color. It's entirely natural that imperfections would occur, and authenticators now rely on these variations in much the same way as the FBI uses fingerprints.

2. Original signs are made of steel, not aluminum. A magnet will be attracted to an authentic sign.

3. Most circular signs are 28, 30, 42, or 48 inches in diameter. Look for telltale signs of use: scratches and deep chips around hang holes, even scratches around the perimeter from frames, rust on exposed steel in place of missing enamel.

For more information about petroliana, consult *Warman's Gas Station Collectibles* by Mark Moran. For more advice on how to intelligently buy petroliana signs, check out *Picker's Pocket Guide - Signs: How to Pick Antiques Like a Pro.*

Vintage Mobil Gas service station jacket and hat, very good condition, some cracking and minor soiling to hat and staining to jacket. .... **$100-$200**

Courtesy of Morphy Auctions, morphyauctions.com

Ajax Tires tin flange sign, marked American Art Works, Coshocton, Ohio, good to very good condition, wear and spots in field and reverse with rust spots, 24" h. x 18" w. **$3,050**

Courtesy of Morphy Auctions, morphyauctions.com

McClure's Magazine Automobile Year Book, New York: Automobile Department of *McClure's Magazine*, The McClure Publications, Inc., 1916. First edition, hardcover, bound in printed paper-covered boards, alphabetical index, index of trade names and sections on care of a car, kinks for car converts, gasoline passenger vehicles, American speedway statistics, table of important sizes of pneumatic tires, inflation table for pneumatic tires, and illustrations of various models of automobiles; light internal wear, light soiling to covers. **$156**

Courtesy of National Book Auctions, www.nationalbookauctions.com

Wayne Model 80 gas pump and globe, floor model pump outfitted with Mobilgas signs and red Mobil Pegasus logo on translucent glass globe, circa 1952, very good condition, chips and scratches to unrestored red paint job, pump 61" h. x 27" w. x 16" d... **$1,830**

Courtesy of Morphy Auctions, morphyauctions.com

Double-sided vintage gasoline pump price sign, enamel on metal, 44" h. x 33-1/2" w... **$187**

Courtesy of Material Culture, www.materialculture.com

Marathon Motor oil one-gallon metal can, early 20th century, all colors good except black on display side near logo, edge wear and scratches, 15" h.**$6,710**

Courtesy of Morphy Auctions, morphyauctions.com

Shell Oil metal can with ribbed sides and welded construction, original lid, marked "Shell Oil", empty, good condition, 21-1/4" h. x 10-3/4" dia. **$71**

Courtesy of North American Auction Co., www.northamericanauctioncompany.com

Standard Oil Matchless Grease 25-pound square metal can, early 20th century, with original lid, empty, good condition, scratches in field. **$518**

Courtesy of Morphy Auctions, morphyauctions.com

Electronic automaton of Union 76 gas station attendant, 20th century, figure turns her head and moves hands up and down, fair condition, 43" h. **$488**

Courtesy of Morphy Auctions, morphyauctions.com

Marx gasoline service station with two pumps, good lithography, excellent condition, 6" w. **$194**

Courtesy of American Antique Auction, www.americanantiqueauctions.net

Tipp & Co. gas station display on metal base with electric display, early 20th century, with entrance and exit signs, two pumps, motor oil cabinet fixture, and two sets of two bulbs to serve as globes on pumps, 5-3/4" h. x 9-2/3" w. x 3-1/3" d. **$1,725**

Courtesy of Ladenburger Spielzeugauktion GMBH, www3.spielzeugauktion.de

Conoco pump island oil display rack with two porcelain die-cut signs on marquee, professionally restored, excellent condition, 42" h. x 13" d. **$1,020**

Courtesy of Rich Penn Auctions, www.richpennauctions.com

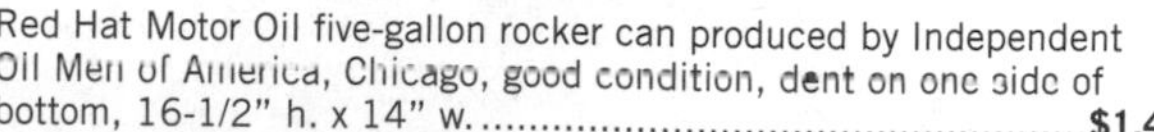

Red Hat Motor Oil five-gallon rocker can produced by Independent Oil Men of America, Chicago, good condition, dent on one side of bottom, 16-1/2" h. x 14" w. **$1,440**

Courtesy of Rich Penn Auctions, www.richpennauctions.com

top lot

U.S. Tires advertising clock titled "Tire-ly Satisfied" produced by William L. Gilbert Clock Co., circa 1912, graphics of early racecar driver with tire surrounding him, clock of lithographed wood, pendulum of lithographed tin, clock in working order and accompanied by original key, all original untouched graphics and pendulum, stamped with marker's mark, excellent condition, light scrapes and mild ware, 18" x 28-1/2". $178,608

COURTESY OF MORPHY AUCTIONS, MORPHYAUCTIONS.COM

Various vintage gas station premiums/giveaways, Mobil Pegasus plate topper, Exxon mug, Amoco radio patches, and tire gauge, among other items, very good to excellent condition. **$180**

Courtesy of Milestone Auctions, www.milestoneauctions.com

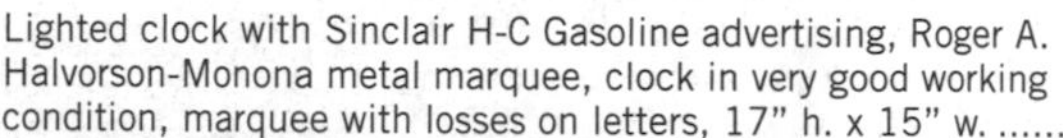

Lighted clock with Sinclair H-C Gasoline advertising, Roger A. Halvorson-Monona metal marquee, clock in very good working condition, marquee with losses on letters, 17" h. x 15" w. **$840**

Courtesy of Rich Penn Auctions, www.richpennauctions.com

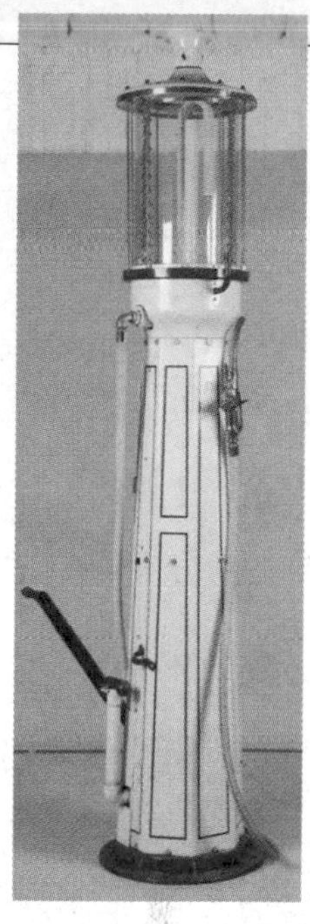

Guaranteed (Fry) Model #71 10-gallon visible gas pump, restored, with new hose, brass nozzle and reproduced Mobil globe, good paint on skins, rough casting, cylinder good, 105" h. **$4,270**

Courtesy of Morphy Auctions, morphyauctions.com

Texaco Gasoline globe with star logo and chimney cab, original paint, mid-20th century, excellent condition, minor flea bites on base, 18" h.. **$23,180**

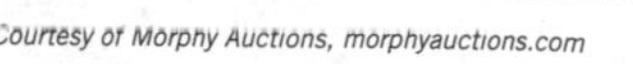

Courtesy of Morphy Auctions, morphyauctions.com

Carved and hand-painted wooden folk art whirligig of gas station attendant filling up early model automobile, 19-1/2" l. **$270**

Courtesy of Stanton Auctions, www.stantonauctions.com

top lot

Musgo Gasoline / Michigan's Mile Maker sign with graphic of Native American Indian chief in full headdress, in original hanging ring, very good condition, small chip at headband and quarter-size chip on reverse, 48" dia. $200,934

COURTESY OF MORPHY AUCTIONS, MORPHYAUCTIONS.COM

Early wooden pump jockey sign, believed to be from a Shell service station, shows station attendant with pump in hand, good condition, 47" w. x 53" h. **$387**

Courtesy of North American Auction Co., www.northamericanauctioncompany.com

Set of eight one-quart glass motor oil bottles with screw-on metal spouts, four with caps, in metal wire carrier with low handle, first half of 20th century, very good condition with light wear and minor rusting on spouts, bottles 14-1/2" h., carrier 9" h. x 18" w. **$300**

Courtesy of Jeffrey S. Evans & Associates, www.jeffreysevans.com

POSTCARDS

IN THE FIRST half of the 20th century, postcards were cheap, often one cent and rarely more than five cents on the racks. Worldwide exchanges were common, making it possible to gain huge variety without being rich.

Those days are gone forever, but collectors today are just as avid about their acquisitions. What postcards are bestsellers today? The people most likely to have the pulse of the hobby are dealers who offer thousands of cards to the public every year.

Ron Millard, longtime owner of Cherryland Auctions, and Mary L. Martin, known for running the largest store in the country devoted exclusively to postcards, have offered some insights into the current state of the market. Both dealers have taken a son into their business, a sure sign of the confidence they have in the future of postcard collecting.

Real photo postcards of the early 1900s are highly rated by both dealers. Martin, who sells at shows as well as through her store, reported that interest in rare real photos is "increasing faster than they can be bought."

Millard, whose Cherryland Auctions features 1,800 lots closing every five weeks, indicated that real photos seem to be "holding steady with prices actually rising among the lower-end real photos as some people shy from paying the huge prices they have been bringing. Children with toys and dolls have been increasing and also unidentified but interesting U.S. views."

Cherryland bidders have also been focused on "advertising cards, high-end art cards, Halloween, early political and baseball postcards." Movie stars, other famous people and transportation, especially autos and zeppelins, also do very well. Lower-priced cards with great potential for rising in value include linen restaurant advertising, "middle range" holidays, and World War I propaganda.

Martin sees hometown views as the most popular category, with real photo social history, dressed animals, and Halloween also in high demand. "We see a lot of interest in military right now, and I don't believe it has really peaked yet," she said. Social history from the 1950s and 1960s also does well.

Will anyone want your postcards when you're ready to sell? It's a valid question, and our two experts have good advice for anyone with a sizable accumulation, say 500 or more postcards.

Auctions are one good option, both for direct purchases and consignments. Millard is always looking

Rare Houdini The Famous Jail Breaker Happy New Year postcard, New York, 1907, color lithographic pictorial of Houdini in chains with Beatrice in corner, sentiment in English and German, undivided back, postmarked from Chicago to London, addressed to Mr. G. Bush, Newgate Prison guard who had befriended Houdini, corners softened, creases, old vertical fold, 5" x 3". **$3,690**

Courtesy of Potter & Potter Auctions, www.potterauctions.com

for quality postcards to offer collectors worldwide. His firm can handle collections of any size from small specialized to giant accumulations, and is willing to travel for large consignments. Active buying is a necessity for dealers to keep their customers supplied, which should reassure collectors that their cards will have a ready market. Contact Millard at CherrylandAuctions@charter.net or www.Cherrylandauctions.com.

Martin suggested that collectors go back to some of the dealers who sold them cards when they're ready to sell. Her firm is always willing to buy back good quality cards. She also sees reputable auction houses as a good avenue. "They should never be sold as a very large group if they can be broken down into different subject matter or topics," she said.

Both experts agree there's an active demand for quality collections. That would exclude postcards in poor condition, a caution for collectors expanding their holdings. Look for the best and pass up damaged and dirty cards.

Billions of postcards were produced in the last century on practically every topic imaginable. As collections become more specialized, new subjects are sure to attract attention. Many outstanding collections were put together with moderate expense by people who were among the first to recognize the value of a new collecting area.

As an example of an area yet to be fully explored, the photographers who made postcards possible haven't been widely collected in their own right. Many were anonymous, but some, like Bob Petley, famous for Western views as well as comic humor, have attracted collectors' attention. The Tucson Post Card Exchange Club has made a specialty of gathering and listing the output of its "favorite son." No doubt there are fresh, new specialties just waiting to be discovered.

Postcard collectors love history, appreciate fine art, enjoy humor, and above all, are imaginative. There's every indication that today's favorite topics will be joined by new and exciting ones in the future.

— *Barbara Andrews*

Jules Verne-signed postcard, 1826, with floral color lithograph illustrated borders, short message in French with signature, very good condition, small creases at corners, chip at edge, used. **$861**

Courtesy of PBA Galleries, www.pbagalleries.com

Robert Robinson Series baseball player postcards, three postcards of baseball players with artwork by Robinson, very good condition, corner bumping throughout, each 5-1/2" x 3-1/2". **$60**

Courtesy of Morphy Auctions, morphyauctions.com

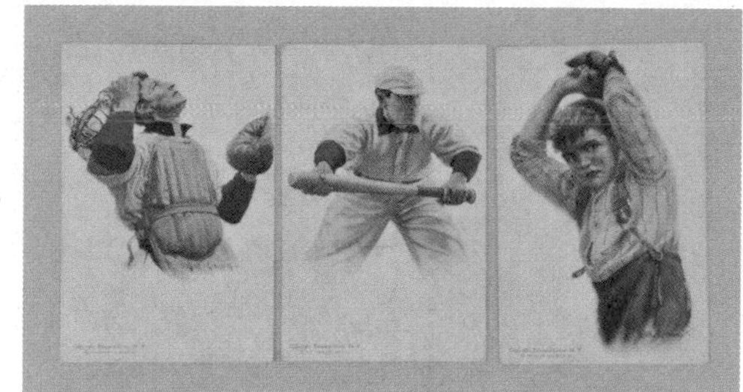

Winsch-Schmucker Halloween postcard, dated 1912, girl in tree with owls, very good-plus condition, minor corner bumping, 6" x 4-3/8". **$90**

Courtesy of Morphy Auctions, morphyauctions.com

1910 Coca-Cola Motor Girl postcard, professionally framed behind glass, very good condition, stain on left of girl, slightly rounded corners, 12" x 10". **$153**

Courtesy of Morphy Auctions, morphyauctions.com

Four Santa in Silk Suit postcards, very good condition, each 5-1/2" x 3-1/2". **$61**

Courtesy of Morphy Auctions, morphyauctions.com

Rare Winsch-Schmucker Halloween postcard, unsigned, dated 1913, very good-plus condition, minor corner bumping, 6" x 4-3/8". **$180**

Courtesy of Morphy Auctions, morphyauctions.com

Framed color postcard of inside of Chas. A. Grove's & Sons Liquor Store, Lancaster, Pennsylvania, advertisement says, " Fine Wines, Liquors, Cordials," very good condition. **$133**

Courtesy of Conestoga Auction Co., www.conestogaauction.com

1928 Shonen Kulubs Babe Ruth postcard, Japanese, rare........... **$272**

Courtesy of Saco River Auction Co., www.sacoriverauction.com

Portrait postcard of Chung Ling Soo, William E. Robinson, British, circa 1912, half-length portrait of magician, his signature printed in English, mock Chinese down right margin, divided back, unused, very good condition, 3-1/2" x 5-1/2"............................... **$246**

Courtesy of Potter & Potter, www.potterauctions.com

"Safety" photograph postcard from 1910 of football player and woman wearing vintage nose guard, handwriting on verso, 3-1/2" x 5-1/2"........... **$38**

Courtesy of Heritage Auctions, ha.com

Two Blackwell's Genuine Bull Durham tobacco postcards, very good condition, minor wear, one with heavier crease, blank backs with some staining, each 6-1/4" x 3-1/2"......................... **$60**

Courtesy of Morphy Auctions, morphyauctions.com

Two postcards of Jack Dempsey and Max Baer matted together, 1959, one with James Montgomery Flagg illustration of Jack Dempsey fighting Jess Willard in 1919, when Dempsey became the world champion; card below with hand-written message from boxing great Max Baer to George Stout, "I am with your pal Dempsey" with signatures of both Dempsey and Baer, excellent condition, no certificate of authenticity, mat 9-1/2" x 11-3/4". **$84**

Courtesy of Heritage Auctions, ha.com

Six military-related articles of correspondence to Bobby Murcer, including postcard from Murcer to his parents, dated 1964 (shown), two items from Oklahoma Senate, and another item from Oklahoma House of Representatives, with letter of provenance from Murcer family. **$46**

Courtesy of Heritage Auctions, ha.com

Beagles postcard of boxing great Jack Johnson, 1919, excellent condition, 3-1/2" x 5-1/2"...... **$239**

Courtesy of Heritage Auctions, ha.com

POSTERS

A POSTER IS a large, usually printed placard, bill, or announcement, often illustrated, that is posted to advertise or publicize something. It can also be an artistic work, often a reproduction of an original painting or photograph, printed on a large sheet of paper.

Vintage posters are usually between 20 and 50 years old and must be original and not copies or newer reproductions.

The value of a vintage poster is determined by condition, popularity of the subject matter, rarity, artistic rendering, and the message it conveys.

"The Cisco Kid," numbered 54 of 341, very good condition, moderate fold lines with wrinkles and some areas of staining, framed 29-1/2" x 17-1/2"....... **$92**

Courtesy of Morphy Auctions, morphyauctions.com

"Lady Luck," 1946, numbered 46 of 669, very good condition, wrinkles, fold lines, and rubs throughout, framed 29-1/2" x 17-1/2"............................... **$61**

Courtesy of Morphy Auctions, morphyauctions.com

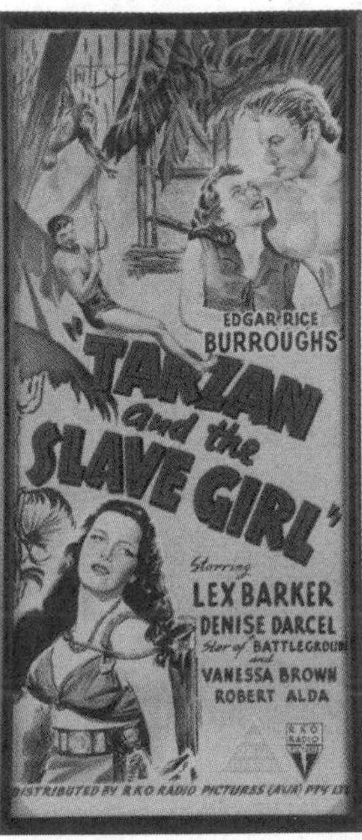

"Tarzan and the Slave Girl," strong colors, very good condition with mild wear, excellent condition, framed 14" x 31-1/4".................... **$244**

Courtesy of Morphy Auctions, morphyauctions.com

MOVIE POSTERS

"Flash Gordon's Trip to Mars," Chapter 6, "Tree-Men of Mars," (Universal, 1938), lobby card, serial, starring Buster Crabbe, Jean Rogers, Charles Middleton, Frank Shannon, Beatrice Roberts, Donald Kerr, Richard Alexander, C. Montague Shaw, Wheeler Oakman, Kenne Duncan, Warner Richmond, Jack Mulhall, Lane Chandler, Anthony Warde, Ben Lewis, Kane Richmond, Earl Askam, Glenn Strange, and Jack "Tiny" Lipson, directed by Ford Beebe, Robert F. Hill, and Frederick Stephani, fine/very fine condition, unrestored with signs of use, 11" x 14". **$239**

Courtesy of Heritage Auctions, ha.com

"It Happened in Flatbush," sight 40-1/2" h. x 27" w., framed 47-1/2" h. x 34" w. **$246**

Courtesy of Kaminski Auctions, www.kaminskiauctions.com

"Conflict" (Warner Brothers, 1945), insert, film noir, starring Humphrey Bogart, Alexis Smith, Sydney Greenstreet, Charles Drake, Rose Hobart, Grant Mitchell, Ann Shoemaker, Patrick O'Moore, Edwin Stanley, and James Flavin, directed by Curtis Bernhardt, fine/very fine condition, unrestored with signs of use, paper and cellophane tape on verso, folded, 14" x 36". ... **$239**

Courtesy of Heritage Auctions, ha.com

◄ "Star Wars" (20th Century Fox, 1977), one sheet, Style A, starring Mark Hamill, Harrison Ford, Carrie Fisher, Alec Guinness, Peter Cushing, Anthony Daniels, Kenny Baker, Peter Mayhew, David Prowse, and James Earl Jones, directed by George Lucas, very fine-minus condition on linen, partially restored, light edge and fold wear, minor creases, small tears, minor pen mark in lower border, 27" x 40-1/2." **$478**

Courtesy of Heritage Auctions, ha.com

▲ "The Empire Strikes Back" (20th Century Fox, 1980), one sheet, Style B, starring Mark Hamill, Harrison Ford, Carrie Fisher, Billy Dee Williams, Anthony Daniels, David Prowse, Frank Oz, Alec Guinness, and James Earl Jones, directed by Irvin Kershner, artwork by Tom Jung, fine-plus condition, folded, unrestored with good color and overall presentable appearance, tears, slight paper loss and lifts, creases, cellophane tape in borders, smudges, minor stains, edge and fold wear, and/or some fold separation, 27" x 41". **$96**

Courtesy of Heritage Auctions, ha.com

◄ "Bathing Beauty" (MGM, 1944), one sheet, Style C, starring Red Skelton, Esther Williams, Basil Rathbone, Bill Goodwin, Harry James and His Music Makers, and Xavier Cugat Orchestra, directed by George Sidney, fine-plus condition on linen, partially restored with overall presentable appearance, slight edge and fold wear, minor fold separations, creases, tears, pinholes, light surface scuffs, and chips in borders, post-restoration stains, small tears, and smudges, 27" x 41"............. **$179**

Courtesy of Heritage Auctions, ha.com

◀ "To Kill a Mockingbird" (Universal, 1963), one sheet, starring Gregory Peck, Mary Badham, Phillip Alford, Robert Duvall, John Megna, Frank Overton, Brock Peters, Estelle Evans, and Paul Fix, directed by Robert Mulligan, fine/very fine condition, folded, unrestored with signs of use, light edge or fold wear, slight fold separations, creases and corner bends, pinholes, or minor smudges, 8" crease in upper right portion of poster, faint bleed-through from ink stamp on verso, 27" x 41"... **$332**

Courtesy of Heritage Auctions, ha.com

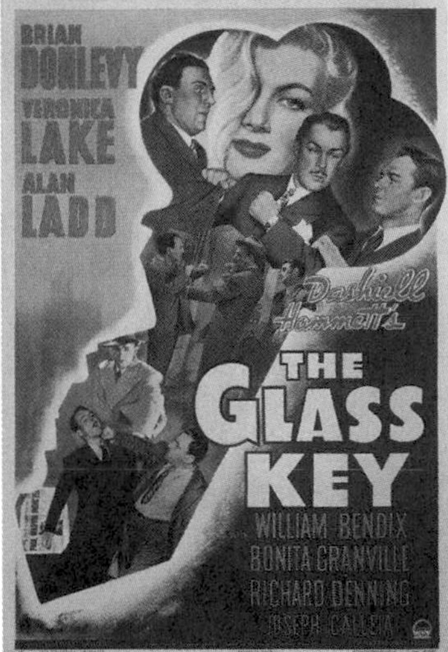

▲ "The Glass Key" (Paramount, 1942), one sheet, starring Veronica Lake and Alan Ladd, based on novel by Dashiell Hammett, desirable and scarce film noir poster, linen backed, bright colors, good graphics, minimal touch-up to fold lines, 27" x 41".......................... **$4,182**

Courtesy of Potter & Potter Auctions, www.potterauctions.com

◀ "The Littlest Rebel" (20th Century Fox, circa 1935), starring Shirley Temple, rare poster created for Rivola West Point theater's "First Showing in N.E. Nebraska / 4 Days Starts / Wed. Jan. 15," marked "Copyright MCMXXXV 20th Century Fox," excellent condition, few spots, professionally matted under glass in gold frame, 30-1/2" x 37".. **$732**

Courtesy of Morphy Auctions, morphyauctions.com

MISCELLANEOUS POSTERS

Mane Katz retrospective exhibition poster, offset lithograph, 1965, framed, 22-1/2" x 22" overall... **$49**

Courtesy of Capo Auction, www.capoauctionnyc.com

Marc Chagall, "Carmen" Metropolitan Opera lithograph, 1966, framed, sight 38-1/2" x 25". **$369**

Courtesy of Capo Auction, www.capoauctionnyc.com

After Marc Chagall (Russian/French, 1887-1985), "Chagall, Galerie Maeght, Juin-Juillet 1962," color lithograph, signed in ink lower right, framed, 34-1/4" h. x 26-1/4" w. overall...................... **$153**

Courtesy of Clars Auction Gallery, www.clars.com

▶ Milton Glaser (American, b. 1924), "Dylan," 1966, color lithograph, printed for Bob Dylan record album as folded insert, framed, 33" h. x 23" w. overall... **$122**

Courtesy of Clars Auction Gallery, www.clars.com

Large Coca-Cola poster, 1942, near mint condition, strong color, slight edge wear, 50-1/4" x 29-3/4"............................. **$3,660**

Courtesy of Morphy Auctions, morphyauctions.com

"Sitting Bull Combination," Strobridge Litho Co., Native American woman dressed in full celebratory outfit, good to very good condition, moderate restoration and repair throughout, mild staining, some areas of discoloration, framed 31" x 21". **$3,965**

Courtesy of Morphy Auctions, morphyauctions.com

1957 Elvis Presley concert poster, excellent condition with some toning, 21-1/2" x 14"..... **$336**

Courtesy of Morphy Auctions, morphyauctions.com

Robert Indiana serigraph, "Love / Indiana / Stable May 66," 32" x 23-3/4". **$242**

Courtesy of William J. Jenack Estate Appraisers & Auctioneers, www.jenack.com

Graficas Valencia Art Deco travel poster, Italian, sight 39" h. x 27" w., framed 54" h. x 42" w. **$800**

Courtesy of Kaminski Auctions, www.kaminskiauctions.com

"World's Champion Rodeo" lithograph poster, early 1900s, Milwaukee Riverside Print Co., Native American war dance and equestrian football, shrink-wrapped on foam board, strong unfaded colors, near mint condition with slight scuffs, 22-3/4" x 58". **$305**

Courtesy of Morphy Auctions, morphyauctions.com

Rare "Free Huey / Black Panther, Peace & Freedom/ Newton / Congress 7th CD / Seale / State Assembly," 1960s, designed by Lisa Lyons, graphic designer for Black Panther Party, unframed, loose, minor edge stains, 17-1/2" x 23". **$1,680**

Courtesy of Thomaston Place Auction Galleries, www.thomastonauction.com

"Federal Art in Cleveland / 1933-1943 / Cleveland Public Library / September 16-November 1," good condition, staining lower right edge, 21-1/8" x 14". **$42**

Courtesy of Rachel Davis Fine Arts, www.racheldavisfinearts.com

PRIMITIVES

IF YOU ASK THREE COLLECTORS (or dealers) of primitives to define the term, you will most certainly get three different answers. This category has long appeared under the description of folk art, and even the legendary Alice Winchester, author, former editor of the magazine *Antiques*, and lifelong student of antiques, did her best to delineate the difference between primitives and folk art in her influential book *The Flowering of American Folk Art*. She describes these objects as thus: "No single term, such as primitive, pioneer, naïve, natural, provincial, self-taught, amateur, is a satisfactory label for the work presented as folk art."

Winchester, however, does point out that all primitives share some common features that set them apart from folk art: Primitives are often independent from cosmopolitan influence and academic training, which often results in simple and unpretentious objects from typically "rural than urban places and from craft rather than fine-art traditions."

Utility is the chief aesthetic of primitive antiques. If one was capable enough to nail four boards together you had a box, which could be used as a wall shelf or the apron of a table or bench. A few more boards (perhaps oak, chestnut, or No. 10 white pine - the wood most often used to build barns) and you could create a cupboard, pie safe, sugar chest, or workbench. Primitives did not require much talent, just a need and the right tools. But those simple truths despoil the simple beauty collectors see in these well-used objects: years of patina only handling may build, scratch marks from thousands of dinners served that only love could provide, ingenuity that only necessity could supply.

A wonderful selection of primitive bowls, often used to allow bread dough to rise or even make coleslaw, tool boxes in original paint, and furnishings are shown for sale in the booth of Michigan country/primitives dealer Beth Pulsipher. She sells online and at specialty shows in Michigan, Ohio, and Illinois, which often attract between 1,000 to 1,500 customers.

Courtesy of Beth Pulsipher

These simple, homegrown items are often the only remnants of the families who worked America's soil and forged her frontier. Not even their portraits are as valued as their primitive bowls, stools, cupboards, spoons, and chairs.

"For some, primitives are ugly and uninteresting," said country/primitive dealer Beth Pulsipher, who sells at specialty shows in Michigan, Ohio, and Illinois [beth.pulsipher@gmail.com]. "But for those who treasure history and practical home-based old antiques, owning primitives fills that need for connecting to an earlier country lifestyle."

Primitives shows have evolved over time from multiday events with hundreds of dealers to five- or six-hour shopping extravaganzas with 40 to 60 hand-selected dealers of the utmost quality. "These shows have very strong followings, bringing in 1,000-1,500 customers," she said. "These short-and-sweet shows are a major change from the traditional multiday general line antiques shows and are quite successful." Pulsipher has also sold country and primitive collectibles through innovative Facebook pages such as "1803 Sugarhouse Auctions" and "Authentic American Folk Art (AAFA)." The pages have assembled more than 9,500 members. Sellers post images of collectibles, and buyers place offers in the comment section below.

Auction results also show strong collector interest, especially in finishes that age well and in original paint – a touch of artistic flair or ingenuity boosts the hammer price considerably. An important 18th century painted pine lantern with oak hoop handle and leather-hinged door, which opens to a crimped tin candlestick under a pierced tin ventilation cover, sold for $8,050 at the auction of Robert Roger's collection of art and antiques held by John McInnis Auctioneers in early 2015. It was an untouched attic find.

"Both primitives and folk art are in a strong market right now," Pulsipher said. "The best pieces are heavily competed for at auction, and there are more primitives dealer specialists than ever. Good quality brings top dollars, and one-of-a-kind 'best' pieces are bringing record prices.

"Still, a collector can find plenty of good primitive antiques in both furniture and in smaller items, with the best shopping being found with specialty primitives dealers and at specialty primitives antiques shows," she said.

Dealers Jim Sheffield, who sell primitives at more than 30 nationwide antiques shows every year with his wife, Sandra, under the name Cabin on the Hill, agreed that small items are brisk sellers. He and Sandra specialize in pantry boxes, crocks, and large bowls retaining original paint.

"Bowls are a big seller," Jim said. "The more original paint the better. They really fit with any décor and just have a warm feel about them. But even those have been hit by reproductions. It's best to always buy from a dealer who sells only originals. The new bowls won't keep values whereas original paint will likely go up in value."

– *Eric Bradley*

Lantern, century 18th century, pine, pierced tin, oak loop handle, leather-hinged door with diamond pane, crimped tin candlestick, original tallow candle, three additional rectangular panes, pierced tin ventilation cover, 16" h. **$8,050**

John McInnis Auctioneers, www.mcinnisauctions.com

Wooden bowl, 6-1/2" h. x 21-1/2" dia. **$316**

Courtesy of Nadeau's Auction Gallery, www.nadeausauction.com

Coffeepot in lighthouse form, signed H. B. Ward, 12" h. **$236**

Courtesy of Nadeau's Auction Gallery, www.nadeausauction.com

General store oak footed keg barrel with brass cap, 12" w. x 25" l., 14" dia. **$175**

Courtesy of Flannery's Estate Services, www.flannerysestateservices.com

▲ Nantucket basket with swing handle and wood base, early 20th century, 9-1/2" dia. **$425**

Courtesy of Eldred's Auctioneers & Appraisers, www.eldreds.com

"Paymaster's" desk, circa 1820, in pine with old brown finish, iron hinges, compartmented interior, single drawer below slant lid with turned knobs, turned legs joined by stretcher base, 37" h. x 24" w. x 18-1/4" d. **$190**

Courtesy of Eldred's Auctioneers & Appraisers, www.eldreds.com

▲ A selection of green pantry boxes from the booth of Cabin on the Hill owned by Jim and Sandra Sheffield. Pantry boxes are brisk sellers but originals are getting more difficult to find.

Courtesy of Eric Bradley

INSIDE INTEL *with* JIM SHEFFIELD

Cabin on the Hill Antiques
Georgetown, Texas
jwandsn@verizon.net,
512-863-0722

WHAT'S HOT: Pantry boxes are strong sellers. "I'm always asked, 'What's a pantry box?' and I tell them, "Consider it early Tupperware." These are hard to find in good condition, but they sell well at shows.

WHAT'S NOT: Pewter has slowed down quite a bit. Good large pieces still sell well, but the market seems softer for small, simple examples.

Two 19th century bowls discovered in southeastern Massachusetts, 8-1/5" dia. and 9-3/4" dia.. **$325**

Courtesy of Eldred's Auctioneers & Appraisers, www.eldreds.com

Cabinet with five drawers, 19th century, in pine under old brown finish, one full-width drawer over four smaller drawers, all with circular wooden pulls, 22-1/2" h. x 30" w. x 10-1/2" d. **$325**

Courtesy of Eldred's Auctioneers & Appraisers, www.eldreds.com

Hanging wall box under old blue paint, late 19th century, "PSH" carved into front, lid attached with primitive tin hinges that lift open to reveal three interior compartments, 8-1/4" h. x 12-1/4" w. x 5-1/2" d.. **$400**

Courtesy of Eldred's Auctioneers & Appraisers, www.eldreds.com

Painting of eagle, first half 19th century, floral and foliate garland surrounds eagle with flowers in its beak, framed 3" h. x 4-1/4" w.................... **$425**

Courtesy of Eldred's Auctioneers & Appraisers, www.eldreds.com

Table in red-painted pine with square tapered legs, 19th century, 27-3/4" h. x 29" l. x 24" w.**$130**

Courtesy of Eldred's Auctioneers & Appraisers, www.eldreds.com

▶ Corner cupboard in walnut under brown paint, early 19th century, shaped cornice over single door with milk glass pull, three interior shelves, remnants of early wallpaper attached to back, 43-1/4" h. x 31-1/2" w. **$160**

Courtesy of Eldred's Auctioneers & Appraisers, www.eldreds.com

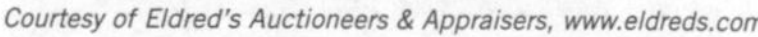

top lot!

Rare and important sugar chest in form of desk, circa 1825-1850, South Carolina, walnut with yellow pine secondary woods, slant lid opening to interior compartment over two large deep dovetailed drawers, on tall feet that are extensions of sides, skirt with carved scroll design on front and sides, light wood inlay arranged in geometric patterns, "eye" designs on case sides, lid and drawer fronts with diamond inlay at key escutcheons on drawers and lid, sliding lid supports on exterior of case sides, old probably original surface, 38" h. x 35-1/2" w. x 16" d. $36,000

COURTESY OF SLOTIN FOLK ART AUCTION, WWW.SLOTINFOLKART.COM

Two wooden bowls/troughs, 41" and 48", and round bowl, 17-1/2" dia. **$186**

Courtesy of Nadeau's Auction Gallery, www.nadeausauction.com

Chair with painted plank seat chair, circa 1820-1840.... **$18**

Courtesy of Nadeau's Auction Gallery, www.nadeausauction.com

Cobbler's bench, 14-1/2" h. x 46" l. **$117**

Courtesy of Nadeau's Auction Gallery, www.nadeausauction.com

Stepback cupboard, 72" h. x 26" w. x 15" d. **$345**

Courtesy of Nadeau's Auction Gallery, www.nadeausauction.com

Sea chest in old green paint, mid-19th century, dovetail construction, carved cleats with heart and star design, intricate sailor-made ropework becket handles, "W.S." painted on front, painted design of hearts, moons, stars and "William. Swain. of. Orleans. County. of. Barnstable. State. of. Massachusetts. 1839." on interior of lid, original strap hinges and interior till, 16-1/2 h. x 35-1/4" w. x 16-3/4" d. **$7,000**

Courtesy of Eldred's Auctioneers & Appraisers, www.eldreds.com

Stool with original paint, signed on bottom, 5" h. x. 10-1/2" l. **$82**

Courtesy of Nadeau's Auction Gallery, www.nadeausauction.com

Stool in original yellow trimmed in red paint, 6" h. x 13" l. **$120**

Courtesy of Nadeau's Auction Gallery, www.nadeausauction.com

Cupboard with grain decoration, molded frame, one door, 58-1/2" h. x 32-1/2" w. 13-1/4" d. .. **$840**

Courtesy of Nadeau's Auction Gallery, www.nadeausauction.com

▲ Blanket chest with lift top in old blue paint, 17" h. x 34" w. **$270**

Courtesy of Nadeau's Auction Gallery, www.nadeausauction.com

◀ Child's chair with heart-carved back, bootjack ends, and old red paint, 19-1/2" h. x 13" w. **$540**

Courtesy of Nadeau's Auction Gallery, www.nadeausauction.com

Cherry sugar chest, circa 1825, 34-1/2" h.... **$2,750**

Courtesy of Stevens Auction Co., www.stevensauction.com

Miniature hutch cupboard, late 19th/early 20th century, made from old cigar and other boxes, upper shelved section above slide-out cutting tray and pull-out flour bin, 21" h. x 14-1/2" w. x 10" d.. **$110**

Courtesy of Eldred's Auctioneers & Appraisers, www.eldreds.com

Brass scale with candleholder on wood base, 22" h. **$156**

Courtesy of Nadeau's Auction Gallery, www.nadeausauction.com

▶ Ladderback great chair with four slats and original rush seat on turned legs, seat 16-1/4" h. **$351**

Courtesy of Nadeau's Auction Gallery, www.nadeausauction.com

QUILTS

EACH GENERATION MADE quilts, comforters, and coverlets, all intended to be used. Many were used into oblivion and rest in quilt heaven, but for myriad reasons, some have survived. Many of them remain because they were not used but stored, often forgotten, in trunks and linen cabinets.

A quilt is made up of three layers: the top, which can be a solid piece of fabric, appliquéd, pieced, or a combination; the back, which can be another solid piece of fabric or pieced; and the batting, the center layer, which can be cotton, wool, polyester, a blend of poly and cotton, or even silk. Many vintage quilts are batted with an old blanket or even another old, worn quilt.

The fabrics are usually cotton or wool or fine fancy fabrics like silk, velvet, satin, and taffeta. The layers of a true quilt are held together by the stitching - or quilting - that goes through all three layers and is usually worked in a design or pattern that enhances the piece overall.

Quilts made from a seemingly single solid piece of fabric are known as wholecloth quilts, or if they are white, as whitework quilts. Usually such quilts are constructed from two or more pieces of the same fabric joined to make up the necessary width. They are often quilted quite elaborately, and the seams virtually disappear within the decorative stitching. Most wholecloth quilts are solid-colored, but prints were also used. Whitework quilts were often made as bridal quilts and many were kept for "best," which means that they have survived in reasonable numbers.

Wholecloth quilts were among the earliest type of quilted bedcovers made in Britain, and the colonists brought examples with them according to inventory lists that exist from colonial times. American quiltmakers used the patterns early in the nation's history, and some were carried with settlers moving west across the Appalachians.

Appliqué quilts are made from shapes cut from fabric and applied, or appliquéd, to a background, usually solid-colored on vintage quilts, to make a design. Early appliqué quilts dating back to the 18th century were often worked in a technique called broderie perse, or Persian embroidery, in which printed motifs were cut from a piece of fabric, such as costly chintz, and applied to a plain, less-expensive background cloth.

Appliqué was popular in thc 1800s, and there are thousands of examples, from exquisite, brightly colored Baltimore Album quilts made in and around Baltimore between circa 1840 and 1860, to elegant four-block quilts made later in the century. Many appliqué quilts are pictorial with floral designs the predominant motif. In the 20th century, appliqué again enjoyed an upswing, especially during the Colonial Revival period, and thousands were made from patterns or appliqué kits that were marketed and sold from 1900 through the 1950s.

Pieced or patchwork quilts are made by cutting fabric into shapes and sewing

Crazy quilt, 19th century, initialed in middle with assorted butterflies and flowers, 81" x 79". **$219**

Courtesy of Vero Beach Auction, www.verobeachauction.com

them together to make a larger piece of cloth. Patchwork became popular in the United States in the early 1800s. The patterns are usually geometric, and their effectiveness depends heavily on the contrast of not just the colors themselves, but of color value as well.

Colonial clothing was almost always made using cloth cut into squares or rectangles, but after the Revolutionary War, when fabric became more widely available, shaped garments were made, and these garments left scraps. Frugal housewives, especially among the westward-bound pioneers, began to use these cutoffs to put together blocks that could then be made into quilts. Patchwork quilts are by far the most numerous of all vintage-quilt categories, and the diversity of style, construction, and effect that can be found is a study all its own.

Dating a quilt is a tricky business unless the maker included the date on the finished item, and unfortunately for historians and collectors, few did. The value of a particular example is affected by its age, of course, and educating yourself about dating methods is invaluable. There are several aspects that can offer guidelines for establishing a date. These include fabrics, patterns, technique, borders, binding, batting, backing, quilting method, and colors and dyes.

In recent years many significant quilt collections have appeared in the halls of museums around the world, enticing both quilters and practitioners of art appreciation. One of the most noted collections to become a national exhibition in 2014 was the Pilgrim/Roy Collection. The selection of quilts included in the "Quilts and Color" exhibition, presented by the Museum of Fine Arts in Boston, was a mix of materials and designs, represented in nearly 60 distinct 19th and 20th century quilts.

For more information on quilts, see *Warman's Vintage Quilts Identification and Price Guide* by Maggi McCormick Gordon.

Patriotic red, white and blue star quilt, circa 1900s, 75" x 78"..**$1,080**

Courtesy of Copake Auction, Inc., www.copakeauction.com

Friendship/memorial Toad in a Puddle pieced quilt, Mid-Atlantic region, possibly Virginia, circa 1850; 36 11-1/2" sq. blocks with central white block with handwritten name, years of 1850, 1851, or 1852, and religious quotations, white ground with two various red print fabrics, straight line and three-petal floral hand quilting, triple-sash border on each side, white binding and backing; various names include David Bear, Miss Rachel Fitts, Miss Mary Anne Burd, Mr. Jeremia Repher, Mrs. Eliza Rush, Mr. Christopher Beard, Enoch G. Warman, Mrs. Elizabeth Melroy, Hanna Marie Curtis, Caroline M. Andrews, Mrs. Margaret Cole, Sarah E. Cole, Christopher Cole, Mrs. Anne Lanning, and Elizabeth Keyser, 81" x 83"...............**$390**

Courtesy of Jeffrey S. Evans & Associates, www.jeffreysevans.com

Crazy quilt with good luck and farming scenes with animals, 19th century, embroidered, 50" x 58"..........................**$115**

Courtesy of Vero Beach Auction, www.verobeachauction.com

Robbing Peter to Pay Paul quilt, 19th century, 88" x 100"............. **$510**

Courtesy of Copake Auction, Inc., www.copakeauction.com

Appliqué quilt with green and red floral, 19th century, 82" x 84".**$270**

Courtesy of Copake Auction, Inc., www.copakeauction.com

Pennsylvania Mennonite Flying Geese quilt, 19th century, 60" sq.............................. **$450**

Courtesy of Copake Auction, Inc., www.copakeauction.com

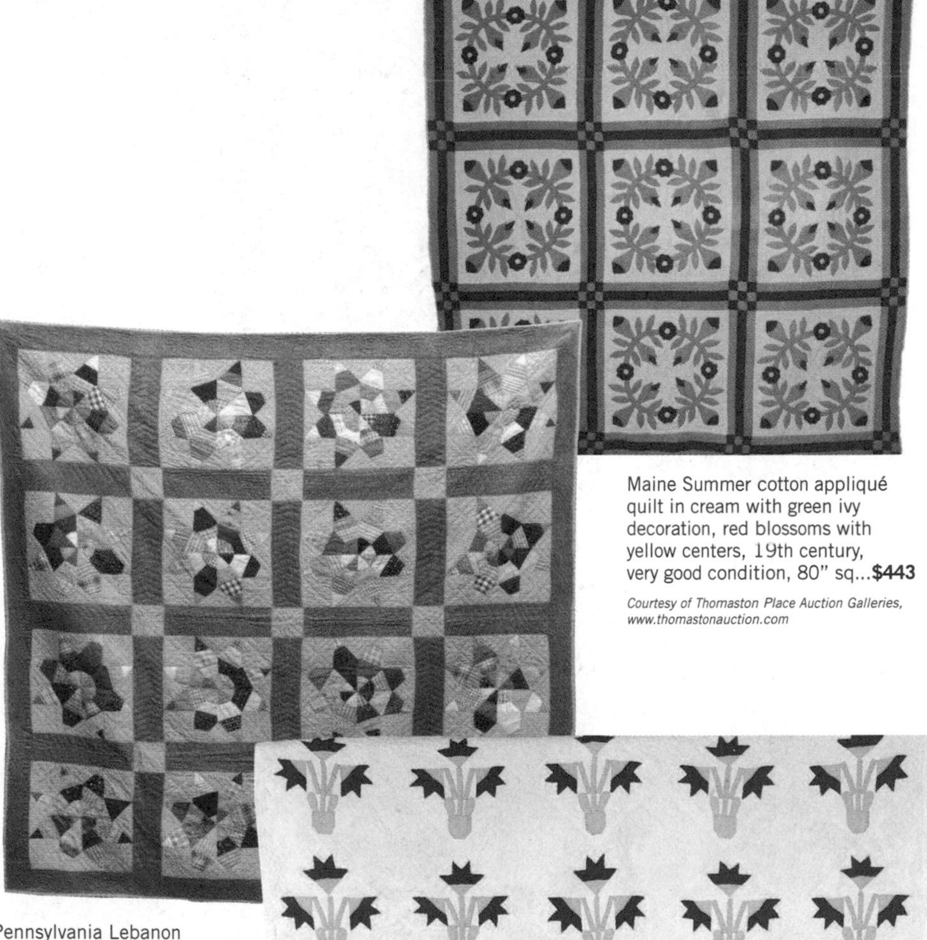

Maine Summer cotton appliqué quilt in cream with green ivy decoration, red blossoms with yellow centers, 19th century, very good condition, 80" sq...**$443**

Courtesy of Thomaston Place Auction Galleries, www.thomastonauction.com

Pennsylvania Lebanon County Stars quilt, 19th century, 80" sq. **$270**

Courtesy of Copake Auction, Inc., www.copakeauction.com

Tulip pattern appliqué quilt, hand-stitched, good condition with wear and fading, 69" x 84"....... **$182**

Courtesy of Conestoga Auction Co., www.conestogaauction.com

Log Cabin quilt, mulberry print cotton backing fabric, very good condition with minor fading, 81" x 82"................. **$272**

Courtesy of Conestoga Auction Co., www.conestogaauction.com

Blue on white arabesque appliqué quilt, hand binding, machine quilted, 92" x 70". **$123**

Courtesy of Capo Auction, www.capoauctionnyc.com

Carolina Lily quilt with trapunto, 19th century, some minor soiling, very good condition, 7' 6" sq................**$575**

Courtesy of Cottone Auctions, www.cottoneauctions.com

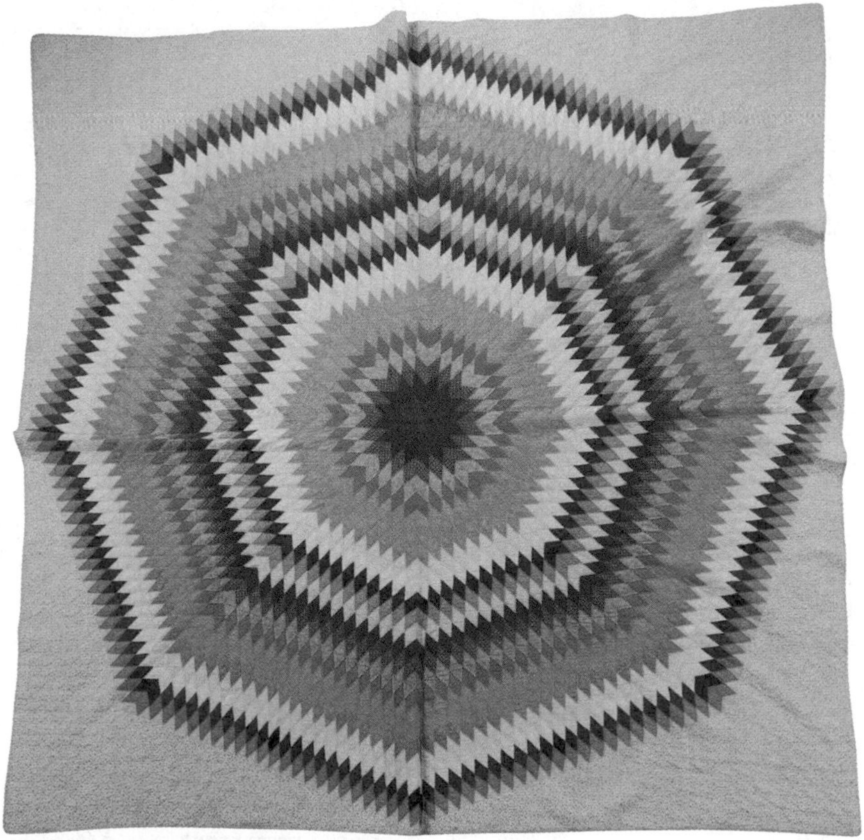

Sunburst quilt, Mid-Atlantic region, probably Virginia, fourth quarter 19th century, printed-fabric borders and backing, 94" sq. **$420**

Courtesy of Jeffrey S. Evans & Associates, www.jeffreysevans.com

Bethlehem Star quilt, 19th century, central star surrounded by others encased in Jacob's Coat framed border, good condition, 88-1/2" l. x 89" w. **$484**

Courtesy of Conestoga Auction Co., www.conestogaauction.com

RECORDS

BEFORE YOU CAN determine a record's worth, you need to grade it. When visually grading records, use a direct light, such as a 100-watt desk lamp, to clearly show all defects. If you're dealing with a record that looks worse than it sounds, play grade it. You also need to assess the condition of each sleeve, cover, label, and insert. Think like the buyer as you set your grades. Records and covers always seem to look better when you're grading them to sell to someone else than when you're on the other side of the table, inspecting a record for purchase. If in doubt, go with the lower grade. And, if you have a still sealed record, subject it to as many of these same grading standards as you can without breaking the seal.

Goldmine Grading

MINT (M): Absolutely perfect. Mint never should be used as a grade unless more than one person agrees the item meets the criteria; few dealers or collectors use this term. There is no rule for calculating mint value; that is best negotiated between buyer and seller.

- Overall Appearance: Looks as if it just came off the manufacturing line.
- Record: Glossy, unmarred surface.
- Labels: Perfectly placed and free of writing, stickers, and spindle marks.
- Cover/Sleeve: Perfectly crisp and clean. Free of stains, discoloration, stickers, ring wear, dinged corners, sleeve splits, or writing.

NEAR MINT (NM) OR MINT MINUS (M-): Most dealers and collectors use NM/M- as their highest grade, implying that no record or sleeve is ever truly perfect. It's estimated that no more than 2% to 4% of all records remaining from the 1950s and 1960s truly meet near-mint standards.

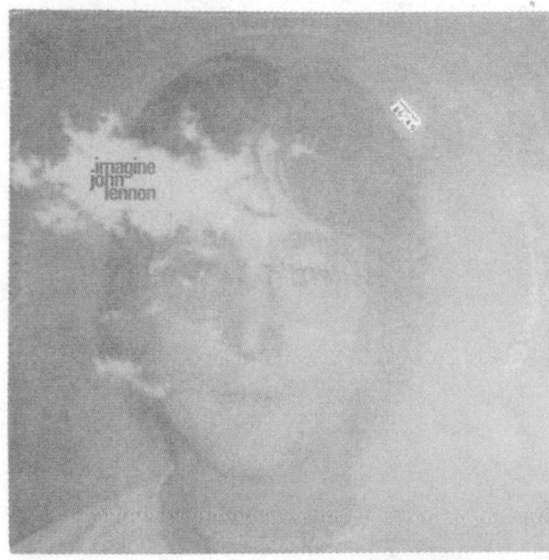

John Lennon, "Imagine" and "Live Peace In Toronto" still-sealed LPs (Apple SW 3379, 1971/Apple 3362, 1969), "Imagine" with original price sticker intact, "Live Peace" with original 13-month calendar shipped with record, album covers and media in mint condition.......... **$500**

Courtesy of Heritage Auctions, ha.com

• Overall Appearance: Looks as if it were opened for the first time. Includes all original pieces, including inner sleeve, lyric sheets, inserts, cover, and record.

• Record: Shiny surface is free of visible defects and surface noise at playback. Records can retain NM condition after many plays provided the record has been stored, used, and handled carefully.

• Labels: Properly pressed and centered on the record. Free of markings.

• Cover/Sleeve: Free of creases, ring wear, cutout markings, and seam splits. Picture sleeves look as if no record was ever housed inside. Hint: If you remove a 45 from its picture sleeve and store it separately, you will reduce the potential for damage to the sleeve.

VERY GOOD PLUS (VG+) OR EXCELLENT (EX+): Minor condition issues keep these records from a NM grade. Most collectors who want to play their records will be happy with VG+ records.

• Overall Appearance: Shows slight signs of wear.

• Record: May have slight warping, scuffs or scratches, but none that affects the sound. Expect minor signs of handling, such as marks around the center hole, light ring wear, or discoloration.

• Labels: Free of writing, stickers, or major blemishes.

• Cover/Sleeve: Outer cover may have a cutout mark. Both covers and picture sleeves may have slight creasing, minor seam wear or a split less than 1" long along the bottom.

VERY GOOD (VG): VG records have more obvious flaws than records in better condition, but still offer a fine listening experience for the price.

• Overall Appearance: Shows signs of wear and handling, including visible groove wear, audible scratches and surface noise, ring wear, and seam splits.

• Record: Record lacks its original glossy finish and may show groove wear and scratches deep enough to feel with a fingernail. Expect some surface noise and audible scratches (especially during a song's introduction and ending), but not enough to overpower the music.

• Labels: May have minor writing, tape, or a sticker.

• Cover/Sleeve: Shows obvious signs of handling and wear, including dull or discolored images; ring wear; seam splits on one or more sides; writing or a price tag; bent corners; stains; or other problems. If the record has more than two of these problems, reduce its grade.

VERY GOOD MINUS (VG–), GOOD PLUS (G+) OR GOOD (G): A true G to VG- record still plays through without skipping, so it can serve as filler until something better comes along; you can always upgrade later. At most, these records sell for 10% to 15% of the near mint value.

• Overall Appearance: Shows considerable signs of handling, including visible groove wear, ring wear, seam splits, and damaged labels or covers.

• Record: The record plays through without skipping, but the surface sheen is almost gone, and the groove wear and surface noise is significant.

• Labels: Worn. Expect stains, heavy writing, and/or obvious damage from attempts to remove tape or stickers.

• Cover/Sleeve: Ring wear to the point of distraction; dinged and dog-eared edges; obvious seam splits; and heavy writing (such as radio station call letters or an owner's name).

FAIR (F) OR POOR (P): Only outrageously rare items ever sell for more than a few cents in this condition, if they sell at all. More likely, F or P records and covers will end up in the trash or be used to create clocks, journals, purses, jewelry, bowls, coasters or other art.

• Overall Appearance: Beat, trashed, and dull. Records may lack sleeves or covers.

• Record: Vinyl may be cracked, scratched, and/or warped to the point it skips.

• Labels: Expect stains, tears, soiling, marks, and damage, if the label is even there.

• Cover/Sleeve: Heavily damaged or absent.

LPS

"Cool Struttin'" by Sonny Clark, Blue Note (BLP 1588), Mono, U.S. pressing, vinyl record: VG-/VG, cover type/grade: standard album jacket VG, 1/4" lower seam split, faint laminate separation on front cover near open edge, moderate staining on back cover......... **$798**

"David Bowie" by David Bowie, Deram (291029), French pressing, vinyl record: VG+, with original luster, minor hairline marks under super-strong light, probably from being placed in and out of inner sleeve, cover: minor shelf wear, spine in good condition. **$395**

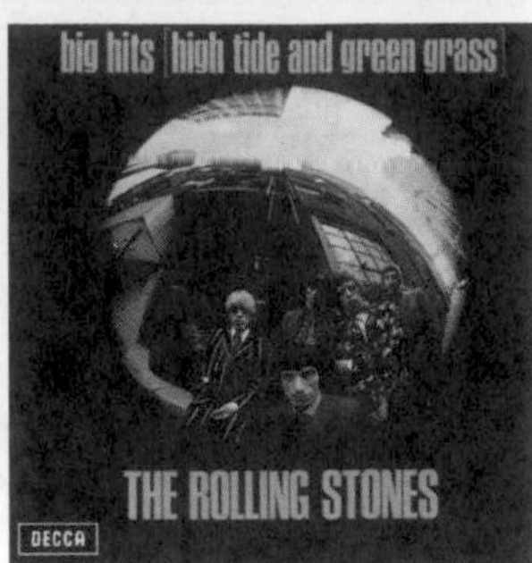

"Big Hits (High Tide and Green Grass)" by The Rolling Stones, Decca (TXL101), 1966 compilation release, rare U.K. first pressing, 14-track mono LP with grooved unboxed Decca logo light blue, gatefold picture sleeve with integral six-page photo booklet, light shelf wear with minor edge scuffing, vinyl remains excellent with spindle trails around center primary evidence of play.................. **$362**

"Dynamite" by Ike and Tina Turner, Original Sue label (Sue-2004), mono, rare, record: VG+, vinyl with light scuffs and scratches, wear visible to label, cover: EX, clean, minor wear.**$125**

"Odessey and Oracle" by The Zombies, date label (TES 4013, 1968), rare, NM, first U.S. pressing of British Invasion classic................. **$349**

"Screaming for Vengeance" by Judas Priest, CBS, Inc. (39926), 1984 picture disc release, autographed by band members with letter of authenticity........................ **$325**

"Blue Train" by John Coltrane, Blue Note (1577), 1957 original LP release in mono, record: VG++, cover: VG+................................ **$390**

"Surrealistic Pillow" by Jefferson Airplane, RCA (LSP 3766), 1967 original U.S. release, factory-sealed, record: M, cover: NM. **$173**

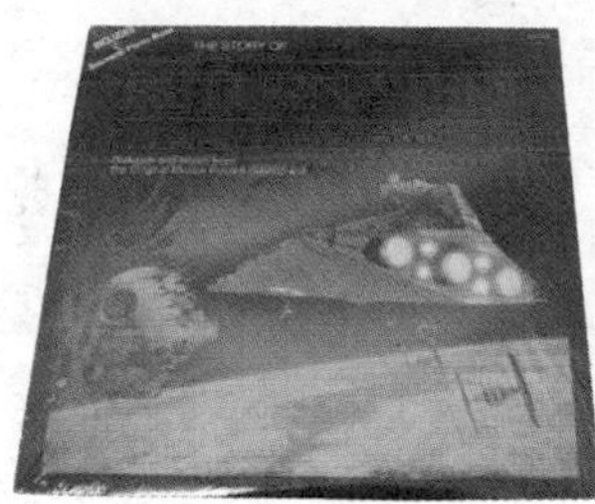

"The Story of Star Wars Return of the Jedi" soundtrack, Disney Buena Vista (62103), 1983 stereo vinyl LP, dialogue and music from original motion picture soundtrack with 16-page full-color souvenir photo book inside, made and distributed in Canada by Walt Disney Music of Canada, LP still sealed, puncture in sleeve near top left corner. **$64**

Courtesy of Continental Hobby House, continental-hobby-house.myshopify.com

"Freedom of Choice" by Devo, autographed, Warner Bros. Records (BSK 3435), signed in black marker on back, in-person in 1980. .... **$100**

Courtesy of Philip Weiss Auctions, www.weissauctions.com

"Dusty in Memphis" by Dusty Springfield, Atlantic (SD 8214), original U.S. pressing, 1969, orange and green label without WEA logo, clean and wear-free. **$105**

BEATLES

"Magical Mystery Tour" by The Beatles, Apple (MAS 2835, 1967), still sealed, pristine copy of rarer mono version, record: M, cover: NM. **$813**

Courtesy of Heritage Auctions, ha.com

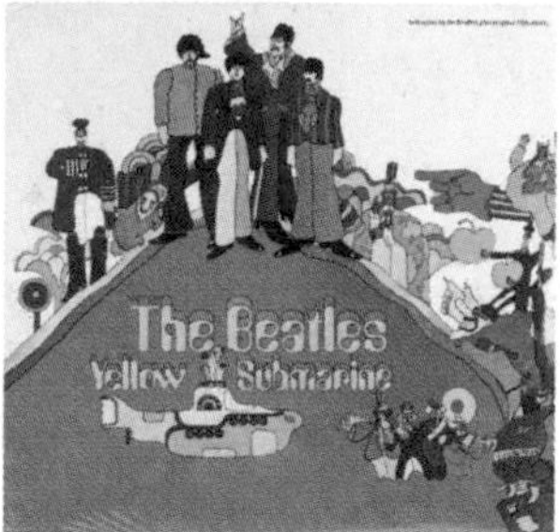

"Yellow Submarine" by The Beatles, Capitol (153, 1969), still sealed, one side of vocal cuts from The Beatles and one side of George Martin instrumentals, all from title movie, record: M (sealed), cover: NM. **$750**

Courtesy of Heritage Auctions, ha.com

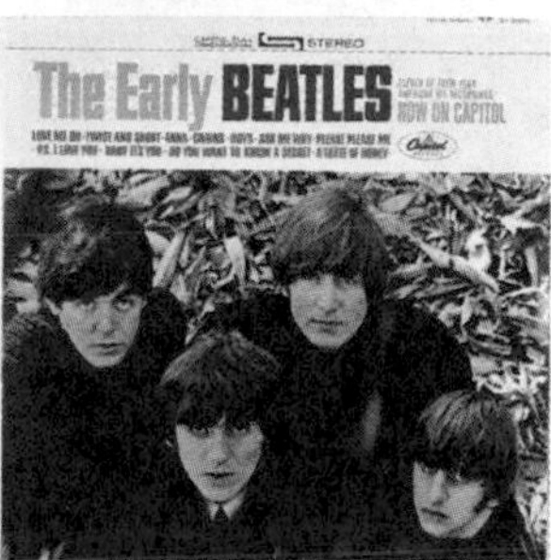

"The Early Beatles" by The Beatles, Capitol (2309, 1965), sealed stereo, Capitol's release of pre-1964 tunes originally offered in United States by Vee-Jay Records on seminal album "Introducing The Beatles," Scranton pressing plant (#3), record: M, cover: NM. **$625**

Courtesy of Heritage Auctions, ha.com

"Love Me Do/P.S. I Love You" by The Beatles, first pressing of U.K. 45 rpm single on Parlophone (4949, 1962), VG-EX. Historic first pressing single backed with "P.S. I Love You" and released in England on Oct. 5, 1962. There were two recordings of this song made the month before at EMI Studios on Abbey Road. The first recording (Sept. 4) had the newest Beatle, Ringo Starr, on drums. One week later, another recording was made with session musician Andy White on drums and Ringo relegated to tambourine. The Ringo recording was the only release done on the Parlophone red label. This also is the first pressing that has the tax stamp "ZT" in the runout groove and does not have "Made in Great Britain," which was pressed from October to mid-November 1962 .... **$625**

Courtesy of Heritage Auctions, ha.com

"Yesterday and Today" by The Beatles, 2nd State Butcher Cover, mono LP on Capitol (T-2553, 1966), partially peeled cover revealing glimpses of less offensive sections of original art, small tear on bottom right of pasted-over cover, with letter Capitol Records issued to critics, DJs, etc., urging them to disregard the original cover; upper right corner never adhered to Butcher Cover, record: EX, cover: VG-EX. **$500**

Courtesy of Heritage Auctions, ha.com

"Abbey Road" by The Beatles, Apple (SO-383, 1969), still sealed, torn plastic on top right corner, ding on top left corner, record: M, cover: NM. **$119**

Courtesy of Heritage Auctions, ha.com

PICTURE SLEEVES AND 45S

"That's All Right/Blue Moon of Kentucky" by Elvis Presley, Sun Records (209), 1954 original pressing, EX. **$800**

The Supremes, "Your Heart Belongs To Me/(He's) Seventeen" picture sleeve from original 1962 Motown (1027) release, 7" record not included **$808**

"Your Love Makes Me Lonely/I Need Your Love" by The Chandlers, Col Soul (HR 1152), Northern Soul 45, record: VG-, chip in dead wax and slight storage warp that does not affect play............ **$390**

"I Need You There/Sad" by The Chessmen, Bismark Records (BK-1012), 1965 U.S. releases of rare Texas garage band, record: VG.......................... **$383**

"Ring-A-Rockin/Fly, Don't Fly On Me" by Neil Sedaka, Legion (L45-133), 1958, 7", record: VG with light surface noise. ...**$78**

"Hit the Road/The Danger Zone" by Ray Charles, ABC label (10244), 1961, 7", VG+ with company sleeve............ **$40**

"Take It Easy/Get You in the Mood" by Eagles, Asylum (AS-11005), 1972, 7", with Glenn Frey autograph, picture sleeve near perfect except for hole in middle, clean record..**$44**

"I Want You Back/Who's Lovin' You" by The Jackson 5, Motown (M 1157), 1969 U.S. 45 release with company Motown sleeve, VG+........................ **$15**

78S

"Calling You/Never Again (Will I Knock On Your Door)" by Hank Williams and The Country Boys, Sterling (201), 1947 U.S. release on shellac, 10", rare, NM. **$405**

"Solo Hop/In a Little Spanish Town" by Glenn Miller and His Orchestra, Columbia (3058), scarce royal blue Columbia from first session under Miller's name, pre-swing jazz sides recorded April 25, 1935, VG. **$100**

"Decoration Blues/Down South" by Sonny Boy Williamson, Bluebird (7665), 1938 U.S. release, shellac, glossy copy with Yank Rachel on mandolin and Big Joe Williams on guitar. **$257**

REPRODUCTIONS

THE DEPTH AND BREADTH OF REPRODUCTIONS, forgeries, fakes, and replicas on today's market is at an all-time high. A glance at eBay.com shows more than 18,000 listings for "reproduction antiques." Companies such as Reproduction Hardware offer replicas spanning three centuries. The nation's flea markets are packed with wholesale imported reproduction inventory from advertising signs to practically anything made of brass.

The cold truth is that every auction house sells reproductions. Respected houses go to meticulous lengths to identify reproductions and point out later replacements (if any) that may affect the piece. The four main collecting categories that have the greatest potential to harm collectors have seen a boon in the number of fakes and reproductions in the last 18 months.

POLITICAL MEMORABILIA

The word the American Political Items Collectors club picked is brummagem. It means cheap, showy, or counterfeit. It's a 17th century word from Birmingham, England, and was originally used to describe counterfeit coins.

Members use the word daily to describe the mountain of fake, fantasy, and reproduction political buttons and memorabilia that flood online auction sites. These items invariably worm their way into a collection and cost collectors lots of money. Some of the reproduced items are obvious – such as a set of shower curtain hooks made with either reproduction Republican or Democratic political buttons – while others are carefully crafted to dupe unwitting collectors out of thousands of dollars.

COINS

In recent years counterfeiters have stepped up efforts targeting third-party companies that are founded on weeding out fakes. Such is the case with counterfeit coins sold in fake holders, or slabs.

Fake holders were first noticed in 2008, but in recent years forgers have increased attempts to counterfeit holders made by the Numismatic Guaranty Co. and the Professional Coin Grading Service. These attempts are illegal and not only infringe on the company's registered trademarks, but also violate both the Hobby Protection Act of 1973 and the Collectible Coin Protection Act of 2014. Fake coins and cases are most often sold out of China on eBay.com, which cooperates by removing listings and blocking sellers whenever a fraudulent holder or coin is discovered.

Counterfeit coin in fake case, 1987 China gold 1/4-oz. Mazu NGC PF 68 Ultra Cameo, cased in near perfect Numismatic Guaranty Co. (NGC) case or "slab" (bidding reached 88 cents before numismatists alerted eBay to the fraud).

ARTWORK

The pitfall for collectors is whether the house or dealer is experienced enough (and honest enough) to identify the object as a reproduction. Some reproductions increase in value over

Original art by Giorgio Comolo, Fantastic Four #74 "re-imagined" cover, 2008, based on original drawn by Jack Kirby in 1961, produced in Ecoline watercolor and ink over graphite on Bristol board, 13-1/4" h. x 19" w. Comolo is an Italian advertising illustrator who produces re-imagined artworks from vintage comics in cooperation with The Jack Kirby Museum and Research Center. **$2,151**

Courtesy of Heritage Auctions, ha.com

time simply due to issues of supply and demand. Commonly reproduced artworks include bronze sculptures, paintings, prints, and Asian carvings and pottery.

In some cases, a reproduction is the only way a collector can ever hope to own a keepsake by a favorite artist. This is especially true in the world of comic art recreations that are, simply stated, an original art reproduction of another artist's classic, famous, or fan-favorite pieces of comic book or original artwork.

"The art of many famous comic artists, such as Frank Frazetta, Jack Kirby, Charles Schulz, Dr. Seuss, or Robert Crumb, is in such demand that the supply is often depleted, or pieces garner such exorbitant prices that reproductions of their art can become acceptable substitutes for the real thing," said Greg Holman, pop culture guru and comics cataloger at Heritage Auctions. "Oftentimes an original piece of comic art will contain much more detail than the printed, colored piece does, and reproductions can be a great way to reveal the artist's original and intricate line work."

Some comic artists have become so proficient at mimicking another artist's work that their reproductions have developed followings of their own; such is the case with Italian artist Giorgio Comolo. Comolo works closely with The Jack Kirby Museum and Research Center, and his original Kirby reproductions can sell for more than $2,000 at auction.

"There are, of course, a few unscrupulous artists and dealers out there [who] do try to pass some of these reproduction pieces off as originals," Holman said, "but a good eye can usually spot inconsistencies in these pieces fairly easily."

SPORTS AUTOGRAPHS

Fake autographs and signatures cost collectors thousands of dollars every year. Professional Sports Authenticator, the largest third-party grading and authentication company in the world, annually releases its list of the "Most Dangerous Autographs" on today's market. Once PSA's panel of experts determines an autograph to be authentic, it marks each specimen with an invisible, permanent DNA marker to track authenticity. These are the most commonly faked and forged signatures of sports and entertainment celebrities:

Babe Ruth
Lou Gehrig
Tie: Mickey Mantle, Ted Williams, Joe DiMaggio
Michael Jordan, retired
Muhammad Ali
Mike Trout, Major League Baseball center fielder for the Los Angeles Angels of Anaheim
Tom Brady, National Football League quarterback for the New England Patriots
Derek Jeter, retired
Stephen Curry, National Basketball Association player for the Golden State Warriors
Sidney Crosby, Canadian professional ice hockey player and captain of the National Hockey League's Pittsburgh Penguins

— *Eric Bradley*

Reproduction Staffordshire porcelain spaniel figure, circa 1950s-1960s, made by Beswick in Staffordshire, England, marks impressed on bottom "Beswick England 1375-5" under glaze, hollow, 7-7/8" h. x 5-3/4" w. **$105**

Courtesy of Giamer Antiques and Collectibles, giamerantiquesandcollectibles.com

Modern reproduction McCoy Jemima or Mammy ceramic cookie jar, figure in white with red scarf, marked "McCoy" on bottom under glaze, imported, 10-3/4" h. **$60**

Reproduction Eames lounge chair and ottoman, new, originally designed by Charles and Ray Eames, 360-degree swivel, "comes in six colors" (original came only in black leather). **$994**

Courtesy of Manhattan Home Design, www.manhattanhomedesign.com

Action figure, "G.I. Joe Exclusive Authentic 1964 Reproduction" action pilot with uniform, hat tag, insignia and field manual, 1/6 scale, in reproduction box, 12" h. **$50**

Courtesy of www.mjstoy.com

Copy of 15th century Italian close helmet, circa 1837-1901, well-made example, hinged at center to allow front and rear halves to open, marked "17" on underside edge of each half, substantial and better-made reproduction, 15" h............ **$2,125**

Courtesy of Heritage Auctions, ha.com

Reproduction aluminum sign, "Ask for Zebo or Zebra Grate Polish," sold in both high gloss and satin coatings, three sizes: extra small, 12" x 12" sq., small, 16" x 16" sq., medium: 20" x 20" sq. ....**$50-$125**

Courtesy of RedBubble.com

Reproduction King of the Swamp alligator mechanical bank, unmarked, fantasy piece, 8" w. x 3" d. x 3-1/2" h., 7 lbs. .... **$20-$50**

▼ Confederate captain frock coat, double-breasted with captain braid on sleeve, captain collar insignia, 14-button front with reproduction Confederate staff buttons, available in several different wools, handmade to order in Idaho (shown in Richmond gray wool with solid navy branch of service color on collar and cuff and navy piping)................ **$369**

Courtesy of C & C Sutlery, www.ccsutlery.com

▼ Dentist Pulling Tooth reproduction cast iron mechanical bank, works, 8-3/4" l.. **$10**

Courtesy of Curran Miller Auctions, curranmiller.com

Reproduction porcelain serving dish with four corners, Japanese-inspired design with images of tigers and ceremonial tables, framed in decorative border, gilt-applied accent, 8-1/2" dia............ **$195**

Stancils Antiques Unlimited, www.stancilsantiquesunlimited.com

Reproduction embossed aluminum sign with "John Deere Farm Implements" printed image, 13" h. x 42" w.. **$50**

Courtesy of GreenCrazy.com

Reproduction demilune mahogany table with two stacked central drawers flanked by two swing-out cabinet doors on either side, drawer labeled "Historic Charleston Reproductions," glass top, 35" h. x 34" w. x 18" d. **$325**

Courtesy of Susanin's Auctioneers & Appraisers, www.susanins.com

Pillar print, "Lady with an umbrella in snow," by Koryusai, reproduction.......... **$50**

Courtesy of Eldred's Auctioneers, www.eldreds.com

Replica arrowheads, hand-chipped "for an authentic look and feel," pack of 25, variety of natural materials including obsidian, from 3/4" to 2-1/2" l. x 1/2" to 1-1/2" w. **$12**

Courtesy of Amazon.com

LEGO counterfeit toy, four characters from Marvel's "Fantastic Four" made in China (LEGO has yet to produce an officially licensed set of mini figures of Marvel Comics' Fantastic Four characters), 1-1/5" h. ....**$10-$20**

Courtesy of Ruben Saldana

Replica of 1932 state of Michigan non-resident pinback fishing license...................**$30**

Courtesy of FirstSportsStore.com

Reproduction tin lantern with punched design on side and vented top, hinged door, "Paul Revere-style: This reproduction antique is an authentic representation of a primitive period lantern – the same kind Paul Revere used to warn that the British were coming!" 13-1/2" h. x 5" w. **$25**

Courtesy of Treasure Gurus, www.treasuregurus.com

Reproduction industrial factory cart sold as coffee table, hardwood planks and cast iron wheels, unfinished, "custom sizes and finishes available, handcrafted from reclaimed solid timbers recycled from old buildings," 53" w. x 28" d. x 18" h. **$1,345**

Courtesy of Mortise & Tenon Custom Furniture, mortiseandtenon.com

▶ Set of six reproduction Sèvres plates with floral monogram of Catherine II of Russia, 10" dia.... **$600**

Courtesy of Eldred's Auctioneers, www.eldreds.com

Reproduction Tiffany leaded glass peacock lamp, bronze base with blue/green glass shade, pull chain, "made with 350 pieces of variegated glass in the blue/green shade with yellow banding and highlights," 23" x 11", 18" dia. **$264**

Courtesy of Aspire Auctions, www.aspireauctions.com

▼ Fully functional replica antique 19th century padlock with two skeleton keys, "antique finish," 3-3/4" l. **$10**

Courtesy of Wild Bill Wholesale, www.wildbillwholesale.com

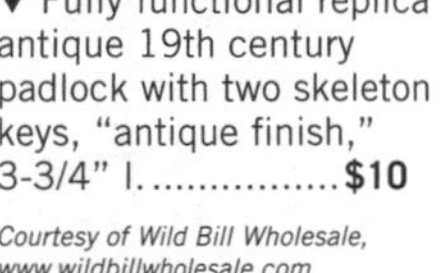

Reproduction pipe with effigy in form of cardinal with platform, catlinite, modern, "marked NW Ohio," 3-7/8" l. **$20**

Courtesy of The Artifact Co., www.theartifactcompany.com

SALESMAN SAMPLES

DOOR-TO-DOOR SALESMEN may be a thing of the past, but salesman samples are a popular collectible of the present, sometimes drawing hefty sums at auction.

You don't have to look too far back in America's manufacturing and commerce history to see how salesmen and their samples transformed modern society. The practice largely came into play in the mid-to-late 19th century, according to Lisa Robinson of The San Lorenzo Valley Museum, in her report "A Brief History of Modern Miniatures."

While it may have been visits from salesmen that first brought small business owners and consumers face-to-face with these miniature modern marvels, salesmen actually took a page out of the playbook of architects, engineers, and filmmakers when tapping into the small-scale samples. For years these other professions had used "scaled models to demonstrate or better understand the operation of full-size or large-scale devices," Robinson said.

One of the people to discover the value of a sample early on was Arthur Vining Davis, general manager of the Aluminum Company of America (ALCOA), according to Walter A. Friedman, author of "Birth of a Salesman" (Harvard Business School website, http://bit.ly/ATCvr091714). It is said Davis worked with fabricators at the company's plant to create sample aluminum kitchen utensils along with pots and pans, so a team of college students would have the samples to use in their door-to-door sales efforts.

The types of samples to show up most often at auctions in recent years include farm machinery (plows, graders, wheat cleaners), stoves, barber chairs, washing machines, and items used by beverage companies (coolers and dispensing devices) to sell units into general stores, among other items.

Early unique reclining Victorian couch, splits and wear to leather with some leather loss, 14" l. **$61**

Courtesy of Morphy Auctions, morphyauctions.com

HOUSEHOLD

Wooden desk with drawers that open, includes small metal tag that reads "Derby Desk Company – Boston, Mass.," excellent condition, water stains on top surface, 16-1/2" x 9" x 7-1/2". **$488**

Courtesy of Morphy Auctions, morphyauctions.com

Four-drawer chest, 20th century, top with slight overhang over ogee-shaped top drawer, three flat drawers with button knobs, bun feet, 14" h. x 14" w. x 8-1/2" d.**$168**

Courtesy of Phoebus Auction Gallery, www.phoebusauction.com

Empire chest with faux-painted Corinthian columns, minor abrasions on top, part of front right foot missing, 13-1/4" w. x 8" d. x 17" h.............**$461**

Courtesy of Roland Auctioneers & Valuers, www.rolandauctions.com

School desk, 19th century, mahogany and brass in two different variations with fold-up seats, unsigned, excellent condition, 16" x 9" x 7-1/2"................**$510**

Courtesy of Mosby & Co. Auctions, www.mosbyauctions.com

Hopewell cast iron furnace embossed "Hopewell Furnace" on both sides, 6-3/4" x 5-3/4" x 2-5/8". **$30**

Courtesy of Stephenson's Auction, www.stephensonsauction.com

Victorian cast iron umbrella stand, shell-form drip pan base, good condition, minor rust damage, 16-1/2" h. x 11" w. x 10-1/2" d. **$42**

Courtesy of Premier Auction Galleries, www.pag4u.com

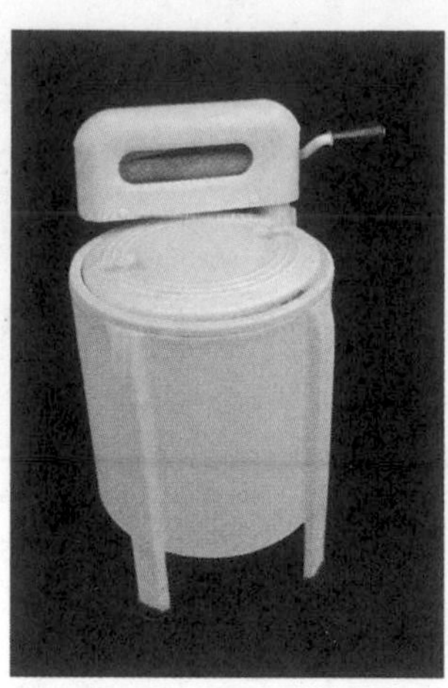

Wringer washing machine, Montello Products Co., Ripon, Wisconsin, possibly repainted, 12-1/4" h....... **$29**

Courtesy of Scheerer McCulloch Auctioneers, Inc., www.smauctioneers.com

Mission-style clock, stickers on back from Wm. L. Gilbert and M. Small Jeweler in Geneva, New York, excellent condition, 14-1/2" h. **$366**

Courtesy of Morphy Auctions, morphyauctions.com

Garland oven range, circa 1950, lacquered wood and steel, hand-painted Garland manufacturer's label to oven door, 17-1/4" w. x 5-3/4" d. x 12" h.................... **$2,816**

Courtesy of Wright, www.wright20.com

Bed used to sell mattresses, 22" l. x 10-1/2" w. **$35**

Courtesy of Vero Beach Auction, www.verobeachauction.com

Marvel cast iron stove by Kenton, 16-1/2" h. x 20-1/2" w. with side panel attached x 7-1/2" d. **$300-$500**

Courtesy of Kaminski Auctions, www.kaminskiauctions.com

Servel refrigerator, 1940s, opens to reveal small illustrated book showing numerous sections of refrigerator, with several working mechanical parts and leather case, excellent condition, 8" h. x 4" l. x 2" w. **$519**

Courtesy of Morphy Auctions, morphyauctions.com

OUTDOORS

1957 picnic table, patent model #D-184,837, very good condition with some soiling and areas of wood loss, 24" l. **$275**

Courtesy of Morphy Auctions, morphyauctions.com

◀ Coca-Cola cooler, 1939, with A Business Builder replacement booklet, excellent restored condition, 10-1/4" h. x 12-1/4" w. x 7-1/4" d. **$1,920**

Courtesy of Rich Penn Auctions, www.richpennauctions.com

! top lot

Old Town canoe, circa 1930, all original green paint, rare, 48" l.................. $19,965

COURTESY OF SACO RIVER AUCTION CO., WWW.SACORIVERAUCTION.COM

◀ Wooden household step ladder, excellent all original condition, 6" x 15" x 9-1/2" extended.................... **$570**

Courtesy of Showtime Auction Services, www.showtimeauctions.com

▲ Wood and metal plow or hay rake, unsigned, very fine to excellent condition, missing one wood piece on front pull bar, 12-1/2" l. x 10-1/2" w. x 6-1/2" h......................... **$3,120**

Courtesy of Mosby & Co. Auctions, www.mosbyauctions.com

Model skiff, circa 1930s, hand-painted, 35"............ **$97**

Courtesy of Saco River Auction Co., www.sacoriverauction.com

Swing set, circa 1950, enameled steel, aluminum, lacquered particle board, string netting, 17-1/2" w. x 15" d. x 14" h...... **$3,840**

Courtesy of Wright, www.wright20.com

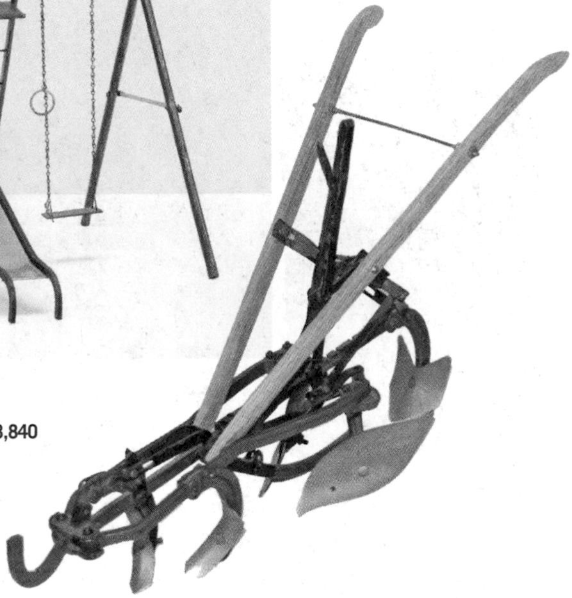

Plow with working parts, unsigned, fine to very fine condition, replaced wooden handles, 12" l. x 7" h...................... **$960**

Courtesy of Mosby & Co. Auctions, www.mosbyauctions.com

Tin running horse dimensional weathervane, 19th century, old red painted surface, good condition with some rust and pitting, 8" h. x 9-1/4" l.................................. **$423**

Courtesy of Conestoga Auction Co., www.conestogaauction.com

Windmill, painted wood and fully articulated moving metal parts, Star Mill Pat. Nov 12 1878, Flint Walling Mfg. Co., Kendallville, Indiana, some tips of vanes missing from wheel, vertical crack across tail, paint and varnish losses, 12" h. x 15" l. **$4,428**

Courtesy of Nest Egg Auctions, www.nesteggauctions.com

Hay baler, Champion, wooden model with nickeled gearing, long rectangular shaft for bale forming, flywheels and gears engage plunger and lifting arm, wood frame with nickel spoke wheels, excellent condition, 19" l. **$9,263**

Courtesy of Bertoia Auctions, www.bertoiaauctions.com

Telephone booth, C.B. French Cabinet Co., Brooklyn, New York, oak with fully paneled exterior, hinged folding door that pushes in, handle on inside to pull to exit, with original decal on bottom along with Western-Electric Co. metal plate, original excellent-plus condition, 14-3/4" h. x 5-1/4" w. x 5-1/2" d. **$2,160**

Courtesy of Rich Penn Auctions, www.richpennauctions.com

Farm road grader, brass, with solo driver's seat, long grader that adjusts, painted red frame with notches, and decal from Texas company on sides, very good condition, 14" l. **$679**

Courtesy of Bertoia Auctions, www.bertoiaauctions.com

Elliot J. Barn gate, excellent all-original condition, 18" x 8" x 3". **$210**

Courtesy of Showtime Auction Services, www.showtimeauctions.com

MISCELLANEOUS

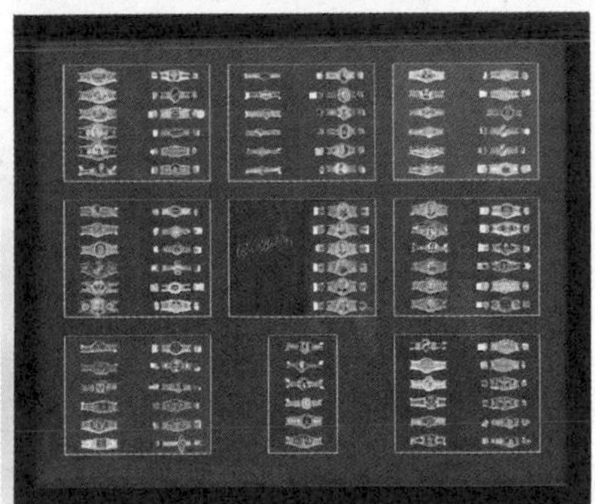

▲ Two-sided cigar labels display from salesman's sample book, 1901 to 1907, 34-1/2" x 30" overall. **$330**

Courtesy of Copake Auction, Inc., www.copakeauction.com

▲ Bronze Vienna beer keg with tap, signed "S X", excellent condition, 10" l. x 5" h.**$122**

Courtesy of Morphy Auctions, morphyauctions.com

▶ Bowser oil pump system dispenser with factory tag #1110, very good condition, working pump, 8" x 5" x 3". **$3,965**

Courtesy of Morphy Auctions, morphyauctions.com

◀ Beer sign with two die-cut tin litho signs, one on top and one on bottom, with cloth or canvas middle section where brewery name was printed, Hausermann Litho, New York and Chicago, excellent condition, middle section with mild soiling, tin signs with two minor paint flecks, 12" x 29-1/2" framed. ... **$1,220**

Courtesy of Morphy Auctions, morphyauctions.com

Galoshes and roller skates, circa 1900, two pairs of rubber galoshes embossed "American Rubber" on sides and pair of metal roller skates, unmarked, very good condition, each 2-3/4" l. ... **$89**

Courtesy of Frasher's Doll Auctions, Oak Grove, Missouri

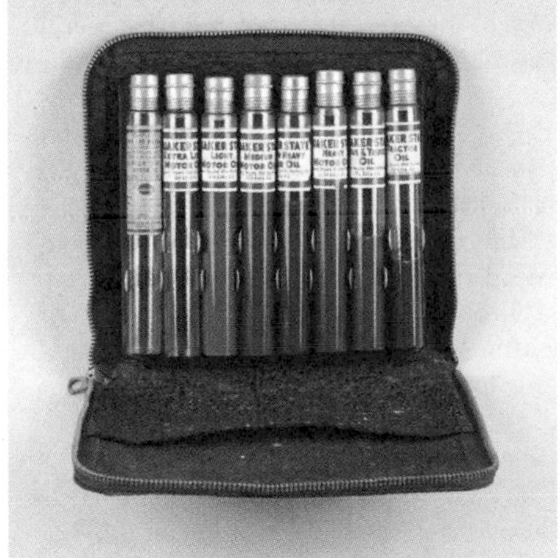

Quaker State oil set, complete with leather case with stamped logo, all bottles in good condition, one label with area of loss, case 8-3/4" x 8". **$67**

Courtesy of Morphy Auctions, morphyauctions.com

SCIENCE & TECHNOLOGY

IT'S THE TYPE of place where the question, "What is that?" is music to the ears.

The three-word question sparked hours of conversation and quite a few transactions at North America's largest and longest-running show devoted to antique scientific equipment and retro-technology, the Antique Science & Retro-Tech Show & Swap Meet in Dallas/Fort Worth. The annual event has a venerated reputation as a source for unusual discoveries, not to mention serving as the venue of the annual World Championship Slide Rule Competition. But at the 21st annual event, held in early 2015, organizers found something nearly as elusive as a Throughton & Simms geodetic theodolite: young collectors.

Photographer Ben D'Avanza hunted for objects to inspire his passion for machining, Triumph motorcycles, and vintage audio. He found a vintage microphone head that will look perfect incorporated in the interior design of his brother's new restaurant.

Casual shoppers like D'Avanza and a growing number of established collections returning to market are just a handful of the reasons why vintage science and technology is a growing segment of the hobby. Much like the objects themselves, collectors' passion for vintage technology can be diverse and intricate. And unlike some categories, vintage tech is still in the early stages of developing strong demand, leaving lots of fresh-to-market discoveries for the historic-minded tinkerer.

Retired software engineer Bob Patton started collecting handheld calculators roughly 25 years ago and has 350 unique models in his collection "but 569 have passed through my hands." He offered highlights from his collection priced from $10 to as much as $100. He sees the interest as rooted in a simpler time: "Any obsolete technology is just nostalgia and a curiosity in old technology," he said. "You can still find things that are valuable; you just need persistence and to look at garage sales, junk stalls, and antiques shops."

Among the collector's items for sale from Patton's inventory was a 1975 Inverton VIP 10 hand-held calculator from Germany. The arithmetic calculator has 10-digit precision and algebraic logic, six functions, 20 keys, and glowing red LED display. The asking price was $100 – a near 10,000% markup from Paton's purchase price. "I found it at an antique shop for 10 cents. The finds are still out there," he said.

Edison Kinetoscope, working replica of 1890 model, 1993, for viewing continuous loops of 35mm film of up to 20 minutes in length, 47" h. **$8,215**

Courtesy of Auction Team Breker, www.breker.com

These finds are not limited to low-run calculators. Science and technology is one of the broadest of all collecting categories and is generally thought to include fossils, fine minerals, medical and navigational devices, globes, and more. As it finds a new generation of collectors – one well-versed in technology from the beginning – the field is inclusive of artworks, computers, portable computing, documents and manuscripts, and oddities. Collections are limited only by budget and imagination. Early specialization based on passion helps the collector avoid fakes, new creations, and inflated prices.

The public's fervent fascination and curiosity with the scientific and technological mind seems especially boundless for pioneers such as Galileo Galilei, Albert Einstein, and Leonardo da Vinci. Visitors flock to exhibits featuring da Vinci's Codex Leicester, the most famous of the inventor's 30 surviving journals. Bill Gates, the founder of Microsoft and one of the world's richest individuals, purchased the Codex from Christie's for $30 million in 1994 and has placed the book on continual display around the world, most recently in the United States.

Letters and documents in Einstein's hand have a devoted collecting base as well. A letter referencing the persecution of the Jews in war-torn Europe sold for $12,500 at auction in late 2014, and a letter sent to Jewish philosopher Erik Gutkind, stating Einstein's belief that God does not exist, sold on eBay for more than $3 million in late 2012.

A 56-page composition notebook completed by Alan Turing, credited as a pioneer of computer science, was auctioned by Bonhams in early 2015 for $1,025,000. Material from Turing's accomplishments is rare, and the previously unknown and one-of-a-kind manuscript came to market just a year after the motion picture "The Imitation Game" made public his important role in cracking Nazi codes during World War II, which shortened the war by at least two years.

SOL-20, processor technology, 1976. .... **$890**

Courtesy of Auction Team Breker, www.breker.com

Demonstration model of "Bell" receiver, cutaway model, 7-1/2" l. **$245**

Courtesy of Auction Team Breker, www.breker.com

Four Remco science kits: Medical Science: Mechanical Heart; Solar System: Planetarium; Electro Magnetism; and Electric Motor. **$31**

Courtesy of Morphy Auctions, morphyauctions.com

! top lot

L'Isle, Guillaume De (1675-1728), Globe Terrestre D'Epoque Louis XIV, dated 1700, with compass and plateau indicating calendar, zodiac signs, and direction. $162,500

COURTESY OF ARADER GALLERIES, WWW.ARADERGALLERIES.COM

СОЮЗ НАУКИ И ТРУДА–ЗАЛОГ НОВЫХ ПОБЕД КОММУНИЗМА

B. A. Mukhin, "The Union of Science and Labor – is the Pledge to New Victories of Communism," Soviet propaganda poster, 1952, 22" x 29-1/4". **$238**

Courtesy of Mroczek Brothers, mbaauction.com

Adding machine of Pierre Fardoil in shape of astrolabe, circa 1700, steel and brass, originally silver-plated, signed "Pierre Fardoil à Paris", 5-1/2" h. **$61,565**

Courtesy of Auction Team Breker, www.breker.com

Milestone Le Pascal, second version, 1898, Japy Frères & Co., France, first motorized roll film camera........................ **$618**

Courtesy of Auction Team Breker, www.breker.com

Maudslay's table steam engine with boiler, mid-19th century, 21-2/3" x 11-3/4" x 26-3/4"... **$3,015**

Courtesy of Auction Team Breker, www.breker.com

4D Magic interim prototype camera, 2000, U.S. Technology Ltd., Hong Kong, one of only 10 produced... **$890**

Courtesy of Auction Team Breker, www.breker.com

Madame P. [Marie] Curie, *Traité de Radioactivité*, Paris: Gauthier-Villars, 1910, first edition. **$1,625**

Courtesy of Heritage Auctions, ha.com

"The Telegraphone" magnetic wire-recording and repeating device, 1909, American Telegraphone Co., model 102, serial No. 125, patent No. 934843.......................... **$4,655**

Courtesy of Auction Team Breker, www.breker.com

Troughton & Simms London brass telescope, late 19th century, 42" l. **$600**

Courtesy of Manor Auctions, www.manorauctions.com

Julien P. Friez & Sons, Inc. science instrument, 1800-1914, maker and supplier of meteorological instruments from Baltimore, excellent condition, 13" x 11" x 6-1/2". **$90**

Courtesy of Showtime Auction Service, www.showtimeauctions.com

Antique mechanical globe planetarium, 1890, 21" l. **$1,320**

Courtesy of Morphy Auctions, morphyauctions.com

Antique scientific barometer, 10-1/4" h. x 16" w. x 9" d. **$277**

Courtesy of Westport Auction, www.westportauction.com

French champleve enamel crystal regulator clock, late 19th century, brass, retailed by Spaulding & Co., eight-day time and strike movement, 11-1/2". **$2,560**

Courtesy of Rago Arts and Auctions, www.ragoarts.com

Surveyor's transit, brass, with bubble level and compass, 12-1/4" l. **$123**

Courtesy of A.H. Wilkins Auctions, ahwilkins.com

Mariner's astrolabe, dated 1555, European, cast brass, 8" dia. **$3,100**

Courtesy of J. James Auctioneers, www.jjamesauctions.com

World War II American scientific bore sighting kit, American Scientific Instrument Co., New York. . **$132**

Courtesy of Milestone Auctions, www.milestoneauctions.com

Mahogany jeweler's scale with instruments, 1910, 19" h. x 19" w. **$185**

Courtesy of Kamelot Auctions, www.kamelotauctions.com

Mortar and pestle, bronze, European, 15th century, mortar 4-1/2" h., pestle 7.4" l. **$430**

Courtesy of Artemis Gallery, www.artemisgallery.com

Dieppe ivory sundial/compass, 1680, 2" x 1-3/4". **$1,930**

Courtesy of Louis J. Dianni Antiques Auctions, louisjdianni.com

SILVER

SILVERSMITHING IN AMERICA goes back to the early 17th century in Boston and New York and the early 18th century in Philadelphia. Boston artisans were influenced by English styles, New Yorkers by Dutch. American manufacturers began to switch to the sterling standard about the time of the U.S. Civil War.

Sterling silver (standard silver) is an alloy made of silver and copper and is harder than pure silver. It is used in the creation of sterling silver flatware - silverware - as well as tea services, trays, salvers, goblets, water and wine pitchers, candlesticks, and centerpieces. Coin silver is slightly less pure than sterling.

Fine silver of some quality improves in value if it's used rather than stored. High-quality silver objects from American name-brand makers such as Gorham, Tiffany, Towle, Stieff, and Reed & Barton remain desirable and represent a solid purchase. Functional pieces will survive longer than those that are purely decorative.

There exist a number of excellent resources on the topic of sterling silver. The most famous continues to be *Discovering Hallmarks on English Silver* by John Bly. This 1968 book was re-released in 2008 by Shire Publishing and remains the mainstay for English hallmarks. Flatware is well covered in *Warman's Sterling Silver Flatware,* 2nd edition, by Phil Dreis. Resources are also available on tablets and tablet personal computers: Dealer Steve Freeman developed a free app for iPad users offering a free library of hundreds of images of English silver maker's marks. The SilverMakers app was released in 2012 and offers an easy way to find marks based on the object's intended use, marks, and even silver content.

Georgian sterling silver teapot, circa 1760s (partially rubbed date mark), London, maker's mark for John Harvey, with turned ebonized finial surmounting domed acanthus-cast hinged lid, over slightly concave top spreading to meet relief-decorated palmette frieze over ovoid body, engraved with crown over motto "Tout Pour L'Eglise" above church house armorial device, stepped circular foot, 7-3/4" h. x 9-1/2" w. x 4-1/2" d., 16.780 troy oz. **$861**

Courtesy of John Moran Auctioneers, www.johnmoran.com

Victorian sterling silver teapot, circa 1890, repoussé bowl, unidentified maker's mark, no visible condition issues, 5" x 3-1/4" x 8-3/4"................. **$113**

Courtesy of Heritage Auctions, ha.com

English Arts & Crafts sterling silver coffee service, Birmingham, 1923-1925, three-piece demi set in hand-hammered sterling silver, each with maker's mark of Alfred E. Jones and stamped "839" to underside, coffeepot, 6-3/4" h. x 5-1/2" w. x 3-1/2" d.; sugar bowl, 1-3/4" h., 3-1/8" dia.; and milk jug, 2-3/4" h. x 3-3/4" w. x 2" d., 12.650 troy oz. **$338**

Courtesy of John Moran Auctioneers, www.johnmoran.com

Mid-century modern Emil Hermann German sterling silver coffeepot with flower accent on lid, 11-1/4" h., 28.4 troy oz.**$518**

Courtesy of Vero Beach Auction, www.verobeachauction.com

◀ Tiffany & Co. Vine pattern sterling silver bonbon spoon in daisy motif, pattern designed in 1871 by Edward C. Moore (1827-1891), New York, with HWMcN monogram, 5-1/4" l., 1.31 troy oz. **$313**

Courtesy of New Orleans Auction Gallery, www.neworleansauction.com

Reed & Barton "Hampton Court" sterling silver six-piece tea and coffee service, hallmarked "Reed & Barton, Sterling, 660, Hampton Court" on bottom, no visible defects, hot water kettle on stand, 9-1/4" x 5-5/8"; coffee pot, 9"; teapot, 7-1/2"; creamer, 5"; and sugar bowl with lid, 6", 126.465 troy oz. **$1,800**

Courtesy of Stephenson's Auction, www.stephensonsauction.com

Late Victorian four-piece sterling silver coffee and tea set, hallmarked London, 1898-1899, by Elkington & Co., each of bulbous oval form, lower half gadrooned, upper half with repoussé floral-scroll band, with everted shell and gadrooned rim and four spherical feet, pots with wooden crested handles and gadrooned finials, bowl and jug with arched silver acanthus handle(s), each monogrammed "PSD" (conjoined), wooden handles with small shrinkage cracks, old repair to coffeepot handle, decorative silver finial above wooden knob on teapot slightly bent, minor scattered small indentations, and light surface scratches throughout, all consistent with age and use, coffeepot, 8-1/2" h. x 9-1/4" l.; teapot, 5-1/2" h. x 11-1/4" l.; open sugar bowl, 4-1/2" h. x 8-1/4" l.; and cream jug, 4-1/2" h. x 6" l.;63.72 total troy oz. **$1,250**

Courtesy of New Orleans Auction Gallery, www.neworleansauction.com

George III sterling tea caddy, 1817, London, Edward Farrell, with squirrel finial over domed rocaille and grape-adorned cover, bombe rectangular body all-over repoussé with rocaille and lion masks, each side centering rocaille-bordered reserve engraved with armorials, two with "Now Thus" motto, maker's mark of Edward Farrell, 5-1/8" h. x 4-3/8" w. x 3-1/8" d., 24.415 troy oz. **$4,613**

Courtesy of John Moran Auctioneers, www.johnmoran.com

◀ Pair of Sanborns sterling silver mustard pots, Mexican, 20th century, each with squat spherical form with applied bird-form handle and finial and glass liner, maker's hallmark stamped to underside, 3-1/8" h., 2-1/2" dia. at widest point, 4.540 troy oz. **$99**

Courtesy of Stefek's Auctioneers & Appraisers, www.stefeksltd.com

Early George III Scottish sterling silver ladle with hemispherical bowl, Old English pattern, hallmarked Edinburgh, 1765-1766, by Robert Clark, with H monogram, 14" l., 5.99 troy oz... **$313**

Courtesy of New Orleans Auction Gallery, www.neworleansauction.com

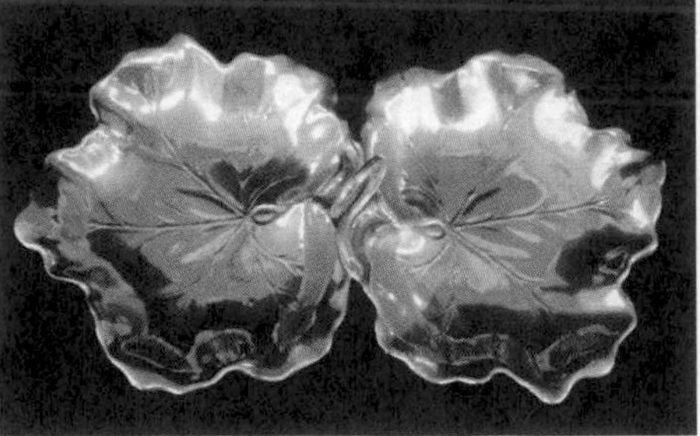

Reed & Barton sterling silver mint dish in form of two leaves with entwined stem handle, circa 1948, marked "Reed & Barton Sterling X102A", 9" x 5-1/4"... **$168**

Courtesy of Phoebus Auction Gallery, www.phoebusauction.com16

top lot!

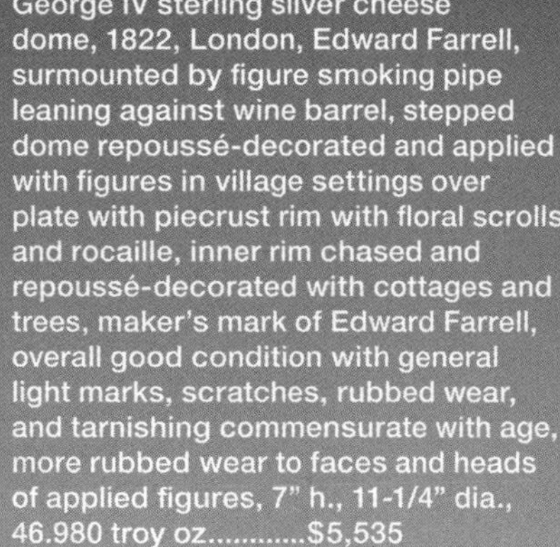

George IV sterling silver cheese dome, 1822, London, Edward Farrell, surmounted by figure smoking pipe leaning against wine barrel, stepped dome repoussé-decorated and applied with figures in village settings over plate with piecrust rim with floral scrolls and rocaille, inner rim chased and repoussé-decorated with cottages and trees, maker's mark of Edward Farrell, overall good condition with general light marks, scratches, rubbed wear, and tarnishing commensurate with age, more rubbed wear to faces and heads of applied figures, 7" h., 11-1/4" dia., 46.980 troy oz............$5,535

COURTESY OF JOHN MORAN AUCTIONEERS, WWW.JOHNMORAN.COM

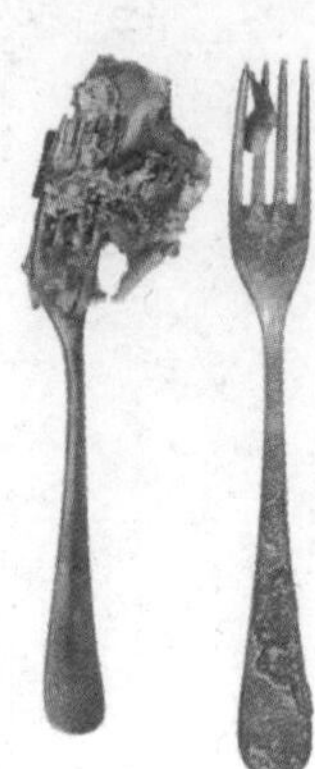

Two silverplate forks retrieved from wreckage of Hindenburg disaster, each with molten metal encrustations, handles depict globe with dirigible superimposed and initials D.Z.R. for "Deutsche Zeppelin Reederei" or German Zeppelin Transport Co., operators of the Hindenburg at the time of its destruction in Lakehurst, New Jersey in 1937, stamped "Bruckmann 100" on stem of forks, 7" and 8-1/4" l. **$5,500**

Courtesy of Heritage Auctions, ha.com

Sterling silver mustard pot with glass liner and two handles, hinged lid with finial, and slot for spoon with clear glass insert, engraved "M.E.M. – D.C.P.S. – 1946-1949" on front base, 7" x 5-1/2," 8.05 troy oz. (sterling only).......... **$246**

Courtesy of Don Presley Auction, www.donpresley.com

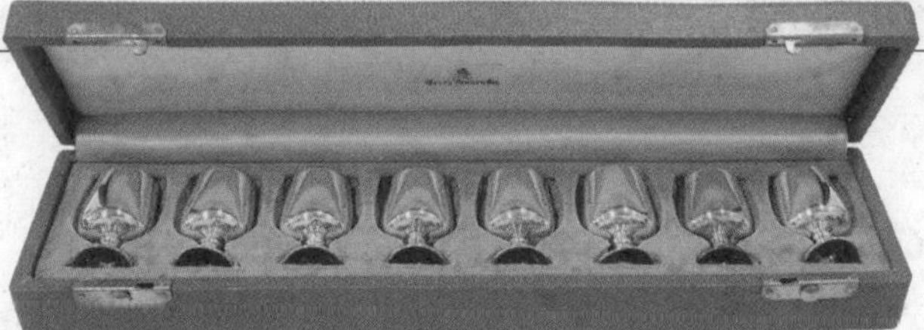

Set of eight B & M sterling silver cordials in Georg Jensen box, 5.47 troy oz. **$374**

Courtesy of Vero Beach Auction, www.verobeachauction.com

Three glass decanters with silver overlay, circa 1900: Long-neck bulbous decanter and stopper with floral reticulation, monogrammed BCS; tall inverted and rounded trumpet-form decanter with fine silver foliate reticulation and matching stopper, monogrammed ALR; stout lipped bulbous decanter and stopper with unengraved cartouche with marks for Alvin-Beiderhase Co., with "999/1000, FINE, L505" stamp, good condition, scuffing to bottoms, sticker residue, cracks to inside neck, tallest 10-1/4" h... **$438**

Courtesy of Heritage Auctions, ha.com

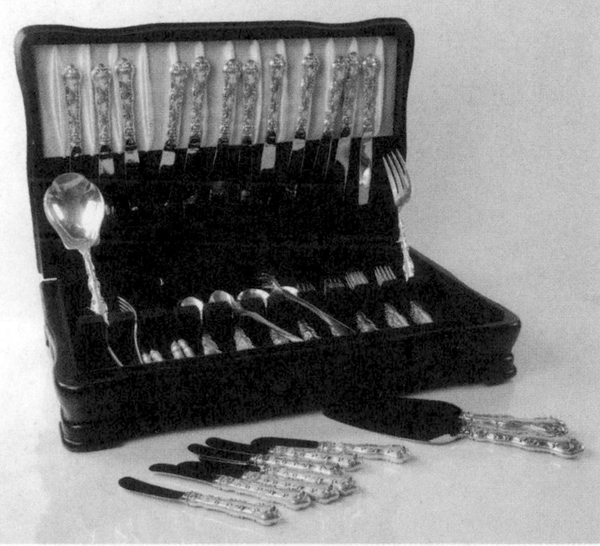

Seventy-two pieces of Gorham sterling silver flatware in Strasbourg pattern: 12 dinner forks (19.22 troy oz.), nine dessert forks (11.72 troy oz.), serving fork and spoon (7.14 troy oz.), 12 soup spoons (15.06 troy oz.), and 12 teaspoons (13.64 troy oz.), good condition.................**$1,250**

Courtesy of Roland Auctioneers & Valuers, www.rolandauctions.com

American sterling silver flower basket, circa 1900, oval with lobed rim and swing handle, paterae and pieced gallery and flower basket rim, "H" monogram, 8-3/4" h. (15-3/4" h. with handle) x 12" l. x 8-5/8" w., 25.51 troy oz. **$750**

Courtesy of New Orleans Auction Gallery, www.neworleansauction.com

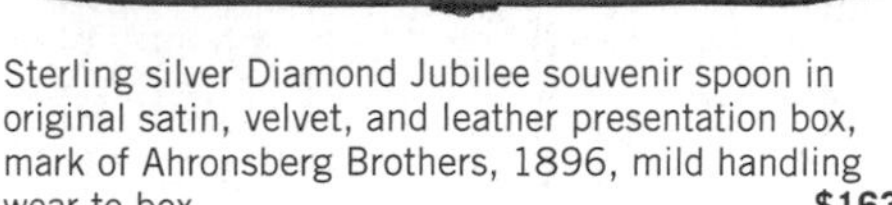

Sterling silver Diamond Jubilee souvenir spoon in original satin, velvet, and leather presentation box, mark of Ahronsberg Brothers, 1896, mild handling wear to box. **$163**

Courtesy of Heritage Auctions, ha.com

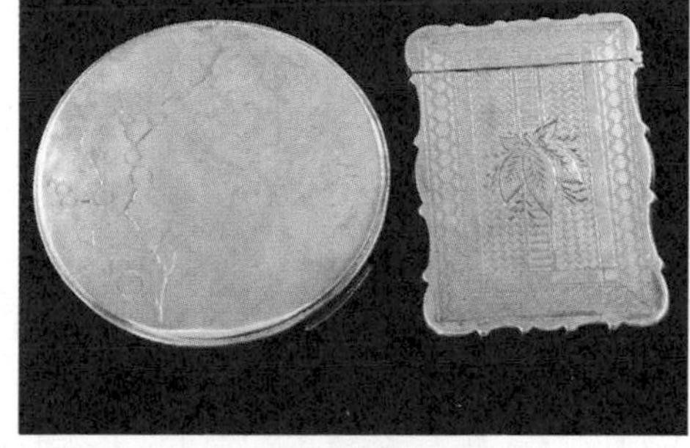

Sterling silver compact and calling card case: compact with mirror, Evald Nielsen "Sterling Silver Denmark 925 S." hallmark, very good condition, some oxidation to mirror, 3-1/2" dia.; and American Victorian calling card case with "W3H 900/1000" hallmark, no monogram, very good condition, 2-1/2" x 3-1/2". **$123**

Courtesy of Nest Egg Auctions, www.nesteggauctions.com

English sterling silver basket, 19th century, 10-1/2" h. x 14-1/2" l. x 12" w., 24.66 troy oz. **$1,476**

Courtesy of Don Presley Auction, www.donpresley.com

▶ Victorian sterling silver christening set, 1886, London, each with maker's mark of John Aldwinckle and Thomas Slater, cased set, each piece engraved with beading, geometric patterning, and scrolling foliage, fork, 6-1/2"; spoon, 6-3/5"; and napkin ring, 1-1/8" d., 1-7/8" dia., 2.840 troy oz......... **$246**

Courtesy of John Moran Auctioneers, www.johnmoran.com

SOUVENIRS

COLLECTIBLE SOUVENIRS ARE so much more than refrigerator magnets and generic t-shirts.

Inspired by the lure of the open road and the mystique of a foreign city, the souvenir is an age-old collectible that touches the heart of collecting itself, and the category is extremely diverse, colorful, and increasingly popular.

Soldiers during World War I and II used the only paper they had at hand, namely foreign currency, to collect signatures of fellow soldiers in their unit or famous political leaders they met during the war. Bills were taped or fastened together in a strip now referred to as "short snorters." The short snorter is also a nickname of a person who crossed the ocean in an airplane, and those who did signed their names on dollar bills. If a soldier is unable to produce this "certificate," then he must buy everyone in the vicinity a small drink, or snort of liquor. These souvenirs are hot collectibles now and can range in price from as low as $30 to as much as $4,000 if the short snorter has signatures from U.S. presidents, astronauts, or entertainers.

On the homefront, citizens occupied their time collecting souvenirs relating to Gen. Douglas MacArthur and various patriotic items urging Americans to "Remember Pearl Harbor" and "Keep 'em Flying." Busts, plaques, banners, mugs, charms, and pins are highly sought after. Sports souvenirs flourished during the 1940s as pennants, programs, and premiums ranged from the practical to the downright ridiculous. Baseball great Joe DiMaggio's Restaurant based in San Francisco created odd souvenir lamps made of seashells that are now worth $300.

CROSSOVER APPEAL

By their very nature, these items are pursued by history buffs as well as those who seek unusual souvenirs. Tokens, plates, teacups, and books are just a few of the souvenir items that appeal to more than one collecting group. Major mass culture events of the 20th century, such as various World's Fairs, Charles Lindberg's flight, and the Apollo 11 moon landing, generated huge demand for mementos, not to mention gift shops for every tourist location across the county. The heyday of American tourism and the good ol' fashioned road trip (1920-1960) stuffed car trunks full of keepsakes from Maine to Hawaii.

One of the most ubiquitous souvenirs ever mass-produced are sterling silver spoons. Created during the mid-19th century, original retail prices of collectible spoons were inexpensive, but the sentimental nature encouraged travelers to save them by the millions. Most sterling spoons are worth less than $50 on today's market, with the top of the market settling at $300. Silver-plated spoons – those often used for state spoons or made by Rogers Bros. – sell for $1 or less. When spoons do appear at auction or in a shop, they are most often sold in a set.

Souvenirs were in demand long before the 20th century. Upper class European young men, from the late 1660s to the mid-1800s, often embarked on a Grand Tour as a rite of passage. The traditional tour was deemed necessary for noblemen and impresarios to experience other cultures, music, and exotic customs. It was important for these gentlemen to tour antiquity collections and amass a respectable amount for their estates. The market for coins, paintings, medals, and replicas of ancient works of art exploded during this time and are now an important segment of the fine and decorative art market, with values generally starting at $1,000.

Souvenirs weren't only reserved for the ruling class. Promoters in Victorian Europe gifted young middle class debutants with gilded dance ball souvenirs to be affixed to dance cards. The little charms were often stamped with a date and were popular from the 1870s to 1900, although they are still made today. These charms are popular collectibles and now trade for $100 to $500.

DIFFERENCE BETWEEN SOUVENIRS AND RELICS

There is a stark difference between objects we call souvenirs and relics, although both serve to memorialize important events, locations, and people. Souvenirs are generally mass-produced objects designed chiefly for tourists. Relics, on the other hand, are objects with a stronger tie to the subject itself. A relic of the Battle of Gettysburg might be a Civil War minnie ball embedded in a chuck of fence post or tree bark left over from the conflict; a Gettysburg souvenir might be a pottery stein depicting artists' scenes and memorial buildings relating to the battle, once available in a gift shop. Both are valued at roughly $200 each.

Deep collecting interest remains for both, with prices particularly on the rise for those objects that have some age or show some quirky appeal – a pair of painted wood clogs decorated with painted U.S. and Netherland flags and designed to hang on the wall. The oddity commemorates the strong relationship among The Netherlands, the United States, and the United Nations, and is valued at $180.

MINIATURE BUILDINGS

The Souvenir Building Collectors Society, a club for those who collect souvenir buildings, has more than 200 members and is over 20 years old. The three-dimensional miniature versions of famous or notable buildings can still be found in gift centers, but vintage versions can sell for as much as $220 if rare, taller than 10 inches, or made from precious metals.

Replica miniature banks were popular premiums during the mid-20th century, and skyscrapers remain popular collectibles.

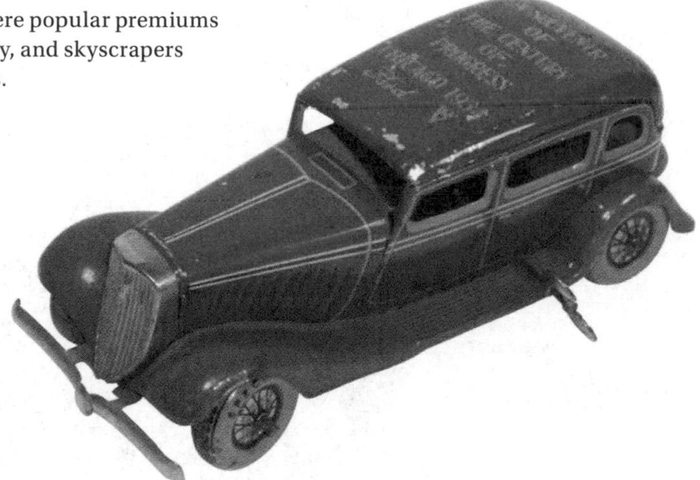

Wind-up metal toy Ford coupe with "A Souvenir of The Century of Progress Chicago 1934" on its roof, marked Japan, possibly by C. K. Graham, excellent working condition, 7-1/2" l. **$650**

Courtesy of Rich Penn, www.richpennauctions.com

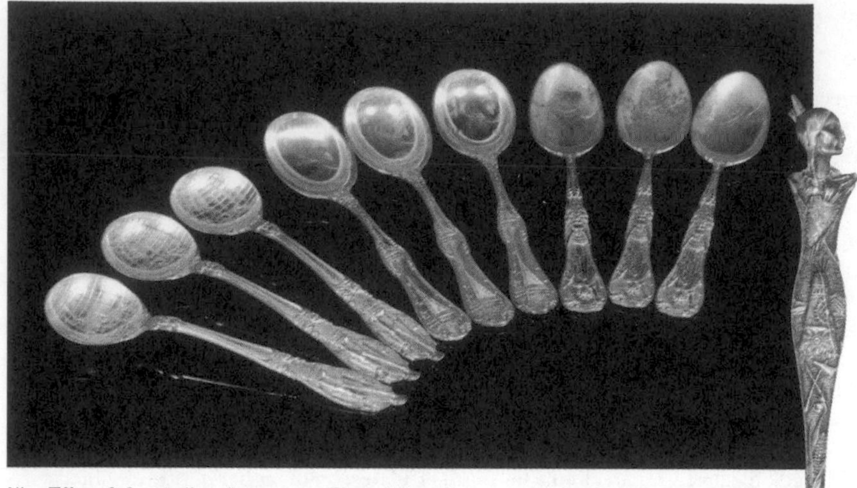

Nine Tiffany & Co. sterling silver spoons: Three Statue of Liberty spoons (5-7/8" l.), three Christopher Columbus spoons designed by John T. Curran (5-3/4" l.), and three George Washington Bridge spoons (5-3/4" l.), approximately 11.3 troy oz. **$369**

Courtesy of Kaminski Auctions, www.kaminskiauctions.com

▶ Sterling silver Lewis & Clark Exposition souvenir spoon, 1905. .... **$30**

Courtesy of Pioneer Auction Gallery, www.pioneerantiqueauction.com

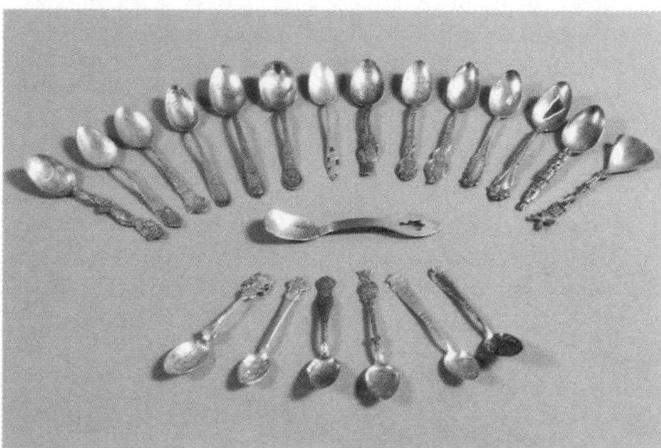

◀ Group of mostly sterling silver souvenir spoons, both American and international destinations including New York, Manchester, Detroit, Holland, and Washington, some of lesser purity silver, approximately 8.4 troy oz. ... **$185**

Courtesy of Skinner, Inc., www.skinnerinc.com

1904 St. Louis World's Fair celluloid tape measure with The Cascades water feature in two different photos on each side, cloth tape retracts with strong action.................. **$50**

Courtesy of Morphy Auctions, morphyauctions.com

Two banks with Native American ▶ Indian chiefs: Bank with tin trap, marked "Yellowstone Park," and bank with key-turn tin trap, marked "Rest Home, Elevation 2249, Mt. Tuscarora Park" with coin and bill slot, near mint condition, larger bank 5" h... **$92**

Courtesy of Morphy Auctions, morphyauctions.com

N.A.G. (Negro Actors Guild) program, Dec. 11, 1938, 46th St., Theatre Place, New York, original pictorial wrappers, covers detached but present, front cover with African-style illustration signed "ESC," 44 unnumbered pages, mostly congratulatory ads, fair to good condition, covers worn, discolored and detached. Formed during the Depression when no black actor or actress had as yet become a Hollywood star, the Negro Actors Guild had among its officers Duke Ellington, Cab Calloway, and Bill "Bojangles" Robinson, with "Honorary Life Memberships" presented to Marian Anderson, Ethel Waters, boxer Joe Louis, and white performers Eddie Cantor and Tyrone Power. **$234**

Courtesy of PBA Galleries, www.pbagalleries.com

Custard glass creamer with hand-painted transfer image of Apache Chief Geronimo, circa 1904-1909, captioned "Geronimo, Indian Chief, / Souvenir of Shawnee, Okla. / E. C. Werner.," excellent condition, 4" h. Geronimo lived the last 15 years of his life at Fort Sill, Oklahoma. This souvenir is likely based on the famous photograph of the Apache chieftain. **$64**

Courtesy of Heritage Auctions, ha.com

▲ Wooden vases from Eagle River, Wisconsin, Native American Indian decals applied, excellent condition, each 6" h. **$75**

Courtesy of Morphy Auctions, morphyauctions.com

Chinese beige ceramic teapot and lid with "New York World's Fair" and official Lamberton U.S.A. souvenir ceramic plate reading "New York World's Fair 1939", plate in good condition, teapot spout worn, plate 11" dia., teapot 9" x 8" h............ **$62**

Courtesy of Roland Auctioneers & Valuers, www.rolandauctions.com

Countertop displays with variety of flags, each display with fancy cast metal footed base with wood top, each in a different style, excellent condition, larger 20" h. **$325**

Courtesy of Morphy Auctions, morphyauctions.com

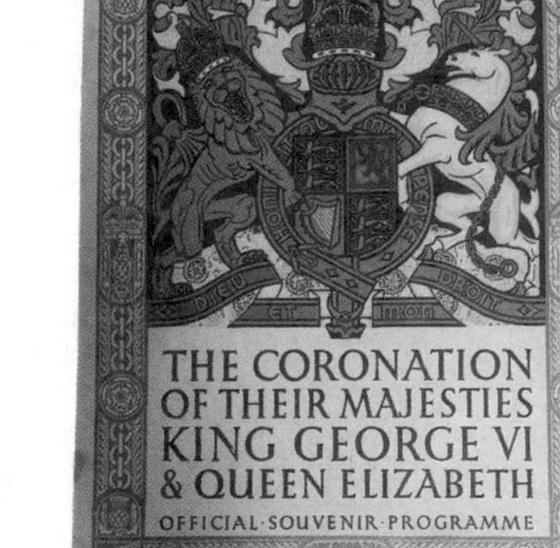

"The Coronation of Their Majesties King George VI & Queen Elizabeth Official Souvenir Programme," 1937.................................... **$24**

Courtesy of Omega Auction Corp., www.omegaauctioncorp.com

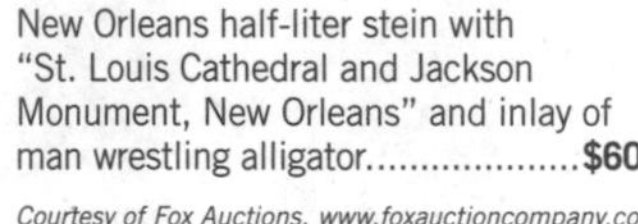

New Orleans half-liter stein with "St. Louis Cathedral and Jackson Monument, New Orleans" and inlay of man wrestling alligator.................... **$60**

Courtesy of Fox Auctions, www.foxauctioncompany.com

Coronation Souvenir Book 1937 of the British monarchy..... **$24**

Courtesy of Omega Auction Corp., www.omegaauctioncorp.com

Tin litho child's cup and saucer with beach scenes from Atlantic City, New Jersey, marked Germany, some paint loss, cup with small dent, saucer 4-3/8" dia., cup 2-1/4" dia..**$12**

Courtesy of Stephenson's Auction, www.stephensonsauction.com

◀ George Dickel Tennessee Sour Mash Whisky souvenir bottle, powder horn-shaped, limited edition to commemorate reopening of distillery, bottled October 1964, 45%, 1-4/5 quart bottle. **$246**

Courtesy of Skinner, Inc., www.skinnerinc.com

Light-up shell art with palm trees and flamingos from Daytona Beach, Florida, excellent condition, 6-1/2" h. **$25**

Courtesy of Morphy Auctions, morphyauctions.com

◀ Rare silk "Souvenir Official Programme Crescent City Jockey Club Winter Meeting," New Orleans, March 15, 1898, printed broadside on pink silk with lineup for six races and musical selections provided by Prof. Wolff's Crescent City Orchestra, on 87th day of racing season, very good condition, creased, light wear, lightly soiled, approximately 14" x 9-2/3".... **$492**

Courtesy of PBA Galleries, www.pbagalleries.com

SPORTS

PEOPLE HAVE BEEN saving sports-related equipment since the inception of sports. Some of it was passed down from generation to generation for reuse; the rest was stored in closets, attics, and basements.

Two key trends brought attention to sports collectibles. First, decorators began using old sports items, particularly in restaurants. Second, collectors began to discover the thrill of owning the "real" thing.

There are collectible items representing nearly every sport, but baseball memorabilia is probably the most well-known segment. The "national pastime" has millions of fans with enthusiastic collectors seeking items associated with players such as Babe Ruth, Lou Gehrig, and others who became legends in their own lifetimes. Although baseball cards, issued as advertising premiums for bubble gum and other products, seem to dominate the field, there are numerous other items available.

Sports collectibles are more accessible than ever before because of online auctions and several auction houses that dedicate themselves to that segment of the hobby. Provenance is extremely important when investing in high-ticket sports collectibles. Being able to know the history of the object may greatly enhance the value, with a premium paid for items secured from the player or directly from his or her estate.

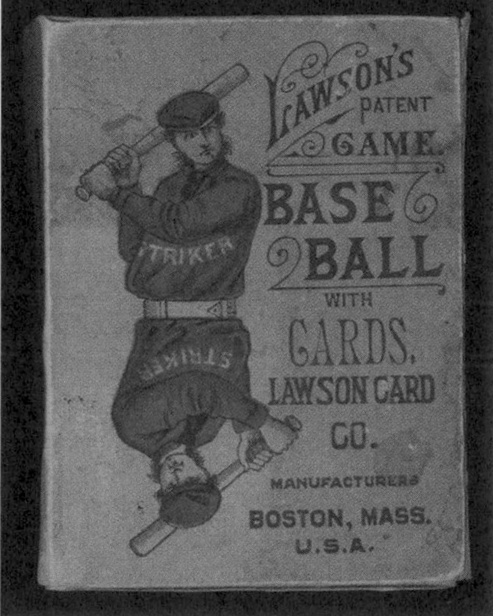

1884 Lawson's Base Ball Game playing card set, Lawson Card Co., Boston, 36-card set with one rules booklet, original box, and two "value of cards" cards...**$840**

Courtesy of Robert Edward Auctions, www.robertedwardsauctions.com

1914 Boston "Miracle" Braves Royal Rooters ribbon pin, gold-colored pin with red ribbon reading "Boston Royal Rooters 1914" in gilt letters, celluloid button attached at base with portrait illustration of Native American Indian brave in full headdress, lettered "Boston Braves Champions 1914" around perimeter, A. Lopez & Bros. of Boston. **$4,800**

Courtesy of Robert Edward Auctions, www.robertedwardsauctions.com

1962 Green Bay Packers NFL Championship wristwatch presented to Jerry Kramer, gold Hamilton with black dial with diamond indices, "Green Bay Packers / 1962 World Champions / NFL" on face, case engraved "Jerry Kramer, Green Bay 13, New York 7" on reverse............. **$45,410**

Courtesy of Heritage Auctions, ha.com

Bill Russell signed Boston Garden replica banner showcasing championship years of Boston Celtics with Russell, 35" x 17"......................... **$120**

Courtesy of Collect Auctions, collectauctions.com

Mike Tyson professional ring bell, bell and hammer affixed to wooden backing. **$160**

Courtesy of Collect Auctions, collectauctions.com

Tommy Anderson game-worn New York Americans NHL jersey, circa 1935-1936, "Alex Taylor & Co." manufacturer's label..... **$16,730**

Courtesy of Heritage Auctions, ha.com

▶1871 Boston Red Stockings baseball pinback, Andy Leonard Collection, likely issued as season pass, 1-1/4" l...................... **$7,170**

Courtesy of Heritage Auctions, ha.com

top lot

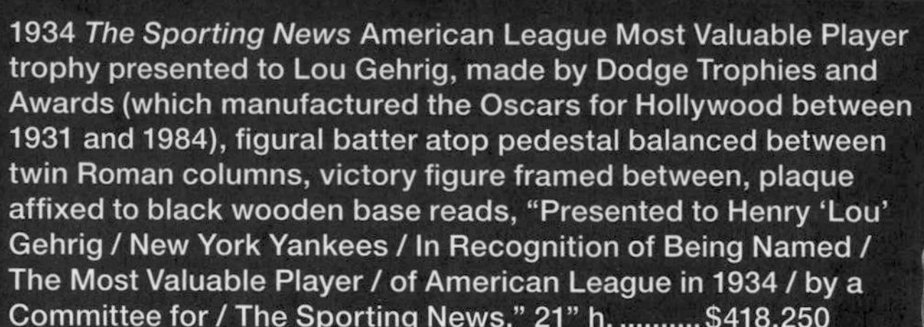

1934 *The Sporting News* American League Most Valuable Player trophy presented to Lou Gehrig, made by Dodge Trophies and Awards (which manufactured the Oscars for Hollywood between 1931 and 1984), figural batter atop pedestal balanced between twin Roman columns, victory figure framed between, plaque affixed to black wooden base reads, "Presented to Henry 'Lou' Gehrig / New York Yankees / In Recognition of Being Named / The Most Valuable Player / of American League in 1934 / by a Committee for / The Sporting News," 21" h. $418,250

COURTESY OF HERITAGE AUCTIONS, HA.COM

Yankee Stadium free-standing triple-seat section, unrestored, from 1973 Yankee Stadium renovation, 58" l. x 13" w. x 30" h. **$4,153**

Courtesy of SCP Auctions, Inc., www.scpauctions.com

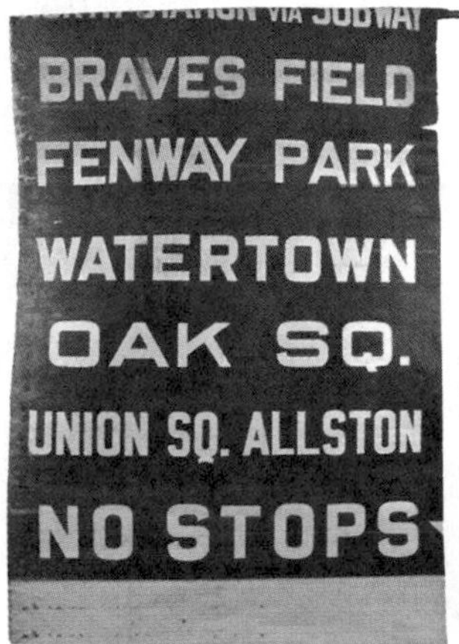

Braves Field/Fenway Park trolley sign, 1915-1952, 14' l. x 5' w. **$1,800**

Courtesy of Robert Edward Auctions, www.robertedwardsauctions.com

Sonny Liston vs. Cassius Clay program from first heavyweight championship fight, 1964, Miami Beach Convention Hall. **$1,420**

Courtesy of SCP Auctions, Inc., www.scpauctions.com

Olympic torch from 1948 London Summer Olympics, one of 1,720 torches made for flame relay, 16" h., circular bowl 6" dia. **$10,367**

Courtesy of SCP Auctions, Inc., www.scpauctions.com

1909 Detroit Tigers match safe with portraits of Ty Cobb, Sam Crawford, and Hughie Jennings, 24 players in all, advertising for Mundus Beer of Detroit on reverse, 2-3/4" x 1-1/2". **$2,040**

Courtesy of Robert Edward Auctions, www.robertedwardsauctions.com

1948 Bowman #69 George Mikan rookie card, graded Gem Mint PSA 10. ....**$403,644**

Courtesy of SCP Auctions, Inc., www.scpauctions.com

Mighty Casey original bronze statue by Mark Lundeen, 7' h., 600-plus lbs. **$12,000**

Courtesy of Robert Edward Auctions, www.robertedwardsauctions.com

Michael Jordan signed Stephen Holland giclée, limited edition No. 41/69, also signed by Holland, 41" x 28".......... **$1,673**

Courtesy of Goldin Auctions, goldinauctions.com

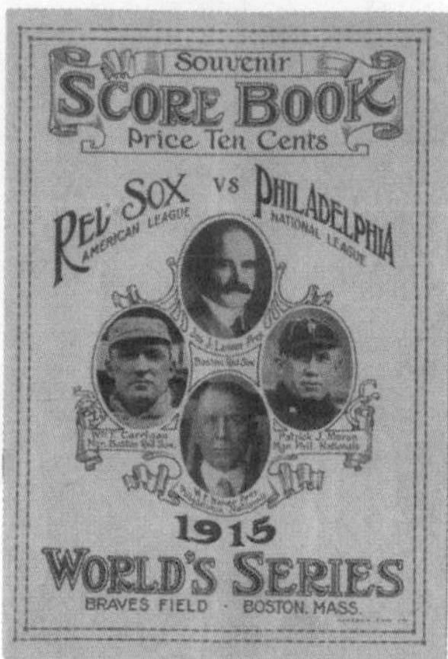

1915 World Series program, Red Sox vs. Philadelphia Phillies.......................... **$2,440**

Courtesy of Goldin Auctions, goldinauctions.com

▲ 1909 Cy Young Welcome Home Cy / Wageman's advertising pinback, 1-1/4" dia................ **$936**

Courtesy of Mile High Card Co., www.milehighcardco.com

◀ 1960 U.S. Hockey Olympic Gold Medal presented to Bill Christian, gilt silver by Herff Jones Co., 55 mm dia., 97 g. **$50,190**

Courtesy of Heritage Auctions, ha.com

▲ "Big" Ed Walsh Old Timers' Day commemorative silver tray honoring veteran White Sox and Yankees baseball stars, 1956, 12" dia. **$1,159**

Courtesy of Goldin Auctions, goldinauctions.com

◀ 1916 Brooklyn Dodgers World Series press pin for games played at Ebbets Field against Boston Red Sox and Babe Ruth, "DIEGES & CLUST MAKERS" on reverse. **$5,020**

Courtesy of SCP Auctions, Inc., www.scpauctions.com

Brooklyn Dodgers pennant, 1940s, possible first appearance of Bums, two sets of tassels next to yellow felt spine, 26" x 8". **$837**

Courtesy of Goldin Auctions, goldinauctions.com

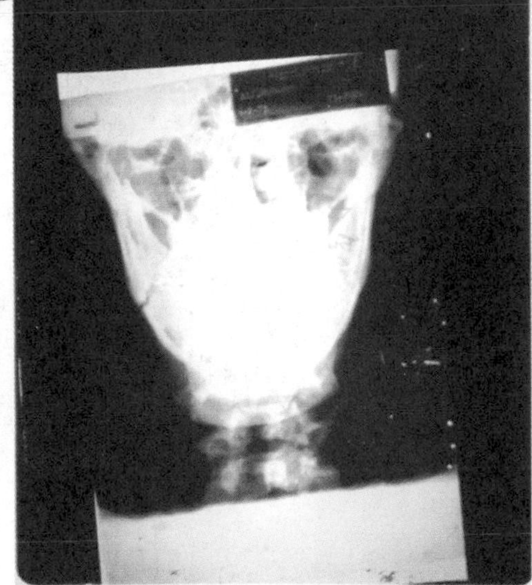

Muhammad Ali broken jaw x-ray from Ken Norton fight, 1973. .... **$1,019**

Courtesy of Collect Auctions, collectauctions.com

Christy Mathewson Type I original photograph by Charles M. Conlon, with numerous back-stampings attributable to news bureau company Underwood & Underwood, 6-1/2" x 8-1/2"........................... **$2,271**

Courtesy of Goldin Auctions, goldinauctions.com

Joe Louis Elasti-Cuff children's boxing gloves, two pairs new in box, 1950s, Sears, Roebuck and Co............**$119**

Courtesy of Collect Auctions, collectauctions.com

R.J. Reynolds Yankee Baseball mechanical die-cut countertop advertising display, 1959, 22" x 16"...................................... **$163**

Courtesy of Mile High Card Co., www.milehighcardco.com

Sporting Life's American League schedule book, 1909, with ad for *Sporting Life* cabinet photos on back. **$239**

Courtesy of Collect Auctions, collectauctions.com

Don Drysdale signed Salvino Statue with original box, limited to 200 examples. **$65**

Courtesy of Mile High Card Co., www.milehighcardco.com

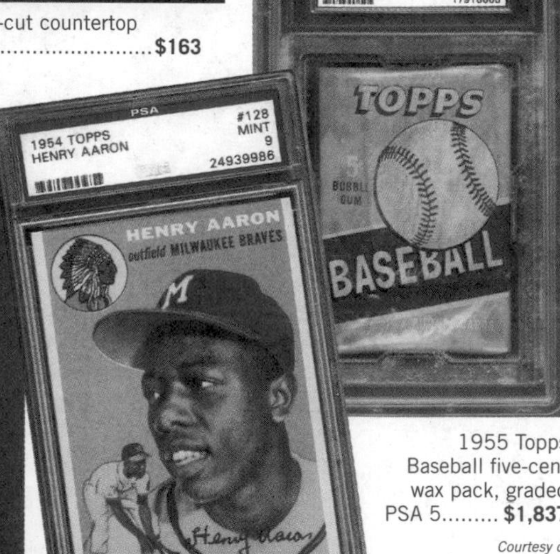

1955 Topps Baseball five-cent wax pack, graded PSA 5......... **$1,837**

Courtesy of Mile High Card Co., www.milehighcardco.com

1954 Topps #128 Henry Aaron baseball card, graded PSA 9 mint condition, population of three at that grade. **$192,527**

Courtesy of Mile High Card Co., www.milehighcardco.com

TOOLS

TOOL COLLECTING IS nearly as old as tools themselves. Certainly it was not long after Stone Age man used his first stone tool that he started watching for that special rock or piece of bone. Soon he would have been putting tools away for the right time or project. The first tool collector was born!

Since earliest man started collecting tools, many other reasons to collect have evolved. As man created one tool, he could then use that tool to make an even better tool.

Very quickly toolmakers became extremely skilled at their craft, and that created a new collecting area – collecting the works of the best makers. In time toolmakers realized that tools were being purchased on the basis of the quality of workmanship alone. With this realization an even more advanced collector was born as toolmakers began making top-of-the-line tools from special materials with fine detailing and engraving. These exquisite tools were never intended for use but were to be enjoyed and collected. Many of the finest tools were of such quality that they are considered works of art.

So many tools exist in today's world that many collectors focus on one special category. Some of the most popular categories to collect fall into the general areas of: function, craft or trade, personal connection, company or brand, patents, and investments.

For more information on tools, check out the "Farm Tools" section in this book. Also see *Antique Trader Tools Price Guide* by Clarence Blanchard.

Early dental cabinet with tools and supplies. **$243**

Courtesy of Keystone Auctions, www.keystoneauctions.com

Homemade tool/tackle chest with assorted tackle and baits. **$60**

Courtesy of Morphy Auctions, morphyauctions.com

Our Very Best Tools Cutlery advertising trade sign, 1910, 70" x 10-1/2"... **$458**

Courtesy of Morphy Auctions, morphyauctions.com

Antique watch/clock maker's tool set, good condition......... **$60**

Courtesy of The Gallery on 1st Street/Chandler's International Auctions, www.chandlersauction.com

Buffalo skinner's kit with tools, 1870s-1890s, 36" belt. **$1,375**

Courtesy of Heritage Auctions, ha.com

Hand-held sugar cane cutter with finger guards, early smith-made tool, ornately decorated, 9" l. **$61**

Courtesy of Keystone Auctions, www.keystoneauctions.com

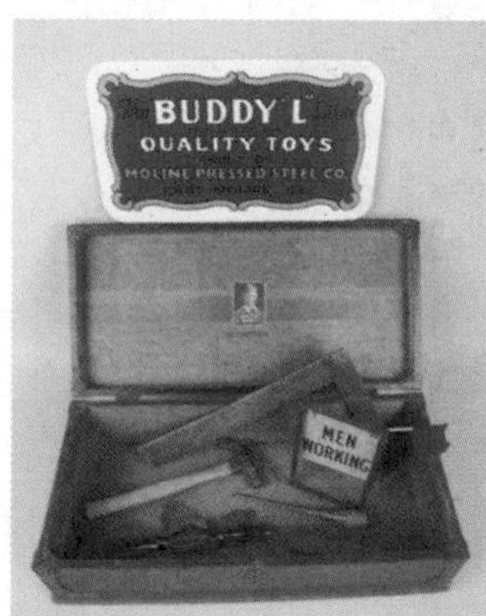

Pressed steel Buddy L toy tool chest, 1927-1929, with non-Buddy L tools, 11" x 23" x 7" **$92**

Courtesy of Morphy Auctions, morphyauctions.com

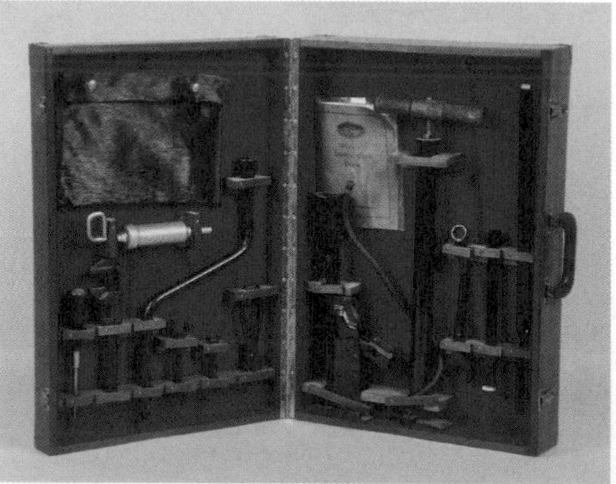

1929 Ford Model A tool kit in display box.......... **$975**

Courtesy of Morphy Auctions, morphyauctions.com

top lot!

Sixty-four fluted ivory-handled turning tools of varying patterns, likely shown in the London Exhibition of the Works of Industry of All Nations by Holtzapffel in 1851, engine-turned silver ferrules and cast threaded rosettes for blade attachment, all stamped Holtzapffel on hardened steel blades, tools show little evidence of being used, in double-door mahogany cabinet with fielded panel interior and doors, cabinet closed 36" h. x 18" w., open 36" w., tools 6-1/2" to 9-1/2" l. $44,280

COURTESY OF SKINNER, INC., WWW.SKINNERINC.COM

Oshkosh Tools pin-up girl advertising calendar, 1963, framed 39-1/2" x 22"......... **$244**

Courtesy of Morphy Auctions, morphyauctions.com

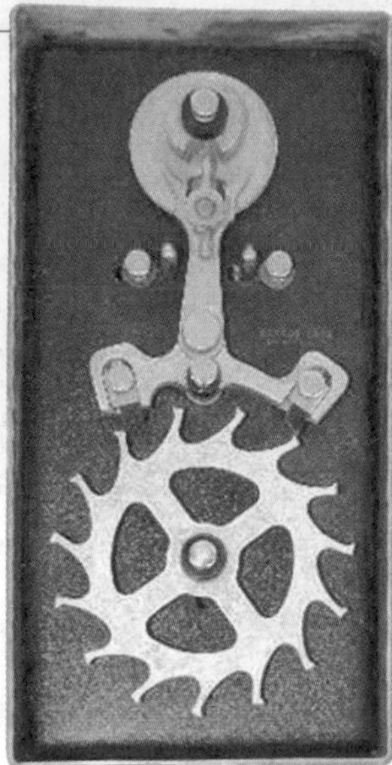

Lever escapement teaching tool, oversized model, Barkus Labs, San Diego, California, 10" l. **$107**

Courtesy of Tom Harris Auctions, www.tomharrisauctions.com

Press lab tool, cast iron, marked "Whitall, Tatum Co., New York, Phila., Boston," 8-1/4" h. **$60**

Courtesy of Morphy Auctions, morphyauctions.com

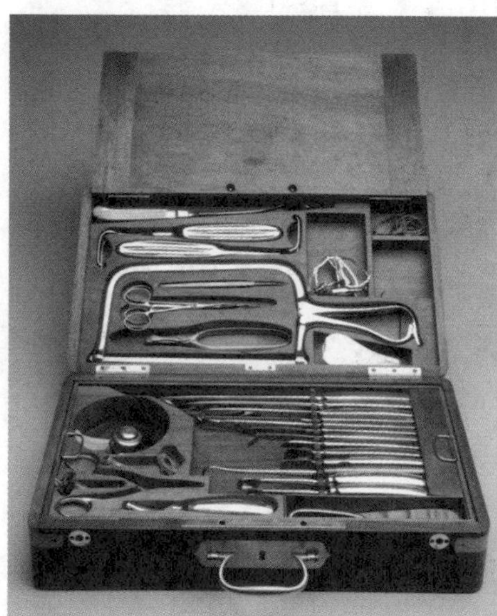

Mathieu Paris surgical kit, stamped "Mathieu" on both instruments and on inner tag, 15-1/4" x 9"............ **$855**

Courtesy of Morphy Auctions, morphyauctions.com

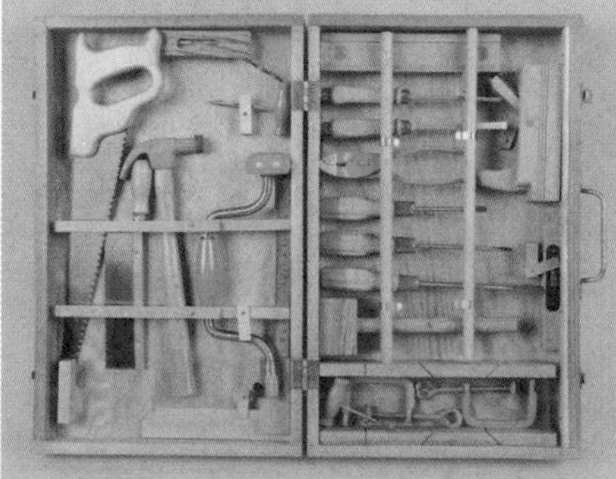

Handy Andy carpenter's tool chest, 1960s, 18" l. **$120**

Courtesy of Morphy Auctions, morphyauctions.com

Providence Tool Co. handcuffs, 10" l. **$120**

Courtesy of Morphy Auctions, morphyauctions.com

▲ Automotive tool, cast iron on wood base, Baker Shoe Press Co., Springfield, Illinois, 11" x 17"......**$60**

Courtesy of Rich Penn Auctions, www.richpennauctions.com

◄ Conestoga wagon tool box, 18th century, painted yellow pine, 15-1/2" x 15-1/2"........... **$300**

Courtesy of Jeffrey S. Evans & Associates, www.jeffreysevans.com

Native American bone tools and needles display, framed, 18-1/2" x 28-1/2".. **$420**

Courtesy of Rich Penn Auctions, www.richpennauctions.com

Blacksmith travelers wheel used for making wagon wheels, hand-forged construction with wooden handle, good condition, 7-1/2" dia., 14-1/2" l............. **$60**

Courtesy of North American Auction Co., www.northamericanauctioncompany.com

Dovetailed pine lidded cutlery/tool carrier, possibly Shaker, 16" x 9"............... **$215**

Courtesy of Skinner, Inc., www.skinnerinc.com

▲ American decorated wrought-iron pie crimper/ pastry wheel, late 18th/early 19th century, 10" l....................... **$1,080**

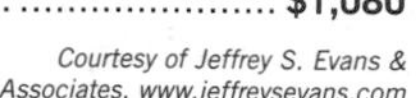

Courtesy of Jeffrey S. Evans & Associates, www.jeffreysevans.com

▲ Unusual camp tool, knife and two-pronged fork in common scabbard, 18" l. **$123**

Courtesy of Kaminski Auctions, www.kaminskiauctions.com

Hardware store sign, Keen Kutter Tools, Murphy & Brown Hardware, Auburn, Nebraska, 9-3/4" x 27-3/4". **$210**

Courtesy of Rich Penn Auctions, www.richpennauctions.com

Soda fountain tool, Sampson press or juicer, 1891, Buffum Tool Co., Louisiana, Missouri, 10-1/2" l. **$180**

Courtesy of Rich Penn Auctions, www.richpennauctions.com

▲ Vintage Agricultural Trustworthy Tools sheet metal display stand, 46" x 4" x 41-1/2" h. **$270**

Courtesy of Copake Auction, Inc., www.copakeauction.com

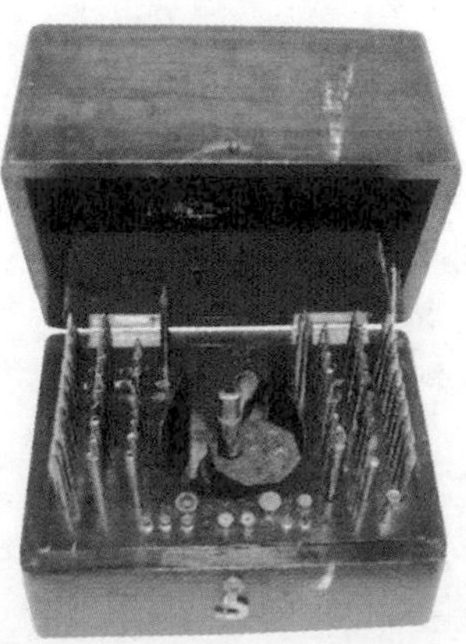

◀ K & D staking set in walnut case, 6" x 7". **$81**

Courtesy of Tom Harris Auctions, www.tomharrisauctions.com

TOYS

IN HIS *PICKER'S POCKET GUIDE: TOYS,* author Eric Bradley said no other hobby touches collectors and people in general quite like toys.

According to Bradley, the people who collect vintage toys are those who are simply revisiting their first collection. In some cases, they never left it. That's the thing about toy collecting: You can find amazing examples in abundant supply from any time period - especially your own.

Sales data shows you'll have lots of company in your toy collecting hobby, but also lots of competition for finer examples. The collectible toy business is one of the largest in both the retail market and the secondary market, and is also perhaps one of the first types of established collecting genres ever defined. It's interesting to note that FAO Schwarz, founded in 1862 as America's first toy store, launched its "Toy Bazaar" antique toy department in the early 1960s to meet collector demand. Toy collecting is an old and venerated hobby, Bradley said.

No figures are kept for the number of vintage collectible toys sold every year, but Bradley said the number sold at auction is growing. At any given time, more than five million toys are for sale or taking bids on eBay. LiveAuctioneers, one of the world's largest auction-hosting websites, shows an estimated half-million toys were sold by brick and mortar auction houses at auction during the last 16 years. In many cases, these sales have set new records as collections finally come to market after decades in private hands, he said.

Among these private collections, Bradley said few reached the size, scope, and value of that owned by Donald Kaufman, whose family founded Kay Bee Toys in 1922, and who decided in 2009 to sell his collection. Kaufman felt collectors would care for the toys better than any museum ever could. It took four auctions to sell the great Kaufman collection of automotive toys for a record $12.1 million. The collection stands as the most valuable of its kind in the history of the world.

You don't need to spend $12 million on toys to have an amazing collection. But it certainly helps to bring a fraction of the passion Kaufman brought to his hobby. You probably have a few toys hanging around the house, and it's never been easier to find unusual examples. Adding to them can become addictive, especially when you find ones you had as a kid...or the ones you always wanted.

Bradley said toy collecting allows for an infinite number of specialized collecting variations. Want cast iron cars made between 1930 and 1940? You could start with the Hubley Manufacturing Co. and collect by size. Only want dolls that were first introduced as paper dolls in the early 1950s? Betsy McCall is your gal. Have an affinity for pre-war metal

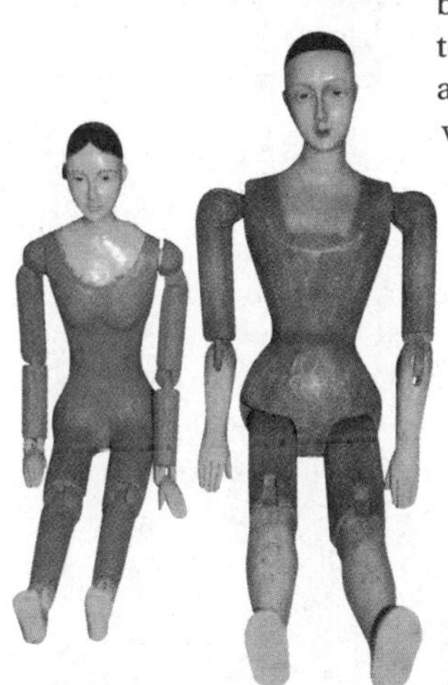

Two antique wood dolls, larger one 23-1/5". **$300**

Courtesy of Tyler Galleries, www.tylergalleries.com

White Wagon Works Teddy toy wagon, stenciled oak, maker marked on rear hub, original stencil decoration throughout, rear brakes and cast iron steering yoke, patent date 12-11-1900, excellent condition, one slat inside missing 3" piece, 36" l. x 14" w. **$180**

Courtesy of Milestone Auctions, www.milestoneauctions.com

squirt guns made in Michigan? Versions made by All Metal Products Co., better known as Wyandotte Toys, can be found for $20 on up, depending on condition. With toys, your collection can be as specialized or as general as you want it to be.

Bradley said toy values are chiefly influenced by demand, rarity, and condition, but there are other factors as well: authenticity, exposure, provenance, quality, and, most importantly, condition.

Authenticity is black or white. There are no gray areas with authenticity: Either the toy is right or it is wrong. It is either authentic or it is a fake.

Exposure influences demand for a work and brings prestige to its owner. When Steve Geppi, the president and CEO of Diamond Comic Distributors, paid $200,000 for the world's most valuable action figure – the first handcrafted prototype of the 1963 G.I. JOE® action figure – the sale made international news and earned a Guinness World Record. Exposure is crucial for building collector demand around a single piece or an entire category.

Provenance explains an established history of ownership. Once a vintage toy has entered the secondary market, it develops a provenance. A famous owner can add at most 15 percent or more on the value of a toy, but there are exceptions and this changes dramatically depending on who owned the toy in the past. When Leonardo DiCaprio sold part of his action figure collection at Morphy Auctions in 2006, values were stronger than expected, thanks to his famous name.

Quality may be a subjective criterion; however, a well-constructed toy is hard to find and fewer still survive for decades or even centuries. The more time you spend looking at quality toys, the easier it is to recognize good craftsmanship when you see it.

Condition is of the utmost importance in today's collector market. The most valuable items are in original condition with minimal restoration or alterations. This "best or nothing" approach to condition has probably been the most influential change in the hobby during the last decade. Values of toys in mid-range to low condition have fallen while values of rare toys in top condition often skyrocket beyond all expectations.

Large wooden knife with fold-out characters of Punch and Judy puppet show, late 19th century, with wooden stand, excellent condition, some handling scuffs, 7-1/4" h. x 6" w. when expanded and propped........... **$100**

Courtesy of Heritage Auctions, ha.com

10 Things You Didn't Know About **Steiff**

1 A seldom-seen Steiff mourning bear, produced in commemoration of the victims of the Titanic, circa 1912, with black fur, shoe button eyes lined with red felt, black stitched nose and claws, and sans an official Steiff button, commanded $34,800 (with buyer's premium) during an auction presented by Morphy Auctions in November 2011.

2 The creator of Steiff bears and animals, Margarete Steiff, fought through a challenging childhood to achieve her goals. As a toddler she survived a high fever, but the illness left her legs paralyzed and chronic pain in her right arm. Despite this, she attended sewing school and earned her seamstress certification at the age of 17. After working in her sisters' tailor shop, she opened her own felt clothing business, and ultimately founded Steiff Manufacture in 1880.

3 Although Steiff is often synonymous with bears, Margarete's first stuffed animal was actually an elephant. The first illustrated Steiff catalog, printed in 1892, not only included stuffed toy elephants, but also monkeys, horses, camels, mice, cats, and rabbits, among others. It was Margarete's nephew, Richard, who designed the first stuffed toy bears in 1902.

4 An early 20th century golden mohair Steiff bear with shoe button eyes, underscore Steiff button, and an intact leather muzzle, measuring 24" in height, realized $10,497 during a March 2014 auction presented by Bertoia Auctions.

5 Steiff collectors are a very active community. The Official Steiff Club, established in 1992, has more than 30,000 members from all corners of the globe. According to the club's events page, more than 15 events dedicated to Steiff plush toys were held in 2015. Plus, the Official Steiff Fan page on Facebook had nearly 8,700 "likes" at the beginning of July 2015.

6 The Steiff Museum, located in Giengen an der Brenz, Germany, and established in 1980, includes an exhibition representing various elements of the more than 130-year Steiff history, a tour of Margarete Steiff's sewing center, a demonstration of the traditional Steiff production process, the Steiff petting zoo, and the largest Steiff store in the world.

7 In 2012, an animated advertising automation manufactured by Margarete Steiff GmbH, Giengen, Germany, circa 1970s, featuring a workshop setting including 14 original Steiff animals, sold for $2,995 at auction, through Auction Team Breker.

8 The recognizable brand tag "Steiff – Button in Ear" was developed by Franz Steiff in 1904 to confirm authentic Steiff bears and to ward off imitations, of which there were many.

9 Inspired by the book *The Roosevelt Bears* by Seymour Eaton, Steiff and other companies began manufacturing clothing for teddy bears. In 1904, the Steiff Teddy B and Teddy G bears, inspired by those in *The Roosevelt Bears*, sold for 5 cents each, and today they can fetch more than $1,000 at auction.

10 Margarete Steiff and company displayed their stuffed animals during the Louisiana Purchase Exposition (St. Louis World's Fair) in 1904. Steiff was awarded a coveted Grand Prize during the Fair.

– Compiled by Antoinette Rahn

Margarete Steiff, founder of what became Margarete Steiff GmbH.

Courtesy of Steiff.com

Antique golden mohair Steiff bear with leather muzzle and shoe button eyes sold for $10,497 in 2014.

Courtesy of Bertoia Auctions, www.bertoiaauctions.com

The seldom-seen Steiff mourning bear, produced in commemoration of the victims of the Titanic, circa 1912, commanded $34,800 at auction in November 2011.

Courtesy of Morphy Auctions, morphyauctions.com

Sources: www.steiff.com, www.antiquetrader.com, www.liveauctioneers.com, www.worthpoint.com

Victorian-era horse on platform rocker, hide-covered with glass eyes and open carved mouth, converts from horse on platform pull toy to rocking horse, very good condition, base and rockers with old paint, some wear to saddle, 46" l., horse 32" h. **$110**

Courtesy of Milestone Auctions, www.milestoneauctions.com

Scale model toy wood and metal carriage, fine condition, mild surface wear, 41" x 15" x 8". .. **$200**

Courtesy of Heritage Auctions, ha.com

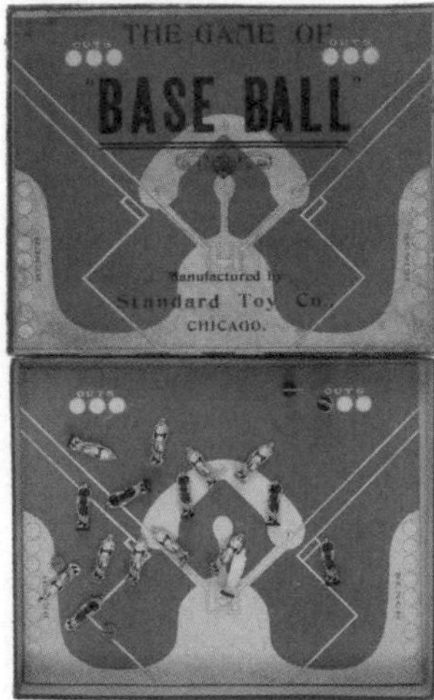

"Base Ball" game by Standard Toy Co., 1920s, spinning wheel determines course of play with die-cut fielders and base runners, lid with general handling wear, soiling and splits at seams of flaps, lower portion of box in better condition with no significant flaws, only known example... **$335**

Courtesy of Heritage Auctions, ha.com

Home Run King tin wind-up toy, Selrite Products, Inc., late 1930s, painted graphics range from action scene on sides of base to playing field on top to pinstriped uniform on batter who springs to life with turn of winding key, "hopper" could be filled with small baseballs (absent), toy lifts up one ball at time for batter to swing at and knock off tee, minimal wear, original packaging in very good condition, batter 7" h. with base. **$657**

Courtesy of Heritage Auctions, ha.com

Amish rag-stuffed cloth doll, circa 1900, originally collected in Pennsylvania, oilcloth head, homespun linen torso, legs made from old stockings, black velvet shoes, original clothing worn out and new clothes created in 1960s by dollmaker's daughter and granddaughter, excellent condition, 15"................... **$400**

Courtesy of Last Chance by LiveAuctioneers, www.liveauctioneers.com

◀ Two tin litho Ferris wheels, The Giant Ride by Ohio Art and 1930s Hercules by J. Chein & Co., age-related losses and wear, 16-1/2".................... **$225**

Courtesy of Vero Beach Auction, www.verobeachauction.com

Arcade cast iron dump truck with green cab, partial door decal, red bed, "219" mark on both cab and bed, good condition, 7-1/4" l............. **$295**

Courtesy of Leonard Auction, Inc., www.leonardauction.com

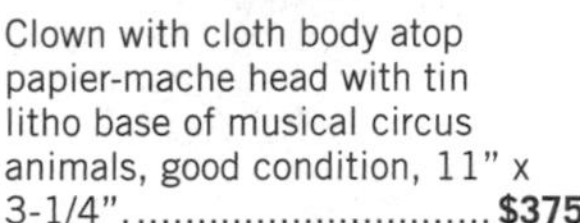

Clown with cloth body atop papier-mache head with tin litho base of musical circus animals, good condition, 11" x 3-1/4".............................. **$375**

Courtesy of Hartzell's Auction Gallery, Inc., www.hartzellsauction.com

Scarce sand toy sailboat by J. Chein & Co., circa 1935, wood hull, tin wheels, litho molds attached to sand sifter sail, good condition, shows wear, hull 16-1/2" l..................... **$160**

Courtesy of Milestone Auctions, www.milestoneauctions.com

Vintage toys, circa 1940s: Rare set of 1940 Ideal jointed wooden dolls, 8" Pinocchio with original box and 9" Jiminy Cricket, both on modern stands for display; Fisher-Price Pinocchio Express wooden pull toy; and Gong Bell Manufacturing Co. wooden Jiminy Cricket pull toy, good to very good condition... **$179**

Courtesy of Heritage Auctions, ha.com

Ideal Novelty Toy Co. Ferdinand Bull jointed composition toy, scattered paint loss, 9" x 9", and Marx Ferdinand Bull tin litho wind-up walker with spinning tail, circa 1938, age crazing and light play wear, 7" l... **$130**

Courtesy of Ron Rhoads Auctioneer, www.ronrhoads-auction.com

Disneyland Musical Map, Walt Disney/Mattel, 1955, rare original of then-newly opened Disneyland, lithograph map with five punch-out 78 rpm records for Adventureland, Frontierland, Fantasyland, Tomorrowland, and Introduction to Disneyland, with black-edge backing board, fine condition, 43" x 15"... **$478**

Courtesy of Heritage Auctions, ha.com

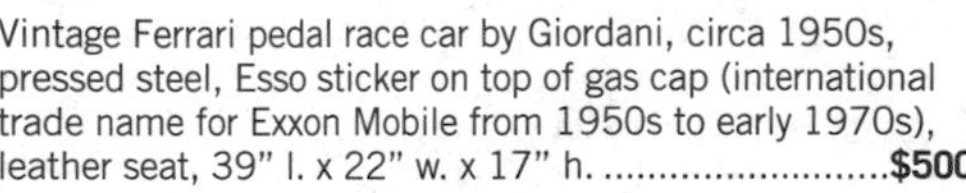

Vintage Ferrari pedal race car by Giordani, circa 1950s, pressed steel, Esso sticker on top of gas cap (international trade name for Exxon Mobile from 1950s to early 1970s), leather seat, 39" l. x 22" w. x 17" h. **$500**

Courtesy of Baer & Bosch Auctioneers, www.baerbosch.com

Toy military vehicle assortment, 21 Solido vehicles and two Tootsietoy miniature cannons, longest 8-1/4" l. **$250**

Courtesy of Leonard Auction, Inc., www.leonardauction.com

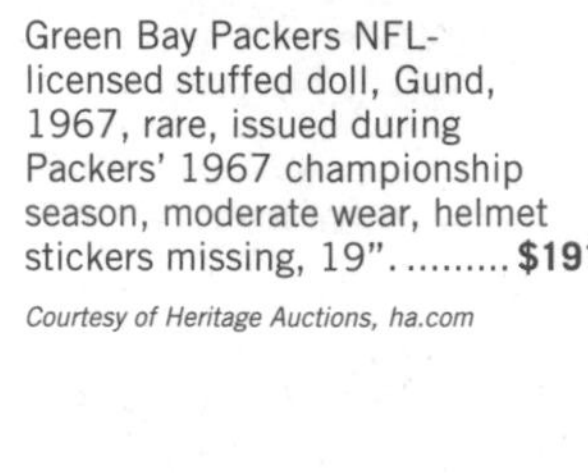

Green Bay Packers NFL-licensed stuffed doll, Gund, 1967, rare, issued during Packers' 1967 championship season, moderate wear, helmet stickers missing, 19". **$191**

Courtesy of Heritage Auctions, ha.com

Lionel model toy train freight car assortment, 17 plastic cars, #3656 stockyard, and partial train set #11460 in box, longest 11" l..................... **$150**

Courtesy of Leonard Auction, Inc., www.leonardauction.com

Early tin toy army truck with cloth canopy, marked U.S.A., good condition, moderate wear to paint, rust on wheels, replaced rear axle needs to be shortened, 13" l................ **$110**

Courtesy of Ron Rhoads Auctioneer, www.ronrhoads-auction.com

◀ Goldfinger-Thunderball Aston-Martin, Gilbert, 1965, tin car in original packaging, hidden machine guns, revolving license plates, ejection seat, very fine condition, original packaging with tear, corner separation, some wear, 4" x 5-1/4" x 12-1/2"............ **$657**

Courtesy of Heritage Auctions, ha.com

"Diamonds are Forever" Moon Buggy # 811 and other vehicles in original packaging, Corgi, 1972-1979, with universal jointed arms and spring-loaded claws in original moon-themed packaging; Drax Jet Ranger Helicopter #930 and Space Shuttle #649 from "Moonraker"; Stromberg Helicopter #926 from "The Spy Who Loved Me"; and Bond's Aston Martin #271; very fine condition, Moon Buggy and Space Shuttle with dings in plastic windows, Aston Martin packaging with crease...... **$1,434**

Courtesy of Heritage Auctions, ha.com

Beatles Banjo, Mastro Industries, 1964, four-stringed toy instrument originally manufactured with instruction manual and packaged on cardboard backing, very fine condition, little damage to face, upper collar around face with crack, early Mastro box of same vintage but probably not box made for this instrument. **$1,375**

Courtesy of Heritage Auctions, ha.com

Walt Disney Roly Poly toy pre-production prototype group, Kohner/Gabriel, circa 1970s, plaster casting of Donald Duck for Roly Poly, 4-1/2" (including selvage at bottom of figure); two slightly different working prototypes of Mickey Mouse Roly Poly (shown); and two Mickey Roly Poly toys in blister packs, one with Kohner logo, other marked Gabriel; with 1976 Gabriel Toy catalog with Mickey and Donald Roly Polys on page 11, and Kohner color flyer with in-house pink Post-it attached, marked "18B"; loose toys in very good to fine condition, plaster Donald in excellent condition, two blister cards with storage wear with mint condition toys inside. **$79**

Courtesy of Heritage Auctions, ha.com

Aquaman bendy toy plaster prototype group, Mego, circa 1973, two cast plaster figures of DC Comics superhero Aquaman, one hand-painted and other unpainted, overall good condition, both in pieces, painted figure with leg and arm broken off but included, unpainted figure with both arms and head broken off but included......................... **$1,315**

Courtesy of Heritage Auctions, ha.com

Space: 1999 Adventure Playset, Amsco, 1975, rare, complete boxed set still shrink-wrapped with high-quality printed images on thick cardstock that fold up to create part of Moonbase Alpha with working elevator, two Eagle space shuttles, Moonbuggy, and several stand-ups of characters from series, mint condition. **$335**

Courtesy of Heritage Auctions, ha.com

Bond-X Automatic Shooting Camera, multiple toymakers, 1966, in original packaging, camera with hidden compartment for bullets, grip, shoulder strap carrying case, bullets, and instructions, very fine-minus condition, minor wear, original packaging with spotting in windows, 3" x 14-1/2" x 23-1/2"........... **$1,195**

Courtesy of Heritage Auctions, ha.com

Star Wars vehicles, Kenner, 1978, die-cast X-Wing Fighter, TIE Fighter, and Land Speeder in original packaging, 12-pack style, all from original release, rare, very fine-plus condition, never opened, minor corner dings, small creases, and slight curvature on packaging, TIE Fighter and Land Speeder with unpunched cards, 7" x 10". **$598**

Courtesy of Heritage Auctions, ha.com

VINTAGE ELECTRONICS

THERE'S PLENTY OF history to collect in the ever-growing and expanding category of vintage electronics. From the dawn of the Electrical Age (which spans 1600-1800) to the household innovations of today, the depth and variety of vintage electronics makes it one of the fastest-growing collectible segments in the hobby.

This is because of an influx of younger collectors (generally mid-20s to mid-40s) who happen to be the first generation to live with mobile, digital technology crucial to modern life. But don't think this category is regulated to "vintage" finds: It's quite amazing to realize that the first book to combine the study of static electricity and the scientific method, *De Magnete* by Sir William Gilbert, was published in 1600 – the same year William Shakespeare oversaw the first production of "A Midsummer Night's Dream."

Despite the innovation and constantly changing adaptations, the principals of electronics have remained unchanged for more than 100 years. Non-collectors might be surprised to learn that the same basic technology that made the original ViewMaster a commercial hit in 1938 is the basis of today's latest virtual reality technology. Presenting two photographs of the same object from slightly different angles is the basis of the Oculus Rift virtual reality device (which may itself be a hot collectible in the next 25 years).

Some of the most sought-after examples of vintage electronics in today's hobby include rare or mint condition video game consoles and games; calculators from the early 1970s; and personal computers from the very early years of the technology, such as the Hewlett Packard 9100A released in 1968 or the KENBAK - 1, which sold for $35,000 at auction in early 2015. By the time you read this chapter, the average cost of a laptop computer is about $600, while the resale value of its 40+ year-old-grandfather starts at about $1,200 and ends at more than $600,000 for one of the scant 63 surviving examples of the Apple 1 computer assembled by Steve Jobs and his friends in 1976.

Vintage electronics falls into the "usable collectible" category; vintage electronics collectors put a premium on usability over decorative value. A good example is the growing popularity of collecting vintage electronics that surround music. Collectors fuel a robust hobby by hunting down obscure and obsolete EL34 tubes made in the early 1960s in West Germany by Telefunken (generally found at $75-$100). The tubes were used in amplifiers made by companies such as Marshall and Hi-Watt and are now prized by collectors and audiophiles who restore amps for the sole purpose of recreating the unique "British-tone" that made the music of The Beatles and Led Zeppelin. Was the music produced by the young Eric Clapton rooted in his imagination and creativity? Absolutely. Were the unique British amps and EL34 tubes crucial in enhancing his harmonic consistency? Without a doubt. So while it might be easy to find parts of a vintage Marshall amp from the days of The British Invasion for about $50 to $200, a near-mint/mint amp in perfect working order will likely cost between $1,500 and $5,500. American examples from the 1950s can command five figures.

One popular niche to appear in the last five years is the emergence of the collection and restoration of vintage boombox stereos, which were a commercial hit in the 1970s and 1980s. Collectors have formed clubs across the country, founded an active Facebook page (Boomboxery), and even an annual event, the First Annual Boomboxery International Blaster Summit in September 2016 in Las Vegas. And this hobby is truly an international one. Collector Rickard Fredholm of Sweden recently refurbished his family's 1981 Sharp 5P-37G boombox, which captured the fascination of his toddler, Lilly.

"My father bought it in 1981 and it has a quite funny history," Fredholm said. "My mother was pregnant in the last months with me and my father had a Toyota Celica 70s model. It was quite a small car and they needed a bigger car like a Volvo 240. He went to her job at the airport and walked into her office and told her that he had a surprise at the parking lot. She thought he had bought a family car...but when she came out she saw the same old Toyota standing there. My father opened the boot and there was this boombox! She wasn't happy at all, and I understand why, but today I'm happy he got it!" Fredholm said.

Collector Rickard Fredholm's toddler, Lilly, is intrigued by a 1981 Sharp 5P-37G boombox. Fredholm is a collector in Sweden, who found time to refurbish his family's vintage boombox, a growing trend around the world.

Courtesy of Rickard Fredholm

When an assortment of low-value vintage electronic parts are so badly damaged they have no collectible value, dealer/artisans like Ed Kautsch of Sanger, Texas, have embraced Steampunk to blend early technological nostalgia with a sculpture's flair. Under his business name of The Steampunk Ballroom (etsy.com/shop/steampunkballroom), his handmade lamps, sculptures, and clocks pay homage to captivating Victorian devices. Kautsch's creations are mostly purchased by young collectors. He sees it as a new and interesting way to introduce a love of collecting vintage objects to the Wi-Fi generation. One of his creations is a functional lamp sculpture titled "Time Machine Experiment No 51" retailing for $165.

"These are made from items that normally wouldn't have much resale value," Kautch said. "But with some time and some imagination, I like to make objects that are not supposed to exist. It's a combination of vintage tech and imagination."

Functional lamp sculpture titled "Time Machine Experiment No 51" by Ed Kautsch.

Courtesy of Eric Bradley

— *Eric Bradley*

Resources: *Retro-Electro: Collecting Technology: From Atari to Walkman*, Pepe Tozzo, Universe Publishing.

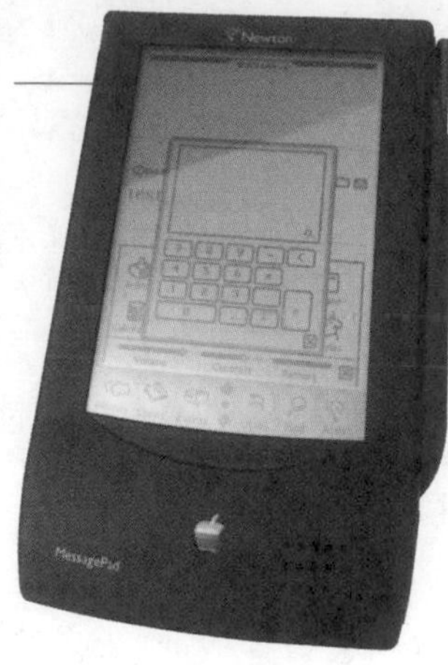

Personal Digital Assistant, 1993, Newton MessagePad, Apple Computer, made in Japan, touch-screen, pen-stylus, original retail $699, CPU:ARM 610 (RISC) @ 20 MHz, RAM: 640K internal, 4MB PCMCIA, OS: Newton OS v1.05, working; collectors seek these because of Newton's unique and interesting ability: Apple's built-in handwriting recognition........................ **$50+**

Courtesy of Owen Morgan

Claybrooke "5 in 1 TV Companion" portable television, Model 13131, 2003, black and white, AM/FM radio, flashlight, compass, antenna, requires 9 C batteries. **$15**

Courtesy of Eric Bradley

Discman compact disc player, 1990, Sony, model D-35, made in Japan, metal body, 8x oversampling digital filter, original retail in 1990 was $400, hard plastic case, AC adapter, original box. Collectors consider it one of the best-sounding small CD players Sony ever produced. **$100**

Courtesy of Dallas Vintage Audio, Bedford, Texas

True View Transportable television set, circa early 1950s, British, 9" GEC 6505A CRT, Osram tubes, built-in loudspeaker, mains wire, faux reptile leather covering, slide-out door. .... **$100+**

Courtesy of Auction Team Breker, www.breker.com

▲ Walkman cassette player, 1985, Sony, Model M-70, made in Japan, rare pink color, new in original box, rare. **$80**

Courtesy of Dallas Vintage Audio, Bedford, Texas

◀ Radio, 1985, Sony, Model SRF-75, made in Japan, Outback Series, made with Elastomer (rubber), water-resistant, variable mega bass control, headphones, canvas strap, original box. **$80**

Courtesy of Dallas Vintage Audio, Bedford, Texas

▲ The Baird Televisor television set, 1928, noted as world's first mechanical television set, designed by John Logie Baird, London, spiral-punched scanning disc by Paul Gottlieb Nipkow, Berlin................. **$2,800**

Courtesy of Auction Team Breker, www.breker.com

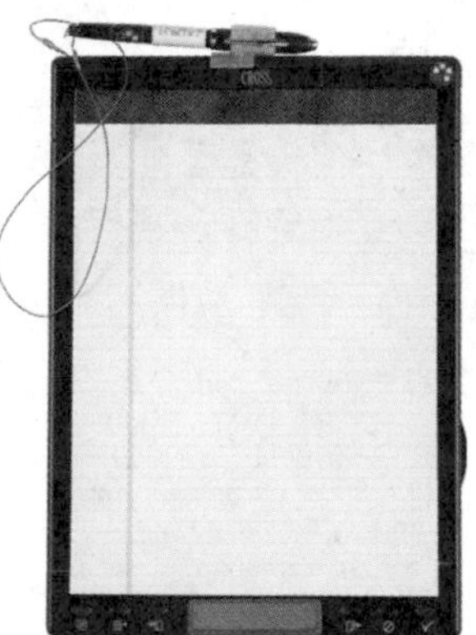

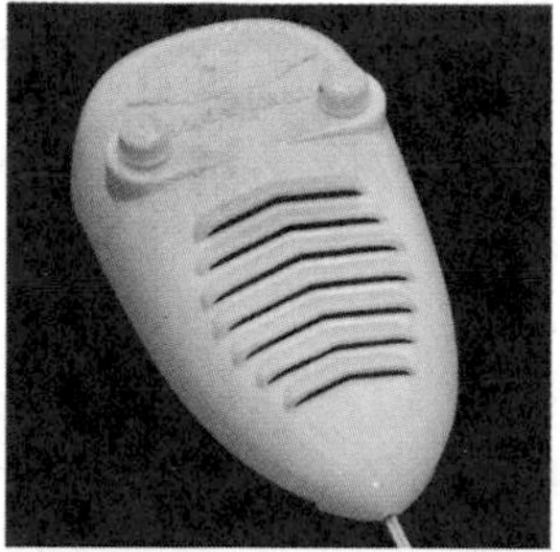

▲ Ozonomat ozone generator, circa 1959, Etuba AG, Munich, Bakelite case, 220V....**$400-$700**

Courtesy of Auction Team Breker, www.breker.com

▲ Beatlephones headphones, 1966, Koss Electronics, original box, made in Milwaukee, 8" w. x 8" l. x 4" h.................................. **$1,062**

Courtesy of Heritage Auctions, ha.com

◀ CrossPad Electronic Notepad, 1997, IBM/Cross, with pen and accessories, used by U.S. Space Program, example with NASA tagging, possibly flown in space, discontinued in 2001, pen transmitted radio signal that told pad where you were writing, 9-1/2" w. x 13" l. x 3/4" h... **$325**

Courtesy of Heritage Auctions, ha.com

▲ Superman Electronic Question and Answer Quizz Machine game, 1966, Lisbeth Whiting Co., Inc., with all Q&A cards and electrodes, box 14" l. x 9" w. x 1-1/2" h..**$180**

Courtesy of Heritage Auctions, ha.com

◀ Electronic Spoken Word educational record, 1963, Bell Telephone Laboratories, vinyl, 33-1/3, computer speech: HEE SAW DHUH KAET (He Saw the Cat), monaural, PB-287, one-sided 7" single in pictorial card sleeve, promotional recording demonstrating newly developed (at the time) computer programming to synthesize human speech. (Listen online at https://www.youtube.com/watch?v=4UjUdPLIQH4). **$200**

Courtesy of Heritage Auctions, ha.com

FENDI flash drive, 2012, designed by Karl Lagerfeld, rubber, mini-gift bag, original box, 2-1/3" l. x 1" d. ..**$150-$250**

Courtesy of FENDI

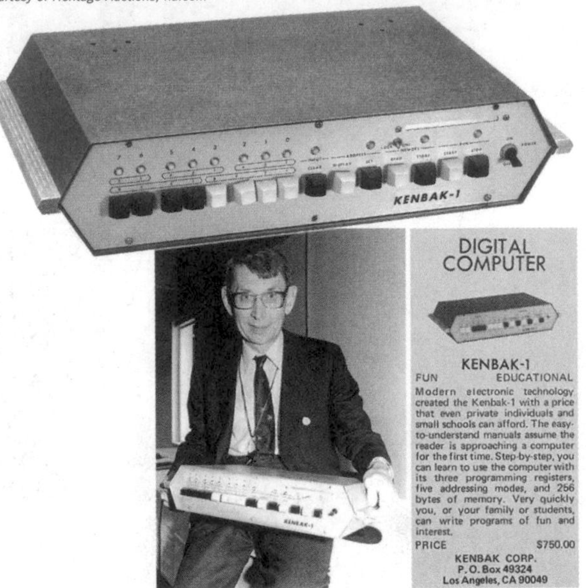

Kenbak-I Digital Computer, No. 0185, 1971, Kenbak Corp., Los Angeles, 8-bit, 256-byte, original chips date-coded 1971, "Kenbak 1000 Rev. B" motherboard designation, power supply, 15 switches and lights, in blue-painted metal case with original chrome side bars and rear label reading "Kenbak Corporation, Los Angeles, Calif., Kenbak-1 Digital Computer, Part 10017, Revision (blank), Serial Number 0185," approximately 19-1/4" w. x 11-1/2" l. x 4-1/4" h. **$44,000**

Courtesy of Auction Team Breker, www.breker.com

Sylvania record player, 1970s, Model 45P13, portable for 45 RPM records, dual speakers. **$25**

Courtesy of Main Street Mining Co., www.mainstreetmining.com

Heat lamp, circa 1970s, 220V, European model of Philips Infraphil, originally introduced in 1946 as medical device to treat muscular pain, colds, bruises. **$35**

Courtesy of FutureForms, etsy.com

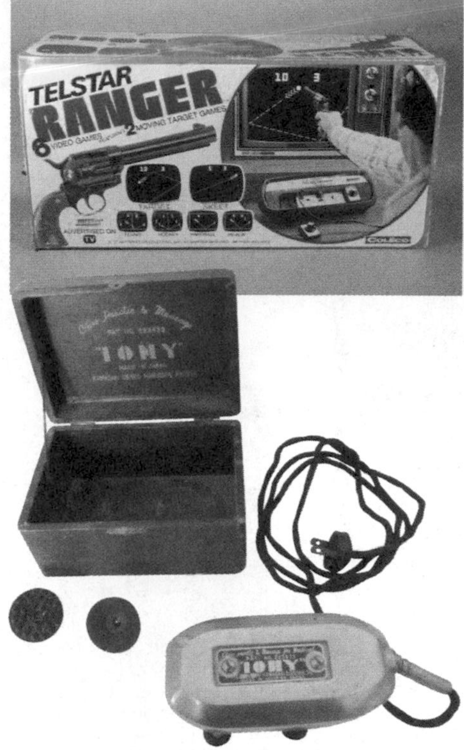

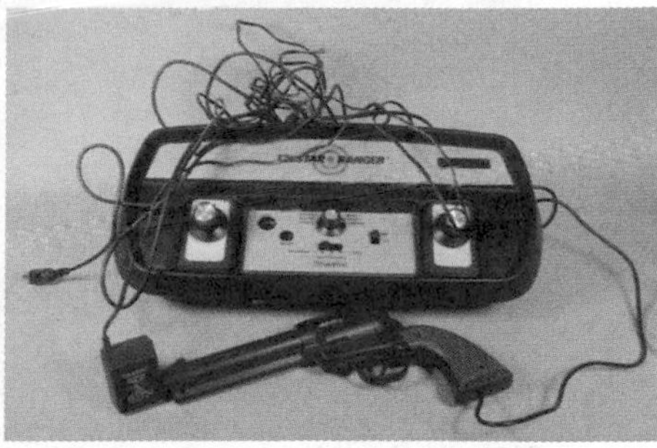

▲Telstar Ranger 6 video games, 1977, Coleco Industries, Inc., Amsterdam, New York, marked "Made in US.A.," two remote controls, gun, original box; plug into TV and play six different games. ....**$50-$100**

Courtesy of Premier Auction Galleries, pag4u.com

IONY electric massager, Kawaski Electric Co., marked "Made in Japan," device with metal plate made in Occupied Japan, rare, box 6-1/4" l. x 4-1/2" h. .... **$30-$35**

Courtesy of Kathy Gardner

Massager, Stim-U-Lax for Barbers, Model 3, nickel-plated, John Oster Mfg. Co., Racine, Wisconsin, 110-120V, original box, 5 1/2" l....... **$25**

Courtesy of The Auction House

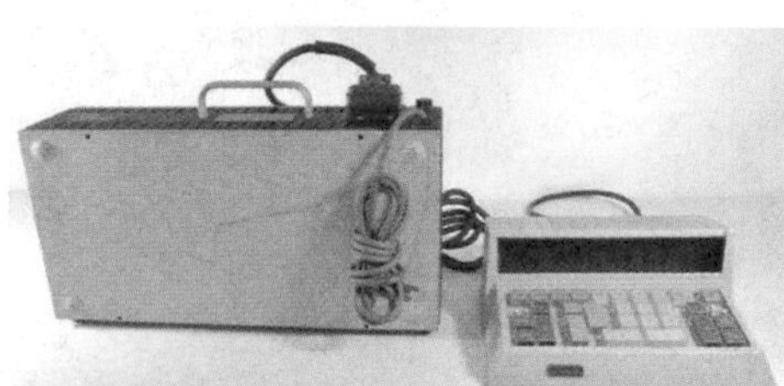

Electronic calculator, Model 320E, 1965, Wang Laboratories Inc., electronic package, keyboard, keyboard cover, 17" l. x 10-1/5" h. x 5" w., 20 lbs. **$170**

Courtesy of Auctions Neapolitan & Gallery, www.auctionsneapolitan.com

▲ Electric demonstration models, circa 1980, maker unknown, used in physics lessons for high frequency and voltage alternating current experiments, transformer, spark gap, 24" h. x 14" w. x 22" d. **$293**

Courtesy of Auction Team Breker, www.breker.com

◀ Calculator, 1967, Casio Computer Ltd., Tokyo, AL-1000, 14 Nixie tube digits, one of first programmable calculators, four functions, square root, memory, 10 circuit boards, magnetic core memory, 230V, working, 15" l. x 17-1/3" w. x 9-1/4" h. **$300**

Courtesy of Auction Team Breker, www.breker.com

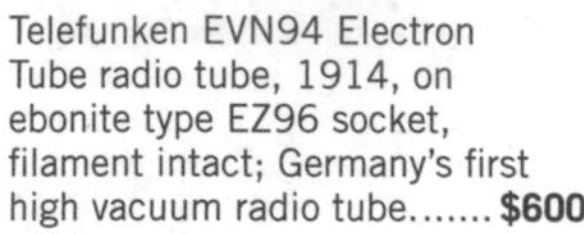

Telefunken EVN94 Electron Tube radio tube, 1914, on ebonite type EZ96 socket, filament intact; Germany's first high vacuum radio tube....... **$600**

Courtesy of Auction Team Breker, www.breker.com

Webster Chicago Electronic Memory recorder, reel to reel wire sound recorder and playback machine, circa 1949, model 180-1, with carrying case, microphone, cords, 7-1/2" x 17" x 11"............... **$30**

Courtesy of The Auction House Sacramento

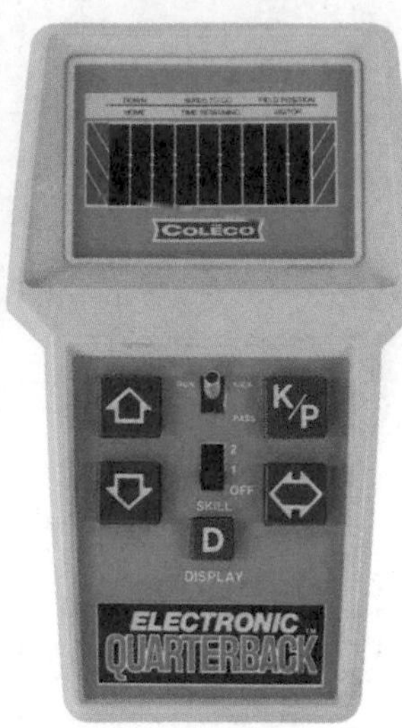

Electronic Quarterback game, 1978, Coleco, power via nine-volt battery or AC adapter (also released by Sears under its own brand with name "Electronic Touchdown"), 6-1/2" l. x 3-1/2" w. x 1-1/8" d...... **$20-60+**

Courtesy of GeekRoom

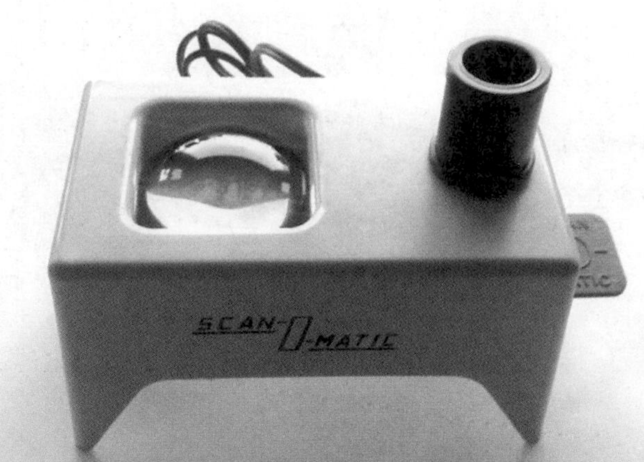

Scan-O-Matic coin magnifier, circa 1960s, device for viewing obverse and reverse of cents, nickels, dimes, and quarters, turn it on, drop coins into feed tube, push slide until coin comes into view under magnifying glass, push again and coin flips over, coin then can be ejected and a new one takes its place, 7-1/2" l. x 5-1/2" h. **$35**

Courtesy of MelroseMemories, etsy.com

"Uniteds 10th Inning" electric pinball machine, circa mid-20th century, 1¢ to play, 39" h. x 16" w. x 28" d. **$649**

Courtesy of Nadeau's Auction Gallery, www.nadeausauction.com

Optica projector, electric powered, with original metal case, 16-1/2" h. .... **$50+**

Courtesy of Nadeau's Auction Gallery, www.nadeausauction.com

"One Armed Bandit" electronic token slot machine from former Sands Hotel in Las Vegas, with tokens, keys and instructions, working, 44" h. x 18" w. x 19" d. **$250**

Courtesy of Eldred's, www.eldreds.com

Minivac 601 game, circa 1960, with instruction booklet, 5" h. x 24" x 13". .... **$100-$350**

Courtesy of Eldred's, www.eldreds.com

Panasonic television, TR-005 Orbitel, 1973, rotates on chrome tripod, 8-1/2" h. **$687**

Courtesy of Heritage Auctions, ha.com

Alarm clocks, walkie-talkie, Game Cube, Super Nintendo, three Micro Cell cameras, games, and shoe shine electronics. **$100**

Courtesy of Nadeau's Auction Gallery, www.nadeausauction.com

VINTAGE PRINTS

THE PRINT-MAKING PROCESS was designed for one reason: to sell reproductions of an artists' work as far as the market would bear. The technology, first launched with simple woodcuts and now being explored with computer-assisted digital printing, revolutionized humankind. Print-making allowed the average person to enjoy expensive works of art.

In fact, vintage prints and frequently copied works are so common now that they are one of the items PBS's "Antiques Roadshow" encourages you to leave at home. The truth is, most-frequently copied prints have only decorative value at best. This doesn't mean all prints have no value – it just means values in this category are influenced by many factors including rarity, condition, artist, exposure, and more. Here's a short list of the most commonly used reproduction methods to help you determine how your vintage print was made.

Most art prints are created by these nine methods:

Engraving, 1823, Declaration of Independence, William Stone, one page broadside, one of 200 produced, marked "ENGRAVED by W. I. STONE for the Dept of State, by order" in upper left corner, followed by "of J. Q. ADAMS, Sect. of State July 4th 1824," 25-1/2" l. x 30-1/2" w. **$597,500**

Courtesy of Heritage Auctions, ha.com

DIGITAL PRINT

The most modern method recognized as a print-making technique, the artist uses a computer and ink-jet printer to create a digital print. This work requires high-quality printers, and most artists use this method to produce a single unique artwork or limited edition prints.

SCREENPRINT (OR SCREEN PRINT)

Favored by many mid-century modern and contemporary artists, the screenprint is commonplace today. It was a medium of choice by Andy Warhol, Ed Ruscha, and Roy Lichtenstein. During the screen printing process, ink is wiped across a screen with a squeegee. The ink passes through the screen exactly in the same location as the artist's image, transferring the printed image onto a selected medium. Also known as silkscreen, serigraphy, and serigraph printing, the process accommodates many different mediums, such as paper, fabric, glass, or canvas.

MONOTYPE

The monotype method is used to produce a single, unique print from a clean and unetched plate. Artists Frank Stella and Sam Francis often used this method to produce colorful abstract art on handmade paper. The image is produced in reverse and then applied to paper using dry pigments, inks, and oils. The monotype is sometimes confused with a monoprint, but a monoprint always contains a pattern or part of an image that is constantly repeated in each print.

ENGRAVING

One of the oldest methods of reproducing original art, engraved prints are commonly found at auctions for as little as $10 to $100. The affordable prices likely represent the number of images produced rather than the artist's painstaking creative process. Engraving was the method of choice to create mass-market images until the 19th century when etching was adopted. To complete an engraving, the artist must incise (scratch) an image directly onto a metal plate using a tool called a burin. The plate is then inked and printed. A single engraving can produce thousands of prints.

For instance, Secretary of State John Quincy Adams commissioned engraver William J. Stone of Washington to produce an exact copy of the original Declaration of Independence onto a copperplate, a process that took him three years to complete. Adams asked Stone to engrave the handwritten version. It is a common but erroneous assumption that the familiar handwritten version reproduced by Stone (with its numerous signatures below) was the original drafted version of the document. However, the first version was printed. Stone's version was not engrossed until July 19 and not signed until early August 1776, but it is his artistic engraving hand that we all now associate with the original version.

Pablo Picasso also employed this process to create sharp, crisp lines to reproduce on his printed images.

ETCHING

Etching replaced engraving in the Middle Ages by allowing an artist to draw a composition on a wax-coated metal plate. The plate is soaked in acid, which corrodes the exposed lines and leaves the wax intact. Prints can be produced by inking the wax layer. Rembrandt van Rijn preferred this method throughout the 17th century, which is astonishing considering you can easily purchase a period print from his original etching for around $1,500.

LINOCUT

You might remember this process from middle school. Using a piece of linoleum, an artist carves out an image that is then inked and pressed against paper. The soft linoleum allows the artist to introduce more nuances to a work by better controlling the depth and angle at which the image is carved. This allows the introduction of more fluid lines.

WOODCUT

Recognized as the oldest printmaking technique, woodcut allows the artist to literally carve an image into a block of wood. The wood is inked and prints are produced, leaving the removed wood in negative. Sometimes the original wood grain is still apparent in a print, which may or may not have been the artist's original intent. Look to artists such as Jim Dine (b. 1935) and M. C. Escher (1898-1972) for quality examples. Escher created his famous mathematically inspired visual illusions and printed them on Japan paper in the 1930s, but few people realize how prolific he was during his most active years. When Escher died in 1972, he left behind a legacy of 448 lithographs and more than 2,000 drawings and sketches.

POSTERS

As a general rule, posters that date to or were printed before World War II almost always have some value. Condition, of course, matters greatly, but that can be overlooked based on historical value, census (how many exist), and eye appeal. This is especially true of tourism and transportation posters and prints produced by economic and tourism agencies. Strangely, an original poster's value can actually increase if it has been reproduced so many times it has become instantly recognizable.

— *Eric Bradley*

Woodcut, "La Sortie, 1990" by Roy Lichtenstein (American, 1923-1997), in colors on museum board, ed. 14/60 (total edition includes 14 artist's proofs), signed, dated and numbered in pencil, 52-5/8" l. x 75" w. **$68,750**

Courtesy of Heritage Auctions, ha.com

Lithograph, "Cigarette Underground" by Irwin D. Hoffman (American, 1901-1989), signed and inscribed to a maestro, 11" l. x 8" w...... **$102**

Courtesy of Mayo Auction & Realty, auctionbymayo.com

Poster, "Odeon Casino" by Joseph Geis (French, 1892-1952), rare, 35" h. x 47" w. **$710**

Courtesy of Mayo Auction & Realty, auctionbymayo.com

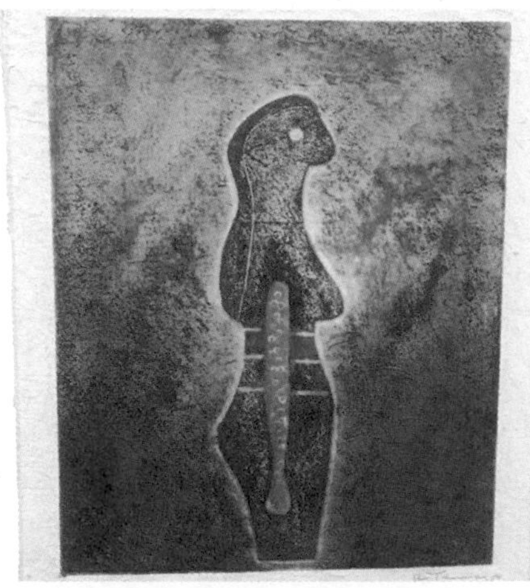

Mixograph, "Untitled" by Rufino Tamayo (Mexican, 1889-1991), signed artist's proof, 16" l. x 13" w. Tamayo is credited with inventing mixograph, which is art printed on paper with texture and depth. **$61**

Courtesy of Mayo Auction & Realty, auctionbymayo.com

▶ Lithograph, "Terezin" by Leo Haas (1901-1983), signed tinted color, done while Haas was a prisoner of war during World War II, 11-11/16" l. x 17-3/4" w. **$128**

Courtesy of Mayo Auction & Realty, auctionbymayo.com

German Nazi SS recruitment poster, 1933, "Leibstandarte" (translated "guard regiment" or "Guard of Corps"), 22" l. x 33-1/2" w. **$106**

Courtesy of Mayo Auction & Realty, auctionbymayo.com

Lithograph, "At Chicago, 1937" by Joseph W. Golinkin (American, 1896-1977), of Louis-Braddock heavyweight fight, from edition of 250, signed, 16" l. x 14" w. **$81**

Courtesy of Mayo Auction & Realty, auctionbymayo.com

Serigraph, "The Dancer" by Erte, signed artist proof, lower right in pencil and marked A/P, 22-3/4" h. x 16-3/4" w. **$160**

Courtesy of Main Street Mining Co., www.mainstreetmining.com

Lithograph, "Babylone d'Allemange (1894)" by Henri de Toulouse-Lautrec (French, 1864-1901), titled, signed, and dated. **$10,200**

Courtesy of Los Angeles Auction House, www.laauctionhouse.com

Woodblock print, Paul Jacoulet La Peche Miraculeusc, (French, 1902-1960), signed Paul Jacoulet lower right, marked "Le Peche Miracluleuse", Izu, Japan, 1939, 18" h. x 14" w. **$425**

Courtesy of Main Street Mining Co., www.mainstreetmining.com

Map, "Nouvelle Carte Particuliere De L'Amerique, The Western or Atlantick" by Henry Popple, four joined sheets, North America colored map showing British Empire in America with French, Spanish, and Dutch settlements, printed for John Covens and Cornelius Mortier, 44-3/4" h. x 40-1/2" w. **$4,500**

Courtesy of Nadeau's Auction Gallery, www.nadeausauction.com

Wallpaper panels, 1834, attributed to Jean Zuber, France, designed after Jean-Julien Deltil (1791-1863), depicting Boston Harbor, 19th century, wharf in foreground with one barrel marked "Boston XII" and ships being unloaded, 63" h. x 94" w. (scene was originally 49' l). Note: First Lady Jacqueline Kennedy installed Zuber's wallpaper from 1834 in the diplomatic reception room of White House.................................. **$4,800**

Courtesy of Nadeau's Auction Gallery, www.nadeausauction.com

Lithograph, "Clipper Ship Sweepstakes" by Currier & Ives, marked "F. F. Palmer Lith" lower left, marked "By N. Currier" lower right, 19-1/2" l. x 24-1/2" w... **$1,080**

Courtesy of Nadeau's Auction Gallery, www.nadeausauction.com

Etching, "Ceci N'est Pas Une Pipe (Kaplan/ Baum 2), 1962" by Rene Magritte (1898-1967), on wove paper, signed, dated and numbered in pencil, with full margins, framed, 4-1/2" l. x 5-3/4" w. **$10,625**

Courtesy of Doyle New York, www.doylenewyork.com

Etching, "Song of the Sea (Holland/Catania/Isen 470), 1936" by Louis Icart, hand-colored color aquatint, signed in pencil with artist's windmill blindstamp, laid on card, 19-1/2" l. x 15-1/2 w. .... **$700+**

Courtesy of Doyle New York, www.doylenewyork.com

Color lithograph, "Two Women (G./R. 108), 1981-82" by Romare Bearden, signed, titled and numbered 114/120 in pencil, colored, framed, 22-7/8" l. x 14-1/4" w. **$2,000**

Courtesy of Doyle New York, www.doylenewyork.com

Etching, "The Persian (B. 152), 1632" by Rembrandt van Rijn, later impression, trimmed, 4-3/8 l. x 3-3/16" w. **$1,500**

Courtesy of Doyle New York, www.doylenewyork.com

Engraving, "Black-bellied Darter, Plotus Anhinga (No 64, Plate CCCXVI), 1836" by John James Audubon (American, 1785-1851), hand-colored with aquatint, J. Whatman, 30" l. x 21-3/4" w................**$27,500**

Courtesy of Heritage Auctions, ha.com

Lithograph, "Jeune Fille Accoudee Au Paravent Fleuri (D. 439), 1924" by Henri Matisse, on chine volant, signed and numbered 27/60 in pencil, framed, 7-3/8" l. x 10-3/8" w. **$10,000**

Courtesy of Doyle New York, www.doylenewyork.com

Monotype, "Indian Portrait" by Joseph Henry Sharp (American, 1859-1953), 11-1/4" l. x 7-1/4" w........................ **$2,629**

Courtesy of Heritage Auctions, ha.com

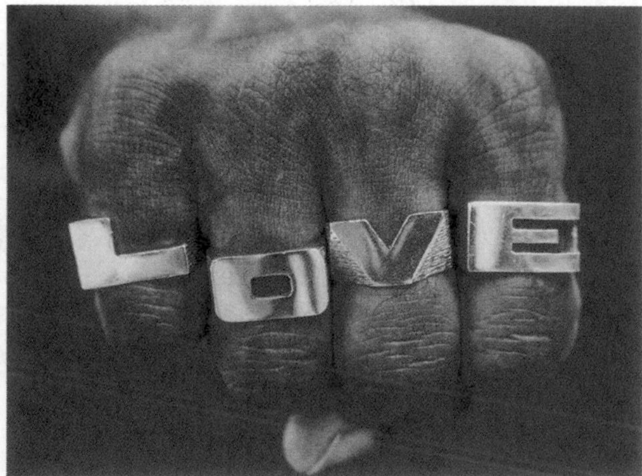

Digital print, "Before Paradise (Love), 2003" by Isaac Julien (British, b. 1960), AP 2/5 (aside from an edition of 24), 17-1/2" l. x 23-3/4" w...**$1,125**

Courtesy of Heritage Auctions, ha.com

Lithograph, "Le Bouquet Rouge et Jaune" by Marc Chagall (French, 1887-1985), on arches paper, artist-signed. **$7,200**

Courtesy of Los Angeles Auction House, www.laauctionhouse.com

Etching, "New York, Brooklyn Bridge" by Luigi Kasimir (1881-1962), aquatint in colors with signature in pencil, 19" h. x 24" w. **$850**

Courtesy of Pangaea Auctions, gopangaea.com

Etching, "N.Y. Sub-Treasury" by Tanna Kasimir-Hoernes (1887-1972), aquatint in colors with signature in pencil, 25" h. x 18" w. **$750**

Courtesy of Pangaea Auctions, gopangaea.com

Etching, "Periscope (U.L.A.E. 218), 1981" by Jasper Johns, color aquatint, on Rives BFK, signed, dated and numbered 57/88 in pencil, published by Petersburg Press, London, with full margins, framed, 34" l. x 24-1/4" w............. **$6,250**

Courtesy of Doyle New York, www.doylenewyork.com

Screenprints, "Endangered Species, 1983" by Andy Warhol (1928-1987), 10 screenprints in colors on Lenox Museum Board, Number 103 from edition of 150 plus 30 artist's proofs, world auction record, 38" l. x 38" w. **$725,000**

Courtesy of Heritage Auctions, ha.com

Woodcut and lithograph, "The Yellow Belt, 2005" by Jim Dine, color, signed and numbered 8/200 in pencil, published by Editions de la Difference, Paris, printed to edges, 26-3/8" l. x 20-3/8" w. **$4,375**

Courtesy of Doyle New York, www.doylenewyork.com

Digital pigment print, "Camptown Races from series Domestic Vacations, 2005" by Julie Blackmon (American, b. 1966), 32" l. x 32" w. **$3,000**

Courtesy of Heritage Auctions, ha.com

Offset lithograph and screenprint, "(i) Pow(er), 2014" by Shepard Fairey (American, b. 1970), on paper, signed, dated, open edition, 36" l. x 24" w., unframed, sold with "(ii) Obama Vote, 2008," inscribed 3736/5000 (II), screenprint on paper, edition of 5,000, 38-1/2" l. x 25" w............................ **$750**

Courtesy of Doyle New York, www.doylenewyork.com

WATCHES

MOST EVERYONE HAS a watch. It can be a graduation gift from high school or college, a family heirloom, or a keepsake to mark an important anniversary or retirement.

Collecting timepieces is not a new fad but one enjoyed by men and women, young and old alike. Essentially, there is something for everyone. Whether you collect by maker, by style, or by the type of movement, you can find watches to fit any budget. By collecting watches, not only do you have a fun collectible, but it also has function.

Over the last 100+ years, millions of watches have been produced. Some were made for the masses, others were made in very small quantities for a select few. Some dealers specialize in watches, but timepieces can also be found at flea markets, garage sales, and auctions, on the Internet, and at antique shops.

Collecting creates an opportunity for you to have a watch for every occasion. You can have a watch to wear to work, one to wear when out on the town, another one to use while participating in sports, and an everyday watch.

The values placed on the watches illustrated in this section are market value, representing what they have recently sold for privately or at auction. Values can fluctuate due to numerous variables. How a watch is sold, where it is sold, and its condition all play a big role in its value.

The Internet has helped collectors identify watches worn by popular celebrities, on the moon, in a car race, in favorite action films, etc. One of the not-so-positive aspects of Internet collecting is the sheer volume of reproductions posing as authentic watches. They turn up everywhere, with links to professionally designed websites offering the best of the best for a discount, or up for bid on an Internet auction. You must keep in mind the old saying, "If it looks too good to be true, it probably is."

For more information on watches, see *Warman's Watches Field Guide* by Reyne Haines.

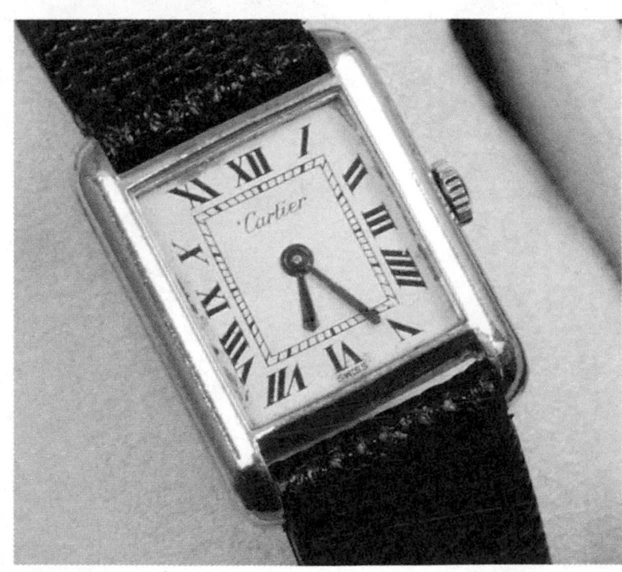

Cartier 18k gold electroplated tank watch, 1970s, Swiss made, mechanical wind-up, leather band, case approximately 25 mm x 19 mm, with Cartier box, minor plate loss to back case, some peeling to dial, buckle replaced.......... **$510**

Courtesy of Stephenson's Auctioneers & Appraisers, www.stephensonsauction.com

Avia wristwatch, circa 1920s, sterling case, 33 mm x 32 mm, snap back; tan metal dial, numerals, skeleton hands; 15-jewel movement, manual wind, triple signed; dial toned, case in very good condition, movement in good condition and running. **$62**

Courtesy of Heritage Auctions, ha.com

Bulova pink gold-filled wristwatch, circa 1936, pink gold-filled case, 30 mm, snap back; pink metal dial, numerals and markers, sub-seconds; 21-jewel movement, manual wind; like new/old stock genuine leather band; light discoloration on dial, case in very good condition, movement in good condition and running. **$163**

Courtesy of Heritage Auctions, ha.com

Hamilton manual-wind wristwatch, circa 1940s, gold-filled case, 38 mm x 22 mm, snap back; Butler white metal dial, applied gold numerals, gold kite hands; 982 B movement, manual wind; like new/old stock genuine lizard band; Butler dial and case in excellent condition, movement in good condition and running. **$81**

Courtesy of Heritage Auctions, ha.com

Elgin manual-wind wristwatch, circa 1912 to 1914, gold-filled case, 32 mm, single hinge back; enamel Arabic dial, blued spade hands, sub-seconds; 13-jewel movement, gilt, 3/4 plate; like new/old stock black leather band; case in excellent condition, movement in good condition and running. **$255**

Courtesy of Heritage Auctions, ha.com

Longines 14k gold manual-wind wristwatch, circa 1920s, 14k gold case, 33 mm, bark finish bezel, three-piece; silver metal dial, gold markers, gold baton hands, sub-seconds; 17-jewel movement, manual wind; like new/old stock genuine leather band; dial, case, and movement in good condition.................... **$250**

Courtesy of Heritage Auctions, ha.com

Rare Illinois Ensign wristwatch, Illinois "Special Model B" signed case, yellow center, white gold filled back and bezel, 35 mm x 28 mm; silver dial, luminous Arabic numerals, offset seconds at 9 o'clock; 15-jewel movement, nickel bridge, movement in good condition and running, dial excellent condition, refinished, case in good condition, some wear on top of lugs. **$200**

Courtesy of Heritage Auctions, ha.com

Omega Seamaster 18k yellow gold wristwatch, original case marked "OMEGA WATCH CO. SWISS MADE, 18K .0750", case not opened, replacement crystal with rub marks, 30 mm dia. movement, worn leatherstrap, 17 mm w., winds and runs. **$861**

Courtesy of Nest Egg Auctions, www.nesteggauctions.com

Monarch (Leonidas) calendar moon phase wristwatch, circa 1950s, three body case, 35 mm, curved lugs, brushed finish to case back; rose gold dial, Arabic numerals, day, month and moon phase apertures, red pointer to outer blue date numerals, luminous Dauphine hands; caliber 1100, 17-jewel movement, straight line lever, monometallic balance, shock absorber; adjustable Champion patented stainless steel band; dial signed Monarch, case and movement signed Leonidas, movement in good condition and running, case and dial in good condition.......**$1,063**

Courtesy of Heritage Auctions, ha.com

▶ Rolex Precision nickel rectangular wristwatch, circa 1925, two body case, curved back, 36 mm x 20 mm; two-tone silver dial, black numerals and minute track, sub seconds; 17-jewel movement, rectangular, straight-line lever escapement; dial in very good condition, refinished, movement in good condition and running, case in good condition, wear on lower back corner.. **$1,375**

Courtesy of Heritage Auctions, ha.com

WOMEN'S WATCHES

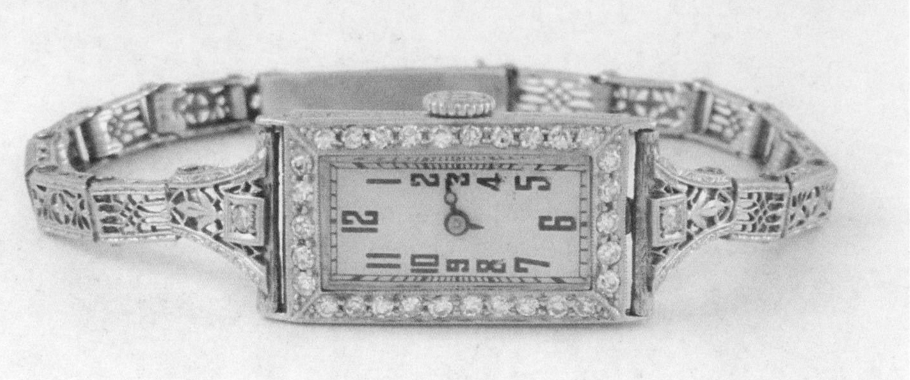

Platinum and diamond wristwatch with filigree band, early 20th century, 30 prong-set diamonds, marked J.E. Caldwell & Co., monogrammed A.C.B on back case, stamped platinum; 17 jewels, Swiss-made mechanical movement; crystal with chips and scratches, dial worn, partial minute hand, case approximately 25 mm x 16 mm, 24.1 gr/15.5 dwt. **$570**

Courtesy of Stephenson's Auctioneers & Appraisers, www.stephensonsauction.com

English yellow and rose gold watch, Chester, 1838, monogrammed EB for Eliza Bowman (1805-1851), with invoice dated Feb. 14, 1859 from A. Romand to Mr. D. Turnbull of Bayou Sara for making key for watch. **$1,920**

Courtesy of Neal Auction Co., www.nealauctions.com

Elgin gold-filled lapel watch with lapel pin, age crack on dial. **$42**

Courtesy of William J. Jenack Estate Appraisers & Auctioneers, www.jenack.com

Swiss Endura watch in bangle-design ivory Bakelite band, winds and runs, 1-1/4" w., approximately 67 g. **$87**

Courtesy of Elite Decorative Arts, www.eliteauction.com

Gruen Switzerland Precision wristwatch in 14k yellow gold with white enamel face with black Arabic numerals and notches, gold hour and minute hands, case number 01444; 15-jewel mechanical movements with adjustments by Gruen Guild Switzerland, movement number 47236; case approximately 1" l. x 1-1/16" w. including crown, approximately 33.4 dwt. **$1,488**

Courtesy of Elite Decorative Arts, www.eliteauction.com

Gold watch with rope twist band, 9k gold ▶ case, 13 mm; back wind and back set; champagne metal dial with gold numerals and markers, manual wind movement, band marked 9k gold, dial discolored, case and bracelet in good condition, movement running, 6-1/4". **$275**

Courtesy of Heritage Auctions, ha.com

Hamilton 14k diamond watch, 16.0 g....... **$431**

Courtesy of Don Presley Auction, www.donpresley.com

Tiffany & Co. diamond and gold open-face pendant watch, round 18k gold case, 18.40 mm, hinged back, dust cover and bale, with European-cut diamonds on reverse, approximately 0.50 carat, reference No. 13925, marked Tiffany & Co.; white dial with black Arabic numerals, black outer minute track, gold Louis XIV hour and minute hands, mineral crystal; manual wind, adjusted, Swiss, No. 13925, Tiffany & Co., New York; signed Tiffany & Co. on case, dial, and movement; very good condition overall, in working order, 18.10 g. **$1,375**

Courtesy of Heritage Auctions, ha.com

! top lot

Historically important and rare Gen. George S. Patton pocket watch, 18k yellow gold five-minute repeater by Patek Philippe & Co., made for Tiffany & Co., split seconds chronograph with register, presented to Patton by his parents on his graduation from U.S. Military Academy in 1909; case No. 112259, four body, gold cuvette engraved "Lieut. George S. Patton U.S.A. from his Father and Mother, June 11th 1909", hinged case back with stylized GSP monogram, rim with gold slide for repeat, gold button for split seconds function, gold lock-out slide to deactivate crown, with original 18k yellow gold chain, 12-1/2" with T-bar, swivel and drop with swing ring; white enamel dial with Arabic numerals, black minute track and 1/5th seconds scale, red numerals at five minutes, subsidiary seconds at 6, 30-minute register at 12, blued steel spade hands; movement No. 112,259, one-quarter plate, nickel finish, straight-line lever escapement, bi-metallic compensated balance with Breguet spring, jeweled to hammer, damascened decoration, 38 jewels, straight index regulator on balance bridge; triple-signed Tiffany & Co., with Patek Philippe & Co.

In his memoirs titled *My Father As I Remembered Him*, dated July 9, 1927, Patton wrote, "The day after graduation Papa, Mama and I went to Tiffany and they bought me a watch. It was a stop watch repeater priced at $600.00 but we got it for $350.00 because it was thicker than the then style. I carried it in Mexico and France, it keeps perfect time and a great watch. Aunt Nannie bought me a chain to go with it. B gave me the locket."

Provenance: From a descendant of Patton, accompanied by signed letter stating in part, "The watch remained in General Patton's possession until his death in 1945. It was given to me by his son, my father, Maj. Gen. George S. Patton IV, in 1987." **$137,000**

COURTESY OF HERITAGE AUCTIONS, HA.COM

WORLD WAR II COLLECTIBLES

DURING THE SEVEN decades since the end of World War II, veterans, collectors, and nostalgia-seekers have eagerly bought, sold, and traded the "spoils of war." Actually, souvenir collecting began as soon as troops set foot on foreign soil. Whether Tommies from Great Britain, Doughboys from the United States, or Fritzies from Germany, soldiers eagerly looked for trinkets and remembrances that would guarantee their place in the historic events that unfolded before them. Helmets, medals, firearms, field gear, daggers, and other pieces of war material filled parcels and duffel bags on the way back home.

As soon as hostilities ended in 1945, the populations of defeated Germany and Japan quickly realized they could make money selling souvenirs to the occupation forces. The flow of war material increased. Values became well established.

Over the years these values have remained proportionally consistent, and though values have increased dramatically, demand has not dropped off a bit. In fact, World War II collecting is the largest segment of the militaria hobby.

Surprisingly, the values of items have been a closely guarded secret. Unfortunately, the hobby has relied on paying veterans and their families far less than a military relic is worth with the hope of selling later for a substantial profit. This attitude has given the hobby a bad reputation.

The advent of the Internet, though, significantly leveled the playing field for sellers and buyers. No longer does a person have to blindly offer a relic for sale to a collector or dealer. Simply logging onto one of several Internet auctions will give the uninitiated an idea of value.

But a little information can be dangerous. The value of military items resides in variation. Whether it is a difference in manufacturing technique, material or markings, the nuances of an item will determine the true value. Don't expect 20 minutes on the Internet - or even glancing through this section - to teach you these nuances. Collectors are a devoted bunch. They have spent years and hundreds, if not thousands, of dollars to establish the knowledge base that enables them to navigate through the hobby.

For more information on World War II collectibles, see *Warman's World War II Collectibles*, 3rd edition, by John Adams-Graf.

◀ USAAF 13th Air Force 5th Bomb Group aerial gunner's painted A2 flight jacket.... **$2,650**

Courtesy of AdvanceGuardMilitaria.com

MILITARY CLOTHING

Assembled uniform and equipment group for RAF crew member..............**$450-$650**

Courtesy of Hermann-Historica.de

U.S. 7th Service Command WAC uniform.......................**$185-$235**

Courtesy of AdvanceGuardMilitaria.com

German field tunic for a captain of a propaganda company. .... **$1,850-$2,000**

Courtesy of Hermann-Historica.de

U.S. double-buckle combat boots......................................**$90-$125**

Courtesy of AdvanceGuardMilitaria.com

HEADGEAR

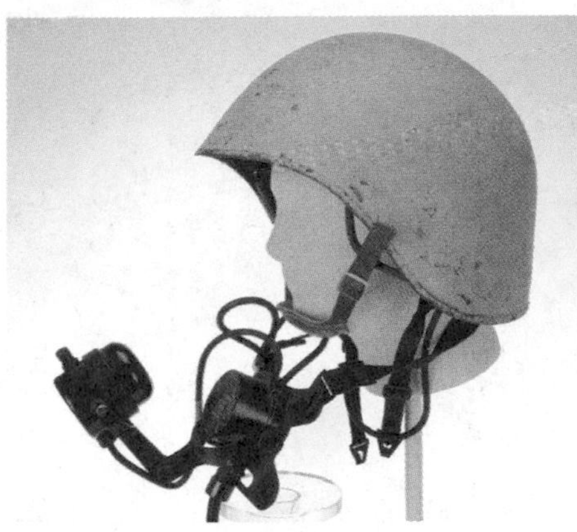

USN MK-2 talker helmet and communications set. ....**$195-$265**

Courtesy of AdvanceGuardMilitaria.com

Japanese army officer's full dress kepi. .....**$350-$400**

Courtesy of AdvanceGuardMilitaria.com

British Royal Air Force group captain's visor cap....................**$200-$265**

Courtesy of AdvanceGuardMilitaria.com

U.S. Army Officer's "Pink" visor cap. **$195-$265**

Courtesy of AdvanceGuardMilitaria.com

◀ German Army "single decal" M35 helmet. .... **$550-$650**

Courtesy of Hermann-Historica.de

▲ Waffen SS officer's visor cap, artillery. ......**$12,000-$14,000**

Courtesy of HistoryHunter.com

ACCOUTREMENTS

German Philips Type 510A table model radio... **$165**

Courtesy of AdvanceGuardMilitaria.com

German Army M31 canteen with wool cover and cup. .... **$65-$100**

Courtesy of AdvanceGuardMilitaria.com

British "Rupert" D-Day dummy paratrooper.... **$3,346**

Courtesy of Heritage Auctions, ha.com

German Waffen-SS enlisted belt and buckle. .... **$550-$650**

Courtesy of Hermann-Historica.de

U.S. Army Pacific Theater camouflage jungle pack.

.... **$200-$245**

Courtesy of AdvanceGuardMilitaria.com

◀ German typewriter with "SS" sig runes key. .... **$600-$750**

Courtesy of Hermann-Historica.de

▲ German Wehrmacht M30 gas mask and carrier, Second style. .... **$115-$165**

Courtesy of AdvanceGuardMilitaria.com

MEDALS

British RAF No. 625 Squadron pilot officer's DFC medal group. **$3,350**

Courtesy of AdvanceGuardMilitaria.com

Hero of the Soviet Union (Gold Star medal).... **$1,850-$2,400**

Courtesy of Hermann-Historica.de

Japanese China Incident war medal. .... **$25-$35**

Courtesy of AdvanceGuardMilitaria.com

British Atlantic Star with France and Germany clasp.... **$80-$95**

Courtesy of AdvanceGuardMilitaria.com

United States Purple Heart medal (no name on reverse) with ribbon bar and lapel button. ... **$65-$95**

Courtesy of AdvanceGuardMilitaria.com

◄ German "Spanish Cross" in bronze with swords. .... **$1,000-$1,250**

Courtesy of Hermann-Historica.de

◄ Third Reich Iron Cross, first class. ....**$200-$400**

Courtesy of AdvanceGuardMilitaria.com

SPECIAL CONTRIBUTORS AND ADVISORS

The following collectors, dealers, sellers, and researchers have supported the ***Antique Trader Antiques & Collectibles Price Guide*** with their pricing and contacts for nearly 30 years. Many continue to serve as a valuable resource to the entire collecting hobby, while others have passed away. We honor all contributors past and present as their hard work and passion lives on through this book.

Andre Ammelounx
Mannie Banner
Ellen Bercovici
Sandra Bondhus
James R. and Carol S. Boshears
Bobbie Zucker Bryson
Emmett Butler
Dana Cain
Linda D. Carannante
David Chartier
Les and Irene Cohen
Amphora Collectors International
Marion Cohen
Neva Colbert
Marie Compton
Susan N. Cox
Caroline Torem-Craig
Leonard Davis
Bev Dieringer
Janice Dodson
Del E. Domke
Debby DuBay
Susan Eberman
Joan M. George
Roselyn Gerson
William A. and Donna J. Gray
Pam Green
Linda Guffey
Carl Heck
Alma Hillman
K. Robert and Bonne L. Hohl
Ellen R. Hill
Joan Hull
Hull Pottery Association
Louise Irvine
Helen and Bob Jones
Mary Ann Johnston
Donald-Brian Johnson
Dorothy Kamm
Edwin E. Kellogg
Madeleine Kirsh
Vivian Kromer
Curt Leiser
Gene Loveland
Mary McCaslin
Pat Moore
Reg G. Morris
Craig Nissen
Joan C. Oates
Margaret Payne
Gail Peck
John Petzold
Dr. Leslie Piña
Joseph Porcelli
Arlene Rabin
John Rader, Sr.
Betty June Wymer
LuAnn Riggs
Tim and Jamie Saloff
Federico Santi
Peggy Sebek
Steve Stone
Phillip Sullivan
Mark and Ellen Supnick
Tim Trapani
Jim Trautman
Elaine Westover
Kathryn Wiese
Laurie Williams
Nancy Wolfe

CONTRIBUTORS BY SUBJECT

Advertising Items: Kristine Manty
Barbie: Steve Evans
Bottles: Michael Polak
Clocks: Kristine Manty/Donald-Brian Johnson
Coins and Currency: Eric Bradley/Arlyn G. Sieber
Country Store: Donald-Brian Johnson/Antoinette Rahn
Disney Collectibles: Tom Bartsch
Fine Art: Eric Bradley
Hunting and Fishing Collectibles: Eric Bradley
Kitchenwares (vintage): Chriss Swaney
Electric Lighting: Joseph Porcelli/Tom Bartsch
Early Lighting: Donald-Brian Johnson
Records: Pat Prince
Salesman Samples: Antoinette Rahn
Souvenirs and Travel Collectibles: Eric Bradley
Sports: Tom Bartsch
Vintage Clothing: Nancy Wolfe and Madeleine Kirsh
World War II: John Adams-Graf

CERAMICS

Amphora-Teplitz: Les and Irene Cohen
Belleek (American): Peggy Sebek
Belleek (Irish): Del Domke
Blue & White Pottery: Steve Stone
Buffalo Pottery: Phillip Sullivan
Doulton/Royal Doulton: Reg Morris, Louise Irvine and Ed Pascoe
Fulper Pottery: Karen Knapstein
Gouda: Antoinette Rahn
Haeger: Donald-Brian Johnson
Ironstone: General - Bev Dieringer; **Tea Leaf:** The Tea Leaf Club International
Limoges: Karen Knapstein
Majolica: Michael Strawser
McCoy: Craig Nissen
Mettlach: Andre Ammelounx
Overbeck: Karen Knapstein
Red Wing: Gail Peck
R.S. Prussia: Mary McCaslin
Satsuma: Melody Amsel-Arieli
Stoneware and Spongeware: Bruce and Vicki Waasdorp
Sumida Gawa: Karen Knapstein
Zsolnay: Federico Santi/John Gacher

GLASS

Animals: Helen and Bob Jones
Carnival Glass: Jim and Jan Seeck
Crackle Glass: Donald-Brian Johnson
Depression Glass: Ellen Schroy
Fenton: Helen and Bob Jones/Mark F. Moran
Fire King: Karen Knapstein
Higgins Glass: Donald-Brian Johnson
Opalescent Glass: James Measell
Phoenix Glass: Helen and Bob Jones
Sugar Shakers: Scott Beale/Karen Knapstein
Wall Pocket Vases: Bobbie Zucker Bryson

PRICING, IDENTIFICATIONS, AND IMAGES PROVIDED BY:

LIVE AUCTION PROVIDERS

AuctionZip
113 West Pitt St., Suite C
Bedford, PA 15522
(814) 623-5059
www.auctionzip.com

Artfact, LLC
38 Everett St., Suite 101
Allston, MA 02134
(617) 746-9800
www.artfact.com

LiveAuctioneers, LLC
2nd Floor
220 12th Ave.
New York, NY 10001
www.liveauctioneers.com

AUCTION HOUSES

A-1 Auction
2042 N Rio Grande Ave., Suite E
Orlando, FL 32804
(407) 839-0004
http://www.a-1auction.net/

Allard Auctions, Inc.
P.O. Box 1030
St. Ignatius, MT 59865
(406) 745-0500
(800) 314-0343
www.allardauctions.com

American Bottle Auctions
2523 J St., Suite 203
Sacramento, CA 95816
(800) 806-7722
americanbottle.com

American Pottery Auction
Vicki and Bruce Waasdorp
P.O. Box 434
Clarence, NY 14031
(716) 759-2361
www.antiques-stoneware.com

Antique Helper Auction House
2764 East 55th Pl.
Indianapolis, IN 46220
(317) 251-5635
www.antiquehelper.com

Apple Tree Auction Center
1616 West Church St.
Newark, OH 43055-1540
(740) 344-4282
www.appletreeauction.com

Artingstall & Hind Auctioneers
9312 Civic Center Dr., #104
Beverly Hills, CA 90210
(310) 424-5288
www.artingstall.com

Arus Auctions
(617) 660-6170
www.arusauctions.com

ATM Antiques & Auctions, LLC
811 SE US Hwy. 19
Crystal River, FL 34429
(352) 795-2061
(800) 542-3877
www.charliefudge.com

Auction Team Breker
Otto-Hahn-Str. 10
50997 Köln (Godorf), Germany
02236 384340
www.breker.com

Backstage Auctions
448 West 19th St., Suite 163
Houston, TX 77008
(713) 862-1200
www.backstageauctions.com

Belhorn Auctions, LLC
2746 Wynnerock Ct.
Hilliard, OH 43026
(614) 921-9441
auctions@belhorn.com
www.belhorn.com
www.potterymarketplace.com

Bertoia Auctions
2141 DeMarco Dr.
Vineland, NJ 08360
(856) 692-1881
www.bertoiaauctions.com

Bonhams
7601 W. Sunset Blvd.
Los Angeles, CA 90046
(323) 850-7500
www.bonhams.com

Briggs Auction, Inc.
1347 Naamans Creek Rd.
Garnet Valley, PA 19060
(610) 566-3138 (Office)
(610) 485-0412 (Showroom)
www.briggsauction.com

Brunk Auctions
P.O. Box 2135
Asheville, NC 28802
(828) 254-6846
www.brunkauctions.com

Bunte Auction Services and Appraisals
755 Church Rd.
Elgin, IL 60123
(847) 214-8423
www.bunteauction.com

Butterscotch Auction Gallery
608 Old Post Rd.
Bedford, NY 10506
(914) 764-4609
www.butterscotchauction.com

Capo Auction
3601 Queens Blvd.
Long Island City, NY 11101
(718) 433-3710
www.capoauctionnyc.com

Charles Miller Ltd.
Suite 6 Imperial Studios
3/11 Imperial Rd.
London, England
SW6 2AG
+44 (0) (207) 806-5530
www.charlesmillerltd.com

Charlton Hall Auctioneers
912 Gervais St.
Columbia, SC 29201
www.charltonhallauctions.com

Cherryland Postcard Auctions
Ronald & Alec Millard
P.O. Box 427
Frankfort, MI 49635
(231) 352-9758
CherrylandPostcards.com

Christie's New York
20 Rockefeller Plaza
New York, NY 10020
www.christies.com

Cincinnati Art Galleries
225 East Sixth St.
Cincinnati, OH 45202
www.cincinnatiartgalleries.com

Clars Auction Gallery
5644 Telegraph Ave.
Oakland, CA 94609
(510) 428-0100
www.clars.com

The Coeur d'Alene Art Auction
8836 North Hess St., Suite B
Hayden, ID 83835
(208) 772-9009
www.cdaartauction.com

John W. Coker, Ltd.
1511 W. Hwy. 11E
New Market, TN 37820
(865) 475-5163
www.antiquesonline.com

Collect Auctions
(888) 463-3063
collectauctions.com

Conestoga Auction Co./ Division of Hess Auction Group
768 Graystone Rd.
Manheim, PA 17545
(717) 898-7284
www.conestogaauction.com

Constantine & Pletcher
1321 Freeport Rd.
Cheswick, PA 15024
(724) 275-7190
Fax: (724) 275-7191
www.cpauction.info

Copake Auction, Inc.
266 Route 7A
Copake, NY 12516
(518) 329-1142
www.copakeauction.com

Cowan's Auctions
6270 Este Ave.
Cincinnati, OH 45232
(513) 871-1670
www.cowanauctions.com

CRN Auctions, Inc.
57 Bay State Rd.
Cambridge, MA 02138
(617) 661-9582
www.crnauctions.com

Dargate Auction Galleries
326 Munson Ave.
McKees Rocks, PA 15136
(412) 771-8700
Fax: (412) 771-8779
www.dargate.com

Rachel Davis Fine Arts
1301 West 79th St.
Cleveland, OH 44102
(216) 939-1190
www.racheldavisfinearts.com

Decoys Unlimited, Inc.
P.O. Box 206
2320 Main St.
West Barnstable,
MA 02668-0206
(508) 362-2766
decoysunlimited.net

DGW Auctioneers & Appraisers
760 Kifer Rd.
Sunnyvale, CA 94086
www.dgwauctioneers.com

Dickins Auctioneers Ltd.
Calvert Rd.
Middle Claydon
Buckingham, England
MK18 2EZ
+44 (129) 671-4434
www.dickinsauctioneers.com

Doyle New York
175 E. 87th St.
New York, NY 10128
(212) 427-2730
www.doylenewyork.com

Dreweatts & Bloomsbury Auctions
24 Maddox St.
London, England W1S 1PP
+44 (207) 495-9494
www.dreweatts.com/

Elite Decorative Arts
1034 Gateway Blvd., #108
Boynton Beach, FL 33426
(561) 200-0893
www.eliteauction.com

Fine Arts Auctions, LLC
324 S. Beverly Dr., #175
Beverly Hills, CA 90212
(310) 990-2150
www.fineartauctionllc.com

Fontaine's Auction Gallery
1485 W. Housatonic St.
Pittsfield, MA 01210
www.fontainesauction.net

Forsythes' Auctions, LLC
P.O. Box 188
Russellville, OH 45168
(937) 377-3700
www.forsythesauctions.com

Fox Auctions
P.O. Box 4069
Vallejo, CA 94590
(631) 553-3841
Fax: (707) 643-3000
www.foxauctionsonline.com

Frasher's Doll Auction
2323 S. Mecklin Sch. Rd.
Oak Grove, MO 64075
(816) 625-3786

J. Garrett Auctioneers, Ltd.
1411 Slocum St.
Dallas, TX 75207
(214) 683-6855
www.jgarrettauctioneers.com

Garth's Arts & Antiques
P.O. Box 369
Delaware, OH 43015
(740) 362-4771
www.garths.com

Glass Works Auctions
Box 180
East Greenville, PA 18041
(215) 679-5849
www.glswrk-auction.com

The Golf Auction
209 State St.
Oldsmar, FL 34677
(813) 340-6179
thegolfauction.com

Gray's Auctioneers & Appraisers
10717 Detroit Ave.
Cleveland, OH 44102
(216) 226-3300
graysauctioneers.com

Great Gatsby's Antiques and Auctions
5180 Peachtree Industrial Blvd.
Atlanta, GA 30341
(770) 457-1903
www.greatgatsbys.com

Grogan & Co.
22 Harris St.
Dedham, MA 02026
(781) 461-9500
www.groganco.com

Guyette & Deeter
24718 Beverly Rd.
St. Michaels, MD 21663
(410) 745-0485
Fax: (410) 745-0487
www.guyetteandschmidt.com

GWS Auctions, LLC
41841 Beacon Hill # E
Palm Desert, CA 92211
(760) 610-4175
www.gwsauctions.com

Ken Farmer Auctions and Appraisals
105 Harrison St.
Radford, VA 24141
(540) 639-0939
www.kfauctions.com

Hake's Americana & Collectibles
P.O. Box 12001
York, PA 17402
(717) 434-1600
www.hakes.com

Hamilton's Antique & Estate Auctions, Inc.
505 Puyallup Ave.
Tacoma, WA 98421
(253) 534-4445
www.joe-frank.com

Norman Heckler & Co.
79 Bradford Corner Rd.
Woodstock Valley, CT 06282
www.hecklerauction.com

Heritage Auctions
3500 Maple Ave.
Dallas, TX 75219-3941
(800) 872-6467
www.ha.com

Hess Fine Auctions
1131 4th St. N.
St. Petersburg, FL 33701
(727) 896-0622
www.hessfineauctions.com

Hewlett's Antique Auctions
PO Box 87
13286 Jefferson St.
Le Grand, CA 95333
(209) 389-4542
Fax: (209) 389-0730
http://www.hewlettsauctions.com/

Holabird-Kagin Americana
3555 Airway Dr., #308
Reno, NV 89511
(775) 852-8822
www.holabirdamericana.com

Homestead Auctions
3200 Greenwich Rd.
Norton, OH 44203
(330) 807-1445
www.homesteadauction.net

Bill Hood & Sons Art & Antique Auctions
2925 S. Federal Hwy.
Delray Beach, FL 33483
(561) 278-8996
www.hoodauction.com

Humler & Nolan
The Auctions at Rookwood
225 E. Sixth St., 4th Floor
Cincinnati, OH 45202
(513) 381-2041
Fax: (513) 381-2038
www.humlernolan.com

iGavel Auctions
229 E. 120th St.
New York, NY 10035
(212) 289-5588
www.igavelauctions.com

Ivy Auctions
22391 Hwy. 76 E.
Laurens, SC 29360
(864) 682-2750
www.ivyauctions.com

Jackson's International Auctioneers & Appraisers
2229 Lincoln St.
Cedar Falls, IA 50613
jacksonsauction.com

James D. Julia, Inc.
P.O. Box 830
203 Skowhegan Rd.
Fairfield, ME 04937
(207) 453-7125
jamesdjulia.com

Jeffrey S. Evans & Associates
2177 Green Valley Ln.
Mount Crawford, VA 22841
(540) 434-3939
www.jeffreysevans.com

John Moran Auctioneers
735 West Woodbury Rd.
Altadena, CA 91001
(626) 793-1833
www.johnmoran.com

Julien's Auctions
9665 Wilshire Blvd., Suite 150
Beverly Hills, CA 90210
(310) 836-1818
www.juliensauctions.com

Kaminski Auctions
564 Cabot St.
Beverly, MA 01915
(978) 927-2223
Fax: (978) 927-2228
www.kaminskiauctions.com/

Kennedy Auctions Service
160 West Court Ave.
Selmer, TN 38375
(731) 645-5001
www.kennedysauction.com

Lang's Sporting Collectibles
663 Pleasant Valley Rd.
Waterville, NY 13480
(315) 841-4623
www.langsauction.com

Legend Numismatics
P.O. Box 9
Lincroft, NJ 07738
(800) 743-2646
www.legendcoin.com

Legendary Auctions
17542 Chicago Ave.
Lansing, IL 60438
(708) 889-9380
www.legendaryauctions.com

Los Angeles Modern Auctions
16145 Hart St.
Van Nuys, CA 91406
(323) 904-1950
www.lamodern.com

Leslie Hindman Auctioneers
1338 West Lake St.
Chicago, IL 60607
(312) 280-1212
www.lesliehindman.com

Louis J. Dianni, LLC Antiques Auctions
May 1-Oct. 15:
982 Main St., Suite 175
Fishkill, NY 12524
Oct. 20-April 15:
1304 SW 160th Ave., Suite 228A
Sunrise, FL 33326
https://louisjdianni.com

Love of the Game Auctions
P.O. Box 157
Great Meadows, NJ 07838
loveofthegameauctions.com

Main Street Mining Co.
2311 East Loop 820 N.
Fort Worth, TX 76118
(817) 616-5001
https://mainstreetmining.com

Manifest Auctions
361 Woodruff Rd.
Greenville, SC 29607
(864) 520-2208
Fax: (864) 520-2210
manifestauctions.com

Manitou Auctions
205 Styer Dairy Rd.
Reidsville, NC 27320
(336) 349-6577
www.manitou-auctions.com

Manor Auctions
2415 N. Monroe St.
Tallahassee, FL 32303
(850) 523-3787
Fax: (850) 523-3786
www.manorauctions.com

Mark Mattox Auctioneer & Real Estate Broker, Inc.
3740 Maysville Rd.
Carlisle, KY 40311
(859) 289-5720
http://mattoxauctions.com/auctions/

Martin Auction Co.
100 Lick Creek Rd.
Anna, IL 62906
(618) 833-3589
www.martinauctionco.com
martinauctioncompany@gmail.com

Martin J. Donnelly Antique Tools
5523 County Rd. 8
Avoca, NY 14809
(607) 566-2617
www.mjdtools.com

Matt Maring Auction Co.
P.O. Box 37
Kenyon, MN 55946
(507) 789-5227
www.maringauction.com

Material Culture
4700 Wissahickon Ave.
Philadelphia, PA 19144
(215) 849-8030
www.materialculture.com

Matthews Auctions
111 South Oak St.
Nokomis, IL 62075-1337
(215) 563-8880
www.matthewsauctions.com

John McInnis Auctioneers & Appraisers
76 Main St.
Amesbury, MA 01913
(978) 388-0400
Fax: (978) 388-8863
www.mcinnisauctions.com

McLaren Auction Service
21507 Highway 99E
Aurora, OR 97002
(503) 678-2441
www.mclarenauction.com

McMasters-Harris Auction Co.
P.O. Box 755
Cambridge, OH 43725
www.mcmastersharris.com

Michaan's Auctions
2751 Todd St.
Alameda, CA 94501
(510) 740-0220
www.michaans.com

Midwest Auction Galleries
925 North Lapeer Rd.
Oxford, MI 48371
(877) 236-8181 or (248) 236-8100
Fax: (248) 236-8396
www.midwestauctioninc.com

Mile High Card Co.
7200 S. Alton Way, Suite A230
Centennial, CO 80112
(303) 840-2784
www.milehighcardco.com

Milestone Auctions
3860 Ben Hur Ave., Unit 8
Willoughby, OH 44094
(440) 527-8060
www.milestoneauctions.com

Dan Morphy Auctions
2000 N. Reading Rd.
Denver, PA 17517
(717) 335-3435
morphyauctions.com

Mohawk Arms, Inc.
P.O. Box 157
Bouckville, NY 13310
(315) 893-7888
www.militaryrelics.com

Mosby & Co. Auctions
5714-A Industry Ln.
Frederick, MD 21704
(240) 629-8139
www.mosbyauctions.com

Neal Auction Co.
4038 Magazine St.
New Orleans, LA 70115
(504) 899-5329
www.nealauction.com

Nest Egg Auctions
30 Research Pkwy.
Meriden, CT 06450
(203) 630-1400
www.nesteggauctions.com

New Orleans Auction Gallery
1330 St. Charles Ave.
New Orleans, LA 70130
www.neworleansauction.com

Nico Auctions
4023 Kennett Pike, Suite 248
Greenville, DE 19807
(888) 390-0201
www.nicoauctions.com

Noel Barrett Vintage Toys @ Auction
P.O. Box 300
Carversville, PA 18913
(215) 297 5109
www.noelbarrett.com

North American Auction Co.
78 Wildcat Way
Bozeman, MT 59718
(800) 686-4216
www.northamericanauctioncompany.com

Northeast Auctions
93 Pleasant St.
Portsmouth, NH 03801
(603) 433-8400
Fax: (603) 433-0415
www.northeastauctions.com

O'Gallerie: Fine Arts, Antiques and Estate Auctions
228 Northeast 7th Ave.
Portland, OR 97232-2909
(503) 238-0202
www.ogallerie.com

Omaha Auction Center
7531 Dodge St.
Omaha, NE 68114
(402) 397-9575
www.omahaauctioncenter.com

Omega Auction Corp.
1669 W. 39th Pl.
Hialeah, FL 33012
(786) 444-4997
www.omegaauctioncorp.com

Pacific Galleries Auction House and Antique Mall
241 South Lander St.
Seattle, WA 98134
(206) 441-9990
Fax: (206) 448-9677
www.pacgal.com

Past Tyme Pleasures
39 California Ave., Suite 105
Pleasanton, CA 94566
www.pasttyme1.com

PBA Galleries
133 Kearny St., 4th Floor
San Francisco, CA 94108
(415) 989-2665
www.pbagalleries.com

Phoebus Auction Gallery
18 East Mellen St.
Hampton, VA 23663
(757) 722-9210
www.phoebusauction.com

Pioneer Auction Gallery
14650 SE Arista Dr.
Portland, OR 97267
(503) 496-0303
www.pioneerantiqueauction.com

Pook & Pook, Inc.
463 East Lancaster Ave.
Downingtown, PA 19335
(610) 269-4040
www.pookandpook.com

Potter & Potter Auctions
3759 N. Ravenswood Ave., #121
Chicago, IL 60613
(773) 472-1442
www.potterauctions.com

Premier Auction Galleries
12587 Chillicothe Rd.
Chesterland, OH 44026
(440) 688-4203
Fax: (440) 688-4202
www.pag4u.com

Don Presley Auction
1319 West Katella Ave.
Orange County, CA 92867
(714) 633-2437
www.donpresley.com

Preston Hall Gallery
2201 Main St., Suite #820
Dallas, TX 75201
(214) 718-8624
www.prestonhallgallery.com

Profiles in History
26901 Agoura Rd., Suite 150
Calabasas Hills, CA 91301
(310) 859-7701
www.profilesinhistory.com

Purcell Auction Gallery
2156 Husband Rd.
Paducah, KY 42003
(270) 444-7599
www.purcellauction.com/

Quinn's Auction Galleries
360 S. Washington St.
Falls Church, VA 22046
(703) 532-5632
www.quinnsauction.com

Rago Arts & Auctions
333 N. Main St.
Lambertville, NJ 08530
(609) 397-9374
www.ragoarts.com

Red Baron's Antiques
8655 Roswell Rd.
Atlanta, GA 30350
(770) 640-4604
www.rbantiques.com

Richard Opfer Auctioneering, Inc.
1919 Greenspring Dr.
Lutherville-Timonium, MD 21093
(410) 252-5035
www.opferauction.com

Rich Penn Auctions
P.O. Box 1355
Waterloo, IA 50704
(319) 291-6688
www.richpennauctions.com

RM Auctions
One Classic Car Dr.
Blenheium, Ontario
N0P 1A0 Canada
+1 (519) 352-4575
www.rmauctions.com

Robert Edward Auctions
P.O. Box 7256
Watchung, NJ 07069
(908) 226-9900
www.robertedwardauctions.com

Rock Island Auction Co.
7819 42 St. West
Rock Island, IL 61201
(800) 238-8022
www.rockislandauction.com

Roland Auction NY
80 E 11th St.
New York, NY 10003
(212) 260-2000
www.rolandauctions.com

RR Auction
5 Route 101A, Suite 5
Amherst, NH 03031
(603) 732-4280
www.rrauction.com

Saco River Auction Co.
2 Main St.
Biddeford, ME 04005
(207) 602-1504
www.sacoriverauction.com

Scheerer McCulloch Auctioneers
515 E Paulding Rd.
Fort Wayne, IN 46816
(260) 441-8636
www.smauctioneers.com

SCP Auctions, Inc.
32451 Golden Lantern, Suite 308
Laguna Niguel, CA 92677
(949) 831-3700
www.SCPauctions.com

Seeck Auction Co.
Jim and Jan Seeck
P.O. Box 377
Mason City, IA 50402
www.seeckauction.com

SeriousToyz
1 Baltic Pl.
Croton on Hudson, NY 10520
(866) 653-8699
www.serioustoyz.com

Showtime Auction Services
22619 Monterey Dr.
Woodhaven, MI 48183-2269
(734) 676-9703
www.showtimeauctions.com

Skinner, Inc.
357 Main St.
Boston, MA 01740
(617) 350-5400
www.skinnerinc.com

Sloans & Kenyon Auctioneers and Appraisers
7034 Wisconsin Ave.
Chevy Chase, MD 20815
(301) 634-2330
www.sloansandkenyon.com

Sotheby's New York
1334 York Ave.
New York, NY 10021
(212) 606-7000
www.sothebys.com

Specialists of the South, Inc.
544 E. Sixth St.
Panama City, FL 32401
(850) 785-2577
www.specialistsofthesouth.com

Stanley Gibbons
399 Strand
London
WC2R 0LX
England
+44 (0)207 836 8444
www.stanleygibbons.com

Carl W. Stinson, Inc.
293 Haverhill St.
Reading, MA 01867
(617) 834-3819
www.stinsonauctions.com

Stefek's Auctioneers & Appraisers
18450 Mack Ave.
Grosse Pointe Farms, MI 48236
(313) 881-1800
www.stefeksltd.com

Stephenson's Auctioneers & Appraisers
1005 Industrial Blvd.
Southampton, PA 18966
(215) 322-6182
www.stephensonsauction.com

Stevens Auction Co.
301 North Meridian St.
Aberdeen, MS 39730-2613
(662) 369-2200
www.stevensauction.com

Strawser Auctions
P.O. Box 332
Wolcottville, IN 46795
www.strawserauctions.com
Sullivan & Son Auction, LLC
1995 E. County Rd. 650
Carthage, IL 62321
(217) 743-5200
www.sullivanandsonauction.com

Swann Auction Galleries
104 E 25th St., # 6
New York, NY 10010-2999
(212) 254-4710
www.swanngalleries.com

Teel Auction Services
619 FM 2330
Montabla, TX 75853
(903) 724-4079
www.teelauctionservices.com

Theriault's – The Doll Masters
P.O. Box 151
Annapolis, MD 21404
(800) 638-0422
www.theriaults.com

Thomaston Place Auction Galleries
51 Atlantic Hwy.
Thomaston, ME 04861
(207) 354-8141
www.thomastonauction.com

John Toomey Gallery
818 North Blvd.
Oak Park, IL 60301
(708) 383-5234
http://johntoomeygallery.com

Tory Hill Auction Co.
5301 Hillsborough St.
Raleigh, NC 27606
(919) 858-0327
www.toryhillauctions.com

Tradewinds Antiques & Auctions
24 Magnolia Ave.
Manchester-by-the-Sea, MA 01944
(978) 526-4085
www.tradewindsantiques.com

Treadway Gallery, Inc.
2029 Madison Rd.
Cincinnati, OH 45208
www.treadwaygallery.com

Turkey Creek Auctions, Inc.
13939 N. Hwy. 441
Citra, FL 32113
(352) 622-4611
(800) 648-7523
www.antiqueauctionsfl.com

Vero Beach Auction
492 Old Dixie Hwy.
Vero Beach, FL 32962
(772) 978-5955
Fax: (772) 978-5954
www.verobeachauction.com

Victorian Casino Antiques Auction
4520 Arville St., #1
Las Vegas, NV 89103
(702) 382-2466
www.vcaauction.com

Wiederseim Associates, Inc.
PO Box 470
Chester Springs, PA 19425
(610) 827-1910
www.wiederseim.com

Philip Weiss Auctions
74 Merrick Rd.
Lynbrook, NY 11563
(516) 594-0731
www.weissauctions.com

William J. Jenack Estate Appraisers & Auctioneers
62 Kings Highway Bypass
Chester, NY 10918
(877) 282-8503
www.jenack.com

Witherell's Art & Antiques
300 20th St.
Sacramento, CA 95811
(916) 446-6490
witherells.com

Woodbury Auction, LLC
50 Main St. N.
Woodbury, CT 06798
(203) 266-0323
www.woodburyauction.com

Woody Auction
317 S. Forrest St.
Douglass, KS 67039
(316) 747-2694
www.woodyauction.com

Wright
1440 W. Hubbard St.
Chicago, IL 60642
(312) 563-0020
www.wright20.com

Zurko Promotions
115 E. Division St.
Shawano, WI 54166
www.zurkopromotions.com

INDEX